ADVANCES IN NEURAL NETWORKS RESEARCH IJCNN 2003

Edited by

Donald C. Wunsch II
University of Missouri-Rolla

Michael Hasselmo
Boston University

Ganesh Kumar Venayagamoorthy
University of Missouri-Rolla

DeLiang Wang
Ohio State University

2003

Pergamon

Amsterdam - Boston - Heidelberg - London -Oxford - Paris
San Diego - San Francisco - Singapore - Sydney - Tokyo

ELSEVIER SCIENCE Ltd
Pergamon (an imprint of Elsevier Science)
The Boulevard, Langford Lane
Kidlington, Oxford OX5 1GB, UK

First edition 2003

Library of Congress Cataloging in Publication Data
A catalog record from the Library of Congress has been applied for.

British Library Cataloguing in Publication Data
A catalogue record from the British Library has been applied for.

Advances in Neural Network Research: IJCNN 2003. Edited by Donald C. Wunsch II, Mike Hasselmo, Ganesh Kumar Venayagamoorthy and DeLiang Wang. Reprinted from Neural Networks, Volume 16, Nos. 5-6 (2003)

Photo on the front cover by Steve Terrill. (www.terrillphoto.com)

ISBN: 978-0-08-044320-1

Transferred To Digital Printing 2012

NEURAL NETWORKS

CONTENTS

2003 Special Issue: Advances in Neural Networks Research – IJCNN'03

D. C. Wunsch II, M. E. Hasselmo, G. K. Venayagamoorthy, D. Wang	**519**	Preface: the best of the best
		Perceptual and Motor Function
A. Ulloa, D. Bullock, B. J. Rhodes	**521**	Adaptive force generation for precision-grip lifting by a spectral timing model of the cerebellum
D. Casasent, X.-w. Chen	**529**	Radial basis function neural networks for nonlinear Fisher discrimination and Neyman–Pearson classification
X. Liu, A. Srivastava, D. Wang	**537**	Intrinsic generalization analysis of low dimensional representations
M. Han, L. Cheng, H. Meng	**547**	Application of four-layer neural network on information extraction
M. Matsugu, K. Mori, Y. Mitari, Y. Kaneda	**555**	Subject independent facial expression recognition with robust face detection using a convolutional neural network
G. Arulampalam, A. Bouzerdoum	**561**	A generalized feedforward neural network architecture for classification and regression
		Cognitive Function and Computational Neuroscience
H. Voicu	**569**	Hierarchical cognitive maps
R. A. Koene, A. Gorchetchnikov, R. C. Cannon, M. E. Hasselmo	**577**	Modeling goal-directed spatial navigation in the rat based on physiological data from the hippocampal formation
H. H. Namarvar, T. W. Berger	**585**	An efficient training algorithm for dynamic synapse neural networks using trust region methods
C. Günay, A. S. Maida	**593**	Temporal binding as an inducer for connectionist recruitment learning over delayed lines
R. A. Santiago, J. McNames, K. Burchiel, G. G. Lendaris	**601**	Developments in understanding neuronal spike trains and functional specializations in brain regions
L. Zhang, J. Mei	**609**	Shaping up simple cell's receptive field of animal vision by ICA and its application in navigation system
T. P. Caudell, Y. Xiao, M. J. Healy	**617**	eLoom and Flatland: specification, simulation and visualization engines for the study of arbitrary hierarchical neural architectures
P. Sussner	**625**	Associative morphological memories based on variations of the kernel and dual kernel methods
		Informatics
H. Ressom, D. Wang, P. Natarajan	**633**	Adaptive double self-organizing maps for clustering gene expression profiles

C. Furlanello, M. Serafini, S. Merler, G. Jurman	**641**	An accelerated procedure for recursive feature ranking on microarray data
		Dynamics
A. Gutierrez-Galvez, R. Gutierrez-Osuna	**649**	Pattern completion through phase coding in population neurodynamics
G. A. Ascoli	**657**	Passive dendritic integration heavily affects spiking dynamics of recurrent networks
A. M. Abdelbar, E. A. M. Andrews, D. C. Wunsch II	**665**	Abductive reasoning with recurrent neural networks
E. Del-Moral-Hernandez	**675**	Neural networks with chaotic recursive nodes: techniques for the design of associative memories, contrast with Hopfield architectures, and extensions for time-dependent inputs
L. A. Feldkamp, D. V. Prokhorov, T. M. Feldkamp	**683**	Simple and conditioned adaptive behavior from Kalman filter trained recurrent networks
		Reinforcement Learning and Control
S. Wermter, M. Elshaw	**691**	Learning robot actions based on self-organising language memory
A. Joshi, J. Weng	**701**	Autonomous mental development in high dimensional context and action spaces
E. N. Sanchez, L. J. Ricalde	**711**	Chaos control and synchronization, with input saturation, via recurrent neural networks
R. Padhi, S. N. Balakrishnan	**719**	Proper orthogonal decomposition based optimal neurocontrol synthesis of a chemical reactor process using approximate dynamic programming
L. Jianyu, L. Siwei, Q. Yingjian, H. Yaping	**729**	Numerical solution of elliptic partial differential equation using radial basis function neural networks
		Theory
B. Widrow, M. Kamenetsky	**735**	Statistical efficiency of adaptive algorithms
E. Mizutani, J. W. Demmel	**745**	On structure-exploiting trust-region regularized nonlinear least squares algorithms for neural-network learning
B. Kosko, S. Mitaim	**755**	Stochastic resonance in noisy threshold neurons
D. Anguita, S. Ridella, F. Rivieccio, R. Zunino	**763**	Quantum optimization for training support vector machines
L. Massey	**771**	On the quality of ART1 text clustering
M. H. Wang, C. P. Hung	**779**	Extension neural network and its applications
D. Tsujinishi, S. Abe	**785**	Fuzzy least squares support vector machines for multiclass problems
J. A. Bullinaria	**793**	Evolving efficient learning algorithms for binary mappings
A. Pezeshki, M. R. Azimi-Sadjadi, L. L. Scharf	**801**	A network for recursive extraction of canonical coordinates
A. Ghodsi, D. Schuurmans	**809**	Automatic basis selection techniques for RBF networks

L. Xu	**817**	Data smoothing regularization, multi-sets-learning, and problem solving strategies
S. A. Mulder, D. C. Wunsch II	**827**	Million city traveling salesman problem solution by divide and conquer clustering with adaptive resonance neural networks
		Applications
A. Zaknich	**833**	A practical sub-space adaptive filter
A. E. Gaweda, A. A. Jacobs, M. E. Brier, J. M. Zurada	**841**	Pharmacodynamic population analysis in chronic renal failure using artificial neural networks—a comparative study
R. Dutta, K. R. Kashwan, M. Bhuyan, E. L. Hines, J. W. Gardner	**847**	Electronic nose based tea quality standardization
A. Eleuteri, R. Tagliaferri, L. Milano, S. De Placido, M. De Laurentiis	**855**	A novel neural network-based survival analysis model
S.-P. Kim, J. C. Sanchez, D. Erdogmus, Y. N. Rao, J. Wessberg, J. C. Principe, M. Nicolelis	**865**	Divide-and-conquer approach for brain machine interfaces: nonlinear mixture of competitive linear models
Y. N. Rao, D. Erdogmus, G. Y. Rao, J. C. Principe	**873**	Stochastic error whitening algorithm for linear filter estimation with noisy data
J.-W. Park, R. G. Harley, G. K. Venayagamoorthy	**881**	New internal optimal neurocontrol for a series FACTS device in a power transmission line
W. Liu, G. K. Venayagamoorthy, D. C. Wunsch II	**891**	Design of an adaptive neural network based power system stabilizer
D. A. Karras, V. Zorkadis	**899**	On neural network techniques in the secure management of communication systems through improving and quality assessing pseudorandom stream generators
H. Szu, S. Noel, S.-B. Yim, J. Willey, J. Landa	**907**	Multimedia authenticity protection with ICA watermarking and digital bacteria vaccination
		Visual Cortex: How Illusions Represent Reality
P. J. Kellman	**915**	Interpolation processes in the visual perception of objects
S. Grossberg	**925**	Laminar cortical dynamics of visual form perception
S. Anstis	**933**	Moving objects appear to slow down at low contrasts
E. Mingolla	**939**	Neural models of motion integration and segmentation

Preface: The Best of the Best

The top-reviewing papers from the 2003 International Joint Conference on Neural Networks (IJCNN) have been expanded and assembled here in book format. In odd-numbered years, IJCNN is led by the INNS, and in even-numbered years, by the IEEE. This year, we decided to offer this select group of IJCNN authors a chance to expand their papers. The chapters of this book appeared as a special issue of the *Neural Networks* journal in July 2003.

IJCNN is the flagship conference of the INNS, as well as the IEEE Neural Networks Society. It has arguably been the pre-eminent conference in the field, even as neural network conferences have proliferated and specialized. As the number of conferences has grown, its strongest competition has migrated away from an emphasis on neural networks. IJCNN has embraced the proliferation of spin-off and related fields (see the topic list, below), while maintaining a core emphasis befitting its name. It has also succeeded in enforcing an emphasis on quality. While being an inclusive conference, IJCNN has strict standards for acceptance, including literature review, quality of English; and reproducibility, accuracy and meaningfulness of results. All papers, even invited papers, were subject to a minimum of two reviews -- and many papers received up to five. We rejected 15% of submitted papers, and only the top 10% of the remaining papers are presented in this issue. These topics cover most of the major areas of research in neural networks, including: self-organizing maps, reinforcement learning, support vector machines, adaptive resonance theory, principal component analysis and independent component analysis, as well as numerous engineering applications and detailed biological models of the function of neural circuits.

IJCNN '03 has, at this writing, surpassed expectations in every capacity. We got all our first choices of plenary speakers: Kunihiko Fukushima, Earl Miller, Terrence Sejnowski, Vladimir Vapnik, and Christoph von der Malsburg; an extraordinary slate of tutorial presenters, and 730 submitted articles -- 33% over projections. Papers are presented in 20-minute format in four parallel sessions, planned to be as topically orthogonal as possible. Poster presentations are given their own generous time slot as well.

If you haven't been to IJCNN lately, you don't know what you are missing. For more information, see www.ijcnn.net or www.inns.org or www.ieee-nns.org. It has been our pleasure to work on creating the program for IJCNN, as well as this book, for you.

Sincerely,

Donald C. Wunsch II, University of Missouri-Rolla
General Chair, IJCNN '03
Michael E. Hasselmo, Boston University
Program Chair, IJCNN' 03
Ganesh Kumar Venayagamoorthy, University of Missouri-Rolla
Program Co-Chair, IJCNN '03
DeLiang Wang, Ohio State University
Program Co-Chair, IJCNN '03

2003 International Joint Conference on Neural Networks
TOPIC LIST

A. PERCEPTUAL AND MOTOR FUNCTION
Vision and image processing
Pattern recognition
 Face recognition
 Handwriting recognition
 Other pattern recognition
Auditory and speech processing
 Audition
Speech recognition
 Speech production
 Other perceptual systems
 Motor control and response
B. COGNITIVE FUNCTION
Cognitive information processing
Learning and memory
Spatial Navigation
Conditioning, Reward and Behavior
Mental disorders
Attention and Consciousness
Language
Emotion and Motivation
C. COMPUTATIONAL NEUROSCIENCE
Models of neurons and local circuits
Systems neurobiology and neural modeling
Spiking neurons
D. INFORMATICS
Neuroinformatics
Bioinformatics
Artificial immune systems
Data mining
E. HARDWARE
Neuromorphic hardware and implementations
Embedded neural networks
F. REINFORCEMENT LEARNING AND CONTROL
Reinforcement learning
Approximate/Adaptive dynamic programming
Control
Reconfigurable systems
Robotics
Fuzzy neural systems
Optimization
G. DYNAMICS
Neurodynamics
Recurrent networks
Chaos and learning theory
H. THEORY
Mathematics of Neural Systems
Support vector machines
Extended Kalman filters
Mixture models, EM algorithms and ensemble learning
Radial basis functions
Self-organizing maps
Adaptive resonance theory
Principal component analysis and independent component analysis
Probabilistic and informationtheoretic methods
Neural Networks and Evolutionary Computation
I. APPLICATIONS
Signal Processing
Telecommunications
Applications
Time Series Analysis
Biomedical Applications
Financial Engineering
Biomimetic applications
Computer security applications
Power system applications
Aeroinformatics
Diagnostics and Quality
Control
Other applications

AVAILABLE AT
www.ComputerScienceWeb.com
POWERED BY SCIENCE DIRECT

PERGAMON

Neural Networks 16 (2003) 521–528

Neural Networks

www.elsevier.com/locate/neunet

2003 Special issue

Adaptive force generation for precision-grip lifting by a spectral timing model of the cerebellum

Antonio Ulloa*, Daniel Bullock, Bradley J. Rhodes

Department of Cognitive & Neural Systems, Boston University, 677 Beacon Street, Boston, MA 02215, USA

Abstract

We modeled adaptive generation of precision grip forces during object lifting. The model presented adjusts reactive and anticipatory grip forces to a level just above that needed to stabilize lifted objects in the hand. The model obeys principles of cerebellar structure and function by using slip sensations as error signals to adapt phasic motor commands to tonic force generators associated with output synergies controlling grip aperture. The learned phasic commands are weight- and texture-dependent. Simulations of the new circuit model reproduce key aspects of experimental observations of force application. Over learning trials, the onset of grip force buildup comes to lead the load force buildup, and the rate-of-rise of grip force, but not load force, scales inversely with the friction of the object.

Keywords: Adaptive timing; Neural model; Synaptic plasticity; Prehension; Learning; Force

1. Introduction

Grasping, lifting, and replacing an object require timed application of *grip forces* (to stabilize the object in the hand during object transport) and *load forces* (to elevate/lower the arm–object system to desired heights in the gravity field). An episode of lifting and lowering an object from and to a table top involves (Johansson, 1996; Johansson & Westling, 1987; Wing, 1996): *pre-lifting*, using the fingers to apply force perpendicular to the object's surface at the points of contact of the fingers with the object; *lifting*, which involves continuing increase of grip force and simultaneous application of load forces sufficient to vertically displace the arm/object system, and to halt its motion at the desired height; *holding* by maintaining grip and load forces; *controlled lowering*, by reducing load forces below the value needed to counteract gravity; and *release*, by rapid simultaneous decrease of grip and load forces following object contact with the table.

After reviewing data on precision grip and prior models of grip force control, this paper presents simulations of a new mathematical model of the neural circuit that enables actors to learn to generate appropriate grip forces to prevent object slippage during lifting. Such learning involves a transition from *reactive* to primarily *anticipatory* application of grip forces that reflect the weight and texture of the object. Also addressed are the problems of reactive load force generation and temporal coordination between load and grip force generation.

2. Data on precision grip

This section outlines: roles of motor cortex and cerebellum in precision grip; trends in the relative timing of exertion of load force versus grip force; and trends in the dependence of grip force on object weight and texture.

2.1. Motor cortex and cerebellum in precision grip

Cell recordings and functional imaging of activity in primary motor cortex (MI) have established close links between MI activity and precision grip force (e.g. Lemon, Johansson, & Westling, 1995; Maier, Bennett, Hepp-Reymond, & Lemon, 1993). Complete lesion of MI and somatosensory cortex impaired monkeys' ability to pick up food that could only be accessed with precision grip (Passingham, 1993). Whereas pre-lesion monkeys used precision grip, post-lesion monkeys retrieved food using whole-hand prehension. Reversible inactivation of MI by

* Corresponding author. Address: National Institutes of Health, Brain Imaging & Modeling Section, 9000 Rockville Pike, 10/3C716, Bethesda, MD 20892, USA. Tel.: +1-301-435-5141; fax: +1-301-480-5625.

E-mail addresses: antonio.ulloa@nih.gov; aup@cns.bu.edu (A. Ulloa), danb@cns.bu.edu (D. Bullock), brhodes@cns.bu.edu (B.J. Rhodes).

0893-6080/03/$ - see front matter © 2003 Elsevier Science Ltd. All rights reserved.
doi:10.1016/S0893-6080(03)00094-7

injection of a GABA agonist produced a similar deficit (Brochier, Boudreau, Pare, & Smith, 1999). Such results exemplify the principle (Passingham, 1993) that MI enables *selective* activation of one or a few effectors, e.g. single joints or fingers, when many effectors could contribute.

Inactivation of the dentate nucleus of the cerebellum, which projects to MI via the thalamus, severely impairs precision grip. After GABA agonist injection in dentate, monkeys used only one finger to retrieve food from a hole, instead of the thumb-index strategy used before (Thach, Goodkin, & Keating, 1992). This effect probably depends partly on disrupted dentate input to MI. Inactivation of the dentate leads to a loss of anticipatory phasic components of MI cell discharges (Vilis & Hore, 1980). Loss of anticipatory components of precision grip, which requires two-finger coordination, may have so degraded the grip that the animal chose the simpler, one-finger, strategy. Consistently (Serrien & Wiesendanger, 1999), patients with unilateral cerebellar damage showed timed, ramp-like anticipatory grip force adjustments on the unaffected side, but maintained high grip forces on the affected side. Switching from an efficient, phasic strategy to a costly tonic strategy may result from loss of the cerebellar adaptive timing needed for the more efficient strategy.

The intermediate zone of cerebellar cortex, which dominates the nucleus interpositus (NIP), also shows strong activity modulation during precision grip. A majority of Purkinje cells in this zone responded with a decrease in tonic activity during maintained grasping (Smith & Bourbonnais, 1981). This decrease would disinhibit the NIP cells, whose resultant excitatory responses could act via the red nucleus, or via motor thalamus and MI, to generate a force increase.

Sufficient repetition of predictable slip events generates anticipatory discharges in NIP-controlling cerebellar cortex neurons. Dugas and Smith (1992) trained monkeys to grasp an object and hold it in a fixed vertical position for 1 s. During a block of trials called slip perturbation trials, a downward force was briefly applied to the object after it had been kept at the correct vertical position for 750 ms. The monkey prevented the object from moving outside a narrow range of vertical heights by phasically stiffening its wrist and firming its grip. On perturbation trials, there was a reflex response evidenced by increases in hand muscle activity and by modulation of discharge in Purkinje and unidentified cells in the paravermal anterior lobe of the cerebellum. Activity increased in muscles with a 30–50 ms latency, and peaked at 50–100 ms *after* the perturbation. About half of the recorded Purkinje cells increased or decreased their simple spike discharges at about 45 ms after the perturbation. Most of the Purkinje cells that responded to the perturbation had cutaneous receptive fields.

After a series of perturbations, a grip force increase, and an *increase* in Purkinje cell activity, developed in *anticipation* of the perturbation, which occurred reliably 750 ms after the cue tone. Grip force began to diverge upward relative to control levels 450 ms before the expected perturbation, and a number of the Purkinje cells increased their discharge at least 50 ms before the grip force divergence. As anticipatory discharges developed, the same cells decreased their reactive, post-perturbation discharge (rendered unnecessary by the effectiveness of the anticipatory response). None of the Purkinje cells exhibited perturbation-related complex spikes, which if present would indicate excitation of Purkinje cells by climbing fiber (CF) discharges. The absence of slip-related CF discharges (in the Purkinje cells studied) may explain why anticipatory *increases* were observed in these Purkinje cell responses rather than anticipatory *reductions*. Many other studies of cerebellar activity have indicated that learned increments in some Purkinje cells' activities typically coincide with learned decrements in others (Berthier & Moore, 1986). Long-term depression (LTD) of excitatory parallel fiber (PF) inputs to Purkinje cells depends on coincidence between two inputs to Purkinje cells: predictive state/context signals carried by PFs and (putative error) signals carried by perturbation-locked CF discharges (Hansel, Linden, & D'Angelo, 2001). Long-term potentiation (LTP) occurs when predictive stimuli excite Purkinje cells in the absence of coincident CF discharges (Hansel et al., 2001). Both LTD and LTP can promote grip force increments if they occur in separate command pathways for opponent muscles. CF discharges in response to cutaneous slip have been reported (Gellman, Gibson, & Houk, 1985).

2.2. Timing and variation of precision grip force

Timing of grip force with respect to load force. In Johansson and Westling (1984), subjects grasped and lifted a 400 g object to about 2 cm above a table top, held it suspended for 10 s, and then replaced it. On some trials, the subjects (Ss) were asked to slowly let the object fall, in order to measure that force level, called the *slip force*, at which the object would slip from the fingers. On typical lift–hold–replace trials, the following *phases* were observed: (1) One of the fingers first touched the object ~50 ms before the first application of grip force. (2) Grip force increased but not load force. This period lasted 80 ± 40 ms. (3) Grip and load forces increased in parallel. (4) Gravity force was overcome, and the object lifted, until it reached the intended height. In this period, grip force reached its maximum value during a transient overshoot of its steady state. (5) Grip and load forces stabilized while Ss held the object in the air. (6) A reduction of load force allowed the object's position to slowly approach the tabletop. (7) At contact, grip and load forces were synchronously terminated.

Rate of rise of grip force during pre-lifting is a function of object weight. The rate of rise of grip force during prelifting is greater for heavier objects (Johansson & Westling, 1988).

Rate of rise of grip force during pre-lifting is a function of object texture. More slippery objects induced faster rates of pre-lift grip force development. In marked contrast, the rate of rise of load force was the same for all textures (Johansson & Westling, 1984).

Grip force during lifting is a joint function of the surface texture and weight of the object lifted (Westling & Johansson, 1984). The static grip force (grip force maintained during the holding stage) was an increasing function of object weight, as was (of course) the minimal force required to prevent slipping (slip force). A greater grip force was used when the material was more slippery.

The time to attain a level of grip force adequate for a given weight/texture is nearly constant for all weights and textures (Johansson & Westling, 1984, 1988). Such constancy greatly reduces variability of behavioral timing.

3. Prior models of grip force control

Johansson (1996) proposed a conceptual model for the application of grip forces and load forces in a lifting task. Briefly, vision provides information on object position, object size, and object shape. This information is used to activate controllers for transporting the hand towards the object while the fingers are being preshaped. Based on visual estimates of weight and friction, a set of tactile responses is predicted to guide planning for the application of initial grip force to the object. Tactile perceptions of weight and texture are fed back and compared to the predicted weight and texture. The mismatch is used to update memory representations of weight and texture for a specific object appearance. This memory is assumed to be retrieved on later occasions to guide anticipatory application of forces (Gordon, Westling, Cole, & Johansson, 1993). If a declining grip force results in slip, a resulting slip alert signal in hand mechanoreceptors triggers a reactive increase in grip force.

Fagergren, Ekeberg, and Forssberg (2000) modeled the transfer function of the peripheral motor system involved in application of grip force. To measure properties of an *active* increase in grip force, subjects were instructed to voluntarily increase grip force in a step-like fashion (from 1 to 50% of maximum voluntary contraction). To test the *reactive* component of grip force, the weight of the object was unexpectedly increased. Once a transfer function for each experiment was identified, a third transfer function was composed to describe a common system involved in active and reactive force generation.

4. A new model of grip force control

Prior treatments of grip force control (Fagergren et al., 2000; Gordon et al., 1993; Johansson, 1996) have not modeled the neural substrates of adaptive control. This section introduces a new, neurobiologically interpretable, model that formalizes the role of MI and the cerebellum in learned transitions from reactive to anticipatory application of grip forces whose magnitudes are texture- and weight-dependent. Control is exercised in aperture coordinates because once the fingers enclose and touch the object, the *targeted* hand aperture can be voluntarily decreased by a further amount. Decreasing the targeted aperture to a value less than object width would cause the fingers to try to move beneath the object's surface, thereby building up a force on it. The size of the applied force would be a function of the size of the decrement (below object width) of target aperture, and of joint stiffness, control of which has been modeled elsewhere (Bullock & Contreras-Vidal, 1993).

4.1. Model circuit and its operation during learning

A model circuit that learns to generate and apply context-dependent grip forces in anticipation of load force application is shown in Fig. 1. It works as follows. Before learning, there is a significant slip error, ε_A, the magnitude of which is needed as an input for the model. As shown at

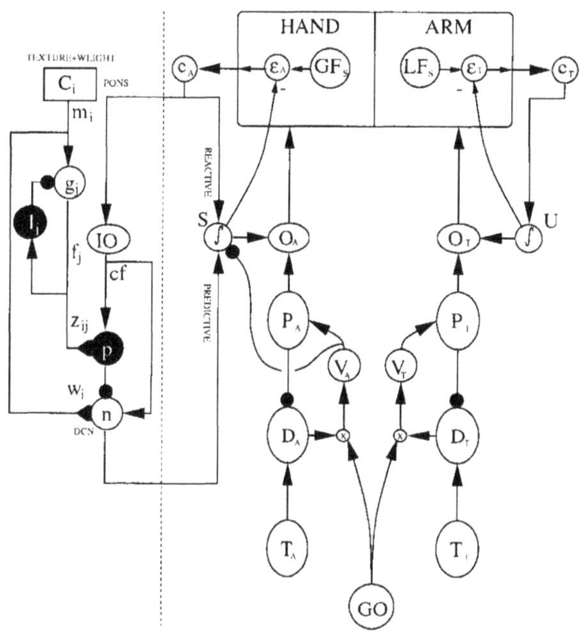

Fig. 1. Circuit for learned transition between reactive and anticipatory grip forces. Elements to the left of the dashed line are components of a cerebellar side-loop that includes inputs from the pons and the inferior olive. Elements to the right of the dashed line are cortical parts of the grip and load force generators and the error estimators. Key: C_i, pontine context representation signals for texture and weight; m_i, mossy fiber signal; g_i, granule cell; l_j, Golgi cell; f_j, parallel fiber signal; IO, inferior olive; cf, climbing fiber; z_{ij} and w_i, weights at adaptive synapses; n, deep cerebellar nuclear (DCN) cell; O_A and O_T, outflow force position vectors for aperture and transport components; S, integrator for grip force adjustments and U, integrator for load force generation; e_A, delayed slip error; e_T, delayed load error; ε_A, slip error; ε_T, load error; GFs, minimal grip force to avoid slip; LFs, appropriate load force to overcome object weight.

the top of Fig. 1, ε_A was computed as the difference between GF_S, the minimal grip force necessary to prevent slip, and the current net adjustment, S, to grip force. Input ε_A is tracked by cell activation variable e_A to form an internal estimate of slip error in the frame of the hand. The figure shows that current net adjustment S is the integral of two phasic inputs: a reactive input from cell e_A and a learned anticipatory input from cell n. The net adjustment S acts on the hand via aperture/force command O_A.

A cerebellar circuit (left side of Fig. 1) enables the model to learn how to preempt performance errors. In addition to providing phasic feedback to charge O_A, cell e_A sends an error signal to the inferior olive, IO, to phasically activate CF signals, *cf*. Because CF branches reach both the cerebellar cortex and the deep cerebellar nuclear (DCN) cells, the *cf* signals excite the Purkinje cell dendritic tree (p) and the DCN cells (n) inhibited by the Purkinje cell.

A context signal, C_i, from the pons, corresponds to the decision to lift the object with the weight-texture combination indexed by i. Signal C_i activates mossy fibers (MF) m_i, each of which in turn generates a spectrum of granule cell activations, g_j. This spectrum of activations, inhibited by Golgi interneuron activities l_j, generates phasic PF activities f_j with different rise times and amplitudes (Bullock, Fiala, & Grossberg, 1994). Adaptive synapses z_{ij} from PFs to Purkinje cells undergo LTD when PF activations are repeatedly paired with CF activations $h(e_A)$. In addition, these synapses undergo long-term potentiation (LTP, slower than LTD) when PF signals f_j are present but there are no correlated CF signals. There are also adaptive synapses, w_i, from MFs to nuclear cells; these synapses undergo LTP when MF activation is paired with CF activation $h(e_A)$; LTD (slower than LTP in these synapses w_i) occurs when MFs are activated without coincident CF activation. Purkinje cells have a baseline activation that normally inhibits the DCN cell. The DCN cell is gradually, and context-dependently, released from this inhibition as the PF-Purkinje cell synapses z_{ij} undergo LTD, because this reduces excitatory inputs to Purkinje cells while inhibitory inputs are maintained. Whenever the C_i cue is presented, the resultant phasic reduction of Purkinje cell inhibition of DCN cells allows the DCN cell activation to express a learned compensation for (what would otherwise be) a forthcoming error. The signal n from the DCN cell reaches the command stage O_A following summation with e_A and integration to form net compensation S. When a command is sent to *increase* the hand aperture T_A, and thus *release* the grip on the object, the integrators must be reset in order to zero the grip force adjustments. Fig. 1 shows that reset in the model is mediated by inhibition of the integrator S whenever there is a positive (opening) aperture velocity command, V_A.

In order to generate a load force that depends on weight-related movement errors in the transport component, a corresponding outflow force position vector in the transport component (O_T in the figure) was introduced, which also receives force adjustments from an integrator, U. As in the Vector Integration To Endpoint model (Bullock, Cisek, & Grossberg, 1998) of MI contributions in arm movement control, O_T cells provide graded force application modulated by integrated feedback of movement error based on signals arising in muscle spindles. Fig. 1 shows that U integrates e_T and e_T tracks the movement error, ε_T. The input ε_T is computed as the difference between the minimal load force, LF_S, adequate for the given object weight, and the current load force, U.

4.2. Technical specifications of the model

Arm transport component. The arm transport component of Fig. 1 obeys the following equations (Cf. Bullock et al., 1998; Ulloa & Bullock, 2003):

$$\dot{D}_T = \alpha(-D_T + T_T - P_T) \quad (1)$$

$$\dot{V}_T = \alpha_V(-V_T + G[D_T]^+) \quad (2)$$

$$\dot{P}_T = V_T \quad (3)$$

and

$$O_T = P_T + U \quad (4)$$

where D_T is the transport difference vector (positive values only when rectified via $[D_T]^+$), $\dot{D}_T$ is the time derivative of D_T, T_T is the internal representation of the position of the target, P_T is the transport present position vector, V_T is a velocity command vector, and GO signal G initiates movement. Parameters α and α_V were set to 30 and 300, respectively. O_T is the outflow force position vector for the transport component, and U integrates the load error:

$$\dot{U} = \alpha_U e_T \quad (5)$$

where α_U was set to 40. In this study, 1D vectors were sufficient to represent stages in the control of the elbow flexion needed to lift the object.

Grip aperture component. The grip aperture component obeyed the following system of equations:

$$\dot{D}_A = \alpha(-D_A + T_A - P_A) \quad (6)$$

$$\dot{V}_A = \alpha_V(-V_A + GD_A) \quad (7)$$

$$\dot{P}_A = V_A \quad (8)$$

and

$$O_A = P_A - S \quad (9)$$

where D_A is the difference vector for hand aperture, T_A is the internal vector representation of the target aperture, P_A is the aperture present position vector, V_A is the aperture velocity vector; O_A is the outflow force-position vector; S is defined by

$$\dot{S} = \alpha_S(e_A + [n]^+ - \beta_S[V_A]^+S) \quad (10)$$

where e_A is the slip error signal (which tracks ε_A) and n is the nuclear (DCN) cell activity. Here again, 1D vectors sufficed for current purposes. The term $-\beta_S[V_A]^+S$ resets the integration of the reactive and predictive adjustments to grip force, by causing a decay in cell S whenever the aperture velocity cell, V_A, is positive. This reset is needed to implement releases of grip force, by eliminating the slip-preventing grip adjustments and allowing the aperture to relax. The rate term α_S was set equal to 40 and β_S to 3.

GO signal. The GO signal generator is defined as:

$$\dot{G} = \alpha_G(-G + G_0(t)) \tag{11}$$

where

$$G_0(t) = g_0 t^{1.4} \tag{12}$$

and $\alpha_G = 30$. G is the GO signal multiplying the difference vector of each component (Eqs. (2) and (7)), and g_0 is a step input from a decision center in the brain.

Slip error. The slip error, ε_A, starts being integrated by e_A at 0.050 s after the onset of the GO signal, to account for the delay between onset of muscle activation and onset of slip signals from mechanoreceptors. The delayed slip error is defined by

$$\dot{e}_A = \alpha_{e_A}(-e_A + \gamma_{e_A}[\varepsilon_A]^+) \tag{13}$$

where $\alpha_{e_A} = 50$. Factor $\gamma_{e_A} = 0.08$ scales the slip error, ε_A, which is approximated by

$$\varepsilon_A \propto \mathrm{GF}_S(u, v) - S. \tag{14}$$

Here GF_S is the minimal grip force needed to prevent slip of an object of weight u and texture v.

Load error. The load force error for the transport component, ε_T, starts being integrated by e_T at 0.050 s after the onset of the GO signal, to account for the delay in detecting load error. The delayed load error is defined by

$$\dot{e}_T = \alpha_{e_T}(-e_T + \gamma_{e_T}[\varepsilon_T]^+) \tag{15}$$

where $\alpha_{e_T} = 50$; $\gamma_{e_T} = 0.25$ scales the error, ε_T, which is approximated by

$$\varepsilon_T \propto \mathrm{LF}_S(u) - U \tag{16}$$

where LF_S is a load force adequate for an object of weight u.

Cerebellar component. This component follows the cerebellar timing model developed by Bullock et al. (1994) for eye blink conditioning (cf. also Rhodes & Bullock, 2002). This is one of the simplest models that give the needed computations, viz.: learning with any interstimulus interval (ISI) in the range [0.1 s, 4 s] and timed generation of a context-specific response of sufficient size to preempt the expected error.

A phasic context signal, C_i, activated at $t = -0.200$ s, excites cell activities, m_i, carried by MFs:

$$\dot{m}_i = -\alpha_m m_i + \beta_m(1 - m_i)(C_i + m_i) \tag{17}$$

where $\alpha_m = 0.2$ and $\beta_m = 10$; the positive feedback in Eq. (17) allows the network to keep a trace of C_i in short-term memory. MFs are directed to two classes of cells, granule cells and DCN cells. Granule cells were defined as

$$\dot{g}_j = \alpha_j((1 - g_j)m_i - \beta_g(g_j + \gamma_g)l_j) \tag{18}$$

where α_j is the rate of activation, drawn from the interval [1.3, 12], of the jth granule cell, where $j = 1, 2, \ldots, 40$, $\beta_g = 4$, and $\gamma_g = 0.1$. Signal l_j is a feedback inhibition of granule cells by Golgi cells:

$$\dot{l}_j = -\alpha_l l_j + \beta_l(1 - l_j)(\gamma_l m_i + f_j) \tag{19}$$

where $\alpha_l = 0.1$, $\beta_l = 5$, and $\gamma_l = 0.02$. The use of f_j in Eq. (19) and l_j in Eq. (18) together imply recurrent signal processing in the cerebellar cortex. The signals f_j conducted by PFs were

$$f_j = \frac{b([g_j - \lambda_f]^+)^2}{1 + c([g_j - \lambda_f]^+)^2} \tag{20}$$

where $b = 12$, $c = 4$, and $\lambda_f = 5$.

Signals f_j are directed to a Purkinje cell through synapses, z_{ij}, which adapt according to

$$\dot{z}_{ij} = f_j((1 - z_{ij}) - \beta_z h(e_A)z_{ij}) \tag{21}$$

where the learning rate $\beta_z = 10$. Thus weights z_{ij} can exhibit slow LTP via term $f_j(1 - z_{ij})$ and faster LTD via term $f_j\beta_z h(e_A)z_{ij}$. The LTD process is gated by CF signal

$$h(e_A) = \begin{cases} e_A & \text{if } \dot{e}_A \geq 0 \\ 0 & \text{otherwise.} \end{cases} \tag{22}$$

This function provides a means to use only the leading edge of the slip error signal e_A. This is justified by evidence (Ito, 1984) that the IO provides this type of filtering. The Purkinje cell firing rate was defined as

$$p = 1 + \frac{1.5\ \mathrm{sgn}(b)b^2}{1 + b^2} \tag{23}$$

where $b = J^+ - J^-$ is the net activity on the dendrites of the Purkinje cells. Here the excitatory term

$$J^+ = \sum_{k=1}^{N} f_k z_{ik} \tag{24}$$

and the inhibitory term

$$J^- = \sum_{k=1}^{N} f_k s_{ik} \tag{25}$$

where $N = 40$. Term J^- represents the influence of basket and stellate cells on the Purkinje cell. For present purposes, the sum in (Eq. 25) had a constant value of 1.0. MFs are also directed to the DCN cell, whose activity, n, was defined by

$$\dot{n} = \alpha_n\left(-n + \sum_{i=1}^{M} m_i w_i - p\right) \qquad (26)$$

where M is the number of different context cues and $\alpha_n = 100$. The adaptive synapses, w_i, from MFs to nuclear cells were adapted according to

$$\dot{w}_i = m_i(\alpha_w w_i + \beta_w(1 - w_i)h(e_A)) \qquad (27)$$

where the forgetting rate $\alpha_w = -0.001$ and the learning rate $\beta_w = 10$.

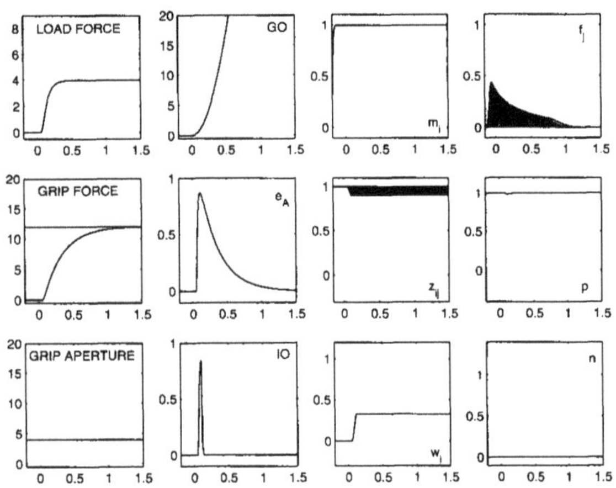

(A)

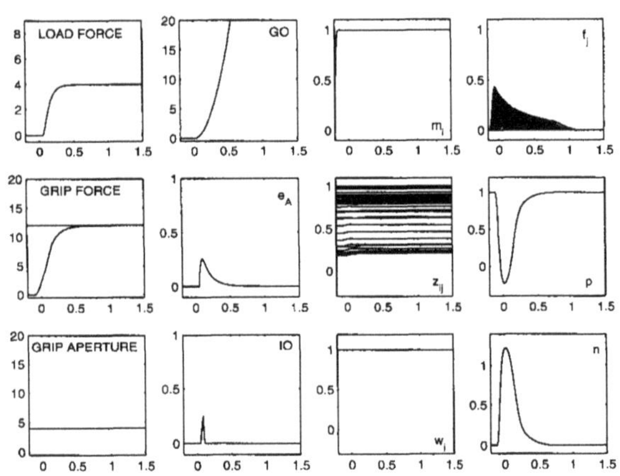

(B)

Fig. 2. (A) Single trial evolution of model variables during early phase of learning adequate grip forces for a 400g silk-covered object. Horizontal axes give time in s; the horizontal line in the grip force plot shows the minimal grip force necessary to prevent slip. Key: e_A, delayed slip error; IO, inferior olive discharge $h(e_A)$; m_i, mossy fiber activity; z_{ij}, adaptive parallel fibers-Purkinje cell synapses; w_i, adaptive mossy fiber-nuclear cell synapse; f_j, activities in parallel fibers; p, Purkinje cell activity; n, nuclear cell activity. In the f_j and z_{ij} plots, there are many separate traces that partially superpose. Separation of the z_{ij} values begins to occur just after the IO discharge. (B) Evolution of model variables during one trial following asymptotic learning of grip force generation for same object as in A.

5. Results

To show activation dynamics of key internal variables, simulations of initial learning (Fig. 2A) and asymptotic phases (Fig. 2B) are shown. The behavioral effect of learning can be seen by comparing the early learning plots in Fig. 2A with the asymptotic performance plots in Fig. 2B. Note that although the GO signal takes off at $t = 0$, load force and grip force take off (during early learning) with a lag corresponding to the delay in the error signals ($t = 0.050$ s). During early learning, grip force is increased in *reaction* to load force, whereas after learning grip force onset *precedes* load force onset. Grip aperture, which equals object width, remains the same in all stages of learning. The slip error (e_A), which is large during learning, becomes small after learning. The panel labeled *IO* shows how the model processes the slip error to use only its leading edge to gate cerebellar learning. The functional generation of the adaptive response is seen by an evolution from no pause in activity to a deep pause in the Purkinje cell activity (p), which controls the DCN cell activation (n). The DCN cell is released from inhibition at the moment of the Purkinje cell pause and in proportion to the depth of the pause. The learning that enables the adaptive response can be appreciated by looking at the weights of the PF-Purkinje cell adaptive synapses (z) and the weights of the MF-nuclear cell adaptive synapses (w). In each case, $w_i = 1.0$ after learning, whereas the below 1.0 deviations of those z_{ij} associated with appropriately timed PF signals scaled directly with the magnitude of the required grip force, and with the depth of the Purkinje cell pause. That the learned w_i values were constant while the learned z_{ij} values varied with object weight and texture (not shown) indicates that the z_{ij} changes were causative for both adaptive timing and scaling of the amplitude of the cerebellar response.

To show that the model is able to simultaneously store and recall grip force adjustments for different weights and textures, simulations were run with various weights and textures. Each combination of weight and texture was represented by a distinct context cue, C_i, and a distinct GF_S (Eq. (14)) was used for each texture-weight combination. The circuit was able to generate anticipatory grip forces that depended upon the presented cue (Fig. 3). After learning converged, the two sets of weights, z_{ij} and w_i, maintain values that preempt the slip onset for each of the presented cues. When the 400 g objects are presented (Fig. 3A), the anticipatory grip forces are adequate for each of the three textures. As in Fig. 2B, the grip force for each texture begins to grow before the onset of load forces. The DCN cell activation and resultant anticipatory grip force are larger the more slippery the surface, but with equal rise times. Therefore, both the rate of rise of grip force and the final grip force value are larger the more slippery the surface. Fig. 3B shows model performance with different weights but

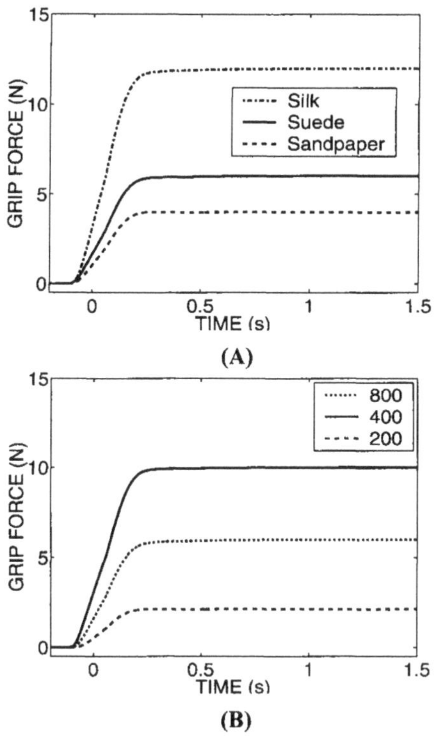

Fig. 3. (A) Simulations of grip force generation for a 400 g object, covered with silk, suede or sandpaper. (B) Simulations of grip force generation for suede-covered objects of three weights (200, 400, and 800 g).

the same texture. Similarly selective, preemptive, error correction can be observed. As in Fig. 2B, the grip force onsets occur in anticipation of load force onset for the three weights. An appropriate grip force is produced, with larger rates of rise and final values for heavier objects, but the grip force rise times for the three weights are equal.

6. Discussion and conclusions

An adaptive circuit was devised to solve the problem of anticipatory application of grip forces when lifting objects of different textures and weights. The cerebellar component of this circuit uses slip signals to adapt the motor commands responsible for exerting just enough force to stabilize the lifted object in the frame of the hand. The adaptive grip force model:

1. Works as a side loop in the aperture control part of a reach–grasp circuit. This circuit makes grip force adjustments in response to slip signals resulting from the application of load forces on the object.
2. Works in anticipation of the activation of the voluntary lifting movement to preempt slippage that would otherwise be produced by that movement. The cerebellar component was able to generate a predictive adjustment to grip force, after the presentation of a context cue corresponding to a visual estimate of object weight and texture. The learned adjustment to grip force was applied in anticipation to load force onset.
3. Resets its compensation when the aperture is voluntarily reset to a larger size, to allow relaxation of the grip aperture.

The cerebellar model of Medina and Mauk (1999) attributed most of the asymptotic memory load in cerebellar learning to the plastic synapse between MFs and DCN cells. Recent data (Hesslow, Svensson, & Ivarsson, 1999) and our results instead suggest that the PF-Purkinje cell synapse can control both timing and amplitude of predictive responses. Our results also accord with the major properties of human grip force adjustment, namely: grip force onset precedes load force onset, grip force and its rate of increase during lifting are functions of object texture and weight, and time to maximum grip force is constant across different weights and textures.

Acknowledgements

A. Ulloa was supported by CONACYT of México (No. 65907); D. Bullock was supported in part by DARPA/ONR N00014-95-1-0409 and NIMH R01 DC02852.

References

Berthier, N., & Moore, J. (1986). Cerebellar Purkinje cell activity related to the classically conditioned nictitating membrane response. *Experimental Brain Research*, *63*, 341–350.

Brochier, T., Boudreau, M. J., Pare, M., & Smith, A. M. (1999). The effects of muscimol inactivation of small regions of motor and somatosensory cortex on independent finger movements and force control in the precision grip. *Experimental Brain Research*, *128*, 31–40.

Bullock, D., Cisek, P., & Grossberg, S. (1998). Cortical networks for control of voluntary arm movements under variable force conditions. *Cerebral Cortex*, *8*, 1–15.

Bullock, D., & Contreras-Vidal, J. (1993). How spinal neural networks reduce discrepancies between motor intention and motor realization. In K. Newell, & D. Corcos (Eds.), *Variability and motor control* (pp. 183–221). Champaign, Il: Human Kinetic Press.

Bullock, D., Fiala, J., & Grossberg, S. (1994). A neural model of timed response learning in the cerebellum. *Neural Networks*, *7*, 1101–1114.

Dugas, C., & Smith, A. (1992). Responses of cerebellar Purkinje cells to slip of a handheld object. *Journal of Neurophysiology*, *67*, 483–495.

Fagergren, A., Ekeberg, O., & Forssberg, H. (2000). Precision grip force dynamics: a system identification approach. *IEEE Transactions on Biomedical Engineering*, *47*, 1366–1375.

Gellman, R., Gibson, A. R., & Houk, J. C. (1985). Inferior olivary neurons in the awake cat: detection of contact and passive body displacement. *Journal of Neurophysiology*, *54*, 40–60.

Gordon, A., Westling, G., Cole, K., & Johansson, R. (1993). Memory representations underlying motor commands used during manipulation of common and novel objects. *Journal of Neurophysiology*, *69*, 1789–1796.

Hansel, C., Linden, D. J., & D'Angelo, E. (2001). Beyond parallel fiber LTD: the diversity of synaptic and non-synaptic plasticity in the cerebellum. *Nature Neuroscience*, *4*, 467–475.

Hesslow, G., Svensson, P., & Ivarsson, M. (1999). Learned movements elicited by direct stimulation of cerebellar mossy fiber afferents. *Neuron*, *24*, 179–185.

Ito, M. (1984). *The cerebellum and neural control*. New York: Raven Press.

Johansson, R. (1996). Sensory control of dexterous manipulation in humans. In A. Wing, P. Haggard, & J. Flanagan (Eds.), *Hand and brain: The neurophysiology and psychology of hand movements* (pp. 381–414). London: Academic Press.

Johansson, R., & Westling, G. (1984). Roles of glabrous skin receptors and sensorimotor memory in automatic control of precision grip when lifting rougher or more slippery objects. *Experimental Brain Research*, *56*, 550–564.

Johansson, R., & Westling, G. (1987). Signals in tactile afferents from the fingers eliciting adaptive motor responses during precision grip. *Experimental Brain Research*, *66*, 141–154.

Johansson, R., & Westling, G. (1988). Coordinated isometric muscle commands adequately and erroneously programmed for the weight during lifting task with precision grip. *Experimental Brain Research*, *71*, 59–71.

Lemon, R., Johansson, R., & Westling, G. (1995). Cortico-spinal control during reach, grasp, and precision lift in man. *Journal of Neuroscience*, *15*, 6145–6156.

Maier, M. A., Bennett, K. M., Hepp-Reymond, M. C., & Lemon, R. N. (1993). Contribution of the monkey corticomoto-neuronal system to the control of force in precision grip. *Journal of Neurophysiology*, *69*, 772–785.

Medina, J., & Mauk, M. (1999). Simulations of cerebellar motor learning: Computational analysis of plasticity at the mossy fiber to deep nucleus synapse. *Journal of Neuroscience*, *19*, 7140–7151.

Passingham, R. (1993). *The frontal lobes and voluntary action*. Oxford: Oxford University Press.

Rhodes, B., & Bullock, D. (2002). A scalable model of cerebellar adaptive timing and sequencing: The recurrent slide and latch (RSL) model. *Applied Intelligence*, *17*, 35–48.

Serrien, D. J., & Wiesendanger, M. (1999). Role of the cerebellum in tuning anticipatory and reactive grip force responses. *Journal of Cognitive Neuroscience*, *11*, 672–681.

Smith, A., & Bourbonnais, D. (1981). Neuronal activity in cerebellar cortex related to control of prehensile force. *Journal of Neurophysiology*, *45*, 286–303.

Thach, W., Goodkin, H., & Keating, J. (1992). The cerebellum and the adaptive coordination of movement. *Annual Review of Neuroscience*, *15*, 403–442.

Ulloa, A., & Bullock, D. (2003). A neural network simulating human reach–grasp coordination by continuous updating of vector positioning commands. *Neural Networks*.

Vilis, T., & Hore, J. (1980). Central neural mechanisms contributing to cerebellar tremor produced by perturbations. *Journal of Neurophysiology*, *43*, 279–291.

Westling, G., & Johansson, R. (1984). Factors influencing the force control during precision grip. *Experimental Brain Research*, *53*, 277–284.

Wing, A. (1996). Anticipatory control of grip force in rapid arm movement. In A. Wing, P. Haggard, & J. Flanagan (Eds.), *Hand and brain: The neurophysiology and psychology of hand movements* (pp. 301–324). London: Academic Press.

AVAILABLE AT
www.ComputerScienceWeb.com
POWERED BY SCIENCE DIRECT

PERGAMON

Neural Networks 16 (2003) 529–535

Neural Networks

www.elsevier.com/locate/neunet

2003 Special issue

Radial basis function neural networks for nonlinear Fisher discrimination and Neyman–Pearson classification

David Casasent[a,*], Xue-wen Chen[b]

[a]Department of Electrical and Computer Engineering, Carnegie Mellon University, Pittsburgh, PA 15213, USA
[b]Department of Electrical and Computer Engineering, California State University, Northridge, CA 91330, USA

Abstract

We propose a novel technique for the design of radial basis function (RBF) neural networks (NNs). To select various RBF parameters, the class membership information of training samples is utilized to produce new cluster classes. This allows emphasis of classification performance for certain class data rather than best overall classification. This allows us to control performance as desired and to approximate Neyman–Pearson classification. We also show that by properly choosing the desired output neuron levels, then the RBF hidden to output layer performs Fisher discrimination analysis, and that the full system performs a nonlinear Fisher analysis. Data on an agricultural product inspection problem and on synthetic data confirm the effectiveness of these methods.

Keywords: Clustering; Linear discriminant analysis; Neural networks; Neyman–Pearson classification; Radial basis function networks

1. Introduction

Radial basis function (RBF) neural networks (NNs) are attractive due to their fast training and simplicity. They have been used in function approximation (Poggio & Girosi, 1990) [1], pattern recognition (Krzyzak, Linder, & Lugosi, 1996), and signal processing (Chen, Mulgrew, & Grant, 1993). An important consideration in designing RBF networks is the hidden layer (Billings & Zheng, 1995; Bruzzone & Prieto, 1998; Chen, Cowan, & Grant, 1991; Moody & Darken, 1989; Musavi, Ahmed, Chan, Faris, & Hummels, 1992; Vogt, 1993). Much work exists (Moody & Darken, 1989; Musavi et al., 1992; Vogt, 1993; Bruzzone & Prieto, 1998) using clustering to select the RBFs to use. The original RBF NNs (Poggio and Girosi, 1990) were concerned with representing nonlinear mapping functions by RBF interpolation; thus clustering methods used were different and many RBF neurons were used. For classification applications, a large number of RBFs are not desirable for on-line computational reasons and for good generalization (similar training and test set scores). Most of the clustering methods (Moody & Darken, 1989; Vogt, 1993) used in RBF NNs did not consider the class of the samples when clustering (this is not attractive for a classification application). For classification applications, other RBF cluster selection methods are needed. For classification applications, others (Bruzzone & Prieto, 1998; Musavi et al., 1992) allow clusters with very few samples (this produces poor mean and variance estimates and poor generalization).

Another issue, which is not considered in most work, is the effect of the choice of the desired outputs on system performance. Different choices result in different performance (Bishop, 1995). For two-class cases, a common choice of the desired outputs is 1 for one class and 0 for the other. With this choice and the mean square error cost function, the output neuron level can be the posterior probability (Richard & Lippmann, 1991) that the input is in class 1 or 2. However, practical networks are often far from ideal estimators due to the fact that the training data is not sufficient to specify the network and that the network is not sufficiently complex to model the posterior distribution accurately. Therefore, the choice [0,1] does not necessarily minimize the probability of error.

There are many applications in which minimizing the probability of error is not the best criterion to design a decision rule because the misclassifications of samples from different class may have different consequences. For example, in agricultural product inspection problems, the goal is to reduce the amount of bad products to some level while not removing more than a certain percentage of the good products. The Neyman–Pearson (N-P) criterion

* Corresponding author. Tel.: +1-412-268-2464; fax: +1-412-268-6345.
E-mail address: casasent@ece.cmu.edu (D. Casasent).

0893-6080/03/$ - see front matter © 2003 Elsevier Science Ltd. All rights reserved.
doi:10.1016/S0893-6080(03)00086-8

minimizes the error for one class while keeping the error for the other class equal to a constant (Fukunaga, 1990; Neyman & Pearson, 1933). If we know the probability density function (PDF) of the input samples, conditioned on each class, we can easily implement the N-P classification by computing the likelihood ratio. Unfortunately, in most cases, the conditional PDF is not available. The standard NN approach to implement an N-P solution (Bankman, Sigillito, Wise, & Smith, 1992; Miao, Azimi-Sadjadi, Tian, Dubey, & Witherspoon, 1998; Sum, Leung, Young, Chan, & Kan, 1999) is to vary the output neuron threshold values so that more samples will be classified into one specific class. This allows a different operating point to be selected, rather than the one with the best total classification accuracy. Most recently, a new confidence-clustering RBF (CC RBF) network to achieve this was advanced and shown to perform better than traditional thresholding methods (Casasent & Chen, 2003). This method allows samples, such as those that are near decision boundaries, to be treated differently from other samples.

In this paper, we consider RBF networks for classification problems. To train RBF networks, first we use a new method to cluster data in different classes, which produces clusters with different expected values of class confidence and removes clusters with few samples. Then, we show how to choose the desired neuron output such that the RBF hidden layer-to-output layer performs Fisher discrimination analysis. We use validation or cross validation techniques to select the optimal parameters to produce the minimum probability of error. To find the preferable operating point (N-P), we combine the above method with CC RBF neural networks. Both synthetic data and agricultural product inspection data are used to verify our methods.

We briefly review RBF NNs in Section 2. The design of our RBF NNs is addressed in Section 3. Test results on a synthetic data case study and on an agricultural product inspection problem are presented in Sections 4 and 5, respectively. Finally, conclusions are given in Section 6.

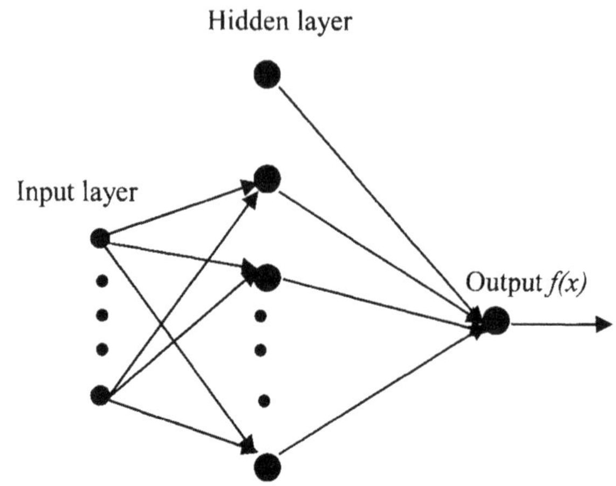

Fig. 1. A basic radial basis function neural network.

2. Radial basis function networks

An RBF network consists of one input layer, one RBF hidden layer, and one output layer, as shown in Fig. 1. Such a network can be considered as a mapping $f : R^N \to R$ according to

$$f(\mathbf{x}) = \sum_{i=0}^{M} \omega_i \varphi(\|\mathbf{x} - \boldsymbol{\mu}_i\| \tag{1}$$

where $x \in R^N$ is the input vector, there are $(M + 1)$ hidden neurons, ω_i are the weights to the output layer, $\varphi(\bullet)$ is the basis function and $\boldsymbol{\mu}_i$ is the center of the i-th RBF, and ω_0 is the bias weight with input $\varphi(\|\mathbf{x} - \boldsymbol{\mu}_0\|) = 1$.

In classification problems, the nonlinear mapping of the hidden layer is usually carried out with the Gaussian function $\varphi(x) = \exp(-x^2/(2\sigma^2)$. For different hidden layer neurons, we use different widths σ. The output of each hidden neuron depends on the distance of the input vector x from its center $\boldsymbol{\mu}_i$ and the width σ_i. Thus, unlike a multilayer perception, only a few hidden layer neurons will be active for a given input.

Training RBF networks requires designing the hidden layer RBFs and calculating the hidden-to-output layer weights. To design the hidden RBF layer in a classification problem, we allocate each RBF neuron to represent a local region of space associated with one cluster of training samples (localized representation) (Haykin, 1994). We use a new supervised clustering algorithm to select the number of RBFs and the $\boldsymbol{\mu}_i$ and σ_i parameters in the hidden layer. Once clustering has determined the number of RBFs and the parameters for the hidden layer neurons, the hidden-to-output layer weights are determined by a pseudo inverse or singular value decomposition method. The least square solution for these weights satisfies

$$(A^{\mathrm{T}}A)\boldsymbol{\omega} = A^{\mathrm{T}}\mathbf{b}, \tag{2}$$

where N is the total number of training samples, A is a $N \times (M + 1)$ matrix with element A_{ij} representing the output of the j-th hidden neuron for the i-th input, $\mathbf{b}$ is the desired output vector, and $\boldsymbol{\omega}$ is the connection weight vector.

3. Designing RBFNN: supervised clustering and fisher discrimination function

In this section, a new strategy for training RBF networks is presented. A supervised clustering algorithm is used to cluster training samples, and the desired output vector is chosen such that linear discrimination analysis is realized between the hidden layer and the output layer. Furthermore, a validation set is used to design RBF networks such that the network is optimal in the sense of probability of errors.

3.1. Supervised clustering

In the case of classification, knowledge of the class membership of training samples is usually available. We use this information in a supervised clustering algorithm in which each cluster contains samples of the same class and in which clusters near decision boundaries do not have a small number of samples (Casasent & Chen, 2003). The supervised two-stage clustering algorithm follows.

We first specify two values, A and B, $A < B$. In stage one, we assign the first sample to cluster 1. For the next sample, we calculate its distance d to the closest cluster center of the correct class. We assign it to that cluster if $d \le A$. If $d \ge B$, we form a new cluster with the sample. If $A < d < B$, no cluster decision is made on the sample in stage one. The centers of all clusters are recalculated when new samples are added to a cluster. We continue until the number of clusters does not change. This first stage results in s clusters (and a number of unassigned samples with $A < d < B$). In the second stage, the unassigned samples are assigned to the closest correct class cluster; samples can and do move between clusters in stage two as the cluster centers change; but, the number of clusters remains at s; adjacent same-class clusters are not merged. The first stage determines s; the number of clusters is thus modest and each cluster is generally a good cluster; we select A to generally produce clusters with a reasonable number of samples per cluster. The choice of B determines the number of clusters, larger B values result in fewer clusters.

3.2. Fisher discrimination function

In classification problems, the task is to assign a class label ω_i ($i = 1, 2$ for two-class problem) to an input vector $\mathbf{x}$. Typically (Krzyzak et al., 1996; Musavi et al., 1992), the desired outputs in RBF networks have values in the range {0,1} or {−1,1}. When a squared-error cost function is used, the network outputs provide good posterior probability estimates of the class of the input, provided that the network is complex enough, the number of training samples are sufficient, and classes are sampled with the correct a priori probabilities in the training samples (Richard & Lippmann, 1991). Unfortunately, in practical problems, those assumptions are always violated, and thus the choice of desired outputs such as {0,1} or {−1,1} does not necessarily minimize the probability of error.

RBF NNs can be considered as two-step classifiers. The first step (from input to hidden layer) performs nonlinear feature mapping. The second step (from hidden to output layer) performs linear discrimination.

We assume a total of N training set samples with N_1 samples in class ω_1 and N_2 samples in classes ω_2, We now show that if we set the desired outputs to N/N_1 for class ω_1 and to $-N/N_2$ for class ω_2, then minimizing mean square error results in hidden-to-output layer weights that perform Fisher discriminant analysis. Therefore, the full RBFNN system performs a nonlinear Fisher discriminant analysis. Without loss in generality, we assume that the first N_1 samples belong to class ω_1, and the last N_2 samples belong to class ω_2. Thus, the matrix A in Eq. (2) is

$$A = \begin{bmatrix} 1 & \varphi_1^{\mathrm{T}} \\ \vdots & \vdots \\ 1 & \varphi_{N_1}^{\mathrm{T}} \\ 1 & \kappa_1^{\mathrm{T}} \\ \vdots & \vdots \\ 1 & \kappa_{N_2}^{\mathrm{T}} \end{bmatrix} \tag{3}$$

In Eq. (3), $\varphi_i^{\mathrm{T}} = [\varphi_i^{(1)}\varphi_i^{(2)}\ldots\varphi_i^{(M)}]$ is the output vector of the M hidden neurons for the i-th sample of class ω_1 and $\kappa_j^{\mathrm{T}} = [\kappa_j^{(1)}\kappa_j^{(2)}\ldots\kappa_j^{(M)}]$ is the output vector of the M hidden neurons for the j-th sample of class ω_2. Thus, each row of A is the vector of hidden neuron outputs for an input training sample. We define the sample mean of class ω_1 as

$$\bar{\varphi}^{\mathrm{T}} = \frac{1}{N_1}\sum_{i=1}^{N_1}\varphi_i^{\mathrm{T}}, \tag{4}$$

and similarly the sample mean of class ω_2 as

$$\bar{\kappa}^{T} = \frac{1}{N_2}\sum_{i=1}^{N_2}\kappa_i^{\mathrm{T}}, \tag{5}$$

The scatter matrix S_{w} is given by

$$S_{\mathrm{w}} = \sum_{i=1}^{N_1}(\varphi_i - \bar{\varphi})(\varphi_i - \bar{\varphi})^{\mathrm{T}} + \sum_{i=1}^{N_2}(\kappa_i - \bar{\kappa})(\kappa_i - \bar{\kappa})^{\mathrm{T}} \tag{6}$$

Eq. (6) can be rewritten as

$$S_{\mathrm{w}} = \sum_{i=1}^{N_1}\varphi_i\varphi_i^{\mathrm{T}} + \sum_{i=1}^{N_2}\kappa_i\kappa_i^{\mathrm{T}} - N_1\bar{\varphi}\bar{\varphi}^{\mathrm{T}} - N_2\bar{\kappa}\bar{\kappa}^{\mathrm{T}}. \tag{7}$$

From Eq. (4),

$$A^{\mathrm{T}}A = \begin{bmatrix} N & N_1\bar{\varphi}^{\mathrm{T}} + N_2\bar{\kappa}^{\mathrm{T}} \\ N_1\bar{\varphi}^{\mathrm{T}} + N_2\bar{\kappa}^{\mathrm{T}} & \sum_{i=1}^{N_1}\varphi_i\varphi_i^{\mathrm{T}} + \sum_{i=1}^{N_2}\kappa_i\kappa_i^{\mathrm{T}} \end{bmatrix}. \tag{8}$$

Using Eq. (7), we can rewrite Eq. (8) as

$$A^{\mathrm{T}}A = \begin{bmatrix} N & N_1\bar{\varphi}^{\mathrm{T}} + N_2\bar{\kappa}^{\mathrm{T}} \\ N_1\bar{\varphi}^{\mathrm{T}} + N_2\bar{\kappa}^{\mathrm{T}} & S_{\mathrm{w}} + N_1\bar{\varphi}\bar{\varphi}^{\mathrm{T}} + N_2\bar{\kappa}\bar{\kappa}^{\mathrm{T}} \end{bmatrix} \tag{9}$$

Our desired output vector is $\mathbf{b}^{\mathrm{T}} = [N/N_1\cdots N/N_1 - N/N_2\cdots - N/N_2]$ with N_1 elements having value N/N_1 and N_2 elements having value $-N/N_2$. From this, we have

$$A^{\mathrm{T}}\mathbf{b} = \begin{bmatrix} 0 \\ N(\bar{\varphi} - \bar{\kappa}) \end{bmatrix}. \tag{10}$$

Substituting Eqs. (9) and (10) into Eq. (2), and recalling that the vectors $(\bar{\varphi} - \bar{\kappa})(\bar{\varphi} - \bar{\kappa})^T\tilde{\omega}$ and $(\bar{\varphi} - \bar{\kappa})$ have the same direction for any $\tilde{\omega}$ where $\omega^T = [\omega_0\ \tilde{\omega}^T]$, we have the weight solution

$$\tilde{\omega} = kS_w^{-1}(\bar{\varphi} - \bar{\kappa}), \tag{11}$$

where k is a scalar. Obviously, this $\tilde{\omega}$ is the Fisher linear discriminant solution. Thus, with the mean squared error cost function and the given choices for the desired outputs, the second half of the RBF network (from hidden to output layer) performs Fisher linear discrimination. The inputs to this hidden-to-output layer are the features obtained by nonlinear mapping. Thus, the resultant RBF system performs nonlinear Fisher discriminant analysis.

3.3. Approximating Neyman–Pearson classification

There are many applications in which the probability of false alarm and the probability of a miss are not equally important. The N-P decision fixes one of the error types to be below a prespecified value while minimizing the other. Theoretically, the N-P decision strategy takes the form of comparing a likelihood ratio to a threshold. However, in many cases, we do not know the likelihood ratio. One way to implement N-P classification in neural networks is to vary the output neuron threshold (Bankman et al., 1992; Miao et al., 1998; Sum et al., 1999). As we will see, this is not an optimal choice. Here we briefly describe a new strategy to approximate N-P classification using RBF networks, refer to (Casasent & Chen, 2003) for full details.

Assume that our goal is to minimize the probability of error for class 1 while keeping the probability of error for class 2 below a constant; i.e. we want to correctly classify more samples in class 1, while keeping the number of misclassified samples in class 2 to not be too large. To achieve this, we redesign the hidden layer of the RBF NN. We first group training set samples into six categories (Casasent & Chen, 2003), which relate to the confidence with which we expect training set samples to be classified. Our supervised clustering algorithm is then separately applied to the samples in each of these categories. This determines the number of hidden layer neurons needed and the RBF parameters for each. Our new hidden layer neurons thus relate to clusters of data with expected performance. The hidden-to-output layer weights are then trained to implement Fisher linear discrimination. We can now adjust the parameters of individual RBF neurons and thus achieve better performance by varying local parameters (in our CC RBF NN, we vary the σ for the RBFs associated with certain clusters or categories). We show that this is better than varying a global parameter (such as the output neuron threshold). This local variation is applicable to the CC RBF NN, since its hidden layer neurons are associated with clusters of data for which samples there is knowledge of their classification confidence. If we change the parameters for one category of RBF neurons, this predominantly affects decisions on only one category of data. This is preferable to varying the output neuron threshold; which uniformly affects all RBFs, since this changes the decision surfaces for all data in all neuron clusters.

4. Experimental results on synthetic data

In this section, we compare the performance of our new training method with that of the traditional method using the k-means clustering algorithm. For the traditional method, the desired outputs are {0,1}. For our proposed training method, the desired outputs are $\{N/N_1, -N/N_2\}$ as discussed in Section 3. In both cases, we use a validation set database to select parameters; i.e. we chose k in k-means and A (and B) in our new clustering method (we set $B = 1.5A$) such that the chosen parameters in both cases gave the minimum probability of error. We generate a training set, a test set, and a validation set, each consisting of 400 samples for class 1 and 150 samples for class 2. The data is synthetic with two features. The distributions of the samples are normal for both classes. Class 1 has a mean vector $[2\ 3]^T$, a standard deviation vector $[0.5\ 0.5]^T$, and a correlation coefficient of 0.75, and class 2 has a mean vector $[2.4\ 2.5]^T$, a standard deviation vector $[0.45\ 0.6]^T$, and a correlation coefficient of 0.80. We find the optimal choices are $k = 20$ and $A = 0.9$, which gave the minimum probability of error for the validation database.

Fig. 2 shows the probability of error for test data as the number of hidden layer neurons is varied in the two methods. For the traditional method, we vary k in k-means to increase the number of RBFs; for our new method, we vary the parameter A. The data show that our method reduces the probability of error, especially when the number of hidden neurons is small. For example, when there are two hidden neurons, our proposed method gives a probability of error that is over 14% less than that of the traditional method. This occurs since our method selects better clusters and because it allows us local control of selected decision

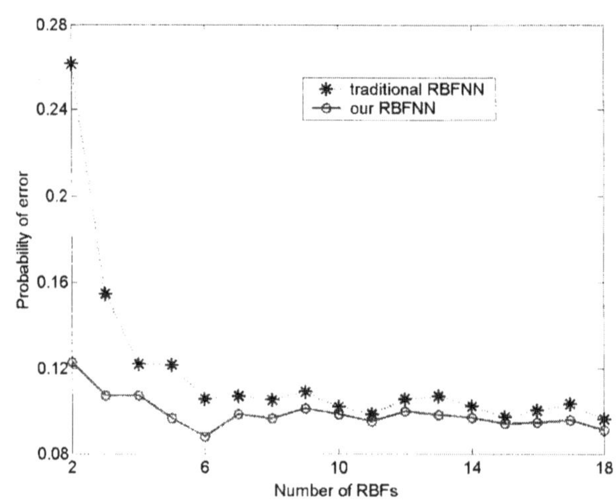

Fig. 2. Probability of error of test data versus number of hidden neurons.

Table 1
Probability of error for different classifiers

Classifier	1-NN	RBFNN	Our RBF	Bayes
Training (%)	12.9	9.5	8.2	7.3
Test (%)	12.5	10.6	8.8	7.6

boundaries. Table 1 lists the corresponding training and test results. We list the results from a Bayes classifier (a quadratic classifier for the known pdf distributions) and from a one nearest neighbor classifier (1-NN). As we see, 1-NN yields the worst probability of error, and Bayes gives the best probability of error of 7.6% on test data (since here the pdfs are known). Our RBF gives a better probability of error by about 2% compared to the traditional RBFNN method. This is a significant improvement, considering the fact that the results from our proposed method (8.8%) are close to the optimum results from a Bayes classifier (7.6%).

We next compare our method with the standard threshold changing method. For the threshold changing method, we first train the system using k-means clusters and then change the threshold of the system outputs to approximate N-P classification. For our method, we select RBF clusters as described in Section 3 and then change the widths of the Gaussian RBFs for the hidden neurons corresponding to clusters formed by samples of class 1 near a decision boundary. We also implemented the N-P method, which should theoretically yield the best results, by computing the likelihood ratio and comparing it to a threshold. Table 2 shows the test results for the three methods with the probability of a miss (probability of error of class 1) equal to 5%. It can be seen that the lowest probability of false alarm (probability of error of class 2) is 22.7%. Using our proposed method, the probability of false alarm is 25.3%, which is close to the lowest one. When using the threshold changing method, the probability of false alarm is about 7% larger than that of our proposed method. In Fig. 3, we plot the receiver operating curve (ROC) for the three methods, where the x axis represents the probability of false alarm for class 2 and the y axis denotes the probability of detection of class 1. In our method, the width of the Gaussian is varied to produce ROC data; in the traditional method, the output neuron threshold is varied. As seen, our method performs better than the standard threshold changing method.

In practice, the pdfs of the data are not known and thus, the Bayes method in Table 1 and the N-P method in Table 2

Table 2
Classification of class 2 test data with the probability of error for class 1 equal to 5%

Methods	Vary T	Vary σ	N-P
Probability of error (class 2) (%)	32	25.3	22.7

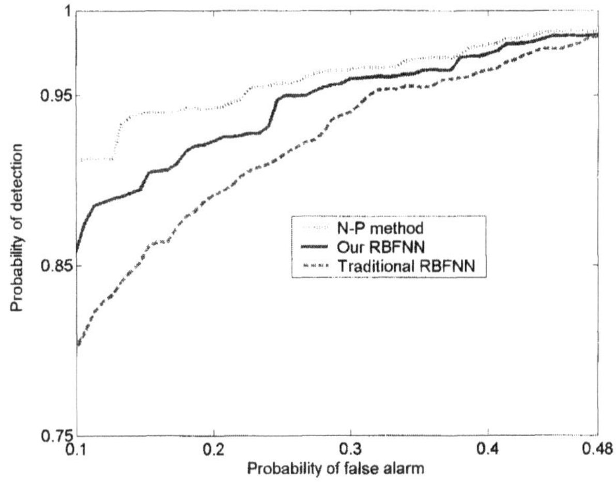

Fig. 3. ROC curves for different classifiers.

and Fig. 3 cannot be employed. For our present synthetic data, the pdfs are known and thus the Bayes and N-P benchmark results are available.

5. A practical problem: agricultural product inspection

We now discuss a practical application of such RBF networks for an N-P classification problem: agriculture product inspection. After initial inspection, pistachio nuts typically contain 3% insect or feeding damage, while USDA standards require about 1% of such damage (Casasent, Talukder, & Lee, 1997). A 66% reduction in damage (from 3 to 1% of the crop), while restricting rejection of good nuts to a commercially acceptable 2% or less, is desirable for quality and aflatoxin reduction. Thus, this is a problem in which we need to select a preferable operating point. Achieving the best overall classification rate is not what is desired. Rather, we want to fix the probability of a miss (good nuts classified as bad nuts) to be 2%, while minimizing the probability of a false alarm (bad nuts classified as good nuts).

The database we consider consists of a training set of 942 nuts (600 good and 342 bad) and a test set of 942 nuts (600 good and 342 bad). Fig. 4a and b shows the images of good nuts and Fig. 4c and d shows the images of bad nuts. The features considered are the mean, variance, skewness, and kurtosis (histogram features) of four different images of each nut (raw, edge, curvature of raw, and curvature of edge images). Therefore, for each nut sample we have 16 features.

For the traditional method, we use k-means to train the RBF network and vary the output threshold to approximate N-P classification. For our new proposed method, we use the procedures described in Section 3. To select parameters such as A, we use a cross validation technique; we divide the training data into six groups, one of them is used to validate and the other five groups are used to train

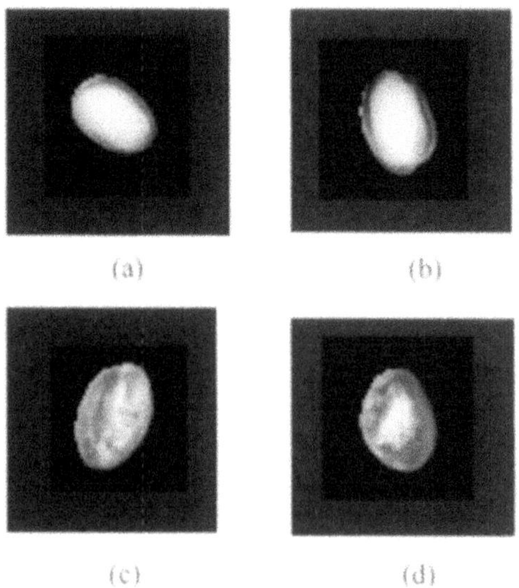

Fig. 4. Images of pistachio nuts, (a) and (b) good nuts, (c) and (d) bad nuts.

the system. This division of the data set is repeated six times and then we present the average probability of error for all six tests. Our results show that for the probability of a miss to be 2%, the probability of a false alarm is 30% for our proposed method and 40% for the traditional method. This result is promising, since the proposed method can reduce bad nuts in the crop from 3 to 1%, which achieves the USDA's goal, while the results using the traditional method do not satisfy the goal. Fig. 5 shows the ROC curve. It is obvious that our new proposed method performs better than the threshold changing method, especially when the probability of detection is in the desired high range of 98–99% (this is the desired probability for the identification of good nuts) and when the probability of a false alarm (a bad nut not detected) is in the desired low 30% range.

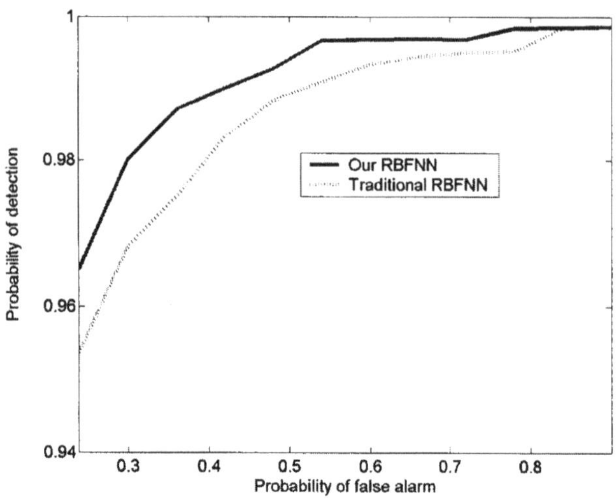

Fig. 5. ROC curves for the traditional method and our new proposed method.

6. Conclusions

In this paper, we advanced new methods for training RBF networks. We derived a new strategy to implement nonlinear Fisher discriminant analysis using an RBF NN by choosing the desired network outputs. This training method, together with the selection of categories of samples based on the confidence of their correct classification, the use of a supervised clustering algorithm, and use of a locally varying parameter (σ_i) to produce N-P classification, resulted in a new RBF NN system for the selection of preferable operating points. It is expected that outliers will form a cluster with a small number of samples (the outliers), which will be discarded in our supervised clustering algorithm. All experimental results on both synthetic data and on an agricultural product inspection problem are promising and merit further attention and tests on other product inspection databases and in other applications.

References

Bankman, I., Sigillito, V., Wise, R., & Smith, P. (1992). Feature based detection of the K-complex wave in the human electroencephalogram using neural networks. *IEEE Transactions on Biomedical Engineering*, *39*(12), 1305–1310.

Billings, S., & Zheng, G. (1995). Radial basis function network configuration using genetic algorithms. *Neural Networks*, *8*, 877–890.

Bishop, M. (1995). *Neural networks for pattern recognition*. Oxford: Clarendon Press.

Bruzzone, L., & Prieto, D. (1998). Supervised training techniques for radial basis function neural networks. *Electronic Letters*, *34*(11), 1115–1116.

Casasent, D., & Chen, X.-W. (2003). New training strategies for RBF neural networks for X-ray agricultural product inspection. *Pattern Recognition*, *36*, 535–547.

Casasent, D., Talukder, A., & Lee, H. (1997). X-ray agricultural product inspection: segmentation and classification. *Proceedings of SPIE*, *3205*, 46–55.

Chen, S., Cowan, C., & Grant, P. (1991). Orthogonal least squares learning algorithm for radial basis function networks. *IEEE Transactions on Neural Networks*, *2*, 302–309.

Chen, S., Mulgrew, B., & Grant, P. (1993). A clustering technique for digital communications channel equalization using radial basis function networks. *IEEE Transactions on Neural Networks*, *4*, 570–579.

Fukunaga, K. (1990). *Introduction to statistical pattern recognition*. New York: Academic Press.

Haykin, S. (1994). *Neural networks. A comprehensive foundation*. New York: Macmillan.

Krzyzak, A., Linder, T., & Lugosi, G. (1996). Nonparametric estimation and classification using radial basis function nets and empirical risk minimization. *IEEE Transactions on Neural Networks*, *7*, 475–487.

Miao, X., Azimi-Sadjadi, M., Tian, B., Dubey, A., & Witherspoon, N. (1998). Detection of mines and minelike targets using principal component and neural-network methods. *IEEE Transactions on Neural Networks*, *9*(3), 454–463.

Moody, J., & Darken, J. (1989). Fast learning in networks of locally-tuned processing units. *Neural Computation*, *1*, 281–294.

Musavi, M. T., Ahmed, W., Chan, K. H., Faris, K. B., & Hummels, D. M. (1992). On the training of radial basis function classifiers. *Neural Networks*, *5*, 595–603.

Neyman, J., & Pearson, E. (1933). On the problem of the most efficient tests of statistical hypothesis. *Philosophical Transactions of the Royal Society A*, *231*, 289–337.

Poggio, T., & Girosi, F. (1990). Network for approximation and learning. *Proceedings of the IEEE*, *78*, 1481–1497.

Richard, M. D., & Lippmann, R. P. (1991). Neural network classifiers estimate Bayesian a posteriori probabilities. *Neural Computation*, *3*, 461–483.

Sum, J., Leung, C., Young, G., Chan, L., & Kan, W. (1999). An adaptive Bayesian pruning for neural networks in a non-stationary environment. *Neural Computation*, *11*(4), 965–976.

Vogt, M. (1993). Combination of radial basis function neural networks with optimized learning vector quantization. *Proceedings of the IEEE, ICNN 3*, 1841–1846.

PERGAMON

AVAILABLE AT
www.ComputerScienceWeb.com
POWERED BY SCIENCE DIRECT

Neural Networks 16 (2003) 537–545

Neural Networks

www.elsevier.com/locate/neunet

2003 Special issue

Intrinsic generalization analysis of low dimensional representations

Xiuwen Liu[a,*], Anuj Srivastava[b], DeLiang Wang[c]

[a]Department of Computer Science, Florida State University, Palmetto St. LOVE Building Rm 250, Tallahassee, FL 32306-4530, USA
[b]Department of Statistics, Florida State University, Tallahassee, FL 32306-4330, USA
[c]Department of Computer and Information Science and Center for Cognitive Science, The Ohio State University, Columbus, OH 43210, USA

Abstract

Low dimensional representations of images impose equivalence relations in the image space; the induced equivalence class of an image is named as its intrinsic generalization. The intrinsic generalization of a representation provides a novel way to measure its generalization and leads to more fundamental insights than the commonly used recognition performance, which is heavily influenced by the choice of training and test data. We demonstrate the limitations of linear subspace representations by sampling their intrinsic generalization, and propose a nonlinear representation that overcomes these limitations. The proposed representation projects images nonlinearly into the marginal densities of their filter responses, followed by linear projections of the marginals. We use experiments on large datasets to show that the representations that have better intrinsic generalization also lead to better recognition performance.

Keywords: Generalisation; Intrinsic generalisation; Spectral histogram; Linear representations

1. Introduction

In recent years, appearance-based methods have become a common choice for building recognition systems based on images. The main motivation is that variations in images of objects can be captured through (a large number of) training images, which avoids the necessity of building complex probability models. Due to the high dimensionality of images, low dimensional representations become necessary in order to develop computationally efficient systems. For example, principal component analysis (PCA) (Hotelling, 1933), also known as Karhunen and Loève transformation (Karhunen, 1947; Loève, 1955), has become a widely used tool for dimension reduction. One of the major limitations of PCA representation is that it is not able to capture statistics higher than the second order. Independent component analysis (ICA) (Comon, 1994[1] see Hyvärinen, Karhunen, & Oja, 2001 for a review) has been used to overcome this limitation by imposing statistical independence among the linear coefficients. By maximizing a discrimination measure among different classes, Fisher discriminant analysis (FDA) offers another popular linear sub-space representation (Fisher, 1936). In computer vision, these representations have been applied to face recognition (Belhumeur, Hepanha, & Kriegman, 1997; Turk & Pentland, 1991; Sirovich & Kirby, 1987).

As the recognition performance of a classifier depends heavily on the choice of training data, it becomes important to study the generalization of a low dimensional representation through the equivalence relation it imposes on the image space. The importance of studying the equivalence classes for generalization is greatly emphasized by Vapnik (2000). In fact, Vapnik named the cardinality of equivalence classes a new concept (to be studied) for learning from small samples (Vapnik, 2000, p. 296). While the cardinality of equivalence classes is important for reducing dimensionality, for recognition performance, it is also important to study the properties of images in a particular equivalence class. Ideally, only images with similar underlying models should be grouped into an equivalence class. We will name this semantics-related aspect of generalization as intrinsic generalization. This isolates an intrinsic aspect of a representation that affects the recognition performance. Our study of intrinsic generalization for linear subspaces of images reveals that these representations group images from different models within the same equivalent class and are inherently sensitive to noise and deformations. By analyzing two problems with linear subspace representations, we propose a way to improve their intrinsic generalization,

* Corresponding author. Tel.: +1-850-644-0050; fax: +1-850-644-0058.
E-mail addresses: liux@cs.fsu.edu (X. Liu), anuj@stat.fsu.edu (A. Srivastava), dwang@cis.ohio-state.edu (D.L. Wang).

[1] As pointed out by Simoncelli and Olshausen (2001), ICA is a misnomer as estimated independent components are not guaranteed to be independent.

0893-6080/03/$ - see front matter
doi:10.1016/S0893-6080(03)00089-3

the advantage of which is demonstrated by recognition results. We emphasize that our goal is to characterize an important aspect of a representation through the study of intrinsic generalization, which leads to an important measure to compare different representations.

This paper is organized as follows. Section 2 gives a definition of generalization and then introduces intrinsic generalization and shows that of linear subspaces. Section 3 briefly describes the spectral histogram representation of images, and spectral histogram subspace analysis (SHSA), and shows the intrinsic generalization of SHSA through object synthesis. Section 4 shows the experimental results on recognition of large datasets. Section 5 concludes the paper with a discussion on a number of related issues.

2. Intrinsic generalization

In this paper, an image $\mathbf{I}$ is defined on a finite lattice $\mathcal{L} \subset \mathbf{Z}$,[2] the intensity at pixel location $\vec{v} \in \mathcal{L}$ is denoted by $\mathbf{I}(\vec{v}) \in \mathcal{G} = [r_1, r_2]$, where r_1, r_2 bound the dynamic range of the imaging sensor, and Ω the set of all images on $\mathcal{L}$. A representation is a mapping defined as $f : \Omega \rightarrow R^K$. For a low dimensional representation, we require $K \ll |\mathcal{L}|$. Before we introduce the notion of intrinsic generalization, we first give a formal definition of generalization of representations.

2.1. Generalization of low dimensional representations

In learning-based recognition of objects from images, a classifier/recognizer is often trained using some training data and is applied to classify/recognize future inputs in the form of test data. A key issue is to extend good performance on test inputs using information limited to the training set; it is commonly known as the generalization problem (Bishop, 1995).

There are several ways of formulating the generalization problem and we have chosen the framework laid out by Bishop (1995). Let the observed images be generated from an unknown probability density P on Ω and the underlying true recognition function be denoted by $h : \Omega \mapsto \mathcal{A}$, where $\mathcal{A}$ is the set of all classes. For any classifier function g, its average generalization ability is defined as the probability that $g(\mathbf{I}) = h(\mathbf{I})$, i.e.

$$G(g) = Pr\{\mathbf{I} | \mathbf{I} \in \Omega, g(\mathbf{I}) = h(\mathbf{I})\}. \quad (1)$$

According to Eq. (1), obtaining good generalization becomes an optimization over all the possible classifier functions. In practice, since the underlying model $P(\mathbf{I})$ and $h(\mathbf{I})$ are generally unknown, several ways have been proposed. One way is to estimate $G(g)$ directly through a set separate from the training one with known class labels such as cross-validation (Bishop, 1995). Another way is to impose additional constraints on $G(g)$ based on some generic heuristics such as Akaike in-formation criterion (Akaike, 1973) and minimum description length (Rissanen, 1978), where a model with more free parameters is penalized. Yet another approach is to optimize an analytical bound based on statistical analysis such as the worst-case performance of all the implementable classifiers of a neural network architecture (Baum & Haussler, 1989). Note that all the existing efforts on generalization have been focused on the generalization of classifiers.

Because of the high dimensionality of images, dimension reduction becomes necessary for computational reasons. In case of using a low dimensional representation f, the average generalization ability then becomes the probability that $\hat{g}(f(\mathbf{I})) = h(\mathbf{I})$ for an input $\mathbf{I}$ randomly sampled according to $P(\mathbf{I})$, where $\hat{g}$ is a classifier based on a low dimensional representation f. In other words, we have

$$\begin{aligned} G(\hat{g},f) &= Pr\{\mathbf{I} | \mathbf{I} \in \Omega, g(f(\mathbf{I})) = h(\mathbf{I})\} \\ &= \sum_{f(\mathbf{I})} Pr\{\mathbf{J} | \mathbf{J} \in \Omega, f(\mathbf{J}) = f(\mathbf{I}) 1\}_{\hat{g}(f(\mathbf{I}))=h(\mathbf{I})}, \end{aligned} \quad (2)$$

where $1_{x=y}$ is an indicator function, and we use $f(\mathbf{I})$ as the range of f on Ω. From Eq. (2), it is clear that f has a significant effect on the generalization of $\hat{g}$. Ideally, we want to group all the images from each class as a single equivalence class (in this case, the classifier is trivial). While this is generally not possible for real applications, we want to group images from each class into a small number of equivalence classes, with each class having a large cardinality, as emphasized by Vapnik (2000). This also reduces the number of necessary training images. However, when making each equivalence class as large as possible, we do not want to include images from other classes, as this will make a good classification performance impossible. This leads to the need of analyzing equivalence class structures of low dimensional representations to achieve a good generalization performance.

2.2. Intrinsic generalization

The previous analysis shows that the equivalence class structures of low dimensional representations are essential for a good generalization performance. In this paper, we focus on studying the images of a particular equivalence class through statistical sampling.

Definition 1. Given a representation f, the intrinsic generalization of an image $\mathbf{I}$ under f is defined as

$$S_f(\mathbf{I}) = \{\mathbf{J} | \mathbf{J} \in \Omega, f(\mathbf{J}) = f(\mathbf{I})\} \subset \Omega. \quad (3)$$

In other words, intrinsic generalization of image $\mathbf{I}$ includes all the images that cannot be distinguished from $\mathbf{I}$ under representation f. The recognition performance based on f depends critically on the intrinsic generalizations of training

[2] http://www.uk.research.att.com/facedatabase.html

images as the images in their intrinsic generalizations are implicitly included in the training set. We define $S_I^0(\mathbf{I})$ as the images sharing the same underlying probability models with $\mathbf{I}$. Ideally, $S_I(\mathbf{I})$ should be as close as possible to $S_I^0(\mathbf{I})$. As $S_I^0(\mathbf{I})$ is generally not available, to explore $S_I(\mathbf{I})$, we employ statistical sampling through the following probability model

$$q(\mathbf{J}, T) = \frac{1}{Z(T)} \exp\{ - D(f(\mathbf{J}), f(\mathbf{I}))/T\}. \quad (4)$$

Here T is a temperature parameter, $D(\cdot,\cdot)$ a Euclidean or other distance measure, and $Z(T)$ is a normalizing function, given as $Z(T) = \sum_{\mathbf{J} \in \Omega} \exp\{ - D(f(\mathbf{J}), f(\mathbf{I}))/T\}$. This model has been used for texture synthesis (Zhu, Liu, & Wu, 2000) and we generalize it to any representation. It is easy to see that as $T \rightarrow 0$, $q(\mathbf{J}, T)$ defines a uniform distribution on $S_I(\mathbf{I})$ (Zhu et al., 2000). The advantage of using a sampler is to be able to generate typical images in $S_I(\mathbf{I})$ so that $S_I(\mathbf{I})$ under f can be examined in a statistical sense.

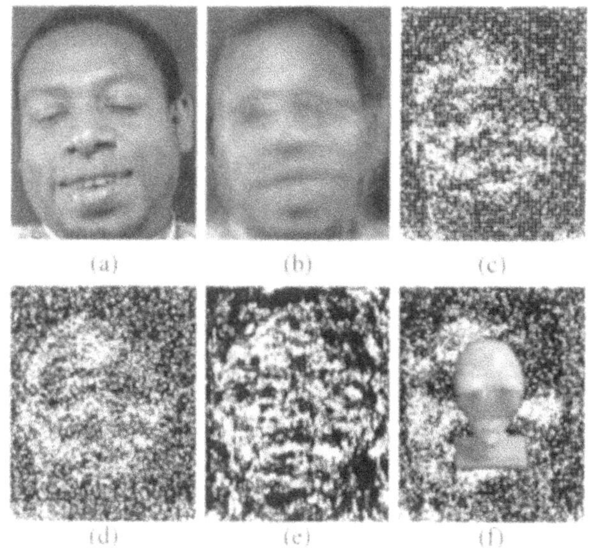

Fig. 1. (a) A face image. (b) Reconstructed image using $K = 50$ principal components. (c)–(f) Four random samples from the set $S_I(\mathbf{I})$, with $\pi(\mathbf{I})$ identical to the one shown in (b).

2.3. Intrinsic generalization of linear subspaces

Linear subspace representations of images, including PCA, ICA, and FDA, assume that f is a linear map, and $S_I(\mathbf{I})$ forms a linear subspace. While these methods are successful when applied to images belonging to a specific nature, e.g. face images, their generalization seems poor if we consider $S_I(\mathbf{I})$ under these linear subspace methods in Ω.

If $S_I^0(\mathbf{I})$ is available then one can analyze the overlap between the sets $S_I^0(\mathbf{I})$ and $S_I(\mathbf{I})$. If not, then one has to resort to some indirect techniques such a random sampling to compare elements of the two sets. Random sampling seems sufficient in that the typical images in $S_I(\mathbf{I})$ are very different from $\mathbf{I}$. To illustrate these ideas, we have used PCA of the ORL face dataset[2], which consists of 40 subjects with 10 images each; we have obtained similar results using other linear subspaces. We calculate the eigen faces corresponding to the 50 largest eigen-values. Under PCA, given an image $\mathbf{I}$, $f(\mathbf{I})$ is the projection of $\mathbf{I}$ along eigen faces. We define the reconstructed image[3] of $\mathbf{I}$ as $\pi(\mathbf{I}) = \sum_{i=1}^{K} < \mathbf{I}, \mathbf{V}_i > \mathbf{V}_i$, where $\mathbf{V}_i$ is the ith eigen face and $\langle\cdot,\cdot\rangle$ is the canonical inner product. Fig. 1(a) shows a face image in the dataset and Fig. 1(b) shows the reconstructed image with $K = 50$. We then use a Gibbs sampler to generate samples of $S_I(\mathbf{I})$ by sampling from $q(\mathbf{J}, \mathrm{T})$ given by Eq. (4). Fig. 1(c)–(f) show four samples of $S_I(\mathbf{I})$ (For Fig. 1(f), the object in the middle is used as boundary condition, i.e. pixels on the object are not updated). In other words, all these images have the same 50 eigen decompositions. Note that $S_I(\mathbf{I})$ is defined on Ω and these images are far from each other in Ω. As expected, the corresponding reconstructed images are identical to Fig. 1(b).

Because $S_I(\mathbf{I})$ consists of images from various underlying probability models, the linear subspace representations can make the subsequent classification intrinsically sensitive to noise and other deformations. To show that, Fig. 2(a) gives three different face images which share exactly the same eigen representation (bottom row). On the other hand, Fig. 2(b) shows three similar images whose eigen representations correspond to three different faces.

We emphasize here that the sampling is very different from reconstruction. The sampling is to draw a typical sample from the set of all the images with a particular low dimensional representation while reconstruction gives one in the set whose coefficients are zero along the dimensions complement to the given subspace. To illustrate this, Fig. 3 shows an example of a one-dimensional subspace in a two-dimensional space. In this case, the reconstructed 'image' of 'x' is the point given by ' + ' in Fig. 3(a) while the sampling can return any point with equal probability along the solid line shown in Fig. 3(b). This shows clearly that the reconstructed image may not provide much information about all the other images having the same low dimensional representation. This has an important implication for building low dimensional generative models. For recognition purpose, it is not sufficient to show that the synthesized image based on a generative model has certain desirable properties as in PCA; to be a good model, all the images in the intrinsic generalization should also exhibit the desirable properties. As generative models become popular in modeling, their intrinsic generalizations should also be studied and analyzed.

These results, while generated using PCA, are valid for an arbitrary linear subspace since the sampling tries to match the representation. The main problems of linear subspace representations, as revealed here, are that these

[3] We assume the mean is taken care of properly.

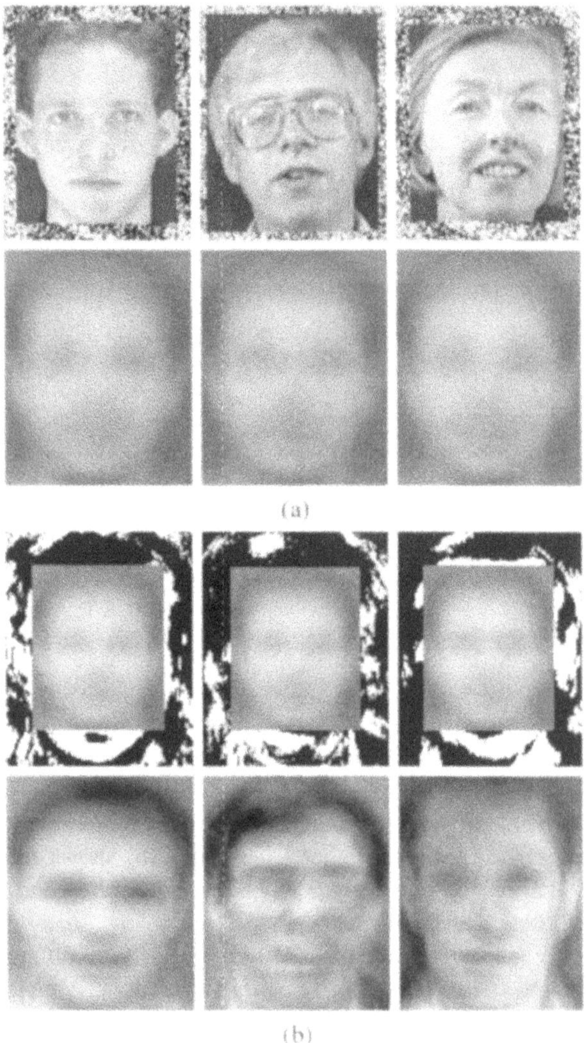

Fig. 2. Examples of different images with identical eigen decompositions and similar images with different eigen decompositions. The top row shows the images and the bottom reconstructed. (a) Three different images with the same eigen representations; (b) three similar images with different eigen representations.

representations cannot account for the fact that most images in the image space are white noise images. Additionally, they cannot incorporate important spatial constraints in images.

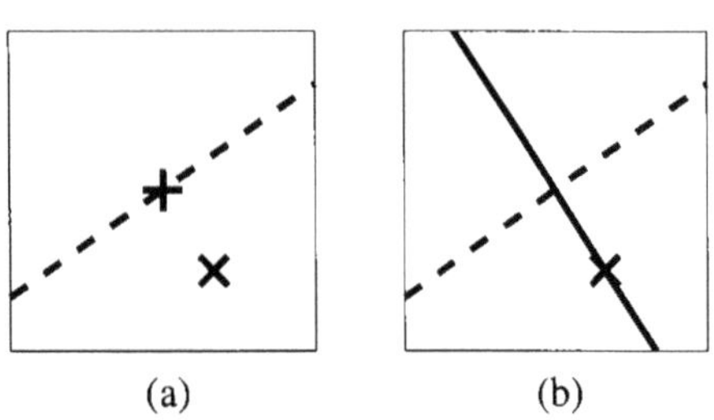

Fig. 3. An illustration example of the difference between sampling and reconstruction. Here the dashed line represents a one-dimensional subspace in a two-dimensional space. For a training example (marked as 'x'), the sampling is to draw a random point along the solid line in (b) while the reconstructed image is a single point given by ' + ' in (a).

3. Spectral histogram subspace analysis

3.1. Spectral histogram representation of images

As discussed earlier, an ideal representation f for $\mathbf{I}$ will be such that $S_I(\mathbf{I}) = S_I^0(\mathbf{I})$. There are two important limitations of the linear methods that need to be addressed: (i) As the vast majority images in Ω are white noise images, a good approximation of $S_I^0(\mathbf{I})$ for an image of object(s) must handle white noise images effectively; otherwise, $S_I(\mathbf{I})$ will concentrate on white noise images. Experiments show that linear representations suffer from this problem. (ii) Another issue is the linear superposition assumption, where each basis contributes linearly independently to the image. In contrast, pixels on objects are dependent and efficient models should exploit this dependency.

The issue of white noise images can be dealt with effectively through the method of types (Csiszar & Korner, 1981) as the white noise images are grouped together under types. However, the direct use of types does not provide enough constraints as only the histogram of images is used. We generalize the type definition by including marginals of filter responses (of the input image) with respect to a set of filters, which also incorporates local pixel dependence through filtering.

The representation of using marginals of filtered images can be justified in many ways: (i) by assuming that *small disjoint regions in the frequency domain are statistically independent*. That is, partition the frequency domain into small disjoint regions and model each region by its marginal distribution. The partitioning of the frequency also leads to spatial filters. (ii) Wavelet decompositions of images are local in both space and frequency, and hence, provide attractive representations for objects in the images. We convolve an image with the filters and compute the histograms of the resulting images. Each image is then represented by a vector consisting of all the marginal distributions. We shall call this representation *spectral histogram representation* (Liu & Wang, 2002), each of these vectors a *spectral histogram*, and the set of all valid vectors the *spectral histogram space*. Elements of a spectral histogram relate to the image pixels in a nonlinear fashion, and hence, avoid the linearity issue mentioned earlier.

This representation has also been suggested through psychophysical studies on texture modeling (Chubb, Econopouly, & Landy, 1994), and has been used in texture modeling and synthesis (Heeger & Bergen, 1995; Liu & Wang, 2002; Zhu, Wu, & Mumford, 1997), texture classification (Liu & Wang, 2003), and face recognition (Liu & Cheng, 2003). Both the histogram of input images (Swain & Ballard, 1991) and joint histograms of local fields (Schiele & Crowley, 2000) have been used for object recognition.

3.2. Spectral histogram subspace analysis

In this method, the strategy is to first represent each image in the spectral histogram space and then apply a linear subspace method, such as PCA, ICA or FDA, in the spectral histogram space[4]. Name these corresponding methods as SHPCA, SHICA, and SHFDA, and call them collectively as SHSA.

To demonstrate the effectiveness of SHSA representations, we explore their intrinsic generalization through sampling. As in the linear subspace case, we use SHPCA for experiments; similar results have been obtained using other linear spectral histogram subspaces.

First, bases in the spectral histogram space are computed based on training images. Given an image, its spectral histogram representation is computed and then projected onto a spectral histogram subspace. We use a Gibbs sampling procedure to generate images that share the same spectral histogram representation. Fig. 4 shows two sets of examples; Fig. 4(a) shows three texture images and Fig. 4(b) shows three objects. These examples show that the spectral histogram subspace representation captures photometric features as well as topological structures, which are important to characterize and recognize images.

4. Experimental results for recognition

To demonstrate the effectiveness of SHSA representations, we use several data sets and compare their performance with that of linear subspace representations. In our experiments, the number of principal components is determined by thresholding the ratio of a component's eigen-value and the largest eigen-value. (If the same threshold is applied to PCA, it tends to keep more components, as the dimension of the input space here is much larger). We have used the same number of components for ICA, FDA, SHICA, and SHFDA as PCA and SHPCA, respectively. Here ICA is calculated using the FastICA algorithm (Hyvärinen, 1999) and FDA based on an algorithm by Belhumeur et al. (1997). We use the nearest neighbor classifier for recognition. To calculate the spectral histogram, we use a fixed set of 21 filters. These filters were chosen automatically from a larger set of Gabor and Laplacian of Gaussian filters using a filter selection algorithm (Liu & Wang, 2001) for the ORL face dataset.

A classifier's performance in a low dimensional space depends on intrinsic generalization of the representation to the test data. The result for a new image of a classifier is determined by the decision region partitions in the feature space and thus in the image space. Given a training set B, we

[4] Note a reconstructed spectral histogram may be outside the spectral histogram space and here we ignore this complication.

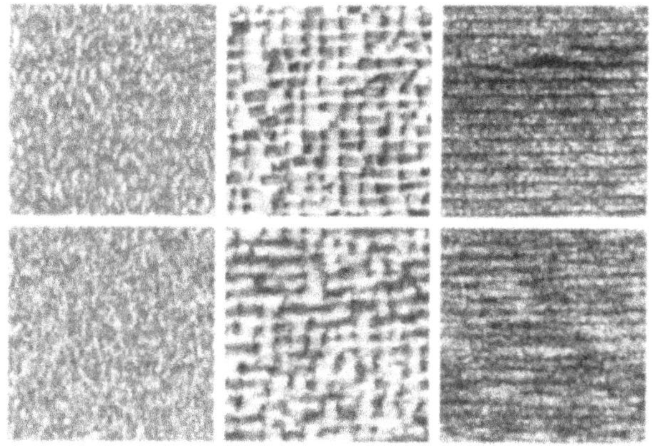

(a)

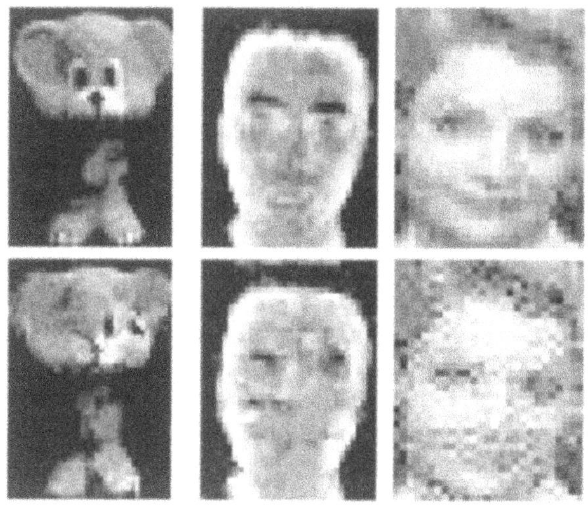

(b)

Fig. 4. Samples from SHPCA intrinsic generalization. In each panel the top row shows the input image and the bottom a typical sample from its intrinsic generalization. (a) Three textures. (b) One object and one face image. Boundary conditions need to be taken with care when sampling from $S_I(\mathbf{I})$.

define the extrinsic generalization set of $\mathbf{I} \in B$ as

$$S_E(\mathbf{I}) = \{\mathbf{J} | \mathbf{J} \in \Omega, L(\mathbf{J}|B) = L(\mathbf{I})\} \backslash \{\mathbf{J} | \mathbf{J} \in \Omega, L(\mathbf{J}|B \backslash \mathbf{I}) = L(\mathbf{I})\}. \quad (5)$$

Here $L(\mathbf{I})$ is the label of $\mathbf{I}$ and $L(\mathbf{J}|B)$ is the label of image $\mathbf{J}$ assigned by the classifier trained on the set B. To separate the effectiveness of a representation from that of the choice of training and test data, we have also used (uniformly) randomly generated bases, which we call random component analysis (RCA) and spectral histogram random component analysis (SHRCA).

First we use the Columbia Object Image Library (COIL-100)[5] dataset, which consists of images of 100 3-D objects with varying pose, texture, shape and size, 21 of which are shown Fig. 5. Pontil and Verri (1998) applied Support Vector Machines method (SVM) to 3D object

[5] Available at http://www.cs.columbia.edu/CAVE

Fig. 5. Twenty one selected objects from the 100 objects in the database.

Table 2
Recognition results for the coil-100 dataset with respect to translation

Methods	Horizontal/vertical translation (%)				
	0/0	2/0	0/2	2/2	4/4
PCA	93.3	81.7	46.4	32.3	4.9
ICA	93.2	81.9	46.8	32.3	5.1
SHPCA	94.7	94.7	94.7	94.7	94.7
SHICA	94.6	94.6	94.6	94.6	94.6

recognition. Yang, Roth, and Ahuja (2000) proposed a learning algorithm, named Sparse Network of Winnows (SNoW) for appearance based recognition and applied their learning algorithm to the full COIL dataset and compared with SVM methods. They tested their method by varying the number of training views. For a fair comparison with the results in Yang et al. (2000), these color images were converted to gray level images and downsampled to size 32×32, which are used in all the experiments described here.

As in Yang et al. (2000), we vary the number of training views per object. Table 1 shows the recognition rates on the dataset using PCA, ICA, FDA, SNoW (Yang et al., 2000) and Linear SVM (Yang et al., 2000) as well as SHSA methods. While the COIL-100 dataset is considered to be easy with enough training data, Table 1 reveals clearly the generalization capability of different representations. Under all the conditions, SHSA methods outperform the other methods. Among the SHSA methods, SHFDA gives the best performance. However, FDA in the image space does not outperform other linear methods; this is because these images are not linearly separable in the image space and linear FDA bases are not effective. This result is consistent with that of Martinez and Kak (2001), which showed that FDA may not outperform PCA in general. Another interesting point of Table 1 is that RCA and SHRCA give comparable results to those of other bases, suggesting that the choice of commonly used different bases within a space may not be that critical for recognition as none of them is considerably better than a random one in term of recognition performance.

While SHSA representations are translation invariant by definition, the linear subspaces of images are not as translation will change the random variables associated with pixels in the images. Theoretically speaking, SHSA representations are not rotation invariant in general as filters are orientation sensitive. It has been shown that Gabor filters can tolerate a certain amount of rotation (Lades et al., 1993). Tables 2 and 3 show the recognition results using PCA, ICA, SHPCA, and SHICA representations with respect to 2-D translations and rotations; similar results have been obtained using other linear subspaces. Here 12 views were used for training and the remaining 60 views were used for testing for each object and borders with background color were added to images so that translations and rotations can be done without clipping the objects. As Table 2 shows, PCA and ICA are very sensitive to translation. While neither PCA, ICA, SHPCA, or SHICA is rotation invariant, SHPCA and SHICA are less sensitive to rotation as shown in Table 3. In addition, for SHPCA and SHICA the correct recognition rate to the closest three does not decrease much, suggesting that SHPCA and SHICA can be used as an effective means to propose candidates for more accurate models.

Eigen faces have been used widely for face recognition applications (Kirby & Sirovich, 1990; Sirovich & Kirby,

Table 1
Recognition results for the coil-100 dataset

Methods	Training/test per object (%)			
	36/36	18/54	8/64	4/68
PCA	98.6	96.7	87.2	75.8
ICA	98.6	96.5	87.9	76.0
RCA	98.6	96.3	87.0	75.4
FDA	97.6	92.6	82.1	56.8
SNoW (Yang et al., 2000)	95.8	92.3	85.1	81.5
Linear SVM (Yang et al., 2000)	96.0	91.3	84.8	78.5
SHPCA	99.4	97.1	89.3	82.9
SHICA	99.4	97.0	89.2	82.7
SHRCA	99.4	96.9	89.1	83.0
SHFDA	99.9	98.9	94.4	87.4

Table 3
Recognition results for the coil-100 dataset with respect to 2D rotation

Methods	Rotation angle (°)				
	0	5	10	15	20
Recognition rate with the correct to be among the first (%)					
PCA	93.3	91.6	83.2	60.8	38.1
ICA	93.2	91.7	82.6	61.8	39.0
SHPCA	94.7	93.4	89.5	79.4	66.3
SHICA	94.6	93.2	89.2	79.0	66.1
Recognition rate with the correct to be among the first three (%)					
PCA	96.9	96.5	93.7	80.8	60.6
ICA	96.9	96.5	93.6	81.3	60.9
SHPCA	97.1	96.9	95.9	92.5	83.0
SHICA	97.0	96.9	95.9	92.3	82.8

Table 4
Recognition results for the ORL face dataset of 100 trials with different number of training/test faces

Methods	Training/test per subject			
	Average rate (%)		Worst rate (%)	
	5/5	3/7	5/5	3/7
PCA	94.5	88.0	89.0	80.7
ICA	94.0	86.0	89.0	75.4
FDA	98.9	96.3	95.5	91.1
RCA	85.6	73.7	79.5	65.7
SHPCA	98.5	94.6	95.0	87.9
SHICA	98.15	94.10	94.00	87.86
SHFDA	99.3	98.5	98.0	95.7
SHRCA	96.2	90.2	92.5	84.6

1987; Turk & Pentland, 1991). We have also applied our method to ORL[6], a standard face dataset. The dataset consists of faces of 40 subjects with 10 images for each. The images were taken at different times with different lighting conditions on a dark background. While only limited side movement and tilt were allowed, there was no restriction on facial expression. The procedure is the same as that for 3D object recognition. We use the same 21 filters and vary the number of the training images per subject and the remaining ones are used for testing. We randomly choose the training images from the dataset to avoid potential bias due to the choice of training faces. The average and worst results of 100 trials from linear subspace representations as well as SHSA ones are shown in Table 4. SHSA performance is significantly better than the corresponding linear subspace in the image space essentially because different lighting conditions and facial expressions make the pixel-wise representation not reliable for recognition (Zhang, Yan, & Lades, 1997). The results obtained here are also significantly better than those obtained in Zhang et al. (1997) on the same dataset.

We have also applied our method to a dataset of 40 real texture images[7] with size of 256×256. This dataset contains different kinds of natural textures. Also some of textures are similar to others in the dataset, making the classification very challenging.

To do the texture classification, we partition each texture image into nonoverlapping patches with size 32×32, resulting in a total of 64 patches per texture type. We then choose a specified number of patches as the training set and the rest are used for testing. As in the face recognition experiment, we randomly choose a given number of patches as training and run our method 100 times. Table 5 shows the average, best, and worst classification results of 100 trials with 32 training patches and 32 test patches per texture type. It is clear that the SHSA representations give significantly better results. Not surprisingly, linear subspaces of images do not give satisfactory results as the pixel-wise difference between textures is not a meaningful distance for textures.

Table 5
Average recognition results for the texture dataset

Methods	Average rate (%)	Best rate (%)	Worst rate (%)
PCA	22.8	24.2	21.1
ICA	23.2	25.4	21.6
FDA	57.5	60.8	17.6
RCA	17.8	19.5	16.5
SHPCA	94.2	95.3	92.8
SHICA	93.8	94.9	92.7
SHFDA	97.9	98.5	97.1
SHRCA	88.3	89.8	87.0

5. Discussion

One of the major obstacles of developing a generic vision system is the generalization of the adopted underlying representation. By studying the intrinsic generalization of a representation, we can better understand and predict its performance under different conditions. To our knowledge, this is the first attempt to provide a quantitative generalization measure intrinsic to a representation; in contrast, generalization is commonly tied to recognition performance, which depends on the choice of the classifier and the choice of training and test data, as shown by the experiments here. Our study on the intrinsic generalization of linear subspace representations in the image space shows that they cannot generalize well as images from different models tend to be grouped into one equivalence class; we emphasize that this result holds for any low dimensional linear subspace in the image space. We have suggested a way to improve the intrinsic generalization by implementing linear subspaces in the spectral histogram space. We have demonstrated substantial improvement in recognition on large datasets.

However, our goal is not to show that SHSA representation is optimal in general. In fact, if classes consist of white noise like images, SHSA representations would be very ineffective. Rather our emphasis is on the importance of the underlying representation for object images. An ideal representation of image $\mathbf{I}$ is $S_I^0(\mathbf{I})$, which can be implemented only when the true underlying object models and the physical imaging process are available; this leads to the analysis-by-synthesis paradigm (Grenander, 1993). When $S_I^0(\mathbf{I})$ is not available explicitly, one needs to approximate it. There is a trivial solution for a good approximation by forcing $S_I(\mathbf{I}) = \{\mathbf{I}\}$. However, the generalization is very poor and it requires literally all possible images in the training set. A good representation should approximate $S_I^0(\mathbf{I})$ well and $|S_I(\mathbf{I})|$ should be as large as possible. These two constraints provide the axes of

[6] http://www.uk.research.att.com/facedatabase.html

[7] Available at http://www-dbv.cs.uni-bonn.de/image/texture.tar.gz

forming a continuous spectrum of different representations and allow us to study and compare them. For example, only marginal distributions are used in the spectral histogram representation; one can describe and synthesize image **I** better by incorporating joint statistics (Portilla & Simoncelli, 2000); however, this obviously decreases $|S_I(\mathbf{I})|$. Within linear subspace methods, one can also decrease $|S_I(\mathbf{I})|$ by imposing additional constraints on bases and coefficients, such as the nonnegative constraints (Lee & Seung, 1999)[8]. Due to the complexity of $S_I^0(\mathbf{I})$, a very close approximation using some low dimensional representations may not be feasible. An alternative is to combine the analysis-by-synthesis paradigm (Grenander, 1993) and a low dimensional representation based approach. The hypothesis pruning by Srivastava, Liu, and Grenander (2002) provides such an example, where a low dimensional representation selects plausible hypotheses for an analysis-by-synthesis model. In this framework, the difference among low dimensional representations is their effectiveness of selecting good hypotheses rather than providing a final answer.

Within the spectral histogram representation, in addition to linear subspace methods, the dimension can also be reduced by choosing a subset of filters. Filter selection for performance optimization has been studied by Liu and Wang (2003). Filters can also be learned by optimizing a heuristic-based measure such as statistical independence (Liu & Cheng, 2003) or by maximizing the recognition performance (Liu & Srivastava, 2003). We have also developed a two-parameter analytical form for the marginals of filter responses (Grenander & Srivastava, 2001; Srivastava et al., 2002), which reduces the dimension of spectral histogram representation significantly.

An important question for recognition applications, which is not addressed here, is which representation is optimal given the choice of the representation space. The experimental results here suggest that the SHFDA in general gives the best performance; however, no optimality can be established theoretically as SHFDA's optimality requires that the underlying probability distributions are Gaussian and linear discrimination functions are used (Liu, Srivastava, & Gallivan, 2003). To find optimal representations, computationally efficient algorithms have recently been developed (Liu et al., 2003; Liu & Srivastava, 2003) and their effectiveness has been demonstrated in the image space and in the spectral histogram space.

Acknowledgements

This research was supported in part by grants NIMA NMA201-01-2010, NSF DMS-0101429, and ARO DAAD19-99-1-0267. D.L.W. was supported in part by an NSF grant (IIS-0081058) and an AFOSR grant (F49620-01-1-0027). The authors would like to thank the producers of the COIL, ORL, and texture datasets for making them publicly available.

[8] Rigorously speaking, the bases with nonnegative constraints do not form linear subspaces anymore.

References

Akaike, H. (1973). Information theory and an extension of the maximum likelihood principle. In B. N. Petrov, & F. Csaki (Eds.), *2nd International Symposium on Information Theory* (pp. 267–281).

Baum, E. B., & Haussler, D. (1989). *Neural Computation*, *1*, 151–160.

Belhumeur, P. N., Hepanha, J. P., & Kriegman, D. J. (1997). Eigenfaces vs. fisherfaces: recognition using class specific linear projection. *IEEE Transactions on Pattern Analysis and Machine Intelligence*, *19*, 711–720.

Bishop, C. M. (1995). *Neural networks for pattern recognition*. Oxford, UK: Oxford University Press.

Chubb, C., Econopouly, J., & Landy, M. S. (1994). Histogram contrast analysis and the visual segregation of IID textures. *Journal of the Optical Society of America A*, *11*, 2350–2374.

Comon, P. (1994). Independent component analysis. A new concept? *Signal Processing*, *36*, 287–314.

Csiszar, I., & Korner, J. (1981). *Information theory: coding theorems for discrete memoryless systems*. New York: Academic Press.

Fisher, R. A. (1936). The use of multiple measures in taxonomic problems. *Annals of Eugenics*, *7*, 179–188.

Grenander, U. (1993). *General pattern theory*. Oxford, UK: Clarendon Press.

Grenander, U., & Srivastava, A. (2001). Probability models for clutter in natural images. *IEEE Transactions on Pattern Analysis and Machine Intelligence*, *23*, 424–429.

Heeger, D. J., & Bergen, J. R. (1995). *Pyramid-based texture analysis/synthesis. In Proceedings of SIGGRAPHS*, pp. 229–238.

Hotelling, H. (1933). Analysis of a complex of statistical variables in principal components. *Journal of Educational Psychology*, *24*, 417–441. see also 498–520.

Hyvärinen, A. (1999). Fast and robust fixed-point algorithm for independent component analysis. *IEEE Transactions on Neural Networks*, *10*, 626–634.

Hyvärinen, A., Karhunen, J., & Oja, E. (2001). *Independent component analysis*. New York: Wiley–Interscience.

Karhunen, K. (1947). On linear methods in probability theory. *Annales Academiae Scientiarum Fennicae, Ser. A1*, *37*, 3–79. English translation, Doc. T-131, The RAND Corp., Santa Monica, CA 1960.

Kirby, M., & Sirovich, L. (1990). Application of the Karhunen-Loève procedure for the characterization of human faces. *IEEE Transactions on Pattern Analysis and Machine Intelligence*, *12*, 103–108.

Loève, M. M. (1955). *Probability theory*. Princeton, NJ: Van Nostrand.

Lades, M., Vorbruggen, J. C., Buhmann, J., Lange, J., von der Malsburg, C., Wurtz, R. P., & Konen, W. (1993). Distortion invariant object recognition in the dynamic link architecture. *IEEE Transactions on Computers*, *42*, 300–311.

Lee, D. D., & Seung, S. (1999). Learning the parts of objects by non-negative matrix factorization. *Nature*, *401*, 788–791.

Liu, X., & Cheng, L. (2003). Independent spectral representations of images for recognition. *Journal of the Optical Society of America*, in press.

Liu, X., Srivastava, A (2003). Stochastic geometric search for optimal linear representations of images. In *Proceedings of the Fourth International Workshop on Energy Minimization Methods in Computer Vision and Pattern Recognition*, in press.

Liu, X., Srivastava, A., Gallivan, K (2003). Optimal linear representations of images for object recognition. In *Proceedings of the IEEE Computer*

Society Conference on Computer Vision and Pattern Recognition, in press.

Liu, X., & Wang, D. L. (2001). Appearance-based recognition using perceptual components. *In Proceedings of the International Joint Conference on Neural Networks*, 1943–1948.

Liu, X., & Wang, D. L. (2002). A spectral histogram model for texton modeling and texture discrimination. *Vision Research*, *42*, 2617–2634.

Liu, X., & Wang, D. L. (2003). Texture classification using spectral histograms. *IEEE Transactions on Image Processing*, in press.

Martinez, A. M., & Kak, A. C. (2001). PCA versus LDA. *IEEE Transactions on Pattern Analysis and Machine Intelligence*, *23*, 228–233.

Pontil, M., & Verri, A. (1998). Support vector machines for 3D object recognition. *IEEE Transactions on Pattern Analysis and Machine Intelligence*, *20*, 637–646.

Rissanen, J. (1978). Modeling by shortest data description. *Automatica*, *14*, 465–471.

Portilla, J., & Simoncelli, E. P. (2000). A parametric texture model based on joint statistics of complex wavelets. *International Journal of Computer Vision*, *40*, 49–71.

Schiele, B., & Crowley, J. L. (2000). Recognition without correspondence using multidimensional receptive field histograms. *International Journal of Computer Vision*, *36*, 31–50.

Simoncelli, E. P., & Olshausen, B. A. (2001). Natural image statistics and neural representation. *Annual Review of Neuroscience*, *24*, 1193–1216.

Sirovich, L., & Kirby, M. (1987). Low-dimensional procedure for the characterization of human faces. *Journal of the Optical Society of America A*, *4*, 519–524.

Srivastava, A., Liu, X., & Grenander, U. (2002). Universal analytical forms for modeling image probabilities. *IEEE Transactions on Pattern Analysis and Machine Intelligence*, *23*, 1200–1214.

Swain, M. J., & Ballard, D. H. (1991). Color indexing. *International Journal of Computer Vision*, *7*, 11–32.

Turk, M., & Pentland, A. (1991). Eigenfaces for recognition. *Journal of Cognitive Neuroscience*, *3*, 71–86.

Vapnik, V. N. (2000). *The nature of statistical learning theory* (2nd ed.). New York: Springer-Verlag.

Yang, M.H., Roth, D., Ahuja, N (2000). Learning to recognize 3D objects with SNoW. In: *Proceedings of the Sixth European Conference on Computer Vision* (pp. 439–454).

Zhang, J., Yan, Y., & Lades, M. (1997). Face recognition: Eigenface, elastic matching, and neural nets. *Proceedings of IEEE*, *85*, 1423–1435.

Zhu, S. C., Liu, X., & Wu, Y. (2000). Exploring texture ensembles by efficient Markov chain Monte Carlo. *IEEE Transactions on Pattern Recognition and Machine Intelligence*, *22*, 554–569.

Zhu, S. C., Wu, Y. N., & Mumford, D. (1997). Minimax entropy principle and its application to texture modeling. *Neural Computation*, *9*, 1627–1660.

PERGAMON

AVAILABLE AT
www.ComputerScienceWeb.com
POWERED BY SCIENCE DIRECT

Neural Networks 16 (2003) 547–553

Neural Networks

www.elsevier.com/locate/neunet

2003 Special issue

Application of four-layer neural network on information extraction

Min Han*, Lei Cheng, Hua Meng

School of Electronic and Information Engineering, Dalian University of Technology, Dalian 116023, China

Abstract

This paper applies neural network to extract marsh information. An adaptive back-propagation algorithm based on a robust error function is introduced to build a four-layer neural network, and it is used to classify Thematic Mapper (TM) image of Zhalong Wetland in China and then extract marsh information. Comparing marsh information extraction results of the four-layer neural network with three-layer neural network and the maximum likelihood classifier, conclusion can be drawn as follows: the structure of the four-layer neural network and the adaptive back-propagation algorithm based on the robust error function is effective to extract marsh information. The four-layer neural network adopted in this paper succeeded in building the complex model of TM image, and it avoided the problem of great storage of remotely sensed data, and the adaptive back-propagation algorithm speeded up the descending of error. Above all, the four-layer neural network is superior to the three-layer neural network and the maximum likelihood classifier in the accuracy of the total classification and marsh information extraction.

Keywords: Remote sensing; Neural network; Information extraction; Marsh

1. Introduction

Remotely sensed images distinguish different landform mainly through the different brightness of pixels. Different brightness of pixels shows the different information of spectrum. According to this, classifying the land cover to categories and then extracting needed category is an important application of the remotely sensed images. Traditionally, the ways to classify the land cover are based on the Bayesian classifier. It is well known that the Bayesian classifier is theoretically optimal if the assumptions about the probability density functions (PDFs) are correct. Poor performance may be obtained if the true PDFs are different from those assumed by the model (Heermann & Khazenie, 1992). The need to have a specific probabilistic model is a major limitation of the Bayesian approach. Maximum likelihood classification is based on the Bayesian classifier. It has the minimum value of classification error probability. We assume all kinds of targets on the ground submit to normal distribution when we conduct the statistic classification of image. According to this assumption, a distribution of a response pattern can be completely presented by the mean vector and variance. The statistic probability of some pixel belonging to each category can be computed through these parameters.

Artificial neural network has been greatly applied in the field of classification and information extraction of remotely sensed image, especially back-propagation neural network classifier. Back-propagation neural network has succeeded in realizing the supervised classification of remotely sensed image (Kanellopoulos & Wilkinson, 1997; Li, 1998). Yang and Zhou (2001) presented a classification method based on knowledge. Compared with traditional method, neural network does not need the probability pattern but becomes a classifier by its adaptive learning ability. It starts with an inherently parallel processing, adaptive learning and nonlinear technique. The problems solved by neural network usually focus on the small data sets less than 200 patterns. However, remotely sensed image has great training data sets usually more than 1000. Therefore, we should select the network structure and learning algorithm carefully when we use neural network to classify the remotely sensed image and extract needed category, so that neural network can solve the problems more efficiently and precisely.

Multilayer feed-forward neural networks realize the complex nonlinear mapping. Single-hidden-layer structure can solve most classification and information extraction problems, but if samples are comparatively complex, that is,

* Corresponding author.
E-mail address: minhan@dlut.edu.cn (M. Han).

0893-6080/03/$ - see front matter © 2003 Elsevier Science Ltd. All rights reserved.
doi:10.1016/S0893-6080(03)00120-5

they are highly in discretization, two-hidden-layer neural network can be adopted (Zhang, 1999). The general back-propagation has some disadvantages, such as long-time training and difficulty of converge, etc. Bruzzone and Serpico (1997) presented a technique—training for two steps—to accelerate the training time. Du, Mei, and Li (1998) introduced conjugate gradient with line search (CGL) to optimize the learning rate. In this paper, the model of remotely sensed image is built with a four-layer feed-forward neural network, and an adaptive back-propagation algorithm based on a robust error function is introduced to avoid the problem of long-time training and difficulty of convergence. Comparing the four-layer neural network with the three-layer neural network and the maximum likelihood method through the analysis of classification process and marsh information extraction results, conclusion can be drawn that the four-layer neural network is able to perform best in the accuracy of the marsh information extraction.

2. Algorithm description of BP neural network

Land cover classification of remotely sensed image should be done before marsh information extraction. The main idea of remotely sensed image classification using neural network is to make the feature of the image as the input signals, to train the neural network following some rule, then to classify output signals. In this paper, a four-layer neural network with two-hidden-layer is used to build the model of remotely sensed data. In Fig. 1 the structure of the four-layer neural network is shown.

In all kinds of algorithms of neural network, the back-propagation algorithm has gained nearly full development. However, it still has several limitations, for example, it easily falls into local minimum, cannot acquire the global optimum solution, its convergence rate is slow and so on. It is difficult to determine the learning rate, but the learning rate is the key to influence the efficiency of the back-propagation learning algorithm (Wang, Li, & Mao, 2001; Zhou, Luo, Yang, Yang, & Liu, 2001). In normal back-propagation learning algorithm, the value of learning rate is constant. However, the optimum learning rate should be adjusted on line; training process is done under the direction of summed squared error function and reaches the minimum through the weight adjustment. This kind of error function is sensitive to the great error (Xia & Bian, 1998). In this paper, a robust error function is adopted to train the neural network, and an adaptive back-propagation algorithm, which is later proved to suit to classify the Thematic Mapper (TM) image of Zhalong wetland in China, is introduced to adjust the learning rate on line. The principle of the learning algorithm is introduced as following.

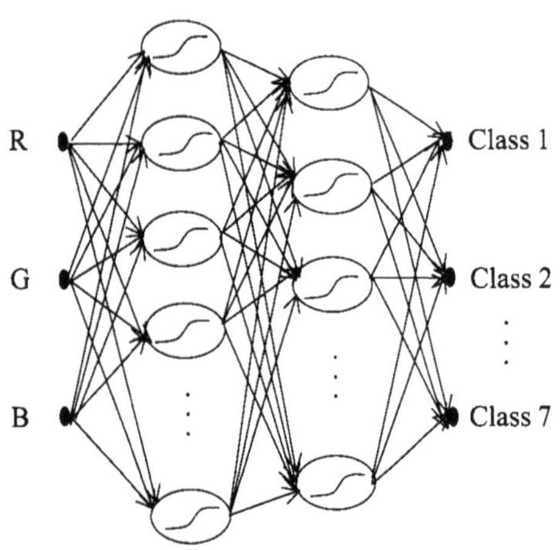

Fig. 1. Structure of four-layer feed-forward neural network.

Firstly, define the new robust error function $\varphi(\varepsilon)$ under the following conditions ($\varepsilon = d_j(k) - y_j(k)$ is called the remain error):

(a) $\varphi(\varepsilon) = 0$, when $\varepsilon = 0$;
(b) $\varphi(\varepsilon)$ is continuous everywhere;
(c) $\varphi(\varepsilon)$ is symmetrical;
(d) $\Phi(\varepsilon) = (\partial\varphi(\varepsilon)/\partial\varepsilon) \geq 0$, when $\varepsilon \geq 0$;
(e) $\lim_{\varepsilon\to\infty} \Phi(\varepsilon) = 0$.

Typically, $\varphi(\varepsilon)$ can be selected as:

$$\varphi(\varepsilon) = \frac{\varepsilon^2}{b + a\varepsilon^2} \tag{1}$$

Then

$$\Phi(\varepsilon) = \frac{\partial\varphi(\varepsilon)}{\partial\varepsilon} = \frac{2b\varepsilon}{(b + a\varepsilon^2)^2} \tag{2}$$

The parameter a, b in equation should be selected according to the actual need. In this paper, we select $a = 1, b = 2$.

From the above equation, we can see that $\Phi(\varepsilon)$ is changing normally when ε is small. However, the increasing speed of $\Phi(\varepsilon)$ drops when ε is bigger, this leads to depress the influence of great error. Therefore, $\varphi(\varepsilon)$ is a robust function. When $a = 0, b = 1$, we have $\Phi(\varepsilon) = \varepsilon^2$, which is the error energy function in normal back-propagation learning algorithm.

Suppose the number of samples is P. Input a sample whose serial number is k, then the algorithm flow can be described as follows.

Step 1: Forward-propagation process. The relation is

$$y_j^l(k) = f\left(\sum_i \omega_{ji}^l(k) y_i^{l-1}(k) - \theta_j^l\right) \tag{3}$$

where $y_j^l(k)$ is the output of the jth unit of the lth layer. $\omega_{ji}^l(k)$ is the weight connecting ith unit of the $(l-1)$th layer and jth unit of the lth layer. θ_j^l is threshold value of the jth unit of the lth layer. $f(\cdot)$ is the active function. The active function of the hidden layer is nonlinear function usually, such as a sigmoid function and a hyperbolic function.

Step 2: Back-propagation process. It is also the adjustment process of the weight. The relation is

$$\omega_{ji}^{l}(k+1) = \omega_{ji}^{l}(k) + \mu(k)\Delta\omega_{ji}^{l}(k) \tag{4}$$

where μ is the adaptive learning rate, $\Delta\omega_{ji}^{l}(k)$ is the adjusted value of the weight. It can be carried out through the gradient descent algorithm.

$$\Delta\omega_{ji}^{l}(k) = \delta_j^{l}(k)y_i^{l-1}(k) \tag{5}$$

For output units, we have

$$\delta_j(k+1) = y_j(k)[1 - y_j(k)]\Phi(\varepsilon_j) \tag{6}$$

For hidden units, we have

$$\delta_j^{l}(k+1) = y_j^{l}(k)[1 - y_j^{l}(k)]\sum_q \delta_q^{l+1}(k)\omega_{qj}^{l+1}(k) \tag{7}$$

Train the neural network by inputting the neural network input–output samples. When P samples have been input, compute the total squared error E, which can be defined as

$$E = \frac{1}{2P}\sum_{k=1}^{P}\sum_{j=1}^{m}\varphi(\varepsilon_j(k)) \tag{8}$$

Step 3: Input P samples again and compare the total error acquired in two epochs. Suppose k is the serial number of circulation. The comparative results could be divided into three situation:

1. If $E_k < E_{k-1}$, that is the error is descending, learning direction is right, learning rate μ can be increased as follows:

   $$\mu_{k+1}^{l} = \beta\mu_k, \qquad \beta \geq 1 \tag{9}$$

   If $\mu_{k+1}^{l} > \mu_{\max}$, $\mu_{k+1} = \mu_{\max}$, otherwise $\mu_{k+1} = \mu_{k+1}^{l}$.
2. If $E_k > E_{k-1}$, it shows that learning step length is too long, then

   $$\mu_{k+1}^{l} = \alpha\mu_k, \qquad \alpha < 1 \tag{10}$$

   If $\mu_{k+1}^{l} < \mu_{\min}$, $\mu_{k+1} = \mu_{\min}$, otherwise $\mu_{k+1} = \mu_{k+1}^{l}$.
3. If $E_k > \lambda E_{k-1}$ $(\lambda > 1)$, make kth learning result unused, decrease the learning rate and train the neural network again.

In a word, TM image model of Zhalong wetland is established by four-layer feed-forward neural network; training process is done under direction of a robust error function and weight value is adjusted by the adaptive back-propagation algorithm.

3. Marsh information extraction of Zhalong wetland using neural network

In this paper, a four-layer feed-forward neural network is adopted to classify the TM image model of Zhalong wetland and then extract marsh information. The information extraction results are compared with three-layer feed-forward neural network and the maximum likelihood classifier.

3.1. Research area and its data

Our research area, that is named Zhalong protected district, lies in the lower reaches of Wuyuer river in the west of Heilongjiang province in China. Its geographic coordinate is 46°52′–47°32′N and 123°47′–124°37′E. Zhalong protected district is an upcountry wetland and ecosystem which is mostly covered by reed marsh, and it is the most complete, original and broad wetland ecosystem in the north of China compared to area of the same latitude. It has been listed in the international important wetland contents. Therefore, it is important to monitor the marsh change. Marsh information extraction from the remotely sensed image is an effective way to acquire the situation of the marsh.

The data we used for land cover classification and information extraction is half of a Landsat TM scene of the surroundings of Zhalong wetland. Date of TM image of Zhalong wetland acquisition is October 5, 2001.

The TM scene contains seven bands. In this research, we use combination of TM band 4, 3 and 2 to create a false color composite as seen in Fig. 2, which is suitable for land

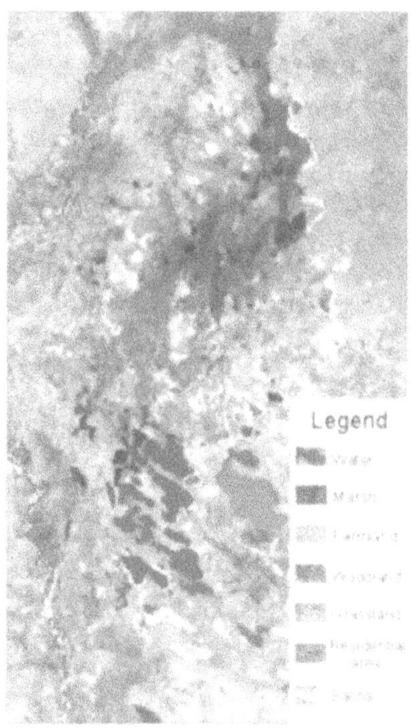

Fig. 2. Bands 4,3,2 composite image.

cover classification. The image was interpreted by comprehensive analysis and compared with map of land use and ability of visual interpreters. Then seven classes were confirmed in the region of TM image, which include water, marsh, farmland, woodland, grassland, residential area and salina.

3.2. Build the neural network model

Select the training and testing data. According to the results of visual interpreter, we select 1500 pixels from the false color composite to train the network and 700 pixels to test the network. The maximum likelihood classifier adopted the same samples. Table 1 shows the sample examples of every class in training sets and the numbers of every class samples, where TM4, TM3 and TM2, respectively, present the sample value of TM band 4, 3 and 2.

Before classification of remotely sensed image using neural network classifier, the samples should be changed into the region of [0, 1]. In this way, the supersaturated phenomenon could be avoided.

Confirm the parameter of input and output units of the network. The number of input units is three according to RGB color, and the number of output units is seven according to the number of categories. Each output unit presents a kind of category. The outputvector can be described as follows: (0.9,0.1,0.1,0.1,0.1,0.1,0.1),(0.1,0.9,0.1,0.1,0.1,0.1,0.1),… (0.1,0.1,0.1,0.1,0.1,0.1,0.9). An input pattern will be divided to *i*th category if it has the highest output value in *i*th unit.

The number of hidden layers and the number of hidden units are obtained by experiments. In the experiments, we found out that single hidden layer network structure cannot get the needed accuracy. When we adopted the two hidden layer network structure, we found out that the number of first hidden layer should be at least twice the number of input layer units. The number of second hidden layer should at least be the larger one of the input units and the output units. If we increase the number of the hidden layer units, accuracy can be improved, but it needs more learning time.

Parameters of the neural network can be obtained by such method. The result is, the number of the input units is three; the number of the hidden layer is two; the number of first hidden layer units is eight; the number of second hidden layer units is seven; the number of the output units is seven; the initial learning rate is 0.1; the initial weight and threshold value is random numbers. The structure of the neural network is shown in Fig. 1.

Compare the classification and extraction results of neural network and maximum likelihood classifier. The classification process of neural network is mainly realized by two steps. The first step is to train the network according to the samples; the second step is to classify the whole remotely sensed data using learning results.

Firstly, we should input the training data into the model of the neural network and train the neural network. The four-layer neural network adopts the adaptive back-propagation learning algorithm introduced in this paper and the three-layer neural network adopts normal back-propagation learning algorithm. The learning error curve of the three-layer neural network and the four-layer neural network are shown in Fig. 3, where error is computed by summed squared error function. We can see the error of four layer neural network falls faster than the three layer neural network, and the convergence error is also lowest than the three layer neural network. Therefore, the two hidden layer structure can reach more accurate degree compared with the single layer structure. At the same time we found out that the error function would not be convergent in simulation if we did not adopt the adaptive learning algorithm. It was noticeable that the robust error function makes the training time shorter comparing with normal summed squared error function.

The error matrix can be obtained from the classification results of test samples. The classification error matrices of four-layer neural network, three-layer neural network and maximum likelihood method are, respectively, shown in Tables 2–4. From the three tables, we can see that the four-layer neural network can get best classification results. Three-layer neural network mistook other classes of land cover as marsh and maximum likelihood classifier had weak ability to judge the grassland and residential area.

Table 1
Sample examples of training sets

Class	Band			Number
	TM4	TM3	TM2	
Water	18	63	93	400
Marsh	112	97	99	200
Farmland	195	190	162	200
Woodland	147	67	92	100
Grassland	73	90	106	300
Residential area	85	133	140	200
Salina	215	255	253	100

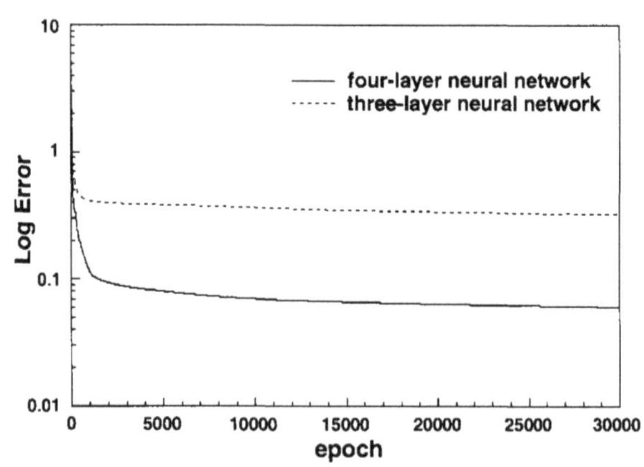

Fig. 3. Learning error curve of four-layer and three-layer neural network.

Table 2
The error matrix of four-layer neural network classification

Practice	Class							Total
	Water	Marsh	Farmland	Woodland	Grassland	Residential Area	Salina	
Water	99	0	0	0	0	2	0	101
Marsh	0	98	0	2	0	0	0	100
Farmland	0	1	100	2	0	0	0	103
Woodland	0	0	0	96	0	0	0	96
Grassland	0	1	0	0	93	3	0	97
Residential area	1	0	0	0	7	95	0	103
Salina	0	0	0	0	0	0	100	100
Total	100	100	100	100	100	100	100	700

Table 3
The error matrix of three-layer neural network classification

Practice	Class							Total
	Water	Marsh	Farmland	Woodland	Grassland	Residential Area	Salina	
Water	97	2	0	0	0	2	0	101
Marsh	1	83	0	0	7	0	0	91
Farmland	0	5	87	1	1	0	0	94
Woodland	0	0	0	94	0	0	0	94
Grassland	0	10	13	5	92	4	0	124
Residential area	2	0	0	0	0	94	0	96
Salina	0	0	0	0	0	0	100	100
Total	100	100	100	100	100	100	100	700

Classification accuracy calculations on pixels are based on the error matrix. Accuracy of each class can be calculated by the error matrix shown in Tables 2–4. As seen in Table 5, four-layer neural network can obtain highest accuracy of each class.

In most cases, the integrated classification accuracy reflects the total effect of classification. The integrated classification accuracy is average classifier accuracy. The integrated classification accuracy of four-layer neural network, three-layer neural network and maximum likelihood classifier is, respectively, 97.29, 92.43 and 89.43%. It shows that the classification result of four-layer neural network is better than three-layer neural network and maximum likelihood classifier in integrated accuracy, which presents that the four-layer neural network adopted in this paper is more suitable to build complicated model of TM image.

After the classification of the whole remotely sensed image using trained neural network and maximum likelihood classifier, the result images of marsh information

Table 4
The error matrix of maximum likelihood classification

Practice	Class							Total
	Water	Marsh	Farmland	Woodland	Grassland	Residential area	Salina	
Water	87	0	0	0	0	4	0	91
Marsh	6	95	4	2	22	0	0	129
Farmland	0	2	95	0	4	0	0	101
Woodland	0	0	0	96	0	0	0	96
Grassland	0	3	1	2	66	9	0	81
Residential area	7	0	0	0	8	87	0	102
Salina	0	0	0	0	0	0	100	100
Total	100	100	100	100	100	100	100	700

Table 5
Accuracy of the three methods

Method	Class							Average accuracy (%)
	Water (%)	Marsh (%)	Farmland (%)	Woodland (%)	Grassland (%)	Residential area (%)	Salina (%)	
Four-layer neural network	99.00	98.00	100.00	96.00	93.00	95.00	100.00	97.29
Three-layer neural network	97.00	83.00	87.00	94.00	92.00	94.00	100.00	92.43
Maximum likelihood	87.00	95.00	95.00	96.00	66.00	87.00	100.00	89.43

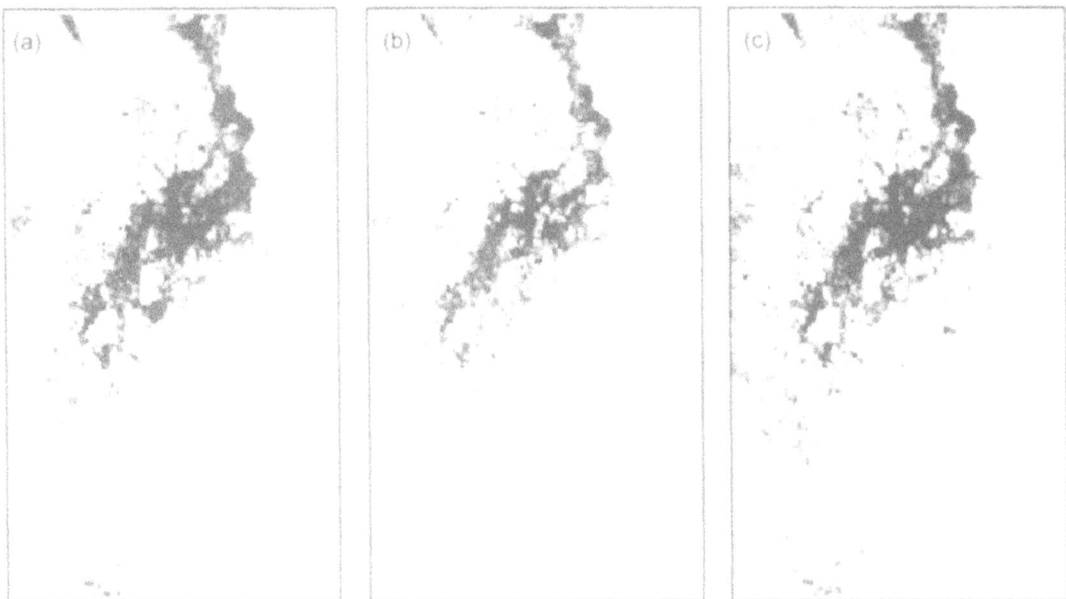

Fig. 4. Marsh information extraction results with three methods: Marsh information extraction with (a) four-layer neural network; (b) three-layer neural network; (c) maximum likelihood classifier.

extraction are obtained and shown in Fig. 4(a)–(c). Since the four-layer neural network can get highest accuracy of each category (including marsh), the accuracy of marsh information extraction is highest.

4. Conclusion

The four-layer neural network and the adaptive back-propagation algorithm based on the robust error function appear to be feasible to classify the TM image of Zhalong wetland and extract marsh information. Compared to three-layer neural network, four-layer neural network could avoid the burden of large storage; Compared to the traditional maximum likelihood classifier, neural network needs not to assume the model of probability but acquires weight value through learning ability then becomes a classifier. Therefore, it avoided the error made by the imprecise probability model. From the simulation results, mistaken and lack classification phenomena of four-layer neural network decreased greatly. Therefore, the classification and information extraction accuracy of four-layer neural network is superior to three-layer neural network and the maximum likelihood classifier; the adaptive back-propagation learning algorithm based on the error robust function avoids the divergence of error function, decreases the general error to a smaller degree and accelerates the learning rate. These lead the marsh information extraction to be conducted successfully. Other neural network structure and algorithm should be taken to try to improve the information extraction accuracy.

Acknowledgements

This research is supported by the project (50139020) of the National Natural Science Foundation of China. All of these supports are appreciated.

References

Bruzzone, L., & Serpico, S. B. (1997). Classification of imbalanced remote-sensing data by neural networks. *Pattern Recognition Letters*, *18*, 1323–1328.

Du, H., Mei, W., & Li, D. (1998). Classification of remote sensing images using BP neural network with dynamic learning rate. *Journal of Beijing Institute of Technology*, *18*(4), 485–488.

Heermann, P. D., & Khazenie, N. (1992). Classification of multispectral remote sensing data using a back-propagation neural network. *IEEE Transactions on Geoscience and Remote Sensing*, *30*(1), 81–88.

Kanellopoulos, I., & Wilkinson, G. (1997). Strategies and best practice for neural network image classification. *Remote Sensing*, *18*(4), 711–725.

Li, Z. (1998). Supervised classification of multispectral remote sensing image using B-P neural network. *Journal of Infrared and Millimeter Waves*, *17*(2), 153–156.

Wang, Y., Li, S., & Mao, J. (2001). *Image processing and recognition with computer*, (pp. 197–205). Beijing: Higher Education Press.

Xia, G., & Bian, X. (1998). BP algorithm based on robust error function. *Journal of Harbin Engineering University*, *19*(3), 33–37.

Yang, C., & Zhou, C. (2001). Investigation on classification of remote sensing image on the basis of knowledge. *Geography and Territorial Research*, *17*(1), 72–77.

Zhang, J. (1999). Construction of a neural network on remote sensing image classification. *Journal of Image and Graphics*, *4(A)*(10), 831–834.

Zhou, C., Luo, J., Yang, X., Yang, C., & Liu, Q. (2001). *Geography understanding and analysis of remotely sensed image*, (pp. 229–239) Beijing: Science Press.

PERGAMON

AVAILABLE AT
www.ComputerScienceWeb.com
POWERED BY SCIENCE DIRECT

Neural Networks

Neural Networks 16 (2003) 555–559

www.elsevier.com/locate/neunet

2003 Special issue

Subject independent facial expression recognition with robust face detection using a convolutional neural network

Masakazu Matsugu*, Katsuhiko Mori, Yusuke Mitari, Yuji Kaneda

Canon Research Center, 5-1, Morinosato-Wakamiya, Atsugi 243-0193, Japan

Abstract

Reliable detection of ordinary facial expressions (e.g. smile) despite the variability among individuals as well as face appearance is an important step toward the realization of perceptual user interface with autonomous perception of persons. We describe a rule-based algorithm for robust facial expression recognition combined with robust face detection using a convolutional neural network. In this study, we address the problem of subject independence as well as translation, rotation, and scale invariance in the recognition of facial expression. The result shows reliable detection of smiles with recognition rate of 97.6% for 5600 still images of more than 10 subjects. The proposed algorithm demonstrated the ability to discriminate smiling from talking based on the saliency score obtained from voting visual cues. To the best of our knowledge, it is the first facial expression recognition model with the property of subject independence combined with robustness to variability in facial appearance.

Keywords: Convolutional neural network; Face detection; Facial expression

1. Introduction

Facial expressions as manifestations of emotional states, in general, tend to be different among individuals. For example, smiling face as it appears may have different emotional implications for different persons in that 'smiling face', perceived by others, for some person does not necessarily represent truly *smiling state* for that person. To the best of our knowledge, only a few algorithms (Ebine & Nakamura, 1999) have addressed robustness to such individuality in facial expression recognition. Furthermore, in order for facial expression recognition to be used for human–computer interaction, for example, that algorithm must have good ability in dealing with variability of facial appearance (e.g. pose, size, and translation invariance). Most algorithms, so far, have addressed only a part of these problems (Földiák, 1991; Wallis & Rolls, 1997). In this study, we propose a system for facial expression recognition that is robust to variability that originates from individuality and viewing conditions.

Recognizing facial expression under rigid head movements was addressed by Black and Yacoob (1995). Neural network model that learns to recognize facial expressions from an optical flow field was reported in Rosenblum, Yacoob, and Davis (1996). Rule-based systems were reported in Black and Yacoob (1997) and Yacoob and Davis (1996), in which primary facial features were tracked throughout the image sequence.

Convolutional neural network (CNN) models (Le Cun & Bengio, 1995) as well as neocognitrons (Fukushima, 1980) known as one of biologically inspired models, have been used for pattern recognition tasks such as face recognition and hand-written numeral recognition. The network includes feature detecting (FD) layers, each of which alternated with a sub-sampling layer (pooling layer) to obtain properties leading to translation and deformation invariance. Recently, Fasel (2002) has proposed a model with two independent CNNs, one for facial expression the other for face identity recognition, which are combined by a MLP.

The proposed model in this study turns out to be much more efficient and compact than Fasel's model. In addition, our model comes with the property of subject independence. Specifically, the proposed system can detect smiling or laughing faces based on difference in local features between a normal face and those not.

In Section 2, we introduce a modular convolutional network architecture for robust face detection and facial expression recognition involving module-based learning based on a variant of BP. In Section 3, we propose a rule-based algorithm that utilizes differences of specific local features, extracted in the CNN, between neutral and emotional faces. We show that the proposed scheme attains not only subject independence but also position independence

* Corresponding author. Tel.: +81-46-247-2111; fax: +81-46-248-0306.
E-mail address: matsugu.masakazu@canon.co.jp (M. Matsugu).

0893-6080/03/$ - see front matter
doi:10.1016/S0893-6080(03)00115-1

in facial expression recognition. In Section 4, we discuss the properties of proposed scheme that adds to the conventional neural networks for facial expression recognition.

2. Robust face detection using CNN

As in the previously proposed model (Matsugu, Mori, Ishii, & Mitarai, 2002), internal representation of face is provided by a hierarchically ordered set of convolutional kernels defined by the local receptive field of FD neurons. Face model is represented as a spatially ordered set of local features of intermediate complexity, such as eyes, mouth, nose, eyebrow, cheek, or else, and all of these features are represented in terms of a fixed set of lower and intermediate features.

The lower and intermediate features constitute some form of a fixed set of figural alphabets in our CNN. Corresponding receptive fields for the detection of these alphabetical features are learned in advance to form a local template in the hierarchical network, and once learned, they would never be changed during possible learning phase for object recognition in upper layers.

Our CNN model is different from the original model (Le Cun and Bengio, 1995) in three ways. First, training of the proposed model proceeds module by module (i.e. for each local feature class) only for FD_k ($k > 1$) layers. Second, we do not train FP (or sub-sampling) layers (FP neurons perform either maximum value detection or local averaging in their receptive fields). Third, we use a detection result of skin color area as input to the face detection module in FD4. The skin area is obtained simply by thresholding hue data of input image in the range of $[-0.078, 0.255]$ for the full range of $[-0.5, 0.5]$.

The training proceeds as follows. In the first step of training, two layers from the bottom, namely FD1 with eight modules and FD2 with four modules, are trained using standard back-propagation with intermediate local features (e.g. eye corners) as positive training data sets. Negative examples that do not constitute the corresponding feature category are also used as false data. Specifically, we trained the FD2 layer, the second from the bottom FD layer to form detectors of intermediate features, such as end-stop structures or blobs (i.e. end-stop structures for left and right side) and two types of horizontally elongated blobs (e.g. upper part bright, lower part bright) with varying size and rotation (up to 30° with rotation in-plane axis as well as head axis). These data used for training are fragments extracted from face images (Fig. 1).

More complex local feature detectors (e.g. eye, mouth detectors, but not restricted to these) are trained in the third (FD3) or fourth (FD4) layer using the patterns extracted from face images with geometric transform as in the FD2 layer. As a result of these training sequences, the top FD layer, FD4, learns to locate faces in complex scenes.

As given in Fig. 2, information concerning locations of eyes and mouth detected by the CNN is fed to the rule-based processing module so that our facial analysis system can deal with variability in position, size, and pose.

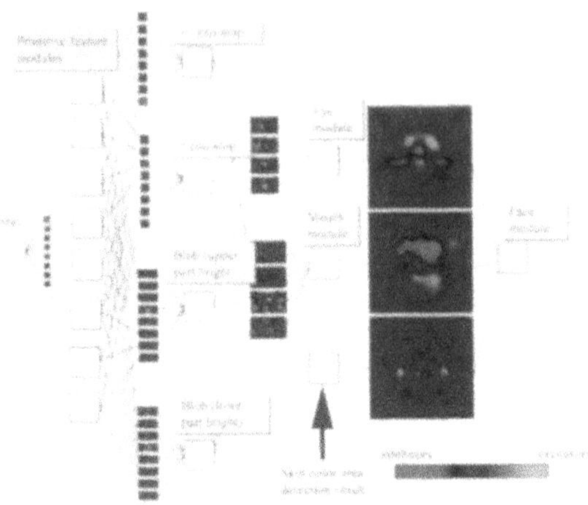

Fig. 1. Convolutional architecture (feature pooling layers are not shown for simplified illustration) for face detection.

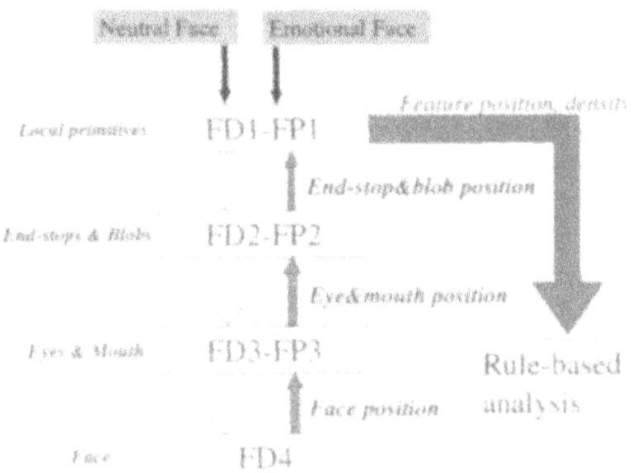

Fig. 2. CNN with feedback mechanism for rule-based analysis.

3. Rule-based analysis of facial expressions using local features detected by CNN

In the following, we propose a rule-based processing scheme to enhance subject independence in facial expression recognition. We found that some of lower level features extracted by the first FD layer of CNN were useful for facial expression recognition. Primary features used in the analysis are horizontal line segments and edge-like structures similar to step and roof edges (extracted by the two modules in FP1 layer circled in Fig. 3) representing parts of eyes, mouth, and eyebrows. For example, changes in distance between end-stops (e.g. left-corner of left eye and left side end-stop of mouth) within facial components and changes in width of line segments in lower part of eyes or cheeks are detected to obtain saliency scores of a specific facial expression. Primary cues related to facial actions adopted in our rule-based facial analysis for the detection of smiling/laughing faces are as follows.

(1) Distance between endpoints of eye and mouth gets *shorter* (lip being raised)
(2) Length of horizontal line segment in mouth gets *longer* (lip being stretched)
(3) Length of line segments in eye gets *longer* (wrinkle around the tail of eye gets longer)

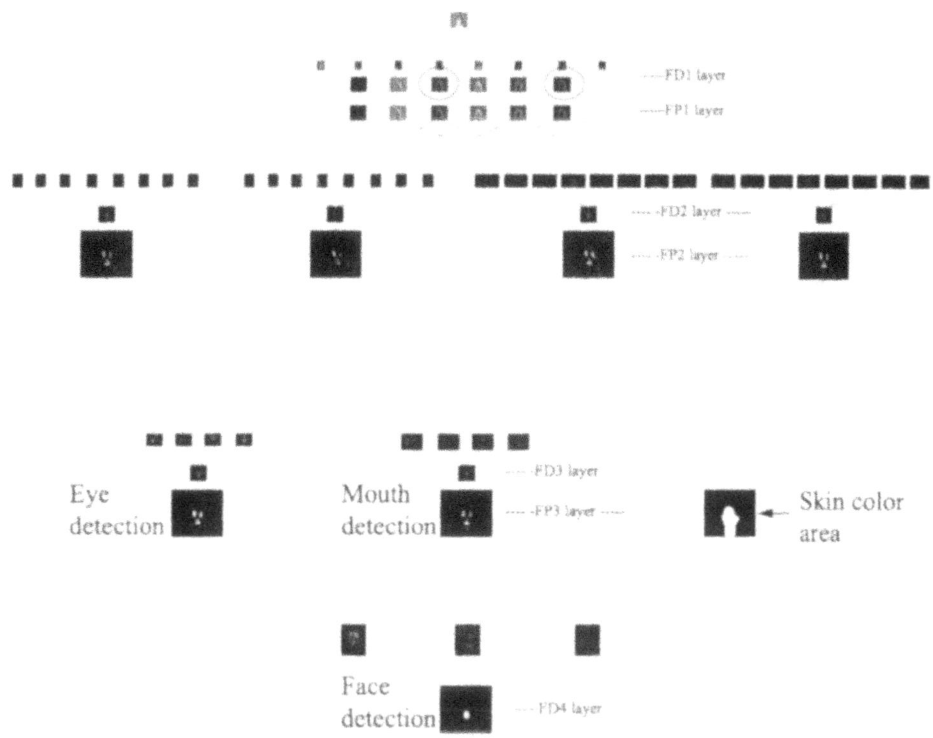

Fig. 3. Face detection by proposed convolutional NN with the results of intermediate feature detection.

(4) Gradient of line segment connecting the mid point and endpoint of mouth gets *steeper* (lip being raised)
(5) No. of step-edges in mouth get *increased* (teeth get appeared)
(6) No. of edges in cheeks *increased* (wrinkle around cheeks gets grown).

Each cue was scored based on the degree of positive changes (i.e. designated changes as given above) to the emotional state (e.g. happiness). For example, given a positive change in some cue by *a%* to the feature value in neutral face, then we give *Ca* points (*C* is some constant) to that feature.

Saliency score of specific emotional state is calculated using a sort of voting scheme with the summation (with weight p_k) of scores s_k for respective cues given as follows

$$S = \sum_k p_k s_k$$

After the voting process, the score S is normalized and thresholded for judging the facial expression (e.g. smiling/laughing or not).

4. Results

4.1. Face detection

In the training of our CNN, the number of facial fragment images used is 2900 for the FD2 layer, 5290 for the FD3, and 14,700 (face) for the FD4 layer, respectively. The number of non-face images, also used for the FD4 layer, is 137. Apparently greater number of facial component images as compared with non-face images is used to ensure robustness to varying rotation, size, contrast, and color balance of face images. So, we used a fixed set of transformed images for a given training sample image.

In particular, we used three different sizes of the fragment images ranging from 0.7 to 1.5 times the original image (i.e. fragments of facial components for modules in FD2 and FD3, entire face without background for FD4). The performance for face images other than the training data set was tested for over 200 face images with cluttered background and varying image-capturing conditions.

Fig. 4. Face detection results in complex scenes.

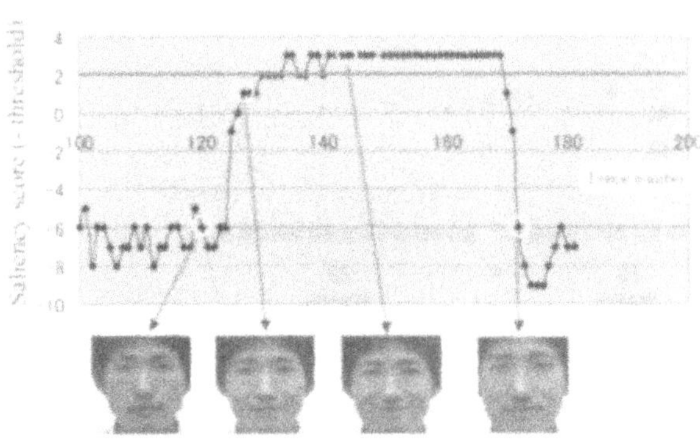

Fig. 5. Normalized saliency score subtracted by constant value for smiling face detection.

As shown in Fig. 4, the tested images of face are of different size (from 30 × 30 to 240 × 240 in VGA image), pose (up to 30° in head axis rotation and also in-plane rotation), and varying contrasts with cluttered background. The convolutional network demonstrated robust face detection with 1% false rejection rate and 6% false acceptance rate with quite good generalization ability.

4.2. Facial expression recognition

Fig. 5 shows a sequence of normalized saliency scores indicating successful detection of smiling faces, around the frame number from 130 to 170, with an appropriate threshold level of 2. The normalization was done by dividing the weighted sum of scores by 10 and subtracting some constant. The weight for each cue was assigned based on individuality factor, tendency of subject dependence. So, cues of larger individuality, found heuristically in advance, was assigned with some smaller weight values (e.g. 40), whereas cues of less individuality was assigned with larger weights (e.g. 45).

As shown in Fig. 6, the proposed system demonstrated the discrimination of smiling from talking state for different persons based on the normalized saliency score. In addition, we obtained results demonstrating reliable detection of smiles with the recognition rate of 97.6% for 5600 still images of more than 10 subjects.

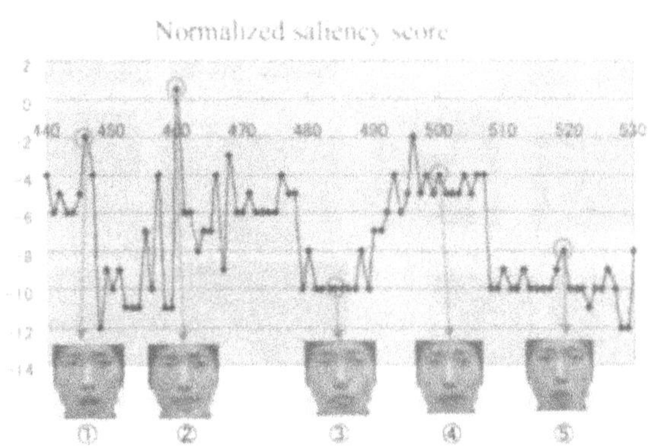

Fig. 6. Talking faces can be discriminated from laughing face. Note that the second face obtained higher score due to similarity to laughing face.

5. Discussion

Robust face detection with invariance properties in terms of translation, scale, and pose, inherent in our non-spiking version of CNN model (Matsugu, 2001; Matsugu et al., 2002) brings robustness to dynamical changes both in head movements and in facial expressions. In particular, because of the topographic property of our network preserving positional information of respective facial features from the bottom to top layers, the translation invariance in facial expression recognition is inherent in our convolutional architecture.

The feedback mechanism from the top to intermediate modules is used to identify corresponding facial features between neutral and emotional states. Specifically, face location as detected by FD4 was used to confine the search area of eye and mouth, and those intermediate facial features as detected in FD3 layer were utilized for tracking primitive local features extracted by the bottom layer FD1, which turned out to be useful for facial expression recognition. Location information of eyes and mouth detected in the CNN are thus transmitted, through the feedback loop from the FP3 layer to the rule-based processing module, to confine the processing area of facial feature analysis in the image based on differences in terms of at least six cues shown in Section 3.

A great number of approaches (see Donato, Bartlett, Hager, Ekman, & Sejnowski, 1999 for review) have been taken for robustness in facial expression recognition. However, most existing models do not have all of those properties for robustness stated in the above, and many of them require explicit estimation of motion parameters.

In contrast to a number of conventional methods, the proposed model for facial expression recognition is much more compact and efficient with the following distinct aspects.

(1) Our model requires only differences in local features, extracted by the CNN, between a neutral face and emotional faces, instead of using differences between adjacent frames.
(2) For the facial analysis, we need only a single set of local features from one neutral face as reference data.
(3) Unlike many other approaches, the proposed system requires no explicit estimation of motion parameters over image sequences.

Additionally important feature of our model in terms of compactness is that we need a single system of CNN, whereas the Fasel's model requires two CNNs in tandem to obtain subject dependent facial expression recognition.

Conversely, it turned out that the proposed system is quite insensitive to individuality of facial expressions mainly by virtue of the rule-based facial analysis. Those cues exploited in the analysis undergo voting process with weighted summation of scores for respective cues in terms of differences of facial features in neutral and emotional states. As a result of this, voting individuality is averaged out to obtain subject independence. In practice, this subject independence is quite preferable since we can dispense with a large database that contains individual facial expressions. However, Fasel's model was not endowed with such property. We believe that it is easy to extend the current framework to other tasks for subject independent facial expression recognition. Although our rule-based facial analysis is useful as it is, we may incorporate fuzzy rules to obtain more robust performance.

In conclusion, our model is the first facial expression recognition system with subject independence combined with robustness with regard to variability in face images in terms of appearance and location.

References

Black, M., & Yacoob, Y. (1995). Tracking and recognizing rigid and non-rigid facial motions using local parametric models of image motion. *Proceedings of IEEE Fifth International Conference on Computer Vision*, 374–381.

Black, M., & Yacoob, Y. (1997). Recognizing facial expressions in image sequences using local parameterized models of image motion. *International Journal of Computer Vision*, *25*, 23–48.

Donato, G., Bartlett, M. S., Hager, J. C., Ekman, P., & Sejnowski, T. (1999). Classifying facial actions. *IEEE Transactions on Pattern Analysis and Machine Intelligence*, *21*, 974–989.

Ebine, H., & Nakamura, O. (1999). The recognition of facial expressions considering the difference between individuality. *Transaction on IEE of Japan*, *119-C*, 474–481. (In Japanese).

Fasel, B. (2002). Robust face analysis using convolutional neural networks. *Proceedings of International Conference on Pattern*.

Földiák, P. (1991). Learning invariance from transformation sequences. *Neural Computation*, *3*, 194–200.

Fukushima, K. (1980). Neocognitron: a self-organizing neural networks for a mechanism of pattern recognition unaffected by shift in position. *Biological Cybernetics*, *36*, 193–202.

Le Cun, Y., & Bengio, T. (1995). Convolutional networks for images, speech, and time series. In M. A. Arbib (Ed.), *The handbook of brain theory and neural networks* (pp. 255–258). Cambridge, MA: MIT Press.

Matsugu, M. (2001). Hierarchical pulse-coupled neural network model with temporal coding and emergent feature binding mechanism. *Proceedings of International Joint Conference on Neural Networks*, 802–807.

Matsugu, M., Mori, K., Ishii, M., & Mitarai, Y. (2002). Convolutional spiking neural network model for robust face detection. *Proceedings of the Ninth International Conference on Neural Information Processing, Singapore*, 660–664.

Rosenblum, M., Yacoob, Y., & Davis, L. S. (1996). Human expression recognition from motion using a radial basis function network architecture. *IEEE Transactions on Neural Networks*, *7*, 1121–1138.

Wallis, G., & Rolls, E. T. (1997). Invariant face and object recognition in the visual system. *Progress in Neurobiology*, *51*, 167–194.

Yacoob, Y., & Davis, L. S. (1996). Recognizing human facial expression from long image sequences using optical flow. *IEEE Transaction on Pattern Analysis and Machine Intelligence*, *18*, 636–642.

PERGAMON

AVAILABLE AT
www.ComputerScienceWeb.com
POWERED BY SCIENCE @ DIRECT

Neural Networks 16 (2003) 561–568

Neural Networks

www.elsevier.com/locate/neunet

2003 Special issue

A generalized feedforward neural network architecture for classification and regression

Ganesh Arulampalam*, Abdesselam Bouzerdoum

Edith Cowan University, 100 Joondalup Drive, Joondalup, WA 6027, Australia

Abstract

This article presents a new generalized feedforward neural network (GFNN) architecture for pattern classification and regression. The GFNN architecture uses as the basic computing unit a generalized shunting neuron (GSN) model, which includes as special cases the perceptron and the shunting inhibitory neuron. GSNs are capable of forming complex, nonlinear decision boundaries. This allows the GFNN architecture to easily learn some complex pattern classification problems. In this article the GFNNs are applied to several benchmark classification problems, and their performance is compared to the performances of SIANNs and multilayer perceptrons. Experimental results show that a single GSN can outperform both the SIANN and MLP networks.

Keywords: Feedforward neural network; Generalized shunting neuron; Perceptron; Shunting inhibition; Classification

1. Introduction

Shunting inhibition is a powerful computational mechanism that plays an important role in sensory neural information processing systems. Since it was proposed as a plausible physiological model in the early 1960s (Furman, 1965; Lettvin, 1962), shunting inhibition has been extensively used to model some important visual and cognitive functions. For example, Grossberg used it to model long-term and short-term memory mechanisms, feature detection, and other cognitive functions (Grossberg, 1973, 1976, 1988). Fukushima employed it for local feature detection as part of the neocognitron (Fukushima, Miyake, & Ito, 1983). Pinter used it to model the adaptation phenomena in receptive field organization and modulation transfer function (Pinter, 1983, 1984, 1985). Bouzerdoum (1993) and Bouzerdoum and Pinter (1992) proposed a model of motion detection in insects based on shunting inhibition. They also introduced a shunting inhibitory cellular neural network and used it to model receptive field profiles of neurons in the early parts of the visual system (Bouzerdoum & Pinter, 1993). Other researchers have also used shunting inhibition, including some of its VLSI implementations.

Despite their widespread use in modelling psychophysical, neurophysiological and cognitive phenomena, to our knowledge, shunting networks have not been used in supervised pattern classification or function approximation, other than in the neocognitron (Fukushima, Miyake, & Ito, 1983) and ART networks (Carpenter & Grossberg, 1988). It is only recently that Bouzerdoum (1999, 2000) proposed an artificial neural network architecture, based on shunting inhibition, that can be trained to perform pattern classification or function approximation; he called it the shunting inhibitory artificial neural network (SIANN). SIANNs are shunting networks that operate in a feedforward mode and use the steady-state solution of the set of ordinary differential equations governing the dynamics of the shunting networks, thereby avoiding the need to obtain a numerical solution for a set of differential equations (Bouzerdoum, 1999, 2000). This allows the network to operate in a static mode like multilayer perceptrons (MLPs). The idea was to exploit the inherent nonlinearity of shunting inhibition to develop powerful, trainable networks, with nonlinear decision surfaces, for classification, nonlinear regression and pattern association.

In the past, lack of efficient training algorithms has restricted the potential applications of shunting inhibitory neural networks. We have developed supervised learning algorithms, based on gradient techniques and the back-propagation algorithm, for SIANNs and applied them to some benchmark pattern classification problems (Arulampalam & Bouzerdoum, 2000, 2001). SIANNs are more powerful than MLPs in that each shunting neuron has

* Corresponding author.
E-mail address: g.arulampalam@ecu.edu.au (G. Arulampalam).

0893-6080/03/$ - see front matter © 2003 Elsevier Science Ltd. All rights reserved.
doi:10.1016/S0893-6080(03)00116-3

a higher capacity than a perceptron neuron and can form linear as well as nonlinear decision boundaries, which allows the network to form complex decision surfaces much more readily.

Although SIANNs performed satisfactorily on benchmark tests, and even outperformed MLPs on some problems, there was a drawback in the original formulation; each input served as the excitatory input to a different neuron, resulting in the number of shunting neurons being equal to the number of inputs. If the number of inputs is large, the number of synaptic weights will be large; this is neither desirable nor necessary. In many problems, SIANNs can generalize very well when the number of shunting neurons is smaller than the number of inputs. Therefore, in Arulampalam and Bouzerdoum (2002) an enhancement to the SIANN structure has been proposed and tested, which allows the number of shunting neurons to be different from the number of external inputs. This has increased the flexibility and efficiency of SIANNs; however, a new question arises as to which inputs should be used as excitatory inputs.

In this paper, the shunting neuron model used in SIANNs is expanded to allow greater flexibility in network structure. The result is a new neuron model that combines the shunting neuron model with the traditional perceptron model. We use this 'generalized' shunting neuron model in feedforward networks, which henceforth is referred to as the generalized feedforward neural network (GFNN). The GFNN is tested on some benchmark classification problems and its performance is compared to that of MLPs and SIANNs. Section 2 describes the generalized shunting neuron (GSN) model and the structure of the GFNN. Section 3 presents the experiments performed using the GFNN classifier. The results are presented in Section 4. Finally, the discussion and the conclusion are presented in Sections 5 and 6, respectively.

2. Generalized feedforward neural network

In this section we develop the GFNN architecture as an extension of SIANNs (Bouzerdoum, 1999, 2000). The SIANN architecture and its basic computing element, the static shunting neuron, are introduced next, followed by the GSN model, then the GFNN architecture.

2.1. The static shunting neuron and SIANNs

The dynamics of a shunting neuron are governed by a non-linear differential equation in which inhibition is mediated by shunting a portion of the excitatory signal. This appears in the differential equation describing the activity of the neuron as a multiplicative term between the state of the neuron and the inhibitory signal (Grossberg, 1973, 1976; Pinter, 1983, 1984). In shunting inhibitory neural networks neighboring neurons exert mutual inhibitory interactions of the shunting type. The activity of each neuron is described by a nonlinear differential equation:

$$\frac{dx_j}{dt} = I_j - a_j x_j - f\left(\sum_i c_{ji} x_i\right) x_j + b_j \tag{1}$$

where x_j represents the activity of the jth neuron; I_j is the input to the jth neuron; a_j is the passive decay rate of the neuron (positive constant); c_{ji} is the connection weight from the ith input to the jth neuron; b_j represents the bias; and f is an activation function bounded from below.

Eq. (2) describes recurrent shunting inhibition, where each neuron receives an external excitatory input and the weighted outputs of the nearby neurons are fed back, through the nonlinear activation function, as inhibitory inputs. The stability of these networks has been investigated by Bouzerdoum (1992) and Bouzerdoum and Pinter (1993), and they have been successfully applied to vision and image processing tasks (Bouzerdoum, 1993; Beare & Bouzerdoum, 1999; Cheung, Bouzerdoum & Newland, 1999).

In the feedforward model, both the excitatory and inhibitory influences are mediated by the external inputs; in other words, the x_i term in Eq. (1) is replaced by I_i :

$$\frac{dx_j}{dt} = I_j - a_j x_j - f\left(\sum_i c_{ji} I_i\right) x_j + b_j \tag{2}$$

The static shunting neuron model is derived from the steady-state solution of Eq. (2). Therefore, the state of the static shunting neuron is given by

$$x_j = \frac{I_j + b_j}{a_j + f\left(\sum_i c_{ji} I_i + c_{jo}\right)} \tag{3}$$

The static model of a shunting neuron is shown diagrammatically in Fig. 1. The shunting neuron has only one unweighted excitatory input, whereas all inhibitory (shunting) inputs are weighted and fed into an activation function. We define the denominator in Eq. (3) as the shunting term for

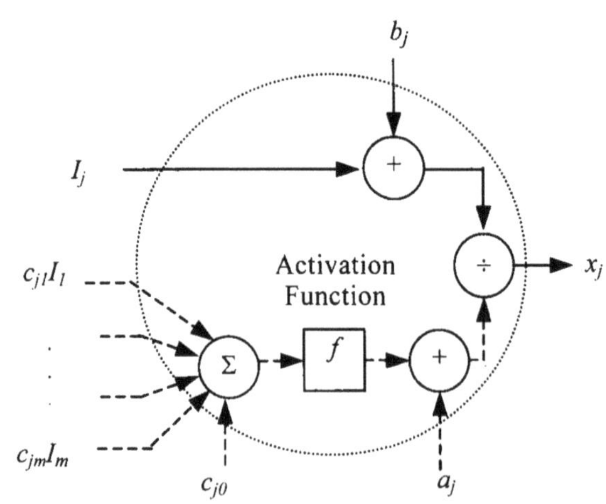

Fig. 1. Static model of a shunting neuron.

the jth neuron, s_j, given by

$$s_j = a_j + f\left(\sum_i c_{ji} I_i + c_{jo}\right) \tag{4}$$

The term s_j is constrained to be positive so as not to encounter a divide by zero error, i.e. $s_j > 0$.

SIANNs are feedforward networks where shunting neurons are arranged in a layer (or layers). The output layer consists of linear or sigmoidal neurons. Fig. 2 shows a feedforward SIANN with a single layer of m shunting inhibitory neurons. The outputs of the shunting neurons are connected to n output neurons.

Originally, the SIANN was proposed as a fully connected structure (Bouzerdoum, 1999, 2000); that is, each input is fed directly into one shunting neuron as an excitatory input, whereas all inputs are weighted and fed in as inhibitory inputs (refer Fig. 2). Therefore, the fully connected SIANN structure has as many shunting neurons as there are inputs. The perceptron layer is used to sum the outputs of the shunting layers and produce the right number of outputs for the network.

Using this basic SIANN structure, the number of neurons in the network is actually determined by the dataset. The number of neurons in the shunting layer(s) is determined by the number of data attributes, whereas the number of neurons in the output layer is determined by the number of class labels. While this removes the need to find an optimal network structure, it was found to be too restrictive. In particular, when the data has a large number of inputs and outputs the resulting structures are inordinately large. This leads to increased computational complexity and training time.

A modified SIANN structure has been described where the number of shunting neurons can vary arbitrarily (Arulampalam & Bouzerdoum, 2002). A network may have less shunting neurons than there are inputs from the previous layer. In these cases, only some of the inputs are excitatory (equal to the number of shunting neurons) and the other inputs act only as inhibitory inputs. For structures where a shunting layer has more neurons than the previous layer outputs, the additional shunting neurons are fed in with a constant bias as excitatory input, but with the normal inputs fed in as inhibitory inputs. This gives more freedom in selecting the optimum network structure.

The results obtained showed that the modified SIANN structure could perform as well as the regular SIANNs using smaller structures. This resulted in savings in terms of computational effort and memory requirements. However, a question arises as to which inputs ought to be used as excitatory inputs. To alleviate this inherent limitation, a generalised shunting neuron (GSN) model is proposed here.

2.2. Generalized shunting neuron model

One of the shortcomings of the shunting neuron model described above was the fact that each neuron can only have one unweighted excitatory input. This means that either the network needs to have as many neurons as there are inputs, or only some inputs can be excitatory. It was concluded in Arulampalam and Bouzerdoum (2002) that one way out of this is to have excitatory inputs summed and passed through an activation function as with a perceptron neuron. In fact, the proposed new neuron model combines the perceptron neuron model with the shunting neuron model as previously described. The output of the GSN can be described as

$$x_j = \frac{g\left(\sum_i w_{ji} I_i + w_{j0}\right) + b_j}{a_j + f\left(\sum_i c_{ji} I_i + c_{j0}\right)} \tag{5}$$

The GSN model is shown diagrammatically in Fig. 3. It should be noted that both the perceptron neuron and the shunting neuron model are special cases of this new model. The perceptron model is a special case of the GSN where

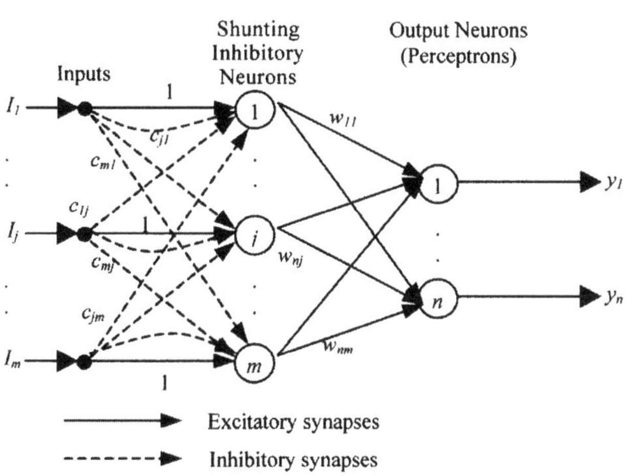

Fig. 2. Feedforward SIANN structure.

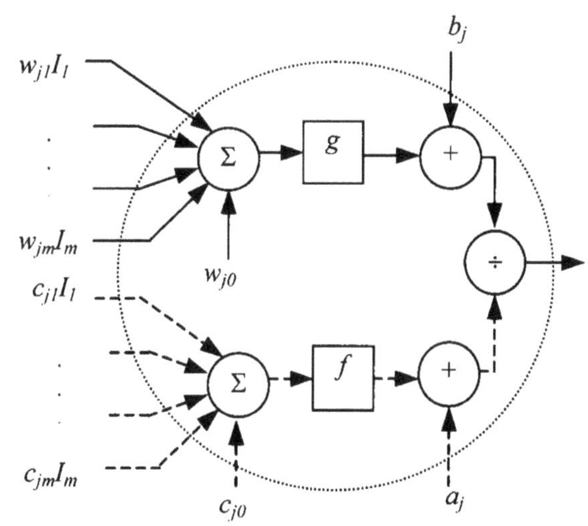

Fig. 3. GSN model.

the denominator weights c are fixed at 0 and a is set to a constant that makes the denominator equal to 1, depending on the activation function f. Furthermore, Eq. (5) reduces to Eq. (3), which models the normal shunting neuron, when $w_{jj} = 1$, all other weights w_{ji} are 0, and g is the linear activation function. We have therefore named this new model the GSN model.

More important, however, is the fact that the input-output transfer characteristic of a GSN is adaptive. Even when the activation functions f and g, in Eq. (5), are fixed, the type of input–output relationship each computing element can have varies depending on its synaptic weights. Fig. 4 shows some input–output transfer functions of a GSN using the logarithmic activation function for both f and g, obtained by simply changing the weights. More complex characteristics can be obtained by mixing different activation functions. By contrast, traditional artificial neural models, such as the RBF (radial basis function) and the perceptron, have their input–output transfer function of a fixed type, e.g., bell-shaped or sigmoid-shaped. This we believe places an artificial constraint on the type of decision surfaces a particular neuron can produce.

Jankowski and Duch have investigated the role of activation functions in neural network performance, and have used a number of transfer functions, such as bicentric and extended conic functions, that can produce complex decision boundaries, thus allowing the number of adaptive units in the network to be reduced (Duch & Jankowski, 2001; Jankowski, 1999; Jankowski & Duch, 2001). Neurons with these activation functions have been used in ontogenic and heterogenous neural networks. The GSN neuron is able to produce similar transfer characteristics, with the added advantage that it requires only $2N + 4$ parameters per neuron instead of $3N$ or $4N$ parameters as given by Jankowski and Duch.

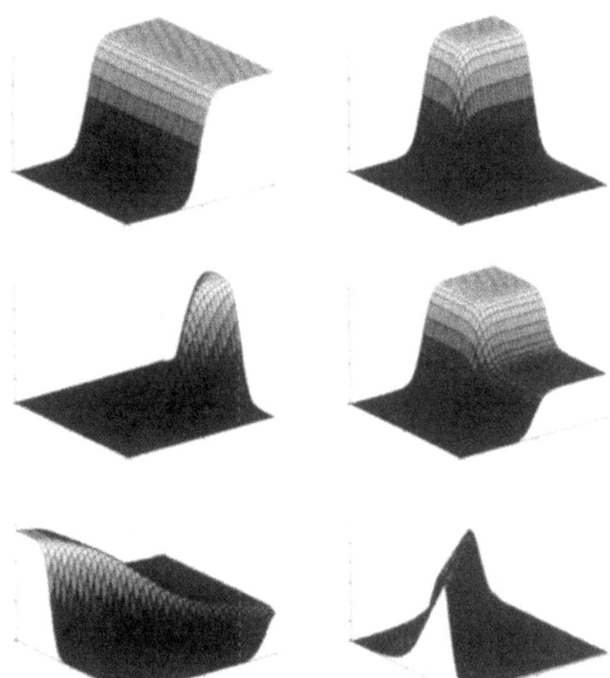

Fig. 4. Input–output transfer characteristics of a GSN obtained the same f and g functions, but different w and c weight vectors.

2.3. The GFNN architecture

The GFNN is a multilayer feedforward neural network architecture consisting of several hidden layers of generalized neurons, and an output layer of generalized, sigmoidal or linear neurons. Neurons in each layer receive inputs only from the preceding layer, calculate their outputs according to Eq. (5), and transmit the resulting signals to the next layer. Note that GFNNs may contain in their hidden layers, as 'special case', shunting or perceptron-type neurons. However, in this paper, we consider only fully connected GFNN structures with only one hidden-layer, containing one or more generalized neurons, and an output layer of linear or logarithmic neurons.

3. Experimental details

3.1. Classification problems

Three datasets were used as benchmark tests for this experiment: one artificial problem, namely the 3-bit parity problem, and two 'real world' datasets—the Pima Indians Diabetes and the Wisconsin Breast Cancer problems. The real-world datasets were obtained from the UCI Machine Learning Repository (Blake & Merz, 1998).

All real-world dataset inputs have been scaled to the range -1 to 1 for the experiment. Each dataset was partitioned into three sets: 50% was used as the training set, 25% as the validation set and 25% as the test set. The 3-bit parity problem has only 8 binary input combinations and all these input patterns were used for training, validation and testing. A trained neural network should be able to correctly classify previously unseen inputs (good generalization). The validation set is used for early stopping so that the networks are not overtrained and are able to generalize well. During training the network weights that result in the minimum validation set error are saved. If the validation set error is not reduced for 50 consecutive epochs, the training is stopped and the final network weights used for testing are those that resulted in the minimum validation set error. All results shown are based on the test set, which contains examples not used in the training process for the real-world datasets.

3.2. Network structures

The datasets were used to train a number of different GFNN, SIANN and MLP networks. The number of layers and number of neurons per layer were varied. GFNN networks tested are either single layer network with only GSNs or a single layer of GSNs with a layer of perceptrons as the output layer. The structures are denoted by G for single layer network and GP for the two-layer network with perceptron output. This will be followed by the size of the layers. For example, G 9-1 denotes a single GSN neuron with nine inputs, whereas GP 8-2-1 denotes a network with eight inputs going into 2 GSN neurons with a single output perceptron. The SIANNs tested were the original fully connected SIANN structures with the number of shunting neurons equal to the number of inputs. MLP structures with similar number of weights to the GFNNs were tested for comparison.

The GSN neurons were tested with various combinations of activation functions for the numerator and denominator. Linear (lin), hyperbolic tangent (tan), logarithmic (log) and exponential (exp) activation functions were used for the numerator. The constraint on the shunting term given in Eq. (4) requires the denominator activation function to have a lower bound. Therefore the linear activation function could not be used for the denominator. The output perceptron neurons had either linear or logarithmic activation functions.

For SIANNs and MLPs, the hidden layers had hyperbolic tangent activation functions, while the output layer neurons had either logarithmic or linear activation functions.

For each network structure, 50 networks with the same structure but with randomly initialized weights were generated. Each set of 50 networks was trained using various training algorithms and the results were averaged over the 50 networks.

3.3. Training algorithms

The training algorithms used are based on the standard backpropagation algorithm. The derivation of gradient-based algorithms for SIANNs and their application to simple classification problems can be found in Arulampalam and Bouzerdoum (2000). The same derivation process was applied to GFNNs and the training algorithms set accordingly.

For this experiment, two 'standard' training algorithms were used, gradient descent with momentum and adaptive learning rate (GDX) (Demuth & Beale, 1992) and the Levenberg-Marquardt (LM) algorithm (Hagan & Menhaj, 1994). In both cases, the update of the parameter a was limited so that the shunting term $s_j > 0.1$ to ensure stability. In order to test the effect of the parameter b, experiments were also carried out with modified training algorithms that did not train the b parameter, which was set to 0 at the start. Where used, these results are marked by superscript a next to the training algorithm.

3.4. Initialization

The weights b, c and w were initialized using a random number generator that generates uniformly distributed values in the range $[-r, r]$. Thimm and Fiesler (1997) have compared initialization schemes for perceptrons and found that schemes of this form perform well over a variety of problems. Initial tests used $r = 1$, but subsequent results indicated that the scheme used by Smieja (1991) performed well over the different problems. In this scheme, the range r is defined by

$$r = \frac{2}{\sqrt{N}} \tag{6}$$

where N is the number of inputs of the particular neuron (fan-in). This initialization scheme ensures that the sigmoid activation functions start in their linear regions and not in saturation, thereby improving training performance.

The parameter a was initialized to a random value between 0 and 1, then offset with a constant so that when added with the lower bound of the denominator activation function it would not be smaller than the limit of 0.1. For example, for a hyperbolic tangent activation function with a lower bound of -1, the constant offset would be 1.1.

4. Experimental results

4.1. 3-bit Parity problem

The 3-bit parity problem is a popular artificial classification problem where the network has to generate the appropriate binary output for a 3-bit binary input so that there are always an even (or odd) number of ones. This 3-dimensional problem is not linearly separable and is one level of complexity higher than the 2-dimensional XOR problem. The eight input combinations can be visualized as the vertices of a unit cube, where no two adjacent vertices are of the same class. A single perceptron neuron can only produce a linear decision boundary (Haykin, 1994), whereas a single shunting neuron can correctly classify the XOR problem (Arulampalam & Bouzerdoum, 2000, 2002). In this paper, a single GSN has been used to successfully classify the 3-bit parity problem, as shown in Table 1.

The results show that a single GSN neuron is capable of solving the 3-bit parity problem consistently (70–94% of networks). The performance of a single neuron is able to surpass that of the SIANNs and MLPs that have more neurons and also more weights.

4.2. Breast cancer dataset

The breast cancer dataset has 699 samples with nine integer inputs and two output classes (benign and malignant). The data has missing values that were replaced by zeros before scaling. While there are better approaches for estimating the missing values (Hathaway

Table 1
Results for 3-bit parity

Training algorithm	Activation functions			Runs with zero error (%)	Avg. epochs		Test error	
	Hidden		Output		All runs	No errors	Mean (%)	Median (%)
	Numerator	Denominator						
GFNN G 3-1 (10 weights)								
LM	Lin	Log		94	123	108	1.50	0
LM	Exp	Log		90	201	155	4.25	0
GDX[a]	Exp	Log		70	403	394	15.00	0
SIANN 3-3-1 (22 weights)								
LM		Tan	Lin	66	620	424	10.25	0
GDX		Tan	Log	78	645	582	3.50	0
MLP 3-2-1 (11 weights)								
LM	Tan		Lin	42	285	142	26.00	25.00
GDX	Tan		Lin	18	828	1000	25.25	25.00
MLP 3-3-1 (16 weights)								
LM	Tan		Log	76	52	40	6.75	0
GDX	Tan		Log	50	730	598	12.25	6.25

[a] Trained with b fixed at 0.

& Bezdek, 2001), we chose this method for the sake of simplicity. Furthermore, the Breast Cancer Dataset is not a very complex one; even with this simple approach perfect classification results are obtained. Table 2 summarizes the results of the best GFNN, SIANN and MLP network structures.

The breast cancer problem appears to be quite simple for the neural networks. Most cases had mean error under 1% with a number of networks achieving 100% test success. The single GSN neuron was capable of achieving perfect results in 90–100% of the cases. The 2-1 GFNN also performed well with more than 66% of networks achieving perfect results. Both these GFNN structures were able to achieve average error rates of below 0.3%, better than anything obtained with the other networks. The SIANN, though the largest in terms of weights and neurons, performed the worst.

4.3. Results for diabetes diagnosis

The diabetes dataset has 768 samples with eight real-valued inputs and two output classes. The summarized results for the best-performing networks are given in Table 3. The diabetes diagnosis problem was a lot harder for the neural networks compared to the breast cancer

Table 2
Results for breast cancer dataset

Training algorithm	Activation functions			Runs with zero error (%)	Avg. epochs		Test error	
	Hidden		Output		All runs	No errors	Mean (%)	Median (%)
	Numerator	Denominator						
GFNN G 9-1 (22 weights)								
LM	Exp	Tan		90	157	167	0.10	0
GDX[a]	Tan	Exp		100	177	177	0.0	0
GFNN GP 9-2-1 (47 weights)								
LM	Log	Tan	Lin	66	401	454	0.28	0
GDX[a]	Log	Exp	Lin	78	193	192	0.14	0
GDX[a]	Lin	Log	Log	68	128	126	0.18	0
SIANN 9-9-1 (118 weights)								
LM		Tan	Log	24	60	54	1.14	1.13
GDX		Tan	Log	12	130	135	1.01	1.13
MLP 9-2-1 (23 weights)								
LM	Tan		Lin	22	64	70	0.84	0.56
GDX	Tan		Lin	66	176	173	0.32	0
MLP 9-4-1 (45 weights)								
LM	Tan		Lin	26	63	60	0.78	0.56
GDX	Tan		Lin	48	200	201	0.40	0.56

[a] Trained with b fixed at 0.

Table 3
Results for diabetes dataset

Training algorithm	Activation functions			Runs with error < 20% (%)	Avg. epochs all runs	Best case test error (%)	Test error	
	Hidden		Output			No errors	Mean (%)	Median (%)
	Numerator	Denominator						
GFNN G 8-1 (20 weights)								
LM	Tan	Log		46	39	18.75	20.50	20.31
GDX[a]	Log	Log		22	201	19.27	20.77	20.83
GFNN GP 8-2-1 (43 weights)								
LM	Tan	Tan	Lin	48	32	18.23	20.43	20.31
GDX	Tan	Log	Log	48	169	17.71	21.27	20.31
SIANN 8-8-1 (97 weights)								
LM		Tan	Log	24	71	18.23	21.27	21.35
GDX		Tan	Log	28	174	17.71	20.78	20.83
MLP 8-2-1 (21 weights)								
LM	Tan		Lin	24	62	19.27	21.27	20.83
GDX	Tan		Log	12	191	19.27	21.48	20.83
MLP 8-5-1 (51 weights)								
LM	Tan		Lin	20	61	17.71	21.95	21.88
GDX	Tan		Log	26	193	18.75	21.03	20.83

[a] Trained with b fixed at 0.

problem. The average test error was generally between 20 and 22%, with best case results as low as 17.7%. This compares well with previously reported results for this problem (Prechelt, 1994; Sherrah, 1998) where the best case error rates were above 20%.

From the results, it can be seen that all three types of networks can consistently achieve about 80% success rate for diabetes prediction, from the given inputs. The difference in average errors is not significant. The 2-1 GFNNs, however, were able to get a greater number of networks achieving less than 20% test error, and in fewer epochs.

5. Discussion

The primary objective of the formulation of the GSN model was to overcome some limitations of SIANNs. In particular, the aim was to be able to reduce the size of the shunting network without having to make arbitrary decisions as to which inputs were more ‘important’ and therefore used as both excitatory as well as inhibitory inputs. From that perspective, the results obtained have far exceeded the initial aims. The GSN model has proven to be a ‘super’ model.

Firstly, it is a superset of both perceptrons and the shunting inhibitory neuron model previously used. Secondly, a single neuron been shown to be able to successfully classify well known benchmark problems, or at least match the best performances of more complex network structures. This is the ultimate in structural simplicity.

The problem of finding the optimal network structure has been removed, or at least significantly reduced. The problem then is to find the combination of activation functions and training algorithm that will produce the best result The GFNNs were tested for all the different permutations of numerator and denominator activation functions. The results obtained indicate performance can vary significantly for different combinations and that the optimal combination is problem dependent. The reason is that various combinations of activation functions can produce different types of transfer characteristics. Certain characteristics will be able to approximate the decision boundary for a given problem more efficiently than others. Due to space constraints, only the results for best combinations of activation functions for each structure–algorithm pair have been shown. Even from the limited results shown it can be seen that the best activation function combination depends not only on the problem but also the network structure.

While the single neuron has performed well on the benchmark problems used here, further work needs to be done in analyzing the performance of GFNNs for more complex problems that may require more than a single neuron. The tests thus far have been limited to one and two-layer networks. If multiple layers are used, the possibility of mixing layers of different neurons types in a single structure will open up myriad possibilities.

6. Conclusion

In this paper we presented a generalized feedforward architecture for classification and regression. It uses as a basic building block a GSN, which includes as special cases the normal shunting inhibitory neuron and the perceptron. Overall, the results show that the GFNN classifiers can solve problems with simple structures. The power of these networks is lies with the neuron model used. The GSN is able to produce complex decision boundaries with a single neuron. This is exemplified by the solving of the 3-bit parity and Breast Cancer problems with a single neuron. The GFNNs were able to match or out-perform SIANNs and MLPs with more neurons and more synaptic weights. The success of the GFNNs depends on the combination of numerator and denominator activation functions used. Different combinations of activation functions can produce various types of transfer characteristics by varying the synaptic weights. GFNNs show the ability to be the basis of a class of powerful new classifiers. Further investigations need to be carried out on more complex problems, the performance of more complex GFNN structures and the choice of activation functions.

References

Arulampalam, G., & Bouzerdoum, A. (2000). Training shunting inhibitory artificial neural networks as classifiers. *Neural Network World, 10*(3), 333–350.

Arulampalam, G., & Bouzerdoum, A. (2001). Application of shunting inhibitory artificial neural networks to medical diagnosis. *Proceedings of the Seventh Australian and New Zealand Intelligent Information Systems Conference (ANZIIS 2001), Perth, Australia*, 89–94.

Arulampalam, G., & Bouzerdoum, A. (2002). Expanding the structure of shunting inhibitory artificial neural network classifiers. *Proceedings of the International Joint Conference on Neural Networks (IJCNN 2002), Honolulu, USA*, 2855–2860.

Beare, R., & Bouzerdoum, A. (1999). Biologically inspired local motion detector architecture. *Journal of Optical Society of American Association, 16*(9), 2059–2068.

Blake, C. L., & Merz, C. J (1998). *UCI Repository of machine learning databases*. University of California, Department of Information and Computer Science: http://www.ics.uci.edu/~mlearn/MLrepository.html

Bouzerdoum, A. (1992). Convergence of symmetric shunting competitive neural networks. In D. Green, & T. Bossomaier (Eds.), *Complex systems: From biology to computation* (pp. 301–312). Amsterdam: IOS Press.

Bouzerdoum, A. (1993). The elementary movement detection mechanism in insect vision. *Philosphical Transactions of the Royal Society of London, B-339*, 375–384.

Bouzerdoum, A. (1999). A new class of high-order neural networks with nonlinear decision boundaries. *Proceedings of the Sixth International Conference on Neural Information Processing (ICONIP '99), Perth, Australia*, 1004–1009.

Bouzerdoum, A. (2000). Classification and function approximation using feed-forward shunting inhibitory artificial neural networks. *Proceedings of the International Joint Conference on Neural Networks (IJCNN 2000), Como, Italy*, 613–618.

Bouzerdoum, A., & Pinter, R. B. (1992). Nonlinear lateral inhibition applied to motion detection in the fly visual system. In R. B. Pinter, & B. Nabet (Eds.), *Nonlinear vision* (pp. 423–450). Boca Raton: CRC Press.

Bouzerdoum, A., & Pinter, R. B. (1993). Shunting inhibitory cellular neural networks: derivation and stability analysis. *IEEE Transactions on Circuits and Systems I: Fundamental Theory and Applications, 40*(3), 215–221.

Carpenter, G. A., & Grossberg, S. (1988). The ART of adaptive pattern recognition by a self-organising neural network. *IEEE Computer, 21*(3).

Cheung, H. N., Bouzerdoum, A., & Newland, W. (1999). Properties of shunting inhibitory cellular neural networks for colour image enhancement. *Proceedings of the Sixth International Conference on Neural Information Processing (ICONIP'99), Perth, Australia*, 1219–1223.

Demuth, H., & Beale, M. (1992). *Neural network toolbox user's guide* (Version 3 ed). The MathWorks Inc.

Duch, W., & Jankowski, N. (2001). Transfer functions: hidden possibilities for better neural networks. *Proceedings of the Ninth European Symposium on Artificial Neural Networks (ESANN), Brugge*, 81–94.

Fukushima, K., Miyake, S., & Ito, T. (1983). Neocognitron: a neural network model for a mechanism of visual pattern recognition. *IEEE Transaction on Systems, Man and Cybernetics, 13*, 826–834.

Furman, G. G. (1965). Comparison of models for subtractive and shunting lateral-inhibition in receptor-neuron fields. *Kybernetik, 2*, 257–274.

Grossberg, S. (1973). Contour enhancement, short term memory, and constancies in reverberating neural networks. *Studies in Applied Mathematics, 52*(3), 213–257.

Grossberg, S. (1976). Adaptive pattern classification and universal recoding: I. Parallel development and coding of neural feature detectors. *Biological Cybernetics, 23*, 121–134.

Grossberg, S. (Ed.), (1988). *Neural networks and natural intelligence*. Cambridge, MA: MIT Press.

Hagan, M. T., & Menhaj, M. B. (1994). Training feedforward networks with the Marquadt algorithm. *IEEE Transactions on Neural Networks, 5*(6), 989–993.

Hathaway, R., & Bezdek, J. C. (2001). Fuzzy c-means clustering of incomplete data. *IEEE Transactions on Systems, Man and Cybernetics, Part B: Cybernetics, 31*(5), 735–744.

Haykin, S. (1994). *Neural networks: A comprehensive foundation*. New York: Macmillan.

Jankowski, N. (1999). *Flexible transfer functions with ontogenic neural networks*. Torun, Poland: Computational Intelligence Lab, DCM NCU.

Jankowski, N., & Duch, W. (2001). Optimal transfer function neural networks. *Proceedings of the Ninth European Symposium on Artificial Neural Networks (ESANN), Brugge*, 101–106.

Lettvin, J. Y. (1962). *Form–function relations in neurons. Res. Quart. Prog. Report*. Cambridge, MA: MIT Press.

Pinter, R. B. (1983). Product term nonlinear lateral inhibition enhances visual selectivity for small objects or edges. *Journal of Theoretical Biology, 100*, 525–531.

Pinter, R. B. (1984). Adaptation of receptive field organization by multiplicative lateral inhibition. *Journal of Theoretical Biology, 110*, 435–444.

Pinter, R. B. (1985). Adaptation of spatial modulation transfer function via nonlinear lateral inhibition. *Biological Cybernetics, 51*, 285–291.

Prechelt, L. (1994). *PROBEN 1—A set of neural network benchmark problems and benchmarking rules (Technical Report 21/94)*. Karlsruhe, Germany: Fakultat fur Informatik, Universitat Karlsruhe.

Sherrah, J (1998). *Automatic feature extraction for pattern recognition*. PhD Thesis, University of Adelaide, Adelaide.

Smieja, F. J. (1991). *Hyperplane spin dynamics, network plasticity and backpropagation learning*. St Augustin, Germany: GMD.

Thimm, G., & Fiesler, E. (1997). High-order and multilayer perceptron initialization. *IEEE Transactions on Neural Networks, 8*(2), 349–359.

PERGAMON

AVAILABLE AT
www.ComputerScienceWeb.com
POWERED BY SCIENCE DIRECT

Neural Networks 16 (2003) 569–576

Neural Networks

www.elsevier.com/locate/neunet

2003 Special issue

Hierarchical cognitive maps

Horatiu Voicu*

Department of Psychological and Brain Sciences, Duke University, P.O. Box 90086, Durham, NC 27708-0086, USA

Abstract

We describe a computational model of spatial navigation based on experimental studies conducted with human participants. The model builds and uses a hierarchical cognitive map of a large environment. Computer simulations show that the model correctly describes experimental results including hierarchical organization of space and distance estimation. Furthermore, the model predicts that reaction time for distance estimation varies nonlinearly with distance.

Keywords: Cognitive maps; Computational model; Spatial navigation

1. Introduction

Research in spatial cognition has shown that humans build internal representations of the environments they explore. These internal representations, also known as cognitive maps, have many properties including sensory fusion, distortion, subjectivity, fragmentation and hierarchical structure.

The hierarchical organization of the cognitive map in humans has been studied in a series of experiments. Hirtle and Jonides (1985) showed that humans who experience the Ann Arbor Campus (Fig. 1A) for at least 2.5 years and use walking as their primary mode of travel, tend to organize their spatial representation in clusters of landmarks. This result has been obtained by analyzing the data produced by a recall task using the ordered tree algorithm (Reitman & Rueter, 1980). The recall task consisted of an enumeration, by each subject, of 32 landmarks in the Ann Arbor Campus. The enumeration was repeated 14 times. The complete lists of landmarks were fed to the ordered tree algorithm, which revealed the structure of the recall data. An example of an ordered tree generated for the Ann Arbor campus is shown in Fig. 2A. The tree reveals the clusters of landmarks found in the recall data. For example, Bell Tower and League form a cluster and they are close in the Ann Arbor Campus.

In order to reveal other aspects of the internal representation of space, Hirtle and Jonides asked subjects to estimate distances between landmarks. A list of triplets of landmarks were chosen so that they satisfy the following conditions: (a) the first and the second landmark in the triplet belong to the same cluster, (b) the first and the third landmark in the triplet belong to different clusters, and (c) the distance between the first and the second landmark is roughly equal to the distance between the first and the third landmark. The pairs of landmarks that belong to the same cluster are called within cluster pairs and the pairs of landmarks that belong to different clusters are called across cluster pairs.

Subjects estimated distances for the across cluster and within cluster pairs. These distances were plotted as a function of real distance (Fig. 3). The results show that estimated distances between landmarks belonging to the same cluster are shorter relative to estimated distances between landmarks that belong to different clusters.

McNamara, Hardy, and Hirtle (1989) conducted a study in which they showed that even when human subjects learn an unstructured environment (e.g. a map layout containing uniformly distributed objects, see Fig. 1B) they still encode the environment using a hierarchical representation of space (Fig. 2B).

Although these studies present evidence for how spatial information is encoded, they do not provide information about how the hierarchical structure is built and used.

In this paper we present a computational model of spatial navigation that builds and uses a hierarchical representation of space. Then, we explain how the model describes experimental data and present a novel prediction related to the dependency between reaction time for distance estimation and real distance.

* Tel.: +1-919-660-5659; fax: +1-919-660-5726.
E-mail address: horatiu.voicu@duke.edu (H. Voicu).

0893-6080/03/$ - see front matter © 2003 Elsevier Science Ltd. All rights reserved.
doi:10.1016/S0893-6080(03)00095-9

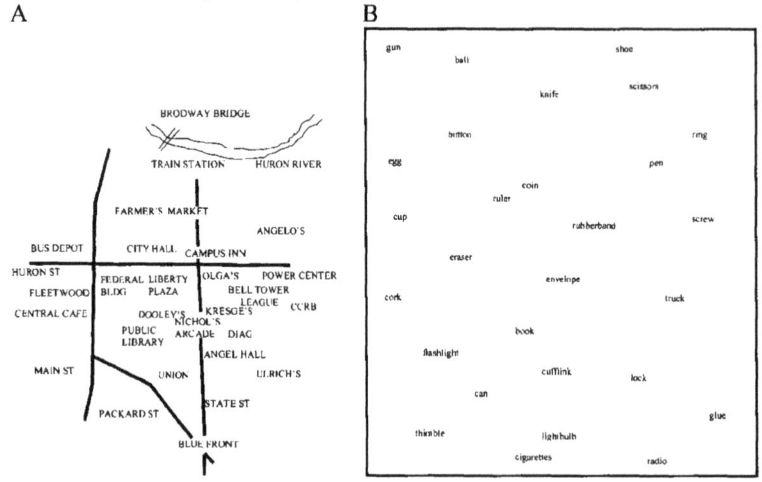

Fig. 1. Environments used for testing the existence of the hierarchical organization of space: Ann Arbor Campus (A) and map layout containing uniformly distributed objects (B) (adapted from Hirtle & Jonides, 1985; McNamara et al., 1989).

2. A spatial navigation model

2.1. Description of the model

The architecture of the model, except the hierarchical cognitive map, is based on a previous model (Voicu & Schmajuk, 2001). It contains five modules: a localization system that provides a unique code for each landmark in the environment, a cognitive map that builds and updates a hierarchical representation of space, a working memory used for path planning, a motor system that translates the path planning information into motor action and a control system that supervises the flow of information between the above modules (Fig. 4).

The localization system recognizes landmarks that are contained in the sector of circle that has the center in the position of the agent, an angle of 60° and a radius equal to one-tenth of the length of the environment. The orientation of the agent is given by the bisecting line of the sector of circle. The representation of the landmarks recognized by the localization system are stored in a short-term memory and provided to the cognitive map.

The working memory stores information retrieved from the cognitive map and used by the motor system to plan and execute paths in the environment.

The cognitive map contains three associative memories, implemented by hetero-associative networks (Kohonen, 1977), that build association between landmarks. As shown in Fig. 5, all networks have recurrent connections and can exchange information. Each associative memory stores spatial information about the environment at a different resolution. The first level stores associations between all the landmarks in the environment. The second level stores associations between landmarks that have the largest number of associations at the first level. The third level stores associations between landmarks that have

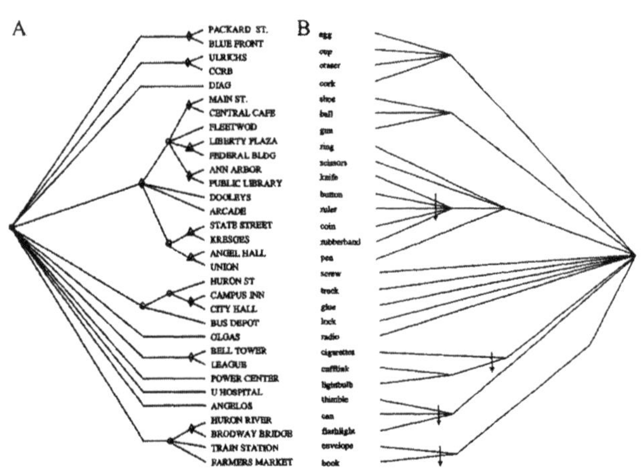

Fig. 2. Ordered trees obtained from environments shown in Fig. 1: Ann Arbor Campus (A) and map layout (B) (adapted from Hirtle & Jonides, 1985; McNamara et al., 1989).

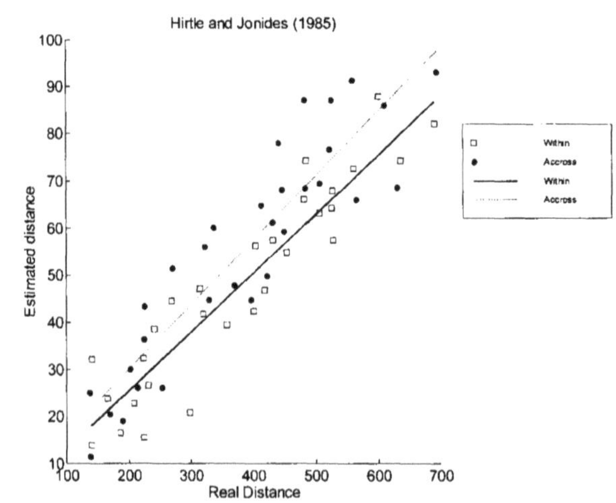

Fig. 3. Estimated distance as a function of real distance (adapted from Hirtle & Jonides, 1985).

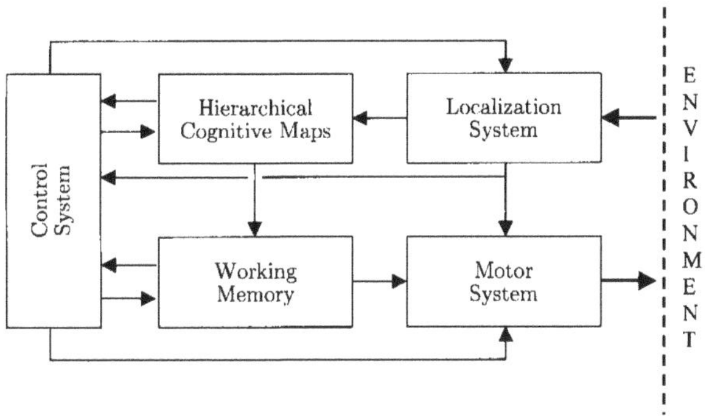

Fig. 4. Block diagram of the model. It shows the interaction between the control system, localization system, cognitive map (see Fig. 5 for a detailed version), working memory, motor system and environment.

the largest number of associations at the second level. This hierarchy is acquired while the agent explores the environment. The cognitive map contains no a priori information related to spatial organization.

Fig. 6 shows a possible example of how the cognitive map stores a hierarchical organization of space. Thin lines represent associations stored in the first level, thick lines represent associations that are stored at the second level and very thick lines represent the associations stored at the third level. Because each level is stored in an independent module, the path planning mechanism (working memory and motor system) is able to use any combination of the multiple representations of the environment.

2.2. Building the hierarchical cognitive map

The agent creates the hierarchical cognitive map in two stages. In the first stage, the agent explores the environment and builds the first level (highest resolution). The agent performs complete explorations of the environment by applying the following two rules: (1) at the beginning of the exploration the agent moves in a random fashion avoiding previously visited places and (2) when the cognitive map contains associations between at least 10 landmarks the agent moves toward landmarks that have the fewest associations.

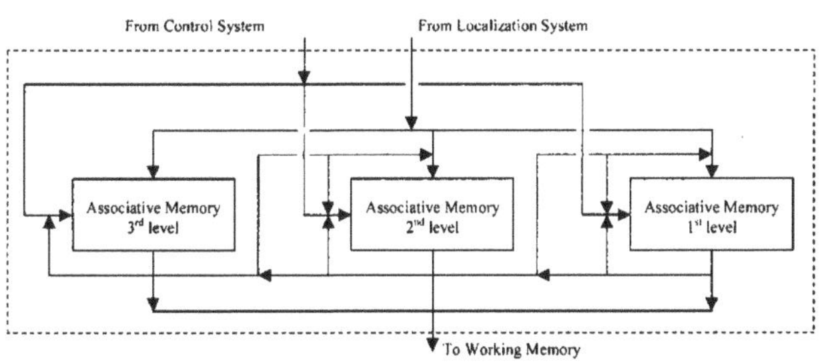

Fig. 5. Architecture of the hierarchical cognitive map. It contains three associative memories that store the connections between landmarks at three different levels.

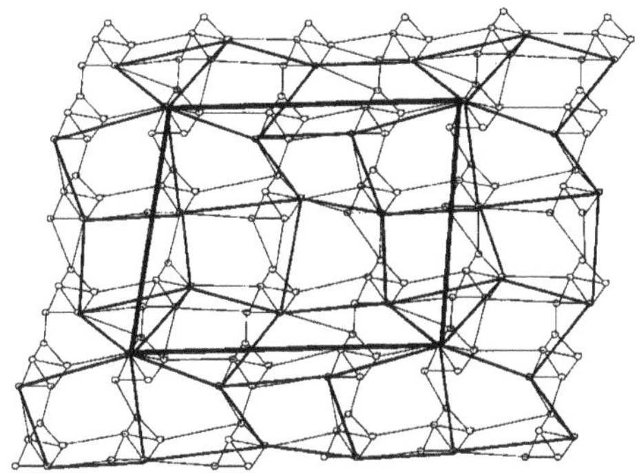

Fig. 6. Example of a multiple level organization of space. Although all nodes are part of a single layer, connections between nodes belong to multiple levels. Thin lines represent first level connections, thick lines represent second level connections and very thick lines represent third level connections.

The cognitive map stores a topological representation of the environment. At the first level, the associations between landmarks are updated using Eq. (1) (Voicu & Schmajuk, 2002)

$$\Delta V_{i,j} = \Delta V_{j,i} = \beta(K - V_{i,j}) \quad (1)$$

where $V_{i,j}$ represents the association between landmarks i and j, K represents the asymptotic value of $V_{i,j}$ and β represents a learning constant. Each time the agent perceives landmarks i and j together, the association between them is updated using Eq. (1) ($K = 1$). Also, the associations between all currently perceived landmarks and the landmarks stored in the short-term memory at a given moment are updated using Eq. (1) ($K = 2$). The role of Eq. (1) is to create memories for the paths visited in the environment. The memory of the paths are stored in the larger associations created by Eq. (1). These larger associations influence the behavior of the agent by attenuating less the activity from the goal location when it spreads along visited paths. The more familiar are the paths to the agent, the less attenuated is the activity spread in the cognitive map. One example that illustrates the role of Eq. (1) is the paradigm concerning detours in open environments (Voicu & Schmajuk, 2002).

In this paradigm an agent navigates between two places (start and goal). If the agent is not familiar with the path between start and goal then when an obstacle is placed in between start and goal the agent circumvents the obstacle and moves directly to the goal location (Fig. 7A). If the agent is familiar with the path between start and goal then when an obstacle is placed on the path, the agent circumvents the obstacle and reaches a place on the known path before reaching the goal location (Fig. 7B). If the agent is very familiar with the path between start and goal then when an obstacle is placed in between start and goal the agent circumvents the obstacle and reaches the closest place on the known path (Fig. 7C). The agent

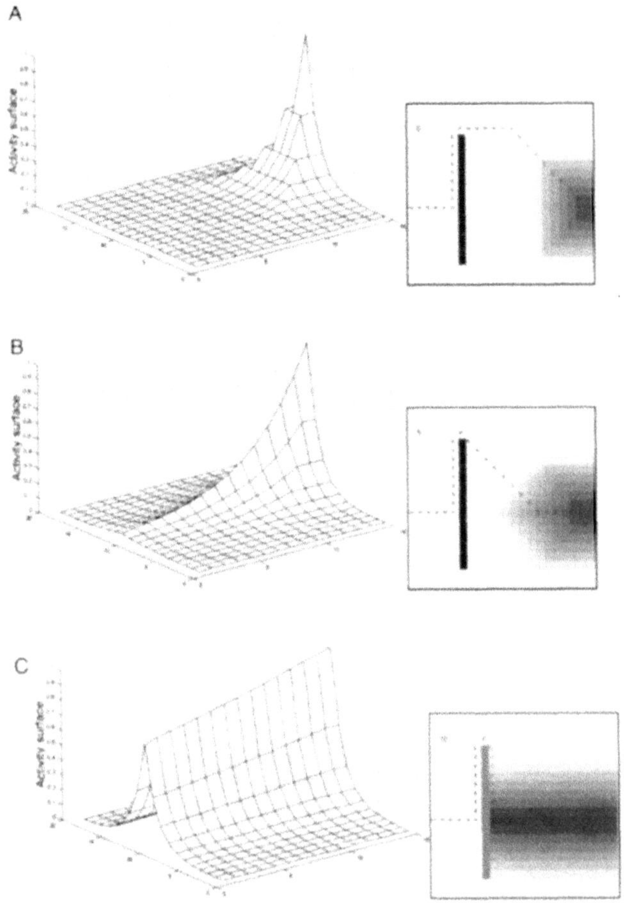

Fig. 7. Open detour paradigm. A: No experience with the path. B: Experienced the path five times. C: Experienced the path 10 times.

shows this behavior because the activity was less attenuated on the known path, making it almost as attractive as the goal location. Fig. 7 shows three instances of a detour in an open environment. Graphs on the left-hand side represent the activity stored in the working memory, which is used to plan paths at the moment the agent encounters the obstacle. The goal location is at (15,10) and the obstacle is on the ordinate axis. The graphs on the right-hand side represent a top view of the environment that includes the trajectory of the agent and the same activity as on the left-hand side graphs only represented in shades of gray. The obstacle is represented as a thin rectangle. In this particular example the environment is represented as a grid.

Once the agent performs several complete explorations of the environment, it starts the second stage of the process of building the hierarchical cognitive map. It begins by selecting from the first level the landmarks that have the largest number of associations. To accomplish this, the agent selects the landmarks that produce the largest values at the output of the first associative memory when activity is spread in the cognitive map for one iteration step from each landmark.

Once all the landmarks that belong to the middle level are known, the network that corresponds to the second level starts making associations between them. This is accomplished by using the information stored in the first level network. From each landmark that belongs to the middle level, activation is spread until a second level landmark is found and the magnitude of the activity is bounded by a given range. Then, an association is stored between the landmark where the activity originated and the landmark where the activity stopped. The value assigned to the association equals the value of the activity in the node where the activity stopped. The same process is repeated for the third level.

2.3. Navigation and path planning

The model uses a goal-activation method (Voicu & Schmajuk, 2000) that consists of activating the goal in the cognitive map, and spreading this activation until the representation of the current location of the agent becomes active. Because this activation is attenuated as it spreads from one landmark to another, landmarks that are closer to the goal are more active than landmarks that are more removed from it. The activation spreads at all levels of the hierarchy. The output of the hetero-associative network is stored in the working memory where the motor system performs gradient ascent to produce action upon the environment. For each associative network the activity is spread using Eq. (2)

$$a_j(t+1) = h\mathring{a}_i V_{i,j} a_j(t) \qquad (2)$$

where $\eta \in (0,1)$ is the attenuation factor, t represents time, a_i represents the activation of neuron i, and $V_{i,j}$ represents the association between landmarks i and j.

3. Computer simulations

The test of the model for the results reported by Hirtle and Jonides (1985) was performed as follows.

3.1. Previous experience of the environment

In the Hirtle and Jonides study, all participants had at least 2.5 years of experience with the Ann Arbor Campus. During this time participants learned the paths between all salient landmarks in the campus including those used in the experiment. Therefore, we assumed that all participants in the study have individual cognitive maps that contain all the landmarks used in the experiment and the paths between them.

In order to create a cognitive map that contains information equivalent to the one used by the human participants, we let the agent explore all the landmarks in the simulated environment shown in Fig. 8.

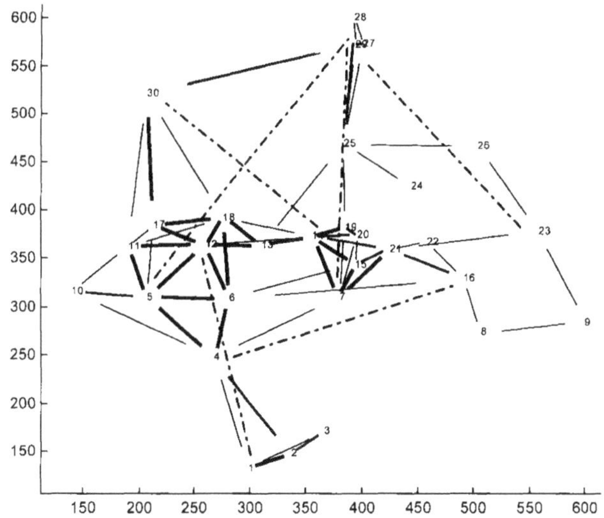

Fig. 8. Simulated version of the Ann Arbor environment. Numbers from 1 to 30 represent the location of the landmarks. Continuous lines represent connections at the first level while dashed lines represent connections at the second level.

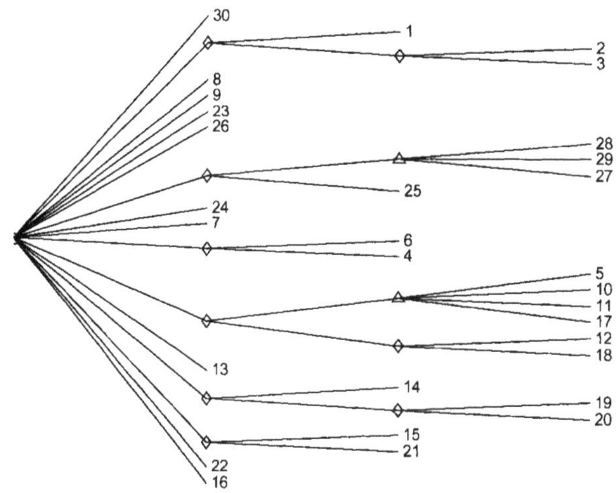

Fig. 9. Ordered tree generated by the model using the Ann Arbor configuration. △: represents unidirectional clusters in which items can be recalled only in one order, ○: represents nondirectional clusters in which items can be recalled in any order; ◇: represent bidirectional clusters in which items can be recalled in one order or its reverse. Numbers denote landmarks.

Fig. 8 also shows the associations formed after the agent exhaustively explores the landmarks for two iterations. Associations between landmarks that have been visited many times are represented with thicker lines. Connections that belong at the second level of the hierarchy are represented with dashed lines. In this particular case there are no connections at the third level.

3.2. The recall task

The recall task mentioned in Section 1, in which participants produce several times the complete list of landmarks starting with different landmarks each time, probably reveals their individual internal representations of the environment. Supposedly, during the generation of the recall list, the subjects imagine moving in space while naming the landmarks they encounter. Landmarks located closer together appear closer on the list. Therefore, the recall list was generated by performing a vicarious navigation in the cognitive map. Because we assume that in the cognitive map the subjects always move to the nearest unvisited landmark (goal), the model produces the recall list by using a nearest neighbor strategy. As in the experimental data, landmarks located closer together also appear closer on the list.

3.3. The ordered tree algorithm

In order to produce several ordered trees like in the experimental study where each subject produced an individual tree, we created several agents that differ in how they build the cognitive map. Each agent, during the acquisition of the cognitive map, starts at different locations in the environment before navigating to all landmarks in the environment. The analysis of the recall data from one agent with the ordered tree algorithm produces the ordered tree shown in Fig. 9. In order to determine whether the ordered trees generated by different agents have the same degree of regularity and structure as the recall data produced by human participants, we calculated the following two measures: the number of possible recall orders (PRO) that the ordered tree can generate and the height of the ordered tree (McNamara et al., 1989). The PRO is calculated by using Eq. (3)

$$\mathrm{PRO}(T) = \log_2\left(2^j \prod_{i=1}^{k} n_i!\right) \tag{3}$$

where T is the ordered tree, j the number of bidirectional nodes, k the number of nondirectional nodes and n_i the number of branches in the ith nondirectional node.

The height of the tree is calculated using Eq. (4)

$$H(T) = \sum_i (2n_i - 3) + j + 1 \tag{4}$$

where j and n_i are defined as above.

The PRO is the logarithm base 2 of the total numbers of recall orders consistent with a particular tree. The lower the PRO value the higher the organization of the information in the recall data. For 30 landmarks PRO can vary between 0 (completely ordered tree) and 107.70 ($= \log_2 30!$, unstructured tree). The height (H) measure calculates the number of transformations necessary to move from a completely ordered tree to the observed tree (McNamara et al., 1989). The larger the height the lower the organization in the recall data. For 30 landmarks the largest value for the height is 57.

The ordered trees obtained in the Hirtle and Jonides and McNamara et al. studies have an average PRO value of 28.06 and average height value of 25.28. The ordered trees obtained from the simulation have an average PRO value of 32.84 and an average height value of 28.57. Statistical analysis shows that there is no significant difference between experimental and simulated ordered trees. This similarity between the empirical and simulated trees suggests that the model is able to produce recall data that has the same degree of regularity and structure as the recall data produced by human participants.

3.4. Distance estimation

The distance estimation task presented in Section 1 is simulated as follows. First, we use the model to estimate the distances between any two landmarks in the environment. This is accomplished by positioning the agent in the place of one landmark and activating the other landmark as a goal. Then, the activity from the goal spreads through the cognitive map, using all levels of the hierarchy, until it reaches the current position of the agent. The estimated distance between the two places is inversely proportional to the value of the activity in the position of the agent.

As mentioned in Section 2.2, the model updates its internal representation of the environment by using Eq. (1). Each time the agent moves from one landmark to another it increases the association between the landmarks. In terms of the distance between these two landmarks, this increase in the association translates into a shortening of the estimated distance. In other words, by navigating repeatedly between two places the estimated distance between them becomes smaller.

The analysis of the estimated distances was performed using a procedure similar to that used by Hirtle and Jonides (1985). First, a list of triplets (O_i, O_j, O_k) is created that satisfies the following conditions: (a) O_i, O_j, and O_k are all landmarks in the environment, (b) O_i and O_j belong to the same cluster in the corresponding ordered tree and O_k belongs to a different cluster, and (c) the distance between O_i and O_k is greater than 90% of the distance between O_i and O_j and less than 103% of the distance between O_i and O_j. The latter constraint, (c), guarantees that the clustering effect is not due to the fact that across cluster distances are on average longer than within cluster distances. The study conducted by Hirtle and Jonides only mentions that the distance between O_i and O_k is roughly equal to the distance between O_i and O_j. The list of pairs (O_i, O_j) is called the within cluster list and the list of pairs (O_i, O_k) is called the across cluster list.

It is important to notice that, for a given environment, the list of triplets depends on the ordered tree used to generate it. Different subjects might have different lists of triplets even if they recall objects from the same environment.

Fig. 10 shows normalized estimated distances between O_i and O_j as a function of real distance between O_i and O_j and estimated distances between O_i and O_k as a function of

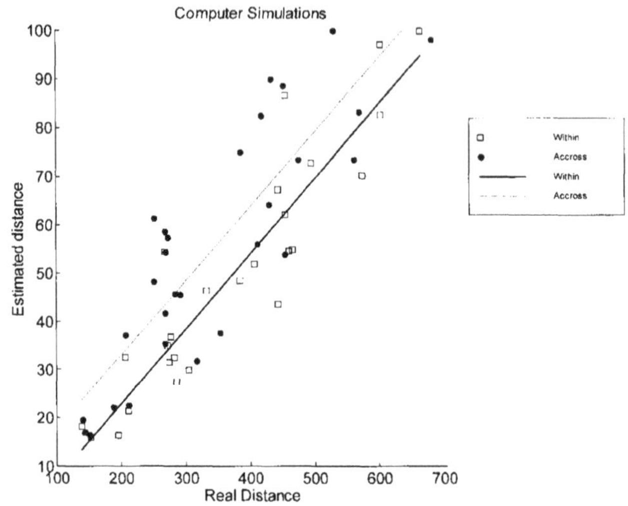

Fig. 10. Computer simulations: estimated distances as a function of real distance. Squares represent within cluster pairs and black circles represent across cluster pairs. Lower line: within cluster regression, Upper Line: across cluster regression.

real distance between O_i and O_k. Normalization involved dividing each estimated distance by the maximum estimated distance and multiplying it by 100.

Like the experimental data, the simulated data shown in Fig. 10 is collected from different agents that build different cognitive maps and produce different ordered trees. For each ordered tree a list of triplets is compiled using the same rules described above. All lists are merged into a single list of triplets that does not contain triplets which have the same across cluster pair or the same within cluster pair. If two triplets have either the same within cluster pair or the same across cluster pair then, the merged list will contain the triplet for which the real distance between the landmarks in the within cluster pair is closer to the real distance between the landmarks in the across cluster pair.

As shown in Fig. 10 the model produces a pattern resembling that found by Hirtle and Jonides (1985): across cluster estimated distances are longer than within cluster estimated distances. This result is produced by the model even though on average the across cluster distances are smaller than the corresponding within cluster distances.

The model produces this result by using an acquired system of strengthened paths. This system is used in all distance estimations performed by the model. On one hand, if the distance to be estimated is between two close landmarks (i.e. they belong to the same cluster) then, the strengthened path used to estimate the distance is the shortest path between the landmarks. On the other hand, if the distance to be estimated is between two distant landmarks (i.e. they do not belong to the same cluster) then, the strengthened path used to estimate the distance is not the shortest path between the two landmarks. Therefore, whereas for within cluster pairs of landmarks the estimated distance is close to the shortest path between the landmarks, for across cluster landmarks the estimated distance is longer than the shortest path between the landmarks. As a consequence, across cluster distances are estimated as longer than within cluster distances.

3.5. Comparing simulated and experimental results

A linear regression analysis of the within and across cluster distances produces the following equations: $y = 0.155x - 8.01$ for within cluster distances and $y = 0.156x + 2.43$ for across cluster distances. It can be noticed that like in the experimental case, the regression lines are almost parallel.

Statistical analysis shows that the correlation between the estimated and actual distance for within cluster pairs and across cluster pairs combined is 0.89. This value is close to that found in previous studies: 0.803 (Hirtle & Jonides, 1985) and 0.89 (McNamara et al., 1989). Also, separate correlations for within cluster pairs (0.92, $N = 24$, $p < 0.01$) and across cluster pairs (0.89, $N = 24$, $p < 0.01$) are significant. Additionally, as in the experimental study, the variance of the estimated distances in the across cluster pair list (experimental: 28.12, simulated: 38.36) is larger than the variance of the estimated distances in the within cluster pair list (experimental: 18.38; simulated: 30.43).

The results were subjected to a paired t-test showing that there is a statistically significant difference between the estimations for within and across clusters ($t(24) = 2.06$, $p < 0.02$).

3.6. Novel prediction

In addition to the ordered trees and distance estimations described above, we have analyzed a theoretical case for which experimental evidence is still lacking. The paradigm consists of measuring reaction times while the agent performs distance estimations.

For a one-dimensional environment that contains 16 places equally displaced we build a hierarchical representation shown in Fig. 11. This hierarchy contains multiple representations of the same environment at different resolutions. On one hand, the time to spread the activity between place 1 and place 16, only by using the representation with the highest resolution, is proportional to the number of connections in between place 1 and place 16, namely 15. On the other hand, the time to spread the activity between place 1 and place 16 when all levels of the hierarchy are used is proportional to twice the depth of the hierarchy, namely 8 ($= 2 \times 4$). This is the number of steps required by the spreading activation from place 16 to reach place 1. We can extrapolate that, in general, whereas reaction time for spreading the activity between two places in the case of a nonhierarchical representation of space is linear with the distance between the two places, in the case of a hierarchical representation of space it varies logarithmically with the distance between the two places (Fig. 12). Therefore, by using low-resolution representations of the environment the agent can speed the spatial planning process.

3.7. Related work

Other models of spatial navigation that use different approaches of building hierarchical cognitive maps have been developed (Car, 1998; Donnart & Meyer, 1996; Kuipers, 2000; Niizuma, Kawano, Tomizawa, Sugiyama, & Degawa, 1992). Although some of them use similar concepts (i.e. multiple levels with different resolutions) they do not address specifically the empirical results reported by Hirtle and Jonides (1985) and McNamara et al. (1989).

A hierarchical structure has also been used by Graham, Joshi, and Pizlo (2000) to build a model that solves the traveling salesman problem (TSP). The TSP is

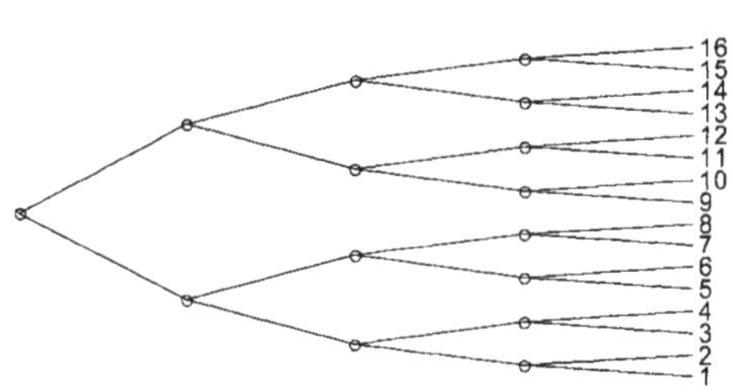

Fig. 11. Multiple level representation of a one-dimensional environment that contains 32 places.

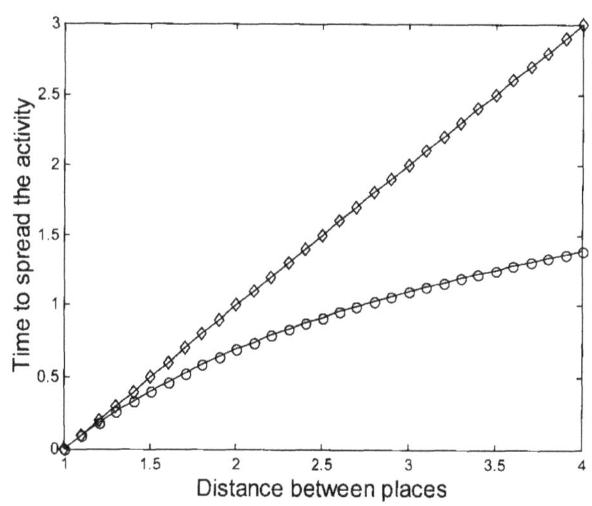

Fig. 12. Linear and logarithmic reaction times as a function of the distance between places. ○: represents time to spread the activity in a hierarchical representation of space; ◇: represents time to spread the activity in a nonhierarchical representation of space.

the problem of finding the shortest tour that connects a number of cities that a salesman is interested to visit. Graham et al. (2000) compared the performance of human subjects, their model and well-known algorithms in the artificial intelligence (AI) literature on TSP. Their results showed that, unlike the AI algorithms, human subjects and the hierarchical model show a linear dependency between the size of the problem, i.e. number of cities, and the error of the solution, i.e. the difference between the solution found by the human subject or the computational model and the actual optimal solution (the shortest tour).

Graham et al. (2000) represent the TSP problem as a high-resolution grid where cells that encode cities have values greater than zero whereas all other cells have a value of zero. By using a process of filtering and compression a succession of smaller grids are produced. Each grid looks like the initial grid only that it has a different resolution. All these grids are used to build step by step a solution to the TSP. First, a partial solution of the problem is produced at the grid with the lowest resolution. Then, this solution is expanded by including partial solutions taken from the grids with higher resolutions.

Notice that although the representation used by Graham et al. (2000) is very similar to ours, the information stored in it is used for different purposes. Whereas their representation is build to solve a particular problem, namely the TSP, our representation is used to explore and navigate large environments.

There are many spatial navigation models that do not use a hierarchical representation of space but are related to the model presented in this paper in terms of how the spatial information is stored and retrieved. These models focus on simulating the function of the rat hippocampus in spatial navigation (Burgess, Donnett, & O'Keefe, 1997; Cannon, Hasselmo, & Koene, 2002; Hasselmo, Hay, Ilyn, & Gorchetchnikov, 2002), building sequences of places and cognitive graphs (Trullier & Meyer, 2000) and performing path integration and cognitive mapping (Samsonovich & McNaughton, 1997).

4. Conclusions

We presented a computational model of spatial navigation characterized by three basic features. First, we show that the network builds a hierarchical representation of space by using several hetero-associative networks that store associations between landmarks in the environment. Each network has a different resolution and represents a different level of the hierarchy. Second, the information stored in the network is used by the motor system to plan paths in the environment. Third, the model describes experimental data that brings evidence for the hierarchical organization of space. In addition, the model predicts that the time to estimate distances varies nonlinearly with distance.

References

Burgess, N., Donnett, J. G., & O'Keefe, J. (1997). Robotic and neuronal simulation of hippocampal navigation. *Philosophical Transactions of the Royal Society B*, *352*, 1535–1543.

Cannon, R. C., Hasselmo, M. E., & Koene, R. A. (2002). From biophysics to behavior: Catacomb2 and the design of biologically plausible models for spatial navigation. *Neuroinformatics*, *1*, 3–42.

Car, A (1998). Hierarchical spatial reasoning: a geocomputation method. *Proceedings of the third international conference on geocomputation*, Bristol, September 17–19.

Donnart, J. Y., & Meyer, J. A. (1996). Hierarchical-map building and self-positioning with MonaLysa. *Adaptive Behavior*, *5*(1), 29–74.

Graham, S. M., Joshi, A., & Pizlo, Z. (2000). The traveling salesman problem: a hierarchical model. *Memory and Cognition*, *28*(7), 1191–1204.

Hasselmo, M. E., Hay, J., Ilyn, M., & Gorchetchnikov, A. (2002). Neuromodulation, theta rhythm and rat spatial navigation. *Neural Networks*, *15*, 689–707.

Hirtle, S. C., & Jonides, J. (1985). Evidence of hierarchies in cognitive maps. *Memory and Cognition*, *13*(3), 208–217.

Kohonen, T. (1977). *Associative memory*. Berlin: Springer.

Kuipers, B. (2000). The spatial semantic hierarchy. *Artificial Intelligence*, *119*, 191–233.

McNamara, T. P., Hardy, J. K., & Hirtle, S. C. (1989). Subjective hierarchies in spatial memory. *Journal of Experimental Psychology: Learning, Memory, and Cognition*, *15*(2), 211–227.

Niizuma, M., Kawano, Y., Tomizawa, M., Sugiyama, M., & Degawa, S. (1992). *Flexible control of autonomous vehicle utilizing hierarchical map and planning*. Japan: Mechatronics and Manufacturing Systems.

Reitman, J. S., & Rueter, H. R. (1980). Organization revealed by recall orders and confirmed by pauses. *Cognitive Psychology*, *12*, 554–581.

Samsonovich, A., & McNaughton, B. L. (1997). Path integration and cognitive mapping in a continuous attractor neural network model. *Journal of Neuroscience*, *17*(15), 5900–5920.

Trullier, O., & Meyer, J. A. (2000). Animat navigation using a cognitive graph. *Biological Cybernetics*, *83*, 271–285.

Voicu, H., & Schmajuk, N. A. (2000). Exploration, navigation and cognitive mapping. *Adaptive Behavior*, *8*(3/4), 207–223.

Voicu, H., & Schmajuk, N. A. (2001). Three-dimensional cognitive mapping with a neural network. *Robotics and Autonomous Systems*, *35*, 21–35.

Voicu, H., & Schmajuk, N. A. (2002). Latent learning, shortcuts and detours: a computational model. *Behavioural Processes*, *59*, 67–86.

PERGAMON

AVAILABLE AT
www.ComputerScienceWeb.com
POWERED BY SCIENCE DIRECT

Neural Networks 16 (2003) 577–584

Neural Networks

www.elsevier.com/locate/neunet

2003 Special issue

Modeling goal-directed spatial navigation in the rat based on physiological data from the hippocampal formation

Randal A. Koene[a,*], Anatoli Gorchetchnikov[b], Robert C. Cannon[c], Michael E. Hasselmo[a]

[a]*Department of Pyschology and Program in Neuroscience, Boston University, Boston, MA 02215, USA*
[b]*Department of Cognitive and Neural Systems, Boston University, Boston, MA 02215, USA*
[c]*Institute of Adaptive and Neural Computation, Division of Informatics, 5 Forrest Hill, Edinburgh EH1 2QL, UK*

Abstract

We investigated the importance of hippocampal theta oscillations and the significance of phase differences of theta modulation in the cortical regions that are involved in goal-directed spatial navigation. Our models used representations of entorhinal cortex layer III (ECIII), hippocampus and prefrontal cortex (PFC) to guide movements of a virtual rat in a virtual environment. The model encoded representations of the environment through long-term potentiation of excitatory recurrent connections between sequentially spiking place cells in ECIII and CA3. This encoding required buffering of place cell activity, which was achieved by a short-term memory (STM) in EC that was regulated by theta modulation and allowed synchronized reactivation with encoding phases in ECIII and CA3. Inhibition at a specific theta phase deactivated the oldest item in the buffer when new input was presented to a full STM buffer. A 180° phase difference separated retrieval and encoding in ECIII and CA3, which enabled us to simulate data on theta phase precession of place cells. Retrieval of known paths was elicited in ECIII by input at the retrieval phase from PFC working memory for goal location, requiring strict theta phase relationships with PFC. Known locations adjacent to the virtual rat were retrieved in CA3. Together, input from ECIII and CA3 activated predictive spiking in cells in CA1 for the next desired place on a shortest path to a goal. Consistent with data, place cell activity in CA1 and CA3 showed smaller place fields than in ECIII.

Keywords: Hippocampal theta oscillation; Spatial navigation; Functional interaction

1. Introduction

The theta rhythm consists of large amplitude 3–12 Hz oscillations recorded in the EEG of the hippocampus of different animal species during exploration and orientation to stimuli (Buzsáki, Leung, & Vanderwolf, 1983). These theta oscillations are associated with rhythmic changes in a number of physiological variables, including neuronal membrane potential (Fox, 1989), synaptic currents in different layers (Brankack, Stewart, & Fox, 1993), the magnitude of synaptic transmission (Wyble, Linster, & Hasselmo, 1997) and the spiking activity of neurons (Fox, Wolfson, & Ranck, 1986). In addition, extensive data demonstrates that long-term potentiation of synaptic strength can be induced more effectively with stimulation at the peak of theta waves, while decreases in strength or no change is observed with stimulation at the trough of the theta wave (Hasselmo, Bodelon, & Wyble, 2002; Hölscher, Anwyl, & Rowan, 1997; Huerta & Lisman, 1993; Pavlides, Greenstein, Grudman, & Winson, 1988). This supports the hypothesis that theta rhythm allows separate phases of encoding and retrieval. In rats, lesions of the fornix remove much of the amplitude of theta rhythm. This impairs the ability to learn reversal tasks, in which a previously rewarded behavior must be replaced with an opposite behavior. For example, rats have difficulty learning a right turn response after initially learning a left turn response (M'Harzi, Palacios, Monmaur, Houcine, & Delacour, 1987). Previous analytical work has shown how performance in behavioral tasks such as the reversal task could depend upon specific phase relationships between physiological variables changing during theta rhythm oscillations (Hasselmo et al., 2002). The simulations presented here further demonstrate the functional role of phase relationships in entorhinal cortex and prefrontal cortex, as well as the functional role of other physiological properties.

* Corresponding author. Tel.: +1-617-358-2769; fax: +1-617-353-1424.
E-mail addresses: randalk@bu.edu (R.A. Koene), anatoli@cns.bu.edu (A. Gorchetchnikov), robert.cannon@ed.ac.uk (R.C. Cannon), hasselmo@bu.edu (M.E. Hasselmo).

0893-6080/03/$ - see front matter © 2003 Elsevier Science Ltd. All rights reserved.
doi:10.1016/S0893-6080(03)00106-0

We have utilized spiking network models of rat entorhinal and hippocampal circuitry to analyze the functional role of theta rhythm oscillations. These models have been developed in two different software packages: CATACOMB, developed by Cannon, Koene, and Hasselmo (2002)) and KInNeSS, developed in the Hasselmo laboratory by Gorchetchnikov. The use of separate models effectively tests the robustness of theoretical hypotheses and allows analysis of individual details of function. In both of these projects, the use of spiking neurons in network simulations to guide movements of a virtual rat in a virtual environment allow the network activity to be analyzed in the same manner as spiking activity recorded from single neurons in awake behaving rats. We will first discuss research using CATACOMB.

Using CATACOMB, a spiking neuron model of rat entorhinal and hippocampal circuitry (Cannon et al., 2002) was implemented to investigate the significance of these phasic changes while performing goal-directed spatial navigation tasks in a T-maze. The roles of neuron populations (ECII, ECIII, CA3, CA1) are based on hypothesized functions of these individual regions in spatial learning and recall tasks. Instead of static data sets, environmental input to model networks changes in accordance with task-specific behaviours that arise from physical simulations driven by the network output (e.g. when exploration of the T-maze leads to the discovery of food-reward). A virtual rat is placed in a novel environment, given an opportunity to learn the environment and then presented with the task to navigate to a goal discovered in that environment.

The task was successfully learned, enabling the virtual rat to find a shortest path to food-reward. Synchronized learning in ECIII and CA3 was achieved with a STM buffer that insured ordered repetition of sequences of place cell spikes without the variability caused by differences in place field traversal times. We improved our knowledge of the connections between physiological and behavioural data through our approach: studying task-specific behavioural problems caused by the dynamic interaction of the neuronal circuitry with the experimental environment. In this manner, we demonstrated the well-known empirical phenomenon of phase precession by recording simulated hippocampal place cell firing. We also found that place fields produced in our model exhibited the typical finer grain in CA1 and less defined, coarser appearance in ECIII. Theta modulation in ECIII and CA3 provided phases of encoding and retrieval that operate in parallel without interference. Theta also regulated episodic repetition in a STM buffer. Phase differences betwen regions undergoing theta modulation ensured the correctly timed propagation of activity. Theta modulation in our model is, therefore, crucial in order to accomplish each of these three aspects of the learning and spatial navigation task.

2. Results

During initial encoding, a virtual rat follows predetermined exploratory trajectories in the environment (Fig. 1). Place cell activity is assigned with variable place field sizes (Barnes McNaghton, Mizumori, Leonard, & Lei--Huey, 1990; Eichenbaum, Dudchenko, Wood, Shapiro, & Tanila, 1999; Frank, Brown, & Wilson, 2000; McNaughton, Barnes, & O'Keefe, 1983; Muller & Kubie, 1989; Quirk, Muller, Kubie, & Ranck, 1992). Associations between sequential place cell activity along the trajectories as well as in the goal location is encoded on recurrent fibres in ECIII and CA3 by LTP. During task performance, retrieval in the spiking neuron network produces output at the CA1 population that guides the direction of movement.

During exploration, the interval between the initial arrival of place cell spikes from adjacent place fields is arbitrary. However, the window of spike intervals that elicit effective LTP is less than 40 ms (Levy & Stewart, 1983) and LTP elicited by the single initial spike input is not reliable enough to produce strong Hebbian learning. Repetition of the ordered presentation of neighbouring place cell spikes is needed within the LTP window. A STM buffer can accomplish this.

There are no initially known patterns and buffering cannot be LTP-dependent, as the establishment of LTP requires in excess of 100 ms (Bi & Poo, 1998). It is hypothesized that intrinsic mechanisms may maintain firing patterns, as initially proposed by Lisman (Lisman & Idiart, 1995). One such mechanism is ADP (calcium sensitive cation currents induced by muscarinic receptor activation (Klink & Alonso, 1997)), as shown below. Synchronized timing can be achieved by regulating repetition through theta modulation. This assures that STM reactivation coincides with an encoding phase in both ECIII and CA3 (Fig. 2). Recurrent inhibition within the buffer can separate the reactivation of sequential items to maintain order (gamma rhythm) (Jensen & Lisman, 1996; Lisman & Idiart, 1995).

2.1. Reactivation in EC at gamma intervals within a phase of theta oscillation may provide short-term memory

Spiking produced by afferent activity during the input phase of the buffer is reactivated by the ADP during subsequent repetition phases. Theta modulation of membrane potential regulates the two phases. Theta oscillations

Fig. 1. Exploratory motions of a virtual rat generate place fields and corresponding spiking activity.

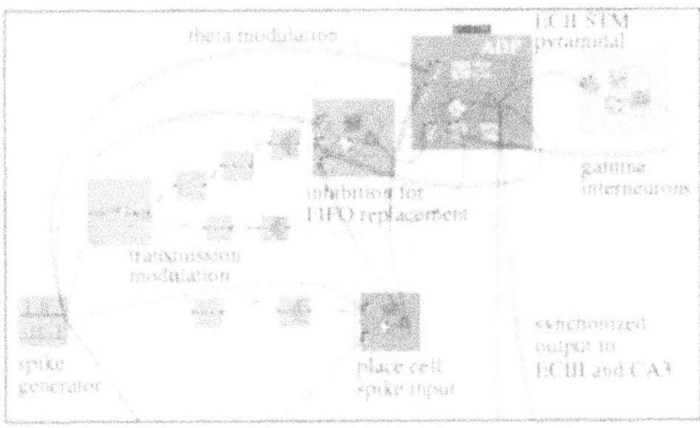

Fig. 2. The STM buffer in ECII converts arbitrary input spikes into synchronously repeated spike pairs for encoding in ECIII and CA3. *Theta modulation* of *ECII pyramidal cell* membrane potentials and phase-locked afferent and recurrent *transmission modulations* impose the repetition frequency and ensure that new input enters the buffer at the theta trough. This rhythmic modulation is regulated by a *spike generator* which simulates data on theta rhythmic firing of neurons in the septum. While the capacity is limited to two items in the current example, our STM model can accommodate up to four items that are reactivated on the depolarizing phase of each theta cycle. Items are separated by *gamma intervals* that are imposed by a population of interneurons. Another population of interneurons provides inhibition at the phase of the first item reactivation when *place cell spike input* arrives at a full STM buffer. This ensures *first-in-first-out* (*FIFO*) *replacement* of STM items.

(8 Hz) are produced by regular activity originating in septal populations (Brazhnik & Fox, 1999) believed to modulate the GABAergic inhibition of pyramidal cells via networks of interneurons (Alonso, Gaztelu, Bruno, & Garcia-Austt, 1987; Skaggs, McNaughton, Wilson, & Barnes, 1996; Stewart & Fox, 1990). Recurrent gamma inhibition produced by interneuronal networks (Bragin, Jando, Nadasdy, & Hetke, 1995) in response to each item spike imposes intervals that maintain the distinct and ordered reactivation of items (Fig. 3).

Noise and slow-AHP gradually decay STM. Prior to such decay, item replacement in the buffer is controlled by inhibition at a specific theta phase when new input is

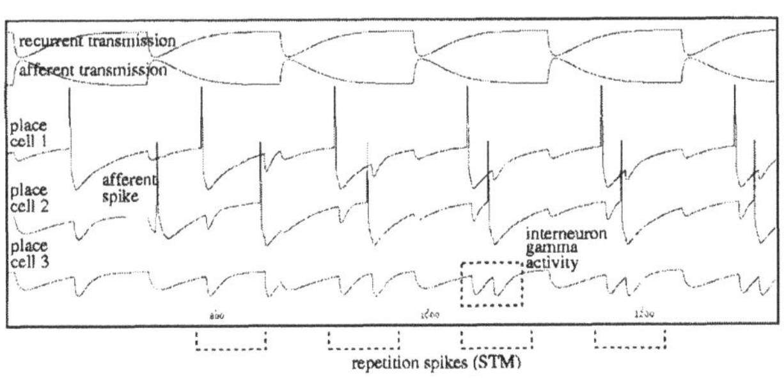

Fig. 3. New input is added to the STM buffer and the sequence is repeated. Reactivation of a buffered sequence occurs when ADP and the strongly depolarizing phase of theta modulation combine to exceed the firing threshold. Lateral inhibition maintains the separation of items in the buffer, as reactivation causes a recurrent interneuronal network to spike at gamma frequency (40 Hz). These recurrent GABAergic synaptic transmissions are enabled during the high value phase of 'recurrent transmission' modulation, while synapses receiving afferent input into the buffer are enabled during the high value phase of 'afferent transmission' modulation.

received. Replacement must retire the earliest item in the buffer (FIFO). Retirement must be rapid to avoid changes in repetition order that could become encoded in ECIII or CA3. This carefully timed inhibition triggered in response to the number of items in the buffer as well as the arrival of a new item spike (shown in Fig. 4) completes the STM model without the problematic input timing and ADP response characteristics required in the Jensen et al. model (Jensen, Idiart, & Lisman, 1996).

An interneuron population receives recurrent synaptic input from the buffer cells as well as input propagated from sources that supply afferent input to the buffer. Synaptic efficacies establish a gating function, such that N recurrent item inputs elicit subthreshold potentials in the interneuronal population, but an additional $N + 1$th afferent input elicits spiking. The consequent GABAergic inhibition on the buffer is synchronized so that its hyperpolarizing effect delays reactivation of the earliest item in the buffer long enough for its ADP to subside (Fig. 4). The first item drops out of the buffer and the new item assumes the last position in the buffered sequence.

The STM buffer bridges large intervals between the appearance of successive place cell spikes and achieves extended repetition of paired spiking so that strong LTP can be established. Sequential binding is, therefore, less dependent on the speed of place field traversal and episodic learning proceeds with correct unidirectional heteroassociativity. The STM provides input that conforms to the encoding requirements of ECIII and CA3.

2.2. *Encoding and retrieval can take place continuously in consecutive phases of theta*

The behavioural task requires ongoing acquisition of new associations without interference from ongoing retrieval using the same synapses. We, therefore, hypothesize that learning and retrieval may take place in separate phases of theta modulation (Hasselmo et al., 2002), 180° apart to avoid interference between the two modes (Fig. 5). This hypothesis is supported by phase differences in different

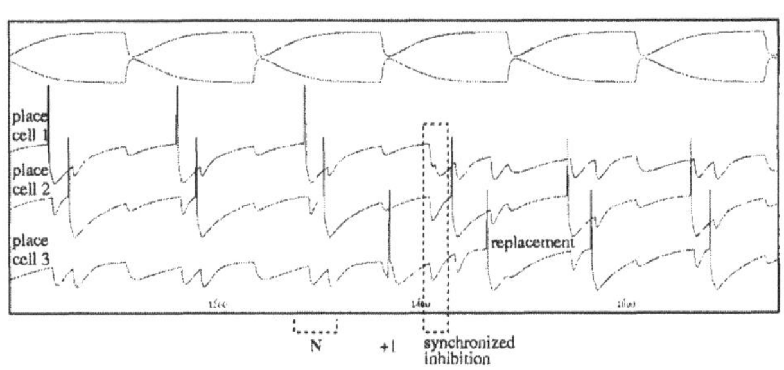

Fig. 4. The STM buffer replaces items in a first-in-first-out (FIFO) manner through targeted inhibition. When activity indicates a full buffer (N spikes), this combines with the arrival of a new item spike to trigger interneurons synchronized to spike so that the GABAergic effect on STM neurons suppresses firing of the first item until its ADP has decayed. The new item reactivates near the peak of theta modulation, thereby assuming the last position in the buffered sequence.

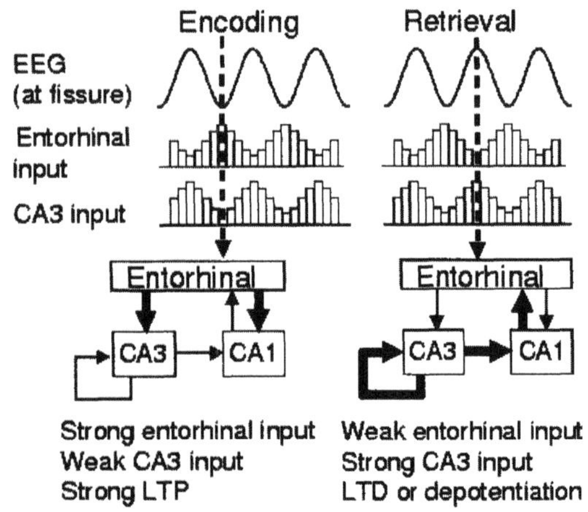

Fig. 5. When afferent synaptic input from EC to CA3 and EC to CA1 is strong encoding is favoured. When recurrent synaptic transmission in CA3 and synaptic input from CA3 to CA1 is strong retrieval is favoured.

synaptic input currents from EC and CA3 observed in current source density measures (Brankack et al., 1993; Stewart & Fox, 1990).

Phase-precession is a phenomenon recorded during in vivo experiments of spatial learning in rats (O'Keefe & Recce, 1993; Skaggs et al., 1996). Data from these experiments shows that the phase of theta at which a place cell fires gradually shifts to earlier phases as a rat traverses a known place field, as well as during learning. In the model, we measured the firing of cells relative to theta rhythm. As the virtual rat enters a place field the corresponding place cell fires at late phases of theta in CA1—predictive spiking. As the virtual rat crosses the place field, place cell firing becomes earlier in theta in CA1—encoding spiking (Fig. 6).

During encoding phases in the model we simulate suppression of recurrent fiber synaptic transmission via increased interneuron activating presynaptic $GABA_B$ channels (Hasselmo et al., 2002). This prevents interference from retrieval of existing associations (Fig. 7). Consistent with experimental data (Hölscher et al., 1997; Wyble, Hyman, Goyal, & Hasselmo, 2001), induction of LTP is

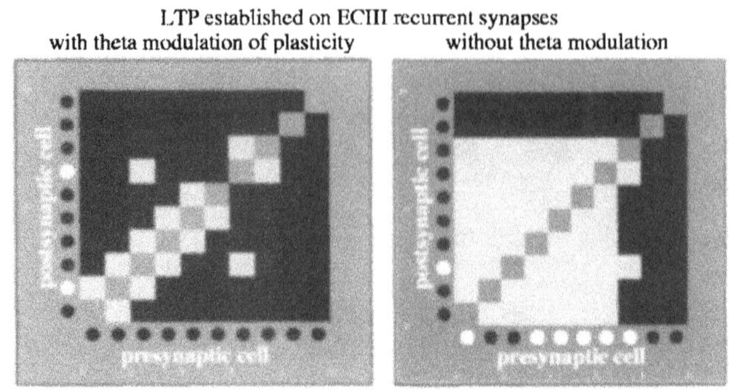

Fig. 7. The matrix of connectivity in the model demonstrates that theta rhythm is essential to the learning of correct paths as represented by ordered episodes of place cell spikes. Left: Good function with theta rhythm. The matrix on the left shows good connectivity resulting from separation of encoding and retrieval into distinct theta phases. This allows path encoding to take place without interference from retrieved spikes. The resulting patterns of synapses strengthened by LTP show pairwise associations between consecutive place cells along paths in the T-maze. Right: Poor encoding without theta. Without theta modulation the order breaks down and erroneous associations are formed between most locations.

rhythmically modulated to occur during the encoding phase, but not during the retrieval phase when recurrent synaptic transmission is strong.

Known locations adjacent to the virtual rat are retrieved in CA3 (Fig. 8), while associative retrieval in ECIII represents known paths (Fig. 9). A PFC STM buffer stores the location of goals that were discovered. PFC and hippocampus must spike synchronously.

CA1 activity (Fig. 10) depends on a combination of sub-threshold contributions from both CA3 (adjacent candidates) and ECIII (association with a path to the goal). Spiking in CA1 activates an interneuronal population that provides recurrent inhibition to CA1. A winner-take-all competition is accomplished (Fig. 11) in which one successful candidate spikes to indicate the next desired place on a shortest path to a goal.

Empirical data indicates that place fields in CA1 are significantly smaller than place fields in EC (Barnes et al., 1990; Frank et al., 2000; Quirk et al., 1992). Measurements

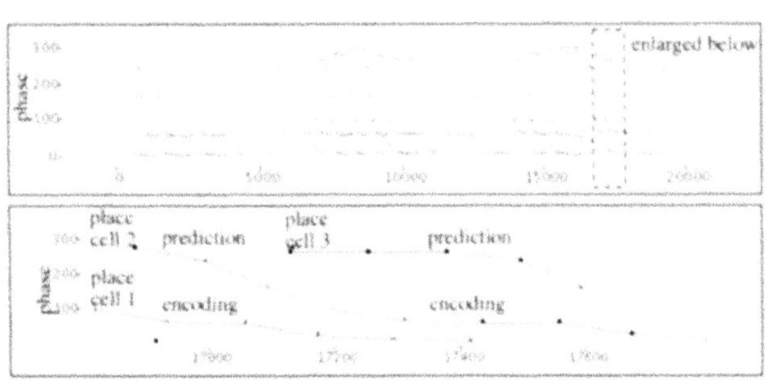

Fig. 6. Encoding and retrieval theta phases simulate theta phase precession. Model results for each place cell in CA1 show that as the corresponding place field is entered, the cell spikes in the retrieval phase of theta modulation. The retrieval allows the virtual rat to predict the next desired location on a path during navigation. As the virtual rat moves, spiking shifts to earlier phases. Spiking of the place cell during this phase allows it to participate in the episodic encoding of new paths.

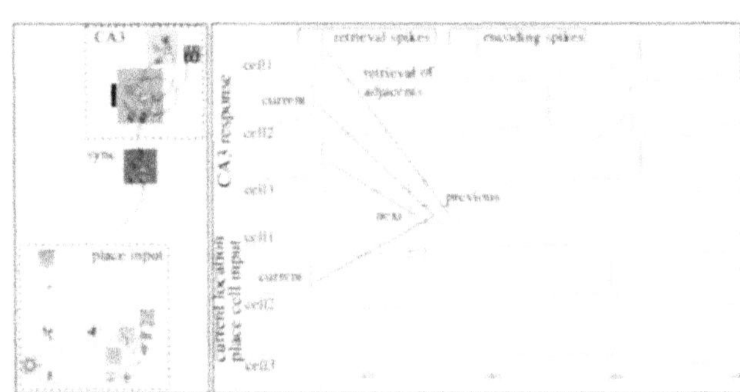

Fig. 8. Current location drives retrieval in CA3. As the virtual rat moves up the stem of the T-maze, a synchronization population ensures that spikes representing current location arrive in CA3 at its retrieval phase. Strong LTP on recurrent fibres then retrieves spikes for known adjacent locations. Lateral inhibition through interneurons in CA3 limits the spread of retrieval. Both the previous and next locations in the stem are retrieved.

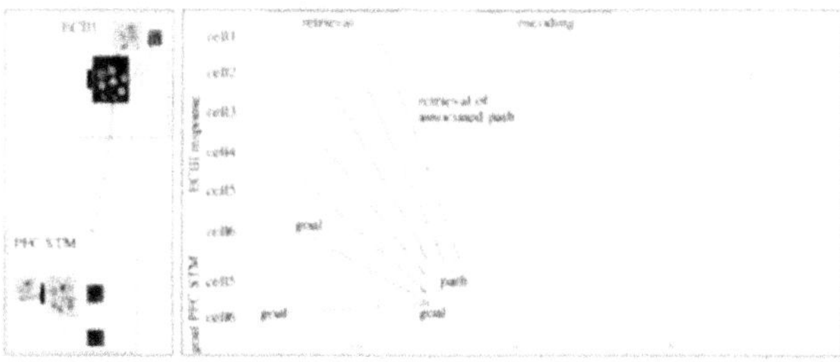

Fig. 9. Known goal locations in the T-maze, stored in PFC, cause spiking in ECIII which spreads from the goal along known paths. The Goal activity elicits spiking in ECIII at its retrieval phase in each theta cycle. Retrieval spreads away from the goal along associated known paths via recurrent fibres previously strengthened by LTP.

in the model show that activity is limited in CA3 and CA1, but broad in ECIII, consistent with that data (Fig. 12) (Cannon et al., 2002).

2.3. Phase differences in theta modulation between prefrontal and medial temporal regions enhance functional interaction

Given the need to propagate retrieval spikes from a source population (e.g. ECII STM) at the encoding phase of a target population (e.g. CA3), it is clear that specific theta phase relationships must exist between the different regions. In Fig. 13, the magnitude of modulation at theta frequency in cellular membrane potentials and synaptic transmission ratios shows the phase differences that allow PFC, ECII, ECIII, CA3 and CA1 regions to interact successfully.

2.4. An alternative model implementation provides additional support for our hypothesis of the role of theta in navigation

Our theoretical model was also evaluated in a different implementation with similar functional properties using the KIn–NeSS simulation package. We selected single-compartment integrate-and-fire neurons in the CATACOMB implementation above. In contrast, in KInNeSS each neuron consists of a dendrite compartment governed by the voltage equation and the standard approximation of the cable equation (Bower & Beeman, 1995), plus a soma compartment based on the canonical model of the type 1 neuron (Ermentrout & Kopell, 1986; Hoppensteadt & Izhikevich, 1998). The details of the cell model are provided elsewhere (Gorchetchnikov & Hasselmo, 2003), while we now emphasize the differences between the two system implementations.

Where a septal source of modulation at theta frequency is assumed in the CATACOMB simulation, septal cell activity in the KInNeSS simulation is derived from recurrent interactions with the hippocampal area via fornix connections. Similar rhythmic behaviour and synchronization at theta frequency emerges in both simulations. This synchronization affects neuronal activity within the hippocampus, as well as phase-locked spiking activity in the hippocampus and PFC. In the simulation above, ECIII learned episodes of place cell activity that represent navigable paths. In the KInNeSS implementation, this requisite knowledge for navigation is provided as sets of restrictions on certain locations. Restrictions range from absolute prohibition (an unreachable location behind a wall) to various degrees of aversion (e.g. a representation of the scent of a predator), established during the exploration of the environment. Unexplored locations remain unrestricted, so that the model can simulate path integration behaviour and attempt to take short-cuts through those locations.

The representation of space in the CATACOMB simulation is continuous in terms of the appearance of place fields during exploration and the motion directed by activity in CA1. In the KInNeSS simulation, space is mapped onto a two-dimensional grid of cells that form the centers of place fields. This approach is based on results by Trullier and Meyer (2000), who demonstrated equivalent performance with both a priori uniformly assigned place fields and place fields that were generated dynamically to

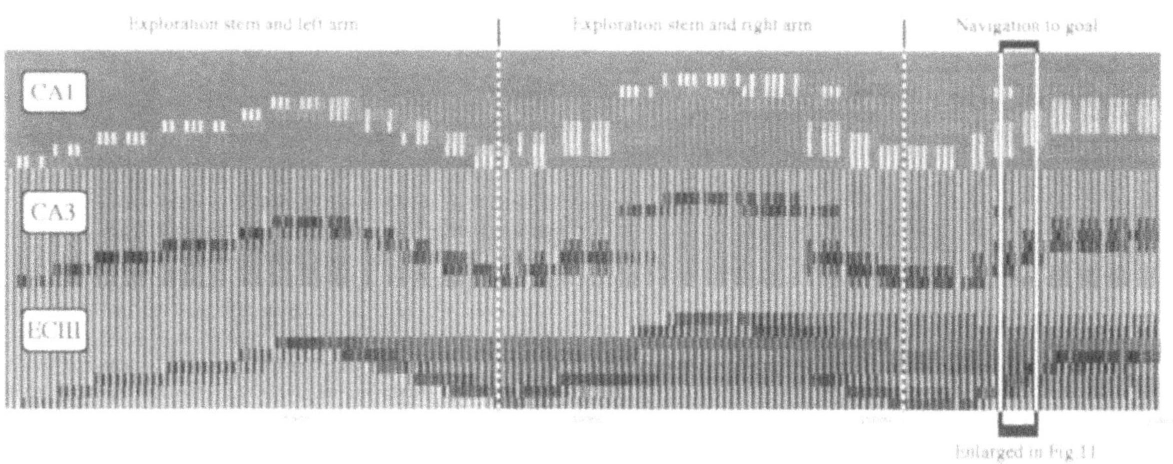

Fig. 10. Spiking in CA1 predicts desired next location on a shortest path to a goal. Retrieval in ECIII of known paths to the goal combines with retrieval in CA3 of known adjacent locations. Where the two most rapidly coincide, a spike is elicited in CA1.

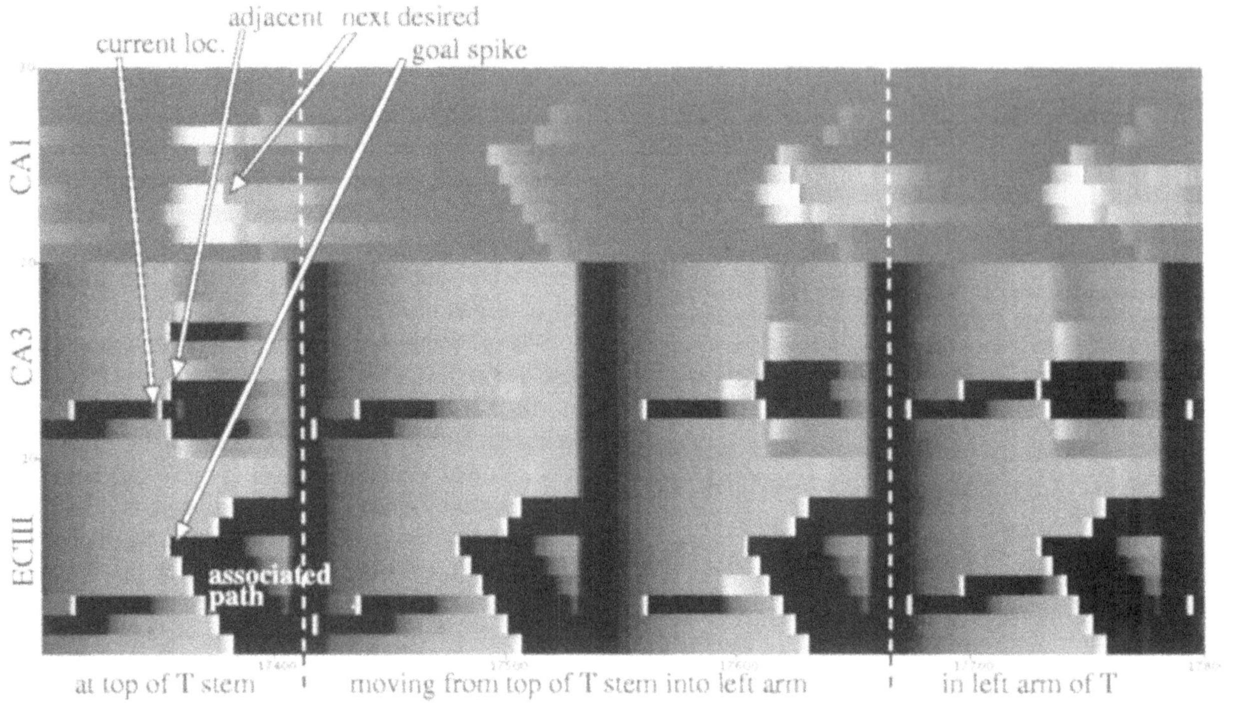

Fig. 11. Retrieved knowledge of paths in the T-maze and of adjacent locations causes predictive spiking that drives movement. The virtual rat is at the top of the T-maze stem. Place cell spiking at the current location retrieves three adjacent locations (down, left, right) Synaptic responses to these spikes in CA3 cause a slowly decaying depolarization in the corresponding cells in CA1. At the same time, a goal-spike received in ECIII elicits retrieval of known paths from the goal location at the end of the left arm of the T-maze to the bottom of the stem, as well as to the end of the right arm. This activity coincides first with the adjacency reponse in CA1 representing the adjacent location in the left arm of the T-maze. The resulting spike in CA1 predicts the next desired location and suppresses further spiking through lateral inhibition. The virtual rat consequently moves into the left arm of the T-maze. There, a new current location spike in CA3 continues the predictions that drive movement.

reflect the complexity of the environment. Similarly, the two different implementations of our theoretical model demonstrate its robust performance, regardless of the method chosen to generate place fields and their layout.

Finally, the KInNeSS simulation enables us to examine performance in the case of multiple goals in a single environment (a linear track, a maze or an open field). Recurrent inhibition in CA1 is critical to the behaviour of the model, as it underlies the competitive choice of a desired move towards the nearest goal. In a linear track or maze with narrow arms, the recurrent CA1 inhibition of the KInNeSS simulation results in optimal winner-take-all competition (Fig. 14). The situation is more complicated

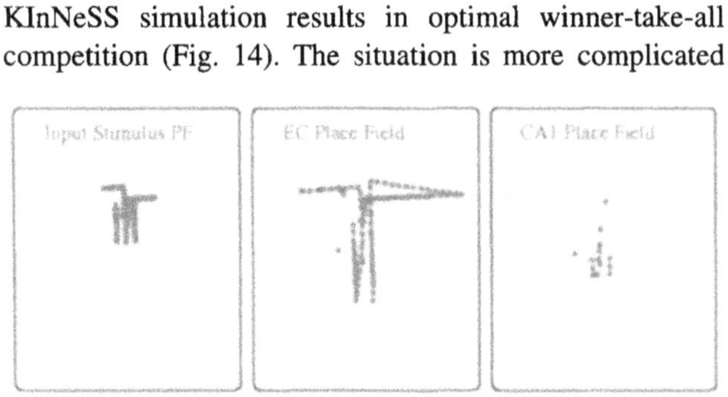

Fig. 12. The model replicates differences in place field sizes observed in experiments. These plots show the locations in the T-maze at which individual example place cells in each region were activated. The place fields generated by spiking activity in ECIII are broad and overlapping. By contrast, the place fields in CA1 are small and well defined.

in the open field, as multiple CA1 cells of neighbouring locations in the general direction of the goal can spike before the onset of the competitive inhibition. This will be resolved through the inclusion of a head-direction system that takes output from CA1 and computes an average direction that can consistently drive the virtual rat's

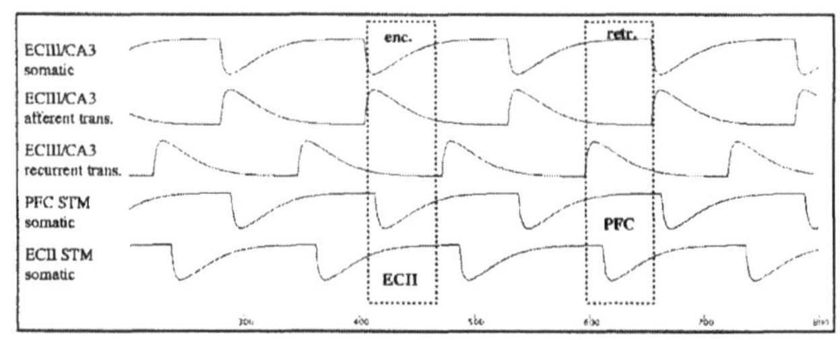

Fig. 13. The function of the model requires specific phase relationships between theta rhythmic modulation of membrane potentials and synaptic transmission in different locations. During encoding (enc.), patterns spike in the STM buffer during the depolarized membrane phase in ECII, and are transmitted to ECIII and CA3 at their encoding phases (less depolarized membrane potential) via afferent synapses in their phase of strong transmission. During retrieval (retr.), the phase of membrane depolarization in PFC activates a goal-representation that is transmitted to ECIII. During retrieval, recurrent fibre synapses are at the phase of full strength and cause spiking in ECIII and CA3 neurons, which are in their phase of somatic depolarization. This leads to the retrieval of known associations. ECIII retrieves known paths associated with the goal-location. These are combined in CA1 with associations retrieved in CA3 that indicate known place fields adjacent to current location of the virtual rat.

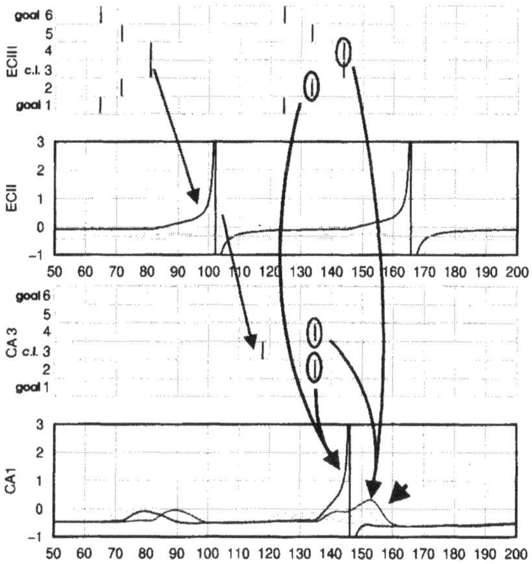

Fig. 14. Competitive decision making between two goals on a linear track with six place fields. ECIII and CA3 panels show raster plots of cells according to their locations on the track and their activity over time. The two goals and current location (c.l.) are indicated. ECII and CA1 panels show the recorded cell activity in respective areas. The spikes in ECIII and CA3 marked with black circles almost coincide in time and produce a rapid response in CA1—a correct choice. The spikes in the gray circles would produce an incorrect choice. They are further separated in time, causing a delayed response in CA1 that is suppressed by recurrent inhibition (black arrowhead).

movements. Empirical measurements support the existence of such head-direction cells in regions receiving input from CA1, such as the parasubiculum (Taube, 1995).

3. Conclusion

The model successfully enabled a virtual rat to learn its environment and to navigate on a shortest path to a food-reward goal encountered during exploration. By modeling with a focus on the behavioural task and interactions with the environment rather than individual regional functions, new insight was gained into significant requirements imposed by the dynamics involved. The manifestation of problems specific to the behaviour allowed us to link behavioural data with physiological data.

These insights support the hypothesis that theta modulation is a functional necessity in an integrative model of a realistic spatial navigation task: (1) It can impose distinct phases of ongoing encoding and retrieval. (2) It can maintain a STM buffer crucial to episodic learning. (3) It synchronizes spiking so that specific phase relationships can be achieved for the propagation of activity between cortical regions. The inspection of simulated spiking neurons resembles recording of place cells from hippocampus in awake behaving rats, allowing phenomena such as phase precession to be investigated and evaluated in terms of existing data. The implementation of a STM buffer made learning less dependent on the speed of motion and the timing of place cell spiking, while it maintained the order in which place cell spikes appeared for sequence learning. Finally, place fields in model CA1 were found to be smaller and more defined than those in ECIII.

In our upcoming work, we are adding a system of neocortical 'minicolumns' that will enable the learning of conditional relationships and task rules. This system will interact with the hippocampus for the retrieval of episodic memory items. A model that extends beyond the hippocampus will allow explicit separation of the components of behavior requiring the hippocampus from those components which are spared after hippocampal lesions.

Acknowledgements

The CATACOMB simulations described here and information about CATACOMB are available on our Computational Neurophysiology website at http://askja.bu.edu.

Supported by NIH R01 grants DA16454, MH60013 and MH61492 to Hasselmo and by Conte Center Grant MH60450.

References

Alonso, A., Gaztelu, J., Bruno, W., Jr, & Garcia-Austt, E. (1987). Crosscorrelation analysis of septohippocampal neurons during theta-rhythm. *Brain Research*, *413*, 135–146.

Barnes, C., McNaughton, B., Mizumori, S., Leonard, B., & Lei-Huey, L. (1990). Comparison of spatial and temporal characteristics of neuronal activity in sequential stages of hippocampal processing. *Progress in Brain Research*, *83*, 287–299.

Bi, G., & Poo, M. (1998). Synaptic modifications in cultured hippocampal neurons: Dependence on spike timing, synaptic strength, and postsynaptic cell type. *Journal of Neuroscience*, *18*(24), 10464–10472.

Bower, J., & Beeman, D. (1995). *The Book of GENESIS. Exploring realistic neural models with the GEneral Neural SImulation System*. New York: Springer.

Bragin, A., Jando, G., Nadasdy, Z., & Hetke, J. (1995). Gamma (40–100 Hz) oscillation in the hippocampus of the behaving rat. *Journal of Neuroscience*, *15*, 47–60.

Brankack, J., Stewart, M., & Fox, S. (1993). Current source density analysis of the hippocampal theta rhythm: associated sustained potentials and candidate synaptic generators. *Brain Research*, *615*(2), 310–327.

Brazhnik, E., & Fox, S. (1999). Action potentials and relations to the theta rhythm of septohippocampal neurons in vivo. *Experimental Brain Research*, *127*, 244–258.

Buzsáki, G., Leung, L., & Vanderwolf, C. (1983). Cellular bases of hippocampal EEG in the behaving rat. *Brain Research*, *287*, 139–171.

Cannon, R., Hasselmo, M., & Koene, R. (2002). From biophysics to behaviour: Catacomb2 and the design of biologically plausable models for spatial navigation. *Neuroinformatics*, *1*(1), 3–42.

Eichenbaum, H., Dudchenko, P., Wood, E., Shapiro, M., & Tanila, H. (1999). The hippocampus, memory, and place cells: Is it spatial memory or a memory space? *Neuron*, *23*, 209–226.

Ermentrout, G., & Kopell, N. (1986). Parabolic bursting in an excitable system coupled with slow oscillation. *SIAM Journal of Applied Mathematics*, *46*, 233–252.

Fox, S. (1989). Membrane potential and impedance changes in hippocampal pyramidal cells during theta rhythm. *Experimental Brain Research, 77*, 283–294.

Fox, S., Wolfson, S., & Ranck, J. (1986). Hippocampal theta rhythm and the firing of neurons in walking and urethane anesthetized rats. *Experimental Brain Research, 62*, 495–508.

Frank, L., Brown, E., & Wilson, M. (2000). Trajectory encoding in the hippocampus and entorhinal cortex. *Neuron, 27*(1), 169–178.

Gorchetchnikov, A., & Hasselmo, M. (2003). Timing of consecutive traveling pulses in a model of entorhinal cortex. *Proceedings of the International Joint Conference on Neural Networks*, in press.

Hasselmo, M., Bodelon, C., & Wyble, B. (2002). A proposed function for hippocampal theta rhythm: Separate phases of encoding and retrieval enhance reversal of prior learning. *Neural Computation, 14*(4), 793–817.

Hölscher, C., Anwyl, R., & Rowan, M. (1997). Stimulation on the positive phase of hippocampal theta rhythm induces long-term potentiation that can be depotentiated by stimulation on the negative phase in area CA1 in vivo. *Journal of Neuroscience, 17*(16), 6470–6477.

Hoppensteadt, F., & Izhikevich, E. (1998). *Weakly connected neural networks*. New York: Springer.

Huerta, P., & Lisman, J. (1993). Heightened synaptic plasticity of hippocampal ca1 neurons during a cholinergically induced rhythmic state. *Nature, 364*, 723–725.

Jensen, O., Idiart, M., & Lisman, J. (1996). Physiologically realistic formation of autoassociative memory in networks with theta/gamma oscillations: Role of fast NMDA channels. *Learning & Memory, 3*, 243–256.

Jensen, O., & Lisman, J. (1996). Novel lists of 7 ± 2 known items can be reliably stored in an oscillatory short-term memory network: Interaction with long-term memory. *Learning & Memory, 3*, 257–263.

Klink, R., & Alonso, A. (1997). Morphological characteristics of layer ii projection neurons in the rat medial entorhinal cortex. *Hippocampus, 7*, 571–583.

Levy, W., & Stewart, D. (1983). Temporal contiguity requirements for long-term associative potentiation/depression in the hippocampus. *Neuroscience, 8*(4), 791–797.

Lisman, J., & Idiart, M. (1995). Storage of 7 ± 2 short-term memories in oscillatory subcylces. *Science, 267*, 1512–1515.

McNaughton, B., Barnes, C., & O'Keefe, J. (1983). The contributions of position, direction, and velocity to single unit activity in the hippocampus of freely-moving rats. *Experimental Brain Research, 52*(1), 41–49.

M'Harzi, M., Palacios, A., Monmaur, P., Houcine, O., & Delacour, J. (1987). Effects of selective lesions of hippocampal connections on learning set in the rat. *Physiology and Behavior, 40*, 181–188.

Muller, R. U., & Kubie, J. (1989). The firing of hippocampal place cells predicts the future position of freely moving rats. *Journal of Neuroscience, 9*, 4101–4110.

O'Keefe, J., & Recce, M. (1993). Phase relationship between hippocampal place units and the hippocampal theta rhythm. *Hippocampus, 3*, 317–330.

Pavlides, C., Greenstein, Y., Grudman, M., & Winson, J. (1988). Long-term potentiation in the dentate gyrus is induced preferentially on the positive phase of theta-rhythm. *Brain Research, 439*(1/2), 383–387.

Quirk, G., Muller, R., Kubie, J., & Ranck, J. Jr (1992). The positional firing properties of medial entorhinal neurons: Description and comparison with hippocampal place cells. *The Journal of Neuroscience, 12*, 1945–1963.

Skaggs, W., McNaughton, B., Wilson, M., & Barnes, C. (1996). Theta phase precession in hippocampal neuronal populations and the compression of temporal sequences. *Hippocampus, 6*, 149–172.

Stewart, M., & Fox, S. (1990). Do septal neurons pace the hippocampal theta rhythm? *Neuron, 13*, 163–168.

Taube, J. (1995). Place cells recorded in the parasubiculum of freely moving rat. *Hippocampus, 5*, 569–583.

Trullier, O., & Meyer, J.-A. (2000). Animat navigation using a cognitive graph. *Biological Cybernetics, 83*, 271–285.

Wyble, B., Hyman, J., Goyal, V., & Hasselmo, M. (2001). Phase relationship of ltp induction and behavior to theta rhythm in the rat hippocampus. *Society for Neuroscience Abstracts, 27*, 53719.

Wyble, B., Linster, C., & Hasselmo, M. (1997). Evoked synaptic potential size depends on the phase of theta rhythm in rat hippocampus. *Society of Neuroscience Abstracts, 23*, 508.

AVAILABLE AT
www.ComputerScienceWeb.com
POWERED BY SCIENCE DIRECT

PERGAMON

Neural Networks 16 (2003) 585–591

Neural Networks

www.elsevier.com/locate/neunet

2003 Special issue

An efficient training algorithm for dynamic synapse neural networks using trust region methods

Hassan H. Namarvar*, Theodore W. Berger

Department of Biomedical Engineering, University of Southern California, OHE-500, Los Angeles, CA 90089-1451, USA

Abstract

We formulate the dynamic synapse neural network from the averaged activity of local population of neurons perspective. We have applied the trust region nonlinear optimization approach to train the network and show the new learning method effectiveness in comparison to the genetic algorithms by optimizing large-scale networks.

Keywords: Dynamic synapse neural network; Trust region nonlinear optimization; Genetic algorithms; Signal processing

1. Introduction

Many artificial neural network models have been proposed to mimic behaviors of biological neural networks (NNs). These models can be categorized into two classes: static and dynamic neural networks. Static neural networks simulate only long-term memory properties of neurons in which input and output are at their steady state. However, static NNs such as McCulloch-Pitts neurons (McCulloch & Pitts, 1943) cannot simulate adaptive properties of neurons or short-term memory, which are very important to spatio-temporal pattern recognition.

To develop more biologically realistic neural network models incorporating some of temporal nonlinear properties of neurons, (Liaw & Berger, 1996) have developed the 'Dynamic Syanpse' Neural Network (DSNN) using the Hebbian learning algorithm. DSNNs are neurocomputational units incorporating experimentally based mathematical models of the nonlinear dynamics and adaptive properties of biological neurons and neural networks. It has been shown that DSNNs have potential strong capabilities in dynamic pattern recognition applications, e.g. speech processing and neural prosthesis (Berger et al., 2001).

We have proposed a training method based on the Genetic Algorithms (GAs) to optimize the DSNN parameters for speech processing, particularly for word recognition (Namarvar, Liaw, & Berger, 2001). Despite our success in recognition of small-set of words for a limited number of speakers, training of large-scale NN with the GAs becomes a challenging problem. The reason is that the GAs suffer an extensive computation burden and very slow convergence, which sometimes make them inappropriate algorithm for certain applications. Later on, we proposed a gradient based learning method for DSNN with continuous input and output (Namarvar, Dibazar, & Berger, 2002). However, training of DSNN for point-process (spike) events-based information remained challenging. Here, we provide a rational approach to this challenge.

In general, the problem of tuning the parameters of a nonlinear dynamic neural network is usually nonlinear and is separated into one-dimensional and multi-dimensional problems, depending on whether the sought function (or functions) is a function of one parameter or many. This problem, especially a multi-dimensional problem, is often ill-posed in the classic sense.

This paper addresses two issues: (a) modifying the DSNN architecture from biological and experimentally mathematical perspective and (b) applying an efficient learning method to optimize the network parameters with point-process input–output (I/O) based on an interior trust-region (TR) nonlinear optimization method. Then we apply the new method to some system identification problems and illustrate the effectiveness of it in comparison to the results obtained from the GA training approach.

* Corresponding author.
E-mail address: heidarin@usc.edu (H.H. Namarvar).

0893-6080/03/$ - see front matter © 2003 Elsevier Science Ltd. All rights reserved.
doi:10.1016/S0893-6080(03)00091-1

2. Material and method

The brain system is a large-scale multi-processor pathway. The sub-systems of the brain such as cerebral cortex and hippocampus are not a single neuron but composed of a large number (millions) population of interconnected neurons. Therefore, we can study the networks of local populations of neurons. In other words, the averaged activity of the local population neurons can be studied.

For example, when neurons activate completely randomly, the averaged activity of population of neurons is almost uniform. It means that measuring of the average activity of field potential provides related information. This information is about probability of firing of individual neurons or releasing of neurotransmitter at individual synaptic clefts from the local population (Fig. 1). Notice that the averaged activity provides only statistical information and does not tell anything about the particular firing of a single neuron. In empirical ANN modeling, we can flexibly interpret results without loss of generality. Here, the notion of local population activity cannot be rigorously defined and it is only taken as an axiom (like the notion of the set in mathematics) (Hoppensteadt & Izhikevich, 1997). Then, we refer to the population of neurons as a neuron and population of pre- and post-synaptic mechanisms simply as a single pre- and post-synaptic mechanism (Fig. 2).

One of the simplest continuous-time forms for excitatory post-synaptic potentials (EPSPs) is an additive differential equation (Hoppensteadt & Izhikevich, 1997):

$$\tau_i \frac{\mathrm{d}x_i}{\mathrm{d}t} = -x_i + S\left(\rho_i + \sum_{j=1}^{n} c_{ij}x_j\right) \qquad x_i \in \Re, \tag{1}$$

$i = 1, \ldots, n$

where each scalar x_i denotes the ith average EPSP activity; $\rho_i \in \Re$ denotes the overall input from external receptors; coefficients c_{ij}, $i \neq j$ describe synaptic efficacy, and the saturation function $S : \Re \rightarrow \Re$ is typically a sigmoidal function:

$$S(x) = \frac{1}{1 + \mathrm{e}^{-x}} \tag{2}$$

with $S(x) \rightarrow 0$ for $x \rightarrow -\infty$ and $S(x) \rightarrow 1$ for $x \rightarrow \infty$, which is consistent with the probability hypothesis.

Fig. 1. Average activity of a local population of neurons relates to the probability of firing of a single ('representative') neuron from the population (Hoppensteadt & Izhikevich, 1997).

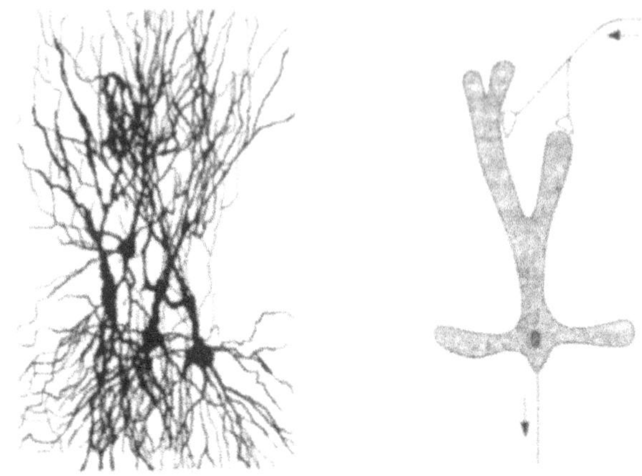

Fig. 2. Equivalent replaced model of an averaged neuron for a local population of neurons (Hoppensteadt & Izhikevich, 1997).

For the steady state I/O transformation, Eq. (1) leads to

$$\begin{cases} 0 = -x_i + S\left(\rho_i + \sum_{j=1}^{n} c_{ij}x_j\right) \Rightarrow x_i = S\left(\rho_i + \sum_{j=1}^{n} c_{ij}x_j\right) \\ \frac{\mathrm{d}x_i}{\mathrm{d}t} \rightarrow 0 \end{cases} \tag{3}$$

which represents for the classical McCulloch–Pitts neuron or multi-layer perceptron (MLP) model.

2.1. DSNN architecture

We use an Integrate-and-Fire (IF) neuron model to convert a continuous input signal into action potential (AP) time events signals. Continuous inputs can arrive from a sensory units, EPSP or output of decomposed signals, like audio signal processing in auditory system that can be artificially simulated using a wavelet filter bank (Mallat, 1999). A first order linear differential equation, a threshold value and an absolute refractory period describe an Integrate-and-Fire (IF) neuron.

$$\tau_{\mathrm{m}} \frac{\mathrm{d}u}{\mathrm{d}t} = -u(t) + KA(t) \tag{4}$$

where $u(t)$ is the membrane potential and τ_{m} is the membrane time constant, $A(t)$ is input and K is a scaling factor. A threshold crossing $u(t^{(f)}) = v$ is used to define the firing time $t^{(f)}$. The form of the spike is not described explicitly immediately after $t^{(f)}$, but we use the Kronecker delta in discrete time domain. The potential is reset to a new value u_{r}.

$$\lim_{\delta \to 0} u(t^{(f)} + \delta) = u_{\mathrm{r}} \tag{5}$$

After an AP occurring at $t^{(f)}$ we force the membrane potential to be zero during a time-period of δ^{abs} (Gestner, 1999).

M first-order pre-synaptic mechanisms describe the dynamics of the pre-synaptic level. For a network with I

inputs and J outputs, we denote $x_1, x_2, \ldots, x_I$ for input signals and $y_1, y_2, \ldots, y_J$ for output signals. The potential of neurotransmitter release is a sum of M pre-synaptic factors; at least one mechanism, i.e. the Mth provides a modulatory feedback. We may write the system equation set as below:

$$F_{ij}^m[n] = A_{ij}^m F_{ij}^m[n-1] + B_{ij}^m x_i[n] \tag{6}$$

$$i = 1, \ldots, I \qquad m = 1, \ldots, M-1 \qquad j = 1, \ldots, J$$

$$n = 1, \ldots, N$$

$$F_{ij}^M[n] = A_{ij}^M F_{ij}^M[n-1] + \sum_{\substack{l=1 \\ l \neq j}}^{J} B_{ijl}^M y_l[n] \tag{7}$$

where F_{ij}^m is the mth mechanism at terminal ij. The total number of I/O data set is denoted by N. A and B are unknown parameters. The modulatory feedback (7) is a weighted sum over all other outputs. The potential of release is expressed as a weighted sum of the activation of presynaptic mechanisms:

$$P_{R_{ij}}[n] = \sum_{m=1}^{M} F_{ij}^m[n] \tag{8}$$

and probability of neurotransmitter release at synaptic cleft can be expressed as

$$Z_{ij}[n] = \varphi(-\alpha_{ij} P_{R_{ij}}[n] - \beta_{ij}) \tag{9}$$

$$\varphi(v) = \frac{1}{1 + e^{-v}} \tag{10}$$

where $\varphi(\cdot)$ is a sigmoidal function.

The rate of change in amplitude of an EPSP stimulus is proportional to Z, and a first order difference equation can describe this phenomenon as:

$$PSP_{ij}[n] = C_{ij} PSP_{ij}[n-1] + D_{ij} Z_{ij}[n] \tag{11}$$

$$V_j[n] = E_j V_j[n-1] + \sum_{i=1}^{I} PSP_{ij}[n] \tag{12}$$

$$Y_j[n] = \varphi(-\psi_j V_j[n] - \zeta_j) \tag{13}$$

$$X_j[n] = \gamma X_j[n-1] + \eta Y_j[n] \tag{14}$$

$$\text{If } X_j[n] > \theta_j \text{ then } O_j[n] = \delta_j[n] \tag{15}$$

where $C, D, E, \psi, \zeta, \gamma$, and η are unknown parameters subject to be estimated. Fig. 3 shows a typical block diagram of the generalized DSNN.

Using reverse correlation analysis, each AP signifies the time course of the stimulus preceding the AP. If this is correct, a reconstruction of the complete time course of the stimulus $s(t)$ from the set of firing times $\Im = \{t^{(1)}, \ldots, t^{(n)}\}$ should be possible (Fig. 4) (Rieke, Warland, de Ruyter van Steveninck, & Bialek, 1996). Therefore, we can use the output membrane potential values as reference information to tune the network parameters.

We have already proposed the GA to train the DSNNs (Namarvar et al., 2001). Despite their success in small-size

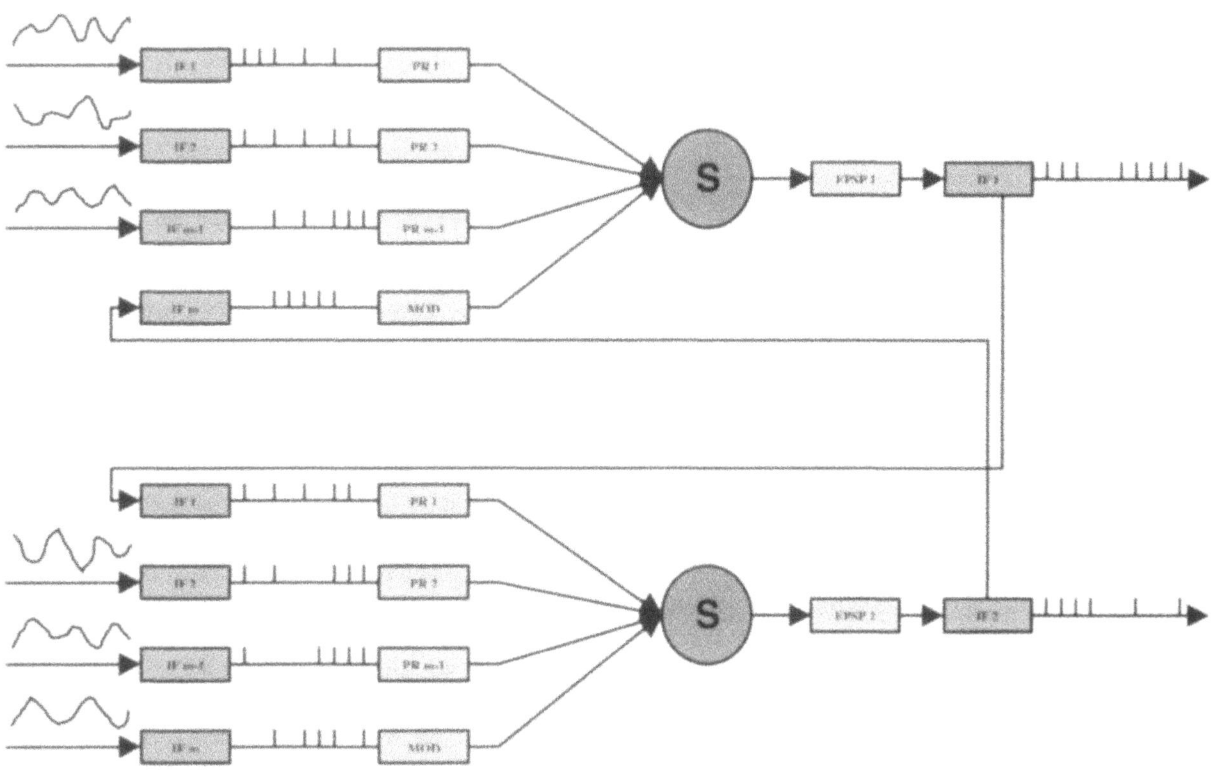

Fig. 3. Block diagram of DSNN. Integrate-and-Fire (IF) neurons are responsible for converting continuous signals into point-process events.

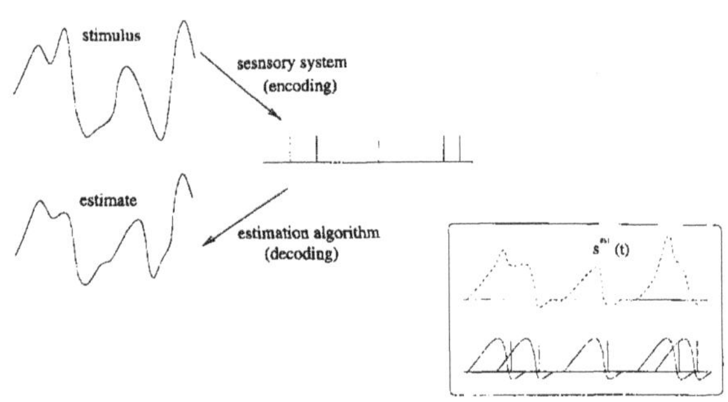

Fig. 4. Reconstruction of a stimulus using the reverse correlation (Rieke et al., 1996).

problem, they have some drawbacks which means they cannot be used in most real applications. For example, they are extremely slow and when a problem size scales up, e.g. greater than 50 parameters, the GA is overwhelmed by the curse of dimensionality. Thus, the algorithm is unable to find anything close to an optimal solution. There is also no way to test whether a given solution is optimal. In practice, the GAs are usually stopped manually or by a predetermined limit on the iterations. To solve the above-mentioned drawbacks, we propose a learning method for DSNN based on an interior, TR approach for nonlinear minimization (Coleman & Li, 1996).

2.2. Trust region approach learning algorithm

An unconstrained minimization problem is stated as:

$$\min\{f(x), \quad x \in \Re^n\} \tag{16}$$

where f maps $\Re^n$ into $\Re$. We assume that f is continuously differentiable. The basic idea is to approximate f with a simple function q, which reasonably reflects the behavior of function f in a neighborhood N around point x. This neighborhood is called the trust region.

Mathematically the TR sub-problem is typically stated as:

$$s_k = x_{k+1} - x_k$$

$$\min\left\{\psi_k(s) = \frac{1}{2}s^{\mathrm{T}}H_k s + s g_k^{\mathrm{T}}, \qquad \|\bar{D}_k s\| \le \Delta_k\right\} \tag{17}$$

$$s \in \Re^n$$

where $g_k \overset{\mathrm{def}}{=} \nabla f(x_k)$, s the gradient of f at the current point x, H_k is a symmetric approximation to the Hessian matrix $\nabla^2 f(x_k)$, $\bar{D}_k$ is a diagonal scaling matrix, Δ_k is a positive scalar representing the trust region size, $\|\cdot\|$ is the 2-norm, and s is a step vector. The algorithms typically to solve this problem involve the computation of a full eigensystem and a Newton process applied to the secular equation:

$$\frac{1}{\Delta} - \frac{1}{\|s\|} = 0 \tag{18}$$

To force the global convergence of the algorithm, (Coleman & Li, 1994) have proposed a method via the steepest descent direction and achieved fast local convergence. A general approach to solve the unconstrained minimization of $f(x)$, based on subproblem (17) is described below. An iteration with $\rho_k^f > \mu$ is said to be successful. Otherwise, the iteration is unsuccessful. The goal of updating algorithm is to force $\rho_k^f > \mu$ and hence ensure sufficient reduction of the objective function.

Algorithm 1: Unconstrained trust region method
Let $0 < \mu < \eta < 1$.
For $k = 0, 1, \ldots$

1. Compute $f(x_k)$ and the subproblem ψ_k, Eq. (17).
2. Define an approximate solution s_k to subproblem.
3. Compute $\rho_k^f = (f(x_k + s_k) - f(x_k))/\psi_k(s_k)$.
4. If $\rho_k^f > \mu$ *then* set $x_{k+1} = x_k + s_k$ *else* set $x_{k+1} = x_k$.
5. Update the scaling matrix $\bar{D}_k$ and Δ_k.

Algorithm 2: Updating trust region size
Let $0 < \gamma_1 < 1 < \gamma_2$.

1. If $\rho_k^f \le \mu$ *then* set $\Delta_{k+1} \in (0, \gamma_1 \Delta_k]$.
2. If $\mu < \rho_k^f < \eta$ *then set*, $\Delta_{k+1} \in [\gamma_1 \Delta_k, \Delta_k]$.
3. If $\rho_k^f \ge \eta$ *then set* $\Delta_{k+1} \in [\Delta_k, \gamma_2, \Delta_k]$.

Trust region methods have also been developed for the solution of nonlinearly constrained optimization problems. It would be quite possible to use any information on the parameters of the DSNN as constrains, if this information was provided on the solution space. However, we have not studied to train the DSNN with constrained bounds here.

3. Simulation and results

In order to compare the efficiency of proposed algorithm to the GA, we study those problems that we already know where at least one specific solution exists. One way to set up such a problem is to predetermine the value of desired DSNN and generate I/O data set based on the generated architecture. Optimization of DSNN parameters refers to optimally estimating the network parameters only through those generated I/O data set by minimizing an objective function over the training data.

Here, we generated 7-dimensional spatio-temporal AP patterns using Mallat's Wavelet decomposition (Mallat, 1999) technique with Daubechies 4th order wavelet kernels (Namarvar et al., 2001), proceeded by m IF neurons. One pre-synaptic and one modulatory feedback mechanisms for each hidden neuron were used. Two hidden neurons and one output neuron completed the architecture of DSNN. In the following, we simply refer to a DSNN with m input, s hidden and l output neuron units as $m - n - l$. The DSNN parameters, W_0, were predetermined to some values in the range of [0,1] for time constants and [0,5] for other coefficients, randomly. The desired output vector of network, $\mathbf{Y}$, was calculated by

$$\mathbf{Y} = \mathrm{DSNN}_l(\mathbf{X}, \mathbf{W}_0) \tag{19}$$

where $\mathbf{X}$ is input vector and $\mathbf{W}_0$ is the predetermined parameter vector. To train a network with unknown parameters using a training data set, we set up second DSNN with the same architecture with parameters $\mathbf{W}$ subject to be estimated.

$$\mathbf{D} = \mathrm{DSNN}_2(\mathbf{X}, \mathbf{W}) \tag{20}$$

The objective function is defined as:

$$\min_{\mathbf{W}} f(\mathbf{W}) = \sum_{i=1}^{N} (d_i - y_i)^2$$

$$= \sum_{i=1}^{N} [\mathrm{DSNN}_2(x_i, \mathbf{W}) - \mathrm{DSNN}_1(x_i, \mathbf{W}_0)]^2 \tag{21}$$

Algorithm (1) and (2) are applied to minimize objective function (21).

Fig. 5 shows 7-dimensional input, the desired membrane potential, and AP output of DSNN_1. Fig. 6 shows the output of DSNN_2 before and after training with the TR optimization method. The GA was also applied to this problem exactly with the same condition, see Fig. 7.

Tables 1a and 1b compares the performance of TR algorithm to those obtained by the GAs. Performance is given in terms of number of network parameters, iterations, minimization function value, i.e. sum-squared error (SSE), and convergence time. As it can be seen from this table in all cases, the TR algorithm extremely outperforms the GAs. For example, the obtained SSE is 20 to 6000 times lower than those obtained by the GAs and convergence time is 20–500 times less than the time

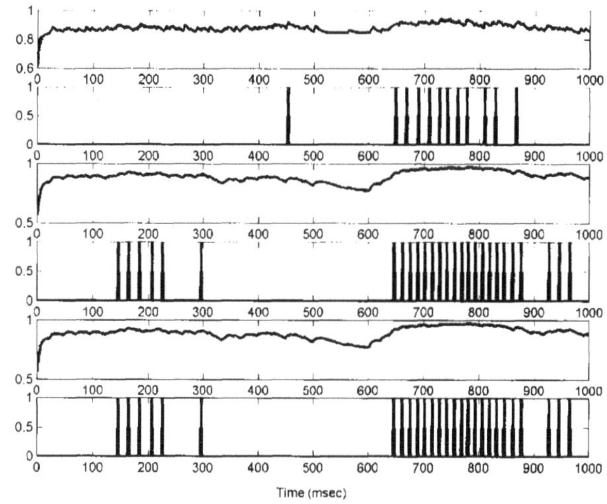

Fig. 6. From top to bottom; (a) the initial membrane potential and spiking output of DSNN with the TR algorithm, (b) the desired membrane potential and output, and (c) the trained membrane potential and output of DSNN with the TR algorithm.

for the GAs. In most cases, the GAs is stuck at a local minimum, so further improvement on the SSE is impossible. That is they never find a desired solution. Even we assume a possibility of linearly improvement on the SSE using the GAs, we would say that the proposed method would be 400–3,000,000 times faster than the GAs. Notice that these numbers are only given here to give a sense about the speed of proposed algorithm. In practice, the TR algorithm is much faster than the GAs. Particularly, if we consider the point-process output as a desired solution, for none of the simulation achieved in this study, the GAs was not able to find a correct desired output pattern. Therefore, in terms of AP I/O transformation, the GAs has not been able to solve the problem, e.g. see Fig. 7.

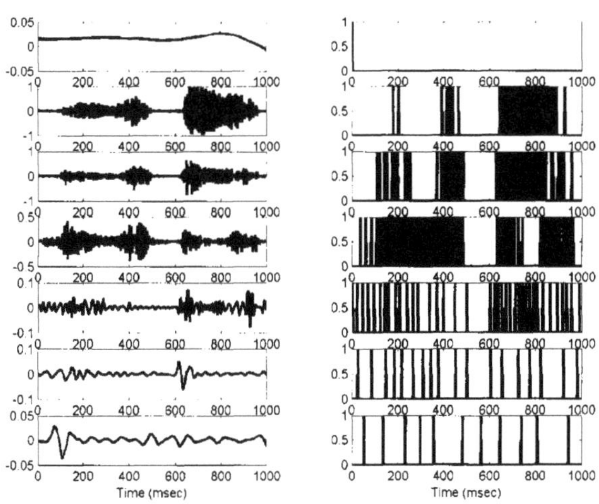

Fig. 5. Seven-dimensional input signal. Decomposed signals using wavelet filter bank (left) and their corresponding point-process (spiking) signals (right).

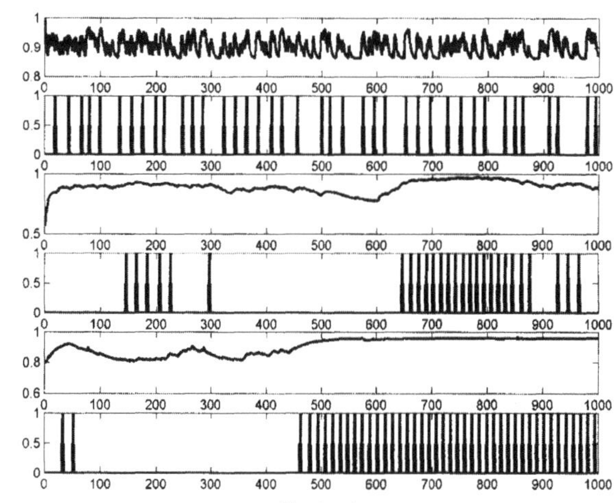

Fig. 7. From top to bottom; (a) the initial membrane potential and spiking output of DSNN with the GAs training, (b) the desired membrane potential and output, and (c) the trained membrane potential and output of DSNN with the GAs.

Table 1a
The performance of the TR algorithm

Arch.	No. of DSNN parameters	SSE of TRA	No. of TRA iterations	TRA time (min)
7-2-1	39	0.0001	4,601	12
7-4-1	77	0.0602	31,201	113
7-6-1	115	0.0027	3,133	14
9-8-1	185	0.0212	41,997	170
11-10-1	271	0.1382	92,685	428

Table 1b
The performance of the GAs

Arch.	No. of DSNN parameters	SSE of GA	No. of GA iterations	GA time (min)
7-2-1	39	0.6	2,436,160	425
7-4-1	77	1.35	10,317,104	2,581
7-6-1	115	2.12	15,834,932	7,472
9-8-1	185	4.56	17,391,205	11,952
11-10-1	271	5.83	20,125,234	21,827

Table 2
The performance of the GAs with a wider range parameter set up

Arch.	No. of DSNN parameters	SSE of GA	No. of GA iterations	GA time (min)
7-2-1	39	1.12	2,781,032	485
7-4-1	77	1.83	12,432,292	3,110
7-6-1	115	3.17	19,562,346	9,230
9-8-1	185	5.39	23,193,826	15,939
11-10-1	271	10.12	30,876,210	33,487

On the other hand, if we cannot estimate the range of parameters for the GAs set-up then the GAs may never converge even to a neighborhood of an optimum solution. In the above set-up, we had provided the GAs with information about the range of parameters. In another case, we initialized the parameters for a wider range, e.g. 10 times wider than a range that could be happened. Table 2 shows the results for this set-up. As it can be seen, the results obtained by the GAs even get worse.

4. Conclusion

Presently, conventional neural networks cannot process information in the way that biological neural networks can. The DSNN is an alternative to traditional ANNs where they employ long-term potentiation (LTP), short-term potentiation (STP) and synaptic plasticity by incorporating nonlinear dynamic properties of synaptic mechanisms and neurotransmitter release. However, due to the high dimensionality and large-scale information processing, finding a unique solution for a data set of multi-input multi-output system is often an ill-posed problem. Therefore, the dynamic networks have been lacking proper learning algorithm to extract complex information from spatio-temporal patterns.

We have presented the general DSNN architecture to model the average local population activity of neurons and applied the learning algorithm based on an interior point TR nonlinear optimization method. The proposed architecture of the DSNN allowing inputs in the form of AP-based time events or continuous membranes potential, which arrive from the output of other local population of neurons, can be easily employed in nonlinear dynamic processing. Here, we only applied the TR optimization method to the AP-based time events I/O signals. Applying this algorithm to combined continuous and point-process I/O signals is possible. The proposed learning method has been more successful in comparison to the GAs training. The TR-learning algorithm is tremendously faster than the GAs (Tables 1a and 1b). The other advantages of the proposed method are: there is no need to determine the stop criterion and specify the range of parameters, while those criteria are very critical for the GAs. In practice, the stop criterion for the GAs is predetermined by limitation on the iterations and the range of parameters is estimated empirically by running the GAs several times with different ranges.

The high regard of trust region methods is partially due to their strong convergence properties, partially due to their naturalness, and partially due to the recent development of reliable, efficient software (Coleman & Li, 1996).

Here, the initial goal was to introduce this idea of general DSNN and use the TR-learning algorithm to optimize the network parameters. DSNNs have some potential applications in signal and image processing, pattern classifications, nonlinear system identification, prediction and neural prosthesis (Berger et al., 2001). There are still theoretical and experimental questions, which are potential interests for subsequent research.

Acknowledgements

This study was supported in part by grants from DARPA CBS, NASA, and ONR.

References

Berger, T. W., Baudry, M., Brinton, R. D., Liaw, J. S., Marmarelis, V. Z., Park, A. Y., Sheu, B. J., & Tanguay, A. R. (2001). Brain-implantable biomimetic electronics as the next era in neural prosthesis. *Proceedings of the IEEE, 89*(7), 993–1012.

Coleman, T. F., & Li, Y. (1994). On the convergence of reflective newton methods for large-scale nonlinear minimization subject to bounds. *Mathematical Programming, 67*(2), 189–224.

Coleman, T. F., & Li, T. F. (1996). An interior trust region approach for nonlinear minimization subject to bounds. *SIAM Journal on Optimization, 6*, 418–445.

Gestner, W. (1999). Spiking neurons. In W. Maass, & W. Bishop (Eds.), *Pulsed neural networks* (pp. 3–53). Cambridge, MA: MIT Press.

Hoppensteadt, F. C., & Izhikevich, E. M. (1997). *Weakly connected neural networks*. New York: Springer.

Liaw, J. S., & Berger, T. W. (1996). Dynamic synapse: A new concept of neural representation and computation. *Hippocampus, 6*, 591–600.

Mallat, S. (1999). *A wavelet tour of signal processing*. New York: Academic Press.

McCulloch, W. S., & Pitts, W. (1943). A logical calculus of the ideas immanent in nervous activity. *Bulletin of Mathematical Biophysics, 5*, 115–133.

Namarvar, H. H., Liaw, J. S., & Berger, T. W. (2001). A new dynamic synapse neural network for speech recognition. *Proceeding of the IEEE International Joint Conference on Neural Networks, 4*, 2985–2990.

Namarvar, H. H., Dibazar, A. A., & Berger, T. W. (2002). The Gauss–Newton learning method for a generalized dynamic synapse neural networks. *Proceedings of the IEEE International Joint Conference on Neural Networks, 2*, 1206–1211.

Rieke, F., & Warland, D. (1996). *Spikes-exploring the neural code*. Cambridge, MA: MIT Press.

PERGAMON

AVAILABLE AT
www.ComputerScienceWeb.com
POWERED BY SCIENCE DIRECT

Neural Networks 16 (2003) 593–600

Neural Networks

www.elsevier.com/locate/neunet

2003 Special issue

Temporal binding as an inducer for connectionist recruitment learning over delayed lines

Cengiz Günay[a], Anthony S. Maida[a,b,*]

[a]Center for Advanced Computer Studies, University of Louisiana at Lafayette, Lafayette, LA 70504, USA
[b]Institute of Cognitive Science, University of Louisiana at Lafayette, Lafayette, LA 70504, USA

Abstract

The *temporal correlation hypothesis* proposes using distributed synchrony for the binding of different stimulus features. However, synchronized spikes must travel over cortical circuits that have varying length pathways, leading to mismatched arrival times. This raises the question of how initial stimulus-dependent synchrony might be preserved at a destination binding site. Earlier, we proposed constraints on tolerance and segregation parameters for a phase-coding approach, within cortical circuits, to address this question [Proceedings of the International Joint Conference on Neural Networks, Washington, DC, 2001]. The purpose of the present paper is twofold. First, we conduct simulation experiments to test the proposed constraints. Second, we explore the practicality of temporal binding to drive a process of long-term memory formation based on a *recruitment learning* method [Biol. Cybernet. 46 (1982) 27].

A network based on Valiant's neuroidal architecture [Circuits of the mind, 1994] is used to demonstrate the coalition between temporal binding and recruitment. Complementing similar approaches, we implement a continuous-time learning procedure allowing computation with spiking neurons. The viability of the proposed binding scheme is investigated by conducting simulation studies which examine binding errors. In the simulation, binding errors cause the perception of illusory conjunctions among features belonging to separate objects. Our results indicate that when tolerance and segregation parameters obey our proposed constraints, the assemblies of correct bindings are dominant over assemblies of spurious bindings in reasonable operating conditions.

Keywords: Synchrony; Temporal correlation; Binding; Recruitment learning; Tolerance window; Phase segregation

1. Introduction

In the brain, functionally and physically separate areas of the sensory cortex (e.g. visual, auditory, somatosensory) analyze different stimulus features in the environment. This raises the question of how these physically distributed feature representations are combined to form coherent unitary percepts. One approach to solving this problem uses the *temporal correlation hypothesis* which posits that binding of disparate feature representations is accomplished by synchronized firing across cortical areas (von der Malsburg, 1995; Singer & Gray, 1995). The viability of this temporal binding model depends on maintaining the synchrony of spikes coding features from the same stimulus and desynchrony of spikes coding features from separate stimuli.

We noted in previous work that some distributed cortical connection topologies appear to be problematic with respect to maintenance of synchrony (Günay & Maida, 2001). We proposed requirements on theoretical *tolerance window* and *phase segregation* parameters of cortical circuits in order to use temporal binding with the *spike response model* (SRM) of Gerstner (1999). The purpose of the current work is twofold: first, to test the suggested parameter requirements with a simulation study; and second, in doing so, to explore the practicality of a *recruitment learning* method that complements temporal binding by creating permanent memories. We hope ultimately our models will help establish a biological grounding for *structured connectionist models* capable of cognitive functions like reasoning (for a review, see Feldman & Bailey, 2000).

1.1. Why recruitment learning?

Temporal binding proposes that only temporary representations are formed. When considering the full range of

* Corresponding author.
E-mail addresses: cengiz@ull.edu (C. Günay), maida@cacs.louisiana.edu (A.S. Maida).

0893-6080/03/$ - see front matter © 2003 Elsevier Science Ltd. All rights reserved.
doi:10.1016/S0893-6080(03)00117-5

cognitive tasks, it is necessary to address the question of how long-term storage is formed (O'Reilly, Busby, & Soto, 2003). Recruitment learning can be used to trigger allocation of long-term or permanent memories (Shastri, 2001; Valiant, 1994). Thus, recruitment may serve as the read-out process for the results of temporal binding processes (i.e. forming binding-detectors). This idea is consistent with the storage and retrieval criterion in the requirements of von der Malsburg (1995) for a binding mechanism.

Recruitment learning was originally proposed by Feldman (1982) (also motivated the *vicinal algorithms* of Valiant (1994)). Recruitment provides a feasible way to represent concepts in randomly connected structures, similar to that of the brain. In particular, the model was motivated by the ratio of connections of cortical pyramidal cells in the brain, where the number of projections from a single neuron is roughly proportional to the square root of the total number of neurons (Wickelgren, 1979).

1.2. Overview of recruitment learning

Briefly, recruitment learning is a concept production scheme which allocates units from a pool of free units that are embedded in a random graph (Feldman, 1982). A concept is a token of information such as a symbol or subsymbol. Novel localist concepts can be allocated by synchronous stimulation of existing concepts. These existing concepts, upon stimulation, coincidentally activate units where signals converge due to random interconnections. The two points to emphasize in recruitment learning are random connections and synchronous activity, both of which have some biological support (Feldman, 1982; Valiant, 1994; Wickelgren, 1979).

The neural representations that we employ can be described as redundant localist representations. Concepts are represented by a small redundant number (~ 10) of randomly distributed units within the network. This number the *replication factor r*. Unlike conventional localist representations, redundancy ensures robustness in case some units are lost.

When projections of two separate concepts target the same area, common units are included in both projection sets due to statistical reasons. These units that receive input from both sources are recruited upon coincident firing of the two concepts. Therefore, it can be said that recruitment depends on the principle of temporal binding. Coincident, or synchronous, activity triggers the memorization mechanism for recruitment, caused by activity above a preset threshold in units at the intersection set of the two projections. These units change their internal states and weights in favor of a permanent memorization. This set of recruited units, in turn, will represent the high-level concept of the conjunction of the two primitive concepts. Our work here is consistent with previous work on recruitment learning (Diederich, 1991; Feldman & Bailey, 2000; Shastri, 2001).

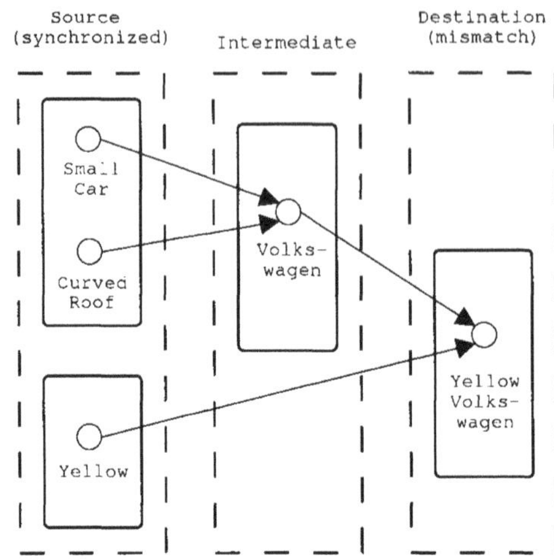

Fig. 1. Connection topology showing possible direct and indirect pathways from an initially synchronized source of activity converging at a destination. Dashed boxes indicate the hypothesized stages of processing, in which each individual solid box indicates the localized processing for a single feature.

1.3. Spike timing: tolerance and segregation

The viability of recruitment learning, since it is triggered by temporal binding, depends on the accuracy of neuron spike timing. It turns out that spike timing is very difficult to maintain in network topologies such as those seen in Fig. 1. Initially synchronous activity may be disrupted after passing through separate direct and indirect converging paths.

This work addresses two related aspects of spike timing in direct/indirect connection topologies: Tolerating delays and preventing crosstalk. In the figure, a hypothetical circuit formed by recruitment learning for recognizing a 'yellow Volkswagen' object is illustrated. On the leftmost part of the figure, the neural firings representing the primitive object properties appear synchronously as the subject focuses attention. This is consistent with stimulus-dependent synchrony behavior (Singer & Gray, 1995). It is reasonable to require an additional level of processing for the potentially more complex shape properties than the color property of the object. This allows the circuit to use features such as 'small car' and 'curved roof' to build the concept of a Volkswagen independent of color. If temporal binding is employed, the signals at the destination need to be synchronous to represent the same object. However, when signal transmission times are considered, the degree of synchrony at the destination is degraded due to signals crossing varying length pathways with varying delays.

A *window of tolerance* as seen in Fig. 2 can be defined for integrating signals with variable delays into the same response. This window corresponds to the maximum time allowed between two incoming spikes that can both contribute to cause an action potential (AP) (Koch, Rapp, & Segev, 1996; Shastri, 2001). However, signals corresponding to different objects need to remain separate, or desynchronized, in order to avoid crosstalk of features

Fig. 2. The tolerance window Γ required to integrate inputs such as shown in Fig. 1. Initially on the left, spikes corresponding to primitive object properties are synchronized. After travelling over separate pathways with different delays, their synchrony is degraded, as seen on the right side. By defining this tolerance window the spikes can still be treated as synchronous. Timings are chosen arbitrarily for illustration.

between objects. In this framework, the notion of desynchrony is defined to associate each object to a different tolerance window. This yields the notion of *segregation* of object representations into *phase* windows (Jensen & Lisman, 1996; Lisman & Idiart, 1995; Schillen & König, 1994; Shastri & Ajjanagadde, 1993; Terman & Wang, 1995).

This phase coding approach is one of the possible methods for desynchronizing responses. This method puts neural activity pertaining to each object in a separate phase window (of a large oscillatory period). This prevents interference as the activity propagates to deeper structures, preserving its integrity with respect to temporal binding. An example with two objects is depicted in Fig. 3. In theoretical and simulation studies, segregation between object representations can be obtained by inhibitory projections. Some propose using global inhibitory projections (Lisman & Idiart, 1995; Terman & Wang, 1995), while others propose using lateral recurrent inhibitory connections (Jensen & Lisman, 1996; Schillen & König, 1994).

In this work, we extend the study of phase segregation by investigating how to maintain synchrony and desynchrony when delays are taken into account. Here, relevance of recurrent inhibitory circuits are secondary, since we are interested in the effect of delays on the synchronous activity coming from upstream areas, converging to a single destination site. Instead, we are seeking to calculate the tolerance and segregation measures required to maintain the phase-coding at the destination read-out site.

We have chosen the connection topology in Fig. 1 as an exemplar for observing effects of delays. In theory, more complex connection topologies can be transformed to this case by hierarchical reduction.

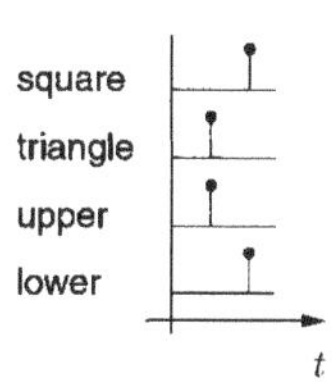

Fig. 3. Activity in separate phase windows for each object in a scene. The scene contains a triangle in the upper part of the visual field and a square in the lower part.

1.4. Related evidence

Psychology and neuroscience studies support the view that temporal binding may be employed in cortical circuits. Primarily, psychological studies identify several classes of visual search tasks where attentional mechanisms serially scan multiple objects in a visual scene (Shiffrin & Schneider, 1977; Treisman, 1996). There is evidence that attending to objects at separate times initiates stimulus-dependent synchronous activity in the primary visual cortex (V1) (Singer & Gray, 1995).

If temporal binding is employed, it is reasonable to assume that synchronous activity representing an object should be sustained as it propagates through various functional areas until the computation terminates. In support of this hypothesis, synchrony has been experimentally observed in different cortical areas (Abeles, 1994; Singer & Gray, 1995). Complementing these observations, analytical and simulation studies of Diesmann, Gewaltig, and Aertsen (1999) show that spike volleys propagating across neuronal pools can become more synchronized. The neurons favor synchrony allowing synchronous volleys to propagate protected, filtering out uncorrelated noise. This observation holds only if a certain degree of connectivity is employed between neurons.

The issue of desynchronization, or segregation of signals pertaining to different objects, has also been explored (Jensen & Lisman, 1996; Lisman & Idiart, 1995; Schillen & König, 1994; Terman & Wang, 1995). However, the phase-coding approach has also been criticised. Knoblauch & Palm (2001) suggested that results of some electromagnetic recording experiments are inconsistent with phase coding. In particular, recordings of activity pertaining to multiple separate stimuli (e.g. bars moving in opposite directions) cause a flat correlogram, whereas phase-coding would predict a non-zero time lag of the central peak.

We propose that the membrane time constant can be dynamically adjusted (possibly by biological processes that vary the membrane resistance), to accommodate the calculated tolerance window. An alternative to varying the membrane time constant may be using persistent firing by inputs occurring at separate times, for creating an overlapping effect on the destination read-out site (Cannon, Hasselmo, & Koene, 2002; Günay & Maida, 2003). Yet another alternative is by adjusting the threshold (excitability) of the destination unit. The calculated segregation, however, needs to be applied at the initial source (possibly by attentional mechanisms). The segregation also predicts the maximum firing frequency in the local circuit. However, there are other views as solution to the problem of variable delays. In particular, it was proposed that introducing synapse-specific delays and integration times adopted during development can accommodate for differences in delays (Senn, Schneider, & Ruf, 2002).

2. Timing constraints

This section extends tolerance and phase segregation constraints presented earlier (Günay & Maida, 2001). For a given connection topology with converging inputs, two requirements were studied: one for the duration of the tolerance window Γ, and a second for the duration of the phase segregation parameter Φ. We first consider the tolerance constraints.

Definition 2.1. A tolerance window Γ_i, for a neuronal unit x_i, is the longest time duration, or interval, during which the unit can integrate a train of incoming spikes that all contribute to emit a single AP. The unit is said to *delay-tolerantly conjoin* the inputs received during this interval.

In this work, Γ_i does not change for different units, therefore we simply use Γ.

Definition 2.2. A neuronal unit x, is said to *cover* a set of distributed sources only in case all synchronized spikes at those sources arrive within the interval Γ.

Lemma 2.3. *Let neuronal unit x receive incoming signals from a set of distributed sources at varying distances. x covers this set of sources if*

$$\Gamma \geq d_{\max} - d_{\min}, \quad (1)$$

where $d_{\max}$ and $d_{\min}$ are the longest and shortest transmission delays from the sources, respectively.

We then start building a *neuroidal* model capable of delay-tolerant conjoining. A neuroid is a neuron-like linear threshold unit (LTU) which also features a finite state machine (Valiant, 1994). We first employ a simple model, where the effect of an incoming spike on the membrane potential is a discrete pulse with constant magnitude.

Theorem 2.4. *Delay-tolerant conjoining of two disparate spikes from sources covered by a neuroidal unit x_i is possible, if each spike causes a Γ-long constant potential of magnitude P on the membrane p_i.*

Proof. Let the first spike reach x_i at time t_1 and second spike at time t_2, where $t_2 - t_1 \leq \Gamma$ according to Definition 2.2. Potentials caused by the disparate spikes on the membrane p_i would overlap for some interval $0 < I \leq \Gamma$. Since x_i is an LTU, the net input p_i will reach $2P$ during the interval I. A threshold T can be set to detect the sum of the overlap value and ignore non-overlapping spikes by choosing $P < T < 2P$. Crossing the threshold can cause an AP and trigger the recruitment of a concept representing the conjunction, satisfying Definition 2.1. □

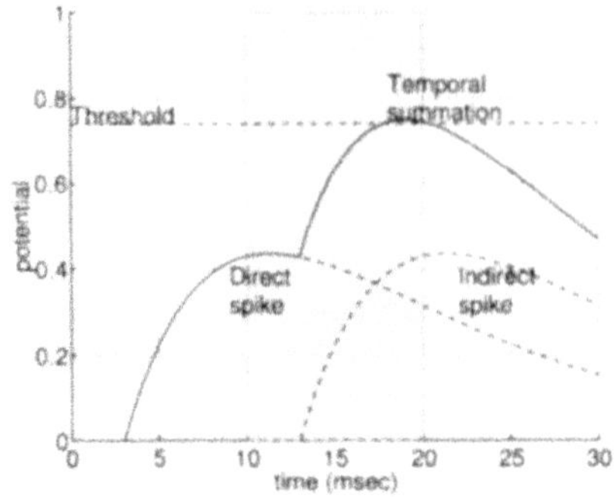

(a) The 10 msec tolerance within the shaded window can be demonstrated with SRM neurons. Early and late arriving spikes cause overlapping *excitatory post synaptic potentials* (EPSPs) that sum to exceed a detection threshold. Obviously, non-overlapping EPSPs do not reach this threshold.

Fig. 4. SRM helps tolerate delayed signals.

Thus far, we used a discrete-time model, consistent with the original proposal for recruitment learning. However, considering timing dynamics of the brain, discrete models can only provide a coarse approximation. A simple integrate-and-fire (I/F) spiking neuron model is more appropriate. For computational reasons we employ the SRM of Gerstner (1999). This model naturally allows delay-tolerant conjoining of disparate signals by generalizing Theorem 2.4 (see Fig. 4).

In the SRM, an EPSP caused by a single spike at $t = 0$ and an axonal delay Δ_i^{ax} is given by the kernel

$$\epsilon_i(t) = \frac{1}{1 - \tau_s/\tau_m}\left[\exp\left(-\frac{t - \Delta_i^{\mathrm{ax}}}{\tau_m}\right) - \exp\left(-\frac{t - \Delta_i^{\mathrm{ax}}}{\tau_s}\right)\right] \mathscr{H}(t - \Delta_i^{\mathrm{ax}}) \quad (2)$$

where $\mathscr{H}(\cdot)$ is the Heaviside step function, τ_s is the synaptic rise time constant, and τ_m is the membrane time constant. The rise and decay behavior of Eq. (2) depend, respectively, on the τ_s and τ_m parameters (Gerstner, 1999).

We then propose parameters for implementing the tolerance window. For delay-tolerant conjoining, a neuroid should emit an AP when the effective parts of two EPSPs caused by separate incoming spikes overlap, whereas the EPSP caused by a single spike should not to cause an AP. The following definition is intended to restrict the SRM to satisfy these necessary conditions.

Definition 2.5. An *effective window* is a time range $t \in \omega$ within the EPSP, where $\epsilon_i(t) > 0.5 \max_t \epsilon_i(t)$.

Theorem 2.6. *Delay-tolerant conjoining of two disparate spikes is possible with a neuroidal unit x_i employing the SRM, if a Γ-long effective window ω can be chosen.*

Proof. Proof of Theorem 2.4 applies when $P = \max_t \epsilon_i(t)$. □

Theorem 2.7. *The region $t \in [\Delta_i^{ax} + \tau_s, \Delta_i^{ax} + \tau_m]$ is an effective window of $\epsilon_i(t)$.*

Proof. Numerical analysis of $\epsilon_i(t)$ in Eq. (2) within the given region satisfies Definition 2.5 when $0.1 < \tau_s/\tau_m < 1$. □

Corollary 2.8. *Delay-tolerant conjoining can be achieved if the membrane time constant*[1] *is chosen as*

$$\tau_m = \tau_s + \Gamma. \tag{3}$$

The second requirement for temporal binding concerns the phase segregation measure for separating activity pertaining to different objects.

Definition 2.9. Phase segregation Φ is the time separation between the synchronized activity pertaining to two different objects represented successively.

We first employ a discrete model as in Theorem 2.4 for delay-tolerant conjoining, for asserting that tolerance windows are exclusive to each object.

Theorem 2.10. *Segregation should obey $\Phi > 2\Gamma$, to prevent crosstalk between elementary features of different objects at a neural unit x covering the sensory sites for these features.*

Proof. Let S_1, S_2 be the sets of spike timings pertaining two successively presented objects o_1, o_2, respectively. Assume, for $t_0, t_1 \in S_1$, the earliest spike arrives at $t_0 = \Delta_1$, and the latest spike arrives at $t_1 = \Delta_1 + \Gamma$. According to Theorem 2.4, the effect of a spike arriving at t_1 will cause a constant potential until $t_1 + \Gamma$. Thus the earliest $t_2 \in S_2$ can arrive at $t_2 > \Delta_1 + 2\Gamma$. According to Definition 2.9, the segregation is the difference between the originating times of spikes pertaining to each object, yielding $\Phi = (t_2 - \Delta_1) - (t_0 - \Delta_1) > 2\Gamma$. □

After defining requirements for segregation in the discrete model, we generalize for the spiking model. We again restrict the SRM EPSP to satisfy these conditions to give a reciprocal of Theorem 2.6.

Lemma 2.11. *Delay-tolerant conjoining of separate groups of spikes pertaining to different objects is possible at a neuroidal unit x_i employing the SRM, if no effective windows of EPSPs from spikes pertaining to different objects overlap in time.*

The part of the SRM EPSP excluded from tolerant conjoining can be given with a time range.

[1] A refinement is made to the earlier paper (Günay & Maida, 2001) where it was proposed that $\tau_m = \Gamma$ is sufficient.

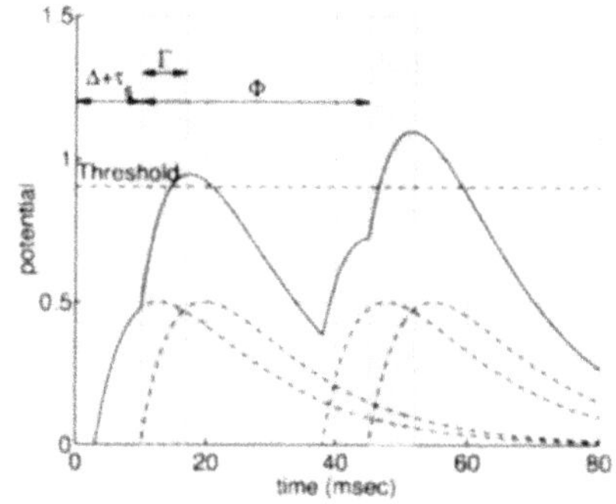

Fig. 5. Phase segregation of SRM EPSPs. Two sets of spikes pertaining to two separate objects are depicted. Shaded areas show the effective windows of the EPSPs that form the tolerance windows.

Theorem 2.12. *There is no effective window in the region of $\epsilon_i(t)$ outside the time range $t \in [\Delta_i^{ax}, \Delta_i^{ax} + 2\tau_m]$.*

Proof. $\epsilon_i(t) = 0$ for $t < \Delta_i^{ax}$, and numerical analysis shows that $\epsilon_i(t) < 0.5 \max_{t'} \epsilon_i(t')$ for $t > 2\tau_m$ when $\tau_s/\tau_m < 0.5$. □

Notice that Theorem 2.12 can be further optimized. We then give the segregation measure adopted for use with the SRM to achieve the effect depicted in Fig. 5.

Theorem 2.13. *The segregation for the SRM should obey*

$$\Phi_{SRM} > \Gamma + 2\tau_m = 3\Gamma + 2\tau_s. \tag{4}$$

Proof. Using $t_0, t_1 \in S_1$ from proof of Theorem 2.10, the arrival time of the earliest spike $t_2 \in S_2$ should be outside any effective windows pertaining to o_1. According to Theorem 2.12, $t_2 > t_1 + 2\tau_m$ should be satisfied in order to avoid overlaps. This yields $\Phi_{SRM} = (t_2 - \Delta_1) - (t_0 - \Delta_1) > t_1 + 2\tau_m - t_0 = \Delta_1 + \Gamma + 2\tau_m - \Delta_1$. □

Corollary 2.14. *The amount of segregation predicts the maximal firing frequency of the destination neuroid by $f < 1/\Phi_{SRM}$.*

Phase segregation or desynchronization can be implemented by having a globally inhibitory projection (Günay & Maida, 2001; Lisman & Idiart, 1995; Schillen & König, 1994; Terman & Wang, 1995), which suppresses the source units for the duration of an inhibitory time constant $\tau_i = \Phi_{SRM}$.

3. Methods and results

We present simulation results to evaluate the hypotheses put forth. The studies are conducted using a simulator for recruitment learning. We predict the following from the simulations. For the tolerance and segregation parameters, the lower bound calculated according to the hypotheses is expected to give acceptable performance.

The tests are conducted by presenting a sequence of hypothetical perceptual objects to the system in each simulation (cf. Fig. 3). The tolerance and segregation parameters are varied between different simulation runs. Multiple simulations are run to collect statistical data, since both the connections within the network, as well as the feature combinations for objects are chosen from a uniform random distribution in each simulation.

The performance of a simulation is evaluated by observing the network's internal organization. We expect to find, at the final layer, units recruited to represent the hypothetical objects presented at the input layers as a combination of features. Each of the concepts for elementary features is represented redundantly with r neuroids (discussed in Section 1.2). In turn, each of the recruited concepts for intermediate representations, and for the objects that occur at the final layer, is expected to have roughly r neuroids.

To test the success of the binding scheme employed, the artifacts of binding errors are investigated. The binding errors cause perception of *illusory conjunctions* among features of separate objects and result in the appearance of spurious concepts to be recruited in the network. Therefore, the quantitative performance measure for a network is given by the quality of both correct and spurious concepts that were formed at the end of the simulation, for providing a comparison. The relative magnitudes of quality can indicate if a threshold can be set to distinguish the correct concepts from spurious ones. For instance, this threshold can be in the form of a winner-take-all mechanism. We assume this is a necessary condition for the network to perform correctly.

3.1. Testbeds for observing timings

The testbeds for verifying the tolerance measure consist of a number of input I_i and middle M_i areas as seen in Fig. 6, where $i = 1, \ldots, k$ and $k \geq 2$. Signals appear synchronously at input areas as the system attends to a sensory stimulus corresponding to a perceptual object. Synchronized signals representing each object is presented to the network successively, segregated by the interval Φ_{SRM} calculated according to Eq. (4). Indirect pathways are created by the signals crossing the middle areas.

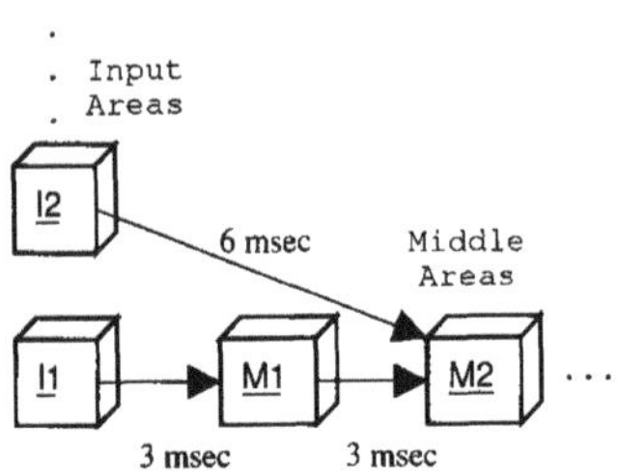

Fig. 6. The type of testbed used to measure the tolerance and segregation required for coherent representations. The middle areas serve to create indirect pathways with more synapses than the direct pathways (compare the path $I_2 \rightarrow M_2$ with $I_1 \rightarrow M_2$). The number of input and middle areas is varied for testing.

Here, we assume that all areas are monolaminar, and there is only one synapse to cross an area. As seen from the figure, axonal delays are designed to conform to the topological organization of the testbed, increasing linearly with distance. Therefore, the difference in pathway length (Lemma 2.3) is caused only by synaptic delays. We vary the number of input and middle areas k to create larger differences in delays. If $k = 2$, this two-layer topology creates a two synapse indirect pathway compared to a single synapse direct pathway to the destination. Therefore, for a topology the tolerance window can be chosen as $\Gamma = (k - 1)\tau_s$, since the shortest path always contains a single synapse.

We chose model parameters estimated according to timing data from visual cortex (Lamme & Roelfsema, 2000). The time it takes to cross an area is assumed to be ~ 10 ms. In turn, axonal delays are estimated to be about $\delta = 3$ ms according to their diameter and physical distance. This leaves $\tau_s = 7$ ms for the synaptic rise time, which is a slower process than the axonal transmission. Employing these parameters, when segregation values are calculated for a two-layer topology similar to the circuit formed by cortical areas V1, V2 and V3, we get 35 ms for segregation. The segregation value predicts the maximum oscillation frequency in this circuit to be 28 Hz, which fall within the gamma band (20–70 Hz). The activity in the gamma frequency band is suggested to be used for object representations.

Each area contains $N = 100$ neuroids with the replication factor $r = 10$ for representing concepts. The connection probability of two neuroids from connected areas is given by $p = \mu/\sqrt{rN}$. This probability is calculated by extending the methodology described in Valiant (1994) for simple random graphs. The parameter μ stands for the amplification factor. We employ $\mu = 6$ for increasing the expectation of the set of recruited neuroids for stability reasons (Günay & Maida, 2003).

The learning algorithm used is a multiplicative weight adjustment method consistent with Hebbian learning. Its state machine and parameters are designed to give a simplified model of permanent recruitment by a one-shot drastic weight modification. Recruitment can also allow creating non-permanent long-term memories via gradual weight adjustment mechanisms. Other parameters used in the simulation include the refractory reset after each spike with a 10 ms time constant.

3.2. Simulations

Results from simulation runs are given in Figs. 7 and 8 over a range of tolerance and segregation values, respectively. In both figures, the solid line gives the quality

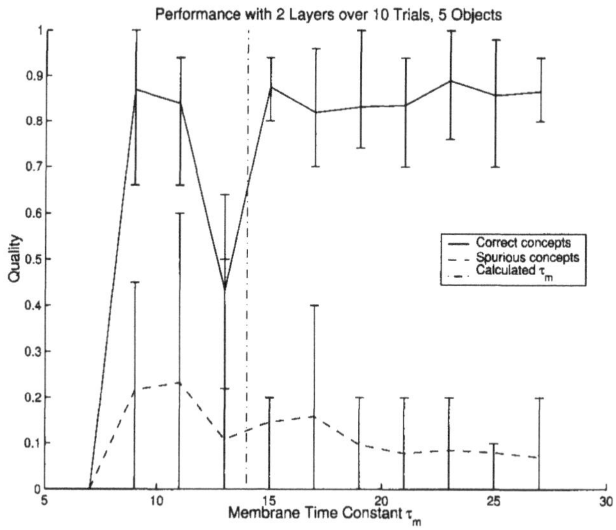

Fig. 7. Concept quality as a function of the membrane time constant τ_m. In the simulations, the tolerance window Γ is varied, implying that τ_m and segregation between activity Φ (the SRM index is dropped for simplicity) is calculated according to Eqs. (3) and (4), respectively. The predicted operating value of Γ is given by Eq. (1).

of correct concepts and the dashed line gives the quality of spurious concepts. A quality value of 1 indicates that all concepts presented to the network were successfully allocated r replicated units. On the other hand, a quality value of 0 indicates that no units were allocated for any of the concepts. Each point is an average of 10 trials, where the minimum and maximum values of the trials are indicated by an error-bar.

Both figures show results from the simplest two-layer testbed. The dash–dotted vertical bars in each figure represent the predicted operating value of the parameter from the theoretical calculations. The spike threshold for

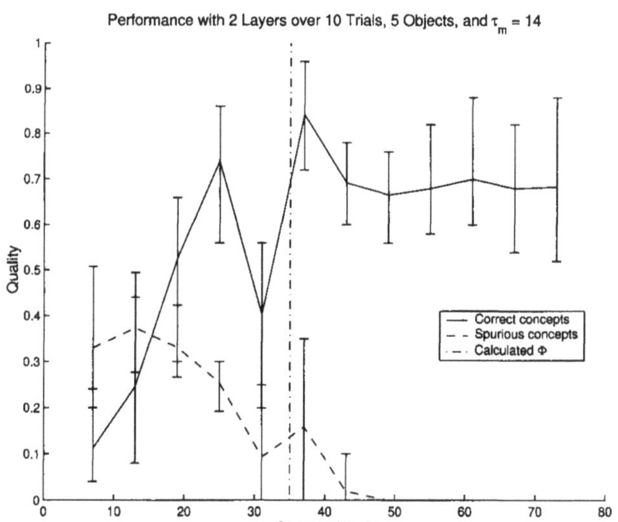

Fig. 8. Concept quality as a function of the segregation amount Φ. In the simulations, the segregation Φ is varied, while the tolerance Γ and τ_m is kept constant at a value calculated according to Eqs. (1) and (3), respectively. The predicted operating value of Φ is given by Eq. (4).

the middle areas is calculated by $T \simeq 2P$ from the proof of Theorem 2.6. The key observation is that the solid line showing the quality of correct objects can be distinguished from spurious objects at the predicted operating value in both cases. For details, see Günay and Maida (2003).

4. Conclusions

Our previous work proposed lower bounds for the temporal window Γ and the phase segregation Φ parameters. Here, we improve these hypotheses, and show their viability with simulations. We offer detailed results and analysis on the robustness of the method in a companion paper (Günay & Maida, 2003). We conclude that tolerance and segregation parameters enable use of temporal binding for recruitment learning in direct/indirect connection topologies. Furthermore, using a spiking neuron model is appropriate for recruitment learning, which is originally proposed with simpler discrete-time neuron models. A recent study is consistent with our view (Shastri, 2001).

We also improved the stability of recruitment with aid of stabilizing mechanism. As a result, our simulations indicate that, up to roughly half of the predicted capacity can be achieved with reasonable performance.

Acknowledgements

The authors would like to thank Prashant Joshi, Ben Rowland, and the anonymous referees for valuable comments and suggestions. This research is partially funded by the University Doctoral Fellowship of the University of Louisiana awarded to the first author.

References

Abeles, M. (1994). Firing rates and well-timed events in the cerebral cortex. In E. Domany, J. L. van Hemmen, & K. Schulten (Eds.), *Models of neural networks (Vol. 2)* (pp. 121–138). *Physics of neural networks*, New York: Springer.

Cannon, R., Hasselmo, M. E., & Koene, R. A. (2002). From biophysics to behavior: Catacomb2 and the design of biologically plausible models for spatial navigation. *Neuroinformatics*, *1*, 3–42.

Diederich, J. (1991). Steps towards knowledge-intensive connectionist learning. In J. A. Barnden, & J. Pollack (Eds.), *Advances in connectionist and neural computation theory (Vol. 1)*, Norwood, NJ: Ablex.

Diesmann, M., Gewaltig, M.-O., & Aertsen, A. (1999). Stable propagation of synchronous spiking in cortical neural networks. *Nature*, *402*, 529–533.

Feldman, J. A. (1982). Dynamic connections in neural networks. *Biological Cybernetics*, *46*, 27–39.

Feldman, J., & Bailey, D. (2000). Layered hybrid connectionist models for cognitive science. In S. Wermter, & R. Sun (Eds.), *Hybrid neural systems (Vol. 1778)* (pp. 14–27). *Lecture notes in computer science*, Berlin: Springer.

Gerstner, W. (1999). Spiking neurons. In W. Maass, & C. M. Bishop (Eds.), *Pulsed neural networks, Chap. 1* (pp. 3–54). Cambridge, MA: MIT Press.

Günay, C., & Maida, A. (2001). The required measures of phase segregation in distributed cortical processing. *Proceedings of the International Joint Conference on Neural Networks, Vol. 1, Washington, DC*, pp. 290–295.

Günay, C., Maida, A (2003). Using temporal binding for robust connectionist recruitment learning over delayed lines. Technical Report TR-2003-2-1, Center for Advanced Computer Studies, University of Louisiana at Lafayette, Lafayette, LA, 70504-4330, USA

Jensen, O., & Lisman, J. E. (1996). Novel lists of 7 ± 2 known items can be reliably stored in an oscillatory short-term memory network: interaction with long-term memory. *Learning and Memory, 3*, 257–263.

Knoblauch, A., & Palm, G. (2001). Pattern separation and synchronization in spiking associative memories and visual areas. *Neural Networks, 14*, 763–780.

Koch, C., Rapp, M., & Segev, I. (1996). A brief history of time (constants). *Cerebral Cortex, 6*, 93–103.

Lamme, V. A. F., & Roelfsema, P. R. (2000). The distinct modes of vision offered by feedforward and recurrent processing. *Trends in Neuroscience, 23*, 571–579.

Lisman, J. E., & Idiart, M. A. P. (1995). Storage of 7 ± 2 short-term memories in oscillatory subcycles. *Science, 267*, 1512–1514.

von der Malsburg, C. (1995). Binding in models of perception and brain function. *Current Opinion in Neurobiology, 5*, 520–526.

O'Reilly, R. C., Busby, R. S., & Soto, R. (2003). Three forms of binding and their neural substrates: alternatives to temporal synchrony. In A. Cleeremans (Ed.), *The unity of consciousness: Binding, integration and dissociation*. Oxford: Oxford University Press.

Schillen, T. B., & König, P. (1994). Binding by temporal structure in multiple feature domains of an oscillatory neuronal network. *Biological Cybernetics, 70*, 397–405.

Senn, W., Schneider, M., & Ruf, B. (2002). Activity-dependent development of axonal and dendritic delays, or, why synaptic transmission should be unreliable. *Neural Computation, 14*, 583–619.

Shastri, L. (2001). Biological grounding of recruitment learning and vicinal algorithms in long-term potentiation. In S. Wermter, J. Austin, & D. J. Willshaw (Eds.), *Emergent neural computational architectures based on neuroscience* (*Vol. 2036*) (pp. 348–367). *Lecture notes in computer science*, Berlin: Springer.

Shastri, L., & Ajjanagadde, V. (1993). From simple associations to systematic reasoning: a connectionist representation of rules, variables, and dynamic bindings using temporal synchrony. *Behavioral and Brain Sciences, 16*(3), 417–451.

Shiffrin, R. M., & Schneider, W. (1977). Controlled and automatic human information processing: II. Perceptual learning, automatic attending, and a general theory. *Psychological review, 84*, 127–190.

Singer, W., & Gray, C. M. (1995). Visual feature integration and the temporal correlation hypothesis. *Annual Review of Neuroscience, 18*, 555–586.

Terman, D., & Wang, D. (1995). Global competition and local cooperation in a network of neural oscillators. *Physica D, 81*, 148–176.

Treisman, A. M. (1996). The binding problem. *Current Opinion in Neurobiology, 6*, 171–178.

Valiant, L. G. (1994). *Circuits of the mind*. Oxford: Oxford University Press.

Wickelgren, W. A. (1979). Chunking and consolidation: a theoretical synthesis of semantic networks. Configuring in conditioning, S–R versus cognitive learning, normal forgetting, the amnestic syndrome, and the hippocampal arousal system. *Psychological Review, 86*, 44–60.

PERGAMON

AVAILABLE AT
www.ComputerScienceWeb.com
POWERED BY SCIENCE DIRECT

Neural Networks 16 (2003) 601–607

Neural Networks

www.elsevier.com/locate/neunet

2003 Special issue

Developments in understanding neuronal spike trains and functional specializations in brain regions

Roberto A. Santiago[a], James McNames[b], Kim Burchiel[c], George G. Lendaris[a,*]

[a]*NW Computational Intelligence Laboratory, System Science, Portland State University,*[1] *USA*
[b]*Biomedical Signal Processing Laboratory, Electrical and Computer Engineering, Portland State University,*[2] *USA*
[c]*Department of Neurological Surgery, Oregon Health Sciences University,*[3] *USA*

Abstract

Understanding information processing at the neuronal level would provide valuable insights to computational intelligence research and computational neuroscience. In particular, understanding constraints on neuronal spike trains would provide indication about the type of syntactic rules used by neurons when processing information. A recent discovery, reported here, was made through analyzing microelectrode recordings (MER) made during surgical procedure in humans. Analysis of MERs of extracellular neuronal activity has gained increasing interest due to potential improvements to surgical techniques involving ablation or placement of deep brain stimulators, done in the treatment of advanced Parkinson's disease. Important to these procedures is the identification of different brain structures such as the globus pallidus internus from the spike train being recorded from the intracranial probe tip during surgery. Spike train data gathered during surgical procedure from multiple patients were processed using a novel feature extraction method reported here. Distinct structures within the spike trains were identified and used to build an effective brain region classifier. The extracted features upon analysis provide some insight into the 'syntactic' constraint on spike trains.

Keywords: Microelectrode recordings; Globus pallidus internus; Spike trains

1. Introduction

Analysis of microelectrode recordings (MERs) of extracellular neuronal activity has importance from both a neurosurgical and neuroscience perspective. For neurosurgery, MER analysis offers potential benefits to surgical techniques involving ablation or placement of deep brain stimulators as in the treatment of Parkinson's disease. From the neuroscience perspective, in vivo recordings of neurons provide an opportunity to analyze the patterns of spike trains and the interactions of neurons in near normal operational conditions. Fundamental to either of these pursuits understands the connection between the spike trains recorded in MERs and the neurons from which they are being recorded. Unlike in vitro experimentation, the cell type producing the recorded spike train is much harder to determine. From the neurosurgical perspective it would be of great advantage to have real time algorithms that would reliably translate MERs into cell source classifications, which in turn could be used to provide accurate estimation and confirmation of intracranial probe placement. The work reported here was done for this end purpose but with the knowledge that any success on this front would also be important for computational neuroscience and for computational intelligence research.

From the neuroscience perspective, the ability to identify cell types from recorded spike trains in vivo would provide some data about the unique information processing happening in a given brain region. Moreover, it would also provided some guidance for modifying current neuronal models such that they capture the information processing specializations found within specific brain regions. Much of the literature studying biological spiking behavior simultaneously treats dendritic processing as highly complex and treats spiking behavior as characterized by a distribution of spike intervals (Koch & Segev, 1989). Many of the spiking neuron models from computational intelligence research use many variations of integrate and fire models for connecting the dendritic processing to

* Corresponding author.
E-mail address: lendaris@sysc.pdx.edu (G.G. Lendaris).
[1] www.nwcil.pdx.edu
[2] www.bsp.pdx.edu
[3] www.ohsu.edu

0893-6080/03/$ - see front matter © 2003 Elsevier Science Ltd. All rights reserved.
doi:10.1016/S0893-6080(03)00123-0

spiking behavior (Maass & Bishop, 1999). Other alternatives exist to integrate and fire, which are inspired both from the biology as well as mathematics (Gerstner & Kistler, 2002). Missing between these two approaches is the ability to ground the computational models onto the biological models such that the characteristics of information processing could be understood. More specifically, in order to get agreement between the computational intelligence models and computational neuroscience models it would be advantageous to estimate the type of distributions that not only correspond to biologically observed spike trains but that also provide some indication of the 'syntactic' constraint placed on the creation of spike trains from the computational perspective. Such distributions would take on the form of joint or conditional probability tables. In the research reported here this type of analysis is done to spike trains and is the source of the information for accurate identification of brain region from the spike train.

In next few sections, the details of the spike train feature extraction algorithm are explained. This is followed a by a review of results on unseen data. In Section 5 the discussion returns to the connections between the feature of spike trains and functional specialization of brain regions.

2. Background

The research reported here was performed in a neurosurgical context. Currently, Oregon Health Science University performs deep brain stimulation procedures. This procedure involves the use of a probe, which is slowly inserted into the patient's brain in a stepwise manner. At each step a reading is taken from the probe, which is sensitive to the spiking of neurons within the local vicinity of the probe tip. The signal from the probe is then sampled and translated into an audio signal as well as visual presentation on an oscilloscope, which the surgeon uses to confirm the brain structure in which the probe tip is located. The insertion path is mapped out presurgically using magnetic resonance imaging. This process is very precise. As such, the signal from the probe is used only for confirmatory information. Still, at time of surgery, the only information available to the surgeon is the intracranial position of the probe tip and the signal recorded by the probe. As such, automated methods to translate this signal into useful information about the brain structures surrounding the probe tip would add another level of consistency and accuracy to deep brain stimulation procedures.

Because of the speed and affordability of digital processing equipment, it now seems feasible to support and improve this surgical procedure. In order to do this, the probe data must first be digitally sampled and filtered for noise. Because this resultant digital signal is of several neurons firing simultaneously, it must undergo processing to isolate spike trains from individual neurons. Surgical recordings were processed postsurgically through a source separation algorithm to be detailed in McNames (2003). This algorithm not only separated the signals from each neuron but also identified spike occurrences. Thus the resulting individual spike train signal was an array of clock times with millisecond or better resolution indicating when a spike was detected. For this research there were a total of 140 spike trains each containing from 2 to 5 s worth of spike train recording. The set of data used was gathered during surgical procedure from 26 patients. These data came in two groupings nominally referred to as the Dirty Data Set (DDS) and the Starr Data Set (SDS). The DDS contained 93 spike trains from several patients which were randomly broken into two subsets, the training DDS (47 spike trains) and the test DDS (46 spike trains). The test DDS was isolated and used to test the effectiveness of the resulting algorithm developed from the training DDS and the Starr DDS. The reason for the label 'Dirty' is due to the unfortunate fact that the data from the DDS was labeled postsurgically; that is, the expert opinion about the brain structure source for each spike train was captured outside the context of the actual surgery. This method for labeling spike train data has the disadvantage of not having the depth and spatial location of the probe to assist with identification. The SDS was gathered under ideal conditions and represents 'perfect' examples of spike trains from individual neurons in the brain regions of interest. There were four major brain structures of interest: Globus Palidus Externus (GPE), Globus Palidus Internus (GPI), the Border (BRD) regions between GPE and GPI, and finally Tremor cells (TRM). This last area, TRM, is not a distinct brain structure but instead describes regions inside the GPI, where the cells fire in a tremor like manner and are linked to the physical tremoring common to Parkinson's disease. Both data sets contained a large amount of spike trains from neurons in GPE. Exact numbers are reported in Section 6.

3. Approach

Spike train analysis has been done for many reasons ranging from understanding the biology of single neurons to the type of medical application motivating this research. Spike train research, regardless of motivation, has the underlying presupposition that the characteristic of spike trains tell us something about the neuron, its operation and/or the information it processes. Most often, this type of research is done in settings, where both input and output of a neuron can be isolated. From this vantage point it is easy to gain a better understanding of the type of information processing being done by a single neuron. Understanding neuron processing involves understanding the mechanisms by which incoming signal is integrated and the process by which a new signal is created and transmitted to other neurons. Historically, these sub-processes have been understood by means of a rate-coding model. That is, a model, where neuronal processing is only concerned with the rate of spike arrival defined over some finite window. Unfortunately, simple rate coding models are not sufficient to explain fast response characteristics of many neuronal circuits, particularly those involved with visual processing (Koch, 1999). Put simply, there is significant presence of neuronal processing that involves dependency only on single spikes or on the time interval between spikes. This latter point is critical since it indicates that the time between spikes, the inter-spike interval (ISI), may contain useful information. This insight has fueled research into understanding methods by which neurons may encode and decode information in these ISIs (Koch, 1999; McNames, 2003). The models from this research are commonly referred to as temporal coding or correlation coding. More complex models have also been developed that describe information encoded across the spikes of more than one neuron. These models are commonly referred to as population coding and pulse coding which each have correlated and non-correlated forms (Koch, 1999).

While these latter coding models are not of much use for single spike train analysis, the entire body of coding research provides information about where to look for information in the spike train of individual neurons (hereafter referred to as single spike trains). The use of coding research in this context is aimed at understanding the timeframe in which the physical properties of a neuron could contribute discernable information in an individual spike train. At the lower end, research supporting rate coding models for neuronal information processing have an upper end of 5–10 ms as the effective length for information encoding/decoding. By way of explanation, since rate coded models rely essentially on counting the number of spikes that arrive during a time period, the critical time factor is the rate at which a spike signal decays on the neuronal membrane of the receiving neuron. As it turns out, the upper bound for the decay in this signal is around 10 ms (Koch, 1999). So assuming that rate coding is at least a partially correct model for neuronal processing, any contribution that an individual neuron makes to this process would be most discernable above this 10 ms threshold. Below this threshold, the spike train behavior is most attributable to the input signal being received from the dendrites. Finding an upper bound is very difficult in light of work in temporal and correlation coding. Precise firing patterns over 200 ms in length have been observed in the visual processing systems of the macaque monkey (Koch, 1999). Moreover, in laboratory setting, neurons can be stimulated to produce firing patterns that are precise and regular for almost indefinite periods. The period of these patterns are as short as 20 ms and as long as 300 ms. The structures involved in these spiking patterns involve both single spikes and sets of spikes separated by very small time intervals, known as bursts. Analysis of single spike and bursting patterns in vivo seem to indicate that 200 ms is the upper bound for discerning any real correlated pattern to spike times (Koch, 1999). In many contexts, though, the nature of the spike train seems random with ISIs exhibiting a Poisson distribution. Some research indicates strongly that the stochastic nature of neuronal processing is far from stationary and may be highly dependent on input stimulus. Again, with the lack of neuronal input data, 200 ms is the apparent upper bound for pattern recognition in just the output spike train. So for the research reported here a window of 10–200 ms was used for analyzing spike trains.

Returning to the surgical context, an important clue was taken from the existing method of train source identification, listening. In terms of description, the sound produced by the MER from the surgical probe is roughly like static with much popping and whirring. Individual spike trains when converted to sound also have a similar characteristic. Discernable are regular patterns of popping intensity; roughly speaking, one can hear bursts and changes in spike frequency. This last comment seems to support research into spike bursting which seeks to isolate and characterize burst events. Given these clues it was hypothesized that within the 10–200 ms window, there should exist discernable patterns of spiking that would happen repeatedly and ultimately would be the source of the characteristics discernable when listening to MER data. As a note, the search for a novel approach to feature extraction was motivated by the lack of strong results from research involving single statistics, power spectrums, smoothing, averaging and histogram approaches (McNames, 2003). These approaches have similar insights and motivations as the research presented here. Moreover, none of these approaches have been able to yield sufficient feature information from individual spike trains to provide a reliable automated spike source identification algorithm.

4. Feature extraction method

The majority of the effort for the present research project was spent analyzing spike trains using a 10–200 ms moving window. This analysis focused on developing a visualization technique for behavior in the moving window. In essence, the research sought features that made visually distinguishing different neuron types very easy. After many attempts only one feature extraction method worked very well and is described here. The method involved the use of two moving windows across a digital spike train (DST). The DST breaks up the duration of a spike train into fixed width intervals with each interval represented by a one or zero. One indicates a spike occurred during that time interval while a zero indicates no spike occurred during that interval. Two adjacent moving windows counted the number of ones in each window, producing a pair of integers. These pairs of integers were used to create a two dimensional histogram. This histogram was used to produce a surface plot, which revealed visually distinguishable features to each of the different types of neurons of interest. Figs. 1–4 are

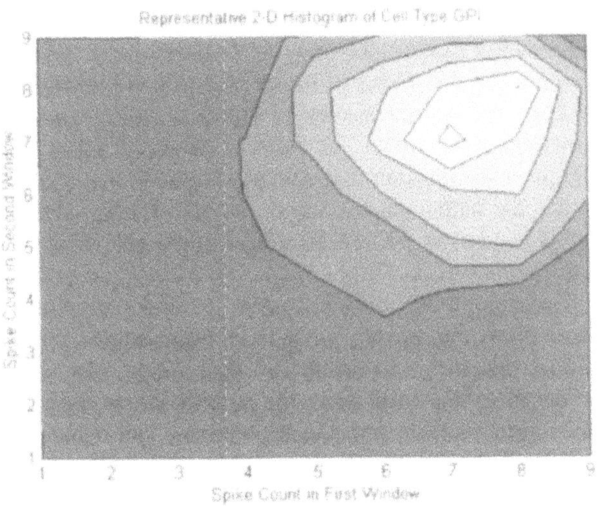

Fig. 1. Example of GPI 2-D histogram.

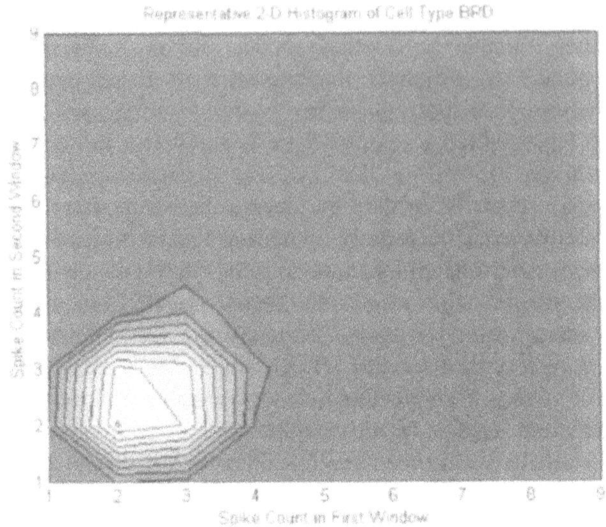

Fig. 3. Example of BRD 2-D histogram.

representative examples of the type of histograms produced by this method. These particular histograms were produced using a sampling rate of 100 Hz and with window sizes of 9 bits. These were not the histograms that were ultimately used for the classification algorithm but because of resolution limitations these histograms demonstrate the types of features that were found and indicated that this method would be useful in the context of classification. It is important to note that while there is much symmetry in each graph, the localization of histogram activity for each type is unique. Moreover, these differing localizations and presence of asymmetries is what inspired looking at these histograms as estimates of joint and conditional distribution and the subsequently as possible indication of syntactic constraints which will be discussed later.

Before moving on, a more detailed explanation of the algorithm is now provided

1. The spike train is converted to a binary digital signal. This involves setting up an array of zeros, where each element represents a time interval. End to end these elements represent the duration length of a given spike train. So for example, each element of the array could represent 1 ms (i.e. the temporal spike train is sampled at 1000 Hz). If a spike train of 5.7 s were being analyzed, this would indicate that the array would have to be 5700 units in length. The array is initialized with all zeros. Continuing with the example, the first spike might occur at 0.1189 s. Translated into milliseconds this time would mean that the first spike of the spike train came after a 118.9 ms pause. Rounding up this number to 119, the 119th element of the array is changed to a one.
2. The binary digital signal is then sampled with two adjacent moving windows of finite length. So for example, a window length of 8 would gather all pairs of 8 bit binary words that occur in the DST.

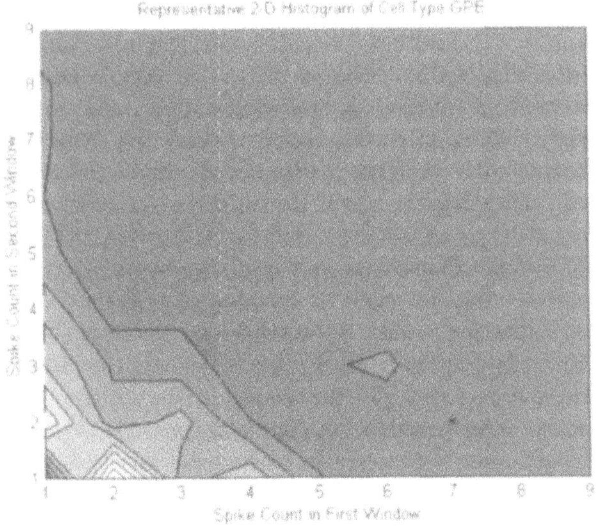

Fig. 2. Example of GPE 2-D histogram.

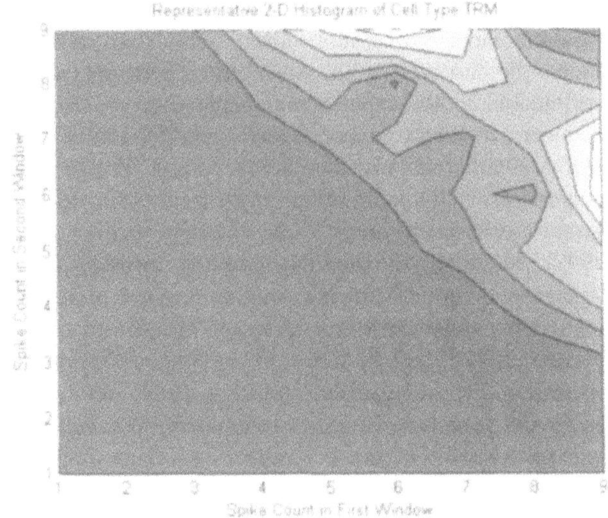

Fig. 4. Example of TRM 2-D histogram.

3. The number of ones in each binary word is counted converting each pair of binary 8 bit words into a pair of decimal integers. So for example if a pair of eight digit words were 01110101 and 10011001, this would be converted to the decimal integer pair of 5 and 4.
4. These integer pairs are then binned together to create a two dimensional histogram.
5. The 0,0 entry in the histogram is then removed. This was done because the most common binary word pairs were all zeros, which yielded no information about the spike train. Additionally the histogram was normalized by dividing by the number of entries and doing a natural logarithmic conversion. This last step was used to avoid problems with histograms generated from different spike trains of significantly different durations. In some cases spike trains were as short as 2 s in duration.

What bears mentioning is the nature of the features seen in the visualization of the histogram. In early experimentation, one dimensional histograms were created using a single moving window. These histograms did not provide enough information for visual identification. The one dimensional histogram is equivalent to looking at the distribution of spike rates. We recall that one of the models of neuron to neuron communication is a rate model that only cares about the number of spikes that occur during a finite time window. The one dimensional histogram essentially analyzes the spike train from that perspective. The two dimensional histogram analyzes the change in the rate of spike arrivals. Although not fully a temporal coding model it does reveal common changes in firing rate.

So for example, a histogram created from a GPE spike train sampled at 1000 Hz with window size of 20 bits may have large numbers associated with the 4,18 and 10,10 bins. This would indicate that if four spikes occur in a 20 ms period it is very likely that it will be followed by 18 spikes in the next 20 ms period. Likewise if 10 spikes occur in a 20 ms period it is likely to be followed by the same rate of spiking. Again, in essence the two dimensional histogram analyzes the changes in spike rate. What it reveals is that changes in spike rate can uniquely characterize the spike trains of different neurons. More analysis is needed to understand all the information revealed in these histograms.

5. Application of support vector machines

The algorithm just described performs well at the task of feature extraction. In order to make this feature extraction applicable to the surgical context it was necessary to choose some form of classifier. Many linear and non-linear classifiers exist. Among the most popular non-linear classifiers that exist are neural networks. While neural networks are effective in many contexts, they often fall short in being able to generalize, or generalize in predictable manners. What is meant by this is that neural network classifiers do not provide any easy methods for predicting performance on unseen test data.

Unlike linear methods that provide characterizations associated with bias and variance, neural networks do not have any analog to these informative statistics. Neural networks were applied to this problem and were found to generalize very poorly. Instead, a support vector machine was employed. Support vector machines have gained much popular acclaim. In essence, they provide a method for calculating optimal hyperplanes for separating points in feature space. In the context of this project, the feature space is the set of values from the histogram. Returning to the example of the histogram created using 1000 Hz sampling rate and 20 bit window, each histogram has $21 \times 21 = 441$ values. These 441 values form a single point in the feature space into which the support vector machine will place hyperplanes to draw boundaries between the points representing GPI, GPE, BRD and TRM cells. More detailed discussion on the operation of support vector machines for classification can be found in Haykin (1999). The application of support vector machines was very successful as will be discussed in Section 6. A set of support vector MATLAB libraries from Ohio State University were used (Ma, Zhao & Ahalt, 2002).

6. Results

Because the test DDS was held separate, early results were generated using a leave one out cross validation method. The support vector classifier was computationally very efficient making this form of testing possible. The first cross validation was performed with the SDS. The spike trains from the SDS were sampled at 400 Hz to create spike trains and a 20 bit window size was used. Table 1 shows a confusion matrix summarizing the results from the cross validation. The results are perfect. As stated before, the SDS was collected under ideal conditions and represents a 'perfect' set of spike train recordings. As such this result indicates that enough features are extracted in the rate change histogram to perform accurate classification in ideal circumstances.

Next, the same cross validation was performed with the training DDS. This data was not gathered under ideal

Table 1
Results of leave one out cross validation testing with the dirty data set

Actual	Predicted			
	GPE	GPI	BRD	TRM
GPE	31		2	
GPI	1	2		1
BRD	2		5	
TRM	2			1

Table 2
Results from test of classification algorithm on unseen data

Actual	Predicted			
	GPE	GPI	BRD	TRM
GPE	30		2	
GPI	2	6		
BRD			3	
TRM	3			

conditions and it is known that at least one of the spike trains is labeled incorrectly. Still, the DDS has some characteristics of data that would be encountered in the surgical context. As such it provides a good bench mark with respect to robustness of this classification method with respect to noise. Table 1 is a confusion matrix summarizing the results of this cross validation.

Finally, the training DDS was used to create a support vector classifier that was applied to the testing DDS. Again, this data set was held independently and was not accessible during the development of the feature extraction algorithm and the subsequent development of the support vector classifier. The confusion matrix describing the classification results with the testing DDS is provided in Table 2. It is important to emphasize that the results in Table 2 are the result of a single pass through the unseen testing data. It is not a leave one out cross validation test as is shown in Tables 1 and 3.

After cross validation, it seemed like the algorithm was performing in a consistent and accurate manner. As a final test, a set of completely unseen data was presented to the classifier. The classifier was 'trained' using data from both the Starr and the Dirty sets. The unseen data set was held by a separate person and was never seen by the researchers prior to the final testing. The classifier was only allowed one single attempt to classify this unseen data. The results of this final test are summarized in Table 2.

It seems apparent that the rate change histogram provides efficient and effective feature extraction for spike trains. The ability to visually identify the different types of neurons was a strong indicator that it would be effective in an automated classification context. The application of support vector machines seems to support this conclusion. The cross validation results from the training DDS and the final results from the testing DDS strongly indicate the feature extraction is fairly resistant to noise but that additional work is needed to cope with irregularities in recorded data, the source of many of the misclassifications. These irregularities are caused by many conditions that are encountered during the surgical procedure. Overall, though, the preliminary results are strong enough to warrant much additional work in further developing this feature extraction technique.

Table 3
Results of leave one out cross validation testing with the starr data set

Actual	Predicted			
	GPE	GPI	BRD	TRM
GPE	13			
GPI		9		
BRD			7	
TRM				8

7. Discussion

Returning to the neuroscience perspective, it is important to seek an explanation as to why this type of classification should even be possible. While it seems that the underlying cellular mechanisms for actions potentials (spikes) are well understood, what is not understood is their role in the processing of information beyond the most general description as a method to transmit information from one cell to another. By way of analogy, understanding the significance of neuron spiking is like trying to understand the significance of transistor switching in digital microprocessors without having an understanding of digital computing theory. More to the point, what these regular patterns indicate about the cells of interest is very ambiguous.

Along these lines there seem to be two general hypothesis that could be explored. First, it might be possible that neurons by their physiology have a specific spiking pattern, which is activated when the membrane potential reaches a threshold. This is slightly different that the standard integrate and fire models of neurons since it includes the ability of neurons to not just simply fire but to fire specific temporal patterns that show conditional statistical regularity. This would provide a foundation for why the histogram visualization shown before should have such consistency.

This model fails, though, to take into account any significant sensitivity to incoming signal. If the recorded spike trains represent primarily the effect of incoming signals, then it implies that regions of the brain have the ability to consistently produce spiking patterns, which are common among all the cells within a region. If this model is true then it would also suggest that the recorded spike trains represent functional specialization within a region. But this model, in the extreme, would suggest functional specialization independent of cell physiology which seems unlikely given what is known about the cell types studied here.

Not enough data exists yet to firmly conclude that either of these models (or some other form in between) is truly correct. This in turn points to deeper research issues surrounding both the nature of what MERs represent and how ablation and stimulation is actually affecting circuits in the brain as understood from a systemic neurophysiological level and not just a behavioral model perspective. The fact that such regular patterns can be discerned in these recorded spike trains indicates that it might be possible to develop neuronal population models that more closely described and explain the functioning of these brain regions.

Further research will look to extend this algorithm to cell types found in the substantia nigra which are much more challenging to recognize. Related research will seek to move these and other source identification techniques into the surgical context to asses their impact on the effectiveness of ablation and deep brain stimulation procedures. Still, further research will also seek to ground these methods in the physiology of neuron populations in search of a clearer understanding of these spike train patterns.

Finally, after studying the types of histograms as shown in Figs. 1–4 it seemed reasonable to conclude that if these histograms are indeed unique to brain region then they indeed did characterize the types of spiking patterns inherent to the information processing occurring in that brain region. In turn, if this were true then these same histograms could be looked at as conditional distributions. Assuming that spike trains are essentially binary digital communication between neurons then the proper syntactic input and output of the neurons within a given region is characterized by this estimated distribution. Returning to the idea of studying digital processors without understanding digital computing theory, the uniqueness of the spike train syntax provides an indication of the type of instruction sets that are encoded into the operation of the neuron. This is a loose hypothesis but the current results seem to significantly support the feasibility of this type of analysis which is one of the foci of the continuing research.

References

Gerstner, W., & Kistler, W. (2002). *Spiking neuron models*. Cambridge, UK: Cambridge University Press.

Haykin, S. S. (1999). *Neural networks: A comprehensive foundation*. Upper Saddle River, NJ: Prentice Hall.

Koch, C. (1999). *Biophysics of computation: Information processing in single neurons*. New York, NY: Oxford University Press.

Koch, C., & Segev, I. (1989). *Methods in neuronal modeling: From synapses to networks*. Cambridge, MA: MIT Press.

Ma, J., Zhao, Y., Ahalt, S (2002). OSU SVM Classifier Matlab Toolbox (ver. 3.00). http://eewww.eng.ohiostate.-edu/maj/osu_svm/

Maass, W., & Bishop, M. (1999). *Pulsed neural networks*. Cambridge, MA: MIT Press.

McNames, J. (2003). *Microelectrode signal analysis techniques for improved localization. Microelectrode recordings in movement disorder surgery*. New York, NY: Thieme Medical Publishers.

PERGAMON

AVAILABLE AT
www.ComputerScienceWeb.com
POWERED BY SCIENCE DIRECT

Neural Networks 16 (2003) 609–615

Neural Networks

www.elsevier.com/locate/neunet

2003 Special issue

Shaping up simple cell's receptive field of animal vision by ICA and its application in navigation system

Liming Zhang*, Jianfeng Mei

Department of Electronics Engineering, Fudan University, Shanghai 200433, China

Abstract

Scientists and experts have explored the mechanism of visual systems for decades for smart image processing and pattern recognition in order to satisfy sophisticated engineering applications. In this paper we apply independent component analyses' (ICA) unsupervised learning to natural images, topography images and other special environment images for demonstrating the simple-cell's process in animal vision. Our results confirm an early biological experiment (Nature 228 (1970) 419) about the growth of simple cells in cat's V1 area. Furthermore, by applying ICA methodology and the simplex algorithm, the unsupervised neural synapse's learning can obtain the receptive fields in visual cortex and can simulate the growth of the visual cortex of young animal in the special environment. These findings imply that an input image can be efficiently represented by ICA bases. An application of image matching in the navigation by ICA is shown that the animal visual system method is indeed better than those classical methods at least more than 5%.

Keywords: Independent component analysis; Gabor Function

1. Introduction

Vision is the most important manner to capture the information from the circumstances for animals. How to process the visual information is a very interesting problem. Many scientists and experts have explored the mechanism of vision and applied these biological methods to image processing and recognition in engineering for many years, because traditional Artificial Intelligence (AI) methods and simple image processing technologies could not work well for these tasks. In this paper, an unsupervised learning algorithm, independent component analysis (ICA), is applied to images, which shows that the unsupervised neural synapse's learning can simulate the response of receptive fields and the growth of simple cells' receptive fields in visual cortex at V1 area.

From the view of morphologic, the primary vision is composed by retina, lateral geniculation nucleus (LGN) and visual cortex. There is little difference of retina and LGN in different kinds of animals. However, simple cell's receptive field is adapted to the variations of environment when animals grow up (Peter & Abbott, 2001; Shuo, 1997). For adult animal, the synapse distribution of simple cell's receptive fields is similar to Gabor functions (Pollen, Nagler, Daugman, Kronauer, & Cavanagh, 1984). In 1996, Bruno Olshausen and Field (Olshausen & Field, 1996) described that some basis-functions, obtained by ICA from natural images, were similar to response of receptive field of simple cells in visual cortex. Bell and Sejnowski presented that these sparse encoding of image could be implemented by ICA (Bell & Sejnowski, 1995, 1997).

In this paper, we show that these ICA filters, the rows of **W**, can perfectly approximate to Gabor functions by simplex method. This is mathematically proved that ICA filters from natural images are similar to the response of simple cell's receptive fields. Another result is that the ICA filter from the topography images is also similar to Gabor function, but the shape of ICA filter-bank is different. Furthermore, we simulate the growth of young animals' visual cortex in special visual environment, which further shows the ICA filter-bank is adaptive with variations of environment as the animal vision. The three simulation results show that the unsupervised learning, ICA, can be considered as a generating model of simple cell's receptive fields when the animal is immature.

One conjecture has been proposed that the unsupervised learning stimulating from environment may be a major manner for the infant, because he or she could not receive any massages from teachers or their parents except their

* Corresponding author.
E-mail address: lmzhang@fudan.edu.cn (L. Zhang).

0893-6080/03/$ - see front matter © 2003 Elsevier Science Ltd. All rights reserved.
doi:10.1016/S0893-6080(03)00133-3

eyes. By unsupervised learning, the receptive fields of vision could be shaped, which only depend on input stimulus from eyes. For the adult period the receptive fields have maturated, so the supervised learning may be a major manner (Szu, 1999).

In order to confirm the above idea, an application of image matching on the navigation of aerospace, using ICA-based model, is shown in this paper finally. The image matching process has two stages: one is unsupervised learning stage simulated the period of infant vision, and the other is supervised learning or projection stage as adult vision. Experimental results attest that the ICA-based model has higher matching rates than traditional image matching methods at least more 5%, which is the evidence of the conjecture.

This paper is organized as follows: Section 2 shows the Gabor function—the model of simple cell's receptive field. In Section 3, we simply introduce the ICA method used in this paper. The three bio-mimic results for ICA filters are shown in Section 4. The image matching system by ICA mimicking the vision system is presented in Section 5. Finally we give the conclusion.

2. Gabor functions

It is known that, in visual system, cells in visual cortex are divided into simple cells, standard complex cells and special complex cells (Peter & Abbott, 2001; Shuo, 1997). And it has been proved that the response of simple cell's receptive field is determined by spatial position and orientation that are similar to the Gabor functions (Pollen et al., 1984). A Gabor function is shown in Eq. (1):

$$g(x,y) = K\exp(-1/2(x_g^2/a^2 + y_g^2/b^2))\cos[-2\pi(U_0x + V_0y) - P]. \tag{1}$$

Here a and b denote the major and minor axis of 2D Gaussian ellipse function respectively; K is normalization parameter, commonly, $K = 1/2\pi ab$, (x,y) is the position coordinate and x_g, y_g, satisfy

$$\begin{cases} x_g = (x - x_0)\cos\theta - (y - y_0)\sin\theta \\ y_g = (x - x_0)\sin\theta - (y - y_0)\cos\theta \end{cases}, \tag{2}$$

where (x_0, y_0) is the central coordinate of Gabor function; θ is angle of rotation; U_0, V_0 denote spatial frequency and P is modulation parameter. In fact, these parameters in Gabor function are related to a simple cell's receptive fields. It is known that different simple cell's receptive field has different parameters. There are many kinds of cells' receptive fields with variant orientations and positions in animal vision. These receptive fields will extract the edges from input image as the key features when the environmental images input to the visual system. These Gabor functions with different parameters to simulate these receptive fields are called Gabor-filters, or Gabor-filter-bank.

3. Independent component analysis

ICA is one of the methods to solve linear equations based on stochastic vector, which is shown as Eq. (3):

$$\mathbf{X} = \mathbf{AS}, \quad \mathbf{X} \in \mathbf{R}^m, \ \mathbf{A} \in \mathbf{R}^{m\times n}, \ \mathbf{S} \in \mathbf{R}^n. \tag{3}$$

Given a stochastic vector $\mathbf{X} = (x_1, x_2, \ldots, x_m)^{\mathrm{T}}$, unknown matrix $\mathbf{A}$ and source signal vector $\mathbf{S} = (s_1, s_2, \ldots, s_n)^{\mathrm{T}}$, in general, Eq. (3) has no solution. However, if the elements of $\mathbf{S}$ are mutually independent and non-Gaussian distribution, and $m \geq n$, we can apply an unsupervised neural network to solve it. If there is a weight matrix $\mathbf{W}$ that satisfies the following equation

$$\mathbf{WX} = \mathbf{WAS} \approx \mathbf{S}, \tag{4}$$

then $\mathbf{A}$ and $\mathbf{S}$ can be derived, which $\mathbf{W} \approx \mathbf{A}^{-1}$ for $m = n$ and $\mathbf{W} \approx \mathbf{A}^{+}$ for $m \neq n$, $\mathbf{A}^{+}$ is pseudo-inverse matrix of $\mathbf{A}$. Here, the row vector of $\mathbf{W}$ is called ICA filter. Accordingly, the corresponding column vectors of $\mathbf{A}$ are named ICA basis function.

There are several algorithms to implement ICA method. In this paper, FastICA proposed by Hyvärinen, (1999) is used, in which the stochastic vector $\mathbf{X}$ is pre-whiten, normalized and the weight vectors are orthogonalized in process. The learning rule of the neural network on the ith unit is

$$\mathbf{W}_i^{+}(t+1) = \langle x(t)g(\mathbf{W}_i(t)^{\mathrm{T}}\mathbf{x}(t))\rangle - \langle g(\mathbf{W}_i(t)^{\mathrm{T}}\mathbf{x}(t))\rangle \mathbf{W}_i(t), \tag{5}$$

$$\mathbf{W}_i(t+1) = \mathbf{W}_i^{+}(t+1)/\|\mathbf{W}_i^{+}(t+1)\|, \tag{6}$$

where $\langle\cdot\rangle$ is expectation and $g(u) = ue^{-u^2/2}$, $\mathbf{W}_i^{+}$ is un-normalized weight vector for the ith unit. In learning phase, weight vector $\mathbf{W}_i^{+}$ of the neural network is updated by Eqs. (5) and (6) for learning image set $\{\mathbf{x}(1), \mathbf{x}(2), \ldots, \mathbf{x}(k)\}$. All weight vectors of the neural network are updated one by one using the same procedure, and then the weight matrix $\mathbf{W} = (\mathbf{W}_1, \mathbf{W}_2, \ldots, \mathbf{W}_n)^{\mathrm{T}}$ is orthogonalized by the following formula:

$$\mathbf{W} \leftarrow (\mathbf{WW}^{\mathrm{T}})^{-1/2}\mathbf{W}. \tag{7}$$

When the iterations of formula (5)–(7) converge, we can obtain the final weight matrix $\mathbf{W}$, rows of whose is orthogonalized each other. The ICA filter-bank $\mathbf{W}'$ is from $\mathbf{W}$ by a sample line transform.

4. Three simulation results by ICA

In this section we apply ICA to three kinds of input images. One kind is natural images; the others are topographic images and horizontal stripe images. Each image is row-stacked to produce a column vector $\mathbf{x}$,

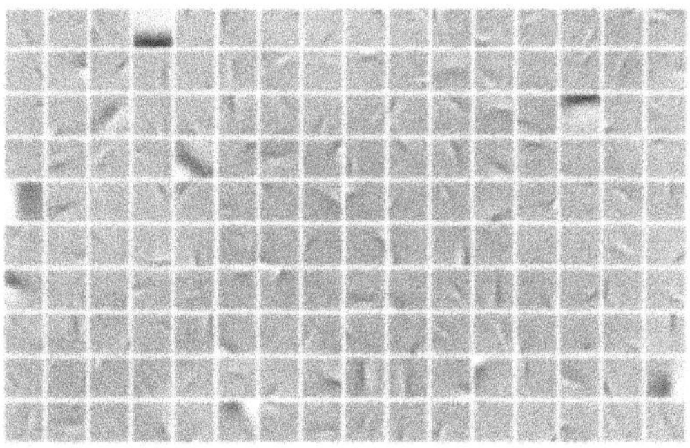

Fig. 1. One-hundred and sixty ICA filters from natural images.

$\mathbf{x} = (x_1, x_2, \ldots, x_m)^T$, and m is the dimensions of the image size. Suppose the series of each kind input image is $\{\mathbf{x}(1), \mathbf{x}(2), \ldots, \mathbf{x}(k)\}$. We hope to find the ICA filter-bank for the three kind images to demonstrate the ICA filter-bank is indeed Gabor-like filter-bank, and it can be adapted to variations of environment as the animal vision does. A simplex method is used to check the approximation between ICA filter from natural images and Gabor filter in the first simulation. Another result is the Gabor-like filter-bank also can obtain from other kind images (topography map), but its shape has some differences. Final simulation result verifies the young cat's growth experiment by using ICA. In the same time, the conjecture of two learning stages is also confirmed.

4.1. ICA filter and Gabor filter

Many ICA simulation results show that the ICA bases or ICA filters is seemly like Gabor function, but there are not mathematically proved. Here, we try to find the approximate error between ICA filter and Gabor function by using simplex method.

The training set is generated of 30 000 samples in size of 16×16, selected from 13 natural images. After ICA training as Eqs. (5)–(7), 160 localized and oriented Gabor-liked filters have been obtained by FastICA, which are shown in Fig. 1. Each patch of Fig. 1 is one of these ICA filters. Denote the function of the ith ICA filter as *ICAi*. We propose the simplex cost function, C_i for the ICAi as follows:

$$C_i = \sum_{x,y} \{K_i \exp(-1/2(x_{gi}^2/a_i^2 + y_{gi}^2/b_i^2))\cos[-2\pi(U_{0i}x + V_{0i}y) - P_i] - \mathrm{ICA}_i(x,y)\}^2. \quad (8)$$

From Eq. (8) we can see that the cost function is the difference between Gabor function in Eq. (1) and the ith ICA filter for all 16×16 pixels.

The basic idea in the simplex method is to build a simplex geometric figure that has 10 vertices, in a 9-dimension parameter space. Each vertex is then characterized by 10 values: nine parameters (K, a, b, x_0, y, θ, U_0, V_0, P) and the cost function C_i.

Using simplex method, each ICA filter can be approximated by a Gabor function with different parameters. The nine parameters of Gabor function and the cost function corresponding to the up-left patch of ICA filter-bank in Fig. 1 are shown in Table 1.

Fig. 2 is 3D representation of ICA-filter, Gabor-filter and the approximate errors. Axis x and y denote horizontal and vertical coordinate axis, respectively, and axis z is the function value. The ICA-filter function of up-left patch in Fig. 1 is shown in Fig. 2(a) and (b) shows an approximated Gabor function with parameters in Table 1. The error value between Fig. 2(a) and (b) is presented in Fig. 2(c).

From Fig. 2, the shape of ICA filter from unsupervised learning is almost the same as Gabor function. It has orientation sensitivity at angle 1.04 rad.

The approximation between ICA filters and Gabor functions by simplex method shows that almost all ICA filters have their corresponding Gabor functions. This result is mathematically proved the relationship between ICA-filter and simple-cell's receptive field in vision system.

4.2. The Gabor-like filter-bank by using ICA on topography image

It was proved that the response of simple cell's receptive field determined by spatial position and orientation are similar to Gabor functions (Pollen et al., 1984) Olshausen et al. showed that applying ICA to the natural images could obtain some ICA-bases or ICA-filters that were localized and oriented Gabor-like functions (Bell & Sejnowski, 1997; Hurri, Hyvärinen & Oja, 1997; Olshausen & Field, 1996). In order to show that the Gabor-like filter can be obtained from other kind image, we do the same work by ICA from topography images.

A high-pass filter is used for enhancing the edges of images before training on the topography images. The training set is composed by 30 000 samples in size of 16×16, selected from 13 topography maps. After ICA training as Eqs. (5)–(7), 160 localized and oriented

Table 1
The parameters and cost function of up-left patch in Fig. 1

K	a	b	x_0	y_0	θ	U_0	V_0	P	C
0.42	0.94	2.90	12.5	8.65	1.04	−0.05	0.10	6.99	0.02

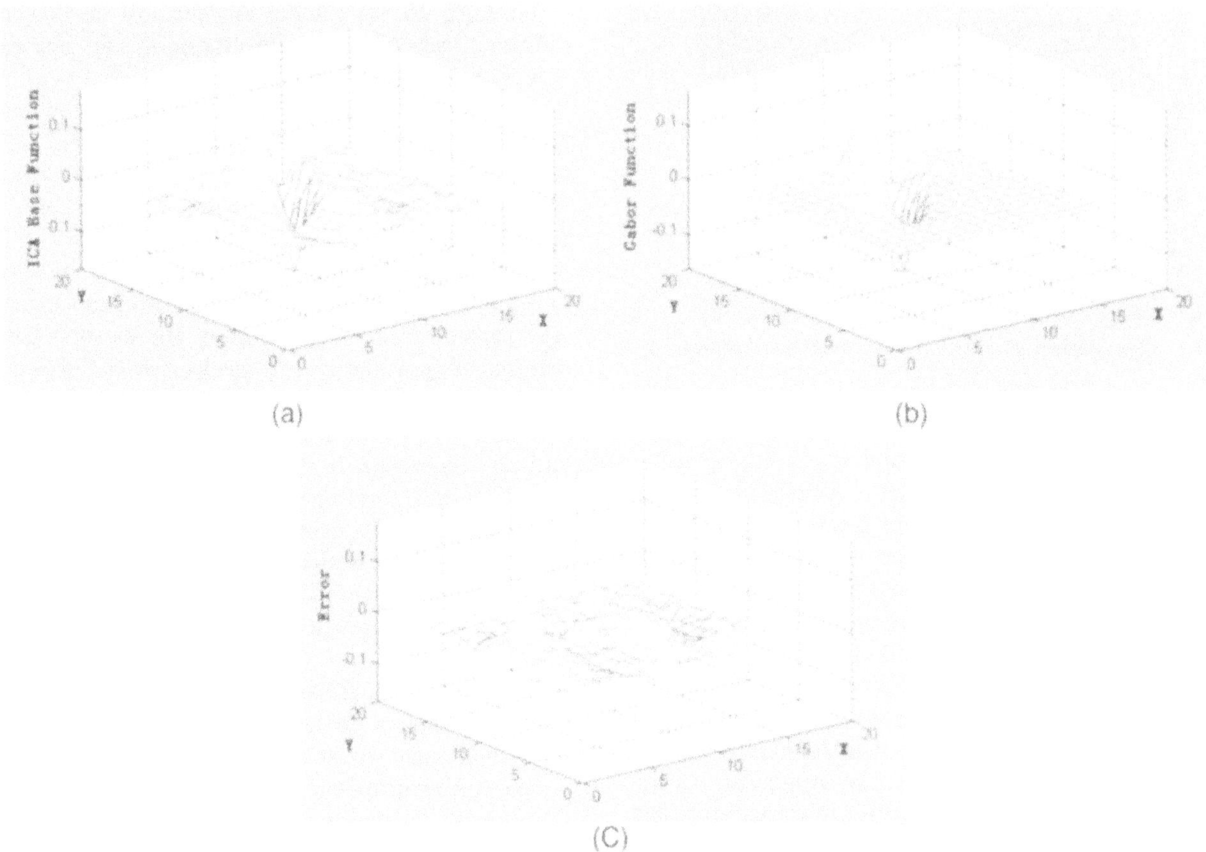

Fig. 2. (a) ICA filter function; (b) Gabor function; (c) the error.

Gabor-liked filters are obtained, which are shown in Fig. 3. Each patch of Fig. 3 is one of these ICA filters.

Comparing Fig. 3 with Fig. 1, the two ICA filter-banks are very like on sparse, localized and oriented, but their shape is different for different training images. The ICA filters from topography pictures have more horizontal and vertical orientations than from natural image. That means the ICA can extract the Gabor-like bank not only from natural images, but also from other kind of images. This result demonstrates that the ICA-filter bank is updating with different input images.

4.3. *Simulation the process of young animal growing up*

In 1970, Blakemore and Cooper (Blakemore & Cooper, 1970) put a young cat in the horizontal stripe visual environment. After its growing up, the simple cell in the cat's visual cortex would almost only respond the stimuli along the horizontal edge. This biological experiment showed that the simple cell's receptive field was adapted to the input environment.

Here, we simulate the growth of the young animals' visual cortex in the special environment by applying ICA. We use a set of horizontal stripe images with different width as the ICA network learning set.

Four horizontal stripe pictures in size of 160×160 with different width are used as the ICA network's input data to simulate the special visual environment that is similar to the young cat's experiment by Blackemore and Cooper. Two horizontal stripe pictures are shown in Fig. 4. Using ICA algorithm in Section 2, 10 000 patches in size of 16×16 are selected randomly from the four pictures to input the ICA network, after training we obtain 20 ICA filters shown in Fig. 5.

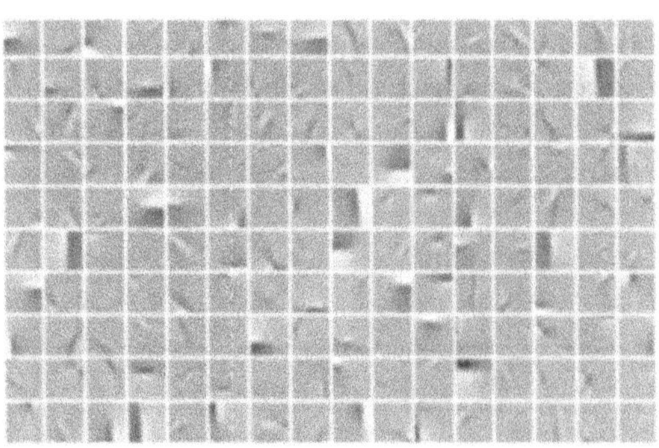

Fig. 3. One-hundred and sixty ICA filters from 13 topography maps.

Fig. 4. Two horizontal stripe images with different width.

Fig. 5. ICA filters in special environment.

From Fig. 5, we can see that all the ICA filters are sensitive to horizontal orientation, which is the same to biological experiment that the young animal grown up in the horizontal stripe environment only has horizontal orientation sensitive cells. The ICA network's learning can also obtain the same result.

The three simulation results show that ICA can mimic the information processing of vision system and refine the key massage from environment, so it can be used to image pattern recognition. Following application example shows its powerful ability in navigation of aerospace.

5. Application

Image matching navigation of aerospace is important application area for some special cases. In general, the real images captured by aircraft are different from previous images of topographic map, because of the noise interference, the change of aircraft height and shooting season, and varying in luminous intensities, etc. So the traditional matching algorithms do not work well. Especially for agro-type's alteration, it is difficult to identify the correct location on different crop in all the seasons. How to grasp the principal features in the topographic images is key problem.

Here, we use unsupervised learning from the topographic map like to infant or young cat learning from the external world to extract ICA filters. In the supervised learning stage, the recognition decision is to compare the coefficients projected on the ICA filter-bank of test image with the target image, as animal vision in the adult stage. The system diagram is shown in Fig. 6.

In the system, the training set includes 5000 random patches from 13 images in size of 160×160 pixels each; each patch's size is 36×36 pixels. There are two training

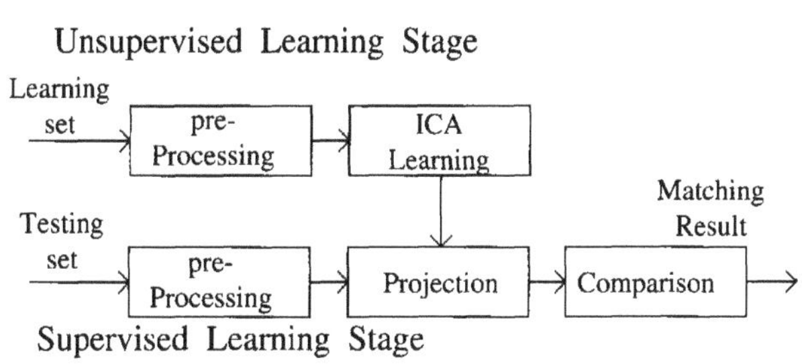

Fig. 6. Diagram of image matching system.

subsets for two kinds of topographic images: city area and farmland area.

Unsupervised learning stage. The unsupervised learning stage includes four steps: (1) pre-processing, (2) dimension reducing for the two kind subsets, (3) ICA algorithm iteration, and (4) ICA filter mixture of the two kind subsets.

Pre-processing includes removing noise, normalizing the gray-scale and removing other useless information from the original image, that the ICA method can extract the features more efficiently. There are three operations involved during the pre-processing phase: high-pass filtering, average value removing and normalization.

The high-pass filtering is to use a 3×3 Laplacian filter. The output is

$$g(x,y) = \sum_{m=x-1}^{x+1} \sum_{n=y-1}^{y+1} f(m,n)h(m-x,n-y). \tag{9}$$

Here, $f(m,n)$ is an input image, $g(x,y)$ is output image by filtering. $h(x,y)$ is the high-pass filter.

After high-pass filtering, the average value of each patch is removed as Eq. (10), because zero-mean is necessary for FastICA algorithm.

$$g(x,y) = f(x,y) - \bar{f}, \qquad \bar{f} = \frac{1}{M^2} \sum_{i=0}^{M-1} \sum_{j=0}^{M-1} f(i,j). \tag{10}$$

Here, M is the dimension of the patches.

The last operation is normalization shown in Eq. (11)

$$g(x,y) = \frac{f(x,y)}{\sqrt{\sum_{i=0}^{M-1} \sum_{j=0}^{M-1} f^2(i,j)}}. \tag{11}$$

The result in preprocess is shown in Fig. 7

After pre-processing, the training patches are selected from the 160×160 image randomly. Each patch is reshaped to a column vector as the input data of ICA networks. The matrix $\mathbf{X}$ is composed by 5000 training patches.

Whitening and dimension reduction. The second step in unsupervised learning stage is whitening and dimension reduction. PCA method is used to whiten the matrix $\mathbf{X}$ in order to remove the correlation between the pixels. Dimension reduction is performed for redundancy

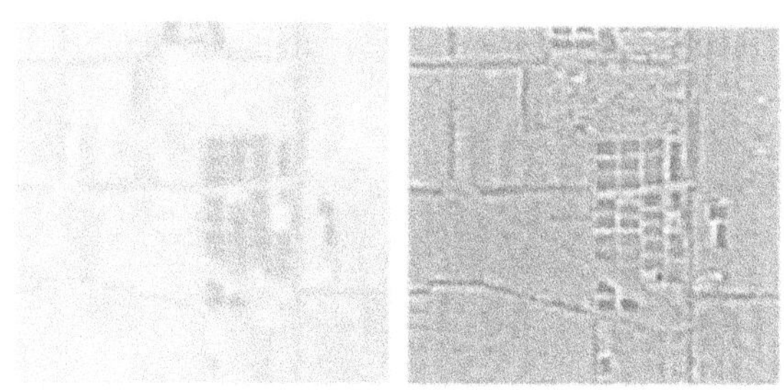

(a) (b)

Fig. 7. Pre-processing of input image for farmland subset. (a) Original topographic image (160×160 pixiels), (b) after pre-processing image.

reduction. In our system, 1296 (36×36) dimensions of original patch are reduced to 600 for farmland subset, and 400 for city subset.

ICA iteration. Two ICA networks are updated their weights as Eqs. (5)–(7) to obtain the ICA filter-banks for farmland images and city-images, respectively, when the training images input. The network is initialized by random weights.

Merge the two kinds of ICA filters. Concerning an unknown testing patch, we do not know its classification previously. Some patches may be including two kind textures. For example, it is normal that in a test patch, there are 30% belonging to city and 70% to farm. So we need to merge the two kinds of ICA filters as a filter-bank. We name the merged ICA filters as mixed filters, so there are 1000 (600 + 400) ICA filters are used to represent an original image.

Supervised training stage. In the supervised training stage, the 1000 ICA filters, representing the information of a city and its neighbors-farmland, have been formed, that like the receptive fields of the simple cells in adult. The test patch image is 36×36 pixels shooting from real world. The reason we use 36×36 patches is that the results show a higher matching rate than we selected 16×16. Here, we only need supervised learning to judge which position is more near the object image in the target image like to adult decision. Fig. 8 shows the process of the image matching system.

In Fig. 8, we only list a part of ICA filters in the mimic visual system in order to economize the space. An object image in size of 36×36, as a test image, is projected on the ICA filters, and the object feature vector is composed by its projected coefficients. In the same way, the feature vector of the patches at the same size (36×36) in the target image (160×160) can also be obtained. By searching all possible patches in the whole target image, the most similar patch to object image can be found, so the position of the object image in a 160×160 target image will be decided. In Fig. 8, the white square in the target image is the position of object image. In supervised learning stage, the object feature vector is teacher. The supervised neural networks can be chosen for judgment.

Two testing experiments are shown here in order to estimate the properties of the bio-mimic system (ICA).

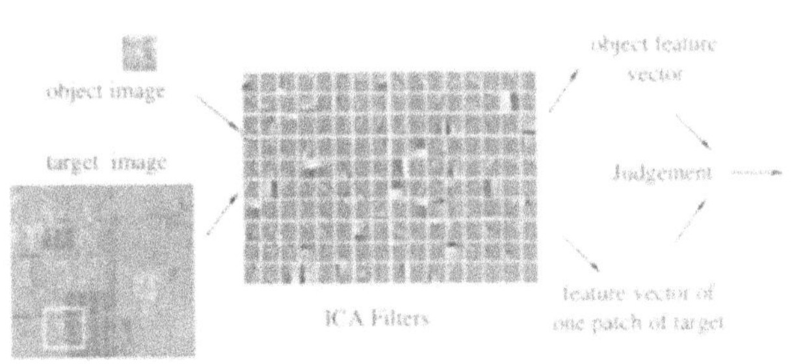

Fig. 8. Image matching process.

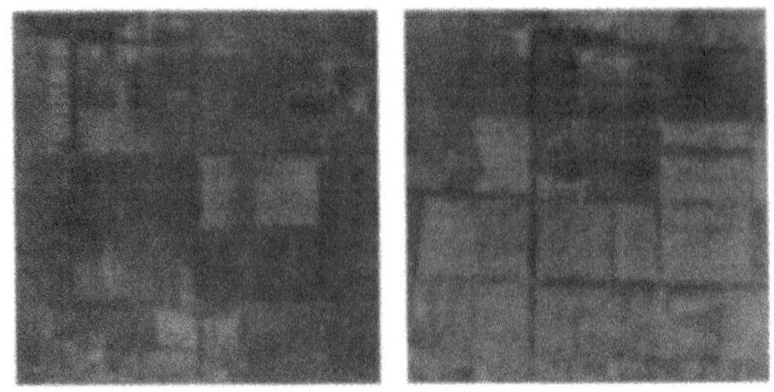

Fig. 9. One pair image for testing our system.

One pair image in size of 160×160 pixels is chosen to compare the performance between different image matching methods shown in Fig. 9.

In the pair image, we select one as target image and the other as the object image pool. In the object image pool, patches in size of 36×36 covering whole image, one by one for per 10 pixels, are chosen as object images. There are 169 object patches for each 160×160 object image pool: $(\lfloor (160 - 36 + 1)/10 \rfloor + 1)^2 = 169$. The correct matching is the position error does not exceed 4 pixels at x and y directions.

In the same conditions, the comparison results of average matching rate, for our bio-mimic system (ICA) and other traditional image matching methods (correlation method (CM), other matching methods after DCT, Walsh and Wavelet transforms) are shown in Table 2. It is obvious that ICA method outperforms other methods.

Another test results are to compare the proposed method with the CM method on 30 image pairs in size of 160×160. The 30 image pairs are divided into three subsets for this experiment. Each one contains 10 image pairs in the simulation system: set 1 covers farmland, and sets 2, 3 are randomly selected from a very large map in size of 3000×4000 pixels. In the same way above, total $169 \times 3 \times 10 = 5070$ patches are chosen as testing samples in our simulation experiments. The testing result is that must be pointed out the correct position in the 30 target images for the 5070 object patches (36×36), and the position error does not exceed 4 pixels at x and y directions.

Table 3 shows the average matching rate for these object images of the three set, and the comparison with traditional method (CM).

It is found that our image matching method based on ICA model is better than the traditional algorithm more than 5%.

Table 2
The comparison results of five methods (correct rate %)

DCT	Walsh	Wavelet	CM	ICA
72.18%	55.4%	44.38%	71.60%	76.33%

Table 3
The matching results of three testing image sets and comparison with traditional method (CM)

	Test Set 1 (%)	Test Set 2 (%)	Test Set 3 (%)
1	71.01	100.00	94.08
2	67.46	94.67	84.62
3	97.63	73.37	89.35
4	81.66	70.41	41.42
5	76.33	57.99	91.12
6	72.19	61.54	69.23
7	81.66	68.05	79.88
8	81.66	25.44	53.25
9	67.46	37.87	67.46
10	62.13	45.56	50.30
Set average	75.92	63.49	72.07
Traditional Method (CM)	68.11	58.05	65.39

6. Conclusion

We reveal the relations between ICA and the mechanism of simple cells in visual cortex by three simulation results in the computer. Two results have confirmed that the ICA filters can approximate to Gabor filters in animal vision and the Gabor-like filters have different parameters to different input images. The other simulation verifies Blakemore and Cooper's experimental results in 1970 about the growth of simple cells in cat's V1 area. Using this model, an aerospace image matching application shows that ICA-based model of simple cell's receptive field has higher matching rate than traditional matching algorithm.

Acknowledgements

This paper is supported by NSF6017.

References

Bell, A. J., & Sejnowski, T. J. (1995). An information-maximization approach to blind separation and blind deconvolution. *Neural Computation*, *7*, 1129–1159.

Bell, A. J., & Sejnowski, T. J. (1997). The 'independent components' of natural scenes are edge filters. *Vision Research*, *37*(23), 3327–3338.

Blakemore, C., & Cooper, G. F. (1970). Development of the brain depends on the visual environment. *Nature*, *228*, 419–478.

Hurri, J., Hyvärinen, A., & Oja, E (1997). Wavelet and natural image statistics. In Proceedings of the Scandinavian Conference on Image Analysis'97, Lappeenranta, Finland.

Hyvärinen, A. (1999). Fast and robust fixed-point algorithms for independent component analysis. *IEEE Transactions on Neural Networks*, *10*(3), 626–634.

Olshausen, B. A., & Field, D. J. (1996). Emergence of simple-cell receptive field properties by learning a sparse code for nature images. *Nature*, *381*, 607–609.

Peter, D., & Abbott, L. F. (2001). *Theoretical neuroscience*. Cambridge, MA: MIT Press, pp. 60–65.

Pollen, D. A., Nagle, M., Daugman, J., Kronauer, R., & Cavanagh, P. (1984). Use of Gabor elementary functions to probe receptive field substructure of posterior inferotemporal neurous in the owl monkey. *Vision Research*, *24*(3), 233–241.

Shou, T. (1997). *Brain mechanism of visual information processing*. Shanghai Science and Technological Publishing House, pp. 1–15.

Szu, H. (1999). ICA: an enabling tech for intelligent sensory processing. *IEEE CAS Newsletters*, 14–41.

PERGAMON

AVAILABLE AT www.ComputerScienceWeb.com POWERED BY SCIENCE DIRECT

Neural Networks 16 (2003) 617–624

Neural Networks

www.elsevier.com/locate/neunet

2003 Special issue

eLoom and Flatland: specification, simulation and visualization engines for the study of arbitrary hierarchical neural architectures

Thomas P. Caudell[a,*], Yunhai Xiao[a], Michael J. Healy[b]

[a]*Department of Electrical and Computer Engineering, University of New Mexico, Albuquerque, NM 87131, USA*
[b]*University of New Mexico and University of Washington, 13544 23rd Place NE, Seattle, WA 98125, USA*

Abstract

eLoom is an open source graph simulation software tool, developed at the University of New Mexico (UNM), that enables users to specify and simulate neural network models. Its specification language and libraries enables users to construct and simulate arbitrary, potentially hierarchical network structures on serial and parallel processing systems. In addition, eLoom is integrated with UNM's Flatland, an open source virtual environments development tool to provide real-time visualizations of the network structure and activity. Visualization is a useful method for understanding both learning and computation in artificial neural networks. Through 3D animated pictorially representations of the state and flow of information in the network, a better understanding of network functionality is achieved. ART-1, LAPART-II, MLP, and SOM neural networks are presented to illustrate eLoom and Flatland's capabilities.

Keywords: eLoom; Flatland; Visualization; Simulation tools

1. Introduction

Neural networks provide a powerful and general technique for inductive learning. They have the potential of accurately describing the behavior of extremely complex systems. Neural networks are characterized by large numbers of simple processing units linked to each other by weighted connections. Usually people use neural network as a black box, without knowing the processes inside the box. Neural networks can be more easily understood when they are represented using graphical attributes such as color, size, and spatial organization. Traditional approaches of visualizing neural networks have focused on displaying a diagram of weight values, or a flowchart of the learning algorithm (Craven & Shavlik, 1992; Edlund & Caudell, 2000; Mesrobian & Skrzypek, 1992; Sundararajan & Saratchandran, 1998). Hinton diagrams provide a compact visual display of the weights and biases related to a particular unit in a network (Hinton & McClelland, 1982), but does not explicitly reveal network topology in relation to the weight data. Many commercial and non-commercial neural network simulators are listed in (http://www.emsl.pnl.gov:2080/proj/neuron/neural/systems/). Matlab provides an integrated neural network toolbox (http://www.mathworks.com/products/neuralnet/). It also has plot functions to show the weight changes, biases, error surface. Stuttgart Neural Network Simulator, developed at University of Stuttgart, Germany, supports many types of networks and training algorithms as well as sophisticated graphical visualization tools under X11 (Petron, 1999). In this paper, eLoom, a new graph specification and simulation tool, and Flatland, a virtual environment development tool, are integrated to produce a dynamic, reconfigurable software environment for the specification, simulation and real time visualization of arbitrary neural networks.

Section 2 describes the simulation and visualization tools. Section 3 shows the simulation and visualization results for two complex neural networks architectures. Section 4 provides a brief discussion and Section 5 ends with the summary and conclusion. Finally, Appendix A gives examples neural architectures.

2. Overview of eLoom and Flatland

eLoom is a graph specification and simulation tool (Caudell, 2002; Caudell & Xiao, 2002). A graph is typically composed of nodes and connections. eLoom supports five component types: modules, nodes, node arrays, directed

* Corresponding author.
E-mail addresses: tpc@eece.unm.edu (T.P. Caudell), yhxiao@eece.unm.edu (Y. Xiao), mjhealy@u.washington.edu (M.J. Healy).

0893-6080/03/$ - see front matter
doi:10.1016/S0893-6080(03)00105-9

connections, directed connection arrays. Nodes and connections may be grouped into arrays and modules, and to support hierarchies modules may contain other modules. All components have user specified simulation functions and data storage methods, as well as representation functions to draw and make sounds for use in visualization systems. eLoom has a text-based specification language using a line-based keywords and parameter/value syntax. Using this language, users can construct arbitrary network structures. The following is a sample eLoom specification file:

```
ms -mn Outstar -fn TestFunc -rfn Module-
RepFunc
  -bsn MODULEBUFFTYPE
n -nn Innode -fn LinearNodeFunc -nfp 2
-fp0 0.0
  -fp1 1.0 -rfn NodeRepFunc
  -bsn NODEBUFFTYPE
na -nan Outarray -d 1 -nc 10 -fn Linear-
NodeFunc
  -fp0 0.0 -fp1 1.0 -rfn NodeArrayRepFunc
  -bsn NODEARRAY-BUFFTYPE
cnaf -can ConnArray -nfr Innode -nato
Outarray
  -fn WeightFunc -nfp 1 -fp0 1.0
  -rfn ConnRepFunc -bsn CONN-BUFFTYPE
me
EOF
```

In this specification, an Outstar network is constructed. A module named *Outstar* is defined first. Modules are used as containers for associated network components. Following this, a node named *Innode* and an array of nodes named *Outarray* are defined. A connection array *ConnArray* connects the *Innode* to *Outarray*. Fig. 1 shows a graphical representation of eLoom components, using an automatic recursive graph layout algorithm to place the nodes, modules around the perimeter of disks. Disks represent either nodes or other modules and are evenly distributed around the disk to minimize connection crossings.

During the execution of a neural network, the flow of activation and connection weights animate, forming various patterns, like an automated loom weaving patterns (hence the name of the software package).

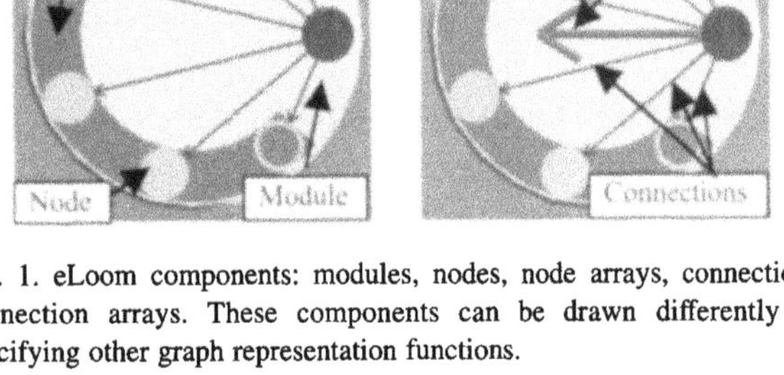

Fig. 1. eLoom components: modules, nodes, node arrays, connections, connection arrays. These components can be drawn differently by specifying other graph representation functions.

eLoom is written in the C programming language and dynamically creates C language structures to store all graph components and modular functions. Fig. 2 shows the organization structure of eLoom. The eLoom Parser reads in a network specification file; then creates the network with its internal data structures. A user specified graph layout function places the components appropriately for display. A scheduler function calls all of the simulation functions, representation functions for each component and begins simulating and visualizing the network. A partition function is used in parallel simulation of the network, and partitions the components onto different processors to distribute the processor load. A save-system-buffer function can save the intermediate simulation results so that the simulation can be paused, and a restore-system-buffer function can resume the simulation later. eLoom also has functions to recreate and save or print the system specifications. By implementing these modular functions with different algorithms, eLoom can easily switch to a different graph layout for display, or a different scheduler for simulation.

Virtual environments provide a synthetic natural surrounding for network graphical representations. The user can interact with the environment through 3D vision, sound, and haptics. The amount of information absorbed from such an environment can be much greater than from a table of numerical results. Currently, eLoom is integrated with the open visualization environment development tool named Flatland.

Flatland is a visualization/virtual reality application development environment, created at the University of New Mexico (http://www.hpcerc.unm.edu/homunculus). It allows the software developer to construct and users to

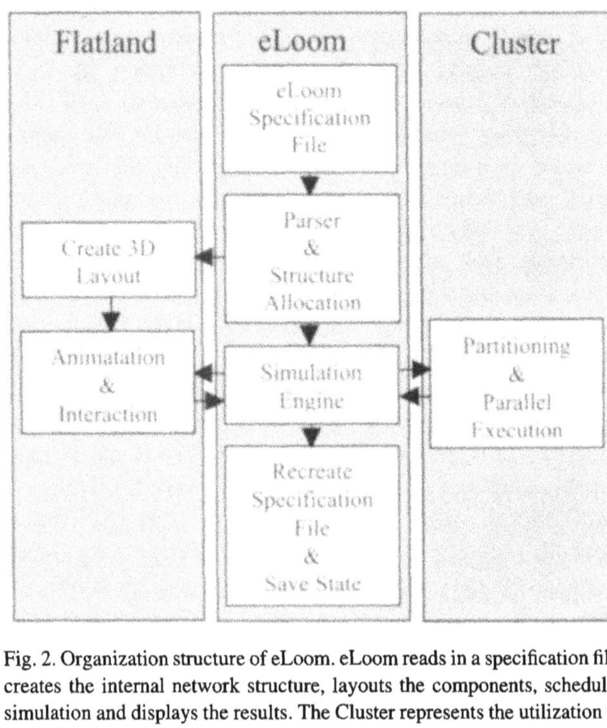

Fig. 2. Organization structure of eLoom. eLoom reads in a specification file, creates the internal network structure, layouts the components, schedules simulation and displays the results. The Cluster represents the utilization of an optional parallel processing system.

interact with arbitrarily complex graphical and aural representations of data and systems. Flatland is written in C/C++ and uses the standard OpenGL graphics language to produce all graphics.

In addition, Flatland uses the standard GLUT library for window, mouse, joystick, and keyboard management. Flatland is object oriented, multithreaded and uses dynamically loaded libraries to build user applications in the virtual environment, and runs under Linux and Irix operating systems. At the core of Flatland is an open, custom, transformation graph data structure (not to be confused with the application graphs specified in eLoom) that maintains and potentially animates the geometric relationships between the objects contained in the graph. Graph objects contain all of the information necessary to draw, sound, and control the entity represented by the object. The transformation graph is one part of a higher-level structure referred to in Flatland as a universe. The universe contains the transformation graph, a flat database of objects in the graph, and a reference to the graph vertex that is currently acting as the root of a hierarchically organized tree. This root is usually the graphical camera viewpoint.

Flatland is intrinsically multi-threaded, allowing the system to make use of computer systems with multi-processors and shared memory. The main thread spawns an OpenGL graphics thread and a Flatland sound thread. The optional tracker allows the user to use the 3D interaction metaphors with their applications and to use head tracking and 3D joysticks or wands. An application in the context of Flatland is a relatively self-contained collection of objects, functions and data that can be dynamically loaded (and unloaded) into the graph of an environment instantaneously. An application is responsible for creating and attaching its objects to the graph, and for supplying all object functionality. An application is added to Flatland through the use of a configuration file. This structured file is read and parsed when Flatland starts, and contains the name and location of the libraries that have been created for the application, as well as a formal list of parameters and an arbitrary set of arguments for the application.

In Flatland, graphics and sound are treated symmetrically. Each object in the graph contains, among other things, a draw function and a sound function. The draw function contains or calls all of the code to draw and animate the graphics that represents the object. From a code developer's perspective, all object graphics are based on and drawn in a local coordinate system. Other structures in the graph handle the placement and orientation of the object's model coordinate relative to other objects in the graph and subsequently the camera. The sound function within an object contains all of the calls or code to make sounds that represents that object. Flatland maintains a library of sound function calls that are designed to resemble OpenGL. Wave sound files are treated like OpenGL display lists and are called sound lists. In addition to opening sound lists, functions exist that allow the author to control the starting, looping, stopping, volume, and 3D location of the sound. All sound is emitted in Flatland from point sources in the 3D space. The developer specifies the location of the sounds in the same model coordinate system used for the graphics.

Although position-tracking technology is not generally available on computers today, Flatland is designed to make use of these. A tracker is a multiple degree of freedom measurement device that can, in real-time, monitor the position and/or orientation of multiple receiver devices in space, relative to a transmitter device of some sort. As such, Flatland launches a tracker thread to sample the available tracker information and make it available for use by applications. In the standard Flatland configuration, trackers are used to locate hand held wands and to track the position of the user's head. Head position and orientation is needed in cases that involve the use of head mounted displays or stereo shutter glasses.

User interaction is a central component of Flatland, and as such, each object is controllable in arbitrary ways defined by the designer. Currently there are four possible methods for the control of objects: (1) GLUT pop up menus in the main viewer window; (2) the console keyboard; (3) Flatland 2D control panels either in the environment or separate windows; and, (4) external systems or simulations. In the future, there will also be available 3D menus and controls in the virtual environment and voice recognition. An array of controls may be defined when an object is coded by the developer. Finally, external systems may control an object, for example, through a threaded simulation, serial communication (trackers), or Unix sockets to another process.

Since eLoom is currently integrated with Flatland, users are able to fly around and interact with the neural network simulation as it executes, using their location relative to the graphical forms to control their point of view and focus of study. Human subjects studies have shown that this form of continuous semantic zooming interface increases a user's understanding of complex program networks (Summers, 2002).

3. Results

Using eLoom, two neural network architectures, Adaptive Resonance Theory (ART) and Laterally Primed Adaptive Resonance Theory (LAPART) are simulated and visualized. The specification files for these architectures, and two others can be found in the Appendix A.

ART was originated by Carpenter and Grossberg (1987). ART version 1 (ART-1) performs clustering of binary vectors. There are three network layers in ART-1: Input, F1, and F2. First binary input pattern Input is presented to F1 layer. F1 layer forwards adaptively filtered copies to the F2 layer, which undergoes winner-takes-all node selection and feeds back to F1, and adjusts the template associated with the winner node. The complete model about ART-1 neural architecture can be found in (Moore, 1988). Fig. 3

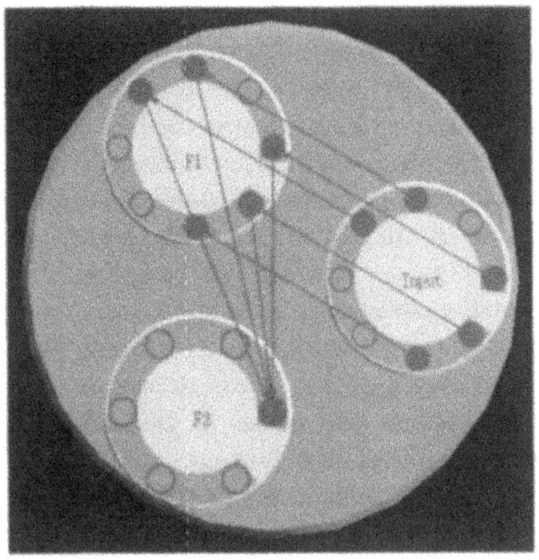

Fig. 3. ART-1 neural network simulation. There are three modules: Input module, F1 module, and F2 module. 10110 is presented to the Input module and a new template 10110 is formed in F2 module in this graph.

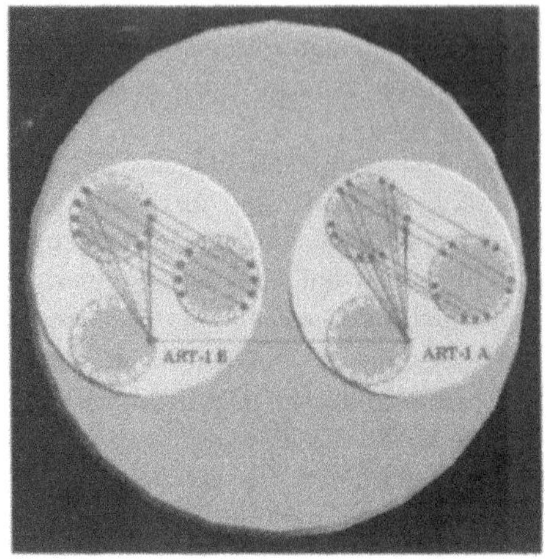

Fig. 5. The LAPART neural networks are shown as two interconnected ART-1 networks:ART-1 A and ART-1 B. Both ART-1 modules get new input pattern and form new template in F2 layer. A new connection from A module to B module becomes activated.

shows a snapshot of ART-1 neural network simulation. During the simulation, Input module reads input pattern from external file first. Then the input pattern is presented to F1 through the connection functions. Then there is a search among the F2 nodes. Either a new template is created or an existing template is updated. The patterns in input module and F1 module are shown by displaying the nodes with filled or unfilled circles. The connections associated with node in F2 module represent the learned template of the winner node.

LAPART neural network architecture is composed of two interconnected ART-1 networks. Each ART-1 module performs pattern clustering within its own self-organizing network. The interconnections between these two ART-1 modules enable LAPART to learn to infer one pattern class from another to form a predictive sequence. Fig. 4 shows a full detail of a LAPART system. A complete, formal model of LAPART inference learning rule can be found in Healy, Caudell, and Smith (1993). In Fig. 5, LAPART neural networks are shown as two ART-1 networks, with connections from F2 nodes in ART-1 A module to F2 nodes in ART-1 B module. In this snapshot, both ART-1 modules get new input pattern and form new temPlate in F2 layer, a new connection from A module to B module becomes activated.

LAPART neural networks are used to train an autonomous robot to move through a set of obstacles (Gao, Healy, & Caudell, 2001). Fig. 6 shows this application in Flatland virtual environment. The foreground shows the robot, obstacles, and a target at the right front corner. A sensor on the front of the robot simulates a one-dimension image camera, providing information regarding the location of obstacles. A binary coding of this information is supplied to the input of the ART-1 A module. The robot control function will generate corresponding control signals, code them into binary format and supply them to ART-1 B

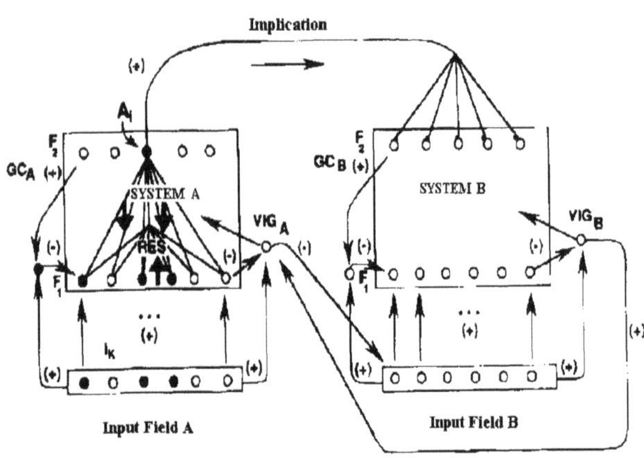

Fig. 4. Full detail of a LAPART system. Each ART-1 system has gain control and vigilance nodes GC_A, VIG_A and GC_B, VIG_B, respectively. VIG_A, activated initially and during each system A reset, inhibits system B's read-in of its input until resonance occurs in A (indicated by RES).

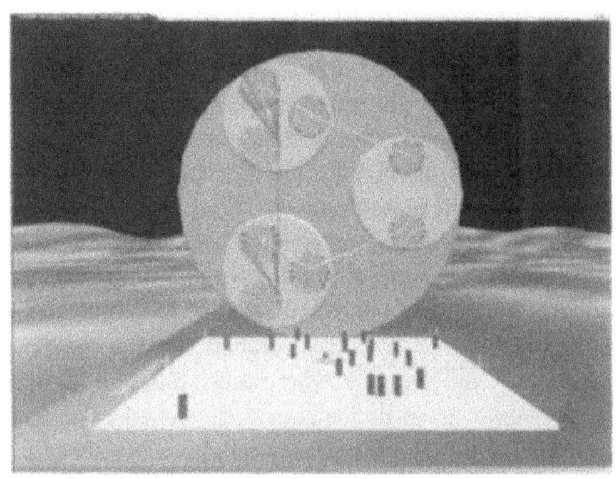

Fig. 6. LAPART simulation of an autonomous robot moving through a set of obstacles in Flatland. The LAPART neural network application is shown in the back. The simulated robot (gray triangle), obstacles (cylinders), and target (cone) are shown in the foreground.

Fig. 7. A close look of a hierarchical network structure visualized by eLoom in Flatland.

module. LAPART networks are shown in the back as disk modules. The disks on the right are Interface module. It contains two sub-modules. One shows the obstacle position information obtained by the sensor. The other shows the control information by the robot control function. The disks on the left top are ART-1 A module and the disks on the left bottom are ART-1 B module. As the robot moves through the obstacles, the change of node outputs and connection weights, and the formation of new templates are reflected in the LAPART modules.

In Flatland, users are able to fly around to view the change of the entire neural network by moving farther from the module, or view only a specific part of the neural network by moving closer to the modules. Fig. 7 shows a close look of a hierarchical network structure in Flatland.

4. Discussion

The simulation of ART-1 and LAPART network is state-transition style. The users can see the propagation of input to Fl layer, a search on F2 layer, and creation of new temPlate or updating existing temPlate. The simulation of ART-1 and LAPART shows the dynamic change of connection weights and node outputs. It gives users an intuitively understanding of the neural network process. By simulating the neural network in Flatland, users can observe patterns of learning and discover relationships between the network and the simulation. When the robot senses an obstacle, the sensor signals changes to indicate the obstacle's position. Users can observe how this change in the simulation model precipitates a change in the input pattern, and discern how each input pattern is processed and classified by the neural network. Users can watch as the neural network searches through its collection of templates and either finds a resonant pattern or creates a new one, thus they can intuitively gain an understanding of the LAPART classification process.

The training of neural networks may take a very long time to converge. eLoom provides functions to save the specification and intermediate simulation buffer. Later eLoom can reconstruct the network and restore the simulation buffer to resume simulation.

As the number of nodes and connections in the neural network becomes larger, the load on a single processor becomes heavier. Thus the simulation speed is limited by the processor. Neural networks are inherently parallel systems. Parallel simulation on multiprocessors will be the solution. In Sundararajan and Saratchandran (1998), a parallel implementation of ART-1 neural networks on processor ring architectures is described. eLoom is designed to support parallel simulation. The partition function partitions eLoom components onto multiprocessors to distribute the load before simulation. The connection functions in eLoom will do the communication task between processors. If the two components at the ends of the connection are on the same processor, the connection function can get the data without communicate to other processors. Otherwise the connection function will request data from other processors. The communication between processors may be large and thus limits the simulation speed. Minimization of the communication between processors is a graph partition optimization problem. By implementing the partition function with different graph partition algorithms, the communication load between processors can be reduced.

5. Summary and conclusion

eLoom is a graph specification and simulation tool. With the eLoom specification language, users can construct arbitrary network architectures often without programming. eLoom supports the use of module library files, which make it easy to specify more complicated network architecture. For example, the specification of LAPART will be very concise if using two ART module libraries. By changing the simulation function, representation function, graph layout function, users can simulate different network models, experience with different representations, get an intuitively view of neural network process.

By visualizing neural networks, researchers are empowered to discover new information about the neural learning process. Within the virtual environment, users can easily and naturally position themselves to best observe the activity in which they are most interested and discover the evolving space of an operating neural network. More interactive features may be added, such as clicking on an ART F2 node, showing the pattern associated with it. Integrated with Flatland, eLoom becomes a powerful engine for modeling arbitrary hierarchical neural architectures.

Acknowledgements

The authors would like to thank the Department of Electrical and Computer Engineering, the High

Performance Computing, Education, and Research Center at the University of New Mexico, The Boeing Company, and the Department of Electrical Engineering at the University of Washington for supporting this research. Thanks to Zengfa Gao for his priory work on robot control with LAPART. Thanks Dr Kenneth Summers' support with Flatland.

Appendix A. Architecture specifications

This appendix provides the specification for ART1 and LAPART-2, plus specifications and visualizations for multilayer perceptrons and self organizing maps.

A.1. ART-1 example (Fig. 3)

```
# ART1.lib: ART1 neural network specifi-
cation library
td -tn ART1Net -?mn ART1 -?Inputmn Input-
Module
  -?nc0 8 -?ncF2 10 -?F1mn F1Module -?F2mn
  F2Module -?IF1can OneOne -?F1F2can
  FullConn
  -?Inputna Input -?F1na F1 -?F2na F2
  -?datafile ART1data -?rho.6 -?period 1
mts -mn ?mn -fn Art1Func -nfp 4 -fp0
?Inputna
  -fp1 -?F1na -fp2 ?F2na -fp3 ?rho -rfn
  ModuleRepFunc -bsn MODULEBUFFTYPE
  -poe ?period
ms -mn ?Inputmn -rfn ModuleRepFunc -poe
?period
  na -nan ?Inputna -d 1 -nc0 ?nc0 -afn
    NodeArray- ReadDataFunc -nafp 1
    -afp0
    ?datafile -bsn NODEBUFF-TYPE -absn
    NODEARRAYBUFFTYPE -rfn NodeRepFunc
    -arfn
    NodeArrayRepFunc
me
ms -mn ?F1mn -rfn ModuleRepFunc -poe
?period
  na -nan ?F1na -d 1 -nc0 ?nc0 -fn
    LinearNodeFunc -nfp 1 -fp0 0.0 -bsn
    NODEBUFFTYPE -absn NODEARRAY-BUFF-
    TYPE -rfn
    NodeRepFunc -arfn NodeArrayRepFunc
me
ms -mn ?F2mn -rfn ModuleRepFunc -poe
?period
  na -nan ?F2na -d 1 -nc0 ?nc0 -fn
    ConstantNodeFunc -nfp 1 -fp0 0.0 -bsn
    NODEBUFFTYPE -absn NODEARRAY-BUFF-
    TYPE -rfn
    NodeRepFunc -arfn NodeArrayRepFunc
me
cmaf -can ?IF1can -camode OneToOne -mfr
  ?Inputmn -nafr ?Inputna -mto ?F1mn
  -nato
  ?F1na -fn WeightBasicFunc -nfp 1 -fp0
  1.0
  -arfn ConnArrayRepFunc -bsn CONNBUFF-
  TYPE
cmaf -can ?F1F2can -mfr ?F1mn -nafr ?F1na
-mto
  ?F2mn -nato ?F2na -fn WeightBasicFunc
  -nfp 1
  -fp0 0.0 -bsn CONNBUFFTYPE -rfn
  ConnRepFunc
  -absn CONNARRAY-BUFFTYPE
mte
EOF
```

A.2. LAPART II example, using ART1 library (Fig. 5)

```
#LAPART II neural network specification
lb -ln ART1.lib
ms -mn LAPART -fn LapartFunc -nfp 3 -fp0
ART1A
  -fp1 ART1B -fp2 0 -rfn ModuleRepFunc
  -bsn
  MODULEBUFFTYPE -poe 1
  mti -tn ART1Net -?mn ART1A -?Inputmn
    InputModuleA -?F1mn F1ModuleA
    -?F2mn
    F2ModuleA -?IF1can OneOneA
    -?F1F2can
    FullConnA -?Inputna InputA -?F1na
    F1A -?F2na
    F2A -?datafile Sensordata -?nc0 32
    -?ncF2 30
    -?rho.8
  mti -tn ART1Net -?mn ART1B -?Inputmn
    InputModuleB -?F1mn F1ModuleB
    -?F2mn
    F2ModuleB -?IF1can OneOneB
    -?F1F2can
    FullConnB -?Inputna InputB -?F1na
    F1B -?F2na
    F2B -?datafile Controldata -?nc0 16
    -?ncF2 20
    -?rho.85
  cmaf -can ConnAB -mfr F2ModuleA -nafr
  F2A -mto
    F2ModuleB -nato F2B -fn WeightBasic-
    Func -nfp
    1 -fp0 0.0 -rfn ConnRepFunc -bsn
    CONNBUFFTYPE
    -absn CONNARRAYBUFFTYPE
me
EOF
```

A.3. Multilayer perceptrons (MLPs) example, a 6 × 12 × 8 × 4 network (Fig. A1)

```
ms -mn MLP -fn BPFunc -nfp 1 -fp0 0.0
  -rfn ModuleRepFunc -bsn MODULEBUFF-
  TYPE
  ms -mn InputLayer -rfn ModuleRepFunc
    na -nan InputArray -d 1 -nc0 6 -afn
      NodeArrayRead-DataFunc -nafp 1
      -afp0
      mlp_data.txt  -rfn  NodeRepFunc
      -arfn
      NodeArrayRepFunc -bsn NODEBUFF-
      TYPE -absn
      NODEARRAYBUFFTYPE
  me
  ms -mn HiddenLayer1 -rfn ModuleRepFunc
    na -nan HiddenArray1 -d 1 -nc0 12 -fn
      LinearNodeFunc -nfp 1 -fp0 0.0 -bsn
      NODEBUFFTYPE  -absn  NODEARRAY-
      BUFFTYPE -rfn
      NodeRepFunc -arfn NodeArrayRep-
      Func
  me
  ms -mn HiddenLayer2 -rfn ModuleRepFunc
    na -nan HiddenArray2 -d 1 -nc0 8 -fn
      LinearNodeFunc -nfp 1 -fp0 0.0 -bsn
      NODEBUFFTYPE  -absn  NODEARRAY-
      BUFFTYPE -rfn
      NodeRepFunc -arfn NodeArrayRep-
      Func
  me
  ms -mn OutputLayer -rfn ModuleRepFunc
    na -nan OutputArray -d 1 -nc0 4 -fn
      ConstantNodeFunc -nfp 1 -fp0 0.0 -bsn
      NODEBUFFTYPE  -absn  NODEARRAY-
      BUFFTYPE -rfn
      NodeRepFunc -arfn NodeArrayRep-
      Func
  me
  cmaf -can ConnArray1 -mfr InputLayer
  -nafr
    InputArray -mto HiddenLayer1 -nato
    HiddenArray1 -fn WeightBasicFunc
    -nfp 1 -fp0
    1.0 -rfn ConnRepFunc -bsn CONNBUFF-
    TYPE
  cmaf -can ConnArray2 -mfr HiddenLayer1
  -nafr
    HiddenArray1  -mto  HiddenLayer2
    -nato
    HiddenArray2 -fn WeightBasicFunc
    -nfp 1 -fp0
    1.0 -rfn ConnRepFunc -bsn CONNBUFF-
    TYPE
  cmaf -can ConnArray3 -mfr HiddenLayer2
  -nafr
    HiddenArray2 -mto OutputLayer -nato
    OutputArray  -fn  WeightBasicFunc
    -nfp 1 -fp0
    1.0 -rfn ConnRepFunc -bsn CONNBUFF-
    TYPE
me
EOF
```

A.4. Self organizing map example, 3, 4 × 4 network (Fig. A2)

```
ms -mn SOM -fn SOMFunc -nfp 1 -fp0 0.0 -rfn
  ModuleRepFunc
  ms -mn InputLayer -rfn ModuleRepFunc
    na -nan InputArray -d 1 -nc0 3 -afn
```

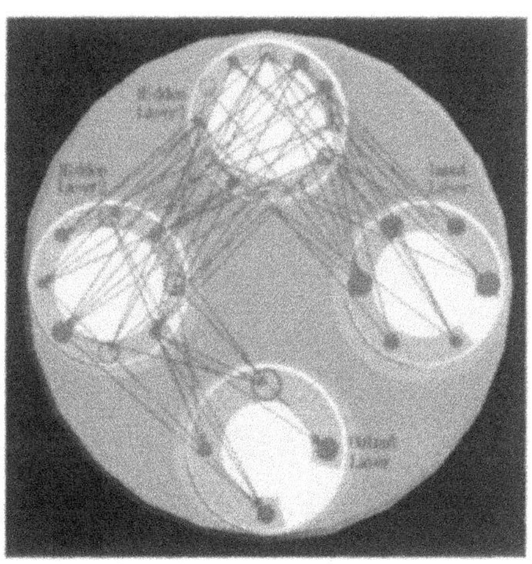

Fig. A1. Multilayer perceptrons neural networks. It shows a 6 × 12 × 8 × 4 MLPs network. The size of nodes reflects the output of the nodes. If the node output is less than some threshold, then a circle is drawn. Small weight connections are not drawn.

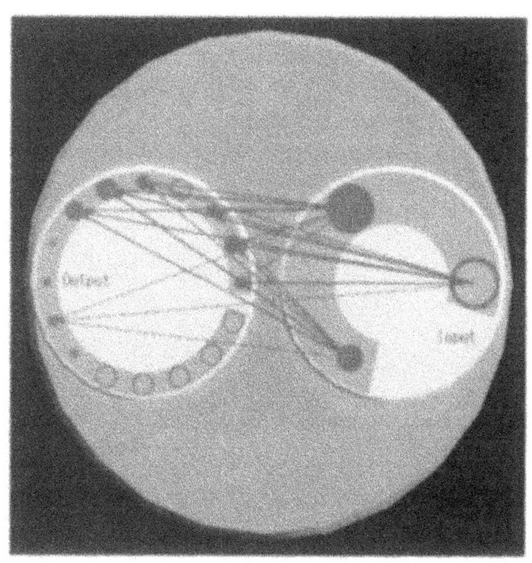

Fig. A2. Self-Organizing Maps neural network. The input space is three neurons, the output space is 4 × 4 neurons. The size of nodes reflects the output of the nodes. If the node output is less than a threshold, it is drawn with a circle. Small weight connections are not drawn.

```
      NodeArrayReadDataFunc  -nafp  1
      -afp0
      SOMdata.txt   -rfn   NodeRepFunc
      -arfn
      NodeArrayRepFunc -bsn NODEBUFF-
      TYPE -absn
      NODEARRAYBUFFTYPE
  me
  ms -mn OutputLayer -rfn ModuleRepFunc
    na -nan OutputArray -d 2 -nc0 4 -nc1 4
    -afn
      NodeArrayInitFunc -nafp 1 -afp0
      0.0 -rfn
      NodeRepFunc -arfn NodeArrayRep-
      Func -bsn
      NODEBUFFTYPE -absn NODEARRAYBUFF-
      TYPE
  me
  cmaf -can ConnArray -mfr InputLayer
  -nafr
    InputArray -mto OutputLayer -nato
    OutputArray
    -fn WeightBasicFunc -nfp 1 -fp0 1.0
    -rfn
    ConnRepFunc -bsn CONNBUFFTYPE
me
EOF
```

References

Carpenter, G., & Grossberg, S. (1987). A massively parallel architecture for a self-organizing neural pattern recognition machine. *Computer Vision, Graphics and Image Processing*, *37*(1), 54–115.

Caudell, T.P (2002). The homunculus project homepage, http://www.ahpcc.unm.edu/homunculus/, Visualization Laboratory, High Performance Computing, Education, and Research Center, The University of New Mexico.

Caudell, T. P., & Xiao, Y. (2002). *eLoom manual*. Homunculus Laboratory, Department of Electrical and Computer Engineering, The University of New Mexico.

Craven, M. W., & Shavlik, J. W. (1992). Visualizing learning and computation in artificial neural networks. *International Journal on Artificial Intelligence Tools*, *1*, 399–425.

Edlund, K. M., & Caudell, T. P. (2000). Realtime visualization of the learning processes in the LAPART neural architecture as it controls a simulated autonomous vehicle. *IEEE-INNS-ENNS International Joint Conference on Neural Networks (IJCNN'00), Como, Italy, July 24–27, 2000, 3*.

Gao, Z. F., Healy, M. J., & Caudell, T. P. (2001). A study of autonomous robot behavior using the LAPART neural architecture. *Proceedings of the IEEE International Joint Conference on Neural Networks, Washington, DC*, 2171–2176.

Healy, M. J., Caudell, T. P., & Smith, S. D. (1993). A neural architecture for pattern sequence verification through inferencing. *IEEE Transactions on Neural Networks*, *4*(1), 9–20.

Hinton, G. E., & McClelland, J. L. (1982). Distributed representations. In D. E. Rumelhart, & J. L. McClelland (Eds.), *Parallel distributed processing: explorations in the microstructure of cognition. Vol.1: Foundations*. Cambridge, MA: MIT Press.

http://www.emsl.pnl.gov:2080/proj/neuron/neural/systems/

Mesrobian, E., & Skrzypek, J. (1992). A software environment for studying computational neural systems. *IEEE Transactions in Software Engineering*, *18*(#7), 575–589.

Moore, B. (1988). ART 1 and pattern clustering. In D. Touretzky, & G. Hinton (Eds.), *Proceedings of the Connectionist Models Summer School at Carnegie-Mellon University*. New York: Morgan Kaufmann.

Petron, E. (1999). Stuttgart neural network simulator: exploring connectionism and machine learning with SNNS. *Linux Journal*, *1999*(63es).

Summers, K.L (2002). *Visualization of programs using proximity to trigger continuous semantic zooming: an experimental study*. PhD Dissertation. Computer Science Department, The University of New Mexico.

Sundararajan, N., & Saratchandran, P. (1998). Parallel Implementation of ART1 Neural Networks on Processor Ring Architectures. In Cheryl Baltes (Ed.), IEEE Computer Society.

PERGAMON

AVAILABLE AT www.ComputerScienceWeb.com POWERED BY SCIENCE DIRECT

Neural Networks 16 (2003) 625–632

Neural Networks

www.elsevier.com/locate/neunet

2003 Special issue

Associative morphological memories based on variations of the kernel and dual kernel methods

Peter Sussner*

Institute of Mathematics, Statistics, and Scientific Computation, State University of Campinas, Campinas, CEP 13081-970, SP, Brazil

Abstract

Morphological associative memories (MAMs) belong to the class of morphological neural networks. The recording scheme used in the original MAM models is similar to the correlation recording recipe. Recording is achieved by means of a maximum (M_{XY} model) or minimum (W_{XY} model) of outer products.

Notable features of autoassociative morphological memories (AMMs) include optimal absolute storage capacity and one-step convergence. Heteroassociative morphological memories (HMMs) do not have these properties and are not very well understood. The fixed points of AMMs can be characterized exactly in terms of the original patterns. Unfortunately, AMM fixed points include a large number of spurious memories.

In this paper, we combine the M_{XX} model and variations of the kernel method to produce new autoassociative and heteroassociative memories. We also introduce a dual kernel method. A new, dual model is given by a combination of the W_{XX} model and a variation of the dual kernel method. The new MAM models exhibit better error correction capabilities than M_{XX} and W_{XX} and a reduced number of spurious memories which can be easily described in terms of the fundamental memories.

Keywords: Morphological neural network; Associative memory; Autoassociative morphological memory; Fixed point; Spurious memory; Error correction capability; Kernel; Dual kernel

1. Introduction

In recent years, a number of different morphological neural network models and applications have emerged (Gader, Khabou, & Koldobsky, 2000; Pessoa & Maragos, 2000; Raducanu, Graña, & Albizuri, 2003; Ritter, Sussner, & Diaz-de-Leon, 1998; Ritter & Sussner, 1996; Sussner, 2003; Won, Gader, & Coffield, 1997). Morphological neural networks can be characterized as neural networks which calculate a maximum or a minimum of a sum at each node. Thus, they are drastically different from 'traditional' neural network models which perform linear operations followed by applications of nonlinear activation functions.

The emphasis of this paper is on morphological associative memories (Ritter et al., 1998; Ritter, Diaz-de-Leon, & Sussner, 1999). The original recording strategies for MAMs are similar to correlation recording (Anderson, 1972; Kohonen, 1972; Nakano, 1972). In the M_{XY} model, the pattern associations $(\mathbf{x}, \mathbf{y})$ are stored in terms of a maximum of outer products. In the dual W_{XY} model, the pattern associations $(\mathbf{x}, \mathbf{y})$ are stored in terms of a minimum of outer products. We have shown that MAMs exhibit many desirable characteristics (Ritter et al., 1998). We proved for example that the AMMs M_{XX} and W_{XX} do not impose any restrictions on the number of pattern associations to be encoded in the memory. Thus, 2^n patterns can be stored in the binary case, where n is the length of memory. In comparison, McEliece et al. showed that the absolute (asymptotic) capacity of the Hopfield associative memory is $n/2 \log n$ if with high probability the unique fundamental memory is to be recovered, except for a vanishingly small fraction of fundamental memories (McEliece, Posner, Rodemich, & Venkatesh, 1987). Moreover, the information storage capacity (number of bits which can be stored and recalled associatively) of the morphological autoassociative memory exceeds the respective number for certain linear matrix associative memories which was calculated by Palm (Palm, 1980). Furthermore, the AMM converges in one step, i.e. every output pattern obtained after one application of the AMM is a fixed point or stable state of the memory. Unfortunately, the number of fixed points is huge (Sussner, 2000b) and the error correction capability of binary AMMs

* Tel.: +55-19-7885959; fax: +55-19-2895808.
E-mail address: sussner@ime.unicamp.br (P. Sussner).

0893-6080/03/$ - see front matter © 2003 Elsevier Science Ltd. All rights reserved.
doi:10.1016/S0893-6080(03)00113-8

is very limited. The heteoassociative models M_{XY} and W_{XY} are more difficult to analyze. A number of theorems indicate the deficiencies of HMMs with respect to storage capacity, spurious memories, and tolerance with respect to noise (Ritter et al., 1998).

We introduced the kernel method to circumvent these difficulties for AMMs and HMMs and achieved significant improvements regarding error correction capability and the number of spurious memories (Ritter et al., 1998; Sussner, 2000a). One of the problems of the kernel method is the fact that the output may vary depending on the particular choice of the kernel. Inspiration for this paper was drawn from the realization that the output is independent on the selection of the kernel according to a certain set of rules if the kernel method is preceded by an application of the M_{XX} model.

In this paper, we show that combinations of the kernel method and the M_{XX} model yield new autoassociative and heteroassociative memories which exhibit less spurious memories and better error correction capabilities than the M_{XX} model. In fact, these new models either produce an expression involving only 'maximum' symbols and the fundamental memories or a pattern which equals the output of a constant pattern. Similar models with similar properties arise from compositions of the W_{XX} model and the dual kernel method which is introduced in this paper. We also provide conditions which can be used for the construction of a kernel and a dual kernel. However, kernels and dual kernels are not guaranteed to exist for all problems, in particular if the number of associations to be stored is large in comparison to the length of the input patterns. Therefore, we introduce variations of the kernel and dual kernel methods depending on sets of intermediate patterns which are subject to less stringent conditions. Combining these approaches with the M_{XX} yields new MAM models which are similar to the combinations of the (dual) kernel method and the M_{XX}/W_{XX}-model discussed before. The only difference lies in the fact that these approaches retain the absolute storage capacity of 2^n of the autoassociative models M_{XX} and W_{XX}.

2. Some minimax algebra background for morphological associative memories

Many models of associative memories allow for a formulation in terms of matrices (Hopfield, 1982; Kohonen, 1972; Kosko, 1988; Wu & Batalama, 2000; Wu & Pados, 2000). The model of associative memories described in this paper employs products of matrices which are defined in the theory of *minimax algebra* (Cuninghame-Green, 1995). Two types of matrix products exist in minimax algebra. For an $m \times p$ matrix A and a $p \times n$ matrix B with entries from $\mathbb{R}$, the matrix $C = A \boxtimes B$, also called the *max product* of A and B, and the matrix $D = A \boxslash B$, also called the *min product* of A and B, are defined by

$$c_{ij} = \bigvee_{k=1}^{p} (a_{ik} + b_{kj}), \qquad d_{ij} = \bigwedge_{k=1}^{p} (a_{ik} + b_{kj}). \tag{1}$$

The algebraic structure $(\mathbb{R}, \vee, \wedge, +)$ represents a division belt in minimax algebra with the self-dual multiplication '$+$'. Thus, it provides for an elegant duality between matrix operations. For any real-valued $m \times n$ matrix A, we define the *conjugate matrix* A^* of A as the $n \times m$ matrix $A^* = -A'$, where A' is the transpose of A. It follows that

$$(A \wedge B)^* = A^* \vee B^* \text{ and } (A \boxslash B)^* = B^* \boxtimes A^*. \tag{2}$$

The maximum and the minimum of two matrices occurring in Eq. (2) are performed element wise. Eq. (2) implies that every statement about morphological neural networks induces a dual statement which simply arises by replacing each $\wedge$ symbol with a $\vee$ symbol and vice versa, and by reversing each inequality.

As an example, consider the following true statements of minimax algebra for appropriately sized matrices A, B, and C (Cuninghame-Green, 1995).

$$(A \boxtimes B) \vee (A \boxtimes C) = A \boxtimes (B \vee C), \tag{3}$$

$$A \boxtimes (B \wedge C) \leq (A \boxtimes B) \wedge (A \boxtimes C). \tag{4}$$

The corresponding dual statements can be found below.

$$(A \boxslash B) \wedge (A \boxslash C) = A \boxslash (B \wedge C), \tag{5}$$

$$A \boxslash (B \vee C) \geq (A \boxslash B) \vee (A \boxslash C). \tag{6}$$

3. Introduction to morphological associative memories

Morphological associative memories were originally conceived as simple matrix memories endowed with recording recipes which are similar to correlation recording. Suppose that we want to record k vector pairs $(\mathbf{x}^1, \mathbf{y}^1), \ldots (\mathbf{x}^k, \mathbf{y}^k)$ using a *morphological associative memory*. Let X denote the matrix in $\mathbb{R}^{n \times k}$ whose column vectors are the vectors $\mathbf{x}^\xi \in \mathbb{R}^n$ and let Y denote the matrix in $\mathbb{R}^{m \times k}$ whose column vectors are the vectors $\mathbf{y}^\xi \in \mathbb{R}^m$, where $\xi = 1, \ldots, k$.

The first recording scheme consists of constructing an $m \times n$ matrix W_{XY} as $W_{XY} = Y \boxslash X^*$. The second, dual scheme consists of constructing an $m \times n$ matrix M_{XY} of the form $M_{XY} = Y \boxtimes X^*$. If the matrix W_{XY} receives a vector $\mathbf{x}$ as input, the product $W_{XY} \boxtimes \mathbf{x}$ is formed. Dually, if the matrix M_{XY} receives a vector $\mathbf{x}$ as input, the product $M_{XY} \boxslash \mathbf{x}$ is formed. If $X = Y$ (i.e. $y^\xi = x^\xi$, for $\xi = 1, \ldots, k$), we obtain the *autoassociative morphological memories* (AMMs) W_{XX} and M_{XX}. Note that the identity $(W_{XY})^* = M_{YX}$ can be deduced from Eq. (2). This fact leads to the following relationship which we will use throughout the paper.

$$W_{XX} \in \{0, -1\}^{n \times n} \Leftrightarrow M_{XX} \in \{0, 1\}^{n \times n}. \tag{7}$$

Example 1

$$X = \begin{pmatrix} 0 & 3 & -3 & 1 \\ 8 & 6 & -4 & 5 \\ 6 & 3 & -3 & -4 \end{pmatrix}, \quad (8)$$

$$W_{XX} = \begin{pmatrix} 0 & -8 & -6 \\ -1 & 0 & -1 \\ -5 & -9 & 0 \end{pmatrix}, \quad (9)$$

$$M_{XX} = (W_{XX})^*, \qquad W_{XX} \boxvee X = X = M_{XX} \boxwedge X. \quad (10)$$

Note that although the number of stored patterns exceeds the length of the patterns in this example, we have perfect recall for undistorted patterns. We will see in the next section that the absolute storage capacity for autoassociative morphological memories is unlimited, i.e. as many patterns as desired can be stored in an AMM with perfect recall.

4. Fundamental properties of binary autoassociative morphological memories

The recall phase of binary AMMs can be described exactly in terms of their fixed points and their basins of attraction (Sussner, 2000b).

Definition 1. *A vector* $\mathbf{x} \in \mathbb{R}^n$ *is called a* fixed point *or* stable state *of* W_{XX} *if and only if* $W_{XX} \boxvee \mathbf{x} = \mathbf{x}$. *Similarly,* $\mathbf{x}$ *is a fixed point of* M_{XX} *if and only if* $M_{XX} \boxwedge \mathbf{x} = \mathbf{x}$.

Definition 2. *An expression consisting of some* $\mathbf{x}^1, \ldots, \mathbf{x}^k$ *and some* $\vee$ *and/or* $\wedge$ *symbols is called a* lattice polynomial *in* $\mathbf{x}^1, \ldots, \mathbf{x}^k$.
To be precise, we adopt the following recursive definition. Every $\mathbf{x}^\xi$, *where* $\xi = 1, \ldots, k$, *is a lattice polynomial in* $\mathbf{x}^1, \ldots, \mathbf{x}^k$. *If* $\mathbf{p}$ *and* $\mathbf{q}$ *are lattice polynomials in* $\mathbf{x}^1, \ldots, \mathbf{x}^k$ *then* $\mathbf{p} \vee \mathbf{q}$ *and* $\mathbf{p} \wedge \mathbf{q}$ *are also lattice polynomials in* $\mathbf{x}^1, \ldots, \mathbf{x}^k$ (Birkhoff, 1993).

Definition 3. *A lattice polynomial consisting only of* $\vee$ *operators and some* $\mathbf{x}^\xi$ *where* $\xi = 1, \ldots, k$ *is called a* $\vee$-clause *in* $\mathbf{x}^1, \ldots, \mathbf{x}^k$. *Similarly, a lattice polynomial consisting only of* $\wedge$ *operators and some* $\mathbf{x}^\xi$ *where* $\xi = 1, \ldots, k$ *is called a* $\wedge$-clause *in* $\mathbf{x}^1, \ldots, \mathbf{x}^k$.

Theorem 1. *Let* $X = [\mathbf{x}^1, \ldots, \mathbf{x}^k] \in \{0, 1\}^{n \times k}$ *such that* $M_{XX} \in \{0, 1\}^{n \times n}$. *A pattern* $\mathbf{y}$ *is a fixed point of* W_{XX} *if and only if* $\mathbf{y}$ *is a lattice polynomial in* $\mathbf{x}^1, \ldots, \mathbf{x}^k$ *or equal to one of the constant patterns* $\mathbf{0}$ *or* $\mathbf{1}$. *A pattern* $\mathbf{z}$ *is a fixed point of* M_{XX} *if and only if* $\mathbf{z}$ *is a lattice polynomial in* $\mathbf{x}^1, \ldots, \mathbf{x}^k$ *or equal to* $\mathbf{0}$ *or* $\mathbf{1}$ (Sussner, 2003).

Theorem 2. *The following equalities are satisfied for all* $X \in \mathbb{R}^{n \times k}$ *and* $\mathbf{x} \in \mathbb{R}^n$ (Sussner, 2000).

$$W_{XX} \boxvee \mathbf{x} = \hat{\mathbf{x}} \text{ and } M_{XX} \boxwedge \mathbf{x} = \check{\mathbf{x}}, \quad (11)$$

where $\hat{\mathbf{x}}$ *denotes the* least upper bound ('sup') *of* $\mathbf{x}$ *in the set of fixed points of* W_{XX} *and where* $\check{\mathbf{x}}$ *denotes the* greatest lower bound ('inf') *of* $\mathbf{x}$ *in the set of fixed points of* M_{XX}. *In other words,* $\hat{\mathbf{x}}$ *acts as an attractor state for* $\mathbf{x}$ *when using* W_{XX} *and* $\check{\mathbf{x}}$ *acts as an attractor state for* $\mathbf{x}$ *when using* M_{XX}.

Theorems 1 and 2 lead to a number of important consequences:

1. The absolute storage capacity of a binary AMM is 2^n for patterns of length n.
2. Every output pattern remains stable under repeated applications of a binary AMM.
3. The fixed points of both W_{XX} and M_{XX} include the original patterns and the ground states $\mathbf{0}$ and $\mathbf{1}$ as well as a large number of spurious states.
4. The memory W_{XX} exhibits tolerance with respect to eroded, i.e. incomplete patterns, and the memory M_{XX} exhibits tolerance with respect to dilated patterns.
5. W_{XX} and M_{XX} are not suited for patterns corrupted by both erosive and dilative noise.

A pattern $\tilde{\mathbf{x}}$ is called an *eroded* version of a pattern $\mathbf{x}$ if and only if $\tilde{\mathbf{x}} \leq \mathbf{x}$. In this case, we say that $\tilde{\mathbf{x}}$ has undergone an *erosive change*. Similarly, a pattern $\tilde{\mathbf{x}}$ is called an *dilated* version of $\mathbf{x}$ if and only if $\tilde{\mathbf{x}} \geq \mathbf{x}$. In this case, we say that $\tilde{\mathbf{x}}$ has undergone a *dilative change*.

Example 2. The following small example will illustrate Theorems 1 and 2. Consider the three pattern images $\mathbf{p}^1$, $\mathbf{p}^2, \mathbf{p}^3$ shown in the top row of Fig. 1. Using the standard row-scan method, each pattern image $\mathbf{p}^\xi$ can be converted into a pattern vector $\mathbf{x}^\xi = (x_1^\xi, \ldots, x_{16}^\xi)$. Note that each $\boldsymbol{x}^\xi$ is a fixed point of both W_{XX} and M_{XX} by Theorem 1 since the fundamental memories are lattice polynomials in $\mathbf{x}^1, \mathbf{x}^2, \mathbf{x}^3$. Some other patterns corresponding to fixed points of W_{XX} and M_{XX} are shown in the bottom row of Fig. 1. If $\mathbf{x}$ corresponds to a pattern in the middle row of Fig. 1 then $W_{XX} \boxvee \mathbf{x}$ corresponds to the pattern below.

5. Kernels and dual kernels

The kernel method has previously been suggested for dealing with patterns which contain both dilative and erosive noise (Ritter, 1998; Sussner, 2000a). Generalizing and simplifying our original definition of a kernel, we provide the following definition.

Definition 4. *An* $n \times k$ *matrix* $Z = [\mathbf{z}^1, \mathbf{z}^2, \ldots, \mathbf{z}^k]$ *is called a* kernel *for* (X, Y) *if and only if there exists a memory* W

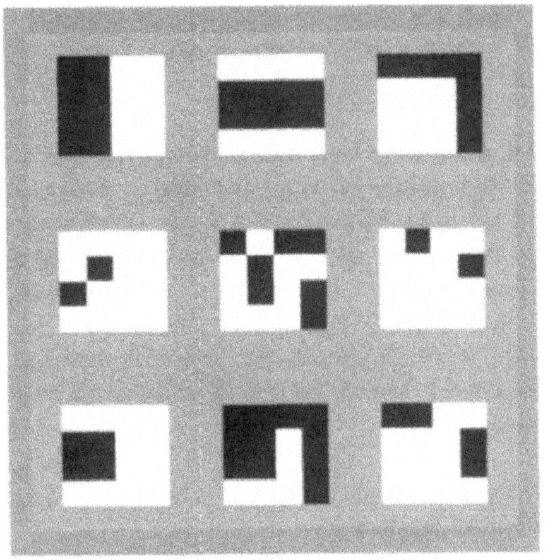

Fig. 1. The top row contains the three patterns used in constructing the morphological memories. The patterns in the bottom row of this figure represent fixed points of both W_{XX} and M_{XX}. In an application of W_{XX}, a pattern **p** in the middle row is attracted to the pattern in the bottom row directly below **p**.

such that

$$W \boxvee (M_{ZZ} \boxwedge X) = Y. \tag{12}$$

If $X = Y$, we say that Z is a kernel for X.

Given a particular problem of associating binary patterns $\mathbf{x}^\xi$ with binary pattern $\mathbf{y}^\xi$, a kernel with respect to (X, Y) can be easily chosen by means of the Theorem 3 below (Sussner, 2000a).

Theorem 3. *Let X, Y, Z be binary patterns with $Z \le X$. If*

$$\mathbf{z}^\gamma \wedge \mathbf{z}^\xi = \mathbf{0} \text{ and } \mathbf{z}^\gamma \not\le \mathbf{x}^\xi \ \forall \gamma, \xi, \gamma \ne \xi, \tag{13}$$

then $W_{ZY} \boxvee (M_{ZZ} \boxwedge X) = Y$. Therefore, Z is a kernel for (X, Y).

The *kernel method* consists of retrieving x^γ from a corrupted version $\tilde{\mathbf{x}}^\gamma$ by means of $W \boxvee (M_{ZZ} \boxwedge \tilde{\mathbf{x}}^\gamma)$. A successful retrieval of $\mathbf{x}^\gamma$ is guaranteed under the following conditions.

Theorem 4. *If Z is a kernel for (X, Y) satisfying the conditions* Eq. (13). *We obtain $W_{ZY} \boxvee (M_{ZZ} \boxwedge \tilde{\mathbf{x}}^\gamma) = \mathbf{y}^\gamma$, if*

$$\tilde{\mathbf{x}}^\gamma \ge \mathbf{z}^\gamma \text{ and } \tilde{\mathbf{x}}^\gamma \not\ge \mathbf{z}^\xi \ \forall \gamma, \xi, \ \gamma \ne \xi. \tag{14}$$

More information on the kernel method can be found in other papers (Sussner, 2000a; Ritter et al., 1998). By duality, every statement in minimax algebra induces a dual statement. Therefore, we define the concept of a *dual kernel* and provide the dual theorems of Theorems 3 and 4. The proofs of Theorems 3 and 4 which appeared in Sussner (2000a) do not make use of our recent results on fixed points and basins of attraction of binary AMMs (Sussner, 2000b; Sussner 2003). Given these results, Theorems 5 and 6 are easier to understand and we consider it instructive to use these results in the proofs. We leave it to the reader to provide similar proofs for Theorems 3 and 4.

Definition 5. *An $n \times k$ matrix $S = (\mathbf{s}^1, \mathbf{s}^2, \ldots, \mathbf{s}^k)$ is called a* dual kernel *for (X, Y) if and only if there exists a memory M such that*

$$M \boxwedge (W_{SS} \boxvee X) = Y. \tag{15}$$

If $X = Y$, we say that S is a dual kernel for X.

The *dual kernel method* consists of retrieving $\mathbf{x}^\gamma$ from a corrupted version $\tilde{\mathbf{x}}^\gamma$ by means of $M \boxwedge (W_{SS} \boxvee \tilde{\mathbf{x}}^\gamma)$.

Theorem 5. *Let X, Y, S be binary patterns with $S \ge X$ If*

$$\mathbf{s}^\gamma \vee \mathbf{s}^\xi = \mathbf{1} \text{ and } \mathbf{s}^\gamma \not\ge \mathbf{x}^x \ \forall \gamma, \xi, \ \gamma \ne \xi, \tag{16}$$

then $M_{SY} \boxwedge (W_{SS} \boxvee X) = Y$. Therefore, S is a dual kernel for (X, Y).

Proof. The proof follows immediately from Lemmas 3 and Lemma 4. First, we assure with Lemma 1 that our results on fixed points and basins of attraction of W_{SS} can be applied. A more general result than Lemma 3 is presented in Lemma 2, which along with Lemma 4 will be used to prove Theorem 6. □

Theorem 6. *If S is a dual kernel for (X, Y) satisfying* Eq. (16) *then we obtain $M_{SY} \boxwedge (W_{SS} \boxvee \tilde{\mathbf{x}}^\gamma) = \mathbf{y}^\gamma$, if*

$$\tilde{\mathbf{x}}^\gamma \le \mathbf{s}^\gamma \text{ and } \tilde{\mathbf{x}}^\gamma \not\le \mathbf{s}^\xi \ \forall \xi, \gamma, \ \xi \ne \gamma. \tag{17}$$

Proof. The proof is a direct consequence of Lemmas 2 and 4. □

Example 3. Consider the set $X = \{\mathbf{x}^1, \mathbf{x}^2, \mathbf{x}^3\}$ of Example 2 displayed in the top row of Fig. 1. Fig. 2 shows a set of patterns corresponding to a kernel for X and to a dual kernel for X.

Lemma 1. *If $S \in \{0, 1\}^{n \times k}$ satisfies $\mathbf{s}^\gamma \vee \mathbf{s}^\xi = \mathbf{1}$ for all γ, ξ such that $\gamma \ne \xi$ then $W_{SS} \in \{0, -1\}^{n \times n}$ and $W_{SS} \boxvee \mathbf{x}$ is either a $\wedge$-clause in $\mathbf{s}^1, \ldots, \mathbf{s}^k$ or equal to $\mathbf{0}$ or $\mathbf{1}$.*

Fig. 2. Let X be as in Example 2. The set of vectors corresponding to the first three patterns represents a kernel for X. The set of vectors corresponding to the next three patterns represents a dual kernel for X.

Proof. Let W denote W_{SS}. By definition we have, $w_{ij} = \wedge_{\xi=1}^{k} (s_i^\xi - s_j^\xi) \in \{-1, 0, 1\}$ for $i, j = 1, \ldots, n$. For the proof of the first part of Lemma 1, it is enough to show that $w_{ij} \leq 0$.
By assumption, $\mathbf{s}^\gamma \vee \mathbf{s}^\xi = \mathbf{1}$ for all $\gamma \neq \xi$. Equivalently, $s_j^\gamma \vee s_j^\xi = 1$ for all $j = 1, \ldots, n$. Hence, $s_j^\gamma = 1$ or $s_j^\xi = 1$ all $j = 1, \ldots, n$ which implies that for every $j = 1, \ldots, n$ there is a $\nu \in \{1, \ldots, k\}$ such that $s_j^\nu = 1$. Therefore, the following equation holds for all $j = 1, \ldots, n$.

$$w_{ij} = \bigwedge_{\xi}^{k} (s_i^\xi - s_j^\xi) \leq s_i^\nu - s_j^\nu = s_i^\nu - 1 \leq 0 \ \forall i = 1, \ldots, n. \tag{18}$$

Let us now prove the second part of Lemma 1. By Theorem 2, $W \boxtimes \mathbf{x} = \hat{\mathbf{x}}$, the supremum of $\mathbf{x}$ in the set of fixed points of W. By Theorem 1, $\hat{\mathbf{x}} \in \{0,1\}^n$ is either constant or a lattice polynomial in $\mathbf{s}^1, \ldots, \mathbf{s}^k$. Let us assume that $\hat{\mathbf{x}} \neq \mathbf{0}, \mathbf{1}$. Since $\mathbb{R}^n$ represents a distributive lattice, $\hat{\mathbf{x}}$ can be written in conjunctive normal form

$$\hat{\mathbf{x}} = C_1 \wedge C_2 \wedge \ldots \wedge C_m, \tag{19}$$

where $C_i = \vee_{\xi \in \Theta_i} \mathbf{s}^\xi$, with $\emptyset \neq \Theta_i \subseteq \{1, \ldots, k\}$ for $i = 1, \ldots, m$ (Birkhoff, 1993).
Let i be arbitrary, fixed. We distinguish between the cases $|\Theta_i| \geq 2$ and $|\Theta_i| = 1$. In the first case, we see that $C_i = \mathbf{1}$ since $\mathbf{s}^\gamma \vee \mathbf{s}^\xi = \mathbf{1}$ for all $\gamma, \xi, \gamma \neq \xi$. If $|\Theta_i| = 1$, we have $C_i = \mathbf{s}^\xi$ for some ξ. Since we excluded the case $\hat{\mathbf{x}} = \mathbf{1}$, we cannot have $C_i = \mathbf{1}$ for all $i = 1, \ldots, m$. Therefore, $\hat{\mathbf{x}}$ can be written as a $\wedge$-clause in $\mathbf{s}^1, \ldots, \mathbf{s}^k$. □

Lemma 2. *Let* $S, X \in \{0,1\}^{n \times k}$ *such that* $S \geq X$ *and let* $\tilde{\mathbf{x}}^\gamma \in \{0,1\}^n$. If Eqs. (16) and (17) *are satisfied then* $W_{SS} \boxtimes \tilde{\mathbf{x}}^\gamma = \mathbf{s}^\gamma$.

Proof. First note that $\tilde{\mathbf{x}}^\gamma \neq \mathbf{0}$ because $\mathbf{s}^\xi \not\geq \tilde{\mathbf{x}}^\gamma$ for all $\xi \neq \gamma$ by Eq. (17). Since W_{SS} has a zero diagonal, $\tilde{\mathbf{x}}^\gamma \leq W_{SS} \boxtimes \tilde{\mathbf{x}}^\gamma$. Moreover, $W_{SS} \boxtimes \tilde{\mathbf{x}}^\gamma \leq W_{SS} \boxtimes \mathbf{s}^\gamma$ because $\tilde{\mathbf{x}}^\gamma \leq \mathbf{s}^\gamma$. The pattern $\mathbf{s}^\gamma$ is a fixed point of W_{SS} by Theorem 1 and differs from $\mathbf{1}$ since $\mathbf{s}^\gamma \not\geq \tilde{\mathbf{x}}^\xi$ for all $\xi \neq \gamma$ by Eq. (17). We obtain the following relationships.

$$\mathbf{0} \neq W_{SS} \boxtimes \tilde{\mathbf{x}}^\gamma \leq W_{SS} \boxtimes \mathbf{s}^\gamma = \mathbf{s}^\gamma \neq \mathbf{1}. \tag{20}$$

We infer from Lemma 1 that $W_{SS} \boxtimes \tilde{\mathbf{x}}^\gamma = \wedge_{\xi \in \Theta} \mathbf{s}^\xi$, where $\emptyset \neq \Theta = \{1, \ldots, k\}$. Therefore, $\tilde{\mathbf{x}}^\gamma \leq \mathbf{s}^\xi$ which according to Eq. (16) only happens in case $\xi = \gamma$. □

Lemma 3. *If* $X \leq S \in \{0,1\}^{n \times k}$ *such that* Eq. (16) *holds then* $W_{SS} \boxtimes X = S$.

Proof. It suffices to show for every $\gamma \in \{1, \ldots, k\}$ that $W_{SS} \boxtimes \mathbf{x}^\gamma = \mathbf{s}^\gamma$. We know that Eq. (16) holds and that $X \leq S$. For $\tilde{\mathbf{x}}^\gamma = \mathbf{x}^\gamma$, Eq. (17) can be confirmed as well. Therefore, Lemma 2 is applicable and yields $W_{SS} \boxtimes \mathbf{x}^\gamma = \mathbf{s}^\gamma$. □

Lemma 4. *Let* $Y \in \{0,1\}^{m \times k}$ *and* $S \in \{0,1\}^{n \times k}$ *such that* $\mathbf{s}^\gamma \not\geq \mathbf{s}^\xi$ *for all* γ, ξ *with* $\gamma \neq \xi$. *We have* $M_{SY} \boxtimes S = Y$ *in either one of the following cases.*

$$\mathbf{s}^\gamma \vee \mathbf{s}^\xi = \mathbf{1} \ \forall \xi, \gamma, \ \xi \neq \gamma, \tag{21}$$

$$\mathbf{y}^\gamma \wedge \mathbf{y}^\xi = \mathbf{0} \ \forall \xi, \gamma, \ \xi \neq \gamma. \tag{22}$$

Proof. By Corollary 2.1 of (Ritter et al., 1998), it is enough to show that for each $i = 1, \ldots, m$ and each $\gamma = 1, \ldots, k$ there exists a $j \in \{1, \ldots, n\}$ such that

$$s_j^\gamma - y_i^\gamma = \bigwedge_{\xi=1}^{k} (s_j^\xi - y_i^\xi). \tag{23}$$

$$s_j^\gamma - y_i^\gamma \Leftrightarrow s_j^\gamma - y_i^\gamma \leq s_j^\xi - y_i^\xi \ \forall \xi = 1, \ldots, k. \tag{24}$$

Let us fix arbitrary i, γ. There is an index j_o with $s_{j_o}^\gamma = 0$ because $\mathbf{s}^\gamma \not\geq \mathbf{s}^\xi$ for all $\xi \neq \gamma$.
First, let us assume that $\mathbf{s}^\gamma \vee \mathbf{s}^\xi = \mathbf{1}$ for all $\xi \neq \gamma$. In this case, we see that $\mathbf{s}_{j_o}^\xi = 1$ for all $\xi \neq \gamma$ which implies $s_{j_o}^\gamma < s_{j_o}^\xi$. In the second case where $\mathbf{y}^\gamma \wedge \mathbf{y}^\xi = 0$ for all $\xi \neq \gamma$, there are two possibilities: $y_i^\gamma = 1$ and $y_i^\xi = \mathbf{0}$ for all $\xi \neq \gamma$ or $y_i^\gamma = 0$ and $y_i^\xi = 1$ for all $\xi \neq \gamma$. Either way, we have $-y_i^\gamma < y_i^\xi$ for all $\xi \neq \gamma$.
Thus, in both cases given by Eqs. (21) and (22), the inequality $s_{j_o}^\gamma - y_i^\gamma \leq s_{j_o}^\xi - y_i^\xi$ holds for all $\xi \neq \gamma$, and obviously also for all $\xi = 1, \ldots, k$. □

Lemma 5. *Let* Y, S *be as in Lemma 4. For all* $\emptyset = \Theta \subseteq \{1, \ldots, k\}$, *we have*

$$M_{SY} \boxtimes \left(\bigwedge_{\xi \in \Theta} \mathbf{s}^\xi \right) = \bigwedge_{\xi \in \Theta} \mathbf{y}^\xi. \tag{25}$$

Proof. For the proof of Lemma 5, we use the previous lemma and repeated applications of Eq. (5).

$$M_{SY} \boxtimes \bigwedge_{\xi \in \Theta} \mathbf{s}^\xi = \bigwedge_{\xi \in \Theta} (M_{SY} \boxtimes \mathbf{s}^\xi) = \bigwedge_{\xi \in \Theta} \mathbf{y}^\xi. \quad \square \tag{26}$$

We finish this section by providing yet another result which we will use for the construction of new morphological associative memories in Section 5. We will employ a hardlimiting funtion $f : \mathbb{R}^m \to \{0,1\}^m$. For every $\mathbf{x} \in \mathbb{R}^m$, we define $f(\mathbf{x})$ as follows.

$$f(\mathbf{x})_i = 1 \Leftrightarrow x_i > 0 \ \forall i = 1, \ldots, m. \tag{27}$$

In Lemma 6, we use the convention $\vee_{\xi \in \emptyset} \mathbf{y}^\xi = \mathbf{0}$ for patterns $\mathbf{y}^\xi \in \{0,1\}^m$.

Lemma 6. *Let* $X \in \{0,1\}^{m \times k}$ *and* $Z \in \{0,1\}^{m \times k}$ *such that* $\mathbf{z}^\gamma \wedge \mathbf{z}^\xi = \mathbf{0}$ *and for all* ξ, γ *with* $\xi \neq \gamma$. *If* Θ *denotes the set* $\{\xi : \mathbf{x} \geq \mathbf{x}^\xi\}$ *then the following statement is true for all binary* $\mathbf{x} \neq \mathbf{1}$.

$$f(M_{XZ} \boxtimes \mathbf{x}) = \bigvee_{\xi \in \Theta} \mathbf{z}^\xi. \tag{28}$$

Proof. Let $\mathbf{y}$ denote $M_{XZ} \boxtimes \mathbf{x}$. For all $i = 1, \ldots, m$, the i-th entry of $\mathbf{y}$ is given by

$$y_i = \bigwedge_{j=1}^{n} \left(\bigvee_{\xi=1}^{k} (z_i^\xi - x_i^\xi) + x_j \right). \tag{29}$$

Depending on the index i we distinguish between two cases. For indices i such that $z_i^\xi = 0$ for all ξ, we have $y_i = \wedge_{j=1}^{k}$

$(\bigvee_{\xi=1}^{k}(-x_j^{\xi})+x_j)$. Since $\mathbf{x}\neq\mathbf{1}$ there exists j_0 such that $x_{j_0}=0$ and therefore $y_i\leq 0$. We are thus able to deduce the following fact.

$$f(\mathbf{y})\leq\bigvee_{\xi=1}^{k}\mathbf{z}^{\xi}. \tag{30}$$

Now consider an index i such that $z_i^{\gamma}=1$ for some $\gamma\in\{1,\ldots,k\}$. Recall that, by assumption, $z_i^{\xi}=0$ for all $\xi\neq\gamma$. We can derive the following equations.

$$y_i=\bigwedge_{j=1}^{n}(z_i^{\gamma}-x_j^{\gamma}+x_j)=1+\bigwedge_{j=1}^{n}(x_j-x_j^{\gamma}). \tag{31}$$

The last expression equals 1 if and only if $\mathbf{x}\geq\mathbf{x}^{\gamma}$. Specifically, we have shown the following relationship for all indices i such that $z_i^{\gamma}=1$ for some γ.

$$y_i=1\Leftrightarrow\mathbf{x}\geq\mathbf{x}^{\gamma}. \tag{32}$$

Using this fact and Eq. (30), the desired equation $f(\mathbf{y})=\bigvee_{\xi\in\Theta}\mathbf{z}^{\xi}$ follows. □

6. Some new models of MAMs

In Section 4, we saw that the set of fixed points of W_{XX} and M_{XX} consists of the lattice polynomials in $\mathbf{x}^1,\ldots,\mathbf{x}^k$ and the ground states $\mathbf{0},\mathbf{1}$. In this section, we propose new binary AMM models with a reduced number of fixed points. A new morphological autoassociative model is based on the kernel method, the dual kernel method, or a similar method and reduces the set of fixed points to a set which consists of $\vee$-clauses or $\wedge$-clauses and possibly memories corresponding to the outputs of $\mathbf{0},\mathbf{1}$. This approach can be generalized to include heteroassociative morphological memories (HMMs) and leads to a reduced number of spurious memories and an increased tolerance with respect to dilative or erosive noise.

Let Z be a kernel for (X,Y) and let S be a dual kernel for (X,Y). Thus, there exist memories W and M such that $W\boxvee(M_{ZZ}\boxwedge X)=Y$ and $M\boxwedge(W_{SS}\boxvee X)=Y$. A pair of new MAM models are given by their action on an input pattern $\mathbf{x}\in\{0,1\}^n$ as follows.

$$W\boxvee(M_{ZZ}\boxwedge(M_{XX}\boxwedge X))=W\boxvee(M_X^Z\boxwedge\mathbf{x}), \tag{33}$$

$$M\boxwedge(W_{SS}\boxvee(W_{XX}\boxvee X))=M\boxwedge(W_X^S\boxvee\mathbf{x}), \tag{34}$$

where $M_X^Z=M_{ZZ}\boxwedge M_{XX}$ and $W_X^S=W_{SS}\boxvee W_{XX}$. For simplicity, we denote the memory given by Eq. (33) by $W\boxvee M_X^Z$ and we denote the memory given by Eq. (34) by $M\boxvee W_X^S$. Note, however, that in general $(W\boxvee M_X^Z)\boxvee\mathbf{x}\neq W\boxvee(M_X^Z\boxwedge\mathbf{x})$ and $(M\boxwedge W_X^S)\boxwedge\mathbf{x}\neq M\boxvee\times(W_X^S\boxvee\mathbf{x})$. Before we analyze $M\boxvee W_X^S$ for different choices of M, we present the following facts about W_X^S. Due to space constraints, we omit the results on the dual approach $W\boxwedge\times M_X^Z$.

Theorem 7. *Let $X,S\in\{0,1\}^{n\times k}$ such that $X\leq S$. Suppose $M_{XX}\in\{0,1\}^{n\times n}$. If S satisfies* Eq. (16) *then the following implication holds for every $\mathbf{x}\in\{0,1\}^n$ and every $\xi=1,\ldots,k$.*

$$W_{XX}\boxvee\mathbf{x}=\mathbf{x}^{\xi}\Rightarrow W_X^S\boxvee\mathbf{x}=\mathbf{s}^{\xi}. \tag{35}$$

Furthermore, $W_X^S\boxvee X=S$ and, for every $\mathbf{x}\in\{0,1\}^n$, the max product $W_X^S\boxvee\mathbf{x}$ is either a $\wedge$-clause in $\mathbf{s}^1,\ldots,\mathbf{s}^k$ or equal to $\mathbf{0}$ or $\mathbf{1}$.

Proof. Suppose that $W_{XX}\boxvee\mathbf{x}=\mathbf{x}^{\xi}$ for some ξ. An application of Lemma 3 shows that $W_X^S\boxvee\mathbf{x}=W_{SS}\boxvee\mathbf{x}^{\xi}=\mathbf{s}^{\xi}$. In particular, in the special case $\mathbf{x}=\mathbf{x}^{\xi}$, it is known by Theorems 1 and 2 that $W_{XX}\boxvee\mathbf{x}=\mathbf{x}^{\xi}$ for all $\xi=1,\ldots,k$. Therefore, $W_X^S\boxvee X=S$.
Finally, we deal with the last statement of Theorem 7. Let us consider an arbitrary $\mathbf{x}\in\{0,1\}^n$. By Lemma 1, $W_{SS}\boxvee\mathbf{y}\in\{0,1\}^n$ is either constant or represents a $\wedge$-clause in $\mathbf{s}^1,\ldots,\mathbf{s}^k$. This statement holds true in particular for $\mathbf{y}=W_{XX}\boxvee\mathbf{x}\in\{0,1\}^n$. Thus, $W_X^S\boxvee\mathbf{x}=W_{SS}\boxvee(W_{XX}\boxvee\mathbf{x})\in\{0,1\}^n$ is either constant or a $\wedge$-clause in $\mathbf{s}^1,\ldots,\mathbf{s}^k$. □

Corollary 1. *Let $X,S\in\{0,1\}^{n\times k}$ and let $Y\in\{0,1\}^{m\times k}$. Suppose $M_{XX}\in\{0,1\}^{n\times n}$. If S satisfies* Eq. (16) *then the following statements are true. The matrix S is a dual kernel for (X,Y) and $M_{SY}\boxwedge(W_X^S\boxvee X)=Y$. For all $\mathbf{x}\in\{0,1\}^n$, the pattern $M_{SY}\boxwedge(W_X^S\boxvee\mathbf{x})$ is a $\wedge$-clause in $\mathbf{x}^1,\ldots,\mathbf{x}^k$ or equal to $M_{SY}\boxwedge\mathbf{0}$ or $M_{SY}\boxwedge\mathbf{1}$. Furthermore, the following implication holds for all $\xi=1,\ldots,k$ and all $\mathbf{x}\in\{0,1\}^n$.*

$$W_{XX}\boxvee\mathbf{x}=\mathbf{x}^{\xi}\Rightarrow M_{SY}\boxwedge(W_X^S\boxvee\mathbf{x})=\mathbf{y}^{\xi}. \tag{36}$$

Proof. Note that S is a dual kernel for (X,Y) by Theorem 5. Also observe that the conditions of Theorem 7 are satisfied. First, an application of Theorem 7 yields $W_X^S\boxvee X=S$. In view of Lemma 3 we obtain

$$M_{SY}\boxwedge(W_X^S\boxvee X)=M_{SY}\boxwedge S=Y. \tag{37}$$

Now let us characterize the output of the memory $M_{SY}\times\boxwedge W_X^S$. By Theorem 7, the max product $W_X^S\boxvee\mathbf{x}$ is either a $\wedge$-clause in $\mathbf{s}^1,\ldots,\mathbf{s}^k$ or equal to $\mathbf{0}$ or $\mathbf{1}$. The last two cases result in $M_{SY}\boxwedge\mathbf{0}$ and $M_{SY}\boxwedge\mathbf{1}$ after applying M_{SY}. Otherwise, we have $W_X^S\boxwedge\mathbf{x}=\bigwedge_{\xi\in\Theta}\mathbf{s}^{\xi}$ for some $\emptyset\neq\Theta\subseteq\{1,\ldots,k\}$. An application of Lemma 5 gives

$$M_{SY}\boxwedge(W_X^S\boxvee\mathbf{x})=M_{SY}\boxwedge\bigwedge_{\xi\in\Theta}\mathbf{s}^{\xi}=\bigwedge_{\xi\in\Theta}\mathbf{y}^{\xi}. \tag{38}$$

Finally, assume that $W_{XX}\boxvee\mathbf{x}=\mathbf{x}^{\xi}$ for some $\xi\in\{1,\ldots,n\}$. Theorem 7 states that $W_X^S\boxvee\mathbf{x}=\mathbf{s}^{\xi}$. Using

Lemma 4, we see that

$$M_{SY} \boxed{\wedge} (W_X^S \boxed{\vee} \mathbf{x}) = M_{SY} \boxed{\wedge} \mathbf{s}^\xi = \mathbf{y}^\xi. \quad (39)$$

□

Remark. In the autoassociative case $Y = X$, Corollary 1 induces results about the fixed points of $M_{SX} \boxed{\wedge} W_X^S$ which are similar to the ones we will present in Corollary 2.

Corollary 2. *Let X, S, W_{XX} be as in* Corollary 1. *Moreover, suppose that $M_{XX} \boxed{\wedge} S = X$. The fixed points of $M_{XX} \boxed{\wedge} W_X^S$ include the fundamental memories $\mathbf{x}^1, \ldots, \mathbf{x}^k$. If $\mathbf{x}$ is a fixed point of $M_{XX} \boxed{\wedge} W_X^S$ then $\mathbf{x}$ is either a $\wedge$-clause in $\mathbf{x}^1, \ldots, \mathbf{x}^k$ or equal to $\mathbf{0}$ or $\mathbf{1}$. If $\mathbf{x}^\xi$ is recalled by W_{XX} then $\mathbf{x}^\xi$ is also recalled by $M_{XX} \boxed{\wedge} W_X^S$.*

Proof. The first and third statement follow immediately from Theorem 7 and the assumption.
It remains to be shown that if $\mathbf{x}$ is a fixed point of $M_{XX} \boxed{\wedge} W_X^S$ then $\mathbf{x}$ is either a $\wedge$-clause in $\mathbf{x}^1, \ldots, \mathbf{x}^k$ or equal to $\mathbf{0}$ or $\mathbf{1}$. Note that every fixed such point can be written as $M_{XX} \boxed{\wedge} (W_X^S \boxed{\vee} \mathbf{x})$ for some $\mathbf{x}$. According to Theorem 7, the max product $W_X^S \boxed{\vee} \mathbf{x}$ is either a $\wedge$-clause in $\mathbf{s}^1, \ldots, \mathbf{s}^k$ or equal to $\mathbf{0}$ or $\mathbf{1}$. Since the diagonal of M_{XX} consists only of zeros, we have $M_{XX} \boxed{\wedge} \mathbf{0} = \mathbf{0}$ and $M_{XX} \boxed{\vee} \mathbf{1} = \mathbf{1}$. If $W_X^S \boxed{\vee} \mathbf{x} = \wedge_{\xi \in \Theta} \mathbf{s}^\xi$ for some non-empty $\Theta \subseteq \{1, \ldots, k\}$ then repeated applications of Eq. (5) can be used to complete the proof of the corollary as follows.

$$M_{XX} \boxed{\wedge} (W_X^S \boxed{\vee} \mathbf{x}) = M_{XX} \boxed{\wedge} \left(\bigwedge_{\xi \in \Theta} \mathbf{s}^\xi \right), \quad (40)$$

$$M_{XX} \boxed{\wedge} (W_X^S \boxed{\vee} \mathbf{x}) = \bigwedge_{\xi \in \Theta} (M_{XX} \boxed{\wedge} \mathbf{s}^\xi) = \bigwedge_{\xi \in \Theta} \mathbf{x}^\xi. \quad (41)$$

□

Theorem 8. *Let $X \in \{0,1\}^{n \times k}$ such that $M_{XX} \in \{0,1\}^{n \times k}$. Let $Y \in \{0,1\}^{m \times k}$, $Z, S \in \{0,1\}^{p \times k}$ and let $\mathbf{x} \in \{0,1\}^n$ be arbitrary. We use the notations $\Theta = \{\xi : \mathbf{x} \geq \mathbf{x}^\xi\}$ and $M_X^{XZ} = M_{XZ} \boxed{\wedge} M_{XX}$ (similarly W_X^{XS} denotes $W_{XS} \boxed{\vee} W_{XX}$).
If $\Theta \neq \emptyset$, $\mathbf{z}^\gamma \not\geq \mathbf{z}^\xi$ and $\mathbf{z}^\gamma \wedge \mathbf{z}^\xi = \mathbf{0}$ for all ξ, γ with $\xi \neq \gamma$ then the following equation holds for all $\mathbf{x} \neq \mathbf{1} \in \{0,1\}^n$.*

$$W_{ZY} \boxed{\vee} f(M_X^{XZ} \boxed{\wedge} \mathbf{x}) = \bigvee_{\xi \in \Theta} \mathbf{y}^\xi. \quad (42)$$

Moreover, the following implication holds for all $\xi = 1, \ldots, k$ and all $\mathbf{x} \in \{0,1\}^n$.

$$M_{XX} \boxed{\wedge} \mathbf{x} = \mathbf{x}^\xi \Rightarrow W_{ZY} \boxed{\vee} f(M_X^{XZ} \boxed{\wedge} \mathbf{x}) = \mathbf{y}^\xi. \quad (43)$$

Proof. For the proof of the first part of Theorem 8, let us consider an arbitrary $\mathbf{x} \neq \mathbf{1}$. By Theorems 1 and 2, the min product $M_{XX} \boxed{\wedge} \mathbf{x}$ equals $\check{\mathbf{x}}$, the infimum of $\mathbf{x}$ in the set which consists of the lattice polynomials in $\mathbf{x}^1, \ldots, \mathbf{x}^k$ and $\mathbf{0}$.

Applying Lemma 6 to $\check{\mathbf{x}}$ results in the following equation.

$$f(M_X^{XZ} \boxed{\wedge} \mathbf{x}) = \bigvee_{\xi \in \Gamma} \mathbf{z}^\xi, \quad (44)$$

where $\Gamma = \{\xi : \check{\mathbf{x}} \geq \mathbf{x}^\xi\}$. We will now show that $\Gamma = \Theta$. On one hand, the set Γ is contained in the set Θ because $\check{\mathbf{x}}$ is a lower bound of $\mathbf{x}$. On the other hand, if $\mathbf{x} \geq \mathbf{x}^\xi$ then $\check{\mathbf{x}} \geq \mathbf{x}^\xi$ due to the facts that the set of lower bounds of $\mathbf{x}$ includes $\mathbf{x}^\xi$ and that $\check{\mathbf{x}}$ is the greatest lower bound. Therefore, we see that $\Theta \subseteq \Gamma$ is also valid.
Note that, due to the conditions imposed on Z, the matrices Z and Y satisfy the requirements for an application of the dual version of Lemma 5. We obtain,

$$W_{ZY} \boxed{\vee} \left(\bigvee_{\xi \in \Theta} \mathbf{z}^\xi \right) = \bigvee_{\xi \in \Theta} \mathbf{y}^\xi. \quad (45)$$

Combining Eqs. (44) and (45) leads to the desired Eq. (42). The statement given in Eq. (43) can be deduced using Lemma 6 and the dual version of Lemma 5. □

Remark. Note that by Corollary 1 and 2, and the dual of Theorem 8, the error correction capability of $M_{SY} \boxed{\wedge} W_X^S$, $M_{XX} \boxed{\wedge} W_X^S$, and $M_{SY} \boxed{\wedge} f(W_X^{XS})$ cannot be inferior to the error correction capability of W_{XX}. In fact, since $M_{SY} \boxed{\wedge} W_X^S$, $M_{XX} \boxed{\wedge} W_X^S$, and $M_{SY} \boxed{\wedge} f(W_X^{XS})$ exhibit less spurious memories than W_{XX}, it seems intuitive to conclude that the new models have an increased tolerance with respect to noise. This hypothesis is confirmed by experimental results. An additional advantage of the approach proposed in Theorem 8 and its dual version is the following. The matrices Z and S do not have to satisfy the stringent conditions of Eqs. (13) and (16). The requirements imposed on Z and S in Theorem 8 and its dual version can always be met, which implies that 2^n associations can be stored in the memory if n is the length of the input patterns.

Example 4. In this experiment, we randomly generated 12 binary vectors of length 32 from a uniform distribution.

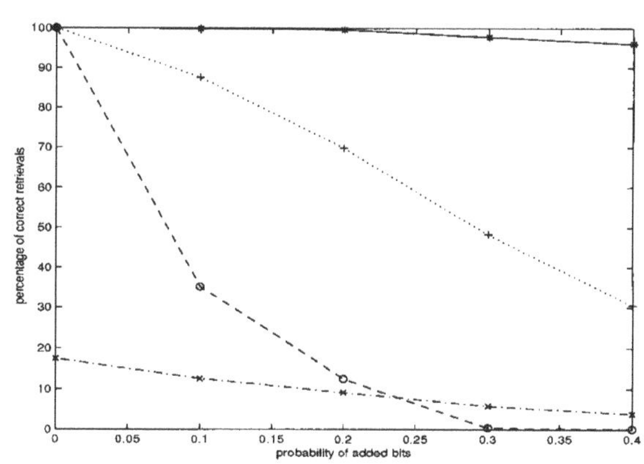

Fig. 3. In this experiment, we randomly added dilative noise with probability p to one of the fundamental memories and recorded the percentage of perfect recalls. The mark type ' $*$ ' refers to $W_{ZX} \boxed{\vee} f(M_X^{XZ})$, ' + ' refers to a projection-recorded DAM, 'O' refers to M_{XX}, and ' × ' refers to the discrete Hopfield net.

We stored each set of 12 fundamental memories $\mathbf{x}^1, \ldots, \mathbf{x}^{12}$ using the binary AMMs M_{XX} and $W_{ZX} \boxtimes f(M_X^{XZ})$, a discrete Hop-field net (Hopfield, 1982), and a projection recorded dynamic associative memory (DAM) (Hassoun, 1993). Then we probed the different memories with a corrupted version $\tilde{\mathbf{x}}^1$ where $\tilde{\mathbf{x}}^1$ was generated from $\mathbf{x}^1$ by randomly introducing dilative noise with probability p. Fig. 3 shows the percentage of perfect recalls of $\mathbf{x}^1$. Note that, in this experiment, the two-layer feed-forward model $W_{ZX} \boxtimes f(M_X^{XZ})$ outperforms the projection-recorded DAM, the M_{XX} model, and the discrete Hopfield net.

A similar experiment can be conducted by corrupting one of the fundamental memories with erosive noise. In this case, the percentage of perfect recalls using $M_{SX} \boxtimes f(W_X^{XS})$ is similar to the one using $W_{ZX} \boxtimes f(M_X^{XZ})$ of Fig. 3.

7. Concluding remarks

In this paper, we present new binary MAM models which combine AMMs with methods which are similar to the kernel or dual kernel method. We were able to achieve significant improvements with respect to the number of spurious memories and the tolerance with respect to dilative or erosive noise in comparison to the AMM models W_{XX} and M_{XX} while maintaining the absolute storage capacity of 2^n of W_{XX} and M_{XX}. In the near future, we plan to employ the new recording strategies developed in this paper in order to deal with arbitrary noise.

References

Anderson, J. A. (1972). A simple neural network generating interactive memory. *Mathematical Biosciences*, *14*, 197–220.

Birkhoff, G. (1993). *Lattice theory* (3rd ed). Providence, RI: American Mathematical Society.

Cuninghame-Green, R. (1995). Minimax algebra and applications. In P. Hawkes (Ed.), (*Vol. 90*) (pp. 1–121). *Advances in electronics and electron physics*, New York: Academic Press.

Gader, P. D., Khabou, M., & Koldobsky, A. (2000). Morphological regularization neural networks. *Pattern Recognition*, *30*(6), 935–945. Special Issue on Mathematical Morphology and Its Applications.

Hassoun, M. H. (1993). Dynamic associative neural memories. In M. H. Hassoun (Ed.), *Associative neural memories: Theory and implementation*. Oxford: Oxford University Press.

Hopfield, J. J. (1982). Neural networks and physical systems with emergent collective computational abilities. *Proceedings of the National Academy of Sciences*, *79*, 2554–2558.

Kohonen, T. (1972). Correlation matrix memory. *IEEE Transactions on Computers*, *21*, 353–359.

Kosko, B. (1988). Bidirectional associative memories. *IEEE Transactions on Systems, Man, and Cybernetics*, *18*, 49–60.

McEliece, R. J., Posner, E. C., Rodemich, E. R., & Venkatesh, S. S. (1987). The capacity of the Hopfield associative memory. *IEEE Transactions on Information Theory*, *1*, 33–45.

Nakano, K. (1972). Associatron: a model of associative memory. *IEEE Transactions on Systems, Man, Cybernetics*, *SMC-2*, 380–388.

Palm, G. (1980). On associative memory. *Biological Cybernetics*, *36*, 19–31.

Pessoa, L. F. C., & Maragos, P. (2000). Morphological regularization neural net-works. *Pattern Recognition*, *30*(6), 945–960. Special Issue on Mathematical Morphology and Its Applications.

Raducanu, B., Graña, M., & Albizuri, X. (2003). Morphological scale spaces and associative memories: results on robustness and practical applications. *Journal of Mathematical Imaging and Vision*, Special Issue on Morphological Neural Networks, *19*(2), in press.

Ritter, G. X., & Sussner, P. (1996). An introduction to morphological neural networks. *Proceedings of the 13th International Conference on Pattern Recognition, Vienna, Austria*, 709–717.

Ritter, G. X., Sussner, P., & Diaz-de-Leon, J. L. (1998). Morphological associative memories. *IEEE Transactions on Neural Networks*, *9*(2), 281–292.

Ritter, G. X., Diaz-de-Leon, J. L., & Sussner, P. (1999). Morphological bidirectional associative memories. *Neural Networks*, *12*, 851–867.

Sussner, P. (2000a). Observations on morphological associative memories and the kernel method. *Neurocomputing*, *31*, 167–183.

Sussner, P. (2000b). Fixed points of autoassociative morphological memories. *Proceedings of the International Joint Conference on Neural Networks, Como, Italy*.

Sussner, P. (2003). Generalizing operations of binary morphological autoassociative memories using fuzzy set theory. *Journal of Mathematical Imaging and Vision*, Special Issue on Morphological Neural Networks, *19*(2), in press.

Won, Y., Gader, P. D., & Coffield, P. C. (1997). Morphological shared-weight neural network with applications to automatic target detection. *IEEE Transactions on Neural Networks*, *8*(5), 1195–1203.

Wu, Y., & Pados, D. A. (2000). A feedforward bidirectional associative memory. *IEEE Transactions on Neural Networks*, *11*(4), 859–866.

Wu, Y., & Batalama, S. N. (2000). An efficient learning algorithm for associative memories. *IEEE Transactions on Neural Networks*, *11*(5), 1058–1066.

PERGAMON

AVAILABLE AT
www.ComputerScienceWeb.com
POWERED BY SCIENCE @ DIRECT

Neural Networks 16 (2003) 633–640

Neural Networks

www.elsevier.com/locate/neunet

2003 Special issue

Adaptive double self-organizing maps for clustering gene expression profiles

H. Ressom*, D. Wang, P. Natarajan

Department of Electrical and Computer Engineering, University of Maine, 201 Barrows Hall, Orono, ME 04469-5708, USA

Abstract

This paper introduces a new model of self-organizing map (SOM) known as adaptive double self-organizing map (ADSOM). ADSOM has a flexible topology and performs data partitioning and cluster visualization simultaneously without requiring a priori knowledge about the number of clusters. It combines features of the popular SOM with two-dimensional position vectors, which serve as a visualization tool to detect the number of clusters present in the data. ADSOM updates its free parameters and allows convergence of its position vectors to a fairly consistent number of clusters provided its initial number of nodes is greater than the expected number of clusters. A novel index is introduced based on hierarchical clustering of the final locations of position vectors. The index allows automated detection of the number of clusters, thereby reducing human error that could be incurred from counting clusters visually. To test ADSOM's consistency in data partitioning, we examine the number of common profiles found in the clusters that were obtained by varying the initial number of nodes. This provides a confidence measure for the clusters formed by ADSOM and illustrates the effect of different initial number of nodes on data partitioning. The reliance of ADSOM in identifying number of clusters is demonstrated by applying it to publicly available yeast gene expression data.

Keywords: Self-organizing maps; Clustering; Cluster validation; Tree-based index

1. Introduction

DNA microarray technology offers insights into biological processes. The technology allows scientists, engineers, medical professionals, and others to identify functionally related genes, classify cancerous and healthy tissues, and study signaling pathways and genetic regulatory networks. However, advanced computational tools are needed for extracting useful information from the high dimensional, spatio-temporal, and noisy gene expression data. Such tools help to organize large data sets and make information retrieval more efficient.

Key and early processing steps in the analysis of gene expression data include clustering groups of genes that manifest similar expression profiles. Genes with similar expression profiles might be transcriptionally regulated through the same transduction pathway. Thus, the rationale for clustering gene expression data is to identify a new transduction pathway or novel genes, which may be co-regulated through the same known pathway.

A wide range of techniques have been proposed for clustering gene expression data. Examples include hierarchical clustering (Eisen, Spellman, Brown, & Botstein, 1998), self-organizing map (SOM) (Tamayo et al., 1999), k-means (Tavazoie, Hughes, Campbell, Cho, & Church, 1999), graph-theoretic approaches (Ben-Dor, Shamir, & Yakhini, 1999), fuzzy ART (Tomida, Hanai, Honda & Kobayashi, 2001), fuzzy c-means (Guthke, Schmidt-Heck, Hahn, & Pfaff, 2000), fuzzy Kohonen and growing cell structures network (Granzow et al., 2001). However, most of the above mentioned clustering algorithms are heuristically motivated, and the issues of determining the 'correct' number of clusters and choosing a 'good' clustering algorithm are not yet rigorously solved.

Clustering gene expression data using hierarchical clustering (Eisen et al., 1998) and SOM has been very popular among the bioinformatics research community. Hierarchical clustering organizes the expression profiles in a hierarchical tree structure, which allows detecting higher order relationships between clusters of profiles. Although hierarchical clustering has been proven valuable for describing gene expression (Eisen et al., 1998; Spellman

* Corresponding author.

0893-6080/03/$ - see front matter © 2003 Elsevier Science Ltd. All rights reserved.
doi:10.1016/S0893-6080(03)00102-3

et al., 1998), it has several shortcomings. The hierarchical trees do not reflect the multiple ways in which expression patterns of genes can be similar. The deterministic nature of hierarchical clustering can cause the data points to be clustered on the basis of local decisions, with no opportunity to reevaluate. As the amount of data increases, this problem can be exacerbated. Mangiameli, Chen, and West (1996) compared SOM with hierarchical clustering method and found that SOM is superior in both robustness and accuracy.

The design of SOM starts with defining a geometric configuration for the partitions in a one- or two-dimensional grid. Then, random weight vectors are assigned to each partition. During training, a gene expression profile is picked randomly. The weight vector closest to the expression profile is identified. The identified weight vector and its neighbors are adjusted to look similar to the expression profile. This process is repeated until the weight vectors converge. During operation, SOM maps gene expression profiles to the relevant partitions based on the weight vectors to which they are most similar. However, in circumstances where the expected number of partitions (clusters) available in gene expression data is unknown, the validation of SOM's clustering result becomes a critical issue. One may heuristically validate the clustering results to identify the approximate number of clusters.

Many validation techniques have been implemented to evaluate clustering results. Yeung, Haynor, and Ruzzo (2001b) introduced figure of merit (FOM); Tibshirani, Walther, and Hastie (2000) applied 'gap statistic'; Jain and Dubes (1998) referred to using 'Hubert and Jaccard index'; Hubert and Arabie (1985) suggested the use of an 'adjusted rand index'; Lubovac, Olsson, Jonsson, Laurio, and Andersson (2001) proposed to use an 'entropy measure'. All these algorithms have been proven valuable by some experiments. However, given the large volume and high-dimension of the gene expression data, the use of such heuristic evaluation technique makes the clustering process extremely time-consuming and complicated.

A number of methods have been proposed in the literature to accomplish data partitioning and cluster validation/visualization either simultaneously or independently. Fraley and Raftery (2002) developed model based clustering that provides functionality for displaying/visualizing cluster results. Ramoni, Sebastiani, and Kohane (2002) introduced Bayesian method of model based clustering of gene expression dynamics. Kaski, Nikkilä, and Kohonen (1998), introduced methods for detecting, visualizing and interpreting clusters generated by SOM. They improved the SOM-based method of U-matrix (Ultsch and Siemon, 1990) for visualization of cluster information. Nikkilä et al. (2002) and Kaski (2001) applied this improved method for the analysis and visualization of gene expression data. Herrero and Dopazo (2002) proposed a combination of SOM and hierarchical method for clustering gene expression data.

Su and Chang (2001) developed a new technique known as double self-organizing map (DSOM). In DSOM, each center in the network has an N-dimensional weight vector and a two-dimensional *position vector*. The position vectors are projection of the weight vectors into a two-dimensional space and serve as a visualization tool for deciding how many clusters are needed, thus combining clustering and cluster visualization in one computational procedure. In other words, with the help of position vectors, DSOM adjusts its network structure during the learning phase so that neurons that respond to similar stimuli will not only have similar weight vectors but also move spatially closer to each other.

Although DSOM addresses the issue of detecting number of clusters, the selection of its free parameters, such as learning rates and neighborhood functions for updating the weight vectors as well as corresponding position vectors, is vital for a proper projection of the position vectors in a two-dimensional space. While some combinations of these parameters make all the position vectors converge too quickly into a small dense area, some other lead the updating process to 'get stuck' after several epochs and result in erroneous number of clusters. Thus, the regulation of these parameters is very important. In addition, the visualization results depend on the distributions of position vectors. If the position vectors are not distinct, it is difficult to determine the correct number of clusters by visualization.

In this paper, we propose an adaptive double self-organizing map (ADSOM), which updates the free parameters involved in DSOM during the training process. This is achieved by carefully analyzing the mathematical relationships between the parameters and the updating processes. This new approach improves the performance of DSOM. Unlike DSOM, ADSOM gives fairly consistent number of clusters provided the initial number of nodes is greater than the expected number of clusters. Furthermore, a novel validation technique, tree-based index is introduced to identify the number of clusters from the final locations of position vectors.

2. Adaptive double self-organizing map algorithm

ADSOM offers a systematic method of adapting its free parameters, in addition to updating its weights and two-dimensional position vectors, during the training process. The free parameters include learning rates, neighborhood functions, and the exponential decaying rates of neighborhood definitions. The proposed approach provides improved convergence compared to DSOM (Su and Chang, 2001), which intends to move the two-dimensional position vectors towards each other if their corresponding N-dimensional weight vectors are close to each other. For example, let there be two nodes with weight vectors $\mathbf{w}_1$ and $\mathbf{w}_2$ and position vectors $\mathbf{p}_1$ and $\mathbf{p}_2$, respectively. Assuming $\mathbf{p}_w(k)$ is the position vector of the winning neuron, $\mathbf{w}_w(k)$, when the kth input vector $\mathbf{x}(k)$ is applied, if $\mathbf{w}_1(k)$ is closer to $\mathbf{x}(k)$ than $\mathbf{w}_2(k)$, which means $\|\mathbf{w}_1(k) - \mathbf{x}(k)\|$ is less than $\|\mathbf{w}_2(k) - \mathbf{x}(k)\|$, one requires that $\mathbf{p}_1(k)$ moves toward $\mathbf{p}_w(k)$ faster than $\mathbf{p}_2(k)$. DSOM does not take this requirement into account during training. As a result, its position vectors sometimes converge to erroneous number of clusters. The proposed ADSOM alleviates this problem by adapting the free parameters to control the movements of the position vectors. In the following, we describe the ADSOM algorithm.

Let $\mathbf{w}_j$ be the N-dimensional synaptic weight vector of node j; $\mathbf{p}_j$ be a two-dimensional position vector corresponding to node j; $\mathbf{p}_w(k)$ and $\mathbf{w}_w(k)$ represent the position and weight vectors of the winning neuron when the kth input vector $\mathbf{x}(k)$ is applied, respectively. Defining

$$\alpha(k) = \max_j \{\|\mathbf{p}_j(k) - \mathbf{p}_j(k-1)\|\}$$

$$A_j(k) = \|\mathbf{w}_j(k) - \mathbf{x}(k)\| - \|\mathbf{w}_w(k) - \mathbf{x}(k)\|$$

$$B_j(k) = \|\mathbf{p}_j(k) - \mathbf{p}_w(k)\|$$

$$t_j(k) = \max_i \left\{ \frac{B_i^m(k) - B_j^m(k)}{A_j^n(k) - A_i^n(k)} \right\}, \quad \forall i, j, \ (j \neq i)$$

with $\alpha(k)$ representing the maximum change of position vectors at epoch k and $t_j(k)$ specifying the ratio $s_x(k)$ to $s_p(k)$ in a given boundary, the weight and position vectors are updated for $j = 1, 2, \ldots, N$ as follows:

$$\mathbf{w}_j(k+1) = \mathbf{w}_j(k) + \eta_1(k)\Lambda_w(k,j)[x(k) - \mathbf{w}_j(k)] \qquad (1)$$

$$\mathbf{p}_j(k+1) = \mathbf{p}_j(k) + \eta_2(k,j)h_w(k,j)[\mathbf{p}_w(k) - \mathbf{p}_j(k)] \qquad (2)$$

where

$$\eta_1(k) = \eta_w \frac{1}{k+1} \qquad (3)$$

$$\Lambda_w(k,j) = \exp\left[-s_w\left(1 + \frac{k}{k_{max}}\right)B_j^2(k)\right] \qquad (4)$$

$$\eta_2(k,j) = \frac{\eta_p}{1+k}\exp\left[-s_p(k)\left(1 + \frac{k}{k_{max}}\right)B_j^m(k)\right] \qquad (5)$$

$$h_w(k,j) = \exp\left\{-s_x(k)\left(1 + \frac{k}{k_{max}}\right)A_j^n(k)\right\} \qquad (6)$$

$$s_p(k+1) = \begin{cases} s_p(k)f\left(\dfrac{\alpha(k)}{\alpha(k-1)} - 1\right) & \text{if } k \geq 2 \\ s_p(k) = \text{constant} > 0 & \text{if } k = 1 \end{cases} \qquad (7)$$

$$\frac{s_x(k)}{s_p(k)} = \begin{cases} \text{unchanged}, & \text{if } \max_j \{t_j(k)\} \leq 0 \\ 1.2\max_j \{t_j(k)\}, & \text{if } \max_j \{t_j(k)\} > 0 \end{cases} \qquad (8)$$

where η_w and η_p are the initial learning rates; s_w is a scalar parameter which regulates how fast the function $\Lambda_w(k,j)$ changes; k_{max} is the maximum number of epochs; $s_p(k)$ and $s_x(k)$ are the values of scalar parameters at epoch k that regulate the speed of the movement of the position vectors; m and n are positive numbers, where $n > m$ (for example, one may choose $n = 2$ and $m = 0.5$); $f(\cdot)$ is a function, which is applied to scale s_p based on the value of α. Assuming y is the argument of $f(\cdot)$, we suggest that $f(y)$ be chosen to satisfy three requirements: (i) For $y \in (-1, +\infty)$, $f(y) \in (0, C)$ where C is a positive constant; (ii) $f(y)$ is a continuous, increasing, and non-linear function; and (iii) $f(0) = 1$. In fact, there are many functions, which have all the properties mentioned above. In this paper, $f(\cdot)$ is chosen to have the form:

$$f(y) = \frac{e}{e-1}(1 - e^{-(y+1)}).$$

Eqs. (1)–(8) are repeated until α is steadily less than a pre-specified threshold β. In our experiments, we defined β as 0.1% of largest distance among all the original position vectors. Moreover, the weight initialization scheme provided by Su, Liu, and Chang (1999) is used to choose the initial weight vectors.

3. Tree-based index for identification of number of clusters from position vectors

Once the final locations of the position vectors are obtained, one can visually determine the number of clusters. To minimize possible human error resulting from counting the number of clusters visually, we developed a novel technique that provides an index for each cluster. The index is calculated based on the outcome of clustering the position vectors using hierarchical method. Consider a $2 \times N$ matrix $\mathbf{T}$ that contains the final locations of all two-dimensional position vectors; where N denotes the total number of position vectors. We calculate the Euclidean distances between each pair of position vectors in T. Based on these distances and subsequent distances between merged clusters, we create a hierarchical cluster tree that grows vertically upwards. During clustering, we store the single linkage distance between two clusters that are merged together through a branch. Hence, the height of each branch corresponds to the distance assigned to it. Consider a horizontal line that cuts c branches of the hierarchical cluster tree perpendicularly, the horizontal line picks c clusters that are embraced by the branches it cuts. An index corresponding to this horizontal line is designated as $\gamma(c)$ and is defined as the sum of the heights of each branch it cuts:

$$\gamma(c) = \sum_{i=1}^{c} z_c(i) \quad c = 2, \ldots N$$

where $z_c(i)$ is the height contributed by the ith branch for the case when a horizontal branch cuts c branches of the tree. The index, referred to as tree-based index, is calculated for $c = 2, \ldots, N$. Note that $\gamma(1) = 0$, since there will be no horizontal line that would cut the tree only once. The value of c at which the index reaches its highest peak is considered as an indicator of the maximum separation between clusters

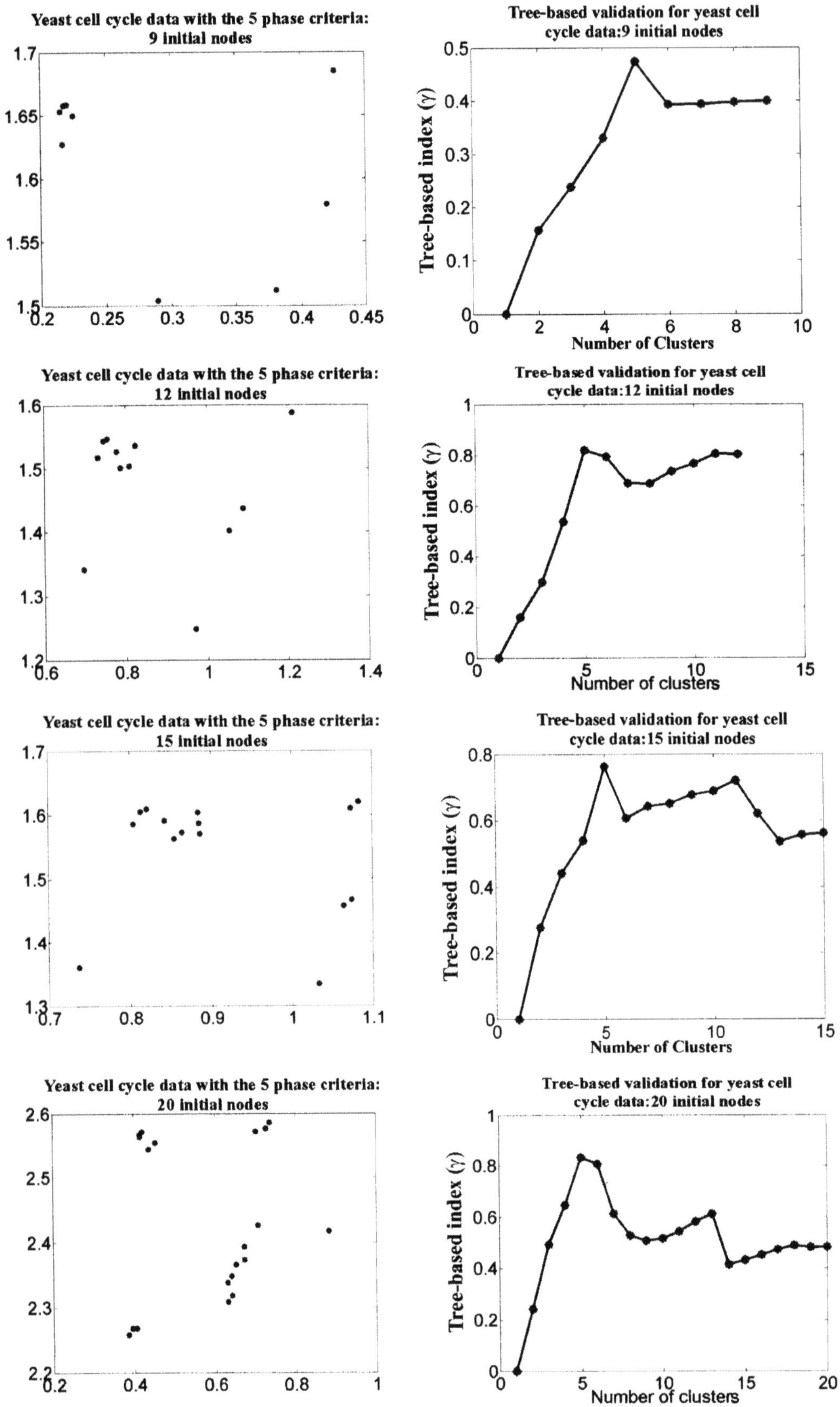

Fig. 1. Final position vectors (left) after using ADSOM to cluster yeast cell cycle data with initial nodes 9, 12, 15 and 20 and the corresponding tree-based validation results (right).

in a two-dimensional space. Hence, it is used as a means to detect the number of clusters.

4. Experimental tests and results

Experimental tests were conducted using publicly available gene expression data. The purpose of the experiments is to employ ADSOM for automated detection of number of cluster numbers. Gene expression data with known and unknown number of clusters are used for this experiment. In the case of known number of clusters, ADSOM's performance in identifying the correct number of clusters is tested. To demonstrate ADSOM's consistency in data partitioning, we counted the number of common profiles found in the clusters that were obtained when the initial number of nodes is varied. The percentage of common profiles provides a confidence measure for the clusters formed by ADSOM and illustrates the effect of different initial number of nodes on data partitioning.

4.1. Yeast cell cycle data with the 5 phase criterion

We used a subset of the gene expression data provided by Cho et al., 1998 that shows the fluctuation of expression levels of approximately 6000 genes over two cell cycles corresponding to (17 time points) mitotic cell cycle of *Saccharomyces cerevisiae* from affymetrix chip.

As in Yeung, Fraley, Murua, Raftery, and Ruzzo (2001a), a subset of 384 genes whose expression levels peak at different time points corresponding to the five phases of cell cycle was used for our experiments. These data were obtained from supplementary web site provided by Yeung et al. (2001a).

Before clustering, the data were normalized to have zero mean and unit variance. ADSOM was applied to cluster this data set with different number of initial weights such as 9, 12, 15 and 20. As depicted in Fig. 1, the final locations of position vectors converge into fewer groups in a two-dimensional space regardless of the initial number of nodes.

We applied the tree-based validation index to estimate the optimal number of clusters from the final locations of the position vectors. As described before, the number of clusters at which the tree-based index reaches its highest peak can be used as an indicator of optimal number of clusters. The results in Fig. 1 indicated that the optimal number of clusters is five regardless of different number of initial nodes. This result agrees with that of Yeung et al. (2001a) and was as expected from a data set corresponding to five phases of the yeast cell cycle.

To test ADSOM's consistency in data partitioning, the number of common genes shared among different clusters formed by varying initial number of nodes is examined. Table 1 shows the number of genes in each cluster as well as the number of common genes found when clustering the yeast cell cycle data with different number of initial nodes (N), i.e. $N = 9$, 12, 15 and 20. The percentage of common genes between clusters formed by $N = 9$ and 12 was 88%, $N = 9$, 12 and 15 was 79.7%; and $N = 9$, 12, 15 and 20 was 70.8%.

4.2. Yeast sporulation data

Gene expression data in the budding yeast *Saccharomyces cerevisiae* from spotted c-DNA microarrays studied during the diauxic shift, the mitotic cell division cycle, sporulation, and temperature and reducing shocks (http://genome-www.stanford.edu/clustering) were considered. In particular, the data corresponding to sporulation were used for this experiment. From the yeast sporulation data, we extracted 218 × 11 gene expression profiles that belong to four classes. Variance normalization was applied to the data. The four classes are ribosomal proteins, respiration, mitochondrial organization, and tricarboxylic-acid pathway. This functional classification was made using information from Munich Information Center for Protein Sequences (MIPS) (Mewes, Albermann, Heumann, Liebl, & Pfeiffer, 1997). ADSOM clustered this yeast data into its four distinct classes without having the knowledge of the actual number of clusters. The beauty of ADSOM algorithm is that it would converge to the actual number of clusters without having to go through tedious cluster validation techniques. To demonstrate this, two experiments were conducted with this data set; once ADSOM was assigned nine initial nodes and once 20 nodes. ADSOM's position vectors that were assigned to these initial nodes converged to four final clusters regardless of the initial number of nodes chosen. Note that the nodes were arranged in the form of a grid prior to training.

Fig. 2 shows the location of final position vectors for initial nodes (a), for 20 initial nodes (b) and the results obtained after applying the tree-based validation index (c). Note that these final four groups that represent the actual and true number of clusters in the data are shown by enclosed boundaries. It also shows which of the initial nine or 20 nodes had to be grouped together in order to make the final four clusters. As can be seen from the Fig. 2,

Table 1
Number of genes as well as number of common genes for yeast cell cycle data using ADSOM with 9, 12, 15 and 20 initial nodes; N, number of initial nodes

Cluster no.	I	II	III	IV	V
No. of genes for $N = 9$	43	89	77	107	68
No. of genes for $N = 12$	38	100	71	100	75
No. of genes for $N = 15$	40	89	73	116	66
No. of genes for $N = 20$	35	93	70	110	76
No. of common genes for $N = 9$ and 12	29	81	71	92	65
No. of common genes for $N = 9$, 12 and 15	28	66	73	83	61
No. of common genes for $N = 9$, 12, 15 and 20	24	55	70	76	53

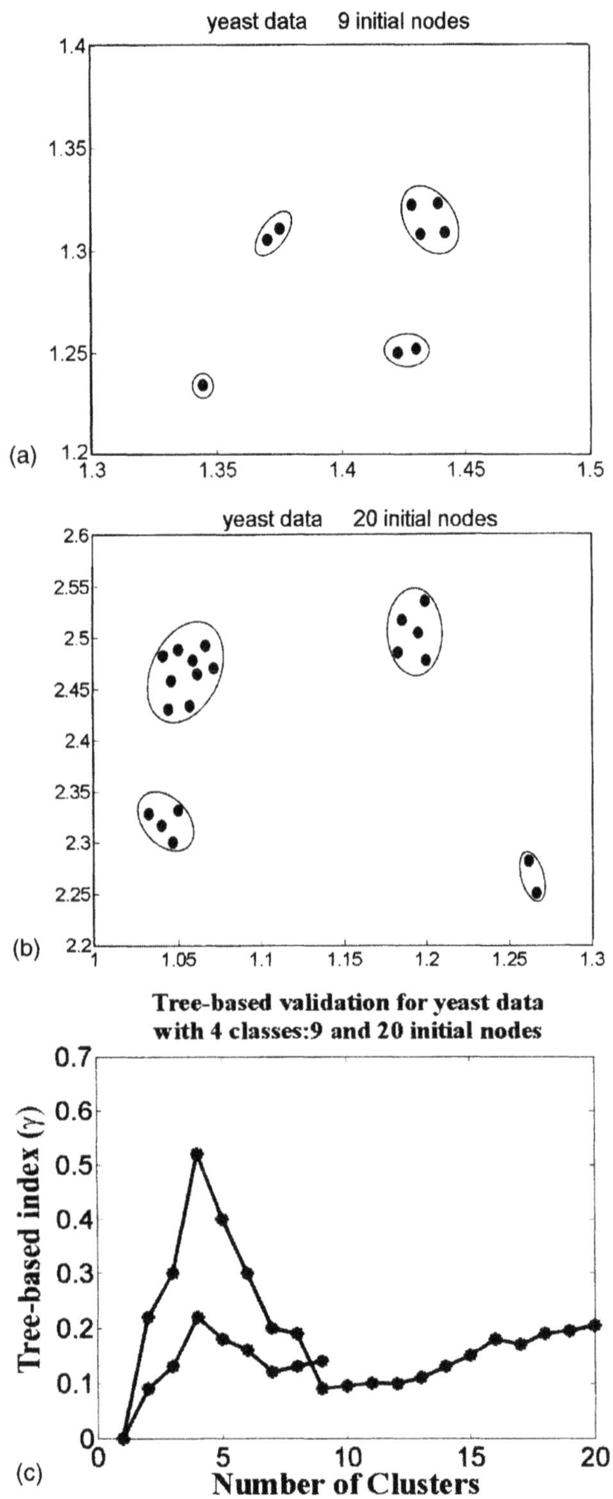

Fig. 2. Final position vectors with initial nodes 9 (a), 20 (b) and tree-based validation results (c) using ADSOM for yeast sporulation data with four classes.

the optimal number of clusters is four regardless of the number of initial nodes (nine and 20).

It was observed that ADSOM resulted in partitioning the data with 70% accuracy. This accuracy was calculated based on the biological classification made by MIPS. In gene expression data, one does not normally have a priori knowledge about the true number of classes, and what distinguishes ADSOM from the currently available techniques is that one doesn't need to have this knowledge to be able to find the true number of classes accurately.

Table 2
Number of genes and common genes for yeast sporulation data using ADSOM with 9 and 20 initial nodes. N, number of initial nodes

Cluster no.	I	II	III	IV
No. of genes for $N = 9$	60	28	19	111
No. of genes for $N = 20$	55	25	21	117
No. of common genes for $N = 9$ and 20	46	24	16	111

To evaluate the consistency of the clustering, the number of common genes in two clusters for different number of initial nodes was investigated. Table 2 illustrates the number of genes obtained in the four clusters formed by ADSOM and the number of common genes between the cluster pair formed with nine and 20 initial number of nodes, respectively. The robustness and consistency of ADSOM in clustering is evident from the large number of common genes (90.4%) in the clusters as shown in the table.

In a separate experiment, the performance of ADSOM for different cluster sizes was investigated. To accomplish this, yeast sporulation data from 2, 3 and 4 MIPS classes were extracted and clustered independently. As shown in Fig. 3, the number of clusters was correctly identified by ADSOM using nine initial nodes.

4.3. Yeast cdc15 and elu

The spotted c-DNA microarray data used for this experiment were those corresponding to cdc15 and elu (http://genome-www.stanford.edu/clustering); cdc15 data consisted of 15 time points following arrest of cdc15 temperature sensitive mutant and elu data contained 14 time points following elutriation. After removing genes

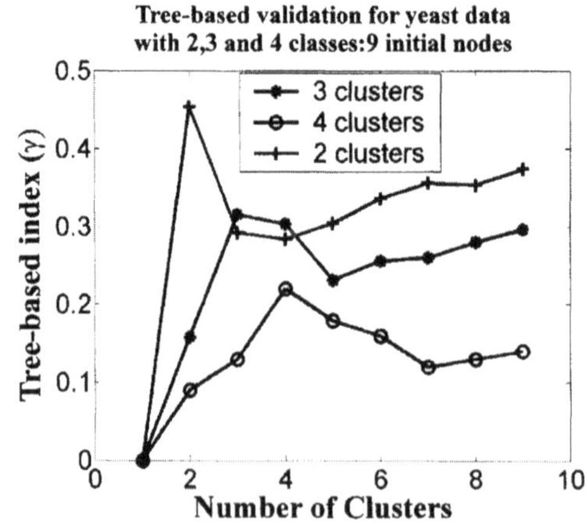

Fig. 3. Tree-based validation results for yeast sporulation data.

Table 3
Number of clusters obtained using ADSOM. N, number of initial nodes

	Yeast cdc 15	Yeast elu
Size of data	1882 × 15	2020 × 14
No. of clusters for $N = 25$	16	16
No. of clusters for $N = 30$	16	16
No. of clusters for $N = 36$	17	16
No. of clusters for $N = 42$	17	17
Average no. of clusters	16.5	16.25

with missing points, there were 1882 genes in cdc15 data and 2020 genes in elu data. Before applying ADSOM, variance normalization was applied to the data. ADSOM was used to cluster each data set with different number of initial weights such as 25, 30, 36 and 42. The tree-based indices corresponding to the final locations of the position vectors were used to identify the number of clusters in both data sets. ADSOM gave fairly consistent number of clusters in the unknown yeast data set, thus demonstrating its effectiveness and reliability. As it can be seen from Table 3, the result of this experiment shows that there are 16 or 17 clusters available in both data sets.

5. Conclusion

In this paper a new model of SOM called ADSOM is presented. It is shown that ADSOM performs clustering and cluster visualization simultaneously without requiring a priori knowledge about the number of clusters.

The reliance of ADSOM in accurately detecting number of clusters is demonstrated by applying it to cluster publicly available yeast gene expression data. The experimental results prove that ADSOM gives a fairly consistent final topology regardless of the initial topology as long as the initial number of nodes is greater than the expected number of clusters. This topological flexibility of ADSOM enables it to provide credible information about the number of clusters present in the data. ADSOM accomplishes this via its position vectors, which serve as a visualization tool for identifying the number of clusters present. In combination with hierarchical clustering, a tree-based index is introduced that allows automated detection of number of clusters, thereby reducing human error that could be incurred from counting clusters visually.

By examining the number of common profiles found in clusters obtained from different initial topologies, ADSOM's consistency in data partitioning is verified. The outcome of this analysis provides a confidence measure for the clusters formed and illustrates the effect of different initial number of nodes on data partitioning.

In summary, ADSOM offers two main advantages. First, it converges to a consistent number of groups regardless of the initial number of nodes. Second, it visually presents the clusters together with corresponding indices for cluster validation while partitioning the data. Hence, ADSOM eliminates the trial-and-error process as well as the heuristic validating process in clustering gene expression data, thus saving significant computational time.

References

Ben-Dor, A., Shamir, R., & Yakhini, Z. (1999). Clustering gene expression patterns. *Journal of Computational Biology*, *6*, 281–297.

Cho, R. J., Campbell, M. J., Winzeler, E. A., Steinmetz, L., Con-way, A., Wodicka, L., Wolfsberg, T. G., Gabrielian, A. E., Landsman, D., Lockhart, D. J., & Davis, R. W. (1998). A genome-wide transcriptional analysis of the mitotic cell cycle. *Molecular Cell*, *2*, 65–73.

Eisen, M. B., Spellman, P. T., Brown, P. O., & Botstein, D. (1998). Cluster analysis and display of genome-wide expression patterns. *Proceedings of the National Academy of Sciences of the United States of America*, *95*, 14863–14868.

Fraley, C., & Raftery, A. E. (2002). Model-based clustering, discriminant analysis, and density estimation. *Journal of the American Statistical Association*, *97*, 611–631.

Granzow, M., Berrar, D., Dubitzky, W., Shuster, A., Azuaje, F. J., & Eils, R. (2001). Tumor classification by gene expression profiling: comparison and validation of five clustering methods (21). *SIGBIO Special Interest Group on Biomedical Computing of the ACM*, New York: ACM Press, pp. 16–22.

Guthke, R., Schmidt-Heck, W., Hahn, D., & Pfaff, M. (2000). Gene expression data mining for functional genomics. *Proceedings of European Symposium on Intelligent Techniques (ESIT 2000), Aachen, Germany* (pp. 170–177).

Herrero, J., & Dopazo, J. (2002). Combining hierarchical clustering and self-organizing maps for exploratory analysis of gene expression patterns. *Journal of Proteome Research*, *1*, 467–470.

Hubert, L., & Arabie, P. (1985). Comparing partitions. *Journal of Classification*, *2*, 193–218.

Jain, A. K., & Dubes, R. C. (1998). *Algorithms for clustering data*. Englewood Cliffs, NJ: Prentice Hall.

Kaski, S. (2001). SOM-based exploratory analysis of gene expression data. In N. Allinson, H. Yin, L. Allinson, & J. Slack (Eds.), *Advances in self-organizing maps* (pp. 124–131). London: Springer.

Kaski, S., Nikkilä, J., & Kohonen, T. (1998). Methods for interpreting a self-organized map in data analysis. In M. Verleysen (Ed.), *Proceedings of ESANN'98, Sixth European Symposium on Artificial Neural Networks, Bruges* (pp. 185–190).

Lubovac, Z., Olsson, B., Jonsson, P., Laurio, K., & Andersson, M. L. (2001). Biological and statistical evaluation of gene expression profiles. In C. E. D'Attellis, V. V. Kluev, & N. E. Mastorakis (Eds.), *Proceedings of Mathematics and Computers in Biology and Chemistry* (pp. 149–155). WSES Press.

Mangiameli, P., Chen, S. K., & West, D. (1996). A comparison of SOM neural network and hierarchical clustering methods. *European Journal of Operational Research*, *93*, 402–417.

Mewes, H. W., Albermann, K., Heumann, K., Liebl, S., & Pfeiffer, F. (1997). MIPS: A database for protein sequences, homology data and yeast genome information. *Nucleic Acid Research*, *25*, 28–30.

Nikkilä, J., Törönen, P., Kaski, S., Venna, J., Castrén, E., & Wong, G. (2002). Analysis and visualization of gene expression data using self-organizing maps. *Neural Networks, Special Issue on New Developments on Self-Organizing Maps*, *15*, 953–966.

Ramoni, M., Sebastiani, P., & Kohane, L. (2002). Cluster analysis of gene expression dynamics. *Proceedings of the National Academy of Sciences of the United States of America*, *99*, 9121–9126.

Spellman, P. T., Sherlock, G., Zhang, M. Q., Iyer, V. R., Anders, K., Eisen, M. B., Brown, P. O., Botstein, D., & Futcher, B. (1998). Comprehensive identification of cell cycle-regulated genes of the yeast *Saccharomyces cerevisiae* by microarray hybridization. *Molecular Biology of the Cell*, *9*, 3273–3297.

Su, M., & Chang, H. (2001). A new model of self-organizing neural networks and its application in data projection. *IEEE Transactions on Neural Networks*, *12*, 153–158.

Su, M., Liu, T., & Chang, H. (1999). An efficient initialization scheme for the self-organizing feature map algorithm. *Proceedings of International Joint Conference on Neural Networks*, *3*, 1906–1910.

Tamayo, P., Slonim, D., Mesirov, J., Zhu, Q., Kitareewan, S., Dmitrovsky, E., Lander, E. S., & Golub, T. R. (1999). Interpreting patterns of gene expression with self-organizing maps: Methods and application to hematopoietic differentiation. *Proceedings of the National Academy of Sciences of the United States of America*, *96*, 2907–2912.

Tavazoie, S., Hughes, J. D., Campbell, M. J., Cho, R. J., & Church, G. M. (1999). Systematic determination of genetic network architecture. *Nature Genetics*, *22*, 281–285.

Tibshirani, R., Walther, G., Hastie, T (2000). *Estimating the number of clusters in a dataset via the gap statistic*. Technical Report 208, Department of Statistics, Stanford University

Tomida, S., Hanai, T., Honda, H., & Kobayashi, T. (2001). Gene expression analysis using fuzzy ART. *Genome Informatics*, *12*, 245–246.

Ultsch, A., & Siemon, H. (1990). Kohonen's self organizing maps for exploratory data analysis. *Proceedings of International Neural Network Conference (INNC'90)*, 305–308.

Yeung, K. Y., Fraley, C., Murua, A., Raftery, A. E., & Ruzzo, W. L. (2001a). Model-based clustering and data transformations for gene expression data. *Bioinformatics*, *17*, 977–987.

Yeung, K. Y., Haynor, D. R., & Ruzzo, W. L. (2001b). Validating clustering for gene expression data. *Bioinformatics*, *17*, 309–318.

AVAILABLE AT
www.ComputerScienceWeb.com
POWERED BY SCIENCE DIRECT

PERGAMON

Neural Networks 16 (2003) 641–648

Neural Networks

www.elsevier.com/locate/neunet

2003 Special issue

An accelerated procedure for recursive feature ranking on microarray data

C. Furlanello*, M. Serafini, S. Merler, G. Jurman

ITC-irst, v. Sommarive 18, Povo, I-38050 Trento, Italy

Abstract

We describe a new wrapper algorithm for fast feature ranking in classification problems. The Entropy-based Recursive Feature Elimination (E-RFE) method eliminates chunks of uninteresting features according to the entropy of the weights distribution of a SVM classifier. With specific regard to DNA microarray datasets, the method is designed to support computationally intensive model selection in classification problems in which the number of features is much larger than the number of samples. We test E-RFE on synthetic and real data sets, comparing it with other SVM-based methods. The speed-up obtained with E-RFE supports predictive modeling on high dimensional microarray data.

Keywords: Entropy-based recursive feature elimination; Microarray; Support Vector Machines

1. Introduction

For microarray data, class prediction generally refers to models of response to treatment with existing or new therapies, or to the detection of disease type or subtype (Chung, Bernard, & Perou, 2002; Slonim, 2002). Significant benefits to patients are expected from these efforts to develop new diagnostic tools as well as from the elucidation of disease functional mechanisms at the molecular level. Microarrays, however, offer unusual challenges to machine learning algorithms, as gene expression data matrices measure thousands of genes (features) at tens or hundreds of samples. Ranking genes according to their importance in contributing to models' predictive accuracy is thus crucial not only as a machine learning problem, but also in the perspective of application.

Support Vector Machines (SVMs) are considered a performing classification method for gene-expression data and were soon embedded with feature selection procedures (Cristianini & Shawe-Taylor, 2000; Guyon, Weston, Barnhill, & Vapnik, 2002; Li, Campbell, & Tipping, 2002; Nguyen & Rocke, 2002; Weston et al., 2000; Xiong, Fang, & Zhao, 2001; Zhang & Wong, 2001).

The procedure we discuss in this paper was motivated by a subtle methodological problem that has emerged in this field, resulting in initial studies on microarray data which reported of very few genes discovered to yield classification models with negligible or zero error rates. As discussed in Ambroise and McLachlan, 2002 and confirmed by our study (Furlanello, Serafini, Merler, & Jurman, 2002), the feature-selection process has to be separated from the performance assessment, otherwise uncorrected estimates of the prediction error are obtained (the selection bias problem). Careful experimental Scheme are thus required by the gene ranking and selection procedures when they depend on the optimization of a classification rule. The process of the evaluation of error for models developed on a reduced number of interesting genes should operate out-of-sample from the data involved in the selection process (Spang et al., 2001). The two processes also need to be intensively based on partition or resampling methods to smooth data variability. As a crucial consequence, the model selection processes (including feature selection) require an intensive replication of the classification-and-ranking steps.

The entropy-based recursive feature elimination (E-RFE) procedure we analyse in this paper was especially designed to provide an accelerated feature ranking process for the predictive modeling analysis in microarray data experiments.

In this paper we discuss the feature selection properties of E-RFE. We also consider the speed-up of E-RFE with respect to the base method (RFE, described in Guyon et al., 2002) and the parametric accelerated variant SQRT-RFE. Furthermore, on the basis of the experiments carried out in Guyon et al., 2002, we also show on synthetic data sets that

* Corresponding author. Tel.: +39-461-314592; fax: +39-461-302040.
E-mail addresses: furlan@itc.it (C. Furlanello), mserafini@itc.it (M. Serafini), merler@itc.it (S. Merler), jurman@itc.it (G. Jurman).

0893-6080/03/$ - see front matter
doi:10.1016/S0893-6080(03)00103-5

the well known 1-RFE method might fail on certain weights distributions. Finally, we demonstrate the method on three real public domain gene expression data sets: Colon cancer (Alon et al., 1999), Lymphoma (Alizadeh et al., 2000), and the more recent Tumour vs. Metastases (Ramaswamy, Ross, Lander, & Golub, 2003; Ramaswamy et al., 2001). Accuracy and computational costs of E-RFE and of the base methods are discussed and compared.

2. Methods

2.1. Details of the E-RFE technique

In this section we define and motivate the E-RFE procedure. First we describe the original Recursive Feature Elimination (RFE) procedure for SVMs (Guyon et al., 2002), a ranking method applied in several gene-expression studies (Ramaswamy et al., 2001). In brief, a SVM realizes a classification function $f(\mathbf{x}) = \sum_{i=1}^{N} \alpha_i y_i K(\mathbf{x}_i, \mathbf{x}) + b$, where the coefficients $\boldsymbol{\alpha} = (\alpha_i)$ and b are obtained by training over a set of examples $S = \{(\mathbf{x}_i, y_i)\}_{i=1,\dots,N}$, $\mathbf{x}_i \in \mathbb{R}^n$, $y_i \in \{-1, 1\}$. In the linear case, the SVM expansion defines the hyperplane $f(\mathbf{x}) = \langle \mathbf{w}, \mathbf{x} \rangle + b$, with $\mathbf{w} = \sum_{i=1}^{N} \alpha_i y_i \mathbf{x}_i$. The idea is to define the importance of a feature for a SVM in terms of its contribution to a cost function $J(\alpha)$. At each step of the RFE procedure, a SVM is trained on the given data set, J is computed and the feature less contributing to J is discarded. In the case of linear SVM, the variation due to the elimination of the ith feature is $\delta J(i) = w_i^2$; in the non-linear case, $\delta J(i) = \frac{1}{2}\boldsymbol{\alpha}' Z \boldsymbol{\alpha} - \frac{1}{2}\boldsymbol{\alpha}' Z(-i)\boldsymbol{\alpha}$, where $Z_{ij} = y_i y_j K(\mathbf{x}_i, \mathbf{x}_j)$.

A ranked list of features is thus obtained, from which the most convenient subset of features may be selected according to predictive accuracy or to other practical criteria.

Note that the SVM model must be retrained again after each elimination, because the importance of a feature of medium–low importance may be promoted by removing a correlated feature. The computational cost of RFE is thus a function of the number of variables (more than 16,000 in one of the data sets considered below). The problem is that the whole RFE process may have to be repeated many times for each stage of the experimental schema. For example, the schema may require a double cross-validation or bootstrap resampling process in order to realize the selection of the optimal model parameters (type or width of SVM kernel) and of the subset of interesting genes (Ambroise & McLachlan, 2002; Furlanello et al., 2002).

In the first loops of the RFE algorithm many weights are generally similar and concentrated nearby zero (see subplot S_3 in Fig. 1). Thus the removal of a chunk of features

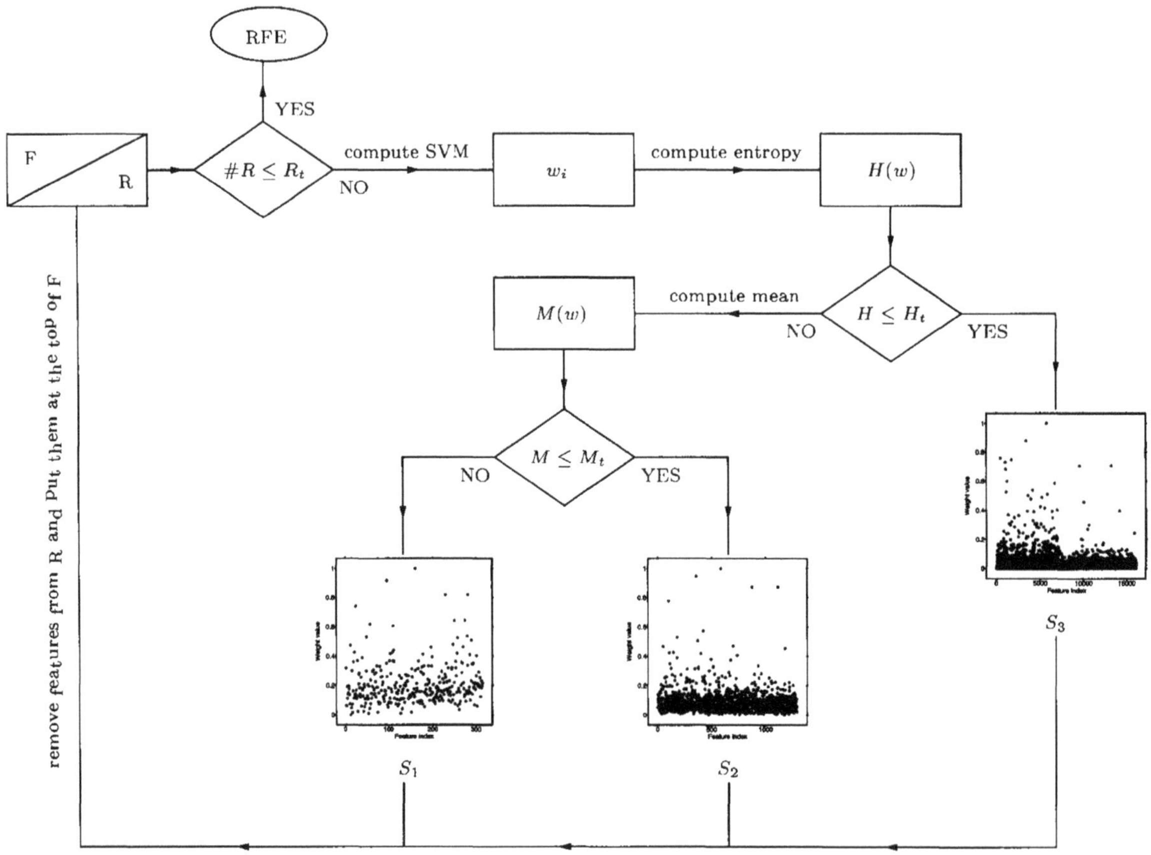

Fig. 1. The E-RFE flowchart. The included subplots S_1–S_3 illustrate three prototype cases of SVM weights distributions (tumor vs. metastases data set).

corresponding to minimum weights may reduce significantly the number of steps, an alternative also indicated in Guyon et al., 2002. However, parametric approaches such as removing $\sqrt{\#R}$ of the $\#R$ remaining features (SQRT-RFE) operate regardless of the specific classification problem: typically they are too slow at the beginning (with many uninteresting genes) and too fast in the final part of the procedure, where each of the remaining genes is potentially important. Another possible choice is sorting of weights without SVM retraining (1-RFE): this non-recursive method does not take into account the possible existing correlation between the features which might change the weight values in the recursive procedures, as shown in Section 3.

The observation of different prototype structures as those of the three subplots in Fig. 1 suggested an ad hoc strategy for an elimination process based on the structure of the weights distribution. Consider the *entropy* function H as a measure of the weights distribution. First we split the range of the weights into n_{int} intervals (with $n_{\text{int}} = \sqrt{n}$), computing for each interval the relative frequencies

$$p_i = \frac{\#(w_i)^2}{\#R}, \qquad i = 1, \dots, n_{\text{int}},$$

with R set of feature indices. Entropy is then defined as:

$$H = -\sum_{i=1}^{n_{\text{int}}} p_i \log_2 p_i.$$

The definition of entropy implies the inequality:

$$0 \le H \le \log_2 n_{\text{int}},$$

whose bounds correspond to the two configurations:

- $H = 0$: one interval contains all the weights;
- $H = \log_2 n_{\text{int}}$: all the intervals contain the same number of weights.

The goal of the E-RFE algorithm is the elimination of chunks of genes at every loop. A scheme of E-RFE is displayed in Fig. 1. A complete description of algorithm is detailed in Appendix A. Elimination is operated according to different internal sub-procedures: the distinction is needed to remove chunks of genes that have a similar (low) weight, preserving the residual distribution structure and allowing for differences between classification problems. Let $\{\text{pw}_i\}_{i\in R}$ be the *projected weights*, i.e. the weights linearly projected in the interval [0,1]; let H be their entropy and H_t a threshold to discriminate between distributions. We set $H_t = \frac{1}{2}\log_2 n_{\text{int}}$ to equally split the entropy range.

When $H > H_t$, the weights are less concentrated than for low entropy configurations: nevertheless, in some cases, many of them may still have approximately the same low value. It is thus necessary to introduce a further discriminating measure. Let M be the mean of the projected weights and M_t a suitable threshold for such a measure. This threshold must be chosen to decide which projected weights should be eliminated: in fact, the situations where $M \le M_t$ are precisely those when many features should be discarded. We use $M_t = 0.2$ according to an empirical fine-tuning with synthetic and real microarray data.

When $H > H_t$ and $M > M_t$, the features whose weight is in the interval $[0, 1/n_{\text{int}}]$ are discarded. In the remaining cases ($H > H_t$ and $M \le M_t$, or $H \le H_t$), we discard the features whose weight is in the leftmost chunk through a bisection procedure. The stopping condition is that no more than half of the features with weights in $[0, \frac{1}{2}M]$ should be discarded. We take a conservative approach by reverting to standard RFE when the number of variables has been reduced below a threshold value R_t, which has to be chosen as a suitable compromise between the computational cost and the estimated size of supposed optimal features subset. For the three microarray data sets, $R_t = 100$ was used, while it was reduced down to $R_t = 5$ for the synthetic data sets.

2.2. Methodology's scheme guidelines

The complete experimental setup we used to evaluate the classification accuracy and provide a feature subset selection mechanism is described in details in Furlanello et al., 2002. It may be summarized as an external stratified partition resampling scheme coupled to an internal K-fold cross-validation, to be applied to E-RFE or to other feature ranking methods at each run. The method is composed by three main procedures:

- *OFS-M*: given a training set TR, a feature ranking method produces a list of ranked features RF, from which an optimal feature set OFS of size n^* is selected. Based on OFS, a model M is developed by a suitable learning method. The optimal number of features n^* is computed by the ONF procedure, while the accuracy of OFS-M is to be validated by the VAL procedure.
- *ONF*: given a training set TR, this procedure is applied to select the optimal number of features based on a ranking method. A resampling procedure is iterated K times, each time producing a $(\text{TR}_k, \text{TS}_k)$ split of TR. A feature ranking method is applied to TR_k producing a ranked list RF_k; a family (M_{ki}, F_{ki}) of models M_{ki} is produced, one for each increasing F_{ki} feature subsets. The M_{ki} models are evaluated on the TS_k test data, computing test errors TE_{ki}, and the average error curve $\text{TE}_i = \frac{1}{K}\sum_{k=1}^{K}\text{TE}_{ki}$ is obtained. An exponential fit procedure is applied, and the n^* value leading to saturation in terms of the exponential curve is returned as the ONF result.
- *VAL*: the OFS-M procedure is validated over B replicated experiments (runs) using a resampling scheme. The model with n^* features is operated on the test set, in order to minimize risk of data overfitting, obtaining a TE^b error. The procedure returns the expected test error $ATE = \frac{1}{B}\sum_{b=1}^{B}\text{TE}^b$ and a resulting feature ranking score

RF given as the multiplicity of the variables in the B replicates.

The first step is to build the (SVM) model through the OFS-M procedure on the whole dataset. As a resampling scheme for the ONF procedure, for compatibility with class cardinalities in the microarray data sets, we use a three-fold cross-validation and we obtain the optimal feature set for the data set. The remaining steps deal with the validation of the above model, the key methodological issue. We set up $B = 50$ experiments according to the following guidelines:

- the resampling scheme used in the VAL procedure consists in splitting the dataset into training and test set with proportion 3/4–1/4; class priors are preserved within the split.
- the resampling procedure used in ONF is a three-fold cross-validation; class priors are preserved within the folds.
- the curve representing the cross-validation error vs. the number of features given in the previous step is fitted by an exponential map $g(x) = a \cdot e^{\frac{b}{x}}$;
- the optimal number n^* of mostly relevant features for the running experiment is chosen as the point where the error difference with respect to the next point is less than 1/1000 of the cross-validation error range (i.e. the difference between the maximum and the minimum cross-validation error).

The total number of extractions (multiplicity) of the n^* selected features from the optimal feature sets over all the B experiments of the VAL procedure additionally provides a measure of relative importance for the selected features. Furthermore, a randomization procedure is used to detect design problems and to test the robustness of the whole process: new data sets are built by randomizing the labels by permutation, then the VAL procedure is applied a suitable number of times on each of those no-information data sets.

In this study, only the feature ranking section of OFS-M was applied for the synthetic datasets. For the three microarray data sets, for the ONF procedure, we use a $K = 3$-fold cross-validation stratified for compatibility with class cardinalities. The feature ranking criteria we used in this paper are E-RFE, RFE, SQRT-RFE, 1-RFE. As a last step the VAL procedure was applied on the microarray data sets.

3. Results

Four synthetic and three microarray data sets from public domain were considered in this paper in order to evaluate the E-RFE feature ranking method.

3.1. Data description

3.1.1. Synthetic datasets

To assess E-RFE in comparison with a more standard SQRT-RFE method, we designed four synthetic data sets for binary classification problems. The data sets correspond to different possible SVM weights distributions. Each of the four data sets consists of 100 examples described by 1000 features. Each data set consists of a number n of significant features and $1000 - n$ not significant features. The n significant features were generated by sampling two n-dimensional Gaussian distributions centered in $\mathbf{1} = (1, \ldots, 1)$ and $-\mathbf{1}$. Covariance matrices were diagonal for all the two distributions; standard deviations were chosen by randomly sampling a uniform distribution ranging between 0.1 and 1 for each dimension. The 100 examples were extracted by sampling 50 points from each of the two Gaussian distributions and assigned to class 1, -1, respectively. Each one of the remaining $1000 - n$ features was generated by randomly sampling 100 points from a uniform distribution ranging between -2 and 2. The data sets are further specified as follows.

- For the HELM data set, the number of significant features is set to $n = 400$. In the first SVM run, we expect many SVM weights to be concentrated nearby 0, but also a relevant number of them distributed in [0,1], leading to a high entropy value and low mean value.
- For the HEHM data set, all the $n = 1000$ features are significant. In the first SVM run, the SVM weights are not concentrated on any point in [0,1]. Hence, we will get high values both for entropy and mean value.
- For the LE data set, the number of significant features is set to $n = 100$. This causes most of the initial weights to be concentrated nearby 0. As a consequence, the entropy of the distribution will be low.
- For the HEHM1 data set, the number of significant features is set to $n = 940$. The initial weights distribution is peculiar: most of the weights are very high so that we still are in a high entropy and high mean, although the pattern is different from that obtained for HEHM.

3.1.2. Microarray datasets

We tested the E-RFE ranking approach on three data sets previously considered in microarray studies.

- the colon cancer data set is described by expression levels of 2000 genes from 62 tissues, 22 normal and 40 tumor cases (Alon et al., 1999) (Affimetrix oligonucleotide technology).
- the lymphoma data set consists of 96 samples, 72 cancer and 24 non-cancer, described by 4026 gene expression levels (Alizadeh et al., 2000) (cDNA).

- the tumor vs. metastases data set is formed from 64 primary adenocarcinomas and 12 metastatic adenocarcinomas, described by 16,063 genes (Ramaswamy et al., 2001) (Affimetrix oligonucleotide technology).

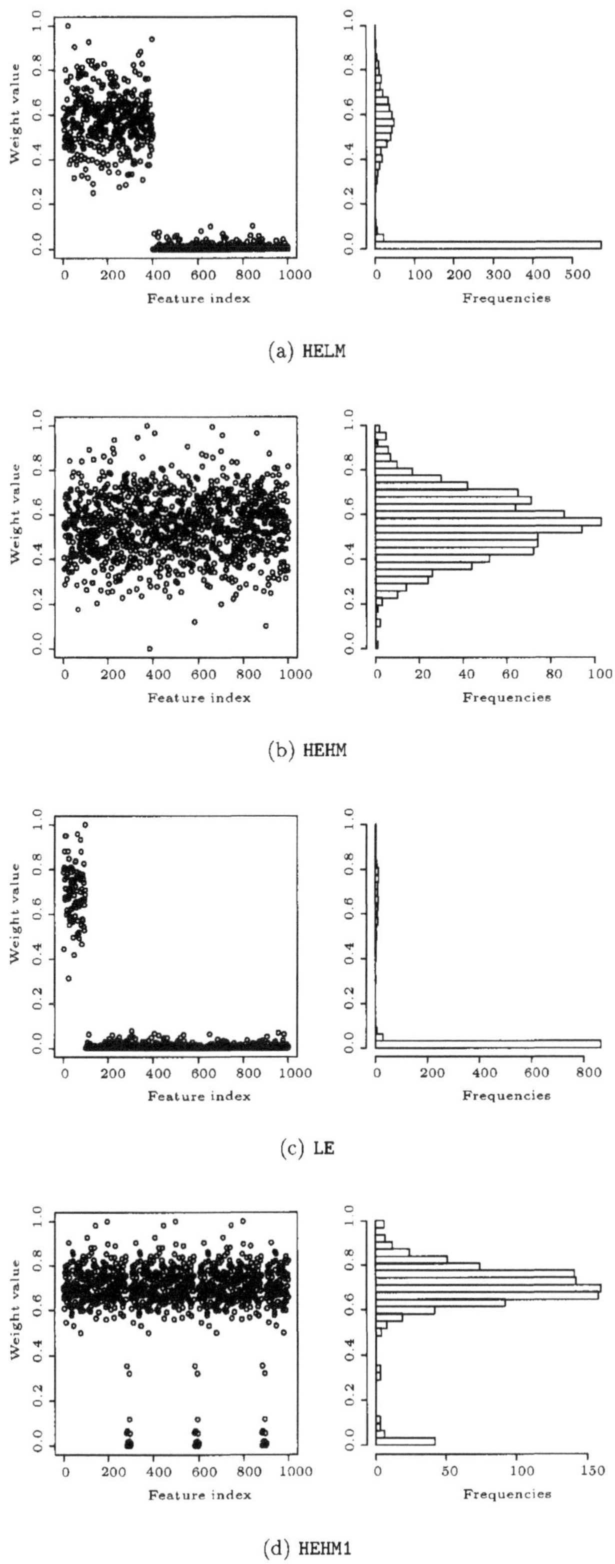

Fig. 2. SVM weights: examples of distributions.

A linear normalization procedure transforming the gene expressions to mean value 0 and standard deviation 1 was applied to each data set.

3.2. Results

3.2.1. Synthetic datasets

We applied the E-RFE procedure to the four synthetic data sets described in Section 3.1.1. In Fig. 2, we report the initial SVM weights and the histograms of their distributions for each data set. In all cases, the SVM is able to recognize the relevant features (by assigning to them a high weight); entropy and mean value of the weights distributions compare with the expected values.

The HELM data set has a high entropy and low mean. In this data set, 400 features out of the total of 1000 are significant: 399 of them were ranked in the first 400 positions, and the 400th was ranked 401th. The number of required steps was 99.

The HEHM data set has a high entropy and a high mean value. In this case all the features are important: a ranking was obtained in 398 steps.

The LE data set has low entropy with few significant variables (100/1000) and they were again precisely recognized: of the 100 relevant features, only the 99th was not selected in the first 100, but ranked 104th. The process was completed in 26 steps.

The HEHM1 data set has low entropy but many significant variables (940/1000). In this case, 939 from the 940 significant features were ranked in the first 940 positions. The number of steps required was 142.

The number of steps required by SQRT-RFE were 63 for all the experiments. In Fig. 3 the number of steps required by the E-RFE and SQRT-RFE methods on the LE data set are compared along with the number of undiscarded features at each step. In particular, it is interesting to notice that E-RFE is capable to recognize the unimportant features in only 5 steps, in which about 900 features were discarded (the dotted horizontal line is at $n = 100$). At that point, the procedure goes on very cautiously eliminating only few features (being all relevant) at each step. Similar results were found for the other datasets.

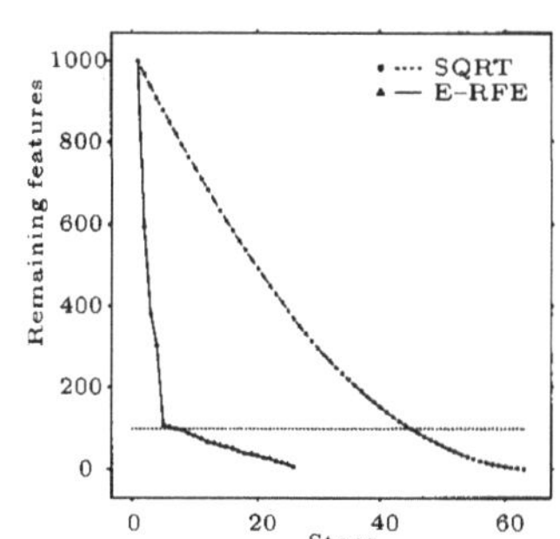

Fig. 3. $H \leq H_t$.

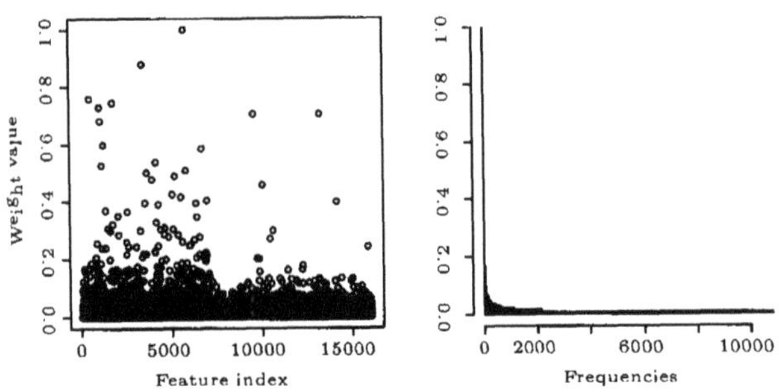

Fig. 4. Tumor vs. metastases: initial weight distribution ($H \leq H_t$).

Table 2
ATE for the lymphoma data set

# Genes	E-RFE	RFE	SQRT-RFE	1-RFE
10	8.0 ± 5.3	7.5 ± 5.2	8.9 ± 5.4	12.7 ± 7.6
20	5.8 ± 4.1	5.8 ± 4.5	5.4 ± 4.6	7.8 ± 6.9
50	3.9 ± 4.0	4.0 ± 3.9	4.7 ± 3.9	5.0 ± 4.0
100	4.1 ± 4.4	4.2 ± 4.3	4.3 ± 4.3	4.5 ± 4.4
300	3.6 ± 3.8	3.7 ± 3.6	3.5 ± 3.7	3.3 ± 3.7
500	3.4 ± 3.5	3.5 ± 3.6	3.5 ± 3.7	3.7 ± 3.8
1000	3.7 ± 3.7	3.6 ± 3.7	3.8 ± 3.7	3.8 ± 3.8
4026	All features: 3.8 ± 3.8			

3.2.2. Microarray datasets

We then applied the complete E-RFE procedure, including error estimation, to the three microarray datasets described in Section 3.1.2.

The initial SVM weights and the histogram of their distribution for the tumor vs. metastases data set are reported in Fig. 4 showing a pattern similar to that observed for the LE data set.

The results of the VAL procedure (see Section 2) applied to the three microarray data sets are summarized in Tables 1–3: the estimated error rate (ATE) and the standard deviation are obtained by averaging the error rate over 50 experiments for the colon cancer, lymphoma and tumor vs. metastases data set, respectively. The estimates are reported for increasing number of features and for the different ranking methods (E-RFE, RFE, SQRT-RFE, 1-RFE). The results for RFE were computed only for the first two datasets.

The procedure for the selection of the optimal number of features n^* was applied to the three microarray data sets. The results are shown in Table 4 in which the average $\bar{n}^*$ is reported along with ATE for different ranking methods. The estimates are obtained by averaging the results of 50 experiments.

In Table 5 we report the elapsed time on a bi-PentiumIII 1GHz for a single run of each of the ranking methods (E-RFE, SQRT-RFE, RFE, 1-RFE) on the three microarray data sets.

3.3. Pitfalls for 1-RFE

As tested on the microarray datasets, the four ranking procedures seem to act and perform similarly, but with quite different running times. So why using a (computationally heavier) recursive algorithm instead of a lighter non-recursive one?

We set up two synthetic experiments in order to show that correlation between features might results in a completely different behaviour between the two class of wrappers. The first experiment is similar to the counter-example described in Guyon et al., 2002 and involves 100 samples equally distributed in the two classes 1 and -1, described by only five features structured as follows. We first generate 3 variables U_i, $i = 1,2,3$ consisting of 50 values uniformly distributed in [0,1] and 50 values uniformly distributed in $[-1,0]$, and three variables $V_j, j = 1,2,3$ uniformly distributed in $[-1,1]$. Then all the points (U_i, V_i) are subjected to a counterclockwise rotation with angle $\frac{\pi}{4}$: the five coordinates $(u_1, u_2, u_3, v_1, v_2)$ of the resulting points (u_i, v_i) are chosen as the data set features. The samples were labelled 1 if the corresponding U_i variables lie in [0, 1] and -1 otherwise. By construction, the two groups of variables u and v are equally important. Because the classifier is not retrained, the non-recursive 1-RFE does not consider the correlation among the variables, so it wrongly ranks all the v features before

Table 1
ATE for the colon cancer data set

# Genes	E-RFE	RFE	SQRT-RFE	1-RFE
10	20.9 ± 10.0	22.0 ± 11.0	19.5 ± 9.8	24.9 ± 11.7
20	19.9 ± 8.9	20.0 ± 9.1	19.3 ± 9.5	18.4 ± 7.2
50	18.5 ± 8.5	18.4 ± 9.0	17.2 ± 8.1	17.5 ± 9.0
100	16.8 ± 7.8	17.3 ± 8.1	17.2 ± 8.2	18.0 ± 8.4
300	17.2 ± 8.2	17.6 ± 8.1	17.6 ± 8.2	18.0 ± 8.2
500	17.9 ± 7.9	17.9 ± 7.9	17.5 ± 7.4	18.0 ± 8.0
1000	16.9 ± 7.5	16.9 ± 7.4	16.8 ± 7.3	16.8 ± 7.4
2000	All features: 16.0 ± 7.5			

Table 3
ATE for the tumor vs. metastases data set

# Genes	E-RFE	RFE	SQRT-RFE	1-RFE
10	17.9 ± 5.2	–	17.3 ± 6.0	20.1 ± 5.4
20	16.7 ± 2.9	–	16.1 ± 3.9	26.7 ± 6.7
50	16.4 ± 3.8	–	16.2 ± 3.5	19.8 ± 6.6
100	16.2 ± 3.7	–	15.8 ± 3.5	16.7 ± 5.0
300	13.7 ± 4.3	–	13.6 ± 4.4	14.0 ± 4.9
500	13.4 ± 4.4	–	13.6 ± 4.8	13.2 ± 5.3
1000	13.3 ± 5.2	–	13.3 ± 5.2	12.5 ± 4.9
16,063	All features: 12.9 ± 5.2			

Table 4
ATE and $\bar{n}^*$ for the microarray data sets

Method	Colon		Lymphoma		Tumor vs. met.	
	ATE	$\bar{n}^*$	ATE	$\bar{n}^*$	ATE	$\bar{n}^*$
E-RFE	17.2	70	3.8	80	16.6	70
RFE	18.1	70	3.9	80	–	–
SQRT-RFE	18.4	70	4.3	80	16.2	70
1-RFE	18.4	80	4.9	80	21.5	25

Table 5
Elapsed time

	E-RFE (s)	RFE (s)	SQRT-RFE (s)	1-RFE (s)
Colon	34	4700	194	11
Lymphoma	128	29612	641	45
Tumor vs. met.	1780	–	12125	484

the u's, while the RFE correctly mixes them as $(v_1, u_3, u_1, v_2, u_2)$. Same behaviour is shown in the second experiment, where we still take 100 equally distributed samples but from just one pair (u_1, v_1) generated as above we produce the 401 features as 201 copies of u_1 and 200 copies of v_1. The two groups have the same importance, nevertheless the 1-RFE again ranks all the u variables more relevant than the v's, while the recursive procedures evaluates them as equally relevant.

4. Conclusions

The experiments on the synthetic data have shown that E-RFE is effective in selecting the important features with different SVM weights distributions, and may adapt to the structure of different classification problems.

On the colon cancer and lymphoma microarray data sets, the prediction accuracy of gene selection and classification with E-RFE is consistent with recently published literature, with similar experimental scheme (Ambroise & McLachlan, 2002). The results on tumor vs. metastases are also consistent with the recent (Ramaswamy et al., 2003), although a different experimental scheme for gene selection and error estimation was used.

The efficiency of E-RFE on the microarray data is evident with respect to both the basic RFE and its alternatives SQRT-RFE and 1-RFE. These data have an initial weights distribution characterized by low entropy and many weights close to zero. Without degradation of accuracy, E-RFE has allowed a much faster gene selection. This property may be important in the development of accurate diagnostic models, which requires estimate of important genes and further optimization of model parameters.

Appendix A

Pseudocode for E-RFE algorithm
Given the training set

$$S = \{(\mathbf{x}_k, y_k)\}_{k=1,\dots,N}, \qquad \mathbf{x}_k \in \mathbb{R}^n, y_k \in \{-1, 1\}$$

Initialize: $R = \{1, \dots, n\}$, subset of remaining features
$F = (\,)$, ranked list of features
while ($\#R > R_t$){
  train SVM on

$$S = \{(\mathbf{x}_k(i)_{i\in R}, y_k)\}_{k=1,\dots,N}$$

  compute $\delta J(i) \quad \forall i \in R$
  linearly transform $\delta J(i)$ into pw_i, ranging on [0,1]
  split [0,1] into n_{int} intervals
  compute

$$p_j = \frac{\#(\mathrm{pw}_i)_{i\in R}}{\#R}, \qquad j = 1, \dots, n_{\mathrm{int}}$$

  compute entropy as

$$H = -\sum_{j=1}^{n_{\mathrm{int}}} p_j \log_2 p_j$$

  compute $M = \mathrm{mean}(\mathrm{pw}_i)$
  if ($H > H_t \& M > M_t$){
    remove from R the features s.t.

$$\mathrm{pw}_i \in \left[0, \frac{1}{n_{\mathrm{int}}}\right]$$

    and put them at the top of F
  }
  else {
    compute $L_i = \log_2 \mathrm{pw}_i \quad \forall i \in R$
    compute $M = \mathrm{mean}(L_i)$
    compute $A = \#\{L_i \le M\}$
    set conv = 0
    while (conv = 0){
      set $M = \frac{1}{2}M$
      compute $\beta = \#\{L_i \le M\}$
      if ($\beta \le \frac{1}{2}A$){
        set conv = 1
      }
    }
    remove from R the β features s.t. $L_i \le M$
    and put them at the top of F
  }
}
while ($R \ne \emptyset$){
  use RFE algorithm
}

The algorithm returns F, ordered list of all variables, and an empty R. For the microarray data experiments, $R_t = 100$, $n_{\mathrm{int}} = \sqrt{\#R}$, $H_t = \frac{1}{2}\log_2 n_{\mathrm{int}}$ and $M_t = 0.2$.

References

Alizadeh, A., Eisen, M., Davis, E., Ma, C., Lossos, I., Rosenwald, A., Boldrick, J., Sabet, H., Tran, T., Yu, X., Powell, J., Yang, L., Marti, G., Jr., J.H., Lu, L., Lewis, D., Tibshirani, R., Sherlock, G., Chan, W., Greiner, T., Weisenburger, D., Armitage, J., Warnke, R., Levy, R., Wilson, W., Grever, M., Byrd, J., Botstein, D., Brown, P., & Staudt, L (2000). Distinct types of diffuse large B-cell lymphoma identified by gene expression profiling. *Nature*, 403, 503–511. Data available on-line at http://llmpp.nih.gov/lymphoma/data.shtml.

Alon, U., Barkai, N., Notterman, D., Gish, K., Ybarra, S., Mack, D., & Levine, A. (1999). Broad patterns of gene expression revealed by clustering analysis of tumor and normal colon tissues probed by oligonucleotide arrays. *Proceedings of the National Academy of Science, USA*, *96*(12), 6745–6750. Data available on-line at http://www.molbio.princeton.edu/oncology/affydata.

Ambroise, C., & McLachlan, G. (2002). Selection bias in gene extraction on the basis of microarray gene-expression data. *Proceedings of the National Academy of Science, USA*, *99*(10), 6562–6566.

Chung, C., Bernard, P., & Perou, C. (2002). Molecular portraits and the family tree of cancer. *Nature Genetics Supplement*, *32*, 533–540.

Cristianini, N., & Shawe-Taylor, J. (2000). *An introduction to support vector machines*. Cambridge: Cambridge University Press.

Furlanello, C., Serafini, M., Merler, S., & Jurman, G (2002). Entropy-based gene ranking without selection bias for the predictive classification of microarray data. Technical Report TR 0212-13, ITC-irst, Trento, Italy.

Guyon, I., Weston, J., Barnhill, S., & Vapnik, V. (2002). Gene selection for cancer classification using support vector machines. *Machine Learning*, *46*, 389–422.

Li, Y., Campbell, C., & Tipping, M. (2002). Bayesian automatic relevance determination algorithms for classifying gene expression data. *Bioinformatics*, *18*, 1332–1339.

Nguyen, D. V., & Rocke, D. M. (2002). Tumor classification by partial least squares using microarray gene expression data. *Bioinformatics*, *18*(1), 39–50.

Ramaswamy, S., Ross, K., Lander, E., & Golub, T. (2003). A molecular signature of metastasis in primary solid tumors. *Nature Genetics*, *33*, 1–6.

Ramaswamy, S., Tamayo, P., Rifkin, R., Mukherjee, S., Yeang, C., Angelo, M., Ladd, C., Reich, M., Latulippe, E., Mesirov, J., Poggio, T., Gerald, W., Loda, M., Lander, E. S., & Golub, T. (2001). Multiclass cancer diagnosis using tumor gene expression signatures. *PNAS*, *98*(26), 15149–15154.

Slonim, D. K. (2002). From patterns to pathways: gene expression data analysis comes of age. *Nature Genetics Supplement*, *32*, 502–508.

Spang, R., Blanchette, C., Zuzan, H., Marks, J., Nevins, J., & West, M. (2001). In E. Wingender, R. Hofestädt, & I. Liebich (Eds.), *Prediction and uncertainty in the analysis of gene expression profiles. Proceedings of the German Conference on Bioinformatics GCB*.

Weston, J., Mukherjee, S., Chapelle, O., Pontil, M., Poggio, T., & Vapnik, V. (2000). *Feature selection for SVMs. In NIPS*, pp. 668–674.

Xiong, M., Fang, X., & Zhao, J. (2001). Biomarker identification by feature wrappers. *Genome Research*, *11*, 1878–1887.

Zhang, X., & Wong, W (2001). Recursive sample classification and gene selection based on SVM: method and software description. Technical report, Department of Biostatistics, Harvard School of Public Health.

PERGAMON

AVAILABLE AT
www.ComputerScienceWeb.com
POWERED BY SCIENCE @ DIRECT

Neural Networks 16 (2003) 649–656

Neural Networks

www.elsevier.com/locate/neunet

2003 Special issue

Pattern completion through phase coding in population neurodynamics

A. Gutierrez-Galvez, R. Gutierrez-Osuna*

Department of Computer Science, Texas A & M University, College Station, TX 77843-3112, USA

Abstract

This article presents an alternative phase coding mechanism for Freeman's KIII model of population neurodynamics. Motivated by experimental evidence that supports the existence of a neural code based on synchronous oscillations, we propose an analogy between synchronization in neural populations and phase locking in KIII channels. An efficient method is proposed to extract phase differences across granule channels from their state-space trajectories. First, the scale invariance of the KIII model with respect to phase information is established. The phase code is then compared against the conventional amplitude code in terms of their bit-wise and across-fiber pattern recovery capabilities using decision-theoretic principles and a Hamming-distance classifier. Graph isomorphism in the Hebbian connections is exploited to perform an exhaustive evaluation of patterns on an 8-channel KIII model. Simulation results show that phase information outperforms amplitude information in the recovery of incomplete or corrupted stimuli.

Keywords: Olfactory system; KIII model; Neural coding; Coherent oscillation; Associative memory

1. Introduction

Neural coding schemes based on firing synchrony are the most compelling hypothesis for a temporal code spatially distributed across large neural populations. These types of codes have been found experimentally in different neocortical areas (Recce, 2001), and play an important role in the integration of visual information (Singer & Gray, 1995) and the codification of odors (Laurent & Davidowitz, 1994; MacLeod & Laurent, 1996). The objective of this paper is to ascertain whether this coding mechanism can be exploited in the KIII model of Freeman and colleagues (Chang, Freeman, & Burke, 1998a; Yao & Freeman, 1990), arguably the most complete neurodynamics model of the olfactory system.

The long term goal of this work is to develop biologically-plausible computational models to process data from chemical sensor arrays, commonly referred to as the electronic nose. An e-nose consists of (1) an array of chemical sensors with broad and overlapping selectivities and (2) a pattern recognition engine capable of associating sensor patterns with the corresponding odor labels (Gardner & Bartlett, 1999). Biologically-inspired approaches have been the focus of attention in recent years (Pearce, 1997) as an alternative to the statistical pattern recognition procedures commonly employed in e-nose data processing (Gutierrez-Osuna, 2002).

Along these lines, our experience with the KIII model (Gutierrez-Osuna & Gutierrez-Galvez, 2002; Gutierrez-Osuna & Sun, 2002) shows that the information provided by the amplitude of the channels tends to degrade when the input patterns have a significant level of overlap, as is oftentimes the case in electronic nose data due to the cross-selectivity of the chemical sensors. This raises the question whether additional robust information can be extracted from the output of the model. In particular, we have observed that the KIII has a tendency to display similar phases in channels that encode for the same odor. This observation, along with experimental evidence for a neural code based on coherent oscillations in neural populations, motivates the study presented in this paper.

2. Temporal coding and coherent oscillations

Work by Adrian (Adrian, 1926, 1928) more than 75 years ago showed that the firing rate of stretch receptor neurons is related to the force being applied to the muscles. This seminal contribution led to the widespread belief that firing rate was the code used by neural systems to transmit information. As a consequence, early neural network models interpreted the output of artificial neurons as an

* Corresponding author. Tel.: +1-979-845-2942; fax: +1-979-847-8578.
E-mail address: rgutier@cs.tamu.edu (R. Gutierrez-Osuna).

0893-6080/03/$ - see front matter © 2003 Elsevier Science Ltd. All rights reserved.
doi:10.1016/S0893-6080(03)00107-2

abstraction of the neural firing rate in their biological counterparts. In recent years, this view has been challenged with ample experimental evidence showing the need to take into consideration the temporal dimension in neural information processing.

Undisputable evidence for a temporal code is best illustrated by the work of Thorpe et al. (van Ruellen & Thorpe, 2000; Thorpe, Delorme, & Van Ruellen, 2001), who have shown that humans and monkeys are able to respond to a visual categorization problem in a very short period of time. In their experiments, an image is briefly flashed and the subject has to decide if it belongs to a target category or not. Considering (i) the pathway of the visual signal as it propagates through the brain, (ii) the minimum time required for a neuron to generate an action potential and (iii) the response time of the subjects in these experiments, it is possible to determine that there is time for only one spike to be generated at every relay station in the visual pathway. This result clashes with a frequency-rate coding hypothesis, and clearly points to the existence of a temporal dimension.

A number of possible temporal coding mechanisms have been proposed, including inter-spike interval codes, time of arrival (latency) codes and synchrony codes (Cariani, 1995). Among these, the synchronous oscillation of ensembles presents the most compelling empirical evidence. Synchronization has been proposed as a potential mechanism to correlate information from different senses or different parts of the brain (Recce, 2001). It has also been found to play a role in visual feature integration (Singer & Gray, 1995). Of particular interest to our work, Laurent et al. (Laurent & Davidowitz, 1994; MacLeod & Laurent, 1996) have found that synchronous oscillations of neuron populations in insects is used as an odor encoding mechanism. Their work has shown that different odors evoke coherent oscillations in different but usually overlapping ensembles of neurons in the olfactory system.

3. The KIII model

The KIII is a neurodynamics model of the olfactory system developed by Freeman and colleagues (Chang et al., 1998a; Yao & Freeman, 1990) over the last 30 years. The output of the model reproduces electroencephalographic (EEG) recordings in the olfactory system by modeling the oscillatory behavior of neuron populations. The topology of the KIII, shown in Fig. 1, is based on the physiological structure of the mammalian olfactory system. Each node in the KIII represents a population of neurons, modeled by a second order differential equation, and each edge models the interaction between two populations. The strength of this interaction is controlled by a weight, which is positive when the connection is excitatory and negative if the connection is inhibitory.

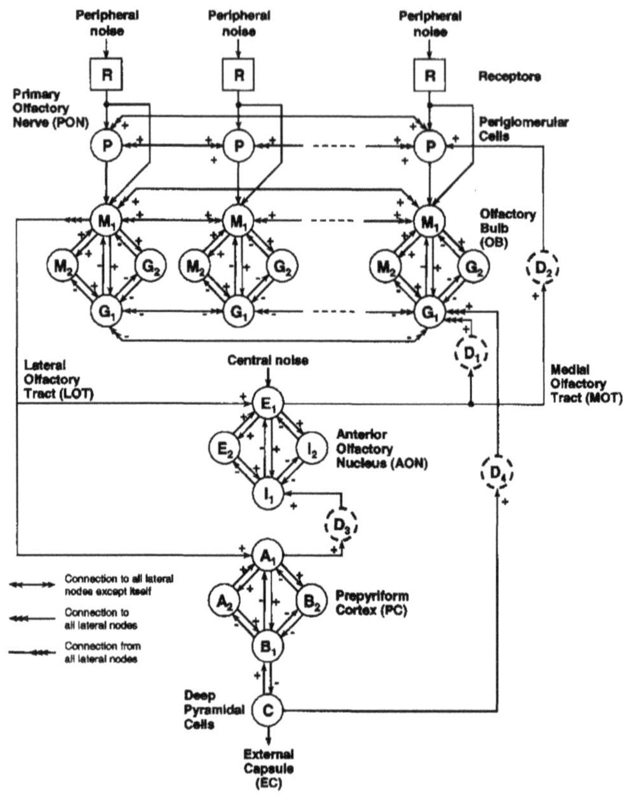

Fig. 1. Structure of the KIII model (from Chang et al., 1998b).

Odor stimuli are presented to the system as patterns, generally binary, through an input layer of receptors. Each receptor is connected to a periglomerular cell and a set of two mitral and two glomerular ensembles, forming a channel. Each of these channels can then be associated with one bit of the binary input stimulus and the corresponding output pattern. The KIII is able to store previously seen patterns by means of Hebbian lateral connections at the M1 mitral layer. This allows the model to work as an associative memory for recovering incomplete or corrupted stimuli.

In the absence of an external stimulus, the KIII channels follow an aperiodic oscillatory behavior known as a basal state. When an input is presented, the system moves into a global attractor in state space, which can also be observed as pseudo-periodic oscillations in the output channels. The amplitude of the oscillations at each channel depends on the activation level of its receptor input, but is also influenced by other receptors as a result of the Hebbian lateral connections. The output pattern of the KIII is commonly assumed to be encoded in the amplitude or RMS of the oscillations of each channel (Yao, Freeman, Burke, & Yang, 1991), which does not exploit the temporal dimension of the KIII dynamics. Considering that the KIII is a model of neuron populations, it is appealing to consider the phase of the oscillations across channels as an analogous of the coherent oscillation coding scheme in biological neural systems. Hence, the goal of this paper is to investigate whether phase information can in fact be used as a coding mechanism and, if so, compare its pattern-recovery performance against the conventional amplitude code.

3.1. Phase coding in the KIII model

In order to efficiently capture phase information, we consider the state-space trajectory of pairs of KIII channels (G1 populations) as a two-dimensional distribution. As shown in Fig. 2, differences in phase (θ) can be mapped into the correlation coefficient (ρ) of the 2D distribution, and vice versa. Two ideal sinusoidal waveforms with the same phase will lead to a correlation coefficient $\rho = 1$ (Fig. 2(a)), whereas a $\theta = 180°$ phase difference result in a correlation coefficient of $\rho = -1$. Intermediate phase differences result in correlation coefficients between those two extremes $[-1,1]$.

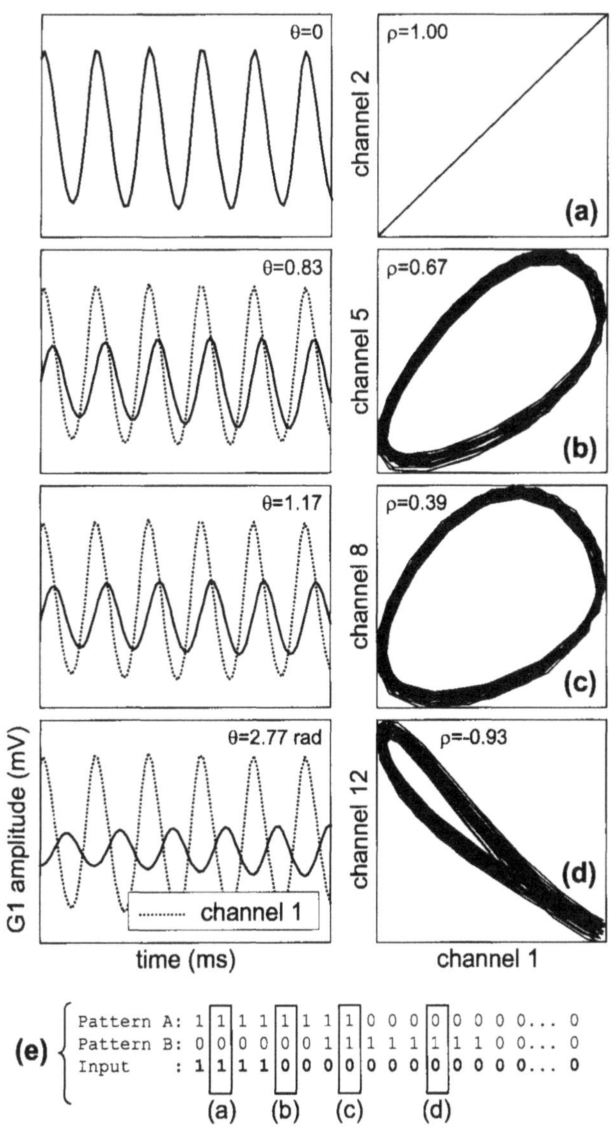

Fig. 2. Extracting phase information from the KIII model.

The waveforms and trajectories in Fig. 2 were obtained by training a 32-channel KIII on two binary patterns, and presenting a distorted version of the first pattern at the inputs. It can be seen that the shape and orientation of the attractors can be associated to different types of errors in the input stimulus. It is also important to note that the correlation coefficient not only captures information about the orientation of the principal eigenvector but also about the area enclosed by the trajectory (i.e. the shape of the attractor).

3.2. KIII implementation

The KIII model with matrix formulation described in Chang, Freeman, & Burke, 1998b was employed in this work. The model was implemented in MATLAB using fourth-order Runge-Kutta ODE integration with a time step of 1.0 ms. Initial conditions for all variables and their derivatives were set to zero. Parameter values for the KIII model are summarized in Table 1. The KIII model presented an aperiodic oscillatory behavior with a $1/f$ power spectra, as shown in Fig. 3 for a 2000 ms simulation of the basal state. Following (Kozma & Freeman, 2001), the more informative part of the signal is located in the gamma frequencies (20–80 Hz). For this reason the G1 signals were band-pass filtered to remove energy outside the gamma band. In what follows, the phase and amplitude are computed on this filtered signal. Comparable results, however, were obtained on the unfiltered signals.

4. Scaling invariance

Invariance of the KIII model with respect to the number of channels has been empirically established (Yao &

Table 1
Parameter values for the KIII model (from (Chang et al., 1998a))

a	0.22	q^C	5.000
b	0.72	w_{M1P}	0.050
q^P	1.824	w^{low}_{M1M1L}	0.599
w_{PPL}	0.900	w^{high}_{M1M1L}	2.100
k_{PR}	0.500	w_{E1M1}	1.311
q^{OB}	5.000	w_{A1M1}	1.710
w_{MM}	1.500	w_{G1G1L}	−0.580
w_{MG}	−2.063	w_{CB1}	−1.543
w_{GM}	2.323	w_{B1C}	0.698
w_{GG}	−2.445	w_{G1D1}	2.349
k_{M1R}	1.000	w_{PD2}	1.087
q^{AON}	5.000	w_{I1D3}	2.553
w_{EE}	1.202	w_{G1D4}	2.305
w_{EI}	−1.426	T^s_1	20.000
w_{IE}	1.372	T^e_1	11.000
w_{II}	−1.571	T^s_2	22.000
q^{PC}	5.000	T^e_2	15.000
w_{AA}	0.823	T^s_3	21.000
w_{AB}	−1.938	T^e_3	12.000
w_{BA}	1.947	T^s_4	30.000
w_{BB}	−2.354	T^e_4	24.000

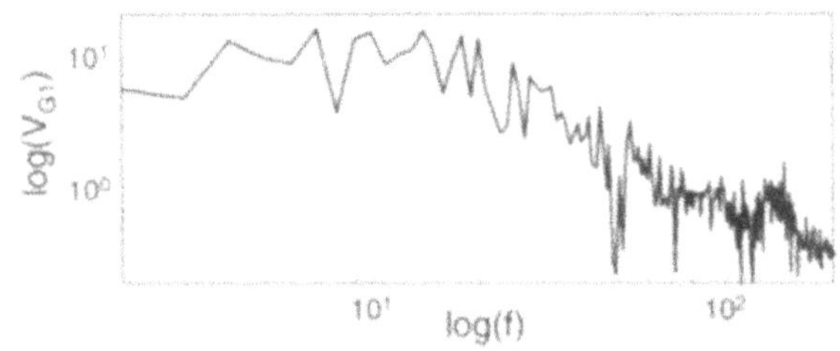

Fig. 3. Power spectra for a 2000 ms simulation of basal state.

Freeman, 1990) in terms of the amplitude and general shape of the oscillations observed at each channel. To determine if these results can be generalized to phase information, we present a thorough study on three KIII models with 16, 32 and 64 channels. The study simulates a two-odor classification problem with varying levels of complexity in terms of (1) the degree of overlap between the two stored patterns and (2) the number of missing or corrupted channels that are presented at the input.

Fig. 4 shows the two input patterns for the 16-channel case. Each pattern consists of four active channels, represented by a 1, and 12 inactive channels, represented by a blank bit. Due to the symmetry of the problem, in what follows the KIII model is always excited with a stimulus from pattern A. To incorporate different degrees of overlap, three patterns sets are considered having 0, 1 and 2 bits of overlap. Each one of these three sets leads to a unique Hebbian associative matrix and, therefore, a separate KIII model. Fig. 4(a) shows the situation where the patterns have an overlap of 2 bits. To simulate incomplete patterns (e.g. caused by sensor degradation), 0, 1 or 2 of the active bits in the stimulus may be set to zero. Fig. 4(b) shows the case where the stimulus for pattern A is incomplete by one bit. Finally, to simulate corrupted patterns (e.g. to due to background odors), 0, 1 and 2 bits not belonging to either pattern may be set to one. Fig. 4(c) shows a stimulus for Pattern A with one corrupted bit. All these different combinations lead to $3 \times 3 \times 3 = 27$ possible scenarios for a 16-channel KIII model. Data for the 32- and 64-channel models is obtained by scaling the stored patterns and input stimuli by a factor of 2 and 4, respectively.

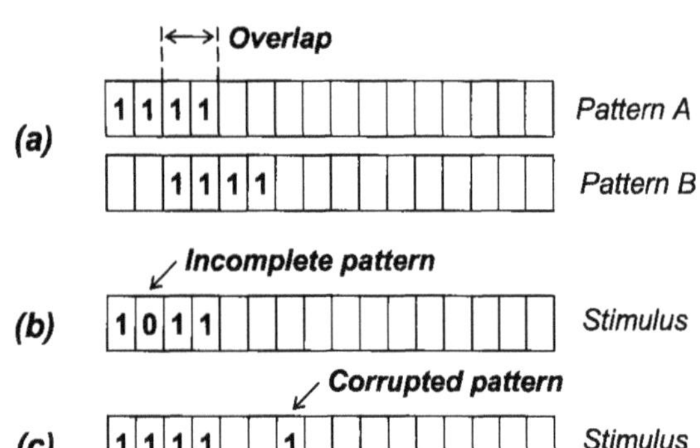

Fig. 4. Overlap between input patterns for a 16-channel KIII (a). Simulating an incomplete (b) and a corrupted (c) input pattern.

Simulation results are presented in Fig. 5 in the form of bi-variate scatter plots. Each point in the scatter plots represents the output of one KIII channel for one stimulus. The abscissa axis is the RMS amplitude of the channel, whereas the ordinate axis is the phase relative to channel 0, which is consistently activated and used as a reference. Four different cases of input-stimulus → desired-response are

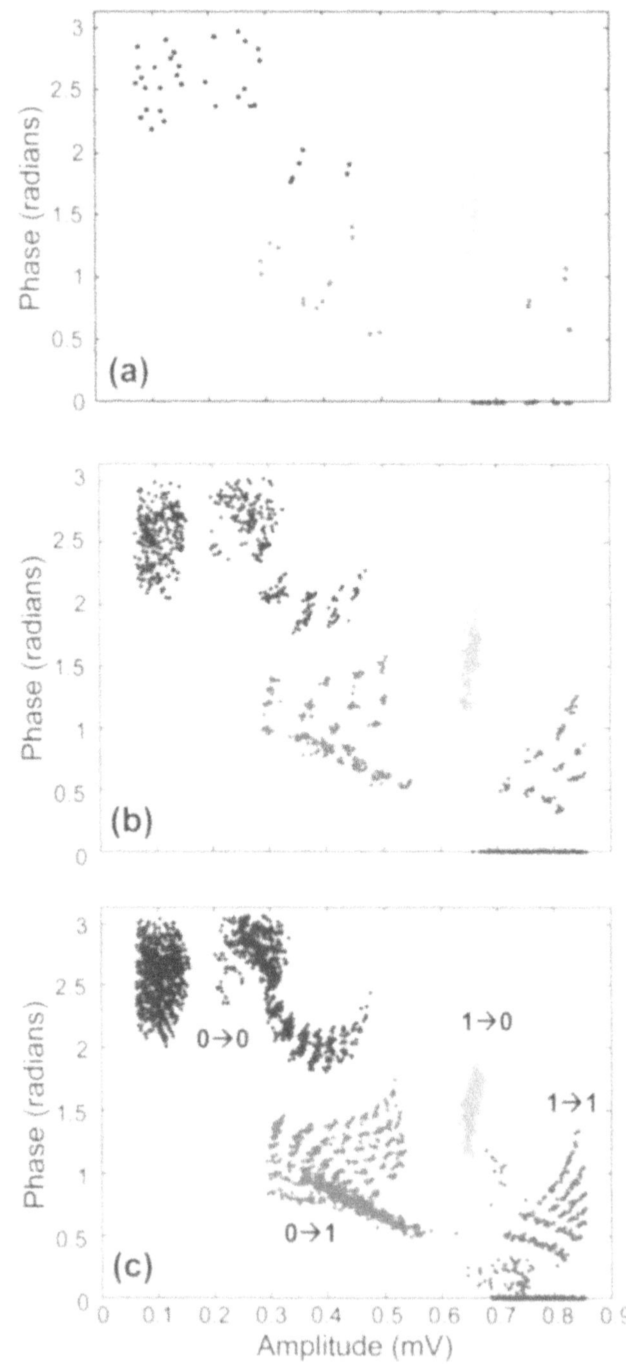

Fig. 5. Scatter plot of amplitude vs. phase codes for different input-stimulus → desired-response cases.

considered in the study, which correspond to two correct and two erroneous input stimuli:

- 1 → 1 (no error): stimulus in a channel that encodes for pattern A;
- 0 → 0 (no error): no stimulus in a channel that does not encode for pattern A;
- 0 → 1 (incomplete pattern): missing stimulus in channel that encodes for pattern A;
- 1 → 0 (corrupted pattern): noisy stimulus in a channel that does not encode for pattern A;

The results in Fig. 5 show that, although a higher number of channels yields a more detailed structure of the amplitude/phase clusters, these scatter plots have a similar structure regardless of the number of channels. This result leads to the conclusion that the KIII model is not only scale invariant with respect to amplitudes, a result previously established in Yao & Freeman, 1990, but also with respect to phase information.

4.1. Bit recovery

An important conclusion can also be extracted from these scatter plots. Fig. 6 shows the marginal univariate distribution of the amplitude and phase codes in the 64-channel model for each of the four input-stimulus → desired-response cases. A Gaussian distribution has been assumed for visualization purposes. It can be observed that the amplitude code is able to recover either incomplete or corrupted bits, but not both, since the 0 → 1 and 1 → 0 densities lie on opposite sides of their desired response. This result indicates that the amplitude of a particular channel tends to be driven primarily by the input stimulus rather than by the lateral connections in the Hebbian matrix. In the case of a phase code, a simple threshold can be obtained to correct the majority of the incomplete or corrupted bits, indicating a higher sensitivity to lateral connections. Bit

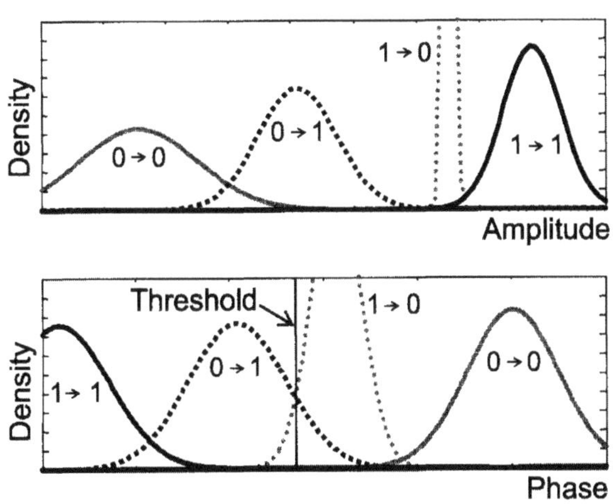

Fig. 6. Univariate density functions for the amplitude and phase codes.

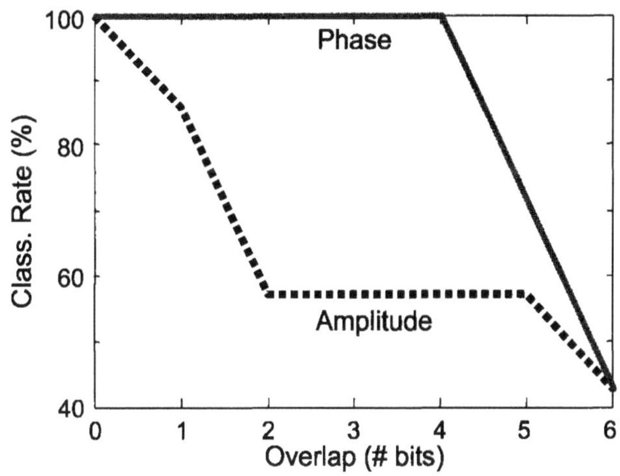

Fig. 7. Performance of a Hamming-distance classifier on the two codes.

recovery is, therefore, more reliable using phase information.

4.2. Pattern recovery: preliminary results

The results in the previous sections demonstrate the significant advantage of a phase code in the recovery of individual errors at the channel level (bit-wise). How do these results translate into classification performance at the across-fiber pattern level? To explore this issue, a Hamming-distance classifier (Lippmann, 1987) was employed at the output of the KIII. Oscillatory activity (phase or amplitude) at each KIII output channel was binarized in a decision-theoretic manner with a Likelihood Ratio Test (van Trees, 1968), where the threshold was obtained by assigning 0 → 0 and 1 → 0 bits into one Gaussian density, and 1 → 1 and 0 → 1 bits into the second one. Inputs and prototype patterns were generated using a 16-channel KIII model with 8 active channels (as opposed to the 4 active channels in Fig. 4) to explore higher levels of overlap between patterns. The number of incomplete or corrupted bits was allowed to range between 0 and 2.

The average classification rate as a function of prototype overlap is shown in Fig. 7, where ties (the input pattern is equidistant from the two prototypes) are counted as miss-classifications. With zero overlap between the two prototypes (1111111100000000 and 0000000011111111), both codes provide 100% classification rate since the Hamming-distance classifier is robust against errors in a few bits. As the overlap between the prototypes grows, discrimination between them becomes more difficult. As a result, bit-wise corrections become increasingly relevant, allowing the phase code to clearly outperform amplitude information.[1]

[1] Not shown in the figure, for overlaps of 7 bits (1111111100000000 and 0111111110000000) and 8 bits (the two prototypes are identical), the performance of both codes drops to 0%.

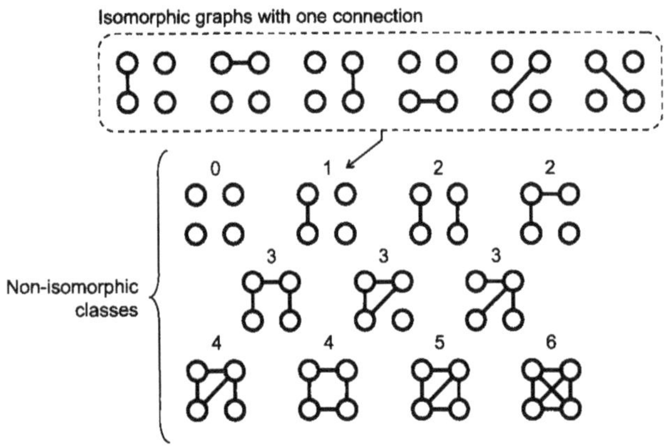

Fig. 8. Reduction of a 4-channel model to 11 non-isomorphic classes. The index above each graph denotes the number of active Hebbian connections.

5. Symmetry of the associative memory matrix

Once the scale invariance of the KIII model with respect to phase information has been validated, the study can now be focused on a lower dimensional model where an exhaustive evaluation of every possible combination of input stimulus and pattern sets is computationally feasible. Although 2- and 4-channel models could be used to this effect, the results in Fig. 5 show that more channels lead to higher resolution. For this reason, an 8-channel model is chosen for the final study.

In order to avoid exploring redundant combinations, the symmetries in the KIII associative-memory matrix will be exploited. Following Yao & Freeman, 1990, the mitral–mitral lateral connections can be computed as:

$$W_{\mathrm{MI}} = \sum_{\forall i} f(p_i p_i^T) \qquad (1)$$

where p_i is the correct input pattern for the ith odor class, and $f(\cdot)$ is a threshold function so that the elements in W_{MI} are binary, either HIGH or LOW[2] (diagonal elements in the matrix are set to zero.) Thus, a HIGH element in the Hebbian matrix represents two KIII channels that are simultaneously active for *at least* one odor pattern. Since different pattern sets can lead to the same Hebbian matrix, an exhaustive evaluation of every possible pattern set can be reduced to the study of all possible matrix configurations.

A representation of the Hebbian matrix as an undirected graph will be used to illustrate the existing symmetries. For simplicity, assume a 4-channel model with only one connection between channels. Since the channels are symmetric, the behavior of the system will be the same regardless of where this connection is located, as shown in Fig. 8. Generalizing this idea, graphs with the same number of connections and the same topology (i.e. isomorphic graphs) have to be considered just once. As a result, a 4-channel model with $2^6 = 64$ possible configurations is reduced to the 11 non-isomorphic graphs in Fig. 8. Similarly, a 8-channel model can be reduced from $2^{28} = 2.7 \times 10^8$ to 1192 cases, for a significant savings in CPU time.

6. Pattern recovery: final results

The final comparison of the two coding schemes will be performed on an 8-channel KIII model, for a total of 1192 non-isomorphic cases. As opposed to the preliminary study in Section 4.1, where performance was studied as a function of degrees of overlap in the pattern set and distortions in the input stimulus, the pattern recovery capabilities in this final study can only be evaluated in terms of the properties of each graph since the relationship between pattern sets and graphs is many-to-one. Two observations will greatly simplify this analysis. First, any two neighboring nodes (those that are connected directly by an edge) represent channels that are simultaneously active for at least one stored pattern. Conversely, any two nodes that are more than one edge away represent channels where two or more patterns overlap. Therefore, it is possible to analyze the across-fiber pattern-recovery performance of the phase and amplitude codes by comparing the activation between nodes connected by a single edge (which represents a true pattern) against the activation between nodes connected by a multi-edge path (which represents an undesirable overlap).

This idea is shown in Fig. 9(a). For a given graph, a single input stimulus is applied to the channel with the highest number of lateral connections (d_0 in the figure), and the activity on the remaining channels is analyzed. Nodes within one edge from d_0 (denoted by d_1) are part of a pattern. Nodes two edges away (denoted by d_2) are the effect of an overlap between two or more patterns. The remaining

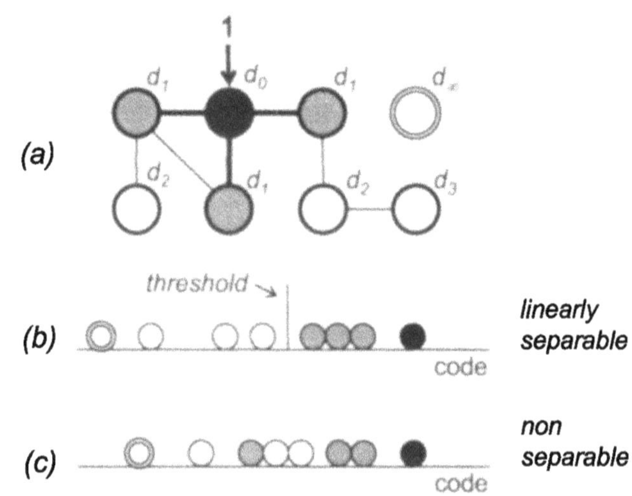

Fig. 9. (a) Pattern and overlap bits for a given Hebbian graph. (b,c) Pattern recovery as a linear separability problem.

[2] LOW and HIGH values are denoted by $W^{\mathrm{low}}_{\mathrm{MIMIL}}$ and $W^{\mathrm{high}}_{\mathrm{MIMIL}}$, respectively, in Table 1.

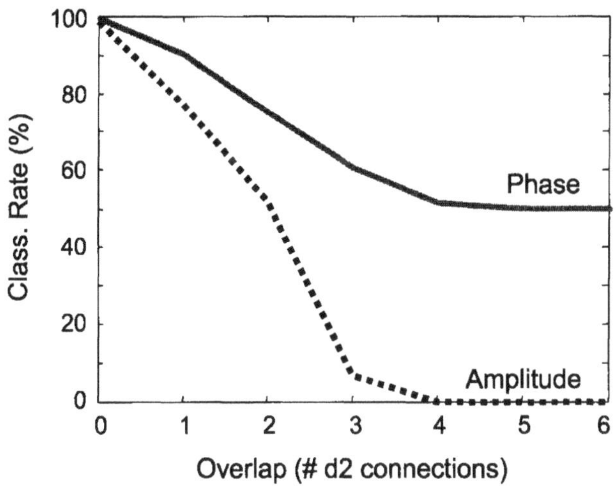

Fig. 10. Overall performance of the phase and amplitude codes as a function of pattern overlap.

nodes (d_3 through d_∞) can be neglected since they involve higher-order overlaps between patterns. Fig. 9(b) shows the situation where the response of d_0 and d_1 nodes is linearly separable from the rest, indicating that a simple threshold function could be used to recover an incomplete pattern from an input stimulus having a single active channel. Fig. 9(c) shows the opposite situation, where the response of d_0 and d_1 nodes is not linearly separable from the rest and, as a result, the incomplete pattern cannot be recovered.

The procedure outlined in Fig. 9 is repeated individually for each of the 1192 non-isomorphic cases in the 8-channel KIII in order to measure the pattern recovery capabilities of the amplitude and phase codes. The results are presented in Fig. 10 as a function of the number of d_2 connections in each graph, which can be related to the overlap (e.g. the complexity) of the corresponding pattern sets. Each point in the plot represents the percentage of graphs where

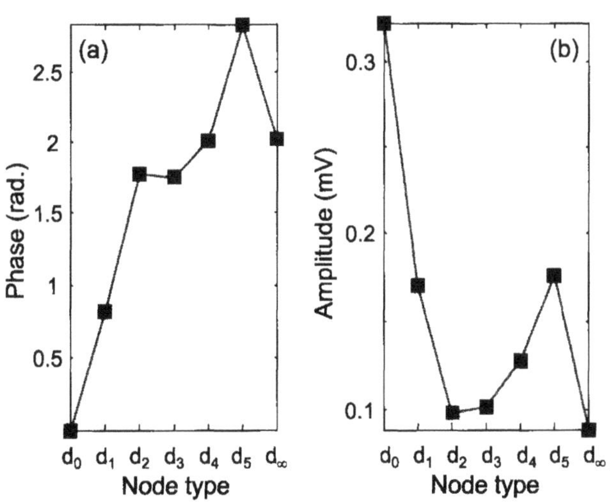

Fig. 11. Phase difference and amplitude as a function of distance (number of edges) to the input node.

the linear separability in Fig. 9(b) is achieved, relative to the total number of graphs. This result shows that the performance of the amplitude code decreases dramatically as the degree of overlap increases, whereas the phase code degrades in a more graceful manner and always provides higher classification rates.

The average phase difference between the input node (d_0) and all remaining nodes is shown in Fig. 11(a). The phase of d_1 nodes is closer to the input node than to the remaining nodes. For comparison, the corresponding average amplitudes are shown in Fig. 11(b). In this case the situation is reversed, with the amplitude of d_1 nodes being farther from the input node than to the other nodes. These results provide additional evidence for the superiority of the phase code.

7. Conclusions

This article has proposed an analogy between coherent oscillations in neural populations and phase locking in the KIII model. We have shown that phase differences between channels can be efficiently captured by treating the state-space trajectory as a two-dimensional distribution and computing its correlation coefficient. Scale invariance of the KIII with respect to this phase information has been empirically validated on three models with 16, 32 and 64 channels. The performance of the phase code has been demonstrated in terms of (1) bit-wise error recovery from a decision-theoretic viewpoint and (2) across-fiber pattern completion with a Hamming-distance classifier.

An exhaustive comparison of the pattern recovery capabilities of the proposed phase coding and the conventional amplitude coding has been presented on an 8-channel model. In order to avoid a combinatorial explosion, redundant pattern and stimulus combinations have been eliminated by means of graph isomorphism. Experimental results show that information embedded in the phase of the KIII channels clearly outperforms the amplitude code.

The present study has focused on binary stimuli, but the KIII has also been shown (Kozma & Freeman, 2001) to work efficiently with continuous inputs. Thus, a natural extension of the work presented in this article is to consider continuous amplitude and phase representations. Additional information other than correlation coefficients (which relate to phase for sinusoidal waveforms) could also be extracted from the KIII dynamic attractors in two- or higher-dimensional state spaces. These areas constitute promising directions for future work.

Acknowledgements

This material is based upon work supported by the National Science Foundation under CAREER Grant No. 9984426/0229598. Ping Sun is acknowledged for earlier work on an implementation of the KIII model.

References

Adrian, E. D. (1926). The impulses produced by sensory nerve ending. *The Journal of Physiology*, *61*, 49–72.

Adrian, E. D. (1928). *The basis of sensation*. New York: Norton.

Cariani, P. (1995). As if time really mattered: temporal strategies for neural coding of sensory information. *Communication and Cognition—Artificial Intelligence*, *12*(1/2), 157–219.

Chang, H., Freeman, J. W., & Burke, B. (1998a). Biologically modeled noise stabilizing neurodynamics for pattern recognition. *International Journal of Bifurcation and Chaos*, *8*(2), 321–345.

Chang, H., Freeman, W. J., & Burke, B. (1998b). Optimization of olfactory model in software to give 1/*f* power spectra reveals numerical instabilities in solutions governed by aperiodic (chaotic) attractors. *Neural Networks*, *11*, 449–466.

Gardner, J. W., & Bartlett, P. N. (1999). *Electronic noses. Principles and applications*. New York: Oxford University Press.

Gutierrez-Osuna, R. (2002). Pattern analysis for machine olfaction: a review. *IEEE Sensors Journal*, *2*(3), 189–202.

Gutierrez-Osuna, R., & Gutierrez-Galvez, A. (2002). Habituation in the KIII olfactory model using gas sensor arrays. *Proceedings of the ninth International Symposium on Olfaction and Electronic Nose* (pp. 171–173). Rome, Italy.

Gutierrez-Osuna, R., & Sun, P. (2002). A biologically-plausible computational architecture for sensor-based machine olfaction. *Proceedings of the ninth International Symposium on Olfaction and Electronic Nose* (pp. 57–59). Rome, Italy.

Kozma, R., & Freeman, W. J. (2001). Chaotic resonance—methods and applications for robust classification of noisy and variable patterns. *International Journal of Bifurcation and Chaos*, *11*(6), 1607–1629.

Laurent, G., & Davidowitz, H. (1994). Encoding of olfactory information with oscillating neural assemblies. *Science*, *265*, 1872–1875.

Lippmann, R. P. (1987). An introduction to computing with neural nets. *IEEE Acoustics, Speech, and Signal Processing Magazine*, 4–22.

MacLeod, K., & Laurent, G. (1996). Distinct mechanisms for synchronization and temporal patterning of odor-encoding neural assemblies. *Science*, *274*, 976–979.

Pearce, T. C. (1997). Computational parallels between the biological olfactory pathway and its analogue 'The Electronic Nose67.

Recce, M. (2001). Encoding information in neuronal activity. In W. Mass, & C. M. Bishop (Eds.), *Pulsed neural networks* (pp. 111–131). Cambridge, MA: MIT Press.

van Ruellen, R., & Thorpe, S. J. (2000). Is it a bird? Is it a plane? Ultra-rapid visual categorization of natural and artifactual objects. *Perception*, *30*, 655–668.

van Trees, H. L. (1968). *Detection, estimation and modulation theory, Part I*. New York: Wiley.

Singer, W., & Gray, C. M. (1995). Visual feature integration and the temporal correlation hypothesis. *Annual Review of Neuroscience*, *18*, 555–586.

Thorpe, S. J., Delorme, A., & Van Ruellen, R. (2001). Spike-based strategies for rapid processing. *Neural Networks*, *14*, 715–725.

Yao, Y., & Freeman, W. J. (1990). Model of biological pattern recognition with spatially chaotic dynamics. *Neural Networks*, *3*, 153–170.

Yao, Y., Freeman, W. J., Burke, B., & Yang, Q. (1991). Pattern recognition by a distributed neural network: An industrial application. *Neural Networks*, *4*, 103–121.

PERGAMON

AVAILABLE AT
www.ComputerScienceWeb.com
POWERED BY SCIENCE DIRECT

Neural Networks 16 (2003) 657–663

Neural Networks

www.elsevier.com/locate/neunet

2003 Special issue

Passive dendritic integration heavily affects spiking dynamics of recurrent networks

Giorgio A. Ascoli*

Krasnow Institute and Psychology Department, George Mason University, 4400 University Dr., Fairfax, VA 22030, USA

Abstract

According to dendritic cable theory, proximal synapses give rise to inputs with short delay, high amplitude, and short duration. In contrast, inputs from distal synapses have long delays, low amplitude, and long duration. Nevertheless, large scale neural networks are seldom built with realistically layered synaptic architectures and corresponding electrotonic parameters. Here, we use a simple model to investigate the spike response dynamics of networks with different electrotonic structures. The networks consist of a layer of neurons receiving a sparse feedforward projection from a set of inputs, as well as sparse recurrent connections from within the layer. Firing patterns are set in the inputs, and recorded from the neuron (output) layer. The feedforward and recurrent synapses are independently set as proximal or distal, representing dendritic connections near or far from the soma, respectively. Analyses of firing dynamics indicate that recurrent distal synapses tend to concentrate network activity in fewer neurons, while proximal recurrent synapses result in a more homogeneous activity distribution. In addition, when the feedforward input is regular (spiking or bursting) and *asynchronous*, the output is regular if recurrent synapses are more distal than feedforward ones, and irregular in the opposite configuration. Finally, the amplitude of network fluctuations in response to asynchronous input is lower if feedforward and recurrent synapses are electrotonically distant from one another (in either configuration). In conclusion, electrotonic effects reflecting different dendritic positions of synaptic inputs significantly influence network dynamics.

Keywords: Neural network model; Dendritic integration; Asynchronous

1. Introduction

Classic neural network models employ basic computational units with no internal structure and a fixed *temporal* window for signal processing (Hopfield, 1982; McCulloch & Pitts, 1943). Cable theory, in contrast, predicts that biological neurons integrate inputs differentially depending on the synaptic position on the dendritic tree. Specifically, the farther is the connection from the soma, the longer are the signal onset and duration, and the lower is the peak value (Rall, 1995). These *electrotonic* effects on dendritic integration are due to the interplay of passive membrane properties (resistance and capacitance). While many neuron classes in the central nervous system possess a variety of active (voltage-gated) channels on their dendrites (Reyes, 2001), there is considerable experimental support for the basic passive mechanisms underlying dendritic integration (Rall et al., 1992). The connectivity of most major natural networks in the mammalian brain is exquisitely organized in layers, such that specific feedforward, recurrent, and feedback projections each contact the target dendrites within precise ranges of electrotonic distances. This layered organization is observed, for example, in all major pathways in the cerebral cortex, hippocampus, and cerebellum (Shepherd, 1998). It is thus likely that dendritic integration and the anatomical organization of synaptic connectivity together constrain network dynamic, and, ultimately, plasticity and function (e.g. Agmon-Snir, Carr, & Rinzel, 1998).

Detailed dendritic passive models of single neurons are widely adopted in computational neuroscience (Segev & London, 2000), often complemented with active mechanisms (Migliore & Shepherd, 2002). For larger scale simulations, simplified integrate-and-fire models are frequently adopted instead (Dayan & Abbott, 2001). Several types of integrate-and-fire models allow the inclusion of electrotonic effects on dendritic processing (e.g. in the form of time constants for signal rise and decay). However, large scale models are seldom built with layered synaptic architectures (e.g. with principal cells receiving proximal feedforward excitation, distal recurrent collaterals, and

* Tel.: +1-703-993-4383; fax: +1-703-993-4325.
E-mail address: ascoli@gmu.edu (G.A. Ascoli).

0893-6080/03/$ - see front matter © 2003 Elsevier Science Ltd. All rights reserved.
doi:10.1016/S0893-6080(03)00090-X

intermediate lateral inhibition) and corresponding electrotonic parameters. The goal of this study is to investigate possible electrotonic effects on the spike response dynamics of networks with organized, layered connectivity. We find that, even in simple cases (feedforward and recurrent excitation), the relative electrotonic position of the inputs dramatically affects the distribution and regularity of activity in the network.

2. Methods

Simulations are based on a spike response model incorporating electrotonic effects. The basic computational unit is a deterministic binary neuron that compares the sum of all active inputs at each time step to the value of a threshold. If the activity sum is over the threshold, and the neuron was not firing in the previous time step (absolute refractory period), then the neuron fires in the given time step. The basic threshold value is uniform throughout the population of neurons, but is dynamically and instantaneously adjusted at each time step to maintain the overall network activity closest to the desired level of 5%. Since the input values are integers (see below) and the network consists of a finite number of neurons, there is generally no threshold value resulting in an activity of *exactly* 5%. Thus, the threshold value is selected to best approximate the target population activity from either direction. This dynamic threshold mechanism may be seen as representing fast feedback inhibition, and is functionally equivalent to the *k-winners-take-all* scheme (O'Reilly & Munakata, 2000). In addition, the threshold value is further increased for each neuron that fired two time steps before, such that its firing probability is halved (relative refractory period).

A given input to a neuron is active depending on the firing state of the corresponding presynaptic neuron. The input is approximated as a square wave characterized by a delay, an amplitude, and a duration ('Dad' synapse). The delay is the number of time steps from presynaptic firing to the onset of the postsynaptic signal. The amplitude is an integer value that is summed with all other active input amplitudes by the postsynaptic neuron at each time step. Finally, the duration is the number of consecutive time steps for which the input is counted by the postsynaptic neuron following the onset (Fig. 1). The values of delay, amplitude, and duration depend on the electrotonic distance of the synapse.

In this work, proximal synapses have a delay of 1 time step, an amplitude of 4, and a duration of 1 time step. Distal synapses have a delay of 2 time steps, an amplitude of 1, and a duration of 4 time steps. The network consists of a set of 1000 inputs projecting to a layer of 1000 neurons with random, sparse (10%) connectivity (feedforward pathway). The neuron (output) layer also projects to itself with random and sparse (10%) connectivity (recurrent pathway). Feedforward (input to output) and recurrent (output to output)

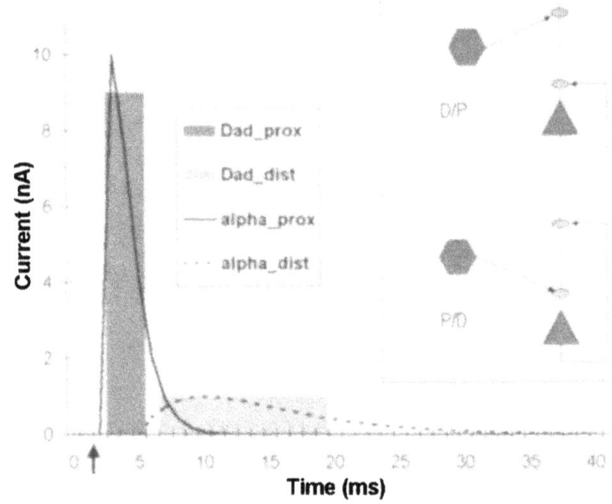

Fig. 1. Examples of typical synaptic currents approximated by alpha functions (full line, proximal; dotted line, distal) and corresponding Dad square waves (dark gray, proximal; light gray, distal). Both current and time scales are for illustration only, and do not correspond to the values used in the simulations. Inset: examples of network configuration (D/P: distal feedforward, proximal recurrent; P/D: proximal feedforward, distal recurrent).

synapses are independently set as proximal or distal, modeling dendritic connections near or far from the soma, respectively. Thus, four architectures are possible: proximal/proximal, proximal/distal, distal/proximal, and distal/distal (with the two attributes referring to feedforward and recurrent synapses, respectively). Two examples are schematized in the inset of Fig. 1.

Firing patterns are set in the set of inputs, and recorded from the neuron layer, for 500 time steps. Six different stimulation patterns are used for the set of inputs, resulting from three firing modes (random, spiking, and bursting), either synchronously or asynchronously. Random firing is aperiodic; spiking is a periodic pattern of one spike followed by 19 silent time steps; and bursting is a periodic pattern of a train of four spikes with inter-spike interval of 2 time steps, followed by 70 silent time steps. In synchronous patterns all inputs fire in phase, while in *asynchronous* patterns the phase of each input is assigned randomly. Thus, in synchronous firing the input activity is sparse (5%) over the whole simulation period, but not at each time step. In contrast, the activity of the neuron layer is maintained as close as possible to 5% at each time step by the dynamic threshold. The dynamics of the neuron layer are mainly characterized here with two parameters: concentration and irregularity. Concentration is a measure of the distribution of network activity among all neurons. For example, given an average network activity of 5%, a high concentration would correspond to 10% of the neurons being active 50% of time steps (with the remaining neurons always silent), while a low concentration would correspond to each and every neuron being active 5% of time steps. Irregularity is a measure of the even separation of spikes in the activity raster. In general, random firing corresponds to high irregularity, while bursting and especially spiking modes correspond to low irregularity. The exact formulae of concentration and irregularity are defined in Eqs. (1) and (2), respectively

$$\text{Concentration} = \sigma_N[\mu_T(F_i)]/\mu_N[\mu_T(F_i)] \quad (1)$$

$$\text{Irregularity} = \mu_N[\sigma_T(\text{ISI}_i)\mu_T(F_i)]/\mu_N[\mu_T(F_i)] \quad (2)$$

where F_i and ISI_i are the set of firing states (0/1 for silent/firing) and inter-spike intervals for the ith neuron, respectively; μ_T and μ_N are the means taken over time and over the set of neurons, respectively; and σ_T and σ_N are the standard deviations taken over time and over the set of neurons, respectively. Thus, $\mu_T(F_i)$ is the mean firing rate of the ith neuron, and concentration corresponds to the coefficient of variation of this quantity over the set of neurons.

Software scripts were written in Matlab (The MathWorks, Natick, MA), and are available upon request. All simulations were run in duplicate under Windows98 on a 500 MHz Pentium III with 256 MB of RAM.

3. Results

A total of 48 simulations were run, two for each combination of stimulus pattern in the set of inputs (synchronous and asynchronous random, spiking, and bursting) and connectivity pattern in the neuron layer (feedforward and recurrent connections corresponding to proximal or distal synapses). The firing state of each neuron, as well as the value of the dynamic threshold, were recorded at each time step. All parameters of Eqs. (1) and (2) were computed from these data. The visualization of the complete raster plots for each of the 24 pairs of repeated simulations showed several emerging trends, all systematically confirmed by both non-identical runs of every pair. First, rasters corresponding to distal synapses in the recurrent connections (independent of the electrotonic distance of feedforward synapses) systematically displayed a more apparent spatial pattern of spikes (e.g. Fig. 2). While neuronal activity in networks with proximal recurrent synapses was centered at the mean of 5%, with a maximum rate of ~ 15%, in networks with distal recurrent synapses most neurons were almost entirely silent, but cells that did fire could reach an activity of >30%.

This feature is quantitatively captured by the concentration parameter, and is summarized for all simulations in Table 1. Note that the concentration ratio between the proximal/distal and distal/proximal connectivity patterns (pd/dp) for each of the firing modes (random, spiking, and bursting) is greater when the input stimulus is synchronous (Table 1).

A closer inspection to the firing patterns of individual neurons revealed additional effects. In particular, certain simulations resulted in more regular temporal patterns of firing than others (see e.g. Fig. 3). The top panel of Fig. 3 resembles traces typical of regular spikers, while the bottom

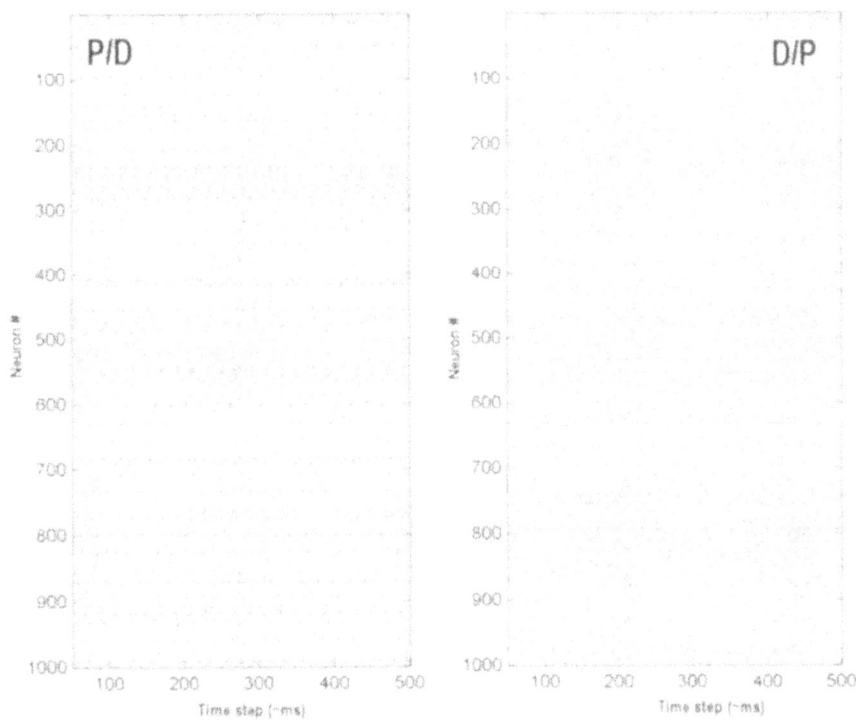

Fig. 2. Activity rasters in response to asynchronous spiking. Left: proximal feedforward, distal recurrent; right: distal feedforward, proximal recurrent. Spikes are more homogeneously distributed among neurons when recurrent synapses are proximal.

Table 1
Firing concentration (see Eq. (1)) in all network architectures (P/P: proximal feedforward, proximal recurrent; through D/D: distal feedforward and recurrent) and stimulation modes. Each simulation was run in duplicate; pair averages were used to calculate the ratio pd/dp between the values of P/D and D/P

Concentration	P/P	P/D	D/P	D/D	pd/dp
Async rand	0.511	0.582	0.629	0.935	0.928
	0.519	0.606	0.651	0.861	
Sync rand	0.564	1.080	0.611	1.020	1.795
	0.566	1.201	0.660	1.070	
Async spike	0.631	0.917	0.627	1.049	1.437
	0.634	0.879	0.623	1.078	
Sync spike	0.586	1.048	0.610	1.219	1.748
	0.580	1.093	0.615	0.991	
Async burst	0.840	0.986	0.804	1.146	1.261
	0.855	0.994	0.766	1.141	
Sync burst	0.680	1.088	0.752	1.108	1.372
	0.696	0.963	0.743	1.141	

panel shows apparently random patterns. This feature is again summarized in tabular format for all simulations using the irregularity parameter (Table 2). If the stimulus from the set of inputs is random and/or synchronous, there is no electrotonic effect on the irregularity in the neuron layer. In contrast, if the input stimulus is regular (spiking or bursting) and asynchronous, then the network activity is more regular when recurrent synapses are electrotonically more distant than feedforward synapses, and less regular in the opposite configuration. Interestingly, the irregularity of the output is intermediate if recurrent and feedforward synapses have the same electrotonic distance (both proximal or both distal). It is important to add that the concentration and irregularity parameters are uncorrelated across the 24 simulations ($R^2 = 0.0616$).

An additional observation regards the temporal plots of the overall network activity (Fig. 4). Although the dynamic threshold mechanism controls the mean firing rate, the network activity fluctuates depending on the number of neurons, which are similarly close to the firing threshold. No electrotonic effects were observed on the activity fluctuations in response to synchronous stimuli. However, in response to asynchronous stimuli, overall network activity layer appeared more constrained (with lower amplitude fluctuations around the mean firing rate), if feedforward and recurrent synapses were electrotonically distant from each other, in either configuration (i.e. proximal/distal or distal/proximal, but not proximal/proximal or distal/distal). As

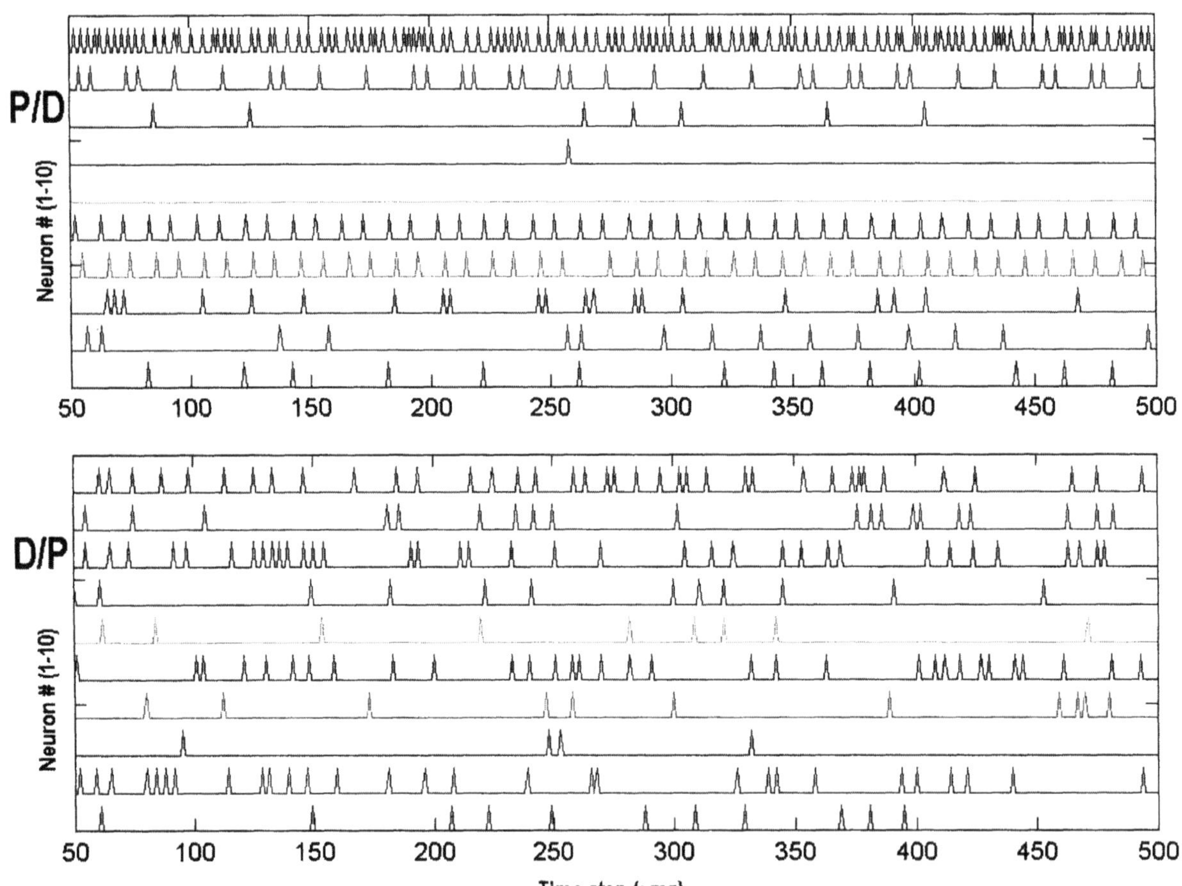

Fig. 3. Examples of spike traces: response to asynchronous spiking. Top: first 10 neurons of the network with proximal feedforward and distal recurrent; bottom: first 10 neurons of the network with distal feedforward and proximal recurrent.

Table 2
Firing irregularity (see Eq. (2)) in all network architectures (P/P: proximal feedforward, proximal recurrent; through D/D: distal feedforward and recurrent) and stimulation modes. Each simulation was run in duplicate; pair averages were used to calculate the ratio pd/dp between the values of P/D and D/P

Irregularity	P/P	P/D	D/P	D/D	pd/dp
Async rand	16.51	16.13	16.18	17.17	0.998
	16.34	16.26	16.26	17.40	
Sync rand	16.59	17.43	16.51	17.34	0.987
	16.89	16.21	17.58	17.59	
Async spike	13.85	7.608	14.89	11.80	0.528
	13.67	8.119	14.88	11.50	
Sync spike	16.42	16.45	15.84	13.85	1.028
	16.02	16.37	16.09	15.85	
Async burst	14.47	10.94	15.63	12.57	0.703
	14.12	10.95	15.51	13.07	
Sync burst	16.82	16.60	16.76	16.32	1.021
	16.64	17.51	16.63	15.93	

an example, in the traces of Fig. 4 corresponding to asynchronous spiking (third row), the high amplitude fluctuations of the first and fourth panel can be contrasted with the low amplitude fluctuations of the second and third panel.

Finally, and not unexpectedly, the temporal pattern of the threshold value in the neuron layer ('inhibition') always closely reflected the stimulus pattern in the set of inputs (Fig. 5). Note that, in the case of synchronous bursting stimulation with distal (but not proximal) feedforward projections, the inhibition traces partially integrate the high frequency component of the bursts into square waves (bottom right panel).

4. Discussion

The spike response model employed in this study approximates synaptic inputs with square waves characterized by three parameters: delay, amplitude, and duration. The electrotonic properties of the relative synaptic positions in a simple feedforward/recurrent network were captured by adopting shorter delay and duration and higher amplitude for proximal than for distal synapses. Network dynamics displayed a wide range of firing concentration, irregularity, and fluctuation around the mean value. This variable behavior appeared to be due to the specific combination of stimulus pattern and

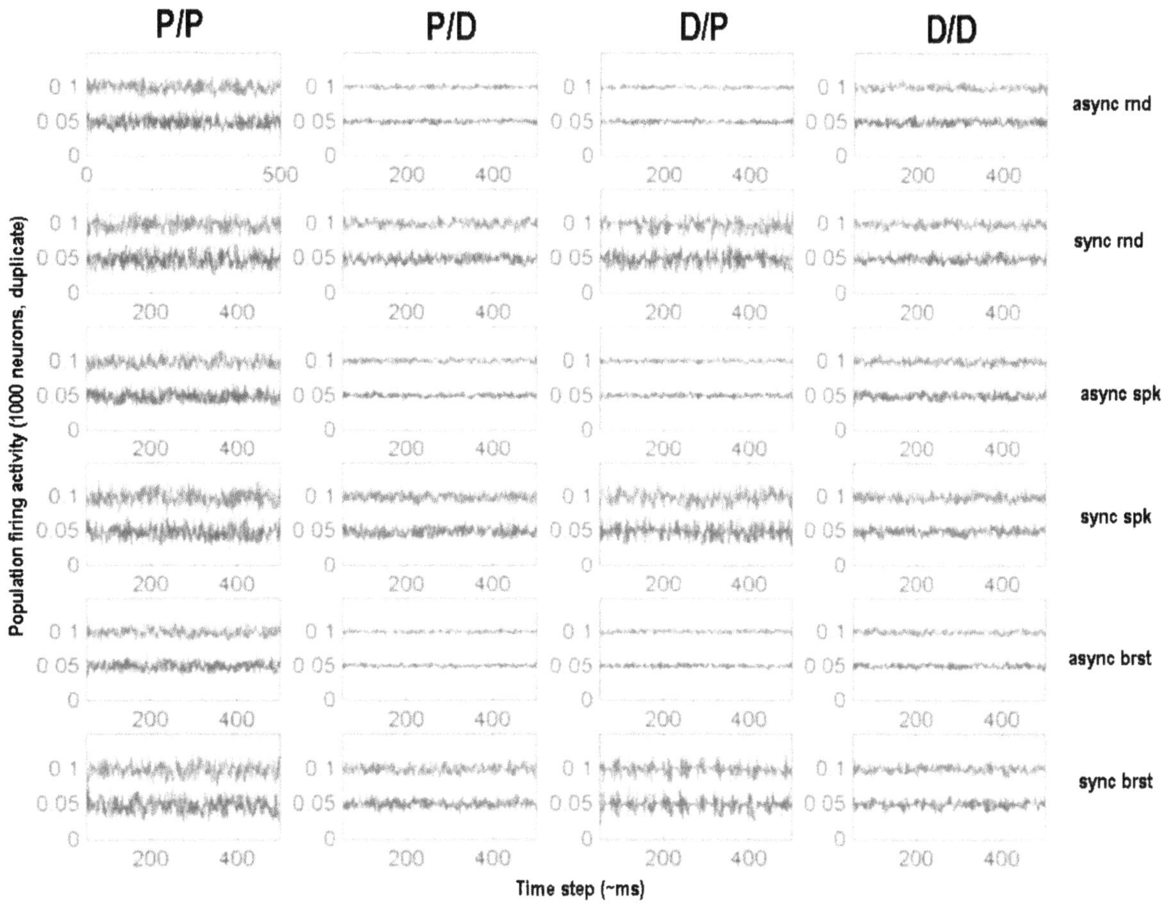

Fig. 4. Population firing in all network architectures and stimulation modes (symbols as in Table 1). Each simulation was run in duplicate (bottom traces in each panel: fraction of active cells, first run; top traces: fraction of active cells +0.05, second run). Note the lower fluctuation amplitude in the P/D and D/P configurations when the stimulus is asynchronous.

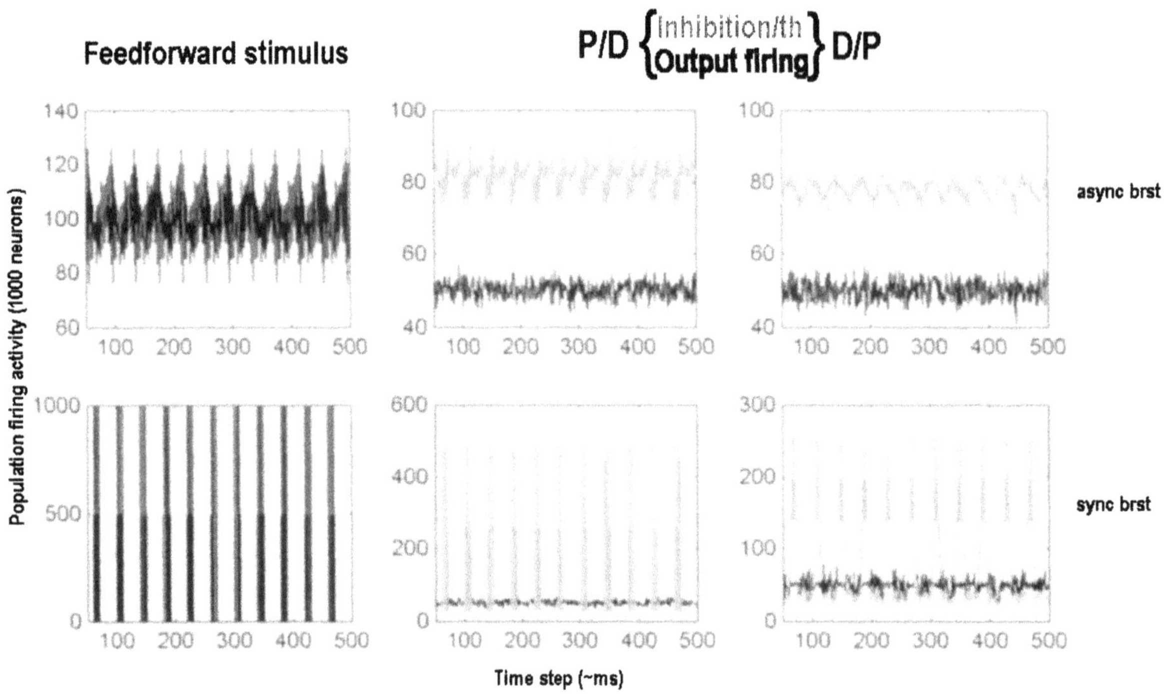

Fig. 5. Feedforward stimulus (left column) and resulting population firing activity (middle and right columns, black trace) and threshold value (middle and right columns, gray traces) for selected examples of stimulus and connectivity patterns. Threshold values, which represent network inhibition, closely reflect stimulus patterns.

electrotonic architecture of the network. In particular, recurrent distal synapses tended to concentrate network activity in fewer neurons, while proximal recurrent synapses resulted in a more homogeneously distributed activity, especially in the presence of synchronous feedforward input. In response to asynchronous spiking or bursting, network activity was regular with recurrent synapses more distal than feedforward ones, and irregular in the opposite configuration. Network fluctuations in response to asynchronous input were dampened when feedforward and recurrent synapses contacted the dendrites in opposite electrotonic positions.

What are the mechanisms underlying these results? Distal connections have a long-lasting effect on neuronal activity. This can provide an explanation for the concentration of network activity in fewer neuron in architectures with distal recurrent synapses. In this configuration (and with random but fixed connectivity), firing of one neuron is a predictor of further firing of the same neuron within a period corresponding to the input duration of recurrent synapses. This explanation was supported by additional simulations with simpler recurrent networks (not shown), in which the effect of electrotonic distance on firing concentration faded completely when the absolute refractory period was extended to match the duration of synaptic input. The peculiar combination of feedforward stimulus pattern and electrotonic configuration controlling irregularity and fluctuation of network activity, in contrast, defies simple explanations.

The firing (spike) duration, as well as the duration of the absolute and relative refractory periods, were all set to one time step in this model. Based on typical Hodgkin–Huxley parameters for central nervous system neurons (Dayan & Abbott, 2001), one could draw a rough correspondence between one simulation time step and 1 ms of biological time. This would result in the equivalence of the chosen activity level (5%) to a mean firing frequency of 50 Hz. In this scale, the parameters selected here for synaptic delay and duration correspond, according to cable theory, to electrotonic distances from the soma of approximately one and five length constants for proximal and distal connections, respectively (Rall, 1995). The relatively sparse connectivity of both feedforward and recurrent pathways is also within a biologically plausible range. Each neuron receives an average of 10 proximal inputs or 40 distal inputs (or a combination of the two) every millisecond. The sparse activity and connectivity typically observed in biological neural networks constitute a difficult challenge for reduced scale models. The spike response model with 'Dad' synapses introduced here provides a formalism almost as simple as McCulloch–Pitts', while allowing the electrotonic representation of layered synaptic architectures. Recent advances in computational neuroanatomy make it now possible to generate anatomically realistic neural network models of relatively large regions of the brain (Ascoli, 1999; 2002a,b). The Dad approximation could thus become a useful modeling formalism for real-scale simulations of biological networks.

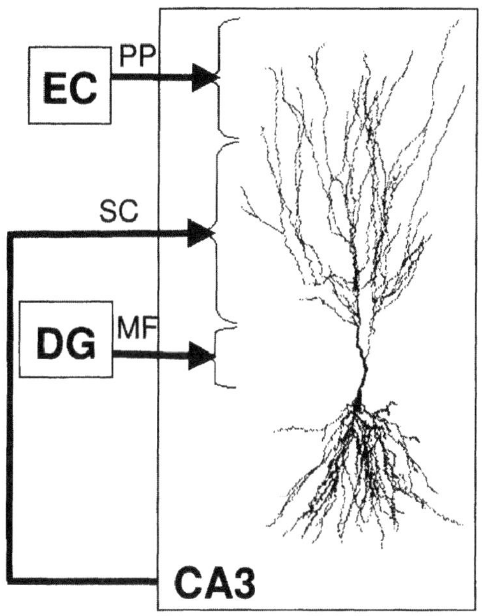

Fig. 6. Schematic architecture of main excitatory inputs to a CA3 pyramidal cell. Recurrent Schaffer collaterals (SC) from CA3 make contacts at electrotonic distances intermediate between the two main feedforward inputs: the mossy fibers (MF) from the dentate gyrus (DG), and the perforant path (PP) from the entorhinal cortex (EC).

The electrotonic effects on the dynamics of networks with more complex synaptic architectures remain to be explored. Even the simple two-layer network architecture examined here, however, is of potential biological relevance. This model can be viewed as an extreme simplification of the CA3 region of the hippocampus (Fig. 6). When the dentate gyrus provides the predominant input to CA3, the recurrent CA3 collaterals are distal relative to the feedforward (mossy fibers) stimulus. Conversely, when the entorhinal cortex constitutes the primary input to CA3, the recurrent CA3 collaterals are proximal relative to the feedforward (perforant path) stimulus.

It may be difficult or impossible to reproduce simple and extreme cases of firing patterns similar to those reported here in an experimental preparation in vivo or even in vitro. In any case, the present simulations are obviously not a faithful representation of the complex physiological and anatomical interactions underlying hippocampal dynamic. Nonetheless, this model represents a proof of principle of the electrotonic influences on network dynamics that could apply to several other synaptic architectures in the central nervous system. It is intriguing that specific active conductances able to counterbalance the individual effects of passive integration on synaptic signals (e.g. I_h, I_{NaP}) are differentially expressed in the dendrites of various neuronal classes (Migliore & Shepherd, 2002; Reyes, 2001). The corresponding extent to which the electrotonic transformation of synaptic signals is 'normalized' by voltage-gated channels in the dendrites varies considerably among the most studied neuronal types, such as motoneurons (Redman & Walmsley, 1983), CA1 pyramidal cells (Magee, 2000), and neocortical neurons (Williams & Stuart, 2002). As firing dynamics are believed to affect and constrain neural network plasticity and performance, the results presented in this paper constitute important clues to the relationship between synaptic architecture and central nervous system function.

Acknowledgements

I am indebted to Drs Kim (Avrama) Blackwell, James Olds, and Thomas Vogl for useful comments on the manuscript, and to the Computational Neuroanatomy Group for many stimulating discussions. Supported by Human Brain Project NS39600, jointly funded by NINDS and NIMH (National Institutes of Health).

References

Agmon-Snir, H., Carr, C. E., & Rinzel, J. (1998). The role of dendrites in auditory coincidence detection. *Nature*, *393*, 268–272.

Ascoli, G. A. (1999). Progress and perspectives in computational neuroanatomy. *Anatomical Record*, *257*, 195–207.

Ascoli, G. A. (Ed.), (2002a). *Computational neuroanatomy: Principles and methods*. Totowa, NJ: Humana Press.

Ascoli, G. A. (2002b). Neuroanatomical algorithms for dendritic modelling. *Network*, *13*, 247–260.

Dayan, P., & Abbott, L. F. (2001). *Theoretical neuroscience: Computational and mathematical modeling of neural systems*. Cambridge, MA: MIT Press.

Hopfield, J. J. (1982). Neural networks and physical systems with emergent collective computational abilities. *Proceedings of the National Academy of Science (USA)*, *79*, 2554–2558.

Magee, J. C. (2000). Dendritic integration of excitatory synaptic input. *Nature Reviews Neuroscience*, *1*, 181–190.

McCulloch, W. S., & Pitts, W. (1943). A logical calculus of the ideas immanent in nervous activity. *Bulletin of Mathematical Biophysics*, *5*, 115–133.

Migliore, M., & Shepherd, G. M. (2002). Emerging rules for the distributions of active dendritic conductances. *Nature Reviews Neuroscience*, *3*, 362–370.

O'Reilly, R. C., & Munakata, Y. (2000). *Computational explorations in cognitive neuroscience*. Cambridge, MA: MIT Press.

Rall, W. (1995). In I. Segev, J. Rinzel, & G. Shepherd (Eds.), *The theoretical foundation of dendritic function: Selected papers*. Cambridge, MA: MIT Press.

Rall, W., Burke, R. E., Holmes, W. R., Jack, J. J., Redman, S. J., & Segev, I. (1992). Matching dendritic neuron models to experimental data. *Physiological Reviews*, *72*, S159–S186.

Redman, S., & Walmsley, B. (1983). The time course and amplitude fluctuations of synaptic potentials evoked in cat spinal motoneurones at identified group Ia synapses. *Journal of Physiology*, *343*, 117–145.

Reyes, A. (2001). Influence of dendritic conductances on the inputoutput properties of neurons properties of neurons. *Annual Reviews of Neuroscience*, *24*, 653–675.

Segev, I., & London, M. (2000). Untangling dendrites with quantitative models. *Science*, *290*, 744–750.

Shepherd, G. M. (1998). *The synaptic organization of the brain* (4th ed.). New York: Oxford University Press.

Williams, S. R., & Stuart, G. J. (2002). Dependence of EPSP efficacy on synapse location in neocortical pyramidal neurons. *Science*, *295*, 1907–1910.

PERGAMON

AVAILABLE AT
www.ComputerScienceWeb.com
POWERED BY SCIENCE DIRECT

Neural Networks 16 (2003) 665–673

Neural Networks

www.elsevier.com/locate/neunet

2003 Special issue

Abductive reasoning with recurrent neural networks

Ashraf M. Abdelbar[a,*], Emad A.M. Andrews[a], Donald C. Wunsch II[b]

[a]*Department of Computer Science, American University in Cairo, 113 Kasr El Aini Street, Cairo, Egypt*
[b]*Department of Electrical and Computer Engineering, University of Missouri, Missouri, Rolla, ND, USA*

Abstract

Abduction is the process of proceeding from data describing a set of observations or events, to a set of hypotheses which best explains or accounts for the data. Cost-based abduction (CBA) is a formalism in which evidence to be explained is treated as a goal to be proven, proofs have costs based on how much needs to be assumed to complete the proof, and the set of assumptions needed to complete the least-cost proof are taken as the best explanation for the given evidence. In previous work, we presented a method for using high order recurrent networks to find least cost proofs for CBA instances. Here, we present a method that significantly reduces the size of the neural network that is produced for a given CBA instance. We present experimental results describing the performance of this method and comparing its performance to that of the previous method.

1. Reasoning under uncertainty

Humans exhibit the ability to assimilate and reason with information that is incomplete, contradictory, or subject to change. Reasoning under uncertainty is the branch of artificial intelligence that is concerned with modeling this facet of human cognition. Conventional first-order logic is inadequate for this task: statements are either known to be true, known to be false, or not known to be one way or the other. Further, once a statement is known to be true (or false), it remains true (or false) forever. One approach to reasoning with uncertainty is higher-order nonmonotonic logic (Ginsberg, 1987; Marek & Truszczynski, 1993; Reiter, 1987; Shoham, 1987). For example, modal logic (Konyndyk, 1986; Popkorn, 1994) augments predicate logic with modal operators, which take whole sentences as arguments. With modal logic, it is possible, for example, to distinguish between a statement which is false but has the potential of being true (such as Jimmy drives a Mercedes) and a statement which is by necessity false (such as Jimmy has three ears).

An alternative to symbol-based nonmonotonic logic is numerical representations of uncertainty. These include Bayesian belief networks (Pearl, 1986, 1988), Dempster-Shafer belief functions (Dempster, 1967; Koffler & Leondes, 1994; Shafer, 1976, 1986; Shafer & Logan, 1987), fuzzy sets (Zadeh, 1979, 1994; Zadeh & Kacprzyk, 1992; Zimmerman, 1991), and rough sets (Pawlak, 1991, 1992; Pawlak, Grzymala-Busse, Slowinski & Ziark, 1995), as well as cost-based abduction (CBA) systems (Charniak & Shimony, 1990, 1994).

2. Cost-based abduction

Abduction is the process of proceeding from data describing observations or events, to a set of hypotheses, which best explains or accounts for the data (Hobbs, Stickel, Martin & Edwards, 1993). Cost-based abduction (Charniak & Shimony, 1990, 1994) is a knowledge representation in which a given world situation is modeled as a 4-tuple $(\mathscr{H}, \mathscr{R}, c, \mathscr{G})$, where $\mathscr{H}$ is a set of hypotheses or propositions, c is a function from $\mathscr{H}$ to the non-negative reals where $c(h)$ is called the assumability cost of hypothesis $h \in \mathscr{H}$, $\mathscr{R}$ is a set of rules of the form

$$R : (h_{i_1} \wedge h_{i_2} \wedge \ldots \wedge h_{i_n}) \rightarrow h_{i_k},$$

where $h_{i_1}, \ldots, h_{i_n}$ (called the antecedents) and h_{i_k} (called the consequent) are all members of $\mathscr{H}$, and $\mathscr{G} \subseteq \mathscr{H}$ is the goal or the evidence. The objective is to find the least cost proof (LCP) for the evidence, where the cost of a proof is taken to be the sum of the costs of all hypotheses that must be assumed in order to complete the proof. Any given hypothesis can be made true in two ways: it can be assumed to be true, at a cost of its assumability cost, or it can be

* Corresponding author.
E-mail address: abdelbar@aucegypt.edu (A.M. Abdelbar).

0893-6080/03/$ - see front matter © 2003 Elsevier Science Ltd. All rights reserved.
doi:10.1016/S0893-6080(03)00114-X

proved. If a hypothesis occurs as the consequent of a rule R, then it can be proved, at no cost, to be true by making all the antecedents of R true, either by assumption or by proof. If a hypothesis does not appear as the consequent of any rule, then it cannot be proved, it can be made true only by being assumed. The cost of a hypothesis can be ∞, which means that it cannot be assumed, it can only be proved. One can assume, without loss of generality, that any hypothesis that appears as the consequent of any rule has an infinite assumability cost.

Charniak & Shimony (1994) have investigated best-first search techniques for CBA, and Santos (Santos, 1991, 1994) presents an algorithm for converting a CBA system into an integer linear program (ILP) which can then be solved by conventional integer linear programming methods (Nemhauser, Rinnooy Kan & Todd, 1989; Schrijver, 1986). Abdelbar (1998) shows how methods for CBA can be applied to the maximum a posteriori (MAP) problem on Bayesian belief networks.

Here, we apply high order recurrent networks (HORN) (Abdelbar, 1999) to the LCP problem through the use of an intermediate representation, penalty logic (PL). (Pinkas, 1992, 1995) defines PL and shows a constructive algorithm for transforming a given PL to an equivalent HORN. We make use of this result by developing a novel method of representing a CBA system with PL. This method is a development on previous work (Abdelbar, Andrews & Tagliarini, 2003), as will be discussed in a later section.

3. Penalty logic and high order networks

3.1. High order recurrent networks

A recurrent neural network is one whose underlying topology of inter-neuronal connections contains at least one cycle. In the case of the Hopfield network (Hopfield, 1982, 1984), the underlying topology is a graph: each weighted connection is either an edge connecting two neurons, or a self-loop involving one neuron. A HORN is a recurrent network whose underlying topology is a hypergraph, i.e., it allows weighted hyperedges which connect more than two neurons. The degree of a hyperedge is the number of neurons it connects; the order of a HORN is the largest hyperedge degree in the topology. We will use the notation $T^{(k)}_{i_1 \ldots i_k}$ to denote the weight of the kth-degree edge connecting neurons $i_1 \ldots i_k$. A HORN is symmetric if

$$T^{(k)}_{i_1 \cdots i_k} = T^{(k)}_{i_{\Pi(1)} \cdots i_{\Pi(k)}}, \tag{1}$$

for any permutation Π of the integers $1, \ldots, k$. In this paper, we are concerned with symmetric HORN's, and, unless otherwise specified, the term HORN should by default be taken to mean symmetric HORN.

The input u_i to a neuron in a kth-order HORN, whose output is V_i, can be characterized by

$$\Delta u_i = \sum_{l=1}^{k} \sum_{i_1 \cdots i \cdots i_l} T^l_{i_1 \cdots i \cdots i_l} \prod_{1 \le j \le l, i_j \ne i} V_{i_j} \tag{2}$$

A kth-order HORN can be viewed as minimizing a kth-order energy function (Pinkas, 1992):

$$\begin{aligned} E = & - \sum_{1 \le i_1 < i_2 < \cdots < i_k \le n} T^{(k)}_{i_1 \cdots i_k} V_{i_1} \cdots V_{i_k} \\ & - \sum_{1 \le i_1 < i_2 < \cdots < i_{k-1} \le n} T^{(k-1)}_{i_1 \cdots i_{k-1}} V_{i_1} \cdots V_{i_{k-1}} \\ & - \cdots - \sum_{1 \le i \le n} T^{(1)} V_i. \end{aligned} \tag{3}$$

The quadratic energy function of the Hopfield network is a special case of Eq. (3); it can be written using the notation of this paper as:

$$E = -\sum_{i \le n} T^{(1)} V_i - \sum_{1 \le i < j \le n} T^{(2)}_{ij} V_i V_j. \tag{4}$$

3.2. Penalty logic

Penalty logic is an extension of propositional logic which associates real-valued penalties with well-formed formulae (wff's) and allows the wff's to be violated at a cost of their associated penalties. A PL $\mathscr{L}$ is a set of pairs $\{\langle \rho_i, \phi_i \rangle\}$, where ϕ_i is a propositional-logic wff called an *assumption* and ρ_i is a real-valued penalty. A truth assignment to the set of propositions which participate in the assumptions of $\mathscr{L}$ is called a *world model*. If a given assumption does not have a value of true under a given world model, then it is said to be *violated*. The *violation rank* of a given world model is the sum of the penalties associated with all the assumptions that are violated by the model.

Consider the following example $\mathscr{L}$ over the set of propositions $\{p, q, r, s\}$.

100	$p\bar{r} \to s$	75	$q\bar{r} \vee \bar{q}r$	500	p
200	$s \leftrightarrow \bar{q}$	50	$\bar{r} \vee \bar{p}$	120	q

Here, the minimum-violation rank world model is $\{p \leftarrow \mathbf{T}, r \leftarrow \mathbf{F}, s \leftarrow \mathbf{F}, q \leftarrow \mathbf{T}\}$, which violates only the first assumption and therefore incurs a total penalty of only 100. The second-lowest violation-rank model is $\{p \leftarrow \mathbf{T}, r \leftarrow \mathbf{T}, s \leftarrow \mathbf{F}, q \leftarrow \mathbf{T}\}$, which violates the second and fifth assumptions, thus incurring a penalty of 125.

3.3. Equivalence between penalty logic and HORN's

Pinkas (1995) shows that there is a two-way equivalence between HORN's and PL, specifically between the problem of finding the minimum energy neuron assignment for a HORN and the problem of finding the minimum violation rank world model for a PL. We briefly sketch the basic elements of this transformation here, but the reader is referred to (Pinkas, 1992) for a fuller descripion.

Given a logical expression s, a characteristic function $H(s)$ is constructed to have its maximum value exactly when s has a value of true. If $s = s_1 \wedge s_2$, then

$$H(s) = H(s_1) \times H(s_2). \quad (5)$$

if $s = s_1 \vee s_2$, then

$$H(s) = H(s_1) + H(s_2) - H(s_1) \times H(s_2). \quad (6)$$

if $s = \neg s_1$, then

$$H(s) = 1 - H(s_1). \quad (7)$$

Finally, if $s = x_1$, where x_1 is an atomic proposition, then

$$H(s) = x_1, \quad (8)$$

where x_1 has values of 1 and 0 in the algebraic function if and only if it has values of true and false, respectively, in the logical function. For example, the expression $a \wedge b \rightarrow c$ would be converted into a characteristic function as follows:

$$H(a\wedge b\rightarrow c) = H(\neg(a\wedge b)\vee c)$$
$$= H(\neg a\vee\neg b\vee c)$$
$$= H(\neg a\vee\neg b) + c - H(\neg a\vee\neg b)c$$
$$= (1-a)+(1-b)-(1-a)(1-b)+c$$
$$-c(1-a)-c(1-b)+c(1-a)(1-b)$$
$$= 1-ab+abc.$$

We can see from the following truth table that $H(s)$ indeed has its maximal points exactly at those truth assignments which satisfy s.

a	b	c	s	H(s)
0	0	0	T	1
0	0	1	T	1
0	1	0	T	1
0	1	1	T	1
1	0	0	T	1
1	0	1	T	1
1	1	0	F	0
1	1	1	T	1

For each ϕ_i in a given $\mathcal{L}$, we first construct $H(\neg\, \phi_i)$,and add the connections corresponding to $\rho_i \times H(\neg\, \phi_i)$ to the HORN.

For example, the PL shown in Eq. (12) would result in the following set of weighted characteristic functions:

$$\begin{aligned}
&1000 \quad (t - tpqs)\\
&1000 \quad (s - spr - squ + sprqu)\\
&1000 \quad (\mathcal{G} - \mathcal{G}tu)\\
&100 \quad (p)\\
&150 \quad (q)\\
&75 \quad (u)\\
&3000 \quad (-\mathcal{G})
\end{aligned} \quad (9)$$

This would produce the following set of HORN hyperedges:

weight	neurons				
-1000	t				
1000	t	p	q	s	
-1000	s				
1000	s	p	r		
1000	s	q	u		
-1000	s	p	r	q	u
1000	$\mathcal{G}$	t	u		
-100	p				
-150	q				
-75	u				
2000	$\mathcal{G}$				

A HORN is then constructed based on these connections, and an activation function based on mean field annealing. For a given neuron i,

$$V_i = \text{sigmoid}(u_i/T), \quad (10)$$

where T is a temperature parameter that starts at an initial value, and is decreased by a fixed percentage factor after each iteration.

4. Transformation

Let $(\mathcal{H}, \mathcal{R}, c, \mathcal{G})$ be an arbitrary CBA instance. We will describe how to construct a corresponding PL $\mathcal{L} = \{\langle\phi_i, \rho_i\rangle\}$ such that the least-cost proof for $(\mathcal{H}, \mathcal{R}, c, \mathcal{G})$ will correspond to the minimum-violation rank world model for $\mathcal{L}$. Each hypothesis in the CBA will become a variable in the PL and will then become a neuron in the HORN. Consider the following example CBA system:

$$p \wedge q \wedge s \rightarrow t$$
$$p \wedge r \rightarrow s$$
$$q \wedge u \rightarrow s$$
$$t \wedge u \rightarrow \mathcal{G}$$
$$c(p) = 100, c(q) = 150, c(u) = 75,$$
$$c(r) = \infty, c(s) = \infty, c(t) = \infty, c(\mathcal{G}) = \infty.$$

Here, the second and third rule constitute an 'implicit OR,' i.e. they represent two different ways in which s can be proven. We begin by converting all implicit OR's into explicit OR's as follows:

$$p \wedge q \wedge s \rightarrow t$$

$$(p \wedge r) \vee (q \wedge u) \rightarrow s$$

$$t \wedge u \rightarrow \mathcal{G}$$

Since each consequent appears on the right hand side of only one rule, and consequents cannot be assumed, the only way the consequent can be true is if the left-hand side is true. We can therefore reverse the flow of the rules as follows:

$$\begin{aligned} &t \rightarrow p \wedge q \wedge s \\ &s \rightarrow (p \wedge r) \vee (q \wedge u) \\ &\mathcal{G} \rightarrow t \wedge u \end{aligned} \tag{11}$$

This can be transformed into a PL by associating a prohibitively high penalty, which we call the rule preservation cost and denote Γ, with each of these non-violable rules. For each of the assumable hypotheses

$$c(p) = 100, c(q) = 150, c(u) = 75,$$

we associate a penalty equal to the assumability cost with the negation of each variable. We also apply a goal enforcement penalty of $c\Gamma$, for some c, to ensure that the goal is also satisfied. For example, if Gamma is set to 1000 and c is set to 3, then the following is the PL that would be produced:

$$\begin{aligned} 1000 &: \quad t \rightarrow p \wedge q \wedge s \\ 1000 &: \quad s \rightarrow (p \wedge r) \vee (q \wedge u) \\ 1000 &: \quad \mathcal{G} \rightarrow t \wedge u \\ 100 &: \quad \neg p \\ 150 &: \quad \neg q \\ 75 &: \quad \neg u \\ 3000 &: \quad \mathcal{G} \end{aligned} \tag{12}$$

One special case that occurs with this method happens when:

- a hypothesis q appears as the consequent of more than one rule in the pre-transformation CBA, (let us call rules with the same consequent *sibling rules*,)
- a hypothesis p appears as a direct antecedent of more than one of the rules which have q as the consequent.

For example, in the rule system below

$$\begin{aligned} &p \wedge q \wedge s \rightarrow t \\ &p \wedge r \rightarrow s \\ &p \wedge u \rightarrow s \\ &r \wedge u \rightarrow t \end{aligned} \tag{13}$$

The hypothesis p appears as an antecedent in two sibling rules with s as the consequent. The characteristic function corresponding to the rule

$$s \rightarrow (p \wedge r) \vee (p \wedge u),$$

is

$$s - prs - pus + p^2rus.$$

Whenever a hypothesis appears as an antecedent in two or more sibling rules, the characteristic function will include terms that include powers of that hypothesis. Such terms are not be legal in a HORN, because a neuron cannot appear more than once in a hyperedge.

We avoid this by preprocessing the CBA, adding auxiliary hypotheses we call *shadow hypotheses*, or *shadows*, to prevent a hypothesis from directly appearing as an antecedent in more than one rule with the same consequent. The rule system above would become

$$\begin{aligned} &p \wedge q \wedge s \rightarrow t \\ &p \wedge r \rightarrow s \\ &p' \wedge u \rightarrow s \\ &r \wedge u \rightarrow t \\ &p \rightarrow p' \end{aligned} \tag{14}$$

where p' is a shadow hypothesis for p. Shadow hypotheses can be reused. For example, consider the CBA below:

$$\begin{aligned} &p \wedge q \wedge s \rightarrow t \\ &p \wedge r \rightarrow s \\ &p \wedge u \rightarrow s \\ &r \wedge u \rightarrow t \\ &p \wedge s \rightarrow v \\ &p \wedge t \rightarrow v \\ &p \wedge q \rightarrow v \end{aligned} \tag{15}$$

Here, p needs one shadow hypothesis for the two s-rules, and it needs two shadows for the three v-rules. We create only two shadows, and one shadow is used in more than one rule:

$$\begin{aligned} &p \wedge q \wedge s \rightarrow t \\ &p \wedge r \rightarrow s \\ &p' \wedge u \rightarrow s \\ &r \wedge u \rightarrow t \\ &p \wedge s \rightarrow v \\ &p' \wedge t \rightarrow v \\ &p'' \wedge q \rightarrow v \\ &p \rightarrow p' \\ &p \rightarrow p'' \end{aligned} \tag{16}$$

Thus, if N_p denotes the number of shadows that need to be added for a given hypothesis p, then

$$N_p = \max_q \{M_p(q)\} - 1, \quad (17)$$

where $M_p(q)$ denotes the number of sibling q-rules in which p appears as an antecedent.

5. Experimental results

We used a test suite of more than 40 randomly generated CBA instances of varying sizes, as shown in Table 1. The random generation procedure takes five parameters:

- number of hypotheses, p_1,
- number of rules, p_2,
- maximum number of antecedents in any rule, p_3,
- the percentage of the hypotheses which should be subgoals, p_4, and
- the guaranteed number of minimum assumable hypotheses, p_5.

The CBA instances generated by the generator have the following properties:

- hypotheses are either assumable or provable: assumable hypotheses have a non-infinite assumability cost and do not appear as consequents of any rule, provable hypotheses are allowed to be consequents and have an assumability cost of ∞.
- to prevent logical cyclicity, all hypotheses are serially numbered, and no hypothesis is allowed to be an antecedent in a rule whose consequent has a lower serial number.

At the start of the process, a number, specified by the parameter p_5, of hypotheses are flagged as being assumable hypotheses. Then, for each rule, the number of antecedents is determined randomly with a uniform distribution between 1 and the parameter p_3. The consequent of the rule is chosen with a uniform distribution over the entire set of hypotheses; if the chosen hypothesis is flagged as an assumable, then the random selection is repeated until a non-flagged hypothesis is found. The set of antecedents is then chosen, uniformly, from within the set of hypotheses whose serial number is less than the chosen consequent.

After all rules are generated, any hypothesis that does not appear as the consequent of any rule is flagged as being assumable. All assumable hypotheses are randomly assigned costs, uniformly, within the range 1–1000. A percentage p_4 of the provable hypotheses is then selected as subgoals: an additional rule is added where all the selected subgoals are the antecedents and $\mathcal{G}$ is the consequent.

A compaction process is then applied to the randomly generated CBA. This process examines every pair of rules R_1 and R_2 : if R_1 and R_2 have the same consequent, but the antecedent set of R_1 is a subset of the antecedent set of R_2, then R_2 is eliminated.

The number of rules in the generated CBA instance, after compaction, can therefore be smaller than the requested number of rules p_2.

Our experimental results and parameter values are shown in Table 1. The initial temperature is always set to 1425 and the temperature decrease factor to 0.999. For most of the experiments shown in Table 1, values within the range of 0.1–0.2 were used for the parameter p_4. Rows for which column I is in italics indicate instances for which the optimal solution was not found by the network. The column headings are as follows:

A	number of hypotheses p_1,
B	number of rules (after compaction),
C	guaranteed number of assumable hypotheses p_5,
D	number of hypotheses, after shadow hypotheses are added,
E	number of rules, after shadow hypotheses are added,
F	number of neurons in produced HORN,
G	number of hyperedges,
H	order of network (equal to maximum hyperedge degree),
I	neural network iterations,
J	rule preservation cost (the goal preservation cost was always set to three times the rule preservation cost).

6. Relation to previous work

The equivalence between PL's and HORN's can be of two types:

- *strong equivalence*: the value of the network's energy function is equal to the violation rank of the corresponding PL plus some constant.
- *weak equivalence*: the global minimum points of the HORN's energy function are identical to the global minimums of the PL's violation rank (but the local minimum points may differ).

Pinkas (1992) shows that a weak equivalence exists between a given PL and the HORN that is produced by the method outlined earlier in this paper. He also shows that a sufficient condition for a strong equivalence to exist is for each wff in the PL to contain no more than three different variables.

In earlier work (Abdelbar et al., 2003), we introduced a transformation from CBA to PL that satisfied this requirement for strong equivalence. This was achieved by the use of auxiliary hypotheses, at the CBA level, to

Table 1
Experimental results and description of CBA instances used

A	B	C	D	E	F	G	H	I	J
8	4	4	8	4	8	19	4	10	10,000
8	5	3	8	5	8	23	5	5	1000
8	6	4	8	6	8	31	4	22	10,000
8	7	4	8	7	8	43	4	6	10,000
8	9	3	9	10	9	67	6	14,309	1000
8	7	4	8	7	8	47	5	8	10,000
8	9	4	17	18	17	303	15	*18,815*	190
8	7	3	8	7	8	32	5	4606	1000
10	7	6	10	7	10	73	6	11	1000
10	14	4	15	19	15	229	11	36,114	2000
10	11	4	11	12	11	114	8	88,439	10,000
10	13	4	17	20	17	185	13	28,736	1000
10	13	5	14	17	14	298	12	14	1000
10	15	4	11	16	11	237	9	26	1000
10	16	4	16	22	16	1104	15	17,984	1000
15	11	6	15	11	15	66	9	4	10,000
15	15	6	22	22	22	215	14	114,201	10,000
15	19	5	23	27	23	301	14	96,225	10,000
15	28	5	29	42	29	1107	19	61,585	10,000
15	30	5	28	43	28	1040	19	62,415	1000
15	37	5	29	51	29	2038	20	*39,022*	920
15	33	5	28	46	28	1103	15	44,300	1000
15	49	5	51	85	51	29,993	39	47,261	400
20	23	9	28	31	28	343	12	111,447	10,000
20	27	9	38	45	38	2124	27	61,946	1000
20	33	9	42	55	42	1987	29	*129,359*	5000
20	37	8	39	56	39	4755	31	26,509	1000
20	34	8	30	44	30	888	17	*48,909*	3500
30	24	21	43	37	43	7430	27	28,618	2000
30	43	16	51	64	51	1757	22	45,765	1000
40	62	21	65	87	65	4483	28	31,411	500
40	67	21	69	96	69	7085	29	34,141	500
40	44	28	73	77	73	7682	31	34,693	1000
40	73	21	61	94	61	14,866	22	*55,547*	2000
50	52	35	79	81	79	8976	31	69,940	1400
50	90	24	73	113	73	7252	21	58,458	1000
50	46	37	66	62	66	3570	29	*39,552*	2200
55	55	31	76	76	76	1502	23	42,665	800
55	56	32	69	70	69	1175	19	86,157	3000
60	55	34	74	69	74	1402	23	16,000	700
60	65	40	90	95	90	2941	25	38,744	700

Column headings are as follows; column A, number of hypotheses p_1; column B, number of rules (after compaction); column C, guaranteed number of assumable hypotheses p_5; column D, number of hypotheses, after shadow hypotheses are added; column E, number of rules, after shadow hypotheses are added; column F, number of neurons in produced HORN; column G, number of hyperedges; column H, order of network (equal to maximum hyperedge degree); column I, neural network iterations; column J, rule preservation cost (the goal preservation cost is set to three times the rule preservation cost); the initial temperature is set to 1425 and the temperature decrease factor is set to 0.999; for most of the experiments shown in the table, values within the range 0.1–0.2 are used for the parameter p_4; rows for which column I is in italics indicate instances for which the optimal solution was not found by the network.

make sure that each rule in the CBA did not contain more than two antecedents, as described in Abdelbar et al. (2003).

In the present work, we have not used auxiliary hypotheses (except to ensure that no variable appears as a direct antecedent in two or more sibling rules), resulting in a significant reduction in the number of neurons in the HORN produced; this size reduction has led to a significant improvement in performance, both in run-time and in solution quality, in spite of the fact that this method no longer satisfies Pinkas' sufficient condition for strong equivalence.

To measure the improvement in performance, we ran the present method on more than 70 of the CBA instances whose results were reported in Abdelbar et al. (2003). This comparison is shown in Table 2; column headings are as follows:

A number of hypotheses,
B number of rules,

Table 2
Comparison between previous and present method

A	B	C	D	E	F	G	H	I	J
4	2	4	4	0	391	2	4	0	31
4	3	6	6	18.07	1,087,374	4	5	0.11	15,900
4	3	6	6	0.05	313	3	4	0	21
4	4	8	8	55.95	1,917,127	6	6	0.06	10,634
4	5	10	10	535.69	16,591,713	8	7	0.22	21,325
4	6	9	9	69.05	2,314,475	9	7	0.281	28,817
4	8	13	13	74.32	1,505,641	13	9	0.471	33,404
5	2	5	5	0.72	15,341	2	5	0	18
5	3	5	5	0.82	22,131	3	5	0	22
5	4	7	7	21.54	1,101,341	4	5	0	22
5	5	9	9	37.18	1,126,697	6	6	0.1	18,687
5	6	11	11	104.32	2,902,261	8	7	0.24	23,710
5	7	14	14	1196.68	17,606,882	12	10	0.661	34,646
5	8	15	15	140.858	3,801,984	14	11	1.743	58,235
6	3	6	6	0.05	458	3	6	0	18
6	4	8	8	80.19	3,466,203	5	7	0.35	46,997
6	5	11	11	168.51	3,878,288	6	7	0.19	2600
6	7	15	15	303.47	5,358,984	10	9	0.531	38,268
6	9	16	16	305.622	4,467,175	12	9	0.38	35,069
7	3	7	7	0.66	12,310	3	7	0	12
7	4	9	9	23.84	1,019,892	5	8	0.151	22,911
7	5	11	11	72.01	2,127,845	6	8	0.15	18,959
7	6	12	12	280.86	5,541,444	7	8	0.23	27,050
7	7	14	14	546.58	6,241,164	9	9	0.41	35,986
7	8	18	18	302.06	3,633,466	12	11	0	25
7	9	20	20	196.45	2,365,931	13	11	0	32
7	10	20	20	191.093	3,802,125	13	10	0.471	34,864
8	4	12	12	0.55	1610	4	8	0	14
8	5	14	14	120.52	2,753,033	5	8	0	8
8	6	13	13	151.55	3,664,209	8	10	0.25	21,197
8	7	15	15	157.69	2,900,206	10	11	0.941	31,824
8	8	17	17	329.76	4,938,781	10	10	0.511	38,860
8	9	25	25	1245.14	4,812,671	14	13	0.731	31,575
8	10	21	21	186.24	1,831,112	13	11	0.431	23,431
8	11	28	28	543.688	2,175,579	18	15	3.094	81,557
8	16	35	35	1050.3	*3,065,039*	25	17	3.375	60,349
9	3	12	12	0.71	4746	3	9	0	5
9	4	13	13	0.6	2068	4	9	0	5
9	5	16	16	0.39	927	5	9	0	7
9	6	18	18	578.4	9,521,052	7	10	0.671	50,640
9	7	21	21	1280.44	10,741,727	8	10	0	8
9	8	20	20	279.11	1,692,142	11	12	0.431	24,621
9	9	24	24	1062	2,462,538	14	14	1.021	42,130
9	10	25	25	137.63	1,250,412	15	14	1.472	58,505
9	15	34	34	965.43	5,559,095	25	19	2.764	44,259
10	3	12	12	4.437	*277,222*	3	10	0	6
10	4	12	12	15.204	750,745	6	12	0.158	13,458
10	5	16	16	108.08	1,996,167	7	12	1.692	104,810
10	6	17	17	183.89	2,921,385	8	12	0.02	1939
10	7	19	19	152.96	*2,374,551*	9	12	0.19	13,630
10	8	17	17	77.03	2,265,829	10	12	1.622	104,245
10	9	22	22	245.233	2,465,984	11	12	0.851	45,064
10	8	22	22	648.57	5,541,624	8	10	0.271	23,372
10	11	26	26	245.233	2,465,984	14	13	0.651	39,767
10	15	33	33	1130.93	6,415,019	21	16	1.002	32,817
10	21	49	49	952.71	1,981,763	32	21	4.21	36,071
11	3	11	11	0.266	21,748	3	11	0	17
11	4	13	13	48.047	2,437,848	4	11	0	5
11	5	17	17	184.765	5,539,860	6	12	1.672	115,357
11	6	21	21	109.624	2,178,685	7	12	0	19
11	7	21	21	312.7	*4,148,292*	9	13	1.683	103,726

(*continued on next page*)

Table 2 (*continued*)

A	B	C	D	E	F	G	H	I	J
11	9	24	24	46.593	860,006	12	14	3.024	116,403
11	10	24	24	177.33	*1,763,956*	12	13	0.751	47,691
11	20	44	44	2387.078	6,022,404	26	17	2.514	58,155
11	25	55	55	2642.109	*6,022,351*	35	21	5.088	56,172
12	3	12	12	2.63	93,608	3	12	0	77
12	5	15	15	167.46	2,766,046	6	13	0	31
12	6	16	16	124.51	2,765,965	7	13	1.462	95,589
12	7	17	17	531.99	5,541,446	8	13	1.793	112,184
12	8	25	25	493.65	2,902,993	8	12	0	3
12	10	29	29	4688.45	17,805,364	11	13	1.803	1,000,536
12	25	68	68	4841.38	5,558,117	36	23	16.737	121,257

Column headings are as follows; column A, number of hypotheses; column B, number of rules; column C, number of rules after auxiliary hypotheses are added (*previous method*); column D, number of neurons (*previous method*); column E, CPU time (*previous method*); column F, neural network iterations (*previous method*); column G, number of rules after shadowing (*present method*); column H, number of neurons (*present method*); column I, CPU time (*present method*); column J, neural network iterations (*present method*); instances for which column F is italicized are instances for which the previous method did not obtain the optimal solution; the present method found optimal solutions for all the instances in the table.

C number of rules after auxiliary hypotheses are added (*previous method*),
D number of neurons (*previous method*),
E CPU time (previous method),
F neural network iterations (*previous method*),
G number of rules after shadowing (*present method*),
H number of neurons (*present method*),
I CPU time (present method),
J neural network iterations (present method).

As can be seen from Table 2, the present method consistently outperformed the previous method. The present method found the optimal solution for all instances in Table 2, including those instances for which the previous method did not find the optimal solution (indicated by italicization in column F).

7. Conclusion

In this and previous work, we have investigated using high order recurrent neural networks to find least-cost proofs for instances of CBA. The method we presented here significantly reduces the size of the neural network produced, with a corresponding improvement in performance as discussed in Section 6, by reducing the number of auxiliary neurons that are used. More detailed and systematic investigation is required to determine how neural network empirical performance is affected by CBA problem parameters such as: ratio of assumable to provable hypotheses, depth of rule system, number of sibling rules, distribution of assumability costs, and number of antecedents per rule, as well as the effect on network performance of growth in the size of the CBA instance.

Acknowledgements

The first author would like to thank his student Lamia Mohamed for invaluable assistance in reviewing and proofreading this manuscript.

References

Abdelbar, A. M. (1998). An algorithm for finding MAPs for belief networks through cost-based abduction. *Artificial Intelligence, 104*, 331.

Abdelbar, A. M. (1999). Designing high order recurrent networks for Bayesian belief revision for Bayesian belief revision. In L. R. Medsker, & L. C. Jain (Eds.), *Recurrent neural networks: design and applications* (pp. 77–98). Boca Raton: CRC Press.

Abdelbar, A. M., Andrews, E. A. M., & Tagliarini, G. A. (2003). Finding least cost proofs using high order recurrent networks. *Proceedings International Joint Conference on Neural Networks*.

Charniak, E., & Shimony, S. E. (1990). Probabilistic semantics for cost-based abduction. *Proceedings AAAI National Conference on Artificial Intelligence*.

Charniak, E., & Shimony, S. (1994). Cost-based abduction and MAP explanation. *Artificial Intelligence, 66*, 345.

Dempster, A. P. (1967). Upper and lower probabilities induced by a multivalued mapping. *Annals of Mathematical Statistics, 38*, 157.

Ginsberg, M. L. (1987). *Readings in nonmonotonic reasoning*. San Mateo: Morgan-Kauffman.

Hobbs, J. R., Stickel, M. E., Martin, P., & Edwards, D. (1993). Interpretation as abduction. *Artificial Intelligence, 63*, 69.

Hopfield, J. J. (1982). Neural networks and physical systems with emergent collective computational abilities. *Proceedings National Academy of Science, 79*, 2554.

Hopfield, J. J. (1984). Neurons with graded response have collective computational properties like those of two-state neurons. *Proceedings National Academy of Science, 81*, 3088.

Kofler, E. T., & Leondes, C. T. (1994). Algorithmic modifications to the theory of evidential reasoning. *Journal of Algorithms, 17*, 269.

Konyndyk, K. (1986). *Introductory modal logic*. Notre Dame: Notre Dame Press.

Marek, V. W., & Truszczynski, M. (1993). *Nonmonotonic logic*. Berlin: Springer.

Nemhauser, G. L., Rinnooy Kan, A. H. G., & Todd, M. J. (1989). *Handbooks in operations research and management science*. Amsterdam: North Holland, Vol. 1.

Pawlak, Z. (1991). *Rough sets*. Dordrecht: Kluwer.

Pawlak, Z. (1992). Rough sets: a new approach to vagueness. In L. Zadeh, & J. Kacprzyk (Eds.), *Fuzzy logic for the management of uncertainty*. New York: Wiley.

Pawlak, Z., Grzymala-Busse, J., Slowinski, R., & Ziark, W. (1995). Rough sets. *Communications of the ACM*, *38*, 88.

Pearl, J. (1986). Fusion, propagation, and structuring in belief networks. *Artificial Intelligence*, *29*, 241.

Pearl, J. (1988). *Probabilistic reasoning in intelligent systems: networks of plausible inference*. San Mateo: Morgan-Kaufmann.

Pinkas, G. (1992). *Logical inference in symmetric connectionist networks. Doctoral thesis*, St Louis, Missouri: Washington University.

Pinkas, G. (1995). Reasoning, nonmonotonicity and learning in connectionist networks that capture propositional knowledge. *Artificial Intelligence*, *77*, 203.

Popkorn, S. (1994). *First steps in modal logic*. Cambridge: Cambridge University Press.

Reiter, R. (1987). Nonmonotonic reasoning. *Annual Review of Computer Science*, 147.

Santos, E., Jr. (1991). On the generation of alternative explanations with implications for belief revision. *Proceedings Seventh Conference on Uncertainty in AI*.

Santos, E., Jr. (1994). A linear constraint satisfaction approach to cost-based abduction. *Artificial Intelligence*, *65*, 1.

Schrijver, A. (1986). *Theory of linear and integer programming*. New York: Wiley.

Shafer, G. (1976). *A mathematical theory of evidence*. Princeton: Princeton University Press.

Shafer, G. (1986). The combination of evidence. *International Journal of Intelligent Systems*, *1*, 155.

Shafer, G., & Logan, R. (1987). Implementing Dempster's rule for heirarchial evidence. *Artificial Intelligence*, *33*, 271.

Shoham, Y. (1987). Nonmonotonic logics: meaning and utility. *Proceedings International Joint Conference on Artificial Intelligence*.

Zadeh, L. (1979). A theory of approximate reasoning. In J. Hayes, D. Michie, & L. I. Mikulich (Eds.), (*Vol. 9*). *Machine intelligence*, New York: Halstead Press.

Zadeh, L. (1994). Fuzzy logic, neural networks and soft computing. *Communications of the ACM*, *37*, 77.

Zadeh, L., & Kacprzyk, J. (1992). *Fuzzy logic for the management of uncertainty*. New York: Wiley.

Zimmerman, H.-J. (1991). *Fuzzy set theory and its applications*. Boston: Kluwer.

PERGAMON

AVAILABLE AT
www.ComputerScienceWeb.com
POWERED BY SCIENCE DIRECT

Neural Networks 16 (2003) 675–682

Neural Networks

www.elsevier.com/locate/neunet

2003 Special issue

Neural networks with chaotic recursive nodes: techniques for the design of associative memories, contrast with Hopfield architectures, and extensions for time-dependent inputs

Emilio Del-Moral-Hernandez*

Department of Electronic Systems Engineering, Polytechnic School of the University of Sao Paulo, Cidade Universitaria, Av. Prof. Luciano Gualberto, Sao Paulo, SP, CEP 05508-900, Brazil

Abstract

This paper addresses the coding and storage of information in neural architectures with bifurcating recursive nodes that exhibit chaotic dynamics. It describes architectures of coupled recursive processing elements (RPEs) used to store binary strings, discusses the choices of network parameters related to the coding of zeros and ones, and analyzes several aspects of the network operation in implementing associative memories through populations of logistic maps. Experiments for the performance evaluation of these memories are described, and results addressing the operation under digital noise (flipped bits) and analog noise added to the prompting pattern are presented and analyzed. Quantitative aspects related to the representation of binary strings through cyclic states are equated, and then related to the planning and analysis of several experiments. A simple pre-processing procedure useful in situations of prompting conditions with analog noise is proposed, and the resultant increase in recovery performance presented. The performance of the RPEs associative networks is contrasted with the performance of Hopfield associative memories, and the situations where the RPEs networks present significant superiority are identified. An extended version of the proposed architecture, which allows to address the issues of time-dependent inputs and analog inputs, is analyzed in detail. Experimental results are presented, and the role of this extended architecture in providing mechanisms for modular RPEs architectures is pointed out.

Keywords: Temporal coding techniques and computation with spatio-temporal patterns; Artificial neural networks; Coding and storage in associative memories; Globally coupled maps; Recursive processing elements; Non-linear dynamics; Chaotic neural networks

1. Introduction

Bifurcating recursive processing elements (RPEs) have the important ability to produce many different dynamical modalities, due to their nature of non-linear dynamical systems. Because of that ability, they are natural elements for the modeling of those biological neural systems in which complex spatio-temporal patterns play some important role (Freeman, 1992; Kaneko, 1992; Kelso, 1995; Kozma & Freeman, 2000, 2001). The issue of how these dynamical modalities can be efficiently used to code and store information is an open and vast area, and it poses many interesting questions to neurobiologists, as well as to researchers in the field of analog computing and artificial neural networks (Aihara, Takabe, & Toyoda, 1990; Ishii et al., 1993; Kaneko, 1992; Kelso, 1995; Kozma & Freeman, 2000, 2001; Lysetskiy, Zurada, & Lozowasky, 2002; Szu & Hsu, 1997; Szu et al., 2003). From the point of view of the potential for the implementation of novel computing machines, neural networks with such class of nodes are particularly fascinating and promising, because of the many possibilities that these rich elements offer by providing ingredients for a large variety of coding and storage methods (Del-Moral-Hernandez, 2000, 2001a). In the following sections, we explore and expand some possibilities for the codification of binary strings in associative architectures composed of bifurcating analog nodes, we show some results of our studies on such networks in situations of noisy prompting (both digital and analog), and we present contrastive performance results with respect to Hopfield architectures.

* Tel.: +55-11-818-5254; fax: +55-11-818-5665.
E-mail address: emilio_del_moral@ieee.org (E. Del-Moral-Hernandez).

0893-6080/03/$ - see front matter © 2003 Elsevier Science Ltd. All rights reserved.
doi:10.1016/S0893-6080(03)00125-4

2. Bifurcating recursive processing elements as nodes of neuro-like associative architectures - network structure and operation

The neural architectures addressed in this paper are composed of Recursive Processing Elements (RPEs) that can bifurcate between many dynamical modalities (RPEs for brevity). While in traditional model neurons the functionality of nodes is described by a non-linear activation function such as the sigmoid, in RPEs the functionality of the nodes is described by a first order parametric recursion R_p acting on discrete time state variables. The prototypical parametric recursion considered in our studies is the logistic map (Del-Moral-Hernandez, 1998, 2001a,b; Farhat & Del-Moral-Hernandez, 1995; Hilborn, 1994; Kaneko, 1993). Although its mathematical simplicity, it exhibits bifurcation and cascading to chaos in its dynamics. Eq. (1) describes the evolution of the state variable x for node i in a network of RPEs, assuming that the recursion R_p corresponds to the logistic map

$$x_{i_{n+1}} = R_{p_i}(x_{i_n}) = p_{i_n} x_{i_n}(1 - x_{i_n}) \quad (1)$$

In Eq. (1), n represents the discrete time, x_{i_n} and $x_{i_{n+1}}$ represent consecutive values of the state variable for node i, R_{p_i} is the parametric recursion (or parametric map) that relates x_{i_n} and $x_{i_{n+1}}$, and p_{i_n} is the bifurcation parameter of the logistic recursion. Another important characterization of the network node is its bifurcation diagram (Del-Moral-Hernandez, 1998; Hilborn, 1994). Fig. 1 shows the bifurcation diagram for the logistic recursion.

We use these recursive elements to compose a network with full connectivity between nodes, allowing the logistic maps to interact with each other, until they reach collective states that represent stored binary patterns. Such a global coupling is implemented through a connectivity matrix $\mathbf{W}_{ij}$, which promotes the driving of the bifurcation parameter p_i of a given node based on the activity of all the state variables x_i (Section 3 gives details on this p_i driving). By using this architecture based on coupled logistic RPEs, we can implement associative memories of binary patterns, and encode zeros and ones by two of the many modalities of dynamic behavior exhibited by the bifurcating recursions (Del-Moral-Hernandez, 2000, 2001b). In the particular studies described here, binary ones and binary zeros are coded through period-2 trajectories performed by the state variables of the logistic nodes. In Fig. 1, the points A and B exemplify one of the period-2 cycles of the logistic recursion, which can be used in such a coding.

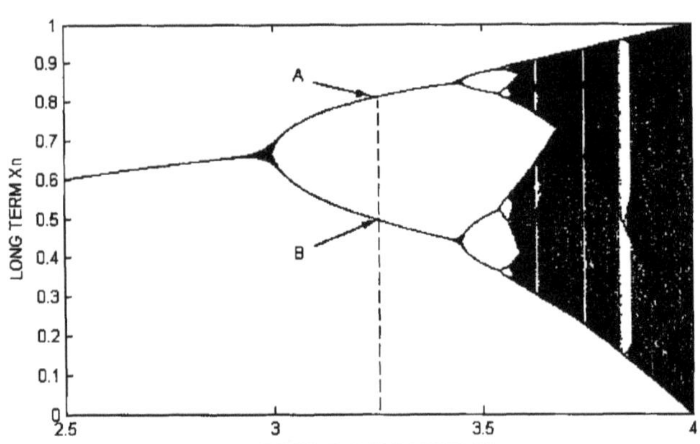

Fig. 1. The bifurcation diagram for the logistic recursion: $x_{n+1} = px_n(1 - x_n)$. The horizontal axis represents the value of the bifurcation parameter p, and the vertical axis represents the values visited in the long-term by the state variable x. The marked points A and B exemplify the specific period-2 cycle that emerges when p is 3.25: in the long-term, x cycles between $A = 0.81$ and $B = 0.50$.

The process of memory prompting and pattern recovery is similar to the one employed in Hopfield Networks. After a prompting pattern defines the initial state of the network (the values x_{i_0}), the coupled logistic elements are free to evolve in time. In this evolution, they possibly exercise different modalities of dynamic behavior (including chaotic trajectories), and eventually reach accommodation when all the nodes' state variables (the x_i) perform period-2 cycles, some of them coding the zeros of a binary string, some of them coding the ones.

3. The process of search for stored patterns

The interaction between nodes, during the search for global dynamic patterns that are compatible with the information stored in matrix $\mathbf{W}_{ij}$, is based on the switching of dynamical modalities of the state variables x_i, for those nodes with high 'disagreement' with respect to the remaining nodes of the network. Such a disagreement (or difference between node activity and network's expectative) is evaluated based on the node's states x_j and the connectivity matrix $\mathbf{W}_{ij}$, which is programmed by the cross-product rule on the stored patterns (Del-Moral-Hernandez, 2001b; Haykin, 1999). Eq. (2) represents the evaluation of the node i disagreement, named here d_i. Eq. (3) describes how the disagreement d_i can promote gradual changes Δp_i in the bifurcation parameter p_i

$$d_i = -(x_i - k_1)(\Sigma_j \mathbf{W}_{ij}(x_j - k_1)) + k_2 \quad (2)$$

$$\Delta p_i = d_i c - d \quad (3)$$

In Eq. (2), k_1 and k_2 are constants, with k_1 being the average for the x variables and k_2 chosen so that the minimal value for d_i is zero. During the network operation, high values for d_i, the disagreement between the node i and the network, indicate that the search for a stored pattern is still in progress and the node i needs to explore different dynamic modalities to facilitate the settling of the network. Due to the richness of the bifurcating node, this exploration of alternative dynamic modalities is easily implemented by proper driving of the bifurcation parameter p_i.

In Eq. (3), the term $d_i c$ promotes the driving of the local variable p_i towards high values, whenever the level of local disagreement with respect to the network is high, while the term $-d$ implements the recovery of p_i towards low values, whenever the quantity d_i becomes low. This driving towards low values of p_i indicates agreement between the local activity and the whole network and possibly means that the recovery of one of the stored patterns is taking place.

The choices of the specific values for the scaling factor c and the dumping factor $-d$ have implications in the speed of the network operation. For the purposes of this paper, this issue does not need to be addressed here in detail. We will just mention that scaling factors in the range 0.1, 0.6, and dumping factors in the range 0.01, 0.06 result in fast and reliable operation of the network; values of c below that range can result in low speeds of operation, while values of c above it can result in low performance of pattern recovery.

In addition to the adaptation expressed in Eq. (3), some kind of limiting mechanism is needed, so as to keep the p_i variables in a convenient range $[\min_p, \max_p]$. Section 4 discusses the choice of these limit values in some detail, together with the issue of coding of zeros and ones.

The outcome of the described global dynamics corresponds to an eventual settling of the network, either recovering stored strings, or returning spurious patterns (including mirror images of each stored pattern). In this settling of the network, its nodes gradually reach period-2 trajectories that encode zeros and ones. In Fig. 2 we have the illustration of the final phases in the process of recovery of one pattern stored in a network of 20 coupled RPEs (Del-Moral-Hernandez, 2001b). In the diagram presented in Fig. 2, named limit set diagram (LSD), the horizontal axis represents the 20 neurons, and the pairs of dots right above a given neuron number (i) represents the period-2 cyclic pattern performed by the state of that neuron (x_i). The circle around one of these two dots indicates the phase of cycling of such a particular period-2 trajectory. This diagram also

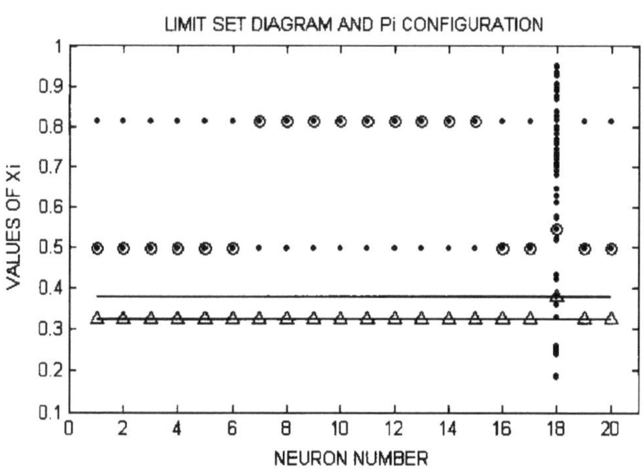

Fig. 2. The illustration of the final steps of pattern recovery in a network of 20 coupled RPEs. In this diagram, the horizontal axis represents the i for the 20 neurons, the dots and circled dots represent the period-2 cyclic pattern performed by the variables x_i, and triangles represent the p_i variables (or more exactly, $p_i/10$, for convenience).

includes the monitoring of the p_i variables: through small triangles, it represents the values of the p_i parameters of all nodes. The horizontal lines, on top of which the triangles are, represent the values $\min_p = 3.25$ and $\max_p = 3.8$ (these p values appear here divided by 10, so we can use the same vertical scale to represent values of x_i and values of p_i). In this example of network operation, most of the nodes (with exception of neuron 18) reached a settling state, with $p_i = \min_p = 3.25$, and x_i oscillating between $A = 0.81$ and $B = 0.5$. For neuron 18, the p_i bifurcation parameter is still not settled, and x_i visits many different values, until the settling is reached and the whole pattern is recovered.

4. Defining the coding of binary zeros and binary ones in period-2 cycles

As mentioned in Section 3, for the proper operation of the network of coupled recursive elements, the evolution of the variables p_i has to be limited. The limit from above, the $\max_p$, guaranties that the allowed maximal value for p_i is not violated ($p < 4$, in the present form of the logistic recursion (Del-Moral-Hernandez, 2001b; Hilborn, 1994). In addition, the variables p_i have to be limited from below, to an amount named here $\min_p$. The choice of the lower limit $\min_p$ has to be compatible with the configuration desired for the network after the recovery is complete. After network settling, with all the p_i variables reaching the value $\min_p$, the trajectory performed by the x_i variables should correspond to the period-2 cycles chosen for the codification of zeros and ones (in the example mentioned in Section 2, this means cycles with x oscillating between values $A = 0.81$ and $B = 0.5$; these same values were assumed in the network represented in Fig. 2). This periodicity 2 is enough for the codification of bits zero and bits one, since cycles oscillating between two values A and B present two possible phases of cycling. For example, the ones can be represented by cycles with the variable x visiting the value A first, then value B, and the zeros can be represented by cycles with the variable x visiting the value B first, then value A. The pairs of values A and B that correspond to allowed period-2 cycles are given by the solutions of Eq. (4), which defines the fixed points for the second order recursion in the logistic map

$$x_{n+2} = x_n \Leftrightarrow x_n = R_p(R_p(x_n)) \tag{4}$$

where

$$R_p(x) = px(1 - x)$$

The analytical solution of Eq. (4) leads to the values A and B associated to a given p. Eq. (5) presents the expressions for A and B. Notice that the condition for those values being real and distinct is that p has to be larger than 3.

$$A\&B = (1 + 1/p \pm (1 - 2/p - 3/p^2)^{1/2})/2 \tag{5}$$

The condition for stability of these period-2 solutions is given by the following inequality (Hilborn, 1994):

$$|R_p'(A)R_p'(B)| < 1 \Leftrightarrow |p^2 - 2p - 4| < 1 \quad (6)$$

This condition guaranties that the oscillations between the values A and B represent an attractor, and it defines the upper limit for values of p that lead to period-2 behavior. This limit is $p < 3.45$. For larger values of p, the inequality in Eq. (6) is not satisfied, the stability of period-2 cycling is lost, and the periodicity of the limit cycle bifurcates from 2 to 4.

Another important amount that we can evaluate from this analysis is the separation between the values A and B involved in the representation of binary zeros and binary ones, which is given by Eq. (7)

$$|A - B| = (1 - 2/p - 3/p^2)^{1/2} \quad (7)$$

This separation $|A - B|$ grows from zero to 0.41 as p (or $\min_p$, if we consider the final configuration of a network of RPEs) grows from 3 to 3.44. The magnitude of this separation has particular importance when we consider the network operation under noisy conditions, as discussed in the following sections. It also relates to the discussion on architecture extensions for the coding of analog quantities, briefly addressed in this Section 8.

5. Error recovery capacity in digital noise environments

Our main goal in this section and the following one is to study how the different choices of $\min_p$ can affect the network's tolerance to digital and analog noise in the prompting initial condition. We will first address the characterization of immunity to digital noise. This situation is relevant for those applications where the coding of binary strings into analog initial conditions is assumed to be perfect, the initial values x_{i_0} are exactly equal to either A or B, and the only source of possible distortion in the prompting patterns occurs in the form of flipped bits, before the analog encoding takes place. This specific type of distortion in the initial condition is named here digital noise. The main tool we used for this characterization of network immunity was the 'Error Plot', shown in Fig. 3. This plot shows how the average Hamming error observed in the (sometimes imperfect) recovery of a stored pattern relates to the level of Hamming distortion of a noisy prompting pattern. Both Hamming quantities are evaluated with respect to the ideal conditions, i.e. no prompting noise, and no recovery mistakes. Fig. 3 shows an error plot obtained for an architecture with $\min_p = 3.25$, and arbitrary levels of digital noise in the initial conditions. Notice that for levels of prompting noise below 35% (less than 35 bits flipped among the 100 nodes) we have virtually no average error in the recovery of the stored pattern. Notice also that the odd symmetry of the error curve with respect to prompting noise 50% is related to the recovery of the mirror images of the prompting patterns. Whenever the number of flipped bits in the noisy prompting condition goes beyond 50%, the evolution of the network tends to lead to the recovery of the mirror image, and the average Hamming error tends to 100%.

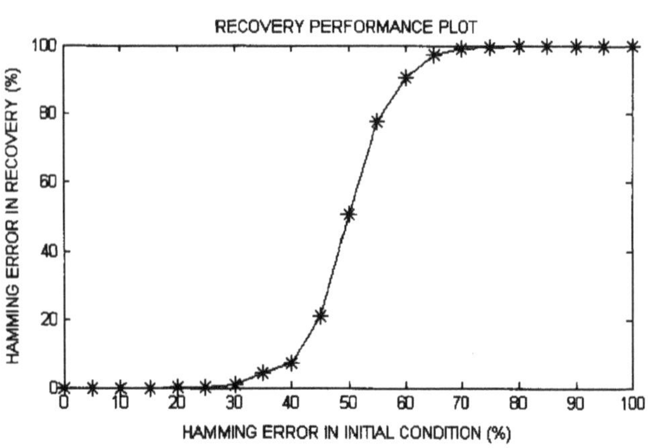

Fig. 3. The graph shows how the level of digital noise in the prompting condition (represented in the horizontal axis) affects the precision in the recovery of stored patterns. Both axis range from 0 to 100% bits.

The discussion in the previous section allowed us to relate the choice of the amount $\min_p$ to the values A and B, which ultimately are the numerical representatives used for the coding of binary ones and binary zeros. The definition of these values is important for the coding of the prompting patterns in terms of initial conditions (values x_{i_0}). In addition, the numerical distance between them tell us how much distinct or similar the representatives of zeros and one are. Because of that, different choices of $\min_p$ within the range of allowed values [3.0, 3.44] can result in different network performance and different levels of pattern recovery ability. Having in mind this potential relationship between $\min_p$ and network performance, we generated error plots for many other values of $\min_p$ besides the 3.25.

In order to have similar conditions for experiments with different choices of $\min_p$ and allow the proper comparison of results, we maintained the same training set (three arbitrarily chosen binary patterns), the same architecture size (100 nodes), and the same ensemble size when evaluating the average Hamming error (50 samples). With the data collected with this series of experiments, it was possible to prepare Table 1, which allows us to contrast the performance of the network in recovering distorted digital patterns, for different choices of the $\min_p$ value, and different levels of distortion in the prompting pattern.

Table 1
Average Hamming errors in recovery (in %), for three different levels of prompting *digital noise* and five different choices of $\min_p$

$\min_p$ choice	3.10	3.20	3.25	3.30	3.40
Separation $\|A - B\|$	0.21	0.29	0.32	0.34	0.39
Digital noise 20% (%)	0.4	1.2	0.2	0.2	0.4
Digital noise 30% (%)	1.0	2.3	1.4	1.4	1.4
Digital noise 40% (%)	8.3	8.6	5.7	10	11

The table presents the average Hamming error observed in the recovery patterns, for five values of $\min_p$ (3.10, 3.20, 3.25, 3.30, and 3.40) and three levels of digital noise in the prompting initial condition (10, 20 and 40% of bits flipped in the initial condition).

We can observe from Table 1 that the case of $\min_p = 3.25$ results in slightly improved performance with respect to the other choices of $\min_p$ here considered. It is interesting to observe that this choice corresponds to a situation in which the Lyapunov exponent of the logistic recursion is more negative than it is for the other values of $\min_p$, implying lower sensibility to initial conditions and faster convergence to the final attractors (Hilborn, 1994). Notice though that, at this point, no theoretical connection between these two facts has yet been established.

6. Analog noise environments and the appearance of strongly preferential patterns

The series of experiments addressed in this section regards the characterization of the network performance in situations in which analog noise is present in the initial conditions of the network. Ideally, each one of the initial conditions x_{i_0} should be either equal to the value A or equal to the value B, the numerical representatives used for the coding of binary ones and binary zeros. Considering situations in which this condition cannot be guaranteed, error plots similar to the ones obtained for digital noise were used to characterize the performance of the network in situations of analog noise. In this study though, the noise in the initial condition cannot be specified in terms of Hamming distances as we did before. Alternatively, we can define the level of analog noise by comparing its average magnitude to the distance $|A - B|$ discussed in Section 4 (Del-Moral-Hernandez, 2001b).

Here again, as in the previous section, we also want to study the relationship between the choice of $\min_p$ and the level of noise that the prompting can support. Table 2 summarizes some results for these experiments dealing with analog noise in the prompting pattern. Similar to Table 1, we show how the average Hamming error observed in the recovery process varies with $\min_p$ and the level of distortion of the prompting pattern. The experiments in this series considered two different levels of uniformly distributed analog noise added to the prompting initial condition ($\langle|\text{noise}|\rangle = 40$ and 50% of $|A - B|$). Notice that the percentages here discussed cannot be directly related to the noise percentages discussed in Section 5, since the nature of the noises in one case and the other are distinct.

Table 2
Average Hamming errors in recovery (in %), for two different levels of prompting *analog noise* and five different choices of $\min_p$

$\min_p$ choice	3.10	3.20	3.25	3.30	3.40
Separation $\lvert A - B\rvert$	0.21	0.29	0.32	0.34	0.39
$\langle\lvert\text{noise}\rvert\rangle/\lvert A - B\rvert = 40\%$ (%)	0.0	0.0	8.4	4.1	3.5
$\langle\lvert\text{noise}\rvert\rangle/\lvert A - B\rvert = 50\%$ (%)	2.0	49	65	17	12

Table 3
Average Hamming errors for *analog noise with clipping*

$\min_p$ choice	3.10	3.20	3.25	3.30	3.40
Separation $\lvert A - B\rvert$	0.21	0.29	0.32	0.34	0.39
$\langle\lvert\text{noise}\rvert\rangle/\lvert A - B\rvert = 40\%$ (%)	0.00	0.00	0.00	0.02	0.08
$\langle\lvert\text{noise}\rvert\rangle/\lvert A - B\rvert = 50\%$ (%)	0.60	0.40	0.22	0.22	0.84

As can be seen from Table 2, the results in this series of experiments produced different relationships between resultant Hamming error and the $\min_p$ choice. For example, for the row of the table in which the ratio between $\langle|\text{noise}|\rangle$ and $|A - B|$ is 40%, as we sweep the value of $\min_p$ from low values to high values, we observe that the final Hamming error changes abruptly, from very low values to values around 8% (when $\min_p = 3.25$). On the other hand, for the row in which the ratio between $\langle|\text{noise}|\rangle$ and $|A - B|$ is 50%, the relationship between $\min_p$ and Hamming error is much smoother. Because of the irregularity of the obtained results, we decided to look more closely to the repertoire of answers issued by the settled network, in experiments with moderate to high levels of analog noisy. The practical way devised to study this issue was through the development of histogram-like tools, for the collection of the recovered patterns and evaluation of their relative frequencies. With this technique, it is possible to verify the unbalanced power of the different attractors, even in situations of moderate levels of analog noise. This analysis indicated the convenience of using some kind of clipping pre-processing on the noisy initial conditions x_{i_0}, so as to restrict them to a range of values roughly defined by the values A and B. Notice that this clipping mechanism does not try to fix the values of the initial conditions in A and B. It just makes sure that the x_{i_0} are in the interior of the segment AB or at least not far from it. The outcome of this simple pre-processing was a dramatic improvement in the performance for analog noise situations. This important result is shown in Table 3, where the Hamming errors in the recovered patterns under high levels of noise were reduced up to one-tenth of the previous results presented in Table 2.

7. Contrasting the performances of RPEs networks and traditional Hopfield architectures

In the past sections, we discussed many design techniques and concepts in coding and storage of binary strings in associative architectures with RPEs nodes, and we presented some results based on concrete implementation of these concepts. We want to show in this section one of the positive results that we can have with the application of the described techniques: the improved recovery abilities of the associative memories based in RPEs, as compared to the traditional

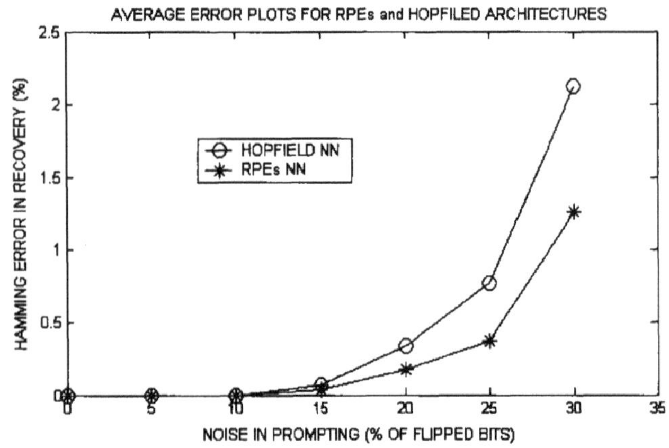

Fig. 4. Error plots for prompting patterns with digital noise (noise level in the horizontal axis), for both associative architectures: RPEs and Hopfield. The plots cover the range of moderate noise factors in the prompting condition, i.e. from 0 to 30% of the bits flipped.

Hopfield architectures. Fig. 4 contrasts the error plots for situations of digital noise (as defined in Section 5), for both associative architectures. These plots cover noise factors ranging from 0 to 30% of bits flipped in the prompting condition. We can clearly see that the average performance of the RPEs network is markedly superior. The Hopfield network generates larger average errors than the RPE network does, by a factor that ranges from 1.5 to 2, what is considerably significant. We have to mention that this advantage of the RPEs can be reversed in favor of the Hopfield network, for levels of prompting noise somewhere around 40% of bits flipped. In any case, for this range of large prompting noise, the performances of the networks decrease severely and, therefore, both networks virtually become of no practical use, no matter which one of them has the best performance. In summary, the results obtained for moderate levels of noise, represented in Fig. 4, show important differences in favor of the RPEs networks.

8. The definition of sensory nodes: the tools for time-dependent inputs, non-binary patterns and modular networks

In the architectures discussed in the previous sections, the network inputs correspond to static patterns: the x_{i_0} initial condition vectors. This represents an important limitation for applications dealing with time-dependent patterns. Also related to this aspect of the static x_{i_0}, we observe that in the RPEs networks discussed above, there is a lack of homogeneity between the natures of inputs and outputs. While the input is a multidimensional static vector, the output of the network corresponds to a multidimensional time series x_{i_n}, as represented in the LSD in Fig. 2. This lack of homogeneity poses difficulties when we think of modular networks, where assemblies of nodes produce output patterns that will be the input patterns to other assemblies of nodes. Therefore, the study of strategies for the consideration of time varying inputs in RPEs networks can have important implications not only in providing tools for the treatment of time-dependent inputs, but also in providing mechanisms for modularity, through a homogeneous framework for the definition of inputs and outputs in RPEs networks.

In order to approach the issues just described, we designed extended architectures in which, in addition to the *associative nodes* (i.e. the ones that compose the networks studied in the previous sections), we also have additional RPEs nodes, named here *sensory* or *input* nodes. These nodes represent an external stimulation to the associative network. Alternatively, we can also name them *interface* nodes or *external* nodes, since they may also represent the output layer of another network, in a modular architecture. The interaction between the activities of the sensory and associative nodes is implemented through a simple extension of the coupling mechanism described in Section 3 and expressed in Eqs. (2) and (3). The necessary adaptation in Eq. (2) for the inclusion of the sensory nodes is represented in Eq. (8)

$$d_i = -(x_i - k_1)(\Sigma_j \mathbf{W}_{ij}(x_j - k_1) + \Sigma_j \mathbf{SW}_{ij}(s_j - k_1)) + k_2 \quad (8)$$

Here, the new elements are s_j, which is the state variable of the sensory RPE number j, and the connection matrix between sensory and associative nodes, the $\mathbf{SW}_{ij}$, which is programmed through the cross-product rule, similarly to what is done for the $\mathbf{W}_{ij}$ programming. With this modification in the evaluation of the disagreement between node i and the network (the d_i), we have that the driving of the p_i variables and the search for stored patterns now also depends on the activities s_i of the sensory nodes. Therefore, the output of this new network does not depend exclusively on its initial state x_{i_0} and its internal dynamics, but it also depends on the continuously changing behavior of the stimulation or external activity. With this, the x_{i_0} pattern does not represent the network input anymore; instead, it represents a summary of its previous history.

For the quantitative evaluation of the extended architecture, we measured its ability in recovering stored patterns under noisy time-dependent inputs. In a first series of experiments, we assumed that the inputs could change from a pattern to another instantaneously (in a single time step). In a more sophisticated model, we considered smooth transitions between one input pattern and the following, with gradual fading of one and gradual emergence of the other. Another scenario included an intermediate phase between patterns, when chaotic behavior was temporarily present. These more complex experiments tried thus to incorporate different elements of what we expect to have in more realistic biological modeling, as well as in contexts of modular architectures, in which the output of one module feeds the input of another, and the switching between an output pattern and the following happens gradually and frequently intermediated by erratic phases. The results of these experiments, showing how the average Hamming

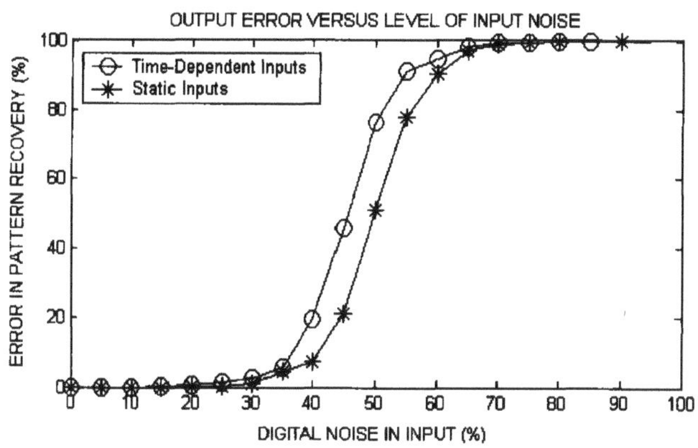

Fig. 5. Evolution of the average Hamming recovery error with the level of input noise, for extended RPEs architectures with sensory nodes and time-dependent inputs. The results obtained for static inputs architectures, from Fig. 3, are reproduced here for comparison.

error in the recovered patterns changes with arbitrary levels of distortion in the time-dependent stimulations s_{i_n}, is represented in Fig. 5, in which the previously obtained results for static inputs (from Fig. 3) were also included, for contrast purposes. We observe that the pattern recovery ability of the extended architecture degrades with the level of input noise faster than the original architecture. This was in fact expected: in time-varying networks, the recovery of patterns involves a constant competition between the attractors exercised previously to each input transition and the attractors related to the new input patterns appearing after the transition.

In addition to the treatment of time-dependent inputs, the inclusion of the sensory nodes and the $\mathbf{SW}_{ij}$ matrix in the original architecture brings another interesting possibility: the natural treatment of non-binary inputs, or more specifically, input patterns of analog nature. By revisiting the bifurcation diagram in Fig. 1 and the discussion on the $|A - B|$ separation developed in Section 4, we can realize that the repertoire of period-2 trajectories exhibited by the logistic map can be fully explored and allow the coding of arbitrary analog quantities in the range $[0, 0.41]$. As a matter of fact, we can also use the phase of cycling of the period-2 attractors as a natural coding for the sign $(\pm)$ of such analog quantity, allowing a bipolar range of values $[0, \pm 0.41]$. Fig. 6 illustrates this strategy, with an LSD representing the activity of 20 sensory nodes, for which this coding of bipolar analog quantities is employed to represent a sine shaped spatial pattern. The main difference that we have when dealing with analog input patterns in the sensory nodes regards the way the $\mathbf{SW}_{ij}$ is programmed: instead of being the result of the cross-product on binary strings, it also involves analog patterns. In both cases though, the entries of the connection matrices express the correlation between node activities x_i and s_j.

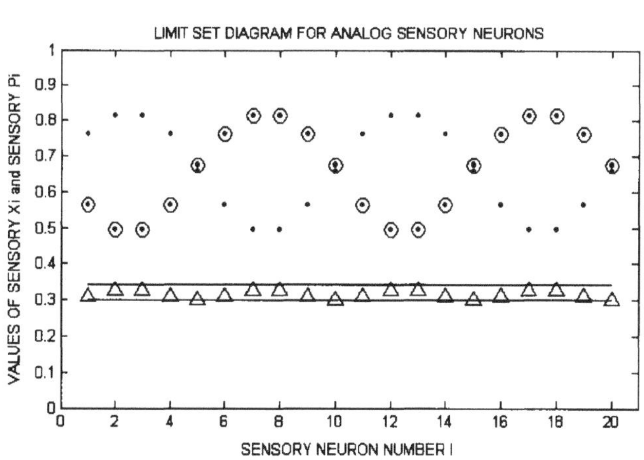

Fig. 6. Coding of bipolar analog inputs through period-2 cycles. The amplitude of cycling ($|A - B|$ discussed in Section 3) encodes the magnitude of sine shaped inputs; the phase of cycling encodes the sign $(\pm)$.

9. Conclusions

The characterization studies in Sections 5 and 6, addressing the RPEs architectures for the recovery of patterns under conditions of noisy prompting, allowed us to have a better understanding of the concepts and design considerations addressed in Sections 2–4. The identification of the emergence of preferential patterns led us to significantly improve the network performance for analog noise environments: the results in Tables 2 and 3 show the clear progress obtained with the clipping pre-processing. The contrastive study with respect to Hopfield networks and its positive results showed the importance of considering RPEs when implementing novel neural architectures.

Finally, the concepts and mechanisms related to *sensory nodes* provided important tools for the application of RPEs in contexts of time-dependent and analog inputs, as well as for the implementation of modular RPEs architectures.

Acknowledgements

I would like to thank the University of São Paulo (Brazil), FAPESP and CNPq, for supporting this work.

References

Aihara, K., Takabe, T., & Toyoda, M. (1990). Chaotic neural networks. *Physica Letters A*, *144*(6/7), 333–340.

Del-Moral-Hernandez, E. (1998). *Artificial neural networks based on bifurcating recursive processing elements*. UMI Dissertation Services: Ann Arbor, MI.

Del-Moral-Hernandez, E. (2000). Bifurcating pulsed neural networks, chaotic neural networks and parametric recursions: conciliating different frameworks in neuro-like computing. *International Joint Conference on Neural Networks*, *6*, 423–428.

Del-Moral-Hernandez, E. (2001a). A novel time-based neural coding for artificial neural networks with bifurcating recursive processing elements. *International Joint Conference on Neural Networks*, *1*, 44–49.

Del-Moral-Hernandez, E. (2001b). Studying neural networks of bifurcating recursive processing elements—quantitative methods for architecture design and performance analysis (2084). *Lecture Notes in Computer Science*. (pp. 546–553). Berlin: Springer-Verlag.

Farhat, N. H., & Del-Moral-Hernandez, E. (1995). *Logistic networks with DNA-like encoding and interactions (930)*. *Lecture Notes in Computer Science*. (pp. 214–222). Berlin: Springer-Verlag.

Freeman, W. J. (1992). Tutorial on neurobiology: from single neuron to brain chaos. *International Journal of Bifurcation and Chaos*, 2(3), 451–482.

Haykin, S. (1999). *Neural networks: A comprehensive foundation* (2nd ed.). Upper Saddle River, NJ: Prentice Hall.

Hilborn, R. C. (1994). *Chaos and nonlinear dynamics: An introduction for scientists and engineers*. New York: Oxford University Press.

Ishii, S., Fukumizu, K., & Watanabe, S. (1993). Associative memory using spatiotemporal chaos. *International Joint Conference on Neural Networks*, *3*, 2638–2641.

Kaneko, K. (1992). Overview of coupled map lattices. *Chaos*, *2*(3), 279–282.

Kaneko, K. (1993). The coupled map lattice: Introduction, phenomenology, Lyapunov analysis, thermodynamics and applications. *In Theory and applications of coupled map lattices*. (pp. 1–49). Chichester: Wiley.

Kelso, J. A. S. (1995). *Dynamic patterns—the self-organization of brain and behavior*. Cambridge, MA: MIT Press.

Kozma, R., & Freeman, W. J. (2000). Encoding and recall of noisy data as chaotic spatio-temporal memory patterns in the style of the brains. *International Joint Conference on Neural Networks*, *5*, 33–38.

Kozma, R., & Freeman, W. J. (2001). Control of mesoscopic/intermediate-range spatio-temporal chaos in the cortex. *American Control Conference*, *1*, 263–268.

Lysetskiy, M., Zurada, J. M., & Lozowasky, A. (2002). Bifurcation-based neural computation. *International Joint Conference on Neural Networks*, *3*, 2716–2720.

Szu, H., & Hsu, C. (1997). Meanfield chaos dynamics with changing chaos threshold value. *International Joint Conference on Neural Networks*, *2*, 651–656.

Szu, H., Telfer, B., Rogers, G., Goboric, D., Hsu, C., Zaghloul, M., & Freeman, W. (2003). Spatiotemporal chaos information processing in neural networks—electronic implementation. WCNN'93.

AVAILABLE AT
www.ComputerScienceWeb.com
POWERED BY SCIENCE DIRECT

PERGAMON

Neural Networks 16 (2003) 683–689

Neural Networks

www.elsevier.com/locate/neunet

2003 Special issue

Simple and conditioned adaptive behavior from Kalman filter trained recurrent networks☆

Lee A. Feldkamp*, Danil V. Prokhorov, Timothy M. Feldkamp

Research and Advanced Engineering, Ford Motor Company, Dearborn, MI, USA

Abstract

We illustrate the ability of a fixed-weight neural network, trained with Kalman filter methods, to perform tasks that are usually entrusted to an explicitly adaptive system. Following a simple example, we demonstrate that such a network can be trained to exhibit input–output behavior that depends on which of two conditioning tasks was performed a substantial number of time steps in the past. This behavior can also be made to survive an intervening interference task.

Keywords: Recurrent neural network; Input–output; Adaptive behavior

1. Introduction

In earlier papers, we questioned the common restriction of the definition of adaptation to systems whose parameters are changed in response to their observed environment. In particular, we have shown (Feldkamp, Puskorius, & Moore, 1996, 1997; Feldkamp & Puskorius, 1997) that the behavior of a fixed-weight recurrent neural network (RNN) can change substantially, according to the pattern of its inputs. We speculate that some or all of the states of the dynamical system represented by the RNN play the role of the parameters of a conventional adaptive system. Our previous demonstrations have fallen generally into two classes: (1) one-step predictions for discrete time dynamical systems (usually low-dimensional chaotic maps) and (2) a single fixed-weight RNN controller for several unrelated multiple-input/multiple-output plants (see Prokhorov, Feldkamp, & Tyukin, 2002, for an overview).

Younger, Conwell, and Cotter (1999) and Hochreiter, Younger, and Conwell (2001) have demonstrated related abilities for specially constructed recurrent networks and have used the term meta-learning for what we call adaptive behavior. We hypothesize that the RNN develops a (possibly distributed) internal state that distinguishes among the various subtasks and is used to choose among the corresponding input–output behaviors stored in the network. (Note that the subtasks need not be discretely different; in Feldkamp et al. (1996, 1997)) we considered prediction for a chaotic time series characterized by a continuous parameter.) We continue to find remarkable the fact that both the decision mechanism and the task execution mechanism can be loaded into a relatively small RNN by training.

An alternative (Annaswamy, 1996) to our hypothesis is that the RNN is merely learning a mapping between a point in a suitably large lag space of its inputs and the desired output. Such an explanation is based on the plausible assertion that the regions of lag space in which the various subtasks 'live' are largely unique.

While we contend that this explanation cannot explain all the results we have observed (especially those involving control), we have felt the need for a simply constructed and reproduced clarifying example. This paper presents an example that demonstrates that an RNN can be trained to develop two different functions of its input, according to which of two prior *conditioning* tasks has been performed. The distinction persists long after the conditioning has been terminated, suggesting that a *strongly hidden state* (Williams, 1990) has been formed and that the network uses this to decide which input–output function to apply. We contend that this capability cannot be attained with a fixed feed-forward network based on time-lagged inputs.

In Section 2, we provide a simple example of adaptive behavior. The task is state estimation in the presence of a nonstationary output function. Then we address the primary topic of this paper, viz. the ability of a trained RNN to condition its behavior on inputs seen a large number of time steps in the past.

☆ This paper contains substantial material from Feldkamp, Prokhorov, & Feldkamp, 2001a.

* Corresponding author.

0893-6080/03/$ - see front matter © 2003 Published by Elsevier Science Ltd.
doi:10.1016/S0893-6080(03)00127-8

2. Example of adaptive behavior

We consider a modified version of the problem treated by van der Merwe and Wan (2003) and Wan and van der Merwe (2001) with several methods, including extended and unscented Kalman filters and various particle filters. The process model is given by

$$x_k = 1 + \phi_1 x_{k-1} + \sin(\omega\pi(k-1)) + \nu_k \qquad (1)$$

where $\phi_1 = 0.5$, $\omega = 0.04$, and the process noise ν is a Gamma random variable (Ga(3,2)) and is largely responsible for the progression of the time series. We generate values for ν using the Matlab function Gamrnd[1] which produces a distribution with a mean of about 6.0 and a standard deviation of about 3.5, but heavily tailed toward high values.

The observation model may switch arbitrarily between the following two forms

$$y_k = 0.2x_k^2 + n_k \qquad (2)$$

and

$$y_k = 0.5x_k - 2 + n_k \qquad (3)$$

where we take the measurement noise n to be uniformly distributed in $[-0.0001, 0.0001]$.

The setting for our example is as follows. As in van der Merwe and Wan (2003), we assume that the form and parameters of the process and observation models are known. We assume that the form of each noise source is known, but that we do not know the actual values of the noise at a given step. Unlike Van der Merwe and Wan (2003), we do not assume knowledge of which observation model is active.[2] The task is to estimate the sequence of values x_k, given the sequence of values of y_k.

The primary difficulty of our version of this problem is not knowing which observation model is active. The only information available to distinguish between the observation models is the magnitude of y_k (for a given x_k the first model yields a larger output). However, a considerable ambiguity remains. A range of output values exists that could have resulted from either observation model, so we do not have a unique mapping from y_k to x_k. (If a unique mapping were to exist, a feed-forward network could be trained to give good results.) The large process noise ν causes jumps in the state variable x_k, though some filtering is provided by its dependence on x_{k-1}. Any approach to this problem must balance information from previous steps with that from the current observation.

The methods described by van der Merwe and Wan (2003) and Wan and van der Merwe (2001) make use of the process and observation models and the form of the process noise model. Likewise, our RNN-based approach uses the same information, but in a different way. Instead of explicitly constructing a filter, we utilize the model information to generate a large amount of training data and then rely on the training process to form a network that combines the past and present information as optimally as possible. In particular, after generating a large set of pairs (x_k, y_k) according to the above equations, switching between observation models with a specified probability, we simply train the RNN with the observed y_k as an input and the desired x_k as output.

We selected a 1-5R-5R-1L network (recurrent multi-player perceptron with one input, two hidden layers of five fully recurrent nonlinear nodes each, one linear output node). Due to the illustrative intent of this exercise, a rigorous search for an optimal architecture was not carried out. We generated 10,000 data instances, with the probability of a switch between observation models taken as 0.01. Though neither distribution was symmetric, the mean of the network input sequence was 26.7 with standard deviation 27.6, while the target sequence had mean value 14.0 and standard deviation 4.17. To facilitate training, we scaled the data; the network input was $y_k^* = 0.01y_k$ and the network target was $x_k^* = 0.1x_k$. We used 20-stream GEKF training (Feldkamp & Puskorius, 1998). We attempted to encourage fast response with a priming length of 1. We trained for 300 cycles of trajectory length 100. Hence we made 300×99 weight updates, each based on 20 instances. The entire training process required about one minute on a fast workstation. The RMS error (original unscaled units) on the training set was approximately 0.52. Errors observed on independently generated testing sets were similar. Much of the RMS error of the RNN may be attributed to regions where switching occurs or appears to be occurring.

Fig. 1 shows the performance of the trained network on an independently generated 100-instance sequence in

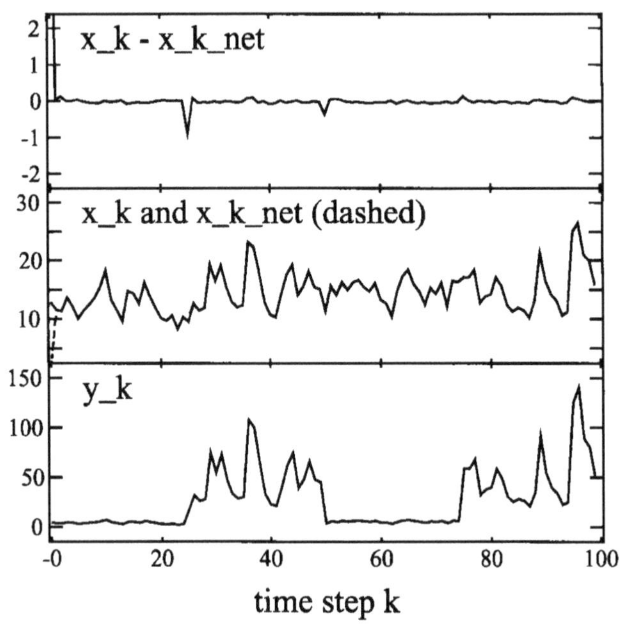

Fig. 1. Performance of a trained RNN in estimating the state variable x_k from observations y_k, where the observation model is switched between two forms every 25 steps. In the middle panel, the desired and estimated x_k are drawn with solid and dashed lines, respectively.

---

[1] This choice differs from the way van der Merwe and Wan (2003) generated such values.

[2] We thank Rudolph van der Merwe for confirming this.

which the observation model was switched every 25 instances. This short segment does not illustrate the full effect of the heavy tails of the process noise distribution on the range of y_k.

The performance of the RNN here cannot be compared directly to the results for the several filters investigated by van der Merwe and Wan (2003), primarily because of different assumptions regarding knowledge of switching between observation models.

We performed three small side experiments. In the first, we trained a feed-forward network of architecture 1-10-10-1L. As expected, the resulting RMS error of 2.08 was much larger than that for the recurrent network. In the second experiment, we removed observation model ambiguity by replacing -2 in the second observation model with -40, thereby degenerating the problem to a static mapping. We obtained an RMS training error of 0.012 for the 1-5R-5R-1L network, significantly reduced from the error of the original problem. Finally, we removed ambiguity in a different way, by providing the network with an input flag that signals which observation model is active. This resulted in an RMS error of about 0.015 on training and independent test sets.

3. Conditioned behavior

3.1. Problem description

We now consider the primary subject of the paper: behavior which must be predicated on what inputs the network has encountered in the possibly distant past.

Suppose we have two conditioning sequences and two associated post-conditioning input–output mappings. Then the desired behavior is the following. While either of the conditioning sequences is being presented as input, we want the network to predict the next value of the sequence, i.e. to make a one-step prediction. If, however, the input sequence consists of random values, we desire the network to output $f_i(x(t))$, $i = 1, 2$, according to which conditioning sequence was more recently presented.

As conditioning sequences, we use the following two variations of the Henon map (the second amounts to a scaled version of the first).

$$x_1(t+1) = 1 - 1.4x_1^2(t) + 0.3x_1(t-1) \quad (4)$$

$$x_2(t+1) = 1.4 - x_2^2(t) + 0.3x_2(t-1) \quad (5)$$

We take the desired mapping of random values to be particularly simple

$$f_1(x) = x \quad (6)$$

$$f_2(x) = -x \quad (7)$$

Thus, if the input x is from a Henon sequence, i.e $x = x_i(t)$, the target output is $y = x_i(t+1)$. If the input x is randomly generated, the target output is $y = f_i(x)$.

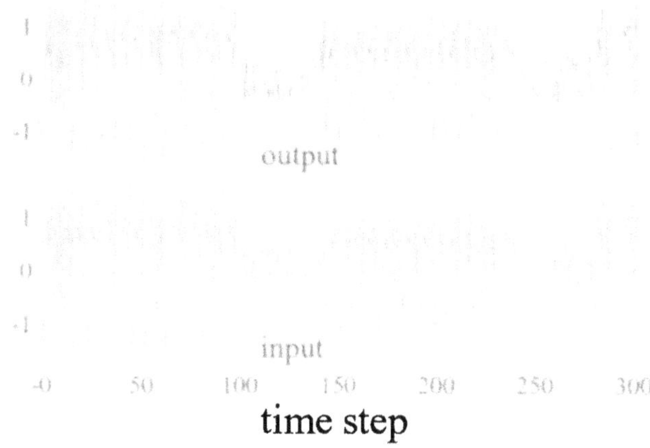

Fig. 2. The beginning of the file used for training, showing two length-100 Henon segments, each followed by length-40 segments of random inputs. A small portion of a third Henon segment appears at the end. In each Henon segment, the target output is the next value of the sequence. In a random segment, the target output is either equal to the input (if Henon version 1 was most recent) or the negative of the input. Here, a segment of Henon version 2 ends at step 100 and Henon version 1 begins at step 141. The output of the trained network is drawn with a dashed line.

An example of the desired behavior is shown in Fig. 2.

3.2. Training procedure

We employed the multistream EKF training method, modified with special assignment of training trajectories as described below. We generated a single training file containing 14,000 instances. This file contains 100 repetitions of the following pattern: 100 instances of a Henon sequence (alternately type 1 or type 2) followed by 40 instances of random inputs and corresponding outputs. The length of the random segments was chosen to exceed the maximum pure delay that could be constructed from the chosen RNN architecture. It was also chosen to be sufficiently large to induce long-term memory of the conditioning sequence, as discussed below. We used 10 streams, with a trajectory length of 330 and a priming length of 10. This length ensures that several transitions between segments are encountered before a new trajectory is started. A starting point was chosen randomly for each stream, subject to the restriction that it be in a conditioning segment and not closer than the priming length from the end of that segment. This restriction was imposed so that the network is not trained on instances for which it does not have sufficient information to give a reasonable output. (There is no basis, even in principle, for a network to produce a correct output if the trajectory starts in a segment in which the inputs are random.) Starting points were balanced between the two types of Henon conditioning sequence.

A recurrent multi-layer perceptron architecture of 1-7R-7R-1L produced the results shown here. In preliminary trials, a larger network was slightly easier to train but did not produce significantly smaller errors. A smaller network (1-5R-5R-1L) did not seem likely to yield a satisfactory solution, though a thorough investigation was not carried out. An EKF learning rate $\eta = 1/R_0 = 0.01$ was employed. The process noise parameter Q_0 was set to 0.01η for 1000 cycles of training, then to $10^{-6}\eta$ for 200 additional cycles. A cycle is comprised of 320 updates (trajectory length−priming length), each based on 10 instances (one from each stream). This means that there were 384,000 updates involving 3,840,000 instances, approximately equivalent to training on each instance 274 times.

Derivatives were obtained with truncated backpropagation through time, BPTT(h), with truncation depth $h = 10$. Longer truncation depths were also tried. Somewhat surprisingly, no significant improvement was noted for $h = 30$, perhaps because the training procedure was constructed to allow 'boot-strapping' as the network learned how to deal with the random segments.

Typically, training reached an RMS error of about 0.1 and less than 250 sign errors out of 14,390 instances tested (errors are not tallied from the instances used for priming). Most of the sign errors may be expected to come from the transitions between segments, as the RNN is accommodating its new context. The training process was successful in the sense that each region of the training file with random inputs is handled with the correct input–output sign relationship.

3.3. Network testing

As noted above, the random regions in the training data were limited to 40 steps. However, as we are interested in what happens for longer segments of random inputs, we prepared data sets in which the random sequence lengths were increased, to 500 in one case and 1000 in the other, with the conditioning sequences decreased to 20 instances.

The network often succeeds in recognizing quickly which Henon sequence is present and in maintaining the correct response to the random input all the way to the end of its segment. The transition from a random segment to a Henon segment is also handled gracefully, with the correct output closely approximated after a few steps.

It is interesting to examine the pattern of hidden-node outputs, i.e. the state variables of the network. Fig. 3 shows the network input and the outputs of the nodes of the second hidden layer. Note that the various segments of data are evident in several of the nodes. Node 2, in particular, assumes four different, roughly constant values, according to which segment is current. Of course, there is no requirement that the identity of the data segments be as transparently reflected in the state variables of the network as it is here.

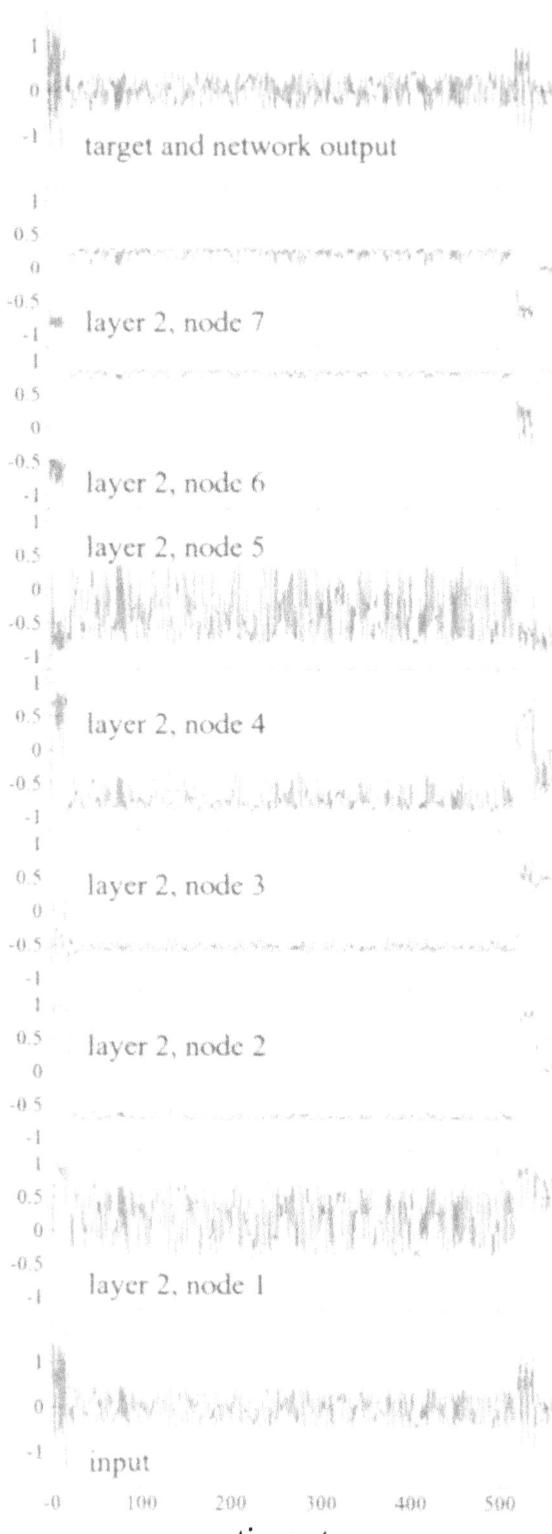

Fig. 3. Network input and output and outputs of the seven nodes of the second hidden layer for a portion of the testing run beginning with a length-20 Henon (version 2) segment followed by an appropriate length-500 random segment. A length-20 version 1 Henon segment and the beginning of the subsequent random segment are also visible. (In the random segments, the sign of the target depends on which conditioning sequence preceded it.) The output for node 2 of layer 2 shows four different levels (the first and third being only slightly different).

It should be noted that we did not explicitly train the network for long-term memory. Therefore, the impressive retention of 500–1000 steps should not have been expected, even though this behavior is a reasonable generalization of the training task. Indeed, in some training trials, especially with trajectory length 100 rather than 330, the retention observed was not as good. In such cases, the response to random inputs that follow one of the Henon sequences would start out correctly but later revert to the opposite response. This suggests an imbalance in the robustness of the hidden state to the network's constantly changing input. It seems likely that eventually any network will experience such a failure; i.e. that robustness in this context is a continuous rather than discrete property. Of course, a training scenario could easily be constructed to encourage long-term retention.

3.4. Conditioning and interference

In the previous example, random segments follow the Henon conditioning sequence directly. It is natural to ask whether the recurrent network can retain memory of which conditioning sequence it has observed if an unrelated task intervenes. To test this, we modified the training problem by creating two additional training files. In the first of these, the first 10 instances after each Henon segment are input–output pairs $(y_3(t), y_3(t+1))$ generated from the following scaled logistic map

$$x_3(t+1) = 3.6x_3(t)(1 - x_3(t)) \tag{8}$$

$$y_3(t) = 2(x_3(t) - 0.65) \tag{9}$$

and followed by a 30-step random segment. In the second added file, the logistic segment is 40 steps and no random segment is present. Note that in logistic segments, the target is a single-step prediction, irrespective of which conditioning sequence had preceded it. The scaling was chosen to give network input values that fall roughly into the same range as those of the random sequences. This was done to make more challenging the network's task of distinguishing between logistic and random sequences.

Training was carried out as described in Section 3.2 with the following modifications. The backpropagation depth was increased to 20 steps to allow for the 10 extra steps between each random segment and its conditioning sequence. The number of streams was increased to 12 to permit a balanced representation of the three files in each update.

This modified training problem was somewhat more difficult than the base problem, but a satisfactory result was obtained well before the training schedule was completed. Fig. 4 shows the network performance on independently generated testing data. The network switches quickly from predicting the Henon map to predicting the scaled logistic map, and then switches to responding to the random sequence with the correct sign.

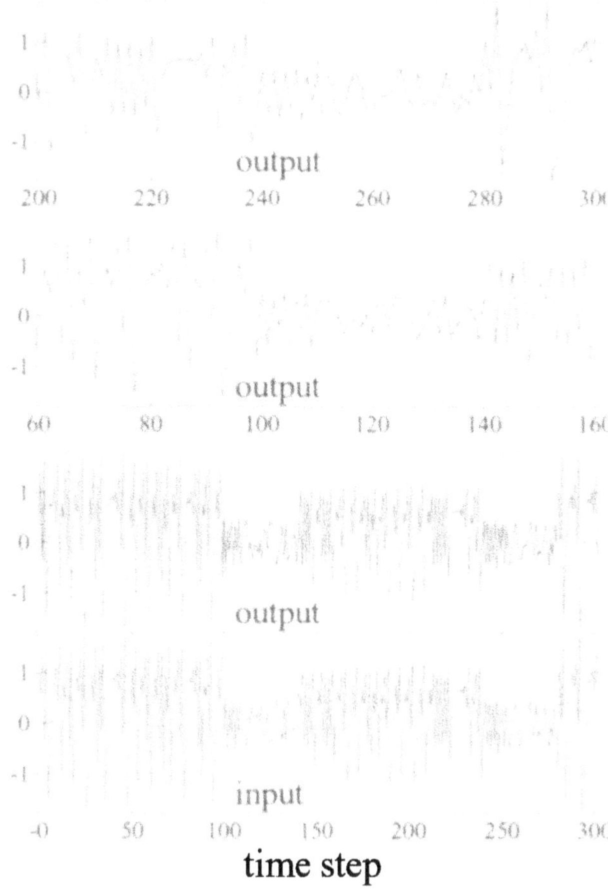

Fig. 4. A portion of the neural network performance on independent testing data for the example of Section 3.4. The bottom two panels show the first 300 instances. The Henon segments (steps 1–100 and 141–240) are each followed by 10 steps of the scaled logistic map, then by 30 steps of the random sequence. The network output is dashed. The upper two panels give expanded views of the outputs in interesting regions.

4. Discussion

The ability of a trained RNN to make accurate one-step predictions for two or more chaotic maps requires the network to pay attention to the current stream of inputs and determine its behavior accordingly. On contrast, in the tasks presented in this paper, the correct response to the random input sequence cannot be determined entirely on the basis of recent inputs, but requires some memory of an event in the possibly distant past to enable selection from two possible correct responses.

Training RNN for the tasks described above with the EKF approach was found to be a robust process; repeated training trials (with different initial network weights) produced consistent results. We also carried out training with two related nonlinear Kalman training approaches, nprKF (Feldkamp, Feldkamp, & Prokhorov, 2001b) and nprKFj (Feldkamp, Feldkamp, & Prokhorov, 2002). With each of these we were usually able to obtain results similar with those of EKF trained RNN on test sequences similar to that of Fig. 4 in terms of the lengths of logistic and random segments. However, we observed that networks trained with nprKFj, which performs joint state and parameter estimation, did not exhibit the substantial long-term memory (more than 200 time steps) that we reported above for EKF trained networks. We speculate that the adjustment of states (i.e. outputs of recurrent nodes) during training reduces the sensitivity to the distant past, in much the same way as does teacher forcing. This observation will be studied further.

One could probably construct a system that performs the present tasks from modules individually trained or designed to carry out the following subtasks: (1) model two Henon maps, (2) determine quickly from the input sequence which Henon map (if either) is present and switch to that model, (3) maintain memory of which Henon map was most recently presented, (4) determine whether a random sequence is present and, if so, switch to the appropriate input–output response. The second example adds the task of modeling the scaled logistic map, differentiating it from a sequence of random numbers in the same range. In this work, we have not used handcrafted network architecture; instead we depend on the training process to induce whatever is required. It seems remarkable that only 14 recurrent nodes suffice.

We offer the following description of the observed behavior of the recurrent network, making use of the speculative concept of *behavioral states*. The latter have aspects of orbital attractors but apply to driven rather than autonomous systems; see (Prokhorov et al., 2002) for a related discussion. We have trained for five desired behaviors: Henon-1 prediction, Henon-2 prediction, random number replication, random number negation, and (scaled) logistic prediction. Because we expect the network to remember the identity of the most recent Henon sequence while behaving as a predictor for the logistic map, we have six behavioral states, which we denote as H1, H2, R1, R2, L1, and L2. States L1 and L2 imply identical network response to scaled logistic inputs but differ in what must be remembered for future use. A diagram of allowed transitions among these states is shown in Fig. 5. Such transitions occur only if the network receives the required input sequence.

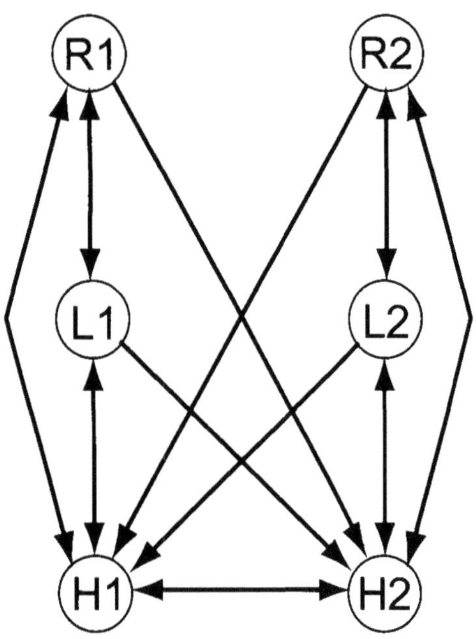

Fig. 5. Transition diagram for the behavioral states of the trained recurrent neural network described in the text. Self transitions for each state are allowed but not shown.

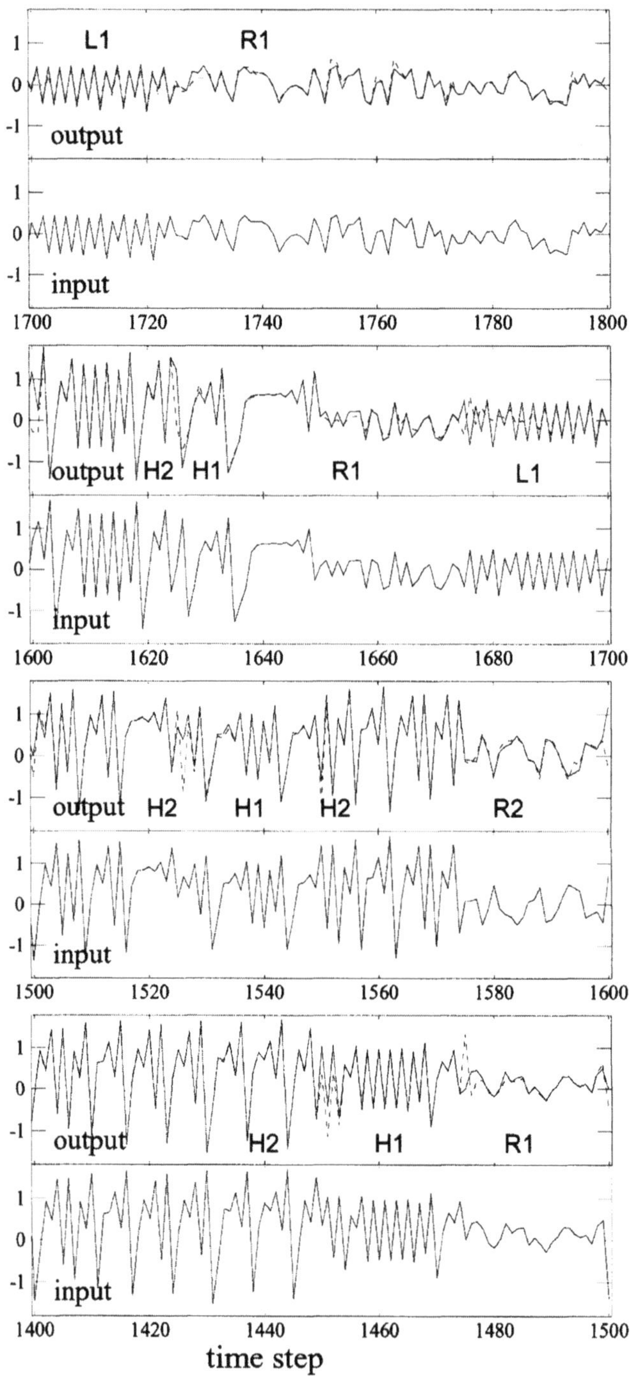

Fig. 6. An illustration of transitions among behavioral states. We show a total of 400 steps, beginning at lower left. A state was chosen randomly every 25 steps, with the same state allowed to repeat. Transitions between different states can usually be detected by a momentary departure of the network's output (dashed curve) from the target.

To illustrate the transitions of Fig. 5, we generated test data in which the desired behavior is chosen randomly every 25 steps. The performance of a network on a portion of this test is shown in Fig. 6. In this case the network was trained with nprKF (Feldkamp et al., 2001b); our standard EKF training produced similar results. Note that the network is displaying the correct behavior for state R1 at step 1800, based on H1 ending at step 1650, in spite of interference from the logistic sequence from steps 1676–1725.

Fig. 5 is drawn on the assumption that the input sequence is always one for which the network has been taught the desired response. If this is not the case, then the diagram must be extended to include at least one additional behavioral state, i.e. one that describes its response to input sequences beyond the repertoire for which it has been trained. On the basis of limited experimentation, we expect this ('garbage') state to transition gracefully to either H1 or H2 when the appropriate input sequence is applied. Following this, normal behavior should be restored. On the other hand, if logistic input is applied to the network in the garbage state, we expect a reasonably good output to be obtained but the choice between L1 and L2 to be uncertain, because the out-of-repertoire input sequence is likely to have corrupted any memory of whether H1 or H2 was more recent. Similarly, the response to random input directly following the garbage state should follow either R1 or R2, the choice depending primarily on any accidental imbalance of 'attraction' conferred by the training process.

5. Conclusions

We have demonstrated interesting and potentially useful capabilities that are within the representational power of even modest size nonlinear dynamical systems, here structured as layered recurrent networks. Furthermore, we claim that these capabilities and many others can be realized by means of powerful training methods.

References

Annaswamy, A., (1996). *On the ability of recurrent neural networks to learn different time series*. Unpublished manuscript.

Feldkamp, L. A., Puskorius, G. V., & Moore, P. C. (1996). Adaptation from fixed weight dynamic networks. *Proceedings of IEEE International Conference on Neural Networks*, 155–160.

Feldkamp, L. A., Puskorius, G. V., & Moore, P. C. (1997). Adaptive behavior from fixed weight networks. *Information Sciences, 98*, 217–235.

Feldkamp, L. A., & Puskorius, G. V. (1997). Fixed weight controller for multiple systems. *Proceedings of the 1997 IEEE International Conference on Neural Networks, 2*, 773–778.

Feldkamp, L. A., & Puskorius, G. V. (1998). A signal processing framework based on dynamic neural networks with application to problems in adaptation, filtering and classification. *Proceedings of the IEEE, 86*, 2259–2277.

Feldkamp, L. A., Prokhorov, D. V., & Feldkamp, T. M (2001a). Conditioned adaptive behavior from a fixed neural network. *Proceedings of the 11th Yale Workshop on Adaptive and Learning Systems* (pp. 78–83).

Feldkamp, L. A., Feldkamp, T. M., & Prokhorov, D. V. (2001b). Neural network training with the nprKF. *Proceedings of International Joint Conference on Neural Networks'01*, 109–114.

Feldkamp, L. A., Feldkamp, T. M., & Prokhorov, D. V. (2002). Recurrent neural network training by nprKF joint estimation. *Proceedings of International Joint Conference on Neural Networks'02*, 2086–2091.

Prokhorov, D. V., Feldkamp, L. A., & Tyukin, I. Y. (2002). Adaptive behavior with fixed weights in RNN: an overview. *Proceedings of International Joint Conference on Neural Networks'02*, 2018–2023.

Hochreiter, S., Younger, S. P., & Conwell, P. (2001). Learning to learn using gradient descent. *Proceedings of ICANN*, 87–94.

Van der Merwe, R., & Wan, E. (2003). Gaussian mixture sigma-point particle filters for sequential probabilistic inference in dynamic state-space models. *Proceedings of IEEE International Conference on Acoustics, Speech and Signal Processing*.

Wan, E., & van der Merwe, R. (2001). The unscented Kalman filter. In S. Haykin (Ed.), *Kalman filtering and neural networks* (pp. 221–280). New York: Wiley.

Williams, R. J. (1990). Adaptive state representation and estimation using recurrent neural networks. In W. T. Miller, III, R. S. Sutton, & P. J. Werbos (Eds.), *Neural networks for control* (pp. 97–114). Cambridge: MIT Press.

Younger, S., Conwell, P., & Cotter, N. (1999). Fixed-weight on-line learning. *IEEE Transaction on Neural Networks, 10*, 272–283.

PERGAMON

AVAILABLE AT
www.ComputerScienceWeb.com
POWERED BY SCIENCE DIRECT

Neural Networks 16 (2003) 691–699

Neural Networks

www.elsevier.com/locate/neunet

2003 Special issue

Learning robot actions based on self-organising language memory

Stefan Wermter*, Mark Elshaw

Centre for Hybrid Intelligent Systems[1], *School of Computing and Technology, University of Sunderland, St Peter's Way, Sunderland, SR6 0DD, United Kingdom*

Abstract

In the MirrorBot project we examine perceptual processes using models of cortical assemblies and mirror neurons to explore the emergence of semantic representations of actions, percepts and concepts in a neural robot. The hypothesis under investigation is whether a neural model will produce a life-like perception system for actions. In this context we focus in this paper on how instructions for actions can be modeled in a self-organising memory. Current approaches for robot control often do not use language and ignore neural learning. However, our approach uses language instruction and draws from the concepts of regional distributed modularity, self-organisation and neural assemblies. We describe a self-organising model that clusters actions into different locations depending on the body part they are associated with. In particular, we use actual sensor readings from the MIRA robot to represent semantic features of the action verbs. Furthermore, we outline a hierarchical computational model for a self-organising robot action control system using language for instruction.

Keywords: Mirror neurons; Robot; Language Memory

1. Introduction

In recent years, there has been much progress in understanding the underlying perceptual and neurocognitive processes in the brain as well as the techniques for these studies (lesion studies, fMRI, MEG and EEG Binder et al., 1997; Braitenberg, 1997; Dogil et al., 2002; Friedman et al., 1998; Joliot et al.,1999; Melcher, 2000; Pulvermüller, 1999; Taylor, 1999). Recent advances in MEG and fMRI techniques have clarified the dynamics of these processes, but it is still a long way for translating these results directly into computational architectures.

Other work has suggested the grounding of visual and auditory perception in neural representations (Dorffner & Prem, 1993; Feldman et al., 1996; Harnad, 1990). However, these results have not been integrated with behavioural studies to any great extent. Recently, a class of neurons has been found in the rostral part of the ventral premotor cortex (area F5) in monkeys that are active both when a monkey handles an object and when it observes an experimenter performing similar actions (Rizzolatti & Arbib, 1998). More recently, PET studies have implicated these 'mirrorneurons' in the gesture recognition system of humans. This system involves Broca's area, a language area in humans, which is generally believed to be the human homologue of area F5 in monkeys. Therefore, we explore the role of mirror neurons and cell assemblies for multimodal integration of action, vision, and language in the MirrorBot project.

Recently, there has been a growing interest in learning for robotics. However, these approaches rarely use neural networks or language instruction. Furthermore, the robots are restricted in their general autonomous behaviour and only learn what has been preprogrammed. Even the 'Talking Heads' approach that incorporates the emergence of language in robots (Steels, 1998) gives little consideration to neuroscience-inspired learning in humans.

Some robots like the tour-guide robot Rhino (Burgard et.al., 2000) have been quite robust in terms of their localization and navigation behaviour; however, they do not interact via language. Although the conversation office robot jjj-2 (Asoh et al., 1997) can be instructed to navigate to certain landmarks and the Minerva tour-guide (Thrun et al., 1999) interacts by using simply preprogrammed speech, they are restricted in their ability to learn. Furthermore, the Kismet interactive robot (Breazeal & Scassellati, 1999) can recognise and represent emotions using a static sophisticated head but does not understand or generate real language.

* Corresponding author. Tel.: +44-191-515-3279; fax: +44-191-515-3553.

E-mail address: stefan.wermter@sunderland.ac.uk (S. Wermter).

[1] http://www.his.sunderland.ac.uk

0893-6080/03/$ - see front matter © 2003 Elsevier Science Ltd. All rights reserved.
doi:10.1016/S0893-6080(03)00100-X

This paper for robot control using language incorporates some neuroscience evidence related to the architectural and processing characteristics of the brain (Wermter, Austin, & Willshaw, 2001). In particular it focuses on the neurocognitive evidence on cortical assemblies and regional modularity for language areas in the brain (Pulvermüller, 2003).

2. Regional distributed modularity

Various distributed neural networks in diverse regions in the brain carry out processing in a parallel distributed manner to perform specific cognitive functions (Reggia, Shkuro, & Shevtsova, 2001). The brain consists of a group of collaborating networks, none of which can deal with a complex task alone (Wermter et al., 2001).

For over a century researchers have considered how language is processed by the brain. As a response therefore there are various models of modular language processing. The classical model of language processing comes from lesion studies in the brain and is based on Broca's and Wernicke's language modules linked via the arcuate fasciculus (Bear, Connors, & Paradiso, 1996).

However, brain regions that are involved in language also include those outside the traditional language areas (Gazzaniga, Ivy, & Mangun, 1998; Purves, 1997). For instance, speech comprehension and information recollection has been observed to involve four regions in the left hemisphere of the cerebral cortex (Binder et al., 1997). Semantic language operations involve the superior temporal sulcus, middle temporal gyrus, angular gyrus and lateral frontal lobe (Friedman et al., 1998).

Recently, cortical assemblies have been identified in the cortex that activate in response to the performance of motor tasks at a semantic level (Pulvermüller, 1999; Rizzolatti, & Arbib, 1998). This evidence supports that these neurons are involved in actions, observing actions and communicating actions. The neurocognitive evidence of Pulvermüller (1999, 2002 and 2003) supports that cell assemblies are activated in different regions of the brain dependent on the word type being processed. This evidence offers the basis for our approach. Pulvermüller 1999 noted that activation was found in both hemispheres of the brain for content words and for vision words in the perisylvian and in the parietal, temporal and/oroccipital lobes. However, function words that have a grammatical role were limited to the perisylvian cortex. For action words that involve moving one's own body the perisylvian cell assemblies were associated with motor, premotor, and prefrontal cortices. Assemblies that depict vision words were found in the perisylvian and visual cortices in parietal, temporal and/or occipital lobes.

It is important to relate the neurons that represent the word with those neurons associated with perception and actions that reflect the semantic information of a word. Hence, if a word is repeatedly presented with a stimulus, the representation of this stimulus is incorporated into the representation for the word. For content words the semantic features that influence the cell assemblies come from various modalities and include the complexity of activity performed, facial expression or sound, the type and number of muscles involved, the colour of the stimulus, the object complexity and movement involved, the tool used, and whether the person can see herself doing this activity.

When examining the processing of action verbs that relate to the leg, face and arm Pulvermüller, Hare, and Hummel (2000) found that cell assemblies are associated through semantic information with the appropriate body part. They found that the average response times for lexical decisions was faster for face-associated words than for arm-associated words and the arm-associated response times faster than the leg ones. There was a significant difference for the prefrontal region and occipital regions and above the motor and premotor cortex.

The prefrontal area was found to be associated mainly with arm verbs and the occipital visual areas for face verbs. Furthermore, it was noted by Rizzolatti, Fogassi, and Gallese, (2001) that when subjects were required to observe actions made by the mouth, hand and foot that the foot was located dorsally and mouth and hand ventrally in the brain. This neurocognitive evidence motivates our approach for self-organising associative memory in multiple regions of the brain.

3. Self-organisation

Self-organising networks offer an unsupervised associative memory approach (Fig. 1). Self-organising networks consist of an input and an output layer, with every input neuron linked to all the neurons in the output layer

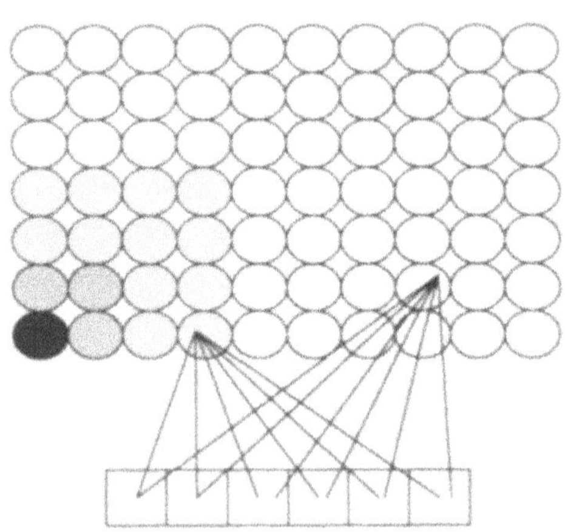

Fig. 1. Architecture of a self-organising network: the darker the neuron on the output layer the higher the activation.

(Kohonen, 1997). The output layer creates a topographical representation that clusters similar inputs together in a two-dimensional neural layer.

A typical self-organising network algorithm has an input vector represented as $\mathbf{i} = [i_1, i_2, ..., i_n]$. The input vector is presented to every output unit of the network. The weights between the links in the network are represented as

$$w_j = [w_{j1}, w_{j2}, ..., w_{jn}] \quad (1)$$

where j identifies unit j in the output layer and n is the nth element of the input. The output of unit j is the weighted sum of its inputs, given by:

$$o_j = \sum w_{jk} i_k = \mathbf{w}_j \cdot \mathbf{i} \quad (2)$$

The weights are usually initialised randomly and hence a unit of the network will react more strongly than others to a specific input representation. The weight vector of this unit as well as the eight neighbouring units are altered based on the following update rule:

$$\Delta \mathbf{w}_{jk} = \alpha(i_k - w_{jk}) \text{ and } w_{jk}(t+1) = w_{jk}(t) + \Delta w_{jk} \quad (3)$$

where α is the learning rate that is usually set between 0.2 and 0.5.

4. Architecture

A structured architecture of self-organising networks is under development to perform robot control based on associating language and actions. This system learns to associate the semantic features that are found in the sensor readings that represent the action with a representation of the word.

As can be seen at the bottom of Fig. 2 the architecture firstly contains a self-organising network to associate the action sensor readings with the appropriate body part by clustering the verbs in different regions. At the next processing level there is a self-organising network for each body part that uses the sensor reading vectors to associate the actual action verbs with different regions. To the right in the architecture, the words that are represented using their phonemes are clustered in a self-organising network. The upper-most self-organising network associates the actions with their appropriate words. Hence, by associating the action representation with the word the robot can describe the action with a word when it receives only the action representation and vice versa perform the action when it is given the word only.

In this system the input is used to produce the output by recreating the action from the sensor readings. The sensor readings provide information on the action such as the velocity of the separate wheels, the gripper activities and how the constituent subactions relate to the states of sensors such as break-beam and table sensors.

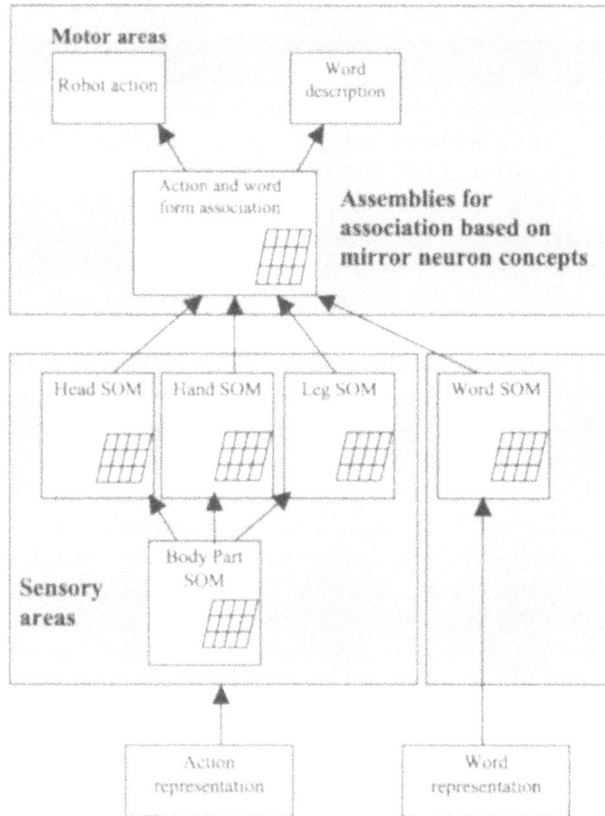

Fig. 2. Overall architecture based on modular distributed and hierarchical self-organising memory.

If the robot receives the 'put' action sensor reading representation, it would be introduced into the trained body part network and activate the hand region of the output layer. The hand self-organising network would then position the sensor readings input in the put region of the output layer. As the robot is describing the word there is no necessary input from the word self-organising network into the association self-organising network. However, as the network has previously learned to associate this action with the appropriate word the put region of the network is activated. The robot will then state using its language synthesis that the action semantic features provided are those for put. This describes the pathway from the internal action representation via the association area to the language description. In a similar, but opposite pathway the word input representation can lead via the association area to the sensory robot action.

This approach offers some brain-inspired regional modularity by having multiple self-organising networks, each performing a subtask of the overall task. These networks are linked in a distributed overall memory organization. Furthermore, at the higher functional level as can be seen from Fig. 2, this architecture includes components that are analogous to brain regions at a higher level. For instance, the SOMs that take the action representations and cluster these are related to the sensory motor cortical areas of the brain. The approach also takes into account the neurocognitive evidence of Pulvermüller et al. in that cell assemblies in different regions are associated with specific action verbs as a functional unit, with the association being based on the action verbs relationship with the appropriate body part.

This architecture links some concepts of the mirror neuron theory. The relationship of mirror neurons to language was pointed out by Rizzolatti and Arbib (1998) who found that neurons located in the F5 area of a primate's brain were activated by both the performance of the action and its observation. The recognition of motor actions comes from the presence of a goal and so the motor system does not solely control the movement (Gallese & Goldman, 1998). The role of these mirror neurons is to associate action representations with vision or language representations. The mirror neuron system was a critical discovery as it shows the role played by the motor cortex in action depiction (Rizzolatti, Fogassi, & Galles 2001). By using the sensor readings as input the mirror neuron concept is considered since the understanding of the action can come from either performing the action or a stored representation is linked to observing the action.

5. Self-organisation on the robot

In our experiments we examine the body parts self-organising map, and the head, hand and leg self-organising maps of the modular system. In our previous study (Elshaw & Wermter, 2001) it was possible to identify that a self-organising network was able to cluster action verbs related to body parts. However, this approach relied upon subjective encodings for the applicable features for the action verbs. In order to have greater objectivity and to incorporate self-organising maps into a robot control system, sensor readings were taken from the MIrror-neuron Robot Agent (MIRA) (Fig. 3). Now sensor readings represent semantic features to describe the action verbs such as the degree of motion and object manipulation. We will now describe the experimental context for testing the architecture.

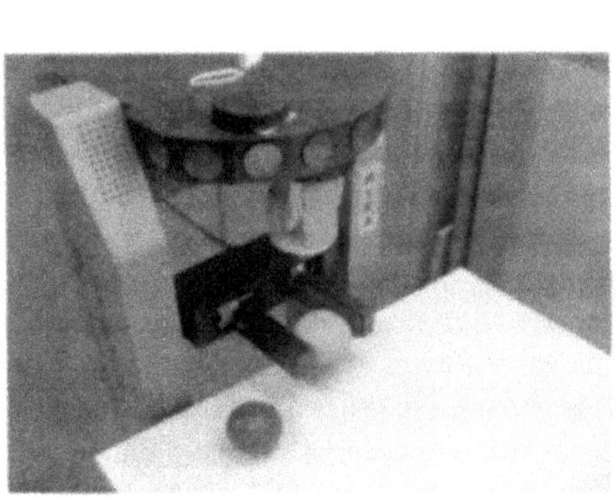

Fig. 3. The MIRA performing the 'pick' action.

5.1. Experimental method

The MIRA robot is based on a PeopleBot platform, and has a PC, microphone and speakers and a PC104 audio board. Wireless communication between the robot and a computer is used. The robot has an adjustable 120-degree pan-tilt camera and fixed-field IR sensors to sense the underside of the table. The robot also has a 2-degree gripper that contains break-beam sensors to detect the object. By using MIRA we take advantage of speech, motion and vision interfaces and explore the development towards a novel neural architecture.

MIRA was set up to perform various actions that are associated in humans with the leg, head or hand. The leg verb actions were 'turn left', 'turn right', 'forward' and 'backward'; head action verbs were 'head up', 'head down', 'head right' and 'head left' and finally the hand verbs were 'pick', put, 'lift', 'drop' and 'touch'. One action can be made of several basic actions. For instance, the hand verb action pick included the following subactions (i) slowly move forward to the table; (ii) tilt camera downwards to see table, (iii) lift gripper to table height; (iv) open gripper; (v) close gripper on object; (vi) stop forward motion; and (vii) lift gripper. This sequence of subactions corresponds in principle (although not in detail) to motor schemata since a complex action is represented as a sequence of basic actions. Sensor readings were taken for such sequences of basic actions.

In order to provide sufficient and varied training and test data the actions were repeated 20 times (15 training and five test) under diverse conditions. For instance, the speed the robot was travelling at and the angle that the camera was tilted or panned to were varied. The sensor readings were taken 10 times a second while MIRA performed these actions including the state of the gripper, the velocity of the wheels and the angle that the robot's camera was at. The full list of the sensor readings is given in Table 1.

To reduce the size of the input for the self-organising network to a manageable level, 10 sets of the readings were taken over time to represent the action. This was achieved by taking the first, last and eight equi-distant sets of readings and combining them to create a single input for a sample. Preprocessing was performed on the data to make it suitable for introduction into the neural networks. As self-organising networks require the input values to be represented numerically 'yes' was represented as 1 and 'no' 0. The gripper break-beam state values were represented as 'no beams broken' 0.25, 'inner broken' 0.5, 'outer broken' 0.75 and 'both broken' 1.

There was a need to normalise the sensor readings for such variables as velocity of left wheel, velocity of right wheel, x coordinate of robot, y coordinate of robot, and the pan and tilt of the camera. Normalisation was done by taking the sensor readings for the specific feature for all samples across the 10 sets of readings and positioning the values

Table 1
Sensor readings taken by robot during actions

Sensor reading	Value
Velocity of left wheel	Real number
Velocity of right wheel	Real number
x coordinate of robot	Real number
y coordinate of robot	Real number
Break-beam state of gripper	No beams broken, inner broken, outer broken, both broken
Gripper state	Gripper fully open, closed, between open and closed
Gripper at highest or lowest position	No Yes
Gripper moving upwards or downwards	No Yes
Table sensors activated	No Yes
Gripper opening or closing	No Yes
Pan of camera	Integer
Tilt of camera	Integer

between 0 and 1 dependent on its relative size. For example, the x coordinate values were normalised using the Eq. (4).

$$\frac{x - \min(x)}{\max(x) - \min(x)} \text{ for } all\ x \quad (4)$$

5.2. Unsupervised learning

For the self-organising network to cluster actions based on the appropriate body part the input layer had 120 units, one for each of the preprocessed sensor readings. The output layers had various sizes (from 8 by 8 units to 13 by13 units) and the networks were trained between 50 and 500 epochs at intervals of 50 epochs. Fig. 4 provides an example self-organising network showing the input and output for a 'put' action training. The number of training and test samples for each of the 13 actions were 15 and 5, respectively. There were 260 samples in total, 195 for training and 65 for testing. The location of each of the training and test samples on the self-organising maps were identified based on the units that had the highest activation.

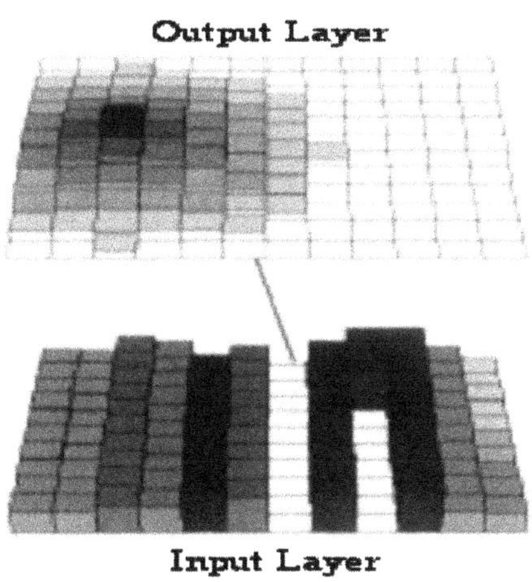

Fig. 4. Example self-organising network showing the input and output for a 'put' training sample.

For the hand, head and leg self-organising networks the inputs were the preprocessed sensor readings, the output layers were varied between 8 by 8 units and 10 by 10 units and they were trained for between 25 and 200 epochs. However, the networks received only sensor readings input for the appropriate body part.

6. Results and discussion

When considering self-organising networks for clustering the actions into their body parts with output layers of between 8 by 8 and 11 by 11 units the networks were only able to produce a split between hand actions and the other two classes. These networks were not able to cluster the leg and head actions into different regions. However, it did indicate an ability to produce a split between simple actions such as 'forward' or 'head right', and more complex actions such as 'put' or 'pick'.

Figs. 5 and 6 show a self-organising network that was 12 by 12 units before training. Before training, it was not possible to differentiate between the hand and leg action samples. Over 90% of the test and training samples for the head actions had the highest activation for the unit that also had the highest activation for 80% of the leg actions. Furthermore, the hand actions were spread out and did not cluster into a single region. However, once this network architecture was trained for 50 epochs there was a clear clustering into the three body parts (Figs. 7 and 8). The hand action words such as 'pick', 'touch', 'lift' were at the bottom of the training and test output layers in the hand body part region, with the head actions slightly below and to the right of the leg region. Although one unit within the head region

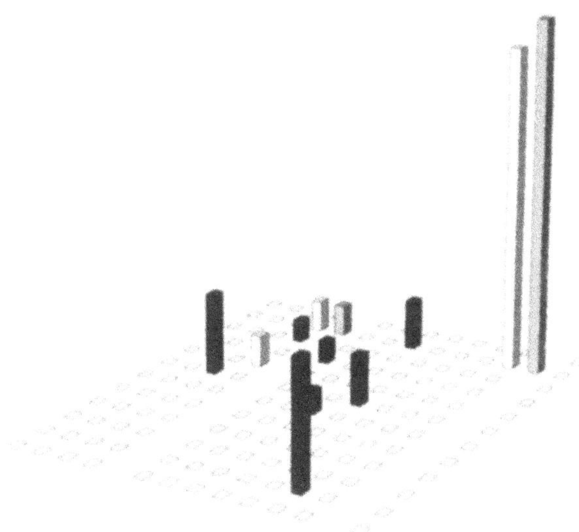

Fig. 5. The percentage of the training samples for the body parts that have highest activation for each unit on a 12 by 12 units network before training. (Black—Hand, White—Head, Grey—Leg).

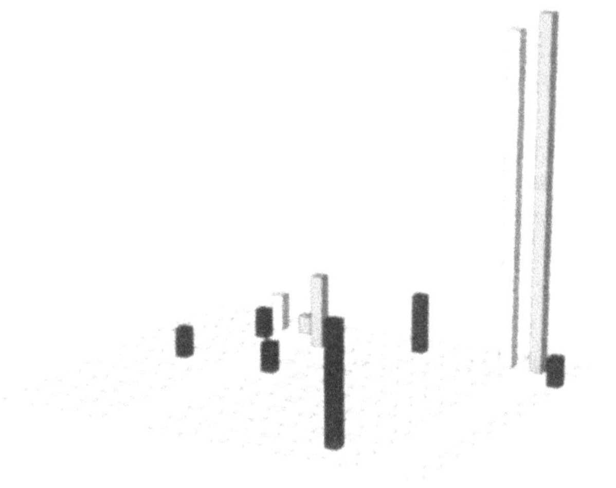

Fig. 6. The percentage of the test samples for the body parts that have highest activation for each unit on a 12 by 12 units network before training. (Black—Hand, White—Head, Grey—Leg).

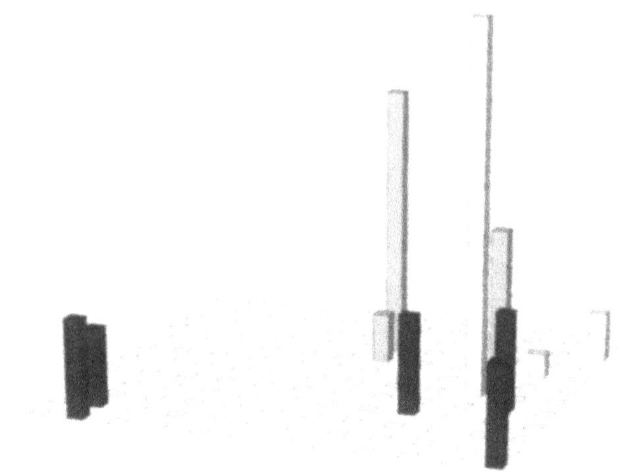

Fig. 8. The percentage of the test samples for the body parts that have highest activation for each unit on a 12 by 12 units network after a training time of 50 epochs. (Black—Hand, White—Head, Grey—Leg).

contained both head and leg action samples with the highest activation, the percentage for head samples was much higher on both test and training data. For the training and test data the percentage of head action samples with the highest activation for that unit was over 60% for training samples and 70% for test samples. Due to the major difference between the head and leg action percentages for this unit, only the head percentage is shown on Figs. 7 and 8.

As can be seen from Table 2 for the training data 100% of the hand and head fell in the appropriate region and 88% of the leg data. For test data the percentage was even better with 100% for hand and head and 90% for leg. It is interesting to note that within the hand verb region there was a good division into the actual action classes. In Figs. 7 and 8 'pick' was located in the lower right of the map, 'put' in the lower left, 'drop' in the unit above 'pick', 'touch' at the top of the hand region and most of the 'lift' samples were located in a unit just below 'touch'. For the other two classes there was some splitting into the individual actions but not on the scale of the hand class.

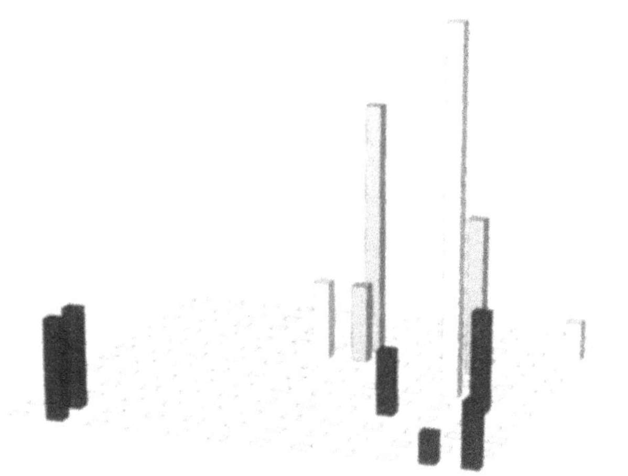

Fig. 7. The percentage of the training samples for the body parts that have highest activation for each unit on a 12 by 12 units network after a training time of 50 epochs. (Black—Hand, White—Head, Grey—Leg).

Hence, such a network can in principle realise the findings of Pulvermüller et al. on the processing of action verbs with different clusters representing the specific body parts. The network was able to identify the semantic features from the actual sensor readings for the individual action verb classes that were specific to the appropriate body part. These features were likely to include the degree of move, whether there was an object involved and the type and number of motors used.

For such an architecture on both training and test data the clusters were in very similar positions on the output layer, which points to the ability of the network to generalise on data it has not seen before. When considering the percentage of test data that fell in the regions identified by the training data the percentages were very high. For the hand actions 100%, head actions 95% and leg actions 88% of the test data fell into the appropriate training region.

Therefore, if the self-organising network was used in the control of a robot it can perform successfully in an online manner clustering semantic features of the action to the appropriate region of the output layer.

Turning to the hand, head and leg self-organising networks, when considering the clustering of the specific body part actions for all three types of action, the size of network that performed best was 8 by 8. For the hand network the training time that produced the best clustering was 50 epochs, for the head network it was 150 epochs and

Table 2
Percentages for the training and test samples that were associated with the appropriate body part clusters for the 12 by 12 units network

Body part	Training samples on training clusters (%)	Test samples on test clusters (%)	Test samples on training clusters (%)
Hand	100	100	100
Head	100	100	95
Leg	88	90	88

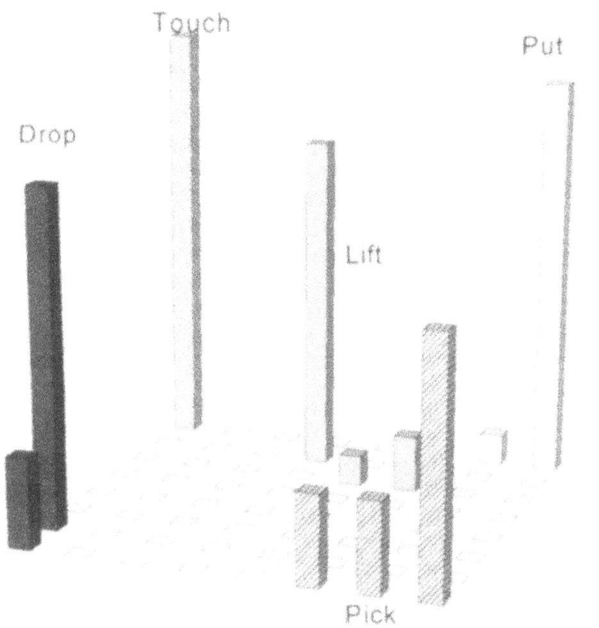

Fig. 9. The percentage of the training samples for the specific hand actions that have the highest activation for each unit on a 8 by 8 units network with a training time of 50 epochs.

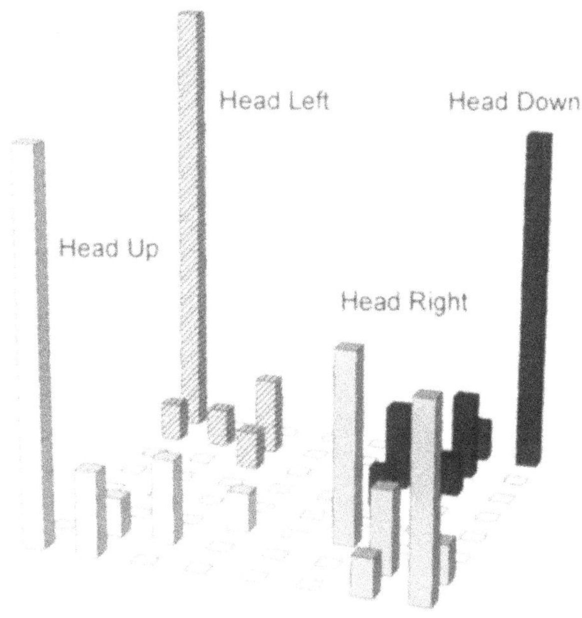

Fig. 11. The percentage of the training samples for the specific head actions that have highest activation for each unit on a 8 by 8 units network with a training time of 100 epochs.

for the leg self-organising network it was 100 epochs. As can be seen from Figs. 9–14 there was clear clustering into different regions for the hand, head and leg actions. For the hand actions on both the training and test data 'touch' was in the top left corner, 'put' in the top right corner, 'drop' in the bottom left corner, 'pick' in the bottom right and 'lift' was in the upper center. Turning to the head self-organising network in Figs. 11 and 12 'head left' was in the upper left region, 'head down' in the upper right, 'head up' in lower left and 'head right' in the lower left region. For the leg self-organising network 'forward' was in the upper left of the map, 'turn left' in the upper right, 'turn right' in the lower left and 'backward' in the lower right corner of the map.

The good performance of the hand, head and leg networks can be observed from Tables 3–5. For the hand network 100% of the 'drop', 'pick', 'lift' and 'touch' and 93% of the 'put' training samples fell into the appropriate

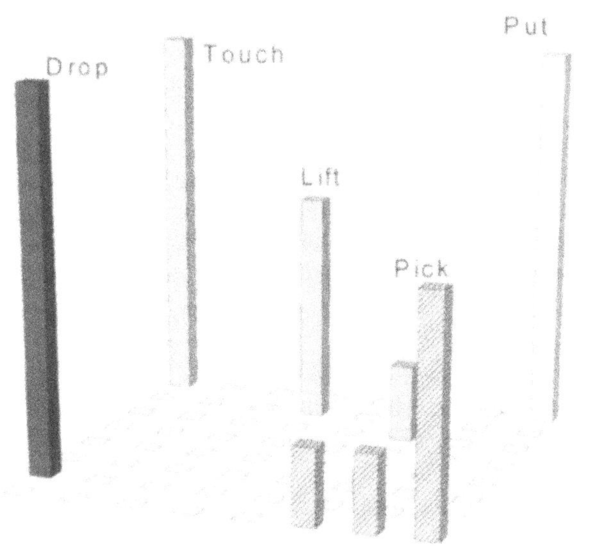

Fig. 10. The percentage of the test samples for the specific hand actions that have highest activation for each unit on a 8 by 8 units network with a training time of 50 epochs.

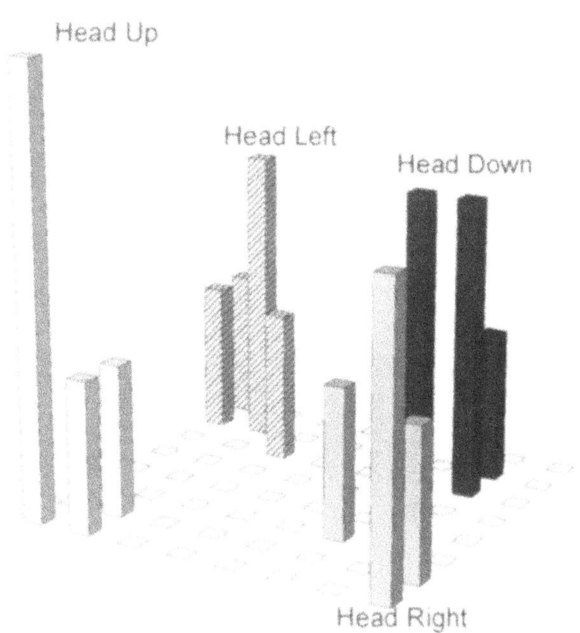

Fig. 12. The percentage of the test samples for the specific head actions that have highest activation for a each unit on a 8 by 8 units network with a training time of 100 epochs.

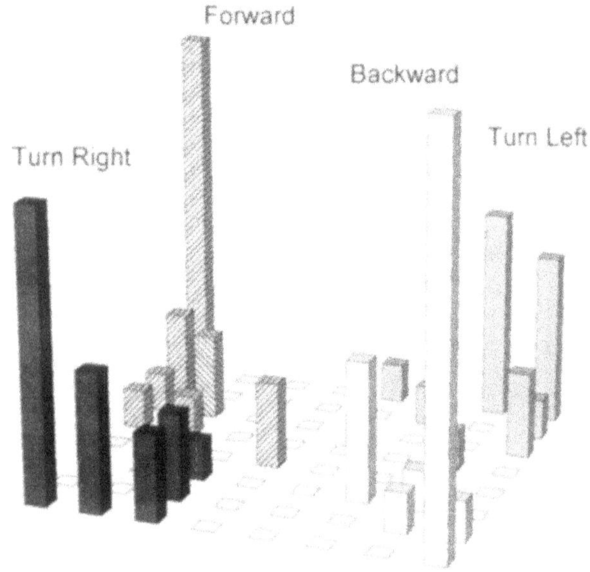

Fig. 13. The percentage of the training samples for the specific leg actions that have the highest activation for each unit on a 8 by 8 units network with a training time of 100 epochs.

training cluster. For the test data it was 100% for all the hand actions. For all head actions they achieved a performance of 100%. When considering the percentage of test data that fell into the regions identified by the training data, the percentages for the hand and head networks was 100%. Finally, as can be seen from Table 5 the leg actions 'backward' and 'turn left' achieved 100% for the training samples in the appropriate training clusters, the test samples on the test clusters and the test samples in the training clusters. Although 'turn right' and 'forward' did not achieve 100% on all three conditions,

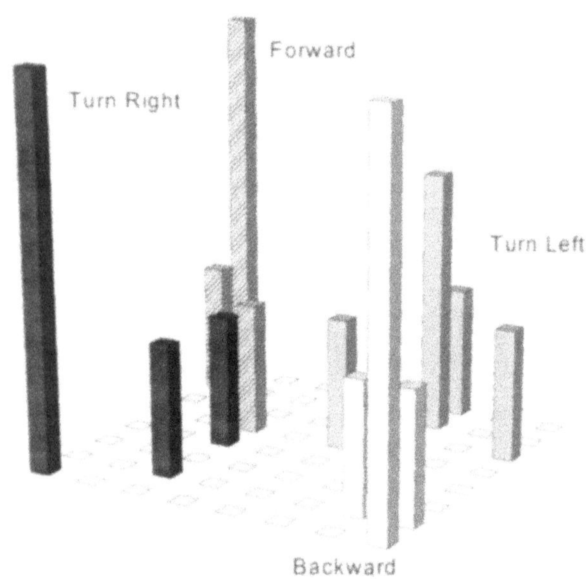

Fig. 14. The percentage of the test samples for the specific leg actions that have highest activation for each unit on a 8 by 8 units network with a training time of 100 epochs.

Table 3
Percentages for the hand training and test samples that were associated with the appropriate clusters for the 8 by 8 units network

Hand actions	Training samples on training clusters (%)	Test samples on test clusters (%)	Test samples on training clusters (%)
Put	93	100	100
Drop	100	100	100
Pick	100	100	100
Lift	100	100	100
Touch	100	100	100

Table 4
Percentages for the head training and test samples that were associated with the appropriate clusters for the 8 by 8 units network

Head actions	Training samples on training clusters (%)	Test samples on test clusters (%)	Test samples on training clusters (%)
Head down	100	100	100
Head left	100	100	100
Head right	100	100	100
Head right	100	100	100

Table 5
Percentages for the leg training and test samples that were associated with the appropriate clusters for the 8 by 8 units network

Leg actions	Training samples on training clusters (%)	Test samples on test clusters (%)	Test samples on training clusters (%)
Backward	100	100	100
Turn right	100	80	80
Turn left	100	100	100
Forward	87	100	80

the performance was still reasonably good. On the training samples on the training clusters 'forward' achieved 87% and 'turn right' 100%, for the test samples on the test clusters 'forward' achieved 100% and 'turn right' 80%, and for test samples on training clusters both actions achieved 80%.

Hence, the performance of the head, leg and hand self-organising networks are in principle suitable for use in a robot control system based on language instruction. This is because it is likely, based on the clear clustering demonstrated, that the sensor reading input will be accurately represented and mapped to the appropriate network region. As this location is the basis for the association between the action and the word this will contribute to the successful identification of the action and its description.

7. Conclusion

We described a model for a robot control system based on language instructions. This model considers that cell assemblies in different regions of the brain are used to process action verbs based on their association with appropriate body parts. By using self-organising networks for each of the three body parts considered it was possible in nearly all cases to cluster the individual actions and to identify them. We directly used sensor readings to represent low level semantic features. While we have not intended to implement a full mirror neuron system in this paper, this paper describes a self-organising approach that controls a robot using language instructions. This approach is based on distributed regional modularity and neurocognitive evidence on clustering action verbs. Such an approach uses sensor readings as the input to the robot and also as the basis for the robot's behaviour. In this sense, we have presented a self-organising language memory for an environmentally grounded robot.

Acknowledgements

This work is part of the MirrorBot project supported by the EU in the FET-IST programme under grant IST- 2001–35282. Thanks to Peter Watt for assistance with data collection and robot experiments.

References

Asoh, H., Huyamizu, S., Isao, H., Motomura, Y., Akaho, S., & Matsu, T (1997). Socially embedded learning of office-conversant robot jjjo-2. *Proceedings of the International Joint Conference on Artificial Intelligence Nagoa.*

Bear, M., Connors, B., & Paradiso, M. (1996). *Neuroscience: Exploring the Brain.*

Binder, J., Frost, J., Hammeke, T., Cox, R., Rao, S., & Prieto, T. (1997). Human brain language areas identified by functional magnetic resonance images. *The Journal of Neuroscience, 17*(1), 280–288.

Braitenberg, V. (1997). Searching for language mechanisms in the brain. *Cybernetics and Systems, 28,* 187–213.

Breazeal, C., & Scassellati, B (1999). A context-dependent attention system for a social robot. In: *Proceedings of the Sixteenth International Joint Conference on Artificial Intelligence (IJCAI99)* (pp. 1146–1151). Stockholm, Sweden.

Burgard, W., Cremers, A. B., Fox, D., Hähnel, D., Lakemeyer, G., Schulz, D., Steiner, W., & Thrun, S. (2000). Experiences with an interactive museum tour-guide robot. *Artificial Intelligence, 114,* 1–2.

Dogil, G., Ackermann, H., Grodd, W., Haider, H., Kamp, H., Mayer, J., Riecker, A., & Wildgruber, D. (2002). The speaking brain: a tutorial introduction to fMRI experiments in the production of speech, prosody and syntax. *Journal of Neurolinguistics, 15*(1), 59–90.

Dorffner, G., & Prem, E (1993). Connectionism, symbol grounding, and autonomous agents. In: *Proceedings of the Fifteenth Annual Conference of the Cognitive Science Society* (pp. 144–148). Boulder.

Elshaw, M., & Wermter, S (2002). A neurocognitive approach to self-organisation of verb actions. In: *Proceedings of the International Joint Conference on Neural Networks* (pp. 24–29). Honolulu, USA.

Feldman, J. A., Lakoff, G., Bailey, D. R., Narayanan, S., Regier, T., & Stolcke, A. (1996). L_0—The first five years of an automated language acquisition project. *AI Review,* 8.

Friedman, L., Kenny, J., Wise, A., Wu, D., Stuve, T., Miller, D., Jesberger, J., & Lewin, J. (1998). Brain activation during silent word generation evaluated with functional MRI. *Brain and Language, 64,* 943–959.

Gallese, V., & Goldman, A. (1998). Mirror neurons and the simulation theory of mind-reading. *Trends in Cognitive Science, 2*(12), 493–501.

Gazzaniga, M., Ivry, R., & Mangun, G. (1998). *Cognitive neuroscience: The biology of the mind.* New York: W.W. Norton and Company Ltd.

Harnad, S. (1990). The symbol grounding problem. *Physica D, 42,* 335–346.

Joliot, M., Papathanassiou, D., Mellet, E., Quinton, O., Mazoyer, N., Courtheoux, P., & Mazoyer, B. (1999). fMRI and PET of self-paced finger movement: Comparison of intersubject sterotaxic averaged data. *Neuroimage, 10,* 430–447.

Kohonen, T. (1997). *Self-organizing maps.* Germany: Springer.

Melcher, J. (2000). Human auditory function studied with fMRI. In: *Proceedings of the Workshop the Nature of Speech Perception.*

Pulvermüller, F. (1999). Words in the brain's language. *Behavioral and Brain Sciences, 22*(2), 253–336.

Pulvermüller, F. (2002). A brain perspective on language mechanisms: From discrete neuronal ensembles to serial order. *Progress in Neurobiology, 67,* 85–111.

Pulvermüller, F. (2003). *The neuroscience of language: On brain circuits of words and serial order.* Cambridge: Cambridge University Press.

Pulvermüller, F., Hare, M., & Hummel, F. (2000). Neurophysiological distinction of verb categories. *Cognitive Neuroscience, 11*(12), 2789–2793.

Purves, D. (1997). *Neuroscience.* Sunderland, MA: Sinauer.

Reggia, J., Shkuro, Y., & Shevtsova, N. (2001). Computational investigation of hemispheric specialization and interactions (pp. 68–82). In S. Wermter, J. Austin, & D. Willshaw (Eds.), *Emergent Neural Computational Architectures Based on Neuroscience.* Heidelberg: Springer.

Rizzolatti, G., & Arbib, M. (1998). Language within our grasp. *Trends in Neuroscience, 21*(5), 188–194.

Rizzolatti, G., Fogassi, L., & Gallese, V. (2001). Neurophysiological mechanisms underlying the understanding and imitation of action. *Nature Review, 2,* 661–670.

Steels, L. (1998). The origins of syntax in visually grounded robotic agents. *Artificial Intelligence, 103*(1-2), 133–156.

Taylor, J. (1999). Towards the networks of the brain: From brain imaging to consciousness. *Neural Networks, 12*(7-8), 943–959.

Thrun, S., Bennewitz, M., Burgard, W., Dellaert, F., Fox, D., Haehnel, D., Rosenberg, C., Roy, N., Schulte, J., & Schulz, D (1999). MINERVA: A second generation mobile tour-guide robot. In: *Proceedings of the IEEE International Conference on Robotics and Automation (ICRA'99).*

Wermter, S., Austin, J., Willshaw, D., & Elshaw, M. (2001). Towards novel neuroscience-inspired computing (pp. 1–9). In S. Wermter, J. Austin, & D. Willshaw (Eds.), *Emergent Neural Computational Architectures Based on Neuroscience.* Heidelberg: Springer.

AVAILABLE AT
www.ComputerScienceWeb.com
POWERED BY SCIENCE @ DIRECT

PERGAMON

Neural Networks 16 (2003) 701–710

Neural Networks

www.elsevier.com/locate/neunet

2003 Special issue

Autonomous mental development in high dimensional context and action spaces

Ameet Joshi[a,*], Juyang Weng[b]

[a]Department of Electrical and Computer Engineering, Michigan State University, East Lansing, MI 48824, USA
[b]Department of Computer Science and Engineering, Michigan State University, East Lansing, MI 48824, USA

Abstract

Autonomous Mental Development (AMD) of robots opened a new paradigm for developing machine intelligence, using neural network type of techniques and it fundamentally changed the way an intelligent machine is developed from manual to autonomous. The work presented here is a part of SAIL (Self-Organizing Autonomous Incremental Learner) project which deals with autonomous development of humanoid robot with vision, audition, manipulation and locomotion. The major issue addressed here is the challenge of high dimensional action space (5–10) in addition to the high dimensional context space (hundreds to thousands and beyond), typically required by an AMD machine. This is the first work that studies a high dimensional (numeric) action space in conjunction with a high dimensional perception (context state) space, under the AMD mode. Two new learning algorithms, Direct Update on Direction Cosines (DUDC) and High-Dimensional Conjugate Gradient Search (HCGS), are developed, implemented and tested. The convergence properties of both the algorithms and their targeted applications are discussed. Autonomous learning of speech production under reinforcement learning is studied as an example.

Keywords: Autonomous mental development; High dimensional; Robotic system

1. Introduction and problem identification

Autonomous Mental Development (AMD) (Weng et al., 2001) is a new paradigm for developing autonomous machine. The machine is controlled by a new kind of program called developmental program ever since its *birth*. Although develop-mental program is different from a traditional program in many ways, the most fundamental difference is that the programmer does not know the tasks that the robot ends up learning after birth. Therefore a developmental program must be able to generate internal representation *on the fly* for virtually any task. The capability of the machine is developed through real time interactions with the physical world. It depends on the five constraints: (1) sensor, (2) effector, (3) computational resource, (4) developmental program and (5) the way the robot is taught.

The other challenges of an AMD robot include

1. Environmental openness.
2. High-dimensional sensors.
3. Completeness in using sensory information.
4. Online processing.
5. Real-time speed.
6. Incremental processing.
7. Perform while learning.
8. Muddy tasks.

There have been studies in humanoid control that involve high dimensional action space e.g. (Vijayakumar & Schaal, 2000; Billard and Mataric, 2000). These studies include strictly action space, without using the perception space. In other words, the robot is able to learn only one action trajectory, but is not able to produce different action trajectories under different contexts. Further, the studies in Vijayakumar and Schaal (2000) and Billard and Mataric (2000) are based on supervised learning. The explosion of both perception and action spaces creates a very practical but unaddressed challenging research issue. Compounding the challenge is the issue of learning modes. For such a high dimensional action space, supervised learning is often not practical, especially for internal actions (actions that are produced by internal effectors that are not reachable externally by human teacher). For example, an external action performed by an arm can be taught in a supervised

* Corresponding author.
E-mail addresses: joshiame@egr.msu.edu (A. Joshi), weng@cse.msu.edu (J. Weng).

0893-6080/03/$ - see front matter © 2003 Elsevier Science Ltd. All rights reserved.
doi:10.1016/S0893-6080(03)00134-5

mode by holding the learner's arm. However, an internal action such as speech production and internal attention cannot be taught in a supervised learning mode. We have to use reinforcement learning. These compounding challenges raised a series of research issues. This paper mainly deals with AMD learning in high dimensional context and action spaces using generalized reinforcement learning mechanisms. Section 2 deals with the modified reinforcement learning model. Sections 3 and 4 explain the methods DUDC and HCGS in detail and Section 5 discusses the results obtained by applying the two methods on real-time robotic system.

2. Modified reinforcement learning

Traditional reinforcement learning deals with modifying a value system attached to the actions based on the rewards (Sutton, 1988; Sutton & Barto, 1998) and possesses a distinct boundary between the environment to be served and the agent (Kaelbling, Littman, & Moore, 1996). However, in the context of humanoid robot, this model is inadequate. The humanoid robot has a body consisting of locomotory organs like hands and feet, sensory organs like ears and eyes and a brain. In order for a robot to function properly, its brain should have precise knowledge of the relative positions of the organs and their limitations. This is achieved by getting internal sensory information from the organs about their states. Fig. 1 shows a picture of the modified reinforcement learning system used in this project. Complete state information is obtained by a combined set of external (environmental) and internal (somatic) sensory state information. The learning policy uses the context retrieved from memory to choose a new action. Traditionally, Q learning is used to

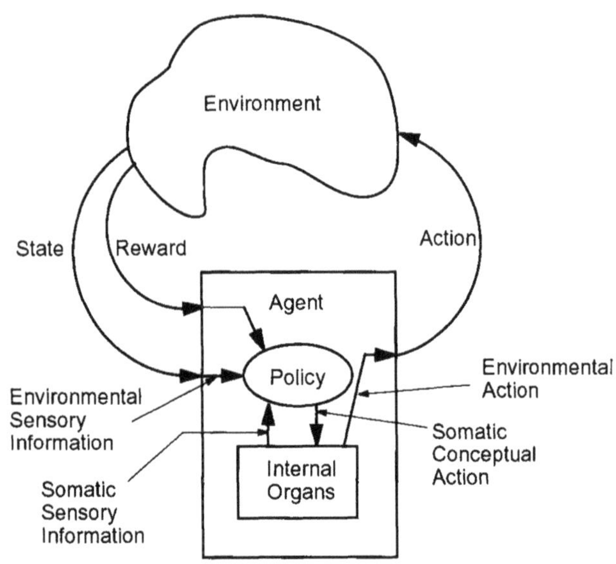

Fig. 1. The modified reinforcement learning model.

produce the desired actions from the current state information. However, due to inadequacy of this method in high dimensional state and action spaces, two new methods, DUDC and HCGS are developed.

3. Learning with direct update on direction cosines (DUDC)

The most important aspect of this method in regards with the standard Q learning is the removal of discrete actions. The action space is high dimensional and numeric. Each action is represented by a single set of direction cosines, $\Psi(i)$ and a step size parameter δ. The direction cosines form a unit vector that specify the direction and the magnitude of the distance traveled is given by the step size δ. The step size is reduced hierarchically based on rewards. The learning of the direction cosines starts afresh with every change in the step size δ. A set of direction cosines $\Psi(i)$ represents an attempt towards the optimal direction in the given search space and in the given hierarchy of step size δ. The objective of the reinforcement learning is to find the optimal set of direction cosines $\Psi(i)$. This explains the quantization imposed on the search space. The value update rules and the policy of action generation are now discussed.

3.1. The value update rule

The value update rule in DUDC is given below.

$$\Psi(i) = \Psi(i) + \alpha r(\Psi'(i) - \Psi(i)) \tag{1}$$

The value of 0.1 is normally used for α, which is known as learning rate. r is the reward obtained from the environment.

3.2. EMMP and action generation

EMMP stands for 'Exploration with Maturation using Multidimensional Perturbation'. Exploration means random change in the given direction. For exploration to be ideal, all the possible directions should be equally likely. The concept of maturation comes with a tradeoff between exploration and exploitation. The direction cosines $\Psi(i)$ are shaped with reinforcement learning. Direct use of direction cosines implies the exploitation. Exploration leads to finding the global optima and exploitation leads to a local optima. Exploration is slowly reduced as the system matures. The mathematical model that is developed with this concept is described below.

$$\kappa = \log\left(1 + \frac{\tau}{40}\right) \tag{2}$$

$$\Omega(i) = \epsilon + \Psi(i)\kappa \tag{3}$$

$$\xi = \left(\sum_{i=1}^{i=10} \Omega^2(i) \right)^{1/2} \quad (4)$$

$$\Psi'(i) = \frac{\Omega(i)}{\xi} \quad (5)$$

With respect to above equations, ϵ is a real valued random number between -1 and $+1$ such that it can take all the values in the range with equal probability. τ is the iteration number, which is incremented with each arrival of context. The number 40 is chosen from the empirical evaluation of various other values. The first step calculates κ, the quantitative measure for the maturity of the system from the number of iterations. The next three steps describe how the new set of direction cosines $\Psi(i)$ is obtained from the old one using the EMMP method. The weights, denoted as $\Omega(i)$, are the intermediate variables used before the normalization. ξ is the normalizing variable. This method uses a variation of the exploration and exploitation tradeoff, which is based on the principles of Boltzmann Exploration. The $\Psi(i)$ represent the original direction cosines and the $\Psi'(i)$ represent the new direction cosines obtained after doing the exploration.

The complete action is obtained by multiplying the direction cosines with the step size δ. The choice of the δ is crucial in the working of the method. For a fixed step size, there is limitation on the maximum proximity towards the target. Hence it is essential to have a hierarchical step size variation which will enable the coarse-to-fine search. With the change of step size the previously learned direction becomes useless, as can be seen from Fig. 2.

3.3. Robust learning

The EMMP method finds the near optimal direction towards the target under the constraint of the given step size. With each reduction in the step size δ, the search becomes finer and scope of the search also reduces. The reduction in δ is solely controlled by the rewards, the details of which are discussed in Section 3.4. In order to take into account the possible errors in the rewards, and make the algorithm converge in spite of erroneous rewards, the following rule is applied to change the step size.

Reversible step size change algorithm:

(1) Initialize δ.
(2) Initialize counter for bad rewards.
(3) Use EMMP for updating the $\Psi(i)$ also keep updating the bad reward counter.
(4) If the number of bad rewards exceed the threshold then increase δ and restart the EMMP.
(5) Stop.

The above algorithm makes sure that the EMMP is not stagnated at certain point in the search space due to the acquisition of a erroneous reward leading to unwanted reduction in δ. This makes the algorithm robust.

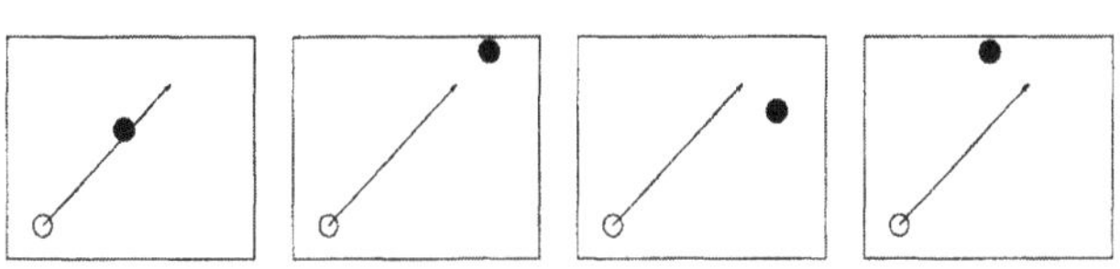

Fig. 2. The solid circle represents the target and the hollow circle is the starting point. The arrow denotes the direction of the previous action and its end denotes the new start position. The different variations of the positions of the new starting point and the target are shown. Although in each case the distance from the target is same, the direction towards the target is entirely different from the starting direction.

3.4. Considerations about rewards

The rewards can be relative or absolute. In former case, a Good reward means that the performance of the system is improved compared to the previous attempt, while in the latter case a *Good* reward means that the performance of the system is within certain predetermined bounds irrespective of the previous performance. In current framework, both types of rewards are expected by the system. The rewards are of three types, *Good reward*, *No reward* and *Bad reward*. The *Good* reward is considered as absolute, and the latter two rewards are considered as relative. A *Good* reward means that the search has reached sufficiently close to the target and the step size can be reduced. A *Bad* reward means that the performance is getting worse compared to previous performance, and the *No reward* means the performance is unchanged or that it has improved compared to the previous attempt, but still not within the predetermined bounds. This structure of rewards is constructed based on real time evaluation, where the rewards are obtained from the human teacher. The formal algorithm of the entire DUDC method is presented below.

DUDC algorithm:

(1) Initialize the start point.
(2) Initialize the direction cosines in all the dimensions. The values are normalized with the norm as unity.
(3) Initialize number of iterations, $n = 1$.
(4) Start iterations.
(5) Get the reward from the iteration.
(6) Use DUDC and EMMP to update $\Psi(i)$ and δ.
(7) Take the action.
(8) Increment the iteration number $n = n + 1$.
(9) Go to step 5. (No Stop.)

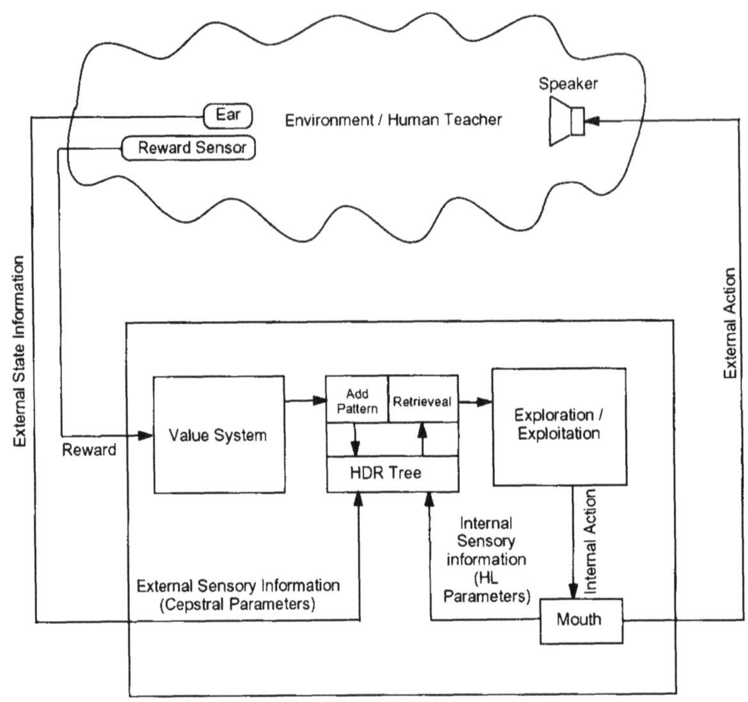

Fig. 3. The system architecture with DUDC.

The system architecture using DUDC is shown in Fig. 3.

4. Learning with high dimensional conjugate gradient search (HCGS)

In this approach, the continuous action space is quantized to form a discrete action space. A variation of vector quantization, called Amnesic Vector Quantization (AVQ) is used.

4.1. AVQ in action space

Using a suitable threshold, actions are quantized into micro-clusters. Each micro-cluster represents a single action and possesses a Q-value. Each context is limited to have a specific number of micro-clusters of actions. The mean value that represents a micro-cluster is updated using the method of Amnesic Average. The amnesic update rule is given in Eq. (6).

$$R^{(n+1)} = \frac{n-1-l(n)}{n}R^{(n)} + \frac{1+l(n)}{n}V \quad (6)$$

In traditional update, where $l(n)=0$ for all n, with accumulation of large number of actions the contribution of new action is reduced to infinitesimal. This is not desirable, and all the system properties need to change with time. The parameter $l(n)$ is an amnesic parameter and is defined as,

$$l(n) = \begin{cases} 0 & \text{if, } n \le n_1 \\ 2(n-n_1)/(n_2-n_1) & \text{if, } n_1 < n \le n_2 \\ 2+(n-n_2)/m & \textit{if, } n > n_2 \end{cases} \quad (7)$$

When the number of updates is less than n_1, the update is same as traditional average. However after that the amnesic parameter $l(n)$ is designed in such a way that more priority is given to the incoming action vector. After n_2 updates the weight of the incoming sample is changed again and it increase with a rate $1/m$. $R^{(n)}$ and $R^{(n+1)}$ denote the nth and $(n+1)$th updated vector, respectively, and V denotes the new action taken in $(n+1)$th iteration. As the system continues the learning process, the micro-clusters are developed and their Q values are updated. These micro-clusters are used to generate the interpolation function for Q value in the composite context of state and action space.

4.2. Interpolation using Q-values

In order to use the Conjugate Gradient (CG) Method (Shewchuk, 1994; Fletcher & Reeves, 1964) to decide the optimal action based on the Q values, it is essential to have an interpolation function representing the distribution of the Q values in the context-action space. CG method needs the interpolation function to be smooth and have a single well-defined local minimum. A new interpolation method with these properties is designed, denoted as 'Density Sensitive Kernel Interpolation' (DSKI). The equation for the interpolated function $G_n(x; x_1, x_2, \ldots, x_n)$ is given below

$$G_n(x; x_1, x_2, \ldots, x_n) = \sum_{i=1}^{n} w_i(x)y(i) \quad (8)$$

Here $x_i \in R^d$, $y_i \in R^k$ and $x_1, x_2, \ldots, x_n$ are n nearest neighbors of $x \in R^d$ from S. S is a set of micro-clusters in R^d representing the approximation of reciprocal of density in R^d. S can also be called as a set of finite number of neurons for each state. The definition of the weights w_i is based on the squared local sparseness σ^2, which is defined as,

$$\sigma^2 = \frac{k}{n}\sum_{i=1}^{n} \|x_i - x\|^2 \tag{9}$$

where, k is called as *kernel variance factor*. The more the value of k, the more is the kernel variance and more flat the interpolated function is. The expression for weights is,

$$w_i = C\exp\left(-\frac{\|x - x_i\|^2}{2\sigma^2}\right), \quad i = 1, 2, \dots n. \tag{10}$$

C is computed such that $\sum_{i=0}^{n} w_i = 1$. $y_i = f(x_i)$ is the function to be approximated. In this case, y_i denotes the Q-value of the action. The typical value of n is 3. The action list contains about 30 samples. The top-11 actions out of 30 existing action micro-clusters are chosen to interpolate the function. Due to inherent limitations of linear line minimization methods they cannot be used to give optimal performance in all the situations. To preserve the generality of the algorithm, line minimization part of the CG algorithm is removed. The initial guess for the step size is calculated based on the density of the samples at the starting point.

4.3. Value update using Q-learning

A queue of n recent states is maintained in memory, called a Prototype Updating Queue (PUQ). With each incoming reward, Q values of the states in PUQ are updated using Eq. (11).

$$Q(s, a) = (1 - \alpha)Q(s, a) + \alpha(\gamma V) \tag{11}$$

where V is the maximum Q value in the currently retrieved state for the first element of PUQ, while for the succeeding states it represents the updated Q value of the previous element in PUQ.

4.4. Boltzmann exploration

The subtle difference between the list of action micro-clusters and the traditional set of actions is that the traditional set encompasses all the possible actions, while the current set does not. The actions outside the list of action micro-clusters can also be taken and they can be even better than the ones in the list. Hence a separate random exploration is used along with the choice of exploitation using CG search. The random exploration uses the upper and lower bounds on the action space along with the inter-dependencies among dimensions of action space to generate a random action. These two choices are feeded to the Boltzmann exploration procedure with probabilities which are based on the status of the action list and maturation.

4.5. Reorganization of the action micro-clusters

During the initial phase of creation of the action micro-clusters, a default distance threshold is used. If the incoming sample has a distance more than the threshold distance from all the existing micro-clusters, a new cluster is created for it. When the list of action micro-clusters is full, the existing micro-clusters are updated with new samples. With each update, the center of the micro-cluster moves towards the new sample. The amnesic average makes sure that even after large number of updates the new samples still make noticeable impact on the micro-cluster in which it is being added.

It is observed that, with the exploitation superseding the exploration, some of the micro-clusters being closer to the target are updated more often than others. Also, due to this, most of the micro-clusters are under utilized. As an implication of this, the required uniform convergence is not observed. After the search reaches certain proximity level towards the target, the algorithm stagnates. In order to address this issue, the re-organization of the micro-clusters is performed after the context is repeated certain number of times.

Let there be n be the number of micro-clusters and $\rho(i)$ denote their centers. The number of updates on ith micro-cluster be $\phi(i)$. The weighted mean of the micro-clusters is given by,

$$\Lambda = \frac{\sum_{i=1}^{i=n} \rho(i)\phi(i)}{\sum_{i=1}^{i=n} \phi(i)} \tag{12}$$

All the micro-clusters are pulled towards it, based on the number of times each one is visited. The update rule for the micro-cluster center is given by,

$$\rho'(i) = \frac{\phi(i)\rho(i) + k\Lambda}{\phi(i) + k} \tag{13}$$

where $\rho'(i)$ is the updated value of initial micro-cluster center $\rho(i)$. The k is a parameter specifying the weight of the Λ and is decided empirically. This is followed by reduction in the search space. Initial search space is denoted by S such that $\rho(i) \subset S$, $i = 1, \dots n$. The new search space is given by S', such that, $\rho'(i) \subset S'$, $i = 1, \dots n$. Also, $S' \subseteq S$.

The reduction in search space ensures that the random exploration is restricted to explore the region which is more likely to contain the global optima. After the reorganization of micro-clusters, number of updates on each micro-cluster is initialized along with their Q-values, $\phi(i) = 0$ and $Q(i) = 0$. This starts the new search in the reduced space. This mechanism basically represents the hierarchical coarse to fine search.

In another approach the top-k clusters with highest Q values are selected and remaining clusters are removed. They are then filled with the new incoming samples.

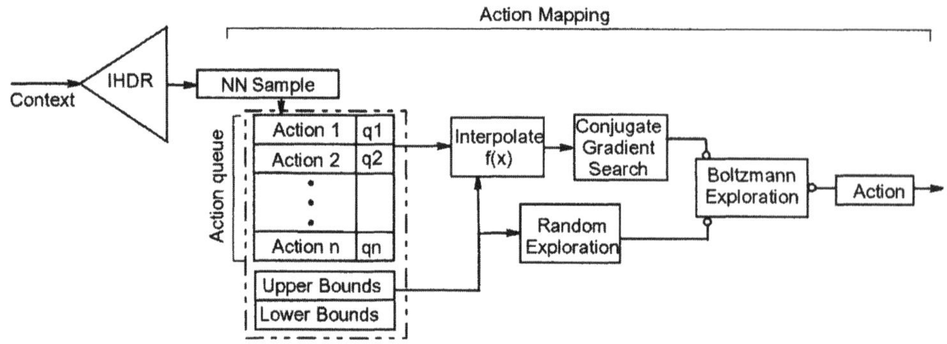

Fig. 4. The learning with HCGS.

The search boundaries are also reduced along with, in order to restrict the random exploration.

The partial block diagram to show the functioning of HCGS, is shown in Fig. 4. The flow chart of the system representing both the approaches is shown in Fig. 5 (Zhang & Weng, 2002). This work is part of the SAIL project, where an entire humanoid robotic system is being developed capable of having vision, and locomotion. The basic block diagram of the system as part of SAIL is shown in Fig. 6. In the entire block diagram of SAIL, the block of sensory mapping consists of all the sensory organs including the vision and locomotion. The details of the system can be found in Zhang and Weng (2001).

5. Results and discussion

We applied the above general mechanisms to a challenging high dimensional internal action learning example: *learning of speech production based on sensory*

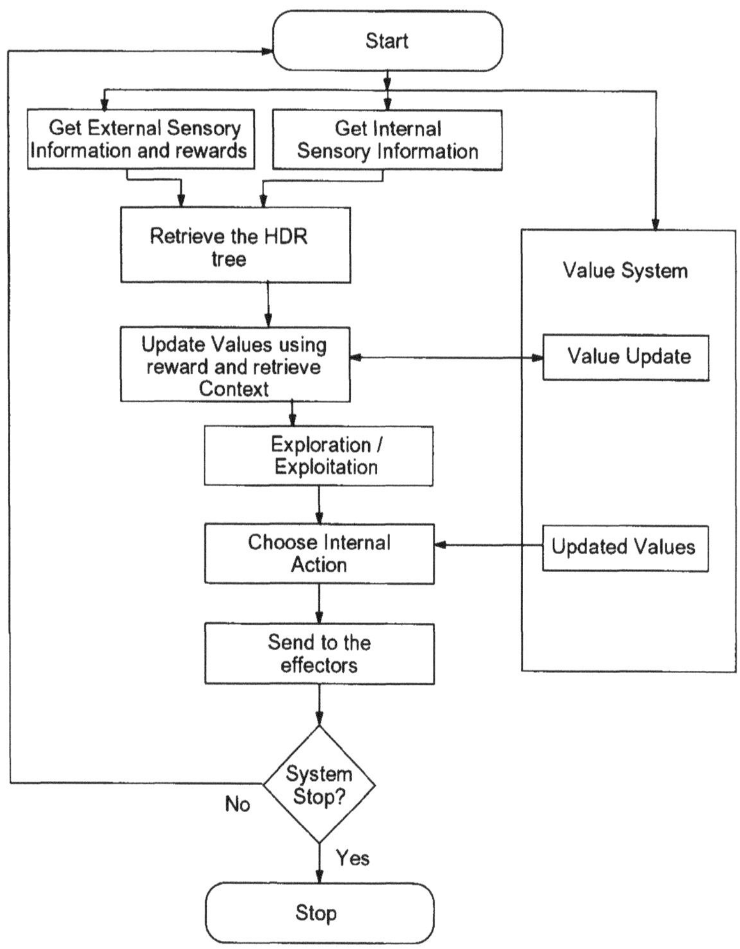

Fig. 5. The flowchart of the program.

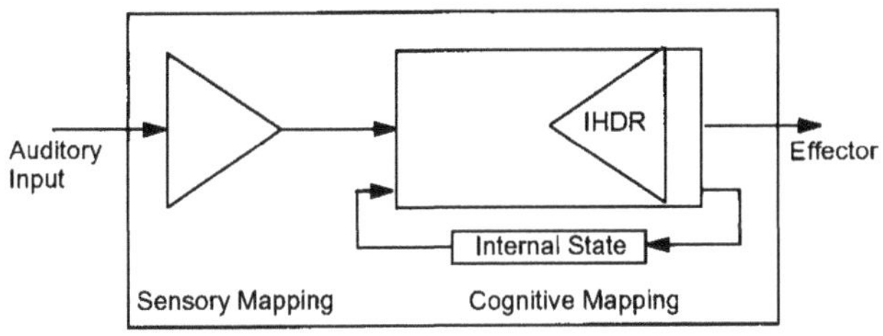

Fig. 6. The block diagram of the system as part of the entire SAIL architecture.

context. No task specific information is programmed into the AMD program. For example, if the teacher wants the robot to repeat what he has pronounced, all he can do is to teach him by giving rewards, as the *repeat* mechanism is not preprogrammed.

5.1. The system architecture

The system based on the architecture as given in Fig. 1, consists of three components, the ear, the mouth and the brain. The mouth is implemented with HL parameters obtained from the Klatt model (Perkell and Klatt, 1986; Stevens and Bickley, 1990; Allen, Hunnicut, & Klatt, 1987; Inc. 1997). For the implementation of the ear, cepstral parameters are used. The raw raw speech (O'Shaughnessy, 1987) is converted into cepstral parameters which are then used by the brain. The temporal behavior of these components is explained in the Fig. 7. The system works with time increment of one second. This restriction arose from the considerations of the parallel operation of the system on a single processor PC and use of multimedia sound card. It should be noted that this restriction does not hamper the basic principle of parallel architecture, as with dedicated components the same algorithm can be extended to arbitrarily small time interval, matching human behavior.

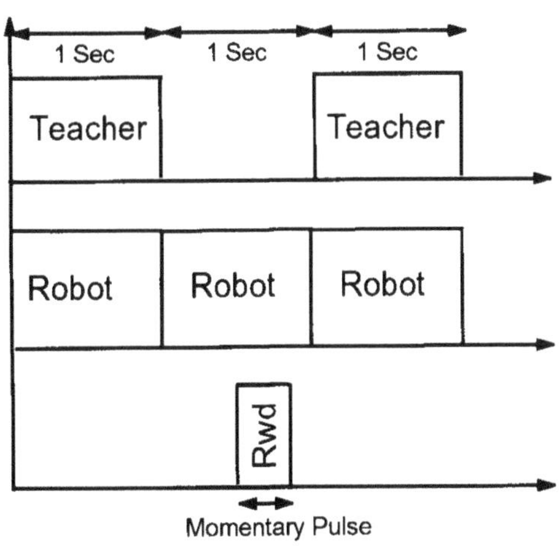

Fig. 7. The temporal behavior of the system.

5.2. Context based learning

The objective here is to respond the voice commands by the teacher. When teacher tells the system to speak certain vowel the system responds to it. The teacher trains the system by providing rewards. For example, the system can be trained to imitate /a/ after the teacher and also it can be trained to speak /e/ when teacher speaks /o/. This generalization makes the learning task independent and is entirely in the hands of the teacher. The rewards shape the system towards desired behavior. The learning is non-supervised (the internal parameters are never controlled by the teacher, no labels are provided), as ideal human learning should be. The details of the context parameters and their acquisition is explained in Section 5.3.

5.3. Obtaining context and normalization

The parameters taken from the ear are cepstral parameters. A set of cepstral parameters correspond to the sound acquired in a time window of 20 ms which is accurate within the bounds (O'Shaughnessy, 1987). The ear continuously keeps converting the incoming raw speech into the cepstral parameters and maintains a queue. The brain has access to this queue for further processing. Out of the ten HL parameters directly obtained from the mouth as internal (somatic) sensory information five parameters are formant frequencies. Formant frequencies possess a considerable overlap among different vowels as can be seen from Fig. 8. To ensure that the desired importance is given to each set of parameters in deciding the context, both the sensory parameters are normalized using their variance obtained from a sample data set.

5.4. Storing and retrieval of the context information

Another important aspect in the working of brain is the storage and retrieval of the sensory information. Brain memory is associative and takes a shape of a statistically generated tree structure, where all the information is stored according to the statistical similarity. The data structure used in this project to model memory is called IHDR (Incremental Hierarchical Discriminant Regression) (Hwang & Weng, 2000; Weng & Hwang, 2000).

5.5. Testing with DUDC

Testing with DUDC is performed in two stages. In the first stage the search algorithm is tested on a variable dimensional synthetic data. Dimensions varying as 2, 5 and 10. Different locations of the target point relative to the starting point are chosen and the results are tabulated in the Table 1. Each experiment is conducted for 100 iterations. The table shows the average values of iterations required for convergence, for each dimensional data. The convergence is defined as the reduction in the distance to the target by factor

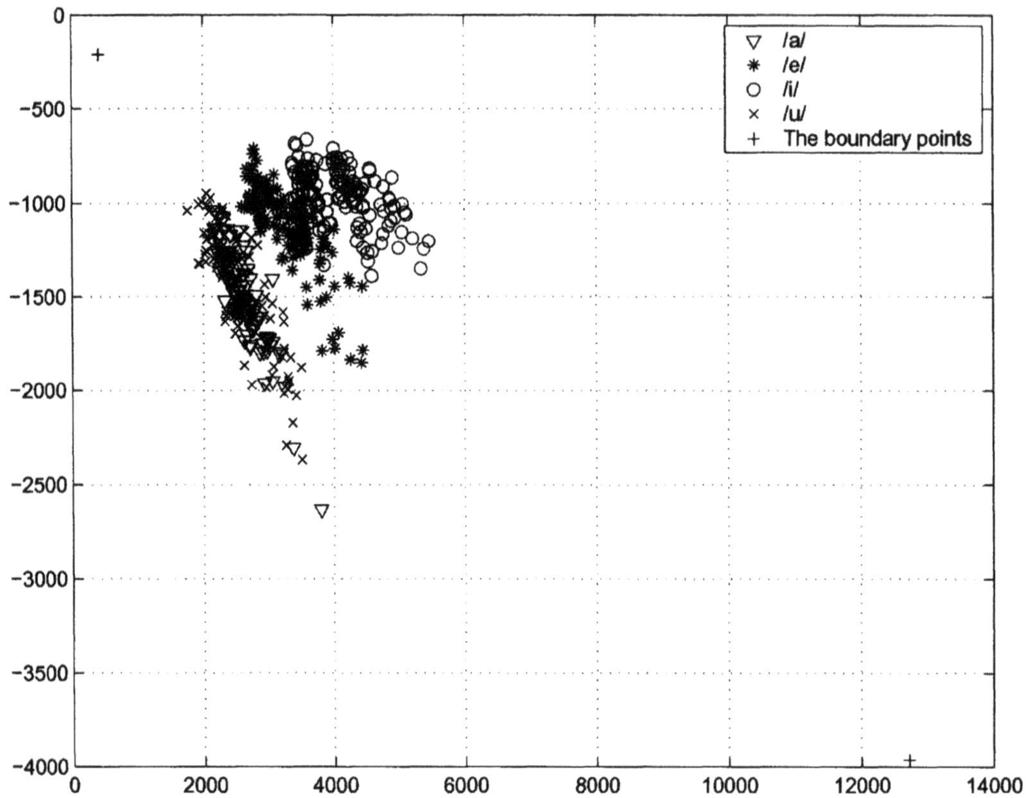

Fig. 8. This figure shows the distribution of the four vowels in the reduced dimensions (using PCA). The point in the left top corner represents one end of the search space and the point in the right bottom corner represents the other end.

of 20 from the starting distance, or 5% proximity compared with the starting point. As expected there is a monotonic rise in the number of steps needed for the convergence with the increase in the dimensionality.

After the first stage of testing with simulated data, the system is tested with a *Synthetic Teacher* (ST). ST is a computer program executing in conjunction with the main system and has access to the internal parameters to generate the rewards. ST is designed to replace the *Human teacher* (HT) for the purpose of automating the process of learning. The rewards given by ST are computed from the euclidian distance to the target and are always accurate. The convergence behavior of the system with ST is shown in Fig. 9. However, it should be noted that, although the ST has access to internal parameters of the system, the internal parameters are not directly altered by it and hence the this framework still satisfies the conditions of the non-supervised learning.

5.6. Testing with HCGS

The testing framework is similar to the one used in DUDC with the use of ST. The number of micro-clusters *nm* in the action list is a crucial parameter in the performance of HCGS. The number of micro-clusters is varied from 10 to 100 and the convergence plots for $nm = 30$ and $nm = 100$ are shown in Fig. 10. The convergence with $nm = 30$ is better compared to $nm = 100$. In either case, the system starts converging and after certain point the convergence gets stagnated. The reason behind this can be explained with following reasoning. Initially as the micro-clusters are formed by random exploration, some of the clusters are

Table 1
The table displaying the average learning rate with variable dimensions and variable error rates in rewards

Dim	Error rate	Target point location	Average no of steps
2	0%	Center	29.91
		Boundary	3.44
		Random	54.48
	25%	Center	35.24
		Boundary	3.84
		Random	44.32
5	0%	Center	257.37
		Boundary	55.66
		Random	319.18
	25%	Center	303.49
		Boundary	50.12
		Random	856.04
10	0%	Center	1248.22
		Boundary	445.27
		Random	1089.82
	25%	Center	1844.08
		Boundary	717.64
		Random	2279.45

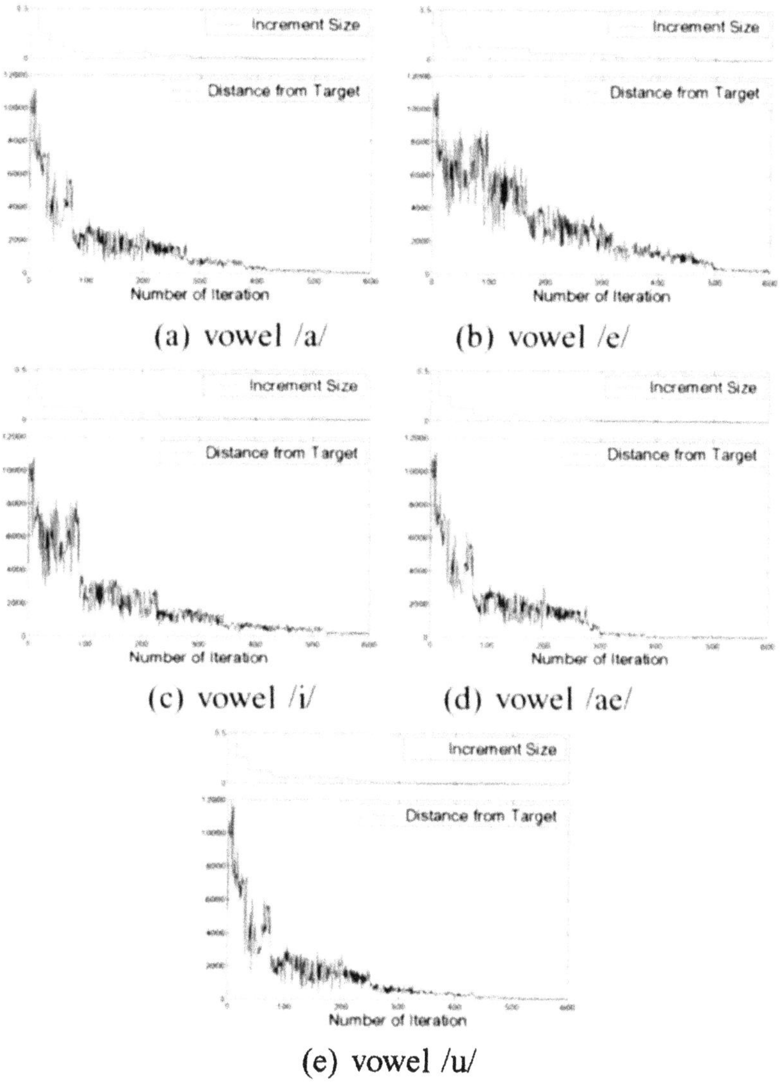

Fig. 9. The convergence plots generated during the learning of different vowels during 600 iterations using ST. The context used in this testing was the direct internal sensory information in the form of HL parameter.

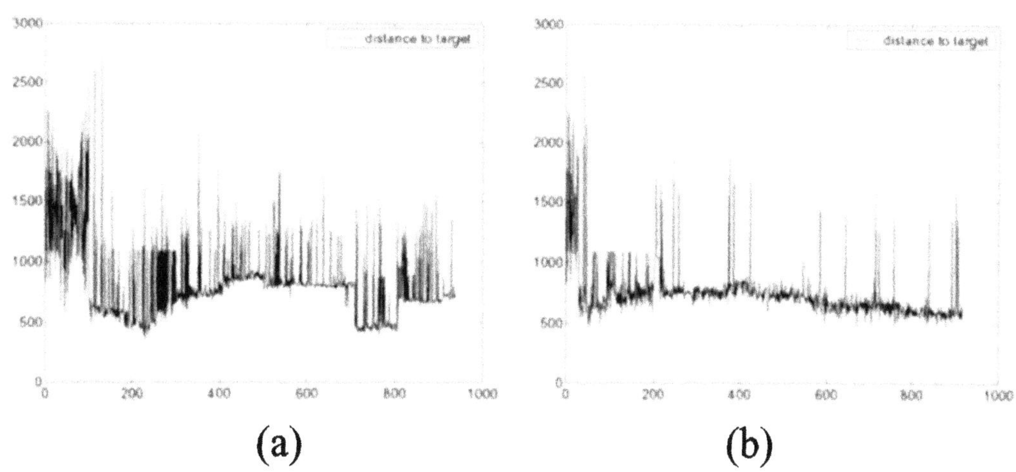

Fig. 10. (a) Shows the convergence with number of micro-clusters as 100 and (b) shows the convergence with number of micro-clusters as 30.

close to the target. With the progress of learning and the movement of micro-clusters, the micro-clusters that are close to the target, are chosen more often and the other clusters remain under-utilized.

Comparing the above results, the DUDC method appears to be superior to the HCGS in computational complexity and rate of convergence. However, it is left as future work to explore the reorganization of the micro-clusters for performance improvement in HCGS. Although current work is targeted towards learning a single action, the generation of smoother transitions from one action to another can be easily obtained using the combination of action and perception space.

6. Conclusions

The methods developed in this project appear promising towards tackling the problem of autonomously developing a robotic system capable of learning to produce high dimensional (e.g. 10D), action interactively and autonomously. The techniques designed and implemented in this work seem capable of realizing the initial development of basic, early behaviors in a high dimensional space through the AMD mode.

In the later stages of the speech learning development the system shows goal-directed behaviors, which facilitates faster learning. It is marked by a representation of the goal from the early learning experience, using the goals to activate actions, changing direction explicitly (e.g. understanding the goal by biting down on one's tongue and giving it a few tries).

The current work is, however, new and very important in bootstrapping higher level goal directed learning in the later development stage.

References

Allen, J., Hunnicut, S., & Klatt, D. (1987). *From text to speech: The MITalk system*. Cambridge: Cambridge University Press.

Billard, A., Mataric, M (2000). *Learning human arm movements by imitation: Evaluation of a biologically-inspired connectionist architecture*. Cambridge, MA, September 7–8.

Fletcher, R., & Reeves, C. (1964). Function minimization by conjugate gradients. *Computational Journal*, *7*, 149–154.

Hwang, W., & Weng, J. (2000). Hierachical discriminant regression. *IEEE Transactions on Pattern Analysis and Machine Intelligence*, *22*(11), 1277–1293.

Kaelbling, L., Littman, M., & Moore, A. (1996). Reinforcement learning: A survey. *Journal of Artificial Intelligence Research*, *4*, 237–285.

O'Shaughnessy, D. (1987). *Speech communication*. New York: Addison-Wesley.

Perkell, J., & Klatt, D. (1986). *Invariance and variability in speech processes*. Hillsade, NJ: Lawrence Erlbaum Associates.

Sensimetrics Inc (1997). *High level parameter speech synthesis system*. Technical Report, Somerville, MA: Sensimetrics Corporation.

Shewchuk J (1994). *An introduction to the conjugate gradient method without agonizing pain*. Technical Report, Carnegie Mellon University.

Stevens, K., & Bickley, C. (1990). Constraints among parameter simplify control of klatt formant synthesizer. *Phonetics*, *1*.

Sutton, R. (1988). Learning to predict by the methods of temporal differences. *Machine Learning*, *3*, 9–44.

Sutton, R., & Barto, A. (1998). *Reinforcement learning, an introduction*. Cambridge, MA: MIT Press.

Vijayakumar, S., Schaal, S (2000). *Real time learning in humanoids: a challenge for scalability of online algorithms*. Cambridge, MA, September 7–8.

Weng, J., & Hwang, W. (2000). An incremental learning algorithm with automatically derived discriminating features. *Proceedings of the Fourth Asian Conference on Computer Vision*, *22*(11).

Weng, J., McClelland, J., Pentland, A., Sporns, O., Stockman, I., Sur, M., & Thelen, E. (2001). Autonomous mental development by robots and animals. *Science, January*.

Zhang, Y., & Weng, J. (2001). Grounded auditory development by a developmental robot. *Proceedings of International Joint Conference of Neural Networks*, 1059–1064.

Zhang, Y., & Weng, J. (2002). Action chaining by a developmental robot with a value system. *Proceedings of International Conference on Development and Learning*.

AVAILABLE AT
www.ComputerScienceWeb.com
POWERED BY SCIENCE DIRECT

PERGAMON

Neural Networks 16 (2003) 711–717

Neural Networks

www.elsevier.com/locate/neunet

2003 Special issue

Chaos control and synchronization, with input saturation, via recurrent neural networks

Edgar N. Sanchez*, Luis J. Ricalde

CINVESTAV, Unidad Guadalajara, Apartado Postal 31-438, Plaza La Luna, Guadalajara, Jalisco C.P. 45091, Mexico

Abstract

This paper deals with the adaptive tracking problem of non-linear systems in presence of unknown parameters, unmodelled dynamics and input saturation. A high order recurrent neural network is used in order to identify the unknown system and a learning law is obtained using the Lyapunov methodology. Then a stabilizing control law for the reference tracking error dynamics is developed using the Lyapunov methodology and the Sontag control law. Tracking error boundedness is established as a function of a design parameter. The new approach is illustrated by examples of complex dynamical systems: chaos control and synchronization.

Keywords: Recurrent neural networks; Trajectory tracking; Adaptive control; Input saturation; Lyapunov function; Stability

1. Introduction

Chaotic behaviour, as a characteristic of a dynamical system, could be desirable or undesirable, depending on the current application; for substance mixing process, a chaotic behaviour might improve the efficiency of the system while for process which involves vibrations, chaos could produce critical structural failures. As a consequence, it is important to be able to manipulate the chaotic nature of the systems, driving stable systems to chaos or whenever it is desirable, stabilizing a chaotic system. It is also important to change the chaotic nature of a system without losing the chaotic behaviour. Controlling this kind of complex dynamical systems has recently attracted a great deal of attention within the engineering society. Different techniques have been proposed to achieve chaos control. For instance, linear state space feedback (Chen & Dong, 1993), Lyapunov function methods (Nijmeijer & Berghuis, 1995), adaptive control (Zeng & Singh, 1997) and bang–bang control (Vincent & Yu, 1991), among many others (Chen & Dong, 1998).

On the other hand, since the seminal paper by Narendra and Parthasarathy (1990), there has been continuously increasing interest in applying neural networks to identification and control of non-linear systems. Lately, the use of recurrent neural networks is being developed, which allows more efficient modelling of the underlying dynamical systems (Poznyak, Yu, Sanchez, & Perez, 1999). Two recent books (Rovitahkis & Christodoulou, 2000; Suykens, Vandewalle, & De Moor, 1996) have reviewed the application of dynamic neural networks for non-linear system identification and control. In Suykens et al. (1996), in particular, off-line learning is used, while Rovitahkis and Christodoulou (2000) analyses adaptive identification and control by means of on-line learning, where stability of the closed-loop system is established based on the Lyapunov function method. In Rovitahkis and Christodoulou (2000), the trajectory tracking problem is reduced to a linear model following problem, with an application to DC electric motors.

The problem of designing robust controllers for non-linear systems with uncertainties which guarantee stability and trajectory tracking has received an increasing attention in the last years. The presence of input saturation limits the ability of freely modifying the dynamics of the system to compensate the effects of the unmodelled dynamics by high gain feedback (El-Farra & Christofides, 2001). This effect is reflected on the loss of stability, undesired oscillations and saturation.

In this paper we extend our previous work (Sanchez, Perez, & Ricalde, 2002) for the trajectory tracking problem to the case where input saturation and uncertainties are present in the non-linear system. The proposed adaptive control scheme is composed of a recurrent neural identifier

* Corresponding author.
E-mail addresses: sanchez@gdl.cinvestav.mx (E.N. Sanchez), lricalde@gdl.cinvestav.mx (L.J. Ricalde).

0893-6080/03/$ - see front matter © 2003 Elsevier Science Ltd. All rights reserved.
doi:10.1016/S0893-6080(03)00122-9

and a controller, where the former is used to build an on-line model for the unknown plant and the latter, to force the unknown plant to track the reference trajectory. An update law for the high order recurrent neural network is proposed via the Lyapunov methodology. A robust learning law to avoid parameter drift in presence of modelling error is also proposed. The control law is developed using the Lyapunov methodology and the Sontag control law (Lin & Sontag, 1991) for stabilizing systems with input saturation and uncertain terms. This control law explicitly depend on the input saturations. Boundedness of the tracking error is proved and an estimation of the closed-loop stability region is given in order to determine the available bounds of the uncertainties and the desired tracking error. The new approach is illustrated by examples of complex dynamical systems: chaos control and synchronization.

2. Mathematical preliminaries

The recurrent neural network to be used is first introduced.

2.1. Recurrent higher-order neural networks

In Kosmatopoulos et al. (1997), recurrent higher-order neural networks (RHONN) are defined as

$$\dot{x}_i = -a_i x_i + \sum_{k=1}^{L} w_{ik} \prod_{j \in I_k} y_j^{d_j(k)}, \quad i = 1, \ldots, n \tag{1}$$

where x_i is the ith neuron state, L is the number of higher-order connections, $\{I_1, I_2, \ldots, I_L\}$ is a collection of non-ordered subsets of $\{1, 2, \ldots, m+n\}$, $a_i > 0$, w_{ik} are the adjustable weights of the neural network, $d_j(k)$ are non-negative integers, and y is a vector defined by

$$y = [y_1, \ldots, y_n, y_{n+1}, \ldots, y_{n+m}]^{\mathrm{T}}$$
$$= [S(x_1), \ldots, S(x_n), S(u_1), \ldots, S(u_m)]^{\mathrm{T}},$$

with $u = [u_1, u_2, \ldots, u_m]^{\mathrm{T}}$ being the input to the neural network, and $S(\cdot)$ a smooth sigmoid function formulated by $S(x) = (1/1 + \exp(-\beta x)) + \varepsilon$. For the sigmoid function, β is a positive constant and ε is a small positive real number. Hence, $S(x) \in [\varepsilon, \varepsilon + 1]$.

As can be seen, Eq. (1) allows the inclusion of higher-order terms. By defining a vector

$$z(x,u) = [z_1(x,u), \ldots, z_L(x,u)]^{\mathrm{T}} = \left[\prod_{j \in I_1} y_j^{d_j(1)}, \ldots, \prod_{j \in I_L} y_j^{d_j(L)} \right]^{\mathrm{T}},$$

Eq. (1) can be rewritten as

$$\dot{x}_i = -a_i x_i + \sum_{k=1}^{L} w_{ik} z_k(x,u), \quad i = 1, \ldots, n$$

or

$$\dot{x}_i = -a_i x_i + w_i^{\mathrm{T}} z_i(x,u), \quad i = 1, \ldots, n \tag{2}$$

where $w_i = [w_{i,1}, \ldots, w_{i,L}]^{\mathrm{T}}$.

In this paper, terms as

$$y = [y_1, \ldots, y_n, y_{n+1}, \ldots, y_{n+m}]^{\mathrm{T}} = [S(x_1), \ldots, S(x_n), u_1, \ldots, u_n]^{\mathrm{T}}$$

are considered. This means that the same number of inputs and states is used. It is also assumed that the input to the neural network enters directly, so Eq. (1) can be rewritten as

$$\dot{x}_i = -a_i x_i + w_i^{\mathrm{T}} z_i(x) + u_i, \quad i = 1, \ldots, n \tag{3}$$

Reformulating Eq. (2) as matrices yields

$$\dot{x} = Ax + Wz(x) + u \tag{4}$$

where $x \in \Re^n$, $W^* \in \Re^{n \times L}$, $z(x) \in \Re^L$, $u \in \Re^n$, and $A = -\lambda I$, $\lambda > 0$.

3. Plant identification

Consider the unknown non-linear plant

$$\dot{x}_p = F_p(x_p, u) \triangleq f_p(x_p) + \mathrm{sat}(u) \tag{5}$$

where $x_p, f_p \in \Re^n$, $g_p \in \Re^{n \times n}$, $u \in \Re^n$ and

$$\mathrm{sat}(u) = \begin{cases} u_{\max} & \text{if } u > u_{\max} \\ u & \text{if } u_{\min} \le u \le u_{\max} \\ u_{\min} & \text{if } u < u_{\min} \end{cases}$$

Taking into account that f_p is unknown, one can modelize Eq. (5) by a recurrent neural network as in Eq. (4). Hence, we will consider the plant model as

$$\dot{x} = Ax + Wz(x_p) + w_{\mathrm{per}} + \mathrm{sat}(u) \tag{6}$$

where the term w_{per} represents the modelling error, and W are the values of the network weights, which minimize the modelling error.

In order to derive an adaptation law which minimize the identification error, we consider the case of no modelling error. We assume that there exist unknown but constant weights W^* such that the plant is completely described by the neural network of the form

$$\dot{x}_p = Ax_p + W^* z(x_p) + \mathrm{sat}(u) \tag{7}$$

where all the elements are as described earlier.

Now, we proceed to analyse the error between the identifier and the real system

$$e_i = x - x_p \tag{8}$$

whose dynamics is given by

$$\dot{e}_i = \dot{x} - \dot{x}_p \qquad \dot{e}_i = Ae_i + \tilde{W}z(x_p) \tag{9}$$

where

$$\tilde{W} = W - W^* \tag{10}$$

In order to perform the stability analysis of Eq. (9), we consider the Lyapunov function candidate

$$V = \frac{1}{2}\|e_i\|^2 + \frac{1}{2\gamma}\mathrm{tr}\{\tilde{W}^{\mathrm{T}}\tilde{W}\}, \quad \gamma > 0 \tag{11}$$

Differentiating along the solutions of Eq. (9), we obtain

$$\dot{V} = -\lambda\|e_i\|^2 + e_i^{\mathrm{T}}\tilde{W}z(x_p) + \frac{1}{\gamma}\mathrm{tr}\{\dot{\tilde{W}}^{\mathrm{T}}\tilde{W}\} \tag{12}$$

The asymptotic stability of the identification error is achieved if we select the weight adaptation law as in Rovitahkis and Christodoulou (2000)

$$\mathrm{tr}\{\dot{\tilde{W}}^{\mathrm{T}}\tilde{W}\} = -\gamma e^{\mathrm{T}}\tilde{W}z(x_p) \tag{13}$$

which can be written element by element as

$$\dot{\hat{w}}_{i,j} = -\gamma e_i z(x_{p_j}), \qquad i = 1,2,\ldots,n, \; j = 1,2,\ldots,L.$$

Substituting the adaptation law in Eq. (12) gives

$$\dot{V} = -\lambda\|e_i\|^2 \le 0$$

then, $\lim_{t\to\infty} e_i(t) = 0$, $\lim_{t\to\infty} \dot{\tilde{W}}(t) = 0$.

However, the assumption of no modelling error is not always satisfied. Hence, the adjusted weight parameters could drift to infinity. In order to avoid the parameter drift the following robust learning law for the neural network weights is proposed (Rovitahkis & Christodoulou, 2000):

$$\dot{\hat{W}} = \begin{cases} -\gamma e_i z(x_{p_j}) & \text{if } |w_i| < w_m \\ -\gamma e_i z(x_{p_j}) - \sigma\gamma w_i & \text{if } |w_i| \ge w_m \end{cases} \tag{14}$$

where σ is a positive constant and w_m is the upper bound for the neural network weights. It can be shown that the robust learning law does not affect the stability of the identification error but improves it, making the Lyapunov function time derivative more negative (Rovitahkis & Christodoulou, 2000).

Once that the identification error is minimized, we consider the trajectory tracking problem for the neural network (and the unknown system) with input saturation, including the modelling error.

4. Trajectory tracking analysis

Consider a non-linear system with input constraints

$$\dot{x}_p = f_p(x_p) + \mathrm{sat}(u) \tag{15}$$

which we modelize by a neural network identifier described in Section 3 and considering the modelling error term as

$$\dot{x} = Ax + Wz(x_p) + w_{\mathrm{per}} + \mathrm{sat}(u) \tag{16}$$

where we assume that the modelling error is bounded.

We will design a robust controller that satisfy

$$|u| \le u_{\max}$$

and enforce asymptotic stability of the tracking error between the plant and the reference signal

$$\dot{x}_r = f_r(x_r, u_r), \quad x_r \in \Re^n \tag{17}$$

namely,

$$e_t := x_p - x_r \tag{18}$$

The time derivative of the tracking error is

$$\dot{e}_t = \dot{x}_p - \dot{x}_r = Ax + Wz(x_p) + w_{\mathrm{per}} + u - f_r(x_r, u_r) \tag{19}$$

this dynamics can be rewritten as

$$\begin{aligned} \dot{e}_t &= Ae_t + Wz(x_p) + (\alpha_r(x_r) + w_{\mathrm{per}}) + u \\ \alpha_r(x_r) &= A(x + x_r - x_p) - f_r(x_r, u_r) \end{aligned} \tag{20}$$

The tracking problem can be analysed as a stabilization problem for the error dynamics (Eq. (20)). To solve this problem, we apply the Lyapunov synthesis method.

4.1. Tracking error stabilization

Once Eq. (20) is obtained, we proceed to study its stabilization. Note that $e_t = 0$, $\tilde{W} = 0$, is an equilibrium point for the system without disturbances.

In order to perform the stability analysis for the system, considering identification and tracking, the following Lyapunov function is formulated:

$$V = \frac{1}{2}\|e_i\|^2 + \frac{1}{2}\|e_t\|^2 + \frac{1}{2\gamma}\mathrm{tr}\{\tilde{W}^{\mathrm{T}}\tilde{W}\} \tag{21}$$

Its time derivative, along the trajectories of Eq. (20) is

$$\begin{aligned} \dot{V} = {} & -\lambda\|e_i\|^2 + e_i^{\mathrm{T}}\tilde{W}z(x_p) + \frac{1}{\gamma}\mathrm{tr}\{\dot{\tilde{W}}^{\mathrm{T}}\tilde{W}\} - \lambda\|e_t\|^2 \\ & + e_i^{\mathrm{T}}Wz(x_p) + e_t^{\mathrm{T}}(\alpha_r(x_r) + w_{\mathrm{per}}) + e_t^{\mathrm{T}}u \end{aligned} \tag{22}$$

Replacing the learning law (Eq. (13) in Eq. (22)) we obtain

$$\begin{aligned} \dot{V} = {} & -\lambda\|e_i\|^2 - \lambda\|e_t\|^2 + e_t^{\mathrm{T}}Wz(x_p) + e_t^{\mathrm{T}}(\alpha_r(x_r) + w_{\mathrm{per}}) \\ & + e_t^{\mathrm{T}}u \\ \triangleq {} & -\lambda(\|e_i\|^2 + \|e_t\|^2) + L_{f_t}^*V + (L_wV)w_{\mathrm{per}} + (L_gV)u \end{aligned} \tag{23}$$

$$L_{f_t}V = e_t^{\mathrm{T}}Wz(x_p) + e_t^{\mathrm{T}}\alpha_r(x_r) \qquad L_wV = e_t^{\mathrm{T}}, \; L_gV = e_t^{\mathrm{T}}$$

Furthermore, similar to El-Farra and Christofides (2001), we assume that the uncertain term $(L_wV)w_{\mathrm{per}}$ is bounded by above as

$$(L_wV)w_{\mathrm{per}} \le |e_t|w_b$$

In order to stabilize the tracking error, let us consider the following modification of the Sontag control law (El-Farra

& Christofides, 2001),

$$u = -\frac{1}{2}R^{-1}(e, \tilde{W})L_gV$$
$$= -\frac{\left(L_fV + (\chi w_b)\left(\frac{|e|^2}{|e|+\phi}\right)\right)}{(L_gV)^2[1+\sqrt{1+(u_{\max}L_gV)^2}]}L_gV$$
$$-\frac{\sqrt{(L_fV + \chi w_b|e|)^2 + (u_{\max}L_gV)^4}}{(L_gV)^2[1+\sqrt{1+(u_{\max}L_gV)^2}]}L_gV \quad (24)$$

where χ, ϕ are adjustable parameters. To simplify the expressions, we name the tracking error as e.

Replacing the control law (Eq. (24) in Eq. (23)) and taking into account the bound for $(L_wV)w_{\text{per}}$, we obtain

$$\dot{V} \le -\lambda(\|e_i\|^2 + \|e\|^2)$$
$$+\frac{(L_fV + w_b|e|)\sqrt{1+(u_{\max}L_gV)^2}}{[1+\sqrt{1+(u_{\max}L_gV)^2}]}$$
$$+\frac{w_b(\phi-(\chi-1)|e|)\left(\frac{|e|^2}{|e|+\phi}\right)}{[1+\sqrt{1+(u_{\max}L_gV)^2}]}$$
$$-\frac{\sqrt{(L_fV + \chi w_b|e|^2 + (u_{\max}L_gV)^4}}{[1+\sqrt{1+(u_{\max}L_gV)^2}]} \quad (25)$$

It is easy to verify that when $|e| > \phi/\chi - 1$, the third term is strictly negative; hence, we proceed to study the case when $|e| \le \phi/\chi - 1$. First, we consider that the modelling error is a disturbance which satisfies a growth bound of the form

$$|L_wV|w_{\text{per}} \le |e|w_b$$

Then, we can obtain the following bound

$$\frac{w_b|L_wV||e|(\phi-(\chi-1)|e|)}{(|e|+\phi)[1+\sqrt{1+(u_{\max}L_gV)^2}]} \le w_b|L_wV||e| \le w_b|e|^2$$
$$\le \frac{w_b\phi^2}{(\chi-1)^2} \triangleq \beta(\phi)\ \forall|e| \le \frac{\phi}{\chi-1}$$

where we assumed that the following inequality holds for a suitable ϕ.

$$(|e|+\phi)[1+\sqrt{1+(u_{\max}L_gV)^2}] \ge \phi$$

Substituting $\beta(\phi)$ in Eq. (25) we obtain

$$\dot{V} \le -\lambda(\|e_i\|^2 + \|e\|^2) + \beta(\phi)$$
$$+\frac{(L_fV + w_b|e|)\sqrt{1+(u_{\max}L_gV)^2}}{[1+\sqrt{1+(u_{\max}L_gV)^2}]}$$
$$-\frac{\sqrt{(L_fV + \chi w_b|e|)^2 + (u_{\max}L_gV)^4}}{[1+\sqrt{1+(u_{\max}L_gV)^2}]} \quad (26)$$

Now, to determine the sign of the last two terms, we consider two cases,

Case 1. $L_fV + w_b|e| \le 0$, substituting this inequality in Eq. (26) yields

$$\dot{V} \le -\lambda(\|e_i\|^2 + \|e\|^2) + \beta(\phi)$$
$$-\frac{\sqrt{(L_fV + \chi w_b|e|^2 + (u_{\max}L_gV)^4}}{[1+\sqrt{1+(u_{\max}L_gV)^2}]}$$

Case 2.

$$0 \le L_fV + w_b|e| \le u_{\max} \quad (27)$$

For this case, we consider the inequality

$$(L_fV + \chi w_b|e|)^2 \le (u_{\max}L_gV)^2$$

Then

$$-\sqrt{(L_fV + \chi w_b|e|^2) + (u_{\max}L_gV)^4}$$
$$\le -(L_fV + w_b|e|)\sqrt{1+(u_{\max}L_gV)^2}$$

Replacing this bound in Eq. (26), we obtain

$$\dot{V} \le -\lambda(\|e_i\|^2 + \|e\|^2) + \beta(\phi)$$
$$+\frac{(1-\chi)w_b|e|\sqrt{1+(u_{\max}L_gV)^2}}{[1+\sqrt{1+(u_{\max}L_gV)^2}]} \quad (28)$$

where we select $\chi > 1$ such that the last term on the right hand is strictly negative.

From Eq. (28), we deduce that exists a class K function α such that

$$\dot{V} \le -\alpha(|e|) + \beta(\phi) \quad (29)$$

Then, by an appropriate selection of ϕ we can make $\beta(\phi)$ small enough such that $\beta\phi \le (1/2)\alpha(|e|)$ in order to obtain

$$\dot{V} \le -\tfrac{1}{2}\alpha(|e|) \quad (30)$$

Hence, the trajectories of V will approach a ball of radius $|e| = \alpha^{-1}(2\beta)$. Therefore, whenever the inequality (27) holds, the trajectories of Eq. (20) will approach an ultimate bound given by $\alpha^{-1}(2\beta)$. Then, the designer can choose the parameters ϕ and χ in order to obtain a suitable tracking error. The design parameter ϕ should be selected small relative to the desired ultimate bound for the tracking error.

Remark 1. Inequality (27) can be used to on-line reducing the bounds for the control input when the tracking error is sufficiently small. This aids to reduce the amplitude of the control effort, which explicitly depend on the input saturations. Hence, the selection of the new reduced bounds should be obtained from simulations to achieve the desired tracking error.

5. Application examples

In order to demonstrate the applicability of the proposed adaptive control scheme with input saturation, the following examples are tested.

5.1. Chaos stabilization

First, we consider a chaotic system stabilization. The unknown system to be stabilized is the Roessler chaotic attractor generated by

$$\dot{x}_{p1} = -x_{p2} - x_{p3} \qquad \dot{x}_{p2} = x_{p1} + a x_{p2}$$
$$\dot{x}_{p3} = -c x_{p3} + b + x_{p1} x_{p3} \tag{31}$$

where a, b, and c are the system physical parameters. Fig. 1 portrays this chaotic attractor for $a = 0.4$, $b = 2$, $c = 4$ and initial conditions $x(0) = (4 \ -10 \ 15)$. We want to stabilize the Roessler system in the origin for a maximum input $u_{max} = 15$. In the simulations, the following recurrent neural network is used:

$$\dot{x} = Ax + Wz(x_p) + \text{sat}(u) \tag{32}$$

with $A = -7.5I$ and with the high order sigmoid vector defined as

$$z(x_p) = [\tanh(kx_{p1})\ \tanh(kx_{p2})\ \tanh(kx_{p3})\ \tanh(kx_{p1})$$
$$\tanh(kx_{p2})\ \tanh(kx_{p1})\tanh(kx_{p3})\ \tanh(kx_{p2})$$
$$\tanh(kx_{p3})\ \tanh^2(kx_{p1})\ \tanh^2(kx_{p2})\ tanh^2(kx_{p3}) \tag{33}$$
$$\tanh(kx_{p1})\tanh^2(kx_{p2})\ \tanh(kx_{p1})\tanh^2(kx_{p3})$$
$$\tanh(kx_{p1})\tanh(kx_{p2})\tanh(kx_{p3})]$$

$k = 0.5$

To avoid parameter drift, we use the robust adaptation law (Eq. (14)) with $\gamma = 25$, $w_{max} = 500$, $\sigma = 50$.

For the control law, we select $w_b = 0.5$, $\chi = 2$ and $\phi = 0.1$. Figs. 2 and 3 display the time evolution for the states. The control law is applied at $t = 5$ s. As can be seen, the control law achieves the stabilization even in presence of uncertainties due to the modelling error and input saturation.

5.2. Chaos synchronization

In this example, the objective is the synchronization of the Roessler's attractor and the Chua's system. We consider the Roessler chaotic attractor defined in Eq. (31) as the unknown system. The goal is to force this chaotic attractor to synchronize the Chua's attractor given by

$$\dot{x} = p(-x + y - \Phi(x)) \quad \dot{y} = x - y + z \quad \dot{z} = -qy \tag{34}$$

where

$$\Phi(x) = \begin{cases} m_0 x - m_1 & \text{if } x \leq -1 \\ m_1 x & \text{if } |x| < 1 \\ m_0 x + m_1 & \text{if } x \geq 1 \end{cases} \tag{35}$$

in this case $p = 10$, $q = 14.87$, $m_0 = 0.68$, $m_1 = -1.27$.

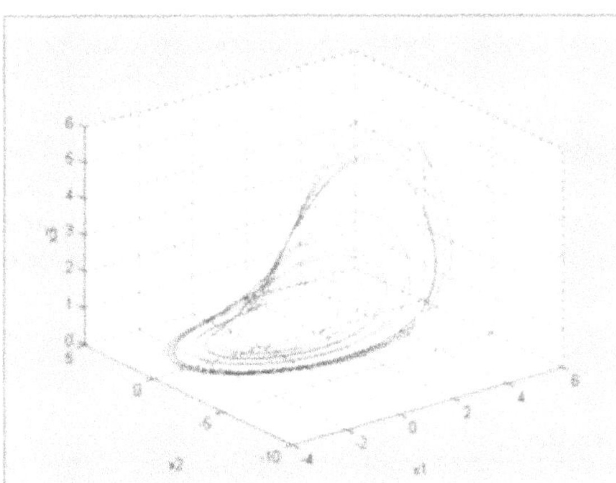

Fig. 1. Roessler chaotic attractor.

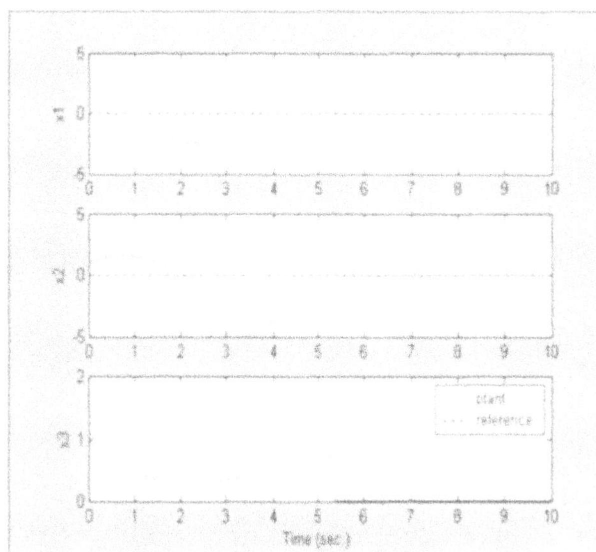

Fig. 2. Chaos stabilization: states time evolution.

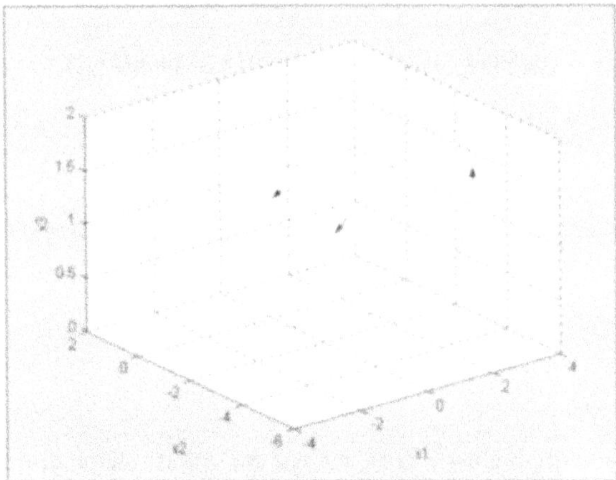

Fig. 3. Chaos stabilization: plant's phase portrait.

The input saturation is defined as $u_{max} = 40$.

We used the neural network (Eq. (32)) with $A = -15I$ and the high order sigmoid vector as defined in Eq. (33). To avoid parameter drift, we use the robust adaptation law (Eq. (14)) with $\gamma = 100$, $w_{max} = 500$, $\sigma = 50$.

For the control law, we select $\chi = 2$, $\phi = 0.02$ and $w_b = 0.25$. For this example, in order to improve the closed-loop performance, we modify the input bounds according to the following relation obtained from simulations,

$$u_{max} = \begin{cases} 5 & \text{if } |e| < 0.05 \\ 10 & \text{if } 0.05 \leq |e| < 0.1 \\ 40 & \text{if } |e| \geq 0.1 \end{cases}$$

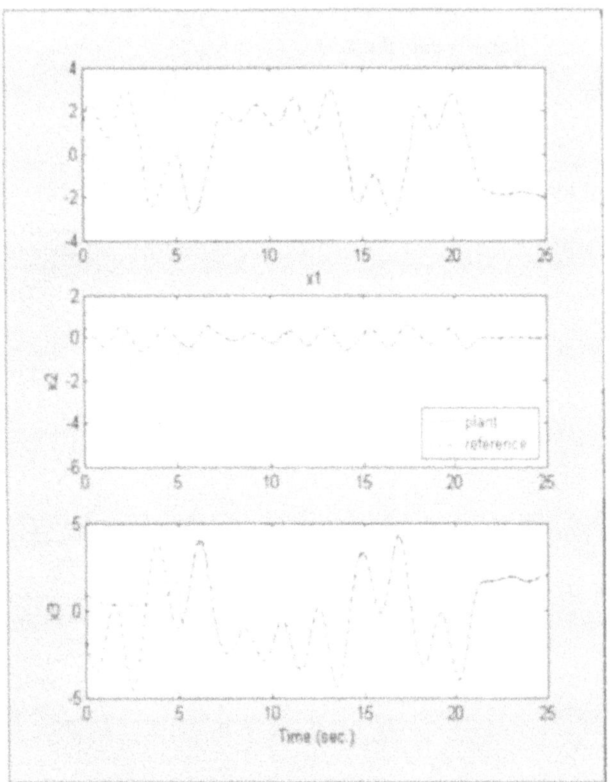

Fig. 4. Chaos synchronization: states time evolution.

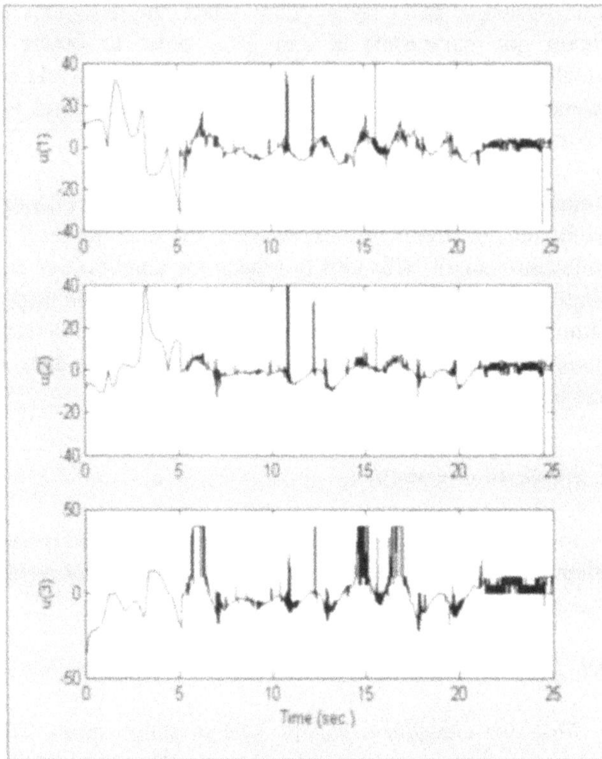

Fig. 5. Chaos synchronization: applied inputs.

We let the Roessler attractor evolve for 5 s. Then we apply the control law in order to synchronize the attractors. The simulation results are shown in Figs. 4 and 5, where state time evolutions and the respective phase portraits are presented. As shown, the unknown system track the reference trajectory with a very small error.

6. Conclusions

A new adaptive control structure based on a recurrent neural networks for trajectory tracking of unknown non-linear systems with input saturation was presented. This structure is composed of a neural network identifier, which builds an online model of the unknown plant, and a control law for trajectory tracking with input saturation. Stability of the identification and tracking error is analysed via Lyapunov control functions.

The applicability of the proposed structure was tested via simulations, by examples of chaos control and synchronization. The results are quite satisfactorily. Continuation of researches along this line is to further relax the required condition of having the same number of inputs and states.

References

Chen, G., & Dong, X. (1993). On feedback control of chaotic continuous-time systems. *IEEE Transaction on Circuits and System, 40*, 591–601.

Chen, G., & Dong, X. (1998). *From chaos to order: methodologies, perspectives, and applications*. Singapore: World Science Publishing Company.

El-Farra, N., & Christofides, P. (2001). Integrating robustness, optimality and constraints in control of nonlinear processes. *Chemical Engineering Science*, *56*, 1841–1868.

Kosmatopoulos, E. B., Christodoulou, M. A., & Ioannou, P. A. (1997). Dynamical neural networks that ensure exponential identification error convergence. *Neural Networks*, *1*(2), 299–314.

Lin, Y., & Sontag, E. (1991). A universal formula for stabilization with bounded controls. *Systems and Control Letters*, *16*, 393–397.

Narendra, K. S., & Parthasarathy, K. (1990). Identification and control of dynamical systems using neural networks. *IEEE Transaction on Neural Networks*, *1*(1), 4–27.

Nijmeijer, H., & Berghuis, H. (1995). On Lyapunov control of Duffing equation. *IEEE Transaction on Circuits and System*, *42*, 473–477.

Poznyak, A. S., Yu, W., Sanchez, E. N., & Perez, J. P. (1999). Nonlinear adaptive trajectory tracking using dynamic neural networks. *IEEE Transaction on Neural Networks*, *10*(6), 1402–1411.

Rovitahkis, G. A., & Christodoulou, M. A. (2000). *Adaptive control with recurrent high-order neural networks*. New York, USA: Springer.

Sanchez, E. N., Perez, J. P., & Ricalde, L. (2002). Recurrent neural control for robot trajectory tracking. *Proceedings of the 15th World Congress International Federation of Automatic Control, Barcelona, Spain*.

Suykens, K., Vandewalle, L., & De Moor, R. (1996). *Artificial neural networks for modelling and control of nonlinear systems*. Boston, USA: Kluwer Academic Publishers.

Vincent, T. L., & Yu, J. (1991). Control of a chaotic system. *Dynamic and Control*, 35–52.

Zeng, Y., & Singh, S. N. (1997). Adaptative control of chaos in Lorenz system. *Dynamic and Control*, *7*, 143–154.

AVAILABLE AT
www.ComputerScienceWeb.com
POWERED BY SCIENCE DIRECT

PERGAMON

Neural Networks 16 (2003) 719–728

Neural Networks

www.elsevier.com/locate/neunet

2003 Special issue

Proper orthogonal decomposition based optimal neurocontrol synthesis of a chemical reactor process using approximate dynamic programming

Radhakant Padhi, S.N. Balakrishnan*

Department of Mechanical and Aerospace Engineering, and Engineering Mechanics, University of Missouri-Rolla, Rolla, MO 65409, USA

Abstract

The concept of approximate dynamic programming and adaptive critic neural network based optimal controller is extended in this study to include systems governed by partial differential equations. An optimal controller is synthesized for a dispersion type tubular chemical reactor, which is governed by two coupled nonlinear partial differential equations. It consists of three steps: First, empirical basis functions are designed using the 'Proper Orthogonal Decomposition' technique and a *low-order* lumped parameter system to represent the infinite-dimensional system is obtained by carrying out a Galerkin projection. Second, approximate dynamic programming technique is applied in a discrete time framework, followed by the use of a dual neural network structure called *adaptive critics*, to obtain optimal neurocontrollers for this system. In this structure, one set of neural networks captures the relationship between the state variables and the control, whereas the other set captures the relationship between the state and the costate variables. Third, the lumped parameter control is then mapped back to the spatial dimension using the same basis functions to result in a feedback control. Numerical results are presented that illustrate the potential of this approach. It should be noted that the procedure presented in this study can be used in synthesizing optimal controllers for a fairly general class of nonlinear distributed parameter systems.

Keywords: Distributed parameter system; Proper orthogonal decomposition; Optimal control; Adaptive critic neural networks; Tubular reactor control

1. Introduction

Process control problems are mostly governed by partial differential equations (PDEs) and are infinite-dimensional in nature. They are also called Distributed Parameter Systems (DPS), as opposed to 'lumped parameter systems' that characterize physical systems such as a car or an airplane. The DPS appear naturally in various application areas such as chemical processes, thermal processes, vibrating structures, fluid flow systems, etc. They inherently have an infinite number of system modes. Since it is impossible to deal with all the modes, some sort of approximation technique is usually applied for the analysis and synthesis procedures related to DPS.

Infinite dimensional operator theory is used in (Curtain & Zwart, 1995) to find closed form solutions for control. However, this approach is difficult to apply to nonlinear DPS. So far this technique has been mainly limited to linear systems (Curtain & Zwart, 1995) and spatially invariant systems (Bameih, 1997). Moreover, the infinite-dimensional control solution needs to be approximated (like truncating an infinite series) for implementation and hence is not completely free from error. This approach of control synthesis is usually known as 'design-then-approximate'. Another approach is 'approximate-then-design'. Here, the PDEs describing the system dynamics are first approximated to yield a finite-dimensional structure. This approximate system is then used for controller synthesis. In this approach, it is relatively easy to design controllers using various concepts. An interested reader can refer to (Burns & King, 1994) for discussions on the relative merits and limitations of the two approaches.

A popular approximate-then-design technique is to find orthogonal basis functions for the PDE solutions and use them with a Galerkin procedure to first create an approximate finite-dimensional lumped parameter model, i.e. a system of Ordinary Differential Equations (ODEs). This model is then used for control design using various tools of lumped parameter control design. If arbitrary basis functions (e.g. Fourier and Chebyshev polynomials) are used in the Galerkin procedure, they can result in

* Corresponding author. Tel.: +1-573-341-4675; fax: +1-573-341-4607.
E-mail address: bala@umr.edu (S.N. Balakrishnan).

0893-6080/03/$ - see front matter
doi:10.1016/S0893-6080(03)00131-X

a high-dimensional ODE system (Sadek & Bokhari, 1998). A better and powerful basis function design is obtained when the Proper Orthogonal Decomposition (POD) technique is used with a Galerkin approximation. In the POD technique, a set of problem-oriented basis functions is first obtained by generating a set of 'snap-shot solutions' through simulations or from the actual process. Using these orthogonal basis functions in a Galerkin procedure, a low-dimensional ODE system can be developed. This technique has widely been used in recent years (Armaou & Christofides, 2002; Banks, Rosario, & Smith, 2000; Burns & King, 1994; Christofides, 2001; Holmes, Lumley, & Berkooz, 1996; Padhi & Balakrishnan, 2002; Ravindran, 1999; Zheng, Hoo, & Piovoso, 2002).

The issue of optimal control synthesis should be addressed next. It is well known that the dynamic programming formulation offers the most comprehensive solution to nonlinear optimal control; however, a huge amount of computational and storage requirements are needed to solve the associated Hamilton–Jacobi–Bellman (HJB) equation (Bryson & Ho, 1975) (also known as the Bellman equation). Werbos (1992) proposed a means to get around this numerical complexity by using 'approximate dynamic programming' (ADP) formulations. His methods approximate the original problem with a discrete formulation. The solution to the ADP formulation is obtained through the two-neural network adaptive critic approach. In one version of the adaptive critic approach called the dual heuristic programming (DHP) one network called the action network represents the mapping between the state variables of a dynamic system and control and the second network, called the critic, outputs the costates with the state variables as its inputs. This ADP process, through the nonlinear function approximation capabilities of neural networks, overcomes the computational complexity that plagued the dynamic programming formulation of optimal control problems. More important, this solution can be implemented on-line, since the control computation requires a few multiplications of the network weights which are trained off-line. This technique was used in Balakrishnan and Biega (1996) to solve an aircraft control problem in a domain of interest. Note that there are various types of adaptive critic designs available in literature. An interested reader can refer to Prokhorov and Wunsch (1997) for more details.

Recently, the techniques of POD and the adaptive critic design have been combined by the authors of this study to develop an innovative computational tool for the optimal control synthesis of nonlinear DPS (Padhi & Balakrishnan, 2002). Besides good numerical results from simulations, this technique has been successfully verified in an *experimental setting* as well, with a relatively simple heat diffusion problem (Prabhat, Balakrishnan, Look, & Padhi, 2003). In this paper, this technique is applied to a more challenging *nonlinear* chemical reactor process. This dispersion type tubular chemical reactor control problem has been discussed in Choe and Chang (1998) and Hlavacek and Hofmann (1970). Possible applications of such reactors include conversion of synthetic (or natural) gas into higher hydrocarbons, carbonization of biomass, synthesis of alkyl-*tert*-alkyl ester, hydro-formation of C2–C25 olefins, etc.

Choe and Chang (1998) have used Green's function to calculate optimal control. Their method for calculating the costate variables that arise in an optimal control formulation is complicated. Even though the authors have found a Green's function for the particular problem, finding an appropriate Green's function and calculating its coefficients is not an easy task in general. More important, their solution is for specific initial condition (initial state profiles) only. In other words, it is an open loop control which will severely degrade the process performance if the initial profile were different. In contrast to this, the approach presented in this paper is applicable to a large number of initial conditions (or profiles). Once the neural networks are trained to capture the relationship between state and control within a domain of interest (which is done off-line) they can be used to compute the control for 'any' value of the state variables within that domain. Moreover since using a set of networks is not computationally intensive it can be implemented on-line. In control terminology this is a feedback solution; a feedback control is desirable because of its beneficial properties like robustness with respect to noise suppression and modeling uncertainties.

We wish to point out that we have solved the same chemical reactor optimal control problem using a different approach earlier (Padhi & Balakrishnan, 2001). In that approach which did not use any model reduction techniques, a controller was used at every step in a finite difference scheme (Gupta, 1995) that was used to discretize the spatial variable. Even though we obtained satisfactory results, there are some implementation issues. Note that one has to take a large number of node points for good finite difference approximations. However, because for each node point critic and action networks were proposed, the number of networks grows with the number of grid points and this would lead to serious problem in training of the networks. As a consequence one has to remain contented with a 'coarse grid approximation'. In contrast, the current approach is grid independent in the sense that lumped parameter state vector does not depend on the number of grid points assumed for the integral evaluations. Second, in the earlier technique the state (and control) values at some point in space other than the node point locations are unknown. If one wants to get value for such a location, interpolation techniques are necessary. The prediction may not be good if the grid approximation is coarse. In contrast, in the proposed methodology by definition the basis functions are supposed to be continuous functions. So values at any point in the space can theoretically be computed without resorting to any interpolation technique. This issue is of significantly less concern in our new approach, since one can have a fine-grid approximation to begin with and therefore, will result in much smaller interpolation errors. Third, in the earlier approach, the state variables used for training were generated with an ∞-norm based procedure. This poses a problem when the grid is refined as the state profiles tend to become more and more discontinuous which does not happen in practice. In contrast, in this paper we propose a method based on L_2 norm (both on state profiles as well as on its spatial derivative(s)), leading to the generation of 'smooth' state profiles for training. Besides capturing the expected state profiles more closely, this process aids the neural network training process substantially as unwanted (discontinuous) state profiles are not considered for training.

2. System model and objective

Dynamics of the chemical reactor problem considered in this research is described by the following set of PDEs (Choe & Chang, 1998):

$$\frac{\partial v_1}{\partial t} = \frac{1}{Pe_1}\left(\frac{\partial^2 v_1}{\partial y^2}\right) - \frac{\partial v_1}{\partial y} + N(v_2)(1 - v_1) \tag{1a}$$

$$\frac{\partial v_2}{\partial t} = \frac{1}{Pe_2}\left(\frac{\partial^2 v_2}{\partial y^2}\right) - \frac{\partial v_2}{\partial y} + BN(v_2)(1 - v_1) - h(v_2 - u) \tag{1b}$$

The boundary conditions are given by

$$\left[\frac{\partial v_1}{\partial y} = Pe_1 v_1\right]_{y=0}, \quad \left[\frac{\partial v_2}{\partial y} = Pe_2 v_2\right]_{y=0}, \quad \left.\frac{\partial v_1}{\partial y}\right|_{y=L} = 0, \quad \left.\frac{\partial v_2}{\partial y}\right|_{y=L} = 0 \tag{2}$$

where v_1, v_2 are the state variables that represent concentration and temperature, respectively. The control variable u represents the cooling water temperature. The terms Pe_1, Pe_2 are the *Peclet* numbers of mass and energy flows, respectively. $N(v_2) = D_a \exp[v_2/(1 + v_2/\varepsilon)]$, where D_a is the *Damkohler* number, ε is the activation energy, B and h are the parameters related to heat of reaction and heat transfer, respectively. $y \in [0, L]$ and $t \in [t_0, t_f]$, where t_0 and t_f are initial and final times, respectively. Values of different parameters describing the process are: $Pe_1 = 1$, $Pe_2 = 1$, $D_a = 1$, $\varepsilon = 20$, $B = 2$, $h = 1$, $m = 2$, $t_0 = 0$ and $L = 1$.

For convenience, we define $v_{1\mathrm{ref}}$ and $v_{2\mathrm{ref}}$ as the steady state values of v_1 and v_2, respectively, while the $h(v_2 - u)$ term is omitted from the v_2 dynamics; this implies that the reactor operates with perfect insulation. Consequently, we observe that $u_{1\mathrm{ref}} = v_{2\mathrm{ref}}$. For computing $u_{1\mathrm{ref}}$ and $v_{2\mathrm{ref}}$, it was assumed that $\partial v_1/\partial t = \partial v_2/\partial t = 0$ (steady-state condition), in addition to $h(v_2 - u) = 0$. Then we use these conditions in Eqs. (1) and (2) and solved the resulting two point boundary value problem (in spatial dimension) for $v_{1\mathrm{ref}}$ and $v_{2\mathrm{ref}}$ using the *shooting method* (Roberts & Shipman, 1972). The computed $v_{1\mathrm{ref}}$ and $v_{2\mathrm{ref}}$ profiles are presented in Fig. 1.

Defining $x_1 \triangleq (v_1 - v_{1\mathrm{ref}})$, $x_2 \triangleq (v_2 - v_{2\mathrm{ref}})$, we rewrite Eq. (1) as

$$\frac{\partial x_1}{\partial t} = \frac{1}{Pe_1}\left(\frac{\partial^2 x_1}{\partial y^2}\right) - \left(\frac{\partial x_1}{\partial y}\right) + f(x_1, x_2) \tag{3a}$$

$$\frac{\partial x_2}{\partial t} = \frac{1}{Pe_2}\left(\frac{\partial^2 x_2}{\partial y^2}\right) - \left(\frac{\partial x_2}{\partial y}\right) + Bf(x_1, x_2) - hv \tag{3b}$$

where

$$f(x_1, x_2) \equiv N(v_{2\mathrm{ref}} + x_2)(1 - v_{1\mathrm{ref}} - x_1) - N(v_{2\mathrm{ref}})(1 - v_{1\mathrm{ref}}) \tag{3c}$$

Here $v \equiv (u - x_2)$ is the new auxiliary control variable. The objective is to find the optimal control $u(t, y)$ which ensures $\{x_1, x_2\} \to \{0, 0\}$ (*i.e.* $\{v_1, v_2\} \to \{v_{1\mathrm{ref}}, v_{2\mathrm{ref}}\}$) as $t \to \infty$. This objective can be met by minimizing the quadratic cost function

$$J = \frac{1}{2}\int_0^\infty \int_0^L [q_1 x_1^2(t, y) + q_2 x_2^2(t, y) + r u^2(t, y)]\mathrm{d}y\,\mathrm{d}t \tag{4}$$

where $q_1, q_2 \geq 0$ and $r > 0$ are weights to be appropriately fixed by the control designer. We have used $q_1 = 5000$, $q_2 = 1$ and $r = 1$. The relatively high value of q_1 was selected mainly because our goal was to drive v_1 towards $v_{1\mathrm{ref}}$ as quickly as possible. One may notice that even though this is a quadratic regulator problem, we cannot apply the infinite-dimensional operator theory based linear quadratic optimal control design technique for DPS (Curtain & Zwart, 1995) since the system dynamics is nonlinear.

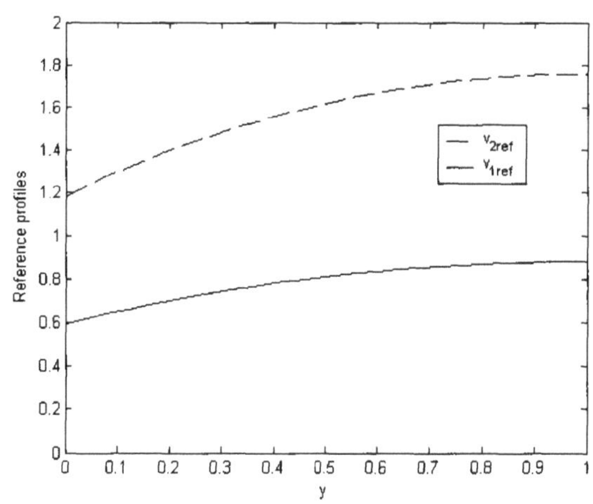

Fig. 1. Reference profiles for state variables.

3. Finite-dimensional approximation

In this section, we describe the design steps for obtaining the POD basis functions and using them in a Galerkin procedure to result in an analogous low-order lumped parameter problem. We also define the domain of interest and outline a procedure to compute initial state profiles as well as snap-shot solutions.

3.1. Proper orthogonal decomposition: design of basis functions

Usually the so-called 'snap-shot' solutions are used as an ensemble of data to design the basis functions. In our case, these are obtained by simulating the system by exciting the system with arbitrary controls for three-unit duration and then collecting some state profiles at random instants of time. More about the snap-shot generation process is discussed later in Section 3.4.

Let $\{U_i(y) : 1 \le i \le N,\ 0 \le y \le L\}$ be a set of N snapshot solutions of the system. The goal of the POD technique is to design a set of basis functions which has the largest mean square projection on the snapshots. In other words, we try to find all such possible basis functions Φ, each of which provides a local maximum for the following figure of merit:

$$I = \frac{1}{N}\sum_{i=1}^{N} |\langle U_i, \Phi\rangle|^2 / \langle \Phi, \Phi\rangle$$

$$= \frac{1}{N}\left[\sum_{i=1}^{N}\left|\int_0^L U_i \Phi \, dy\right|^2 \Big/ \int_0^L \Phi\Phi \, dy\right] \tag{5}$$

The solution approach is to seek a function $\Phi = \sum_{i=1}^{N} w_i U_i$, the coefficients w_i are to be determined such that Φ maximizes I in Eq. (5). In the process we obtain N orthonormal basis functions Φ_i, $i = 1, \ldots, N$. Depending on the energy content, this eigen spectrum is truncated to retain only $\tilde{N} \le N$ eigen functions that will be used in the Galerkin projection.

An interested reader can see Holmes et al. (1996) and Ravindran (1999), for detail discussions on the basis function design procedure. It may be noted, however, that the POD technique is a generalization of a familiar method known as Principal Component Analysis (PCA) to continuous square integrable functions. The PCA technique is widely used as a tool in pattern recognition, image processing, etc. (Haykin, 1994). An important property of the POD basis functions is that they are optimal in the sense that for a given number of modes n, the projection on the subspace spanned by leading n POD basis functions contains the greatest possible energy on an average (Holmes et al., 1996; Chapter 3, Section 3.3).

For the process control problem, the basis functions for x_1 and x_2 were designed independently. In order to determine the proper order of the system, the ratios

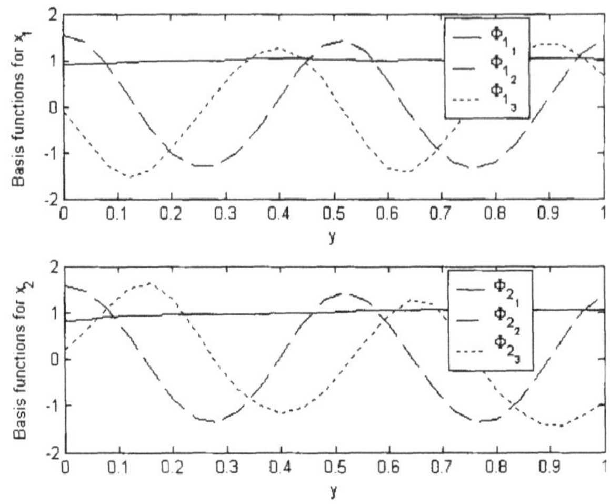

Fig. 2. POD basis functions for state variables.

$\sum_{j=1}^{\tilde{N}_1} \lambda_{1_j} / \sum_{j=1}^{N} \lambda_{1_j}$ and $\sum_{j=1}^{\tilde{N}_2} \lambda_{2_j} / \sum_{j=1}^{N} \lambda_{2_j}$ were plotted for different values of $\tilde{N}_1$, $\tilde{N}_2$ and it was observed that 99% of the ratio was accounted for by the first three eigenvalues for both the state variables. Hence, we fixed $\tilde{N}_1 = \tilde{N}_2 = 3$ and assumed that the six basis functions captured the essential characteristics contained in the snap shots with sufficient accuracy. The basis functions for state variables x_1 and x_2 in the chemical reactor control problem are shown in Fig. 2.

3.2. Finite-dimensional approximation: Galerkin projection

The state variables $x_1(t, y)$, $x_2(t, y)$ and auxiliary control variable $v(t, y)$ can be written in terms of the basis functions as

$$x_1(t, y) = \sum_{j=1}^{\tilde{N}_1} \hat{x}_{1_j}(t)\Phi_{1_j}(y) \tag{6a}$$

$$x_2(t, y) = \sum_{j=1}^{\tilde{N}_2} \hat{x}_{2_j}(t)\Phi_{2_j}(y)$$

$$v(t, y) = \sum_{j=1}^{\tilde{N}_1} \hat{v}_{1_j}(t)\Phi_{1_j}(y) + \sum_{j=1}^{\tilde{N}_2} \hat{v}_{2_j}(t)\Phi_{2_j}(y) \tag{6b}$$

Note that the basis functions for the state variables as well as the control are the same. This is because it is assumed in this study that the control spans a subset of the state variables as it is in a feedback form and therefore, the basis functions to represent the states are adequate to describe the control variable. Note that no mean state profiles were assumed in the expansion since our formulation is based on the state deviations.

For convenience, we define $\hat{X}_1 \triangleq [\hat{x}_1, \ldots, \hat{x}_{\tilde{N}_1}]^T$, $\hat{X}_2 \triangleq [\hat{x}_2, \ldots, \hat{x}_{\tilde{N}_2}]^T$, $\hat{V}_1 \triangleq [\hat{v}_1, \ldots, \hat{v}_{\tilde{N}_1}]^T$ and $\hat{V}_2 \triangleq [\hat{v}_2, \ldots, \hat{v}_{\tilde{N}_2}]^T$. By substituting Eqs. (6a) and (6b) in Eq. (3a), and taking the inner product with the basis function Φ_{2_j}, $i = 1, \ldots, N$ and carrying out some algebra we obtain

$$\dot{\hat{X}} = \hat{A}_1\hat{X}_1 + \hat{F}_1(\hat{X}_1,\hat{X}_2) \tag{7a}$$

where

$$\hat{A}_{1_{ij}} \triangleq -\left[\Phi_{1_i}(0)\Phi_{1_j}(0) + \frac{1}{Pe_1}\int_0^L \Phi'_{1_i}\Phi'_{1_j}\,dy + \int_0^L \Phi'_{1_i}\Phi'_{1_j}\,dy\right]$$

$$\hat{F}_{1_i} \triangleq \int_0^L f(x_1,x_2)\Phi_{1_i}\,dy \tag{7b}$$

Similarly, by substituting Eq. (6) in Eq. (3b), and taking the inner product with the basis function Φ_{2_i}, $i = 1,\ldots,\tilde{N}$ and carrying out some algebra we obtain

$$\dot{\hat{X}}_2 = \hat{A}_2\hat{X}_2 + \hat{F}_2(\hat{X}_2,\hat{X}_2) + \hat{B}_1\hat{V}_1 + \hat{B}_2\hat{V}_2 \tag{8a}$$

where

$$\hat{A}_{2_{ij}} \triangleq -\left[\Phi_{2_i}(0)\Phi_{2_j}(0) + \frac{1}{Pe_2}\int_0^L \Phi'_{2_i}\Phi'_{2_j}\,dy + \int_0^L \Phi'_{2_i}\Phi'_{2_j}\,dy\right] \tag{8b}$$

$$\hat{F}_{2_i} \triangleq B\int_0^L f(x_1,x_2)\Phi_{2_i}\,dy, \quad \hat{B}_{1_{ij}} \triangleq h\int_0^L \Phi_{2_i}\Phi_{1_j}, \quad \hat{B}_2 \triangleq hI_{\tilde{N}_2}$$

$$\hat{Q}_1 \triangleq q_1 I_{\tilde{N}_1}, \quad \hat{Q}_2 \triangleq q_2 I_{\tilde{N}_2}, \quad \hat{R}_{11} \triangleq rI_{\tilde{N}_1}, \quad \hat{R}_{22} \triangleq rI_{\tilde{N}_2}$$

$$\hat{R}_{12_{ij}} \triangleq r\int_0^L \Phi_{1_i}\Phi_{2_j}\,dy, \qquad \hat{R}_{21_{ij}} \triangleq r\int_0^L \Phi_{2_i}\Phi_{1_j}\,dy$$

Eqs. (9) and (10) define an analogous optimal control problem in the reduced-order lumped parameter framework. In other words, we now have a low order finite-dimensional ODE system (9) with a cost function expressed in terms of finite-dimensional state variables and control (10), starting from an infinite dimensional PDE system (3) with a cost function expressed in terms of infinite-dimensional state variables and control (4).

3.3. Domain of interest

In the controller synthesis presented later in Section 5, we choose a set of states for which the networks are to be trained. We define this set as *domain of interest*. This set has to be defined in such a way that the elements in it approximately cover the domain of states that are supposed to be encountered in actual operation of the system. For the reactor problem, we define the domain of interest as

$$S_i = \left\{\begin{Bmatrix} x_1(y) \\ x_2(y) \end{Bmatrix} : \begin{Bmatrix} \|x_1(y)\| \le \|v_{1\mathrm{ref}}\| \\ \|x_2(y)\| \le \|v_{2\mathrm{ref}}\| \end{Bmatrix}, \begin{Bmatrix} \|x'_1(y)\| \le 10\|v'_{1\mathrm{ref}}\| \\ \|x'_2(y)\| \le 10\|v'_{2\mathrm{ref}}\| \end{Bmatrix}, \begin{Bmatrix} \|x''_1(y)\| \le 100\|v''_{1\mathrm{ref}}\| \\ \|x''_2(y)\| \le 100\|v''_{2\mathrm{ref}}\| \end{Bmatrix}\right\} \tag{11}$$

It should be noted that the integrals in Eqs. (7) and (8) can be computed numerically. Moreover since the intervals of integrations are finite, any derivative of the integrals (with respect to $\hat{X}$ and $\hat{U}$) can be carried inside the integral sign and the numerical computations of the derivatives are also possible. Hence this approach is applicable for general nonlinear systems without having to first evaluate the integrals symbolically and then computing them.

By defining $\hat{X} \triangleq [\hat{X}_1^T\ \hat{X}_2^T]^T$ and $\hat{V} \triangleq [\hat{V}_1^T\ V_2^T]^T$, we can write

$$\dot{\hat{X}} = \hat{A}\hat{X} + \hat{F}(\hat{X}) + \hat{B}\hat{V} \tag{9a}$$

where

$$\hat{A} \triangleq \begin{bmatrix} \hat{A}_1 & 0 \\ 0 & \hat{A}_2 \end{bmatrix}, \qquad \hat{B} \triangleq \begin{bmatrix} 0 & 0 \\ \hat{B}_1 & \hat{B}_2 \end{bmatrix} \tag{9b}$$

Similarly, after carrying out some algebra we can write

$$J = \frac{1}{2}\int_0^{t_f\to\infty} (\hat{X}^T\hat{Q}\hat{X} + \hat{V}^T\hat{R}\hat{V})\,dt \tag{10a}$$

where

$$\hat{Q} \triangleq \begin{bmatrix} \hat{Q}_1 & 0 \\ 0 & \hat{Q}_2 \end{bmatrix}, \qquad \hat{R} \triangleq \begin{bmatrix} \hat{R}_{11} & \hat{R}_{12} \\ \hat{R}_{21} & \hat{R}_{22} \end{bmatrix} \tag{10b}$$

where $x' \equiv \partial x/\partial y$, $x'' \equiv \partial^2 x/\partial y^2$, etc. We use L_2 norms. The conditions on $x_1(y)$ and $x_2(y)$ lead to 'smooth' profiles. We expect that in practice the profiles representing the initial conditions will remain within S_I.

3.4. Generation of initial state profiles and snap shot solutions

To generate a possible initial condition from S, first observe that Fourier series is a universal function approximator for piece-wise continuous functions and it always leads to smooth function generation. Therefore, we write

$$x_i(0,y) = a_{i_0} + \sum_{n=1}^{N}\left[a_{i_n}\cos\left(\frac{2n\pi y}{L}\right) + b_{i_n}\sin\left(\frac{2n\pi y}{L}\right)\right] \tag{12}$$

where N is chosen as a sufficiently large number (in our case, $N = 50$) and $i = 1, 2$ represent the two states. A straightforward computation then leads to

$$\|x_i(0,y)\|^2 = 2La_{i_0}^2 + \sum_{n=1}^{N}(a_{i_n}^2 + b_{i_n}^2)L \tag{13}$$

$$\|x_i'(0,y)\|^2 = \sum_{n=1}^{N}\left(\frac{2n\pi}{L}\right)^2 (a_{i_n}^2 + b_{i_n}^2)L$$

$$\|x_i''(0,y)\|^2 = \sum_{n=1}^{N}\left(\frac{2n\pi}{L}\right)^4 (a_{i_n}^2 + b_{i_n}^2)L$$

We computed random values for the coefficients so that the conditions in Eq. (11) are satisfied. These are then used in Eq. (12) to compute state profiles which may represent possible initial conditions. Further details of this procedure are omitted for brevity. After generating an initial condition, the snap shot solutions were obtained with the following steps.

- An arbitrary control profile was generated similar to obtaining $x_2(0,y)$ profiles.
- An arbitrary long value of final time ($t_f = 3$ in our case) was selected-long enough to capture typical reactor characteristics.
- The system dynamics was simulated from the generated initial conditions, holding the control profile constant, from $t = 0$ to $t = t_f$.
- Fifty state profile solutions resulting from this simulation were collected randomly at arbitrary instants of time and assumed to represent snap shots of system dynamics.

The above process was repeated forty times, resulting in a collection of 2000 snap shot solutions.

4. Approximate dynamic programming

In this section, the general discussion on the optimal control of the DPS is presented in an ADP framework. Detailed derivations of these conditions can also be found in Balakrishnan and Biega (1996) and Werbos (1992), which are repeated here for the sake of clarity and completeness.

4.1. Problem description and optimality conditions

We consider a scalar cost function, to be minimized, of the form

$$J = \sum_{k=1}^{N-1} \Psi_k(\hat{X}_k, \hat{V}_k) \tag{14}$$

where $\hat{X}_k$ and $\hat{V}_k$ represent the $n \times 1$ state vector and $m \times 1$ control vector, respectively, at time step k. N represents the number of discrete time steps. Note that when N is large, Eq. (14) represents the cost function for an infinite horizon problem. Following the above representation of the cost function, we denote the *cost function from time step k* as

$$J_k = \sum_{\tilde{k}=1}^{N-1} \Psi_{\tilde{k}}(\hat{X}_{\tilde{k}}, \hat{V}_{\tilde{k}}) \tag{15}$$

We can rewrite the cost from k in terms of the cost from $(k+1)$, J_{k+1} and Ψ_k the cost to go from k to $(k+1)$ (called the utility function) as

$$J_k = \Psi_k + J_{k+1} \tag{16}$$

We define the $n \times 1$ *costate* vector at time step k as

$$\lambda_k \equiv \frac{\partial J_k}{\partial \hat{X}_k} \tag{17}$$

Then the necessary condition for optimality for optimal control is

$$\frac{\partial J_k}{\partial \hat{V}_k} = 0 \tag{18}$$

However

$$\frac{\partial J_k}{\partial \hat{V}_k} = \left(\frac{\partial \Psi_k}{\partial \hat{V}_k}\right) + \left(\frac{\partial J_{k+1}}{\partial \hat{V}_k}\right) = \left(\frac{\partial \Psi_k}{\partial \hat{V}_k}\right) + \left(\frac{\partial \hat{X}_{k+1}}{\partial \hat{V}_k}\right)^{\mathrm{T}} \lambda_{k+1} \tag{19}$$

Combining Eqs. (18) and (19), we arrive at

$$\left(\frac{\partial \Psi_k}{\partial \hat{V}_k}\right) + \left(\frac{\partial \hat{X}_{k+1}}{\partial \hat{V}_k}\right)^{\mathrm{T}} \lambda_{k+1} = 0 \tag{20}$$

The co-state propagation equation can be derived as

$$\lambda_k = \frac{\partial J_k}{\partial \hat{X}_k} = \left(\frac{\partial \Psi_k}{\partial \hat{X}_k}\right) + \left(\frac{\partial J_{k+1}}{\partial \hat{X}_k}\right) = \left[\left(\frac{\partial \Psi_k}{\partial \hat{X}_k}\right) + \left(\frac{\partial X_{k+1}}{\partial \hat{X}_k}\right)^{\mathrm{T}} \lambda_{k+1}\right] + \left(\frac{\partial \hat{V}_k}{\partial \hat{X}_k}\right)^{\mathrm{T}}\left[\left(\frac{\partial \Psi_k}{\partial \hat{V}_k}\right) + \left(\frac{\partial \hat{X}_{k+1}}{\partial \hat{V}_k}\right)^{\mathrm{T}} \lambda_{k+1}\right] \tag{21}$$

However using Eq. (20) on the optimal path, Eq. (21) simplifies to

$$\lambda_k = \left(\frac{\partial \Psi_k}{\partial \hat{X}_k}\right) + \left(\frac{\partial \hat{X}_{k+1}}{\partial \hat{X}_k}\right)^{\mathrm{T}} \lambda_{k+1} \tag{22}$$

4.2. Optimality equations for chemical reactor problem

We can write the state equation in a discrete form as

$$\hat{X}_{k+1} = F(\hat{X}_k, \hat{V}_k) \tag{23}$$

We notice that a discrete equivalent of the cost function (10a) can be written as

$$J = \sum_{k=1}^{(N-1)\to\infty} (\hat{X}_k^T Q_D \hat{X}_k + \hat{V}_k^T R_D \hat{V}_k) \quad (24)$$

where $Q_D \equiv Q\Delta t$ and $R_D \equiv R\Delta t$. From Eqs. (15) and (24), we have

$$\Psi_k = \hat{X}_k^T Q_D \hat{X}_k + \hat{V}_k^T R_D \hat{V}_k \quad (25)$$

Using Eqs. (23) and (25) in Eqs. (20) and (22), we can write the optimal control and costate propagation equations as:

$$\hat{V}_k = -\hat{R}^{-1}\hat{B}^T \lambda_{k+1} \quad (26)$$

$$\lambda_k = G(\hat{X}_k, \hat{V}_k, \lambda_{k+1}) \quad (27)$$

We point out that explicit forms of the functions F and G depend on the type of discretization procedure. A simple way is to introduce *Euler* integration approximation (Gupta, 1995) with a small step size in time Δt. With the availability of relationships in Eqs. (23), (26) and (27), we can proceed to synthesize the neural networks as discussed in Section 5.

5. DHP with adaptive critics

In this section, the procedure of neural network based optimal control synthesis will be presented.

5.1. Neural network synthesis

Assuming the action networks to be optimal for t_k and critic network to be optimal for t_{k+1}, we synthesize the *critic networks* for t_k as follows (Fig. 3).

1. Generate a set of $\hat{X}_k$ values from the domain of interest. For each $\hat{X}_k$, follow the steps below.
   a. Get $\hat{V}_k$ from the action networks
   b. Get $\hat{X}_{k+1}$ from the *state* Eq. (23)
   c. Input $\hat{X}_{k+1}$ to the trained set of critic network to get λ_{k+1}
   d. Calculate target critic λ_k^* from *costate* Eq. (27)
2. Train the set of critic networks with input $\hat{X}_k$ and output λ_k^* for the critic network, using all the input–output data together.

Similarly assuming the critic network to be optimal for $\hat{X}_k$, we synthesize the *action networks* for t_k as follows (Fig. 4).

1. Generate a set of $\hat{X}_k$ values from the domain of interest. For each $\hat{X}_k$, follow the steps below.
   a. Get $\hat{V}_k$ from the action networks
   b. Get $\hat{X}_{k+1}$ from the *state* Eq. (23)
   c. Input $\hat{X}_{k+1}$ to the trained set of critic network to get λ_{k+1}
   d. Get the target optimal control $\hat{V}_k^*$ from Eq. (26)
2. Train the set of action networks with input $\hat{X}_k$ and output $\hat{V}_k^*$, using all the input–output data together.

Levenberg–Marquardt method (Hagan, Demuth, & Beale, 1996) was used in the back propagation technique for training. We took 2000 input–output data points together to avoid the possibility of networks getting trapped in a local minimum. After training the networks with 2000 data points for 50 epochs, the action/critic network was checked for convergence with another 2000 different data points. The convergence conditions of $\|\hat{V}^* - \hat{V}\|/\|\hat{V}^*\| < 0.1$ in case of action networks and $\|\lambda^* - \lambda\|/\|\lambda^*\| < 0.1$ in case of critic networks were used in training. Otherwise, the training process was repeated with different sets of data points.

Once the process of action synthesis is over, we revert to the critic synthesis again and vice-versa. The alternate critic and action network training process is continued till no noticeable change in the output is observed in the outputs of successive training steps. This mutual convergence indicates that the action networks represent the optimal relationship between the state and control. For details on training process, the reader is referred to Balakrishnan and Biega (1996). For more on the topic of adaptive critic (DHP) design process, the reader is

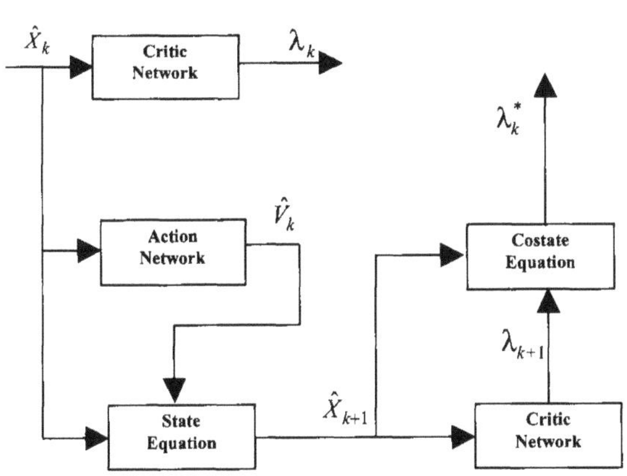

Fig. 3. Schematic of critic network synthesis.

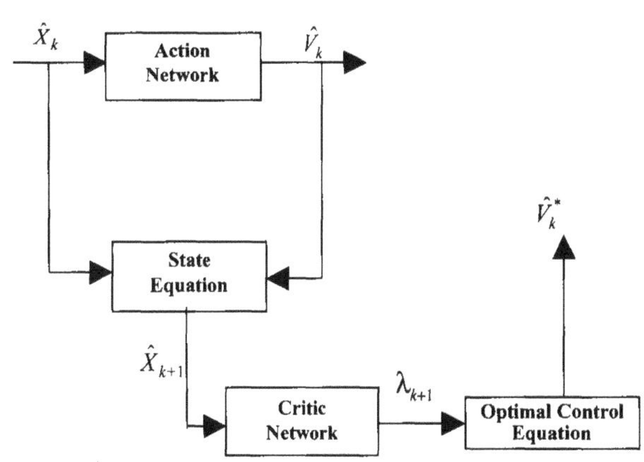

Fig. 4. Schematic of action network synthesis.

referred to Werbos (1992) and Prokhorov and Wunsch (1997).

5.2. *Neural network structures*

In this study, we used six multi-layer feed forward networks of the form $\pi_{6,8,1}$ for the critics and six similar networks for the controller. Here, $\pi_{6,8,1}$ denotes a neural network with 6 neurons in the input layer to account for the six states in the reduced order system, 8 neurons in the hidden layers and 1 neuron in the output layer. Choosing separate networks for each costate and control was needed for faster convergence in this difficult nonlinear problem. We used tangent sigmoid functions for all the hidden layers and linear function for the output layer. No optimization was carried out for the 'best' neural architecture. Numerical results in Section 5 demonstrate that our network structures were appropriate.

5.3. *Initialization of neural networks*

Initialization of the network weights plays an important role in the convergence process. In order to have appropriate initial weights, we linearized Eq. (9) about $\hat{X} = 0$, $\hat{V} = 0$. We then discretized it and used standard *Linear Quadratic Regulator* (*LQR*) theory to obtain the control and costate solutions and train the networks.

6. Numerical results

Histories of state variables and control from various simulations are presented in Figs. 5–7. It should be noted that $y = 0$ and $y = 1$ correspond to the boundary points. The system dynamics equations for the reactor (1) and (2) are given in terms of normalized variables, in which time is normalized with respect to the *residence time* (i.e. the time for which the fluid stays within the reactor). For this reason, we have simulated the system only up to $t_f = 1$, even though we have synthesized the optimal control based on an *infinite-time* formulation. However, simulations beyond $t_f = 1$ keep the state variables at the steady state values (already reached by that time). For clarity of figures, we have plotted the values of the state and control variables obtained at a step size $\Delta t = 0.01$, eventhough we have simulated the system with $\Delta t = 0.001$.

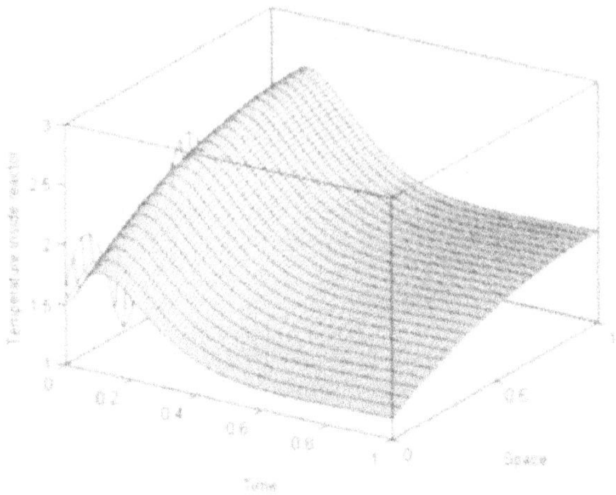

Fig. 6. Temperature in the reactor for conversion as in Fig. 5 from a random initial profile.

We picked random initial profiles of conversion and temperature and let the neuro-controller (cooling water temperature) drive the system. The resulting state variables (conversion and temperature) are plotted in Figs. 5 and 6. It is clear that the state variables are driven towards the final profiles. Moreover, as desired, they reach the desired steady-state profiles quickly (in about 50% of the residence time). The associated control (cooling water temperature) is shown in Fig. 7, which indicates that the control values are not high and the control profile is fairly

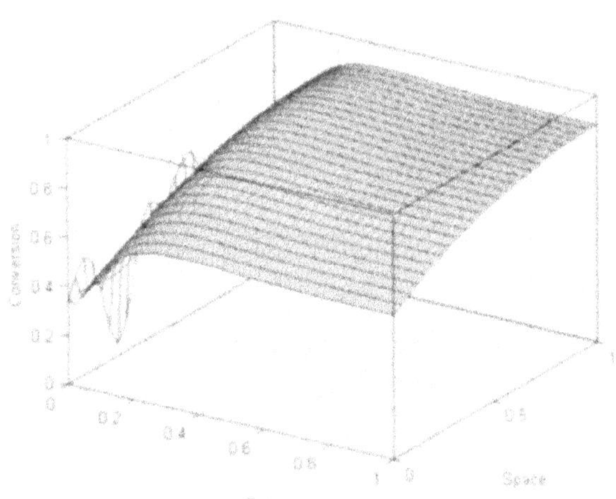

Fig. 5. Development of conversion in the reactor from a random initial profile.

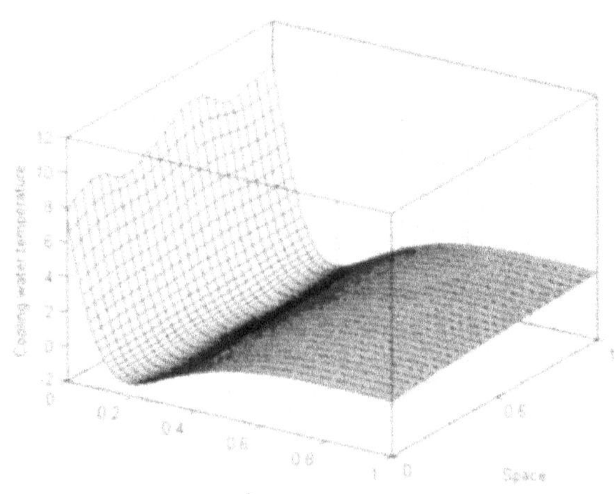

Fig. 7. Cooling water temperature (control) for conversion in Fig. 5 and temperature in Fig. 6.

smooth across the spatial dimension, a desirable characteristic for implementation.

Even though we have presented only a representative case for state and control histories, similar results were observed from a very large number of initial profiles (it was observed in every case we simulated). This indicates that the action networks, with proper training, in fact imbed optimal control solutions for a very large number of initial conditions (state profiles).

For the sake of completion, we wish to point out that one has to be careful in selecting a proper step-size in time Δt for numerical integration. It has to be sufficiently small to avoid instability in numerical integration (Gupta, 1995), which was observed to be dependent on Δy value. Because of its small value, there might arise some reservation about it from the sampling time consideration. However, if the residence time in large, this value of Δt leads to a large enough sampling time. For example, if the residence time is 30 min (which is a realistic assumption) then for $\Delta t = 0.001$ the actual sampling time becomes 1.8 s, large enough for the computational requirements.

It is apparent that that in general we cannot have a large number of sensors and actuators in any real-life applications. In the current simulations we had 51 grid points and assumed same number of sensors and actuators. Furthermore, we assumed that the sensors and actuators are located at the same position (otherwise known as collocated sensors and actuators). This may not be realistic. However, we would like to point out that the issue of large number of sensors as well as the problem of sensor and actuator collocation can be handled properly by incorporating an appropriate sensor location procedure (Burns & King, 1994). Similarly, the issue of large number of actuators can be handled by appropriately formulating the problem considering only finite number of controls and then synthesizing the control. This can be done by incorporating the *direc-delta* functions, as done in (Padhi & Balakrishnan, 2002).

7. Conclusions

Combining the techniques of POD and adaptive critic design, we have successfully synthesized an optimal controller for a nonlinear dispersion-type tubular reactor process. Simulation results are promising. The desired adiabatic steady state profiles are reached quickly (in about 50% of the resident time). This increases the conversion efficiency of the reactor. More important, the controller is able to drive a large number of initial state profiles in the domain of interest towards the desired profiles. For this reason the synthesized action neural network embeds the optimal control solution in a state feedback form, which is highly desired in practical implementation. The technique presented in this paper can also be viewed as a general computational tool for the optimal control of nonlinear DPS. In other words, the procedure of synthesizing the networks remains the same. Only the relevant state, costate and optimal control equations change depending on the problem under consideration.

Acknowledgements

This research was supported by NSF grants ECS 9976588 and ECS 0201076. The authors also express their gratitude to the anonymous reviewers, whose constructive criticisms lead to a substantial improvement of this paper.

References

Armaou, A., & Christofides, P. D. (2002). Dynamic optimization of dissipative PDE systems using empirical eigenfunctions. *Proceedings of the American Control Conference*, 1040–1048.

Balakrishnan, S. N., & Biega, V. (1996). Adaptive-critic based neural networks for aircraft optimal control. *Journal of Guidance, Control and Dynamics*, *19*(4), 893–898.

Bameih, B. (1997). The structure of optimal controllers of spatially-invariant distributed parameter systems. *Proceedings of the Conference on Decision and Control*, 1056–1061.

Banks, H. T., Rosario, R. C. H. del, & Smith, R. C. (2000). Reduced-order model feedback control design: numerical implementation in a thin shell model. *IEEE Transactions on Automatic Control*, *45*(7), 1312–1324.

Bryson, A. E., & Ho, Y. C. (1975). *Applied optimal control*. London: Taylor & Francis.

Burns, J. A., & King, B. B. (1994). *Optimal sensor location for robust control of distributed parameter systems. Proceedings of the Conference on Decision and Control*, pp. 3967–3972.

Choe, Y. S., & Chang, K. S. (1998). A new merging method of optimal control synthesis for distributed parameter systems. *Journal of Chemical Engineering of Japan*, *31*(1), 111–115.

Christofides, P. D. (2001). *Nonlinear and robust control of partial differential equation systems: Methods and applications to transport-reaction processes*. Basel: Birkhauser.

Curtain, R. F., & Zwart, H. J. (1995). *An introduction to infinite dimensional linear systems theory*. Berlin: Springer.

Gupta, S. K. (1995). *Numerical methods for engineers*. New Delhi:Wiley Eastern Ltd. and New Age International Ltd.

Hagan, M. T., Demuth, H. B., & Beale, M. (1996). *Neural network design*. Boston:PWS Publishing Company.

Haykin, S. (1994). *Neural networks*. New York:Macmillan.

Hlavacek, V., & Hofmann, H. (1970). Steady state axial heat and mass transfer in tubular reactors: an analysis of the uniqueness of the solution. *Chemical Engineering Science*, *25*, 173–185.

Holmes, P., Lumley, J. L., & Berkooz, G. (1996). *Turbulence, coherent structures, dynamical systems and symmetry*. Cambridge: Cambridge University Press.

Padhi, R., & Balakrishnan, S. N. (2001). A systematic synthesis of optimal process control with neural networks. *Proceedings of the American Control Conference*, 1910–1915.

Padhi, R., & Balakrishnan, S. N. (2002). *Proper orthogonal decomposition based optimal control design of heat equation with discrete actuators using neural networks. Proceedings of the 15th IFAC World Congress*.

Prabhat, P., Balakrishnan, S. N., Look, D. C., & Padhi, R. (2003). *Proper orthogonal decomposition based modeling and implementation of a neurocontroller for a hear diffusion system. Proceedings of the American Control Conference.*

Prokhorov, D. V., & Wunsch, D. C., II (1997). Adaptive critic designs. *IEEE Transactions on Neural Networks*, *8*(5), 997–1007.

Ravindran, S. S (1999). Proper orthogonal decomposition in optimal control of fluids. *NASA Technical Report*, NASA/TM-1999-209113.

Roberts, S. M., & Shipman, J. S. (1972). *Two point boundary value problems: Shooting methods*. New York:American Elsevier.

Sadek, S., & Bokhari, M. A. (1998). Optimal control of a parabolic distributed parameter systems via orthogonal polynomials. *Optimal Control Applications and Methods*, *19*, 205–213.

Werbos, P. J. (1992). Approximate dynamic programming for real-time control and neural modeling. In White D. A., & Sofge D. A. (Eds.), *Handbook of intelligent control*. New York:Van Nostrand Reinhold.

Zheng, D., Hoo, K. A., & Piovoso, M. J. (2002). Finite dimensional modeling and control of distributed parameter systems. *Proceedings of the American Control Conference*, 4337–4382.

AVAILABLE AT
www.ComputerScienceWeb.com
POWERED BY SCIENCE DIRECT

PERGAMON

Neural Networks 16 (2003) 729–734

Neural Networks

www.elsevier.com/locate/neunet

2003 Special issue

Numerical solution of elliptic partial differential equation using radial basis function neural networks

Li Jianyu[a,b,*], Luo Siwei[a], Qi Yingjian[a], Huang Yaping[a]

[a]*Computer Science Department, Northern Jiaotong University, Beijing 100044, People's Republic of China*
[b]*Information and Engineering College, Beijing Broadcasting Institute, Beijing, People's Republic of China*

Abstract

In this paper a neural network for solving partial differential equations is described. The activation functions of the hidden nodes are the radial basis functions (RBF) whose parameters are learnt by a two-stage gradient descent strategy. A new growing RBF-node insertion strategy with different RBF is used in order to improve the net performances. The learning strategy is able to save computational time and memory space because of the selective growing of nodes whose activation functions consist of different RBFs. An analysis of the learning capabilities and a comparison of the net performances with other approaches have been performed. It is shown that the resulting network improves the approximation results.

Keywords: Radial basis function neural networks; Partial differential equation; Multi-quadrics

1. Introduction

Many problems in science and engineering are reduced to a set of differential equations (DEs) through a process of mathematical modeling. It is not easy to obtain their exact solutions, so numerical methods must be resorted to. There are a lot of techniques available such as the finite difference method (FDM) (Smith, 1978) and the finite element method (FEM) (Hughes, 1987). These methods require the definition of a mesh (domain discretisation) where the functions are approximated locally. The construction of a mesh in two or more dimensions is a non-trivial problem. Usually, in practice, only low-order approximations are employed resulting in a continuous approximation of the function across the mesh but not its partial derivatives. The discontinuity of the approximation of the derivative can adversely affect the stability of the solution. While higher-order schemes are necessary for more accurate approximations of the spatial derivatives, they usually involve additional computational cost. To increase the accuracy of the low-order scheme, it is required that the computational mesh be refined with a higher density of elements in the regions near the contours. This, however, is also achieved at the expense of increased computational cost.

Another method to find an approximate particular solution is achieved by using radial basis function (RBF). Since Kansa (1990a, b) derived a modified RBFs method suitable for solving parabolic, hyperbolic, and elliptic partial differential equations (PDE), the method has been successfully applied for solving PDEs of various types. Later, Franke and Schaback (1997, 1998), Wendland (1999), Wu (1998) and Wu and Schaback (1994) contributed some theories on the solvability and error bounds in applying the RBFs to solve the PDEs. The advantage of RSFs is that they involve a single independent variable regardless of the dimension of the problem. They prove particularly attractive when the domain cannot be expressed as product domains of lower dimensions. In all the interpolation methods for scattered data sets, RBFs outperforms all the other methods regarding accuracy, stability, efficiency, memory requirement, and simplicity of the implementation. In a similar study, Stead (1984) examined the accuracy of partial derivative approximations over scattered data sets, also concluding that RBFs performed more accurately compared to other considered methods. Of the RBFs tested by Franke, Hardy's multi-quadrics (MQ) were ranked the best in accuracy, followed by Duchon's thin plate spline (TPS).

Even though the TPS has been considered as a good interpolating multi-variate function, they do, however, only converge linearly (Powell, 1994). On the other hand, the MQ

* Corresponding author. Present address: Computer Science Department, Northern Jiaotong University, Beijing 100044, People's Republic of China.

0893-6080/03/$ - see front matter © 2003 Published by Elsevier Science Ltd.
doi:10.1016/S0893-6080(03)00083-2

functions converge exponentially and always produce a minimal semi-norm error as proved by Madych and Nelson (1990). However, despite MQs excellent performance, it contains a free parameter, c^2, often referred to as the shape parameter. When c is small, the resulting interpolating surface is pulled tightly to the data points, forming a cone-like basis functions. As c increases, the peak of the cone gradually flattens. Moreover, when the problems to be solved are different, the choice of the optimal RBFs will change. So the network performance is decided not only by the number of the nodes, but also by the RBFs' type. Although, much work has been done in the past, there is one feature that the activation functions of the net are of the same RBF type. In this paper, we focus on the research of how to choose the activation function and how to increase the number of nodes as small as possible.

The approach reported in the present paper uses a growing-network paradigm. Our main goal is to use only as few knots as necessary (selected according to some quality criterion) to achieve a desired accuracy for the fit. We will describe the algorithm, which is based on adaptively inserting knots with different RBFs. The main algorithm includes two more algorithms: one for adapting the networks parameters and the other for inserting new neurons. The approach different from others' (Esposito, Marinaro, Oricchio, & Scarpetta, 2000) is that all parameters are trained and the activation functions of the added nodes can be different RBFs.

For the parameter adaptation we follow the idea of two-stage iterative gradient method (Jianyu, Siwei, & Yingjian, 2002). In this sense, the parameters of centers and width and the parameters of the output weights are trained, respectively, and interactively. New neurons are inserted when the error does not decrease any more by adjusting the parameters.

The outline of this paper is as follows. In Section 2 we introduce RBF Networks method for approximation of function and its derivatives. In Section 3 we formulate the two-stage gradient learning algorithm. Section 4 discusses node insertion. Section 5 reports the net performance on Dirichlet and Neumann problems and the comparisons of results obtained to those already reported in literature. We close the paper with conclusions and discussion in Section 6.

2. Methods for approximation of function and its derivatives

Some of the common types of RBF are as follows:

Linear function: $\phi_k = 1 + r_k$.
Duchon radial cubics: $\phi_k = r_k^3$.
Radial quadratic plus cubic: $\phi_k = 1 + r_k^2 + r_k^3$.
TPS: $\phi_k = r_k^2 \ln r_k$
Hardy MQ: $\phi_k = (r_k^2 + C^2)^{n/2}$ with C being a user specified constant and n being a positive integer.
Inverse MQ: $\phi_k = 1/\sqrt{(r_k^2 + C^2)}$.
Gaussian: $\exp(-r_k^2/C^2)$.

In this paper, many kinds of RBFs will be used to construct the optimal network. In order to express our algorithm clearly and concisely, we will only use the MQ RBFs.

The chosen MQ is given by

$$\phi^{(i)}(\|x - c^{(i)}\|) == \sqrt{(r^2 + a^{(i)2})}, \tag{1}$$

where, $a^{(i)} > 0$, and the parameters $c^{(i)}$, $a^{(i)}$ are the ith RBFs' center and width. Let us consider an RBF-network as a function approximator:

$$u(x) = \sum_{i=1}^{m} w^{(i)} \phi^{(i)}(x) = \sum_{i=1}^{m} w^{(i)} \sqrt{(r^2 + a^{(i)2})}, \tag{2}$$

where m is the number of the RBFs (the hidden neurons).

Given in Eq. (2), the derivatives of the function $u(x)$ are calculated by

$$u_{j\cdots l}(x) = \frac{\partial^k u}{\partial x_j \cdots \partial x_l} = \sum_{i=1}^{m} w^{(i)} \frac{\partial^k \phi^{(i)}}{\partial x_j \cdots \partial x_l}. \tag{3}$$

The derivatives (e.g. up to second order with respect to x_j) are calculated by

$$u_j(x) = \sum_{i=1}^{m} w^{(i)} h^i(x), \tag{4}$$

$$u_{jj}(x) = \sum_{i=1}^{m} w^{(i)} \bar{h}^i(x), \tag{5}$$

where

$$h^i(x) = \frac{\partial \phi^{(i)}}{\partial x_j} = \frac{(x_j - c_j^{(i)})}{(r^2 + a_j^{(i)2})^{0.5}}, \tag{6}$$

$$\bar{h}^i(x) = \frac{\partial h^{(i)}}{\partial x_j} = \frac{r^2 + a^{(i)^2} - (x_j - c_j^{(i)^2})}{(r^2 + a_j^{(i)2})^{1.5}}. \tag{7}$$

3. Two-stage gradient learning algorithm

First, let us begin to consider the 2D Poisson's equation over the domain Ω

$$\Delta u = p(x), \qquad x \in \Omega, \tag{8}$$

where Δ is the Laplace operator, x is the spatial position, p is a known function of x and u is the unknown function of x to be found. Eq. (8) is subject to Dirichlet and/or Neumann boundary conditions over the boundary $\partial\Omega$

$$u = p_1(x), \qquad x \in \partial\Omega_1, \tag{9}$$

$$n \times \nabla u = p_2(x), \qquad x \in \partial\Omega_2, \tag{10}$$

where n is the outward unit normal; ∇ is the gradient operator; $\partial\Omega_1$ and $\partial\Omega_2$ are the boundary of the domain such as $\partial\Omega_1 \cup \partial\Omega_2 = \partial\Omega$ and $\partial\Omega_1 \cap \partial\Omega_2 = \phi$; p_1 and p_2 are known functions of x.

Numerical solutions of PDEs such as Eqs. (8)–(10) is intimately connected with approximating function and its derivatives. It is proposed here that the solution u and its derivatives can be approximated in terms of basis functions (2), (4), and (5). The design of networks is based on the information provided by the given PDE and its boundary conditions.

Now we begin to introduce our method. With the model u being decomposed into m basis functions in a given family, the unknown parameters $w^{(i)}$, $c^{(i)}$, $b^{(i)}$, $i = 1, 2 \cdots m$ are to be found by minimizing the following sum square error (SSE)

$$l = F(w, c, a) = \sum_{i=1}^{n} [u_{11}(x^{(i)}) + u_{22}(x^{(i)}) - p(x^{(i)})]^2 + \sum_{j=1}^{k} [u(x^{(j)}) - p_1(x^{(j)})]^2 + \sum_{j=1}^{k} [n_1 u_1(x^{(j)}) + n_2 u_2(x^{(j)}) - p_2(x^{(j)})]^2, \quad (11)$$

where $w = (w^{(1)}, w^{(2)}, \ldots, w^{(m)})$, $c = (c^{(1)}, c^{(2)}, \ldots, c^{(m)})$, $a = (a^{(1)}, a^{(2)}, \ldots, a^{(m)})$ and $x^{(i)} \in \Omega$, $x^{(j)} \in \partial\Omega$, $i = 1, 2, \ldots n$, $j = 1, 2, \ldots, k$ are some given discrete points.

The algorithm is a gradient descent type which is calculated in two stages, once to optimize the weights $w^{(i)}$ and once to optimize the centers and the widths $c^{(i)}$, $a^{(i)}$ as follows

Step 1: fix $c^{(i)}$, $a^{(i)}$, the purpose is to find $w^{(i)}$ that minimizes the SSE by the following formula

$$w_t^{(i)} = w_{t-1}^{(i)} - \eta_{t-1} \frac{\partial l(c_{t-1}^{(i)}, a_{t-1}^{(i)}, w_{t-1}^{(i)})}{\partial w_{t-1}^{(i)}}. \quad (12)$$

Step 2: fix $w_t^{(i)}$, the purpose is to find $c^{(i)}$, $a^{(i)}$ that minimizes the SSE by

$$c_t^{(i)} = c_{t-1}^{(i)} - \beta_{t-1} \frac{\partial l(c_{t-1}^{(i)}, a_{t-1}^{(i)}, w_t^{(i)})}{\partial c_{t-1}^{(i)}}, \quad (13)$$

$$a_t^{(i)} = a_{t-1}^{(i)} - \alpha_{t-1} \frac{\partial l(c_t^{(i)}, a_{t-1}^{(i)}, w_t^{(i)})}{\partial a_{t-1}^{(i)}}, \quad (14)$$

where η_{t-1}, β_{t-1}, α_{t-1} are the learning rates at time $t-1$. The aforementioned steps are carried on in turn. We call it interactive gradient algorithm.

It has been known that the learning rates are very important for the convergence of the network parameters. If it is small, the convergence is slight; if it is large, the parameters oscillate and do not converge. But how to choose the best learning rates is problem-dependent. η_{t-1} at time of $t-1$ is determined by minimizing the SSE (11) in which $w^{(i)}$ is replaced by:

$$w_{t-1}^{(i)} - \eta_{t-1} \frac{\partial l}{\partial w_{t-1}^{(i)}}, \quad (15)$$

and can be obtained directly.

β_{t-1}, α_{t-1} can be decided by a recurrent procedure. For example, for some positive number, $a > 0$, set, $\beta_{t-1} = a$, the proper learning rate β_{t-1} is determined by the following formula:

$$\beta_{t-1} = \begin{cases} \dfrac{a}{10}, & \text{if } l(c_t^{(i)}, a_t^{(i)}, w_t^{(i)}) > l(c_{t-1}^{(i)}, a_{t-1}^{(i)}, w_t^{(i)}) \\ 10a, & \text{if } l(c_t^{(i)}, a_t^{(i)}, w_t^{(i)}) < l(c_{t-1}^{(i)}, a_{t-1}^{(i)}, w_t^{(i)}) \end{cases} \quad (16)$$

There are two features in this algorithm compared with the conventional gradient descent algorithm: (a) the learning rates are decided properly; (b) in Eqs. (13) and (14), $c_t^{(i)}$ is determined by $c_{t-1}^{(i)}, a_{t-1}^{(i)}, w_t^{(i)}$, not by $c_{t-1}^{(i)}, a_{t-1}^{(i)}, w_{t-1}^{(i)}$; $a_t^{(i)}$ is determined by $c_t^{(i)}, a_{t-1}^{(i)}, w_t^{(i)}$, not by $c_{t-1}^{(i)}, a_{t-1}^{(i)}, w_{t-1}^{(i)}$.

Sometimes it is difficult to determine the centers and the widths by two-stage gradient method when the governing equation is non-linear. They are determined by the following formulae:

$$c_{t+1}^{(i)} = c_t^{(i)} + N(0, \sigma) c_t^{(i)}, \qquad a_{t+1}^{(i)} = a_t^{(i)} + N(0, \sigma) a_t^{(i)}, \quad (17)$$

where $N(0, \sigma)$ is a random number chosen from a Gaussian probability distribution with mean zero and variance σ. If the SSE of the net is less than the previous one, then the centers and the widths changes according to Eq. (17). Otherwise, the old values are kept and the value σ is initialized to a fix value and then modified according to the following rule:

$$\sigma(t+1) = \begin{cases} b_1 \sigma(t), & \text{if the SSE } l(t+1) \le l(t),\ b_1 > 1; \\ b_2 \sigma(t), & \text{if SSE } l(t+1) \ge l(t),\ b_2 < 1. \end{cases} \quad (18)$$

4. Node insertion

Let us assume that we are given a large number of data and need to fit them with different RBFs within a given tolerance. The idea is to start with a very few nodes of set N in the domain, and then, as long as the SSE exceeds the tolerance, repeatedly insert a node at that data location whose SSE component is the largest. Here is the Algorithm in detail.

Algorithm. Node insertion

1. Let data points $X = \{x^{(1)}, x^{(2)}, \ldots, x^{(n)}\}$, and object output data $y^{(i)}$, $i = 1, 2, \ldots, n$ and a tolerance ε (TOL) be given. If $x^{(i)}$ lies in the domain Ω, $y^{(i)}$ will be $p(x^{(i)})$. If $x^{(i)}$ belongs to the boundary, $y^{(i)}$ will be $p_1(x^{(i)})$ or $p_2(x^{(i)})$.
2. Choose m_0 initial nodes whose centers are some subset of X and let $m = m_0$, and calculate the SSE.

3. While SSE > TOL do 'weight' each data point $x^{(i)}$ according to its error component, i.e. let

$$e^{(i)} := [u_{11}(x^{(i)}) + u_{22}(x^{(i)}) - p(x^{(i)})]^2, \text{ or } [u(x^{(j)}) - p_1(x^{(j)})]^2, \text{ or } [n_1 u_1(x^{(j)}) + n_2 u_2(x^{(j)}) - p_2(x^{(j)})]^2, \; i = 1,2,\dots,n; \; j = 1,2,\dots,k. \tag{19}$$

4. Find the data point $x^{(v)} \notin N$ with maximum weight $e^{(v)}$ and insert it as a node, i.e. $N = N \cup \{x^{(v)}\}$,

$$m = m + 1 \text{ and } w_0^{(v)} = 0 \tag{20}$$

5. Train the parameters of the new inserted node by two-stage gradient algorithm.
6. Train the parameters of all nodes by two-stage gradient algorithm.

5. Numerical examples

Although our technique is fit to solve differential equation (ODE and PDE), we focus on discussing the PDE problems.

A measure of the average error of the solution or the norm of the error of the solution, N_e, is defined as

$$N_e = \frac{\sqrt{\sum_i^q [u(x^{(i)}) - u_e(x^{(i)})]^2}}{\sqrt{\sum_{j=1}^q u_e(x^{(i)})^2}}, \tag{21}$$

where $u(x^{(i)})$ and $u_e(x^{(i)})$ are the calculated and exact solution at the point i, respectively, and q is the number of the training data.

5.1. Linear second order elliptic PDE

Example 1. The problem here is to determine a function $u(x_1, x_2)$ satisfying the following PDE

$$\frac{\partial^2 u}{\partial x_1^2} + \frac{\partial^2 u}{\partial x_2^2} = \sin(\pi x_1)\sin(\pi x_2), \tag{22}$$

on the rectangle $0 \le x_1 \le 1$, $0 \le x_2 \le 1$ subject to the Dirichlet condition $u = 0$ along the whole boundary of the domain. The exact solution is given by

$$u_e(x_1, x_2) = -\frac{1}{2\pi^2}\sin(\pi x_1)\sin(\pi x_2). \tag{23}$$

This problem is solved using RBF by Mai-Duy and Tran-Cong (2001). The authors used the following configure 5 × 5 (i.e. 5 × 5 hidden nodes in the hidden layer), 10 × 10 and 20 × 20 to solve the problem using the following data point densities 5 × 5, 10 × 10 and 20 × 20. In the present approach, with the configure of only 21 nodes and 25 data points, we get the accuracy $N_e = 5.32 \times 10^{-3}$. It is obviously less than the accurate 10^{-2} of Mai-Duy and Tran-Cong (2001) with 25 nodes. The results are shown in Fig. 1.

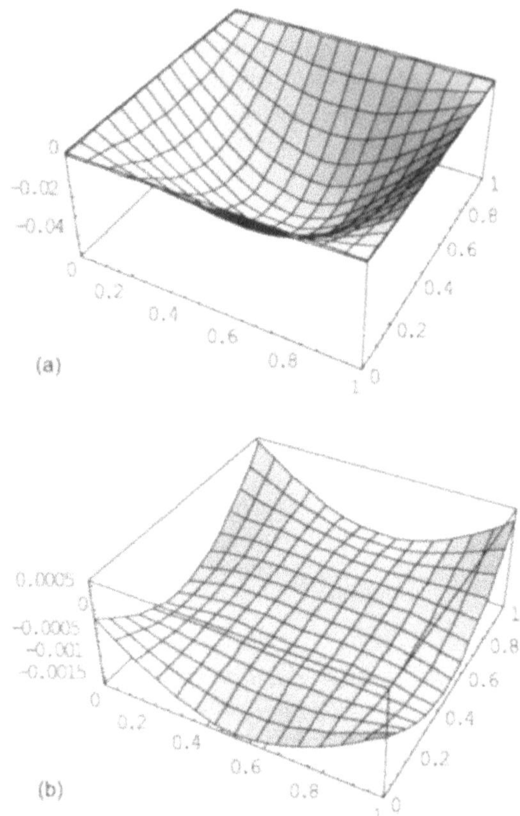

Fig. 1. Net approximation results for the Dirichlet problem of (22), (a) plot of the exact solution, (b) plot of the approximation error curve with 21 RBFs (9 MQ and 12 Gaussian) on 25 data points.

Example 2. In this example, the boundary conditions of the problem include both Dirichlet and Neumann type. Consider the following PDE

$$\frac{\partial^2 u}{\partial x_1^2} + \frac{\partial^2 u}{\partial x_2^2} = (\lambda^2 + \mu^2)\exp(\lambda x_1 + \mu x_2) \tag{24}$$

on the rectangle $0 \le x_1 \le 1$, $0 \le x_2 \le 1$ with the following boundary conditions

$$u = \exp(\lambda x_1 + \mu x_2), \quad x_2 = 0 \text{ and } x_2 = 1$$
$$u_1 = \lambda \exp(\lambda x_1 + \mu x_2), \quad x_1 = 0 \text{ and } x_1 = 1 \tag{25}$$

The exact solution is

$$u_e = (x_1, x_2) = \exp(\lambda x_1 + \mu x_2), \tag{26}$$

here λ and μ are chosen to be 2 and 3, respectively. This problem was solved using MQ approximation scheme by Kansa (1990b). The author used a total of 30 nodal points, including 23 scattered points in the interior and

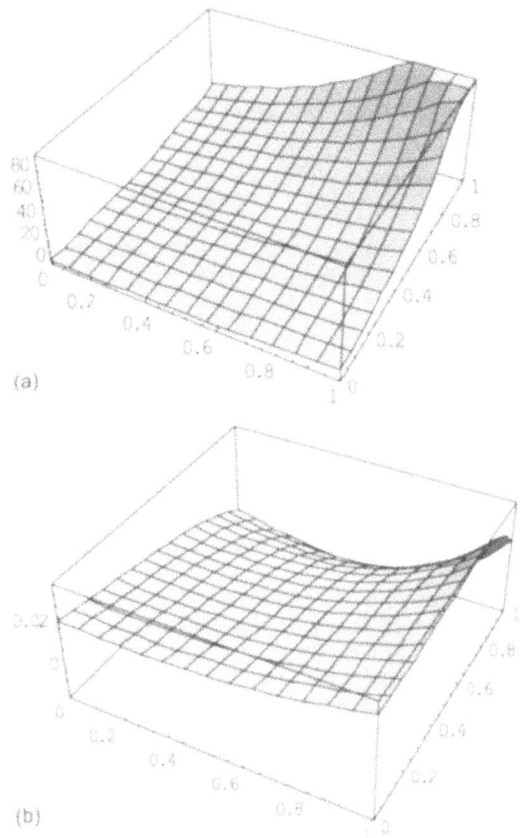

Fig. 2. Net approximation results for the Dirichlet problem of (24), (a) plot of the exact solution, (b) plot of the approximation error curve with 27 RBFs (13 MQ and 14 Gaussian) on 40 data points.

18 along the boundary. The reported results showed that the norm of error is 1.66×10^{-2}. In the present approach, with the configure of 27 nodes and 40 data points, we get a greater accuracy $N_e = 2.2 \times 10^{-4}$. The results are shown in Fig. 2.

5.2. Non-linear second order elliptic PDE

In recent years, many authors have studied the classical solution of the Dirichlet problem in a bounded convex domain Ω in R^n, $n \geq 2$ with smooth boundary $\partial\Omega$:

$$\begin{cases} f(\lambda(D^2u)) = \psi(x,u) & \text{in } \Omega \\ u = \phi(x) & \text{on } \partial\Omega \end{cases}, \qquad (27)$$

where $D^2u = \{u_{ij}\}$ is the Hessian matrix, $\lambda(D^2u)$ are the eigenvalues $\lambda = (\lambda_1, \lambda_2, \ldots, \lambda_n)$ of the Hessian matrix, D^2u, and $f = (\lambda_1, \lambda_2, \ldots, \lambda_n)$ is a smooth symmetric function of $\lambda_1, \lambda_2, \ldots, \lambda_n$. See for instance, Caffarelli, Nirenberg, and Spruck (1987), Cheng and Yau (1977), Lions, Trudinger, and Urbas (1986), and Nell and Trudiger (1995). The equation is assumed to be elliptic for the functions under consideration, i.e.

$$\frac{\partial f}{\partial \lambda_i} > 0, \quad \forall i \qquad (28)$$

and to satisfy

$$f \text{ is a concave function.} \qquad (29)$$

The function f will be required to satisfy other conditions. It is assumed to be defined in an open convex cone $\Gamma \subset R^n$, and $\Gamma \neq R^n$, with vertex at the origin, containing the positive cone:

$$\{\lambda \in R^n | \text{each component } \lambda_i > 0\}. \qquad (30)$$

Eqs. (28)–(30) guarantees the Dirichlet problem has only one solution.

But there are few results of numerical solution. In this work, we are going to study the numerical solution of Monge–Ampere equation which is a special case of Eq. (27).

The Dirirchlet problem for Monge–Appere equation is as follows:

$$\begin{cases} \det D^2u = \varphi & \text{in } \Omega, \\ u = \phi & \text{on } \partial\Omega \end{cases} \qquad (31)$$

where Ω is a bounded convex domain in R^n, $n \geq 2$, D^2u is the Hessian matrix of u and det represents the determination of D^2u.

With the earlier assumptions and explanations, the following problem will be studied.

Table 1
Results for the Dirichlet problem of $\det D^2u = 4$

x	y	Exact	Numerical
0.090431	0.0051258	0.008203	0.068002
0.907687	−0.262936	0.893031	0.811486
−0.49403	0.415965	0.417092	0.460829
0.212206	0.213663	0.090683	0.168499
−0.550199	−0.708161	0.804211	0.72451
0.063556	−0.51718	0.271514	0.335523
0.523413	0.256127	0.339562	0.349226
−0.370998	−0.232061	0.191492	0.309568
−0.606749	−0.562723	0.684801	0.704808
−0.838913	0.171053	0.733034	0.696195
0.158338	−0.218039	0.072612	0.147352
−0.660485	−0.121274	0.450948	0.475388
0.992115	0.125333	1	0.891162
0.637424	0.770513	1	0.904439
0.187381	0.982287	1	1.09248
−0.309017	0.951057	1	1.06037
−0.728969	0.684547	1	1.06959
−0.992115	0.125333	1	1.10944
−0.929776	−0.368125	1	0.904333
−0.535827	−0.844328	1	0.931287
−0.062791	−0.998027	1	0.947677
0.309017	−0.951057	1	0.941198
0.728969	−0.684547	1	0.983203
0.968583	−0.24869	1	1.12118

Example 3.

$$\begin{cases} \det D^2 u = 4 & \text{in } \Omega \\ u = 1 & \text{on } \partial\Omega \end{cases}, \tag{32}$$

where Ω is a unit circular domain. The exact solution is

$$u_e(x_1, x_2) = x_1^2 + x_2^2. \tag{33}$$

It should be pointed out that Eq. (30) is necessary. Without it, Example 3 will have at least another solution

$$u_e(x_1, x_2) = 2 - (x_1^2 + x_2^2). \tag{34}$$

If we study the numerical solution of Eq. (32) satisfying Eqs. (28)–(30), we have to modify the SSE as follows:

$$l = F(w,c,a) = \sum_{i=1}^{n} [\det D^2 u(x^{(i)}) - 4]^2 + \sum_{j=1}^{k} (u(x^{(j)}) - 1)^2 + \omega\left(\sum_{i=1}^{n} [u_{11}(x^{(i)}) - 1]^2 + \sum_{i=1}^{n} [u_{22}(x^{(i)}) - 1]^2\right) \tag{35}$$

where ω ($\omega = 0.01$) is a positive constant and $x^{(i)}$, $x^{(j)}$, $i = 1,\ldots,n, j = 1,\ldots,k$ are, respectively, points inside the domain and on the boundary. Numerical results are displayed in Table 1 with 52 nodes and 110 data points (60 in the domain and 50 on the boundary).

6. Conclusions

In this paper, a new incremental algorithm for growing RBF networks and a two-stage learning strategy for training the net parameters are reported. The novelty of the algorithm has different aspects. First of all, all learning procedure is accomplished by a two-stage gradient method, which not only optimizes the weights of the net, but also optimizes the centers and widths of the Neurons. Moreover, the activation function of the added neuron can be different RBF. The results show that the strategy is better than the algorithm whose neurons are the same RBF type.

The network here allows us to obtain a fast and accurate reconstruction of some solutions of DEs starting from randomly sampled data sets. The incremental architecture allows us to achieve good approximation results without wasting memory space (only a few neurons are needed) and computational time. This is due to the ability of the net to save training time by selectively growing the net structure and by keeping the action of the different activation functions localized.

A comparison to other incremental algorithms reported in literature has showed that the learning strategy proposed here is able to achieve better performance (compared to other approaches) both in terms of net size and computational time.

It should be pointed out that there is no mathematical theory to guarantee which RBF type should be chosen when adding a new node. The proper choice of such functions requires some skill and experience on the user's side. Further developments of the present algorithm and their application in numerical solutions of DEs are under way and the results will be reported in future (Definitions).

Acknowledgements

This work is supported by the Chinese Natural science fund (Grant No. 69973002).

References

Caffarelli, L., Nirenberg, L., & Spruck, J. (1987). The Dirichlet problem for non-linear second order elliptic equations (1): Monge–Ampere equations. *Communication on Pure and Applied Mathematics, 37*, 369–402.

Cheng, S. Y., & Yau, S. Y. (1977). On the regularity of the Monge–Ampere equation. *Communication on Pure and Applied Mathematics, 30*, 41–68.

Esposito, A., Marinaro, M., Oricchio, D., & Scarpetta, S. (2000). Approximation of continuous and discontinuous mappings by a growing neural RBF-based algorithm. *Neural Networks, 13*, 651–665.

Franke, C., & Schaback, R. (1997). Convergence orders of meshless collocation methods using radial basis functions. *Advances in Computational Mathematics, 8*(4), 381–399.

Franke, C., & Schaback, R. (1998). Solving partial differential equations by collocation using radial basis functions. *Applied Mathematics and Computation, 93*(1), 73–82.

Hughes, T. J. R. (1987). *The finite element method.* New Jersey: Prentice Hall.

Jianyu, L., Siwei, L., & Yingjian, Q. (2002). Interactive gradient algorithm for radial basis function networks. *The Sixth International Conference on Signal Processing*, 1187–1190.

Kansa, E. J. (1990a). Multi-quadrics—a scattered data approximation scheme with applications to computational fluid dynamics—II. *Computers in Mathematical Applications, 19*(8/9), 127–145.

Kansa, E. J. (1990b). Multi-quadrics—a scattered data approximation scheme with applications to computational fluid dynamics—II. *Computers in Mathematical Applications, 19*(8/9), 147–161.

Lions, P.-L., Trudinger, N. S., & Urbas, J. I. E. (1986). The Neumann problem for equations of Monge–Ampere type. *Communication on Pure and Applied Mathematics, XXXIX*, 539–563.

Madych, W. R., & Nelson, S. A. (1990). Multi-variable interpolation and conditionally positive definite functions-II. *Mathematical Computations, 54*, 211–230.

Mai-Duy, N., & Tran-Cong, T. (2001). Numerical solution of differential equations using multi-quadric radial basis function networks. *Neural Networks, 14*, 185–199.

Powell, M. J. D. (1994). The uniform convergence of TPS interpolation in two dimensions. *Numerische Mathematik, 68*(1), 107–128.

Smith, G. D. (1978). *Numerical solution of partial differential equations: Finite difference methods.* Oxford: Clarendon Press.

Stead, S. (1984). Estimation of gradients from scattered data. *Rocky Mountain Journal of Mathematics, 14*, 265–279.

Trudiger, N. (1995). On the Dirichlet problem for Hessian equations. *Acta Mathematica, 175*, 151–164.

Wendland, H. (1999). Meshless Galerkin methods using radial basis functions. *Mathematical Computations, 68*(228), 1521–1531.

Wu, Z. (1998). In Z. Chen, C. A. Micchelli, & Y. Xu (Eds.), *Advances in computational mathematics: Guangzhou* (pp. 202*Lectures notes on pure and applied mathematics*, New York: Marcel Dekker.

Wu, Z., & Schaback, R. (1994). Shape preserving properties and convergence of univariate multi-quadic quasi-interpolation. *Acta Mathematice Applicatae Sinica, 10*(4), 441–446.

PERGAMON

AVAILABLE AT
www.ComputerScienceWeb.com
POWERED BY SCIENCE DIRECT

Neural Networks 16 (2003) 735–744

Neural Networks

www.elsevier.com/locate/neunet

2003 Special issue

Statistical efficiency of adaptive algorithms

Bernard Widrow*, Max Kamenetsky

ISL, Department of Electrical Engineering, Stanford University, Rm. 273, Packard Electrical Bldg. 350 Serra Mall, Stanford, CA 94305, USA

Abstract

The statistical efficiency of a learning algorithm applied to the adaptation of a given set of variable weights is defined as the ratio of the quality of the converged solution to the amount of data used in training the weights. Statistical efficiency is computed by averaging over an ensemble of learning experiences. A high quality solution is very close to optimal, while a low quality solution corresponds to noisy weights and less than optimal performance.

In this work, two gradient descent adaptive algorithms are compared, the LMS algorithm and the LMS/Newton algorithm. LMS is simple and practical, and is used in many applications worldwide. LMS/Newton is based on Newton's method and the LMS algorithm. LMS/Newton is optimal in the least squares sense. It maximizes the quality of its adaptive solution while minimizing the use of training data. Many least squares adaptive algorithms have been devised over the years, but no other least squares algorithm can give better performance, on average, than LMS/Newton.

LMS is easily implemented, but LMS/Newton, although of great mathematical interest, cannot be implemented in most practical applications. Because of its optimality, LMS/Newton serves as a benchmark for all least squares adaptive algorithms. The performances of LMS and LMS/Newton are compared, and it is found that under many circumstances, both algorithms provide equal performance. For example, when both algorithms are tested with statistically nonstationary input signals, their average performances are equal. When adapting with stationary input signals and with random initial conditions, their respective learning times are on average equal. However, under worst-case initial conditions, the learning time of LMS can be much greater than that of LMS/Newton, and this is the principal disadvantage of the LMS algorithm. But the strong points of LMS are ease of implementation and optimal performance under important practical conditions. For these reasons, the LMS algorithm has enjoyed very widespread application. It is used in almost every modem for channel equalization and echo cancelling. Furthermore, it is related to the famous backpropagation algorithm used for training neural networks.

Keywords: LMS; Newton algorithm; Least squares; Efficiency

1. Introduction

Learning systems take on many forms. Of special interest here are the adaptive linear combiner of Fig. 1 and the adaptive transversal filter of Fig. 2. The linear combiner is the basic building block of almost all neural networks and adaptive filters. The linear combiner and the adaptive filter have found very wide application in practice (Widrow, Mantey, Griffiths, & Goode, 1967; Widrow, Glover, McCool, Kaunitz, Williams, Hearn, Zeidler, Dong & Goodlin, 1975; Widrow & Stearns, 1985; Widrow & Walach, 1996; Ghogho, Ibnkahla, & Bershad, 1998; Proakis, 2001). For example, the present-day Internet would not exist without adaptive filters in every modem.

A learning system is generally characterized as an operator on signals, images, sounds, etc. that has adjustable parameters and that has a mechanism, an adaptive algorithm, for automatically adjusting the parameters in order to optimize the operator's performance. The adjustable parameters in Figs. 1 and 2 are adjustable weights, indicated by circles with arrows through them. The input signals are stochastic, and information obtained from the inputs is used by the adaptive algorithm to adjust the weights. The algorithm is thus a consumer of data. An efficient algorithm minimizes the usage of data while maximizing the quality of the solution, i.e. achieving parameter adjustments close to optimum. Minimizing data usage and maximizing solution quality are generally antagonistic. Minimizing data usage corresponds to fast adaptive convergence. But fast convergence based on a small amount of data could lead to a solution of poor quality. This tradeoff is present in all learning systems.

* Corresponding author.

E-mail addresses: widrow@stanford.edu (B. Widrow); maxk@stanford.edu (M. Kamenetsky).

0893-6080/03/$ - see front matter © 2003 Elsevier Science Ltd. All rights reserved.
doi:10.1016/S0893-6080(03)00126-6

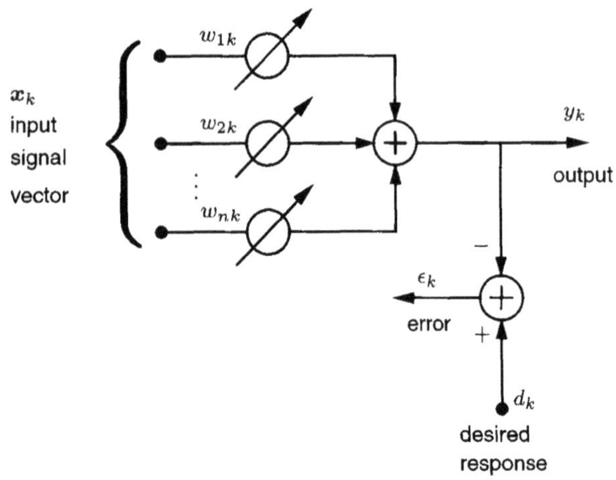

Fig. 1. Adaptive linear combiner.

2. The LMS and LMS/Newton algorithms

When referring to the linear combiner of Fig. 1, the set of weights is designated by the weight vector

$$w_k = \begin{bmatrix} w_{1k} \\ w_{2k} \\ \vdots \\ w_{nk} \end{bmatrix}, \tag{1}$$

and the set of input signals to the weights is the input vector

$$x_k = \begin{bmatrix} x_{1k} \\ x_{2k} \\ \vdots \\ x_{nk} \end{bmatrix}. \tag{2}$$

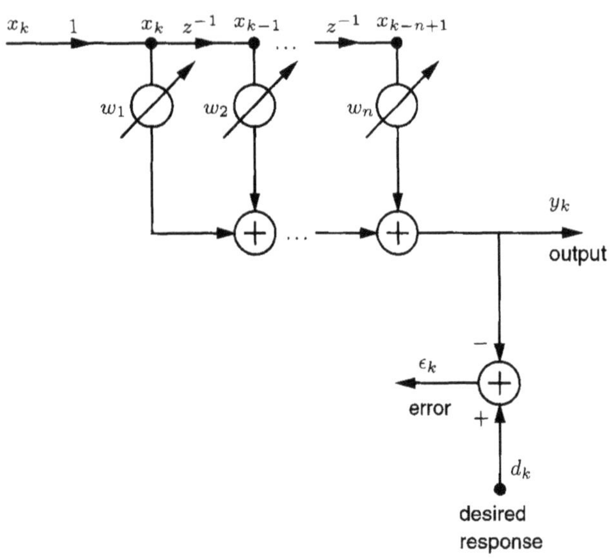

Fig. 2. Adaptive transversal digital filter.

The output signal y_k is the inner product of x_k and w_k :

$$y_k = x_k^T w_k = w_k^T x_k. \tag{3}$$

The subscripts k are a time index.

The desired response d_k is an input training signal that is obtained in practice from the physical context of the application. Many examples of how desired responses may be obtained are shown in Widrow and Stearns (1985) for a variety of practical applications, such as prediction, noise cancelling, sensor array processing, and so forth. The error signal in Fig. 1 is ϵ_k, the difference between the desired response and the actual output signal:

$$\epsilon_k = d_k - y_k. \tag{4}$$

Certain statistical properties of the inputs to the linear combiner are of importance. Assuming that the input and the desired response are stationary, the input autocorrelation matrix, designated by $\mathbf{R}$, is defined as

$$\mathbf{R} \triangleq E[\mathbf{x}_k \mathbf{x}_k^T], \tag{5}$$

and the crosscorrelation vector between the input $\mathbf{x}_k$ and the desired response d_k is defined as

$$\mathbf{p} \triangleq E[d_k \mathbf{x}_k]. \tag{6}$$

For a given weight vector, with stationary input $\mathbf{x}_k$ and desired response d_k flowing into the linear combiner, the mean square error (MSE) is

$$\xi \triangleq E[\epsilon_k^2] = E[d_k^2] - 2\mathbf{p}^T w + w^T \mathbf{R} \mathbf{w}, \tag{7}$$

where we dropped the subscript k from the vector w because we do not yet wish to adjust the weights. The MSE is thus a quadratic function of the weights. If there were only two weights, the MSE could be plotted as in Fig. 3.

With many weights, the surface, known as the performance surface, is a hyperparaboloid. The gradient of this

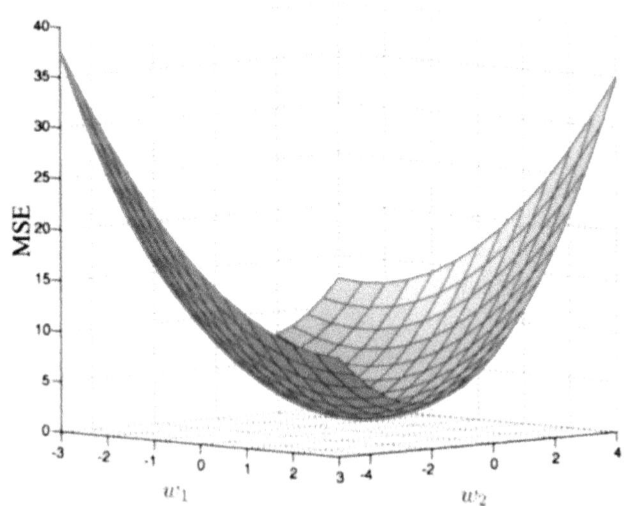

Fig. 3. Sample MSE for a two-weight system.

surface, is a vector obtained by differentiation of Eq. (7):

$$\nabla \triangleq \begin{bmatrix} \frac{\partial \xi}{\partial w_1} \\ \vdots \\ \frac{\partial \xi}{\partial w_n} \end{bmatrix} = -2\mathbf{p} + 2\mathbf{R}\mathbf{w}. \tag{8}$$

Assuming R is not singular, the optimal solution w^* is found by setting the gradient to zero:

$$w^* = \mathbf{R}^{-1}\mathbf{p}. \tag{9}$$

This weight vector is the best linear least squares solution and is commonly known as the Wiener solution. The MSE corresponding to the Wiener solution is designated by ξ_{min}.

The Wiener solution is of great theoretical interest, but it cannot be used directly in many practical circumstances because one would not know the statistics $\mathbf{R}$ and $\mathbf{p}$. Input data samples are available, and they can be used on an iterative basis as they arrive for the adjustment or adaptation of the weights. The weight adjustment process that is the simplest and most widely used in the world today is the Widrow-Hoff LMS algorithm, derived in 1959 (Widrow & Hoff, 1960). This algorithm is based on the method of steepest descent, using instantaneous gradients. It is interesting to note that the backpropagation algorithm of Werbos (1974) also utilizes the method of steepest descent using instantaneous gradients in adapting the weights of a neural network. Backpropagation is a remarkable generalization of the LMS algorithm. It is the most widely used algorithm for adapting neural networks.

Steepest descent can be written as

$$w_{k+1} = w_k + \mu(-\nabla_k). \tag{10}$$

The next weight vector, w_{k+1}, equals the present weight vector, w_k, plus a change which is proportional to the negative gradient. The proportionality constant is μ, and this is a design parameter that controls stability and rate of convergence. The LMS algorithm is obtained from Eqs. (10) and (4) as

$$\begin{cases} w_{k+1} = w_k + 2\mu\epsilon_k\mathbf{x}_k, \\ \epsilon_k = d_k - x_k^{\mathrm{T}} w_k. \end{cases} \tag{11}$$

The gradient for each iteration is instantaneous and is given by $-2\epsilon_k\mathbf{x}_k$, as shown in Widrow and Stearns (1985).

When using steepest descent to find the minimum of a quadratic function of the weights, the weights progress geometrically toward the Wiener solution. In fact, each weight converges toward its Wiener value with a progression that is a sum of geometric progressions. Each of the geometric progressions has an individual 'time constant' (the unit of time is the iteration cycle). It has been shown (Widrow & Stearns, 1985) that there are as many distinct time constants as there are distinct eigenvalues of the $\mathbf{R}$ matrix. These time constants depend on the eigenvalues of $\mathbf{R}$ and correspond to natural modes of the adaptive algorithm. The relative amplitudes of the modes are different from one weight to another and depend on the initial conditions of the weight vector, i.e. its initial setting.

Since one rarely has a priori knowledge of the orientation of the initial weight vector setting with respect to the eigenvectors of the $\mathbf{R}$ matrix, it is difficult to predict the relative amplitudes of the modes and therefore difficult to predict the rate of convergence of the LMS algorithm. In spite of this drawback, LMS is very widely used.

A more predictable algorithm is Newton's method. Assuming that $\mathbf{R}$ is not singular, it can be written as

$$w_{k+1} = w_k + \mu\lambda_{\text{ave}}\mathbf{R}^{-1}(\nabla_k). \tag{12}$$

Here, the negative gradient is premultiplied by $\mu\lambda_{\text{ave}}\mathbf{R}^{-1}$, where λ_{ave} is the average of the eigenvalues of $\mathbf{R}$. Based on Eq. (12) and using the instantaneous gradient $-2\epsilon_k\mathbf{x}_k$, the LMS/Newton algorithm can be written as

$$\begin{cases} w_{k+1} = w_k + 2\mu\lambda_{\text{ave}}\mathbf{R}^{-1}\epsilon_k\mathbf{x}_k, \\ \epsilon_k = d_k - \mathbf{x}_k^{\mathrm{T}} w_k. \end{cases} \tag{13}$$

With Newton's method, there is only one natural mode, corresponding to one time constant. The learning rate of Newton's method is independent of the weight vector's initial conditions. It is interesting to note that Eq. (13) is identical to Eq. (11) when all of the eigenvalues of $\mathbf{R}$ are equal.

So, the good news about LMS/Newton is that its rate of convergence is predictable and does not depend on initial conditions. The bad news is that one cannot implement this algorithm in practice because $\mathbf{R}^{-1}$ is generally unknown. LMS, based on steepest descent, has disadvantages, but it is simple and easy to implement. Also, as will be shown, it performs equivalently to LMS/Newton under many important conditions.

3. Learning with a finite set of data samples

The LMS/Newton algorithm is not only very predictable in its convergence behavior, but it is also highly efficient in its use of input data. It will be shown that in the least squares sense, no other algorithm can be more efficient in its data usage than LMS/Newton.

In order to study the question of efficiency for the LMS/Newton algorithm, it is useful to contemplate training the linear combiner with a finite number of data samples. One data sample consists of an $\mathbf{x}$ vector and its associated desired response. Assume that a set of N training input samples and associated desired responses is drawn from a given distribution. Define a matrix $\mathbf{X}$ for these training samples as the set of N $\mathbf{x}$-vectors:

$$X \triangleq [x_1 \quad x_2 \quad \ldots \quad x_N]^{\mathrm{T}}. \tag{14}$$

Define a desired response vector for these samples as

$$\mathbf{d} \triangleq [d_1 \quad d_2 \quad \dots \quad d_N]^{\mathrm{T}}. \tag{15}$$

For a given weight vector w, the set of output responses is

$$\mathbf{y} \triangleq [y_1 \quad y_2 \quad \dots \quad y_N]^{\mathrm{T}} = \mathbf{X}\mathbf{w}. \tag{16}$$

Define an error vector for these samples as

$$\boldsymbol{\epsilon} \triangleq [\epsilon_1 \quad \epsilon_2 \quad \dots \quad \epsilon_N]^{\mathrm{T}} = \mathbf{d} - \mathbf{y}. \tag{17}$$

The objective is to find a set of weights that will minimize the sum of the squares of the errors for the training sample, i.e. minimize $\boldsymbol{\epsilon}^{\mathrm{T}}\boldsymbol{\epsilon}$. Assuming $\mathbf{X}$ is full rank, one obtains the optimal least squares solution either by differentiating $\boldsymbol{\epsilon}^{\mathrm{T}}\boldsymbol{\epsilon}$ with respect to $\boldsymbol{w}$ and setting the result to zero or by invoking the orthogonality condition (Kailath, Sayed, & Hassibi, 2000; Widrow & Stearns, 1985). The resulting least squares solution is

$$w_{\mathrm{LS}} = (\mathbf{X}^{\mathrm{T}}\mathbf{X})^{-1}\mathbf{X}^{\mathrm{T}}\mathbf{d}. \tag{18}$$

One could directly calculate this solution from the data, or the same result could be obtained by training the weights with the LMS algorithm or any other least squares algorithm, recirculating the training data over and over until the weights converge and stabilize. It should be noted that if the number N were increased without bound, the finite least squares solution of Eq. (18) would converge in the mean-square sense to the true Wiener solution for the given distribution of training samples and desired responses.

In practice, one would have only a finite number of data samples available for training. The question is, given N training samples, how well does the optimal solution of Eq. (18) perform compared to the Wiener solution when operating on an infinite set of samples drawn from the same distribution? The true Wiener solution yields the minimum MSE. The least squares solution based on N training samples produces more MSE than the true Wiener solution. There is an excess MSE. If a different set of N data samples were randomly selected from the same distribution, a different optimal solution (18) would result, with a different excess MSE. Given an ensemble of randomly selected data sets, each with N samples of data, there would be an ensemble of optimal solutions (18) with an ensemble of excess MSEs. One could take an ensemble average of the excess MSEs and normalize with respect to the minimum MSE of the true Wiener solution. This dimensionless ratio is called the misadjustment due to training with N data samples:

$$M \triangleq \frac{\text{(average excess MSE)}}{\text{(minimum MSE)}} = \frac{\text{(number of weights)}}{\text{(number of training samples)}} = \frac{n}{N}. \tag{19}$$

A derivation of this result is given in Widrow and Kamenetsky (2003) and Widrow, McCool, Larimore, and Johnson (1976). It was first reported by Widrow and Hoff at a WESCON conference in 1960 (Widrow & Hoff, 1960). Years of experience with adaptive filters and neural networks lead one to accept a misadjustment of 10% as a reasonable design value. This gives a performance that is only 10% worse than that of the optimal Wiener solution. When training a linear combiner, a 10% misadjustment is obtained when the number of training samples is equal to 10 times the number of weights. When training a neural network having only one neuron, the number of training patterns would be equal to 10 times the number of weights. When training an adaptive filter with a steady flow of stationary input data, the parameter μ should be chosen so that the training time or convergence time (several time constants of the learning curve) would be equal to 10 times the length of its impulse response in order to have a misadjustment of 10%. There is no similar law for multilayered neural networks trained with backpropagation, but one may speculate that for a network with many inputs and a single output, regardless of the number of neurons and layers, training with a number of patterns equal to 10 times the number of inputs should give good performance.

4. Learning with LMS/Newton

Consider the linear combiner, with stationary input data flowing in real time. Starting from an initial (non-optimal) weight vector and adapting with the LMS/Newton algorithm, the weight vector will geometrically (exponentially) relax toward the Wiener solution, with noise superposed. The noise originates from adapting with instantaneous gradients. (Estimating the gradient with a single data sample produces a noisy gradient). As the weights relax toward the Wiener solution, the MSE also relaxes exponentially toward the level of the minimum mean square error $\xi_{\min}$, with noise superposed. Because of gradient noise, the weights do not converge on the Wiener solution, but undergo Brownian motion about it. The MSE is almost always greater than $\xi_{\min}$ and never goes below it, because of the noise in the weights while adapting. A plot of MSE versus number of iterations is shown in Fig. 4, where ξ_{asy} is the asymptotic MSE, and ξ_{excess} is the difference between it and the minimum MSE $\xi_{\min}$. This type of plot is called the 'learning curve'. Note that, in general, $\xi_{\mathrm{excess}} > 0$ because the misadjustment is not zero, and thus, the asymptotic MSE ξ_{asy} is greater than $\xi_{\min}$, which is reflected in Fig. 4.

After gross adaptive transients have died out (after about four exponential time constants), the weights are in a steady state Brownian motion and the MSE hovers randomly above $\xi_{\min}$, exhibiting 'excess mean square error'. The misadjustment for this situation is defined as the average of the excess mean square error divided by $\xi_{\min}$:

$$M \triangleq \frac{\text{(average excess MSE)}}{\text{(minimum MSE)}}. \tag{20}$$

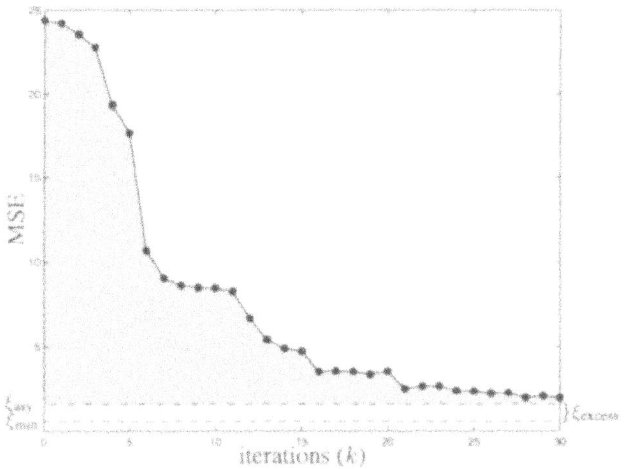

Fig. 4. Sample learning curve with gradient noise.

The bigger one makes μ, the faster the algorithm converges, and the greater is the misadjustment. It has been shown (Widrow & Kamenetsky, 2003; Widrow & Stearns, 1985; Widrow & Walach, 1984) that a good approximation for the misadjustment is

$$M = \mu \mathrm{Tr}(\boldsymbol{R}) = \frac{n}{4\tau_{\mathrm{MSE}}}, \tag{21}$$

where Tr(**R**) is the trace of **R**, and τ_{MSE} is the time constant of the mean square error learning curve. The unit of time is the iteration cycle. Time is marked by number of iteration cycles, and since a new input training sample is used with each iteration cycle, time can equivalently be marked by number of training samples used.

5. Optimality of LMS/Newton in a stationary environment

The LMS/Newton algorithm exponentially weights its input data over time as it establishes its weight values. The settling time of the adaptive process is of the order of four time constants of the MSE learning curve. At any moment, the weights are determined by adaptation that has taken place over essentially the last four time constants worth of data. Thus, in a steady flow situation, the training data 'consumed' or 'absorbed' at any time by the LMS/Newton algorithm is essentially comprised of the most recent $4\tau_{\mathrm{MSE}}$ samples. From Eq. (21), the misadjustment of the LMS/Newton algorithm can therefore be expressed as

$$M = \frac{n}{4\tau_{\mathrm{MSE}}} = \frac{\text{(number of weights)}}{\text{(number of independent training samples)}}. \tag{22}$$

When learning with a finite set of data samples, the optimal weight vector is the best least squares solution for that set of samples, and it is often called the 'exact least squares solution'. This solution, given by Eq. (18), makes the best use of the finite number of data samples, in the least squares sense. All of the data are weighted equally in affecting the solution. This solution will of course vary from one set of samples to another, and it has a misadjustment of

$$M = \frac{\text{(number of weights)}}{\text{(number of independent training samples)}}. \tag{23}$$

For the same consumption of data, it is apparent that LMS/Newton and exact least squares yield the same misadjustment. Although we are comparing 'apples with oranges' by comparing a steady flow algorithm with an algorithm that learns with a finite number of data samples, we nevertheless find that LMS/Newton is as efficient as exact least squares when we relate the quality of the weight-vector solution to the amount of data used in obtaining it. Since the exact least squares solution makes optimal use of the data, so does LMS/Newton.

6. Transient learning with stationary input data

The LMS/Newton algorithm makes optimal use of its training data. Its learning curve is exponential with a single time constant. For practical purposes, its convergence time is of the order of four time constants, although in principle, convergence would take forever. Fast convergence is desirable because, during the initial learning transient, the MSE is excessive. The LMS algorithm has a learning curve which is a sum of exponentials. But, when all of the eigenvalues of the **R** matrix are equal, LMS has a single exponential learning curve that is identical to that of LMS/Newton; and LMS is therefore optimal. Generally, the eigenvalues are not equal, and LMS has a different kind of learning curve than LMS/Newton.

After learning transients die out, the steady state misadjustment for LMS/Newton is

$$M = \mu \mathrm{Tr}(\mathbf{R}), \tag{24}$$

and the steady state misadjustment for LMS is

$$M = \mu \mathrm{Tr}(\mathbf{R}). \tag{25}$$

The derivations of Eqs. (24) and (25) are given in Widrow and Kamenetsky (2003) and Widrow and Stearns (1985).

These misadjustment formulas are approximations of the true misadjustment. It should be noted that more precise formulas for misadjustment have been derived by, among others, Butterweck (2001), Dabeer and Masry (2002), Widrow and Walach (1996, App. A), and Yousef and Sayed (2001). However, the formulas in Eqs. (24) and (25) have been used for many years and have proven to be excellent approximations for small values of M (less than 25%).

A fair and reasonable way to compare two algorithms is to adjust their rates of convergence so that they would have the same steady state misadjustment. One could always make an algorithm 'look good' with fast adaptation, but this causes excessive misadjustment. To compare LMS with LMS/Newton, their μ-parameters should be set to the same value.

Fig. 5 shows plan views of a quadratic MSE surface, Fig. 5(a) indicating adaptive steps for Newton's method and Fig. 5(b) showing corresponding steps for the method of steepest descent with equivalent initial conditions. These steps correspond to three adaptive transient experiments, each starting from a different point on the same contour of constant MSE and operating with the same value of μ. The steps using Newton's method are always directed toward the bottom of the quadratic bowl, whereas those of steepest descent follow the local gradient, orthogonal to the contours of constant MSE.

Fig. 6 shows learning curves corresponding to the adaptive steps illustrated in Fig. 5. All three learning curves derived from Newton's method are identical, since the initial starting conditions are located on the same constant MSE contour, and all three time constants are the same. Fig. 6 shows all three learning curves as a single curve labeled 'Newton's method'. The three steepest descent curves are distinct, having individual time constants. The curves corresponding to initial conditions falling on an eigenvector (a principal axis of the elliptical contours) are pure exponentials, whereas the curve corresponding to the initial condition between the eigenvectors is a sum of two exponentials.

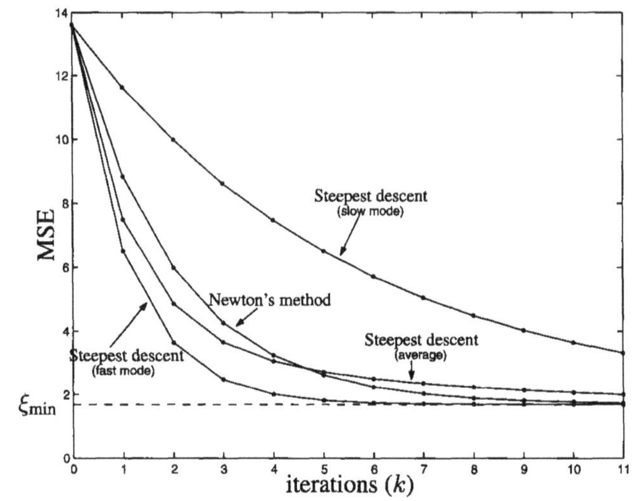

Fig. 6. Steepest descent and Newton's method learning curves.

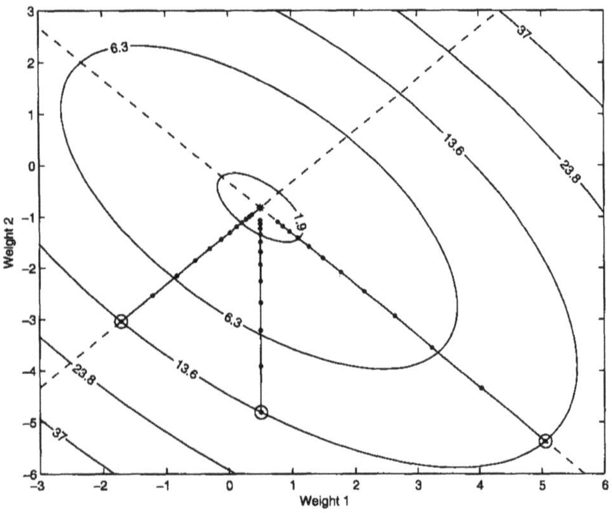

(a)

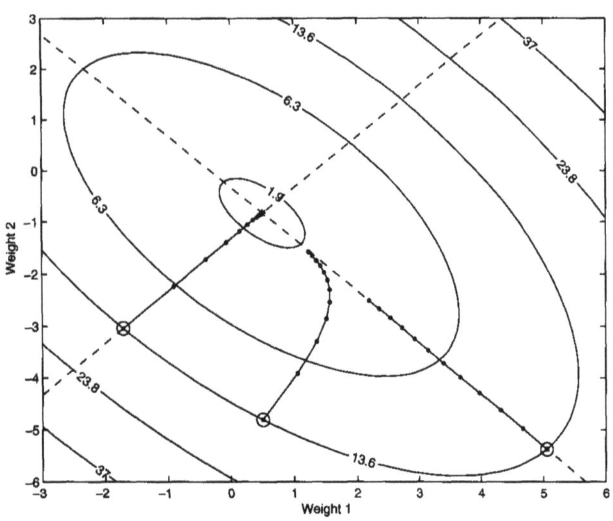

(b)

Fig. 5. Illustration of Newton's method versus steepest descent: (a) Newton's method, (b) steepest descent. The Wiener solution is indicated by $*$. The three initial conditions are indicated by O.

Which algorithm converges faster? For some initial conditions, LMS converges faster than LMS/Newton. For other initial conditions, LMS is slower than LMS/Newton. Yet for other initial conditions, LMS has multiple modes, some faster than LMS/Newton and some slower than it. The question is: which is faster, LMS or LMS/Newton?

7. Excess error energy

The question 'which is faster' prompts a new look at the learning curve and at the issue of learning time. Regarding the learning curves of Fig. 7, it is clear that during the transient, the MSE is excessive. One strives to reduce this MSE to ξ_{min} as fast as possible. The area under the curve and above ξ_{min}, the shaded area, is defined as the excess error energy. This area is a sum of MSE over time. One would like this area to be as small as possible.

The learning curve shown in Fig. 7(a) is an exponential having a single time constant. The area under this curve, the excess error energy, is equal to the amplitude of the exponential (its initial excess MSE) multiplied by the time constant. The learning time for this curve may be considered to be four time constants. This is somewhat arbitrary, but reasonable. Accordingly, the learning time for the single

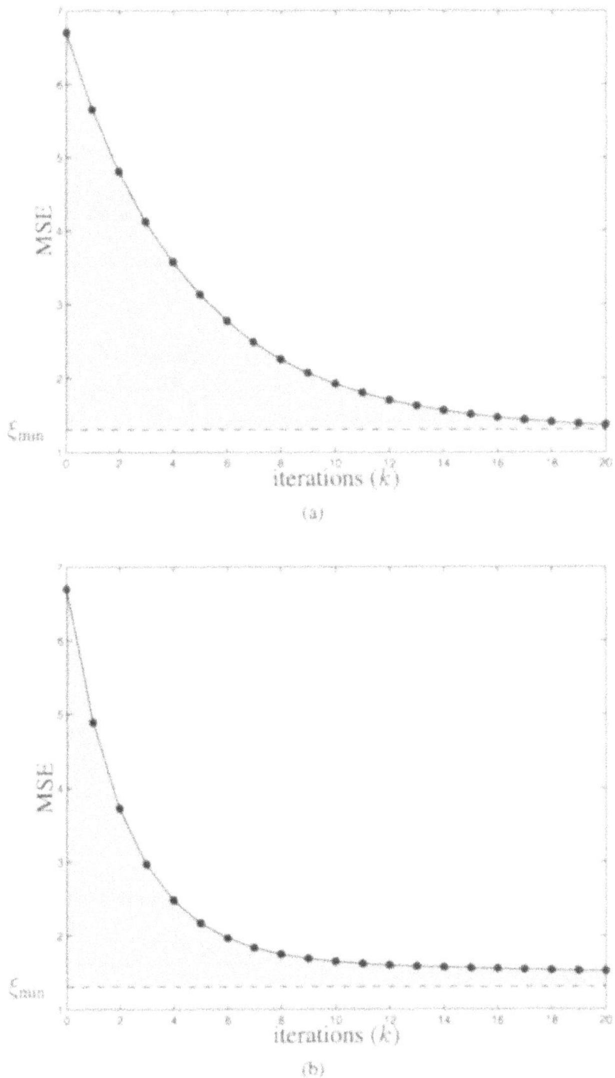

Fig. 7. Idealized learning curves (no gradient noise): (a) single-exponential, (b) two-exponential. The shaded area represents the excess error energy.

exponential is defined as

$$(\text{learning time}) \triangleq 4 \times \frac{(\text{excess error energy})}{(\text{initial excess MSE})}. \tag{26}$$

The learning curve shown in Fig. 7(b) is a sum of two exponentials. Its excess error energy is the same as that of the single exponential learning curve of Fig. 7(a), and the initial excess MSE of both curves is the same. The learning times of both curves are therefore the same and are both given by Eq. (26). In general, the learning time of a learning curve which is a sum of any number of exponentials will be defined hereby as given by Eq. (26). Starting from the same initial MSE, the convergence times of two different learning curves are defined as being identical if their respective excess error energies are equal. Excess error energy is proportional to learning time as it is defined here.

The question remains, which has the greater learning time, LMS or LMS/Newton? Referring to Fig. 6, one can see that LMS/Newton has a fixed learning time, but the learning time of LMS depends on initial conditions. Sometimes LMS is faster than LMS/Newton, sometimes slower. Under worst-case initial conditions, LMS can have a much greater learning time than LMS/Newton. However, it has been shown (Widrow & Kamenetsky, 2003) that with random initial conditions, the average learning time with LMS is identical to the unique learning time of LMS/Newton. LMS/Newton is optimal and its performance is the benchmark. It is important to realize that the average performance of LMS is identical to that of LMS/Newton, when comparing both algorithms starting from the same randomly chosen initial conditions. One must be careful to note that this does *not* mean that the learning curves of LMS and LMS/Newton are identical, even when averaged over initial conditions. On the contrary, it can be shown that the average initial convergence of LMS is faster than that of LMS/Newton, whereas the average final convergence of LMS is slower than that of LMS/Newton (Widrow & Kamenetsky, 2003). However, their average learning times and average excess error energies are the same.

8. LMS and LMS/Newton in a nonstationary environment

With statistically stationary inputs, the quadratic performance surface is fixed, and the Wiener solution is fixed. With nonstationary inputs, this surface changes randomly, and the Wiener solution is not fixed but is a randomly moving target. There is an analogy between, on the one hand, transient adaptation from an ensemble of random initial conditions toward a fixed Wiener target and, on the other hand, steady state adaptation toward a randomly moving Wiener target. In this section, a comparison is made of the performances of the LMS algorithm and the LMS/Newton algorithm when adapting with nonstationary inputs of a simple form.

Filtering nonstationary signals is a major area of application for adaptive systems. When the statistical character of an input signal changes gradually, randomly, and unpredictably, a filtering system that can automatically optimize its input-output response in accord with the requirements of the input signal could yield superior performance relative to that of a fixed, non-adaptive system. The performance of the conventional steepest descent LMS algorithm is compared here with LMS/Newton (which, as demonstrated above, possesses optimality qualities), when both algorithms are used to adapt transversal filters with nonstationary inputs. The nonstationary situations to be studied are highly simplified, but they retain the essence of the problem that is common to more complicated and realistic situations.

The example considered here involves modeling or identifying an unknown time-varying system by an adaptive LMS transversal filter of length n. The unknown system is

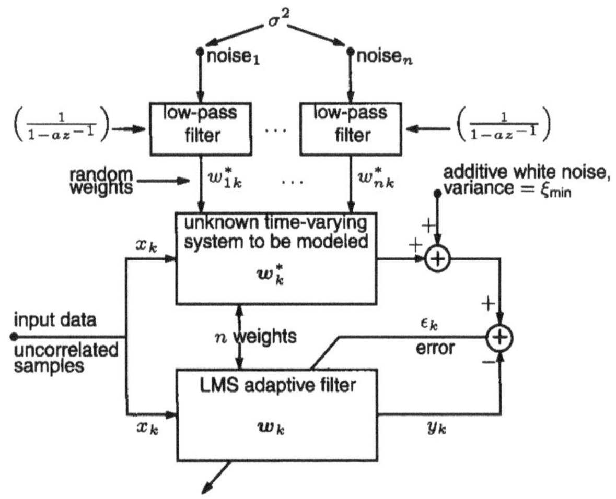

Fig. 8. Modeling an unknown time-varying system.

assumed to be a transversal filter of the same length n whose weights (impulse response values) vary as independent stationary ergodic first-order Markov processes, as indicated in Fig. 8. The input signal x_k is assumed to be stationary and ergodic. Additive output noise, assumed to be stationary and ergodic, of mean zero and of variance $\xi_{\min}$, prevents a perfect match between the unknown system and the adaptive system. The minimum MSE is, therefore, $\xi_{\min}$, and it is achieved whenever the weights of the adaptive filter, $\mathbf{w}_k$, match those of the unknown system. The latter are at every instant the optimal values for the corresponding weights of the adaptive filter and are designated as $\mathbf{w}_k^*$, the time index indicating that the unknown 'target' to be tracked is time-varying.

The components of $\mathbf{w}_k^*$ are generated by passing independent white noises of variance σ^2 through identical one-pole low-pass filters. The components of $\mathbf{w}_k^*$ therefore vary as independent first-order Markov processes. The formation of $\mathbf{w}_k^*$ is illustrated in Figs. 8 and 9.

According to the scheme of Fig. 8, minimizing the MSE causes the adaptive weight vector $\mathbf{w}_k$ to attempt to best match the unknown $\mathbf{w}_k^*$ on a continual basis. The **R** matrix, dependent only on the statistics of $\mathbf{x}_k$, is constant even as $\mathbf{w}_k^*$ varies.

The desired response of the adaptive filter, d_k, is nonstationary, being the output of a time-varying system. The minimum MSE, $\xi_{\min}$, is constant. Thus the MSE function, a quadratic bowl, varies in position while its eigenvalues, eigenvectors, and $\xi_{\min}$ remain constant.

In order to study this form of nonstationary adaptation both analytically and by computer simulation, a model comprising an ensemble of nonstationary adaptive processes has been defined and constructed as illustrated in Fig. 9. Throughout the ensemble, the unknown filters to be modeled are all identical and have the same time-varying weight vector $\mathbf{w}_k^*$. Each ensemble member has its own independent input signal going to both the unknown system

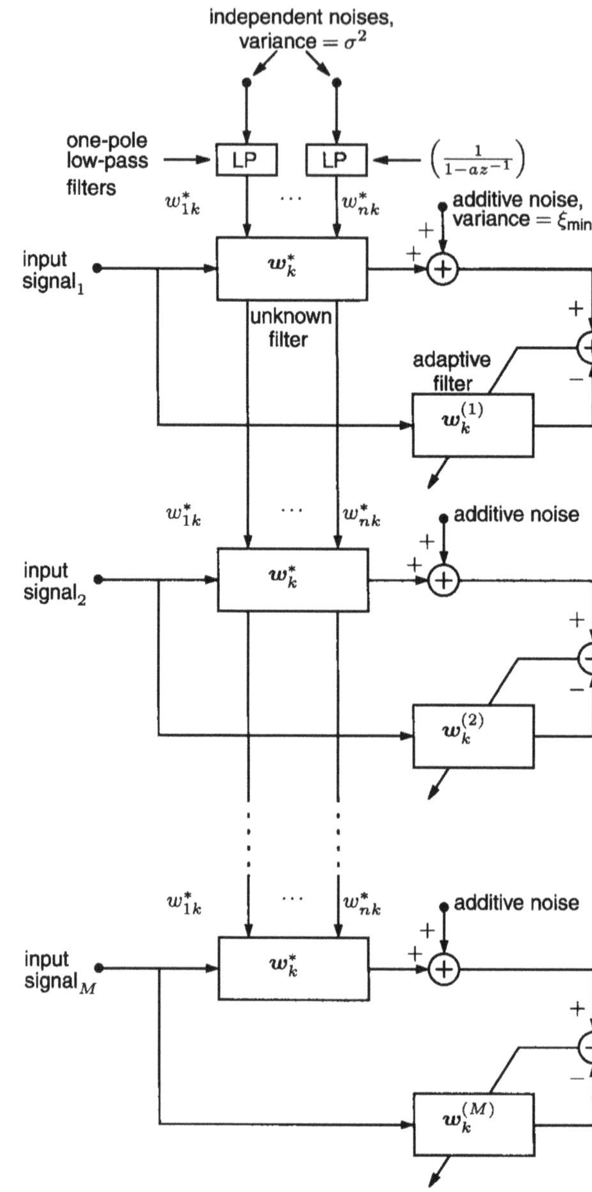

Fig. 9. An ensemble of nonstationary adaptive processes.

and the corresponding adaptive system. The effect of output noise in the unknown systems is obtained by the addition of independent noises of variance $\xi_{\min}$. All of the adaptive filters are assumed to start with the same initial weight vector $\mathbf{w}_0$; each develops its own weight vector over time in attempting to pursue the moving Markovian target $\mathbf{w}_k^*$.

For a given adaptive filter, the weight-vector tracking error at the kth instant is $\mathbf{v}_k \triangleq \mathbf{w}_k - \mathbf{w}_k^*$. This error is due to both the effects of gradient noise and weight-vector lag and may be expressed as

$$\mathbf{v}_k = \mathbf{w}_k - \mathbf{w}_k^* = \underbrace{(\mathbf{w}_k - E[\mathbf{w}_k])}_{\text{weight-vector noise}} + \underbrace{(E[\mathbf{w}_k] - \mathbf{w}_k^*)}_{\text{weight-vector lag}}. \tag{27}$$

The expectations are averages over the ensemble. Eq. (27) identifies the two components of the error. Any difference between the ensemble mean of the adaptive weight vectors and the target value $\boldsymbol{w}_k^*$ is due to lag in the adaptive process, while the deviation of the individual adaptive weight vectors about the ensemble mean is due to gradient noise.

Weight-vector error causes an excess MSE. The ensemble average excess MSE at the kth instant is

$$(\text{average excess MSE})_k = E[(\boldsymbol{w}_k - \boldsymbol{w}_k^*)^{\mathrm{T}}\mathbf{R}(\boldsymbol{w}_k - \boldsymbol{w}_k^*)]. \quad (28)$$

Using Eq. (27), this can be expanded as follows:

$$\begin{aligned}(\text{average excess MSE})_k \\ &= E[(\boldsymbol{w}_k - E[\boldsymbol{w}_k])^{\mathrm{T}}\mathbf{R}(\boldsymbol{w}_k - E[\boldsymbol{w}_k])] + E[(E[\boldsymbol{w}_k]) \\ &\quad - \boldsymbol{w}_k^*)^{\mathrm{T}}\mathbf{R}(E[\boldsymbol{w}_k] - \boldsymbol{w}_k^*)] + 2E[(\boldsymbol{w}_k - E[\boldsymbol{w}_k])^{\mathrm{T}} \\ &\quad \times R(E[\boldsymbol{w}_k] - \boldsymbol{w}_k^*)].\end{aligned} \quad (29)$$

Expanding the last term of Eq. (29) and simplifying since $\boldsymbol{w}_k^*$ is constant over the ensemble,

$$\begin{aligned}&2E[\boldsymbol{w}_k^{\mathrm{T}}\mathbf{R}E[\boldsymbol{w}_k] - \boldsymbol{w}_k^{\mathrm{T}}\mathbf{R}\boldsymbol{w}_k^* - E[\boldsymbol{w}_k]^{\mathrm{T}}\mathbf{R}E[\boldsymbol{w}_k] + E[\boldsymbol{w}_k]^{\mathrm{T}}\mathbf{R}\boldsymbol{w}_k^*] \\ &= 2(E[\boldsymbol{w}_k]^{\mathrm{T}}\mathbf{R}E[\boldsymbol{w}_k] - E[\boldsymbol{w}_k]^{\mathrm{T}}\mathbf{R}E[\boldsymbol{w}_k] - E[\boldsymbol{w}_k]^{\mathrm{T}} \\ &\quad \times \mathbf{R}\boldsymbol{w}_k^* + E[\boldsymbol{w}_k]^{\mathrm{T}}\mathbf{R}\boldsymbol{w}_k^*) = 0.\end{aligned} \quad (30)$$

Therefore, Eq. (29) becomes

$$\begin{aligned}(\text{average excess MSE})_k \\ &= E[(\boldsymbol{w}_k^* - E[\boldsymbol{w}_k])^{\mathrm{T}}\mathbf{R}(\boldsymbol{w}_k - E[\boldsymbol{w}_k])] + E[(E[\boldsymbol{w}_k] \\ &\quad - \boldsymbol{w}_k^*)^{\mathrm{T}}\mathbf{R}(E[\boldsymbol{w}_k] - \boldsymbol{w}_k^*)].\end{aligned} \quad (31)$$

The average excess MSE is thus a sum of components due to both gradient noise and lag:

$$\begin{aligned}(\text{average excess MSE due to lag})_k \\ &= E[(E[\boldsymbol{w}_k] - \boldsymbol{w}_k^*)^{\mathrm{T}}\mathbf{R}(E[\boldsymbol{w}_k] - \boldsymbol{w}_k^*)] \\ &= E[(E[\boldsymbol{w}'_k] - w'*_k)^{\mathrm{T}} \wedge (E[\boldsymbol{w}'_k] - w'*_k)]\end{aligned} \quad (32)$$

$$\begin{aligned}(\text{average excess MSE due to gradient noise})_k \\ &= E[(\boldsymbol{w}_k - E[\boldsymbol{w}_k]^{\mathrm{T}})\mathbf{R}(\boldsymbol{w}_k - E[\boldsymbol{w}_k])] \\ &= E[(\boldsymbol{w}'_k - E[\boldsymbol{w}'_k])^{\mathrm{T}} \wedge (\boldsymbol{w}'_k - E[\boldsymbol{w}'_k])],\end{aligned} \quad (33)$$

where $\boldsymbol{w}'_k \triangleq \mathbf{Q}^{\mathrm{T}}\boldsymbol{w}_k$, $w'*_k \triangleq \mathbf{Q}^{\mathrm{T}}\boldsymbol{w}_k^*$, $\wedge$ is a diagonal matrix of the eigenvalues of $\mathbf{R}$, and $\mathbf{Q}$ is the modal matrix of $\mathbf{R}$. The total misadjustment is therefore a sum of two components, that due to lag and that due to gradient noise. These components of misadjustment have been evaluated by Widrow et al. (1976). The total misadjustment for adaptation with the LMS algorithm is

$$\begin{aligned}M_{\text{sum}} &= (\text{misadjustment due to gradient noise}) \\ &\quad + (\text{misadjustment due to lag}) \\ &= \mu\mathrm{Tr}(\boldsymbol{R}) + \frac{n\sigma^2}{4\mu\xi_{\min}}.\end{aligned} \quad (34)$$

Since M_{sum} is convex in μ, an optimal choice of μ that minimizes M_{sum} can be obtained by differentiating M_{sum} with respect to μ and setting the derivative to zero. Optimization takes place when the two terms of Eq. (34) are made equal. When this happens, the loss in performance from adapting too rapidly (due to gradient noise) is equal to the loss in performance from adapting too slowly (due to lag).

It is interesting to note that M_{sum} in Eq. (34) depends on the choice of the parameter μ and on the statistical properties of the nonstationary environment but does not depend on the spread of the eigenvalues of the $\boldsymbol{R}$ matrix. It is no surprise, therefore, that when the components of misadjustment are evaluated for the LMS/Newton algorithm operating in the very same environment, the expression for M_{sum} for LMS/Newton turns out to be

$$\begin{aligned}M_{\text{sum}} &= (\text{misadjustment due to gradient noise}) \\ &\quad + (\text{misadjustment due to lag}) \\ &= \mu\mathrm{Tr}(\boldsymbol{R}) + \frac{n\sigma^2}{4\mu\xi_{\min}},\end{aligned} \quad (35)$$

which is the same as Eq. (34). From this we may conclude that the performance of the LMS algorithm is equivalent to that of the LMS/Newton algorithm when both are operating with the same choice of μ in the same nonstationary environment, wherein they are tracking a first-order Markov target. The optimum value of μ is the same for LMS/Newton as for LMS. Since LMS/Newton is optimal, we may conclude that the LMS algorithm is also optimal when operating in a first-order Markov nonstationary environment. And LMS is likely to be optimal or close to it when operating in many other types of nonstationary environments, although this has not yet been proven.

9. Conclusion

An adaptive algorithm is like an engine whose fuel is input data. Two algorithms adapting the same number of weights and operating with the same misadjustment can be compared in terms of their consumption of data. The more efficient algorithm consumes less data, i.e. converges faster. On this basis, the LMS/Newton algorithm has the highest statistical efficiency that can be obtained. The LMS/Newton algorithm therefore can serve as a benchmark for statistical efficiency against which all other algorithms can be compared.

The role played by LMS/Newton in adaptive systems is analogous to that played by the Carnot engine in thermodynamics. They both do not exist physically. But their performances limit the performances of all practical systems, adaptive and thermodynamic, respectively.

The LMS/Newton algorithm uses learning data most efficiently. No other least squares learning algorithm can be more efficient. The LMS algorithm performs identically to LMS/Newton when all eigenvalues of the input autocorrelation matrix (the $\boldsymbol{R}$ matrix) are equal. In most practical cases, however, the eigenvalues are not equal. Regardless of eigenvalue spread, the LMS algorithm performs equivalently, on average, to LMS/Newton in nonstationary environments and under transient learning conditions with random initial conditions. However, under 'worst case' initial conditions, LMS can converge much more slowly than LMS/Newton. Under 'best case' initial conditions, LMS converges much faster than LMS/Newton. On average, their convergence rates are equivalent in terms of their excess error energies. Along with its simplicity, ease of implementation, and robustness, the equivalent performance between LMS and LMS/Newton is one of the major reasons for the popularity of the LMS algorithm. Dr. Widrow has discussed this with Dr Paul Werbos, and both conclude that the backpropagation algorithm is popular for similar reasons.

References

Butterweck, H. J. (2001). A wave theory of long adaptive filters. *IEEE Transactions on Circuits and Systems-I: Fundamental Theory and Applications*, *48*(6), 739–747.

Dabeer, O., & Masry, E. (2002). Analysis of mean-square error and transient speed of the LMS adaptive algorithm. *IEEE Transactions on Information Theory*, *48*(7), 1873–1894.

Ghogho, M., Ibnkahla, M., & Bershad, N. J. (1998). Analytic behavior of the LMS adaptive line enhancer for sinusoids corrupted by multiplicative and additive noise. *IEEE Transactions on Signal Processing*, *46*(9), 2386–2393.

Kailath, T., Sayed, A. H., & Hassibi, B. (2000). *Linear estimation*. Upper Saddle River, NJ: Prentice Hall.

Proakis, J. G. (2001). *Digital communications* (4th ed). New York: McGraw-Hill, Chapter 11.

Werbos, P. J (1974). *Beyond regression, new tools for prediction and analysis in the behavioral sciences*. PhD thesis, Harvard University, Cambridge, MA.

Widrow, B., Glover, J. R., Jr., McCool, J. M., Kaunitz, J., Williams, C. S., Hearn, R. H., Zeidler, J. R., Dong, E., Jr., & Goodlin, R. C. (1975). Adaptive noise cancelling. Principles and applications. *Proceedings of the IEEE*, *63*(12), 1692–1716.

Widrow, B., & Hoff, M. E. (1960). Adaptive switching circuits. *IRE WESCON Convention Record*, *4*, 96–104.

Widrow, B., & Kamenetsky, M. (2003). On the efficiency of adaptive algorithms. In S. Haykin, & B. Widrow (Eds.), *Least-mean-square adaptive filters*. New York: Wiley.

Widrow, B., Mantey, P., Griffiths, L., & Goode, B. (1967). Adaptive antenna systems. *Proceedings of the IEEE*, *55*(12), 2143–2159.

Widrow, B., McCool, J., Larimore, M. G., & Johnson, C. R., Jr. (1976). Stationary and nonstationary learning characteristics of the LMS adaptive filter. *Proceedings of the IEEE*, *64*(8), 1151–1162.

Widrow, B., & Stearns, S. D. (1985). *Adaptive signal processing*. Upper Saddle River, NJ: Prentice Hall.

Widrow, B., & Walach, E. (1984). On the statistical efficiency of the LMS algorithm with nonstationary inputs. *IEEE Transactions on Information Theory*, *IT-30*(2), 211–221.

Widrow, B., & Walach, E. (1996). *Adaptive inverse control*. Upper Saddle River, NJ: Prentice Hall.

Yousef, N. R., & Sayed, A. H. (2001). A unified approach to the steady-state and tracking analyses of adaptive filters. *IEEE Transactions on Signal Processing*, *49*(2), 314–324.

AVAILABLE AT
www.ComputerScienceWeb.com
POWERED BY SCIENCE DIRECT

PERGAMON

Neural Networks 16 (2003) 745–753

Neural Networks

www.elsevier.com/locate/neunet

2003 Special issue

On structure-exploiting trust-region regularized nonlinear least squares algorithms for neural-network learning

Eiji Mizutani[a,*], James W. Demmel[b]

[a]*Department of Computer Science, National Tsing Hua University, Hsinchu 300, Taiwan, ROC*
[b]*Department of Mathematics and Computer Science Division, University of California at Berkeley, CA 94720, USA*

Abstract

This paper briefly introduces our numerical linear algebra approaches for solving structured nonlinear least squares problems arising from 'multiple-output' neural-network (NN) models. Our algorithms feature trust-region regularization, and exploit sparsity of either the 'block-angular' residual Jacobian matrix or the 'block-arrow' Gauss-Newton Hessian (or Fisher information matrix in statistical sense) depending on problem scale so as to render a large class of NN-learning algorithms 'efficient' in both memory and operation costs. Using a relatively large real-world nonlinear regression application, we shall explain algorithmic strengths and weaknesses, analyzing simulation results obtained by both direct and iterative trust-region algorithms with two distinct NN models: 'multilayer perceptrons' (MLP) and 'complementary mixtures of MLP-experts' (or neuro-fuzzy modular networks).

Keywords: Trust-region methods; Krylov subspace; Block-angular and block-arrow matrices; Neuro-fuzzy modular networks

1. Introduction

We consider problems to optimize the n-dimensional parameter vector $\boldsymbol{\theta}$ of a given NN model, attempting to achieve good generalization on test (out-of-sample) data, while minimizing the sum over d training (in-sample) data of squared residuals: $E(\boldsymbol{\theta}) = \frac{1}{2}\sum_{p=1}^{d}\|\mathbf{y}_p(\boldsymbol{\theta}) - \mathbf{t}_p\|_2^2 = \frac{1}{2}\sum_{p=1}^{d}\|\mathbf{r}_p(\boldsymbol{\theta})\|_2^2 = \frac{1}{2}\|\mathbf{r}(\boldsymbol{\theta})\|_2^2$. Here, $\mathbf{r}_p(\boldsymbol{\theta})$ is the residual vector on datum p between $\mathbf{y}_p(\boldsymbol{\theta})$ (model's output vector) and $\mathbf{t}_p$ (its desired output vector); these are an F-dimensional vector when the model has F final output nodes, whereas $\mathbf{r}(\boldsymbol{\theta})$ is the m $(= Fd)$-dimensional residual vector composed of r_i $(= y_i - t_i)$, $i = 1, \ldots, m$. The gradient vector and the Hessian matrix of $E(\boldsymbol{\theta})$ have special forms, given by $\mathbf{g} \equiv \mathbf{J}^T\mathbf{r}$ and $\mathbf{H} \equiv \mathbf{J}^T\mathbf{J} + \mathbf{S}$, respectively, where $\mathbf{J}$ is the $m \times n$ **(residual) Jacobian matrix** of $\mathbf{r}$ and $\mathbf{S}$ denotes the matrix of second-derivative terms of $\mathbf{r}$; i.e. $\mathbf{S} \equiv \sum_{i=1}^{m} r_i \nabla^2 r_i$. Table 1 summarizes representative NN-learning algorithms, depending on how $\mathbf{g}$ (gradient) and $\mathbf{H}$ (Hessian) are evaluated: Class-A is a group of online-mode learning algorithms that take a step on each datum, whereas Class-B algorithms, a group of 'nonlinear' conjugate gradient (CG) and quasi-Newton methods, compute the gradient vector $\mathbf{g}$ in batch mode but approximate the entire Hessian $\mathbf{H}$ without exploiting such a special structure as $\mathbf{J}^T\mathbf{J} + \mathbf{S}$ by taking steps (i.e. running estimates). In contrast, Class-C algorithms evaluate the Gauss-Newton Hessian $\mathbf{J}^T\mathbf{J}$ [or Fisher information matrix for natural gradient (Amari, 1998)] explicitly or implicitly in batch mode (with or without approximation to $\mathbf{S}$) at the current point $\boldsymbol{\theta}_{\text{now}}$.

A class of modern nonlinear least squares algorithms solve the following **trust-region subproblem** (Conn et al., 2000; Moré, 1983) to determine an effective step $\Delta\boldsymbol{\theta}$:

$$\min_{\Delta\boldsymbol{\theta}} q(\Delta\boldsymbol{\theta}) \text{ subject to } \|\Delta\boldsymbol{\theta}\|_2 \le R \qquad (1)$$

where $q(\Delta\boldsymbol{\theta}) \equiv E(\boldsymbol{\theta}) + \mathbf{g}^T\Delta\boldsymbol{\theta} + (1/2)\Delta\boldsymbol{\theta}^T\mathbf{H}\Delta\boldsymbol{\theta}$, called the *local quadratic model* to the objective function $E(\cdot)$, and R denotes the **trust-region radius.** Exact computation of $\mathbf{S}$ is expensive; so, $\mathbf{S}$ could be approximated with quasi-Newton methods (see NL2SOL in Dennis et al. (1981) and Mizutani (1999)). When $\mathbf{S}$ is omitted from $\mathbf{H}$ $(\mathbf{H} = \mathbf{J}^T\mathbf{J})$, the subproblem (1) reduces to either (a) or (b) below:

$$\text{(a)} \ \min_{\Delta\boldsymbol{\theta}} \tfrac{1}{2}\|\mathbf{r} + \mathbf{J}\Delta\boldsymbol{\theta}\|_2 \quad \text{subject to } \|\Delta\boldsymbol{\theta}\|_2 \le R \qquad (2)$$

$$\text{(b)} \ \min_{\Delta\boldsymbol{\theta}} \tfrac{1}{2}\{\|\mathbf{r} + \mathbf{J}\Delta\boldsymbol{\theta}\|_2 + \mu\|\Delta\boldsymbol{\theta}\|_2\} = \min_{\Delta\boldsymbol{\theta}} \tfrac{1}{2}\left\{\left\|\left[\frac{\mathbf{J}}{\sqrt{\mu}\mathbf{I}}\right]\Delta\boldsymbol{\theta} + \left[\frac{\mathbf{r}}{\mathbf{0}}\right]\right\|_2\right\},$$

* Corresponding author.
E-mail addresses: eiji@wayne.cs.nthu.edu.tw (E. Mizutani), demmel@cs.berkeley.edu (J.W. Demmel).

0893-6080/03/$ - see front matter © 2003 Elsevier Science Ltd. All rights reserved.
doi:10.1016/S0893-6080(03)00085-6

Table 1
Classification of nonlinear optimization algorithms

Hessian evaluation	Gradient computation	
	Online mode	Batch mode
Online estimate by taking steps	Class A EKF, natural gradient, incremental Gauss–Newton	Class B Quasi-Newton (e.g. DFB, BFGS, PSB, SR1), Nonlinear CG, (e.g. Polak-Ribiere)
Batch estimate at θ_{now}	N/A	Class C Newton (direct) (e.g. direct dogleg in Sec. 2-2.), Inexact Newton (iterative) (e.g. Krylov-dogleg in Sec. 2-3.)

where the constrained minimization (a) is redefined with the **Levenberg-Marguardt parameter** μ (as the Lagrange multiplier) as (b); scalar μ is known as **Tikhonov parameter** in the regularization literature, and related to *ridge regression* in 'linear' least squares. The identity matrix $\mathbf{I}$ in (b) could be replaced with a diagonal matrix $\mathbf{D}$ for scaling (Moré, 1983). Clearly, the classical Levenberg-Marquardt method, a typical Class-C method, solves the subproblem (2), but it is much less robust due to its μ-only control than *trust-region methods* that control R (with or without μ-control) based on how well the local model $q(\cdot)$ predicts the behavior of $E(\cdot)$. In reality, **dogleg algorithms** are often employed to obtain an approximate solution step $\Delta\boldsymbol{\theta}$ to the trust-region subproblem (2) with (restricted) Cauchy step $\Delta\boldsymbol{\theta}_{RC}$ and (regularized/damped) Gauss–Newton (GN) step $\Delta\boldsymbol{\theta}_{\text{GN}}$, yielding the next:

$$\begin{cases} \text{if } R \le \|\Delta\boldsymbol{\theta}_{\text{C}}\|, & \text{set } \Delta\boldsymbol{\theta} = \Delta\boldsymbol{\theta}_{RC} \stackrel{\text{def}}{=} -R\frac{\mathbf{g}}{\|\mathbf{g}\|}, \\ \text{if } R \ge \|\Delta\boldsymbol{\theta}_{\text{GN}}\|, & \text{set } \Delta\boldsymbol{\theta} = \Delta\boldsymbol{\theta}_{\text{GN}} \stackrel{\text{def}}{=} -\mathbf{J}^{+}\mathbf{r}, \\ \quad \text{else} & \text{set } \Delta\boldsymbol{\theta} = \Delta\boldsymbol{\theta}_{\text{Dogleg}} \stackrel{\text{def}}{=} (1-\beta)\Delta\boldsymbol{\theta}_{\text{C}} + \beta\Delta\boldsymbol{\theta}_{\text{GN}}. \end{cases} \tag{3}$$

Here, $\Delta\boldsymbol{\theta}_{\text{C}} \stackrel{\text{def}}{=} -(\mathbf{g}^T\mathbf{g}/\mathbf{g}^T\mathbf{H}\mathbf{g})\ \mathbf{g}$ is the full Cauchy step that minimizes $q(\cdot)$ in the steepest descent direction; $\mathbf{J}^{+}$ is the pseudoinverse of $\mathbf{J}$; and scalar β $(0<\beta<1)$, which regulates the *intermediate* 'dogleg step' $\Delta\boldsymbol{\theta}_{\text{Dogleg}}$ between $\Delta\boldsymbol{\theta}_{\text{C}}$ and $\Delta\boldsymbol{\theta}_{\text{GN}}$ along a piecewise-linear *dogleg trajectory*, is easily determinable as:

$$\beta = \frac{R^2 - \Delta\boldsymbol{\theta}_{\text{C}}^T\Delta\boldsymbol{\theta}_{\text{C}}}{(\Delta\boldsymbol{\theta}_{\text{GN}} - \Delta\boldsymbol{\theta}_{\text{C}})^T\Delta\boldsymbol{\theta}_{\text{C}} + \sqrt{p}},$$

where $p = (\Delta\boldsymbol{\theta}_{\text{GN}} - \Delta\boldsymbol{\theta}_{\text{C}})^T(\Delta\boldsymbol{\theta}_{\text{GN}} - \Delta\boldsymbol{\theta}_{\text{C}})R^2 + (\Delta\boldsymbol{\theta}_{\text{GN}}^T\Delta\boldsymbol{\theta}_{\text{C}})^2 - (\Delta\boldsymbol{\theta}_{\text{GN}}^T\Delta\boldsymbol{\theta}_{\text{GN}})(\Delta\boldsymbol{\theta}_{\text{C}}^T\Delta\boldsymbol{\theta}_{\text{C}})$. In this way, the solution step $\Delta\boldsymbol{\theta}$ is subject to *trust-region regularization* (Conn et al., 2000; Moré, 1983; Dennis et al., 1981; Mizutani & Demmel, 2002, 2003a). Notice that the trust-region mechanism realizes an important Levenberg-Marquardt concept: If the step is not satisfactory, then *that failed step is shorten and deflected towards the steepest descent direction simultaneously*, prohibiting any *uphill* movement. That is, the algorithms are *deterministic* (not stochastic), and the gradient vector should be computed in batch mode or with (sufficiently large) data block (i.e. block mode).

In what follows, we highlight two robust 'direct' and 'iterative' batch-mode learning trust-region algorithms in Class C: Roughly speaking, the *direct batch-mode learning* needs $O(mn^2)$ operations and $O(n^2)$ storage to perform a 'direct' matrix decomposition (only when $R > \|\Delta\boldsymbol{\theta}_{\text{C}}\|$ holds) to determine $\Delta\boldsymbol{\theta}_{\text{GN}}$ (see Algorithm 1) for seeking a regularized solution $\Delta\boldsymbol{\theta}$, whereas the *iterative batch/block-mode learning* (Mizutani & Demmel, 2000, 2003a) typically employs *Krylov subspace* methods, a standard *numerical linear algebra approach* as a substitute for direct matrix factorizations in large-scale problems, to reduce both work and storage by a factor of $O(n)$ (see Algorithm 2). Both algorithms exploit special structures of the residual Jacobian matrix $\mathbf{J}$ with two different NN models: a general-purpose MLP model and a 'complementary mixtures of MLP-experts' model (see Fig. 1). The latter was introduced as a constrained model because good generalization could be attained with certain constraints imposed on NN architectures (e.g. weight-sharing), as well as with effective

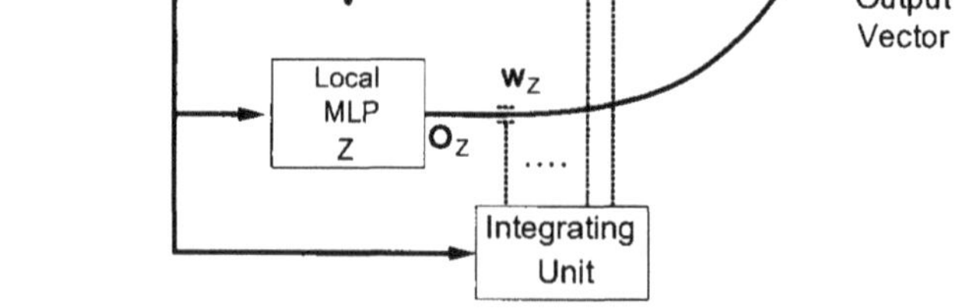

Fig. 1. A typical (neuro-fuzzy) modular network architecture that consists of Z modules (or local-expert MLPs) produces the final outputs $\mathbf{y} = \sum_{i=1}^{Z} w_i\mathbf{o}_i$ wherein w_i is *the ith* (normalized) scalar weight (or firing strength) on the outputs $\mathbf{o}_i$ of expert i $(i = 1, ..., Z)$.

regularization methods (including early stopping), which may introduce small (harmless) bias. Our structure-exploiting algorithms are largely applicable to all the three classes of most algorithms in Table 1.

2. Neural networks nonlinear least squares

A variety of NNs could be employed as a nonlinear model, giving rise to what we call *neural networks nonlinear least squares problems* that often have a **separable** parameter structure (e.g. linear and nonlinear separation); therefore, exploiting such a special architecture often leads to a very efficient algorithm even with *single-output* NNs.

2.1. Block-angular residual Jacobian matrix

With most multiple F-output nonlinear models (except *fully-connected* NNs), the residual Jacobian matrix $\mathbf{J}$, readily obtainable from the *backpropagation* (BP) derivative-computing process, has the following $m \times n$ **block angular** matrix (e.g. see Mizutani & Demmel, 2002; Golub & LeVeque, 1978; Kaufman & Sylvester, 1992; pages 224–227 in Björck (1996)):

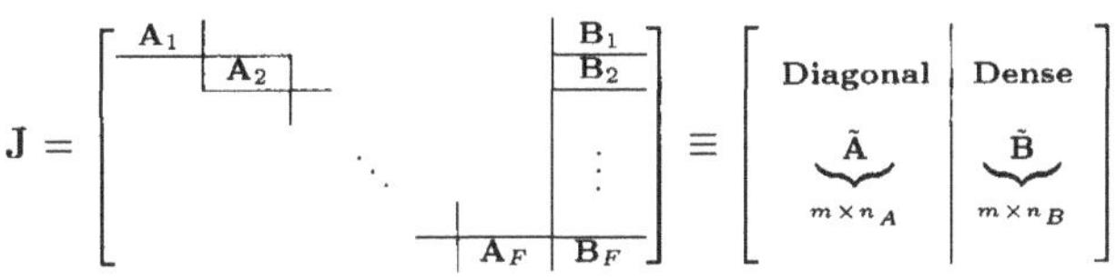

(4)

due to model's parameter separability: $\boldsymbol{\theta}^T = [\boldsymbol{\theta}^{A^T} | \boldsymbol{\theta}^{B^T}] = [\boldsymbol{\theta}_1^{A^T}, \ldots, \boldsymbol{\theta}_k^{A^T}, \ldots, \boldsymbol{\theta}_F^{A^T} | \boldsymbol{\theta}^{B^T}]$. Here, $\boldsymbol{\theta}^A$ denotes n_A **terminal parameters** on direct connections to F terminal nodes, each of which is assumed to have C_k parameters (denoted by $\boldsymbol{\theta}_k^A$) directly connected to each node k $(k = 1, \ldots, F)$; hence, $n_A = \sum_{k=1}^{F} C_k$. The rest of n_B $(\equiv n - n_A)$ parameters $\boldsymbol{\theta}^B$ are not directly connected to any terminal node (hence, n_B **hidden parameters**). For instance, in an S-H-F MLP (with S-input H-hidden F-output nodes), we have $n_A = F(H+1)$, $n_B = H(S+1)$, and $C_1 = C_2 = \cdots = C_F = H + 1 (\equiv C_A)$ including threshold parameters; so $n_A = FC_A$, which we shall assume in what follows without loss of generality. In Eq. (4), $\mathbf{A}_k$ and $\mathbf{B}_k$ are $d \times C_A$ and $d \times n_B$ Jacobian matrices, respectively, of the d-dimensional residual vector $\mathbf{r}_k$ evaluated at terminal node k. There are F diagonal $d \times C_A$ $\mathbf{A}_k$ blocks in the $m \times n_A$ **matrix** $\tilde{\boldsymbol{A}}$ because $(F-1)C_A$ parameters excluding $\boldsymbol{\theta}_k^A$ have no effect on $\mathbf{r}_k$. In other words, each $\boldsymbol{\theta}_k^A$ only contributes to minimizing $\mathbf{r}_k$, but the other n_B hidden parameters $\boldsymbol{\theta}^B$ are associated with all the residuals $\mathbf{r}_k$ $(k = 1, \ldots, F)$ evaluated at all F terminal nodes; hence, the $m \times n_B$ **matrix** $\tilde{\boldsymbol{B}}$ **is dense**. Therefore, the posed problem is **overdetermined** when $m > n$ (namely, $d > C_A + \frac{1}{F} n_B$) holds. In addition, when the terminal nodes have *linear identity functions*, all $\mathbf{A}_k$ blocks become identical $\mathbf{A}_1 = \mathbf{A}_2 = \cdots = \mathbf{A}_F$, whose elements are the outputs of the *nodes directly linking to terminal nodes* (e.g. H hidden nodes and a bias node in S–H–F MLPs); so, need to use only one diagonal block.

To be more specific, we illustrate the structure of the $m \times n$ residual Jacobian matrix $\mathbf{J}$ obtainable from a single-hidden-layer '1-2-3 MLP' model, wherein $S = 1; H = 2; F = 3$ (three outputs); there are $n_A = FC_A = 9$ *terminal* parameters and $n_B = 4$ *hidden* parameters (including threshold parameters); hence, the total number of parameters $n = n_A + n_B = 13$. When five data $(d = 5)$ are processed, totally 15 (= Fd) residuals are obtained because three (scalar) residuals, one per output, are computed on each datum p $(p = 1, \cdots, 5)$. Accordingly, one might form the associated 15×13 Jacobian matrix of the 15-dimensional residual vector sequentially row by row, as shown next:

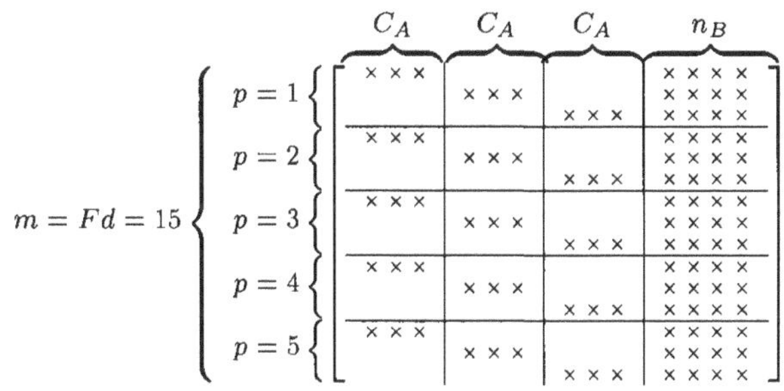

where × denotes some non-zero entry. Because of this obvious sparsity, we should avoid storing and operating on the zero entries. For this purpose, we next permute rows of the above residual Jacobian matrix so as to conform to the *block angular form* in Eq. (4), as shown below:

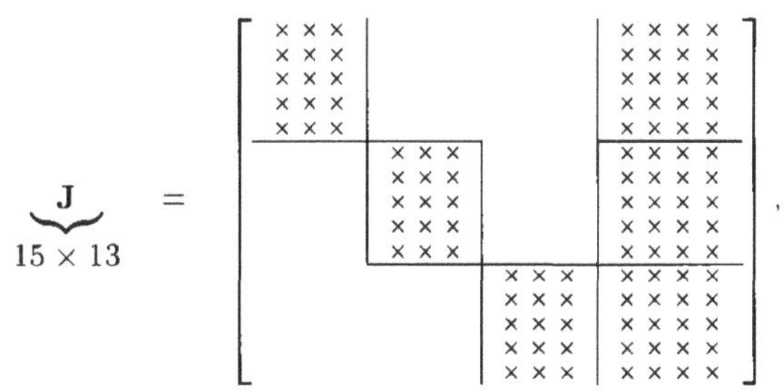

where there are three 5×3 diagonal blocks $\mathbf{A}_k$ $(k = 1, 2, 3)$, and three 5×4 vertical blocks $\mathbf{B}_k$. The key is to form those **dense** blocks $\mathbf{A}_k$ and $\mathbf{B}_k$ alone (during the BP process) either explicitly for *direct* methods (see Algorithm 1 later) or implicitly for *iterative* methods (see Algorithm 2).

As another (multiple F-output) NN model, we consider a 'complementary mixtures of cooperative MLP experts' model [or a neuro-fuzzy modular network (Mizutani & Nishio, 2002) that comprises Z local-expert MLPs (see Fig. 1): By analogy, each residual Jacobian matrix $\mathbf{J}^i$ associated with each expert-MLP i $(i = 1, \ldots, Z)$ has the same block-angular form as in Eq. (4), consisting of $d \times C_A^i$ blocks $\mathbf{A}_k^i$ and $d \times n_B^i$ blocks $\mathbf{B}_k^i$ $(k = 1, \ldots, F)$. Therefore, we can permute columns of the *global* Jacobian matrix $[\mathbf{J}^1 | \mathbf{J}^2 | \cdots | \mathbf{J}^Z]$ of all Z MLPs in order to obtain the block-angular global Jacobian matrix below (even if those MLPs have different sizes):

$$\begin{bmatrix} \mathbf{A}_1^1\mathbf{A}_1^2\ldots\mathbf{A}_1^Z & & & & \mathbf{B}_1^1\mathbf{B}_1^2\ldots\mathbf{B}_1^Z \\ & \mathbf{A}_2^1\mathbf{A}_2^2\ldots\mathbf{A}_2^Z & & & \mathbf{B}_2^1\mathbf{B}_2^2\ldots\mathbf{B}_2^Z \\ & & \ddots & & \vdots \\ & & & \mathbf{A}_F^1\mathbf{A}_F^2\ldots\mathbf{A}_F^Z & \mathbf{B}_F^1\mathbf{B}_F^2\ldots\mathbf{B}_F^Z \end{bmatrix}, \tag{5}$$

which is tantamount to Eq. (4) with $d \times C_A$ ($C_A = \sum_{i=1}^{Z} C_A^i$) blocks $\mathbf{A}_k = [\mathbf{A}_k^1\mathbf{A}_k^2\ldots\mathbf{A}_k^Z]$ and $d \times n_B$ ($n_B = \sum_{i=1}^{Z} n_B^i$) blocks $\mathbf{B}_k = [\mathbf{B}_k^1\mathbf{B}_k^2\ldots\mathbf{B}_k^Z]$ ($k = 1, \ldots, F$). It is very important to use the global Hessian across all the expert MLPs for optimization purposes because of the nature of **complementary learning**, wherein Z expert MLPs are put together so that only the combined final outcome $\mathbf{y} = \sum_{i=1}^{Z} w_i\mathbf{o}_i$ must come close to the targets $\mathbf{t}$; so, each expert's outputs $\mathbf{o}_i$ may not necessarily be close to $\mathbf{t}$. See more algorithmic variants for the neuro-fuzzy modular networks in Mizutani & Demmel (2002), which shows trade-offs between the amount of Hessian information and convergence performance using a small-scale real-world problem.

2.2. Block-arrow least squares algorithms

From Eqs. (4) and (5), the Gauss–Newton (GN) Hessian $\mathbf{J}^T\mathbf{J}$ (or Fisher information matrix) is given by the $n \times n$ symmetric **block arrow** matrix (due to its appearance):

$$\underbrace{\mathbf{J}^T\mathbf{J}}_{n\times n} = \begin{bmatrix} \mathbf{A}_1^T\mathbf{A}_1 & & & & \mathbf{A}_1^T\mathbf{B}_1 \\ & \mathbf{A}_2^T\mathbf{A}_2 & & & \mathbf{A}_2^T\mathbf{B}_2 \\ & & \ddots & & \vdots \\ & & & \mathbf{A}_F^T\mathbf{A}_F & \mathbf{A}_F^T\mathbf{B}_F \\ \mathbf{B}_1^T\mathbf{A}_1 & \mathbf{B}_2^T\mathbf{A}_2 & \cdots & \mathbf{B}_F^T\mathbf{A}_F & \tilde{\mathbf{B}}^T\tilde{\mathbf{B}} \end{bmatrix} \tag{6}$$

$$\stackrel{\text{def}}{=} \begin{bmatrix} n_A \times n_A \;\; \tilde{\mathbf{A}}^T\tilde{\mathbf{A}} & n_A \times n_B \;\; \tilde{\mathbf{A}}^T\tilde{\mathbf{B}} \\ n_B \times n_A \;\; \tilde{\mathbf{B}}^T\tilde{\mathbf{A}} & n_B \times n_B \;\; \tilde{\mathbf{B}}^T\tilde{\mathbf{B}} \end{bmatrix},$$

where the $n_A \times n_A$ normal **matrix** $\tilde{\mathbf{A}}^T\tilde{\mathbf{A}}$ consists of F diagonal $C_A \times C_A \mathbf{A}_k^T\mathbf{A}_k$ blocks, and $\tilde{\mathbf{B}}^T\tilde{\mathbf{B}} \equiv \sum_{k=1}^{F} \mathbf{B}_k^T\mathbf{B}_k$.

It is crucial to exploit the block-angular $\mathbf{J}$ (with rows and columns appropriately permuted) and to *work on each block individually*, by avoiding **fill-in** (creation of *new* non-zeros) that can occur in the following operations:

1. forming half of a *symmetric arrow* Hessian matrix $\mathbf{H}$;
2. performing a matrix factorization on $\mathbf{H}$;
3. inverting full (or approximate) $\mathbf{H}$ since $\mathbf{H}^{-1}$ is *dense*.

For example, if we perform (modified) Cholesky factorization on an arrow matrix with its *arrowhead pointing in different directions* from 'downwards to the right' (e.g. upwards to the left, as shown below), then the resultant lower-triangular Cholesky factor becomes *dense* (i.e. needs extra storage) due to *fill-in* resulting from matrix factorization (see pp. 83-90 in Demmel (1997)):

$$\underbrace{\mathbf{H}_L'}_{sparse} = \begin{bmatrix} * & * & * & * \\ * & * & & \\ * & & * & \\ * & & & * \end{bmatrix} \Rightarrow \underbrace{\mathbf{L}'}_{\text{dense}} = \begin{bmatrix} * & & & \\ * & * & & \\ * & * & * & \\ * & * & * & * \end{bmatrix}.$$

On the other hand, if we form an arrow matrix $\mathbf{H}$ with *its arrowhead pointing downwards to the right* (see Eq. (6)) and apply Cholesky to it, then we can store the *Cholesky factor* in the same space as the nonzero entries of $\mathbf{H}$. More specifically for the *block-arrow* matrix $\mathbf{H}$ (= $\mathbf{J}^T\mathbf{J}$) in Eq. (6), we work on each diagonal block in $\tilde{\mathbf{A}}^T\tilde{\mathbf{A}}$ individually; that is, each block is Cholesky-factored as $\mathbf{A}_k^T\mathbf{A}_k = \mathbf{U}_k^T\mathbf{U}_k$ with the $C_A \times C_A$ upper-triangular matrix $\mathbf{U}_K$, then the resultant $n \times n$ lower triangular Cholesky factor $\mathbf{L}$ (in $\mathbf{H} = \mathbf{L}\mathbf{L}^T$) maintains the same *sparsity*:

$$\mathbf{H} = \begin{bmatrix} * & & & & * \\ & * & & & * \\ & & * & & * \\ & & & * & * \\ * & * & * & * & * \end{bmatrix} \Rightarrow \mathbf{L} = \begin{bmatrix} \mathbf{U}_1^T & & & \\ & \mathbf{U}_2^T & & \\ & & \ddots & \\ & & & \mathbf{U}_F^T & \\ \mathbf{Z}_1 & \mathbf{Z}_2 & \ldots & \mathbf{Z}_F & \mathbf{X} \end{bmatrix}$$

where $\mathbf{Z}_k = (\mathbf{B}_k^T\mathbf{A})\mathbf{U}_k^{-1}$ ($k = 1, \ldots, F$), and $\mathbf{X}$ is the $n_B \times n_B$ lower triangular Cholesky factor of the $n_B \times n_B$ Schur complement of $\tilde{\mathbf{A}}^T\tilde{\mathbf{A}}$ in $\mathbf{J}^T\mathbf{J}$ (see Eq. (6)). This method, applicable to multiple F-output overdetermined problems ($m > n$) even if approximate $\mathbf{S}$ is added to $\mathbf{J}^T\mathbf{J}$, can be used to determine the (modified) GN-step $\Delta\boldsymbol{\theta}_{\text{GN}}$ only when $R > \|\Delta\boldsymbol{\theta}_{\text{C}}\|$ for seeking the trust-region step $\Delta\boldsymbol{\theta}$ in Eq. (3); the algorithmic details are summarized next:

Algorithm 1: (Modified) Cholesky-based block-arrow least squares algorithm [with or without μ in Eq. (2)]:

(a) Form half of each block $C_A \times C_A$ matrix $\mathbf{A}_k^T\mathbf{A}_k$ ($k = 1, \ldots, F$) by rank-one updates, processing the $d \times C_A$ matrix $\mathbf{A}_k$ one row on each datum; similarly, at the same time, form $n_B \times C_A$ $\mathbf{B}_k^T\mathbf{A}_k$ and $n_B \times n_B$ $\tilde{\mathbf{B}}^T\tilde{\mathbf{B}} = \sum_k^F \mathbf{B}_k^T\mathbf{B}_k$ by rank-one updates, processing the $d \times n_B$ matrix $\mathbf{B}_k$ one row per datum;
(b) Perform Cholesky on each block $\mathbf{A}_k^T\mathbf{A}_k$ (i.e. $\mathbf{A}_k^T\mathbf{A}_k = \mathbf{U}_k^T\mathbf{U}_k$) for $k = 1, \ldots, F$ (or on $\mathbf{A}_k^T\mathbf{A}_k + \mu^2 I$);
(c) Obtain the $n_B \times C_A$ matrix $\mathbf{Z}_k = (\mathbf{B}_k^T\mathbf{A}_k)\mathbf{U}_k^{-1}$ by solving the transposed (multiple righthand side) triangular system (here, no need to invert $\mathbf{U}_k$);
(d) Compute the Schur complement of $\tilde{\mathbf{A}}^T\tilde{\mathbf{A}}$ in $\mathbf{J}^T\mathbf{J}$: $\mathbf{V} = \tilde{\mathbf{B}}^T\tilde{\mathbf{B}} - \sum_{k=1}^{F} \mathbf{Z}_k\mathbf{Z}_k^T(+\mu^2\mathbf{I})$;
(e) Perform Cholesky on the Schur complement matrix $\mathbf{V}$ to get $\mathbf{V} = \mathbf{X}\mathbf{X}^T$;
(f) Solve the two *sparse* block triangular systems $\mathbf{L}\mathbf{L}^T \Delta\boldsymbol{\theta}_{\text{GN}} = -\mathbf{g}$ to obtain $\Delta\boldsymbol{\theta}_{\text{GN}}$. □

The dominant costs in *flops*, cheaper than that of algorithm in Golub and LeVeque (1978), are given by: $m(C_A + n_B)^2 + 2FC_A^2 n_B + 1/3(FC_A^3 + n_B^3)$, where $m = Fd$. To save memory space, we form only half of each diagonal block ($\mathbf{A}_k^T\mathbf{A}_k$ and $\tilde{\mathbf{B}}^T\tilde{\mathbf{B}}$) plus off-diagonal blocks $\mathbf{B}_k^T\mathbf{A}_k$ alone (i.e. no need to form zero blocks). Furthermore, if the terminal node functions are linear, then parameters $\boldsymbol{\theta}^A$ are linear and all diagonal blocks $\mathbf{A}_k$ become identical (say, $\mathbf{A}$); so, we need to form half of one block $\mathbf{A}^T\mathbf{A}$ alone in step (a) and factor it *only once* in step (b) (Mizutani & Demmel, 2002). The associated leading terms in *flops* reduce to: $(2Fn_B + d)C_A^2 + mn_B^2 + 2mC_An_B + 1/3(C_A^3 + n_B^3)$.

If we apply the reduced Householder QR factorization (see page 121 in Demmel (1997)) to $\mathbf{A}_k$ as $\mathbf{A}_k = \mathbf{Q}_k\mathbf{U}_k$, then $\mathbf{Z}_k = \mathbf{B}_k^T\mathbf{Q}_k$ $(k = 1, \ldots, F)$. This QR-based block-arrow algorithm avoids forming normal matrices $\mathbf{A}_k^T\mathbf{A}_k$ but needs to store Jacobian blocks $\mathbf{A}_k$, working faster than Cholesky-based Algorithm 1 only when $d < C_A + n_B$ (still overdetermined as long as $d > C_A + \frac{1}{F}n_B$ holds) due to the dominant costs: $F(2dC_A^2 - \frac{2}{3}C_A^3) + Fdn_B^2 + 2FdC_An_B + FC_A^2n_B + \frac{1}{3}n_B^3$. For a *large-scale* problem, such direct methods with either Cholesky on $\mathbf{J}^T\mathbf{J}$ or QR on $\mathbf{J}$ may be prohibitive; in such cases, we could proceed with *iterative batch-mode learning* schemes (e.g. using projection onto Krylov subspaces).

2.3. Truncated CG-based iterative Krylov-dogleg algorithm

Among many Krylov subspace methods (see Section 6.6 in Demmel (1997)), we consider a *linear* conjugate gradient (CG) with *trust-region regularization*; namely, the *Steihaug-Toint-type truncated* CG (CGNR/CGLS in our context), which works even for *nonconvex* problems (see pages 202-218 in Conn et al. (2000)), for solving *inexactly* the GN normal system: $\mathbf{J}^T\mathbf{J}\Delta\boldsymbol{\theta}^{CG} = -\mathbf{J}^T\mathbf{r}$ by the *inner iterative process*: $\Delta\boldsymbol{\theta}_i^{\mathrm{CG}} = \Delta\boldsymbol{\theta}_{i-1}^{\mathrm{CG}} + (\boldsymbol{\delta}_{i-1}^T\boldsymbol{\delta}_{i-1}/\mathbf{d}_i^T\mathbf{z})\mathbf{d}_i$ where $\boldsymbol{\delta}_i$ denotes the ith linear-system residuals ($\boldsymbol{\delta}_i \equiv -\mathbf{J}^T\mathbf{J}\Delta\boldsymbol{\theta}_i^{\mathrm{CG}} - \mathbf{J}^T\mathbf{r}$); $z \equiv \mathbf{J}^T\mathbf{J}\mathbf{d}_i$; and $\mathbf{d}_i$ is the ith CG-direction n-dimensional vector that can be decomposed as: $\mathbf{d}_i^T = [\mathbf{d}_{i,1}^{aT}, \ldots, \mathbf{d}_{i,k}^{aT}, \ldots, \mathbf{d}_{i,F}^{aT} | \mathbf{d}_i^{bT}]$ in accord with the aforementioned separable parameter structure $\boldsymbol{\theta}^T = [\boldsymbol{\theta}_1^{A^T}, \ldots, \boldsymbol{\theta}_k^{A^T}, \ldots, \boldsymbol{\theta}_F^{A^T} | \boldsymbol{\theta}^{B^T}]$; hence, each $\mathbf{d}_{i,k}^a$ is a C_A-vector, and $\mathbf{d}_i^b$ is an n_B-vector. Here, without forming $\mathbf{J}^T\mathbf{J}$ explicitly, $\mathbf{J}^T\mathbf{J}\mathbf{d}_i$ is evaluated in two-step *implicit matrix-vector product* as $\mathbf{z} = \mathbf{J}^T(\mathbf{J}\mathbf{d}_i)$ by exploiting block-angular $\mathbf{J}$ in Eq. (4), working on each block, $\mathbf{A}_k$ and $\mathbf{B}_k$, in a row-wise manner below:

Algorithm 2: Implicit (i.e. matrix-free) matrix-vector multiplication step with an F-output NN model at inner iteration i (starting with $\mathbf{z} = \mathbf{0}$ when $p = 1$):

for $p = 1$ to d (i.e. one sweep of all training data d):
  (a) do forward pass to compute F final outputs $\mathbf{y}_p(\boldsymbol{\theta})$ on datum p;
  for $k = 1$ to F (at each terminal node k):
    (b) do backward pass to obtain the pth row of $\mathbf{A}_k$ as the C_A-vector $\mathbf{a}_p^T$, and the pth row $\mathbf{b}_k$ as the n_B-vector $\mathbf{b}_p^T$;
    (c) compute $\alpha\mathbf{a}_p$ and $\alpha\mathbf{b}_p$, where scalar α is defined as $\mathbf{a}_p^T\mathbf{d}_{i,k}^a + \mathbf{b}_p^T\mathbf{d}_i^b$, and then add them to their corresponding elements of $\mathbf{z}$;
  end for k.
end for p. □

As noted earlier, if the terminal node functions are *linear*, all F diagonal blocks $\mathbf{A}_k$ become identical; so, the row vector $\mathbf{a}_p^T$ (e.g. the vector of C_A outputs, H hidden-node outputs and one bias-node constant output, in an S–H–F MLP) needs to be computed only once on each datum p. The inner process terminates (say, at iteration j) when the iterated CG point falls outside the trust region (i.e. $\|\Delta\boldsymbol{\theta}_{\mathrm{CG}}^j\| \geq R$) or when the linear-system residuals becomes small enough (i.e. $\|\boldsymbol{\delta}_j\| < \gamma\|\mathbf{J}^T\mathbf{r}\|$, where γ is called a forcing term used in a class of inexact or truncated Newton methods; e.g. see Ch. 6 in Nocedal and Wright (1999)). In our context, γ could be fixed ($\gamma = 0.01$ in our application) owing to R-control. Note that if $\|\Delta\boldsymbol{\theta}_{\mathrm{CG}}^1\| \geq R$ (when $j = 1$), the step reduces to the restricted Cauchy step $\Delta\boldsymbol{\theta}_{\mathrm{RC}}$ in Eq. (3). The resulting jth CG step $\Delta\boldsymbol{\theta}_{\mathrm{CG}}^j$ is used as an approximate solution to the trust-region subproblem (2), and it belongs to the Krylov subspace $[-\mathbf{J}^T\mathbf{r}, -(\mathbf{J}^T\mathbf{J})\mathbf{J}^T\mathbf{r}, \ldots, -(\mathbf{J}^T\mathbf{J})^{j-1}\mathbf{J}^T\mathbf{r}]$, which is known to be spanned by the j largest approximate *right singular vectors* of $\mathbf{J}$. Thus, the obtained Krylov-dogleg trust-region step has only components in the directions of those singular vectors, resulting in an approximate **truncated SVD solution** in the j-dimensional Krylov subspace; so, the method intrinsically has regularizing effects. Therefore, without controlling μ (i.e. R-only control), the iterative Krylov-dogleg (with Alogrithm 2) behaves like the direct dogleg method (using Algorithm 1) with μ and R both controlled. Moreover, the overall memory requirement of iterative dogleg is O(n) because at most five n-vectors are enough to implement Algorithm 2, wherein each of steps (a) and (b) costs *at least* $2dn$ [although step (a) may take more time than step (b); see Mizutani and Dreyfus (2001), and step (c) costs $4ml_u$, where $l_u = C_A + n_B < n = FC_A + n_B$. Since Algorithm 2 is dominant in operation cost of the inner process, the overall cost of iterative dogleg, cheaper per epoch than that of algorithm in Toint (1987), is O(ml_u) (*linear* in F) as long as the number of inner iterations is kept small owing to the trust-region bound (Mizutani & Demmel, 2000).

2.4. Direct methods versus iterative methods

Naturally, an important question arises under a certain circumstance: Which is better, a direct method or an iterative method? One might compute mn^2, the most dominant term in operation counts of the normal-equation approach (when $m > n$) to estimate roughly the *time per epoch* (i.e. one-batch time required for a step $\Delta\boldsymbol{\theta}$ after processing all d training data): If that time is acceptable, then employ a direct method; otherwise, resort to an iterative method. Basically, this is an answer to that question, but suppose n is large (e.g. $n = 200,002$) with a given arbitrarily large d : Is an iterative solver 'always' the method of choice in optimizing NN models? In reality, it is not easy to answer for the reasons that follow.

First, the required amount of time for the *inner iterative process* (or the time per epoch) is 'unpredictable,' although the *time per epoch* with direct methods *straight-forwardly* increases as n increases. All we can say about the inner iterative process is that as n increases, the *time per inner iteration* monotonically increases by a factor of $O(n)$ [to be shown later in Fig. 2(c)]. Typically, *the number of inner iterations per epoch is small at an early stage of learning, but may become larger as learning proceeds.* Also, it can decrease due to various factors:

- choice of preconditioner (e.g. for linear-CG), because more elaborate preconditioner reduces linear-system residuals $\boldsymbol{\delta}$ more efficiently at each iteration;
- control of the upper bound on trust radius R, because smaller R allows larger linear-system residuals $\boldsymbol{\delta}$;
- control of forcing terms γ (as in inexact Newton) because larger γ allows larger linear-system residuals $\boldsymbol{\delta}$;
- possible *high redundancy* in large training data, because one sweep of such data sets implicitly corresponds to multiple inner iterations (hence, our block-mode iterative dogleg can converge faster than online-BP on redundant data; Mizutani & Demmel, 2003a);
- control of learning capacity of NN models (e.g. by increasing hidden nodes) to be shown in Section 3.

Unfortunately, all these factors are application-oriented.

Second, even if $d < n$, the posed problem may still be *overdetermined* since $Fd = m > n$ may hold. Therefore, it is important to check how large F is and to investigate parameter separability residing in a given NN model. It is worth noting an intriguing finding in large-scale problems that if the posed problem is *highly-multiple output*; say, $F = 100,000$, with a very hypothetical '1-1-100,000 MLP' model ($n = 200,002$), our direct method (with Algorithm 1) can work faster than iterative methods because of very small $n_B = C_A = 2$. Recall our cost analysis in *flops* described in Sections 2.2 and 2.3: The dominant operation costs of both Algorithms 1 and 2 are **linear** in F, resulting from exploiting sparsity. On the contrary, if 'unskillful' direct methods that ignore *sparsity* (e.g. see pages 68–69 in Masters (1995), wherein $\mathbf{J}^T\mathbf{J}$ was stored with zeros arbitrarily in it, and then SVD was applied (not to $\mathbf{J}$)] are employed, then their dominant cost always becomes **cubic** in F, because $mn^2 = Fd(FC_A + n_B)^2$.

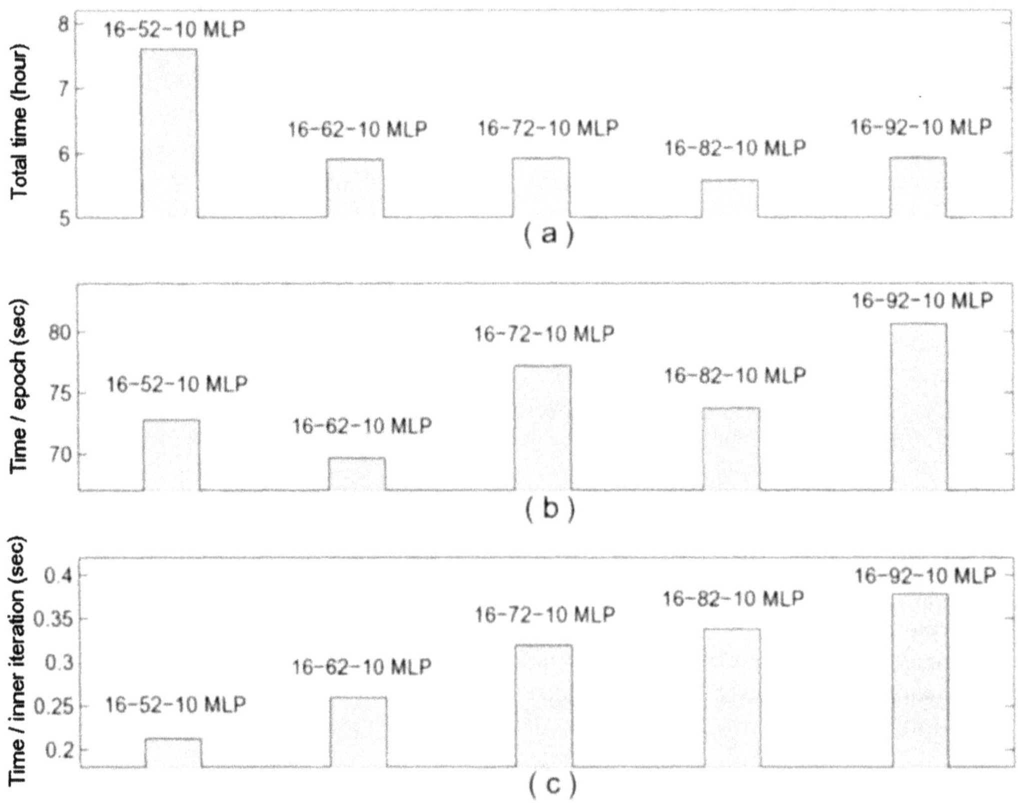

Fig. 2. Comparision (averaged over 20 trials) in various time measures of five MLP models that differ only in the number of hidden nodes optimized by Krylov-dogleg (with Algorithm 2): (a) Average total time (hour) until RMSE ≤0.002; (b) Average time per epoch (second); (c) Average time per inner iteration (second); see details in Table 2.

3. Experiments and discussion

We demonstrated both direct-dogleg (with Algorithm 1) and iterative-dogleg (with Algorithm 2) trust-region methods, using a real-world application *color recipe prediction*, a real challenge in the color industry, which is a problem of determining mixing proportions of available colorants to reproduce the same color as a given reference color sample; it is required to relate surface spectral reflectance of a target color sample to a list of colorant proportions for matching that target color. For experiments, we prepared 1000 training data ($d = 1000$) with 302 checking data to optimize several MLP models and a 'complementary mixtures of MLP-experts' model (see Fig. 1) for learning the desired mapping from 16 inputs (16 surface spectral reflectance signals) to *ten outputs* ($F = 10$) (10 colorant proportions); hence, $m = Fd = 10,000$. Since all MLPs below have nonlinear sigmoidal functions at the terminal layer, both $\boldsymbol{\theta}^A$ (n_A terminal parameters) and $\boldsymbol{\theta}^B$ (n_B hidden parameters) are nonlinear; so, diagonal blocks $\mathbf{A}_k k = 1, \ldots, 10$) in Eqs. (4) or (5) are different. All the experiments that follow were conducted on a 1.6 GHz Pentium-IV PC with FreeBSD 4.5 and gcc-2.95.3 compiler (with-O2 optimization flag), and the results were averaged over 20 trails for each NN model, which was optimized until 'training RMSE ≤ 0.002 (application requirement)' satisfied, when we say that 'convergence' (relatively early stop) occurs. First, using five different-size single MLP models, we show intriguing algorithmic behaviors of the iterative Krylov-dogleg (with Algorithm 2), as mentioned in Section 2.4: the average time per epoch can decrease even as $n (= n_A + n_B)$ *increases* (see Fig. 2(b)) because the 'average number of inner iterations per epoch' (see column 6 in Table 2) can decrease as model's *learning capacity* increases. This never happens with any *direct method* because its dominant cost depends on 'straightforward' linear-equation solving, although the total epochs required to coverage often much fewer than those with the iterative method (compare 'Stopped epoch' between Algorithms 1 and 2 later in Table 3). Notice that the required epochs usually decrease as model's learning capacity increases, which is common to both direct and iterative methods; see column 4 in Table 2.

To improve performance of the single-MLP models, one might employ *two* layers of hidden nodes (rather than *one large* hidden layer), which increases n_B while reducing n_A (hence, detriment to *nice separability* of parameters); consequently, rendering both Algorithms 1 and 2 less efficient (i.e. slower). Alternatively, one might introduce *direct connections* between the input and terminal output layers, which increases C_A (terminal parameters), the column size of $\mathbf{A}_k$, retaining nice parameter separability. Yet another approach (if applicable) is to use a 'complementary mixtures of MLP-experts' model (in Fig. 1) that combines smaller-size MLPs *complementarily* with neither parameters increased nor their nice separability lost, and thus improve learning speed by optimizing them 'simultaneously' with Algorithm 1 or 2. An important design issue of the 'complementary mixtures' model was to select a subset of inputs fed to the integrating unit for input-partition because if all the 16 inputs are used for partitioning, we end up having at least 2^{16} (too many) experts. Therefore, the surface spectral reflectance signals were converted to the *hue angle* as input to the integrating unit that consists of five bell-shaped basis (or fuzzy membership) functions; in this case, the input subspace is partitioned in a fuzzy fashion into five color regions (red, yellow, green, blue, and violet) for five 16-16-10 MLP-experts [$Z = 5$; $n = 2210$ ($C_A = 85$; $n_B = 1360$) in Eq. (5)], each of which receives all the 16 spectral signals as input. With this five-MLP mixtures model, Algorithm 1 (for direct dogleg) yields the *cost reduction ratio* 0.42 (in the leading operation counts $mn^2 + \frac{1}{3}n^3$) and *memory reduction ratio* 0.87 to store the 'symmetric' block-arrow Hessian, compared with inefficient direct methods that ignore the block-arrow structure, whereas Algorithm 2 (for iterative dogleg) yields the reduction ratio 0.65 [in both operation cost in step (c) and memory] compared with unskillful iterative (not direct) methods. Roughly, the same reductions in both work and storage can be expected with a 16-82-10 MLP model, which converged fastest among five models (see Table 2), because its $\mathbf{J}$ has a very similar block-angular form [$n = 2224$ ($C_A = 83$; $n_B = 1394$)]; so, we compare these two distinct models to understand performance difference coming from their architectural difference. Table 3 shows their performance results. For our speed comparison purpose, we also

Table 2
Algorithmic behaviors (averaged over 20 trials) of Krylov-dogleg (using Algorithm 2) with five single-MLP models; see Fig. 2

MLP model structure	n (= no. of parameters)	Total convergence			Inner iterative process		Checking RMSE
		Time (h)	Epoch	Time/epoch (s)	itr./epoch	Time/itr. (s)	
16-52-10	1414	7.6	375.9	72.8	342.5	0.21	0.015
16-62-10	1684	5.9	305.4	69.6	268.6	0.26	0.015
16-72-10	1954	5.9	276.1	77.2	241.9	0.32	0.015
16-82-10	2224	5.6	272.5	73.8	218.3	0.34	0.015
16-92-10	2494	5.9	264.6	80.6	213.1	0.38	0.014

Table 3
Performance comparison (averaged over 20 trails) between a single 16-82-10 MLP model and a 'mixtures of five 16-16-10 MLPs' model

	16-82-10 MLP model ($n = 2224$)			Five-MLP mixtures model ($n = 2210$)		
	BP	Algorithm1	Algorithm2	BP	Algorithm1	Algorithm2
Stopped epoch	2,916,495.2	90.1	272.5	1,914,834.0	81.0	147.3
Total time (h)	145.8	6.3	5.6	123.1	5.6	2.7
Time/epoch (s)	0.18	251.1	73.8	0.23	246.7	65.2
No. of inner itr.	N/A	N/A	218.3	N/A	N/A	193.8
Checking RMSE	0.020	0.013	0.015	0.015	0.017	0.016

tested the online-mode BP (or incremental gradient) algorithm with a fixed momentum (0.8) because if it works, it's probably fastest; yet, the single-MLP model took roughly six days (nearly 3 million epochs), whereas the five-MLP mixtures model took over five days: These results with time-consuming online-BP were averaged over only 10 trails. Note in online-BP results that the time per epoch with the mixtures model was greater than that with the single-MLP model, because the former model involved a greater number of expensive evaluations of transcendental functions (e.g. exp) than the latter in *forward pass*, which usually takes more time than *backward pass* in BP (Mizutani & Dreyfus, 2001). (If all the terminal node functions are linear, then the reverse inequality may hold.) Overall, in this problem setting ($m = 10,000$; $n \approx 2200$), iterative-dogleg was a winner, and the five-MLP mixtures model appeared to have greater learning capacity (faster learning in this case) than the same-size single-MLP model, although they did not differ much in *generalization* performance but the mixtures model is often better in generalization owing to localized parameter-tunings (Mizutani & Nishio, 2002).

4. Conclusion and future work

Identifying certain key features unique to a posed multiple-output NN model often gives rise to a block separable nonlinear least squares problem that commonly entails such sparse data structures as block-angular residual Jacobian and symmetric block-arrow Hessian matrices. Consequently, our structure-exploiting Algorithms 1 and 2, which avoid storing and operating on the zero entries, are applicable to a wide class of NN-learning algorithms that employ the Hessian matrix implicitly or explicitly (e.g. natural gradient and quasi-Newton methods), and thus they are practically very useful in reducing the *time per epoch* as well as the total time to meet a stopping criterion. Specifically, the trust-region block-arrow direct solver [with either Cholesky (Algorithm 1) or QR] often takes much fewer epochs to converge than iterative solvers; hence, recommendable for small- and medium-scale problems. For large-scale problems, our iterative (matrix-free) version (with Algorithm 2) works economically, reducing both work and storage by a factor of O(n) (a large improvement for n very large) via implicit matrix-vector product to extract Hessian information in Krylov subspaces (*iterative batch-mode learning*). With this version, it would be of interest to implement large *ensemble learning* for *simultaneous MLP-model averaging* using the same architecture in Fig. 1 with two distinct residuals $\mathbf{y} - \mathbf{t}$ and $\boldsymbol{\omega}_i - \mathbf{t}$ ($i = 1, \ldots, Z$) used simultaneously [by hidden-node teaching in Mizutani et al. (2000)]; for instance, an equally-weighted MLP-mixtures model with $w_i = \frac{1}{z}$ held fixed can be employed for *simple model averaging* (or *committee methods*) over Z muliple MLP-predictors at the same time [see Ch.8 in Hastie et al. (2002) for model averaging]. In this mode of ensemble model averaging, more sparsity will be involved in Matrix (5). Furthermore, Alogrithm 2 can be accelerated with a simpler method of Pearlmutter (1994) when row vectors of the residual Jacobian matrix are not needed explicitly, although Alogrithm 2 makes it easier to apply other numerical linear algebra approaches (e.g. preconditioning; Mizutani & Demmel, 2003b).

Acknowledgements

The work was supported in part by the Ministry of Education, Taiwan ROC under Grant 89-E-FA04-1-4.

References

Amari, S.-I. (1998). Natural gradient works efficiently in learning. *Neural Computation, 10*, 251–276.

Björck, A. (1996). *Numerical methods for least squares problems*. SIAM.

Conn, A. R., Gould, N. I. M., & Toint, P. L. (2000). *Trust-region methods. MPS/SIAM series on optimization*, SIAM.

Demmel, J. (1997). *Applied numerical linear algebra*. SIAM.

Dennis, J. E., Gay, D. M., & Welsch, R. E. (1981). An adaptive nonlinear least-squares algorithm. *ACM Transactions on Mathematical Software*, 7(3), 348–368.

Golub, G. H., & LeVeque, R. J (1978). Extensions and uses of the variable projection algorithm for solving nonlinear least squares problems. *Technical Report SU 326*, Department of computer Science, Stanford University (also ARO Report 79-3).

Hastie, T., Tibshirani, R., & Friedman, J. (2002). *The elements of statistical learning*. Berlin: Springer.

Kaufman, L., & Sylvester, G. (1992). Separable nonlinear least squares with multiple right-hand sides. *SIAM Journal on Matrix Analysis and Applications*, *13*(1), 68–89.

Masters, T. (1995). *Advanced algorithms for neural networks: a C++ sourcebook*. New York: Wiley.

Mizutani, E. (1999). Powell's dogleg trust-region steps with the quasi-Newton augmented Hessian for neural nonlinear least-squares learning. *Proceedings of the IEEE International Conference on Neural Networks, Washington, DC*, *2*, 1239–1244.

Mizutani, E., Dreyfus, S. E., & Nishio, K. (2000). On derivation of MLP backpropagation from the Kelley-Bryson optimal-control gradient formula and its application. *Proceedings of the IEEE International Conference on Neural Networks, Como, Italy*, *2*, 167–172.

Mizutani, E., & Demmel, J. W. (2000). On iterative Krylov-dogleg trust-region steps for solving neural networks nonlinear least squares problems. In T. Leen, T. Dietterich, & V. Tresp (Eds.), *Advances in neural information processing systems, Vol. 13 (NIPS 2000)* (pp. 605–611). Cambridge, MA: MIT Press.

Mizutani, E., & Dreyfus, S. E. (2001). On complexity analysis of supervised MLP-learning for algorithmic comparisons. *Proceedings of the INNS-IEEE International Joint Conference on Neural Networks, Washington, DC*, *1*, 347–352. Available at http://www.ieor.berkeley.edu/people/faculty/dreyfus-pubs/IJCNN01.ps.

Mizutani, E., & Demmel, J. W. (2002). On separable nonlinear least squares algorithms for neuro-fuzzy modular network learning. *Proceedings of the International Joint Conference on Neural Networks, Honolulu USA*, 2399–2404.

Mizutani, E., & Nishio, K. (2002). Fuzzy mixtures of complementary local experts: towards neuro-fuzzy modular networks. *Proceedings of the IEEE International Conference on Fuzzy Systems (FUZZ-IEEE), Honolulu USA*, *2*, 1192–1197.

Mizutani, E., & Demmel, J.W. (2003a). On augmenting neural-network learning capacity for large-scale classification benchmarks by iterative batch/block-mode trust-region Krylov-dogleg algorithms. To appear in Proceedings of the Third Int'l DCDIS Conf. on Engineering Applications and Computational Algorithms. Guelph CANADA, May.

Mizutani, E., & Demmel, J.W. (2003b). Iterative scaled trust-region learning in Krylov subspaces via Pearlmutter's implicit spares Hessian-vector multiply. (Working manuscript).

Moré, J. J. (1983). Recent developments in algorithms and software for trust region methods. In A. Bachem, M. Grotschel, & B. Korte (Eds.), *Mathematical programming: the state of the art* (pp. 258–287). Berlin: Springer.

Nocedal, J., & Wright, S. J. (1999). *Numerical optimization. Springer series in operations*, Berlin: Springer.

Pearlmutter, B. A. (1994). Fast exact multiplication by the Hessian. *Neural Computation*, *6*(1), 147–160.

Toint, P. L. (1987). On Large scale nonlinear least squares calculations. *SIAM Journal on Scientific Computing*, *8*(3), 416–435.

PERGAMON

AVAILABLE AT
www.ComputerScienceWeb.com
POWERED BY SCIENCE DIRECT

Neural Networks 16 (2003) 755–761

Neural Networks

www.elsevier.com/locate/neunet

2003 Special issue

Stochastic resonance in noisy threshold neurons

Bart Kosko[a,*], Sanya Mitaim[b]

[a]*Department of Electrical Engineering, Signal and Image Processing Institute, University of Southern California, Los Angeles, CA 90089-2564, USA*
[b]*Department of Electrical Engineering, Faculty of Engineering, Thammasat University, Klong Luang, Pathumthani 12121, Thailand*

Abstract

Stochastic resonance occurs when noise improves how a nonlinear system performs. This paper presents two general stochastic-resonance theorems for threshold neurons that process noisy Bernoulli input sequences. The performance measure is Shannon mutual information. The theorems show that small amounts of independent additive noise can increase the mutual information of threshold neurons if the neurons detect subthreshold signals. The first theorem shows that this stochastic-resonance effect holds for all finite-variance noise probability density functions that obey a simple mean constraint that the user can control. A corollary shows that this stochastic-resonance effect occurs for the important family of (right-sided) gamma noise. The second theorem shows that this effect holds for all infinite-variance noise types in the broad family of stable distributions. Stable bell curves can model extremely impulsive noise environments. So the second theorem shows that this stochastic-resonance effect is robust against violent fluctuations in the additive noise process.

Keywords: Stochastic resonance; Noise processing; Threshold neurons; Infinite-variance noise; Mutual information

1. The benefits of noise

Noise can sometimes help neural or other nonlinear systems. Fig. 1 shows that small amounts of Gaussian pixel noise improves the standard 'baboon' image while too much noise degrades the image.

Small amounts of additive noise can also improve the performance of threshold neurons or of neurons with steep signal functions when the neurons process noisy Bernoulli sequences. Several researchers have found some form of this "stochastic resonance" (SR) effect (Bulsara & Zador, 1996; Collins, Chow, Capela, & Imhoff, 1996; Collins, Chow, & Imhoff, 1995; Douglass, Wilkens, Pantazelou, & Moss, 1993; Gammaitoni, 1995; Godivier & Chapeau-Blondeau, 1998; Hess & Albano, 1998; Jung, 1995; Jung & Mayer-Kress, 1995; Stocks, 2001) when either mutual information or input–output correlation (or signal-to-noise ratio) measures a neuron's response to a pulse stream of noisy subthreshold signals. But these studies have all used simple *finite*-variance noise types such as Gaussian or uniform noise. They further assume that the noise is both symmetric and two-sided (hence zero mean). We show that SR still occurs if the noise violates these assumptions.

The two theorems below establish that the mutual-information form of the SR effect occurs for almost all noisy threshold neurons. The first theorem holds for any finite-variance noise type that obeys a simple mean condition. A corollary shows that the SR effect still occurs for right-sided noise from the popular family of gamma probability density functions. Fig. 3 shows some simulation instances of this corollary. The second theorem holds for any infinite-variance noise type from the broad family of stable distributions. All signals are subthreshold.

Infinite variance does not imply infinite dispersion. Stable probability densities have finite dispersions but have infinite variances and infinite higher-order moments. The dispersion controls the width of the bell curve for symmetric stable densities (see Fig. 4). Fig. 2 shows a simulation instance of the second theorem. Infinite-variance Cauchy noise corrupts the subthreshold signal stream but still produces the characteristic nonmonotonic signature of SR. The theorem on infinite-variance noise implies that the SR effect is robust against impulsive noise: a threshold neuron can extract some information-theoretic gain even from noise streams that contain occasional violent spikes of noise. The noise stream itself is a local form of free energy that neurons can exploit.

The combined results support Linsker's hypothesis (Linsker, 1988, 1997) that neurons have evolved to

* Corresponding author.

0893-6080/03/$ - see front matter © 2003 Elsevier Science Ltd. All rights reserved.
doi:10.1016/S0893-6080(03)00128-X

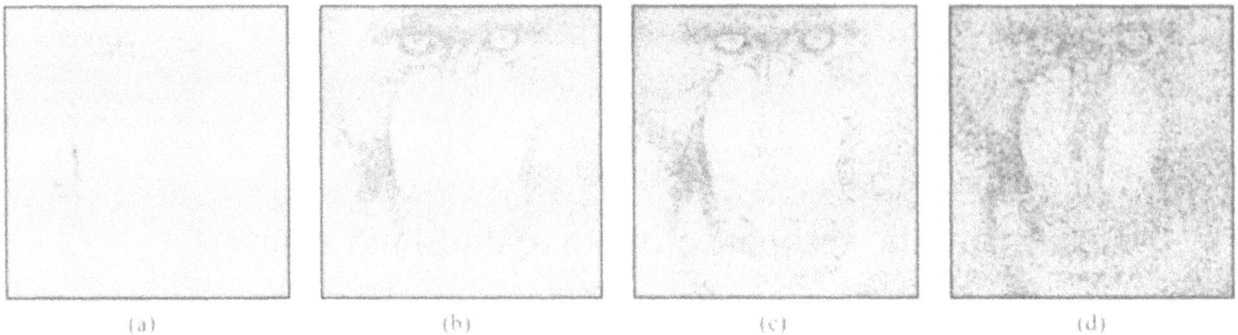

Fig. 1. Gaussian pixel noise can improve the quality of an image through a stochastic-resonance or dithering process (Gaimmaitoni, 1995; Wannamaker, Lipshitz & Vanderkooy, 2000). The noise produces a nonmonotonic response: A small level of noise sharpens the image features while too much noise degrades them. These noisy images result when we apply a pixel threshold to the 'baboon' image. The system first quantizes the original gray-scale baboon image into a binary image of black and white pixels. It gives a white pixel as output if the input gray-scale pixel equals or exceeds a threshold θ. It gives a black pixel as output if the input gray-scale pixel falls below the threshold $\theta : y = g((x+n) - \theta)$ where $g(x) = 1$ if $x \geq 0$ and $g(x) = 0$ if $x < 0$ for an input pixel value$x \in [0,1]$ and output pixel value $y \in \{0,1\}$. The input image's gray-scale pixels vary from 0 (black) to 1 (white). The threshold is $\theta = 0.04$. Thresholding the original baboon image gives the faint image in (a). The Gaussian noise n has zero mean for images (b)–(d). The noise variance σ_n^2 grows from (b) to (d): $\sigma_n^2 = 1.00 \times 10^{-2}$ in (b), $\sigma_n^2 = 2.25 \times 10^{-2}$ in (c), and $\sigma_n^2 = 9.00 \times 10^{-2}$ in (d).

maximize the information content of their local environment. The new twist to the hypothesis is that maximizing a threshold neuron's mutual information requires deliberate use of environmental noise.

2. Threshold neurons and Shannon's mutual information

We use the standard discrete-time threshold neuron model (Bulsara & Zador, 1996; Gammaitoni, 1995; Hopfield, 1982; Jung, 1995; Kosko, 1991; Kosko & Mitaim, 2001)

$$y_t = \mathrm{sgn}(s_t + n_t - \theta) = \begin{cases} 1 & \text{if } s_t + n_t \geq \theta \\ 0 & \text{if } s_t + n_t < \theta \end{cases} \tag{1}$$

where $\theta > 0$ is the neuron's threshold, s_t is the bipolar input Bernoulli signal (with arbitrary success probability p such that $0 < p < 1$) with amplitude $A > 0$, and n_t is the additive white noise with probability density $p(n)$.

The threshold neuron uses subthreshold binary signals. The symbol '0' denotes the input signal $s = -A$ and output signal

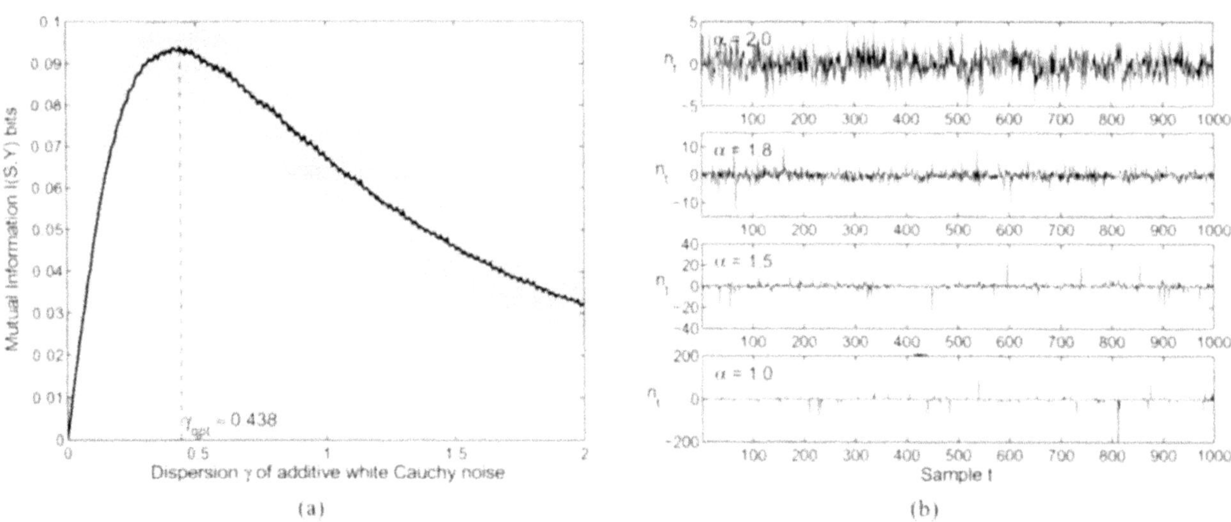

Fig. 2. SR with infinite-variance Cauchy noise. (a) The graph shows the smoothed input-output mutual information of a threshold neuron as a function of the dispersion of additive white Cauchy noise n_t. The dispersion γ controls the width of the Cauchy bell curve. The vertical dashed lines show the absolute deviation between the smallest and largest outliers in each sample average of 100 outcomes. The neuron has a nonzero noise optimum at $\gamma_{\text{opt}} \approx 0.438$ and thus shows the SR effect. The noisy signal-forced threshold neuron has the form of Eq. (1). The Cauchy noise n_t adds to the bipolar input Bernoulli signal s_t. The neuron has threshold $\theta = 1$. The input Bernoulli signal has amplitude $A = 0.8$ with success probability $p = \frac{1}{2}$. Each trial produced 10,000 input–output samples $\{s_t, y_t\}$ that estimated the probability densities to obtain the mutual information. (b) Sample realizations of symmetric (bell-curve) alpha-stable random variables with zero location ($a = 0$) and unit dispersion ($\gamma = 1$). The plots show realizations when $\alpha = 2$,1.8,1.5, and 1. Note the scale differences on the y-axes. The alpha-stable variable n becomes more impulsive as the parameter α falls. The algorithm in (Chambers, Mallows, & Stuck, 1976; Tsakalides & Nikias, 1996) generated these realizations.

$y = 0$. The symbol '1' denotes the input signal $s = A$ and output signal $y = 1$. We assume subthreshold input signals: $A < \theta$. Then the conditional probabilities $P_{Y|S}(y|s)$ are

$$P_{Y|S}(0|0) = Pr\{s + n < \theta\}|_{s=-A} = Pr\{n < \theta + A\}$$

$$= \int_{-\infty}^{\theta+A} p(n)\mathrm{d}n \quad (2)$$

$$P_{Y|S}(1|0) = 1 - P_{Y|S}(0|0) \quad (3)$$

$$P_{Y|S}(0|1) = Pr\{s + n < \theta\}|_{s=A} = Pr\{n < \theta - A\}$$

$$= \int_{-\infty}^{\theta-A} p(n)\mathrm{d}n \quad (4)$$

$$P_{Y|S}(1|1) = 1 - P_{Y|S}(0|1) \quad (5)$$

and the marginal density is

$$P_Y(y) = \sum_s P_{Y|S}(y|s)P_S(s) \quad (6)$$

Other researchers have derived the conditional probabilities $P_{Y|S}(y|s)$ of the threshold system with Gaussian noise with bipolar inputs (Bulsara & Zador, 1996) and Gaussian inputs (Stocks, 2001). We neither restrict the noise density to be Gaussian nor require that the density have finite variance even if the density has a bell-curve shape.

We use Shannon mutual information (Cover & Thomas, 1991) to measure the noise enhancement or SR effect (Bulsara & Zador, 1996; Deco & Schürmann, 1998; Godivier & Chapeau-Blondeau, 1998; Inchiosa, Robinson, & Bulsara, 2000; Stocks, 2001). The discrete Shannon mutual information of the input S and output Y is the difference between the output unconditional entropy $H(Y)$ and the output conditional entropy $H(Y|X)$:

$$I(S,Y) = H(Y) - H(Y|S) \quad (7)$$

$$= -\sum_y P_Y(y)\log P_Y(y) + \sum_s \sum_y P_{SY}(s,y)\log P_{Y|S}(y|s) \quad (8)$$

$$= -\sum_y P_Y(y)\log P_Y(y) + \sum_s P_S(s)\sum_y P_{Y|S}(y|s)\log P_{Y|S}(y|s) \quad (9)$$

$$= \sum_{s,y} P_{SY}(s,y)\log\frac{P_{SY}(s,y)}{P_S(s)P_Y(y)} \quad (10)$$

So the mutual information is the expectation of the random variable $\log[P_{SY}(s,y)/(P_S(s)P_Y(y))]$

$$I(S,Y) = E\left[\log\frac{P_{SY}(s,y)}{P_S(s)P_Y(y)}\right] \quad (11)$$

Here $P_S(s)$ is the probability density of the input S, $P_Y(y)$ is the probability density of the output Y, $P_{Y|S}(y|s)$ is the conditional density of the output Y given the input S, and $P_{SY}(s,y)$ is the joint density of the input S and the output Y. Simple bipolar histograms of samples can estimate these densities in practice.

Mutual information also measures the pseudo-distance between the joint probability density $P_{SY}(s,y)$ and the product density $P_S(s)P_Y(y)$. This holds for the Kullback (Cover & Thomas, 1991) pseudo-distance measure

$$I(S,Y) = \sum_s \sum_y P_{SY}(s,y)\log\frac{P_{SY}(s,y)}{P_S(s)P_Y(y)} \quad (12)$$

Then Jensen's inequality implies that $I(S,Y) \geq 0$. Random variables S and Y are statistically independent if and only if $I(S,Y) = 0$. Hence $I(S,Y) > 0$ implies some degree of dependence. We use this fact in the following proofs.

3. Proof of stochastic resonance for threshold neurons

We now prove that almost all finite-variance noise densities produce the SR effect in threshold neurons with subthreshold signals. This holds for all probability distributions on a two-symbol alphabet. The proof shows that if $I(S,Y) > 0$ then eventually the mutual information $I(S,Y)$ tends toward zero as the noise variance tends toward zero. So the mutual information $I(S,Y)$ must *increase* as the noise variance increases from zero. The only limiting assumption is that the noise mean $E[n]$ does not lie in the signal-threshold interval $[\theta - A, \theta + A]$.

Theorem 1. *Suppose that the threshold neuron* (1) *has noise probability density function $p(n)$ and that the input signal S is subthreshold ($A < \theta$). Suppose that there is some statistical dependence between input random variable S and output random variable Y (so that $I(S,Y) > 0$). Suppose that the noise mean $E[n]$ does not lie in the signal-threshold interval $[\theta - A, \theta + A]$ if $p(n)$ has finite variance. Then the threshold neuron* (1) *exhibits the nonmonotone SR effect in the sense that $I(S,Y) \to 0$ as $\sigma \to 0$.*

Proof. Assume $0 < P_S(s) < 1$ to avoid triviality when $P_S(s) = 0$ or 1. We show that S and Y are asymptotically independent: $I(\sigma) \to 0$ as $\sigma \to 0$. Recall that $I(S,Y) = 0$ if and only if S and Y are statistically independent (Cover & Thomas, 1991). So we need to show only that $P_{SY}(s,y) = P_S(s)P_Y(y)$ or $P_{Y|S}(y|s) = P_Y(y)$ as $\sigma \to 0$ for some signal symbols $s \in \mathcal{S}$ and $y \in \mathcal{Y}$. The two-symbol alphabet set $\mathcal{S}$ gives

$$P_Y(y) = \sum_s P_{Y|S}(y|s)P_S(s) \quad (13)$$

$$= P_{Y|S}(y|0)P_S(0) + P_{Y|S}(y|1)P_S(1) \quad (14)$$

$$= P_{Y|S}(y|0)P_S(0) + P_{Y|S}(y|1)(1 - P_S(0)) \quad (15)$$

$$= (P_{Y|S}(y|0) - P_{Y|S}(y|1))P_S(0) + P_{Y|S}(y|1) \quad (16)$$

So we need to show only that $P_{Y|S}(y|0) - P_{Y|S}(y|1) = 0$ as $\sigma \to 0$. This condition implies that $P_Y(y) = P_{Y|S}(y|1)$ and $P_Y(y) = P_{Y|S}(y|0)$. We assume for simplicity that the noise density $p(n)$ is integrable. The argument below still holds if $p(n)$ is discrete and if we replace integrals with appropriate sums.

Consider $y =$ '0'. Then Eqs. (2) and (4) imply that

$$P_{Y|S}(0|0) - P_{Y|S}(0|1) = \int_{-\infty}^{\theta+A} p(n)\mathrm{d}n - \int_{-\infty}^{\theta-A} p(n)\mathrm{d}n \tag{17}$$

$$= \int_{\theta-A}^{\theta+A} p(n)\mathrm{d}n \tag{18}$$

Similarly for $y =$ '1':

$$P_{Y|S}(1|0) = \int_{\theta+A}^{\infty} p(n)\mathrm{d}n \tag{19}$$

$$P_{Y|S}(1|1) = \int_{\theta-A}^{\infty} p(n)\mathrm{d}n \tag{20}$$

Then

$$P_{Y|S}(1|0) - P_{Y|S}(1|1) = -\int_{\theta-A}^{\theta+A} p(n)\mathrm{d}n \tag{21}$$

The result now follows if

$$\int_{\theta-A}^{\theta+A} p(n)\mathrm{d}n \to 0 \text{ as } \sigma \to 0 \tag{22}$$

Let the mean of the noise be $m = E[n]$ and the variance be $\sigma^2 = E[(x-m)^2]$. Then $m \notin [\theta - A, \theta + A]$ by hypothesis.

Now suppose that $m < \theta - A$. Pick $\epsilon = \frac{1}{2}\mathrm{d}(\theta - A, m) = \frac{1}{2}(\theta - A - m) > 0$. So $\theta - A - \epsilon = \theta - A - \epsilon + m - m = m + (\theta - A - m) - \epsilon = m + 2\epsilon - \epsilon = m + \epsilon$. Then

$$P_{Y|S}(0|0) - P_{Y|S}(0|1) = \int_{\theta-A}^{\theta+A} p(n)\mathrm{d}n \tag{23}$$

$$\leq \int_{\theta-A}^{\infty} p(n)\mathrm{d}n \tag{24}$$

$$\leq \int_{\theta-A-\epsilon}^{\infty} p(n)\mathrm{d}n \tag{25}$$

$$= \int_{m+\epsilon}^{\infty} p(n)\mathrm{d}n \tag{26}$$

$$= Pr\{n \geq m + \epsilon\} \tag{27}$$

$$= Pr\{n - m \geq \epsilon\} \tag{28}$$

$$\leq Pr\{|n - m| \geq \epsilon\} \tag{29}$$

$$\leq \frac{\sigma^2}{\epsilon^2} \text{ by Chebyshev inequality} \tag{30}$$

$$\to 0 \text{ as } \sigma \to 0 \tag{31}$$

A symmetric argument shows that for $m > \theta + A$

$$P_{Y|S}(0|0) - P_{Y|S}(0|1) \leq \frac{\sigma^2}{\epsilon^2} \to 0 \text{ as } \sigma \to 0 \quad \square \tag{32}$$

Corollary. *The threshold neuron Eq.* (1) *exhibits SR for the additive gamma noise density*

$$p(n) = \begin{cases} \dfrac{n^{\alpha-1} e^{-n/\beta}}{\Gamma(\alpha)\beta^{\alpha}} & n \geq 0 \\ 0 & \end{cases} \tag{33}$$

otherwise under the hypotheses of Theorem 1. Parameters α and β are positive constants and Γ is the gamma function

$$\Gamma(x) = \int_0^{\infty} y^{x-1} e^{y}\, \mathrm{d}y \tag{34}$$

$x > 0$. Gamma random variables have finite mean $\alpha\beta$ and functionally related finite variance $\alpha\beta^2$. Gamma family of random variables includes the popular special cases of exponential, Erlang, and chi-square random variables. All these random variables are right-sided. Fig. 3 shows simulation realizations of this corollary. This appears to be the first demonstration of the SR effect for *right-sided* noise processes.

We now proceed to the more general (and more realistic) case where infinite-variance noise interferes with the threshold neuron. The SR effect also occurs in other systems with impulsive infinite-variance noise (Kosko & Mitaim, 2001; Mitaim & Kosko, 1998). We can model many types of impulsive noise with *symmetric* alpha-stable bell-curve probability density functions with parameter α in the characteristic function $\varphi(\omega) = \exp\{-\gamma|\omega|^{\alpha}\}$. Here γ is the *dispersion* parameter (Breiman, 1968; Feller, 1966; Grigoriu, 1995; Nikias & Shao, 1995). Fig. 4 shows examples of symmetric (bell-curve) alpha-stable probability density functions with different α tail thicknesses and different bell-curve dispersions γ.

The parameter α controls tail thickness and lies in $0 < \alpha \leq 2$. Noise grows more impulsive as α falls and the bell-curve tails grow thicker. The (thin-tailed) Gaussian density results when $\alpha = 2$ or when $\varphi(\omega) = \exp\{-\gamma\omega^2\}$. So the standard Gaussian random variable has zero mean and variance $\sigma^2 = 2$ (when $\gamma = 1$). The parameter α gives the thicker-tailed Cauchy bell curve when $\alpha = 1$ or $\varphi(\omega) = \exp\{-|\omega|\}$ for a zero *location* ($a = 0$) and unit dispersion ($\gamma = 1$) Cauchy random variable. The moments of stable distributions with $\alpha < 2$ are finite only up to the order k for $k < \alpha$. The Gaussian density alone has finite variance and higher moments. Alpha-stable random variables characterize the class of normalized sums of independent random variables that converge in distribution to a random variable (Breiman, 1968) as in the famous Gaussian special case called the "central limit theorem."

Alpha-stable models tend to work well when the noise or signal data contains 'outliers'—and all do to some degree.

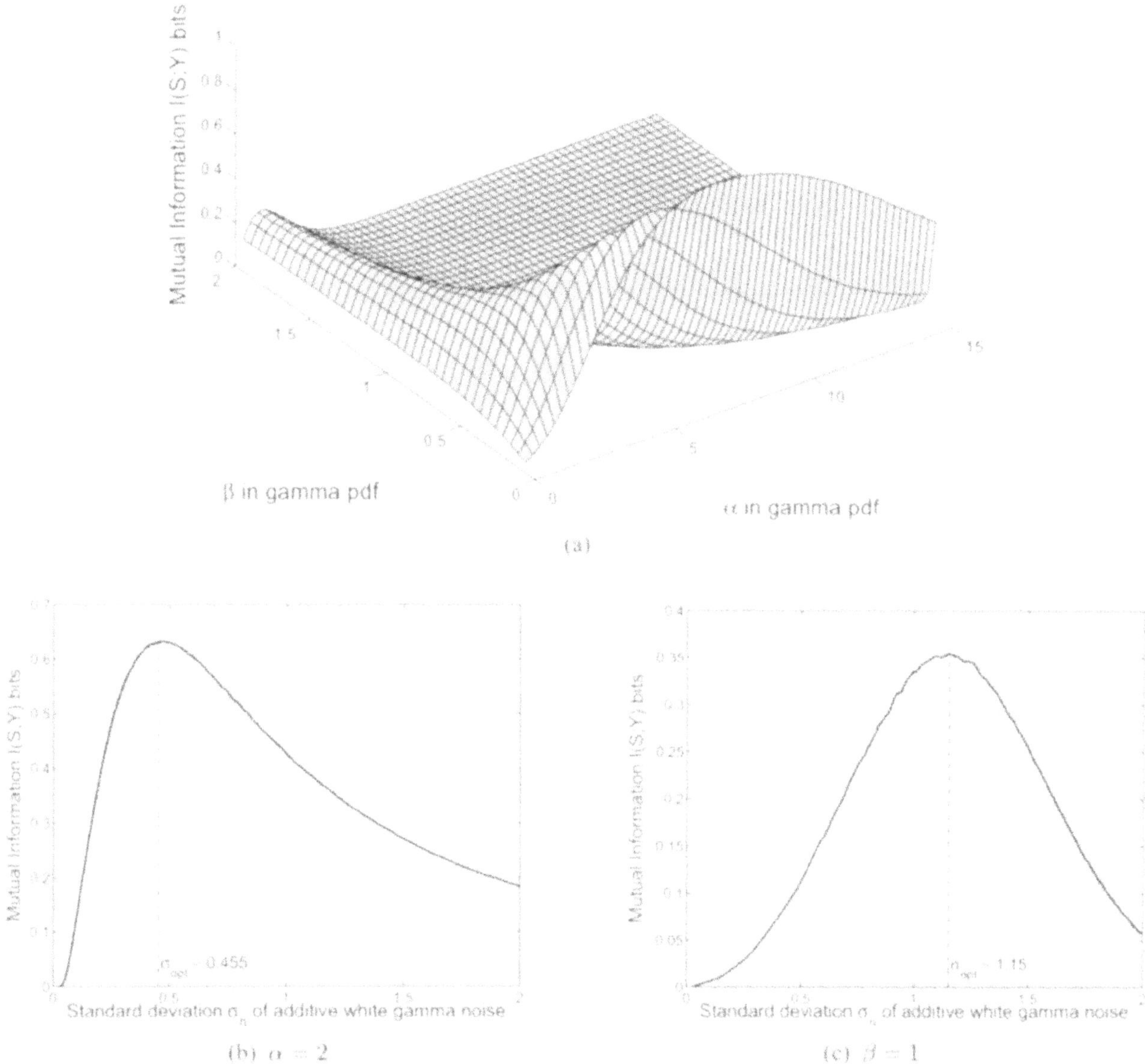

Fig. 3. SR with (finite-variance) gamma noise. The noisy signal-forced threshold neuron has the form of Eq. (1). The gamma noise n_t adds to the bipolar input Bernoulli signal s_t. The neuron has threshold $\theta = 1$. The input Bernoulli signal has amplitude $A = 0.8$ with success probability $p = \frac{1}{2}$. Each trial produced 10,000 input–output samples $\{s_t, y_t\}$ that estimated the probability densities to obtain the mutual information. The algorithm in (Ahrens & Dieter, 1974, 1982) generated realizations of the gamma random variable. (a) The graph shows the smoothed input–output mutual information of a threshold neuron as a function of the parameters α and β of additive white gamma noise n_t. The neuron's mutual information has a nonzero noise optimum $\sigma_{opt} > 0$ for each $\alpha > 0$. It also has a nonzero noise optimum $\sigma_{opt} > 0$ for each $\beta > 0$. (b) The graph shows the cross-section of the mutual-information surface for $\alpha = 2$. (c) The graph shows the cross-section for $\beta = 1$. Note that the mean and variance of the gamma noise are $m_n = \alpha\beta$ and $\sigma_n^2 = \alpha\beta^2$.

Models with $\alpha < 2$ can accurately describe impulsive noise in telephone lines, underwater acoustics, low-frequency atmospheric signals, fluctuations in gravitational fields and financial prices, and many other processes (Kosko, 1996; Nikias & Shao, 1995). Note that the best choice of α is an *empirical* question for bell-curve phenomena. Bell-curve behavior alone does not justify the (extreme) assumption of the Gaussian bell curve.

Theorem 2 applies to *any* alpha-stable noise model. The density need not be symmetric. A general alpha-stable probability density function f has characteristic function φ (Akgiray & Lamoureux, 1989; Bergstrom, 1952; Grigoriu, 1995; Nikias & Shao, 1995):

$$\varphi(\omega) = \exp\left\{ia\omega - \gamma|\omega|^{\alpha}\left(1 + i\beta \text{sign}(\omega)\tan\frac{\alpha\pi}{2}\right)\right\} \text{ for } \alpha \neq 1 \tag{35}$$

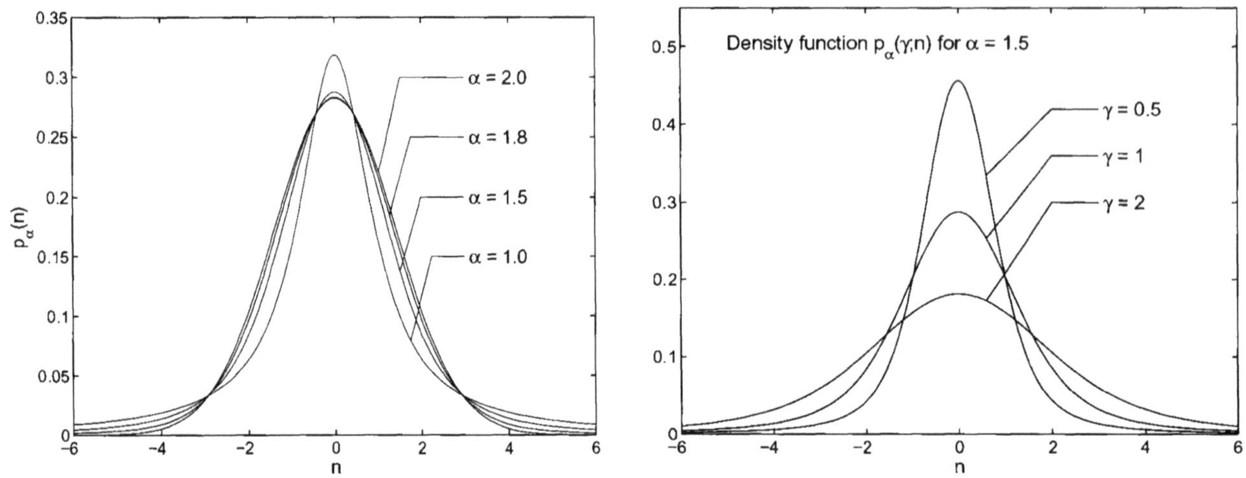

(a) (b)

Fig. 4. Samples of standard symmetric ($\beta = 0$) alpha-stable probability densities. (a) Density functions with zero location ($\alpha = 0$) and unit dispersion ($\gamma = 1$) for $\alpha = 2, 1.8, 1.5$, and 1. The densities are bell curves that have thicker tails as α decreases and thus that model increasingly impulsive noise as α decreases. The case $\alpha = 2$ gives a Gaussian density with variance two (or unit dispersion). The parameter $\alpha = 1$ gives the Cauchy density with infinite variance. (b) Density functions for $\alpha = 1.5$ with dispersions $\gamma = 0.5, 1$, and 2.

and

$$\varphi(\omega) = \exp\{ia\omega - \gamma|\omega|(1 - 2i\beta\ln|\omega|\text{sign}(\omega)/\pi)\} \text{ for } \alpha = 1 \tag{36}$$

where

$$\text{sign}(\omega) = \begin{cases} 1 & \text{if } \omega > 0 \\ 0 & \text{if } \omega = 0 \\ -1 & \text{if } \omega < 0 \end{cases} \tag{37}$$

and $i = \sqrt{-1}$, $0 < \alpha \le 2$, $-1 \le \beta \le 1$, and $\gamma > 0$. The parameter α is the characteristic exponent. Again the variance of an alpha-stable density does not exist if $\alpha < 2$. The location parameter a is the "mean" of the density when $\alpha > 1$. β is a skewness parameter. The density is symmetric about a when $\beta = 0$. Theorem 2 still holds even when $\beta \ne 0$. The dispersion parameter γ acts like a variance because it controls the width of a symmetric alpha-stable bell curve. There are no known closed forms of the α-stable densities for most α's.

The proof of Theorem 2 is simpler than the proof in the finite-variance case because all stable noise densities have a characteristic function with the exponential form in Eqs. (35) and (36). So zero noise dispersion gives φ as a simple complex exponential and hence gives the corresponding density as a delta spike that can fall outside the interval $[\theta - A, \theta + A]$.

Theorem 2. *Suppose $I(S, Y) > 0$ and the threshold neuron* Eq (1) *uses alpha-stable noise with location parameter $a \notin [\theta - A, \theta + A]$. Then the neuron* (1) *exhibits the nonmonotone SR effect if the input signal is subthreshold.*

Proof. Again the result follows if

$$\int_{\theta-A}^{\theta+A} p(n)\mathrm{d}n \to 0 \text{ as } \gamma \to 0 \tag{38}$$

The characteristic function $\varphi(\omega)$ of alpha-stable noise density, $p(n)$ has the exponential form Eqs. (35) and (36). This reduces to a simple complex exponential in the zero-dispersion limit:

$$\lim_{\gamma \to 0} \varphi(\omega) = \exp\{ia\omega\} \tag{39}$$

for *all* α's, skewness β's, and location a's. So Fourier transformation gives the corresponding density function in the limiting case ($\gamma \to 0$) as a translated delta function

$$\lim_{\gamma \to 0} p(n) = \delta(n - a) \tag{40}$$

Then

$$P_{Y|S}(0|0) - P_{Y|S}(0|1) = \int_{\theta-A}^{\theta+A} p(n)\mathrm{d}n \tag{41}$$

$$= \int_{\theta-A}^{\theta+A} \delta(n - a)\mathrm{d}n \tag{42}$$

$$= 0 \tag{43}$$

because $a \notin [\theta - A, \theta + A]$. □

Fig. 2 gives a typical example of the SR effect for highly impulsive noise with infinite variance. Here the noise type is Cauchy ($\alpha = 1$) and thus frequent and violent noise spikes interfere with the signal.

4. Conclusions

Noise affects neural systems in complex ways. The above theorems show that almost all noise types produce SR in threshold neurons that use subthreshold signals and small amounts of noise. This includes right-sided finite-variance noise such as gamma noise. The theorems do not guarantee that the predicted increase in mutual information will be significant. They guarantee only that some increase will occur. Other work (Kosko & Mitaim, 2001) suggests that the increase will decrease in significance as the impulsiveness of the noise process increases. All our simulations showed a significant and visible SR effect.

These results help explain the widespread occurrence of the SR effect in mechanical and biological threshold systems (Braun, Wissing, Schäfer, & Hirsch, 1994; Douglass et al., 1993; Fauve & Heslot, 1983; Melnikov, 1993; Levin & Miller, 1996; Russell, Willkens, & Moss, 1999). The broad generality of the results suggests that SR should occur in any nonlinear system whose input–output structure approximates a threshold system and that includes most model neurons. The infinite-variance result further implies that such widespread SR effects should be robust against violent noise impulses. The combined results support the hypothesis (Linsker, 1988, 1997) that neurons have evolved to maximize their local information if they process subthreshold signals in the presence of noise. This need not hold for suprathreshold signals.

Acknowledgements

National Science Foundation Grant No. ECS-0070284 and Thailand Research Fund Grant No. RSA4680001 supported this research.

References

Ahrens, J. H., & Dieter, U. (1974). Computer methods for sampling from gamma, beta, poisson and binomial distributions. *Computing*, *12*, 223–246.

Ahrens, J. H., & Dieter, U. (1982). Generating gamma variates by a modified rejection technique. *Communications of the ACM*, *25*(1), 47–54.

Akgiray, V., & Lamoureux, C. G. (1989). Estimation of stable-law parameters: A comparative study. *Journal of Business and Economic Statistics*, *7*, 85–93.

Bergstrom, H. (1952). On some expansions of stable distribution functions. *Arkhiv Mathematics*, *2*, 375–378.

Braun, H. A., Wissing, H., Schäfer, K., & Hirsch, M. C. (1994). Oscillation and noise determine signal transduction in shark multimodal sensory cells. *Nature*, *367*, 270–273.

Breiman, L. (1968). *Probability*. Reading, MA: Addison-Wesley.

Bulsara, A. R., & Zador, A. (1996). Threshold detection of wideband signals: A noise-induced maximum in the mutual information. *Physical Review E*, *54*(3), R2185–R2188.

Chambers, J. M., Mallows, C. L., & Stuck, B. W. (1976). A method for simulating stable random variables. *Journal of the American Statistical Association*, *71*(354), 340–344.

Collins, J. J., Chow, C. C., Capela, A. C., & Imhoff, T. T. (1996). Aperiodic stochastic resonance. *Physical Review E*, *54*(5), 5575–5584.

Collins, J. J., Chow, C. C., & Imhoff, T. T. (1995). Stochastic resonance without tuning. *Nature*, *376*, 236–238.

Cover, T. M., & Thomas, J. A. (1991). *Elements of information theory*. New York: Wiley.

Deco, G., & Schürmann, B. (1998). Stochastic resonance in the mutual information between input and output spike trains of noisy central neurons. *Physica D*, *117*, 276–282.

Douglass, J. K., Wilkens, L., Pantazelou, E., & Moss, F. (1993). Noise enhancement of information transfer in crayfish mechanoreceptors by stochastic resonance. *Nature*, *365*, 337–340.

Fauve, S., & Heslot, F. (1983). Stochastic resonance in a bistable system. *Physics Letters A*, *97*(1–2), 5–7.

Feller, W. (1966) (*Vol. II*). *An introduction to probability theory and its applications*. New York: Wiley.

Gammaitoni, L. (1995). Stochastic resonance and the dithering effect in threshold physical systems. *Physical Review E*, *52*(5), 4691–4698.

Godivier, X., & Chapeau-Blondeau, F. (1998). Stochastic resonance in the information capacity of a nonlinear dynamic system. *International Journal of Bifurcation and Chaos*, *8*(3), 581–589.

Grigoriu, M. (1995). *Applied non-gaussian processes*. Englewood Cliffs, NJ: Prentice Hall.

Hess, S. M., & Albano, A. M. (1998). Minimum requirements for stochastic resonance in threshold systems. *International Journal of Bifurcation and Chaos*, *8*(2), 395–400.

Hopfield, J. J. (1982). Neural networks and physical systems with emergent collective computational abilities. *Proceedings of the National Academy of Science*, *79*, 2554–2558.

Inchiosa, M. E., Robinson, J. W. C., & Bulsara, A. R. (2000). Information-theoretic stochastic resonance in noise-floor limited systems: The case for adding noise. *Physical Review Letters*, *85*, 3369–3372.

Jung, P. (1995). Stochastic resonance and optimal design of threshold detectors. *Physics Letters A*, *207*, 93–104.

Jung, P., & Mayer-Kress, G. (1995). Stochastic resonance in threshold devices. *Il Nuovo Cimento*, *17D*(7–8), 827–834.

Kosko, B. (1991). *Neural networks and fuzzy systems: A dynamical systems approach to machine intelligence*. Englewood Cliffs, NJ: Prentice Hall.

Kosko, B. (1996). *Fuzzy engineering*. Englewood Cliffs, NJ: Prentice Hall.

Kosko, B., & Mitaim, S. (2001). Robust stochastic resonance: signal detection and adaptation in impulsive noise. *Physical Review E*, *64*(051110).

Levin, J. E., & Miller, J. P. (1996). Broadband neural encoding in the cricket cercal sensory system enhanced by stochastic resonance. *Nature*, *380*, 165–168.

Linsker, R. (1988). Self-organization in a perceptual network. *Computer*, *21*(3), 105–117.

Linsker, R. (1997). A local learning rule that enables information maximization for arbitrary input distributions. *Neural Computation*, *9*(8), 1661–1665.

Melnikov, V. I. (1993). Schmitt trigger: A solvable model of stochastic resonance. *Physical Review E*, *48*(4), 2481–2489.

Mitaim, S., & Kosko, B. (1998). Adaptive stochastic resonance. *Proceedings of the IEEE: Special issue on intelligent signal processing*, *86*(11), 2152–2183.

Nikias, C. L., & Shao, M. (1995). *Signal processing with alpha-stable distributions and applications*. New York: Wiley.

Russell, D. F., Willkens, L. A., & Moss, F. (1999). Use of behavioural stochastic resonance by paddle fish for feeding. *Nature*, *402*, 291–294.

Stocks, N. G. (2001). Information transmission in parallel threshold arrays. *Physical Review E*, *63*(041114).

Tsakalides, P., & Nikias, C. L. (1996). The robust covariation-based MUSIC (ROC-MUSIC) algorithm for bearing estimation in impulsive noise environments. *IEEE Transactions on Signal Processing*, *44*(7), 1623–1633.

Wannamaker, R.A., Lipshitz, S.P., & Vanderkooy, J. (2000). Stochastic resonance as dithering. *Physical Review E*, *61*(1), 233–236.

AVAILABLE AT
www.ComputerScienceWeb.com
POWERED BY SCIENCE DIRECT

PERGAMON

Neural Networks 16 (2003) 763–770

Neural Networks

www.elsevier.com/locate/neunet

2003 Special issue

Quantum optimization for training support vector machines

Davide Anguita*, Sandro Ridella, Fabio Rivieccio, Rodolfo Zunino

DIBE—Department of Biophysical and Electronic Engineering, University of Genoa, Via Opera Pia 11A 16145 Genova, Italy

Abstract

Refined concepts, such as Rademacher estimates of model complexity and nonlinear criteria for weighting empirical classification errors, represent recent and promising approaches to characterize the generalization ability of Support Vector Machines (SVMs). The advantages of those techniques lie in both improving the SVM representation ability and yielding tighter generalization bounds. On the other hand, they often make Quadratic-Programming algorithms no longer applicable, and SVM training cannot benefit from efficient, specialized optimization techniques. The paper considers the application of Quantum Computing to solve the problem of effective SVM training, especially in the case of digital implementations. The presented research compares the behavioral aspects of conventional and enhanced SVMs; experiments in both a synthetic and real-world problems support the theoretical analysis. At the same time, the related differences between Quadratic-Programming and Quantum-based optimization techniques are considered.

Keywords: Quantum optimization; Support vector machine; Quadratic-programming; Robust classification

1. Introduction

The support vector machine (SVM) (Cortes & Vapnik, 1995) is a well-known and effective method for regression and pattern classification, and often leads to outstanding performances in real-world applications. The success of SVMs mainly derives from setting up the training process so as to optimize the run-time generalization performances of the resulting classifiers.

The key feature of Vapnik's formulation (Vapnik, 1998) lies in posing the maximum-margin search process as a quadratic-programming (QP) optimization problem. In spite of the intricacies brought about by highly constrained (and often poorly conditioned) QP, effective tools are available for fast QP optimization (Chang & Lin, 2003). This has ultimately boosted the practical impact of SVM classifiers.

At the same time, a vast literature in the area of Computational Learning Theory reports the search for newer, tighter bounds to the classifiers' generalization errors. In this respect, sample-based methods that use maximal-discrepancy techniques to estimate model complexity (Bartlett, Boucheron, & Lugosi, 2002; Bartlett & Mendelson, 2002) seem to represent a promising line of research. The notably tight generalization bounds attained in (Bartlett & Mendelson, 2002) result from combining two specialized approaches: a Rademacher estimate of model complexity and an advanced, nonlinear criterion for weighting empirical classification errors.

The research presented in this paper exploits these recent achievements as a single basic approach to SVM training. The paper first demonstrates the advantage of the error-weighting criterion for SVM training: the overall classifier is made robust to peculiar distributions that might divert the conventional error-weighting criterion.

On the other hand, a crucial issue raised by the nonlinear error-weighting approach is that the SVM training process cannot any longer be formulated as a conventional QP problem. Several optimization methods exist for the general case (Fletcher, 1987; Powell, 1989), yet the lack of an efficient algorithm such as QP can turn optimization into a problem with NP complexity.

This scenario leads one to envision to exploit novel technologies for effective optimization. Quantum computing (QC) (Nielsen & Chuang, 2000) represents a promising paradigm, whose importance has increased very rapidly in the last decades, mainly for the recent definition of specialized algorithms to solve complex problems, such as large-number factorization and exhaustive search.

A basic feature that makes quantum approaches appealing to applied research is that QC involves a digital representation of processed information. This proves especially useful in training SVMs for two reasons: first, the overall problem is inherently digital in both quantum

* Corresponding author. Fax: +39-010-353-2175.
E-mail address: anguita@dibe.unige.it (D. Anguita).

0893-6080/03/$ - see front matter
doi:10.1016/S0893-6080(03)00087-X

and classical computers; secondly, the optimization process has to scan exhaustively the set of possible bit configurations in the search space.

Therefore, the paper explores the possibility of using quantum-optimization algorithms for SVM training when conventional QP techniques are no longer applicable. The effectiveness of QC-based optimization is evaluated in synthetic and real-world problems, and the performances are compared with those of a Montecarlo random-search method.

2. Error weighting for training SVM classifiers

The reason that justifies the success of the SVM model lies in its structural approach. SVM training aims to find a function capable of incurring few errors on the training sample, while featuring a promising generalization ability.

Let Φ be a mapping function from the input space X into a higher-dimensional space; then the general form for a hyperplane in the mapped space is:

$$f(\mathbf{x}) = \sum_{i=1}^{\mathrm{np}} \alpha_i y_i \Phi(\mathbf{x}_i)\Phi(\mathbf{x}) + b \tag{1}$$

where the function is expressed as a weighted sum of the input samples, $\{\mathbf{x}_i,\ i = 1,\ldots,\mathrm{np}\}$, and the α_i are positive bounded quantities. If we regard Eq. (1) as a classification surface and label by y_i the class associated with each input point $\mathbf{x}_i$, the general statement of the problem sketched above is:

$$\min_{\mathbf{w},\xi,b}\left\{\frac{1}{2}\|\mathbf{w}\|^2 + C\sum_{i=1}^{\mathrm{np}}\xi_i\right\}$$

$$\text{subject to} \tag{2}$$

$$y_i(\mathbf{w}\Phi_i + b) = 1 + \mu_i - \xi_i \qquad \forall i = 1\ldots\mathrm{np}$$

$$\mu_i, \xi_i \geq 0$$

where

$$\mathbf{w} = \sum_{i=1}^{\mathrm{np}} \alpha_i y_i \Phi_i \tag{3}$$

C is a constant, μ_i are used to balance the equation in the case of a correct classification, and ξ_i is an analog measure of the error on each data-point. One of the main results of Statistical Learning Theory (Vapnik, 1998) is that the first term considered in Eq. (2) is proportional to the VC-dimension, hence its minimization enhances the generalization ability of the hyperplane in Eq. (1).

It is possible to demonstrate (Fletcher, 1987) that Eq. (2) has the same solution as a constrained QP optimization problem (the dual one) with respect to the α_i; in such a problem these variables are bounded by C and linearly constrained by the following relation:

$$\sum_{i=1}^{\mathrm{np}} \alpha_i y_i = 0 \tag{4}$$

In order to find the solution of the dual problem it is crucial to meet the Karush–Kuhn–Tucker (KKT) conditions:

$$\begin{cases} \alpha_i \mu_i = 0 \\ (C - \alpha_i)\xi_i = 0 \end{cases} \qquad \forall i = 1\ldots\mathrm{np} \tag{5}$$

The formulation of the dual problem only involves the computation of the inner product of the Φ_i. The functions for which

$$k(\mathbf{x}_i, \mathbf{x}_j) = \Phi(\mathbf{x}_i)\Phi(\mathbf{x}_j) \tag{6}$$

are called *Kernel Functions*. These functions, together with the α_i, define the SVM expansion in Eq. (1), which becomes

$$f(\mathbf{x}) = \sum_{i=1}^{\mathrm{np}} \alpha_i y_i k(\mathbf{x}_i, \mathbf{x}) + b \tag{7}$$

thus allowing a non-linear class separation.

Among the several available methods to estimate the classification error, the ones with the tightest bounds seem to be those performing a sample-based complexity estimation (Bartlett & Mendelson, 2002). This estimate involves the computation of the *Rademacher Complexity*, as follows:

$$R_{\mathrm{np}}(F) = E_{\mathrm{P}(X)}\left[E_\sigma\left[\sup_{f\in F}\left|\frac{2}{\mathrm{np}}\sum_{i=1}^{\mathrm{np}}\sigma_i f(\mathbf{x}_i)\right|\,\middle|\,\mathbf{x}_i,\ldots,\mathbf{x}_{\mathrm{np}}\right]\right] \tag{8}$$

where F is a class of functions mapping the domain of the input samples into $\Re$, $E_{\mathrm{P}(X)}$ is the expectation with respect to the probability distribution of the input data, and E_σ is the expectation with respect to σ_i, which are independent uniform random variables taking the values $\{+1, -1\}$.

One can regard $R_{\mathrm{np}}(F)$ as a measure of the ability of the class to which Eq. (7) belongs to classify the input samples if associated with a random class: as the fitting ability of the function increases, so does its complexity.

Eq. (8) can be used to derive the following bound to the generalization error of a classifier (Bartlett & Mendelson, 2002); this bound holds with probability $(1 - \delta)$:

$$P(y\cdot f(\mathbf{x}) \leq 0) = \hat{E}_{\mathrm{np}} h(y\cdot f(\mathbf{x})) + 2L\cdot R_{\mathrm{np}}(F) + \sqrt{\frac{\ln(2/\delta)}{2\mathrm{np}}} \tag{9}$$

where $\hat{E}_{\mathrm{np}}$ is the error on the input data measured through a *loss function* $h(\cdot)$ having the Lipschitz constant L, that is:

$$\hat{E}_{\mathrm{np}} h(y\cdot f(\mathbf{x})) = \frac{1}{\mathrm{np}}\sum_{i=1}^{\mathrm{np}} h(y_i\cdot f(\mathbf{x}_i)) \tag{10}$$

The loss function $h(\cdot)$ is used to shape the relative weight of the analog error as follows:

$$\xi_i = h(y_i\cdot f(\mathbf{x}_i)) \tag{11}$$

In the classical SVM formulation by Vapnik, the form of the $h(\cdot)$ function is:

$$h_V(y \cdot f(\mathbf{x})) = \begin{cases} 0 & \text{if } y \cdot f(\mathbf{x}) \geq 1 \\ 1 - y \cdot f(\mathbf{x}) & \text{if } y \cdot f(\mathbf{x}) \leq 1 \end{cases} \quad (12)$$

Bartlett and Mendelson (2002) suggested the following better function to account for classification errors:

$$h_{BM}(y \cdot f(\mathbf{x})) = \begin{cases} 0 & \text{if } y \cdot f(\mathbf{x}) \geq 1 \\ 1 - y \cdot f(\mathbf{x}) & \text{if } 0 \leq y \cdot f(\mathbf{x}) \leq 1 \\ 1 & \text{if } y \cdot f(\mathbf{x}) \leq 0 \end{cases} \quad (13)$$

which has $L = 1$ and saturates to one for any misclassified pattern. Obviously, $h_V(u) \geq h_{BM}(u) \forall u$. As an important consequence, the formulation of the loss function as per Eq. (13) inhibits the use of well-known linearly constrained Quadratic Programming algorithms.

3. A case study on the effects of outliers

We introduce a one-dimensional dataset for the purpose of illustrating the effects of the linear penalty ξ_i used in Eq. (2) to take into account possible classification errors.

The dataset is built as follows: the points belonging to one class, say, the positive one, are concentrated in the origin; the negative-labeled ones are concentrated in $x = -1$. One outlier for the latter class is also present in $x = +\lambda$ (Fig. 1). Supposing the negative class to be composed of N_1 samples plus the outlier and the positive class to be composed of N_2 samples, the dataset can be described as follows:

$$\begin{aligned} y_n &= -1 \Rightarrow x_n = -1 \wedge x_n = +\lambda & n &= 1, \ldots N_1 + 1 \\ y_p &= +1 \Rightarrow x_p = 0 & p &= 1, \ldots N_2 \end{aligned} \quad (14)$$

Writing Eq. (2) for this specific setting and restricting our analysis to the one-dimensional case of a linear kernel (Φ is

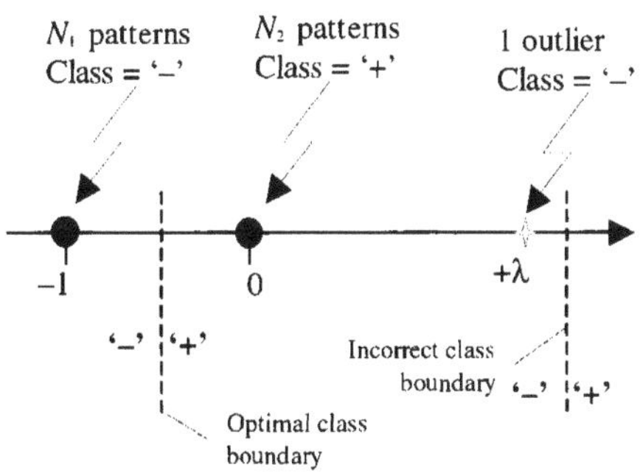

Fig. 1. Outliers might affect class-decision surfaces during SVM training.

the identity) gives:

$$\min_{w,b} \frac{w^2}{2} + C(N_1\xi_1 + N_2\xi_2 + \xi_3)$$

subject to

$$\begin{cases} w - b = 1 + \mu_1 - \xi_1 \\ b = 1 + \mu_2 - \xi_2 \\ -w\lambda - b = 1 + \mu_3 - \xi_3 \end{cases} \quad (15)$$

From the definition Eq. (3) it follows that:

$$w = N_1\alpha_1 - \lambda\alpha_3 \quad (16)$$

The goal is now to find when the analog error caused by the outlier is large enough to draw the separation threshold beyond the positive class, thus causing its misclassification. The required conditions are $w = 0$ and $b = -1$. From Eq. (15) it follows:

$$\begin{cases} -b = 1 + \mu_1 - \xi_1 \\ b = 1 + \mu_2 - \xi_2 \\ -b = 1 + \mu_3 - \xi_3 \end{cases} \quad (17)$$

and from Eq. (16) we have:

$$N_1\alpha_1 = \alpha_3\lambda \quad (18)$$

The positiveness of the constraints on μ_l and ξ_i provides:

$$\begin{cases} \mu_1 = \xi_1 = \mu_3 = \xi_3 = \mu_2 = 0 \\ \xi_2 = 2 \end{cases} \quad (19)$$

and the KKT conditions require:

$$\alpha_2 = C = \frac{N_1\alpha_1 + \alpha_3}{N_2} \quad (20)$$

where the last equality follows from Eq. (4).

Using relations Eqs. (18) and (20), we rewrite the inequality constraints on α_i as:

$$\begin{cases} \alpha_3 = C\dfrac{N_2}{1+\lambda} \leq C \\ \alpha_1 = \dfrac{\alpha_3\lambda}{N_1} = \dfrac{\lambda}{1+\lambda}\dfrac{N_2}{N_1}C \leq C \end{cases} \quad (21)$$

thus the relations that allow the feasibility of the solution are:

$$\begin{cases} N_2 \leq 1 + \lambda \\ \lambda N_2 \leq (1+\lambda)N_1 \end{cases} \quad (22)$$

The present problem has been maliciously set in order to focus the reader's attention on the difference between minimizing the (integer) number of errors and minimizing a bound on the number of errors. Indeed, under the conditions in Eq. (21), the classical SVM fails to find a reasonable solution. It is straightforward to prove that by using the loss function defined in Eq. (13) the optimal solution can be obtained with $w = 2$ and $b = 1$ when:

$$\begin{cases} 2 \le C(N_2 - 1) \\ 2(1 + \lambda^{-2}) \le C(N_1 - 1) \end{cases} \quad (23)$$

Section 4 illustrates how to approach the NP-hard problem of minimizing the number of errors by the computational paradigm of QC.

4. Quantum computing for SVM training

4.1. Quantum-based representation of states

Research on QC has experienced an enormous growth in the last decades. Due to both the subject complexity and the huge amount of existing literature, the following, synthetic treatment of QC can only provide an informal hint at the current scenario.

The state of a classical computer is supported by the mutually exclusive binary quantities '0'and '1'; any consistent state of the machine has to be represented digitally. In QC, instead, a machine may exist in a 'superposition of states' (Nielsen & Chuang, 2000), provided it is allowed to evolve undisturbed. Thus one states that a single digital quantity (a 'qbit'), ψ, can take on both states '0' and '1' at the same time. Each state is characterized by a complex number giving the probability amplitude of the state:

$$|\Psi\rangle = \sum_{i=1}^{n} \omega_i |\Psi_i\rangle \quad (24)$$

where Dirac's conventional 'ket' notation is used for the state qbits ψ_i; the probability amplitudes, ω_i, must satisfy:

$$\sum_{i=1}^{n} \|\omega_i\|^2 = 1 \quad (25)$$

The property by which the internal status of a system is described in a nontrivial probabilistic fashion is called *coherence*; according to quantum-mechanics laws, a machine can persist in a coherent state only if it does not interact in any way with the external environment. Incidentally, such a requirement is probably the major obstacle to the physical realization of quantum computers (Di Vincenzo, 1995).

As inspecting the internal system state inevitably involves some physical interaction with the system itself, an important consequence of the indetermination principle is that any measurement operation on a quantum computer disrupts coherence.

This property also allows indirect interpretation of Eqs. (24) and (25). Assume that only one qbit encodes the overall system state. The possible outcomes of a measurement operation (called 'eigenstates') can just be $|0\rangle$ and $|1\rangle$, and the state itself is written as $|\Psi\rangle = \varpi_0|0\rangle + \varpi_1|1\rangle$ according to Eq. (24). Thus $\|\varpi_0\|^2$ and $\|\varpi_1\|^2$ give the probabilities that, after the measurements, the system will be found in the related states. The extension of this property to the multi-qbit case is straightforward by combining all possible elementary eigenstates into a quantum register $|\Psi\rangle$; each binary configuration will exhibit an associated probability.

Therefore, the crucial representation advantage in QC is that for a system with n state bits, a coherent quantum computer just uses n qbits to represent the whole system state, whereas, a classical computer requires $N = 2^n$ locations for storing all possible configurations. The fact that a quantum computer can hold simultaneously and linearly the exponential number of states of a classical machine seems to hint at the fact that QC might tackle NP-problems by providing P-complex solutions.

4.2. Quantum algorithms

Such a powerful representation paradigm also called for specific computational paradigms and algorithms. A quantum computer transforms the internal, usually superposed states; thus its functioning can be formally described by a set of state transformations, and every quantum operator ('gate') can be analytically expressed in the form of a matrix.

The basic constraint on any admissible quantum gate is the unitary nature of the associated matrix; this derives from the coherence requirement, and ultimately relates to the possibility of reversible computation (Deutsch, 1985).

From the most general perspective that is adopted in the present treatment, within the above constraints most quantum-computing algorithms follow a few common steps.

First, one initializes all qbit registers into a predetermined classical state (typically, '0'). In the specific case of quantum approaches to optimization problems, qbits store the optimized variables. Applying the Walsh-Hadamard operator (Nielsen & Chuang, 2000) prepares the initial state of the quantum machine as

$$|\Psi_0\rangle = \frac{1}{\sqrt{2^n}} \bigotimes_{i=1}^{n} (|0\rangle + |1\rangle) \quad (26)$$

where $\otimes$ denotes the state direct product (Nielsen & Chuang, 2000). Thus $|\Psi_0\rangle$ comprehends all possible states, which are equally probable.

Then one feeds the cost-function algorithm with $|\Psi_0\rangle$, thus obtaining a superposition of all possible cost values. The computing machine can work out the cost-function values by using the same logic circuitry that supports classical computers. Indeed, basic results from quantum theory ensure that any computation feasible on digital Turing Machines can also be performed on Quantum Computers (Deutsch, 1985). Such a computational approach points out the basic advantage deriving from superposed states: a Quantum Computer can explore all of the cost configurations in a single computational run. By contrast, a classical computer would face an exponential computational overhead.

In the subsequent (possibly iterated) steps, unitary operators modify quantum registers, and alter the probabilities of the various states. The art in developing quantum algorithms thus consists in cleverly designing proper unitary operators, such that the sought-for solutions progressively emerge as the most likely states in the registers of the quantum machine.

The last step of quantum algorithms involves inspecting quantum registers. This operation is highly critical, as the measurement operation lets register qbits collapse into classical binary quantities, but also projects the quantum state into a new state and actually loses coherence and the representational power conveyed by superposition. Due to these critical issues, the timing of the measuring phase must be carefully designed and selected during the algorithm progress.

4.3. Quantum optimization

Grover's algorithm (Grover, 1996) tackles the (NP-complete) problem of searching an input string within an unsorted database. It is one of the best-known QC techniques proposed so far, and exhibits all of the above features. At start-up, Grover's approach requires a single computation of the matching function on the superposition of all equally probable input entries prepared as per Eq. (26). Then an iterative process makes the sought-for input entry emerge progressively from among other entries. The process uses a series of special transformations of the quantum-machine state that are repeated for a finite number of steps.

The repetitions involved in Grover's algorithm proceed at the internal clock rate of the quantum machine, and cannot be compared with the conventional number of iterations of optimization procedures. For an input string including n bits and $N = 2^n$ possible states, the number of repetitions grows as $O(\sqrt{N})$.

Thus Grover's method does not break the NP-completeness barrier, yet it has represented a popular basis for a large variety of algorithms. For the purposes of the research presented here, a quantum method for minimization is described in (Durr & Hoyer, 1996). The number, R, of repetitions for that algorithm to convergence is given by:

$$R = 22.5\sqrt{N} + 1.4\lg^2 N \sim 22.5\sqrt{N} \tag{27}$$

Theory shows that a single run of the minimization algorithm (Durr & Hoyer, 1996) finds out a valid solution with probability at least 1/2. Therefore, to increase the success probability one just applies the basic algorithm in a series of $k > 1$ different runs. With this approach, the total number of repetitions, i.e., the computational cost for the quantum machine, is:

$$R^{(k)} = k \cdot R \tag{28}$$

and the associated probability of success becomes:

$$P_q^{(k)} \geq 1 - \frac{1}{2^k} \tag{29}$$

To sum up, to use QC for SVM training first requires one to express the SVM model in a digital representation (including both the free parameters and the cost-function computation). The set of digital parameters to be optimized are stored in as many associated qbits, that are prepared in an initial, equally probable superposition Eq. (26). Feeding the initial state to the cost-function supports an exhaustive scanning of the cost space. The resulting optimization problem is eventually solved by the minimization algorithm, whose quantum computational cost and success probability are given by Eqs. (28) and (29), respectively.

Now one might want to analyze the specific advantages of the quantum approach. The comparison involves the quantum-minimization algorithm and a Montecarlo random-search process, which represents the ultimate resort for NP-complete problems in the lack of effective optimization techniques.

Assume that the minimization problem has M different solutions; in a search space with N possible configurations, the probability of success of a Montecarlo search after r test iterations is expressed as:

$$P_m^{(r)} = 1 - \left(1 - \frac{M}{N}\right)^r \tag{30}$$

To compare the two optimization methods on a fair basis, one should try a Montecarlo search for $R^{(k)}$ times; the quantum approach exhibits an advantage whenever $P_m^{(R(k))} < P_q^{(k)}$; by using Eqs. (29) and (30) one easily obtains:

$$22.5M < \sqrt{N} \ln 2 \tag{31}$$

Interestingly, the expression (31) does not depend on the number, k, of test runs of the quantum algorithm. Rather, the resulting condition exclusively depends on the specific problem complexity, involving the number of solutions and the search-space extension. In particular, one observes that condition (31) is most often fulfilled in common practice, as the measure of the number of optimized bits is usually much larger than that of the problem minima.

As a consequence, the applicative interest in QC paradigms also stems from the fact that their relative effectiveness increases with the difficulty of the specific problem at hand.

5. Experimental results

The different effects of using the loss functions (12) and (13) have been studied experimentally by testing a linear classifier on two non-linearly separable datasets. Each testbed exhibits a different displacement of the misclassified patterns from the separating plane; thus one can analyze how such patterns do affect the eventual classifier configuration in two different cases: in the presence of outliers and when errors lie close to the separation surface.

To inspect the practical effectiveness of a quantum digital implementation, one defines the Digital Cost Function (*DCF*) as per Eq. (2), where the loss function is $h_{BM}(u)$:

$$\mathrm{DCF} = \frac{\|\mathbf{w}\|^2}{2} + C\sum_{i=1}^{np} h_{BM}(y_i(\mathbf{w}\cdot\mathbf{x}_i + b)) \tag{32}$$

In order to define the number, M, of acceptable solutions of the optimization process, those associated with a DCF value lower than 101% of the best achievable cost have been considered as 'good solutions'.

5.1. Iris dataset

This testbed is the non-linearly separable version, including the 'Virginica' and 'Versicolor' classes respectively, each represented by 50 2-D patterns. First, a linear SVM was trained by using the algorithm (Chang & Lin, 2003), featuring the classic $h_V(u)$ loss function with an error penalization $C = 1000$; the resulting separating plane scored six errors.

Then, a digital SVM was trained under the same parameter $C = 1000$ to analyze the performance of a linear classifier implementing the loss function $h_{BM}(u)$. The weights and bias were coded as 10-bit. Such a digital SVM scored three errors; Fig. 2 shows the separating planes resulting from the two different implementations.

Although the dataset does not contain any outlier, the solutions differ in terms of both the number of misclassified patterns and the weight set $\mathbf{w}$: the only errors lie within the overlapping zone between the two classes. This difference can be explained by examining the two terms composing Eq. (2).

The SVM implementing $h_V(u)$ tends to maximize margin and the related errors lie as close as possible to the separation surface; indeed, the specific loss function linearly penalizes the distance from the separating surface. As a result, the solution minimizes complexity and weakly penalizes each of the six errors, which are embedded into the margin itself.

By contrast, the lower error scored by the digital implementation derives from the non-linear weighting of errors that lie away from the margin: in this case, the loss function saturates no matter how distant the error is, thus allowing the better decision surface.

As to quantum optimization, with the notation adopted in Section 4 one has $N = 1{,}073{,}741{,}824$ and $M = 1$; the probability of finding an acceptable solution is $M/N = 9.3 \times 10^{-10}$, thus meeting condition (31).

In a different, intriguing experiment, one might modify the original dataset to introduce the presence of outliers. To this purpose, one flips the classes of two patterns lying far from the separation surface (this simulates the presence of noise in the measurement of the targets).

The resulting artificial dataset was used to train the two SVMs under Eqs. (12) and (13), yielding the classifiers as per Fig. 3. The graph confirms the robustness of $h_{BM}(u)$, as the flipped targets do not alter the position of the separation line, whereas the classic SVM classifier is significantly affected.

5.2. Breast cancer dataset

This dataset includes 699 patterns with 9 features; each pattern is classified as benign or malignant. After excluding 16 samples featuring missing values, all features were normalized in the range [− 1,1].

Previous results (Drago & Ridella, 1998) show that the information carried by the whole dataset is well represented by just two features, i.e. features 6 and 8. Therefore, the present analysis reduces the Breast Cancer dataset to a 2-D problem, which allows useful information to be drawn from a visual inspection. A classical SVM Eq. (7) with a linear

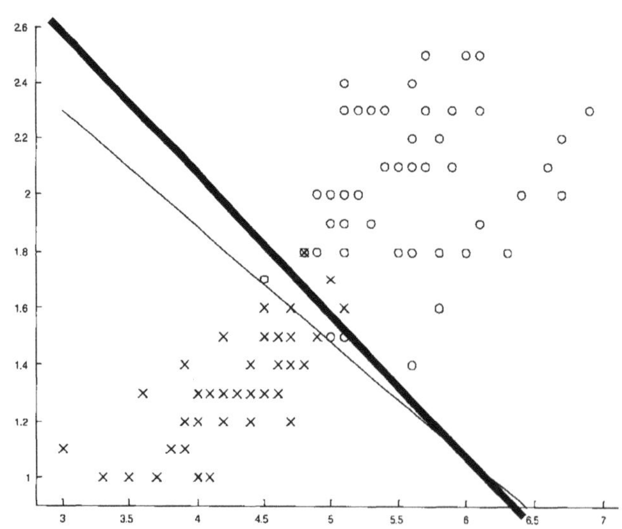

Fig. 2. Iris dataset. The thick-line separation is obtained by a classical SVM implementation while the thin-line represent the solution found by a digital implementation having $h_{BM}(u)$ as loss function.

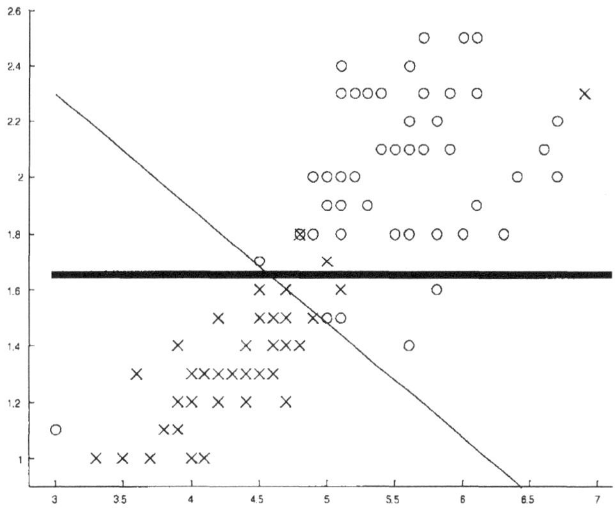

Fig. 3. Modified Iris dataset. The thick-line separation is obtained by a classical SVM implementation; the thin line represents the solution found by a digital implementation having $h_{BM}(u)$ as loss function.

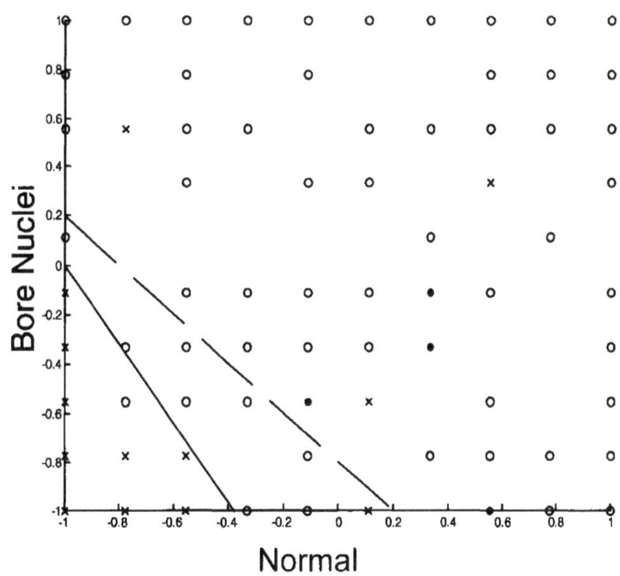

Fig. 4. BCancer. In the ' × ' marks, patterns malignant cases exceed benign ones (viceversa for circles). Filled circles indicate tie cases. The dashed-and solid boundaries relate to a classic and digital-cost SVM, respectively.

kernel and $C = 1000$ scored an empirical error rate of 5.124%; the separation surface is shown in Fig. 4. This result was obtained by using the algorithm (Chang & Lin, 2003), and had to be compared with that obtained by using the loss function $h_{BM}(u)$.

To that purpose, the analysis considered a digital SVM implementation, whose weights and bias were coded as 8-bit values. The optimization process minimizes DCF with respect to $\mathbf{w}$ and b; Fig. 4 presents the class-separation boundary associated with the minimum of Eq. (32), scoring a misclassification error of 4.25%. An histogram-based analysis of the results (Fig. 5) shows that about 6% of the DCF values are less than twice the minimum of the DCF itself.

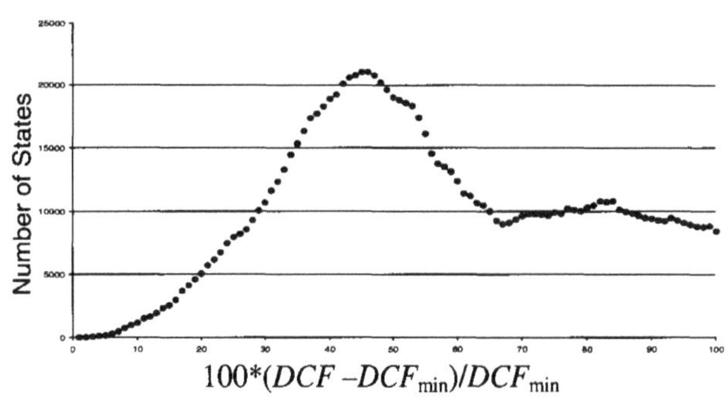

Fig. 5. Breast cancer dataset. Histogram of the values for the digital cost function.

When implementing the digital optimization problem on a quantum machine, in the notation adopted in Section 4, one has $N = 16,777,216$, $M = 6$. The latter value was obtained by keeping valid solutions those which did not displace more than 1% from the minimum of DCF. Thus the probability of finding a good solution is $M/N = 3.6 \times 10^{-7}$, which fulfils condition Eq. (31).

6. Conclusions

The power and effectiveness of SVMs in their original formulation as a general pattern-processing paradigm is not being questioned. However, computer based implementations that take into account the digital nature of represented quantities, and refined formulations that shrink generalization bounds can invalidate the applicability of efficient QP training algorithms.

Scanning a digital bit space without a gradient-based method can turn the optimization task into an NP-complete exhaustive-search problem. This ultimately shifts the interest toward novel and promising computational paradigms such as QC.

The main *pro* for such an approach derives from the principle of quantum superposition of states, which enables an inherent parallelism in information processing that is not achievable by classical computing machinery. On the other hand, two *cons* seem to hold back an excessive enthusiasm for quantum approaches: first, quantum machinery is reportedly not a mature technology yet, hence one should not expect to have quantum optimization available for practical purposes in the near future. Secondly, no proof has been given so far that QC can break the NP-completeness barrier in a real, interesting problem.

In view of these issues, a basic conclusion might anyway be drawn from the research presented in this paper: QC can yet prove effective for an important problem such as training SVMs for digital implementations. The reported analysis also shows that the computational benefits conveyed by quantum optimization increase when the problem complexity increases.

The presented simulations on a real-world problem open new vistas over the possibility of tuning SVM classifiers that are apt to direct and effective realizations in digital circuitry.

References

Bartlett, P., Boucheron, S., & Lugosi, G. (2002). Model selection and error estimation. *Machine Learning*, *48*(1–3), 85–113.

Bartlett, P., & Mendelson, S. (2002). Rademacher and Gaussian complexities: risk bounds and structural result. *Journal of Machine Learning Research*, *3*, 463–482.

Chang, C. C., Lin, C. J., (2003). *LIBSVM: a library for Support Vector Machines*. Retrieved on Mar'03 from: http://www.csie.ntu.edu.tw/~cjlin/papers/libsvm.pdf

Cortes, C., & Vapnik, V. (1995). Support vector networks. *Machine Learning*, *20*, 273–297.

Deutsch, D. (1985). Quantum theory, the church-turing principle, and the universal quantum computer. *Proceedings of the Royal Society of London*, *A400*, 97–117.

Di Vincenzo, D. (1995). Two-bit gates are universal for Quantum Computation. *Physics Review A*, *51*, 1015–1022.

Drago, G. P., & Ridella, S. (1998). Pruning with interval arithmetic perceptron. *Neurocomputing*, *18*(1–3), 229–246.

Durr, C., Hoyer, P., (1996). *A Quantum Algorithm for Finding the Minimum*. Retrieved March, 4, 2003 from: http://arxiv.org/abs/quant-ph/9607014.

Fletcher, R. (1987). *Practical methods of optimization* (2nd ed). New York: Wiley.

Grover, L. K. (1996). A fast quantum mechanical algorithm for database search. *Proceedings of the 28th Annual ACM Symposium Theory of Computing*, 212–219.

Nielsen, M. A., & Chuang, I. L. (2000). *Quantum computation and quantum information*. Cambridge, GB: Cambridge University Press.

Powell, M. J. D., (1989). *TOLMIN: A fortran package for linearly constrained optimization calculations*. DAMTP Report NA2, University of Cambridge, England.

Vapnik, V. (1998). *Statistical learning theory*. Chichester, GB: Wiley.

PERGAMON

AVAILABLE AT
www.ComputerScienceWeb.com
POWERED BY SCIENCE DIRECT

Neural Networks 16 (2003) 771–778

Neural
Networks

www.elsevier.com/locate/neunet

2003 Special issue

On the quality of ART1 text clustering

Louis Massey

Royal Military College of Canada, Kingston, Ont., Canada K7K 7B4

Abstract

There is a large and continually growing quantity of electronic text available, which contain essential human and organization knowledge. An important research endeavor is to study and develop better ways to access this knowledge. Text clustering is a popular approach to automatically organize textual document collections by topics to help users find the information they need. Adaptive Resonance Theory (ART) neural networks possess several interesting properties that make them appealing in the area of text clustering. Although ART has been used in several research works as a text clustering tool, the level of quality of the resulting document clusters has not been clearly established yet. In this paper, we present experimental results with binary ART that address this issue by determining how close clustering quality is to an upper bound on clustering quality.

Keywords: Adaptive resonance theory; Text clustering; Text categorization

1. Introduction

We consider the application of clustering to the self-organization of a textual document collection. *Clustering* is the operation by which similar objects are grouped together in an unsupervised manner (Jain, Murty, & Flynn, 1999; Kaufman & Rousseeuw, 1990). Hence, when clustering textual documents, one is hoping to form sets of documents with similar content. Instead of exploring the whole collection of documents, a user can then browse the resulting clusters to identify and retrieve relevant documents. As such, clustering provides a summarized view of the information space by grouping documents by topics. Clustering is often the only viable solution to organize large text collections into topics. The advantage of clustering is realized when a training set and classes definitions are unavailable, or when creating them is either cost prohibitive due to the collection shear size or unrealistic due to the rapidly changing nature of the collection.

We specifically study text clustering with Adaptive Resonance Theory (ART) (Carpenter & Grossberg, 1995; Grossberg, 1976) neural networks. ART neural networks are known for their ability to perform on-line and incremental clustering of dynamic datasets. Contrary to most other types of artificial neural networks such as the popular Back-propagation Multi-Layer Perceptron (MLP) (Rumelhart, Hinton, & Williams, 1986), ART is unsupervised and allows for plastic yet stable learning. ART detects similarities among data objects, typically data points in an N-dimensional metric space. When novelty is detected, ART adaptively and autonomously creates a new category. Another advantageous and distinguishing feature of ART is its ability to discover patterns at various levels of generality. This is achieved by setting the value of a parameter known as vigilance and denoted by ρ, $\rho \in (0, 1]$. ART stability and plasticity properties as well as its ability to process dynamic data efficiently make it an attractive candidate for clustering large, rapidly changing text collections in real-life environments. Although ART has been investigated previously as a means of clustering text data, due to numerous variations in ART implementations, experimental data sets and quality evaluation methodologies, it is not clear whether ART performs well in this type of application. Since ART seems to be a logical and appealing solution to the rapidly growing amount of textual electronic information processed by organizations, it would be important to eliminate any confusion surrounding the quality of the text clusters it produces. In this paper, we present experimental results with a binary ART neural network (ART1) that address this issue by determining how close clustering quality achieved with ART is to an expected upper bound on clustering quality. We will consider other versions of ART in future work.

E-mail address: massey-l@rmc.ca (L. Massey).

0893-6080/03/$ - see front matter Crown Copyright © 2003 Published by Elsevier Science Ltd. All rights reserved.
doi:10.1016/S0893-6080(03)00088-1

2. Related work

We consider one of the many applications of text clustering in the field of Information Retrieval (IR) (VanRijsbergen, 1979), namely clustering that aims at self-organizing textual document collections. This application of text clustering can be seen as a form of classification by topics, hence making it the unsupervised counterpart to Text Categorization (TC) (Sebastiani, 2002). Text self-organization has become increasingly popular due to the availability of large document collections that change rapidly and that are quasi-impossible to organize manually. A typical example is the organization of web documents according to some topics hierarchy like the Yahoo™ hierarchy (Heuser & Rosenstiel, 2000). Even TC becomes unsuitable in such environments because supervised learning of classifiers is not plastic and thus requires retraining upon detection of novelty. Representative work on text clustering includes, among many others, (Cutting, Karger, Pedersen, & Tukey, 1992; Kohonen et al., 2000; Steinbach, Karypis, & Kumar, 2000). There has also been interesting work done on incremental and on-line text clustering with non-neural approaches (see for instance (Can (1993) and Wong and Fu (2000)).

MacLeod and Robertson (1991) were as far as we know the first researchers to consider ART for text clustering. They used a modified version of ART1 in which the similarity computation and weight updates involved domain and task specific knowledge. The inclusion of this knowledge makes the ART implementation more complex but may advantage it over a basic form of ART1. We intend to test this type of ART network in future work, but for now we are interested in establishing the baseline quality that can be achieved with a more basic implementation. The relatively small Keen and Cranfield text collections (800 and 1400 documents, respectively), were used to test MacLeod's algorithm. ART clustering quality was evaluated with the F measure computed on the results of provided queries. This approach to cluster evaluation does not allow for a comprehensive evaluation of the resulting cluster structure, since it only considers the set of queries. The clustering quality results were not very good with $F_1 = 0.25$ and 0.15 (minimum quality value is 0 and maximum 1), but were comparable with other non-neural clustering results published on the same data sets. Merkl (1995) compared ART with Self-Organizing Maps (SOM) (Kohonen, 2001) for the clustering of a small collection of documents and concluded that SOM forms better clusters based on a visual qualitative evaluation. We want to avoid such a subjective evaluation. Moreover, we think that SOM has several weaknesses compared to ART that make it unsuitable for document clustering in a real-life environment characterized by high volume of dynamic data. Indeed, it is unstable under growth while ART provides inherent stability and plasticity. Furthermore, the multiple iterations required to attain convergence with SOM are incompatible with a real-time environment.

On the other hand, some research concluded that ART text clustering resulted in good quality clusters. Vlajic and Card (1998) used a modified ART2 network to create a hierarchical clustering of a small number of web pages. They report that clustering was 'appropriate in all cases, when compared to human performance [...]', but provide no quantitative result. In previous work, we also considered hierarchical clustering, but with ART1 and with a small database of document titles (Massey, 2002a). Clustering quality was deemed adequate based on the percentage of overlap between clusters and expected classification. Our evaluation measure and text collection were non-standard. Rajaraman and Tan (2001) apply fuzzy ART to the task of Topics Detection and Tracking, in which the aspect of topic detection is performed by ART text clustering. They use a small set of 1468 news articles and attempt to measure the ability of the ART network to detect novelty. However, once again only qualitative results are presented. Finally, Kondadadi and Kozma (2002) compare KMART, their soft clustering version of ART, to Fuzzy-ART and k-means. The text data consists of 2000 documents downloaded from the web as well as another 2000 newsgroup documents. Quality evaluation is based on a one-to-one match of the documents in the clusters with the documents in the specified category. K-MART and Fuzzy-ART results are encouraging with above 50% matching for 100–500 document subsets of the original text collections, while k-means stays in the range of 22–35% matching. However, this evaluation method is optimistic since it does not account for false positives (i.e. documents that are present in a cluster but do not match documents in the corresponding desired topic).

Our interest in this paper is the study of unsupervised text organization, hence supervised versions of ART (Carpenter Grossberg, & Reynolds, 1991a) applied to text categorization (Petridis, Kaburlasos, Fragkou, & Kehagias, 2001) will not be considered.

3. Experimental settings

We selected two well-established cluster quality evaluation measures: Jaccard (JAC) (Downton & Brennan, 1980) and Fowlkes–Mallows (FM) (Fowlkes & Mallows, 1983):

$$\mathrm{JAC} = a/(a + b + c) \tag{1}$$

$$\mathrm{FM} = a/((a + b)(a + c))^{1/2} \tag{2}$$

where

a is the pair-wise number of true positives, i.e. the total number of document pairs grouped together in the expected solution and that are indeed clustered together by the clustering algorithm;

b is the pair-wise number of false positives, i.e. the number of document pairs not expected to be grouped together but that are clustered together by the clustering algorithm;

c is the pair-wise number of false negatives, i.e. the number of document pairs expected to be grouped together but that are not clustered together by the clustering algorithm.

We also use a measure that computes the F1 clustering quality value. It uses the same underlying pair-wise counting procedure as Jaccard and Fowlkes–Mallow to establish a count of false negatives and false positives, but combines those values following the F-measure (VanRijsbergen, 1979) formulae:

$$F_\beta = (\beta^2 + 1)pr/[\beta^2 p + r] \quad (3)$$

where $p = a/(a + b)$ is known as the precision and $r = a/(a + c)$ as recall. β is set to 1 to give equal weighting to precision and recall. We must note that other text clustering work, such as (Larsen and Aone (1999) and Wong and Fu (2000)), have evaluated clustering quality with F_1 computed on the best cluster-class match. Our initial experiments with this approach indicated that it might unfairly inflate quality. We have not conducted an indepth analysis of this divergence at this point in time, but we will as part of future work.

The 'ModApte' split (Apte, Fred Damerau, & Weiss, 1994) of the Reuter-21578 Distribution 1.0[1] data set is used for our experiments. This data sets is known to be challenging because of skewed class distribution, multiple overlapping categories, and its real-life origin (Reuter newswires during the year 1987, in chronological order). We evaluate clustering results against the desired solution originally specified by Reuter's human classifiers. We only use the desired solution information to evaluate clustering results, i.e. after the clusters have been formed. Reuter is a benchmark data set for TC. Using this data set specific split and the F_1 quality measure makes comparison with published TC results (Yang & Liu, 1999) on the same split possible. This is an important and we believe innovative aspect of our experimental approach: TC F_1 quality results are used as an upper bound for cluster quality since learning in a supervised framework with labeled data provides the best possible automated text classification (with current technology). Thus, clustering can be expected to approach this level of quality but not exceed it since it relies solely on the information present in the data itself. This way of evaluating clustering quality allows one to clearly establish the level of quality obtained by a clustering algorithm as a percentage of the upper bound quality.

We use the k-means (MacQueen, 1967) clustering algorithm to establish a lower bound for quality. Our rationale is that since k-means represents one of the simplest possible approaches to clustering, one would expect that any slightly more advanced algorithm would exceed its clustering quality. The parameter k is set to the number of topics (93) specified by the domain experts who manually organized the Reuter text collection. K-means initial cluster centroids are determined randomly and clustering results are averaged over 10 trials to smooth out extreme values obtained from good and bad random initialization. Our hope is that ART clusters would exceed significantly the quality obtained with k-means and approach the quality of supervised TC.

In this set of experiments, we use the simplest form of ART, binary ART1 in fast learning mode, to establish what should be the baseline level of quality attainable by ART neural networks. ART1 networks consist of two layers of neurons: N input neurons and M output neurons, where N is the input size and M the number of clusters. Neurons are fully connected with both feed-forward and feedback weighted links. The feed-forward links connecting to the output neuron j are represented by the real vector $\mathbf{W}_j$ while the feedback links from that same neuron are represented by the binary vector $\mathbf{T}_j$. The latter stores the prototype representing cluster j. We specifically use Moore's ART1 implementation (Moore, 1988), as follows:

1. Initialize network weights and provide parameter values:
   $0 < \rho \leq 1$ (the vigilance parameter) and $L > 1$
   $\mathbf{W}_j = 1/(1 + N)$ for all forward connection weights
   $\mathbf{T}_j = 1$ for all feedback connection weights
2. Set the output neurons activation $u_j = 0$ for $j = 1...M$ and present a document $\mathbf{X}_k$ to the network
3. Compute output activations: $u_j = \mathbf{X}_k \cdot \mathbf{W}_j$ for $j = 1...M$ and where $\cdot$ is the inner product.
4. Competition between output units: select the most similar category represented by output neuron j^* with maximal activation.
5. Vigilance test: determine if j^* is close enough to $\mathbf{X}_k$:
   $\|\mathbf{X}_k \wedge \mathbf{T}_{j^*}\| / \|\mathbf{X}_k\| \geq \rho$
   where '$\wedge$' is the logical AND operation
   If true, go to step 6 (resonance mode); otherwise, go to step 8 (search mode).
6. Update weights for winning node:
   $\mathbf{T}'_{j^*} = \mathbf{T}_{j^*} \wedge \mathbf{X}_k$
   $\mathbf{W}'_{j^*} = \mathbf{L}(\mathbf{T}_{j^*} \wedge \mathbf{X}_k)/(\mathbf{L} - 1 + \|\mathbf{T}_{j^*} \wedge \mathbf{X}_k\|)$
7. Return to step 2 with a new document.
8. $u_{j^*} = -1$ (remove category j^* from current search) and return to step 4.

The vigilance parameter $\rho \in (0, 1]$ determines the level of abstraction at which ART discovers clusters. Moreover, the minimal number of clusters present in the data can be determined by *minimal vigilance* (Massey, 2002b), computed

[1] Available from http://www.daviddlewis.com/resources/testcollections/reuters21578/

as $\rho_{min} < 1/N$ where N is the number of features (words) used to represent a document. We chose a value of $\rho_{min} = 0.0005$ as the initial vigilance parameter and we increment it until we find the best clustering quality. We stop increasing vigilance when more than 200 clusters are obtained because such a large number of clusters would simply result in information overload for a user and therefore not achieve the intended objective of text clustering.

A binary vector-space (Salton & Lesk, 1968) representation was created for the Reuter ModApté test set. Only the test set was clustered for compatibility reasons with TC results and also because in unsupervised learning, one must assume that a training set is unavailable. A standard stop word list was used to remove frequent words and a simple feature reduction by term selection based on term frequency was applied to reduce the dimensionality of the original documents feature space. This approach was judged very effective for TC by Yang and Pedersen (1997)).

4. Experimental results

We eliminated words that appear in 10, 20, 40 and 60 or less documents. In the first case, a total of 2282 term features were retained while in the last only 466 were. Our experiments indicated that less radical feature selection not only increased the number of features and consequently processing time, but also resulted in lower quality clusters in some cases (Fig. 1). Best quality is achieved at vigilance value of 0.05, with 106 clusters, a number close to the expected number of topics specified by the domain experts who labeled the data (93). Vigilance levels past 0.1 result in over 250 clusters, which is not desirable for users as explained previously.

The results shown in Fig. 1 were obtained with a single pass in the data. In reality, ART converges to a stable representation after at most $N - 1$ presentations of the data (Georgiopoulos, Heileman, & Huang, 1990). By stable, it is meant that if the same document is presented several times to the network, it should be assigned to the same category, and presenting the same inputs over and over should not change the cluster prototype values. Unstable clusters are problematic since an identical document submitted at different times may end up in different clusters. Furthermore, we show in Fig. 2a that cluster quality increases after ART has stabilized. Only four iterations were required to attain a stable representation, which is much less than the theoretical upper bound of $N - 1$. However, in real world, high-volume operations this could still be a problem as little idle time in the system operation may be available to stabilize topics representation.

We have processed the documents in their natural order, i.e. the chronological order in which they have been created and thus the order in which they would be submitted to a classification system. This simulates the real-world environment where there is no control over the order in which documents are created. As with any on-line clustering algorithm, ART gives different results depending on the order of presentation of the data. This is expected since clustering decisions are taken for each sequentially submitted document, compared to batch clustering that considers all data at once. We submitted the data set in 15 different random orders to ART and averaged clustering quality for each order. Fig. 2b shows that other orders of presentation are much worse than the natural, chronological order of the documents in Reuter. This is encouraging because if quality was higher for other orders of presentation, one would face the problem of finding the best order among the very large number of possibilities or design a way to combine results from different orders. It is possible that other text collections face this problem. Maybe it just happens that Reuter natural order is simply compatible with the desired solution, while in other cases this may not happen. After all, there are many ways to organize large text collections. Some versions of ART use a similarity measure claimed to make it less susceptible to order variations (Sadananda & Sudhakara Rao, 1995). Our initial experiments with Sadananda and Sudhakara Rao's similarity measures are inconclusive at this point in time. However, their proposed similarity measure will in some circumstances not allow the vigilance test (step 5 of the algorithm) to pass even for a newly created category node. Hence, novelty integration becomes impossible unless the vigilance

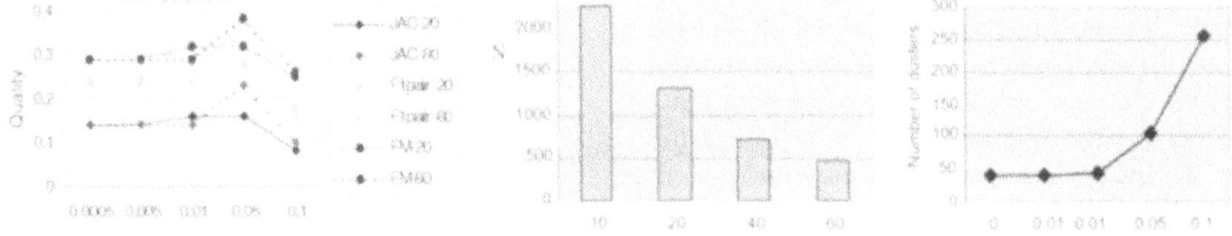

Fig. 1. (a) More radical term selection (removing words appearing in 60 documents or less) results in better clustering quality in some cases, (at vigilance 0.05), compared to removing terms appearing in only 20 documents or less. (b) More radical feature selection also results in much smaller data set dimentionality which in turn allows for more rapid processing. (c) Vigilance 0.05 finds a number of cluster close to the expected number of 93. Vigilance of 0.1 creates too many clusters for users.

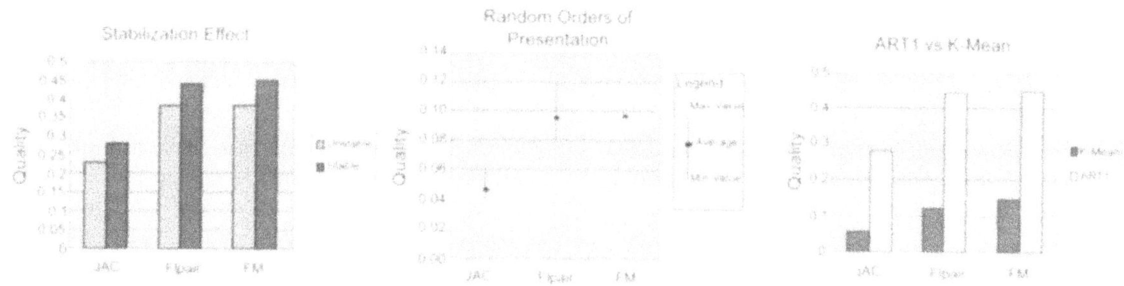

Fig. 2. All results shown for vigilance 0.05. (a) Stabilization improves ART clustering quality. (b) Random orders of presentation even when stabilized give much worse clusters than the natural order of the documents in Reuter. (c) ART clusters (in natural order, stabilized) are of better quality than *k*-means ($k = 93$).

test is not performed for new category nodes. This amounts to a simple modification to the algorithm listed in this paper.

Fig. 2c. shows that ART1 cluster quality clearly exceeds the lower bound established by *K*-means. However, clustering quality achieved by ART with random orders of presentation is comparable to *K*-means. This implies that if the natural order of presentation does not correspond to the chosen organization of the data, ART1 will not do better than *K*-means. We now compare ART1 clustering quality to the upper bound expected for cluster quality: the best TC results obtained with Support Vector Machines (SVM) and k-Nearest Neighbors (kNN) published in Yang and Liu (1999) (Fig. 3). ART1 achieves 51.2% of the TC quality. Comparing to 16.3% level of quality for *k*-means, the lower bound, ART1 does much better but is still only about half-way to the optimal expected quality. There is also a potential for lower quality with other orders of presentation. We must however point out that the solution we use to evaluate clusters is merely one among many other useful ways to organize the text collection. Hence, we merely evaluate the ability of ART to recover the specified solution. A users study may better validate the structure discovered by ART, but such studies are costly and also subjective.

We also built a small program that simulates ART cluster prototype updating behavior and attempts to assign each document to its desired topic. We found that 2.2% of documents could not be assigned to their designated topic. Thus, even in the best conditions, perfect clustering is not possible with ART1 with this data set in natural order since right from the start about 2% quality is lost to the order of presentation. This can be explained as follows: a document is assigned to a topic if it has a sufficiently number of overlapping features, as determined by the vigilance parameter. Furthermore, over time as documents are submitted to the network, the number of active features in prototype vectors decreases, which makes matching a document with its desired topic more unlikely. This is caused by the prototype updating mechanism that intersects documents assigned to a topic with that topic prototype. So, in our simulation, if no feature of a document overlap with the prototype for the document desired topic, it means that the expected solution cannot be satisfied with ART1 and with this order of presentation. Better prototype updating may be required to improve quality, such as (MacLeod & Robertson, 1991), which used the union of a document and its prototype features.

Finally, while conducting our experiments, we noticed an interesting phenomenon: clusters do not necessarily form at the specified level of abstraction. In other words, ART sometimes discovers topics generalizing or specializing desired topics. A generalization is a cluster that includes two or more *classes* (a class being a group of documents representing a desired topic). A specialization on the other hand is a class that includes two or more clusters. In a sense, such behavior can be expected from clustering algorithms since they rely solely on similarity among data items rather than on directions by a domain expert. Fig. 4 shows a portion of the confusion table built from the *matches* between clusters and classes to illustrate generalizations and specializations. A match is the number of documents a class and a cluster have in common. We note from Fig. 4 that:

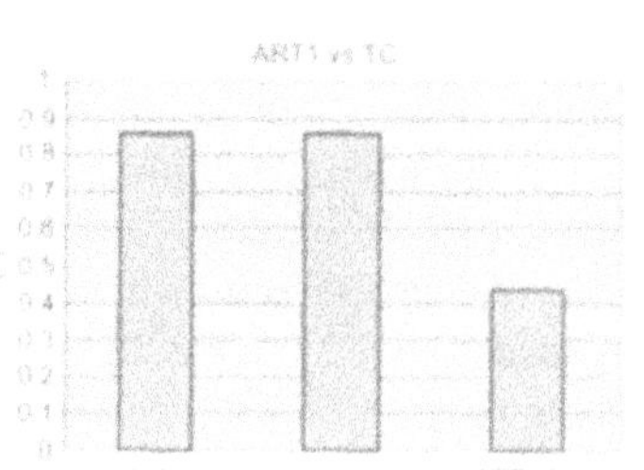

Fig. 3. ART1 clustering F_1 with stabilization at vigilance 0.05 for data in its natural order (ART1 Nat). For both TC methods (SVM and *k*-NN), the micro-averaged F1 values is used for compatibility with our F1pair measure.

- cluster 0 is dominated by 169 documents from class 25 (topic earnings) out of a total of 1087 (16%) documents expected to belong to that class;

0	1	2	3	9	10	11	12	14	15	16	17	18	24	25
6	13	3	1		2	1	0	5	0	11	0	0	6	169
11	32	7	1		1	9	1	19	1	29	13	9	8	741
0	0	1	0		0	0	0	0	0	14	2	2	0	1
97	92	154	26		7	77	5	42	27	598	121	88	5	97

Fig. 4. A shortened version of the confusion table: computed clusters 0-3 on rows and desired classes 0–25 on columns. The first row shows the class number. Highlighted values indicate best match.

- cluster 1 is dominated by 741 documents from class 25 (earnings) out of a total possible of 1087 (68%);
- cluster 3 is dominated by 598 documents from class 16 (acquisitions) out of a total possible of 719 (83%), but there is also a strong presence from class 0 (trade), class 1 (grain), class 2 (crude), class 11 (shipping) and class 18 (interest rate).

Hence, one can consider that clusters 0 and 1 actually correspond to class 25 (earnings) with 910 of the 1087 documents, so topic earnings is specialized. Cluster 3 corresponds to classes 16 (acquisitions), class 0 (trade), class 1 (grain), class 2 (crude), class 11 (shipping), and class 18 (interest rate) for a total of 1106 of 1395 documents. So all these classes are generalized by cluster 3. Other class-cluster matches may be deemed to simply lower generalization and specialization quality. We designed a quality evaluation methodology that, contrary to existing clustering evaluation measures, does not penalize generalizations and specializations. For each class, it looks for all clusters that match the class. This allows for the discovery of specializations. Then, for each of the matching cluster, it also looks for all matching class, which accounts for generalizations. Extraneous documents in the latter case are the clustering errors and a F_1 value is computed based on these errors. Fig. 5 shows quality evaluation with this measure, which we call Sub-Graph Dispersion (SGD) because a sub-graph is created for each class when looking for matches. If one considers generalizations and specializations of the expected solution as acceptable, higher quality can be computed at lower vigilance, but the quality of generalizations and specialization decreases as vigilance increases. This method of evaluation needs to be refined before final conclusions on the true impact of learning at different levels of abstraction on clustering quality can be drawn. For instance, all matches are currently considered but some negatively affect quality and should not be included as being part of generalizations or specializations.

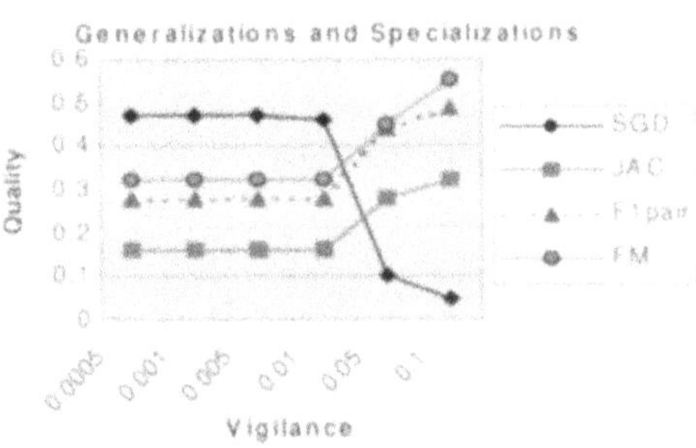

Fig. 5. Increased quality is computed by SGD at lower vigilance by not penalizing generalizations and specializations. Stabilized results shown.

5. Conclusions and future work

Text clustering work conducted with ART up to now has used many different forms of ART-based architectures, as well as different and non-comparable text collections and evaluation methods. This situation resulted in confusion as to the level of clustering quality achievable with ART. As a first step towards resolving this situation, we have tested a simple ART1 network implementation and evaluated its text clustering quality on the benchmark Reuter data set and with the standard F_1 measure. K-means clustering quality was used as the lower bound on quality while published results with supervised TC were used as an upper bound on quality.

Our experiments have demonstrated that text clusters formed by ART1 achieve 51% of TC upper bound and exceed the lower bound considerably. Consequently, about half of the evidence needed to recover the expected document organization solution is available directly from the data under the form of inter-document similarity rather than from costly and time consuming handcrafting of a large labeled training data set. Whether this level of quality is sufficient is a task specific question and ultimately a matter of cost/quality trade-off: it is a choice between higher quality supervised document categorization obtained at high development and maintenance cost versus lower quality clusters obtained at basically no cost. At least we provide here a clear picture of the quality aspect by establishing the baseline quality to be expected with ART. Although ART clusters were of medium quality, ART has the unique advantage of proceeding entirely without human intervention, plus offers the interesting properties of plasticity and stability. Should novelty be detected by the network, a new topic would automatically be created as part of normal system operation. This contrasts with supervised TC, which would require downtime for re-training and related human intervention to prepare a new training set. Therefore, despite lower quality, there may be some situations where ART-based text clustering is a necessity. Furthermore, clustering quality can be increased if one considers discovery of topics at other levels of abstraction as acceptable. Hence, an important area of future research is to explore evaluation measures that do not penalize specializations and generalizations. We are also looking into better feature selection that may also help improve cluster quality. For instance, preliminary experiments with TF-IDF, a well known Information Retrieval measure of term importance, are encouraging in that respect. Moreover, more advanced ART architectures with nonbinary representation (such as ART2 (Carpenter, Grossberg, & Rosen, 1991b), fuzzy ART (Carpenter, Grossberg, & Rosen, 1991c), MacLeod's ART (MacLeod & Robertson, 1991) and FOSART (Baraldi & Alpaydin, 2002)) may further improve cluster quality. We are currently investigating these avenues. As well, in the Reuter collection, topics are not mutually exclusive, while ART1 clustering is. ART based soft clustering such as with KMART (Kondadadi & Kozma, 2002) will thus be explored as yet another possible way to improve clustering.

ART stability and plasticity properties as well as its ability to process dynamic data efficiently make it an attractive candidate for clustering large, rapidly changing text collections in real-life environments. However, in this paper we have only evaluated the static clustering case with some glimpses at the issues that may arise in a more realistic, dynamic environment. For instance, there is a requirement for idle time to allow for stabilization in a text clustering system. We are currently conducting a full assessment of ART's text clustering performance in a simulated realistic environment.

Comparison with other clustering methods has not been our objective. We rather focused on establishing the level of quality achieved by ART within the range defined by a lower and an upper bound. We believe this gives a better appreciation of the level of quality by setting it in a wider framework. Some investigators have evaluated clustering quality with other algorithms on Reuter-21578 and with the F_1 measure, but have used non-standard splits (Larsen & Aone, 1999; Steinbach et al., 2000). So our results cannot be compared directly with theirs. We plan to eventually evaluate other clustering methodologies—particularly incremental clustering algorithms—to compare their clustering quality and ability to function in a dynamic environment to ART's. As well, testing on other text collections is needed to verify if quality results apply to document sets displaying various characteristics.

References

Apte, C., Fred Damerau, F., & Weiss, S. M. (1994). Automated learning of decision rules for text categorization. *ACM Transactions on Information Systems, 12*(2), 233–251.

Baraldi, A., & Alpaydin, E. (2002). Constructive feedforward art clustering networks—Part II. *IEEE Transactions on Neural Networks, 13*, 3.

Can, F. (1993). Incremental clustering for dynamic information, processing. *ACM Transactions on Information Systems, 11*(2), 143–164.

Carpenter, G. A., & Grossberg, S (1995). Adaptive Resonance Theory (ART). In Handbook of brain theory and neural networks, Arbib, M.A.: MIT Press.

Carpenter, G. A., Grossberg, S., & Reynolds, J. H. (1991a). Artmap: supervised real-time learning and classification of nonstationary data by a self-organizing neural network. *Neural Networks, 4*, 565–588.

Carpenter, G. A., Grossberg, S., & Rosen, D. B. (1991b). Art2-a: an adaptive resonance algorithm for rapid category learning and recognition. *Neural Networks, 4*, 493–504.

Carpenter, G. A., Grossberg, S., & Rosen, D. B. (1991c). Fuzzy art: fast stable learning and categorization of analog patterns by an adaptive resonance system. *Neural Networks, 4*, 759–771.

Cutting, D. Karger, D., Pedersen, J., & Tukey, J (1992). Scatter-gather: a cluster-based approach to browsing large document collections. In *Proceedings of SIGIR'92.*

Downton, M., & Brennan, T (1980). Comparing classifications: an evaluation of several coefficient of partition agreement. In *Proceedings of the meeting of the classification society, Boulder, CO.*

Fowlkes, E., & Mallows, C. (1983). A method for comparing two hierarchical clusterings. *Journal of American Statistical Association, 78*, 553–569.

Georgiopoulos, M., Heileman, G. L., & Huang, J. (1990). Convergence properties of learning in ART1. *Neural Computation, 2*(4), 502–509.

Grossberg, S. (1976). Adaptive pattern classification and universal recording: I. Parallel development and coding of neural feature detectors. *Biological Cybernetics, 23*, 121–134.

Heuser, U., & Rosenstiel, W (2000). Automatic construction of local internet directories using hierarchical radius-based competitive learning. In *Proceedings of the fourth world multiconference on systemics, cybernetics and informatics (SCI 2000), Orlando/Florida, Vol. IV (Comunications Systems and Networks)* (pp. 436–441).

Jain, A. K., Murty, M. N., & Flynn, P. J. (1999). Data clustering: a review. *ACM Computing Surveys, 31*, 3.

Kaufman, L., & Rousseeuw, P. J. (1990). *Finding groups in data: An introduction to cluster analysis*. New York: Wiley/Interscience.

Kohonen, T. (2001). *Self-organizing maps. Springer series in information.*

Kohonen, T., Lagus, K., Salojärvi, J., Honkela, J., Paatero, V., & Saarela, A. (2000). Self organization of a document collection. *IEEE Transactions on Neural Networks, 11*, 3.

Kondadadi, R., & Kozma, R (2002). A modified fuzzy art for soft document clustering. In *Proceedings of the international joint conference on neural networks, Honolulu, HA.*

Larsen, B., & Aone, C (1999). Fast and effective text mining using linear-time document clustering. In *Proceedings of the fifth ACM SIGKDD international conference on Knowledge discovery and data mining* (pp. 16–22).

MacLeod, K. J., & Robertson, W. (1991). A neural algorithm for document clustering. *Information Processing and Management, 27*(4), 337–346.

MacQueen, J (1967). Some methods for classification and analysis of multivariate observations. In *Proceedings of the fifth Berkeley symposium on mathematical statistics and probability. Vol. 1, Statistics.*

Massey, L (2002a). Structure discovery in text collections. In *Proceedings of the sixth international conference on knowledge-based intelligent information & engineering systems (KES'2002), Italy.*

Massey, L (2002b). Determination of clustering tendency with art neural networks. In *Proceedings of recent adavances in soft-computing (RASC02), Nottingham, UK.*

Merkl, D (1995). Content-based software classification by selforganization. In *Proceedings of the IEEE international conference on neural networks (ICNN'95), Perth, Australia* (pp. 1086–1091).

Moore, B (1988). ART and pattern clustering. In *Proceedings of the 1988 connectionist models summer school* (pp. 174–183).

Petridis, V., Kaburlasos, V. G., Fragkou, P., & Kehagias, A (2001). Text classification using the sigma-FLNMAP neural network. In *Proceedings of international joint conference on neural networks, Washington, DC.*

Rajaraman, K., & Tan, A.-H (2001). Topic detection, tracking and trend analysis using self-organizing neural networks. In *Proceedings of the fifth Pacific-Asia Conference on knowledge discovery and data mining (PAKDD'01), Hong Kong* (pp. 102–107).

Rumelhart, D. E., Hinton, G. E., & Williams, R. J. (1986). Learning internal representations by error propagation. In D. E. Rumelhart, & J. L. McClelland (Eds.), *(Vol. 1)* (pp. 318–364). *Parallel distributed processing: Explorations in the microstructure of cognition, Foundations*, Cambridge, MA: MIT Press.

Sadananda, R., & Sudhakara Rao, G. R. M (1995). ART1: model algorithm characterization and alternative similarity metric for the novelty detector. In *Proceedings IEEE international conference on neural networks, Vol. 5* (pp. 2421–2425).

Salton, G., & Lesk, M. E. (1968). Computer evaluation of indexing and text processing. *Journal of the ACM, 15*(1), 8–36.

Sebastiani, F. (2002). Machine learning in automated text categorization. *ACM Computing Surveys, 34*(1), 1–47.

Steinbach, M., Karypis, G., & Kumar, V (2000). A comparison of document clustering techniques. In *Proceedings sixth ACM SIGKDD international conference on knowledge discovery and data mining, Boston, MA*.

VanRijsbergen, C. J. (1979). *Information retrieval*. London: Butterworths.

Vlajic, N., & Card, H.-C (1998). Categorizing web pages using modified ART. In *Proceedings of IEEE 1998 Canadian conference on electrical and computer engineering*.

Wong, W.-C., Fu, A., & W.-C (2000). Incremental document clustering for web page classification. In *Proceedings of IEEE 2000 international conference on information society in the 21st century: emerging technologies and new challenges, Japan*.

Yang, Y., & Liu, X (1999). A re-examination of text categorization methods. In *Proceedings of international ACM conference on research and development in information retrieval (SIGIR-99)* (pp. 42–49).

Yang, Y., & Pedersen, J. O (1997). A comparative study on feature selection in text categorization. In *Proceedings of ICML-97, 14th international conference on machine learning, Nashville, USA* (pp. 412–420).

AVAILABLE AT www.ComputerScienceWeb.com
POWERED BY SCIENCE DIRECT

PERGAMON

Neural Networks 16 (2003) 779–784

Neural Networks

www.elsevier.com/locate/neunet

2003 Special issue

Extension neural network and its applications

M.H. Wang*, C.P. Hung

Department of Electrical Engineering, National Chin-Yi Institute of Technology, 35, 215 Lane, Sec. 1, Chung Shan Road, Taiping, Taichung, Taiwan, ROC

Abstract

In this paper, a novel extension neural network (ENN) is proposed. This new neural network is a combination of extension theory and neural network. It uses an extension distance (ED) to measure the similarity between data and cluster center. The learning speed of the proposed ENN is shown to be faster than the traditional neural networks and other fuzzy classification methods. Moreover, the new scheme has been proved to have high accuracy and less memory consumption. Experimental results from two different examples verify the effectiveness and applicability of the proposed work.

Keywords: Neural networks; Extension neural network; Extension theory

1. Introduction

Neural networks are parallel systems used for solving regression and classification problems in many fields (Carpenter, Grossberg, & Rosen, 1991; Kohonen, 1988; Rumelhart & McClelland, 1986; Specht, 1990). They can estimate a relation function between the inputs and outputs from a learning process, and also can discover the mapping form feature space into space of classes. Classification or cluster analysis is one of the most important applications of neural networks. The goal of classification is to partition a set of patterns into a group of desired subsets. There are many popular methods for applying neural networks to pattern recognition such as, multiplayer perceptrons (MLP) (Rumelhart & McClelland, 1986), Kohonen neural networks (KNN) (Kohonen, 1988), probabilistic neural network (PNN) (Specht, 1990), learning vector quantization (LVQ) (Bezdek & Pal, 1995), counter propagation networks (CPN) (Hecht-Nielaen, 1987), and adaptive resonance theory (ART) networks (Carpenter et al., 1991). There have been many successful applications in many fields.

The MLP is a continuous input and output pattern recognition, it experts in supervised learning. The most popular training method is error-back-propagation. The drawbacks are that it is not a good strategy to decide the number of neurons in hidden layers and it is time-consuming in training. The KNN is unsupervised training pattern recognition. It employs a winner-take-all learning strategy to store similar patterns in one neuron. KNN has good applications in phonetic or image pattern recognition, but it is not a good strategy to decide the learning parameters and the region of neighborhood. The ART network is an unsupervised learning and adaptive pattern recognition system. It can quickly and stably learn to categorize input patterns and permit an adaptive process for significant and new information. On the other hand, many methods have been proposed to design fuzzy classification systems for dealing with fuzzy classification problems (Hong & Chen, 1999, 2000; Wang, Liu, Hong, & Tseng, 1999; Yu and Chen, 2002). The fuzzy approaches can take human expertise, and have been successfully applied in this field. However, there are some intrinsic shortcomings, such as the difficulty of acquiring knowledge and maintaining a database.

In our world, there are some classification problems whose features are defined in a range. For example, boys can be defined as a cluster of men from age 1 to 14 and the permitted operation voltages of a specified motor may be between 100 and 120 V. For these problems, it is not easy to implement an appropriate classification method using current neural networks. Therefore, a new neural network topology, called the extension neural network (ENN) is proposed to solve these problems in this paper. In other words, the ENN permits classification of problems, which have range features, supervised learning, or continuous input and discrete output. This new neural network is

* Corresponding author. Tel.: +886-4-23924505-7233; fax: +886-4-23924419.

E-mail address: wangmh@chinyi.ncit.edu.tw (M.H. Wang).

0893-6080/03/$ - see front matter © 2003 Elsevier Science Ltd. All rights reserved.
doi:10.1016/S0893-6080(03)00104-7

a combination of the extension theory (Cai, 1983; Huang & Chen, 1999; Wang & Chen, 2001) and the neural network, the ENN uses a modified extension distance (ED) to measure the similarity between data and cluster center; it permits adaptive process for significant and new information, and gives shorter learning times than traditional neural networks. Moreover, this ENN has shown higher accuracy, less memory consumption in application.

2. Review of extension theory

Extension theory was originally invented by Cai to solve contradictions and incompatibility problems in 1983 (Cai, 1983). The extension set extends the fuzzy set from [0,1] to $(-\infty, \infty)$. As a result, it allows us to define a set that includes any data in the domain.

2.1. Matter-element theory

(1) Definition of matter-element

Defining the name of a matter by N, one of the characteristics of the matter by c, and the value of c by v, we can use an ordered ternary $R = (N, c, v)$ as the fundamental element to state a matter and call it a matter-element in extension theory. For example, $R =$ (Wang, Weight, 80 kg) can be used to state that Wang's weight is 80 kg. If the value of the characteristic has a classical domain or a range, we define the matter-element for the classical domain as follows:

$$R = (N, c, W) = (N, c, \langle w^{\mathrm{L}}, w^{\mathrm{U}} \rangle) \tag{1}$$

Where w^{L} and w^{U} are the lower bound and upper bound of classical domains, respectively.

(2) Multi-dimensional matter-element

If $R = (N, C, V)$ is a multi-dimensional matter-element, $C = [c_1, c_2, ..., c_n]$ a characteristic vector and $V = [v_1, v_2, ... v_n]$ a value vector of C, then a multi-dimensional matter-element is defined as follows:

$$R = (N, C, V) = \begin{bmatrix} N, c_1, v_1 \\ c_2, v_2 \\ \vdots \\ c_n, v_n \end{bmatrix} = \begin{bmatrix} R_1 \\ R_2 \\ \vdots \\ R_n \end{bmatrix} \tag{2}$$

Where $R_i = (N, c_i, v_i) (i = 1, 2 ... n)$ is the sub-matter-element of R.

2.2. Summary of extension set theory

(1) Definition of extension set

If U is a space of objects and x a generic element of U, then an extension set A in U is defined as a set of ordered pairs:

$$A = \{(u, y) | u \in U, y = K(x) \in (-\infty, \infty)\} \tag{3}$$

Where $y = K(x)$ is called the relational function for extension set A. The $K(x)$ maps each element of U to a membership grade between $-\infty$ and ∞. The higher the degree, the closer the element belongs to the set.

(2) Primitively extended relation function

Let $X_o = \langle a, b \rangle$, $X = \langle c, d \rangle$ and $X_o \in X$, then the extended relation function can be defined as follows:

$$K(x) = \frac{\rho(x, X_o)}{D(x, X_o, X)} \tag{4}$$

where

$$\rho(x, X_o) = \left| x - \frac{a+b}{2} \right| - \frac{b-a}{2} \tag{5}$$

$$D(x, X_o, X) = \begin{cases} \rho(x, X) - \rho(x, X_o) & x \notin X_o \\ -1 & x \in X_o \end{cases} \tag{6}$$

When $K(x) \geq 0$, it can describe the degree to which x belongs to X_o and $K(x) < 0$ can describe the degree to which x does not belong to X_o. Apparently, those values that are not inside the set are not discussed in the fuzzy set. When $-1 < K(x) < 0$, this domain is called an extension domain, which means that the element x still has a chance to become an element of the set.

3. Extension neural network

The proposed ENN is a combination of the neural network and the extension theory. The extension theory proves a novel distance measurement for classification processes, and the neural network can embed the salient features of parallel computation power and learning capability. In other words, the ENN permits classification of problems, which have range features, supervised learning, or continuous input and discrete output.

3.1. Structure of ENN

The schematic structure of the ENN is depicted in Fig. 1. It comprises both the input layer and the output layer. The nodes in the input layer receive an input feature pattern and use a set of weighted parameters to generate an image of the input pattern. In this network, there are two connection values (weights) between input nodes and output nodes; one connection represents the lower bound for this classical domain of the features, and the other connection represents the upper bound. The connections between the j-th input node and the k-th output node are w_{kj}^{L} and w_{kj}^{U}.

This image is further enhanced in the process characterized by the output layer. Only one output node in the output layer remains active to indicate a classification of the input pattern. The operation mode of the proposed ENN can be

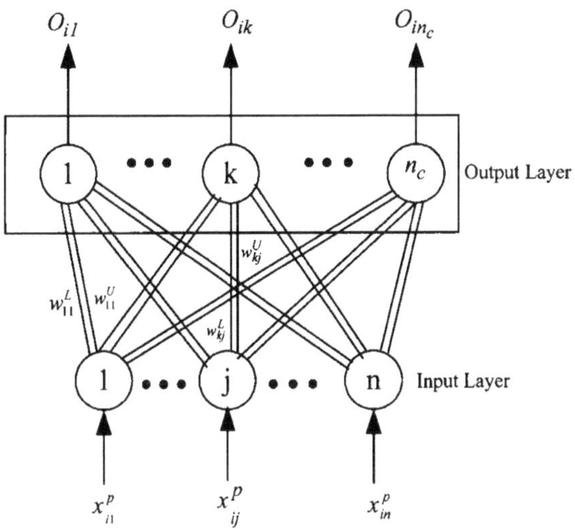

Fig. 1. The structure of extension neural network (ENN).

separated into the learning phase and the operation phase. The learning algorithm of the ENN is discussed in the next section.

3.2. Learning algorithm of the ENN

The learning of the ENN can be seen as supervised learning; the purpose of learning is to tune the weights of the ENN to achieve good clustering performance or to minimize the clustering error. Before the learning, several variables have to be defined. Let training pattern set be $X \equiv \{X_1, X_2, \ldots, X_{N_p}\}$, where N_p is the total number of training patterns. The i-th pattern is $X_i^p \equiv \{x_{i1}^p, x_{i2}^p, \ldots, x_{in}^p\}$, where n is the total number of the feature of patterns, and the category of the i-th pattern is p. To evaluate the clustering performance, the total error number is set as N_m, and the total error rate E_T is defined below:

$$E_T = \frac{N_m}{N_p} \tag{7}$$

The detailed supervised learning algorithm can be described as follows:

Step 1: Set the connection weights between input nodes and output nodes by the matter-element model of extension theory:

$$R_k \begin{bmatrix} N_k, c_1, V_{k1} \\ c_2, V_{k2} \\ \vdots \\ c_n, V_{kn} \end{bmatrix} \quad k = 1, 2, \ldots, n_c \tag{8}$$

In the extension theory, c_j is the j-th characteristic (feature) of N_k and $V_{kj} = \langle w_{kj}^{\mathrm{L}}, w_{kj}^{\mathrm{U}} \rangle$ are the classical domains of the k-th cluster (N_k) about the j-th feature c_j. The range of classical domains can be directly obtained from previous requirement, or determined from training data as follows:

$$w_{kj}^{\mathrm{L}} = \underset{i \in N_p}{\mathrm{Min}} \{x_{ij}^k\} \tag{9}$$

$$w_{kj}^{\mathrm{U}} = \underset{i \in N_p}{\mathrm{Max}} \{x_{ij}^k\} \tag{10}$$

Step 2: Calculate the initial cluster center of every cluster

$$Z_k = \{z_{k1}, z_{k2}, \ldots, z_{kn}\} \tag{11}$$

$$z_{kj} = (w_{kj}^{\mathrm{L}} + w_{kj}^{\mathrm{U}})/2 \tag{12}$$

for $k = 1, 2 \ldots n_c; j = 1, 2 \ldots n$

Step 3: Read the i-th training pattern and its cluster number p

$$X_i^p = \{x_{i1}^p, x_{i2}^p, \ldots, x_{in}^p\}, \qquad p \in n_c \tag{13}$$

Step 4: Use the proposed ED to calculate the distance between the training pattern X_i^p and the k-th cluster as follows:

$$\mathrm{ED}_{ik} = \sum_{j=1}^{n} \left[\frac{|x_{ij}^p - z_{kj}| - (w_{kj}^{\mathrm{U}} - w_{kj}^{\mathrm{L}})/2}{|(w_{kj}^{\mathrm{U}} - w_{kj}^{\mathrm{L}})/2|} + 1 \right] \tag{14}$$

for $k = 1, 2, \ldots, n_c$

The proposed distance is a modification of ED (Cai, 1983). It can be graphically presented as Fig. 2 it can describe the distance between the x and a range $\langle w^{\mathrm{L}}, w^{\mathrm{U}} \rangle$. From Fig. 2, we can see that different ranges of classical domains can arrive at different distances due to different sensitivities. This is a significant advantage in classification applications. Usually, if the feature covers a large range, the requirement of data is fuzzy or low in sensitivity to distance. On the other hand, if the feature covers a small range, the requirement of data is precision or high sensitivity to distance.

Step 5: Find the k^*, such that $\mathrm{ED}_{ik^*} = \mathrm{Min}\{\mathrm{ED}_{ik}\}$. If $k^* = p$ then go to Step 7; otherwise Step 6.

Step 6: Update the weights of the p-th and the k^*-th clusters as follows:

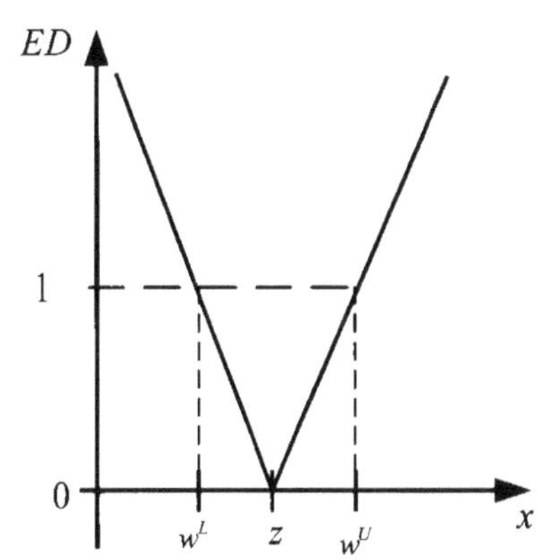

Fig. 2. The proposed extension distance (ED).

(a) Update the centers of the p-th and the k^*-th clusters:

$$z_{pj}^{\text{new}} = z_{pj}^{\text{old}} + \eta(x_{ij}^{p} - z_{pj}^{\text{old}}) \tag{15}$$

$$z_{k^*j}^{\text{new}} = z_{k^*j}^{\text{old}} - \eta(x_{ij}^{p} - z_{k^*j}^{\text{old}}) \tag{16}$$

(b) Update the weights of the p-th and the k^*-th clusters:

$$\begin{cases} w_{pj}^{\text{L(new)}} = w_{pj}^{\text{L(old)}} + \eta(x_{ij}^{p} - z_{pj}^{\text{old}}) \\ w_{pj}^{\text{u(new)}} = w_{pj}^{\text{u(old)}} + \eta(x_{ij}^{p} - z_{pj}^{\text{old}}) \end{cases} \tag{17}$$

$$\begin{cases} w_{k^*j}^{\text{L(new)}} = w_{k^*j}^{\text{L(old)}} - \eta(x_{ij}^{p} - z_{k^*j}^{\text{old}}) \\ w_{k^*j}^{\text{u(new)}} = w_{k^*j}^{\text{u(old)}} - \eta(x_{ij}^{p} - z_{k^*j}^{\text{old}}) \end{cases} \tag{18}$$

Where η is a learning rate. The result of tuning two cluster's weights is shown in Fig. 3 clearly indicating the change of ED_A and ED_B. The cluster of pattern x_{ij} is changed from cluster A to B due to $ED_A > ED_B$. From this step, we can clearly see that the learning process is only to adjust the weights of the p-th and the k^*-th clusters. Therefore, the proposed method has a speed advantage over other supervised learning algorithms, and can quickly adapt to new and important information.

Step 7: Repeat Step 3 to Step 6, if all patterns have been classified, then a learning epoch is finished.

Step 8: Stop, if the clustering process has converged, or the total error rate E_T has arrived at a preset value, otherwise, return to Step 3.

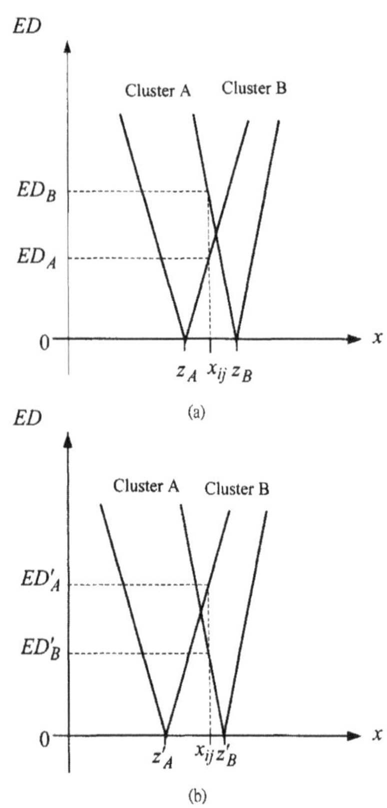

Fig. 3. The results of tuning cluster weights: (a) original condition; (b) after tuning.

3.3. Operation phase of ENN

Step 1: Read the weight matrix of ENN

Step 2: Calculate the initial cluster centers of every cluster using Eqs. (11) and (12)

Step 3: Read the tested pattern

$$X_t = \{x_{t1}, x_{t2}, \ldots, x_{tn}\} \tag{19}$$

Step 4: Use the proposed ED to calculate the distance between the tested pattern and every existed cluster by Eq. (14)

Step 5: Find the k^*, such that $\text{ED}_{ik^*} = \text{Min}\{\text{ED}_{ik}\}$, and set the $O_{ik^*} = 1$ to indicate the cluster of the tested pattern.

Step 6: Stop, if all the tested patterns have been classified, otherwise go to Step 3.

4. Experimental results

In this paper, the Iris data classification problem (Chien, 1978) and vibration diagnosis problems (Li, Sun, Liao, Chen & Hu, 1999; Li, Sun, Hu, Yue, Tang & Wang, 2000) are used to illustrate the effectiveness of the proposed ENN.

4.1. Iris data classification

There are 150 instances in the Iris data; it can be divided into three categories with the distinguishing variables being the length and width of sepal and petal. In this case, the structures of the proposed ENN are three output nodes and four input nodes. To prove the efficiency of the proposed ENN, two test cases is given in the following:

Case 1: If the system randomly chooses 75 instances from the Iris data as the training data set, and let the rest of the instances of the Iris data are the testing data set. Fig. 4 shows the learning curves of the proposed ENN with different learning rates. It is clear that the training time of the proposed ENN is quite economical with about 4 epochs for $\eta = 0.1$ and about 13 epochs for $\eta = 0.01$. Table 1 shows the comparison of the experimental results of the proposed ENN with other typical neural networks. It should

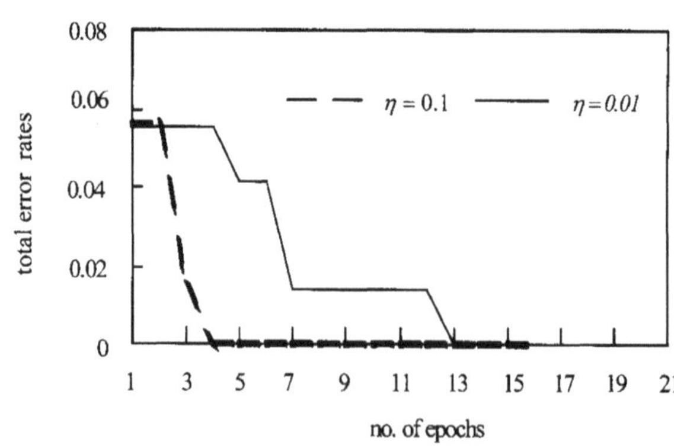

Fig. 4. The learning curves of Iris data classification problem.

Table 1
Comparison of the classification performance of various neural networks

Model	Structure	No. of connections	Learning times (epochs)	Training error	Testing error
Perceptron	4-3	12	200	0.173	0.213
MLP	4-4-3-3	37	50	0.027	0.040
PNN	4-75-3	525	1	0.0	0.053
LVQ	4-15-3	105	20	0.8	0.053
CPN	4-20-3	140	60	0.107	0.160
ENN	4-3	24	4	0.0	0.040

MLP, Multilayer perceptron; PNN, probabilistic neural network; LVQ, learning vector quantization; CPN, counter propagation network; ENN, extension neural network; training set comprised 75 data points and testing set comprised the remaining data points.

be noted that structure of the proposed ENN is the very simple, only 7 nodes and 24 connections is needed. Moreover, the proposed ENN-based also permits fast adaptive process for a large amount of training data or new information, because the learning of ENN is only to tuning low-bound and upper bound of the excited connections. It can be seen from the Table 1 that the proposed ENN has a shorter learning time than the traditional neural networks. As well, the accurate rates are quite high with about 100 and 96% for training and testing patterns, respectively. On the other hand, the proposed ENN can take expert experiences before learning, and can also produce meaningful output after learning, because the optimal classified boundary of the features are clearly determined.

Case 2: If the training data set contains 150 training instances (i.e., the full Iris data) and the testing data set is equal to the training data set containing 150 training instances. Table 2 compares the performance of the proposed ENN with several other fuzzy classification methods on the same data set. It can be seen that the proposed ENN is at least as good as the other methods, but it has a shortest learning times. Moreover, the proposed ENN permits fast adaptive process for significant and new information, and it is easy to acquire knowledge and maintain the classification database.

4.2. Vibration diagnosis of generator sets

The vibration diagnosis of generator set is based on the principle that components in engineering systems and plants produce vibration during operation. If a generator set is operating properly, vibration conditions are usually small and constant, but when faults grow or some of the dynamic processes in the machine change, the vibration signature also changes. Therefore, diagnostic information can be supplied by the spectrum of the vibration signal. In agreement with past studies (Li et al., 1999, 2000), the typical six values (amplitude of <0.4f, 0.4f–0.5f, f, 2f, 3f, and >3f) are selected for vibration fault diagnosis, and the detailed trained data are shown in Table 3. To compare diagnosis performance, the diagnosis results with different two different classification methods (Li et al., 1999, 2000),

Table 2
Comparison of the average classification accuracy rate for different method

Methods	Learning times (epochs)	Average classification accuracy rate
Hong and Chen's method	200	96.67%
Hong and Chen's method	200	97.33%
Wang-et al., method	200	97.33%
Yu and Chen's method	200	97.33%
Proposed ENN method	4	97.33%

Table 3
Tested data of generator sets

Gen. no.	Input data						Fault types
	<0.4f	0.4f–0.5f	1f	2f	3f	>3f	
1	3.35	46.6	12.15	1.94	2.3	3.67	F_1
2	4.43	51	11.02	3.02	1.3	2.43	F_1
3	3.29	50	11.61	1.24	0.9	1.3	F_1
4	5.72	46.3	12.31	3.62	1.5	0.59	F_1
5	6.32	45.8	15.23	3.56	2.3	3.19	F_1
6	1.51	3.29	52.92	6.59	2.5	2.54	F_2
7	2.43	1.19	54.49	4.64	0.8	1.78	F_2
8	0.54	2.92	48.82	6.64	3.9	1.51	F_2
9	0.81	1.73	52	6.43	3.6	1.89	F_2
10	1.24	1.35	49.79	4.64	1.0	2.27	F_2
11	1.78	1.46	22.46	23.8	19	8.59	F_3
12	0.92	1.24	30.08	22	16	5.67	F_3
13	0.65	2.11	21.98	26.2	18	11.1	F_3
14	1.13	0.92	24.46	22.3	15	15.8	F_3
15	0.92	1.40	26.08	26	20	11.4	F_3

F_1, Oil-resonance fault; F_2, imbalance fault; F_3, misalignment fault.

Table 4
Learning results using different neural networks

Classifiers	MLP	AWN	ENN
Structure	6-13-3	6-13-3	6-3
Learning speed (epochs)	2561	900	2
Accuracy	100%	100%	100%

AWN, Adaptive wavelets network.

i.e. MLP and AWN, are shown in Table 4. The two traditional neural networks were capable of pointing toward faults, but both need to learn about 2561 and 900 epochs before fault diagnosis. Contrary, the proposed ENN only need to learn 2 epochs with equivalent accuracy, and the structure of the proposed ENN is simpler than the other neural networks.

5. Conclusions

This paper presents a novel ENN based on the extension theory and neural network. Compared with traditional neural networks and other fuzzy classification methods, it permits an adaptive process for significant and new information, and gives shorter learning times. The proposed ENN can solve some special classification problems that the feature is defined in a range. Moreover, the proposed ED, the different ranges of classical domain can arrive at different distances due to different sensitivities, which is a significant advantage in classification applications. From the tested examples, the proposed ENN has been proved to have the advantage of less learning time, higher accuracy and less memory consumption. Future studies will be carried out to develop an unsupervised learning algorithm of the proposed ENN, and to extend this classification technique to control and develop fault diagnosis systems.

Acknowledgements

The authors gratefully acknowledge the support of the National Science Council, Taiwan, ROC, under the grant no. NSC-91-2213-E-167-014.

References

Bezdek, J. C., & Pal, N. R. (1995). Two soft relative of learning vector quantization. *Neural Networks*, *8*, 729–743.

Cai, W. (1983). The extension set and incompatibility problem. *Journal of Scientific Exploration*, *1*, 81–93.

Carpenter, G., Grossberg, S., & Rosen, D. B. (1991). ART 2-A: an adaptive resonance algorithm for rapid category learning and recognition. *Neural Networks*, *4*, 493–504.

Chien, Y. T. (1978). *Interactive pattern recognition*. New York, USA: Marcel Dekker, pp. 223–225.

Hecht-Nielaen, R. (1987). Counter-propagation networks. *ICNN-87*, *2*, 19–32.

Hong, T. P., & Chen, J. B. (1999). Finding relevant attributes and membership functions. *Fuzzy Sets and Systems*, *103*, 389–404.

Hong, T. P., & Chen, J. B. (2000). Processing individual fuzzy attributes for fuzzy rule induction. *Fuzzy Sets and Systems*, *112*, 127–140.

Kohonen, T. (1988). *Self-organization and associative memory* (2nd ed.). Berlin, Germany: Springer.

Li, H., Sun, C. X., Liao, R. J., Chen, W. G., & Hu, X. S. (1999). Improved BP algorithm in vibration fault diagnosis of steam turbine-generator set. *Journal of Chongqing University*, *22*, 47–52.

Li, H., Sun, C. X., Hu, X. S., Yue, G., Tang, N. F., & Wang, K. (2000). Study of method on Adaptive wavelets network for vibration fault diagnosis of steam turbine-generation set. *Transactions of China Electrotechnical Society*, *15*, 52–57.

Rumelhart, D. E., & McClelland, J. L. (1986). *Parallel distributed processing explorations in the microstructure of cognition*. Cambridge: Bradford Books, MIT Press.

Specht, D. F. (1990). Probabilistic neural networks and the polynomial adaline as complementary techniques for classification. *IEEE Transactions on Neural Networks*, *1*, 111–121.

Wang, C. H., Liu, J. F., Hong, T. P., & Tseng, S. S. (1999). A fuzzy inductive strategy for modular rules. *Fuzzy Sets and Systems*, *103*, 91–105.

Wang, M. H., & Chen, H. C. (2001). Application of extension theory on the fault diagnosis of power transformers. *Proceeding of the 22nd Symposium on Electrical Power Engneering, Taiwan*, 797–800.

Yu, C. H., & Chen, S. M. (2002). A new method for handling fuzzy classification problems based on clustering techniques. *Proceeding of the Seventh Conference on Artificial Intelligence and Applications*, 107–112.

AVAILABLE AT
www.ComputerScienceWeb.com
POWERED BY SCIENCE DIRECT

PERGAMON

Neural Networks 16 (2003) 785–792

Neural Networks

www.elsevier.com/locate/neunet

2003 Special issue

Fuzzy least squares support vector machines for multiclass problems

Daisuke Tsujinishi, Shigeo Abe*

Graduate School of Science and Technology, Kobe University, Rokkodai, Nada, Kobe, Japan

Abstract

In least squares support vector machines (LS-SVMs), the optimal separating hyperplane is obtained by solving a set of linear equations instead of solving a quadratic programming problem. But since SVMs and LS-SVMs are formulated for two-class problems, unclassifiable regions exist when they are extended to multiclass problems.

In this paper, we discuss fuzzy LS-SVMs that resolve unclassifiable regions for multiclass problems. We define a membership function in the direction perpendicular to the optimal separating hyperplane that separates a pair of classes. Using the minimum or average operation for these membership functions, we define a membership function for each class. Using some benchmark data sets, we show that recognition performance of fuzzy LS-SVMs with the minimum operator is comparable to that of fuzzy SVMs, but fuzzy LS-SVMs with the average operator showed inferior performance.

Keywords: Least squares support vector machines; Multiclass problems; Membership functions

1. Introduction

Support vector machines proposed by Vapnik (1998) are trained by solving a quadratic optimization problem. Least squares support vector machines (LS-SVMs) proposed by Suykens and Vandewalle (1999) are trained by solving a set of linear equations. But since SVMs and LS-SVMs are formulated for two-class classification problems, an extension to multiclass problems is not unique. There are roughly four types of support vector machines that handle multiclass problems:

(1) one-against-all support vector machines (Vapnik, 1998),
(2) pairwise support vector machines (Kreßel, 1999),
(3) error-correcting-output code (ECOC) support vector machines (Dietterich & Bakiri, 1995),
(4) all-at-once support vector machines (Vapnik, 1998).

According to Vapnik's formulation, in one-against-all support vector machines, a k-class problem is converted into k two-class problems and for the ith two-class problem, class i is separated from the remaining classes. But by this formulation unclassifiable regions exist if we use the discrete decision functions. One way to solve this problem is to use continuous decision functions. Another is to introduce fuzzy membership functions as proposed in Inoue and Abe (2000).

In pairwise support vector machines, the k-class problem is converted into $k(k-1)/2$ two-class problems which cover all pairs of classes. But by this method also unclassifiable regions exist. Similar to Inoue and Abe (2000) unclassifiable regions can be resolved by introducing membership functions (Abe & Inoue, 2002).

In this paper, to resolve unclassifiable regions in LS-SVMs, we introduce fuzzy membership functions in the similar way as discussed in Abe and Inoue (2002), in which the membership function for a class is defined using the minimum operator. Here, we use the average operator as well as the minimum operator. By the minimum operator, the contour surface is parallel to the decision functions, thus the fuzzy SVM always outperforms the SVM. But this is not guaranteed for the average operator. In ECOC to resolve unclassifiable regions, the continuous Hamming distance is used. We can show that the average operator is complementary to the continuous Hamming distance.

Our purpose is to resolve the unclassifiable regions of LS-SVMs by the introduction of membership functions and then to clarify which operator is suited for LS-SVMs by computer experiments using several benchmark data sets.

This paper is organized as follows. In Section 2, we describe the architectures of the SVM and the LS-SVM. In Section 3, we discuss fuzzy LS-SVMs that resolve

* Corresponding author.
E-mail addresses: abe@eedept.kobe-u.ac.jp (S. Abe), tujinisi@frenchblue.scitec.kobe-u.ac.jp (D. Tsujinishi).

0893-6080/03/$ - see front matter © 2003 Elsevier Science Ltd. All rights reserved.
doi:10.1016/S0893-6080(03)00110-2

unclassifiable regions in multiclass problems. And in Section 4 we show performance comparison of fuzzy SVMs and fuzzy LS-SVMs using some benchmark data sets.

2. Least squares support vector machines

In this section, we describe SVMs and LS-SVMs for two-class problems and the training method of LS-SVMs.

2.1. Architecture of SVMs

Let m-dimensional training data be $\mathbf{x}_i$ ($i = 1, \ldots, M$) and their class labels be y_i, where $y_i = 1$ and $y_i = -1$ for Classes 1 and 2, respectively. If these input data are linearly separable in the feature space, we can determine the following decision function:

$$D(\mathbf{x}) = \mathbf{w}^{\mathrm{t}}\mathbf{g}(\mathbf{x}) + b, \tag{1}$$

where $\mathbf{g}(\mathbf{x})$ is a mapping function that maps $\mathbf{x}$ into the l-dimensional space, $\mathbf{w}$ is an l-dimensional vector and b is a scalar. To separate data linearly, the decision function satisfies the following condition:

$$y_i(\mathbf{w}^{\mathrm{t}}\mathbf{g}(\mathbf{x}_i) + b) \geq 1 \quad \text{for } i = 1, \ldots, M. \tag{2}$$

If the problem is linearly separable in the feature space, there are an infinite number of decision functions that satisfy Eq. (2). Among them we require that the hyperplane has the largest margin between two classes. Here the margin is the minimum distance from the separating hyperplane to the input data and this is given by $|D(\mathbf{x})|/\|\mathbf{w}\|$. And we call the separating hyperplane with the maximum margin optimal separating hyperplane.

Assuming that the margin is ρ, the following condition needs to be satisfied:

$$\frac{y_i D(\mathbf{x}_i)}{\|\mathbf{w}\|} \geq \rho \quad \text{for } i = 1, \ldots, M. \tag{3}$$

We fix the product of ρ and $\|\mathbf{w}\|$:

$$\rho\|\mathbf{w}\| = 1. \tag{4}$$

Then, in order to obtain the optimal separating hyperplane with the maximum margin, we must find $\mathbf{w}$ with the minimum $\|\mathbf{w}\|$ that satisfy Eq. (3). From Eq. (4), this leads to solving the following optimization problem. Namely, minimize

$$\tfrac{1}{2}\mathbf{w}^{\mathrm{t}}\mathbf{w} \tag{5}$$

subject to the constraints:

$$y_i(\mathbf{w}^{\mathrm{t}}\mathbf{g}(\mathbf{x}_i) + b) \geq 1 \quad \text{for } i = 1, \ldots, M. \tag{6}$$

When training data are not linearly separable, we introduce slack variables $\xi_i (> 0)$ into Eq. (2) as follows:

$$y_i(\mathbf{w}^{\mathrm{t}}\mathbf{g}(\mathbf{x}_i) + b) \geq 1 - \xi_i, \qquad \xi_i \geq 0 \quad \text{for } i = 1, \ldots M. \tag{7}$$

The optimal separating hyperplane is determined so that the maximization of the margin and the minimization of the training error are achieved. Namely, minimize

$$\frac{1}{2}\mathbf{w}^{\mathrm{t}}\mathbf{w} + \frac{C}{2}\sum_{i=1}^{n}\xi_i^p \tag{8}$$

subject to the constraints:

$$y_i(\mathbf{w}^{\mathrm{t}}\mathbf{g}(\mathbf{x}_i) + b) \geq 1 - \xi_i, \qquad \xi_i \geq 0 \quad \text{for } i = 1, \ldots, M, \tag{9}$$

where C is a parameter that determines the tradeoff between the maximum margin and the minimum classification error and p is 1 or 2. When $p = 1$, the SVM is called L1 soft margin SVM (L1-SVM), and when $p = 2$, L2 soft margin SVM (L2-SVM). In the conventional SVM, optimal separating hyper-plane is obtained by solving the above quadratic programming problem.

2.2. Architecture of LS-SVMs

In contrast to the SVM, the LS-SVM is trained by minimizing

$$\frac{1}{2}\mathbf{w}^{\mathrm{t}}\mathbf{w} + \frac{C}{2}\sum_{i=1}^{M}\xi_i^2 \tag{10}$$

subject to the equality constraints:

$$y_i(\mathbf{w}^{\mathrm{t}}\mathbf{g}(\mathbf{x}_i) + b) = 1 - \xi_i \quad \text{for } i = 1, \ldots, M. \tag{11}$$

In the LS-SVM, we use equality constraints instead of inequality ones employed in the conventional SVM. Therefore, the optimal solution can be obtained by solving a set of linear equations instead of solving a quadratic programming problem.

To derive the dual problem of Eqs. (10) and (11), we introduce the Lagrange multipliers as follows:

$$Q(\mathbf{w}, b, \alpha, \xi) = \frac{1}{2}\mathbf{w}^{\mathrm{t}}\mathbf{w} + \frac{C}{2}\sum_{i=1}^{M}\xi_i^2 - \sum_{i=1}^{M}\alpha_i\{y_i(\mathbf{w}^{\mathrm{t}}\mathbf{g}(\mathbf{x}_i) + b) - 1 + \xi_i\},$$

where $\boldsymbol{\alpha} = (\alpha_1, \ldots, \alpha_M)^{\mathrm{t}}$ is Lagrange multipliers, which can be positive or negative in case of LS-SVM formulation. The conditions for optimality are derived by differentiating the above equation with respect to $\mathbf{w}$, ξ_i, b, and α_i and equating the resulting equations to zero:

$$\mathbf{w} = \sum_{i=1}^{M}\alpha_i y_i \mathbf{g}(\mathbf{x}_i), \tag{12}$$

$$\sum_{i=1}^{M}\alpha_i y_i = 0, \tag{13}$$

$$\alpha_i = C\xi_i. \tag{14}$$

In a matrix form, Eqs. (11)–(14) are expressed by

$$\begin{bmatrix} \boldsymbol{\Omega} & \mathbf{Y} \\ \mathbf{Y}^{\mathrm{t}} & 0 \end{bmatrix} \begin{bmatrix} \boldsymbol{\alpha} \\ b \end{bmatrix} = \begin{bmatrix} \mathbf{1} \\ 0 \end{bmatrix}, \tag{15}$$

where $\boldsymbol{\Omega}$, $\mathbf{Y}$ and $\mathbf{1}$ are, respectively,

$$\boldsymbol{\Omega}_{ij} = y_i y_j \mathbf{g}(\mathbf{x}_i)^{\mathrm{t}} \mathbf{g}(\mathbf{x}_j) + \frac{\delta_{ij}}{C}, \tag{16}$$

$$\mathbf{Y} = (y_1, \ldots, y_M)^{\mathrm{t}}, \tag{17}$$

$$\mathbf{1} = (1, \ldots, 1)^{\mathrm{t}}. \tag{18}$$

Here,

$$\delta_{ij} = \begin{cases} 1 & i = j, \\ 0 & i \neq j. \end{cases}$$

2.3. Training of LS-SVMs

An LS-SVM is trained by solving Eq. (15). From Eq. (16), $\boldsymbol{\Omega}$ is positive definite. Thus,

$$\boldsymbol{\alpha} = \boldsymbol{\Omega}^{-1}(\mathbf{1} - \mathbf{Y}b). \tag{19}$$

Substituting Eq. (19) into the second matrix equation in Eq. (15), we obtain

$$b = \frac{\mathbf{Y}^{\mathrm{t}} \boldsymbol{\Omega}^{-1} \mathbf{1}}{\mathbf{Y}^{\mathrm{t}} \boldsymbol{\Omega}^{-1} \mathbf{Y}}. \tag{20}$$

Here, since $\boldsymbol{\Omega}$ is positive definite, $\boldsymbol{\Omega}^{-1}$ is also positive definite. In addition, since $\mathbf{Y}$ is non zero vector, $\mathbf{Y}^{\mathrm{t}}\boldsymbol{\Omega}^{-1} \mathbf{Y} > 0$. Thus, b is always obtained.

Substituting Eq. (20) into Eq. (19), we obtain $\boldsymbol{\alpha}$. In solving Eq. (20), we use the Cholesky factorization.

Applying the Cholesky factorization to matrix $\boldsymbol{\Omega}$, it is decomposed into the product of two symmetric matrix as $\boldsymbol{\Omega} = LL^{\mathrm{t}}$. Here, L and L^{t} are lower and upper triangular matrixes, respectively, and each element of L is given by

$$l_{op} = \left(q_{op} - \sum_{n=1}^{p-1} l_{pn} l_{on} \right) / l_{pp}$$

$$\text{for } o = 1, \ldots, m, \ \ p = 1, \ldots, o - 1, \tag{21}$$

$$l_{aa} = \sqrt{q_{aa} - \sum_{n=1}^{a-1} l_{an}^2} \ \text{ for } a = 1, \ldots, m. \tag{22}$$

Although $\boldsymbol{\Omega}$ is positive definite, the Cholesky factorization becomes unstable if $\boldsymbol{\Omega}$ is near positive semi-definite. Then, to prevent this, if

$$q_{aa} = \sum_{n=1}^{a-1} l_{an}^2 \leq \eta \tag{23}$$

where $\eta = (> 0)$, we set

$$l_{aa} = \sqrt{\eta}. \tag{24}$$

In this paper, we set η at 10^{-5}.

Then letting

$$\boldsymbol{\Omega}\mathbf{a} = LL^{\mathrm{t}}\mathbf{a} = \mathbf{Y}, \tag{25}$$

where $\mathbf{a}$ is an M-dimensional vector, we can solve Eq. (25) without matrix inversion. Using $\mathbf{a}$, b given by Eq. (20) reduces to

$$b = \frac{\mathbf{a}^{\mathrm{t}}\mathbf{1}}{\mathbf{Y}^{\mathrm{t}}\mathbf{a}}. \tag{26}$$

Similarly, we can obtain $\boldsymbol{\alpha}$.

2.4. Kernel functions

One of the characteristic of the SVM is that it uses the technique called kernel trick. In Eq. (16), defining

$$K(\mathbf{x}, \mathbf{x}') = \mathbf{g}(\mathbf{x})^{\mathrm{t}} \mathbf{g}(\mathbf{x}'), \tag{27}$$

where $K(\mathbf{x}, \mathbf{x}')$ is a kernel function, we can avoid treating variables in the feature space. In the following study, we use the kernel functions as follows:

- dot product kernels: $K(\mathbf{x}, \mathbf{x}') = \mathbf{x}^{\mathrm{t}}\mathbf{x}'$;
- polynomial kernels: $K(\mathbf{x}, \mathbf{x}') = (\mathbf{x}^{\mathrm{t}}\mathbf{x}' + 1)^d$, where d is a positive integer;
- RBF kernels: $K(\mathbf{x}, \mathbf{x}') = \exp(-\gamma \|\mathbf{x} - \mathbf{x}'\|^2)$, where γ is a positive parameter.

If the problem has a very large number of input variables, the value of a kernel function becomes so small or large that training of support vector machines becomes difficult.

For a polynomial kernel with degree d, the maximum value is $(m + 1)^d$ if the range of input variables is [0, 1]. Thus, when m is very large, we normalize polynomial kernels as follows:

$$K(\mathbf{x}, \mathbf{x}') = \frac{(\mathbf{x}^{\mathrm{t}}\mathbf{x}' + 1)^d}{(m + 1)^d}. \tag{28}$$

Similarly, for RBF kernels, the maximum value of $\|\mathbf{x} - \mathbf{x}\|^2$ is m. Thus we normalize RBF kernels as follows:

$$K(\mathbf{x}, \mathbf{x}') = \exp\left(-\frac{\gamma}{m} \|\mathbf{x} - \mathbf{x}'\|^2 \right). \tag{29}$$

3. Multiclass classification

The formulation of SVMs is based on a two-class classification problem. Since SVMs determine the decision boundary directly, an extension to multiclass problem is not unique. Vapnik (1998) uses one-against-all classification, in which one class is separated from the remaining classes. By this formulation, however, we need to solve a set of linear equations with the number of variables equal to the number of training data. Therefore, long training time is necessary for training a problem with a large number of training data.

Considering the computational burden in training, here we use pairwise classification (Kreßel, 1999). In one-against-all and pairwise classifications, unclassifiable regions exist (Abe & Inoue, 2002; Inoue & Abe, 2000). Thus similar to Abe and Inoue (2002) we introduce fuzzy membership functions to resolve unclassifiable regions in pairwise classification.

In pairwise classification we require a binary classifier for each possible pair of classes and the number of the total pairs is $k(k-1)/2$ for a k-class problem. The decision function for the pair of classes i and j is given by

$$D_{ij}(\mathbf{x}) = \mathbf{w}_{ij}^{t}\mathbf{g}(\mathbf{x}) + b_{ij}, \tag{30}$$

where $D_{ij}(\mathbf{x}) = -D_{ji}(\mathbf{x})$. Then for the datum $\mathbf{x}$ we calculate

$$D_i(\mathbf{x}) = \sum_{j \neq i,\ i=1}^{k} \mathrm{sign}(D_{ij}(\mathbf{x})), \tag{31}$$

where

$$\mathrm{sign}(a) = \begin{cases} 1 & a > 0, \\ 0 & \text{otherwise,} \end{cases}$$

and this datum is classified into the class

$$\operatorname*{argmax}_{i=1,\ldots,k} D_i(\mathbf{x}). \tag{32}$$

If Eq. (32) is satisfied for one i, $\mathbf{x}$ is classified into class i. But if Eq. (32) is satisfied for plural is, $\mathbf{x}$ is unclassifiable. In Fig. 1, if $\mathbf{x}$ is in the shaded region, $D_i(\mathbf{x}) = 1$ for $i = 1, 2, 3$. Thus, from Eq. (32), $\mathbf{x}$ is unclassifiable. Therefore, the shaded region in the figure is unclassifiable.

To avoid this, similar to Abe and Inoue (2002), we introduce the fuzzy membership function. First, we define the one-dimensional membership function $m_{ij}(\mathbf{x})$ in the direction perpendicular to the optimal separating hyperplane $D_{ij}(\mathbf{x})$ as follows:

$$m_{ij} = \begin{cases} 1 & \text{for } D_{ij}(\mathbf{x}) \geq 1, \\ D_{ij}(\mathbf{x}) & \text{otherwise.} \end{cases} \tag{33}$$

Here, we allow negative degree of membership to make any data except those on the decision boundary be classified.

In Abe and Inoue (2002), the minimum operator is used for defining the membership function, $m_i(\mathbf{x})$, of $\mathbf{x}$ for class i. Here, we use the average operator as well as the minimum operator. The average operator is complementary to the continuous Hamming distance used in error correcting output codes (Dietterich & Bakiri, 1995).

Using the minimum operator the membership function, $m_i(\mathbf{x})$, of $\mathbf{x}$ for class i is given by

$$m_i(\mathbf{x}) = \min_{j=1,\ldots,k} m_{ij}(\mathbf{x}). \tag{34}$$

Using the minimum operator, the shape of the membership function is a truncated polyhedral pyramid (Abe, 2001) in the feature space, and the contour surface, in which the degree of membership is the same, is parallel to the decision function as shown in Fig. 2.

Using the average operator the membership function, $m_i(\mathbf{x})$, of $\mathbf{x}$ for class i is given by

$$m_i(\mathbf{x}) = \frac{1}{k-1} \sum_{j \neq i,\ j=1}^{k} m_{ij}(\mathbf{x}). \tag{35}$$

Using the average operator, the shape of the membership function is a truncated polyhedral pyramid but some part of the contour surface is not parallel to the decision function as shown in Fig. 3.

Using either Eq. (34) or Eq. (35), the data $\mathbf{x}$ is classified into the class

$$\operatorname*{argmax}_{i=1,\ldots,k} m_i(\mathbf{x}). \tag{36}$$

Comparing the minimum and average operators, the regions where $m_i(\mathbf{x}) = 1$ are the same, but the regions where $m_i(\mathbf{x}) < a$ and $a < 1$, are different. We can show that the decision boundaries with the minimum operator are the same with those given by Eq. (31) for classifiable regions but the decision boundaries for the average operator are not. Thus the recognition rate using the minimum operator is

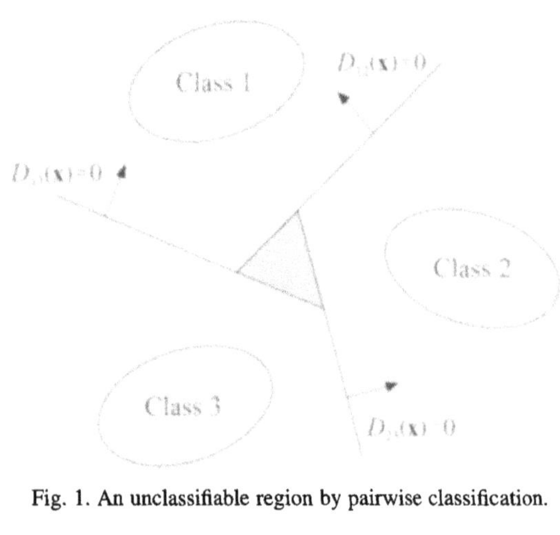

Fig. 1. An unclassifiable region by pairwise classification.

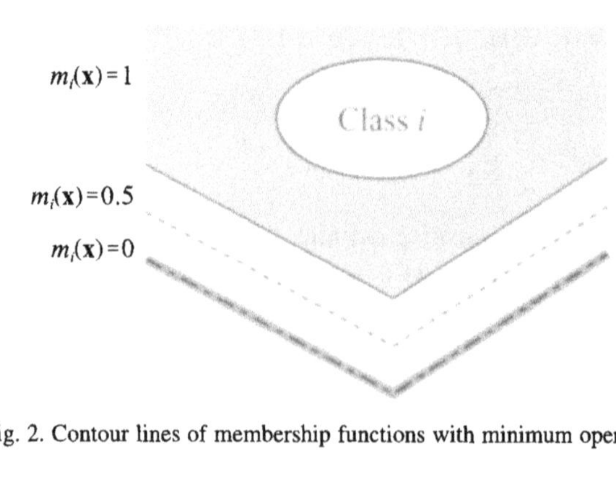

Fig. 2. Contour lines of membership functions with minimum operator.

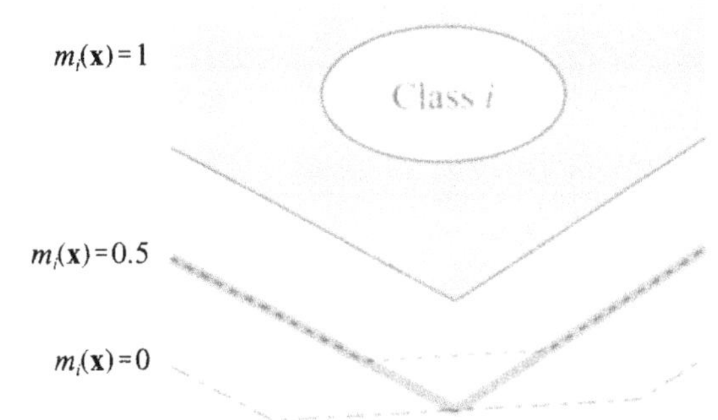

Fig. 3. Contour lines of membership functions with average operator.

always better than or equal to that by the conventional pairwise SVM. But this does not hold for the average operator.

Using the minimum operator, the unclassifiable region shown in Fig. 1 is resolved as shown in Fig. 4.

4. Performance evaluation

4.1. Condition of experiments

Using the iris data (Bezdek, Keller, Krishnapuram, Kuncheva, & Pal, 1999; Fisher, 1936), the numeral data for license plate recognition (Takenaga et al., 1991), the thyroid data (Weiss & Kapouleas, 1999), the blood cell data (Hashizume, Motoike, & Yabe, 1988), and the hiragana data (Abe, 2001) listed in Table 1, we compared the performance of the fuzzy LS-SVM (FLS-SVM) with minimum and average operators, the conventional LS-SVM, and the conventional L1 soft margin FSVM. The LS-SVM was used to show the improvement of the recognition rates by the FLS-SVM.

For the hiragana-105 and hiragana-50 data sets, the numbers of input valuables are over 50. Thus, we normalized the kernels. The value of the margin parameter C affects the recognition rates of the training and test data, but we evaluated the performance fixing C at 5000. We used

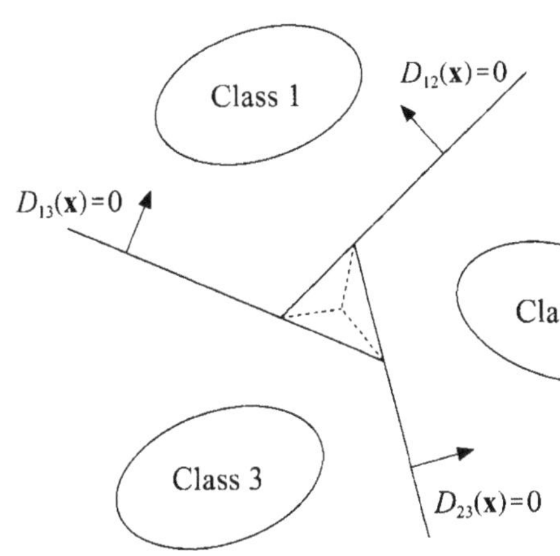

Fig. 4. Resolution of the unclassifiable region by the minimum operator.

Table 1
Benchmark data specification

Data	Inputs	Classes	Training data	Test data
Iris	4	3	75	75
Numeral	12	10	810	820
Thyroid	21	3	3772	3428
Blood cell	13	12	3097	3100
Hiragana-50	50	39	4610	4610
Hiragana-105	105	38	8375	8356
Hiragana-13	13	38	8375	8356

the dot product, polynomial, and RBF kernels. The simulations were done on a Pentium III 1 GHz PC.

4.2. Results and discussions

Table 2 shows the results of the conventional FSVM, the LS-SVM, and the FLS-SVM with minimum and average operators. The highest recognition rates of the test data are shown in boldfaces. The FSVM performed best for 13 cases and the FLS-SVM with the minimum operator performed best for 16 cases. The FLS-SVM always outperforms the LS-SVM, which does not resolve unclassifiable regions. This is because the decision boundaries for the classifiable regions of the LS-SVM are the same with those of the FLS-SVM with the minimum operator. But this is not true for the FLS-SVM with the average operator. Performance of the FLS-SVM with the average operator is unstable; for some cases the performance is inferior to that of the LS-SVM.

4.3. Iris data

The Fisher iris data are widely used for evaluating classification performance of classifiers. They consist of 150 data with four features and three classes; 50 data per class. We used the first 25 data of each class as the training data and the remaining 25 data of each class as the test data.

From Table 2, the LS-SVM and the FLS-SVM show the same performance. This means that there are no data in the unclassifiable regions. The LS-SVM and the FLS-SVM outperformed the FSVM. But the FLS-SVM with the average operator is inferior to the LS-SVM and the FLS-SVM.

4.4. Numeral data

The numeral data were collected to identify Japanese license plate of running cars. They include numerals, hiragana and kanji characters. The original image taken from a TV camera was preprocessed and each numeral was transformed into 12 features such as the number of holes and the curvature of a numeral at some point.

In Table 2, the recognition rates by the FSVM for $d = 3$, 4 are very low. This may be caused by a convergence problem since the recognition rates of the training data are low. The FSVM and the FLS-SVM with the minimum

Table 2
Performance of FSVM and FLS-SVM

Data	Kernel		FSVM		LS-SVM		FLS-SVM (Min)		FLS-SVM (Avg)	
			Test (%)	Train. (%)	Test (%)	Train. (%)	Test (%)	Train. (%)	Test (%)	Train. (%)
Iris	Dot		93.33	100	**97.33**	100	**97.33**	100	92.00	100
	Poly	$d = 2$	94.67	100	**98.67**	100	**98.67**	100	96.00	100
		$d = 3$	94.67	100	**96.00**	100	**96.00**	100	**96.00**	100
Numeral	Dot		**99.63**	100	99.27	99.51	99.39	99.75	99.15	94.04
	Poly	$d = 2$	**99.88**	100	97.56	100	98.17	100	98.54	100
		$d = 3$	89.88	92.47	98.17	100	**98.78**	100	98.66	100
		$d = 4$	89.63	92.35	98.42	100	**98.78**	100	98.66	100
Thyroid	Dot		**97.49**	98.65	93.35	93.37	93.79	94.04	93.73	93.90
	Poly	$d = 2$	**97.58**	99.44	94.75	96.10	95.10	96.42	95.27	95.27
		$d = 3$	**96.79**	99.87	93.20	97.85	93.85	97.93	93.70	98.20
		$d = 4$	**95.95**	98.46	90.67	98.62	92.12	98.65	92.01	98.81
	RBF	$\gamma = 0.5$	**97.41**	98.57	94.55	95.84	94.72	95.56	94.49	95.33
		$\gamma = 1$	**97.20**	98.78	94.55	95.71	95.94	94.78	94.75	95.81
Blood cell	Dot		90.90	96.71	92.48	94.74	**92.61**	94.80	88.32	90.38
	Poly	$d = 2$	92.19	99.32	93.52	97.55	**93.71**	97.58	92.72	94.84
		$d = 3$	91.97	99.94	92.16	99.26	**93.25**	99.26	93.13	99.16
		$d = 4$	**92.84**	98.39	90.13	99.84	92.10	99.84	92.16	99.84
	RBF	$\gamma = 0.5$	92.94	97.32	94.07	96.48	**94.10**	96.51	92.16	94.51
		$\gamma = 1$	92.97	98.03	93.84	96.87	**93.97**	96.93	92.84	95.35
Hiragana-50a	Dot		**98.31**	100	96.51	99.96	97.53	99.96	93.43	98.48
	Poly	$d = 2$	98.94	100	98.50	100	**99.11**	100	97.46	100
		$d = 3$	98.92	100	98.48	100	**99.15**	100	97.20	100
		$d = 4$	98.98	100	98.92	100	**99.07**	100	96.51	100
Hiragana-105	Dot		**99.93**	100	99.83	99.90	99.88	100	98.25	98.97
	Poly	$d = 2$	**100**	100	**100**	100	**100**	100	99.99	100
Hiragana-13	Dot		**99.35**	99.95	98.55	99.45	98.85	99.57	92.40	96.17
	Poly	$d = 2$	99.62	100	99.64	99.96	**99.70**	99.96	97.57	99.98
		$d = 3$	99.56	100	99.69	100	**99.79**	100	99.61	100

operator show comparable performance. For three cases out of four, the minimum operator performed better than the average operator did.

4.5. Thyroid data

Thyroid data include 15 digital features and more than 92% of the data belong to one class. Thus the recognition rate smaller than 92% is useless.

The recognition rates of both training and test data by the FLS-SVM with minimum and average operators are much lower than those of the FSVM. The reason is not clear but this may be caused by the fact that almost all the input variables are discrete and that almost all the training data belong to one class. The results of the average operator are almost the same as those of the minimum operator.

4.6. Blood cell data

Blood cell classification involves classifying optically screened white blood cells into 12 classes using 13 features. This is a very difficult problem; class boundaries for some classes are ambiguous because the classes are defined according to the growth stages of white blood cells.

The FLS-SVM with minimum and average operators performed better than the FSVM on average and the FLS-SVM with the minimum operator performed better than the FLS-SVM with the average operator except for the polynomial kernel with degree 2.

4.7. Hiragana data

Hiragana-50 and hiragana-105 data are gathered from Japanese license plate. The original gray-scale images of hiragana characters were transformed into 5×10 and 7×15-pixel images, respectively, with the gray-scale range being from 0 to 255. Then by performing gray-scale shift, position shift, and random noise addition to the images, the training and test data were generated. For the hiragana-105 data to reduce the number of input variables, i.e., $7 \times 15 = 105$, the hiragana-13 data were generated by calculating the 13 central moments (Cash & Hatamian, 1989). For the hiragana-105 and hiragana-50 data, we normalized the kernels.

Table 3
Training time

Kernel		FSVM (s)	FLS-SVM (s)
Dot		3	86
Poly	$d = 2$	3	91
	$d = 3$	3	96
	$d = 4$	3	100
RBF	$\gamma = 0.5$	4	98
	$\gamma = 1$	4	98

For the hiragana-50, 105, and 13 data, the FLS-SVM with the minimum operator and the conventional FSVM show comparable performance except for dot product kernels. In case of the average operator, in most cases results are not good. Especially, they are very bad for dot product kernels.

4.8. Training speed

Table 3 shows the training time of the FLS-SVM and conventional FSVM for the blood cell data. In training the FSVM, we used the primal-dual interior-point method with variable chunking. Starting from 50 training data, 50 data were added successively. In training the FLS-SVM, we used the Cholesky factorization method to solve the set of linear equations. The FLS-SVM requires 25–30 times longer training time than the FSVM. This is because the matrix $\boldsymbol{\Omega}$ shown in Eq. (15) becomes large if the number of input data become large. Therefore, as indicated in Suykens and Vandewalle (1999), we need to use iterative methods for speedup.

4.9. Influence of the outliers

Since LS-SVMs use equality constraints instead of inequality constraints, they are vulnerable to outliers (Suykens & Vandewalle, 1999). Only the difference between LS-SVMs and L2-SVMs is that the former uses equality constraints while the latter uses the inequality constraints. Thus, we compared their recognition performance when outliers were included.

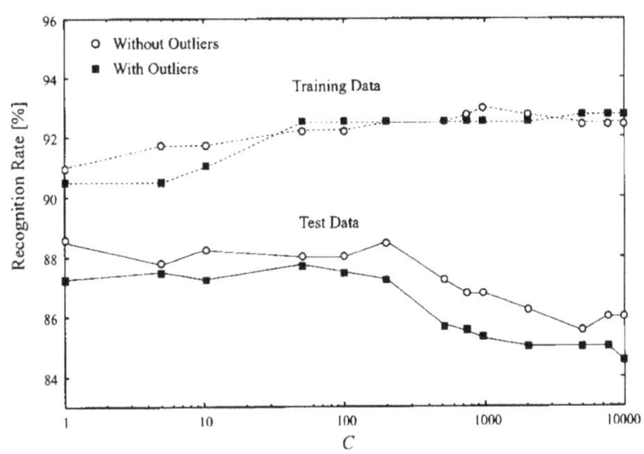

Fig. 5. Influence of outliers to LS-SVM.

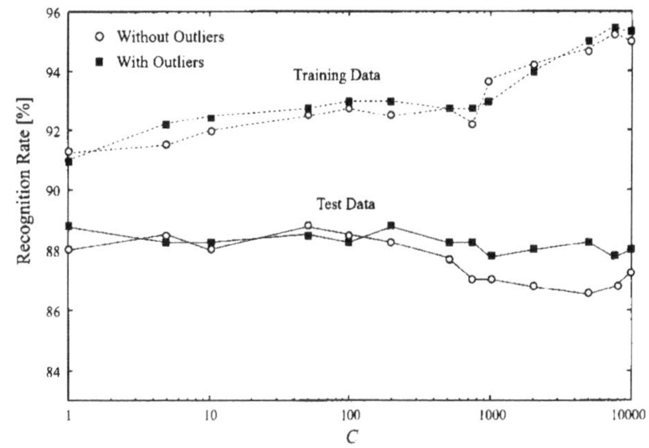

Fig. 6. Influence of outliers to L2-SVM.

For evaluation, we used the blood cell data belonging to Classes 2 and 3, which overlap heavily and are difficult to be classified. As outliers, we added 10 data belonging to classes other than 2 and 3 to Class 2 training data. We used the polynomial kernel with degree 2.

Figs. 5 and 6 show the recognition rates against the margin parameter C for the LS-SVM and L2-SVM, respectively. In the figures, the dotted lines show the recognition rates of the training data and the solid lines show those of the test data. We calculated the recognition rate of the training data excluding outliers.

In Fig. 5, the recognition rates of the training data for the LS-SVM did not change much for $100 < C < 10000$ even if the outliers were included. But the recognition rate of the test data dropped rapidly, especially when outliers were included.

In Fig. 6, the recognition rates of the training data for the L2-SVM increased as the value of C was increased and there is no much difference between the recognition rates with and without outliers. In addition, the recognition rate of the test data with outliers was almost constant for the change of C and for a large value of C, it is better than that without outliers. Comparing Figs. 5 and 6, we can see that the L2-SVM is more robust than the LS-SVM for outliers.

5. Conclusions

In this paper, we discussed fuzzy LS-SVMs that resolve unclassifiable regions for multiclass problems. In defining membership functions for a class, we used minimum and average operators.

We evaluated the effectiveness of our method using several benchmark data sets. In most cases the fuzzy LS-SVMs with the minimum operator showed comparable performance with the fuzzy support vector machine but the fuzzy LS-SVMs with the average operator showed the worst performance.

References

Abe, S. (2001). *Pattern classification, neuro-fuzzy methods and their comparison*. London: Springer.

Abe, S., & Inoue, T. (2002). Fuzzy support vector machines for multiclass problems. *Proceedings of the Tenth European Symposium on Artificial Neural Networks (ESANN 2002)*, 113–118.

Bezdek, J. C., Keller, J. M., Krishnapuram, R., Kuncheva, L. I., & Pal, N. H. (1999). Will the real iris data please stand up? *IEEE Transactions on Fuzzy Systems*, *7*(3), 368–369.

Cash, G. L., & Hatamian, M. (1989). Optical character recognition by the method of moments. *Computer Vision, Graphics, and Image Processing*, *39*, 291–310.

Dietterich, T. G., & Bakiri, G. (1995). Solving multiclass learning problems via error-correcting output codes. *Journal of Artificial Intelligence Research*, *2*, 263–286.

Fisher, R. A. (1936). The use of multiple measurements in taxonomic problems. *Annals of Eugenics*, *7*, 179–188.

Hashizume, A., Motoike, J., & Yabe, R. (1988). Fully automated blood cell differential system and its application. *Proceedings of the IUPAC Third International Congress on Automation and New Technology in the Clinical Laboratory, Kobe, Japan*, 297–302.

Inoue, T., & Abe, S. (2000). Fuzzy support vector machines for pattern classification. *Proceedings of the International Joint Conference on Neural Networks (IJCNN'01)*, 1449–1454.

Kreßel, U. H.-G. (1999). Pairwise classification and support vector machines. In B. Schölkopf, C. J. C. Burges, & A. J. Smola (Eds.), *Advances in kernel methods: Support vector learning* (pp. 255–268). Cambridge, MA: MIT Press.

Suykens, J. A. K., & Vandewalle, J. (1999). Least squares support vector machine classifiers. *Neural Processing Letters*, 293–300.

Takenaga, H., Abe, S., Takatoo, M., Kayama, M., Kitamura, T., & Okuyama, Y. (1991). Input layer optimization of neural networks by sensitivity analysis and its application to recognition of numerals. *Electrical Engineering in Japan*, *111*(4), 130–138.

Vapnik, V. (1998). *Statistical learning theory*. New York: Wiley.

Weiss, S. M., & Kapouleas, I. (1999). An empirical comparison of pattern recognition, neural nets, and machine learning classification methods. *Proceedings of the 16th International Joint Conference on Artificial Intelligence (IJCAI-99), Workshop ML3*, 55–60.

AVAILABLE AT
www.ComputerScienceWeb.com
POWERED BY SCIENCE @ DIRECT

PERGAMON

Neural Networks 16 (2003) 793–800

Neural Networks

www.elsevier.com/locate/neunet

2003 Special issue

Evolving efficient learning algorithms for binary mappings

John A. Bullinaria

School of Computer Science, The University of Birmingham, Birmingham B15 2TT, UK

Abstract

Gradient descent training of sigmoidal feed-forward neural networks on binary mappings often gets stuck with someout puts totally wrong. This is because a sum-squared-error cost function leads to weight updates that depend on the derivative of the output sigmoid which goes to zero as the output approaches maximal error. Although it is easy to understand the cause, the best remedy is not so obvious. Common solutions involve modifying the training data, deviating from true gradient descent, or changing the cost function. In general, finding the best learning procedures for particular classes of problem is difficult because each usually depends on a number of interacting parameters that need to be set to optimal values for a fair comparison. In this paper I shall use simulated evolution to optimise all the relevant parameters, and come to a clear conclusion concerning the most efficient approach for learning binary mappings.

Keywords: Neural network; Learning algorithms; Evolution; Binary mappings

1. Introduction

It is inevitable that the most efficient neural network learning algorithm for a given problem will depend on the problem class being considered. Simple gradient descent based learning algorithms using sum-squared-error cost functions work well for a wide range of problems, but are well known to run into difficulties when used with sigmoidal feed forward neural networks that need to learn binary mappings. This is because the weight updates depend linearly on the derivative of the output activation function, and for sigmoidal activation functions that derivative tends to zero as the sigmoids saturate at either the correct or the maximally incorrect output. This means it is theoretically possible for the network to get stuck with some outputs totally wrong, and in practice this is actually quite common in realistic applications. Early on in training some patterns (e.g. the most regular or frequent) will dominate the weight changes and force the other patterns into errors. By the time the errors on the dominant patterns have reduced to small values, the other patterns are stuck. We could consider abandoning the sigmoids and use linear output units instead, but then we would lose the natural interpretation of the outputs in terms of posterior probabilities (Bishop, 1995; Golden, 1988).

Perhaps the most obvious solution that keeps the sigmoids, which dates back to the re-discovery of the back propagation learning algorithm, is to simply offset the target outputs (Rumelhart, Hinton, & Williams, 1986). Instead of using the actual binary targets of 0 and 1, one offsets them slightly to 0.1 and 0.9 (say) so the sigmoids never saturate and the weight update signals no longer go to zero when the wrong target is reached. We effectively restrict the outputs to the near linear central region of the sigmoids. If we then setout put response thresholds at 0.2 and 0.8 (say) it will make no difference to the binary network responses, but it mayhave other side effects, such as slowing down the training, and destroying the interpretation of the output values.

Another early solution to the problem involves offsetting the sigmoid derivatives (a.k.a. sigmoid prime) directly by adding a small constant (say 0.1) to them (Fahlman, 1988). This Sigmoid Prime Offset (SPO) approach will clearly prevent the weight update signals from going to zero when the wrong target is reached, but it also means that the learning algorithm is no longer performing true gradient descent on the cost function, and it is not obvious what effect that will have on the speed of learning.

It will obviously be rather important for both of these approaches to choose good values for the offset parameters, that are large enough to be sure of preventing the outputs from getting stuck at the wrong values, but small enough to result in minimal loss of learning efficiency. Some degree of experimentation, and perhaps a liking for round numbers, has led to offsets of 0.1 being more or less standard for all problems. However, it is not clear that these really are the optimal values, nor is it clear which form of offset is best to use. The problem is that the best values of the other learning

0893-6080/03/$ - see front matter © 2003 Elsevier Science Ltd. All rights reserved.
doi:10.1016/S0893-6080(03)00093-5

algorithm parameters (such as the learning rates and momentum) and the magnitude of the chosen offset will depend on each other, and also on the type of offset used.

To complicate matters further, another proposed solution has been to replace the sum-squared-error gradient descent cost function with the cross-entropy cost function (Hinton, 1989; Van Ooyen & Nienhuis, 1992). This is known to be amore appropriate cost function for classification problems with network outputs that are to be interpreted as specifying probability distributions over binary vectors (Bishop, 1995; Hinton, 1989). In this case the sigmoid derivative simply cancels out of the weight update equation, and so we never have the problem of it going to zero for totally wrong outputs. However, again we have a problem comparing this against the two offset approaches because the optimal learning algorithm parameters are likely to be different.

Whichever approach is used to avoid getting stuck with the wrong outputs, one should presumably then continue the training with the right cost function and no offsets if we want to recover the interpretation of non-binary output activations as probabilities. Once all the output errors are relatively small, there is much less chance of patterns being forced back into error and getting stuck again. The big question is: which approach provides the most efficient (i.e. fastest) learning to get us to that final stage, and how do we determine the appropriate learning and offset parameters?

We are fortunate that increasing computational resources have, over recent years, rendered it feasible to optimize such learning parameters using evolutionary strategies (Yao, 1999), and thus ensure than we are comparing each approach when performing as best they can. In the remainder of this paper I shall describe the Target Offset, Sigmoid Prime Offset, and Cross Entropy approaches in more detail, and present the results from a series of evolutionary simulations that optimize each case for a representative pair of binary mappings. We end with a clear conclusion concerning which approach is best.

2. The neural network models

The procedures for training feed-forward neural networks by gradient descent are now well known (Bishop, 1995; Hinton, 1989), so I shall simply summarize my notation here. We define an appropriate cost or error function E, and compute a smoothed iterative series of updates

$$\Delta w_{ij}(n) = -\eta_{\mathrm{L}} \frac{\partial E}{\partial w_{ij}} + \alpha \Delta w_{ij}(n-1)$$

for each weight w_{ij} which reduce that function, where n is the epoch of training. Past experience indicates that networks learn better if they have different learning rates η_{L} for each connection layer, and each bias set. So, to ensure that each network learns at its full potential, each has five learning parameters: the learning rate η_{IH} for the input to hidden layer, η_{HB} for the hidden layer biases, η_{HO} for the hidden to output layer, and η_{OB} for the output biases, and the momentum parameter α. The initial network weights $w_{ij}(0)$ are generated randomly with a uniform distribution from the range $[-iw_{\mathrm{L}}, +iw_{\mathrm{L}}]$. Naturally, different initial weight range parameters iw_{L} are allowed for the input to hidden layer connections, the hidden layer biases, the hidden to output layer connections, and the output biases.

With the standard sum squared error (SSE) cost function

$$E = \frac{1}{2} \sum_j |t_j - o_j|^2$$

the output layer weight derivatives are

$$\frac{\partial E}{\partial w_{ij}} = h_i(t_j - o_j)[(1 - o_j)o_j]$$

where t_j are the binary target network outputs, o_j are the actual outputs, and h_i are the hidden unit activations. The term in square brackets is the problematic sigmoid derivative that goes to zero as the sigmoids saturate. We thus consider

$$\frac{\partial E}{\partial w_{ij}} \approx h_i(t_j - o_j)[(1 - o_j)o_j + spo2]$$

where *spo2* is the sigmoid prime offset that would be zero if the derivative were performed exactly. We can also allow the possibility of a similar sigmoid prime offset *spo1* at the hidden layer. The second approach we consider is to off set the output targets and take them to be *toff* and 1 − *toff*, rather than 0 and 1, with appropriate outputs beyond these targets deemed errorless.

The third approach is to employ a better network cost function. For the cross-entropy (CE) cost function

$$E = -\sum_j [t_j \log(o_j) + (1 - t_j)\log(1 - o_j)]$$

the output layer weight derivatives simplify to

$$\frac{\partial E}{\partial w_{ij}} = h_i(t_j - o_j)$$

Clearly, we should need no offsets here, and indeed there is no place for an *spo2*, but we can still check to see if there is any advantage in having a non-zero *spo1* at the hidden layer, or an output target offset *toff*.

3. Evolving the models

The goal here is to optimise our neural network models using evolution by natural selection. We can simulate such a process for the systems discussed above by taking a whole population of individual instantiations of each model and allowing them to learn, procreate and die in a manner approximating these processes in real (biological) systems.

The genotype of each individual will depend on the genotypes of its two parents, and contain all the appropriate innate parameters. Then, throughout its life, the individual will learn from its environment how best to adjust its weights to perform most effectively. Each individual will eventually die, perhaps after producing a number of children.

For biological evolution, the ability of an individual to survive or reproduce will depend on a number of factors which can vary in a complicated manner on that individual's performance over a range of related and unrelated tasks (food gathering, fighting, fleeing, and so on). For current purposes it is appropriate and sufficient to assume a simple relation between our single task performance and the survival or procreation fitness. Whilst any monotonic relation should result in similar evolutionary trends, we often find that, in simplified simulations, the details can have a big effect on what evolves and what gets lost in the noise.

A more natural approach to procreation, mutation and survival will be followed than many evolutionary simulations have used in the past, such as those described by Yao (1999). Rather than simultaneously training all members of the current population and picking the fittest to breed and form the next generation, the populations will contain competing learning individuals of all ages, each with the potential for dying or procreation at each stage. The alternative earlier approaches typically set the number of epochs of training per generation and base the fitness on the remaining error, or base the fitness on the number of epochs required to reduce the error to a set value. Both of these procedures are problematic in that they involve parameters (the number of epochs or the target fitness) that are difficult to fix when the ability to learn is changing from generation to generation.

In my approach, each individual will learn from their own experience with the environment (i.e. set of training/-testing data) and have their fitness determined each simulated year. A fitness biased random subset of the least fit individuals, together with a flat random subset of the oldest individuals, will then die. These are replaced by children, each having one parent chosen randomly from the fittest members of the population, who randomly chooses a mate from the rest of the whole population. Each child inherits characteristics from both parents such that each innate free parameter is chosen at random somewhere between the values of its parents, with sufficient noise (or mutation) that there is a reasonable possibility of the parameter falling outside the range spanned by the parents. There are many other aspects of biological evolution that could be incorporated into our simulations, but this simplified approach proves adequate. A similar regime has already been employed successfully elsewhere to study genetic assimilation and the Baldwin effect in the evolution of adaptable control systems (Bullinaria, 2001a), and the evolution of modularity in neural network systems (Bullinaria, 2001b).

In the simulations, each genotype includes all the innate parameters needed to specify the details of the associated individual network, namely the architecture, the initial connection weights, the learning algorithm, the learning rates, the offsets, and so on. In real biological evolution, all these parameters will be free to evolve. For simulations that are designed to explore particular issues, it makes sense to fix some of these parameters to avoid the complication of unforeseen interactions (and also to speed up the simulations).

In my earlier study of the Baldwin effect (Bullinaria, 2001a), for example, it made sense to keep the architecture fixed and to allow the initial innate connection weights and learning rates to evolve. In my study of modularity (Bullinaria, 2001b) it was more appropriate to have each individual start with random initial connection weights and allow the architecture and learning rates to evolve. Here we shall have a fixed fully connected feed-forward architecture with one hidden layer and random initial weights, and allow all the learning algorithm parameters to evolve, i.e. the four learning rates, the momentum, and the offsets. Then, since the appropriate ranges for the random initial weights may well depend on the evolved learning parameters, and vice versa, we must allow the four initial weight distributions to evolve as well. In total, we thus have up to 12 evolvable parameters in each genotype: four to control the individual's distribution of random initial weights, five to control its learning rates, and up to three to determine the offsets. All the other network parameters, such as the number of hidden units, were fixed across the whole population.

4. Simulation results

We can clearly expect some degree of problem dependence with the simulation results, so two representative sets of training data were used:

'What'—A simplified pattern recognition task that mapssimple images (5×5 binary matrices) to a representation of 'what' (a 9 bit binary vector with one bit 'on'). Following earlier studies (Rueckl, Cave & Kosslyn, 1989; Bullinaria, 2001b), 9 patterns consisting of different 3×3 arrays with 5 cells 'on' were used as images, and these could appear in any of 9 positions in the full input array, giving 81 training patterns in all.

'QuasiReg'—A quasi-regular mapping from 9 binary input units to 9 binary output units. There were 60 training patterns in all, 48 regular (permuted identity maps) and 12 irregular (random maps). The irregular patterns will naturally be harder to learn than the regulars, and hence prime candidates for learning problems of the type discussed above.

Obtaining reliable results relies on fixing all the evolutionary parameters appropriately according to the details of theproblem and the speed and coarseness of the simulations. For example, if all the individuals were able to learn the given task perfectly by the end of their first year, and we only tested their performance once per year, then the advantage of those that learn in two months over those that take 10 would be lost, and our simulated evolution would not be very realistic, nor would it encourage faster learning. Since the networks are allowed to evolve their own learning rates, this had to be controlled by fixing the number of hidden units at 36 (which is plenty, but not excessive, for our two tasks), and restricting the number of presentations of the training data set to two per simulated year for each individual. A fixed population size of 100 was chosen as a trade-off between maintaining genetic diversity and running the simulations reasonably quickly. The death rates were chosen to result in reasonable age distributions, and to prevent the population from becoming dominated by skilled adults who killed off most of the children before they had the chance to learn how to perform well. This meant about 10 deaths per year due to competition, and another three individuals over the age of 20 dying each year due to old age. The mutation parameters were chosen to speed the evolution as much as possible by maintaining genetic diversity without introducing an excessive amount of noise into the process. These parameter choices inevitably led to coarser simulations than one would ideally like, but otherwise the simulations would have taken too long to complete.

For any evolutionary simulation, the choice of fitness function is obviously a crucial factor. Relating it to the gradient descent cost function was not feasible, because it prevents fitness comparisons between the sum-squared-error and cross-entropy cases, and because the target offsets just grow so large that any output value is deemed errorless. The natural fitness measure here is in terms of the total or average number of network output bits that are significantly wrong (e.g. more than 0.2 from their binary targets) over the whole training set. This works well, but the distribution of errors actually becomes very skewed over the population, so the fitness measure was chosen to be $1/\log(1 + \text{ErrorCount})$.

Previous evolutionary studies (Bullinaria, 2001a,b) have shown that the results of evolution can depend strongly on the initial conditions, i.e. on the distributions of innate parameters across the initial population. In particular, the populations tend to settle into near optimal states more quickly and reliably if they start with a wide distribution of initial learning rates, rather than expecting the mutations to carry the system from a state in which there is little learning at all. Consequently, in all the following experiments, the initial population learning rates η_L were chosen randomly from the range [0.0, 4.0], the momentum parameters α randomly from the range [0.0, 1.0], and the random initialweight ranges iw_L from the range [0.0, 4.0]. The results are then consistent enough for us to present typical runs, rather than averages which tend to obscure the interesting details.

The starting point is to evolve the standard learning algorithms with no offsets. Figs. 1 and 2 show how the initial weight distribution sizes and learning rates evolve for the 'What' task with the SSE and CE cost functions. Note the wide differences in the emerging values for the different network components, and also for the different cost functions. We see that even after 45,000 simulated years, some parameters are still drifting to ever lower values, but are already so low that they have very small effect on what the networks are learning. It is clear that the common practice of setting the same initial weight distributions and learning rates throughout a given network is unlikely to result in the optimal performances we can arrive at with an evolutionary approach.

Naturally it is the resultant learning abilities that we are primarily interested in. In Fig. 3 we have plots of the performance against age for the final evolved populations. The left graph shows that, as expected, the evolved SSE population from Fig. 1 is unable to learn the task to perfection. In fact, a more detailed analysis shows that, by the simulated age of 30, approximately 96% of

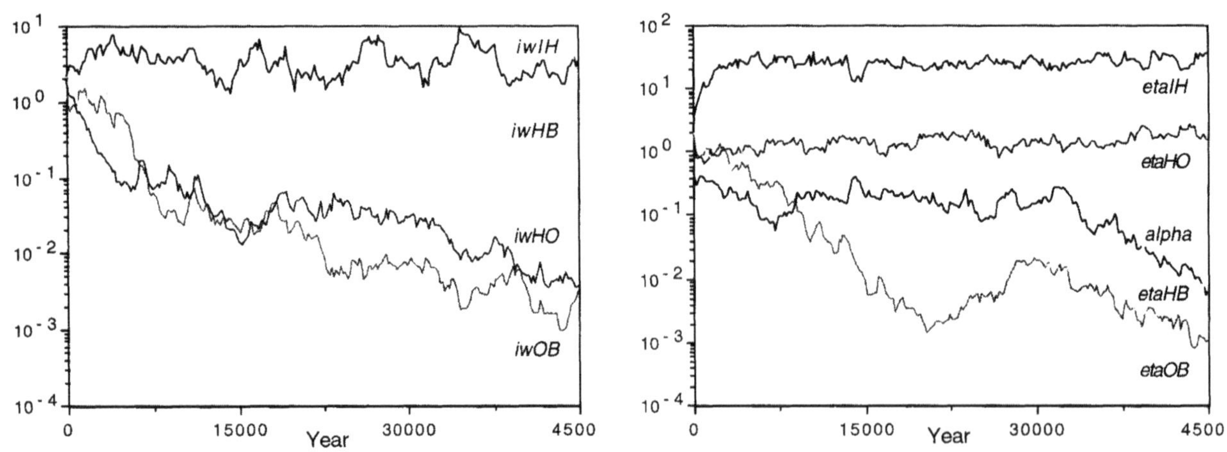

Fig. 1. Evolution of the initial weight ranges and learning rates for the SSE cost function and 'What' training data.

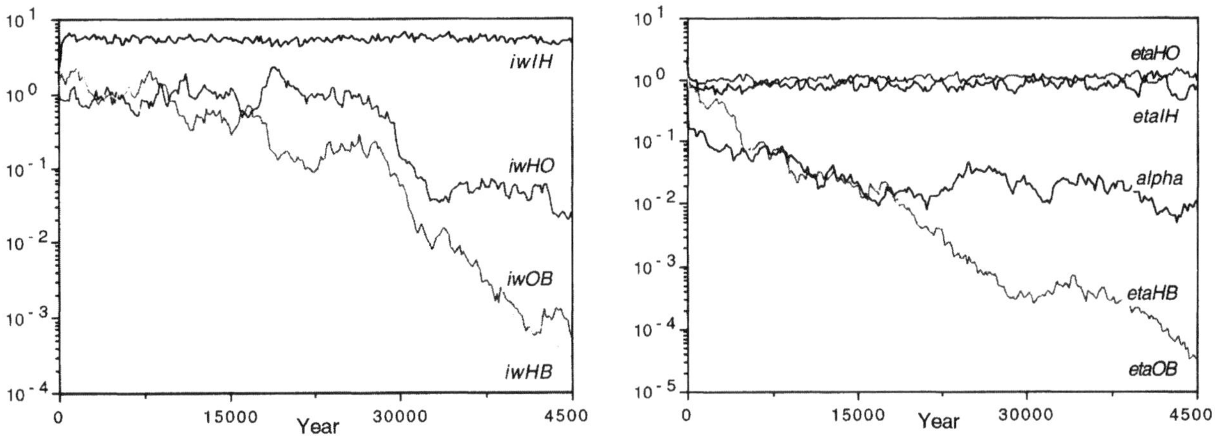

Fig. 2. Evolution of the initial weight ranges and learning rates for the CE cost function and 'What' training data.

the remaining output unit errors are greater than 0.99, which confirms that the main cause of the learning problems is the outputs getting stuck with totally wrong values. The right graph of Fig. 3 shows how the evolved CE population corresponding to Fig. 2 has no such problem, and is typically able to learn the given task by about 10 simulated years of age.

As discussed above, we can hope to do better, particularly in the SSE case, by evolving appropriate offsets. In Fig. 4 we can see what the evolutionary pressures do produce in practice. For both the SSE and CE cost functions, we find that the hidden layer sigmoid derivative offsets *spo1* and the output target offsets *toff* take on very low (effectively zero) values, indicating that their presence does not help. In the SSE case, we see that the other potential offset, the output layer sigmoid derivative offset *spo2*, takes on very large values (around 50 after 45,000 simulated years and still rising). This was rather surprising given the relatively small offsets of around 0.1 that are traditionally used (Fahlman, 1988). What happens is that the offset ends up totally swamping the sigmoid derivative to result in weight updates that are good approximations to the standard CE weight updates, but with the learning rates multiplied by *spo2*. Normally, multiplying the learning rates by such large numbers would be detrimental to learning, but because the base learning rates η_L are also allowed to evolve, they adjust themselves in inverse proportion to *spo2* to give appropriate effective learning rates at each stage. In effect, the SSE cost function has discovered how to evolve into the better CE cost function, with its superior learning performance.

We clearly need to check that this result is not dependent on the particular training set used. The set of simulations corresponding to Figs. 1–3 were therefore repeated with the 'QuasiReg' task. Similar patterns emerged for the evolution of the initial weights and learning rates, and Fig. 5 shows the learning performance for the individuals in the evolved populations. Again the CE cost function results in all the individuals learning the task easily, but the SSE population is unable to learn the task to perfection. Here approximately 92% of the remaining output unit errors are greater than 0.99 at the simulated age of 30, so again the main cause of

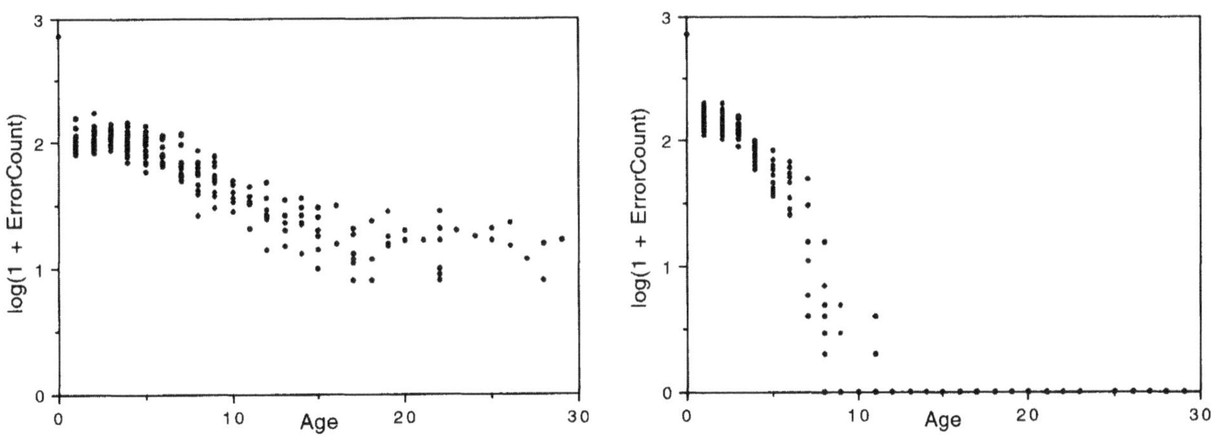

Fig. 3. Learning of the 'What' training data by the evolved populations for SSE (left) and CE (right) cost function.

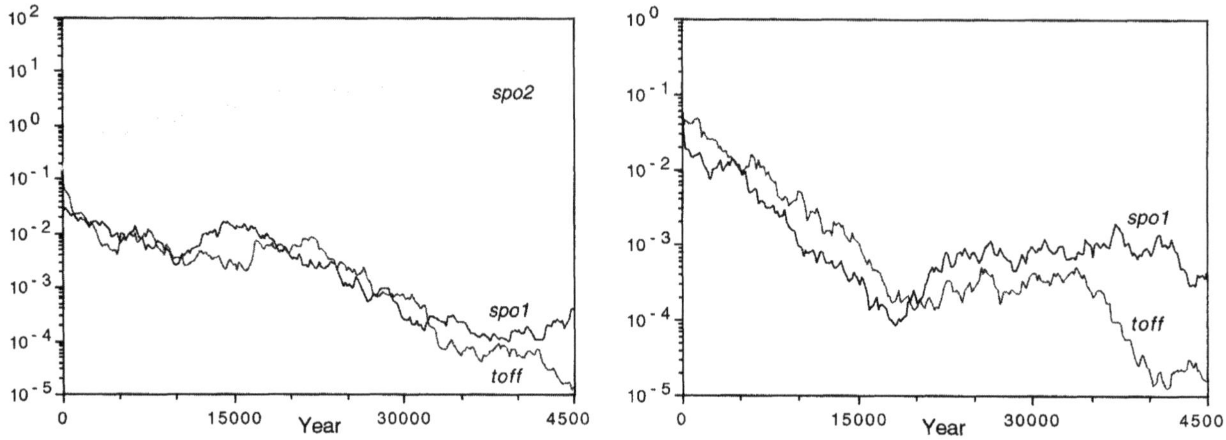

Fig. 4. Evolution of the offsets for the SSE (left) and CE (right) cost functions with the 'What' training data.

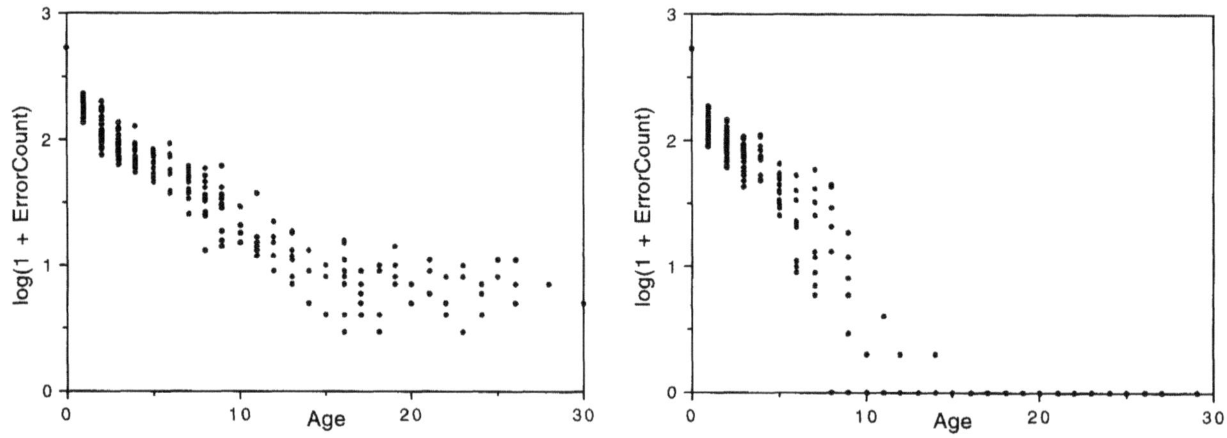

Fig. 5. Learning of the 'QuasiReg' training data by the evolved populations for SSE (left) and CE (right) cost function.

the learning problems appears to be outputs getting stuck with totally wrong values.

As before, we can hope to improve the learning by allowing appropriate offsets to evolve. The results shown in Fig. 6 are not as clear cut as we had for the 'What' training data in Fig. 4, but the same general pattern emerges. The target offset *toff* and hidden layer sigmoid derivative offset *spo1* take on effectively zero values indicating that they are not useful, while the output layer sigmoid derivative offset *spo2* takes on the ever increasing values that allows the SSE

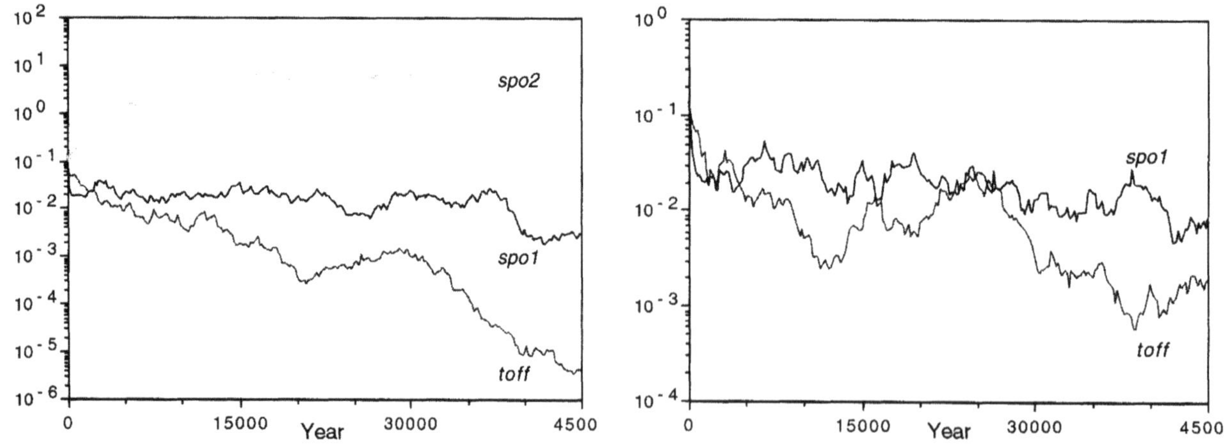

Fig. 6. Evolution of the offsets with SSE (left) and CE (right) cost functions for the 'QuasiReg' training data.

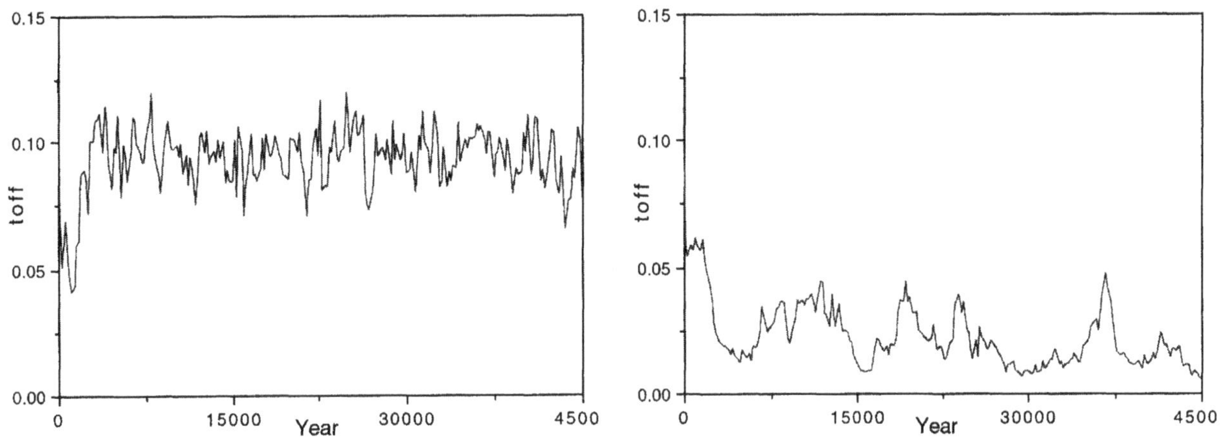

Fig. 7. Evolution of target offsets for SSE when SPO is not available for the 'What' (left) and 'QuasiReg' (right) tasks.

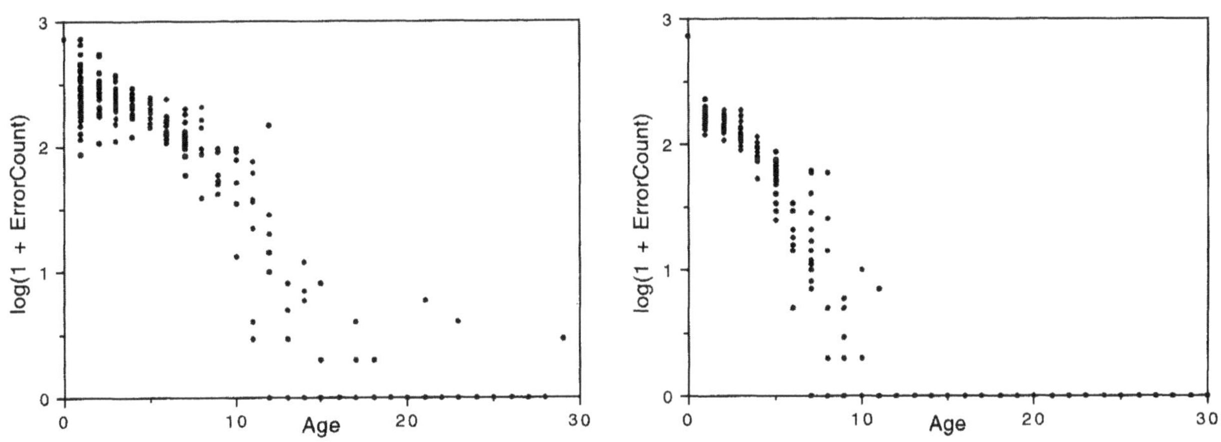

Fig. 8. Learning of the 'What' training data by the evolved SSE populations for zero SPO (left) and large SPO (right).

cost function to evolve into the better performing CE cost function as we found previously.

The final situation we need to consider is that in which we do not allow the evolution of sigmoid derivative offsets, and thus prevent the ability of the SSE networks to evolve into CE networks. Will significant target offsets evolve in this situation? Not surprisingly, simulations of the CE case result in the target offsets evolving towards zero values as before. For the SSE case we obtain the problem dependent results shown in Fig. 7. For the 'What' task we find that *toff* evolves to take on values around 0.1, which is exactly the value traditionally used (Bullinaria, 2001b; Rumelhart et al., 1986; Rueckl et al., 1989). Learning in this case takes around 15 simulated years, as shown on the left in Fig. 8, which is significantly slower and less reliable than the CE case seen in Fig. 2, and the SSE case with evolved SPO shown on the right in Fig. 8. For the 'QuasiReg' task, on the other hand, Fig. 7 reveals that a significant *toff* does not evolve. This is presumably because it does not offer sufficient improvement over the no offset case. Even carrying out the evolution with *toff* fixed at the 'standard' value of 0.1 fails to produce a population that can successfully learn the task.

5. Conclusion

This paper has demonstrated how an evolutionary approach can be used to generate efficient neural network learning algorithms by discovering appropriate initial weight distributions and learning parameters. Explicit simulations for two representative binary mappings were carried out for both the SSE and CE cost functions. The evolved CE networks learned quickly and reliably, while the SSE networks ran into a well known problem in which some outputs get stuck with totally wrong values. The same evolutionary approach enabled the optimization of two common techniques for avoiding such problems in SSE networks, namely the introduction of target offsets and/or sigmoid derivative offsets. Not surprisingly, for the CE case, evolution caused the unnecessary offset parameters to approach zero. For the SSE networks, evolution failed to produce offsets in the range traditionally used, but rather generated values that transformed the networks into increasingly good approximations of the CE networks that have no such learning problems.

This study has two clear conclusions. First, appropriate evolutionary strategies provide an extremely powerful approach for optimizing neural network systems. Second, when performing gradient descent training of neural networks on binary mapping, it is better to employ the CE cost function rather than using approaches that attempt to fix the problems inherent in using the SSE cost function.

References

Bishop, C. M. (1995). *Neural networks for pattern recognition*. Oxford, UK: Oxford University Press.

Bullinaria, J. A. (2001a). Exploring the Baldwin effect in evolving adaptable control systems. In R. F. French, & J. P. Sougné (Eds.), *Connectionist models of learning, development and evolution* (pp. 231–242). London: Springer.

Bullinaria, J. A (2001). Simulating the evolution of modular neural systems. In *Proceedings of the 23rd annual conference of the cognitive science society* (pp. 146–151), Mahwah, NJ: Lawrence Erlbaum Associates

Fahlman, S. E. (1988). Faster learning variations of back propagation: An empirical study. In D. Touretzky, G. E. Hinton, & T. J. Sejnowski (Eds.), *Proceedings of the 1988 connectionist models summer school* (pp. 38–51). San Mateo, CA: Morgan Kaufmann.

Golden, R. M. (1988). A unified framework for connectionist systems. *Biological Cybernetics*, *59*, 109–120.

Hinton, G. E. (1989). Connectionist learning procedures. *Artificial Intelligence*, *40*, 185–234.

Rueckl, J. G., Cave, K. R., & Kosslyn, S. M. (1989). Why are 'What' and 'Where' processed by separate cortical visual systems? a computational investigation. *Journal of Cognitive Neuroscience*, *1*, 171–186.

Rumelhart, D. E., Hinton, G. E., & Williams, R. J. (1986). Learning internal representations by error propagation. In D. E. Rumelhart, & J. L. McClelland (Eds.), (*Vol. 1*) (pp. 318–362). *Parallel distributed processing*, Cambridge, MA: MIT Press.

Van Ooyen, A., & Nienhuis, B. (1992). Improving the convergence of the back propagation algorithm. *Neural Networks*, *5*, 465–471.

Yao, X. (1999). Evolving artificial neural networks. *Proceedings of the IEEE*, *87*, 1423–1447.

AVAILABLE AT
www.ComputerScienceWeb.com
POWERED BY SCIENCE DIRECT

PERGAMON

Neural Networks 16 (2003) 801–808

Neural Networks

www.elsevier.com/locate/neunet

2003 Special issue

A network for recursive extraction of canonical coordinates

Ali Pezeshki*, Mahmood R. Azimi-Sadjadi, Louis L. Scharf

Department of Electrical and Computer Engineering, Colorado State University, Fort Collins, CO 80523-1373, USA

Abstract

A network structure for canonical coordinate decomposition is presented. The network consists of two single-layer linear subnetworks that together extract the canonical coordinates of two data channels. The connection weights of the networks are trained by a stochastic gradient descent learning algorithm. Each subnetwork features a hierarchical set of lateral connections among its outputs. The lateral connections perform a deflation process that subtracts the contributions of the already extracted coordinates from the input data subspace. This structure allows for adding new nodes for extracting additional canonical coordinates without the need for retraining the previous nodes. The performance of the network is evaluated on a synthesized data set.

Keywords: Canonical coordinates; Singular value decomposition; Deflation; Iterative learning

1. Introduction

Canonical correlation analysis (Hotelling, 1936; Anderson, 1958) provides a minimal description of the correlation between two data channels by concentrating the linear dependence of the channels into a small set of canonical variables. Canonical correlations are maximal invariants to uncoupled linear transformations of two-channel data. The corresponding canonical coordinates resolve the channels into coordinates that are only pairwise correlated. Canonical coordinates have been used to decompose Wiener filters and Gaussian communication channels into their canonical modes where each mode corresponds to a scalar Gaussian channel, or Wiener filter (Scharf & Thomas, 1998; Scharf & Mullis, 2000). They provide an elegant framework for analyzing linear dependence and mutual information between two data channels. In this coordinate system, the linear dependence and mutual information between the original channels are decomposed into those of canonical coordinates of the channels, which are determined by the corresponding canonical correlations. The canonical correlation associated with each pair of canonical coordinates determines the contribution of that pair to the linear dependence and mutual information between the channels (Scharf & Mullis, 2000).

The conventional method of finding canonical coordinates involves computation of square-root-inverses of covariance matrices followed by a singular value decomposition (SVD) of a coherence matrix. These operations become computationally intractable and inefficient especially for large dimensional data. In addition all the singular values and singular vectors of the coherence matrix have to be evaluated even though only the most significant singular values and their associated singular vectors are used in most applications. These deficiencies make the conventional scheme inefficient for real-time applications. Consequently, to perform the canonical coordinate decomposition efficiently, a method is required to extract the most significant canonical coordinate pairs and the corresponding canonical correlations recursively, and without any matrix inversion, matrix square root computation or direct SVD operations.

Neural networks have been proven to be powerful tools for performing linear and nonlinear transformations. Several neural network-based approaches have been reported for extracting principal components of a stochastic vector process directly from the input data set. Oja (1982) proved that a linear model with a single node trained with a normalized Hebbian rule can extract the dominant principal component of a stationary vector process. Sanger (1989) and Foldiak (1989), extended Oja's work to the multi-node case in order to simultaneously extract the first m principal components of a vector process. Diamantaras and Kung (1994) exploited

* Corresponding author.
E-mail address: ali@engr.colostate.edu (A. Pezeshki).

0893-6080/03/$ - see front matter
doi:10.1016/S0893-6080(03)00112-6

the idea of using lateral connections with anti-Hebbian learning to recursively extract the principal components. In a different approach, based on recursive least squares (RLS) learning, Bannour and Azimi-Sadjadi (1995) proposed another structure for recursive extraction of principal components. Readers are referred to Diamantaras and Kung (1996) for a review of other related work in this area. Kung and Diamantaras (1994) also introduced a network structure for computing the reduced-rank Wiener filter. A network-based approach has been reported in Lai and Fyfe (1999) for performing canonical correlation analysis. However, this network only finds the most significant canonical coordinate pair and the corresponding canonical correlation.

In this paper a network and a set of updating rules for performing canonical coordinate decomposition is presented. First, the problem of finding the first canonical coordinate pair is formulated as a constrained minimization problem. Then, given the first r canonical coordinate pairs, the problem of finding the $(r+1)$th pair is formulated as one of finding the first canonical coordinate pair after the contributions of the first r pairs are deflated from the input data subspace. This formulation is used to propose a network structure that consists of two single-layer linear subnetworks. The weights of the subnetworks are trained using a stochastic gradient descent learning algorithm. Each subnetwork includes a set of lateral connections that whiten the output. The structure of each subnetwork is similar to the structure of the single network proposed by Diamantaras and Kung (1994). The lateral connections are trained to deflate the contributions of the already extracted canonical coordinates from the input data subspace. This structure allows for adding new nodes for extracting a new canonical coordinate without the need for retraining the previous nodes. This is very useful since in most cases the number of canonical coordinates or canonical correlations required is not known a priori. In these cases a test of linear dependence or mutual information may be performed to determine whether additional canonical coordinate pairs need to be extracted. A simulation example is given to demonstrate the validity of the proposed network and the corresponding learning rules.

2. A review on canonical coordinate decomposition

Let us follow the development of Scharf and Mullis (2000) and consider the two random vectors, $\mathbf{x} \in \mathbb{R}^{m\times 1}$ and $\mathbf{y} \in \mathbb{R}^{n\times 1}$ with m being the smaller dimension ($m \leq n$). Assume that $\mathbf{x}$ and $\mathbf{y}$ have zero means and share the composite covariance matrix

$$E\left[\begin{pmatrix}\mathbf{x}\\ \mathbf{y}\end{pmatrix}(\mathbf{x}^T \quad \mathbf{y}^T)\right] = \begin{bmatrix} R_{xx} & R_{xy} \\ R_{yx} & R_{yy}\end{bmatrix} \tag{1}$$

This composite covariance matrix has the following block tridiagonal decomposition

$$\begin{bmatrix} F^T & 0 \\ 0 & G^T\end{bmatrix}\begin{bmatrix} R_{xx}^{-1/2} & 0 \\ 0 & R_{yy}^{-1/2}\end{bmatrix}\begin{bmatrix} R_{xx} & R_{xy} \\ R_{yx} & R_{yy}\end{bmatrix} \cdot\begin{bmatrix} R_{xx}^{-T/2} & 0 \\ 0 & R_{yy}^{-T/2}\end{bmatrix}\begin{bmatrix} F & 0 \\ 0 & G\end{bmatrix} = \begin{bmatrix} I & K \\ K & I\end{bmatrix} \tag{2}$$

where $R_{xx}^{-1/2}R_{xx}R_{xx}^{-T/2} = I$, $R_{xx}^{1/2}R_{xx}^{T/2} = R_{xx}$, and F, G and K are chosen to be the SVD of the coherence matrix $C = R_{xx}^{-1/2}R_{xy}R_{yy}^{-T/2}$. That is

$$C = R_{xx}^{-1/2}R_{xy}R_{yy}^{-T/2} = FKG^T \text{ and } F^TCG = K, \qquad F^TF = I,\ G^TG = I,\ K = \mathrm{diag}[k_1, k_2, \ldots, k_m] \tag{3}$$

The diagonal matrix K is the canonical correlation matrix of canonical correlations k_i. The canonical correlations are arranged in descending order ($1 \geq k_1 \geq \ldots \geq k_m > 0$).

The canonical coordinates of $\mathbf{x}$ and $\mathbf{y}$ are defined as

$$\begin{bmatrix}\mathbf{u}\\ \mathbf{v}\end{bmatrix} = \begin{bmatrix} F^T & 0 \\ 0 & G^T\end{bmatrix}\begin{bmatrix} R_{xx}^{-1/2} & 0 \\ 0 & R_{yy}^{-1/2}\end{bmatrix}\begin{bmatrix}\mathbf{x}\\ \mathbf{y}\end{bmatrix} \tag{4}$$

Correspondingly, the matrices

$$W^T = F^TR_{xx}^{-1/2} \text{ and } D^T = G^TR_{yy}^{-1/2} \tag{5}$$

map $\mathbf{x}$ and $\mathbf{y}$ to their corresponding canonical coordinates $\mathbf{u}$ and $\mathbf{v}$. Thus we may rewrite the canonical coordinate map of Eq. (4) as

$$\begin{bmatrix}\mathbf{u}\\ \mathbf{v}\end{bmatrix} = \begin{bmatrix} W^T & 0 \\ 0 & D^T\end{bmatrix}\begin{bmatrix}\mathbf{x}\\ \mathbf{y}\end{bmatrix} \tag{6}$$

The composite vector of canonical coordinates, $[\mathbf{u}^T\ \mathbf{v}^T]^T$ has covariance matrix

$$E\left[\begin{pmatrix}\mathbf{u}\\ \mathbf{v}\end{pmatrix}(\mathbf{u}^T \quad \mathbf{v}^T)\right] = \begin{bmatrix} R_{uu} & R_{uv} \\ R_{vu} & R_{vv}\end{bmatrix} = \begin{bmatrix} W^TR_{xx}W & W^TR_{xy}D \\ D^TR_{yx}W & D^TR_{yy}D\end{bmatrix} = \begin{bmatrix} I & K \\ K & I\end{bmatrix} \tag{7}$$

The canonical correlation matrix K is the cross covariance matrix of $\mathbf{u}$ and $\mathbf{v}$. That is

$$E[\mathbf{u}\mathbf{v}^T] = K = W^TR_{xy}D = F^TR_{xx}^{-1/2}R_{xy}R_{yy}^{-T/2}G \tag{8}$$

The squared canonical correlations k_i^2 decompose the linear dependence H between $\mathbf{x}$ and $\mathbf{y}$, which is measured by the Hadamard ratio

$$H = \det\{I - KK^T\} = \prod_{i=1}^{m}(1 - k_i^2) \tag{9}$$

In the case where $\mathbf{x}$ and $\mathbf{y}$ are marginally Gaussian, the squared canonical correlation decompose the mutual information $I(\mathbf{x},\mathbf{y})$ between $\mathbf{x}$ and $\mathbf{y}$

$$I(\mathbf{x},\mathbf{y}) = -\frac{1}{2}\log\det\{I - KK^T\} = -\frac{1}{2}\sum_{i=1}^{m}\log(1 - k_i^2) \tag{10}$$

The conventional method of canonical coordinate decomposition, i.e. Eq. (4), requires the computation of the SVD of the coherence matrix $C = R_{xx}^{-1/2}R_{xy}R_{yy}^{-T/2}$ and the products $F^TR_{xx}^{-1/2}$ and $G^TR_{yy}^{-1/2}$, which involve computation of matrix square-root-inverses. In addition, the conventional method does not allow for recursive extraction of a subset of canonical coordinates at a lower computational cost. These deficiencies of the conventional method motivate our next discussion.

3. A network for recursive extraction of canonical coordinates

This section presents a network structure and a set of updating rules to recursively extract the canonical coordinates of two data channels. The updating rules are derived so that no matrix inversion or square root computation is required. The network may be trained in either batch or sequential mode and thus may be used for online applications as well.

Let $\mathbf{w}_i \in \mathbb{R}^{m\times 1}$ and $\mathbf{d}_i \in \mathbb{R}^{n\times 1}$ denote the ith columns of W and D. Then, the ith canonical coordinates of $\mathbf{x}$ and $\mathbf{y}$ and their corresponding canonical correlation are

$$u_i = \mathbf{w}_i^T\mathbf{x},\ v_i = \mathbf{d}_i^T\mathbf{y}, \text{ and } k_i = E\{u_iv_i\} = \mathbf{w}_i^TR_{xy}\mathbf{d}_i \tag{11}$$

From here on, we refer to $\mathbf{w}_i$ and $\mathbf{d}_i$ as the ith canonical coordinate mapping vectors. From Eq. (7), we have

$$\begin{aligned} E[u_iu_j] &= \mathbf{w}_i^TR_{xx}\mathbf{w}_j = \delta(i-j) \\ E[v_iv_j] &= \mathbf{d}_i^TR_{yy}\mathbf{d}_j = \delta(i-j) \\ E[u_iv_j] &= \mathbf{w}_i^TR_{xy}\mathbf{d}_j = k_i\delta(i-j) \end{aligned} \tag{12}$$

where $\delta(\cdot)$ is the Kronecker delta. Noting that $k_1 = \mathbf{w}_1^TR_{xy}\mathbf{d}_1$ is the largest canonical correlation, the problem of finding the first canonical coordinate mapping vectors, $\mathbf{w}_1$ and $\mathbf{d}_1$, may be formulated as the maximization problem

$$\max_{\mathbf{w}_1,\mathbf{d}_1} \mathbf{w}_1^TR_{xy}\mathbf{d}_1 \tag{13}$$

subject to the constraints

$$\mathbf{w}_1^TR_{xx}\mathbf{w}_1 = 1 \text{ and } \mathbf{d}_1^TR_{yy}\mathbf{d}_1 = 1 \tag{14}$$

Using the method of Lagrange multipliers we may rewrite the constrained optimization problem defined by Eqs. (13) and (14) as minimizing the objective function J_1 of the form

$$\begin{aligned} J_1 = &-\mathbf{w}_1^TR_{xy}\mathbf{d}_1 + (\mathbf{w}_1^TR_{xx}\mathbf{w}_1 - 1)\frac{\lambda_{1,1}}{2} \\ &+ (\mathbf{d}_1^TR_{yy}\mathbf{d}_1 - 1)\frac{\lambda_{1,2}}{2} \end{aligned} \tag{15}$$

where $\lambda_{1,1}$ and $\lambda_{1,2}$ are Lagrange multipliers that enforce the constraints in Eq. (14).

Now, assume that the first $r < m$ columns of W and D have already been found. Let $W_r \in \mathbb{R}^{m\times r}$ and $D_r \in \mathbb{R}^{n\times r}$ be the matrices that, respectively, contain the first r columns of W and D. That is

$$W_r = [\mathbf{w}_1, \ldots, \mathbf{w}_r] \text{ and } D_r = [\mathbf{d}_1, \ldots, \mathbf{d}_r] \tag{16}$$

The first r canonical coordinates of $\mathbf{x}$ and $\mathbf{y}$ are then given by

$$\mathbf{u}_r = [u_1, \ldots, u_r]^T = W_r^T\mathbf{x} \text{ and } \mathbf{v}_r = [v_1, \ldots, v_r]^T = D_r^T\mathbf{y} \tag{17}$$

By deflating the contribution of the first r canonical coordinates $\mathbf{u}_r$ and $\mathbf{v}_r$ from the input channels, we may formulate the problem of finding the $(r+1)$th pair of canonical coordinates as one of finding the first canonical coordinate pair of the deflated input channels. This may be done by replacing R_{xy} in Eq. (15) with its deflated version $(I - R_{xx}W_rW_r^T)R_{xy}(I - R_{yy}D_rD_r^T)^T$ (See Appendix for the proof). Thus, the $(r+1)$th pair of canonical coordinate mapping vectors $\mathbf{w}_{r+1}$ and $\mathbf{d}_{r+1}$ may be found by minimizing the objective function

$$\begin{aligned} J_{r+1} = &-\mathbf{w}_{r+1}^T(I - R_{xx}W_rW_r^T)R_{xy}(I - R_{yy}D_rD_r^T)^T\mathbf{d}_{r+1} \\ &+ (\mathbf{w}_{r+1}^TR_{xx}\mathbf{w}_{r+1} - 1)\frac{\lambda_{r+1,1}}{2} \\ &+ (\mathbf{d}_{r+1}^TR_{yy}\mathbf{d}_{r+1} - 1)\frac{\lambda_{r+1,2}}{2} \end{aligned} \tag{18}$$

where $\lambda_{r+1,1}$ and $\lambda_{r+1,2}$ are Lagrange multipliers that guarantee the unit variance property of the new pair of coordinates,

$$\begin{aligned} E\{u_{r+1}^2\} &= \mathbf{w}_{r+1}^TR_{xx}\mathbf{w}_{r+1} = 1 \\ E\{v_{r+1}^2\} &= \mathbf{d}_{r+1}^TR_{yy}\mathbf{d}_{r+1} = 1 \end{aligned} \tag{19}$$

Taking the partial derivatives of J_{r+1} with respect to $\mathbf{w}_{r+1}$ and $\mathbf{d}_{r+1}$ yields

$$\begin{aligned} \frac{\partial J_{r+1}}{\partial \mathbf{w}_{r+1}} &= -(I - R_{xx}W_rW_r^T)R_{xy}(I - R_{yy}D_rD_r^T)^T\mathbf{d}_{r+1} \\ &\quad + R_{xx}\mathbf{w}_{r+1}\lambda_{r+1,1} \\ \frac{\partial J_{r+1}}{\partial \mathbf{d}_{r+1}} &= -(I - R_{yy}D_rD_r^T)R_{yx}(I - R_{xx}W_rW_r^T)^T\mathbf{w}_{r+1} \\ &\quad + R_{yy}\mathbf{d}_{r+1}\lambda_{r+1,2} \end{aligned} \tag{20}$$

At the solution the constraints in Eq. (19) are satisfied. Moreover, $\mathbf{w}_{r+1}$ and $\mathbf{d}_{r+1}$ are, respectively, orthogonal to $R_{xx}W_r$ and $R_{yy}D_r$. That is

$$\mathbf{w}_{r+1}^T R_{xx} W_r = 0 \text{ and } \mathbf{d}_{r+1}^T R_{yy} D_r = 0 \tag{21}$$

Using Eqs. (19) and (21) the optimal values of Lagrange multipliers in Eq. (18) are found to be

$$\lambda_{r+1,1} = \lambda_{r+1,2} = \lambda_{r+1} = \mathbf{w}_{r+1}^T R_{xy} \mathbf{d}_{r+1} = k_{r+1} \tag{22}$$

From Eq. (6) the $(r+1)$th canonical coordinate pair of $\mathbf{x}$ and $\mathbf{y}$ is given by

$$u_{r+1} = \mathbf{w}_{r+1}^T \mathbf{x} \text{ and } v_{r+1} = \mathbf{d}_{r+1}^T \mathbf{y} \tag{23}$$

Using Eqs. (17) and (21) we may rewrite Eq. (23) as

$$\begin{aligned} u_{r+1} &= \mathbf{w}_{r+1}^T (I - R_{xx} W_r W_r^T)\mathbf{x} = \mathbf{w}_{r+1}^T \mathbf{x} - \mathbf{q}_r^T \mathbf{u}_r \\ v_{r+1} &= \mathbf{d}_{r+1}^T (I - R_{yy} D_r D_r^T)\mathbf{y} = \mathbf{d}_{r+1}^T \mathbf{x} - \mathbf{p}_r^T \mathbf{v}_r \end{aligned} \tag{24}$$

where

$$\mathbf{q}_r^T = \mathbf{w}_{r+1}^T R_{xx} W_r \text{ and } \mathbf{p}_r^T = \mathbf{d}_{r+1}^T R_{yy} D_r \tag{25}$$

The pair of equations in Eq. (24) may be used to define a network structure for extracting the $(r+1)$th pair of canonical coordinates, given the first r pairs. Each equation in Eq. (24) defines a single layer subnetwork that features a feedforward set of weights from the input to the output and a set of lateral connections that connects the first r nodes to the $(r+1)$th node. Fig. 1 shows the structure of this network. In this structure, W_r and D_r are the weight matrices that map $\mathbf{x}$ and $\mathbf{y}$ to their first r canonical coordinates $\mathbf{u}_r$ and $\mathbf{v}_r$. Given these weights, the network may be trained, by minimizing J_{r+1} in Eq. (18), to extract the $(r+1)$th canonical coordinate pair and the corresponding mapping vectors. The weight vectors $\mathbf{w}_{r+1}$ and $\mathbf{d}_{r+1}$ are trained to maximize the correlation between the outputs u_{r+1} and v_{r+1} and make them unity variance. The lateral weight vector $\mathbf{q}_r$ is trained to orthogonalize $\mathbf{u}_r$ (the first r canonical coordinates of $\mathbf{x}$) to u_{r+1} (the $(r+1)$th canonical coordinate of $\mathbf{x}$). Similarly, the lateral weight vector $\mathbf{p}_r$ is trained to orthogonalize $\mathbf{v}_r$ to $\mathbf{v}_{r+1}$. The lateral connections perform a deflation process that subtracts the contributions of the already extracted coordinates from the linear subspaces of $\mathbf{x}$ and $\mathbf{y}$. This structure allows for adding new nodes for extracting additional canonical coordinates without the need for retraining the previous nodes.

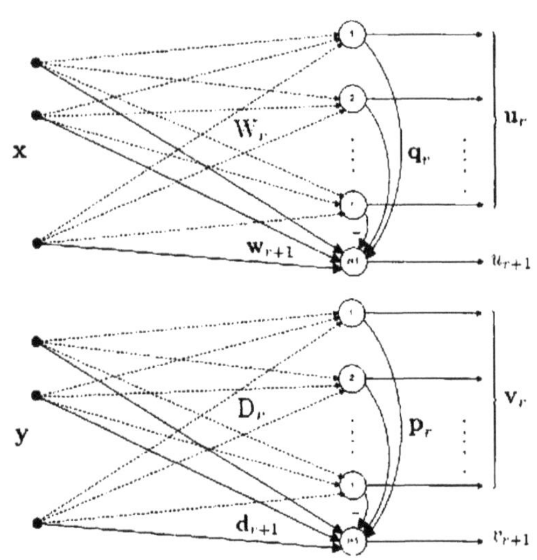

Fig. 1. The structure of the network for recursive extraction of canonical coordinates of $\mathbf{x}$ and $\mathbf{y}$.

Using the stochastic gradient descent learning algorithm, with instantaneous values of covariance matrices inserted into Eq. (20), we may derive the following updating rules for $\mathbf{w}_{r+1}$, and $\mathbf{d}_{r+1}$

$$\begin{aligned} \mathbf{w}_{r+1}(j+1) = \mathbf{w}_{r+1}(j) + [(&\mathbf{x}(j+1) - S_r(j+1)\mathbf{u}_r(j+1) \\ &\cdot v_r(j+1) - \mathbf{x}(j+1)\mathbf{x}(j+1)^T \mathbf{w}_{r+1}(j)\lambda_{r+1} \\ &\times (j+1)]\beta(j+1) \\ \mathbf{d}_{r+1}(j+1) = \mathbf{d}_{r+1}(j) + [(&\mathbf{y}_{(j+1)} - T_r(j+1)\mathbf{v}_r(j+1) \\ &\cdot u_r(j+1) - \mathbf{y}(j+1)\mathbf{y}(j+1)^T \mathbf{d}_{r+1}(j)\lambda_{r+1} \\ &\times (j+1)]\beta(j+1) \end{aligned} \tag{26}$$

where j is the index of iteration. Matrices S_r and T_r are updated to asymptotically approximate $R_{xx}W_r$ and $R_{yy}D_r$, respectively. From Eq. (22), the Lagrange multiplier $\lambda_{r+1} = \lambda_{r+1,1} = \lambda_{r+1,2}$ shall be updated to asymptotically approximate $\mathbf{w}_{r+1}^T R_{xy} \mathbf{d}_{r+1} = k_{r+1}$. Thus the updating rules for S_r, T_r, and λ_{r+1} are

$$\begin{aligned} S_r(j+1) &= \frac{j}{j+1} S_r(j) + \frac{1}{j+1} \mathbf{x}(j+1)\mathbf{u}_r^T(j+1) \\ T_r(j+1) &= \frac{j}{j+1} T_r(j) + \frac{1}{j+1} \mathbf{y}(j+1)\mathbf{v}_r^T(j+1) \\ \lambda_{r+1}(j+1) &= \frac{j}{j+1} \lambda_{r+1}(j) + \frac{1}{j+1} \mathbf{w}_{r+1}^T(j)\mathbf{x}(j+1) \\ &\quad \cdot \mathbf{y}^T(j+1)\mathbf{d}_{r+1}(j)] \end{aligned} \tag{27}$$

Finally using Eq. (25) the learning rules for the lateral weight vectors $\mathbf{q}_r$, and $\mathbf{p}_r$ may be written as

$$\begin{aligned} \mathbf{q}_r(j+1) &= S_r^T(j+1)\mathbf{w}_{r+1}(j+1) \\ \mathbf{p}_r(j+1) &= T_r^T(j+1)\mathbf{d}_{r+1}(j+1) \end{aligned} \tag{28}$$

Thus we may summarize the step-by-step training algorithm for extracting the $(r+1)$th canonical coordinate pair for $r = 0, 1, \dots, m-1$ and the corresponding mapping vectors as

$$\mathbf{u}_r(j+1)=W_r^T\mathbf{x}(j+1) \text{ and } \mathbf{v}_r(j+1)=D_r^T\mathbf{y}(j+1)$$

$$u_{r+1}(j+1)=\mathbf{w}_{r+1}^T(j+1)\mathbf{x}(j+1)-\mathbf{q}_r^T(j)\mathbf{u}_r(j+1)$$

$$v_{r+1}(j+1)=\mathbf{d}_{r+1}^T(j+1)\mathbf{y}(j+1)-\mathbf{p}_r^T(j)\mathbf{v}_r(j+1)$$

$$\lambda_{r+1}(j+1)=\frac{1}{j+1}[j\lambda_{r+1}(j) + \mathbf{w}_{r+1}^T(j)\mathbf{x}(j+1)\mathbf{y}^T(j+1)\mathbf{d}_{r+1}(j)]$$

$$S_r(j+1)=\frac{1}{j+1}[jS_r(j)+\mathbf{x}(j+1)\mathbf{u}_r^T(j+1)]$$

$$T_r(j+1)=\frac{1}{j+1}[jT_r(j)+\mathbf{y}(j+1)\mathbf{v}_r^T(j+1)]$$

$$\mathbf{w}_{r+1}(j+1)=\mathbf{w}_{r+1}(j)+[(\mathbf{x}(j+1)-S_r(j+1)\mathbf{u}_r(j+1))\mathbf{v}_r(j+1) -\mathbf{x}(j+1)\mathbf{x}(j+1)^T\mathbf{w}_{r+1}(j)\lambda_{r+1}(j+1)]\beta(j+1)$$

$$\mathbf{d}_{r+1}(j+1)=\mathbf{d}_{r+1}(j)+[(\mathbf{y}(j+1)-T_r(j+1)\mathbf{v}_r(j+1))\mathbf{u}_r(j+1) -\mathbf{y}(j+1)\mathbf{y}(j+1)^T\mathbf{d}_{r+1}(j)\lambda_{r+1}(j+1)]\beta(j+1)$$

$$\mathbf{q}_r(j+1)=S_r^T(j+1)\mathbf{w}_{r+1}(j+1)$$

$$\mathbf{p}_r(j+1)=T_r^T(j+1)\mathbf{d}_{r+1}(j+1) \tag{29}$$

The initial values $\mathbf{w}_{r+1}(0)\in\mathbb{R}^{m\times 1}$, $\mathbf{d}_{r+1}(0)\in\mathbb{R}^{n\times 1}$, $\mathbf{q}_r(0)\in\mathbb{R}^{r\times 1}$, $\mathbf{p}_r(0)\in\mathbb{R}^{r\times 1}$, $S_r(0)\in\mathbb{R}^{m\times r}$, $T_r(0)\in\mathbb{R}^{n\times r}$, and λ_{r+1} may be chosen randomly. The learning rate β may be varied or kept fixed (Haykin, 1991). After convergence, the linear dependence captured by the first $(r+1)$ pair of canonical coordinates is

$$H_r=\prod_{i=1}^{r+1}(1-k_i^2)=\prod_{i=1}^{r+1}(1-\lambda_i^2) \tag{30}$$

and in case that $\mathbf{x}$ and $\mathbf{y}$ are marginally Gaussian, the mutual information preserved by the first $(r+1)$ pair of canonical coordinates becomes

$$I_r(\mathbf{x},\mathbf{y})=-\frac{1}{2}\sum_{i=1}^{r+1}\log(1-k_i^2)=-\frac{1}{2}\sum_{i=1}^{r+1}\log(1-\lambda_i^2) \tag{31}$$

Since in most applications, the number of canonical coordinate pairs to be extracted is not known a priori, we may run a test based on Eqs. (30) or (31) to determine if the amount of linear dependence or mutual information preserved, meets a pre-specified threshold. If the threshold is not reached, we may add another node to the network to extract the next pair of canonical coordinates.

4. Simulation results

In this section, the proposed network is used to recursively extract the canonical coordinate mappings for a synthesized data set. The performance of the network is demonstrated by presenting the plots of squared error between the actual canonical coordinate mappings, computed using the direct method in Eq. (5), and the ones estimated by the network, along with the plots of squared error for canonical correlations. Let $\hat{\mathbf{w}}_i$ and $\hat{\mathbf{d}}_i$, respectively, denote the estimate of the ith pair of the actual canonical coordinate mappings $\mathbf{w}_i$ and $\mathbf{d}_i$. We define $e_{\mathbf{w}_i}^2$ and $e_{\mathbf{d}_i}^2$ as the squared estimation error of the ith canonical coordinate mappings $\mathbf{w}_i$ and $\mathbf{d}_i$. That is

$$e_{\mathbf{w}_i}^2 = \|\mathbf{w}_i - \hat{\mathbf{w}}_i\|^2 \text{ and } e_{\mathbf{d}_i}^2 = \|\mathbf{d}_i - \hat{\mathbf{d}}_i\|^2$$

Also, $e_{\mathbf{k}_i}^2 = (k_i - \hat{k}_i)^2$, is defined as the squared estimation error of the ith canonical correlation k_i. The actual canonical correlation k_i is found from the SVD in Eq. (3). From Eq. (22), it is seen that the ith canonical correlation k_i is estimated by the Lagrange multiplier λ_i. The data set is formed from 500 samples of two data channels $\mathbf{x}\in\mathbb{R}^{4\times 1}$, $\mathbf{y}\in\mathbb{R}^{5\times 1}$ governed by the linear model

$$\mathbf{x} = H_x\eta_x \text{ and } \mathbf{y} = H_y\eta_y + H_{yx}\mathbf{x}$$

The matrices $H_x\in\mathbb{R}^{4\times 4}, H_y\in\mathbb{R}^{5\times 5}$ and $H_{yx}\in\mathbb{R}^{5\times 4}$ are used to synthesize $\mathbf{x}$ and $\mathbf{y}$ from $\eta_x\in\mathbb{R}^{4\times 1}$ and $\eta_y\in\mathbb{R}^{5\times 1}$, which are two independent white Gaussian vectors. The network is trained for 2500 epochs using the training algorithm in Eq. (29), without knowledge of the generating mechanism for $\mathbf{x}$ and $\mathbf{y}$. The learning rate is varied linearly from $\beta = 5\times 10^{-3}$ to 5×10^{-6} in 2500 steps. All the initial values in Eq. (29) are randomly selected.

Fig. 2(a)–(d) show the squared estimation errors $e_{\mathbf{w}_i}^2, i\in[1,4]$ vs. the epoch index for 10 independent initializations of the network. It is seen that in all the cases the squared error approaches zero within a misadjustment error (Haykin, 1996) and thus the weights of the upper subnetwork (Fig. 1) converge to the actual canonical coordinate mapping vectors that map the first data channel $\mathbf{x}$ into its canonical coordinates $\mathbf{u}$.

The plots of the squared estimation errors $e_{\mathbf{d}_i}^2, i\in[1,4]$ vs. epoch index for the 10 initializations are shown in Fig. 3. The convergence behaviors are very similar to those in Fig. 2. In all the cases the squared error approaches zero within a misadjustment error and thus the weights of the lower subnetwork (Fig. 1) converge to the actual canonical coordinate mapping vectors that map the second data channel $\mathbf{y}$ into its canonical coordinates $\mathbf{v}$.

Fig. 4 shows the squared estimation errors $e_{\mathbf{k}_i}^2, i\in[1,4]$ vs. the epoch index for the 10 initializations. The plots show that the squared error decays to zero in all the cases. The estimate of the ith canonical correlation k_i is given by the Lagrange multiplier λ_i. These plots indicate that λ_i's converge to the actual canonical correlations k_i's.

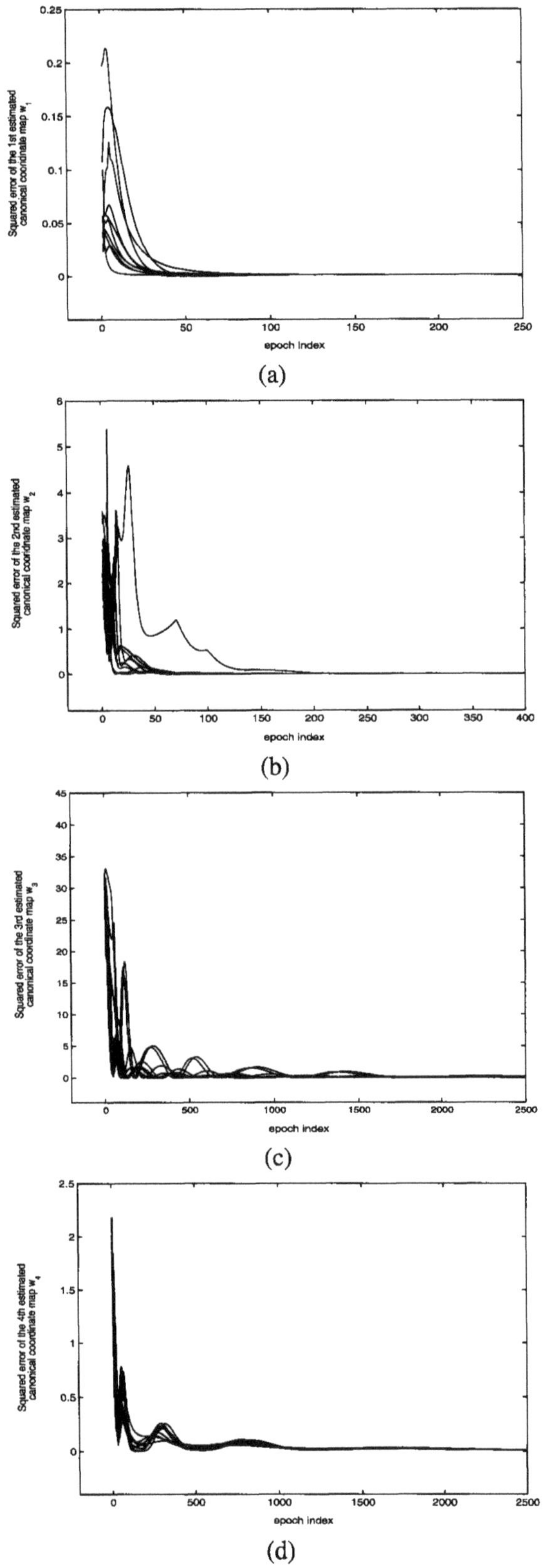

Fig. 2. The squared error for $\mathbf{w}_i$'s, $i \in [1,4]$ vs. the epoch index for 10 independent initializations of the network (a) $i=1$; $e^2_{\mathbf{w}_1} = \|\mathbf{w}_1 - \hat{\mathbf{w}}_1\|^2$. (b) $i=2$; $e^2_{\mathbf{w}_2} = \|\mathbf{w}_2 - \hat{\mathbf{w}}_2\|^2$. (c) $i=3$; $e^2_{\mathbf{w}_3} = \|\mathbf{w}_3 - \hat{\mathbf{w}}_3\|^2$. (d) $i=4$; $e^2_{\mathbf{w}_4} = \|\mathbf{w}_4 - \hat{\mathbf{w}}_4\|^2$. In all the cases the squared error approaches zero and the weights of the upper subnetwork (Fig. 1) converge to the actual canonical coordinate mapping vectors that map the first data channel $\mathbf{x}$ into its canonical coordinates $\mathbf{u}$.

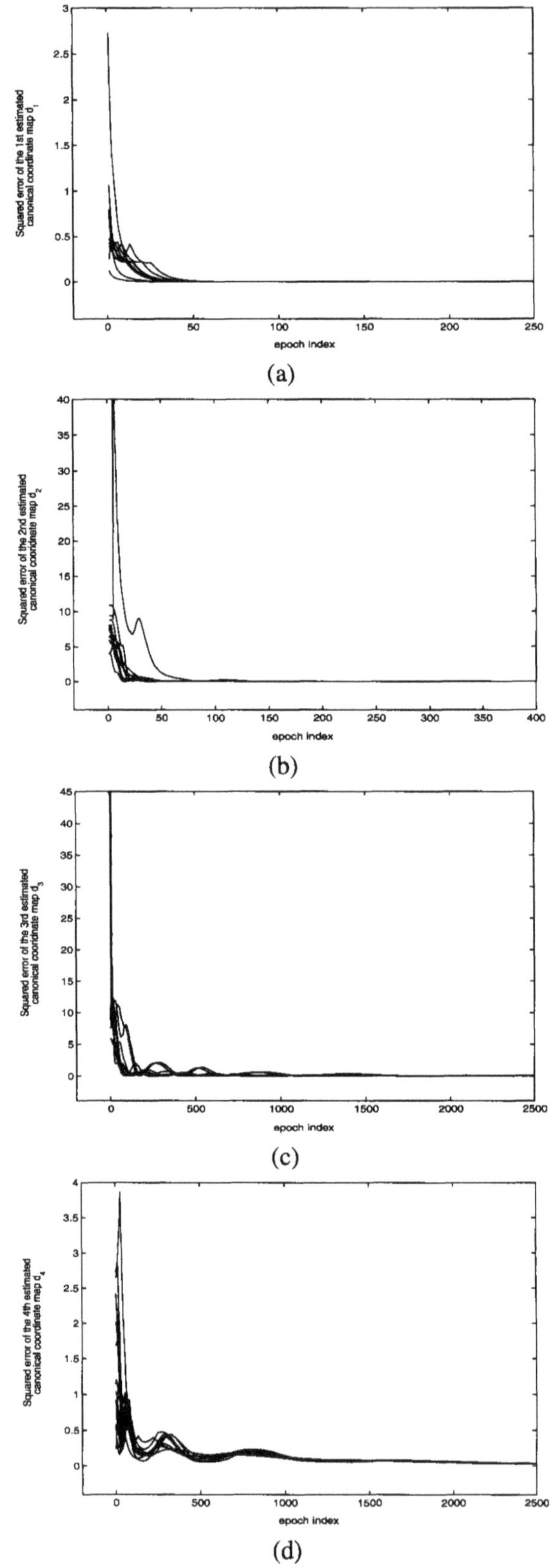

Fig. 3. The squared error for $\mathbf{d}_i$'s $i \in [1,4]$ vs. the epoch index for 10 independent initializations of the network (a) $i=1$; $e^2_{\mathbf{d}_1} = \|\mathbf{d}_1 - \hat{\mathbf{d}}_1\|^2$. (b) $i=2$; $e^2_{\mathbf{d}_2} = \|\mathbf{d}_2 - \hat{\mathbf{d}}_2\|^2$. (c) $i=3$; $e^2_{\mathbf{d}_3} = \|\mathbf{d}_3 - \hat{\mathbf{d}}_3\|^2$. (d) $i=4$; $e^2_{\mathbf{d}_4} = \|\mathbf{d}_4 - \hat{\mathbf{d}}_4\|^2$. In all the cases the squared error approaches zero and the weights of the lower subnetwork (Fig. 1) converge to the actual canonical coordinate mapping vectors that map the second data channel $\mathbf{y}$ into its canonical coordinates $\mathbf{v}$.

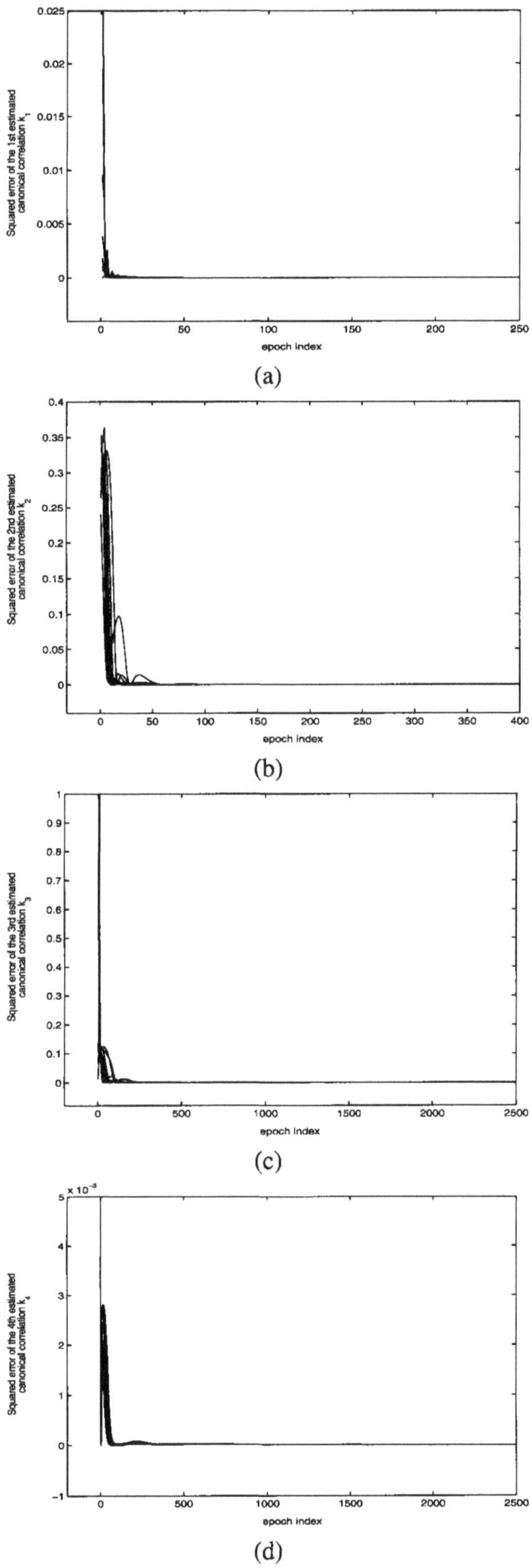

Fig. 4. The squared error for k_i's, $i \in [1,4]$ vs. the epoch index for 10 independent initializations of the network (a) $i = 1$; $e^2_{k_1} = (k_1 - \hat{k}_1)^2$. (b) $i = 2$; $e^2_{k_2} = (k_2 - \hat{k}_2)^2$. (c) $i = 3$; $e^2_{k_3} = (k_3 - \hat{k}_3)^2$. (d) $i = 4$; $e^2_{k_4} = (k_4 - \hat{k}_4)^2$. The estimate of k_i is given by the Lagrange multiplier λ_i. The plots show that λ_i converges to the actual canonical correlation k_i in all the cases.

5. Conclusion

A new network for recursive extraction of canonical coordinates of two data channels is introduced. The network is based on a constrained minimization problem that exploits a deflation process. The deflation process is performed by incorporating lateral connections into the subnetworks. The learning rules are derived using a stochastic gradient descent algorithm. The structure of the network along with the learning rules allow for adding a new node to the network in order to extract a new canonical coordinate pair without the need to retrain the previous nodes. Unlike conventional methods, no matrix inversion, matrix square root computation, or direct SVD is required during the training. A simulation example demonstrates the validity of the proposed network and learning rules. The results confirm that the extracted canonical coordinate mappings indeed approximate the true ones.

Acknowledgements

This work is supported by the Office of Naval Research (ONR) under the contract number N00014-02-1-0006.

Appendix A

Here we show that the constrained minimization problem in Eq. (18) indeed formulates the problem of finding the $(r+1)$th pair of canonical coordinate mappings $\mathbf{w}_{r+1}$ and $\mathbf{d}_{r+1}$. The assumption is that the matrices W_r and D_r, which contain the first r columns of W and D (the first r pair of canonical coordinate mappings), have already been found.

Let us start by partitioning F, G and K into

$$F = [F_r\ F_{\bar{r}}],\quad G = [G_r\ G_{\bar{r}}],\quad \text{and}\ K = \begin{bmatrix} K_r & 0 \\ 0 & K_{\bar{r}} \end{bmatrix} \tag{32}$$

where matrices F_r and G_r contain the first r and matrices $F_{\bar{r}}$ and $G_{\bar{r}}$ the last $m-r$ columns of F and G. The diagonal matrices $K_r = \text{diag}[k_1, \ldots, k_r]$ and $K_{\bar{r}} = \text{diag}[k_{r+1}, \ldots, k_m]$, respectively, contain the first r and last $m-r$ canonical correlations. Then from Eq. (3), we have

$$C = R_{xx}^{-1/2} R_{xy} R_{yy}^{-T/2} = FKG^T = F_r K_r G_r^T + F_{\bar{r}} K_{\bar{r}} G_{\bar{r}}^T \tag{33}$$

and

$$\begin{bmatrix} F_r^T F_r & F_{\bar{r}}^T F_r \\ F_r^T F_{\bar{r}} & F_{\bar{r}}^T F_{\bar{r}} \end{bmatrix} = \begin{bmatrix} I_r & 0 \\ 0 & I_{\bar{r}} \end{bmatrix}$$
$$\begin{bmatrix} G_r^T G_r & G_{\bar{r}}^T G_r \\ G_r^T G_{\bar{r}} & G_{\bar{r}}^T G_{\bar{r}} \end{bmatrix} = \begin{bmatrix} I_r & 0 \\ 0 & I_{\bar{r}} \end{bmatrix} \tag{34}$$

where I_r and $I_{\bar{r}}$ are the $r \times r$ and $(m-r) \times (m-r)$ identity matrices. The SVD in Eq. (33), may be rewritten as

$$R_{xy} = R_{xx}^{1/2} F_r K_r G_r^T R_{yy}^{T/2} + R_{xx}^{1/2} F_{\bar{r}} K_{\bar{r}} G_{\bar{r}}^T R_{yy}^{T/2} \quad (35)$$

Using Eqs. (33) and (34), it may easily be verified that the first term on the right hand side of Eq. (35) has three equivalent representations. That is

$$\begin{aligned} R_{xx}^{1/2} F_r K_r G_r^T R_{yy}^{T/2} &= R_{xx}^{1/2} F_r F_r^T R_{xx}^{-1/2} R_{xy} \\ &= R_{xy} R_{yy}^{-T/2} G_r G_r^T R_{yy}^{T/2} \\ &= R_{xx}^{1/2} F_r F_r^T R_{xx}^{-1/2} R_{xy} R_{yy}^{-T/2} G_r G_r^T R_{yy}^{T/2} \end{aligned} \quad (36)$$

Using this property, we may rewrite Eq. (35) as

$$\begin{aligned} &(I - R_{xx}^{1/2} F_r F_r^T R_{xx}^{-1/2}) R_{xy} (I - R_{yy}^{1/2} G_r G_r^T R_{yy}^{-1/2})^T \\ &= R_{xx}^{1/2} F_{\bar{r}} K_{\bar{r}} G_{\bar{r}}^T R_{yy}^{T/2} \end{aligned} \quad (37)$$

We now partition W and D into $W = [W_r\ W_{\bar{r}}]$ and $D = [D_r\ D_{\bar{r}}]$, where the matrices $W_{\bar{r}} = [\mathbf{w}_{r+1}, \ldots, \mathbf{w}_m]$ and $D_{\bar{r}} = [\mathbf{d}_{r+1}, \ldots, \mathbf{d}_m]$ contain the last $m-r$ columns of W and D. Then, from Eq. (5) we have

$$\begin{aligned} F_r &= R_{xx}^{T/2} W_r, \quad F_{\bar{r}} = R_{xx}^{T/2} W_{\bar{r}}, \\ G_r &= R_{yy}^{T/2} D_r, \quad G_{\bar{r}} = R_{yy}^{T/2} D_{\bar{r}} \end{aligned} \quad (38)$$

Using Eq. (38), we may rewrite Eq. (37) as

$$(I - R_{xx} W_r W_r^T) R_{xy} (I - R_{yy} D_r D_r^T)^T = R_{xx} W_{\bar{r}} K_{\bar{r}} D_{\bar{r}}^T R_{yy} \quad (39)$$

Pre-multiplying Eq. (39) by $\mathbf{w}_{r+1}^T$, post-multiplying it by $\mathbf{d}_{r+1}$, and noting that $\mathbf{w}_{r+1}^T R_{xx} W_{\bar{r}} = [1, 0, \ldots, 0]$ and $\mathbf{d}_{r+1}^T R_{yy} D_{\bar{r}} = [1, 0, \ldots, 0]$ results in

$$\mathbf{w}_{r+1}^T (I - R_{xx} W_r W_r^T) R_{xy} (I - R_{yy} D_r D_r^T)^T \mathbf{d}_{r+1} = k_{r+1} \quad (40)$$

Considering that k_{r+1} is the largest diagonal element of $K_{\bar{r}}$ we may formulate the problem of finding $\mathbf{w}_{r+1}$, $\mathbf{d}_{r+1}$ as

$$\max_{\mathbf{w}_{r+1}, \mathbf{d}_{r+1}} \mathbf{w}_{r+1}^T (I - R_{xx} W_r W_r^T) R_{xy} (I - R_{yy} D_r D_r^T)^T \mathbf{d}_{r+1}$$

subject to the constraints

$$\mathbf{w}_{r+1}^T R_{xx} \mathbf{w}_{r+1} = 1 \text{ and } \mathbf{d}_{r+1}^T R_{yy} \mathbf{d}_{r+1} = 1.$$

References

Anderson, T. W. (1958). *An introduction to multivariate statistical analysis*. New York: Wiley.

Bannour, S., & Azimi-Sadjadi, M. R. (1995). Principal component extraction using recursive least squares learning. *IEEE Transactions on Neural Networks*, *6*, 457–469.

Diamantaras, D. I., & Kung, S. Y. (1994). Multi-layer neural networks for reduced-rank approximation. *IEEE Transactions on Neural Networks*, *5*, 684–697.

Diamantaras, K. I., & Kung, S. Y. (1996). *Principal component neural networks: theory and applications* (1st ed). New York: Wiely.

Foldiak, P. (1989). Adaptive network for optimal linear feature extraction. *Proceedings of the International Joint Conference on Neural Networks, IJCNN', Washington, DC, 89*, I401–I406.

Haykin, S. (1991). *Neural networks: a comprehensive foundation* (2nd ed). Upper Saddle River, NJ: Printice Hall.

Haykin, S. (1996). *Adaptive filter theory* (3rd ed). Upper Saddle River, NJ: Printice Hall.

Hotelling, H. (1936). Relation between two sets of variates. *Biometrica*, *28*, 321–377.

Kung, S. Y., & Diamantaras, K. I. (1994). Adaptive principal component extraction (apex) and applications. *IEEE Transactions on Signal Processing*, *42*, 1202–1217.

Lai, P. L., & Fyfe, C. (1999). A neural network implementation of canonical correlation analysis. *Neural Networks*, *12*, 1391–1397.

Oja, E. (1982). A simplified neuron model as principal component analyzer. *Journal of Mathematical Biology*, *15*, 267–273.

Sanger, T. D. (1989). Optimal unsupervised learning in a single-layer linear feedforward neural network. *Neural Networks*, *2*, 459–473.

Scharf, L. L., & Mullis, C. T. (2000). Canonical coordinates and the geometry of inference, rate and capacity. *IEEE Transactions on Signal Processing*, *48*, 824–831.

Scharf, L. L., & Thomas, J. T. (1998). Wiener filters in canonical coordinates for transform coding, filtering, and quantizing. *IEEE Transactions on Signal Processing*, *46*, 647–654.

PERGAMON

AVAILABLE AT
www.ComputerScienceWeb.com
POWERED BY SCIENCE @DIRECT

Neural Networks 16 (2003) 809–816

Neural Networks

www.elsevier.com/locate/neunet

2003 Special issue

Automatic basis selection techniques for RBF networks

Ali Ghodsi*, Dale Schuurmans

School of Computer Science, University of Waterloo, 200 University Avenue West, Waterloo, Ont., Canada N2L 3G1

Abstract

This paper proposes a generic criterion that defines the optimum number of basis functions for radial basis function (RBF) neural networks. The generalization performance of an RBF network relates to its prediction capability on independent test data. This performance gives a measure of the quality of the chosen model. An RBF network with an overly restricted basis gives poor predictions on new data, since the model has too little flexibility (yielding high bias and low variance). By contrast, an RBF network with too many basis functions also gives poor generalization performance since it is too flexible and fits too much of the noise on the training data (yielding low bias but high variance). Bias and variance are complementary quantities, and it is necessary to assign the number of basis function optimally in order to achieve the best compromise between them. In this paper we use Stein's unbiased risk estimator to derive an analytical criterion for assigning the appropriate number of basis functions. Two cases of known and unknown noise have been considered and the efficacy of this criterion in both situations is illustrated experimentally. The paper also shows an empirical comparison between this method and two well known classical methods, cross validation and the Bayesian information criterion, BIC.

Keywords: Radial basis function network; Model selection; Stein's unbiased risk estimator; Bayesian information criterion

1. Introduction

Radial basis function (RBF) networks have attracted a lot of interest in the past. One reason is that they form a unifying link between function approximation, regularization, noisy interpolation, classification and density estimation. It is also the case that training RBF networks is usually faster than training multi-layer perceptron networks.

RBF network training usually proceeds in two steps: First, the basis function parameters (corresponding to hidden units) are determined by clustering. Second, the final-layer weights are determined by least squares which reduces to solving a simple linear system. Thus, the first stage is an unsupervised method which is relatively fast, and the second stage requires the solution of a linear problem, which is also fast.

One of the advantages of RBF neural networks, compared to multi-layer perceptron networks, is the possibility of choosing suitable parameters for the units of hidden layer without having to perform a non-linear optimization of the network parameters. However, the problem of selecting the appropriate number of basis functions remains a critical issue for RBF networks. The number of basis functions controls the complexity, and hence the generalization ability of RBF networks. An RBF network with too few basis functions gives poor predictions on new data, i.e. poor generalization, since the model has limited flexibility. On the other hand, an RBF network with too many basis functions also yields poor generalization since it is too flexible and fits the noise in the training data. A small number of basis functions yields a high bias, low variance estimator, whereas a large number of basis functions yields a low bias but high variance estimator. The best generalization performance is obtained via a compromise between the conflicting requirements of reducing bias while simultaneously reducing variance. This trade-off highlights the importance of optimizing the complexity of the model in order to achieve the best generalization.

In this paper, we propose a criterion for selecting the number of RBFs in an RBF network, and compare it with two well studied classical model selection method, cross validation and the Bayesian information criterion (BIC).

To develop a theoretically well motivated criterion for choosing an appropriate number of basis functions, we derive a generalization of Stein's unbiased risk estimator (SURE) (Ker-Chau, 1985) which defines a generic criterion that determines the optimum number of basis functions to use in a given problem.

* Corresponding author.
E-mail addresses: aghodsib@cs.uwaterloo.ca (A. Ghodsi), dale@cs.uwaterloo.ca (D. Schuurmans).

0893-6080/03/$ - see front matter © 2003 Elsevier Science Ltd. All rights reserved.
doi:10.1016/S0893-6080(03)00118-7

In Section 2 of this paper we review RBF networks and their training algorithm. We then explain the under-fitting and over-fitting effects caused by using an inappropriate number of basis functions for RBF networks in Section 3. In Section 4 we derive a generalization of SURE, and in Section 5 show how it can be applied to RBF networks. Experimental results of the proposed criterion and its compression with other methods are presented in Section 6.

2. Radial basis function networks

RBF networks are a major class of neural network model, where the distance between the input vector and a prototype vector determines the activation of a hidden unit. RBF methods became a popular technique in the mid 1980s for performing exact interpolation of a set of data points in a high-dimensional space (Powell, 1987). The basic technique provides an interpolating function which passes through every data point: Consider a mapping from a d-dimensional input space to a one-dimensional target space y, where the data set consists of N input vectors x_i, with corresponding targets y_i, $i = 1,\dots,N$. An exact interpolation is achieved by introducing a set of N basis functions, one for each data point, and then setting the weights for the linear combination of basis functions. Here, basis functions are non-linear functions, $\Phi(\|x - x_i\|)$, of the input vectors x_i, and a linear combination of these basis functions can be written as

$$\sum_{i=1}^{N} w_i \Phi(\|x - x_i\|)$$

The interpolation problem can then be written in a matrix form as

$$\Phi W = y$$

where the square matrix Φ has elements $\Phi_{ii'} = \Phi(\|x_i - x_{i'}\|)$. This linear system of equations can be solved to yield

$$W = \Phi^{-1} y$$

For the case of Gaussian basis functions we have

$$\Phi(x) = \exp\left(\frac{x^2}{2v^2}\right)$$

where v is a parameter that controls the smoothness of the interpolating function.

A RBF neural network model (Broomhead & Lowe, 1988; Moody & Darken, 1989) can be obtained by a number of modifications to the exact interpolation procedure as follows: First, the number, M, of basis functions is usually much less than the number, N, of data points. Second, the centers of the basis functions no longer need to be given by input data vectors, and appropriate centers can alternatively be determined during the training process. Third, unlike the exact interpolation procedure, each basis function can have its own width parameter, v_j, whose value is also determined in the training process. Finally, by applying these changes to the original (exact) interpolation formula we obtain the following form for the RBF neural network mapping

$$y_k(X) = \sum_{j=1}^{M} w_{kj} \Phi_j(X) + w_{k0} \tag{1}$$

By including an extra basis function Φ_0 whose activation is set to 1, the biases w_{k0} can be absorbed into the final summation. Another useful variation is the normalized RBF representation:

$$y_k(X) = \frac{\sum_{j=1}^{M} w_{kj} \Phi_j(X)}{\sum_{r=1}^{M} \Phi_r(X)}$$

This normalized representation is closely related to TSK fuzzy inference systems (Sugeno & Yasakawa, 1993; Takagi & Sugeno, 1985).

Several forms of basis function have been considered in previous research on RBF models, the most common being the Gaussian:

$$\Phi_j(X) = \exp\left(-\frac{\|X - \mu_j\|^2}{2v_j^2}\right)$$

where X is the d-dimensional input vector with elements x_i, and μ_j is the center of basis function Φ_j (Fig. 1)

In practice, training RBF networks proceeds through two steps. The first step determines the first layer of weights, in which the basis function parameters μ_j and σ_j are selected based on the X-values of the training samples (via unsupervised learning techniques). The basis functions are then kept fixed while the second-layer weights w_i are estimated via linear least squares.

Typical approaches for the first phase include using the generalized Lloyd algorithm and Konhonen's self-organized maps. Another common approach is to model the input distribution as a Gaussian mixture model and then estimate the center and width parameters of the Gaussian mixture components via the EM algorithm (Bishop, 1995). For the second phase one can consider the RBF network mapping in Eq. (1). If we absorb the bias parameters into the weights, this can be written in matrix notation as

$$Y = W\Phi \tag{2}$$

where Y is a matrix of output values, and $W = (w_{kj})$ is a matrix of second-layer weights to be estimated.

This is a classical least squares estimation problem. A necessary condition for $\|Y - W\Phi\|^2$ to be minimized is that W must satisfy

$$W = (\Phi^{\mathrm{T}}\Phi)^{-1}\Phi^{\mathrm{T}} Y$$

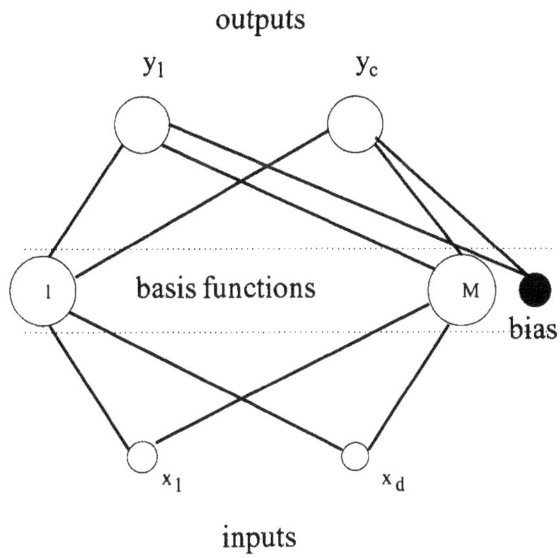

Fig. 1. A graphical form of a radial bassis function neural network architecture. Basis functions act like hidden units. The corresponding elements μ_{ji} of the vector μ_j is represented by the line connecting basis function Φ_j to the inputs. The weights w_{kj} are shown as lines from the basis functions to the output units. An extra basis function whose output is fixed at 1 serves as the bias for each output unit.

3. Over-fitting, under-fitting and model selection

Model selection is the task of choosing a model of optimal complexity for a given problem. Learning a RBF network from data is a parameter estimation problem. One difficulty with this problem is selecting parameters that show good performance on both training and testing data. In principle, a model is selected to have parameters associated with the best observed performance on training data, although our goal really is to achieve good performance on unseen testing data. Not surprisingly, a model selected on the basis of training data does not necessarily exhibit comparable performance on the testing data. When squared error is used as the performance index, a zero-error model on the training data can always be achieved by using a sufficient number of basis functions. However, training error, *err*, and testing error, *Err*, do not demonstrate a linear relationship. In particular, a smaller training error does do not necessarily result in a smaller testing error. In practice, one often observes that, up to a certain point, the model error on testing data tends to decrease as the training error decreases. However, if one attempts to decrease the training error too far by increasing model complexity, the testing error often can take a dramatic increase.

The basic reason behind this phenomenon is that in the process of minimizing training error, after a certain point, the model begins to over-fit the training set. Over-fitting in this context means fitting the model to training data at the expense of losing generality. In the extreme form, as we mentioned in the previous section, a set of N training data points can be modeled exactly with N RBFs. Such a model follows the training data perfectly. However, the model is not representative features of the true underlying data source, and this is why it fails to correctly model new data points.

In general, the training error rate err will be less than the testing error on the new data, Err. A model typically adapts to the training data, and hence the training error err will be an overly optimistic estimate of the generalization error Err. An obvious way to estimate generalization error is to estimate the degree of optimism *OP* inherent in a particular estimate, and then add a penalty term to the training error to compensate, i.e. such that Err = err + OP. The method described in Section 4 works in this way.

4. Estimating the optimism

4.1. Stein's unbiased risk estimator

Let

- $\hat{f}(X)$ denote the *prediction model*, which is estimated from a training sample by the RBF neural network model.
- $f(X)$ denote the *real model.*
- $\text{MSE}(\hat{f}) = E(\hat{f} - f)^2$.
- err denote the *training error*, which is the average loss over the training sample.
- Err denote the *generalization error*, which is the expected prediction error on an independent test sample.

Recall that the training error, err $= \sum_{i=1}^{N} (\hat{y} - y)^2$, is an estimate of the expectation of the squared error on the training data, $E(\hat{y} - y)^2$, while the generalization error (test error) Err is an estimate of mean squared error, $\text{MSE} = (\hat{f} - f)^2$, where $\hat{f}(X)$ is the estimated model and $f(X)$ is the true model.

Now suppose $y_i = f(x_i) + \varepsilon_i$, where ε is additive Gaussian noise $N(0, \sigma^2)$. We need to estimate $\hat{f}$ from training data $D = \{(x_i, y_i)\}_i^n$. Consider

$$E[(\hat{y}_0 - y_0)^2] = E[(\hat{f} - f - \varepsilon)^2]$$

$$= E[(\hat{f} - f)^2] + E[\varepsilon]^2 - 2E[\varepsilon(\hat{f} - f)] \quad (3)$$

$$E[(\hat{y}_0 - y_0)^2] = E[(\hat{f} - f)^2] + \sigma^2 - 2E[\varepsilon(\hat{f} - f)] \quad (4)$$

Here, the last term can be written as:

$$E[2\varepsilon(\hat{f} - f)] = 2E[(y_0 - f)(\hat{f} - f)] \equiv \text{cov}(y_0, \hat{f})$$

We consider two different cases.

Case 1. Consider the case in which a new data point has been introduced to the estimated model, i.e. $(x_0, y_0) \notin D$. Since y_0 is a new point, $\hat{f}$ and y_0 are independent. Therefore $\text{cov}(y_0, \hat{f}) = 0$ and (4) in this case can be written as:

$$E[(\hat{f} - f)^2] = \sigma^2 E(\hat{y}_0 - y_0)^2 \quad (5)$$

This is the justification behind the technique of cross validation. In cross validation, to avoid overfitting or underfitting, a validation data set is used which is independent from the estimated model. The optimal model parameters should be selected to have the best performance index associated with this data set. Since this data set is independent from the estimated model, it is a fair estimate of $E(\hat{f}-f)^2$ and consequently of generalization error *Err* as indicated in Eq. (5).

Case 2. A more interesting case is the case in which we do not use new data points to assess the performance of the estimated model, and the traing data is used for both estimating and assessing a model $\hat{f}$. In this case the cross term in Eq. (4) cannot be ignored because $\hat{f}$ and y_0 are not independent. Therefore the cross term, which is $\mathrm{cov}(y_0,\hat{f})$, is not zero. However the cross term can be estimated by Stein's lemma (Ker-Chau, 1985; Stein, 1981). which was originally proposed to estimate the mean of a Guassian distribution (Stein, 1981).

According to Stein's lemma if $X \sim N(\theta,\sigma^2)$ and $g(x)$ is a differentiable function, such that $E[|g'(x)|] < \infty$ then $E(g(x)(x-\theta)) = \sigma^2 E(g'(x))$. So we let

$$g(\varepsilon) = \hat{f} - f = \hat{f} - y - \varepsilon$$

and $x = \varepsilon$. Then by applying Stein's lemma we obtain

$$E(\varepsilon(\hat{f}-f)) = \sigma^2 E(g'(\varepsilon)) = \sigma^2 E\left(\frac{\mathrm{d}\hat{f}}{\mathrm{d}y}\right)$$

Summing over all y we get

$$\mathrm{Err} = \sum_{i=1}^{M}(\hat{y}-y)^2 - N\sigma^2 + 2\sigma^2\sum_{i=1}^{N}\frac{\mathrm{d}\hat{f}(x_i)}{\mathrm{d}y_i}$$

$$= \mathrm{err} - N\sigma^2 + 2\sigma^2\sum_{i=1}^{N}\frac{\mathrm{d}\hat{f}(x_i)}{\mathrm{d}y_i} \qquad (6)$$

This is known as Stein's Unbiased Risk Estimator (SURE).

4.2. The Bayesian information criterion

A well studied method for estimating the degree of optimism OP is the BIC statistic, which is also known as the Schwarz criterion (Schwarz, 1978). BIC is a classical model selection criterion motivated in quite a different way from SURE. However it yields a very similar result. BIC has the generic form of

$$\mathrm{BIC} = -2\log lik + (\log N)p$$

where in the case of linear models p is the dimensionality of inputs.

Under the Gaussian model, assuming the variance σ^2 is known, Schwarz's procedure can be written as:

$$\mathrm{BIC} = (N/2\sigma^2)\left[\mathrm{err} + \frac{P}{N}(\log N)\sigma^2\right] \qquad (7)$$

5. Optimum number of basis functions for RBF networks

Based on SURE, the optimum number of basis functions should be assigned to have the minimum generalization error Err in Eq. (6). From the least squared solution of Eq. (2) we have

$$W = (\Phi^{\mathrm{T}}\Phi)^{-1}\Phi^{\mathrm{T}}Y$$

$$\hat{f} = \Phi W = \Phi(\Phi^{\mathrm{T}}\Phi)^{-1}\Phi^{\mathrm{T}}Y = HY \qquad (8)$$

where H depends on the input vector x_i but not on y_i. Note that in practice, Eq. (2) is solved using singular value decomposition to avoid problems due to possible ill-conditioning of the matrix Φ.

From Eq. (8) we can easily obtain the required derivative of $\hat{f}(x_i)$ with respect to y_i.

$$\sum_{i=1}^{N}\frac{\mathrm{d}\hat{f}(x_i)}{\mathrm{d}y_i} = \sum_{i=1}^{N}H_{ii}$$

Now, substituting this into Eq. (6) we obtain

$$\mathrm{Err} = \mathrm{err} - N\sigma^2 + 2\sigma^2\sum_{i=1}^{N}H_{ii}$$

Here we observe that $\sum_{i=1}^{N}H_{ii} = \mathrm{Trace}(H)$, the sum of the diagonal elements of H. Thus, we can obtain the further simplification that $\mathrm{Trace}(H) = \mathrm{Trace}(\Phi(\Phi^{\mathrm{T}}\Phi)^{-1}\Phi^{\mathrm{T}}) = \mathrm{Trace}(\Phi^{\mathrm{T}}\Phi)\Phi^{\mathrm{T}}\Phi)^{-1}) = \mathrm{Trace}(I) = p$, where p is the dimension of Φ. Since Φ is a projection of input matrix X onto a basis set spanned by M, the number of basis functions, one can show generally $p = M + 1$.

To use this method to find the optimum number of basis functions, we simply choose the model that obtains the smallest Err over the set of models considered. Given a set of models $\hat{f}_M(x)$ indexed by the number of basis functions, M, denote the training error for each model by $\mathrm{err}(M)$. We then obtain

$$\mathrm{Err}(M) = \mathrm{err}(M) - N\sigma^2 + 2\sigma^2(M+1) \qquad (9)$$

where N is the number of training samples and the noise, σ,^{2} can be estimated from the mean squared error of the model.

Based on the discussion in this section applying BIC to RBF networks is trivial. One just needs to substitute p with $M+1$ in Eq. (7) to obtain:

$$\mathrm{BIC}(M) = (N/2\sigma^2)[\mathrm{err}(M) + \frac{M+1}{N}(\log N)\sigma^2] \qquad (10)$$

5.1. Estimating unknown noise

The proposed criterion in Eq. (9) depends on the standard deviation of additive noise σ. In practice, however, the noise and therefore its standard deviation are often unknown. When this is the case, noise can be estimated from the training data as

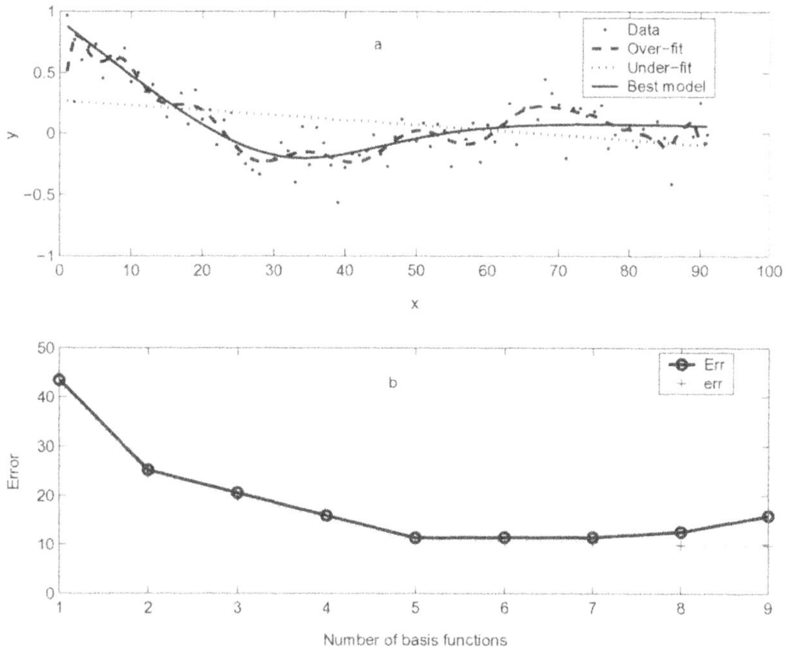

Fig. 2. (a) Overfitting, underfitting, and the best estimated model for $y = \sin(x)/x$. (b) Err obtained in Eq. (9) used to find the optimum number of basis functions for model $y = \sin(x)/x$.

$$\hat{\sigma}^2 = \frac{1}{N-p}\sum_i^n (\hat{y} - y) \tag{11}$$

In this case, one can use (11) in conjunction with (9) in one of two possible ways. In the first approach, noise is estimated via (11) using a high-variance/low-bias estimator, and then this estimate is plugged into (9) to select optimal model complexity. Under the second approach, noise is estimated via (11) for each model complexity. Therefore different estimation are used in Eq. (9) for each model complexity. In this paper we use the earlier approach to conduct empirical compression.

6. Experimental results

To explore the effectiveness of our complexity control method, we considered the problem of fitting a RBF network model to a set of points (Fig. 2). The goal is to minimize the squared generalization error Err. To determine the efficacy of the method we compared its performance to the well studied standard cross validation and BIC (Craven & Wahba, 1979).

We first conducted a simple series of experiments by fixing a uniform distribution on the unit interval [0,1], and then fixing various target functions $f: [0,1] \rightarrow R$. To generate training samples, a sequence of values $x_1, \ldots, x_t$ is drawn from [0,1], the target function values $f(x_1, \ldots, f(x_t)$ are computed, and independent Gaussian noise is added to each value. In the first step of RBF network training, centers μ_j and width parameter v_j are estimated using subtractive clustering (Chiu, 1994), an unsupervised training technique.

For a given training sample, the series of best fit functions corresponding to a number of basis functions $M = 1, 2, \ldots$ are computed. Given this sequence, the cross validation strategy will choose some particular model $\hat{f}^*_M$

Table 1
Fitting different target functions with $\sigma = 0.25$

Method	Target function Step ($x \geq 0.5$)	$\sin(\frac{1}{x})$	$\sin^2(2\pi x)$
σ_SURE	1.021	1.082	1.041
$\hat{\sigma}$_SURE	1.022	1.089	1.056
BIC	1.020	1.082	1.038
CV	1.074	1.083	1.029

The table reports ratio of test errors relative to best possible test error achieved by different methods. A smaller ratio is better. Results are reported at training sample sizes $N = 10$ and averaged over 100 repeated trials in each case. The first row corresponding to sure when σ is known and the second row shows sure when σ is estimated. BIC is evaluated when σ is known.

Table 2
Fitting different target functions with $\sigma = 0.25$

Method	Target function Step ($x \geq 0.5$)	$\sin(\frac{1}{x})$	$\sin^2(2\pi x)$
σ_SURE	1.0044	1.0068	1.0166
$\hat{\sigma}$_SURE	1.0049	1.0063	1.0169
BIC	1.0030	1.0063	1.0169
CV	1.0044	1.005	1.0181

The table reports ratio of test errors relative to best possible test error achieved by different methods. A smaller ratio is better. Results are reported at training sample size $N = 100$ and averaged over 100 repeated trials in each case. The first row corresponding to sure when σ is known and the second row shows sure when σ is estimated. BIC is evaluated when σ is known.

Table 3
Fitting different target functions with $\sigma = 0.25$

Method	Target function Step ($x \geq 0.5$)	$\sin(\frac{1}{x})$	$\sin^2(2\pi x)$
σ_SURE	1.0254	1.0686	1.0701
$\hat{\sigma}$_SURE	1.0292	1.0891	1.0672
BIC	1.0252	1.0681	1.0649
CV	1.0544	1.0721	1.0635

The table reports ratio of test errors relative to best possible test error achieved by different methods. A smaller ratio is better. Results are reported at training sample size $N = 10$ and $\sigma = 0.5$ and averaged over 100 repeated trials in each case. The first row corresponding to sure when σ is known and the second row shows sure when σ is estimated. BIC is evaluated when σ is known.

on the basis of the observed empirical errors on the validation data set (generated the same way as training data). Our technique will alternatively chose the model corresponding to minimum Err in Eq. (9) and BIC will select the model corresponding to min BIC in Eq. (10).

To determine the effectiveness of these strategies, the ratio of the test error of the model selected by them to the best test error on a new test data set among the models in sequence $M = 1, 2, \ldots$ is measured.

Tables 1–8 show the results obtained for fitting various functions. These results are obtained by repeatedly generating training samples of a fixed size, and recording the ratio of test error achieved relative to the best possible test error, for each technique (BIC, CV and SURE).

In another experiment we considered a highly nonlinear function distorted by Gaussian noise

$$z = 3(1 - x)^2 e^{(-(x^2)-(y+1)^2)} - 10\left(\frac{x}{5} - x^3 - y^5\right)e^{(-x^2-y^2)} - \frac{1}{3}e^{(-(x+1)^2-y^2)} + \varepsilon$$

$$\varepsilon \sim N(0, 0.25)$$

We call this function peaks. Here the goal is to estimate the true smooth function based on noisy observations (Figs. 3 and 4). In this experiment, our proposed criterion SURE and cross validation CV chose 35 basis functions,

Table 4
Fitting different target functions with $\sigma = 0.25$

Method	Target function Step ($x \geq 0.5$)	$\sin(\frac{1}{x})$	$\sin^2(2\pi x)$
σ_SURE	1.0056	1.0052	1.0120
$\hat{\sigma}$_SURE	1.0068	1.0045	1.0142
BIC	1.0031	1.0037	1.0112
CV	1.0050	1.0051	1.0132

The table reports ratio of test errors relative to best possible test error achieved by different methods. A smaller ratio is better. Results are reported at training sample size $N = 100$ and $\sigma = 0.5$ and averaged over 100 repeated trials in each case. The first row corresponding to sure when σ is known and the second row shows sure when σ is estimated. BIC is evaluated when σ is known.

Table 5
Fitting different target functions with $\sigma = 0.25$

Method	Target function Step ($x \geq 0.5$)	$\sin(\frac{1}{x})$	$\sin^2(2\pi x)$
σ_SURE	−0.3	0.57	−0.42
$\hat{\sigma}$_SURE	−0.1	0.24	−0.15
BIC	−0.33	0.54	−0.48
CV	−0.18	−0.22	−0.62

Table reports the difference between the optimum number of RBF functions and the number of RBF functions chosen by different techniques. Results are reported at training sample sizes $N = 10$ and averaged over 100 repeated trials in each case.

Table 6
Fitting different target functions with $\sigma = 0.25$

Method	Target function Step ($x \geq 0.5$)	$\sin(\frac{1}{x})$	$\sin^2(2\pi x)$
σ_SURE	0.14	0.37	0.41
$\hat{\sigma}$_SURE	0.41	0.07	0.57
BIC	−0.11	0.1	0.19
CV	0.51	0.15	0.57

Table reports the difference between the optimum number of RBF functions and the number of RBF functions chosen by different techniques. results are reported at training sample size $N = 100$ and $\sigma = 0.25$ and averaged over 100 repeated trials in each case.

Table 7
Fitting different target functions with $\sigma = 0.25$

Method	Target function Step ($x \geq 0.5$)	$\sin(\frac{1}{x})$	$\sin^2(2\pi x)$
σ_SURE	−0.33	0.09	0.01
$\hat{\sigma}$_SURE	−0.11	−0.4	0.18
BIC	−0.34	−0.01	−0.07
CV	−0.19	−0.32	0.19

Table reports the difference between the optimum number of RBF functions and the number of RBF functions chosen by different techniques. results are reported at training sample size $N = 100$ and $\sigma = 0.25$ and averaged over 100 repeated trials in each case.

Table 8
Fitting different target functions with $\sigma = 0.25$

Method	Target function Step ($x \geq 0.5$)	$\sin(\frac{1}{x})$	$\sin^2(2\pi x)$
σ_SURE	0.01	0.07	−0.19
$\hat{\sigma}$_SURE	0.22	−0.05	0.39
BIC	−0.19	−0.15	−0.53
CV	0.38	0.3	0.26

Table reports the difference between the optimum number of RBF functions and the number of RBF functions chosen by different techniques. results are reported at training sample size $N = 100$ and $\sigma = 0.25$ and averaged over 100 repeated trials in each case.

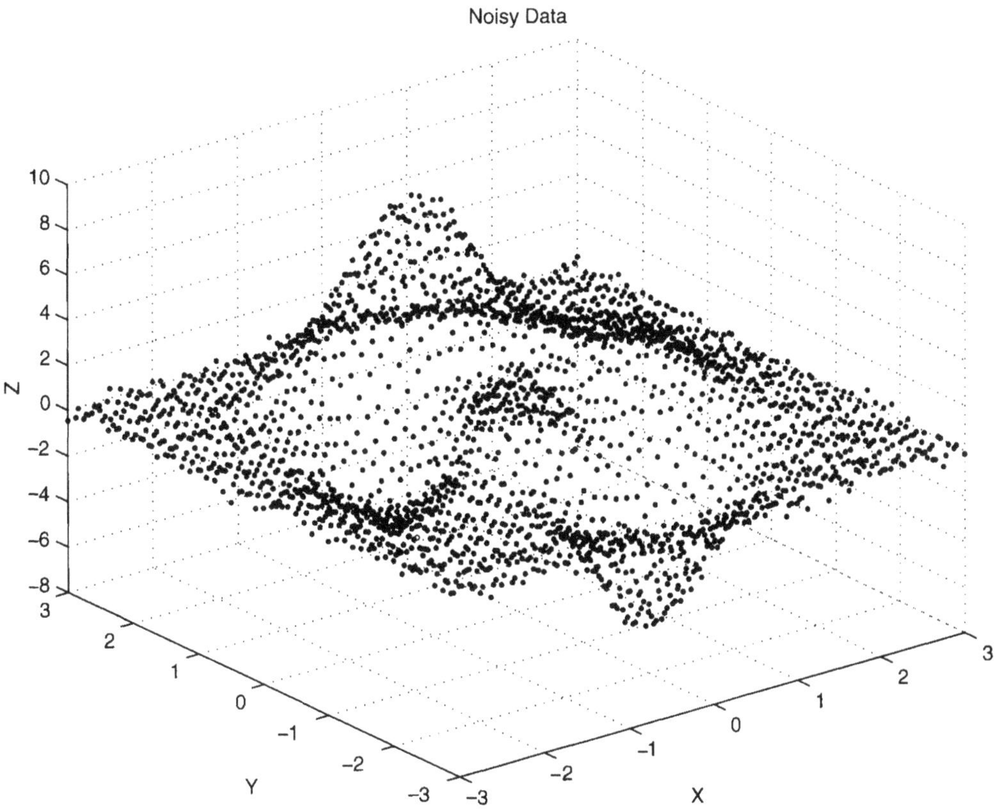

Fig. 3. Data generated in 3D dimensional space by nonlinear function 'Peaks', and distorted by additive Gaussian noise $N(0, 0.25)$.

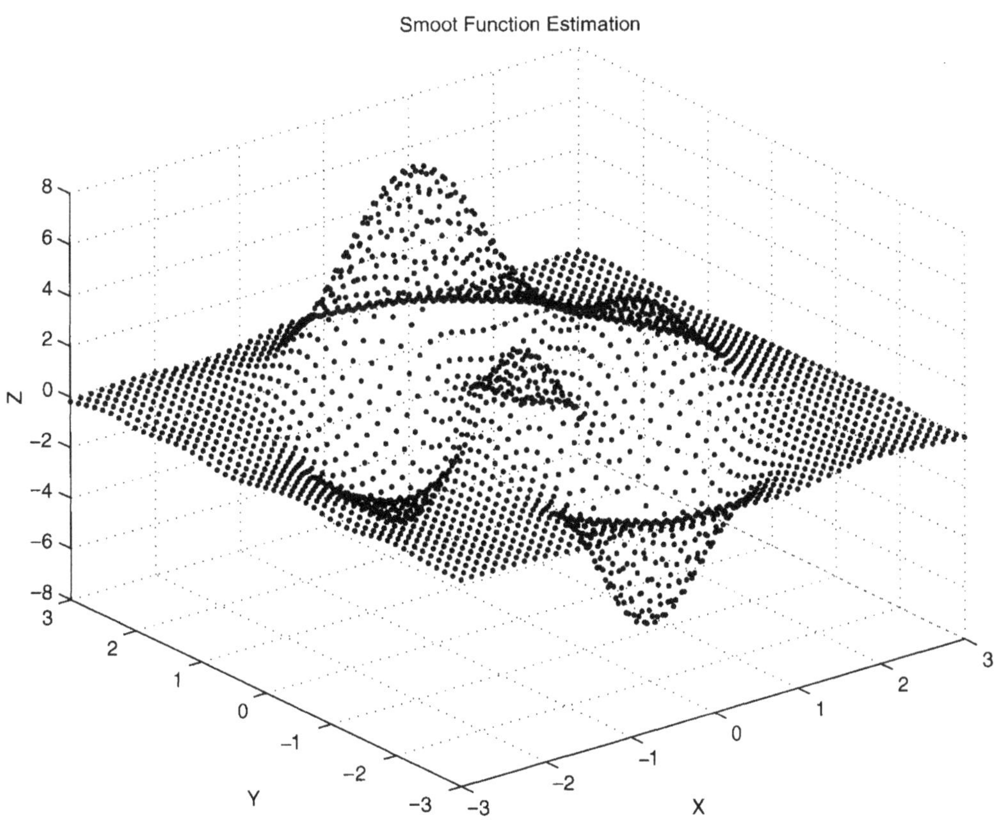

Fig. 4. The smooth true function 'Peaks' has been recovered from noisy observation. Err obtained in Eq. (9) used to find the optimum number of radial basis functions for the model.

and therefore they achieved the same generalization error on the test data. However, the SURE technique does not require an extra validation set to choose the number of basis functions, and in fact used half the data available to CV in this case. Therefore, we claim that it achieved more effective performance on this example.

The degree of optimism OP in BIC is similar to SURE. They produce the same result if the factor 2 in SURE is replaced by log N. This means that when $N > e^2$, BIC penalizes complex models more and gives preference to simpler models that SURE.

7. Conclusion

We have proposed a new approach to choosing the optimum number of basis functions for RBF networks. Our approach minimizes a theoretically unbiased estimate of generalization error of the model. Our experimental results validate the effectiveness of this approach. A comparison cross validation illustrates that the generalization error of the models selected by our approach can be less than models selected by cross validation. Importantly, this is achieved while requiring much less computation than cross validation. The utility of our method is greatest when there is insufficient data to hold out a validation set for cross validation.

Our method based on SURE and BIC behave similarly in our experiments. However one can show analytically that BIC generally gives preference to simpler models because it penalizes complex models more harshly.

References

Bishop, C. M. (1995). *Neural networks for pattern recognition*. Oxford: Oxford University Press.

Broomhead, D. S., & Lowe, D. (1988). Multivariable functional interpolation and adaptive networks. *Complex Systems*, *2*, 321–355.

Chiu, S. L. (1994). Fuzzy model identification based on cluster estimation. *Journal of Intelligent and Fuzzy Systems*, *2*, 267–278.

Craven, P., & Wahba, G. (1979). Smoothing noisy data with spline functions. *Numerical Mathematics*, *31*, 377–403.

Ker-Chau, L. (1985). From Stein's unbiased risk estimates to the method of generalized cross validation. *Annals of Statistics*, *13*(4), 1352–1377.

Moody, J., & Darken, C. J. (1989). Fast learning in networks of locally-tuned processing units. *Neural Computation*, *1*(2), 281–294.

Powell, M. J. D. (1987). Radial basis functions for multivariable interpolation: a review. In J. C. Mason, & M. G. Cox (Eds.), *Algorithms for approximation* (pp. 143–167). Oxford: Clarendon Press.

Schwarz, G. (1978). Estimating the dimension of a model. *Annals of Statistics*, *6*, 461–464.

Stein, M. C. (1981). Estimation of the mean of a multivariate normal distribution. *Annals of Statistics*, *9*(6), 1135–1151.

Sugeno, M., & Yasukawa, T. (1993). A fuzzy-logic-based approach to qualitative modeling. *IEEE Transaction on Fuzzy System*, *1*, 7–31.

Takagi, T., & Sugeno, M. (1985). Fuzzy identification of systems and its application to modeling and control. *IEEE Transaction on System Man and Cybernetics*, *SMC-15*(3), 116–132.

AVAILABLE AT
www.ComputerScienceWeb.com
POWERED BY SCIENCE DIRECT

PERGAMON

Neural Networks 16 (2003) 817–825

Neural Networks

www.elsevier.com/locate/neunet

2003 Special issue

Data smoothing regularization, multi-sets-learning, and problem solving strategies

Lei Xu*

Department of Computer Science and Engineering, Chinese University of Hong Kong, Shatin, NT, Hong Kong, China

Abstract

First, we briefly introduce the basic idea of data smoothing regularization, which was firstly proposed by Xu [Brain-like computing and intelligent information systems (1997) 241] for parameter learning in a way similar to Tikhonov regularization but with an easy solution to the difficulty of determining an appropriate hyper-parameter. Also, the roles of this regularization are demonstrated on Gaussian-mixture via smoothed versions of the EM algorithm, the BYY model selection criterion, adaptive harmony algorithm as well as its related Rival penalized competitive learning. Second, these studies are extended to a mixture of reconstruction errors of Gaussian types, which provides a new probabilistic formulation for the multi-sets learning approach [Proc. IEEE ICNN94 I (1994) 315] that learns multiple objects in typical geometrical structures such as points, lines, hyperplanes, circles, ellipses, and templates of given shapes. Finally, insights are provided on three problem solving strategies, namely the competition-penalty adaptation based learning, the global evidence accumulation based selection, and the guess-test based decision, with a general problem solving paradigm suggested.

Keywords: Data smoothing; Tikhonov regularization; Gaussian mixture; Multiple objects; Problem solving

1. Introduction

It is well understood that regularization is of key important for parametric modeling or neural networks learning on a finite set of samples. Several regularization techniques have been studied in the literature. They are closely related to the well known Tikhonov regularization (Tikhonov & Arsenin, 1977; Girosi, 1995), featured by adding to the fitting error with a regularizing term that is weighted by a so called hyper-parameter. Conceptually, this hyper-parameter can be further determined via one of several methods, including estimating generalization error bound, cross validation, Bayesian approach, and minimum description length, etc. In implementation, however, they not only suffer extensive computational cost but also are able to provide a rough solution only.

It is also well known for several decades, e.g. in the literatures of signal processing or control theory, that adding a noise with an appropriate variance to a finite set of samples will help parameter estimation or system modeling. In the literature of neural networks, it has been shown that training with noise is equivalent to Tikhonov regularization (Bishop, 1995).

When the size of noise samples are infinite or large enough, it follows from probability theory that adding noise to samples is equivalent to the convolution of the empirical density obtained directly from samples with a smoothing kernel function. This nature is directly used in a non-parametric density estimation under the name Parzen window estimation. When the kernel is a Gaussian function, we have

$$p_h(u) = \frac{1}{N}\sum_{t=1}^{N} G(u|u_t, \Sigma_h), \qquad \Sigma_h = h^2 I, \tag{1}$$

where and throughout this paper, $G(u|m, \Sigma)$ denotes a Gaussian density with a mean vector m and covariance matrix Σ. Particularly, $p_h(u)$ returns back to the empirical density when $h = 0$. That is,

$$p_0(u) = \frac{1}{N}\sum_{t=1}^{N} \delta(u - u_t). \tag{2}$$

Therefore, this h is usually called smoothing parameter and takes a role similar to the above noise variance and the hyper-parameter in Tikhonov regularization. Though

* Tel.: +852-2609-8423; fax: +852-2603-5024.
E-mail address: lxu@cse.cuhk.edu.hk (L. Xu).

0893-6080/03/$ - see front matter © 2003 Elsevier Science Ltd. All rights reserved.
doi:10.1016/S0893-6080(03)00119-9

many studies have been made theoretically on how to estimating an appropriate smoothing parameter (Devroye et al., 1996), in implementation they share difficulties similar to that discussed for determining a hyper-parameter.

The idea of data smoothing regularization came firstly in (Xu, 1997a–c) from using the Parzen window estimator by Eq. (1) in place of directly using empirical density by Eq. (2) on parameter learning of the Bayesian Ying Yang (BYY) system such that the effect of a finite size of samples is regularized via the smoothing role of an appropriate smoothing parameter h that is decided during learning. The BYY harmony learning was firstly proposed in 1995 (Xu, 1995a, 1996b) and systematically developed in the past several years (Xu, 2000a,b, 2001a,b, 2002, 2003). This BYY harmony learning acts as a general statistical learning framework such that not only a number of existing major learning problems and learning methods are revisited as special cases from a unified perspective, but also a harmony learning theory is developed with a new learning mechanism that makes model selection implemented either *automatically* during parameter learning or *subsequently after* parameter learning via a new class of model selection criteria obtained from this mechanism, with new insights and a series of new results. Further details are referred to Xu (2002, 2003).

After briefly introducing the basic idea of data smoothing regularization in Section 2, this paper will focus on its role in two types of finite mixture models via both the maximum likelihood (ML) learning and the BYY harmony learning. In Section 3, the roles of data smoothing regularization are demonstrated on Gaussian-mixture via smoothed versions of the EM algorithm, the BYY model selection criterion, adaptive harmony learning as well as its related Rival Penalized Competitive Learning (RPCL). In Section 4, these studies are extended to a mixture of reconstruction errors of Gaussian types as a new probabilistic formulation for the multi-sets learning approach (Xu, 1994) that learns multiple objects via typical geometrical structures such as points, lines, hyperplanes, circles, ellipses, and templates of given shapes. Moreover, insights are provided in Section 5 on three problem solving strategies, namely the competition-penalty adaptation based learning, the global evidence accumulation based selection, and the guess-test based decision, with a general problem solving paradigm suggested.

2. Data smoothing regularization

2.1. Data smoothing regularization

Given a parametric model $q(\mu|\theta)$, learning with data smoothing regularization is made via maximizing the following criterion (Xu, 1998a, 1999, 2002, 2003):

$$L_D(\theta, h) = L_h(\theta) + Z(h), \tag{3}$$

where $L_h(\theta)$ is a smoothed version of the likelihood function $L_0(\theta)$ as follows:

$$\begin{aligned} L_h(\theta) &= \int p_h(u)\ln q(u|\theta)\mathrm{d}u, \\ L_0(\theta) &= \int p_0(u)\ln q(u|\theta)\mathrm{d}u = \frac{1}{N}\sum_{t=1}^{N}\ln q(u_t|\theta), \end{aligned} \tag{4}$$

with the empirical density $p_0(u)$ replaced by $p_h(u)$. We have the following general form (Xu, 1999, 2002, 2003):

$$\begin{aligned} L_h(\theta) &\approx L_0(\theta) - 0.5R_h(\theta), \\ R_h(\theta) &= -\frac{1}{N}\sum_t Tr\left[\Sigma_h \frac{\partial^2 \ln q(u|\theta)}{\partial u\,\partial u^{\mathrm{T}}}\right]_{u=u_t}. \end{aligned} \tag{5}$$

It follows from $\Sigma_h = h^2 I$ that

$$R_h(\theta) = h^2\pi_q,\ \pi_q = -\frac{1}{N}\sum_t Tr\left[\frac{\partial^2 \ln q(u|\theta)}{\partial u\,\partial u^{\mathrm{T}}}\right]_{u=u_t}. \tag{6}$$

which provides a Tikhonov-type regularization (Tikhonov & Arsenin, 1977; Girosi, 1995) on $L_h(\theta)$ and the role h is equivalent to the hyper-parameter in (Bishop, 1995).

The new thing in Eq. (3) is that h can be decided by $\max_{\theta,h} L_h(\theta)$ due to the role of $Z(h)$, which can be one of two choices (Xu, 1998a, 1999, 2002, 2003):

$$Z(h) = \begin{cases} -\int p_h(u)\ln p_h(u)\mathrm{d}u, & \text{(a)}, \\ -\ln\sum_{t=1}^{N} p_h(u_t), & \text{(b)}. \end{cases} \tag{7}$$

In both the cases, it contains a dominated term $R_h(\theta)$ that increases as h increases. On the other hand, it follows from Eqs. (5) and (6) that $L_h(\theta)$ is maximized as $h \to 0$ since π_q is always non-negative. As a result, the trade-off of two aspects results in an appropriate value for h.

The two types of $Z(h)$ lead to two types of data smoothing regularization. It follows from Eq. (5) that

$$\begin{aligned} Z(h) &= 0.5\ln|\Sigma_h| + G(h) + \ln N + c_z,\quad c_z \text{ is constant}, \\ G(h) &= \begin{cases} \dfrac{-1}{N}\sum_{\tau=1}^{N}\ln\left[\sum_{t=1}^{N} \mathrm{e}^{-d_h(u_t,u_\tau)}\right], & \text{(a)}, \\ -\ln\sum_{\tau=1}^{N}\left[\sum_{t=1}^{N} \mathrm{e}^{-d_h(u_t,u_\tau)}\right], & \text{(b)}. \end{cases} \\ d_h(u_t, u_\tau) &= 0.5(u_t - u_\tau)^{\mathrm{T}}\Sigma_h^{-1}(u_t - u_\tau). \end{aligned} \tag{8}$$

As observed in Xu (2002), two types of regularization in Eq. (8) tends to being equivalent as the size N of samples increases to be large enough. The case (a) is more suitable when $q(u|\theta)$ is modeled directly via the smoothed likelihood

$L_h(\theta)$ in Eq. (3) but with no consideration on model selection. While the case (b) is more suitable for making the harmony learning with model selection (Xu, 2001a, 2002, 2003) on a Bayesian Ying–Yang system that represents $q(u|\theta)$ as its marginal density.

Moreover, it follows from Eq. (3) that the learning can be implemented by alternatively (Xu, 1998a–c)

$$\begin{aligned}&\text{(a) Estimating } \theta \text{ via } \max_\theta L_h(\theta) \text{ with } h \text{ fixed,}\\ &\text{(b) Estimating } h \text{ via } \max_h L_D(\theta, h) \text{ with } \theta \text{ fixed.}\end{aligned} \tag{9}$$

e.g. the step (b) can be made via the gradient ascent iteration:

$$h^{\text{new}} = h^{\text{old}} + \eta \Delta h, \qquad \Delta h = \frac{dL_D(\theta, h)}{dh}. \tag{10}$$

Alternatively, Δh can also simply given by (Xu, 1999)

$$\Delta h = \begin{cases} \eta, & \text{if } L_D(\theta, h+\eta) > L_D(\theta, h), \\ -\eta, & \text{if } L_D(\theta, h-\eta) > L_D(\theta, h), \\ 0, & \text{otherwise.} \end{cases} \tag{11}$$

In the following we further introduce the details of Eq. (9) in two typical situations:

(1) $\Sigma_h = h^2 I$ in Eq. (1). It applies to the cases that all the components in an observed sample vector should be equally smoothed, e.g. the case of estimating a density $q(x|\theta)$ or equivalently a joint density $q(x, z|\theta)$ that becomes the same as the former by $u = [x, z]$. In the case, we have Eq. (6). It further follows from Eqs. (5) and (8), $\max_h L_D(\theta, h)$ can be made via (Xu, 2002)

$$\frac{dL_D(\theta, h)}{dh} \approx -h\pi_q + d/h + dh_{u,0}^2/h^3,$$

$$h_{u,0}^2 = \frac{1}{d}\sum_{\tau=1}^{N}\sum_{t=1}^{N} p_{t,\tau}\|u_t - u_\tau\|^2,$$

$$p_{t,\tau} = \begin{cases} \dfrac{1}{N}\dfrac{e^{-d_h(u_t,u_\tau)}}{\sum_{t=1}^{N} e^{-d_h(u_t,u_\tau)}}, & \text{(a)}, \\[2ex] \dfrac{e^{-d_h(u_t,u_\tau)}}{\sum_{\tau=1}^{N}\sum_{t=1}^{N} e^{-d_h(u_t,u_\tau)}}, & \text{(b)}, \end{cases} \tag{12}$$

where d is the dimension of u. Thus, the estimation of h can be made via solving a positive root of $v^2\pi_q + vd + h_0^2 d = 0$ with $v = h^2$ and h_0^2 regarded approximately as a constant. That is,

$$h^2 = \frac{2h_{u,0}^2}{1 + \sqrt{1 + 4h_{u,0}^2 d^{-1}\pi_q}}. \tag{13}$$

which can be either used directly or as an initial value for Eq. (10).

(2) $\Sigma_h = \text{diag}[h_x^2 I_x, h_z^2 I_z]$ in Eq. (1) with h denoting a vector $[h_x, h_z]^{\text{T}}$. It applies to the cases that the components in an observed sample vector can be divided into two parts (Xu, 1999). Each part has a quite different statistical property and thus should be smoothed separately, where I_x, I_z denotes the unit matrix in the space of x, z, respectively. Correspondingly, $q(x, z|\theta) = q(z|x, \theta_{z|x})q(x|\theta_x)$ also has different structures on z, x. In the case, Eq. (6) is replaced with

$$\begin{aligned} R_h(\theta) &= 0.5h_x^2[\pi^x_{q(z|x)} + \pi^x_{q(x)}] + 0.5h_z^2\pi^z_{q(z|x)}, \\ \pi^x_{q(x)} &= -\frac{1}{N}\sum_t Tr\left[\frac{\partial^2 \ln q(x|\theta_x)}{\partial x\, \partial x^{\text{T}}}\right]_{x=x_t}, \\ \pi^x_{q(z|x)} &= -\frac{1}{N}\sum_t Tr\left[\frac{\partial^2 \ln q(z|x, \theta_{z|x})}{\partial x\, \partial x^{\text{T}}}\right]_{x=x_t, z=z_t}, \\ \pi^z_{q(z|x)} &= -\frac{1}{N}\sum_t Tr\left[\frac{\partial^2 \ln q(z|x, \theta_{z|x})}{\partial_z\, \partial_z^{\text{T}}}\right]_{x=x_t, z=z_t}. \end{aligned} \tag{14}$$

Moreover, Eq. (12) is replaced by

$$\begin{aligned} \frac{dL_D(\theta, h)}{dh_x} &\approx -h_x[\pi^x_{q(z|x)} + \pi^x_{q(x)}] + \frac{d_x}{h_x} + \frac{dh_{x,0}^2}{h_x^3}, \\ \frac{dL_D(\theta, h)}{dh_z} &\approx -h_z\pi^z_{q(z|x)} + \frac{d_z}{h_z} + \frac{dh_{z,0}^2}{h_z^3}. \end{aligned} \tag{15}$$

where d_x, d_z are the dimension of x, z, respectively, and $h_{x,0}^2$, $h_{z,0}^2$ are obtained from $h_{u,0}^2$ with u replaced by x, z, respectively. Thus, the root by Eq. (13) becomes

$$\begin{aligned} h_x^2 &= \frac{2h_{x,0}^2}{1 + \sqrt{1 + 4h_{x,0}^2 d_x^{-1}[\pi^x_{q(z|x)} + \pi^x_{q(x)}]}}, \\ h_z^2 &= \frac{2h_{z,0}^2}{1 + \sqrt{1 + 4h_{z,0}^2 d_z^{-1}\pi^z_{q(z|x)}}}. \end{aligned} \tag{16}$$

The above studies apply to both the case of estimating a joint density $q(z|x, \theta_{z|x})q(x|\theta_x)$ and the case of estimating a conditional density $q(z|x, \theta_{z|x})$ for supervised learning on the regression function $E(z|x) = \int zq(z|x, \theta_{z|x})dz$. Typical examples of the latter include three layer forward net, RBF nets and mixture of experts. To do so, we can set $q(x|\theta_x)$ to be either of the following two choices:

$$q(x|\theta_x) = \begin{cases} p_{h_x}(x), & \text{(a) by Eq. (1),} \\ p_o(x), & \text{(b) the unknown true density.} \end{cases} \tag{17}$$

Thus, we approximately have

$$\pi^x_{q(x)} = \begin{cases} -d/h_x^2, & \text{(a) by Eq. (1)} \\ -Tr[S^{-1}], & \text{(b) the unknown true density,} \end{cases} \tag{18}$$

where S is the sample covariance matrix estimated directly from samples of x (Xu, 1999). Thus, the maximum likelihood learning on $q(z|x, \theta_{z|x})$ with data smoothing regularization can be implemented via $\max_{\theta,h} L_h(\theta)$ with $\pi^x_{q(x)}$ substituted into Eqs. (14)–(16).

Being different from that in Eq. (8) of the case (a), an alternative estimate of $Z(h)$ is also given as follows (Xu, 1999, 2000b):

$$Z(h) = 0.5 \ln|\Sigma_h| - G(h) - 0.5d\frac{h_0^2 - e_0^2}{h^2},$$
$$e_0^2 = \frac{1}{dN}\sum_{\tau=1}^{N}\left\|u_t - \sum_{t=1}^{N} Np_{t,\tau}u_\tau\right\|^2, \quad (19)$$

where $p_{t,\tau}$ is same as in Eq. (12). We can get both $dL_D(\theta, h)/dh$ in Eq. (12) and h^2 in Eq. (13) simply with h_0^2 replaced by e_0^2. Similarly, we can get $e_{x,0}^2$, $e_{z,o}^2$ with u_t replaced by x_t, z_t, and then get $dL_D(\theta, h)/dh_x$ and $dL_D(\theta, h)/dh_z$ in Eq. (15) and h_x^2, h_z^2 in Eq. (16) with $h_{x,0}^2$, $h_{z,0}^2$ replaced by $e_{x,0}^2$, $e_{z,0}^2$. The difference between $Z(h)$ in Eq. (19) from that of the case (a) in Eq. (7) is whether the second order information within $p_h(u)$ is considered.

2.2. Historic remarks

The data smoothing learning by Eq. (3) with $Z(h)$ by the cases (a) in Eq. (7) came firstly from the implementation of BYY parameter learning via minimizing the Kullback–Leiber (KL) divergence between the Yang machine and Ying machine in the case of the backward architecture (Xu, 1995a, 1996b). With $p_h(x)$ by Eq. (1), it was firstly proposed under the name of data smoothing by Eq. (16) in Xu (1997b) and Eq. (3.10) in Xu (1997a) that an appropriate h is also learned via minimizing the KL divergence, which becomes equivalent to

$$\min_{\theta,h} \mathrm{KL}(\theta, h), \qquad \mathrm{KL}(\theta, h) = \int p_h(x)\ln\frac{p_h(x)}{q(x|\theta)}dx, \quad (20)$$

which was firstly presented by Eq. (7) in Xu (1997c). Obviously, it can be rewritten into Eq. (3) with $Z(h)$ given by the case (a) of Eq. (7). In a BYY system, $q(x|\theta) = \int q(x|y)q(y)dy$ is the marginal density represented by the Ying machine. Generally, being independent of the BYY system, $q(x|\theta)$ can be any parametric model for density estimation. Also in Xu (1997b), the data smoothing regularization is suggested on $q(z|x, \theta_{z|x})$ for supervised learning of three layer forward net and mixture of experts.

A preliminary systematic study on data smoothing regularization was provided in Xu (1998a), including (a) two ways to tackle the integral in $L_h(\theta)$; (b) the alternative strategy of Eq. (9); (c) extensions to estimating $q(z|x, \theta_{z|x})$ for supervised learning with three layer forward net, RBF nets and mixture of experts; (d) the role of h in the model selection by BYY harmony learning. Further progresses in all the four aspects were presented in Xu (1999), including (1) handling the integral in $L_h(\theta)$ in help of

$$\int G(x|x_t, h^2I)F(x)dx \approx F(x_t) + 0.5h^2Tr[H_F], \quad (21)$$

with H_F being the Hessian matrix of $F(x)$; (2) the use of Δh in Eq. (11) and the use of Eq. (21) in handling $-\int p_h(x) \ln p_h(x)dx$; (3) the use of Eq. (1) with $\Sigma_h = \mathrm{diag}[h_x^2 I_x, h_z^2 I_z]$ for estimating $q(z|x, \theta_{z|x})$; (d) the suggestion of the case (b) in Eq. (18) for learning of three layer forward net, RBF nets and mixture of experts.

A systematic summary can be found in Xu (2000b) on the studies of Eq. (3) with $Z(h)$ by the case (a) in Eq. (7). The data smoothing learning by Eq. (3) with $Z(h)$ by the case (b) in Eq. (7) was firstly proposed in Xu (2001b). The detailed equations as those introduced in Section 2.1 were firstly provided in Xu (2001a) and further discussions in comparison with the case (a) are made in Xu (2002, 2003).

3. Gaussian mixture and multi-sets-mixture

3.1. Gaussian mixture and smoothed EM algorithm

Specifically we start at considering a Gaussian mixture:

$$q(x|\theta) = \sum_{\ell=1}^{k} \alpha_\ell G(x|m_\ell, \Sigma_\ell). \quad (22)$$

Give a known k, as proposed in Xu (1997b), the estimation of can be implemented by the following smoothed EM algorithm:

$$E\text{ step}: p_{\ell,t} = \alpha_\ell G_t(\theta_\ell)/\sum_{\ell=1}^{k}\alpha_\ell G_t(\theta_\ell),$$
$$G_t(\theta_\ell) = G(x_t|m_\ell, \Sigma_\ell), \qquad \theta_\ell = \{m_\ell, \Sigma_\ell\} \quad (23)$$
$$M\text{ step}: \alpha_\ell = \frac{1}{N}\sum_{t=1}^{N} p_{\ell,t}, \qquad m_\ell = \frac{1}{N\alpha_\ell}\sum_{t=1}^{N} p_{\ell,t}x_t,$$
$$e(x_t, m_\ell) = x_t - m_\ell,$$
$$\Sigma_\ell = h^2 I + \frac{1}{N\alpha_\ell}\sum_{t=1}^{N} p_{\ell,t}e(x_t, m_l)e^{\mathrm{T}}(x_t, m_\ell),$$

which is different from the EM algorithm (Dempster, Laird & Rubin, 1977; Redner & Walker, 1984) with a smoothing parameter h^2 added to the diagonal elements of Σ_ℓ. Also, it follows from Eq. (5) that

$$\pi_q = -\frac{1}{N}\sum_{t=1}^{N}\sum_{\ell=1}^{k} p_{\ell,t}Tr[\Sigma_\ell^{-1}] = -\sum_{\ell=1}^{k}\alpha_\ell Tr[\Sigma_\ell^{-1}], \quad (24)$$

and the estimation of h^2 is made by Eq. (13) and can be further elaborated via Eq. (10).

When k is unknown, we need also to select an appropriate value for it. The task is called model selection, which is usually made on selecting a best value for k via

$\min_k J(k)$, with $J(k)$ called model selection criterion. In Xu (1997d), a criterion is proposed from the BYY harmony learning, without considering data smoothing regularization. Considering data smoothing regularization in the case of a finite size of samples, this criterion is further extended into (Xu, 2002):

$$J(k) = \sum_{\ell=1}^{k} \alpha_\ell \ln \frac{|\Sigma_\ell|^{0.5}}{\alpha_\ell} + 0.5h^2 \sum_{l=1}^{k} \alpha_\ell Tr[\Sigma_\ell^{-1}], \quad (25)$$

which returns to the one in Xu (1997d) if $h = 0$. As experimentally shown in Hu and Xu (2003), $J(k)$ with data smoothing can select the correct value of k on a data of a small size of samples, while the $J(k)$ by Eq. (25) with $h = 0$ (i.e. without data smoothing) sometimes fail to find the correct value of k. On a data set of enough number of samples, the above $J(k)$ without or with data smoothing can both select the correct value of k. On the same data set of a large size, however, typical existing criteria of the Akaike's information criterion (Akaike, 1974), the Schwarz's Bayesian inference criterion (Schwarz, 1978) or equivalently the minimum description length criterion (Rissanen, 1999) all result in wrong solutions.

Via the BYY harmony learning, k may also be selected in parallel automatically during estimating θ. For the Gaussian mixture by Eq. (22), the resulted algorithm is a modification of Eq. (23) with the E step simplified into the following hard-cut form

$$p_{\ell,t} = \begin{cases} 1, & \ell = \arg\max_j [\alpha_j G_t(\theta_j)], \\ 0, & \text{otherwise} \end{cases} . \quad (26)$$

As long as k is initially a number large enough, the competitive role of Eq. (26) will make α_j, that corresponds to an extra Gaussian, become very small or zero (Xu, 2001b, 2002). Thus, the corresponding Gaussian can be discarded with an appropriate number k determined automatically.

The winner-take-all (WTA) nature of Eq. (26) may cause the learning process to be stuck at a local solution (Xu 2001b), especially on a finite size of samples. This problem is compensated by the regularization of h^2 during the M-step.

The problem caused by this WTA can also be solved by another type of regularization called normalization that introduces a new conscience de-learning mechanism similar to the RPCL (Xu, Krzyzak, & Oja, 1993), which gets

$$c = \arg\min_j d_{j,t}, \qquad r = \arg\min_{j \neq c} d_j, t,$$

$$d_{j,t} = -\ln[\alpha_j G_t(\theta_j)], \qquad p_{\ell,t} = \begin{cases} 1, & \text{if } \ell = c, \\ -\gamma, & \text{if } \ell = r, \\ 0, & \text{otherwise,} \end{cases} \quad (27)$$

where γ approximately takes a value between [0.1, 0.05]. The first winner will learn while the second winner (or called rival) will be de-learned by a small degree. Though, RPCL learning was originally proposed in a heuristic way. It has been further found that it can be regarded as a simplification or a variant of BYY harmony learning with normalization regularization. The details are referred to Xu (2001b, 2002).

The RPCL learning algorithm, an adaptive version of Eq. (23) for maximum likelihood (ML) learning, and BYY harmony (H)-learning with the E step replaced by Eq. (26) can be unified into the following procedure:

$$(a)\ p_{\ell,t} = \begin{cases} \text{by Eq. (23),} & \text{ML-Learning,} \\ \text{by Eq. (26),} & \text{Harmony-Learning,} \\ \text{by Eq. (27)} & \text{RPCL-Learning,} \\ p(\ell|x_t) - \gamma q(\ell|x_t), & \text{A general form.} \end{cases}$$

where $p(\ell|x_t) \geq 0$,

$$\sum_{\ell=1}^{k} p(\ell|x_t) = 1; \quad q(\ell|x_t) \geq 0, \quad \sum_{\ell=1}^{k} q(\ell|x_t) = 1. \quad (28)$$

$$(b)\ \alpha_\ell = \beta_\ell^{2\text{new}} \Big/ \sum_{\ell=1}^{k} \beta_\ell^{2\text{new}},$$

$$\beta_\ell^{\text{new}} = \beta_\ell^{\text{old}} + \eta(p_{\ell,t} - \alpha_\ell^{\text{old}} \sum_{\ell=1}^{k} p_{\ell,t})/\beta_\ell^{\text{old}},$$

$$(c)\ m_\ell^{\text{new}} = m_\ell^{\text{old}} + \eta p_{\ell,t} e_{\ell,t}, \; e_{\ell,t} = x_t - m_\ell,$$

$$\Sigma_\ell = S_\ell S_\ell^{\text{T}}, \; S_\ell^{\text{new}} = S_\ell^{\text{old}} + \eta p_{\ell,t} G_{\Sigma_\ell}^{\text{old}} S_\ell^{\text{old}},$$

$$G_{\Sigma_\ell} = \Sigma_\ell^{-1} e_{\ell,t} e_{\ell,t}^{\text{T}} \Sigma_\ell^{-1} - \Sigma_\ell^{-1}.$$

where the updating rules on α_ℓ, Σ_ℓ guarantee the satisfaction, even when $p_{\ell,t} < 0$, that $\alpha_\ell \geq 0$, $\sum_{\ell=1}^{k} \times \alpha_\ell = 1$ and Σ_ℓ is non-negative definite. The general form of $p_{\ell,t} = p(\ell|x_t) - \gamma q(\ell|x_t)$ includes the other three cases as its special cases. When $\gamma = 0$, we get the ML-Learning case for $p(\ell|x_t) = p_{\ell,t}$ by Eq. (23) and the Harmony-Learning case for $p(\ell|x_t) = p_{\ell,t}$ by Eq. (26). When γ approximately takes a value between [0.1, 0.05], we get the RPCL-Learning when $p(\ell|x_t) = \bar{\delta}_{\ell,c}$, $q(\ell|x_t) = \bar{\delta}_{\ell,r}$ with c, r by Eq. (27) and

$$\bar{\delta}_{i,j} = \begin{cases} 1, & i = j, \\ 0, & i \neq j. \end{cases}$$

The general form also leads to the mentioned BYY harmony learning with normalization regularization when $p(\ell|x_t) = \bar{\delta}_{\ell,c}$ and

$$q(\ell|x_t) = \begin{cases} \dfrac{\alpha_j G(x_i(m_j, \Sigma_j))}{\sum_{\ell \in L_k} \alpha_\ell G(x_t|m_\ell, \Sigma_t)}, & j \in L_k, \\ 0, & \text{otherwise;} \end{cases}$$

where L_k consists of the first k labels of $\{1, \ldots, k\}$ that correspond the first k largest values of $\alpha_j G(x|m_j, \Sigma_j)$.

It leads to the RPCL learning again when $k = 2$ (Xu, 2001b and 2002).

3.2. Best modeling via a parametric set

Instead of representing multiple data sets with each Gaussian density for a data set, a multi-sets-mixture is more suitable for the fields of computer vision and image recognition, where we often encounter the tasks of detecting objects in typical shapes such as lines, circles, and ellipses, as well as pre-specified shapes. In these cases, we need to model multiple data sets with samples of each data set coming from an object of a given shape. Except for the simplest cases such as points and lines, a Gaussian density is not able to represent such a data set. The multi-sets-mixture or called multi-sets modeling is proposed for modeling these objects (Xu, 1994, 1995b).

Samples from each object consists of one deterministic part plus random noise. The deterministic part is described by a finite or continuous set $S(\theta)$ of real points in R^d, subject to a parametric set θ of a finite number of unknown parameters. Each $S(\theta)$ represents a shape such as a line, a curve, and an ellipsis, as well as a pre-specified shape.

Subject to such a set $S(\theta)$, a sample x is represented by

$$\hat{x} = \arg\min_{y\in S(\theta)} \varepsilon(x,y), \qquad \varepsilon(x,y) = \mathscr{C}(e(x,y)), e(x,y) = x - y, \tag{29}$$

where $\hat{x}$ is called the best reconstruction of x by $S(\theta)$, and $e(x,\theta) = e(x,\hat{x})$ is called the reconstruction error of $S(\theta)$ per sample x. Moreover, $\varepsilon(x,y)$ is a given measure for the discrepancy $e(x,y)$ such that $\varepsilon(x,y) \geq 0$ and $\varepsilon(x,y) = 0$ if and only if $e(x,y) = 0$ or $x = y$. The best modeling of $S(\theta)$ on a given set of samples is made by determining θ such that

$$\min_\theta \sum_{t=1}^N \min_{y\in S(\theta)} \varepsilon(x_t, y), \tag{30}$$

The most widely used $\varepsilon(x,y)$ is

$$\varepsilon(x,y) = e(x,y)^{\mathrm{T}}\Sigma^{-1}e(x,y), \tag{31}$$

which is called the Mahalanobis distance with Σ being positively defined. It returns to the square distance between x, y when $\Sigma = I$. In this case, we call $\hat{x}$ the least square reconstruction of x by $S(\theta)$, with

$$\varepsilon_2(x,\theta) = \|e(x,\theta)\|^2 = \min_{y\in S(\theta)} \|e(x,y)\|^2. \tag{32}$$

which is generally a minimizing procedure. However, $e(x,\theta)$ gets an explicit expression in the following special cases:

(a) a point $S(\theta) = \{a\}$: $e(x,\theta) = x - a$; (33)

(b) a line $S(\theta) = \{x : x - a \textit{ parallels } w - a\}$,

$$e(x,\theta) = [I - (w-a)(w-a)^{\mathrm{T}}](x-a);$$

(c) a plane $S(\theta) = \{x : (x-a)^{\mathrm{t}}(w-a) = 0\}$,

$$e(x,\theta) = \frac{(w-a)^{\mathrm{T}}(w-a)}{\|w-a\|};$$

(d) a subspace $S(\theta)$ spanned by W at the origin a,

$$e(x,\theta) = (I - W(W^{\mathrm{t}}W)^{-1}W^{\mathrm{t}})(x-a);$$

(e) a circle $S(\theta) = \{x : \|x-a\|^2 = c^2\}$,

$$e(x,\theta) = \|x-a\| - c;$$

(f) an ellipse

$$S(\theta) = \{x = [u,v]^{\mathrm{T}} : \frac{(u-u_0)^2}{a^2} + \frac{(v-v_0)^2}{b^2} = 1\},$$

$e(x,\theta) = x - \hat{x}$, with $\hat{x}$ as in Eq.(29).

$S(\theta)$ in the cases (b) and (c) consists of a line or a hyperplane, respectively, passing through a point a, and $S(\theta)$ in the case (d) consists of a *linear manifold*—a shifted subspace that locates at a point a. $S(\theta)$ in the case (e) consists of a *sphere* of radius c that locates at a. The corresponding error $\varepsilon_2(x,\theta)$ is actually the shortest distance of the point x to the line, hyperplane, linear manifold, sphere, and ellipse, respectively.

For the cases (a), (b), (c) and (d), the implementation of Eq. (30) can be made with an analytical solution, with a being the mean vector, w being the direction of either principal or minor component of the sample set, and W spans a principal subspace. For the case (e) and case (f), the implementation of Eq. (30) can be implemented via an iterative procedure, e.g. gradient descent. For all the cases, the implementation of Eq. (30) can also be made adaptively with the parameter θ updated per sample x_t via the descent direction of the gradient $\nabla_\theta\varepsilon_2(x_t,\theta)$.

More generally, given a set of samples $\mathscr{Y} = \{y_\tau\}_{\tau=1}^N$ that represents a contour of a specific shape, we have

$$S(\theta) = \{\lambda R(\phi)(y_\tau + a) : \forall y_\tau \in \mathscr{Y}\} \tag{34}$$

for a shape resulted from a displacement a, a rotation of an angle ϕ and a scaling by λ, where $R(\phi)$ is a rotation matrix and $\theta = \{a, \phi, \lambda\}$. Correspondingly, fitting the shape by Eq. (30) becomes

$$\min_\theta \sum_{t=1}^N \min_{y_\tau\in\mathscr{Y}} \|x_t - \lambda R(\phi)(y_\tau + a)\|^2. \tag{35}$$

3.3. Multi-sets-mixture and adaptive learning

When samples come from multiple objects, a number of $S(\theta_\ell)$, $\ell = 1,\cdots,k$ are needed. As shown in (Xu, 1994, 1995b), the multiple counterparts by the cases of (a), (b), (c) and (d) in Eq. (33) actually perform the mean square error k-means clustering, local principal component analysis (PCA), minor principal component analysis (MCA), local principal subspace analysis (PSA), and as well as its complementary local MSA.

Directly considering x, a multi-sets will correspond a mixture of non-Gaussian densities that is not easy to implement (Xu, 1995b, 1996a). However, considering the reconstruction error $e(x, \theta_\ell)$ from a Gaussian, we have the following Gaussian mixture

$$p(e|\theta) = \sum_{\ell=1}^{k} \alpha_\ell G(e|0, \Sigma_\ell), \quad (36)$$

which is a further extension of the mixture of exponential densities in (Xu, 1996a).

For each sample x_t, we get $e_{\ell,t} = e(x_t, \theta_\ell)$ for each $S(\theta_l)$ with the probability $p_{\ell,t} = p(\ell|x_t)$, and make learning with data smoothing regularization by maximizing

$$L_D(\theta, h) = \sum_{\ell=1}^{k}\left[\frac{1}{N}\sum_{t=1}^{N} p_{\ell,t}L_{\ell,t}(h) + Z_\ell(h)\right],$$
$$L_{\ell,t}(h) = \int G(e|e_{t,\ell}, h^2 I)\ln[\alpha_\ell G(e|0, \Sigma_\ell)]de, \quad (37)$$

where $Z_\ell(h)$ is same as in Eq. (8) with $e_{t,\ell}$ in place of u_t.

With h^2 fixed, learning can be modeled via the smoothed EM algorithm by Eq. (23) with $G_t(\theta_\ell) = G(e_{\ell,t}|0, \Sigma_\ell)$ and $e(x_t, m_\ell)$ replaced by $e(x_t, \theta_\ell)$, as well as

$$m_\ell = \frac{1}{N\alpha_\ell}\sum_{t=1}^{N} p_{\ell,t}x_t$$

replaced by

$$\theta_\ell = \arg\max_{\hat{\theta}_\ell} \frac{1}{N}\sum_{t=1}^{N} p_{\ell,t}e(x_t, \hat{\theta}_\ell)^{\mathrm{T}} \sum_\ell^{-1} e(x_t, \hat{\theta}_\ell). \quad (38)$$

which is usually solvable for those cases in Eq. (33) (Xu, 1994, 1995b).

Then, h^2 is updated by Eq. (10) or Eq. (11) or Eq. (13), with π_q still given by Eq. (24) and $\mathrm{d}L_D(\theta, h)/\mathrm{d}h$ by Eq. (12) but getting

$$p_{t,\tau} = \begin{cases} \dfrac{1}{N}\dfrac{\sum_{j=1}^{k} p_{j,t}\exp\left(\dfrac{-\|e_{j,t} - e_{jt}\|^2}{h^2}\right)}{\sum_{t=1}^{N}\sum_{j=1}^{k} p_{j,t}\exp\left(\dfrac{-\|e_{j,t} - e_{jt}\|^2}{h^2}\right)}, & \text{(a)}, \\[2ex] \dfrac{\sum_{\ell=1}^{k}\sum_{j=1}^{k} p_{j,\tau}p_{\ell,t}\exp\left(\dfrac{-\|e_{l,t} - e_{j\tau}\|^2}{h^2}\right)}{\sum_{\tau=1}^{N}\sum_{t=1}^{N}\sum_{\ell=1}^{k}\sum_{j=1}^{k} p_{j,\tau}p_{\ell,t}\exp\left(\dfrac{-\|e_{l,t} - e_{j\tau}\|^2}{h^2}\right)} & \text{(b)}, \end{cases}$$

Moreover, after parameter learning we can select k by the minimum of $J(k)$ via Eq. (25). Also, similar to the case of Eq. (22), we can replace the E step by Eq. (26) such that an appropriate number k is determined automatically during learning. With $G_t(\theta_\ell)=G(e_{\ell,t}|0,\Sigma_\ell)$ and $e_{\ell,t}=e(x_t,\theta_\ell)$, we get various types of adaptive algorithms as in Eq. (28). Particularly, when $\Sigma_\ell=\sigma_\ell^2 I$, the step (c) in Eq. (28) is simplified as follows

$$\sigma_\ell^{\mathrm{new}} = \sigma_\ell^{\mathrm{old}} - \frac{\eta p_{\ell,t}}{\sigma_\ell^{\mathrm{new}}}\left[1 - \frac{\|e(x,\theta_\ell)\|^2}{\sigma_\ell^{2\mathrm{old}}}\right],$$
$$\sigma_\ell^{2\mathrm{new}} = \sigma_\ell^{\mathrm{new}} * \sigma_\ell^{\mathrm{new}}, \quad (39)$$
$$\theta_\ell^{\mathrm{new}} = \theta_\ell^{\mathrm{old}} + \eta\nabla_{\theta_\ell}\|e(x,\theta_\ell)\|^2.$$

A preliminary case of Eqs. (28) and (39) at $\alpha_\ell=1/k$ and $\Sigma_\ell=\beta I$ for a given $\beta>0$ was proposed in (Xu, 1998c) for RPCL learning on a multi-sets.

4. Guess-test decision, competiton-penalty adaptation, and global evidence accumulation

The tasks of learning or modeling or problem solving in general can be understood mathematically as a mapping from the observation space $\mathcal{X}$ to a set Θ of hypotheses. A set $\{x_t\}$ comes from $\mathcal{X}$ with each $x \in \mathcal{X}$ called a sample or an evidence. The set Θ is either a finite or infinite set that represents a family of models with a given form of mathematical function and a parameter vector θ such that each fixed value of θ is an element or called a point of Θ, i.e. $\theta \in \Theta$ is a hypothesis that represents a specific mathematical model. A mapping from $\{x_t\}$ to one or several points in Θ indicates that one or several hypotheses are drawn as conclusions from the evidences in $\{x_t\}$. Generally, there are three fundamental strategies for these tasks:

(a) *Competition-penalty adaptation*. As discussed in this paper, we have $\theta_\ell \in \Theta$, $\ell = 1, \ldots, k$ that compete to adapt $\{x_t\}$ in $\mathcal{X}$ via making each θ_ℓ of the k variables move in Θ. All the movements are motivated to minimize a given cost function $C(\{x_t\}, \{\theta_\ell\})$ in a way that the trace of each moving variable is a continuous trace of improvements from a current hypothesis locally to a nearby hypothesis. Finally, the trace is trapped at a hypothesis that any moving to its nearby points has no improvement. Then, this hypothesis is taken as a conclusion. The advantage of this process is easy in implementation with only a small computing cost and memory. Also, it is adapted once an new evidence comes and we always have k hypotheses as current interpretations available. A main disadvantage is thus that the movements are made locally to neighbors only and thus likely trapped at conclusions of local optimal instead of being the best. Moreover, a strong competition among the k variables of θ_k will make the situation even worse. Usually one or more type of penalty is companied with this competition to reduce its negative effect.

(b) *Global evidence accumulation based selection*. As used by the well known Hough Transform (Hough, 1962), each point in Θ is considered as a candidate hypothesis. Each evidence x_t casts one vote to a subset of points in Θ as possible hypotheses. After voted by all evidences in $\{x_t\}$, those points that receive the number of votes large enough are taken as conclusions. The advantage of the approach is the conclusion is made via a global voting based on all evidences in $\{x_t\}$. The disadvantages is that the cost is very expensive in casting and storing all the votes, usually increasing exponentially with the dimension of θ.

(c) *Guess-test based decision.* As used by the RANSAC approach (Fischler and Bolles, 1981), a point θ of Θ is guessed from a few evidences in $\{x_t\}$, then a given testing criterion is used to check how many samples in $\{x_t\}$ are fitted by the model with this θ and how well this fitting. The guess is either taken as a conclusion if the test is passed or discarded if failed. Then, the next guess-test circle repeats. This approach has little memory cost. However, a simple algorithm that bases on only a few evidences is easy to give a wrong guess and too many wrong guess will cost a lot of computations. In contrast a complicated algorithm needs many computing cost but may not be able to considerably increase the accuracy of guessing. Similarly, a simple testing criterion will create many wrong solutions while a complicated criterion will waste a lot of computing times. Moreover, a testing made on a hypothesis may only give a local solution, instead of an optimal solution. Hence, many open issues remain, especially on making a testing on multiple hypotheses.

It can be observed that the above processes of learning, voting a subset of candidates, and guessing share a common point of providing certain hypotheses as candidates. A difference is that these hypotheses are simply taken as conclusions for (a) but will be further evaluated for (b) and (c). Also, though (b) and (c) share a common point that both evaluate candidate hypotheses before taking any conclusion, a difference is whether conclusions are based either on comparison after enough evidence accumulated for (b) or on a testing immediately following a guessing for (c).

Three strategies can all be regarded as the particular cases of **a general problem solving paradigm** that consists of

(i) Drawing candidate hypotheses from samples $\{x_t\}$,
(ii) Accumulating votes on the candidate hypotheses,
(iii) Selecting most likely hypotheses via comparison,
(iv) Testing the most likely hypotheses that become conclusions or rejected;
(v) Refining the conclusions (e.g. via local adaptation).

For a specific problem solving strategy, some of the above five ingredients may disappear, and the strength of each ingredient may be different. For examples, the above (a) consists of only the ingredient (i), made via a sophisticated learning process. The above (b) consists of the first three ingredients with (i) being enumerating simply each sample in $\{x_t\}$. The above (c) consists of the ingredient (iv) and the ingredient (i) that is simply random sampling.

By putting the focuses and strengths differently on the five ingredients, we may combine the advantages of the above (a) (b) and (c) and reduce the effect of their disadvantages. For an example, the Random Hough Transform (Xu & Oja, 1993) improves the disadvantages of the Hough Transform (Hough, 1962) via modifying the ingredient (i) to reduce the burden of the ingredient (ii) as well as via adding the ingredient (iv) to improve accuracy. For another example, we can implement the above (a) of learning that starts at different initializations to take the role of the ingredient (i), followed by all or a part of all the rest ingredients. Particularly, with learning on a mixture of multi-sets by Eqs. (34) and (35) as the ingredient (i), we can get an improved version of the generalized Hough Transform (Ballard, 1981).

5. Conclusions

The data smoothing based regularization not only provides an easy implementing solution to the difficulty of determining an appropriate hyper-parameter in Tikhonov like regularization for parameter learning, but also takes an important role in BYY harmony learning both on penalizing the WTA effect of the least complexity nature and on improving the performance of model selection criteria in the cases of a small size of samples. The roles are detailed via Gaussian-mixture with the smoothed EM algorithm, the smoothed BYY model selection criterion, adaptive algorithm as well as its related RPCL learning. Moreover, the studies are further extended to a reconstruction error based Gaussian mixture for multi-sets learning with data smoothing based regularization, which are suitable to tasks of modeling and recognizing multiple objects of typical geometrical shapes. Finally, insights are provided on three problem solving strategies, namely the competition-penalty adaptation based learning, the global evidence accumulation based selection, and the guess-test based decision, under the general problem solving paradigm.

Acknowledgements

The work described in this paper was fully supported by a grant from the Research Grant Council of the Hong Kong SAR (project No: CUHK4336/02E).

References

Akaike, H. (1974). A new look at the statistical model identification. *IEEE Transactions on Automatic Control*, *19*, 714–723.

Ballard, D. H. (1981). Generalizing the Hough transform to detecting arbitary shapes. *Pattern Recognition*, *13*(2), 111–122.

Bishop, C. M. (1995). Training with noise is equivalent to Tikhonov regularization. *Neural Computation*, *7*, 108–116.

Dempster, A. P., Laird, N. M., & Rubin, D. B. (1977). Maximum-likelihood from incomplete data via the EM algorithm. *Journal of Royal Statistical Society*, *B39*, 1–38.

Devroye, L., Györfi, L., & Lugosi, G. (1996). *A probability theory of pattern recognition*. Berlin: Springer.

Fischler, M. A., & Bolles, R. C. (1981). Random sample consensus: A paradigm for modeling fitting with applications to image analysis and automated cartography. *Communications of ACM*, *24*, 381–395.

Girosi, F., Jones, M., & Poggio, T. (1995). Regularization theory and neural architectures. *Neural Computation*, *7*, 219–269.

Hough, P. V. C (1962). *Method and means for recognizing complex patterns*. US Patent No. 3069654, December 18

Hu, X. L., & Xu, L. (2003). A comparative study of several cluster number selection criteria. *Proceedings of IDEAL03, March 21–23, Hong Kong*, in press.

Redner, R. A., & Walker, H. F. (1984). Mixture densities, maximum likelihood, and the EM algorithm. *SIAM Review*, *26*, 195–239.

Rissanen, J. (1999). Hypothesis selection and testing by the MDL principle. *Computer Journal*, *42*(4), 260–269.

Schwarz, G. (1978). Estimating the dimension of a model. *Annals of Statistics*, *6*, 461–464.

Tikhonov, A. N., & Arsenin, V. Y. (1977). *Solutions of ill-posed problems*. Baltimore, MD: Winston.

Xu, L. (1994). Multisets modeling learning: An unified theory for supervised and unsupervised learning. *Proceedings of IEEE ICNN94, June 26–July 2, 1994, Orlando, FL*, *I*, 315–320.

Xu, L. (1995a). Bayesian–Kullback coupled Ying–Yang machines: Unified learnings and new results on vector quantization. *Proceedings of ICONIP95, Oct 30–Nov 3, 1995, Beijing, China*, 977–988.

Xu, L. (1995b). A unified learning framework: Multisets modeling learning. *Proceedings of the 1995 World Congress on Neural Networks, July 17–21, 1995, Washington, DC*, *I*, 35–42.

Xu, L. (1996a). Bayesian–Kullback Ying–Yang learning scheme: Reviews and new results. *Proceedings of ICONIP96, Sept 24–27, 1996, Hong Kong*, *1*, 59–67.

Xu, L. (1996b). A unified learning scheme: Bayesian–Kullback Ying–Yang machine. *Advances in Neural Information Processing Systems*, *8*, 444–450.

Xu, L. (1997a). Bayesian Ying–Yang system and theory as a unified statistical learning approach: (I) Unsupervised and semi-unsupervised learning. In S. Amari, & N. Kassabov (Eds.), *Brain-like computing and intelligent information systems* (pp. 241–274). Berlin: Springer.

Xu, L. (1997b). Bayesian Ying–Yang system and theory as a unified statistical learning approach: (II) From unsupervised learning to supervised learning and temporal modeling. In K. W. Wong, I. King, & D. Y. Leung, (Eds.), *Theoretical aspects of neural computation: A multidisciplinary perspective* (pp. 25–42). Berlin: Springer.

Xu, L. (1997c). Bayesian Ying–Yang system and theory as a unified statistical learning approach: (II): Models and algorithms for dependence reduction, data dimension reduction, ICA and supervised learning. In K. W. Wong, I. King, & D. Y. Leung, (Eds.), *Theoretical aspects of neural computation: A multidisciplinary perspective*. Berlin: Springer.

Xu, L. (1997d). Bayesian Ying–Yang machine, clustering and number of clusters. *Pattern Recognition Letters*, *18*(11), 1167–1178.

Xu, L. (1998a). Bayesian Ying–Yang system and theory as a unified statistical learning approach (VII): Data smoothing. *Proceedings of ICONIP'98, Oct 21–23, 1998, Kitakyushu, Japan*, *1*, 243–248.

Xu, L. (1998b). BKYY three layer net learning, EM-like al-gorithm, and selection criterion for hidden unit number. *Proceedings of ICONIP'98, Oct 21–23, 1998, Kitakyushu, Japan*, *2*, 631–634.

Xu, L. (1998c). Rival penalized competitive learning, finite mixture, and multisets clustering. *Proceedings of IJCNN98, May 5–9, 1998, Anchorage, Alaska*, *II*, 2525–2530.

Xu, L. (1999). BYY data smoothing based learning on a small size of samples. *Proceedings of IJCNN'99, Washington, DC, USA, July 10–16*, *1*(6), 546–551.

Xu, L. (2000a). Temporal BYY learning for state space approach, hidden Markov model and blind source separation. *IEEE Transactions on Signal Processing*, *48*, 2132–2144.

Xu, L. (2000b). BYY learning system and theory for parameter estimation, data smoothing based regularization and model selection. *Neural, Parallel and Scientific Computations*, *8*, 55–82.

Xu, L. (2001a). BYY harmony learning, independent state space and generalized APT financial analyses. *IEEE Transactions on Neural Networks*, *12*(4), 822–849.

Xu, L. (2001b). Best harmony, unified RPCL and automated model selection for unsupervised and supervised learning on Gaussian mixtures, ME-RBF models and three-layer nets. *International Journal of Neural Systems*, *11*(1), 3–69.

Xu, L. (2002). BYY harmony learning, structural RPCL, and topological self-organizing on mixture models. *Neural Networks*, *15*, 1125–1151.

Xu, L. (2003). BYY learning, regularized implementation, and model selection on modular networks with one hidden layer of binary units. *Neurocomputing*, *51*, 277–301.

Xu, L., Krzyzak, A., & Oja, E. (1993). Rival penalized competitive learning for clustering analysis, RBF net and curve detection. *IEEE Transactions on Neural Networks*, *4*, 636–649.

Xu, L., & Oja, E. (1993). Randomized Hough transform (RHT): Basic mechanisms, algorithms and complexities. *Computer Vision, Graphics, and Image Processing: Image Understanding*, *57*(2), 131–154.

PERGAMON

AVAILABLE AT
www.ComputerScienceWeb.com
POWERED BY SCIENCE DIRECT

Neural Networks 16 (2003) 827–832

Neural Networks

www.elsevier.com/locate/neunet

2003 Special issue

Million city traveling salesman problem solution by divide and conquer clustering with adaptive resonance neural networks

Samuel A. Mulder[a,*], Donald C. Wunsch II[b]

[a]Applied Computational Intelligence Lab, Department of Computer Science, University of Missouri–Rolla, Rolla, MO 65401, USA
[b]Applied Computational Intelligence Lab, Department of Electrical and Computer Engineering, University of Missouri–Rolla, Rolla, MO 65401, USA

Abstract

The Traveling Salesman Problem (TSP) is a very hard optimization problem in the field of operations research. It has been shown to be NP-complete, and is an often-used benchmark for new optimization techniques. One of the main challenges with this problem is that standard, non-AI heuristic approaches such as the Lin–Kernighan algorithm (LK) and the chained LK variant are currently very effective and in wide use for the common fully connected, Euclidean variant that is considered here. This paper presents an algorithm that uses adaptive resonance theory (ART) in combination with a variation of the Lin–Kernighan local optimization algorithm to solve very large instances of the TSP. The primary advantage of this algorithm over traditional LK and chained-LK approaches is the increased scalability and parallelism allowed by the divide-and-conquer clustering paradigm. Tours obtained by the algorithm are lower quality, but scaling is much better and there is a high potential for increasing performance using parallel hardware.

Keywords: Traveling salesman problem; Lin–Kernighan algorithm; Adaptive resonance theory

1. Introduction

The Traveling Salesman Problem (TSP) is one of the most studied problems in computer science literature. It is an example of the important class of problems known as NP-complete problems. An NP-complete problem is one that is solvable in polynomial time by a non-deterministic algorithm, but not necessarily by a deterministic one. Another way of considering this class of problems is to say that a correct solution may be checked in polynomial time, but no known algorithm can solve the problem in that time. These problems are interesting because it is possible to draw parallels between any two NP-complete problems and show that finding an algorithm to solve one in polynomial time gives you an algorithm to solve the other. They are also interesting because it has never been proven that NP-complete problems cannot be solved in polynomial time, so it remains as an open question. The most general form of the TSP is to find a Hamiltonian cycle given an arbitrary graph. All known algorithms to solve this problem take greater than polynomial time, but if we have a solution we can check it in $O(n)$ time. The more specific case of the TSP considered in this paper is also NP-complete, but is more complicated to check.

The traveling salesman family of problems is an area in which neural networks have previously been unable to compete with the best non-neural approaches, in accuracy, speed, or scaling. (See (Vishwanathan & Wunsch, 2001) for a critique of the then-state-of-the-art in neural network approaches to TSP. Improvements in the past 2 years notwithstanding, accuracy, speed and scaling were significant limitations.) Accuracy remains an important limitation. In fact, it seems doubtful whether neural networks will ever exceed the accuracy of algorithms like the Lin–Kernighan solution (Lin & Kernighan, 1973) in solving this class of problems. Clustering algorithms in general are limited in the accuracy they can achieve on the TSP Table 1. If highly accurate tours are required, then Lin–Kernighan and variants (Applegate, Cook, & Rohe, 2000) seem likely to remain the algorithms of choice. In situations where accuracy is not the primary determinant, however, neural networks may show some promise. This is especially relevant for situations where significant modifications to (Lin & Kernighan, 1973) and (Applegate et al., 2000) may be required, as opposed to minor modifications and retraining, which is often all that is needed for a neural network.

* Corresponding author.
E-mail addresses: smulder@umr.edu (S.A. Mulder), dwunsch@ece.umr.edu (D.C. Wunsch II).

0893-6080/03/$ - see front matter © 2003 Elsevier Science Ltd. All rights reserved.
doi:10.1016/S0893-6080(03)00130-8

Our goal then is to evaluate what advantages a neural clustering algorithm can bring to bear on the problem and decide how to best exploit those advantages. Adaptive resonance theory (ART) provides a very rapid and effective neural clustering model. Functionally, it operates similarly to k-means clustering, with an optimal k determined dynamically by the vigilance factor. The divide and conquer paradigm gives us the flexibility to hierarchically break large problems into arbitrarily small clusters depending on what trade-off between accuracy and speed is desired. In addition, the sub-problems provide an excellent opportunity to take advantage of parallel systems for further optimization. Even without parallel processing, the algorithm developed in this paper has demonstrated that better scaling is possible using a divide and conquer approach.

1.1. Traveling salesman problem

Given a complete undirected graph $G = (V, E)$, where V is a set of vertices and E is a set of edges each relating two vertices with an associated non-negative integer costs $c(u, v)$, the most general form of the TSP is equivalent to finding any Hamiltonian cycle over G where such a cycle is known as a tour. The more common form of the problem is the optimization problem of trying to find the shortest Hamiltonian cycle. Both of these problems have been proven to be NP-complete in (Cormen, Leiserson, & Rivest, 1996). These problems are very useful to consider because they map so easily to many real-world applications in a wide range of fields from network routing to cryptography (Agarwala, Applegate, Maglott, Schuler, & Schaffler, 2000; Bailey, McLain, & Beard, 2003; Turino, 2002).

The variation of the TSP that we (and most neural network approaches to this topic) consider is even more limited. We look only at graphs that can be mapped to a two-dimensional Euclidean coordinate system, where the edge weight between two nodes is the distance between them. This system implies that the triangle inequality holds: $c(u, w) \leq c(u, v) + c(v, w)$. We also require that the XY coordinates of each node be given. This variation can be shown to still be NP-complete and therefore to map onto the more general problem (Papadimitriou, 1977). The Euclidean form of the TSP has been widely studied (Aurora, 1998; Braun & Buhmann, 2002; Cochrane & Cochrane, 1999).

1.2. Adaptive resonance theory

ART was first introduced by Carpenter and Grossberg (1988). The unsupervised variants provide a simple, effective neural clustering algorithm. The original algorithm, designated ART1, used binary input sequences. The variation developed for this solution uses two-input integer sequences where the integers are the XY coordinates of a node. In this form, ART is functionally similar to k-means clustering except that k is increased dynamically as new patterns are introduced.

1.3. Local search techniques

By far the most successful algorithms in tackling large-scale (1000 + cities) TSPs have been the family of algorithms known as local search heuristics (Johnson & McGeoch, 2002). The basic idea of local search is to start with some tour, either randomly generated or generated by some fast but low quality method, and make iterative improvements, hopefully driving it towards the optimal. In many ways this resembles the neural network technique of starting with random initial weights and then making incremental improvements via a technique like steepest descent, in an attempt to minimize errors. In the case of the TSP, the error to be minimized may be seen as the tour length. The local search class of algorithms considers a series of minor changes to determine whether they reduce the tour length.

A simple local search technique that has been easy to implement is to consider the result of swapping any two edges currently in the tour with two new edges in such a way that a valid tour still exists. In a permutation representation of the tour, this change can be seen as the operation of flipping a segment of the tour. By repeatedly searching for the flip that minimizes the tour length, and stopping when no flips can be found that reduce the tour length, a shorter tour may be discovered. Once no shorter tour can be found through this method, the tour is said to be locally optimal. This specific algorithm is referred to in the literature as 2-Opt. There is a general class of algorithms of this nature that involve substituting a fixed number of edges with new edges such that a valid tour is maintained. These are referred to as k-Opt algorithms. An $(n + 1)$-Opt algorithm, where n is the number of cities in the problem, will always find the optimal solution, i.e. the optimal solution is at most $n + 1$ edges away from the current tour (Rego & Glover, 2002)

Considering the time complexity of k-Opt algorithms, it immediately becomes obvious that large values of k are not practical. A naïve implementation of 2-Opt requires $O(n^2)$ time, and in general a k-Opt algorithm requires $O(n^k)$ time. A number of improvements to this family of algorithms have been considered to reduce this running time. The primary improvement in terms of running time has been the use of bounded neighbor lists. With this modification, the nearest h neighbors are calculated for each city, and the search for edges to swap is restricted to this list of neighbors for each city. This neighbor list may be generated in a number of different ways, but in the general case require time $O(n^2 \log h)$, which may be reduced to $O(n \log n)$ in the case of Euclidean TSPs using k–d trees (Johnson & McGeoch, 2002). The main problem with this improvement is that it limits the quality of tours generated, since it restricts which edges are considered for improvement. In practice, the speed-up is so large and the difference in solution is so small that this improvement is almost universally applied. Cases may be constructed, however, where it causes very poor tours to be found.

1.4. The Lin–Kernighan local optimization algorithm

The current best results on large-scale TSP instances come from variations on an algorithm proposed by Lin and Kernighan (1973), (Rego & Glover, 2002). This algorithm takes a randomly selected tour and optimizes it by stages until a local minimum is found. This result is saved and a new random tour selected to begin the process again. Given enough time, the optimal tour can be found for any instance of the problem, although in practice this is limited to small instances for an absolute result due to time constraints. Even with extremely large instances, however, reasonably short tours can be found (Johnson & McGeoch, 2002).

The optimizations performed by the Lin–Kernighan (LK) algorithm use the concept of λ-optimality. If n is the number of cities in a TSP, then we know that given any tour we can reach an optimal tour by swapping at most n edges. Using λ-optimality, we consider the optimal tour that can be reached by swapping only λ edges. As λ grows, the chance that the λ-optimal tour is actually optimal increases. Unfortunately, the processing time required to find λ-optimal tours is intractable for large λ. The largest commonly used values for λ are 2 and 3, although some attempts have been made with λ as 4 or 5 (Lin & Kernighan, 1973).

The algorithm proposed by Lin and Kernighan examines variable λ optimization. In brief, an initial 2-edge swap is chosen. The algorithm then examines whether it would be profitable to make a 3-edge swap, and continues increasing the number of edges as long as the total swap remains an improvement over the initial tour. This process is repeated with each node being considered in turn as a starting point for the initial 2-edge swap until no further improvements can be found. The original algorithm then started with a different random tour and worked from the beginning, always saving the best tour seen. This original algorithm is what is used in our current algorithm. Applying more advanced variants of LK will likely yield even better results (Johnson & McGeoch, 2002).

Table 1
Algorithm Pseudocode

```
Read data from file
Apply ART algorithm to cluster data
For each cluster
   Apply LK optimization
   Apply intersection removal
   Apply LK optimization
   Merge with final tour
End for
Save final tour and time
```

2. Algorithm-divide and conquer

The algorithm developed in this paper combines ART and the LK local optimization algorithm to divide and conquer instances of the TSP. We begin by reading in the cities, stored in TSP–LIB format (Moscoto, 2002). The ordering of the cities in memory represents the current tour at any time. This is known as a permutation representation and obviously only works with fully connected variants of the TSP, as an arbitrary permutation of a non-fully connected graph would not necessarily represent a valid tour. This permutation representation is chosen because weight-matrix representations become intractable for large values of n, i.e. a 250k-city problem would require around 62.5 GB of memory to store an edge-weight matrix. Since the problem is Euclidean, it is sufficient to store (X, Y) coordinates for each city and calculate distances on the fly.

The first stage of the algorithm involves sorting the cities into clusters using the ART algorithm described previously. Our variation of ART uses the vigilance parameter to set a maximum distance from the current pattern. A vigilance parameter between 0 and 1 is considered and used as a percentage of the global space to determine the vigilance distance. Values were chosen based on the number and size of individual clusters desired, but typical values ranged from 0.80 to 0.97. The learning rate was set to 0.02. The clusters at this point were still in a random order. The individual clusters were then each passed to a version of the LK algorithm also described above. Since the size of the tours was controlled and kept under a thousand cities, we allowed the LK search depth to be infinite as long as the total improvement for a given swap series remained positive. We also did not restrict the neighborhood size as specified in the original algorithm. This required more time than a limited depth search, but resulted in better overall tour quality. After a first pass through the LK algorithm, a simple intersection removal algorithm was applied. This algorithm is based on the idea that any tour containing an intersection between two edges is demonstrably sub-optimal. Typically after LK is run, few intersections remain, but those that do remain often involve edges crossing large distances. Swapping these edges changes the global search space sufficiently that a new run of LK can often find additional improvement. In short, the intersection removal algorithm is capable of making double-bridge swaps that the LK algorithm is unable to discover. This double-bridge property is the same as that used in the chained LK algorithms described in (Applegate et al., 2000).

Now we are faced with the problem of combining a number of sub-tours back into one complete tour. This may be accomplished by adding the cluster tours into a combined tour, one at a time. Obviously the order in which the tours are added back is important. To minimize the cost added by inter-tour edges, it is important to add tours that are adjacent to the current combined tour. Our method for accomplishing this is to add the tours in order of increasing distance from the origin. It is not clear whether this is the optimal solution, and this is an area for future research. The other major factor involved with merging the tours is running time. Since this a potentially global operation, care must be exercised in the nature of the algorithm. For example, attempting to find an optimal linking between the two tours could be at least an $O(n_g^2)$ algorithm, which is unacceptable, because the n involved would be the total number of cities, not just the cities in a tour. To avoid the $O(n_g^2)$ global operation, we first find the centroid of the cluster to be added. This is just the average of the X and Y coordinates of each city in the cluster, and is easily calculated in $O(n_c)$, where the n involved is the size of an individual cluster. We then find the k nearest cities to that centroid in the combined tour. Clearly, this operation requires $O(n_g)$ time. Next, we consider each of the k cities from the main tour to determine the cost of inserting the cluster tour in place of the following edge. This involves the comparison of k cities to n_c cities to determine the lowest cost matching, yielding a running time of $O(k^* n_c)$, where $k \ll n_g$. Finally, the cluster tour is inserted into the merged tour at the best location discovered.

3. Results

The results from our experiments were very encouraging. In all these results, the cities were distributed randomly (uniform distribution), generated by the generation algorithm provided at the TSPLIB web site (Moscoto, 2002). All experiments were run on a 2 GHz AMD Athlon MP processor with 512 M of DDR RAM. In Tables 2 and 3 below, we compare our clustered variation of the LK algorithm to the original LK algorithm. The LK algorithm used for these comparisons is that same algorithm that we implemented and used on the clusters of our main algorithm. Since the focus of these experiments was to determine the effects of clustering, the LK implementation is not heavily optimized and the running times reflect are only to be used in comparison to each other. In this implementation of the LK algorithm, neighborhoods were not used. Instead, the algorithm compared all possible swaps at a given level. This resulted in relatively slow running times. Further below, a more representative LK implementation is benchmarked against our technique. However, in Tables 2 and 3 results, some noteworthy items are already apparent.

Table 2
original Lin–Kernighan algorithm implemented by author

TSP size	Tour length	Time (s)
1000	2.63808e7	5
2000	3.64058e7	21
4000	5.07807e7	82
20000	1.12221e8	4814

Table 3
Clustered Lin–Kernighan

TSP size	Tour Length	Time (s)	Off LK (%)
1000	2.69785e7	1	2
2000	3.80334e7	3	4
4000	5.35437e7	8	5
20000	1.17e8	98	4

Table 4
Concorde chained LK

TSP size	Tour length	Time (s)
10000	7.20532e7	38
20000	1.01468e8	85
250000	3.58274e8	1380

Obviously the clustered variation is scaling much better than the original, and tour quality is remaining within 5% or so. Also, with the clustered version we can smoothly trade time for quality in either direction by adjusting the vigilance factor.

In the second set of experiments, we compare our algorithm with an improved version of the LK algorithm, the Concorde software package. This version incorporates the limited neighborhood structure that most implementations of the LK algorithm use, as well as additional optimizations. Concorde is widely regarded as the fastest TSP solver, for large instances, currently in existence. Concorde is described in more detail in (Applegate, Bixby, Chvatal, & Cook, 2001). Essentially, it uses the chained LK algorithm. Search depth for LK is greatly limited, but high quality is obtained by repeatedly applying double-bridge transformations and optimizing. The Concorde (Table 4) package also applies a simple algorithm to generate an initial tour of fair quality before beginning that provides a large speed boost to the LK algorithm. These techniques could also be implemented in our clustered variation giving similar speed and quality improvements. For now we are just interested in the scalability of the relative algorithms.

In Table 5, we can clearly see that while our algorithm is below the quality of tour that the chained-LK algorithm produces, it is scaling nicely. Our quality-of-result numbers, reported in the last column of Table 5, are comparable with previously published neural net results for much smaller TSP problems, see (Vishwanathan & Wunsch, 2001). In fact, our algorithm gives us additional flexibility in terms of changing the vigilance factor to generate different numbers of clusters. To illustrate this, Table 6 shows the results of the 250k city problem as the vigilance parameter is adjusted.

Table 5
Clustered Lin–Kernighan

TSP size	Tour length	Time (s)	Off CLK (%)
10000	8.21277e8	57	14
20000	1.17e8	98	15
250000	4.27169e8	693	19

Table 6
Clustered Lin–Kernighan 250k city problem

Vigilance	Tour length	Time (s)	% off CLK
0.95	4.09444e8	2451	14
0.96	4.18222e8	1077	17
0.97	4.27169e8	693	19
0.98	4.47744e8	778	25

As is clear from the table, increasing the vigilance parameter increases the speed at the expense of tour quality. We also observe the limit of 0.97 for this particular problem past, which the time begins to increase instead of decrease. This is the point where the individual constant factors involved with processing each cluster begin to outweigh the advantages of having smaller clusters. The actual vigilance parameter chosen depends largely on the quality of tour needed and the time available.

As a further experiment, a version of the program was developed which used a neighborhood structure similar to that used in the Concord package, as well as other algorithm optimizations described in (Johnson & McGeoch, 2002). This resulted in significant speed and quality increases are seen in the comparison provided by Tables 7 and 8. It also gives an opportunity to illustrate the potential scalability of our technique. At the 1,000,000-city level, our solution is just 11% off of the Concorde algorithm results, but only takes 16% as long to run. (Because of the much longer run time of the Concorde algorithm, some intermediate size problems are omitted, thus the blank spaces in the last column of Table 7 and the shorter Table 8.)

Table 7
New clustered LK algorithm results for randomly distributed TSP

Cities (#)	Tour length	Time	Vigilance	Off (%)
1000	2.58499E + 07	0.422	0.7	10.40
2000	3.61019E + 07	1.031	0.7	10.64
4000	5.07564E + 07	2.484	0.7	
6000	6.20307E + 07	5.141	0.72	
8000	7.13997E + 07	8.328	0.72	10.97
10,000	7.96673E + 07	11.359	0.75	10.57
20,000	1.12156E + 08	24.641	0.8	10.53
30,000	1.37686E + 08	35.407	0.82	
50,000	1.78731E + 08	61.985	0.83	
85,000	2.33053E + 08	104.094	0.85	
100,000	2.53306E + 08	122.407	0.86	
250,000	3.99968E + 08	315.078	0.92	11.64
500,000	5.64177E + 08	667.375	0.95	
750,000	6.91278E + 08	1015.890	0.96	
1,000,000	7.93896E + 08	1468.165	0.97	11.03

Table 8
Concorde results for randomly distributed TSP

Cities (#)	Tour length	Time
1000	2.34148E + 07	1.670
2000	3.26303E + 07	3.500
8000	6.43398E + 07	26.570
10,000	7.20532E + 07	37.620
20,000	1.01468E + 08	84.830
250,000	3.58274E + 08	1379.540
1,000,000	7.15058E + 08	9013.530

4. Conclusions

Our main result is the potential of combining neural clustering with traditional local search techniques. A significant speedup was shown by using clustering in combination with the original Lin–Kernighan algorithm. This speedup was offset by a 2–5% loss in tour quality that is the result of the inherent limitations of clustering when applied to the TSP. Clustering approaches will typically be unable to locate a global minimum because they assume a certain structure on the underlying data that may be sub-optimal. In most real-world situations, however, finding the absolute global minimum is not a requirement. Most applications prefer speed to tour quality within limitations. While our current implementation doesn't beat the latest chained-LK techniques, with heavy optimization, developed over many years of research, it does scale better, and gives additional flexibility when trading tour quality for speed. The modified version of the algorithm, incorporating many of the latest improvements in the LK algorithm, appears to scale on the order of $O(n^*\lg n)$. Scaling was shown through one million cities. In addition, since the number of global operations is limited in our algorithm, it should scale smoothly with parallel hardware and show significant improvement over current solutions.

Acknowledgements

The authors gratefully acknowledge support from the National Science Foundation and M.K. Finley endowment.

References

Agarwala, R., Applegate, D.L., Maglott, D., Schuler, G.D., & Schaffler, A.A (2000). *A fast and scalable radiation hybrid map construction and integration strategy*. http://www.ncbi.nlm.nih.gov/genome/rhmap/

Applegate, D., Bixby, R., Chvatal, V., & Cook, W (2001). *Concorde—A code for solving traveling salesman problems*. http://www.math.princeton.edu/tsp/concorde.html

Applegate, D., Cook, W., & Rohe, A (2000). *Chained Lin–Kernighan for large traveling salesman problems*. Technical report http://www.keck.caam.rice.edu/reports/chained lk.ps

Aurora, S. (1998). Polynomial time approximation schemes for {Euclidean} traveling salesman and other geometric problems. *Journal of the ACM*, *45*(5), 753–782.

Bailey, C. A., McLain, T. W., & Beard, R. W. (2003). Fuel saving strategies for dual spacecraft interferometry missions. *Journal of the Astronatical Science*, in press.

Braun, M. L., & Buhmann, J. M. (2002). The noisy Euclidean traveling salesman problem and learning. *Advances in neural information processing systems*. Cambridge, MA: MIT Press.

Carpenter, G., & Grossberg, S. (1988). The art of adaptive pattern recognition by a self-organizing neural network. *IEEE Computer, March*, 47–88.

Cochrane, E. M., & Cochrane, J. M. (1999). Exploring competition and co-operation for solving the Euclidean traveling salesman problem by using the self-organizing map. *Artificial Neural Networks*, *1*, 180–185.

Cormen, T., Leiserson, C., & Rivest, R. (1996). *Introduction to algorithms*. Cambridge, MA: MIT Press, pp. 954–960.

Johnson, D., & McGeoch, L. (2002). Experimental analysis of heuristics for the STSP. In G. Gutin, & A. Punnen (Eds.), *The traveling salesman problem and its variations* (pp. 369–487). Boston: Kluwer Academic Publishers.

Lin, S., & Kernighan, B. W. (1973). An effective heuristic algorithm for the traveling salesman problem. *Operations Research*, *21*, 498–516.

Moscoto, P (2002). *TSPBIBHome Page*. http://www.densis.fee.unicamp.br/~moscato/TSPBIB_home.html

Papadimitriou, C. H. (1977). The Euclidean traveling salesman problem is NP-complete. *Theoretical Computer Science*, *4*, 237–244.

Rego, C., & Glover, F. (2002). Local search and metaheuristics. In G. Gutin, & A. Punnen (Eds.), *The traveling salesman problem and its variations* (pp. 309–368). Boston: Kluwer Academic Publishers.

Turino, J (2002). *ASIC DFT and BIST Alternatives*. http://www.chipcenter.com/asic/tn004.html

Vishwanathan, N., & Wunsch, D (2001). A Hybrid Approach to the TSP. *IEEE International Joint Conference on Neural Networks, Washington, DC*.

AVAILABLE AT
www.ComputerScienceWeb.com
POWERED BY SCIENCE DIRECT

PERGAMON

Neural Networks 16 (2003) 833–839

Neural Networks

www.elsevier.com/locate/neunet

2003 Special issue

A practical sub-space adaptive filter

A. Zaknich

Centre for Intelligent Information Processing Systems (CIIPS), University of Western Australia, Crawley, WA 6009, Australia

Abstract

A Sub-Space Adaptive Filter (SSAF) model is developed using, as a basis, the Modified Probabilistic Neural Network (MPNN) and its extension the Tuneable Approximate Piecewise Linear Regression (TAPLR) model. The TAPLR model can be adjusted by a single smoothing parameter continuously from the best piecewise linear model in each sub-space to the best approximately piecewise linear model over the whole data space. A suitable value in between ensures that all neighbouring piecewise linear models merge together smoothly at their boundaries. This model was developed by altering the form of the MPNN, a network used for general nonlinear regression. The MPNNs special structure allows it to be easily used to model a process by appropriately weighting piecewise linear models associated with each of the network's radial basis functions. The model has now been further extended to allow each piecewise linear model section to be adapted separately as new data flows through it. By doing this, the proposed SSAF model represents a learning/filtering method for nonlinear processes that provides one solution to the stability/plasticity dilemma associated with standard adaptive filters.

Keywords: Sub-space; Adaptive filter; Modified probabilistic neural network; General regression neural network; Approximate piecewise linear regression; Integrated sensory intelligent system; Common bandwidth radial basis function

1. Introduction

Standard linear or nonlinear filter systems have no specific mechanism built into them that prevents old learning to be progressively lost as new data, representing new operating states, flows through them. In a learning context this is referred to as the stability-plasticity dilemma. Typical adaptive filter systems are deliberately designed to readapt, in this way, to new operating states as they occur. However, this can pose a problem if large changes are occurring faster than the system can adequately readapt to them. For these special circumstances, it would be very desirable to have an efficient adaptive learning system that retains all the features and benefits of the standard adaptive system but that is also able to retain a useful degree of old learning. In this way, as the process switches to a new distant state very quickly the system can immediately start adapting from the closest learned state available from previous experiences. For stationary processes the system would eventually build a complete model of the whole process as it experiences the full range of operating states. Continued adaptation then only occurs as a result of noise fluctuations. For nonstationary processes the system would eventually build up a set of learned starting points available for each new adaptation instance, which is better than an initial zero or random start.

The system specification described above can be achieved by making a suitable extension to the Tuneable Approximate Piecewise Linear Regression (TAPLR) model (Zaknich & Attikiouzel, 2000), which is based on the Modified Probabilistic Neural Network (MPNN) structure (Zaknich, 1998). The MPNN structure has a set of weighted Radial Basis Functions (RBFs), having common bandwidths, that cover the input data space. It is possible to associate a separate adaptive linear filter model with each RBF and to only adapt the filter that is within the sphere of influence of that RBF at any given point in time. In the standard MPNN the centres of each RBF in the input space are typically computed as the mean of all the input training vectors within a local vicinity of the RBF. Each RBF in the network has a scalar weight Z_i associated with it that typically represents the density of training points (points used to compute its centre) within each RBFs sphere of influence. In the proposed multiple Sub-Space Adaptive Filter (SSAF) model vector points used to develop the RBFs are not necessarily directly related to the filter input vectors and their associated desired filter outputs. The adaptation mechanism can be controlled by any measurable state vector meaningful

0893-6080/03/$ - see front matter © 2003 Elsevier Science Ltd. All rights reserved.
doi:10.1016/S0893-6080(03)00096-0

to the filtering process. Also, the weighting factor Z_i can be used for a number of different possible purposes depending on the needs of the design. It can represent training density as before, represent a priori probability of occurrence of data in its RBFs region for filter operation, or be set to be proportional to the distance of separation of neighbouring RBFs, in order to provide an appropriate weighting between neighbouring linear filter models.

A number of other multiple model approaches similar to the proposed method have been developed in recent years. One of these is based on a combination of piecewise polynomials (Heredia & Arce, 2000). This method also uses an additive combination of multiple kernels, which constitute localised models to cover the data space. The main difference is related to kernel shape parameter selection. In the proposed SSAF model the kernels are all RBFs having a common bandwidth (a single smoothing parameter σ). Heredia and Arce's method finds appropriate parameters for its more complex kernels via linear optimisation. Another somewhat similar approach is the off-line multiple model approach used by (Simani, Fantuzzi, Rovatti, & Beghelli, 2000). They do not use local kernels, but they do combine multiple affine models to cover the data space and force continuity constraints among local affine models by solving an optimization problem. Their parameter estimation algorithm is based on the well established Frisch scheme (Frisch, 1934).

A promising on-line approach that arranges linear filters and thresholds in a tree structure was previously proposed by (Gelfand & Ravishankar, 1993). They developed a stochastic gradient based training algorithm to adapt both filter coefficients and thresholds at the nodes of the tree as well as to prune the tree. Their method performs a sequential, hierarchical partitioning of the input space into polygonal domains and a pruning procedure selects a suitable tree size. Although this method does offer robust estimation and fast adaptation of linear filters it suffers from the problem that training at parent nodes is not completed prior to training at offspring nodes. Therefore, data at non-root node filters have a complicated nonstationary and dependent character, and consequently stabilisation with penalty methods is required. Nevertheless, it is a conceptually simple and computationally efficient method (Gelfand, Krogmeiern, & Balasubramanian, 1995).

The SSAF model has many applications but its application to audio and underwater acoustic signal modelling, equalisation and filtering systems is of particular interest. This is because SSAF model can be used to provide a convenient and practical model of system responses and signal propagation through either a changing homogeneous or nonhomogeneous three-dimensional (3D) medium based on measured data. In these types of applications it is possible that only properties of arbitrary locales of the medium change at any time, in which case training and filters in other locales need not be affected. Consequently, these types of environments can be very difficult to analytically model throughout, especially when their properties are changing over space and time in quite complex ways.

The main contribution of this paper is a practical and conceptually simple method for smoothly coupling and selecting multiple linear (or affine) or nonlinear adaptive filter models using common bandwidth RBFs to cover the operating data space. Although the method is not strictly optimal it does provide a convenient way of fine tuning based on a single smoothing parameter, being the common bandwidth of the RBFs.

This paper provides reviews of the MPNN and APLR models in Sections 2 and 3 as a background for the development of the SSAF model in Section 4. Hints for suitable applications are provided with two representative problem developments in Section 5. Section 6 discusses some relevant issues related to the method, including suitable training strategies as well as possible extensions of the idea.

2. Review of the MPNN model

The MPNN was developed for application to general signal processing problems (Zaknich, 1998). It is effectively a generalisation of Specht's General Regression Neural Network (GRNN) (Specht, 1991) and is related to his Probabilistic Neural Network (PNN) classifier (Specht, 1990). The MPNN and GRNN have fundamental similarities with the method of (Moody & Darken, 1989); the method of RBFs (Powell, 1985); and a number of other nonparametric kernel based regression techniques inspired by the work of (Nadaraya, 1964) and (Watson, 1964).

If it can be assumed that for each local region in the input vector space, represented by the centre vector $\mathbf{c}_i$, there is a corresponding scalar output y_i that it maps into, then a convenient general model to use for all forms of the MPNN and the GRNN is

$$\hat{y}(\mathbf{x}) = \frac{\sum_{i=1}^{M} Z_i y_i f_i(\|\mathbf{x}-\mathbf{c}_i\|, \sigma)}{\sum_{i=1}^{M} Z_i f_i(\|\mathbf{x}-\mathbf{c}_i\|, \sigma)} \tag{1}$$

where

$f_i(\|\mathbf{x}-\mathbf{c}_i\|, \sigma)$ is a common bandwidth RBF

$\mathbf{c}_i$	centre vector i in the input space
σ_i	single learning parameter chosen during training
y_i	scalar training output i related to $\mathbf{c}_i$
M	number of RBF centre vectors $\mathbf{c}_i$
Z_i	number of training vectors $\mathbf{x}_j$ associated with $\mathbf{c}_i$
L	total number of training vector pairs= $\sum_{i=1}^{M} Z_i$.

Eq. (1) represents the GRNN if all the $Z_i = 1$, the y_i are real valued, the centre vectors $\mathbf{c}_i$ are replaced with individual training vectors $\mathbf{x}_i$ and $M = L$. A Gaussian RBF, with a bandwidth of σ (typically modelling the noise standard deviation), is often used for $f_i(\mathbf{x})$ as defined by

$$f_i(\|\mathbf{x} - \mathbf{c}_i\|, \sigma = \exp\frac{-(\mathbf{x} - \mathbf{c}_i)^{\mathrm{T}}(\mathbf{x} - \mathbf{c}_i)}{2\sigma^2} \quad (2)$$

Eq. (2) can be more conveniently represented by

$$f_i(d_i, \sigma) = \exp\left(\frac{-d_i^2}{2\sigma^2}\right) \quad (3)$$

where

$$d_i = \|\mathbf{x} - \mathbf{c}_i\| = \sqrt{(\mathbf{x} - \mathbf{c}_i)^{\mathrm{T}}(\mathbf{x} - \mathbf{c}_i)},$$

One simple way the MPNN set of training vector pairs $\{(\mathbf{c}_i, y_i)|i = 1, ..., M\}$ can be formed is through a form of vector quantisation, where the input space is firstly partitioned into uniform hypercubes. Then, $\mathbf{c}_i$ is made to be the mean of all training input vectors $\mathbf{x}_j$ in each hypercube that map to y_i. The value y_i is computed as the mean of the corresponding outputs y_j. These outputs must be sufficiently close to each other to be adequately represented by their mean. In this way a local group of vectors in the input space can be replaced with a single centre vector that maps to a single mean output value. The value Z_i is simply the number of associated vectors $\mathbf{x}_j$ averaged to make centre vector $\mathbf{c}_i$. If training samples are taken randomly from the process, Z_i could be interpreted as being proportional to the a priori probability of occurrence. A number of different hypercube sizes can be systematically tested to choose the best one. There are various strategies for constructing the network based on Eq. (1) depending on the application and its requirements (Zaknich, 1998).

Training then simply involves finding the single optimal learning parameter σ giving the minimum Mean Squared Error (MSE) of the network output minus the desired output for a representative testing set of known sample vector pairs $\{(\mathbf{x}_k, \mathbf{y}_k)|k = 1, ..., \mathrm{NUM}\}$. In typical applications there is a unique bandwidth σ that produces the minimum MSE between the network output and the desired output for the testing set (independent of the training set) and can be found quite easily by trial and error. Since the relation between σ and MSE is usually smooth with a broad minimal MSE section the value of σ is often not overly critical for adequate performance.

The MPNN model can be described as a semiparametric model and produces more efficient networks than the nonparametric GRNN model, but it can still be quite large and inefficient. A way to make the MPNN smaller without compromising accuracy is to convert it to an Approximate Piecewise Linear Regression (APLR) model as described in Section 3.

3. Review of the approximate piecewise linear regression model

The APLR model (4) can be formed by first partitioning the input space into uniform hypercubes as is done for the MPNN. When the centre vectors $\mathbf{c}_i$ are found the Z_i number of corresponding input vectors $\mathbf{x}_j$ are used to create a set of best fit least squares linear regression models $l_i(\mathbf{x})$ associated with each of the centres. The outputs y_i in Eq. (1) are then replaced with the outputs of the linear models $l_i(\mathbf{x})$ for all input vectors during operation. When this is done the linear model outputs provide more accurate mappings from the input to the output space within each hypercube than to the fixed means y_i of the MPNN. Consequently, the input space hypercubes can be made much larger and fewer, resulting in a much smaller network size (smaller M) for comparable accuracy.

In the APLR model the adjustment of σ during training controls the degree of weighting of each linear model associated with each centre. Input vectors closest to a centre will activate the associated linear model more than for those further away. For very small σ the linear model associated with the centre closest to the current input point will dominate, resulting in a linear response in the local space of that centre. For very large σ the network output will approach an unweighted biased average of all the linear models. Somewhere in between an optimal model will result that provides approximately linear operation close to each centre, and possibly deviating significantly from linearity close to centre boundaries. At the boundaries a smooth merging of neighbouring linear models occurs

$$\hat{y}(\mathbf{x}) = \frac{\sum_{i=1}^{M} Z_i l_i(\mathbf{x}) f_i(\|\mathbf{x} - \mathbf{c}_i\|, \sigma)}{\sum_{i=1}^{M} Z_i f_i(\|\mathbf{x} - \mathbf{c}_i\|, \sigma} \quad (4)$$

where

$\mathbf{x}$	arbitrary input space vector
$\mathbf{c}_i$	centre vector i in the input space
σ	single learning parameter chosen during training
$l_i(\mathbf{x})$	linear output model related to centre $\mathbf{c}_i$
M	number of RBF centre vectors $\mathbf{c}_i$
Z_i	number of training $\mathbf{x}_j$ associated with $\mathbf{c}_i$
L	total number of training vector pairs= $\sum_{i=1}^{M} Z_i$.

A simple one-dimensional (1D) illustration of an APLR model, typical of a loudspeaker amplitude frequency response, is shown by Figs. 1 and 2. Fig. 1 shows an arbitrary continuous and differentiable function $g(x)$, which is modelled by five ($M = 5$) linear (actually affine)

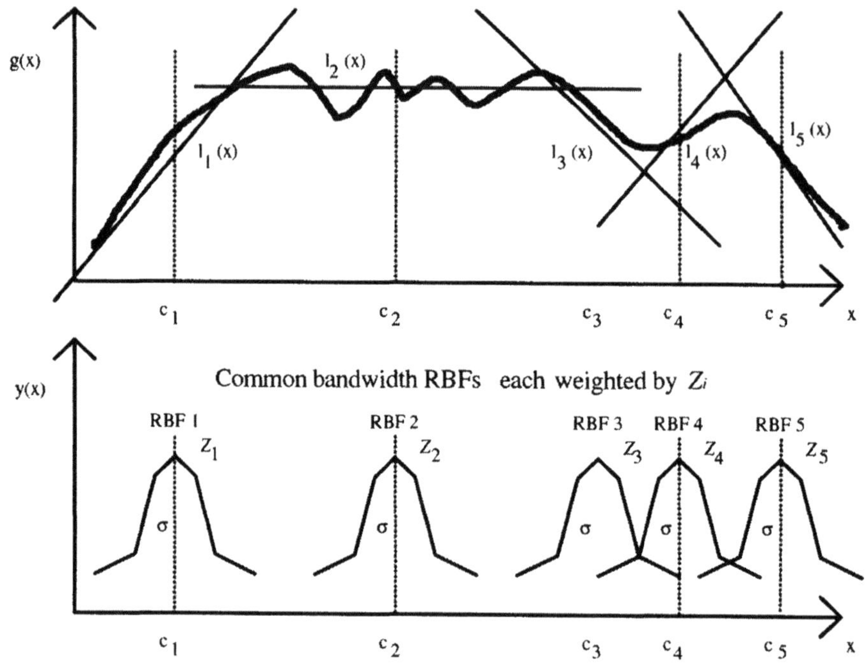

Fig. 1. Illustrative 1D example of the APLR model.

sections ($i = 1, \ldots, 5$) each associated with its own RBF_i and centre c_i in the input space x. Fig. 2 shows what the resulting APLR model might look like after selection of suitable σ and Z_i values. In this example the Z_i values would be proportional to the distances of separation between RBFs. For example, Z_1 would be larger than say, Z_4 because RBF_1 needs to span more space that RBF_2 in order to provide appropriate weighting between respective linear models $l_1(x)$ and $l_4(x)$ and their respective neighbouring models.

Linear model $l_2(x)$ in Fig. 1 provides more smoothing than the others and consequently contributes more overall regression error to the result. This may still be acceptable for a given design specification, but if not it is just a matter of adding more linear (or affine) models to region 2 to improve regression accuracy. Another quite acceptable solution may be to make model $l_2(x)$ a suitable order of polynomial or even a Multi-Layer Perceptron (MLP). There is nothing in the APLR structure that prevents the mixing of linear and nonlinear models in appropriate sections. However, retaining a set of linear models throughout may provide a simpler design at the expense of model efficiency. It can be easily appreciated that each of the models $l_i(x)$ may either be computed off-line and fixed and/or simply adapted as new training data becomes available.

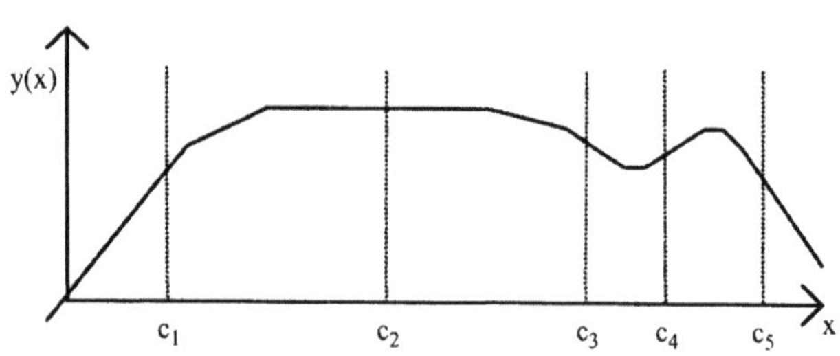

Fig. 2. APLR model regression result.

4. The sub-space adaptive filter model

A slight modification to the APLR model (Zaknich & Attikiouzel, 2000) in conjunction with an adaptive mechanism forms the basis to the proposed SSAF model. We now define the linear models $l_i(x)$ in Eq. (5) as filter models. The main difference between Eqs. (4) and (5) is that in Eq. (5) the RBFs are formed in a chosen process state space $\mathbf{z}$, which is not necessarily the same as the input space $\mathbf{x}$, but in practice often is. The process state space $\mathbf{z}$ represents some general aspect of the process that can be measured, monitored and used to determine when a particular filter model $l_i(\mathbf{x})$ should take effect. Z_i becomes a filter model weight that can be arbitrarily adjusted or set independently of training vector numbers (proportional to a priori probability density of training vectors)

$$\hat{y}(\mathbf{x}, \mathbf{z}) = \frac{\sum_{i=1}^{M} Z_i l_i(\mathbf{x}) f_i(\|\mathbf{z} - \mathbf{cz}_i\|, \sigma}{\sum_{i=1}^{M} Z_i f_i(\|\mathbf{z} - \mathbf{cz}_i\|, \sigma)} \tag{5}$$

where

$\mathbf{x}$ arbitrary filter input space vector
$\mathbf{z}$ arbitrary process state vector associated with $\mathbf{z}$. Often $\mathbf{z} \equiv \mathbf{x}$

$\mathbf{cz}_i$	RBF centre vector i in the process state space
σ	single learning parameter chosen during tuning
$l_i(\mathbf{x})$	linear filter model output related to centre $\mathbf{cz}_i$
M	number of RBF centre vectors $\mathbf{cz}_i$
Z_i	weight associated with model $l_i(\mathbf{x})$ and $\mathbf{cz}_i$.

The SSAF model is created from Eq. (5) by adding a suitable adaptation mechanism similar to that of the MPNN (Zaknich & deSilva, 1997). Refer to Fig. 3. In MPNN the network parameters associated with a particular RBF_i were adapted, for a given input/output pair, only if

$$f_i(\|\mathbf{x}-\mathbf{c}_i\|,\sigma) \geq f_k(\|\mathbf{x}-\mathbf{c}_k\|,\sigma), \qquad \forall \neq i.$$

For the SSAF model the adaptation condition, for a given input/output pair and process state vector $\mathbf{z}$, is defined by Eq. (6). The SSAF model is basically the adaptive version of the Integrated Sensory Intelligent System (ISIS) model described in Zaknich (2003). In Zaknich (2003) the ISIS model is used to model a nonlinear detector to solve an underwater Doppler shifted chirp signal detection problem

$$f_i(\|\mathbf{z}-\mathbf{cz}_i\|,\sigma) \geq f_k(\|\mathbf{z}-\mathbf{cz}_k\|,\sigma), \qquad \forall \neq i \tag{6}$$

In most designs it would be expected that σ is determined and fixed before adaptation begins, else it can be periodically or continually adjusted as the data flows through the system. The range of σ value for acceptable performance is often quite broad and as such is not necessarily an overly critical parameter. Its main purpose is to ensure a sufficiently smooth interconnection between neighbouring linear filter models.

There are many possible standard linear adaptive filters and associated adaptation mechanisms that may be used for the models $l_i(\mathbf{x})$ (Diniz, 1997; Garas, 2000; Hayes, 1996; Haykin, 1996; Haykin, 1999; Stergiopoulos, 2001), depending on design requirements. Most applications may be adequately served by using Finite Impulse Response (FIR) filters with a suitable variant of the Least Mean Square adaptation algorithm. For applications that may require more efficient filter models and a faster adaptation capability the Recursive Least Squares adaptation algorithm, or one of its variants, used in conjunction with linear recursive filters may provide a better solution. The use of adaptive versions of time-frequency filters would also add a very useful dimension to design possibilities.

The SSAF model is actually very similar in form to an adaptive multiple FIR filter used for sub-band echo cancellation (Vaseghi, 1996). This filter splits the input signal into a M frequency sub-bands having equal bandwidths. Each sub-band can be down sampled without loss of information, and assigned a separate smaller FIR filter. The main advantage of doing this is that the set of reduced length filters operating in parallel can now converge much faster than a single long FIR filter would. The SSAF is really a kind of more general form of this, where the chosen sub-space is not restricted to frequency bands but can be any definable division of space that can be somehow related to the filter's operating domain.

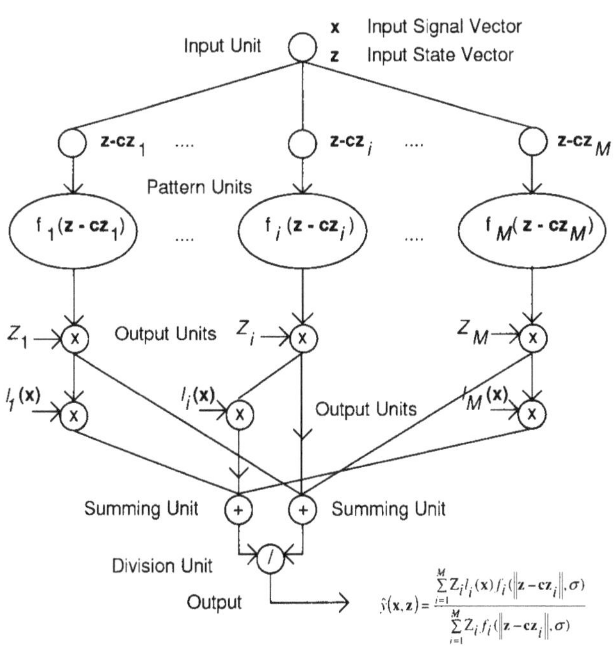

$$\hat{y}(\mathbf{x},\mathbf{z}) = \frac{\sum_{i=1}^{M} Z_i l_i(\mathbf{x}) f_i(\|\mathbf{z}-\mathbf{cz}_i\|,\sigma)}{\sum_{i=1}^{M} Z_i f_i(\|\mathbf{z}-\mathbf{cz}_i\|,\sigma)}$$

Fig. 3. SSAF model.

5. Some relevant applications

The SSAF model has been developed with its application to 3D audio and underwater acoustic signal modelling, equalisation and filtering firmly in mind. These processes are very difficult to model analytically, especially when the properties of the acoustic medium can and do vary nonlinearly with position and time. Consequently, problems such as these are characterised by the need to develop and adapt practical models from data measurements. Two example problems to illustrate SSAF utility are loudspeaker modelling and adaptive equalisation, and acoustic signal propagation through the ocean. In both these applications the state space vector represents the three spatial dimensions and is used to segment and identify the 3D sub-spaces of operation. Also, any model adjustments are restricted to local RBF sub-spaces based on local measurements while still maintaining good interpolation between the other sub-models.

A loudspeaker 3D frequency response model can be built up by initially measuring the responses at a number of suitable points in space in front of the loudspeaker. The SSAF model can then be used to both smoothly interpolate the response between measured responses over the whole space of interest as well as be adapted away from there according to any dynamic equalisation requirements. Although loudspeaker amplitude vs frequency contours can vary at a single spot in 3D space as well as over space in front of the speaker they change relatively smoothly over frequency and space. This means that relatively few spots in front of the speaker need to be initially measured to build an effective 3D loudspeaker response model.

The shape of Fig. 2 is similar to a typical loudspeaker amplitude response at one spot in front. Eq. (5) can be used to very easily model and smooth this type of shape using standard one-twelfth octave frequency amplitude measurements taken at a one meter distance from the loudspeaker. Centres are placed at the one-twelfth octave frequency positions and each linear model $l_i(\mathbf{x})$ at that point is taken to be a constant equal to the respective measurement. Weighting factors Z_i are set to values defined by Eq. (7), to span the exponentially increasing gaps between centres. The smoothing factor σ can then be used for final tuning

$$Z_i = [(2)^{1/12}]^{i-1}, \qquad i = 1, \dots, M \tag{7}$$

This loudspeaker response model can form the basis of an adaptive room equalisation system that can make separate filter adaptations within each one-twelfth octave frequency sub-band. Loudspeakers are typically minimum phase systems and consequently their phase characteristics can be computed directly from the magnitude of the amplitude response (Poularikas, 1996) obviating the need for extra data memory.

The timely maintenance of an accurate velocity of sound model to cover a 3D region of sonar operation in the ocean is important in order to calculate good subsequent signal propagation models (Urick, 1983). The main variation of sound velocity occurs with depth due to thermal variations occurring during the course of the day. In this case the SSAF model can be used to maintain a good 3D velocity of sound model and keep it adapted during the course of system operation. Often it is sufficient to have a sound velocity model only as a function of depth to achieve good first order results. Measurements of sound velocity may be made at various depths and locations by various means and used to adapt the main model in the sections delineated by the RBFs. These measurements can be done periodically using depth probes or preferably by a sub-ocean vehicle and acoustically transmitted back to the system.

Fig. 4 Shows a typical ocean sound velocity vs depth profile (Urick, 1983). If depth is divided up into an appropriate number of levels an affine adaptive model can be associated with each level using Eqs. (5) and (6). Weighting for each depth span can be controlled by setting factors Z_i proportional to the respective depth spans between model centres. As new velocity values are measured at any depth the appropriate model is adapted to maintain accuracy while an appropriate value of σ keeps joins at the model boundaries sufficiently smooth.

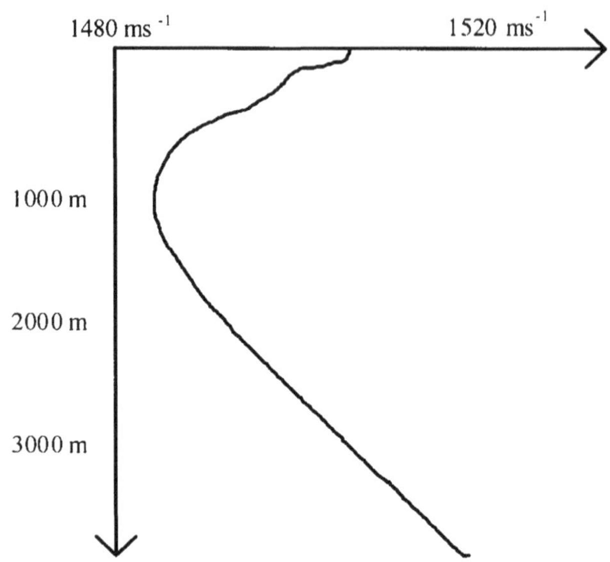

Fig. 4. Ocean sound velocity vs depth profile.

6. Discussion and conclusions

This paper has introduced the SSAF model, based on the MPNN, which provides some significant benefits for practical design of complex adaptive filtering systems. The SSAF can be seen as a development that provides a simple and practical means of solving some important complex adaptive filtering problems. However, in order to apply it successfully it still requires some intelligent design decisions by a human designer. The designer must decide the role and set the values for the Z_i, decide how many RBFs to use and where to place them to adequately cover a chosen process state space.

These decisions can be automated in a similar way as is typically done for the MPNN. However, a more efficient mechanism needs yet to be developed that may begin to approach some optimal solution, within specified design constraints. For example, such a design must be able to automatically reduce the SSAF down to a single RBF and linear adaptive filter model when solving a linear problem. For nonlinear problems it needs to be able to reduce down to a minimal set of RBFs and adaptive filter models that adequately cover the whole operating space for a given design specification. The methods of (Verselinovic & Leenaerts, 1996) and (Mattavelli, Amaldi, & Gruter, 1996) can offer some useful insight as they both deal with the automatic generation of piecewise linear models. The method of (Verselinovic & Leenaerts, 1996) is intended for the modelling of nonlinear multivariable scalar functions and uses a specified relative error to guide model generation in a way that trades off between model size and accuracy. A simple combinatorial optimisation approach is used in (Mattavelli, Amaldi, & Gruter, 1996) that provides natural partitions of time series state-spaces for a given error tolerance. The partitioning of the data space and allocation of centres can also be done using methods related to Vector Quantisation and unsupervised artificial neural networks (Kohonen, 1990). An unsupervised on-line clustering method previously applied to the MPNN (Young, Zaknich, & Attikiouzel, 2001) may also provide useful solutions.

In this paper linear filter models are preferred but there is no reason why quadratic or higher order Volterra filters can not also be used in any required combination. The only drawback may be that many more piecewise model parameters must be stored for each RBF. This may not really be much of a drawback if it allows a process to be better approximated with fewer RBFs regions, i.e. smaller M.

A further very useful way to exploit the MPNN structure is to use it to smoothly piece together and merge a set of adaptive MLP filters or models throughout a nonlinear data space. This provides a method of decoupling MLP models such that as data statistics change in a local region only the MLP related to that region needs to be adapted. Not only does this allow the total model to adapt much faster but it also preserves the training of each of the, now much less complex, unaffected local MLPs and helps with the stability-plasticity dilemma.

Another interesting development may be to consider using Support Vector Machines (SVMs) (Cherkassky & Mulier, 1998; Vapnik, 2000) to replace models $l_i(\mathbf{x})$. SVMs are able to turn nonlinear problems into optimal linear ones by projection of the problem into a very high dimensional space. This could mean that each RBF can more adequately cover a greater space since the filtering process need not be approximately linear in the vicinity of each RBF to produce an accurate enough overall model. Using the SVM approach may then obviating the need for more complex nonlinear optimisation solutions for nonlinear sections.

References

Cherkassky, V., & Mulier, F. (1998). *Learning from data*. New York: Wiley.

Diniz, P. S. R. (1997). *Adaptive filtering: Algorithms and practical implementation*. Dordrecht: Kluwer Academic Publishers.

Frisch, R. (1934). *Statistical confluence analysis by means of complete regression systems* (3rd ed). Economic Institute, University of Oslo.

Garas, J. (2000). *Adaptive 3D sound systems*. Dordrecht: Kluwer Academic Publishers.

Gelfand, S.B., Krogmeier, J.V., Balasubramanian, R (1995). A tree-structured piecewise linear filter with recursive least-squares adaptation. *Proceedings of the 29th asilomar conference on signals systems and computers (Vol. 1)* (pp. 673–675)

Gelfand, S. B., & Ravishankar, C. S. (1993). A tree-structured piecewise linear adaptive filter. *IEEE Transactions on Information Theory*, *39*(6), 1907–1922.

Hayes, M. H. (1996). *Statistical digital signal processing and modelling*. New York: Wiley.

Haykin, S. (1996). *Adaptive filter theory*. Englewood Cliffs, NJ: Prentice-Hall.

Haykin, S. (1999). *Neural networks, a comprehensive foundation* (2nd ed). Upper Saddle River, NJ: Prentice-Hall.

Heredia, A., & Arce, G. R. (2000). Nonlinear filters based on combinations of piecewise polynomials with compact support. *IEEE Transactions on Signal Processing*, *48*(10), 2850–2863.

Kohonen, T. (1990). Self-organising map. *Proceedings of the IEEE*, *78*, 1464–1480.

Mattavelli, M., Vesin, J. M., Amaldi, E., & Gruter, R. (1996). A new approach to piecewise linear modelling of time series. *IEEE Digital Signal Processing Workshop Proceedings*, 502–505.

Moody, J., & Darken, C. (1989). Fast learning in networks of locally-tuned processing units. *Neural Computation*, *1*(2), 281–294.

Nadaraya, E. A. (1964). On estimating regression. *Theory Probability Applications*, *9*, 141–142.

Poularikas, A. (1996). *The transforms and applications handbook*. Boca Raton, FL/New York: CRC/IEEE Press, pp. 535–538.

Powell, M.J.D (1985). *Radial basis functions for multivariate interpolation: A review*. Technical report DAMPT 1985/NA12. Department of Applied Mathematics and Theoretical Physics, Cambridge University, England.

Simani, S., Fantuzzi, C., Rovatti, R., Beghelli, S (2000). Non-linear dynamic modelling in noisy environment using multiple model approach. *Proceedings of the American control conference (Vol. 4)* (pp. 2332–2336).

Specht, D. F. (1990). Probabilistic neural networks. *International Neural Network Society, Neural Networks*, *3*, 109–118.

Specht, D. F. (1991). A general regression neural network. *IEEE Transactions on Neural Networks*, *2*(6), 568–576.

Stergiopoulos, S. (2001). *Advanced signal processing handbook: Theory and implementation for radar, sonar, and medical imaging real-time systems*. Boca Raton, FL: CRC Press.

Urick, R. J. (1983). *Principles of underwater sound* (3rd ed). New York: McGraw-Hill.

Vapnik, V. N. (2000). *The nature of statistical learning theory* (2nd ed). Berlin: Springer.

Verselinovic, P., Leenaerts, D (1996). A method for automatic generation of piecewise linear models. Proceedings of the 1996 IEEE international symposium on circuits and systems 'connecting the world' (Vol. 3) (pp. 24–27).

Vaseghi, S. V. (1996). *Advanced signal processing and digital noise reduction*. New York/Stuttgart: Wiley/Teubner, (pp. 339–341).

Watson, G. S. (1964). Smooth regression analysis. *Sankhya Series A*, *26*, 359–372.

Young, J., Zaknich, A., & Attikiouzel, Y. (2001). Center reduction algorithm for the modified probabilistic neural network equalizer. *IEEE International Joint Conference on Neural Networks (IJCNN), Washington, DC*, 1966–1970.

Zaknich, A., & deSilva, C. J. (1997). Adaptive learning Scheme for the modified probabilistic neural network. *IEEE Third International Conference on Algorithms and Architectures for Parallel Processing, Melbourne, Australia*, 597–610.

Zaknich, A. (1998). Introduction to the modified probabilistic neural network for general signal processing applications. *IEEE Transactions on Signal Processing*, *46*(7), 1980–1990.

Zaknich, A., & Attikiouzel, Y. (2000). A tuneable approximate piecewise linear model derived from the modified probabilistic neural network. *IEEE Signal Processing Workshop on Neural Networks for Signal Processing (NNSP), Sydney, Australia*, *1*, 45–53.

Zaknich, A. (2003). *Neural networks for intelligent signal processing (Vol. 4). Series on advanced biology and logic-based intelligence*, World Scientific Publishing, (pp. 256–273).

AVAILABLE AT
www.ComputerScienceWeb.com
POWERED BY SCIENCE DIRECT

PERGAMON

Neural Networks 16 (2003) 841–845

Neural Networks

www.elsevier.com/locate/neunet

2003 Special issue

Pharmacodynamic population analysis in chronic renal failure using artificial neural networks—a comparative study

Adam E. Gaweda[a,*], Alfred A. Jacobs[a], Michael E. Brier[a,b], Jacek M. Zurada[c]

[a]*Kidney Disease Program, University of Louisville, Louisville, KY 40202, USA*
[b]*Department of Veteran Affairs, University of Louisville, Louisville, KY 40202, USA*
[c]*Depatment of Electrical and Computer Engineering, University of Louisville, Louisville, KY 40202, USA*

Abstract

This work presents a pharmacodynamic population analysis in chronic renal failure patients using Artificial Neural Networks (ANNs). In pursuit of an effective and cost-efficient strategy for drug delivery in patients with renal failure, two different types of ANN are applied to perform drug dose-effect modeling and their performance compared. Applied in a clinical environment, such models will allow for prediction of patient response to the drug at the effect site and, subsequently, for adjusting the dosing regimen.

Keywords: Pharmacodynamic modeling; Multilayer perceptron network; Radial basis; Autoregressive model

1. Introduction

Anemia is a nearly universal sequel in an End-Stage Renal Disease (ESRD) patient. Until the advent of Erythropoietin (EPO), ESRD patients faced severe anemia and cardiovascular complications, or the requirement for multiple transfusions and the risk of a variety of blood borne pathogens. The addition of this expensive drug to the already burdensome cost of the Medicare ESRD program has created a fiscal crisis. The Dialysis Outcomes Quality Initiative of the National Kidney Foundation recommends hematocrit maintained within the narrow range of 33–36%. To this end, several strategies (protocols) exist for the dosing of EPO. These protocols adjust the dose amount or the dosing frequency based on the current hematocrit, its 3 month rolling average, as well as previous EPO doses. This process is labor intensive and requires trained personnel to assess monthly hematocrit and iron levels and to make adjustments or assessments every 2 or 4 weeks. Furthermore, such process is not optimal with respect to the cost of the EPO. It is therefore of great significance that the available computational tools be utilized to support the medical personnel in this difficult task and to optimize the treatment cost.

Several attempts at the automation of the EPO delivery have already been reported (Bellazzi, 1992; Bellazzi, Siviero, & Bellazzi, 1994). A multicompartmental model of erythropoiesis and a set of integro-differential state-space equations served as a basis to formulate a parametric description of the process. Parametric identification, performed using Bayesian framework, was then performed on the population data (Bellazzi, 1992). This approach was subsequently enhanced by a fuzzy rule-based control strategy (Bellazzi et al., 1994) to improve the cost-efficiency of the drug delivery process. Unfortunately, as of today, neither one of these methodologies have achieved acceptance in the clinical environment.

The advances in the area of Computational Intelligence, especially the resurgence of Artificial Neural Networks (ANN), have influenced the area of pharmacokinetic and pharmacodynamic (PK/PD) modeling. A number of publications presenting applications of ANN models to PK/PD analysis can be found in the literature (Brier, Zurada, & Aronoff, 1995; Veng-Pedersen & Modi, 1992, 1995). One particular application area which benefits from the data-driven learning capabilities of ANNs is the drug-effect modeling (Veng-Pedersen & Modi, 1992, 1995). It is well known from control theory that an effective control strategy can be achieved only of an adequate system model is available. Hence, an efficient and cost-effective dosing protocol for EPO must be based on an accurate model of patient response to EPO. Only very recently, a few efforts have been undertaken to utilize ANN models in individualized EPO dosing (Jacobs, Lada, Zurada, Brier,

* Corresponding author.

0893-6080/03/$ - see front matter © 2003 Elsevier Science Ltd. All rights reserved.
doi:10.1016/S0893-6080(03)00084-4

& Aronoff, 2002; Guerrero et al., 2002). Such individualized models are applicable when a large data record associated with the specific patient is available. In the clinical environment it is sometimes important to have access to a population model, i.e. a model built upon data from a large population of patients. Such model not only provides useful information about the population of patients, but can also be applied to a patient without a sufficient treatment history, in which case it would be very difficult to provide an individualized model.

This work presents an approach to PK/PD population analysis and modeling of hematocrit response in ESRD patients. Two types of ANN models are studied here, Multi-Layer Perceptron (MLP) network and Radial Basis Function (RBF) network. Their performance is mutually compared based on a modification of a popular validation method. It is also compared to the performance obtained by a linear autoregressive model (ARX). Finally, a statistical significance testing is performed, in order to establish the validity of the obtained results.

2. Method

2.1. Data

Two hundred and nine patients undergoing hemodialysis at the University of Louisville Chronic Dialysis Unit during the period 1/1/96 to 10/31/2001 were studied. Data abstraction was approved by the Human Studies Committee of both, the Department of Veteran Affairs and University of Louisville. Patients were excluded from study only for sickle cell disease, and HIV infection. Demographic, clinical, and laboratory data were abstracted from clinical and laboratory databases. Each data entry contains the following fields: patient number, week, hematocrit, EPO dose for a given week, Ferritin level, Iron saturation, Albumin level, Parathyroid hormone level, Kt/V (hemodialysis quality index), and IV iron dose for a given week. It has been suggested (Bellazzi, 1992) and demonstrated empirically (Jacobs et al., 2002) that the current level of hematocrit and the weekly EPO dose are the most significant factors in influencing the future hematocrit level. Following this finding, the presented analysis focuses on these two variables. Table 1 shows patient demographics as well as mean and standard deviation values of the most relevant variables.

Table 1
Patient characteristics

Race (B/W)	130/35
Gender (M/F)	95/71
Age, years (mean ± SD)	55 ± 15
Study period, weeks (mean ± SD)	157 ± 71
Hematocrit (mean ± SD)	35.2 ± 5.2
Erythropoietin dose (U/week) (mean ± SD)	11,800 ± 12,000

In the clinical environment, hematocrit levels are determined every 2–6 weeks. To address the resulting problem of non-uniform sampling, a linear interpolation between the available samples was first performed. The time series obtained this way was subsequently resampled on a weekly basis. The purpose of using the linear method was to replicate the smooth dynamics of red blood cell production and to prevent the occurrence of peaks, often seen with higher order interpolation methods. Finally, the monthly average hematocrit levels and their standard deviations were derived from the resampled weekly data.

The process of red blood cell production resulting from EPO infusion consists of several stages in which mature red blood cells are derived from a stem cell (Fisher, 2003). The length of this process is estimated as 12 weeks and is subject to intra- and inter-individual variation. To account for this phenomenon, average monthly hematocrit levels over past 2 months, together with their standard deviations, as well as average doses of erythropoietin over past 2 months are used as input variables for the proposed model.

2.2. Multilayer perceptron network model

The first ANN model applied in this study was a MLP network. It contains a single hidden layer with hyperbolic tangent activation functions and a linear output layer. The choice of a single hidden layer is based on the hypothesis that such configuration is sufficient for universal approximation. In the functional form, the MLP model can be represented as:

$$\mathrm{hct}_{\mathrm{avg}}(k+1)=\mathrm{MLP}[\mathrm{hct}_{\mathrm{avg}}(k),\mathrm{hct}_{\mathrm{SD}}(k),\mathrm{hct}_{\mathrm{avg}}(k-1),\mathrm{hct}_{\mathrm{SD}}(k-1),\mathrm{EPO}_{\mathrm{avg}}(k),\mathrm{EPO}_{\mathrm{avg}}(k-1)] \quad (1)$$

In this expression $\mathrm{hct}_{\mathrm{avg}}$ is the average monthly hematocrit level, $\mathrm{hct}_{\mathrm{SD}}$ is a monthly standard deviation of hematocrit level, and $\mathrm{EPO}_{\mathrm{avg}}$ is the monthly average erythropoietin dose. The number of the hidden layer neurons was selected using heuristics combined with a trial and error approach. It was established that 10 hidden neurons proved sufficient for accurate prediction. Any increase of this number did not significantly improve the prediction accuracy. Hence, the MLP network has a 6:10:1 structure.

The population analysis was performed using a patient-specific variant of the leave-one-out validation. This means that for each single patient, their data were left out and the MLP model was trained upon the remaining data. The trained model was then evaluated against the previously unseen data records of the left-out patient.

The simulations were performed in MATLAB using Neural Network Toolbox. Due to its robustness and fast convergence, the Levenberg–Marquardt method was used for training. This method adjusts the network weights using the following formula.

$$\mathbf{w}_{l+1} = \mathbf{w}_l - [\mathbf{J}^T\mathbf{J} + \mu\mathbf{I}]^{-1}\mathbf{J}^T\mathbf{e} \quad (2)$$

where $\mathbf{w}$ are the network weights, $\mathbf{J}$ is the Jacobian matrix that contains first derivatives of the network output with respect to the weights, $\mathbf{e}$ is the vector of network errors, and $\mathbf{I}$ is the identity matrix. The coefficient μ controls the step size of the weight update and is varied based on the error convergence. When μ is large, the method becomes gradient descent with a small step size, whereas for μ close to zero, it acts as Newton's method with an approximate Hessian. In the described simulations, the training was concluded after exceeding the maximum number of epochs (100), or after no error decrease was detected (small μ). To improve the optimization, the input data were uniformly rescaled to the interval $[-1;1]$.

2.3. Radial basis function network model

The second ANN model applied in this study was a RBF network. It contains a single layer of Gaussian basis functions and a linear output layer. In the functional form, the RBF model can be represented as

$$\begin{aligned}\mathrm{hct}_{\mathrm{avg}}(k+1) = \mathrm{RBF}[&\mathrm{hct}_{\mathrm{avg}}(k), \mathrm{hct}_{\mathrm{SD}}(k), \mathrm{hct}_{\mathrm{avg}}(k-1), \\ &\mathrm{hct}_{\mathrm{SD}}(k-1), \mathrm{EPO}_{\mathrm{avg}}(k), \mathrm{EPO}_{\mathrm{avg}}(k-1)] \quad (3)\end{aligned}$$

The RBF network applied in this study contains a maximum of 10 function neurons. The process of selecting the centers of the basis functions relies on the functional equivalence between RBF networks and Fuzzy Rule-based Inference Systems (Jang & Sun, 1993). It has been established that optimal fuzzy rules cover extrema of the approximated function (Kosko, 1995) and that these extrema can be found by identifying the maxima of the absolute approximation error. Based on these foundations, the following iterative procedure for center selection has been employed in this work:

Given: data set $Z = [X\,y]$ of size N, where X is the input and y the output portion of the data, basis function spread s, and the maximum number of basis functions $h_{\max}$

1. Create a mean predictor $\tilde{y} = \bar{y}$
2. Evaluate the mean predictor on data Z, i.e. compute errors $e_i = |y_i - \bar{y}|$, $i = 1, \ldots, N$
3. Find maximum error $e_{\max} = \max(e_i)$
4. Establish first basis function with center at X_k, s.t. $e_k = e_{\max}$, set $h = 1$.
5. Estimate output weights of the RBF network using lest squares.
6. Evaluate the RBF network on data Z, i.e. compute errors $e_i = |y_i - y_{\mathrm{RBF}}(X_i)|$.
7. Find maximum error $e_{\max} = \max(e_i)$
8. Add new basis function with center at, X_k, s.t. $e_k = e_{\max}$, set $h = h + 1$.
9. Estimate output weights of the RBF network using least squares.
10. Stop if $h = h_{\max}$, otherwise go to 6.

Out of $h_{\max}$ RBF networks the one with the best performance is selected. To select the optimal value of the basis function spread, s, the procedure was repeated for several different spreads, ranging from 0.5 to 2.0. It must be emphasized, though, that the input data was uniformly rescaled to the interval $[-1;1]$.

The so obtained RBF network model was further optimized using the very same Levenberg–Marquardt method, as in the case of the MLP model.

2.4. Linear model

An autoregressive model with exogenous inputs (ARX) was developed as a point of reference to evaluate the performance of the previously developed ANN models. The ARX model has the following form

$$\begin{aligned}\mathrm{hct}_{\mathrm{avg}}(k+1) = a_0 &+ a_1\mathrm{hct}_{\mathrm{avg}}(k) + a_2\mathrm{hct}_{\mathrm{SD}}(k) \\ &+ a_3\mathrm{hct}_{\mathrm{avg}}(k-1) + a_4\mathrm{hct}_{\mathrm{SD}}(k-1) \\ &+ a_5\mathrm{EPO}_{\mathrm{avg}}(k) + a_6\mathrm{EPO}_{\mathrm{avg}}(k-1) \quad (4)\end{aligned}$$

The coefficients a_i, $(i = 0, \ldots, 6)$ for this model were obtained using least squares estimation.

2.5. Performance measures

For each model, Root Mean Square Error (RMSE) and Normalized Root Mean Square Error (NRMSE) was computed to evaluate its performance

$$\mathrm{RMSE} = \sqrt{\frac{\sum_{i=1}^{N}(y_i - \tilde{y}_i)^2}{N}} \quad (5)$$

$$\mathrm{NRMSE} = \sqrt{\frac{\sum_{i=1}^{N}(y_i - \tilde{y}_i)^2}{\sum_{i=1}^{N}(y_i - y_m)^2}} \quad (6)$$

where y_i is the actual output, $\tilde{y}_i$ is the model output, and y_m is the mean value of y_i, $(i = 1, \ldots, N)$. While the RMSE assesses the quality of approximation, the NRMSE evaluates the relative improvement with respect to mean prediction.

3. Results

Using the aforementioned patient-specific variant of leave-one-out validation, 209 MLP network models and 209 RBF network models were constructed. The average validation RMSE obtained in this way was 1.93% for

Table 2
Comparison between neural network models and the linear model

	MLP	RBF	ARX
RMSE (mean ± SD)	1.93 ± 0.60	2.02 ± 0.65	2.11 ± 0.70
NRMSE (mean ± SD)	0.60 ± 0.25	0.65 ± 0.28	0.68 ± 0.35

the MLP and 2.02% for the RBF model. Using the width of the target hematocrit range (33–36%), one can conclude that this is an acceptable performance. This is particularly true when we consider the fact that no patient specific attributes (age, weight, gender, race) were utilized in the analysis.

A comparison of the errors produced by all the models is presented in Table 2. Mean values and Standard Deviations of RMSE and NRMSE over whole patient population are shown. Both ANN models improve upon the linear model (lower mean error values) and are more consistent (smaller Standard Deviations).

Finally, a statistical significance analysis was performed on the results to establish the significance of difference between the obtained performances. Analysis of variance with repeated measures was performed using SPSS version 11 on both the RMSE and NRMSE for each subject. A post test is shown comparing the errors between ARX, MLP, and RBF. Table 3 shows the results of the significance analysis performed for the RMSE, whereas Table 4 shows the results for the NRMSE. These results imply that the MLP is significantly better than the other two models. The difference in performance between the RBF model and the ARX can also be adjudged as significant.

Fig. 1 presents the performance of the obtained models for a selected patient. The continuous lines represent the model predicted output, whereas the dotted ones represent the actual values. It should be pointed out that the predicted and the actual curve significantly overlap for the MLP model which illustrates its better performance as compared to the RBF and the ARX models. In the case of the latter one, one can almost observe a time shift of one prediction step between the actual and the predicted hematocrit. The RMSE values for this particular patient are as follows

Table 3
Pairwise comparison for RMS error

Model 1	Model 2	Mean difference ($P < 0.5$)	Significance
MLP	RBF	−0.093	0.000
	ARX	−0.181	0.000
RBF	ARX	−0.087	0.001
	MLP	0.093	0.000
ARX	MLP	0.181	0.000
	RBF	0.087	0.001

Table 4
Pairwise comparison for NRMS error

Model 1	Model 2	Mean difference ($P < 0.5$)	Significance
MLP	RBF	−0.050	0.000
	ARX	−0.081	0.000
RBF	ARX	−0.030	0.002
	MLP	0.050	0.000
ARX	MLP	0.081	0.000
	RBF	0.050	0.002

- MLP:RMSE = 1.55; NRMSE = 0.37 (2.7-fold improvement over mean prediction)
- RBF:RMSE = 1.71; NRMSE = 0.41 (2.4-fold improvement over mean prediction)

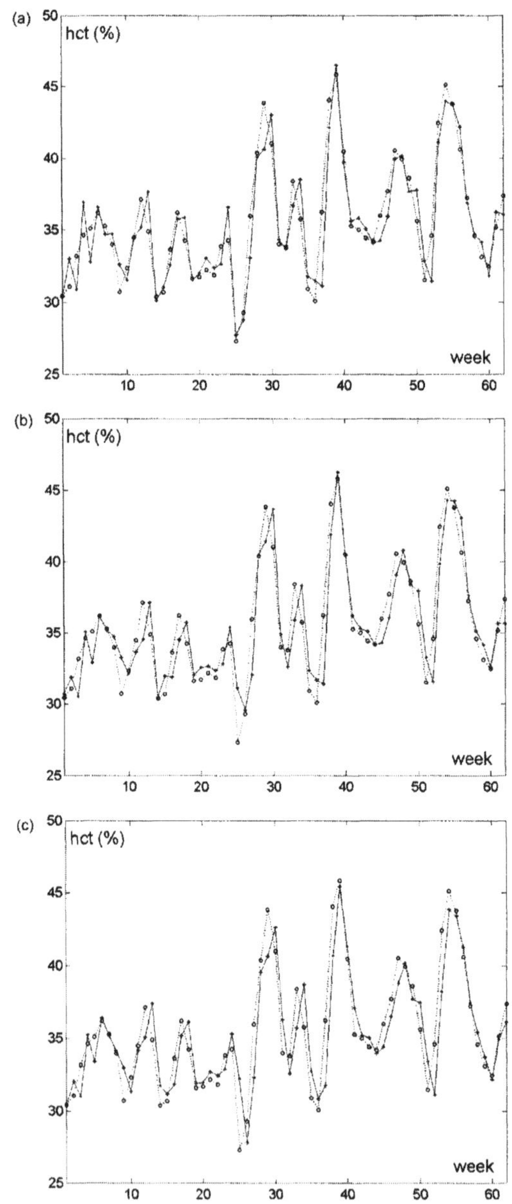

Fig. 1. Illustration of hematocrit prediction for an individual patient: (a) MLP, (b) RBF, (c) ARX.

- ARX:RMSE = 1.80; NRMSE = 0.44 (2.2-fold improvement over mean prediction)

4. Conclusions

An ANN-based approach to pharmacodynamic population analysis of patients with renal failure has been presented. Two different ANN architectures, MLP and RBF network, have been studied and their performance compared and statistically evaluated for significance. The analysis revealed superiority of the MLP model, as well as supremacy of both ANN models over the linear, autoregressive model. In further stages, the developed ANN models of patient response to EPO treatment will form a component of a hybrid intelligent control system for EPO delivery. Given a large population of patients, it has been shown that ANN models are capable of satisfactorily predict the response of an unseen patient. The obtained result is of paramount importance in the clinical environment, because it suggests that the employment of an intelligent drug delivery system to a large number of dialysis patients is feasible.

Acknowledgements

This material is based upon work supported by the Office of Research and Development, Medical Research Service, Department of Veteran Affairs.

References

Bellazzi, R. (1992). Drug delivery optimization through Bayesian networks: an application to erythropoietin therapy in uremic anemia. *Computers and Biomedical Research*, *26*, 274–293.

Bellazzi, R., Siviero, C., & Bellazzi, R. (1994). Mathematical modeling of erythropoietin therapy in uremic anemia. Does it improve cost-effectiveness? *Haematologica*, *79*, 154–164.

Brier, M. E., Zurada, J. M., & Aronoff, G. R. (1995). Neural network predicted peak and trough gentamicin concentrations. *Pharmaceutical Research*, *12*(3), 406–412.

Fisher, J. W. (2003). Erythropoietin: physiology and pharmacology update. *Experimental Biology and Medicine*, *228*(1), 1–14.

Guerrero, J. D. M., Olivas, E. S., Camps Valls, G., Serrano Lopez, A. J., Perez Ruixo, J. J., & Jimenez Torres, N. V. (2003). Use of neural networks for dosage individualisation of erythropoietin in patients with secondary anemia to chronic renal failure. *Computers in Biology and Medicine*, in press.

Jacobs, A. A., Lada, P., Zurada, J. M., Brier, M. E., & Aronoff, G. R. (2001). Predictors of hematocrit in hemodialysis patients as determined by artificial neural networks. *Journal of American Society of Nephrology*, *12* (Program and Abstract issue), p. 387A.

Jang, J. R., & Sun, C. (1993). Functional equivalence between radial basis function and fuzzy inference systems. *IEEE Transactions on Neural Networks*, *4*, 156–159.

Kosko, B. (1995). Optimal fuzzy rules cover extrema. *International Journal of Intelligent Systems*, *10*(2), 249–255.

Veng-Pedersen, P., & Modi, N. B. (1992). Neural networks in pharmacodynamic modeling. Is current modeling practice of complex kinetic systems at a dead end? *Journal of Pharmacokinetics and Biophamraceutics*, *20*(4), 397–412.

Veng-Pedersen, P., & Modi, N. B. (1995). Application of neural networks in pharmacodynamics. In D. Z. D'Argenio (Ed.), (2) (pp. 101–120). *Advanced methods of pharmacokinetic and pharmacodynamic systems analysis*, New York: Plenum Press.

AVAILABLE AT
www.ComputerScienceWeb.com
POWERED BY SCIENCE @ DIRECT

PERGAMON

Neural Networks 16 (2003) 847–853

Neural Networks

www.elsevier.com/locate/neunet

2003 Special issue

Electronic nose based tea quality standardization

Ritaban Dutta[a,*], K.R. Kashwan[b], M. Bhuyan[b], E.L. Hines[a], J.W. Gardner[a]

[a]Department of Engineering, University of Warwick, Coventry CV4 7AL, UK
[b]Department of Electronics, Tezpur University (A Central University), Napaam, Tezpur (Assam) 784028, India

Abstract

In this paper we have used a metal oxide sensor (MOS) based electronic nose (EN) to analyze five tea samples with different qualities, namely, drier month, drier month again over-fired, well fermented normal fired in oven, well fermented overfired in oven, and under fermented normal fired in oven. The flavour of tea is determined mainly by its taste and smell, which is generated by hundreds of Volatile Organic Compounds (VOCs) and Non-Volatile Organic Compounds present in tea. These VOCs are present in different ratios and determine the quality of the tea. For example Assamica (Sri Lanka and Assam Tea) and Assamica Sinesis (Darjeeling and Japanese Tea) are two different species of tea giving different flavour notes. Tea flavour is traditionally measured through the use of a combination of conventional analytical instrumentation and human or ganoleptic profiling panels. These methods are expensive in terms of time and labour and also inaccurate because of a lack of either sensitivity or quantitative information. In this paper an investigation has been made to determine the flavours of different tea samples using an EN and to explore the possibility of replacing existing analytical and profiling panel methods. The technique uses an array of 4 MOSs, each of, which has an electrical resistance that has partial sensitivity to the headspace of tea. The signals from the sensor array are then conditioned by suitable interface circuitry. The data were processed using Principal Components Analysis (PCA), Fuzzy C Means algorithm (FCM). We also explored the use of a Self-Organizing Map (SOM) method along with a Radial Basis Function network (RBF) and a Probabilistic Neural Network classifier. Using FCM and SOM feature extraction techniques along with RBF neural network we achieved 100% correct classification for the five different tea samples with different qualities. These results prove that our EN is capable of discriminating between the flavours of teas manufactured under different processing conditions, viz. over-fermented, over-fired, under fermented, etc.

Keywords: Electronic nose; Tea flavour; Odours

1. Introduction

1.1. Olfactory system and chemical senses

To humans, the sensation of flavour is due to three main chemoreceptor systems. These are gustation (sense of taste by tongue), olfaction (sense of smell by nose) and trigeminal (sense of irritation). Taste is used to detect non-volatile chemicals, which enter the mouth while the sense of smell is used to detect volatile compounds. Receptors for the trigeminal sense are located in mucous membranes and in the skin, they also respond to many volatile chemicals and it is thought to be especially important in the detection of irritants and chemically reactive species. In the perception of flavour all three chemoreceptor systems are involved but olfaction plays by far the greatest role with other two senses contributing much less to the overall perception (Dutta, Hines, Gardner, Udrea, & Boilot, 2003).

The smell sensation is a chemical and neural process wherein odorant molecules stimulate the olfactory receptor cells that are located high up in the nose in the olfactory epithelium. Odours are of two types, simple and complex. Nature of stimulus and not the quality of sensation distinguish these. A simple odour is one which consists of only one type of odorant molecule whereas a complex odour is a mixture of many, different types of odorant molecules. All naturally occurring odours are complex mixtures. Odorants are typically small hydrophobic, organic molecules containing one or two functional groups. The size, shape and polar properties of the molecules determine its odour properties.

Broad patterns of response are shown by the mammalian olfactory system consisting of a large number of non-specific receptors—with about 300 different olfactory binding proteins having been identified—in a total of about 50 million. These cells send their signals to secondary nodes and then cells located in the olfactory bulb. There is a marked convergence at this stage with between 1000 and

* Corresponding author.

0893-6080/03/$ - see front matter © 2003 Elsevier Science Ltd. All rights reserved.
doi:10.1016/S0893-6080(03)00092-3

20,000 primary receptor cells connecting to each secondary cell followed by limited divergence (Pearce, Gardner, Friel, Bartlett, & Blair, 1993). This suggests that the secondary cells be involved in the integration of information, i.e. impulses simultaneously from many input cells. The nature of the primary cells is non-specific in their responses whereas the secondary cells respond to distinct categories of odours. Secondary cells interact with each other and with higher cells as well. Thus the system is a complex non-linear one with both and excitation and local inhibition helping to produce a high degree of sensitivity (ppb or better) and specificity.

The sensors employed here in the electronic nose (EN) are metal oxide films coated across the gap between two thin gold electrodes to form a chemoresistor. Conducting metal chemoresistors respond to a variety of Volatile Organic Compounds present in tea (Dutta et al., 2003; Pearce et al., 1993).

1.2. Tea processing and its flavour

Due to large number of organic compounds present in tea, it is difficult to process tea to an absolute standard. The volatile compounds present in tea determine its quality. Table 1 (Bhuyan & Borah, 2001) describes different volatile compounds present in black tea. In conventional tasting, it is very difficult to keep a consistency in the standard of tea quality from batch to batch during a production process. The quality is ensured by a human taste panel, which may vary due to different factors.

The aroma and flavour are two quality factors of tea, which depend upon the number of volatile compounds present and their ratios. Human panel tasting is inaccurate, laborious and time consuming due to adaptation, fatigue, infection and state of mind. An EN can be a better alternative to conventional methods for tea tasting and quality monitoring during production process. An EN is an increasingly fast, reliable and robust technology. Tea industries all over the world presently use certain standard terminology of tea flavour, however, there is no mention about a quantitative description or score on these flavour terms. The Tocklai Tea Research Association, Assam, (India) has adopted standard terminology but some of them overlap. Twenty-five non-overlapping flavour terms have been identified (Bhuyan & Borah, 2001) (Fig. 1) out of about 40 generally used flavour notes. An EN may provide amore objective platform to augment the conventional methods for tea tasting and quality monitoring during production process.

1.3. Purpose of electronic nose

As stated above, an attractive and alternative strategy for monitoring the quality of tea samples manufactured under different processing conditions potentially can be achieved by sensing the organic aromatic volatiles emitted by tea samples, using EN systems (Benady, Simon, & Miles, 1995; Simon, Hetzroni, Bordelon, Miles, & Charles, 1996). EN systems appear to be very promising for a number of reasons. The main ones are that EN systems are based on inexpensive, non-specific solid-state sensors, which are sensitive to the gases that are emitted by tea samples. Furthermore, once an EN has been 'trained', it does not require a skilled operator and can potentially obtain the results in the order of few tens of seconds. In the EN system, a pattern recognition engine enables the system to perform

Table 1
Ratios of main volatile compounds to total volatile compound in black tea

Compound	Sri Lanka		India					Japan
	Rt[b]	Uva	Var. Assamica	Hybrid of Assamica* Sinesis				Beniho mare
			Assam Dimbula	Darjeeling				
				(1)	(2)	(1)	(2)	
t-2-Hexenal	0.40	3.10	2.60	4.90	3.10	0.70	0.30	1.50
cis-3-Hexenal	0.53	2.80	4.30	0.20	3.80	1.40	0.10	6.10
t-2-Hexenyl formate	0.65	9.50	11.80	11.9	5.00	5.70	3.10	5.20
Linalool oxide (furanoid-*cis*)	0.77	3.40	3.20	3.50	3.60	8.20	4.70	3.80
Linalool oxide (furanoid-*trans*)	0.83	10.30	8.80	8.00	12.0	16.7	12.0	12.0
Linalool	1.00	24.00	15.50	18.3	32.8	15.6	13.7	9.30
Phenylacetaldehyde	1.20	0.20	0.50	4.00	5.00	1.10	1.80	1.00
Linalool oxide	1.40	0.30	0.40	0.40	trace	trace	1.00	6.00
Pyranoid-*cis*	1.50	18.60	18.80	9.00	13.2	9.80	5.30	4.90
Methysalcylate	1.67	1.3	2.20	3.30	1.60	7.30	15.9	21.7
Geraniol	1.71	1.00	1.90	4.30	1.00	1.70	2.00	2.60
Benzylalcohol 2-phenylethanol	1.78	0.20	0.90	4.30	1.00	2.00	6.70	7.50
cis-Jasmone + β-ionone	1.83	0.20	0.10	7.4	1.50	0.50	4.40	0.30

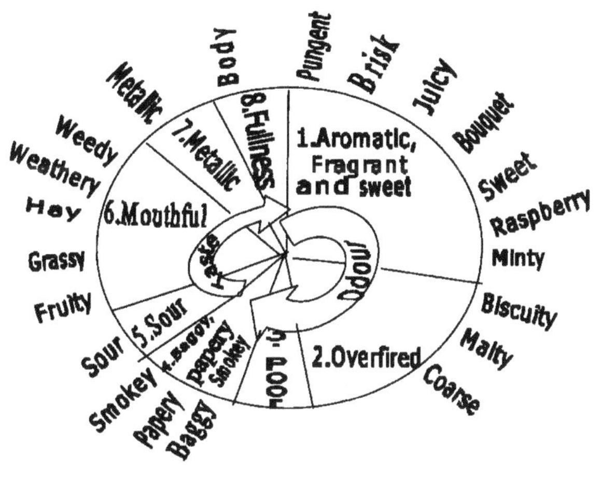

Fig. 1. Flavour wheel used to illustrate the international flavour terminology for tea. There are about 40 flavour terms out of which only 24 non-overlapping terms have been used.

complex aroma analysis of the sensor signals. Artificial neural networks (ANNs) have been extensively used to perform this pattern recognition, and good results have been reported previously in the classification of foodstuffs, such as eggs (Dutta et al., 2003), beverages (Gardner, Hines, & Tang, 1992), coffees (Gardner, Shurmer, & Tan, 1992), fish and meat (Schweizer-Berberich, Vaihinger, & Göpel, 1994; Winquist, Hornsten, Sundgren, & Lündstrom, 1993). The back propagation trained Multilayer Perceptron (MLP) paradigm is the most popular pattern recognition method in aroma analysis today. Other promising techniques include Learning Vector Quantization (LVQ), Probabilistic Neural Network (PNN) and Radial Basis Function (RBF). In this paper, we report on the use of an EN, employing an array of four tin oxide sensors, in combination with different pattern recognition engines (MLP, LVQ, PNN and RBF) to predict the quality of tea. This paper includes sections concerned with experimental procedure, data analysis, comparative evaluation of results and conclusions.

2. Experimental description

2.1. Materials

We had received five tea samples manufactured under different processing conditions from Assam, India. These five different tea samples with different qualities are as follows, (1) Drier month tea sample; (2) Drier month again over-fired tea sample; (3) Well fermented normal fired in oven tea sample; (4) Well fermented over-fired in oven tea sample; (5) Under fermented normal fired in oven tea sample. Each sample, without any additional manipulation, was placed over the period of the experiments. Monitoring is the important issue here because we wished to keep the experiment as simple as possible. We recorded temperature and humidity so that we could attempt to 'correct' for their effects if necessary.

2.2. Test procedure and data acquisition

The sensor system comprises four tin oxide odour sensors from the same manufacturer (Table 2) housed in a sensor chamber (Dutta et al., 2003). The sensors were chosen on the basis of sensitivity of the sensors to different gases; the selected sensors are designed to respond to gases such as the cooking vapours, ammonia, hydrogen sulphide, alcohol, toluene, xylene, etc. as specified by the manufacturer. The electrical conductance of the sensors varies in the presence of reducing/oxidizing gases. A thin plastic tube was connected from the input to the sensor chamber to one of the two holes in the cover of both plastic vessels (tea vessel and reference vessel). A diaphragm pump (Vacuum Pump Manufacturing Co. Ltd, UK) was used to facilitate sampling of the headspace of the vessels (Fig. 2) (Dutta et al., 2003). The headspace of the vessel containing the tea samples (5 tea samples with 5 different qualities were used for experiment) and the reference vessel were sampled in sequence as follows:

- *Tea vessel.* A sample measurement typically took 5 min to complete. The flow rate was 2 l/min. The air removed from the vessel by the pump was replaced by air from the room (Fig. 2).
- *Reference vessel.* Here, the tube from the input to the sensor chamber was connected to a plastic vessel which was full of pure water. Air from the room was pumped into the sensor chamber through this vessel. In this way the sensors were allowed to return to their baseline level over a period of some 20 min after sampling the headspace of the tea vessel. This was to make sure that the EN system was responding to the tea aromas rather than to any residual smell of the plastic vessel or only to the different environment in the reference plastic vessels (5 l). Fig. 2 shows the experimental set-up. The vessels had two small holes in their covers, to allow the headspace to be analyzed with the EN equipment. The ambient conditions (temperature and humidity) of the room in which the tea samples were kept were

Table 2
Summary details of commercially available metal oxide sensors used in our EN system

Sensor	Manufacturer	Sensitivity to
TGS 880	Figaro Engineering Inc.	Cooking vapours
TGS 826	Figaro Engineering Inc.	Toxic gases (ammonia (NH_3))
TGS 825	Figaro Engineering Inc.	Toxic gases (hydrogen sulphide (H_2S))
TGS 822	Figaro Engineering Inc.	Organic solvents (alcohol, toluene, xylene, etc.)

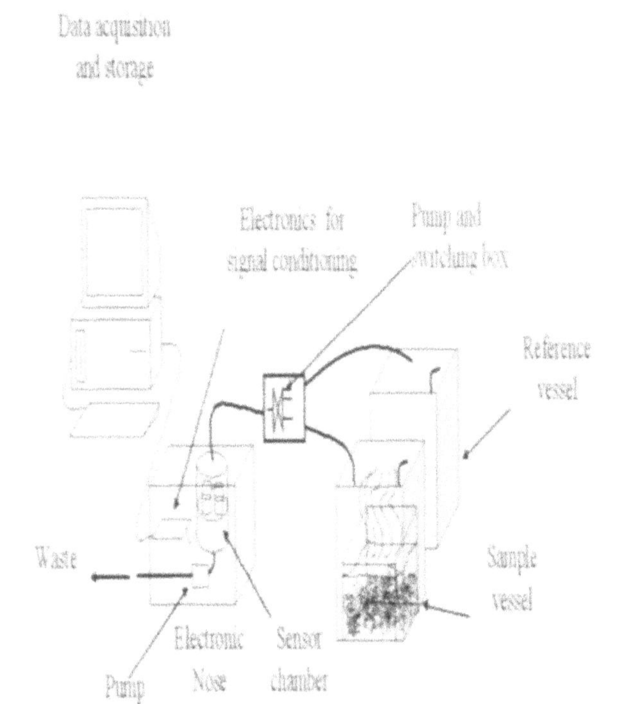

Fig. 2. Set-up for the Warwick MOS based electronic nose system for tea experiment.

monitored for the duration of the experiments. The temperature and humidity variations in the laboratory were typically 25 ± 1 °C and 30 ± 1%, over the period of the experiments.

One measurement comprises taking, alternatively, a headspace sample from the tea vessel followed by the reference vessel. During the process of the measurements, a sample of each sensor's resistance was taken every 5 s and stored in a data file for subsequent processing (Fig. 2). This process was repeated for each of the 5 tea samples in turn.

2.3. Interface electronics

The data acquisition and storage system was controlled usingLabVIEW© software (National Instruments Inc.) (National Instruments Corporation, 1998). A PC-LPM-16 PnP Data acquisition card was used for online data gathering (National Instruments Corporation, 1998).

2.4. Experimental data

In summary five different data-sets were gathered chronologically as follows:

- Data-set 1 (for 'under fermented normal fired in oven' sample)
- Data-set 2 (for 'well fermented over-fired in oven' sample)
- Data-set 3 (for 'well fermented normal fired in oven' sample)
- Data-set 4 (for 'drier month again over-fired' sample)
- Data-set 5 (for 'drier month' sample)

For each class of tea, 150 data vectors were gathered over a period of 10 consecutive days from 150 data gathering cycles. The number of days and samples were limited by practical circumstances though data collection continued 24 h per day, seven days per week, using our online EN data logger system.

3. Data processing

3.1. Signal pre-processing

The choice of the data pre-processing algorithm has been shown elsewhere to affect the performance of the pattern recognition stage (Dutta et al., 2003). In this case a difference model (i.e. static change in sensor resistance) was used: $dR = R_{air} - R_{odour}$. The complete tea data-set was then normalized, by dividing each dR by the maximum value, to set their range to [0, 1].

3.2. Data clustering

The use of Principal Components Analysis (PCA), Self-Organizing Map (SOM) and Fuzzy C Means (FCM) cluster analysis (Dutta et al., 2003; www.mathwork.com) to explore clustering within the data-sets is now discussed. Different 'cluster classification' methods were applied to verify that the categories established by each method were not arbitrary.

3.3. PCA analysis

PCA is a linear method that has been shown to be effective for discriminating the response of an EN to simple and complex odours (Dutta et al., 2003; Gardner, 1991; www.mathwork.com). The results of PCA, using the normalized data as described in the previous sub-section, are shown in Fig. 3. Three principal components were kept, which accounted for 99.8556% of the variance in the data-set (PC #1, PC #2 and PC#3 accounted for 97.9693, 1.0708 and 0.8155% of the variance, respectively, where PC #4 accounted for 0.14444%). Five qualities appear to be evident. It is also clearly evident that the sensors are linearly correlated. Since a reasonable correlation exists between categories, it can be assumed that the categories established by PCA are consistent with the five different qualities of the five tea samples (Fig. 3). The multivariate data analysis suggests there is considerable spread in the data. This spread may be due to a drifting in the sensors' responses.

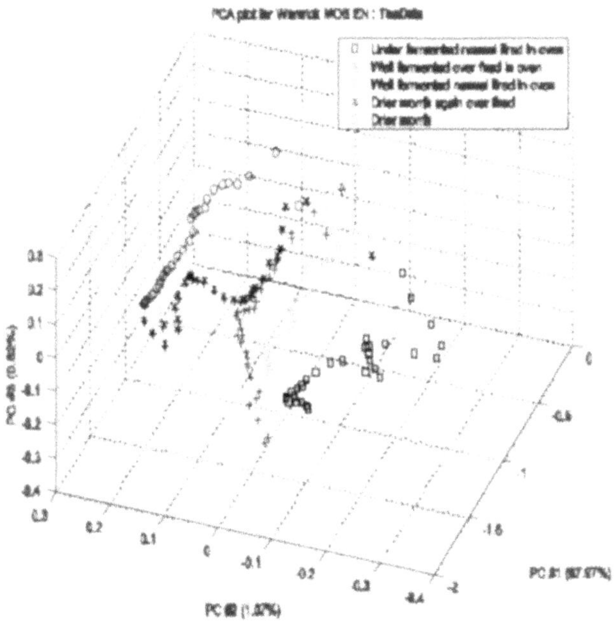

Fig. 3. PCA plot for the tea sample data.

3.4. Combined SOM, FCM and 3D-Scatter plot analysis: a new approach

An innovative data clustering approach was investigated for these tea data by combining the 3D-Scatter plot, FCM and SOM network (Gardner & Persaud, 2000; Jang, Sun, & Mizutani, 1997; Kohonen, 1989). It is depicted in Fig. 4. In multisensor space, normalized data-sets were represented using 3D-Scatter plots. From the FCM approach, a cluster center is found for each group by minimizing a dissimilarity function (Gardner, 1991; Kohonen, 1989). These cluster centers were plotted in multisensor space. So combining the 3D-Scatters plot and FCM, cluster centers were properly located in multisensor space and also within the data (Dutta et al., 2003). Thereafter a [5x1] SOM network was trained with the whole data-sets. After 500 epochs it was clear that the five nodes were approaching to the five cluster centers (estimated using FCM), which is more clearly evident from Fig. 4. So, using these three data clustering algorithms simultaneously, better 'classification' of data into different clusters was achieved (Fig. 4).

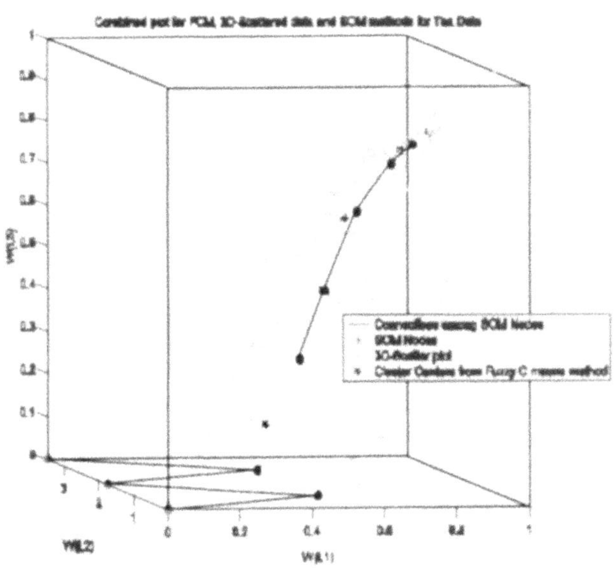

Fig. 4. Combined 3D-Scatter, FCM and SOM plot for tea sample data.

4. Comparative evaluation of neural network classification performance

4.1. Neural networks

The data-sets were analyzed using four supervised ANN classifiers, namely the MLP, LVQ, PNN and RBF paradigms (Dutta et al., 2003; Mao, 2002; www.mathwork.com). Training of the neural networks was performed with 50% of the whole data-set. The remaining 50% of the whole data was used for testing the neural networks. The aim of this comparative study was to identify the most appropriate ANN paradigm, which can be trained with best accuracy, to predict the 'Quality of tea samples'. Table 3, summarizes the architectures of the neural networks, which we used for our experimental training and testing for tea quality determination.

4.2. Dynamic drift correction using additional network training

Drift is a dynamic process, caused by physical changes in the sensors and the chemical background, which gives an unstable signal over the time (Distante, Artursson, Siciliano, Holmberg, & Lundström, 2000). EN data are usually affected by several disturbances in part due to the non-idealities of sensors and in part due to the effects of the environment as far as the composition of the gaseous sample is concerned. In some practical applications, the sample cannot be completely insulated from the surrounding environment and its drift (due to temperature and relative humidity changes) may be so large to completely obscure the intrinsic resolution of the sensor array. The problem could be solved at data analysis level making some assumptions on the nature of the disturbances (Natale, Martinelli, & D'Amico, 2002). Most gas sensors do not give stable responses over a long period of time. So sensor drift is addressed as one of the most serious impairments affecting chemical and biochemical sensors. One possible solution to this problem is to view sensor array as time-varying dynamic systems, whose variation have to be tracked by adaptive estimation algorithm (Holmberg, Davide, Natale, D'Amico, Winquist, & Lundström, 1997).

In this paper we have considered the two major drift effects from environmental temperature and humidity

Table 3
Architecture of different neural networks and results obtained in terms of 'percentage correct classification'

Neural networks	Architecture	Classification (%)
Learning Vector Quantization	3 hidden neurons were used for this network. Output class percentage was [0.2 0.2 0.2 0.2 0.2] and learning rate was 0.0125. (www.mathwork.com)	89
Multilayer Perceptron	For this network transfer function was HARDLIM and learning function was LEARNP (www.mathwork.com)	88
Probabilistic Neural Network	It was very similar to RBF network with a competitive output layer and SPREAD constant was set as 1.0 (www.mathwork.com)	94
Radial Basis Function network	Radial basis networks consist of two layers: a hidden radial basis layer and an output linear layer. For this network SPREAD constant was set as 1.0 (www.mathwork.com)	100

variations. Variations of temperature and humidity were monitored and stored throughout the experiment periods. To consider these temperature and humidity drifts effects on the original gathered data sensors' responses, we added two extra input nodes to our neural network. As these environmental parameters were stored along with the four sensors' responses it was appropriate to input them together into the neural network. ANNs trained with temperature and humidity were thus able to adjust their weights using information about environmental effects along with sensors' responses. With these additional network inputs, tea samples were better classified and we achieved up to 100% accuracy (see later sections).

4.3. MLP net

A MLP network (with learning rate equal to 0.3 and a momentum term equal to 0.4) with 6 inputs, 5 hidden and 5 output neurons was able to reach a success rate 88% in classification.

4.4. LVQ net

The networks had 6 input and 5 output neurons and a variable number of nodes in the competitive layer. Two main stages were followed:

- Initially the network was trained with a learning rate equal to 0.01 and the conscience factor was set equal to 1.
- In this next stage, once a 'relatively good' solution has been found by modifying the boundaries between zones where misclassifications occur, the solution is further refined. The learning rate was set to 0.0129. The LVQ algorithm was able to correctly classify 89% of the response vectors.

4.5. RBF and PNN

Neurons are added to the network until the sum-squared error falls beneath an error goal (0.000001) or a maximum number (150) of internal neurons was reached. It is important that the spread parameter is large enough so that the radial basis neurons respond to overlapping regions of the input space, but not so large that all the neurons respond in essentially the same manner (Mao, 2002; www.mathwork.com). For both the networks the spread parameter was set to value of 1.0. The PNN was able to classify correctly 94% of the response vectors whereas the RBF network's level of correct classification was up to 100%.

5. Conclusion

In this paper an effort has been made to discriminate between the flavours of different tea samples using an EN and hence explore the possibility of replacing existing analytical and profiling panel methods. Odour patterns from five different sets of tea samples were gathered with an EN instrument. Five different tea categories were identified with the help of PCA, FCM and SOM of the sensor responses (Dutta et al., 2003; Mao, 2002). From this result it is evident that our metal oxide sensor based Warwick EN was capable of discriminating between the flavours of teas manufactured under different processing conditions, viz. over-fermented, over-fired, under fermented, etc. along with linear data processing techniques like PCA. Then MLP, LVQ, RBF and PNN neural networks were applied to the classification of the state of the tea samples. An accuracy of 100% was reached in the classification using RBF network compared with 94% using a PNN (Gardner & Persaud, 2000; www.mathwork.com). It was found that these performances compared favourably with those achieved with trained MLP (88%) and LVQ (89%). Finally, the training time of RBF and PNN were found to be faster than MLP and LVQ. In this paper we have considered the two major drift effects from environmental temperature and humidity variations. Variations of temperature and humidity were monitored and stored throughout the experiment periods. To consider these temperature and humidity drifts effects on the original gathered data sensors' responses, we added two extra input nodes to our neural network. As these environmental parameters were stored along with the four sensors' responses it was appropriate to input them together into the neural network. The ANN trained with temperature and humidity was able to adjust its weights and hence compensate for changes in the ambient conditions. For example, tea samples were better classified and achieved up to an accuracy of 100% with a RBF network (Dutta et al., 2003).

In conclusion, we believe that a RBF networked based Warwick Metal Oxide EN provides an attractive means of discriminating among the flavours of teas manufactured under different processing conditions, viz. namely drier month, drier month again over-fired, well fermented normal fired in oven, well fermented over-fired in oven and under fermented normal fired in oven.

Acknowledgements

The authors would like to thank Warwick University for their financial support, and Aruneema Das for proof reading this manuscript.

References

Benady, M., Simon, J. E., & Miles, G. E. (1995). Fruit ripeness determination by electronic sensing of aromatic volatiles. *Transactions of the ASAE*, *38*(1), 251–257.

Bhuyan, M., & Borah, S. (2001). *Use of Electronic Nose in Tea Industry*. EAIT.

Distante, C., Artursson, T., Siciliano, P., Holmberg, M., & Lundström, I. (2000). Odour identification under drift effect. *Electronic Noses and Olfaction 2000* (pp. 89–95). Institute of Physics Publishing (IoP).

Dutta, R., Hines, E. L., Gardner, J. W., Udrea, D. D., & Boilot, P. (2003). Non-destructive egg freshness determination: an electronic nose based approach. *Measurement Science and Technology (IoP)*, *14*, 190–198.

Gardner, J. W. (1991). Detection of vapours and odours from a multisensor array using pattern recognition. Part 1: principal components and cluster analyses. *Sensors and Actuators B*, *4*, 108–116.

Gardner, J. W., Hines, E. L., & Tang, H. C. (1992). Detection of vapours and odours form a multisensor array using pattern recognition techniques: artificial neural networks. *Sensors and Actuators B*, *9*, 9–15.

Gardner, J. W., & Persaud, K. C. (2000). *Electronic Noses and Olfaction 2000*. Institute of Physics Publishing (IoP).

Gardner, J. W., Shurmer, H. V., & Tan, T. T. (1992). Application of an electronic nose to the discrimination of coffees. *Sensors and Actuators B*, *6*, 71–75.

Holmberg, M., Davide, F. A. M., Natale, C. D., D'Amico, A., Winquist, F., & Lundström, I. (1997). Drift counteraction in odour recognition applications: lifelong calibration method. *Sensor and Actuator B*, 185–194.

Jang, J. S. R., Sun, C. T., & Mizutani, E. (1997). *Neurofuzzy and Soft Computing: A Computational Approach to Learning and Machine Intelligence*. Upper Saddle River NJ: Prentice Hall, (3rd ed.) (pp. 423–433).

Kohonen, T. (1989). *Self-Organization and Associative Memory* (3rd ed.). Heidelberg: Springer, (pp. 185–209).

Mao, K. Z. (2002). RBF neural network center selection based on Fisher ration class separability measure. *IEEE Transaction on Neural Network*, *13*(5), 1211–1217.

Natale, C. D., Martinelli, E., & D'Amico, A. (2002). Counteraction of environmental disturbances of electronic nose data by independent component analysis. *Sensors and Actuators B*, *82*, 158–165.

National Instruments Corporation (1998). *LabVIEW version 5 Data Manual*. Austin, TX: National Instruments.

Pearce, T. C., Gardner, J. W., Friel, S., Bartlett, P. N., & Blair, N. (1993). Electronic nose for monitoring the flavour of beers. *Analyst*, 118.

Schweizer-Berberich, P. M., Vaihinger, S., & Göpel, W. (1994). Characterization of food freshness with sensor arrays. *Sensors and Actuators B*, *18*, 282–290.

Simon, J. E., Hetzroni, A., Bordelon, B., Miles, G. E., & Charles, D. J. (1996). Electronic sensing of aromatic volatiles for quality sorting of blueberries. *Journal of Food Science*, *61*(5), 967–970.

Winquist, F., Hornsten, E. G., Sundgren, H., & Lündstrom, I. (1993). Performance of an electronic nose for quality estimation of ground meat. *Measurement Science and Technology (IoP)*, *4*, 1493–1500.

www.mathwork.com.

AVAILABLE AT
www.ComputerScienceWeb.com
POWERED BY SCIENCE DIRECT

PERGAMON

Neural Networks 16 (2003) 855–864

Neural Networks

www.elsevier.com/locate/neunet

2003 Special issue

A novel neural network-based survival analysis model

Antonio Eleuteri[a,b,*], Roberto Tagliaferri[c,d], Leopoldo Milano[b,e], Sabino De Placido[f], Michele De Laurentiis[f]

[a]DMA, Università di Napoli 'Federico II', Naples, Italy
[b]INFN Sez. Napoli, Naples, Italy
[c]DMI, Università di Salerno, Salerno, Italy
[d]INFM Unità di Salerno, Salerno, Italy
[e]Dipartimento di Scienze Fisiche, Università di Napoli 'Federico II', Naples, Italy
[f]Dipartimento di Endocrinologia ed Oncologia Molecolare e Clinica, Università di Napoli 'Federico II', Naples, Italy

Abstract

A feedforward neural network architecture aimed at survival probability estimation is presented which generalizes the standard, usually linear, models described in literature. The network builds an approximation to the survival probability of a system at a given time, conditional on the system features. The resulting model is described in a hierarchical Bayesian framework. Experiments with synthetic and real world data compare the performance of this model with the commonly used standard ones.

Keywords: Survival analysis; Conditioning probability estimation; Neural networks; Bayesian learning; MCMC methods

1. Introduction

Survival analysis is used when we wish to study the occurrence of some event in a population of subjects and the time until the event is of interest. This time is called *survival time* or *failure time*. Survival analysis is often used in many fields of study. Examples include: time until failure of a light bulb and time until occurrence of an anomaly in an electronic circuit in industrial reliability, time until relapse of cancer and time until pregnancy in medical statistics, duration of strikes in economics, length of tracks on a photographic plate in particle physics.

In literature we find many different modeling approaches to survival analysis. Conventional parametric models may involve too strict assumptions on the distributions of failure times and on the form of the influence of the system features on the survival time, assumptions which usually extremely simplify the experimental evidence, particularly in the case of medical data (Kalbfleisch & Prentice, 1980). In contrast, semi-parametric models do not make assumptions on the distributions of failures, but make instead assumptions on how the system features influence the survival time. Finally, non-parametric models only allow for a qualitative description of the data.

Neural networks (NN) have been recently used for survival analysis, but most of the efforts have been devoted to extending Cox's model (Faraggi & Simon, 1995; Bakker & Heskes, 1999; Lisboa & Wong, 2001; Liestøl, Andersen, & Andersen, 1994), or in making piecewise or discrete approximations of the hazard functions (Neal, 2001; Biganzoli, Boracchi, & Marubini, 2002), or treating the problem as a classification one (De Laurentiis, De Placido, Bianco, Clark, & Ravdin, 1999) or by ignoring the censoring, which may introduce significant bias into the estimates, as criticized in Ripley and Ripley (1998) and Schwarzer, Vach, and Schumacher (2000). We refer to the latter two excellent surveys for the description of the many limitations which arise in the current use of NNs, limitations due to the use of heuristic approaches which do not take into account the peculiarities of survival data, and/or ignore fundamental issues such as regularization.

In this paper we describe a novel NN architecture which overcomes all the limitations of currently available NN models without making assumptions on the underlying survival distribution and which is proven to be flexible enough to model the most complex survival data. We describe our model in a Bayesian framework, which, as advocated by Raftery, Madigan, and Volinsky (1994) in

* Corresponding author. Address: INFN Sez, Napoli, Naples, Italy.
E-mail addresses: eleuteri@na.infn.it (A. Eleuteri), robtag@unisa.it (R. Tagliaferri).

0893-6080/03/$ - see front matter
doi:10.1016/S0893-6080(03)00098-4

the context of survival analysis, helps taking into account model uncertainty, which can help to improve the predictive performance of a model.

The paper is organized as follows. In Section 2 we describe the fundamentals of survival analysis and pose the censoring problem. In Section 3 we describe two of the most used standard modeling techniques, which will be used in comparison to our model. In Section 4 we describe the architecture of our NN. In Section 5 we describe our model in a hierarchical Bayesian framework and a Monte Carlo estimator of the survival function is shown. In Section 6 some experimental results are shown, in comparison with some commonly used modeling techniques.

2. Survival analysis

Let $T(\mathbf{x})$ denote an absolutely continuous random variable (rv) describing the failure time of a system defined by a vector of features $\mathbf{x}$. If $F_T(t|\mathbf{x})$ is the cumulative distribution function for $T(\mathbf{x})$, then we can define the *survival function*:

$$S(t|\mathbf{x}) = P\{T(\mathbf{x}) > t\} = 1 - F_T(t|\mathbf{x}) = 1 - \int_0^t f_T(u|\mathbf{x})\mathrm{d}u \quad (1)$$

which is the probability that the failure occurs after time t.

The requirements for a function $S(t|\mathbf{x})$ to be a survival function are, uniformly w.r.t. $\mathbf{x}$:

(1) $S(0|\mathbf{x}) = 1$ (there cannot be a failure before time 0),
(2) $S(+\infty|\mathbf{x}) = 0$ (asymptotically all events realize),
(3) $S(t_1|\mathbf{x}) \geq S(t_2|\mathbf{x})$ when $t_1 \leq t_2$.

From the definitions of survival and density of failure, we can derive the *hazard function* which gives the probability density of an event occuring around time t, given that it has not occured before t. It can be shown that the hazard has this form (Kalbfleisch & Prentice, 1980):

$$\lambda(t|\mathbf{x}) = \frac{f_T(t|\mathbf{x})}{S(t|\mathbf{x})}. \quad (2)$$

In many studies (e.g. in medical statistics or in quality control), we do not observe realizations of the rv $T(\mathbf{x})$. Rather, this variable is associated with some other rv $V \sim r$ such that the observation is a realization of the rv $Z = q(T, V)$. In this case we say that the observation of the time of the event is *censored*. If V is independent of T, we say that censoring is *uninformative*.

Depending on the form of the function q, we have different forms of censoring. Two of the most common ones in applications are *right censoring*, when $q \equiv \min(\cdot,\cdot)$ and *left censoring*, when $q \equiv \max(\cdot,\cdot)$.

Survival data can then be represented by triples of the form $(t, \mathbf{x}, y)$ where $\mathbf{x}$ is a vector of features defining the process, t is an observed time, and y is an indicator variable:

$$y = \begin{cases} 1 & \text{if } t \text{ is an event time} \\ 0 & \text{if } t \text{ is a censored time} \end{cases}. \quad (3)$$

We can define the sampling density $l(y|t, \mathbf{x})$ of a survival process (assuming, e.g. right censoring) by noting that, if we observe an event ($y = 1$), it directly contributes to the evaluation of the sample density; if we do not observe the event ($y = 0$), the best contribution is to evaluate $S(t|\mathbf{x})$. We have then:

$$l(y|t, \mathbf{x}) = S(t|\mathbf{x})^{1-y} f_T(t|\mathbf{x})^y. \quad (4)$$

The joint sample density for a set of independent observations $D = \{(t_k, \mathbf{x}_k, y_k)\}$ can then be written as:

$$L = \prod_k l(y_k|t_k, \mathbf{x}_k). \quad (5)$$

Since the censoring is supposed uninformative, it does not influence inference on the failure density, but gives contribution to the sample density.

Note that censored data models can be seen as a particular class of missing data models in which the densities of interest are not sampled directly (Robert & Casella, 1999).

3. Standard models for survival analysis

In the next sections we will describe some of the most commonly used models, both for homogeneous (time-only) and heterogeneous modeling.

3.1. The Kaplan–Meier non-parametric estimator

The Kaplan–Meier (KM) estimator is a non-parametric maximum likelihood estimator of the survival function. It is piecewise constant, and it can be thought of as an empirical survival function for censored data. In its basic form, it is only homogeneous.

Let k be the number of events in the sample, $t_1, t_2, \ldots, t_k$ the event times (supposed unique and ordered), e_i the number of events at time t_i and r_i the number of times (event or censored) greater than or equal to t_i. The estimator is given by the formula:

$$S_{\mathrm{KM}}(t) = \prod_{i:t_i<t} \frac{r_i - e_i}{r_i}. \quad (6)$$

It can be shown that the KM. estimator maximizes the generalized likelihood over the space of all distributions, so its evaluation on large data sets gives a good qualitative description of the true survival function. However, it should be noted that it is noisy when the data are few, in particular when the events are rare, since it is piecewise constant. Therefore KM estimates from datasets sampled from the same distribution but with different number of samples can differ quite a lot.

3.2. Proportional hazards models

The most used survival specification which takes into account system features is to allow the hazard function to have the form:

$$\lambda(t|\mathbf{x}) = \lambda(t)\exp(\mathbf{w}^{\mathrm{T}}\mathbf{x}) \tag{7}$$

where $\lambda(t)$ is some homogeneous hazard function (called the *baseline hazard*) and $\mathbf{w}$ are the feature dependent parameters of the model. This is called a *proportional hazards* (PH) model. The two most used approaches for this kind of model are:

- Choose a parameterized functional form for the baseline hazard, then use Maximum Likelihood (ML) techniques to find values for the parameters of the model;
- do not fix the baseline hazard, but make a ML estimation of the feature dependent part of the model, and a non-parametric estimation of the baseline hazard. This is called Cox's model (Kalbfleisch & Prentice, 1980).

NNs have simply been used to estimate the feature dependent part of the model; however, the main drawback remains, which is the assumption of proportionality between the time-dependent and feature-dependent parts of the model.

4. A neural network model

In this section we define a NN which, given a data set of system features and times, provides a model for the survival function (and implicitly, by suitable transforms, of the other functions of interest, e.g. failure density and hazard).

It is well known (Bishop, 1996) that a sigmoid is the appropriate activation function for the output of a NN to be interpretable as a probability. If $V(a) = (1 + \exp(-a))^{-1}$ is such a sigmoid function (a is the net input to the activation), by taking into account Eq. (1) and using $S = 1 - V$ we can define the activation function of the NN as:

$$S(a) = \frac{1}{1 + \exp(a)}. \tag{8}$$

This is not sufficient to define a survival function, since we must also enforce the requirements in Section 3.

(1) $S(0|\mathbf{x}) = 1$ and $S(+\infty|\mathbf{x}) = 0$. We set one of the activation functions of the hidden layer to be the $h(t|w_{t_1}) \equiv a_t = \log(tw_{t_1})$ function. We call this hidden unit the *time unit*. Note that the only input feeding into this unit through the weight w_{t_1} is the time input (neither biases nor other inputs feed this unit).

The other activation functions (denoted by g) are assumed to be squashing functions. Since these functions are all bounded (and the integration functions for hidden and output nodes is assumed to be the scalar product), this ensures us that the required conditions are satisfied if the first-layer weight w_{t_1} connecting the input t is non-negative and the second-layer weight w_{t_2} connecting the h unit to the output is also non-negative. In this way the net input to the output activation goes to negative infinity or zero, so that the output saturates to 1 or 0, respectively. Note that the input t is also connected to the squashing hidden units with variable strength weights so that interactions with other input features are taken into account. As shown in the next sections, these weights must also be constrained in some way.

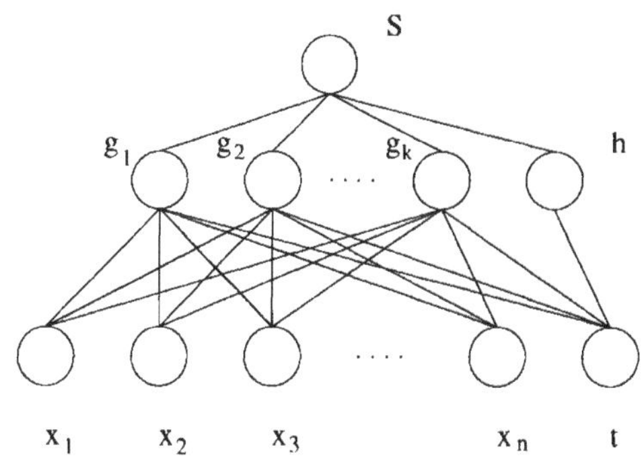

Fig. 1. Architecture of SNN.

(2) $S(t|\mathbf{x})$ must be non-increasing as t increases. We must look at the functional form of the network output. Since it must be a non-increasing function of a, we must ensure that a is a non-decreasing function of t. We have:

$$a \equiv a_N + a_t = \sum_{j=1}^{N} w_j g(a_j) + w_{t_2} \log(w_{t_1} t) \tag{9}$$

where g is the activation function in the hidden layer, w_j is a weight of the second layer[1] and N is the number of squashing hidden units (we have not included the biases in the summation). If we suppose that the $g(a_j)$ are non-decreasing, then a is non-decreasing if and only if the weights w_j are non-negative. We must now impose that the $g(a_j)$ are non-decreasing. Since they are monotonic non-decreasing functions, then we must impose that their arguments are non-decreasing functions of t. This can be accomplished if we impose that the weights associated with the time input are non-negative. In short, all the weights on paths connecting the time input to the network output must be non-negative. In Fig. 1 the architecture of the Survival Neural Network (SNN) is shown (the bias connections are not shown).

Note that the use of an unbounded activation function as hidden time unit does not put discontinuities in the function

[1] From here on, to simplify the notation, when we must refer to expressions involving all the weights in a layer (including the weights into and out of the time unit), we will denote generic second-layer weights with a single index, and generic first-layer weights with two indices.

defined by the network, since it can be easily verified that Eq. (8) is equivalent to:

$$S = \frac{1}{1 + (w_{t_1} t)^{w_{t_2}} \exp(a_N)} \quad (10)$$

which, however, has not the form of a standard MLP network function.

5. Hierarchical Bayesian modeling

In the conventional ML approach to training, a single weight vector is found which minimizes an error function; in contrast, the Bayesian scheme considers a probability distribution over weights.

We made many tests with ML approaches, training a single network with constrained optimization algorithms, and then using ensembles of such networks. The results, however, were always less than satisfactory and uniformly worse than those obtained in a Bayesian framework. For an in-depth discussion on Bayesian learning in the context of NNs we refer to Neal (1996).

As pointed out by Watanabe (2001), Bayesian learning methods are necessary when we deal with hierarchical statistical models like NNs, which are non-identifiable and non-regular. The use of networks with a large number of hidden units implies that neither the distribution of the ML estimator nor the a posteriori probability density of weights converges to the normal distribution, even in the case of infinite data sets. This implies that model selection methods like Akaike's Information Criterion (AIC), Bayesian Information Criterion (BIC) and Minimum Description Length (MDL) cannot be used in the context of complex NNs.

Since SNN is a very complex network, we shall build a Bayesian statistical model, which is composed by a parametric statistical model (the sample density) and a prior distribution over the weights.

We can then describe the learning process as an updating of a prior distribution $p(\mathbf{w})$, based on the observation of the data D through the joint sample density $p(D|\mathbf{w})$. This process can be expressed by Bayes' theorem:

$$p(\mathbf{w}|D) = \frac{p(D|\mathbf{w})p(\mathbf{w})}{\int p(D|\mathbf{w})p(\mathbf{w})\mathrm{d}\mathbf{w}}. \quad (11)$$

The joint sample density is given in Eq. (5), in which S is the function realized by the network and f_T is given by minus the Jacobian of the network, which can be efficiently evaluated with a backpropagation procedure.

5.1. Choosing the prior distribution

The prior over weights should reflect any knowledge we have about the mapping we want to build. For the SNN model, we must then take into account the fact that we want a smooth mapping and that we have both constrained and unconstrained weights; furthermore, we should take into account the specialized rôle the weights have in the network depending on their position. We can thus define the following weight groups:

- Unconstrained weights:
  - a group for each of the covariate input, comprising the weights out of that input into the hidden squashing units;
  - one group for the biases feeding the hidden squashing units;
  - one group for the output bias.
- Constrained weights:
  - one group for the weights out of the input time unit feeding the hidden squashing units;
  - one group for the weight out of the input time unit feeding the hidden time unit;
  - one group for the weight out of the hidden time unit;
  - one group for the weights out of the hidden squashing units;

If n is the number of inputs then we have $n + 5$ groups.

We assign a distribution to each group, governed by its set of parameters (hyperparameters). Since the weights are a priori statistically independent, then the prior over the whole set of weights will be the product of the priors over each group.

(1) *Priors for unconstrained weights.* We can give a zero mean Gaussian prior to unconstrained weights, so as to favor small weights and consequently smooth mappings. This kind of prior, due to its simplicity and analytical properties has been extensively used in the literature (Neal, 1996; MacKay, 1992; Bishop, 1996).

By assigning a different prior to the weights out of each covariate input allows us to use the Automatic Relevance Determination (ARD) technique (MacKay, 1992; Neal, 1996), which can give hints on the relevance of inputs to non-linear relations with the output. Furthermore, the weights out of each input can be scaled to reflect the different scales of the different inputs.

The Gaussian prior over the unconstrained weights has the following form:

$$p(\mathbf{w}_u|\boldsymbol{\alpha}_u) \propto \prod_{k \in \mathcal{G}_u} \exp\left(-\frac{\alpha_k}{2} \sum_{i_k=1}^{W_k} w_{i_k}^2\right) \quad (12)$$

where $\mathbf{w}_u$ is the vector of unconstrained weights, $\mathcal{G}_u$ is the set of the unconstrained weight groups, W_k is the cardinality of the k-th group and $\boldsymbol{\alpha}_u$ is the vector of hyperparameters (inverse variances).

(2) *Priors for constrained weights.* The positivity constraints on some groups forces us to choose a distribution with positive support. The most simple distribution with good analytical properties and which expresses well our prior requirements on positivity and smoothness is

the exponential distribution. The exponential prior over the constrained weights has this form:

$$p(\mathbf{w}_c^{(e)}|\boldsymbol{\alpha}_c^{(e)}) \propto \prod_{k\in\mathcal{G}_c^{(e)}} \exp\left(-\alpha_k \sum_{i_k=1}^{W_k} w_{i_k}\right) \mathbb{I}(\mathbf{w}_c^{(e)}) \quad (13)$$

where $\mathbf{w}_c^{(e)}$ is the vector of constrained weights, $\mathcal{G}_c^{(e)}$ is the set of the unconstrained weight groups, W_k is the cardinality of the k-th group, $\boldsymbol{\alpha}_c^{(e)}$ is the vector of hyperparameters (inverse means) and $\mathbb{I}(\cdot)$ is the indicator function over the positive half-space in which the weights are constrained. It can be shown that this prior is appropriate for all constrained weights, except those out of the hidden squashing units.

(3) *Limit behaviour for priors with finite variance.* We now analyze the prior over the survival functions implied by an exponential prior on the weights out of the hidden squashing units when the network inputs are fixed to a given value. From Eq. (9), we see that a contribution to the overall sum is given by the weighted sum of N squashing hidden units. The terms in the sum are a priori independent and identically distributed. We can evaluate the expected value of each squashing hidden unit's contribution by noting that the w_j are a priori independent of the activations g_j (from here on, we omit the indices since the distribution is the same for all j):

$$\mu_{wg} \equiv \mathbf{E}[wg] = \mathbf{E}[w]\mathbf{E}[g] \equiv \mu_w\mu_g. \quad (14)$$

The expectation of the contribution is finite because μ_g is finite since the activation is a bounded function.

We can also evaluate the variance of each squashing hidden unit contribution:

$$\begin{aligned}\sigma_{wg}^2 &\equiv \mathbf{E}[(wg)^2] - \mathbf{E}[wg]^2 = \mathrm{E}[w^2]\mathrm{E}[g^2] - \mu_w^2\mu_g^2 \\ &= (\sigma_w^2 + \mu_w^2)(\sigma_g^2 + \mu_g^2) - \mu_w^2\mu_g^2 \\ &= \sigma_w^2(\sigma_g^2 + \mu_g^2) + \mu_w^2\sigma_g^2. \end{aligned} \quad (15)$$

The variance of the contribution is finite because σ_g^2 is finite since the activation is a bounded function.

We can then apply the Central Limit Theorem and conclude that for large N the total contribution converges to a Gaussian distribution with parameters:

$$\mu = N\mu_w\mu_g \qquad \sigma^2 = N[\sigma_w^2(\sigma_g^2 + \mu_g^2) + \mu_w^2\sigma_g^2]. \quad (16)$$

This result extends Neal's analysis in Neal (1996) to non-Gaussian distributions with finite variance. To obtain a finite limit for the location parameter which does not saturate the output activation, we must scale μ_w according to N, by choosing $\mu_w = \rho_e N^{-1}$, for fixed ρ_e. However, this choice is troublesome. In fact, for the exponential distribution we have $\mu_w = \sigma_w$, so that the variance of the contribution is, for large N :

$$\lim_{N\to\infty} N\left[\left(\frac{\rho_e}{N}\right)^2(\sigma_g^2 + \mu_g^2) + \left(\frac{\rho_e}{N}\right)^2\sigma_g^2\right] = 0. \quad (17)$$

This behaviour is not desirable, since we get a degenerate distribution centered on $\rho_e\mu_g$. To get a non-degenerate distribution we should let the location grow as N grows, which is undesirable since we do not want to saturate the output of the network. Furthermore, since all the weights would tend to assume the same value, we would lose the possibility that the network represents hidden features of the data (Neal, 1996).

We could think to solve the problem by choosing a different distribution with continuous positive support. However, the problem is more general than it might appear. In fact, what we said before is true whenever the mean and the standard deviation of the distribution are in a proportionality relation. And this is true for many common distributions such as: the gamma family (which includes the exponential and Maxwell distributions), truncated normal, inverse gamma, Fisher, χ^2, Weibull.

(4) *Limit behaviour for stable priors.* A possible solution is to use distributions which are not in the normal domain of attraction of the Gaussian, that is densities whose limiting sums do not tend to the Gaussian density. It turns out that all the densities with finite variance are in the normal domain of attraction of the Gaussian.

Densities which are not in the normal domain of attraction of the Gaussian are said to be *stable*, and are characterized by an index α such that, if $X_1, \ldots, X_n$ are independent identically distributed with the same index, then $(X_1 + \cdots + X_n)/n^{1/\alpha}$ is stable with the same index (note that Gaussian densities are stable with $\alpha = 2$). For an in-depth discussion on stable processes we refer to Samorodnitsky and Taqqu (1994). We shall concentrate our attention on the Lévy density, for which $\alpha = 1/2$. The joint distribution of the weights out of the squashing hidden units is:

$$p(\mathbf{w}_c^{(L)}|\gamma) \propto \exp\left(-\sum_{i=1}^{N}\left(\frac{\gamma}{2w_i} + \frac{3}{2}\log w_i\right)\right)\mathbb{I}(\mathbf{w}_c^{(L)}). \quad (18)$$

To obtain a well defined limit as N grows large, we need to scale the parameter: $\gamma = \rho_L N^{-2}$, with fixed ρ_L.

With this choice of the prior, we will have a stable non-degenerate distribution whatever the number N of squashing hidden units is. Furthermore, since this density is heavy tailed, the larger the value of the γ parameter is, the higher the probability that many weights have values in a wide range, favoring complex models and the representation of hidden features in the data (Neal, 1996).

5.2. Markov chain Monte Carlo methods for sampling the posterior

The best prediction we can obtain given a new input and the observed data D can be written in the following way:

$$\begin{aligned} p(y|(\mathbf{x}, t), D) &= \int p(y, \mathbf{w}, \boldsymbol{\alpha}|\mathbf{x}, t), D)\mathrm{d}\mathbf{w}\,\mathrm{d}\boldsymbol{\alpha} \\ &= \int p(y|(\mathbf{x}, t), \mathbf{w})p(\mathbf{w}, \boldsymbol{\alpha})|D)\mathrm{d}\mathbf{w}\,\mathrm{d}\boldsymbol{\alpha} \end{aligned} \quad (19)$$

where $p(y|(\mathbf{x}, t), \mathbf{w})$ is the predictive model of the network. This can be seen as the evaluation of the expectation of the network function with respect to the posterior distribution of the network weights. In our case the integral cannot be solved analytically, so we must use a numerical approximation scheme.

The posterior density in Eq. (11) can be efficiently sampled by using a Markov chain Monte Carlo (MCMC) method, which consists in generating a sequence of weight vectors, and then using it to approximate the integral in Eq. (19) with the following the Monte Carlo estimator (M is the number of samples from the posterior):

$$p(y|\mathbf{x}, t), D) \approx \frac{1}{M} \sum_{i=1}^{M} p(y|\mathbf{x}, t), \mathbf{w}_i) \tag{20}$$

which is guaranteed to converge by the Ergodic Theorem to the true value of the integral as M goes to infinity.

The MCMC method we used for generating the sequence of weight vectors is the Slice Sampling method. For a detailed discussion see Neal (2000).

5.3. Gibbs sampling

As we have seen, the priors over the weights used in the inference of the posterior are themselves parametrized. Instead of setting the values of these hyperparameters to arbitrary values, we can make them part of the inference process, by sampling from Eq. (11). This can efficiently be done by using the Gibbs sampling process. In a first step the hyperparameters are kept constant, and we use an MCMC method to sample from Eq. (11). The second step consists in keeping the weights constant, while the hyperparameters are sampled from the following distribution:

$$\begin{aligned} p(\boldsymbol{\alpha}|\mathbf{w}, D) &= \frac{p(\boldsymbol{\alpha}, \mathbf{w}, D)}{p(\mathbf{w}, D)} \\ &= \frac{p(D|\mathbf{w})p(\mathbf{w}|\boldsymbol{\alpha})p(\boldsymbol{\alpha})}{p(D|\mathbf{w})p(\mathbf{w})} \propto p(\mathbf{w}|\boldsymbol{\alpha})p(\boldsymbol{\alpha}). \end{aligned} \tag{21}$$

This process can be done efficiently if we choose a hyperprior $p(\boldsymbol{\alpha})$ which is conjugate to the hyperposterior $p(\boldsymbol{\alpha}|\mathbf{w}, D)$ (i.e. they both belong to the same family (Robert, 2001)). It is possible to show that in the case of Gaussian, exponential and Lévy priors, by choosing gamma hyperprior distributions, the resulting hyperposteriors are gamma distributions.

It can be proven that this hierarchical extension is beneficial in many respects, one of which is the increased robustness of the model. For a detailed discussion on the topic of hierarchical Bayesian modeling we refer to Robert (2001) and Neal (1996) for applications to NNs.

6. Experiments

In this section we show the performance of the SNN model on two data sets, a synthetic heterogeneous problem and a real heterogeneous medical problem. All the software for the simulations has been written by the authors in the MATLAB© language. In each experiment two models were fitted: a Cox PH model and a SNN model with 50 hidden units. KM estimates were then evaluated for each model.

The Cox PH model was trained using standard ML estimation while the SNN model was trained with the MCMC slice sampling algorithm with Gibbs sampling of the hyperparameters. The first 400 samples were omitted from the chain. Then, 700 samples were generated by alternating between normal and overrelaxed steps. Finally, the last 100 samples were used to obtain the Monte Carlo estimator of the SNN output, based on an inspection of the energies of the chain. Note that in a real use of the algorithm, a simple inspection of the energies might not be sufficient to assess convergence; instead, a formal test of convergence, like the *Estimated Potential Scale Reduction* diagnostic (Robert & Casella, 1999) should be used.

6.1. Synthetic heterogeneous data

In this experiment we considered a mixture of Weibull and gamma densities with parameters dependent on the variables x_1, x_2 :

$$\begin{aligned} f_T(t|\mathbf{x}) =& x_2 \mathscr{W}e(x_1^2, \sin(x_1)^3 + 2) + (1 - x_2) \\ & \times \mathscr{G}a((x_1 + 1)^2, \exp(\cos(x_1) + 2)). \end{aligned} \tag{22}$$

This data set was built to test the SNN model in the case in which the proportional hazards assumption is not verified. The covariates x_1 and x_2 were first sampled from a bivariate Gaussian with mean vector (0, 0) and full covariance matrix such that the correlation coefficient of the variables was -0.71. Next, the variable x_2 was transformed to a binary indicator: values greater than or equal to 0 were set to 1, values less than 0 were set to 0. After the transformation the correlation coefficient was -0.57. Then, 7000 samples were generated from the mixture, with about 27% uniformly right censored data in the interval [0,80]. The data were then uniformly split in two disjoint data sets: a training set of 4000 samples and a testing set of 3000 samples (with the same percentage of censored data in each set).

To get a clear understanding of how well the SNN model is capturing the behaviour of the censored data, we made a comparison with KM estimates. The test data was stratified in five quantities based on the survival estimates of the models at $t = 8.4$ (median time). Then, the mean (with respect to the covariates) survival probabilities were estimated, togheter with KM estimates of the quantiles induced by the models. If a model is

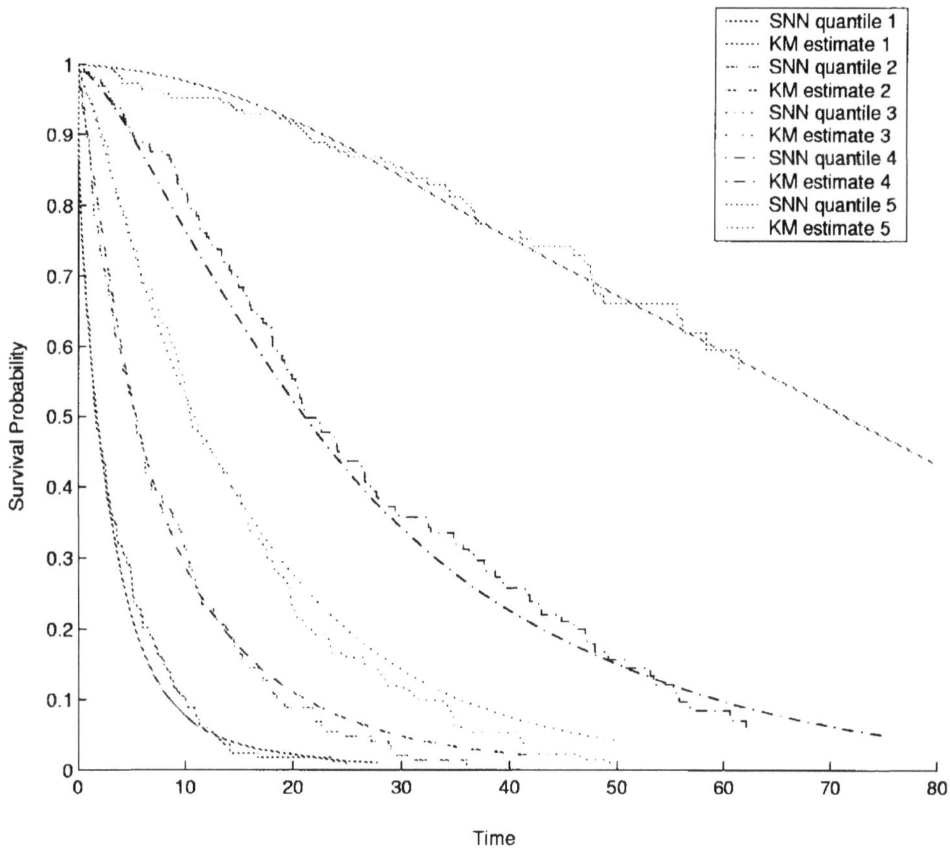

Fig. 2. SNN model of a synthetic survival function with covariates (evaluated on the test set).

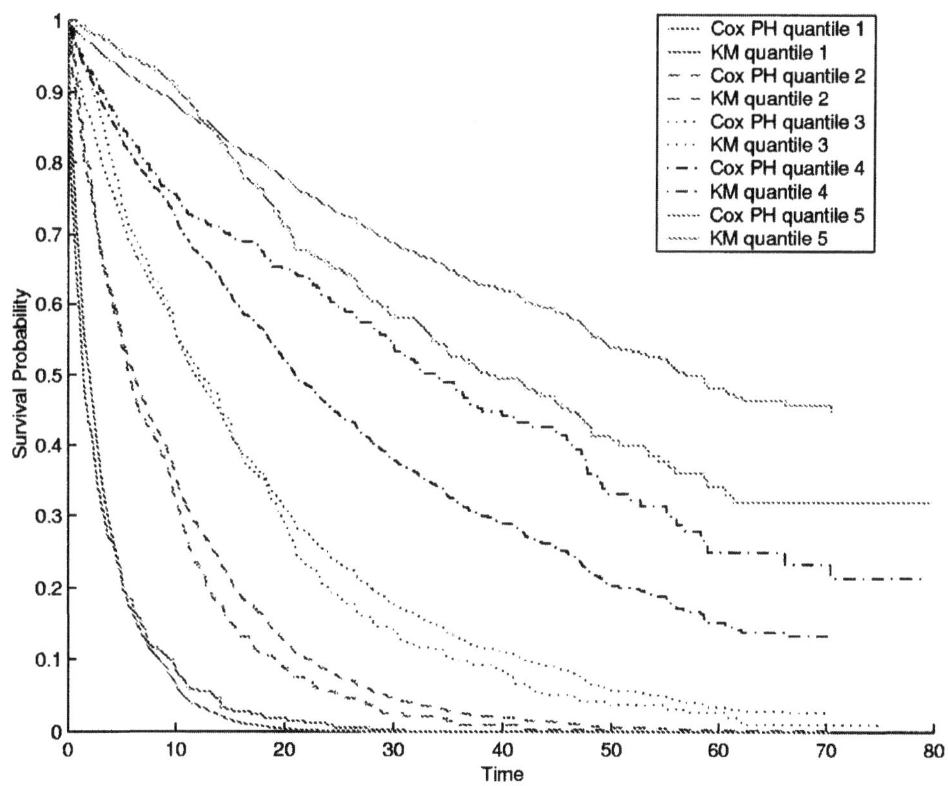

Fig. 3. Cox PH model of a synthetic survival function with covariates (evaluated on the test set).

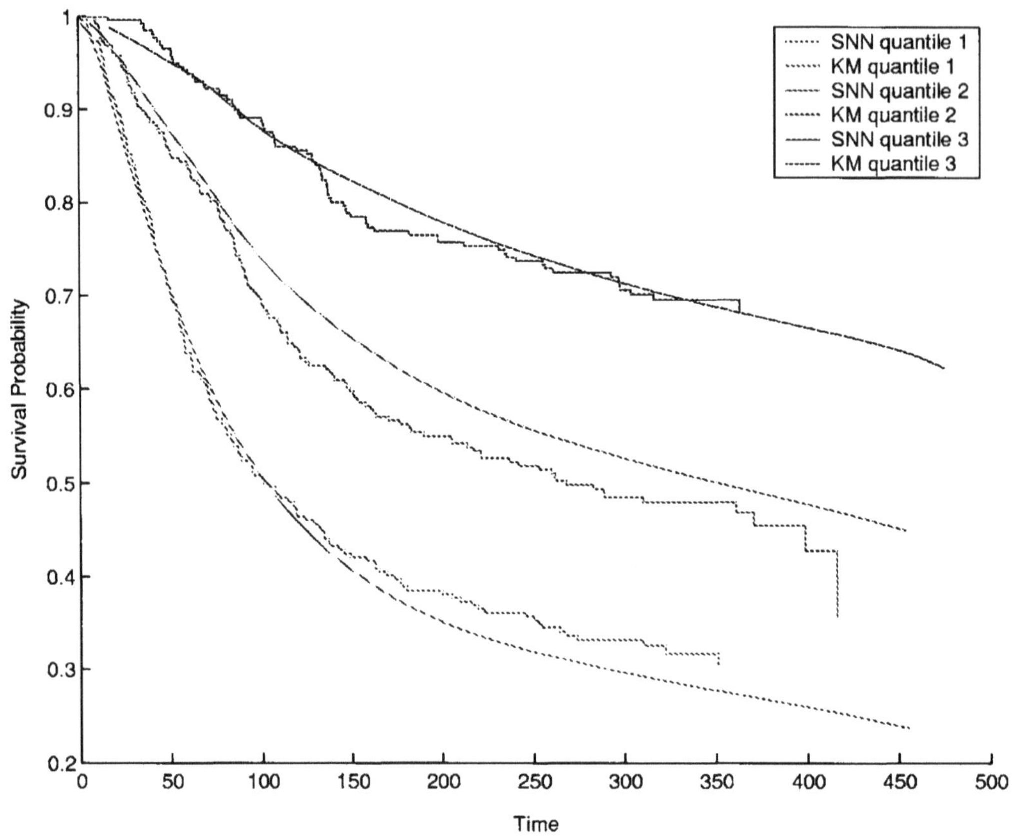

Fig. 4. SNN model of a real survival function with covariates (evaluated on the test set).

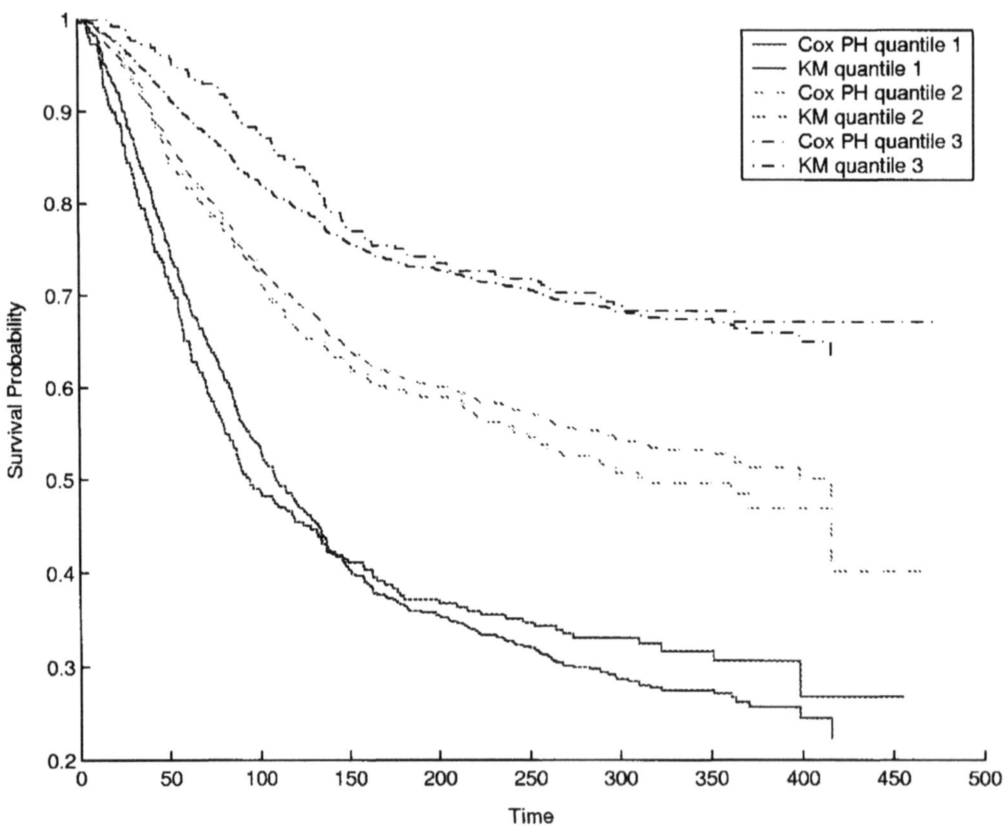

Fig. 5. Cox PH model of a real survival function with covariates (evaluated on the test set).

able to capture the distribution of the data we expect the output of the model and KM estimates to be similar. As can be seen in Figs. 2 and 3, the SNN model shows good performance on all quantiles, while the Cox PH model shows good performance only on bad prognosis quantiles. As we expected, the proportional hazards model could not describe well the data.

6.2. Real heterogeneous data

These data are taken from trials of chemotherapy for stage B/C colon cancer.[2] It is composed of 1776 samples, with 12 covariates. The dataset was split into a training set of 1076 samples, and a test set of 700 samples. About 49% of the data are censored, which makes the analysis of the data a complex task.

The test data was stratified in three quantiles based on the survival estimates of the models at $t = 217$ weeks. Then, the mean (with respect to the covariates) survival probabilities were estimated, togheter with KM estimates of the quantiles induced by the models. If the model can capture the distribution of the data we expect the output of the model and KM estimates to be similar. As can be seen in Figs. 4 and 5, the SNN and Cox PH model both exhibit good discriminatory power, also if the Cox estimate is noisy, since it is piecewise constant. This test shows that the SNN model is able to work with real-world data for which the proportional hazards assumption is roughly verified.

7. Conclusions and perspectives

In this paper we have described a novel NN architecture that addresses survival analysis in a neural computation paradigm.

Starting from the requirements on the survival function, we have defined a feedforward NN which satisfies those requirements with appropriate choice of hidded unit activations and constraints on the weight space.

The proposed model does not make any assumption on the form of the survival process, and does not use discretizations or piecewise approximations as other NN approaches to survival analysis do.

Experiments on synthetic and real survival data demonstrate that the SNN model can approximate complex survival functions. On synthetic survival data it outperformed the PH model, since the data did not verify the proportional hazards assumptions by construction. On real survival data which verifies the PH assumptions it showed very similar performance to the Cox PH model, thus showing the capability to model also proportional hazards, real-word data.

As an empirical proof of effectiveness, we have also shown that the SNN model closely follows the time evolution of the KM non-parametric estimator on large data sets, for which the KM estimator is known to give very accurate descriptions of the survival process.

The development of DNA microarrays and other techniques to produce high-quality, highly informative and complex datasets will require correspondingly complex modeling techniques. We believe that the neural computation paradigm if correctly employed can be a powerful tool to analyze complex datasets, and the SNN model shows that complex data can be analyzed in a robust Bayesian framework.

Acknowledgements

This work was partially supported by MIUR Progetto di Rilevanza Nazionale, MIUR-CNR, AIRC.

References

Bakker, B., & Heskes, T. (1999). A neutral-Bayesian approach to survival analysis. *Proceedings of IEE Artificial Neural Networks*, 832–837.

Biganzoli, E., Boracchi, P., & Marubini, E. (2002). A general framework for neural network models on censored survival data. *Neural Networks*, *15*, 209–218.

Bishop, C. M. (1996). *Neural networks for pattern recognition*. Oxford: Clarendon Press.

De Laurentiis, M., De Placido, S., Bianco, A. R., Clark, G. M., & Ravdin, P. M. (1999). A prognostic model that makes quantitative estimates of probability of relapse for breast cancer patients. *Clinical Cancer Research*, *19*, 4133–4139.

Faraggi, D., & Simon, R. (1995). A neural network model for survival data. *Statistics in Medicine*, *14*, 73–82.

Kalbfleisch, J. D., & Prentice, R. L. (1980). *The statistical analysis of failure time data*. New York: Wiley.

Liestøl, K., Andersen, P. K., & Anderson, U. (1994). Survival analysis and neural nets. *Statistics in Medicine*, *13*, 1189–1200.

Lisboa, P. J. G., & Wong, H. (2001). Are neural networks best used to help logistic regression? An example from breast cancer survival analysis. *IEEE Transactions on Neural Networks*, 2472–2477.

MacKay, D. J. C. (1992). A practical Bayesian framework for back-propagation networks. *Neural Computation*, *4*(3), 448–472.

Neal, R. M. (1996). *Bayesian learning for neural networks*. New York: Springer.

Neal, R. M (2000). *Slice Sampling*. Technical Report No. 2005, Department of Statistics, University of Toronto.

Neal, R. M (2001). *Survival Analysis Using a Bayesian Neural Network*. Joint Statistical Meetings report, Atlanta.

Raftery, A. E., Madigan, D., & Volinsky, C. T. (1994). Accounting for model uncertainty in survival analysis improves predictive performance. *Bayesian Statistics*, *5*, 323–349.

Ripley, B. D., & Ripley, R. M. (1998). Neural Networks as statistical methods in survival analysis. In R. Dybowsky, & V. Gant (Eds.), *Artificial neural networks: Prospects for medicine*. Landes Biosciences.

[2] The data are distributed with the freeware R statistical software, available at http://www.r-project.org

Robert, C. P. (2001). *The Bayesian choice* (2nd ed). New York: Springer.

Robert, C. P., & Casella, G. (1999). *Markov chain Monte Carlo methods.* New York: Springer.

Samorodnitsky, G., & Taqqu, M. S. (1994). *Stable non-Gaussian random processes: Stochastic models with infinite variance.* New York: Chapman and Hall.

Schwarzer, G., Vach, W., & Schumacher, M. (2000). On the misuses of artificial neural networks for prognostic and diagnostic classification in oncology. *Statistics in Medicine*, *19*, 541–561.

Watanabe, S (2001). *Learning Efficiency of Redundant Neural Networks in Bayesian Estimation.* Technical Report No. 687, Precision and Intelligence Laboratory, Tokyo Institute of Technology.

PERGAMON

AVAILABLE AT www.ComputerScienceWeb.com POWERED BY SCIENCE DIRECT

Neural Networks 16 (2003) 865–871

Neural Networks

www.elsevier.com/locate/neunet

2003 Special issue

Divide-and-conquer approach for brain machine interfaces: nonlinear mixture of competitive linear models

Sung-Phil Kim[a,*], Justin C. Sanchez[a], Deniz Erdogmus[a], Yadunandana N. Rao[a], Johan Wessberg[b], Jose C. Principe[a], Miguel Nicolelis[b]

[a]*Department of Electrical Engineering, University of Florida, Gainesville, FL 32611, USA*
[b]*Department of Neurobiology, Duke University, Durham, NC 27710, USA*

Abstract

This paper proposes a divide-and-conquer strategy for designing brain machine interfaces. A nonlinear combination of competitively trained local linear models (experts) is used to identify the mapping from neuronal activity in cortical areas associated with arm movement to the hand position of a primate. The proposed architecture and the training algorithm are described in detail and numerical performance comparisons with alternative linear and nonlinear modeling approaches, including time-delay neural networks and recursive multilayer perceptrons, are presented. This new strategy allows training the local linear models using normalized LMS and using a relatively smaller nonlinear network to efficiently combine the predictions of the linear experts. This leads to savings in computational requirements, while the performance is still similar to a large fully nonlinear network.

Keywords: Brain machine interfaces; Multiple local linear models; Competitive learning

1. Introduction

Brain machine interfaces (BMI) are a developing technology that aims to directly transfer the subject's intent of movement to a machine. Our goal is to engineer devices that are able to interpret neural activity originating in the motor, premotor, and posterior parietal cortices and generate accurate predictions of hand position. We envision the application of these devices in BMI, where movement can be restored in individuals suffering from neurological disorders.

Recently, a number of groups have demonstrated that linear and nonlinear adaptive system identification approaches can lead to BMI that effectively predict the hand position of primates using only neural signals (Chapin, Moxon, Markowitz, & Nicolelis, 1999; Moran & Schwartz, 1999; Serruya, Hatsopoulos, Paninski, Fellows, & Donoghue, 2002; Wessberg et al., 2000). The topologies studied thus far include FIR filters, time-delay neural networks (TDNN), Kalman filter and extensions, and recursive multilayer perceptrons (RMLP). In the BMI experimental paradigm, large arrays of microelectrodes are implanted in the cortical areas listed above and the corresponding neural activity is recorded. Spike-detection and sorting algorithms are used to process these analog potentials to determine the firing times of single neurons. Typically, the spike-time information is summarized into bin counts using short windows (100 ms in this paper). In all previous work, the approach had been to try to determine a functional/dynamical mapping between these bin counts and the hand position. In this paper, we follow the same approach.

An important consideration in designing BMI is the feasibility of the approach taken. The target applications necessitate real-time implementations with minimal computational and hardware requirements. On one hand, linear models are usually the best in terms of their computational requirements. On the other hand, a simple linear model is often insufficient to accurately capture the complex input–output relationships between neural activity and hand position. Recently, our group has conducted a performance comparison between linear and nonlinear modeling approaches, and the latter was found to be favorable (Sanchez et al., 2002).

In this paper, our aim is to demonstrate that the target input–output mapping can be discovered using a *divide-and-conquer* approach. In this approach, we combine the simplicity of training linear models with the performance boost that can be achieved by nonlinear methods.

* Corresponding author.

0893-6080/03/$ - see front matter © 2003 Published by Elsevier Science Ltd.
doi:10.1016/S0893-6080(03)00108-4

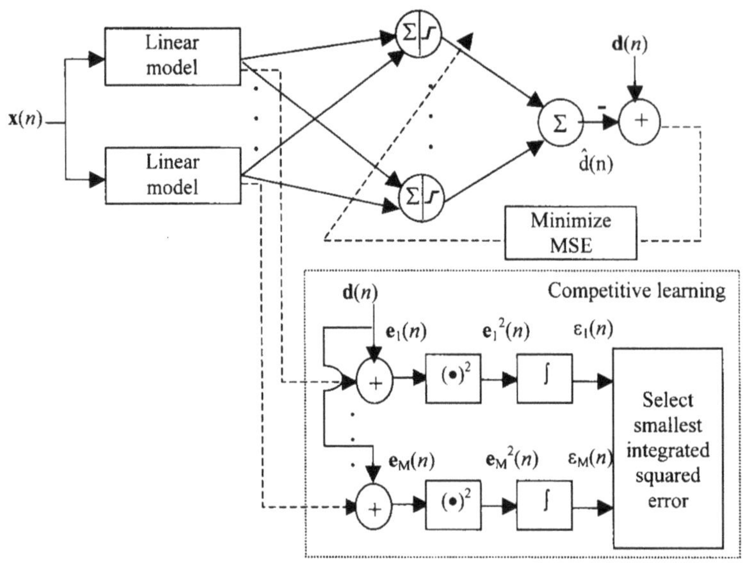

Fig. 1. An overall architecture of the proposed model. The box illustrates the selection of the winner using integrated squared errors from each linear model. Outputs from M trained linear models are fed to a MLP, which is trained using the conjugate gradient algorithm. $d(n)$ denotes the desired response.

Specifically, a two-stage structure is used where the first stage consists of a bank of competitively trained linear filters and the second stage consists of a single hidden layer MLP (see Fig. 1). Performance comparisons with simple linear, TDNN, and RMLP approaches are provided.

2. The models

In this section, we describe the modeling approaches that will be considered in the experimental comparisons of study. The main focus will be on the nonlinear mixture of competitive linear models (NMCLM). However, a brief description of the other three topologies will also be provided for completeness.

2.1. Nonlinear mixture of competitive linear models

The overall architecture is identical to a single nonlinear layer TDNN. However, the training procedure undertaken here is significantly different. This modeling method uses the divide-and-conquer approach. Our reasoning is that, a complex nonlinear modeling task can be elucidated by dividing it into simpler linear modeling tasks and combining them properly (Farmer & Sidorowich, 1987). Previously, this approach was successfully applied to nonstationary signal segmentation, assuming that a nonstationary signal is a combination of piecewise stationary signals (Fancourt & Principe, 1996). Hypothesizing that the neural activity will demonstrate varying characteristics for different localities in the space of the hand trajectories, we expect the multiple model approach, in which each linear model specializes in a local region, to provide a better overall input–output mapping. However, here the problem is different since the goal is not to segment a signal but to segment the joint input/desired signal space.

The local linear models can be conceived as a committee of experts each specializing in one segment of the hand trajectory space. The MLP is introduced to the system in order to nonlinearly combine the predictions generated by all the linear models. For BMI applications, it has the further advantage that it does not require a selection scheme in testing, which can only be accurately done using the desired output. For example, in a prosthetic arm application, the desired hand position is not available in practice.

The topology allows a two-stage training procedure that can be performed sequentially in off-line training: first, competitive learning for the local linear models and then error backpropagation learning for the MLP. It is important to note that in this scheme, both the linear models and the MLP are trained to approximate the same desired response, which is the hand trajectory of the primate.

The training of the multiple linear models is accomplished by competitively (hard or soft) updating their weights in accordance with previous approaches using the normalized-least-mean-squares (NLMS) algorithm (Haykin, 1996). The winning model is determined by comparing the (leaky) integrated squared errors of all competing models and selecting the model that exhibits the least integrated error for the corresponding input (Fancourt & Principe, 1996). In competitive training, the leaky integrated squared error for the ith model is given by

$$\varepsilon_i(n) = (1-\mu)\varepsilon_i(n-1) + \mu e_i^2(n), \qquad i = 1, \dots, M \tag{1}$$

where M is the number of models, and μ is the time constant of the leaky integrator. If hard competition is employed, then only the weight vector of the winning model is updated. Specifically, the hard competition update rule for the weight vector of the winning model is

$$\mathbf{w}_{\text{winner}}(n+1) = \mathbf{w}_{\text{winner}}(n) + \frac{\eta e_{\text{winner}}(n)\mathbf{x}(n)}{\gamma + \|\mathbf{x}(n)\|^2} \quad (2)$$

where $\mathbf{w}_{\text{winner}}$ is the weight vector, $\mathbf{x}(n)$ is the current input, $e_{\text{winner}}(n)$ is the instantaneous error of the winning model, η is the learning rate and γ is the small positive constant. If soft competition is used, a Gaussian weighting function centered at the winning model is applied to all competing models.

Every model is then updated proportional to the weight assigned to that model by this Gaussian weighting function

$$\mathbf{w}_i(n+1) = \mathbf{w}_i(n) + \frac{\eta(n)\Lambda_{i,j}(n)e_i(n)\mathbf{x}(n)}{\gamma + \|\mathbf{x}(n)\|^2}, \quad (3)$$

$i = 1, ..., M$

where $\mathbf{w}_i$ is the weight vector of the ith model, jth model is the winner, and $\Lambda_{i,j}(n)$ is the weighting function

$$\Lambda_{i,j}(n) = \exp\left(-\frac{d_{i,j}^2}{2\sigma^2(n)}\right) \quad (4)$$

where $d_{i,j}$ is the Euclidean distance between index i and j, which is equal to $|j-i|$, $\eta(n)$ is the annealed learning rate, and $\sigma^2(n)$ is the kernel width, which decreases exponentially as n increases. The learning rate also decreases exponentially with time.

Soft competition preserves the topology of the input space, updating the models neighboring the winner; thus it is expected to result in smoother transitions between models specializing in topologically neighboring regions (of the state space). However, in the experimental results that will be provided in Section 3, we will utilize the hard competition rule since comparisons on the data sets utilized in these experiments did not show any significant difference in generalization performance (possibly due to the nature of the data set used in these experiments).

The competitive training of the first layer of linear models to match the hand trajectory using the neural activity creates a set of basis signals from which the following single hidden layer MLP can generate a more accurate overall prediction than any one of the individual competing linear models (thus the name nonlinear mixture of competitive linear models).

2.2. *Alternative modeling approaches*

The rich variety of alternative modeling approaches for BMI design is evident from the relevant literature and the works of independent groups. In this paper, results are compared with the following three approaches: single moving average (MA) model, single hidden layer TDNN, single recursive hidden layer RMLP. Below, a brief description of each topology is provided for the sake of completeness.

Single moving average model. This approach tries to model the mapping from neural activity to hand position using a linear combiner, which is structurally equivalent to each one of the multiple local linear models used in the competitive framework of Section 2.1. It creates a prediction of the hand position by a product of its weight matrix $\mathbf{W}$ and its input vector $\mathbf{x}(n)$ at time n, i.e. $\hat{\mathbf{d}}(n) = \mathbf{W}^{\mathrm{T}}\mathbf{x}(n)$. The input vector consists of L lags of the bin counts for each of the neurons that measurements are taken from. The desired hand trajectory $\mathbf{d}(n)$, depending on the experiment, has one, two, or three dimensions. Optimal weights are determined either from the Wiener-Hopf equations or by gradient descent learning (Haykin, 1996).

Time-delay neural network. This approach models the mapping from neural activity to hand position using a nonlinear combination of delayed bin counts from every neuron. The memory is preset to the length of the tap-delay lines used in the input layer. The single hidden layer uses sigmoid nonlinearities. The output of the TDNN is given by $\hat{\mathbf{d}}(n) = \mathbf{W}_2 f(\mathbf{W}_1^{\mathrm{T}}\mathbf{x}(n) + \mathbf{b}_1) + \mathbf{b}_2$, where $\mathbf{W}_1$, $\mathbf{W}_2$, $\mathbf{b}_1$, $\mathbf{b}_2$ are the weights of the TDNN that are trained with error backpropagation (Haykin, 1994).

Recurrent multilayer perceptron. This network is built from a hidden layer of nonlinear processing elements (PEs) with state feedback and linear outputs. Different from a TDNN, the input vector $\mathbf{x}(n)$ of this network consists only of the instantaneous values of the bin counts from the neurons. In addition, its hidden layer has a fully connected feedback to itself with a feedback weight matrix $\mathbf{W}_{\mathrm{f}}$, which is capable of adjusting its time-resolution to various levels depending on the requirements of the optimization criterion. The output of the RMLP is obtained by the following recursive equation: $\hat{\mathbf{d}}(n) = \mathbf{W}_2 f(\mathbf{W}_1\mathbf{x}(n) + \mathbf{W}_{\mathrm{f}}\mathbf{y}_1(n-1) + \mathbf{b}_1) + \mathbf{b}_2$. The hidden layer state vector is denoted by $\mathbf{y}_1$. This network is trained using the backpropagation through time algorithm (Principe, Euliano, & Lefebvre, 2000).

3. Simulations and analysis

In this section, experimental results obtained with the multiple models trained with hard competition are presented and the performance is compared with the single linear model, TDNN, and RMLP.

3.1. *Data collection*

Synchronous, multichannel neuronal spike trains were collected at Duke University using owl monkeys (*Aotus trivirgatus*). Microwire electrodes were implanted in cortical regions where motor associations are known (Wessberg et al., 2000). The firing times of individual neurons were recorded while the primate performed a 3D reaching task that consists of a reach to food and followed by placing it in the mouth. The primate's hand position was also recorded (with a shared time clock) and digitized with a 200 Hz sampling rate. The neuronal firings were binned in nonoverlapping windows of 100 ms, which represents the local firing rate for each neuron. These spike counts were directly used as inputs to the model to estimate hand positions. The digitized hand position signal was down-sampled to 10 Hz to synchronize with spike counts in time. In order to take the reaction time into account, the spike trains were delayed by 0.23 s with respect to the hand position.

3.2. Experimental environments

The spike counts from 104 neurons, a set of 20,000 consecutive time bins (2000 s), were used to train the models. After training, the weights of all models are fixed to their *optimal values* identified from the training set and the performance of the models are evaluated on an independent test set of 3000 consecutive bins (300 s).

Single moving average model. The MA model accepts an input vector that consists of 10 delayed versions of the bin counts of 104 neurons, and has three outputs (x, y, z). The 10 tap memory depth (1 s) is based on the suggestion of Wessberg et al. (2000). The model is trained with NLMS with a step size of 0.01.

Nonlinear mixture of competitive linear models. This topology consists of 10 competing linear models for each coordinate (x, y, z) and a single hidden layer MLP with 30 inputs (three coordinates × 10 models), 30 hidden PEs with tanh nonlinearity, and three linear output PEs to predict the x, y, and z coordinates of the primate's hand. The number of multiple linear models and the number of hidden PEs were chosen empirically by examining the prediction performance on the test set. Each linear model is the same as the MA model. In the competition, the leaky integrator used a forgetting factor of $\mu = 0.1$. This corresponds to an approximate memory depth of 1 s, which is consistent with the memory depth of the linear models (Fancourt & Principe, 1996). The model was trained using NLMS for the local linear models and backpropagation for the MLP, both using a step size of 0.01. Training of the MLP is repeated with 100 random initial conditions and the minimum mean square error (MSE) solution is accepted.

Time-delay neural network. In the experiments, a TDNN (1040:30:3) is trained with the 104 neurons and their 10 delay bin counts as the input. The 30 hidden PEs use tanh nonlinearities and the output have three linear PEs. Effectively, this is the same topology as the competitive linear models and MLP combination, except it is trained completely based on error backpropagation with MSE criterion.

Recursive multilayer perceptron. The RMLP used here is a 104:5:3 network whose input consists of 104 instantaneous bin counts from all neurons. The hidden layer uses nonlinear PEs with tanh activation. Training is performed using Neurosolutions®, where 3 s trajectories are employed for gradient calculations.

3.3. Results

The accuracy of these estimations are evaluated using several measures: the correlation coefficient (CC) is used to quantify the linear relationship between the estimated and actual trajectories; the signal to error ratio (SER) between actual and estimated hand trajectories is used to account for the deficiency of CC in identifying the bias and scaling errors in trajectories; the cumulative error metric (CEM) is used to provide a global statistical picture of how well the models perform in terms of following the actual trajectory; the number of movement *hits* and *misses* a model obtains.

Specifically, the SER is defined as the ratio of the powers of the actual hand trajectory and the error of the estimated trajectory (Sanchez et al., 2002). The CC and SER are computed using 4 s overlapping windows (each reaching movement takes approximately 4 s). The CEM is defined as the probability that the L_2-norm (or radius in 3D space) of the error vector is less than or equal to some r : $\mathrm{CEM}(r) = P(\|e\|_2 \le r)$ (Sanchez et al., 2003). This is, in fact, the empirical cumulative distribution function of the error radius. During a reaching movement, a model is said to hit the movement if 70% of the time, the instantaneous error norm is less than half of the norm of the hand position vector. Otherwise, the model is said to miss the movement.

The performances of all models are summarized in Table 1 using these measures. In the test set, there are a total of 10 reaching movements. The hit and miss counts are provided in the first two rows. The SER and CC values are segmented in movement and rest. The average and standard deviation of SER and CC for moving and resting portions are reported separately. For a fair comparison, this averaging is performed over only the six common movements that the TDNN, RMLP and multiple models hit.

The z-coordinates of the estimated hand positions with each model for the test set are shown along with the actual hand position in Fig. 2a. Also, in Fig. 2b, we present the changes in SER over time. It is observed that the SER increases when the hand is moving, and decreases when the hand is at rest, for all models. The multiple models achieve

Table 1
Performances of the four models compared (number in parenthesis are the free parameters). The average and the standard deviation were computed for the correlation coefficient (CC) and the SER over samples and three dimensions

Measures	Single MA (3123)	TDNN (31,323)	RMLP (568)	NMCLM (32,253)
No. of hits	2	8	7	7
No. of misses	8	2	3	3
CC: move	0.83 ± 0.07	0.86 ± 0.10	0.88 ± 0.11	0.89 ± 0.07
SER: move (dB)	4.69 ± 1.19	6.64 ± 1.99	7.40 ± 2.00	7.02 ± 2.47
CC: rest	0.06 ± 0.27	0.04 ± 0.25	0.06 ± 0.25	0.07 ± 0.26
SER: rest (dB)	−0.19 ± 4.27	2.95 ± 5.69	7.13 ± 4.01	4.53 ± 4.99

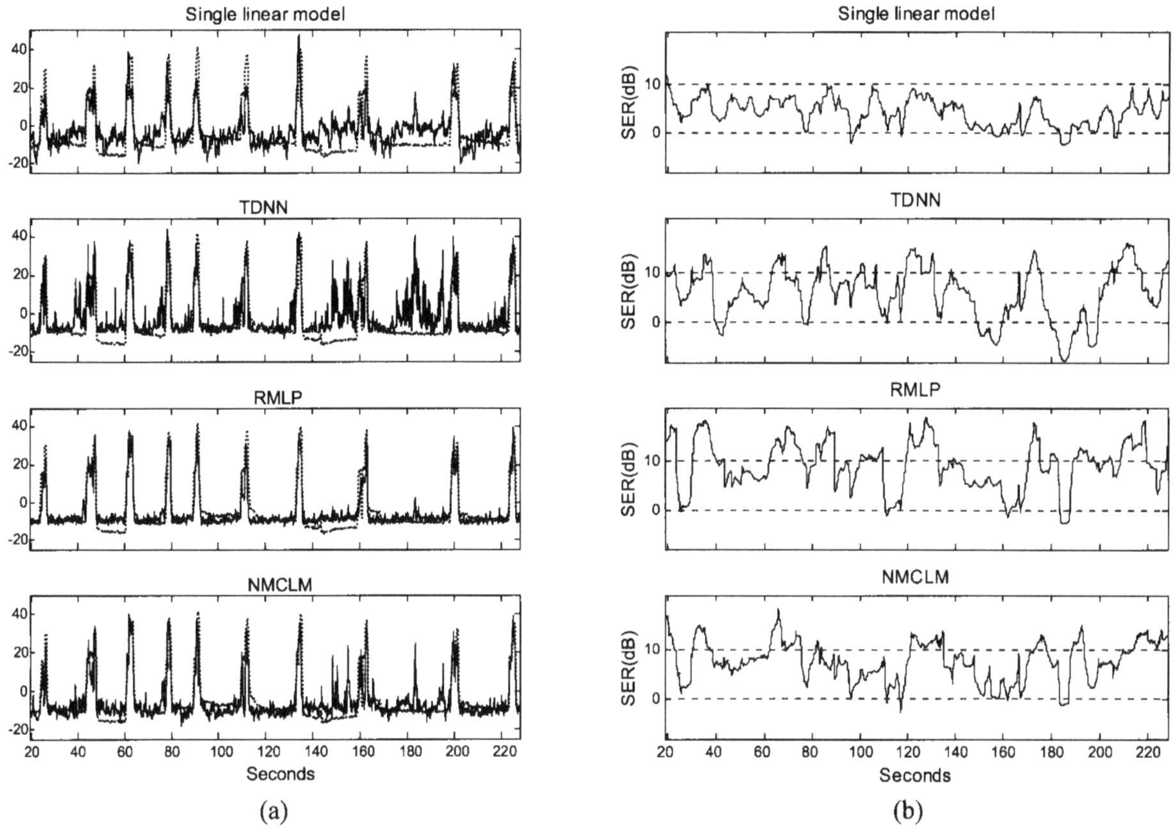

Fig. 2. (a) The z-coordinate of the actual hand trajectory (dotted) and that of the estimated hand trajectories (solid) on testing data for the single linear MA model, TDNN, RMLP, and the NMCLM, respectively. (b) The signal to error ratio (SER) for the z-coordinate in dB using a 4 s sliding window over time.

higher SER levels than the TDNN when the hand is at rest. The RMLP, however, performs better than the multiple models on average.

In Fig. 3, the CEM curves of all models are presented for the entire test set and for only the six common movements. Overall, the RMLP and the multiple models exhibit better performance in these curves compared to the TDNN and the single linear model. On the other hand, when we only consider movements, three models (RMLP, TDNN, and multiple models) produce similar performance.

We further investigate the localization properties of the multiple linear models in the hand trajectory space. In order to demonstrate this, two example reaching movements (taken from the training set) are shown in Fig. 4. For each trajectory, winners at every sample are indicated by different markers. It can be observed that the winning models localize in different regions of the movement. For instance, the 10th model specializes in the portion of the trajectory from mouth to the rest position, while the seventh model learns the trajectory from the rest position to the food.

3.4. Evaluation of training performance

The topology proposed in NMCLM is basically equivalent to a three-layer network: the first layer of weights consists of the competitive model coefficients, the second and third layer of weights are simply the weights of the following MLP. In this topology, the first hidden layer and the output layer have linear PEs, whereas the second hidden layer has nonlinear PEs. In the NMCLM approach, the first layer weights are trained competitively to predict the desired signal, whereas the MLP is optimized using standard error backpropagation.

In order to quantify the performance of this training procedure from an information-theoretic point-of-view, we evaluate the mutual information (Cover & Thomas, 1991), $I(\mathbf{z}_C, \mathbf{d})$, between the outputs of the competitive models, $\mathbf{z}_C$, and the desired output, $\mathbf{d}$. Using a Parzen window estimator for mutual information (Erdogmus, 2002) on 10 segments of the hand trajectory (each of length 1000 samples), the average and standard deviation of $I(\mathbf{z}_C, \mathbf{d})$ is found to be 8.97 nats ($\pm$ 1.21 nats). The maximum mutual information allowed by this model and data, obtained by estimating $I(\mathbf{z}_C, \hat{\mathbf{d}})$ is 9.83 nats ($\pm$ 1.19 nats). Percentage-wise, the information contained in the competitive model outputs pertaining to the desired output is thus 92% ($\pm$ 6%). From this, we conclude that the information loss in the first layer is just 8% ($\pm$ 6%).

For comparison, a second network with the same topology is trained as follows: The MLP weights are

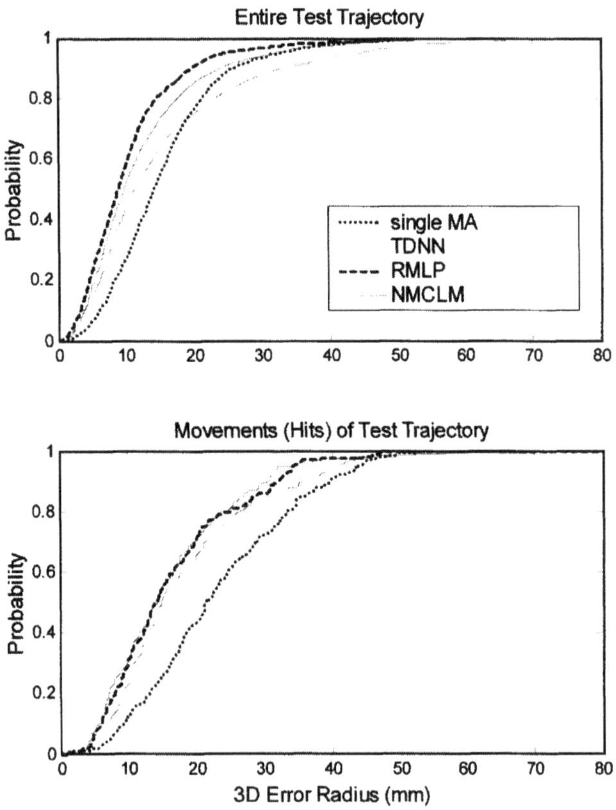

Fig. 3. Comparison of the CEM of the four models evaluated for the entire test set (top), and for the six common reaching movements (bottom).

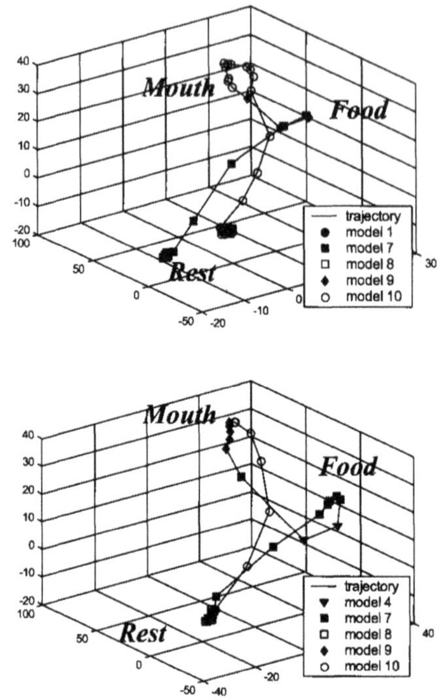

Fig. 4. Demonstration of the localization of multiple linear models for two different reaching movements. Each symbol represents a different winning model during training.

borrowed from the one trained with competition (in order to ensure *identical* information loss at this stage). The first layer weights are then trained using standard backpropagation through these MLP weights, instead of using competition. This second network, therefore, uses the minimum MSE solution for the first layer weights. Similarly, the mutual information $I(\mathbf{z}_B, \mathbf{d})$ between the output of the first layer of this network $\mathbf{z}_B$, and the desired output d is calculated to be 7.42 nats ($\pm$1.35 nats). For this network, the maximum mutual information is 10.90 nats ($\pm$0.40 nats). These correspond to an information-transfer percentage of 68% ($\pm$11%). Therefore, the information loss in the first layer of the second network is 32% ($\pm$11%).

5. Discussions

In this paper, we have investigated the performance of a nonlinear mixture of competitively trained multiple linear models in predicting the hand position of a primate using neural activity recorded from cortical areas related to arm movement. This approach possesses significant advantages compared to both the single MA model and the standard TDNN, although it is essentially a combination of both. The multiple models follow a divide-and-conquer approach to identify the nonlinear mapping from neuronal data to hand positions. Its performance did not exceed that of an RMLP, probably because the RMLP has the most parsimonious architecture (568 free parameters).

The biggest difficulty with any of these BMI models is the enormous set of free parameters produced by the large neural input vector (104 dimensions). For example, the TDNN and the NMCLM presented above had more than 30,000 weights. Training the first layer of the TDNN with backpropagation is a difficult task due to the attenuation of the error by the hidden layer PEs. By competitively training the first layer of linear models, on the other hand, the training complexity is made more practical, since standard LMS-type linear filter adaptation rules can be employed. However, the problem of large data requirements still remains, and we conclude that we did not have enough data to train these models sufficiently well. The performance of the single MA model is the worst of the group, which means that the constraint of linearity for this specific reaching task is taxing performance (in spite of having 'only' 10% of the TDNN weights). From the CEM of Fig. 3, we can conclude that the precision in tracking a trajectory needs further improvements to be useful.

The performance of the NMCLM can be improved further in several respects. First and foremost, pruning the linear model is a viable alternative because not all the neurons are important all the time. A simple test with weight decay on the single MA model shows that we are able to prune less important inputs significantly. For instance, the portion of weights whose magnitudes are less than 0.1, increases from 22.4 to 36.3%. It consequently helps generalization in testing such that the SER increases to 5.56 dB (± 1.11 dB) (compared to 4.69 ± 1.19 dB) for the movement, and 2.88 dB (± 2.76 dB) for the rest (compared to − 0.19 dB ± 4.27 dB).

In a purely competitive framework, one could use the output generated by only the winning linear model. However, the selection of the winner in the testing phase is not possible since the desired output is not available. Nevertheless, it is interesting to investigate how much performance loss occurs due to the use of the MLP as compared to the selection of the winner alone. To this end, we have calculated the CC and SER for the purely competitive prediction scheme for the same test set used in the experiments (assuming that the desired hand position is available for the selection). For the six reaching movements that have been considered throughout the experiments, the CC is 0.94 (± 0.03) (compared to 0.89 ± 0.07 with the mixture), and the SER is 9.79 dB (± 1.62 dB) (compared to 7.02 ± 2.47 dB with the mixture). Hence, we conclude that there is room for improvement in the selecting of the winner in testing.

From the models presented, the NMCLM is the only one that uses explicit competition to divide the trajectory among models. This is an advantage if we are interested in creating a system that models each piece of the trajectory, as may be required in the future for BMIs with a large repertoire of trajectories. The other approach to segmentation that we are testing is a Hidden Markov Model (HMM) (Darmanjian et al., 2003). For a two segment task (rest and movement), the segmentation performance of the HMM is high, but it still requires lots of data for training (1620 free parameters when the input data is quantized in 128 levels). Each HMM can then be coupled with an MA model and fitting performance can be increased up to 20% with respect to the single MA model (we are in the process of validating this approach). However, it is still unclear how to extend the technique to finer segmentation (e.g. rest to food, food to mouth, mouth to rest).

Overall, the multiple model approach produced better CC and SER than both the TDNN and the single linear filter at a reasonable additional cost in terms of training complexity. Additionally, it produced a CC profile identical to the RMLP. However, the SER of RMLP is on average slightly higher than the multiple models. This can be attributed to the additional error variance that the multiple models exhibit in predicting the hand position at rest. This may motivate replacing the MLP in the topology with an RMLP in future work.

Acknowledgements

This work is supported by DARPA grant # N-66001-02-C-8022.

References

Chapin, J. K., Moxon, R. S., Markowitz, M. A., & Nicolelis, M. A. (1999). Real-time control of a robot arm using simultaneously recorded neurons in the motor cortex. *Nature Neuroscience*, *2*(7), 664–670.

Cover, T., & Thomas, J. (1991). *Elements of information theory*. New York: Wiley.

Darmanjian, S., Kim, S. P., Nechyba, M. C., Morrison, S., Principe, J. C., & Nicolelis, M. A (2003). Bimodal brain-machine interface for motor control of robotic prosthetic. Submitted for publication

Erdogmus, D (2002). *Information theoretic learning: Renyi's entropy and its applications to adaptive system training*. PhD Dissertation. Department of Electrical and Computer Engineering, University of Florida, Gainesville, FL

Fancourt, C., & Principe, J. C. (1996). Temporal self-organization through competitive prediction. *Proceedings of ICASSP'96*, 3325–3329.

Farmer, J. D., & Sidorowich, J. J. (1987). Predicting chaotic time series. *Physical Review Letters*, *50*, 845–848.

Haykin, S. (1994). *Neural networks: A comprehensive foundation*. New York: McMillan.

Haykin, S. (1996). *Adaptive filter theory*. Upper Saddle River, NJ: Prentice-Hall.

Moran, D. W., & Schwartz, A. B. (1999). Motor cortical activity during drawing movements: population representation during spiral tracing. *Journal of Neurophysiology*, *82*(5), 2693–2704.

Principe, J. C., Euliano, N. R., & Lefebvre, W. C. (2000). *Neural and adaptive systems: Fundamentals through simulations*. New York: Wiley.

Sanchez, J. C., Erdogmus, D., Rao, Y. N., Principe, J. C., Nicolelis, M. A., & Wessberg, J. (2003). Learning the contributions of the motor, premotor, and posterior parietal cortices for hand trajectory reconstruction in a brain machine interface. *IEEE EMBS Neural Engineering Conference*.

Sanchez, J. C., Kim, S. P., Erdogmus, D., Rao, Y. N., Principe, J. C., Wessberg, J., & Nicolelis, M. A. (2002). Input–output mapping performance of linear and nonlinear models for estimating hand trajectories from cortical neuronal firing patterns. *Proceedings of NNSP'02*, 139–148.

Serruya, M. S., Hatsopoulos, N. G., Paninski, L., Fellows, M. R., & Donoghue, J. P. (2002). Brain-machine interface: instant neural control of a movement signal. *Nature*, *416*, 141–142.

Wessberg, J., Stambaugh, R., Kralik, J. F., Beck, P. D., Laubach, M., Chapin, J. K., Kim, J., Biggs, J., Srinivasan, M. A., & Nicolelis, M. A. (2000). Real-time prediction of hand trajectory by ensembles of cortical neurons in primates. *Nature*, *408*(6810), 361–365.

AVAILABLE AT
www.ComputerScienceWeb.com
POWERED BY SCIENCE DIRECT

PERGAMON

Neural Networks 16 (2003) 873–880

Neural Networks

www.elsevier.com/locate/neunet

2003 Special issue

Stochastic error whitening algorithm for linear filter estimation with noisy data

Yadunandana N. Rao*, Deniz Erdogmus, Geetha Y. Rao, Jose C. Principe

Computational NeuroEngineering Laboratory, Department of Electrical and Computer Engineering, University of Florida, Gainesville, FL 32611, USA

Abstract

Mean squared error (MSE) has been the most widely used tool to solve the linear filter estimation or system identification problem. However, MSE gives biased results when the input signals are noisy. This paper presents a novel stochastic gradient algorithm based on the recently proposed error whitening criterion (EWC) to tackle the problem of linear filter estimation in the presence of additive white disturbances. We will briefly motivate the theory behind the new criterion and derive an online stochastic gradient algorithm. Convergence proof of the stochastic gradient algorithm is derived making mild assumptions. Further, we will propose some extensions to the stochastic gradient algorithm to ensure faster, step-size independent convergence. We will perform extensive simulations and compare the results with MSE as well as total-least squares in a parameter estimation problem. The stochastic EWC algorithm has many potential applications. We will use this in designing robust inverse controllers with noisy data.

Keywords: Error whitening criterion; Total-least squares; LMS; Mean squared error; Error whitening

1. Introduction

It was been a widely acknowledged fact that the mean squared error (MSE) criterion is optimal for linear filter estimation when there are no noisy perturbations on the data (Haykin, 1996). In adaptive filter theory, the Wiener solution for the MSE criterion is used to derive recursive algorithms like RLS and the more popular stochastic gradient based LMS algorithm (Haykin, 1996). An important property of the Wiener solution is that if the adaptive filter is sufficiently long enough, then the prediction error signal for stationary data is white (Haykin, 1996). This very nice property is true only when the input data is noise-free. It has been long recognized that the MSE-based filter optimization approaches are unable to produce the optimal weights associated with the noise free data due to the biasing of the input covariance matrix by the additive noise (Douglas, 1996). For many real-world applications, the 'noise-free' assumption is easily violated and using MSE-based methods for parameter estimation will result in severe degradation in performance. Researchers have proposed several techniques to combat and suppress the bias in MSE-based methods. For instance, the subspace methods coupled with the Wiener solution can result in superior filter estimates. However, finding the right subspace dimension and the optimal subspace projections is a non-trivial problem. Moreover, subspace based Wiener filtering methods can only reduce the bias; they can never remove the bias completely. An important statistical tool called total least squares (TLS) (Golub & Van Loan, 1989) can be utilized to eliminate this bias completely. The major stumbling block for the TLS that severely limits its practicability is the requirement that the variances of the noisy perturbations on the input and desired signals be identical (Douglas, 1996; Rao & Principe, 2002). Recently, we proposed a novel criterion called the error whitening criterion (EWC) (Principe, Rao, & Erdogmus, 2003; Rao, Erdogmus, & Principe, 2003) that presents a different approach to whiten the error sequence at the output of an adaptive filter even in the presence of noisy inputs. This criterion enforces zero autocorrelation of the error signal beyond a certain lag; hence the name EWC.

In Section 2, we will motivate the theory of EWC; briefly state some of its interesting properties and then present an online stochastic gradient algorithm called EWC-LMS. In Section 3, we will discuss the convergence of this algorithm to the optimal EWC solution. Section 4

* Corresponding author.

0893-6080/03/$ - see front matter © 2003 Published by Elsevier Science Ltd.
doi:10.1016/S0893-6080(03)00109-6

talks about extensions to the EWC-LMS algorithm for increased robustness and faster convergence. In Section 5, we will present case studies and compare the performance of the stochastic EWC algorithm with TLS and the regular LMS algorithms. In the same section, will also demonstrate the usefulness of this algorithm in an inverse controller design application. Discussions and conclusions are in Section 6.

2. Error whitening criterion

The classical Wiener solution tries to minimize the zero-lag autocorrelation of the error, i.e. $E(e_k^2)$. In the presence of additive white noise, the zero-lag input autocorrelation is always biased by the noise power. Therefore, when we minimize the MSE, we always end up with a biased parameter estimate. This bias increases with increasing noise power. So, instead of working with zero-lag correlations, we propose to analyze the error autocorrelation at a non-zero lag. Consider the problem of identifying a linear system characterized by the parameter vector $\mathbf{w}_T \in \Re^N$ as shown in Fig. 1. Suppose noisy training data pair $(\hat{\mathbf{x}}_k, \hat{d}_k)$ is provided, where $\hat{\mathbf{x}}_k \in \Re^N = \mathbf{x}_k + \mathbf{v}_k$ and $\hat{d}_k \in \Re^1 = d_k + u_k$ with $\mathbf{x}_k$ as the noise-free input vector at discrete time index k; $\mathbf{v}_k$, the additive white noise vector entering the input; d_k being the noise-free desired signal and u_k as the additive white noise entering the desired signal. We further assume that the noises entering the system $\mathbf{v}_k$ and u_k are uncorrelated with the data pair and also uncorrelated with each other. Let the weight vector (filter) that generated the noise-free data pair $(\mathbf{x}_k, d_k)$ be $\mathbf{w}_T$, of dimension N. Without loss of generality, we will assume that the length of $\mathbf{w}$, the estimated weight vector is greater than N. Since $d_k = \mathbf{x}_k^T\mathbf{w}_T$, the error is simply given by $\hat{e}_k = \mathbf{x}_k^T(\mathbf{w}_T - \mathbf{w}) + u_k - \mathbf{v}_k^T\mathbf{w}$. The corresponding error autocorrelation at some arbitrary lag L can be determined as

$$\rho_{\hat{e}}(L) = [\mathbf{w}_T - \mathbf{w}]^T E[\mathbf{x}_k\mathbf{x}_{k-L}^T][\mathbf{w}_T - \mathbf{w}] + \mathbf{w}^T E[\mathbf{v}_k\mathbf{v}_{k-L}^T]\mathbf{w} \quad (1)$$

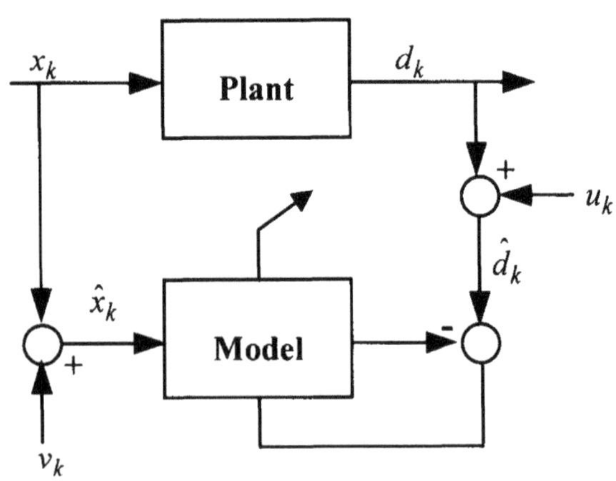

Fig. 1. System identification block diagram.

From Eq. (1), it is obvious that if $L \geq M$, where M is the length of the true filter $\mathbf{w}$, $E[\mathbf{v}_k\mathbf{v}_{k-L}^T] = \mathbf{0}$. Assuming that the matrix $E[\mathbf{x}_k\mathbf{x}_{k-L}^T]$ exists and is full rank, $\rho_{\hat{e}}(L) = 0$ only when $\mathbf{w} = \mathbf{w}_T$. Therefore, if we make the error autocorrelation at any lag $L \geq M$ zero, then the estimated weight vector will be exactly equal to the true weight vector. This is the motivation behind the EWC, which partially whitens the error signal by making $\rho_{\hat{e}}(L) = 0$ for $L \geq M$. Since the goal is to make $\rho_{\hat{e}}(L) = 0$, a suitable cost function to derive a stochastic gradient algorithm is $|\rho_{\hat{e}}(L)|$. Using Bluestein's identity (Taylor & Mellott, 1998), we can write $\hat{e}_k\hat{e}_{k-L}$ as

$$\hat{e}_k\hat{e}_{k-L} = 0.5[\hat{e}_k^2 + \hat{e}_{k-L}^2 - (\hat{e}_k - \hat{e}_{k-L})^2] \quad (2)$$

Taking the expectations on both sides and recognizing the fact that $E(\hat{e}_k^2) = E(\hat{e}_{k-L}^2)$, we get

$$E(\hat{e}_k\hat{e}_{k-L}) = E(\hat{e}_k^2) - 0.5E(\hat{e}_k - \hat{e}_{k-L})^2 \quad (3)$$

For convenience, we define $\hat{\dot{e}}_k = (\hat{e}_k - \hat{e}_{k-L})$ and use a constant β instead of -0.5. We can rewrite Eq. (3) as

$$E(\hat{e}_k\hat{e}_{k-L}) = E(\hat{e}_k^2) + \beta E(\hat{\dot{e}}_k^2) \quad (4)$$

The cost function for the EWC can now be formally stated as

$$J(\mathbf{w}) = |E(\hat{e}_k^2) + \beta E(\hat{\dot{e}}_k^2)| \quad (5)$$

The form in Eq. (5) is appealing because, it includes the MSE as a special case when $\beta = 0$. With $\beta = -0.5$, the above cost function becomes $|\rho_{\hat{e}}(L)|$ which when minimized would result in the unbiased estimate of the true weight vector. Another interesting result is that the sensitivity of $\rho_{\hat{e}}(L)$, given by, $\partial\rho_{\hat{e}}(L)/\partial\mathbf{w} = -2[\mathbf{w}_T - \mathbf{w}]E[\mathbf{x}_k\mathbf{x}_{k-L}^T]$ is zero if $(\mathbf{w}_T - \mathbf{w}) = \mathbf{0}$. Thus, if $(\mathbf{w}_T - \mathbf{w})$ is not in the null space of $E[\mathbf{x}_k\mathbf{x}_{k-L}^T]$ or if $E[\mathbf{x}_k\mathbf{x}_{k-L}^T]$ is full rank, then only $(\mathbf{w}_T - \mathbf{w}) = \mathbf{0}$ makes $\rho_{\hat{e}}(L) = 0$ and $\partial\rho_{\hat{e}}(L)/\partial\mathbf{w} = \mathbf{0}$ simultaneously. This property has a useful implication. Consider any cost function of the form $J(\mathbf{w})^p$, $p > 0$. Then the performance surface is not necessarily quadratic and the stationary points of this new cost are given by $J(\mathbf{w}) = 0$ or $\partial J(\mathbf{w})/\partial\mathbf{w} = \mathbf{0}$. Using the above property, we immediately see that both $J(\mathbf{w}) = 0$ and $\partial J(\mathbf{w})/\partial\mathbf{w} = \mathbf{0}$ yield the same solution. Optimization on Eq. (5) without the absolute value operator is impossible using a constant sign gradient algorithm, as the stationary point can then be a global maximum, minimum or a saddle point (Principe et al., 2003). The stochastic instantaneous gradient of the EWC cost function in Eq. (5) is

$$\partial J(\mathbf{w})/\partial\mathbf{w} = -2\,\mathrm{sign}(\hat{e}_k^2 + \beta\hat{\dot{e}}_k^2)(\hat{e}_k\hat{\mathbf{x}}_k + \beta\hat{\dot{e}}_k\hat{\dot{\mathbf{x}}}_k) \quad (6)$$

where $\hat{\dot{e}}_k = (\hat{e}_k - \hat{e}_{k-L})$ and $\hat{\dot{\mathbf{x}}}_k = (\hat{\mathbf{x}}_k - \hat{\mathbf{x}}_{k-L})$ as defined before. The stationary point is a global minimum and using gradient descent, we can write the EWC-LMS algorithm as

$$\mathbf{w}_{k+1} = \mathbf{w}_k + \eta \operatorname{sign}(\hat{e}_k^2 + \beta\hat{\dot{e}}_k^2)(\hat{e}_k\hat{\mathbf{x}}_k + \beta\hat{\dot{e}}_k\hat{\dot{\mathbf{x}}}_k) \quad (7)$$

where $\eta > 0$ is a small step-size parameter. Note that when $\beta = 0$, Eq. (7) reduces to the renowned LMS algorithm (Widrow & Stearns, 1985). We are specifically interested in using Eq. (7) with $\beta = -0.5$. In Section 3, we will present the convergence analysis of Eq. (7) and derive some useful results.

3. Convergence analysis

Theorem 1. *In the noise-free case (deterministic signals), EWC-LMS given in* (7) *converges to the stationary point* $\mathbf{w}_* = \mathbf{w}_T$ *provided that the step size satisfies the following inequality at every update*

$$0 < \eta < \frac{2|e_k^2 + \beta\dot{e}_k^2|}{\|e_k\mathbf{x}_k + \beta\dot{e}_k\dot{\mathbf{x}}_k\|^2}\ \forall k \quad (8)$$

Proof. From the arguments presented in Section 2 and owing to the quadratic nature of the EWC performance surface, it is clear that the EWC-LMS algorithm in Eq. (7) has a single stationary point (global minimum) $\mathbf{w}_* = \mathbf{w}_T$. The formal proof is trivial and is omitted here. Consider the weight error vector defined as $\boldsymbol{\varepsilon}_k = \mathbf{w}_* - \mathbf{w}_k$. Subtracting both sides of Eq. (7) from $\mathbf{w}_*$, we get $\boldsymbol{\varepsilon}_{k+1} = \boldsymbol{\varepsilon}_k - \eta \operatorname{sign}(e_k^2 + \beta\dot{e}_k^2)(e_k\mathbf{x}_k + \beta\dot{e}_k\dot{\mathbf{x}}_k)$. Taking the norm of this error vector we get

$$\|\boldsymbol{\varepsilon}_{k+1}\|^2 = \|\boldsymbol{\varepsilon}_k\|^2 - 2\eta \operatorname{sign}(e_k^2 + \beta\dot{e}_k^2)\boldsymbol{\varepsilon}_k^{\mathrm{T}}(e_k\mathbf{x}_k + \beta\dot{e}_k\dot{\mathbf{x}}_k) + \eta^2\|e_k\mathbf{x}_k + \beta\dot{e}_k\dot{\mathbf{x}}_k\|^2$$

In case of noise-free data, $\boldsymbol{\varepsilon}_k^{\mathrm{T}}\mathbf{x}_k = e_k$ and $\boldsymbol{\varepsilon}_k^{\mathrm{T}}\dot{\mathbf{x}}_k = \dot{e}_k$. Using these two equations we get

$$\|\boldsymbol{\varepsilon}_{k+1}\|^2 = \|\boldsymbol{\varepsilon}_k\|^2 - 2\eta|e_k^2 + \beta\dot{e}_k^2| + \eta^2\|e_k\mathbf{x}_k + \beta\dot{e}_k\dot{\mathbf{x}}_k\|^2 \quad (9)$$

By allowing the error vector norm to decay asymptotically by making $\|\boldsymbol{\varepsilon}_{k+1}\|^2 < \|\boldsymbol{\varepsilon}_k\|^2$, we obtain the bound in Eq. (8). The error vector will eventually converge to zero, i.e. $\lim_{k\to\infty} \times \|\boldsymbol{\varepsilon}_k\|^2 \to 0$, which implies that $\lim_{k\to\infty} \mathbf{w}_k \to \mathbf{w}_* = \mathbf{w}_T$. □

Observe that when $\beta = 0$, the upper bound on the step-size in Eq. (8) reduces to $0 < \eta < 2/\|\mathbf{x}_k\|^2$, which is nothing but the step-size bound for LMS in the case of deterministic signals.

Theorem 2. *In the noisy data case, EWC-LMS given in* (7) *with* $\beta = -0.5$ *converges to the stationary point* $\mathbf{w}_* = \mathbf{w}_T$ *in the mean provided that the step size is bound by the inequality*

$$0 < \eta < \frac{2|E(\hat{e}_k^2 - 0.5\hat{\dot{e}}_k^2)|}{E[\|\hat{e}_k\hat{\mathbf{x}}_k - 0.5\hat{\dot{e}}_k\hat{\dot{\mathbf{x}}}_k\|]^2} \quad (10)$$

Proof. Again, it is clear that the only stationary point of Eq. (7) with $\beta = -0.5$ is $\mathbf{w}_* = \mathbf{w}_T$ even in the presence of noise where $\mathbf{w}_T$ is the true weight vector that generated the noise-free data pair $(\mathbf{x}_k, d_k)$. Following the same steps as in the proof of the previous theorem, the dynamics of the error vector norm can be determined by the difference equation

$$\|\boldsymbol{\varepsilon}_{k+1}\|^2 = \|\boldsymbol{\varepsilon}_k\|^2 - 2\eta \operatorname{sign}(\hat{e}_k^2 + \beta\hat{\dot{e}}_k^2)\boldsymbol{\varepsilon}_k^{\mathrm{T}}(\hat{e}_k\hat{\mathbf{x}}_k + \beta\hat{\dot{e}}_k\hat{\dot{\mathbf{x}}}_k) + \eta^2\|\hat{e}_k\hat{\mathbf{x}}_k + \beta\hat{\dot{e}}_k\hat{\dot{\mathbf{x}}}_k\|^2 \quad (11)$$

Using Eq. (11), a recursive expression for the error vector norm at an iteration index k in terms of the initial error vector norm $\|\boldsymbol{\varepsilon}_0\|^2$ can be written as

$$\|\boldsymbol{\varepsilon}_k\|^2 = \|\boldsymbol{\varepsilon}_0\|^2 - 2\eta\sum_{j=0}^{k-1} \operatorname{sign}(\hat{e}_j^2 + \beta\hat{\dot{e}}_j^2)\boldsymbol{\varepsilon}_j^{\mathrm{T}}(\hat{e}_j\hat{\mathbf{x}}_j + \beta\hat{\dot{e}}_j\hat{\dot{\mathbf{x}}}_j) + \eta^2\sum_{j=0}^{k-1}\|\hat{e}_j\hat{\mathbf{x}}_j + \hat{\dot{e}}_j\hat{\dot{\mathbf{x}}}_j\|^2 \quad (12)$$

With the absolute value operator replacing the sign, we get

$$\|\boldsymbol{\varepsilon}_0\|^2 - \|\boldsymbol{\varepsilon}_k\|^2 + \eta^2\sum_{j=0}^{k-1}\|\hat{e}_j\hat{\mathbf{x}}_j + \beta\hat{\dot{e}}_j\hat{\dot{\mathbf{x}}}_j\|^2 < 2\eta\sum_{j=0}^{k-1}|\boldsymbol{\varepsilon}_j^{\mathrm{T}}(\hat{e}_j\hat{\mathbf{x}}_j + \beta\hat{\dot{e}}_j\hat{\dot{\mathbf{x}}}_j)| \quad (13)$$

Dividing Eq. (13) on both sides by k and letting $k \to \infty$, we have

$$\eta E\|\hat{e}_j\hat{\mathbf{x}}_j + \beta\hat{\dot{e}}_j\hat{\dot{\mathbf{x}}}_j\|^2 < \lim_{k\to\infty}\frac{1}{k}\frac{\|\boldsymbol{\varepsilon}_k\|^2}{\eta} + 2E|\boldsymbol{\varepsilon}_j^{\mathrm{T}}(\hat{e}_j\hat{\mathbf{x}}_j + \beta\hat{\dot{e}}_j\hat{\dot{\mathbf{x}}}_j)|$$

and hence

$$\tfrac{\eta}{2}E\|\hat{e}_j\hat{\mathbf{x}}_j + \beta\hat{\dot{e}}_j\hat{\dot{\mathbf{x}}}_j\|^2 < E|\boldsymbol{\varepsilon}_j^{\mathrm{T}}(\hat{e}_j\hat{\mathbf{x}}_j + \beta\hat{\dot{e}}_j\hat{\dot{\mathbf{x}}}_j)| \quad (14)$$

Note that we have used the facts that

$$\lim_{k\to\infty}\frac{1}{k}\sum_{j=0}^{k-1} f(\cdot) = E[f(\cdot)]$$

(ergodicity) and $\eta > 0$. If Eq. (14) holds, then it is trivial to show that $E\|\boldsymbol{\varepsilon}_{k+1}\|^2 < E\|\boldsymbol{\varepsilon}_k\|^2$. Note that the expectation operator depicts averaging over the entire input data with the weight fixed at the iteration index specified in the error vector norm. Thus, we can only state that the mean error norm decreases over time. Note that, the right-hand side of Eq. (14) is still hard to compute due to the absolute value operator. However, using Jensen's inequality for convex functions, $E|X| \geq |E(X)|$, we can deduce a loose upper bound for the step-size as

$$0 < \eta < 2\frac{|E[\boldsymbol{\varepsilon}_j^{\mathrm{T}}(\hat{e}_j\hat{\mathbf{x}}_j + \beta\hat{\dot{e}}_j\hat{\dot{\mathbf{x}}}_j)]|}{E\|\hat{e}_j\hat{\mathbf{x}}_j + \beta\hat{\dot{e}}_j\hat{\dot{\mathbf{x}}}_j\|^2} \tag{15}$$

Now, we can simplify Eq. (15) further. The evaluation of the terms $E(\boldsymbol{\varepsilon}_k^{\mathrm{T}}\hat{e}_k\hat{\mathbf{x}}_k)$ and $E(\boldsymbol{\varepsilon}_k^{\mathrm{T}}\hat{\dot{e}}_k\hat{\dot{\mathbf{x}}}_k)$ are tedious and is omitted here. It can be shown that

$$E(\boldsymbol{\varepsilon}_k^{\mathrm{T}}\hat{e}_k\hat{\mathbf{x}}_k) = \boldsymbol{\varepsilon}_k^{\mathrm{T}}\mathbf{R}\boldsymbol{\varepsilon}_k - \boldsymbol{\varepsilon}_k^{\mathrm{T}}\mathbf{V}\mathbf{w}_k \tag{16}$$

$$E(\boldsymbol{\varepsilon}_k^{\mathrm{T}}\hat{\dot{e}}_k\hat{\dot{\mathbf{x}}}_k) = \boldsymbol{\varepsilon}_k^{\mathrm{T}}(2\mathbf{R} - \mathbf{R}_L)\boldsymbol{\varepsilon}_k - 2\boldsymbol{\varepsilon}_k^{\mathrm{T}}\mathbf{V}\mathbf{w}_k$$

where $\mathbf{R} = E[\mathbf{x}_k\mathbf{x}_k^{\mathrm{T}}]$, $\mathbf{R}_L = E[\mathbf{x}_k\mathbf{x}_{k-L}^{\mathrm{T}} + \mathbf{x}_{k-L}\mathbf{x}_k^{\mathrm{T}}]$, $\mathbf{V} = E[\mathbf{v}_k \mathbf{v}_k^{\mathrm{T}}]$. Since we assumed that the noise is white, $\mathbf{V} = \sigma_v^2 I$, where σ_v^2 represents the variance of the input noise. Now, with $\beta = -0.5$,

$$E(\boldsymbol{\varepsilon}_k^{\mathrm{T}}\hat{e}_k\hat{\mathbf{x}}_k) - 0.5(\boldsymbol{\varepsilon}_k^{\mathrm{T}}\hat{\dot{e}}_k\hat{\dot{\mathbf{x}}}_k) = 0.5\boldsymbol{\varepsilon}_k^{\mathrm{T}}\mathbf{R}_L\boldsymbol{\varepsilon}_k \tag{17}$$

Using $\boldsymbol{\varepsilon}_k = \mathbf{w}_* - \mathbf{w}_k = \mathbf{w}_{\mathrm{T}} - \mathbf{w}_k$ and $d_k = \mathbf{x}_k^{\mathrm{T}}\mathbf{w}_{\mathrm{T}}$, Eq. (17) can be further reduced to

$$E(\boldsymbol{\varepsilon}_k^{\mathrm{T}}\hat{e}_k\hat{\mathbf{x}}_k) - 0.5E(\boldsymbol{\varepsilon}_k^{\mathrm{T}}\hat{\dot{e}}_k\hat{\dot{\mathbf{x}}}_k) = E(e_k e_{k-L})$$

$$= E(\hat{e}_k^2 - 0.5\hat{\dot{e}}_k^2) \tag{18}$$

Substituting the numerator of Eq. (15) with the above result, we immediately get the upper bound in Eq. (10). If the step-size chosen satisfies this condition, then $E\|\boldsymbol{\varepsilon}_{k+1}\|^2 < E\|\boldsymbol{\varepsilon}_k\|^2$ and the error vector norm asymptotically converges to zero in the mean. Thus, $\lim_{k\to\infty} E\|\boldsymbol{\varepsilon}_k\|^2 \to 0$ and $\lim_{k\to\infty} E(\mathbf{w}_k) \to \mathbf{w}_* = \mathbf{w}_{\mathrm{T}}$. □

We would like to mention that the upper bound on step-size given by Eq. (10) is computable using only the data samples. For the LMS algorithm ($\beta = 0$), if the input and desired signals are noisy, the upper bound on the step-size is dependent on the true weight vector as well as on the variance of the noise, which makes it impractical. Since the EWC-LMS algorithm with $\beta = -0.5$ minimizes $|\rho_{\hat{e}}(L)|$, the effect of finite step-sizes on the steady state $|\rho_{\hat{e}}(L)|$ would be a good performance index. This is analogous to the excess-MSE in LMS (Haykin, 1996).

Theorem 3. *With $\beta = -0.5$, the steady state excess error autocorrelation at lag $L \geq M$, i.e. $|\rho_{\hat{e}}(L)|$ is always bound by*

$$|\rho_{\hat{e}}(L)| \leq \frac{\eta}{2}E(\hat{e}_\infty^2)[\mathrm{Tr}(\mathbf{R} + \mathbf{V})] + 2\eta[\sigma_u^2 + \|\mathbf{w}_\infty\|\|\mathbf{w}_*\|\mathrm{Tr}(\mathbf{V})] \tag{19}$$

where $\mathbf{R} = E[\mathbf{x}_k\mathbf{x}_k^{\mathrm{T}}]$, and $\mathbf{V} = E[\mathbf{v}_k\mathbf{v}_k^{\mathrm{T}}]$ and $\mathrm{Tr}(\cdot)$ denotes the matrix trace. The noise variances in the input and desired signals are represented by σ_v^2 and σ_u^2, respectively.

Proof. Following the footsteps of the previous proofs, we start with the error dynamics equation given by Eq. (11). Since we are interested in the dynamics near convergence (steady state) we let $k \to \infty$. Applying the expectation operator to both sides of Eq. (11) will give

$$E\|\boldsymbol{\varepsilon}_{k+1}\|^2 = E\|\boldsymbol{\varepsilon}_k\|^2 - 2\eta E[\mathrm{sign}(\hat{e}_k^2 - 0.5\hat{\dot{e}}_k^2)\boldsymbol{\varepsilon}_k^{\mathrm{T}}(\hat{e}_k\hat{\mathbf{x}}_k - 0.5\hat{\dot{e}}_k\hat{\dot{\mathbf{x}}}_k)] + \eta^2 E\|\hat{e}_k\hat{\mathbf{x}}_k - 0.5\hat{\dot{e}}_k\hat{\dot{\mathbf{x}}}_k\|^2 \tag{20}$$

Expanding the terms $\boldsymbol{\varepsilon}_k^{\mathrm{T}}\hat{e}_k\hat{\mathbf{x}}_k$, $\boldsymbol{\varepsilon}_k^{\mathrm{T}}\hat{\dot{e}}_k\hat{\dot{\mathbf{x}}}_k$ and simplifying we get

$$\begin{aligned} E\|\boldsymbol{\varepsilon}_{k+1}\|^2 =& E\|\boldsymbol{\varepsilon}_k\|^2 + \eta^2 E\|\hat{e}_k\hat{\mathbf{x}}_k - 0.5\hat{\dot{e}}_k\hat{\dot{\mathbf{x}}}_k\|^2 \\ &+ 2\eta E[\mathrm{sign}(\hat{e}_k^2 - 0.5\hat{\dot{e}}_k^2)[\mathbf{w}_*^{\mathrm{T}}(\mathbf{v}_k\mathbf{v}_k^{\mathrm{T}} - 0.5\dot{\mathbf{v}}_k\dot{\mathbf{v}}_k^{\mathrm{T}})\mathbf{w}_k]] \\ &+ 2\eta E[\mathrm{sign}(\hat{e}_k^2 - 0.5\hat{\dot{e}}_k^2)(u_k^2 - 0.5\dot{u}_k^2)] \\ &- 2\eta E|\hat{e}_k^2 - 0.5\hat{\dot{e}}_k^2| \end{aligned} \tag{21}$$

Letting $E\|\boldsymbol{\varepsilon}_{k+1}\|^2 = E\|\boldsymbol{\varepsilon}_k\|^2$ as $k \to \infty$, we see that

$$\begin{aligned} &E|(\hat{e}_k^2 - 0.5\hat{\dot{e}}_k^2)| \\ &= \frac{\eta}{2}E\|\hat{e}_k\hat{\mathbf{x}}_k - 0.5\hat{\dot{e}}_k\hat{\dot{\mathbf{x}}}_k\|^2 + \eta E[\mathrm{sign}(\hat{e}_k^2 - 0.5\hat{\dot{e}}_k^2) \\ &\quad \times [\mathbf{w}_*^{\mathrm{T}}(\mathbf{v}_k\mathbf{v}_k^{\mathrm{T}} - 0.5\dot{\mathbf{v}}_k\dot{\mathbf{v}}_k^{\mathrm{T}})\mathbf{w}_k + u_k^2 - 0.5\dot{u}_k^2]] \end{aligned} \tag{22}$$

By Jensen's inequality, $E|(\hat{e}_k^2 - 0.5\hat{\dot{e}}_k^2)| \geq |E(\hat{e}_k^2 - 0.5\hat{\dot{e}}_k^2)|$, and therefore we have

$$\begin{aligned} |\rho_{\hat{e}}(L)| \leq& \frac{\eta}{2}E\|\hat{e}_k\hat{\mathbf{x}}_k - 0.5\hat{\dot{e}}_k\hat{\dot{\mathbf{x}}}_k\|^2 + \eta E[\mathrm{sign}(\hat{e}_k^2 - 0.5\hat{\dot{e}}_k^2) \\ &\times [\mathbf{w}_*^{\mathrm{T}}(\mathbf{v}_k\mathbf{v}_k^{\mathrm{T}} - 0.5\dot{\mathbf{v}}_k\dot{\mathbf{v}}_k^{\mathrm{T}})\mathbf{w}_k + u_k^2 - 0.5\dot{u}_k^2]] \end{aligned} \tag{23}$$

Note that, we used the relation $\rho_{\hat{e}}(L) = E(\hat{e}_k^2 - 0.5\hat{\dot{e}}_k^2)$ in the above equation. The first term on the RHS of Eq. (23) can be easily evaluated by invoking the assumption that $\|\hat{\mathbf{x}}_k\|^2$ and $\hat{e}_k^2$ are uncorrelated in steady state

$$E\|\hat{e}_k\hat{\mathbf{x}}_k - 0.5\hat{\dot{e}}_k\hat{\dot{\mathbf{x}}}_k\|^2 = E(\hat{e}_k^2)[\mathrm{Tr}(\mathbf{R}) + \mathrm{Tr}(\mathbf{V})] \tag{24}$$

The above assumption is commonly used in computing the steady-state excess-MSE for stochastic LMS algorithm (Al-Naffouri & Sayed, 2001). Importantly, this assumption is less restrictive and more natural when compared to the independence theory that was frequently used in the past (Haykin, 1996). The second term in RHS of Eq. (23) is involved and has no closed form expression even with Gaussianity assumptions that are typically made in the analysis of sign-LMS algorithm (Al-Naffouri & Sayed, 2001). Even the validity of Gaussianity assumption is questionable as discussed by Eweda (Eweda, 2000) who proposed additional, reasonable constraints on the noise probability density function to overcome the Gaussianity and independence assumptions (Eweda, 2000) that lead to a more generic misadjustment upper bound for the sign-LMS algorithm. Nevertheless, the analyses of stochastic algorithms (with or without sign) in the existing literature explicitly assume that the input signal is 'noise-free' that simplifies the problem to a great extent. In this paper we particularly deal with input noise and refrain from making any assumptions in deriving an upper bound for excess error autocorrelation. We proceed by rewriting Eq. (23) using the identity $E[\mathrm{sign}(a)b] \le E|b|$ as

$$|\rho_{\hat{e}}(L)| \le \frac{\eta}{2}E(\hat{e}_k^2)[\mathrm{Tr}(\mathbf{R})+\mathrm{Tr}(\mathbf{V})] + \eta E|[\mathbf{w}_*^{\mathrm{T}}(\mathbf{v}_k\mathbf{v}_k^{\mathrm{T}} - 0.5\dot{\mathbf{v}}_k\dot{\mathbf{v}}_k^{\mathrm{T}})\mathbf{w}_k + u_k^2 - 0.5\dot{u}_k^2]| \quad (25)$$

We know that $|a+b| \le |a| + |b|$ and $E(u_k u_{k-L}) = 0$. Therefore,

$$E|[u_k^2 - 0.5\dot{u}_k^2]| \le E(u_k^2) + 0.5E(\dot{u}_k^2) = 2\sigma_u^2 \quad (26)$$

Similarly,

$$E|\mathbf{w}_*^{\mathrm{T}}(\mathbf{v}_k\mathbf{v}_k^{\mathrm{T}} - 0.5\dot{\mathbf{v}}_k\dot{\mathbf{v}}_k^{\mathrm{T}})\mathbf{w}_k| \le E|\mathbf{w}_*^{\mathrm{T}}\mathbf{v}_k\mathbf{v}_k^{\mathrm{T}}\mathbf{w}_k| + 0.5E|\mathbf{w}_*^{\mathrm{T}}\dot{\mathbf{v}}_k\dot{\mathbf{v}}_k^{\mathrm{T}}\mathbf{w}_k| \quad (27)$$

Since the individual terms $\mathbf{w}_*^{\mathrm{T}}\mathbf{v}_k\mathbf{v}_k^{\mathrm{T}}\mathbf{w}_k$ and $\mathbf{w}_*^{\mathrm{T}}\dot{\mathbf{v}}_k\dot{\mathbf{v}}_k^{\mathrm{T}}\mathbf{w}_k$ are not necessarily positive we use the Cauchy–Schwartz inequality to continue further

$$\mathbf{w}_*^{\mathrm{T}}\mathbf{v}_k\mathbf{v}_k^{\mathrm{T}}\mathbf{w}_k \le \|\mathbf{w}_k\|\|\mathbf{w}_*\|\|\mathbf{v}_k\|^2,$$
$$\mathbf{w}_*^{\mathrm{T}}\dot{\mathbf{v}}_k\dot{\mathbf{v}}_k^{\mathrm{T}}\mathbf{w}_k \le \|\mathbf{w}_k\|\|\mathbf{w}_*\|\|\dot{\mathbf{v}}_k\|^2 \quad (28)$$

we know that $E[\mathbf{v}_k\mathbf{v}_{k-L}^{\mathrm{T}}]$ is $\mathbf{0}$ for $L \ge M$. Therefore,

$$E|\mathbf{w}_*^{\mathrm{T}}\mathbf{v}_k\mathbf{v}_k^{\mathrm{T}}\mathbf{w}_k| + 0.5E|\mathbf{w}_*^{\mathrm{T}}\dot{\mathbf{v}}_k\dot{\mathbf{v}}_k^{\mathrm{T}}\mathbf{w}_k| \le 2\|\mathbf{w}_*\|\|\mathbf{w}_k\|\mathrm{Tr}(\mathbf{V}) \quad (29)$$

Using Eqs. (26) and (29) in Eq. (25), and letting $k \to \infty$, we get the result in Eq. (19). The term $E(\hat{e}_\infty^2)$ represents the residual MSE and is given by

$$E(\hat{e}_\infty^2) = \boldsymbol{\varepsilon}_\infty^{\mathrm{T}}\mathbf{R}\boldsymbol{\varepsilon}_\infty + \sigma_u^2 + \mathbf{w}_\infty^{\mathrm{T}}\mathbf{V}\mathbf{w}_\infty \le \|\boldsymbol{\varepsilon}_\infty\|^2\lambda_{\max} + \sigma_u^2 + \|\mathbf{w}_\infty\|\sigma_v^2$$

where $\lambda_{\max}$ is the maximum eigenvalue of $\mathbf{R}$. □

Observe that by reducing the step-size, one can arbitrarily reduce the steady-state excess error autocorrelation at lag $L \ge M$. Extensive simulations have confirmed this fact and the results have been reported by Principe et al. (2003).

4. Algorithm extensions

EWC-LMS is a stochastic gradient algorithm and like all stochastic algorithms, it has tradeoffs between speed of convergence and accuracy of the asymptotic solution. Choosing the right step-size to ensure a desired tradeoff is a non-trivial problem. Recursive algorithms can be derived for EWC, but incur additional computational costs. In this section, we will explore some simple extensions that can improve the robustness and speed of convergence of EWC-LMS.

Normalization with eigenvalue of Hessian. It is a well-known fact, that, a gradient algorithm operating around the vicinity of the stable stationary point converges if the step-size is upper bound by $2/|\lambda_{\max}|$, where $|\lambda_{\max}|$ denotes the absolute maximum eigenvalue of the Hessian matrix of the performance surface. Since, the cost function of EWC is quadratic in nature, the Hessian matrix is simply given by, $\mathbf{H} = \mathbf{R} + \beta\mathbf{S}$, where $\mathbf{R} = E[\mathbf{x}_k\mathbf{x}_k^{\mathrm{T}}]$ and $\mathbf{S} = E[\dot{\mathbf{x}}_k\dot{\mathbf{x}}_k^{\mathrm{T}}]$. For notational convenience, we will assume that the signals are noise-free, and this will not affect the discussions to follow. Since we use $\beta = -0.5$, the Hessian matrix $\mathbf{H}$ can have mixed eigenvalues and this complicates the algorithms for online estimation of the absolute maximum eigenvalue. From the triangle inequality (Golub & Van Loan, 1989)

$$\|\mathbf{H}\|_2 \le \|\mathbf{R}\|_2 + |\beta|\|\mathbf{S}\|_2\sqrt{\lambda_{\max}(\mathbf{R})} + |\beta|\sqrt{\lambda_{\max}(\mathbf{S})} \quad (30)$$

where $\|\cdot\|_2$ denotes the matrix norm. Since, both $\mathbf{R}$ and $\mathbf{S}$ are positive-definite matrices, we can write

$$\|\mathbf{H}\|_2 \le \sqrt{\mathrm{Tr}(\mathbf{R})} + |\beta|\sqrt{\mathrm{Tr}(\mathbf{S})} \le \sqrt{E\|\mathbf{x}_k\|^2} + |\beta|\sqrt{E\|\dot{\mathbf{x}}_k\|^2} \quad (31)$$

In the stochastic framework, we can include this in the update equation in Eq. (7) to give us a step-size normalized EWC-LMS update rule given by

$$\mathbf{w}_{k+1} = \mathbf{w}_k + \frac{\eta\,\mathrm{sign}(e_k^2 + \beta\dot{e}_k^2)(e_k\mathbf{x}_k + \beta\dot{e}_k\dot{\mathbf{x}}_k)}{(\|\mathbf{x}_k\| + |\beta|\|\dot{\mathbf{x}}_k\|)^2} \quad (32)$$

Note that when $\beta = 0$, Eq. (32) reduces to the well-known normalized LMS (NLMS) algorithm (Haykin, 1996).

Normalized gradient EWC-LMS. Another way of improving the convergence speed of EWC-LMS is to use the upper bound in Eq. (10) for the step-size in a stochastic framework. This is a weak upper bound for guaranteed convergence, and including this in the update equation, we get

$$\mathbf{w}_{k+1} = \mathbf{w}_k + 2\frac{(e_k^2 + \beta\dot{e}_k^2)(e_k\mathbf{x}_k + \beta\dot{e}_k\dot{\mathbf{x}}_k)}{(\|e_k\mathbf{x}_k + \beta\dot{e}_k\dot{\mathbf{x}}_k\|^2 + \delta)} \quad (33)$$

Note that in Eq. (33), the sign of the gradient is now given explicitly by the instantaneous EWC cost term itself. The term δ, a small positive constant compensates for the numerical instabilities when the signal has zero power or when the error goes to zero, which can happen in the noiseless case even with finite number of samples. Once again, we would like to state that with $\beta = 0$, Eq. (33) defaults to NLMS algorithm. The caveat is that, both Eqs. (32) and (33) do not satisfy the principle of minimum disturbance or they do not correspond to minimum norm update unlike the NLMS algorithm (Haykin, 1996). We have verified the faster convergence of the normalized EWC algorithms in Eqs. (32) and (33) with extensive simulations. The results are omitted here owing to space constraints. The drawback with the update equation in Eq. (33) is the increased misadjustment with noises injected in the training data. This is in agreement with the fact that misadjustment in the NLMS algorithm is high when compared with the standard LMS for noisy signals. This can be further controlled by inserting a small decaying step-size instead of the constant step-size of 2 in Eq. (33). It is easy to show that $\mu = 2$ is the largest possible step-size for guaranteed convergence of Eq. (33).

EWC with multiple lags. The EWC-LMS algorithm we have proposed ensures that the error autocorrelation at any single lag $L \geq M$ is minimized. With decreasing SNR values (< -10 dB), the Hessian matrix $\mathbf{H} = \mathbf{R} + \beta\mathbf{S}$ (with $\beta = -0.5$) is mostly determined by the noise covariance matrix. This can degrade the performance of the EWC-LMS and we might be forced to use very small step-sizes (slow convergence) to achieve good results. This problem can be alleviated by incorporating multiple lags in the EWC cost function. Instead of minimizing the error autocorrelation at a single lag, we can add similar constraints at additional lags. The corresponding stochastic EWC-LMS algorithm is then given by

$$\mathbf{w}_{k+1} = \mathbf{w}_k + \sum_{l=M}^{l=M+\Delta} \eta_l \operatorname{sign}(\hat{e}_k^2 + \beta\hat{e}_{kl}^2)(\hat{e}_k\hat{\mathbf{x}}_k + \beta\hat{e}_{kl}\hat{\mathbf{x}}_{kl}) \quad (34)$$

Note that Δ is the total number of lags (constraints) for the error autocorrelation. We have verified that Eq. (34) is more robust than the single lag EWC-LMS algorithm. However, the additional robustness comes at an increase in the computational cost. In the case when $\Delta = M$, the complexity of Eq. (34) becomes $O(M^2)$. Further analysis on Eq. (34) is beyond the scope of this paper and will be given in a later paper.

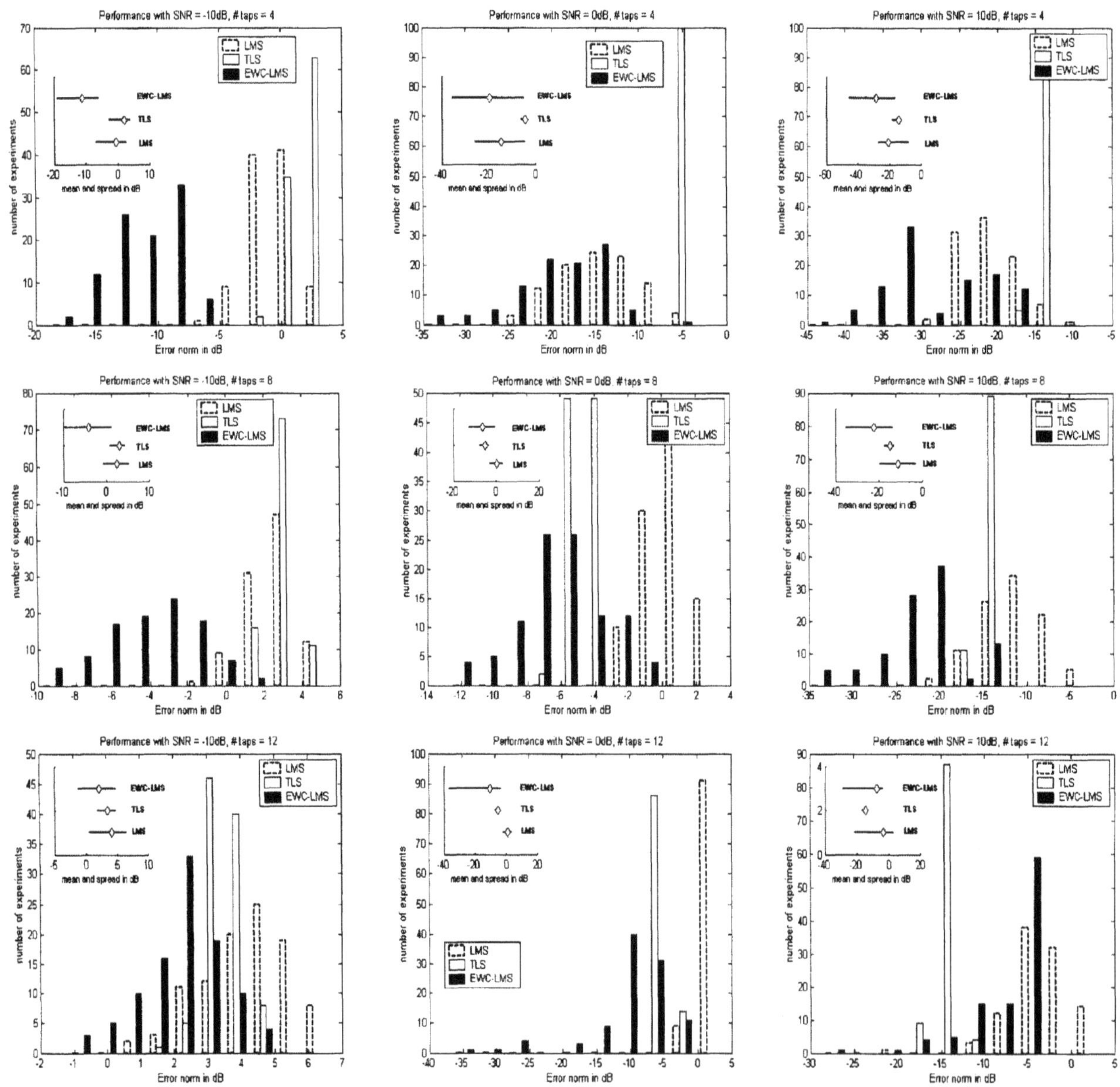

Fig. 2. Histogram plots of the error vector norm for EWC-LMS, LMS algorithms and the numerical TLS solution.

5. System identification and inverse control

System identification using EWC-LMS. We will now verify the noise rejecting capability of EWC-LMS algorithm when $\beta = -0.5$ in a system identification problem. A noise-free, sufficiently colored input signal of 50,000 samples is passed through an *unknown* system to form the noise-free desired signal. Uncorrelated white Gaussian noise is added to the input signal. Clean desired signal is used, as the noise in the desired averages out automatically in stochastic LMS type algorithms. The input SNR was set at − 10, 0 and 10 dB. We chose the order of the unknown system to be 4, 8 and 12 and performed 100 Monte Carlo runs calculating the error vector norm in each case using

$$\text{error norm} = 20 \log 10[\|\mathbf{w}_T - \mathbf{w}_*\|] \quad (35)$$

where $\mathbf{w}_*$ is the solution given by EWC-LMS after one complete presentation of the training data and $\mathbf{w}_T$ represents the unknown system. We ran the regular LMS algorithm as well as the numerical TLS method (batch type). The step-sizes for both LMS and EWC-LMS algorithms were varied to get the best possible results in terms of the error vector norm given by Eq. (35). Fig. 2 shows the histograms of the error vector norms for all three methods. The inset plots in Fig. 2 show the summary of the histograms for each method. EWC-LMS performs significantly better than LMS at low SNR values (− 10 and 0 dB), while performances are on par for SNR greater than 10 dB. Batch type numerical TLS method gives best results when the SNR is high. As we have stated before, TLS suffers if the noise variances in input and desired are not the same.

Inverse modeling and control. System identification is the first step in the design of an inverse controller. Specifically, we wish to design a system that controls the plant to produce a predefined output. Fig. 3 shows a block diagram of model reference inverse control (Widrow & Walach, 1995). In this case, the adaptive controller is designed so that the controller-plant pair would track the response generated by the reference model for any given input (command). Clearly, we require the plant parameters (which are typically unknown) to devise the controller. Once we have a model for the plant, the controller can be easily designed using conventional MSE minimization techniques. In this example, we will assume that the plant is an all-pole system with transfer function $P(z) = 1/(1 + 0.8z^{-1} - 0.5z^{-2} - 0.3z^{-3})$. The reference model is chosen to be an FIR filter with five taps. The block diagram for the plant identification is shown in Fig. 4. Notice that the output of the plant is corrupted with additive white noise due to measurement errors. The SNR at the plant output was set to 0 dB. We then ran the EWC-LMS and LMS algorithms to estimate the model parameters given noisy input and desired signals. The model parameters thus obtained are used to derive the controller (Fig. 3) using standard backpropagation of error. We then tested the adaptive controller-plant pair for trajectory tracking by feeding the controller-plant pair with a non-linear time series and observing the responses. Ideally, the controller-plant pair must follow the trajectory generated by the reference model. Fig. 5(top) shows the tracking results for both controller-plant pairs along with the reference output. Fig. 5(bottom) shows a histogram of the tracking errors. Note that the errors with EWC-LMS controller are all concentrated around zero, which is desirable. In contrast, the errors produced with the MSE based controller are significant and this can be worse if the SNR levels drop further. Fig. 6 shows the magnitude and phase responses of the reference models along with the generated controller-model pairs. Note that, the EWC controller-model pair matches very closely with the desired transfer function, whereas MSE controller-model pair produces a significantly

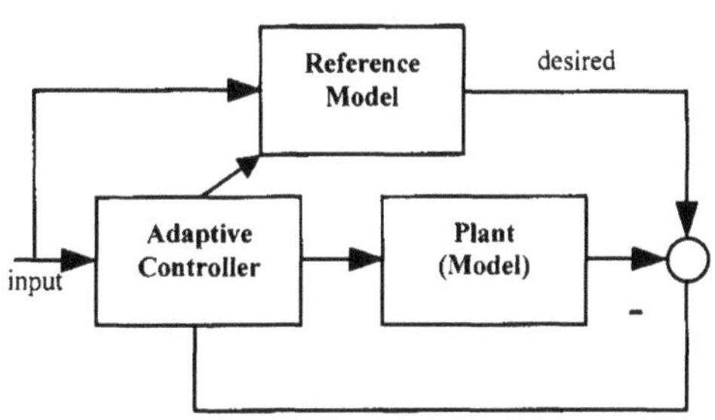

Fig. 3. Block diagram for model reference inverse control.

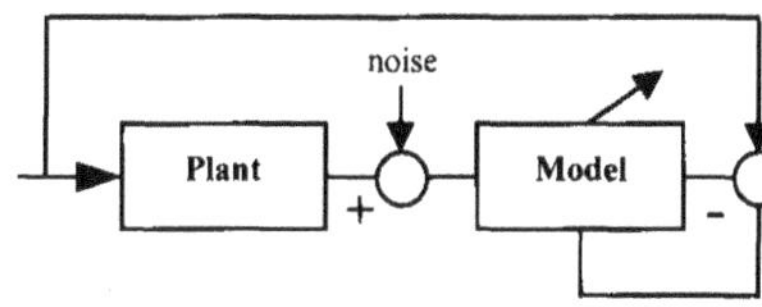

Fig. 4. Block diagram for inverse modeling.

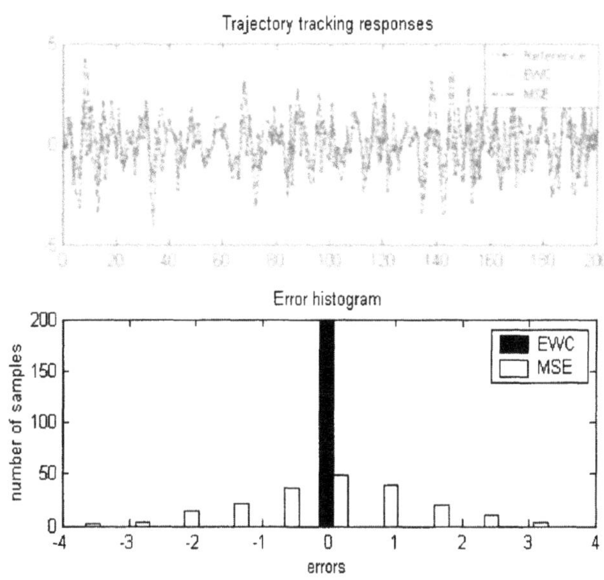

Fig. 5. Tracking results and error histograms.

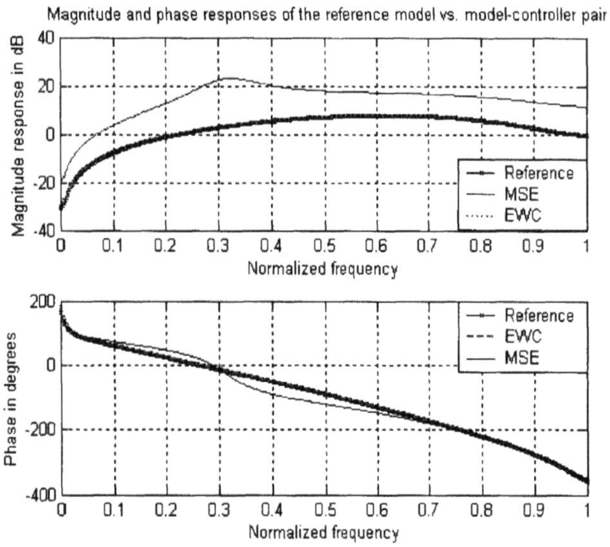

Fig. 6. Magnitude and phase responses of the reference model and designed model-controller pairs.

different transfer function. This clearly demonstrates the advantages offered by EWC.

6. Conclusions

In this paper, we presented a stochastic gradient algorithm for the recently proposed EWC, which includes MSE as a special case. MSE and TLS methods give highly biased parameter estimates if additive white noise with arbitrary variance is present in the input. However, EWC can be used to accurately estimate the underlying parameters of a linear system in the presence of additive white noise. We discussed some interesting properties of this new criterion, and then proposed an on-line, stochastic gradient algorithm with linear complexity in the number of parameters. Convergence of the stochastic gradient algorithm was derived making minimal assumptions and upper bounds on the step-size and the steady-state excess error autocorrelation were determined. We then proposed some extensions for improving the convergence speed and robustness of the EWC-LMS algorithm. Extensive Monte-Carlo simulations were carried out to show the superiority of the new criterion in a FIR system identification problem. We then successfully applied this method for designing a linear inverse controller and obtained superior results when compared with MSE based methods. Currently, further research is in progress to extend the criterion to handle colored noise and non-linear system identification.

Acknowledgements

This work was partially supported by the National Science Foundation under Grant NSF ECS-9900394.

References

Al-Naffouri, T. Y., & Sayed, A. H. (2001). Adaptive filters with error nonlinearities: mean-square analysis and optimum design. *EURASIP Journal of Applied Signal Processing*, *4*, 192–205.

Douglas, S. C. (1996). Analysis of an anti-hebbian adaptive FIR filtering algorithm. *IEEE Transactions on Circuits and Systems. II: Analog and Digital Signal Processing*, *43*(11).

Eweda, E. (2000). Convergence analysis of the sign algorithm without the independence and gaussian assumptions. *IEEE Transactions on Signal Processing*, *48*(9).

Golub, G. H., & Van Loan, C.F. (1989). *Matrix computations*. Baltimore, MD: Johns Hopkins University Press.

Haykin, S. (1996). *Adaptive filter theory*. Upper Saddle River, NJ: Prentice Hall.

Principe, J. C., Rao, Y. N., & Erdogmus, D. (2003). Error whitening wiener filters: theory and algorithms. In S. Haykin, & B. Widrow (Eds.), *Advances in LMS filters, Chap. 10*. New York, NY: Wiley.

Rao, Y. N., Erdogmus, D., & Principe, J. C. (2003). Error whitening criterion for linear filter adaptation. *Proceedings of IJCNN'03, Oregon*, in press.

Rao, Y. N., & Principe, J. C (2002). Efficient total least squares method for system modeling using minor component analysis. *Proceedings of NNSP'02* (pp. 259–268).

Taylor, F. J., & Mellott, J. (1998). *Hands-on digital signal processing*. New York, NY: McGraw Hill.

Widrow, B., & Stearns, S. D. (1985). *Adaptive signal processing*. Englewood Cliffs, NJ: Prentice Hall.

Widrow, B., & Walach, E. (1995). *Adaptive inverse control*. Englewood Cliffs, NJ: Prentice Hall.

AVAILABLE AT
www.ComputerScienceWeb.com
POWERED BY SCIENCE DIRECT

PERGAMON

Neural Networks 16 (2003) 881–890

Neural Networks

www.elsevier.com/locate/neunet

2003 Special issue

New internal optimal neurocontrol for a series FACTS device in a power transmission line

Jung-Wook Park[a,*], Ronald G. Harley[a], Ganesh K. Venayagamoorthy[b]

[a]School of Electrical and Computer Engineering, Georgia Institute of Technology, Atlanta, GA 30332-0250, USA
[b]Department of Electrical and Computer Engineering, University of Missouri-Rolla, Missouri-Rolla, MO 65409-0249, USA

Abstract

In this paper, the proportional-integral (PI) based conventional internal controller (CONVC) of a power electronic based series compensator in an electric power system, is replaced by a nonlinear optimal controller based on the dual heuristic programming (DHP) optimization algorithm. The performance of the CONVC is compared with that of the DHP controller with respect to damping low frequency oscillations. Simulation results using the PSCAD/EMTDC software package are presented.

Keywords: Neurocontroller; Dual heuristic programming; Power system

1. Introduction

In the last decade, flexible AC transmission system (FACTS) devices (Hingorani & Gyugyi, 2002; Makombe & Jenkins, 1999; Noroozian, Ängquist, Ghandhari, & Andersson, 1997; Schauder et al., 1998) have been progressively developed for controlling power flow in a power transmission system, improving the transient stability, damping power system oscillations, and providing voltage stability by using high power semiconductor technology based inverters connected to the electric power grid. Recently, the static synchronous series compensator (SSSC) (Gyugyi, Schauder, & Sen, 1997; Rigby & Harley, 1998; Sen, 1998) among the FACTS device family has attracted considerable attention for damping of low frequency power oscillations in the lines by using controllable series voltage compensation.

The internal control strategy for the inverter of a SSSC as well as other FACTS devices has traditionally been based on linear proportional-integral (PI) regulators. These conventional PI linear controllers (CONVC) operate well at one particular operating point where they have been designed. In other words, their transient and dynamic performances are degraded at any other operating point, or their gains have to be re-tuned for the new operating points.

Artificial neural networks (ANNs) can offer an efficient alternative to overcome the above limitation of the CONVC for the internal control. However, only a few researchers (Dash, Mishra, & Panda, 2000; Mohaddes, Gole, & McLaren, 1999) have reported on FACTS device control using ANNs in the literature due to the difficulty of implementing an effective and fast internal control of the inverter with the ANNs.

The recently developed adaptive critic designs (ACDs) (Park, Harley, & Venayagamoorthy, 2002; Prokhorov & Wunsch, 1997; Si & Wang, 2001; Venayagamoorthy, Harley, & Wunsch, 2002; Werbos, 1992) based techniques avoid the possibility of instability of the neurocontroller, and also find an optimal control (Bertsekas, 2001; White & Jordan, 1992).

This paper proposes a novel intelligent internal control approach using the multilayer perceptron neural network (MLPNN) as an optimal nonlinear neurocontroller.

The background of the dual heuristic programming (DHP) algorithm, which has the best robust control capability among the ACDs family, is presented. Based on the DHP algorithm, a novel nonlinear optimal neurocontroller (called DHPNC) is designed as an alternative for internal control of the SSSC, thereby replacing the PI based regulators for the currents but not for the DC link voltage.

* Corresponding author.
E-mail addresses: jungwookpark@ieee.org (J.-W. Park), rharley@ece.gatech.edu (R.G. Harley), ganeshv@ece.umr.edu (G.K. Venayagamoorthy).

0893-6080/03/$ - see front matter © 2003 Elsevier Science Ltd. All rights reserved.
doi:10.1016/S0893-6080(03)00121-7

The performances of the DHPNC and CONVC are compared with respect to the damping of power oscillations by time-domain simulations in the PSCAD/EMTDC software environment.

2. Static synchronous series compensator

The SSSC converter can control the reactive and/or active power on an AC system by changing both phasor angle and magnitude of the converter's output voltage with a fast control action. Especially, the exchange of active power, which is the particular characteristic of the SSSC, is accomplished by controlling the DC voltage inside the SSSC (Hingorani & Gyugyi, 2002).

2.1. Modeling of SSSC

The single machine infinite bus (SMIB) system shown in Fig. 1 is used to compare the damping control capabilities of the proposed DHPNC and CONVC for the SSSC. The plant consists of the synchronous generator (160 MV A, 15 kV (L–L)), turbine–governor system, automatic voltage regulator (AVR)–exciter system, transmission line connected to an infinite bus, and the SSSC connected in series with transmission line. The parameters of the synchronous generators and transmission line are given in Anderson and Fouad (1994).

The EXACIA (IEEE alternator supplied rectifier excitation systems) and H_TURI/GOV1 (IEEE type hydro turbine–governor) models in PSCAD/EMTDC software package are used as the AVR/exciter system and turbine/governor, respectively.

For the mathematical model of the SSSC, the associated equation can be represented with the lumped series transmission line reactance x_e' (transmission line x_e plus leakage reactance of series-connected transformer) and transmission series resistance r_e (the inverter is regarded simply to have no conduction losses) in per unit as follows

$$\frac{\mathrm{d}}{\mathrm{d}t}\begin{bmatrix} i_{sa} \\ i_{sb} \\ i_{sc} \end{bmatrix} = \begin{bmatrix} -\frac{r_e\omega_s}{x_e'} & 0 & 0 \\ 0 & -\frac{r_e\omega_s}{x_e'} & 0 \\ 0 & 0 & -\frac{r_e\omega_s}{x_e'} \end{bmatrix}\begin{bmatrix} i_{sa} \\ i_{sb} \\ i_{sc} \end{bmatrix} + \begin{bmatrix} \frac{\omega_s}{x_e'}(v_{sa}+v_{ca}-v_{ra}) \\ \frac{\omega_s}{x_e'}(v_{sb}+v_{cb}-v_{rb}) \\ \frac{\omega_s}{x_e'}(v_{sc}+v_{cc}-v_{rc}) \end{bmatrix} \tag{1}$$

where ω_s is the synchronous speed of the power system, v_s is the sending-end voltage (terminal voltage in practice), i_s is the current in transmission line, v_r is the receiving-end voltage in the infinite bus, and v_c is the injected series compensation voltage.

Using the synchronously rotating reference frame based transformation (Makombe & Jenkins, 1999), in which the d-axis is always coincident with the instantaneous voltage vector v and the q-axis leads the d-axis by 90°, the three-phase circuit equations in Eq. (1) can be transformed to the following d–q axis vector resprentation

$$\frac{\mathrm{d}}{\mathrm{d}t}\begin{bmatrix} i_d \\ i_q \end{bmatrix} = \begin{bmatrix} -\frac{r_e\omega_s}{x_e'} & \omega \\ -\omega & -\frac{r_e\omega_s}{x_e'} \end{bmatrix}\begin{bmatrix} i_d \\ i_q \end{bmatrix} + \begin{bmatrix} \frac{\omega_s}{x_e'}(|v_s|+v_{cd}-v_{rd}) \\ \frac{\omega_s}{x_e'}(v_{cq}-v_{rq}) \end{bmatrix} \tag{2}$$

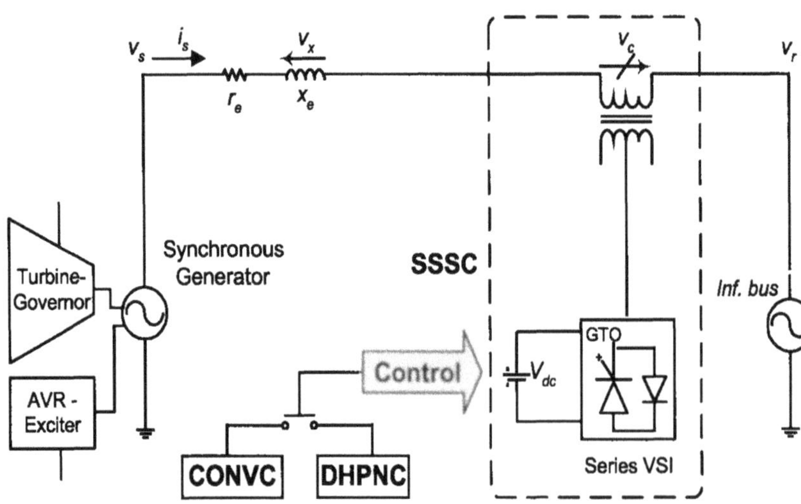

Fig. 1. Plant: 160 MV A, 15 kV (L–L) SMIB test system.

Neglecting the series inverter harmonics, the AC side injected voltage v_c in Fig. 1 can be expressed with relation to the capacitor voltage V_{dc} on the DC link as follows

$$v_{cd} = mV_{dc}\cos(\alpha), \qquad v_{cq} = mV_{dc}\sin(\alpha) \tag{3}$$

where α is the phase voltage difference between the voltages v_c and v_s (the v_c leads the v_s), and m is the modulation index of the series inverter. The dynamics of the DC capacitor voltage is given by

$$\frac{dV_{dc}}{dt} = \frac{1}{C}\frac{P_{dc}}{V_{dc}} = \frac{1}{C}\frac{V_{dc}i_{dc}}{V_{dc}} = \frac{1}{C}\frac{(v_{cd}i_d + v_{cq}i_q)}{V_{dc}}$$
$$= \frac{1}{C}[m\{\cos(\alpha)i_d + \sin(\alpha)i_q\}] \tag{4}$$

2.2. Conventional control strategy

The main goal of the SSSC is to inject the series voltage in quadrature with the line current and to maintain the DC voltage V_{dc}. For this purpose, the $P-Q$ (real and reactive power) automatic power flow control mode (Hingorani & Gyugyi, 2002) in Fig. 2 is used.

In Fig. 2, an instantaneous three-phase set of line voltages, v_a, v_b, and v_c is used to calculate the transformation angle, θ provided by the vector phase-locked loop for synchronous operation of the series voltage source inverter shown in Fig. 1.

As shown in Eq. (2), the three-phase set of measured line currents at the AC terminal of the SSSC is decomposed into its real/direct component, i_d, and reactive/quadrature.component, i_q. These actual signals (i_d and i_q) and the reference $d-q$ current signals (i_d^* and i_q^*) are compared, respectively.

The error signal Δi_q for the reactive power exchange is passed through the PI regulator PI-i_q. The signal Δi_p for the real power exchange and maintenance of a constant V_{dc}, is passed through the PI-i_p. The Δi_p consists of the Δi_d and error signal $\Delta V'_{dc}$ (which passes through the PI-V_{dc}).

The V_{dc}^* is the desired value for V_{dc}. The value of V_{dc}^* is determined by selecting a suitable value of the modulation index within its range of 0 to 1. Finally, the estimated signals ($\tilde{v}_{cq}$ and $\tilde{v}_{cd}$) in Fig. 2 are used to compute the angle α and modulation index m to drive the gate turn-off (GTO) thyristor of the inverter.

3. DHP based neurocontroller design

ACDs proposed by Werbos (1992) are new optimization techniques to handle the nonlinear optimal control problem using ANNs.

The adaptive critic method finds the optimal control in the *infinite horizon problem* to minimize/maximize the user-defined heuristic cost-to-go function **J** for a system, by successively adapting two ANNs, namely the *action network* (which dispenses the control signals) and the *critic network* (which learns to approximate the cost-to-go function **J**). This process is called the *approximate dynamic programming* (ADP) for the value iteration **J**. The adaptation process starts with a nonoptimal, arbitrarily chosen, control by the action network; the critic network then guides the action network towards the optimal solution at each successive adaptation. During the adaptations, neither of the networks needs any 'information' of an optimal trajectory, only the desired cost needs to be known (Prokhorov & Wunsch, 1997).

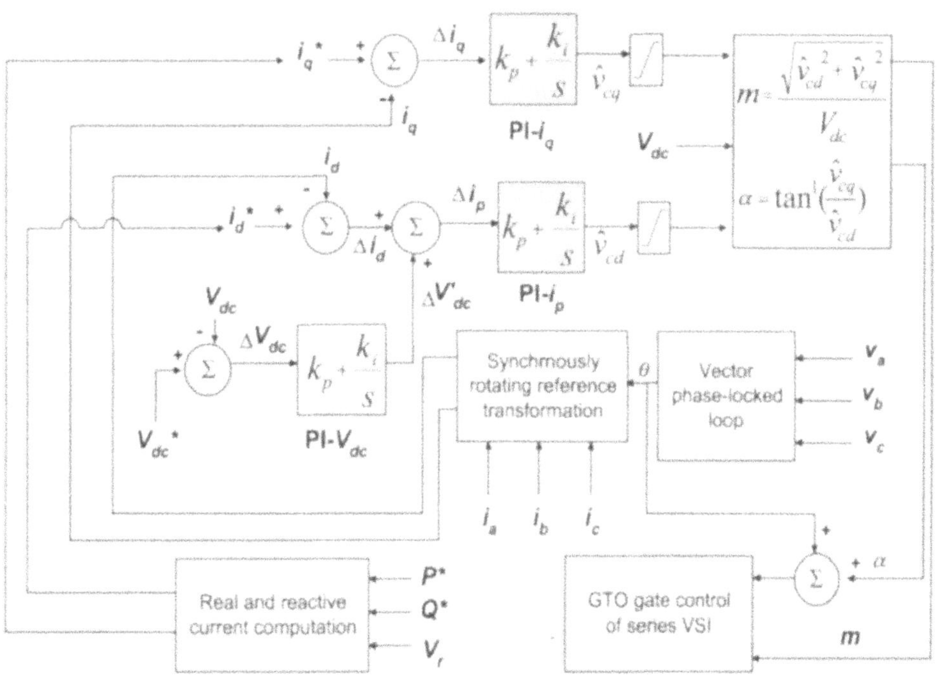

Fig. 2. $P-Q$ automatic power flow control diagram for the internal control of the SSSC.

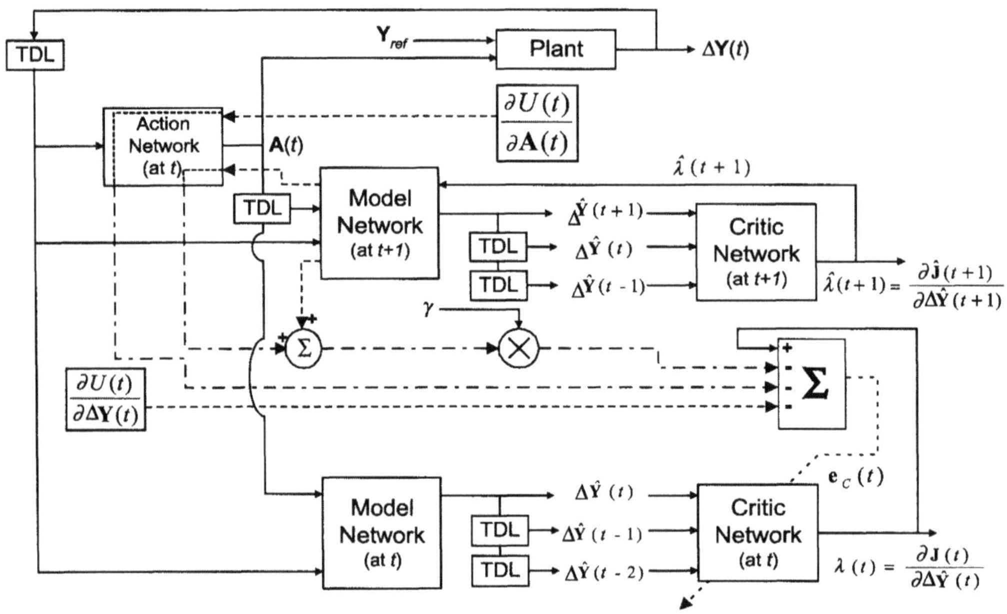

Fig. 3. Critic network adaptation in DHP: This diagram shows the implementation of Eq. (8). The same critic network is shown for two consecutive times, t and $t+1$. The discount factor γ is chosen to be 0.5. Backpropagation paths are shown by dotted and dash-dot lines. The output of the critic network $\hat{\lambda}(t+1)$ is backpropagated through the model network from its outputs to its inputs, yielding the first term of Eq. (7) and $\hat{\lambda}\mathbf{J}(t+1)/\partial\mathbf{A}(t)$. The latter is backpropagated through the action network from its outputs to its inputs forming the second term of Eq. (7). Backpropagation of the vector $\partial U(t)/\partial\mathbf{A}(t)$ through the action network results in a vector with components computed as the last term of Eq. (8). The summation of all these signals produces the error vector $\mathbf{e}_C(t)$ used for training the critic network.

The DHP technique (among the ACDs family) has the strong control capability in that the critic network of the DHP approximates the derivatives of the function $\mathbf{J}$ with respect to the states of the plant to be controlled. The DHP algorithm described in this paper uses three different multilayer (three layer) perceptron neural networks (MLPNNs), namely one for each of the critic, model, and action networks.

The weight vector V of the MLPNN is adjusted/trained using the gradient descent based backpropagation algorithm. By trial and error, 14 neurons are used in the hidden layer of the MLPNN for the model network, and 10 neurons for each of the critic and action networks.

3.1. Critic network

As mentioned before, the DHPNC is designed to replace the PI regulators PI-i_q and PI-i_p in Fig. 2. The input reference vector $\mathbf{J}_{ref}$ into the SSSC and output vector $\Delta\mathbf{J}$ from the SSSC are

- $\mathbf{J}_{ref}(t)$, input reference vector to the SSSC $= [i_p^*(t), i_d^*(t), V_{dc}^*(t)]$.
- $\Delta\mathbf{J}(t)$, output vector from the SSSC $= [\Delta i_q(t), \Delta i_p(t)]$.

The configuration for the critic network adaptation in the DHP is shown in Fig. 3. The inputs and outputs of the action and model networks used in the critic network adaptation are shown in Figs. 4 and 5.

The critic network estimates the derivatives of function $\mathbf{J}$ with respect to the vector of observables of the plant (identified by the model network), which is the $\Delta\tilde{\mathbf{Y}}(t) = [\Delta\tilde{\iota}_q(t), \Delta\hat{\iota}_p(t)]$ (input vector of the critic network), and it learns to minimize the following error measure over time

$$\|E_c\| = \sum_t \mathbf{e}_C^T(t)\mathbf{e}_C(t) \quad (5)$$

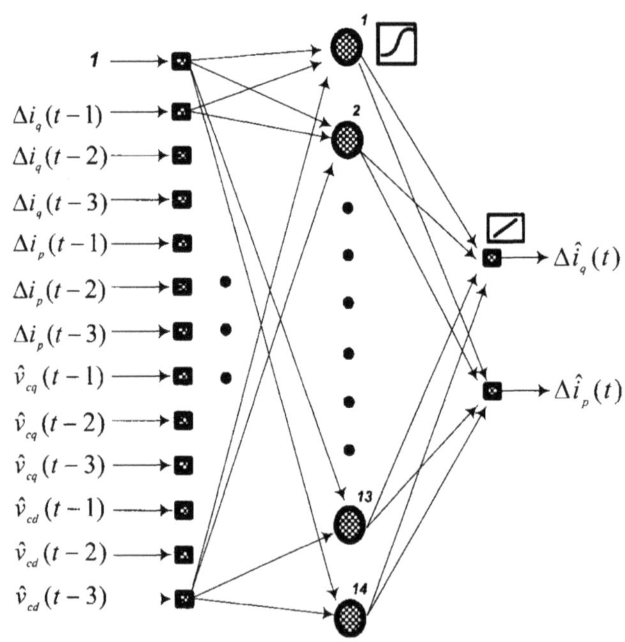

Fig. 4. Input–output mapping of the model network at t used in the critic network adaptation in Fig. 3.

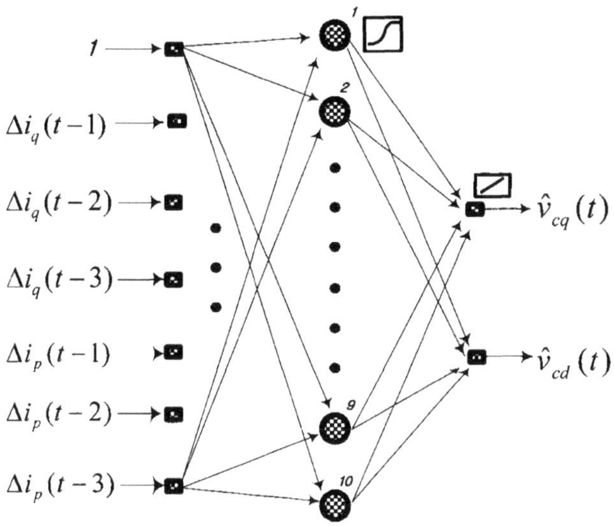

Fig. 5. Input–output mapping of the action network at t used in the critic network adaptation in Fig. 3.

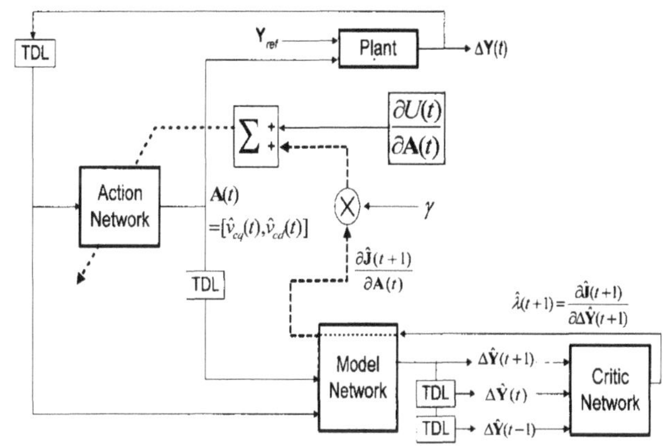

Fig. 6. Action network adaptation in DHP: The discount factor γ is chosen to be 0.5. Backpropagation paths are shown by dotted lines. The output of the critic network $\hat{\lambda}(t+1)$ at time $(t+1)$ is backpropagated through the model network from its outputs to its inputs (output of the action network), and the resulting vector multiplied by the discount factor ($\gamma = 0.5$) and added to $\partial U(t)/\partial \mathbf{A}(t)$. Then, an incremental adaptation of the action network is carried out by Eqs. (10) and (11).

$$\mathbf{e}_{\mathrm{C}}(t) = \frac{\partial \mathbf{J}[\Delta\hat{\mathbf{Y}}(t)]}{\partial \Delta\hat{\mathbf{Y}}(t)} - \gamma \frac{\partial \hat{\mathbf{J}}[\Delta\hat{\mathbf{Y}}(t+1)]}{\partial \Delta\mathbf{Y}(t)} - \frac{\partial U[\Delta\mathbf{Y}(t)]}{\partial \Delta\mathbf{Y}(t)} \tag{6}$$

After exploiting all relevant pathways of backpropagation as shown in Fig. 3, where the paths of derivatives and adaptation of the critic network are depicted by dotted and dash-dot lines, the error signal $\mathbf{e}_{\mathrm{C}}(t)$ is used for training to update the weights of the critic network. The jth component of the second term in Eq. (6) can be expressed by the output of critic network at time $t+1$, $\hat{\lambda}_i(t+1) = \partial\hat{\mathbf{J}}[\Delta\hat{\mathbf{Y}}(t+1)]/\partial\Delta\hat{\mathbf{Y}}_i(t+1)$ as follows

$$\frac{\partial \hat{\mathbf{J}}[\Delta\hat{\mathbf{Y}}(t+1)]}{\partial \Delta\mathbf{Y}_j(t)} = \sum_{i=1}^{n} \hat{\lambda}_i(t+1) \frac{\partial \hat{\mathbf{Y}}_i(t+1)}{\partial \Delta\mathbf{Y}_j(t)} + \sum_{k=1}^{m}\sum_{i=1}^{n} \hat{\lambda}_i(t+1) \times \frac{\partial \Delta\hat{\mathbf{Y}}_j(t+1)}{\partial \mathbf{A}_k(t)} \frac{\partial \mathbf{A}_k(t)}{\partial \Delta\mathbf{Y}_j(t)} \tag{7}$$

where n and m are the numbers of outputs of the model and the action networks, respectively.

By using Eq. (7), each component of the vector $\mathbf{e}_{\mathrm{C}}(t)$ from Eq. (6) is determined by

$$\mathbf{e}_{\mathrm{C}j}(t) = \frac{\partial \mathbf{J}[\Delta\hat{\mathbf{Y}}(t)]}{\partial \Delta\hat{\mathbf{Y}}_j(t)} - \gamma \frac{\partial \hat{\mathbf{J}}[\Delta\hat{\mathbf{Y}}(t+1)]}{\partial \Delta\mathbf{Y}_j(t)} - \frac{\partial U[\Delta\mathbf{Y}(t)]}{\partial \Delta\mathbf{Y}_j(t)} - \sum_{k=1}^{m} \frac{\partial U[\Delta\mathbf{Y}(t)]}{\partial \mathbf{A}_k(t)} \frac{\partial \mathbf{A}_k(t)}{\partial \Delta\mathbf{Y}_j(t)} \tag{8}$$

Using Eq. (8), the expression for the weights' update for the critic network is as follows

$$\Delta\mathbf{V}_{\mathrm{C}}(t) = -\eta_{\mathrm{C}} \mathbf{e}_{\mathrm{C}}^{\mathrm{T}}(t) \frac{\partial \mathbf{e}_{\mathrm{C}}(t)}{\partial \mathbf{V}_{\mathrm{C}}(t)} \tag{9}$$

where η_{C} is a positive learning rate and $\mathbf{V}_{\mathrm{C}}$ contains the weights of the DHP critic network.

3.2. Action network

The adaptation of the action network in Fig. 3 is shown in Fig. 6, which propagates $\hat{\lambda}(t+1)$ back through the model network to the action network. The goal of this adaptation is expressed in Eq. (10), and the weights of the action network are updated by Eq. (11)

$$\frac{\partial U[\Delta\mathbf{Y}(t)]}{\partial \mathbf{A}(t)} + \gamma \frac{\partial \hat{\mathbf{J}}[\Delta\hat{\mathbf{Y}}(t+1)]}{\partial \mathbf{A}(t)} = 0, \qquad \forall t. \tag{10}$$

$$\Delta\mathbf{V}_{\mathrm{A}}(t) = -\eta_{\mathrm{A}} \left[\frac{\partial U[\Delta\mathbf{Y}(t)]}{\partial \mathbf{A}(t)} + \gamma \frac{\partial \hat{\mathbf{J}}[\Delta\hat{\mathbf{Y}}(t+1)]}{\partial \mathbf{A}(t)} \right]^{\mathrm{T}} \frac{\partial \mathbf{A}(t)}{\partial \mathbf{V}_{\mathrm{A}}(t)} \tag{11}$$

where η_{A} is a positive learning rate and $\mathbf{V}_{\mathrm{A}}$ contains the weights of the DHP action network.

The discount factor γ of 0.5 and the user-defined utility function $U(t)$ in Eq. (12) are used in Eqs. (8) and (10) during adaptation of the critic and action networks

$$U(t) = [\Delta i_q(t) + \Delta i_q(t-1) + \Delta i_q(t-2)]^2 + [\Delta i_{\mathrm{p}}(t) + \Delta i_{\mathrm{p}}(t-1) + \Delta i_{\mathrm{p}}(t-2)]^2 \tag{12}$$

3.3. Model network

Fig. 7 shows how the model network (identifier) is trained to identify the dynamics of the plant in Fig. 1. The nonlinear autoregressive moving average with exogenous inputs (NARMAX) model is used as the structure for the on-line identification. The components of vectors $\mathbf{Y}_{\mathrm{ref}}(t)$, $\Delta\mathbf{Y}(t)$, $\mathbf{A}(t)$, and $\Delta\hat{\mathbf{Y}}(t)$ are already noted in subsection *A* above (Figs. 4 and 5).

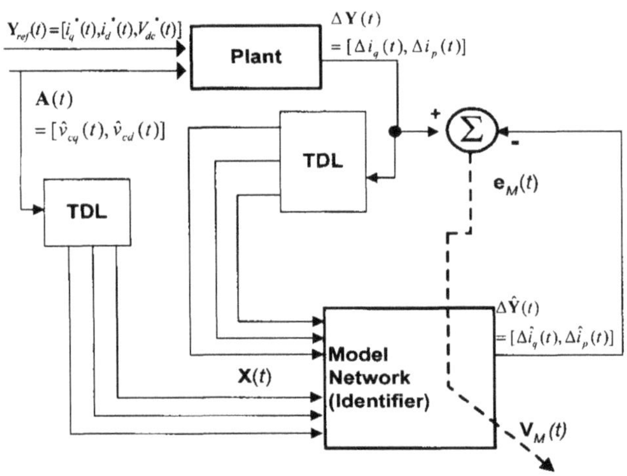

Fig. 7. NARMAX model for on-line training of the model network.

The residual vector, $\mathbf{e}_\mathrm{M}(t)$ given in Eq. (13) is used for updating the model network's weights $\mathbf{V}_\mathrm{M}$ in Eq. (14) during training by the backpropagation algorithm

$$\mathbf{e}_\mathrm{M}(t) = \Delta\mathbf{Y}(t) - \Delta\hat{\mathbf{Y}}(t)$$

$$= [\Delta i_q(t) - \Delta\hat{i}_q(t), \Delta i_\mathrm{p}(t) - \Delta\hat{i}_p(t)], \tag{13}$$

$$\Delta\mathbf{V}_\mathrm{M}(t) = -\eta_\mathrm{M}\mathbf{e}_\mathrm{M}^\mathrm{T}(t)\frac{\partial\mathbf{e}_\mathrm{M}(t)}{\partial\mathbf{V}_\mathrm{M}(t)} \tag{14}$$

where η_M is a positive learning rate and $\mathbf{V}_\mathrm{M}$ is the weights of the DHP model network.

The training of the critic, action, and model networks in the DHP algorithm is carried out by different kinds of small pseudo-random binary signals (PRBSs) signals (Park et al., 2002), and the training procedures are explained in Park et al. (2002), Prokhorov & Wunsch (1997) and Venayagamoorthy, Harley, & Wunsch (2003).

Note that the model network is trained before the training of the action and critic networks, and the DHPNC with the fixed (converged) weights for the critic and action networks is used to control the plant for real-time operation. In other words, they have been successfully trained to their optimization purposes, which are the value iteration (to minimize the value of derivatives of the function **J**) for the critic network and policy iteration (to solve the optimal control **u** in optimal policy) for the action network (Bertsekas, 2001).

4. Case studies

4.1. Dynamic performance for fault at receiving end

To evaluate the damping performance of the proposed neurocontroller for the control of the SSSC, 100 and 120 ms three phase short circuits are applied to the infinite bus (receiving end) at $t = 1$ *s*. The generator operates with a rotor angle of 53.6° ($P_t = 1.0$ pu, $Q_t = 0.59$ pu) in a steady-state operating point. The results are shown in Figs. 8–12, where 'Uncompensated' and 'CONVC' denote the response of generator controlled without SSSC and with the PI controlled SSSC, respectively.

From Fig. 8, it can be observed that the transmission line current is leads the compensating injection voltage v_c by almost 90° (considering the r_e) in steady-state such that the SSSC controlled by both the CONVC and DHPNC can establish the same effect as the series capacitive

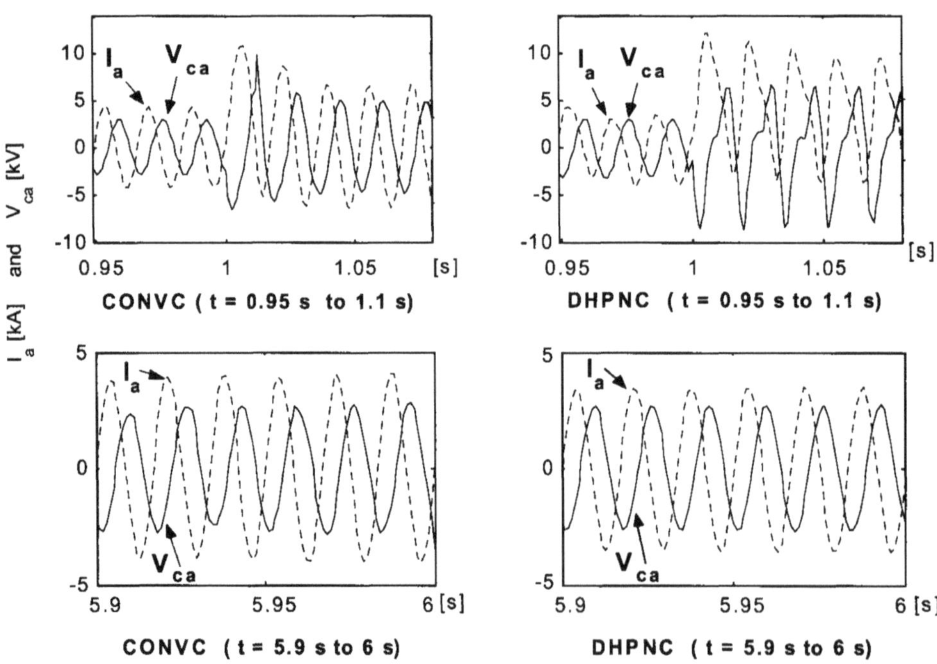

Fig. 8. Line current i_a (kA) and injected voltage v_ca (kV).

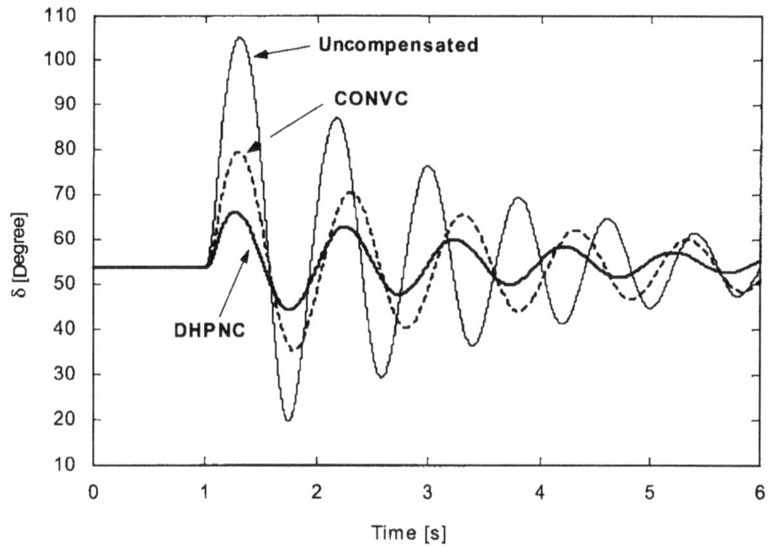

Fig. 9. A 100 ms three phase short circuit test δ (°).

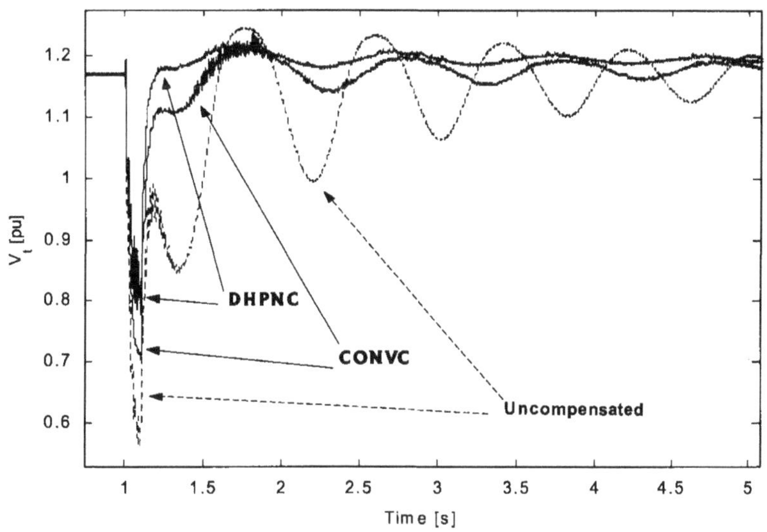

Fig. 10. A 100 ms three phase short circuit test: V_t (pu).

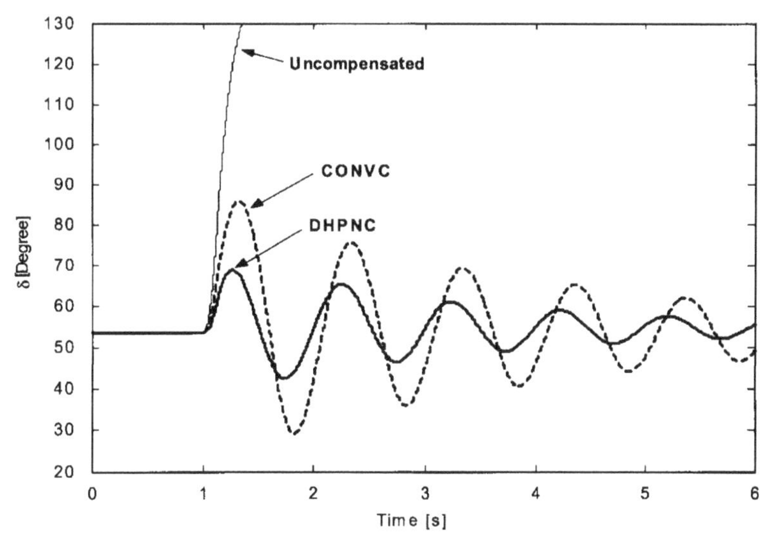

Fig. 11. A 120 ms three phase short circuit test: δ (°).

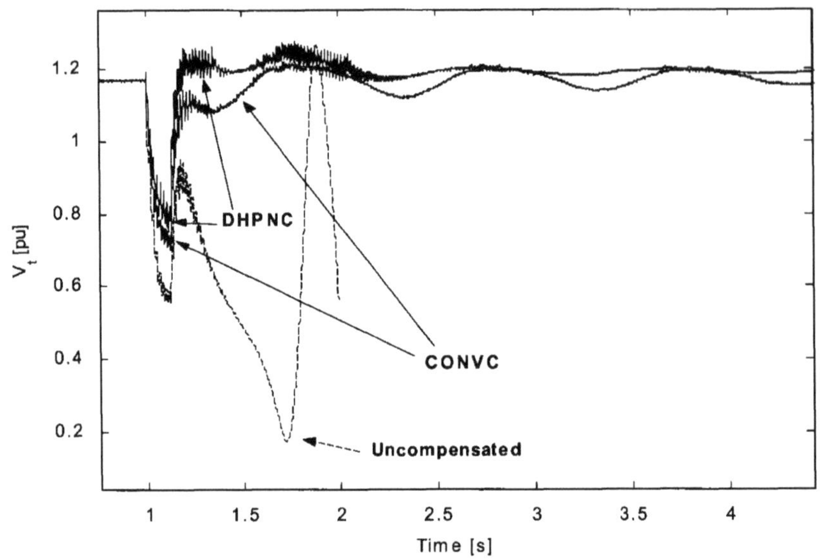

Fig. 12. A 120 ms three phase short circuit test: V_t (pu).

compensation resulting in increasing the line current (i_s) and transmitted power (P).

From Figs. 9–10, the DHPNC damping control is more effective compared to the CONVC. Also, it is clear from Figs. 11 and 12 that the generator controlled without the SSSC goes unstable and loses synchronism when the fault duration is 120 ms.

In contrast, the DHPNC and CONVC restore the generator to a stable mode, and the DHPNC damping control is more effective compared to the CONVC, which means that the DHPNC allows the generator to be operated closer to its stability limit during steady state and thus would make it possible in a practical plant for the generation of more mega watts of power per dollar of invested capital.

4.2. Dynamic performances for single line-to-ground fault at machine terminal and multiple short circuits at both receiving and sending ends

To further evaluate the damping performance of the DHPNC, a 150 ms single (a-phase) line-to-ground short circuit is applied at the generator terminals (the sending end in the SMIB system in Fig. 1) at $t = 1$ s. The generator operates at the same steady-state operating condition as the previous test.

The result in Fig. 13 shows that the DHPNC once gain has the best damping performance compared to the CONVC as well as the uncompensated.

The same controllers are again evaluated for multiple different types of short circuits at different points. A 100 ms

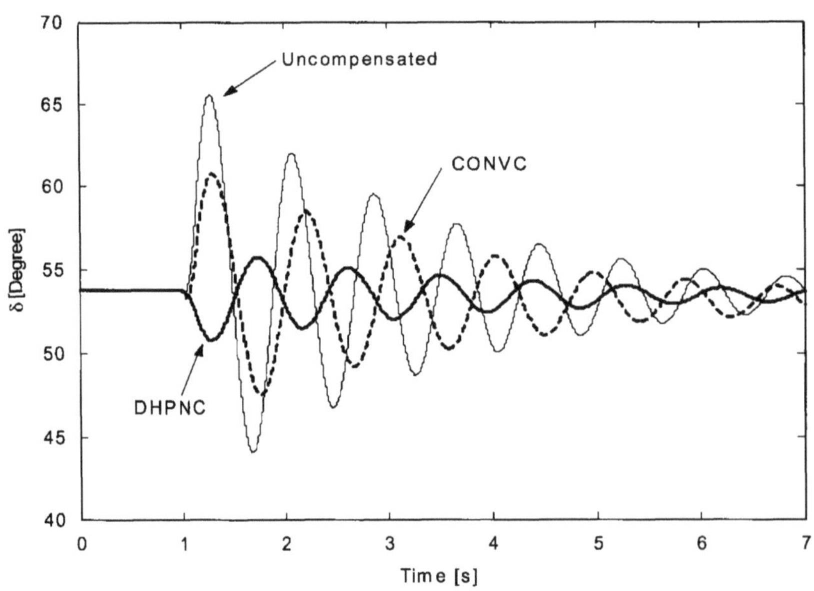

Fig. 13. A 150 ms single (a-phase) line-to-ground short circuit fault occurs at $t = 1$ s: δ (°).

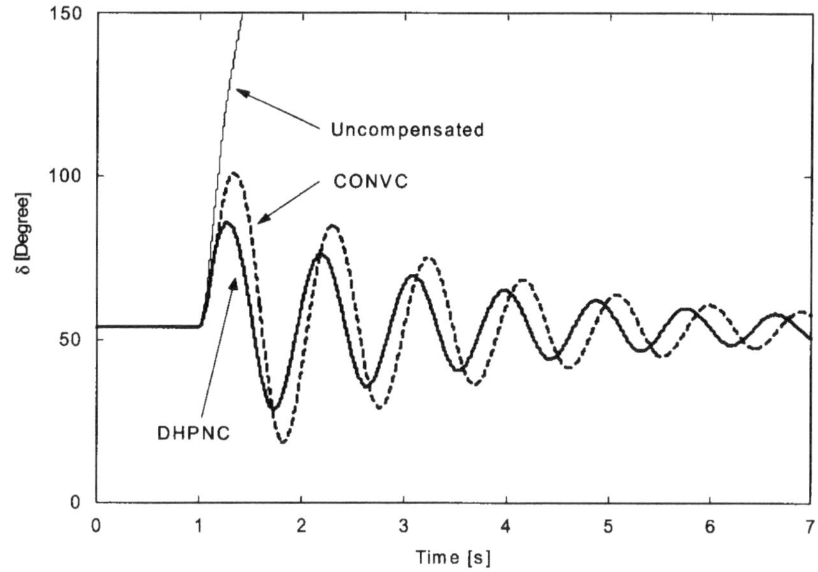

Fig. 14. Multiple short circuits test at both receiving and sending ends: δ (°).

three phase short circuit is applied at the infinite bus at $t = 1$ s. Meanwhile, a 150 ms single (a-phase) line-to-ground fault is applied at the generator terminals at $t = 1.05$ s.

The result in Fig. 14 shows that the CONVC and DHPNC restore the system to a stable mode, but that the uncompensated system goes unstable.

4.3. Selection of sampling rates during simulation

The numerical integration time step of PSCAD/EMTDC is 50 μs in order to obtain a switching frequency of 1980 Hz (33 times the fundamental) for the gate turn-off thyristors (GTOs). A sampling rate of 50 μs is used for the DHPNC because the outputs ($\hat{v}_{cq}$ and $\hat{v}_{cd}$ in Fig. 2) of the DHPNC should be generated fast enough to compute the angle α and modulation index m to drive the GTOs of the inverter. Moreover, the simulation results with 10 times slower sampling rates (500 μs) do not show any severe degradation in performance of the DHPNC.

5. Conclusions

This paper has proposed a novel DHP based design of a nonlinear optimal neurocontroller (DHPNC) for the internal control of a SSSC used in a transmission line of an electric power grid. The multiplayer perceptron neural network (MLPNN) is used as function approximator for the critic, action, and model networks to implement the DHP algorithm.

The PSCAD/EMTDC simulation results show that the DHPNC has a better performance than the PI based conventional controller (CONVC) with respect to damping low frequency power oscillations and minimizing the terminal voltage variations.

The use of fixed parameters in the DHPNC for real-time control not only has an important significance in terms of reducing the number of computations in dealing with the infinite optimal control problem by using the ANNs, but also proves robustness of the ACDs based controllers.

Acknowledgements

Financial support by the National Science Foundation (NSF), USA under Grant No. ECS-0080764 for this research is gratefully acknowledged.

References

Anderson, P. M., & Fouad, A. A. (1994). *Power system control and stability*. New York: IEEE Press.

Bertsekas, D. P. (2001). *Dynamic programming and optimal control*. Belmont, MA: Athena Scientific.

Dash, P. K., Mishra, S., & Panda, G. (2000). A radial basis function neural network controller for UPFC. *IEEE Transaction on Power Systems*, *15*(4), 1293–1299.

Gyugyi, L., Schauder, C. D., & Sen, K. K. (1997). Static synchronous series compensator: a solid-state approach to the series compensation of transmission lines. *IEEE Transaction on Power Delivery*, *12*(1), 406–417.

Hingorani, N. G., & Gyugyi, L. (2002). *Understanding FACTS: concepts and technology of flexible AC transmission systems*. New York: IEEE Press.

Makombe, T., & Jenkins, N. (1999). Investigation of a unified power flow controller. *IEEE Proceedings on Generation Transmission Distribution*, *146*(4), 400–408.

Mohaddes, M., Gole, A. M., & McLaren, P. G. (1999). A neural network controlled optimal pulse-width modulated STATCOM. *IEEE Transaction on Power Delivery*, *14*(2), 481–488.

Noroozian, M., Ängquist, L., Ghandhari, M., & Andersson, G. (1997). Improving power system dynamics by series-connected FACTS devices. *IEEE Transaction on Power Delivery*, *12*(4), 1635–1641.

Park, J.-W., Harley, R. G., & Venayagamoorthy, G. K. (2002). Adaptive critic based optimal neurocontrol for synchronous generator in power system using MLP/RBF neural networks. *37th IEEE Annual Industry Application Society (IAS) Meeting*, *2*, 1447–1454.

Prokhorov, D. V., & Wunsch, D. C. (1997). Adaptive critic designs. *IEEE Transaction on Neural Networks*, *8*(5), 997–1007.

Rigby, B. S., & Harley, R. G. (1998). An improved control scheme for a series-capacitive reactance compensator based on a voltage-source inverter. *IEEE Transaction on Industry Applications*, *34*(2), 355–363.

Schauder, C. D., et al. (1998). Operation of the unified power flow controller (UPFC) under practical constraints. *IEEE Transaction on Power Delivery*, *13*(2), 630–639.

Sen, K. K. (1998). SSSC: static synchronous series compensator: theory, modeling, and application. *IEEE Transaction on Power Delivery*, *13*(1), 241–246.

Si, J., & Wang, Y.-T. (2001). On-line learning control by association and reinforcement. *IEEE Transaction on Neural Networks*, *12*(2), 264–276.

Venayagamoorthy, G. K., Harley, R. G., & Wunsch, D. C. (2002). Comparison of heuristic dynamic programming and dual heuristic programming adaptive critics for neurocontrol of a turbogenerator. *IEEE Transaction on Neural Networks*, *13*(3), 764–773.

Venayagamoorthy, G. K., Harley, R. G., & Wunsch, D. C. (2003). Dual heuristic programming excitation neurocontrol for generators in a multimachine power system. *IEEE Transaction on Industry Applications*, *39*(2).

Werbos, P. J. (1992). Approximate dynamic programming for real-time control and neural modeling. In D. White, & D. Sofge (Eds.), *Handbook of intelligent control* (pp. 493–526). New York: Van Nostrand Reinhold.

White, D. A., & Jordan, M. I. (1992). Optimal control: A foundation for intelligent control. In D. White, & D. Sofge (Eds.), *Handbook of intelligent control* (pp. 185–214). New York: Van Nostrand Reinhold.

PERGAMON

AVAILABLE AT
www.ComputerScienceWeb.com
POWERED BY SCIENCE DIRECT

Neural Networks 16 (2003) 891–898

Neural Networks

www.elsevier.com/locate/neunet

2003 Special issue

Design of an adaptive neural network based power system stabilizer

Wenxin Liu*, Ganesh K. Venayagamoorthy, Donald C. Wunsch II

Department of Electrical and Computer Engineering, University of Missouri–Rolla, Rolla, MO 65409, USA

Abstract

Power system stabilizers (PSS) are used to generate supplementary control signals for the excitation system in order to damp the low frequency power system oscillations. To overcome the drawbacks of conventional PSS (CPSS), numerous techniques have been proposed in the literature. Based on the analysis of existing techniques, this paper presents an indirect adaptive neural network based power system stabilizer (IDNC) design. The proposed IDNC consists of a neuro-controller, which is used to generate a supplementary control signal to the excitation system, and a neuro-identifier, which is used to model the dynamics of the power system and to adapt the neuro-controller parameters. The proposed method has the features of a simple structure, adaptivity and fast response. The proposed IDNC is evaluated on a single machine infinite bus power system under different operating conditions and disturbances to demonstrate its effectiveness and robustness.

Keywords: Neural networks; Neuro-identifier; Neuro-control; Power system stabilizer; Indirect adaptive control; On-line training

1. Introduction

Currently most of the generators are equipped with voltage regulators to automatically control the terminal voltage. It is known that the voltage regulator action had a detrimental impact upon the dynamic stability of the power system. Oscillations of small magnitude and low frequency often persist for long periods of time and in some cases even present limitations on power transfer capability (Larsen & Swann, 1981).

In the analysis and control of power system stability, two distinct types of system oscillations are usually recognized. One type is associated with generators at a generating station swinging with respect to the rest of the power system. Such oscillations are referred to as 'intra-area mode' oscillations. The s type of oscillations is associated with the swinging of many machines in the one area of the system against machines in other areas. This is referred to as 'inter-area mode' oscillations. Power system stabilizers (PSS) are used to generate supplementary control signals for the excitation system in order to damp both types of oscillations.

The widely used conventional power system stabilizers (CPSS) are designed using the theory of phase compensation in the frequency domain and are introduced as a lead-lag compensator. The parameters of CPSS are determined based on the linearized model of the power system. To have the CPSS provide good damping over a wide operating range, its parameters need to be fine tuned in response to both types of oscillations. Since power systems are highly nonlinear systems, with configurations and parameters that change with time, the CPSS design based on the linearized model of the power system cannot guarantee its performance in a practical operating environment. Thus, an adaptive PSS which considers the nonlinear nature of the plant and adapts to the changes in the environment is required for the power system.

To improve the performance of CPSSs, numerous techniques have been proposed for their design, such as using intelligent optimization methods (simulated annealing, genetic algorithm, tabu search) (Abdel-Magid, Abido, & Mantaway, 2000; Abido, 2000; Do Bomfim, Taranto, & Falcao, 2000), fuzzy logic (El-Metwally, Hancock, & Malik, 1996; Hariri & Malik, 1996), neural networks and many other nonlinear control techniques (Chapman, Ilic, King, Eng, & Kaufman, 1993; Nambu & Ohsawa, 1996; Soos & Malik, 2002). The intelligent optimization algorithms are used to determine the optimal parameters for CPSS by optimizing an eigenvalue based cost function in an offline mode. Since the method is based on a linearized model and the parameters are not updated online, therefore they lack satisfactory performance during practical operation. The rule-based fuzzy logic control methods are well known for the difficulty in obtaining and adjusting the parameters of the rules especially online. Recent research indicates that more emphasis has been placed on the combined usage of fuzzy systems and other

* Corresponding author.

0893-6080/03/$ - see front matter © 2003 Elsevier Science Ltd. All rights reserved.
doi:10.1016/S0893-6080(03)00129-1

technologies such as neural networks to add adaptability to the design (Hiyama & Tomsovic, 1999). Currently, most of the nonlinear control based methods use simplified models to decrease complexity of the algorithms. Considering the complexity of practical power systems, more realistic model with less computation time is required for effective robust control over a wide range of operating conditions.

Since neural networks have the advantages of high computation speed, generalization and learning ability, they have been successfully applied to the identification and control of nonlinear systems. The work on the application of neural networks to the PSS design so far includes online tuning of CPSS parameters (Hsu & Chen, 1991; Segal, Kothari, & Madnani, 2000), the implementation of inverse model control (Park, Hyun, & Lee, 1996b; Zhang, Malik, Hope, & Chen, 1994), direct control (Shamsollahi & Malik, 1999) and indirect adaptive control (Changaroon, Srivastava, & Thukaram, 2000; He & Malik, 1997; Kobayashi & Yokoyama, 1996; Park, Choi, & Lee, 1996a; Shamsollahi & Malik, 1997). The online tuning of CPSS parameters and the inverse model control do not update the weights of neural networks online so their performances highly depend on the quality of offline training samples which are difficult to obtain. Since the plant model is not used in the direct adaptive neural network control structure, computation time is greatly decreased. But there is no accurate way to directly evaluate the performance of the controller, especially when the system parameters are changing over time; therefore, this is not the most effective control technique.

Paper (Shamsollahi & Malik, 1997) has shown that an indirect adaptive PSS can be designed using two input signals, the speed deviation and the power deviation to a neural network controller. In this paper, the authors show that it is possible to design an effective online trained PSS using only the speed deviation as an input to a neuro-controller. The indirect neural network control design consists of two neural networks, namely the neuro-controller and the neuro-identifier. The neuro-controller is used to generate the stabilizing supplementary control signal to the plant and the neuro-identifier is used to provide a dynamic model of the plant to evaluate and update the weights of the neuro-controller. Since both the neuro-identifier and the neuro-controller are updated online, the controller can adapt to changes in the system configuration and condition.

The power system model is described in Section 2. The design of the indirect adaptive neural network controller is described in Section 3. The training process of the indirect neural network controller (IDNC) is described in Section 4. Some simulation results are provided in Section 5.

2. Power system model

The single machine infinite bus power system (SMIB) model used to evaluate the IDNC is shown in Fig. 1.

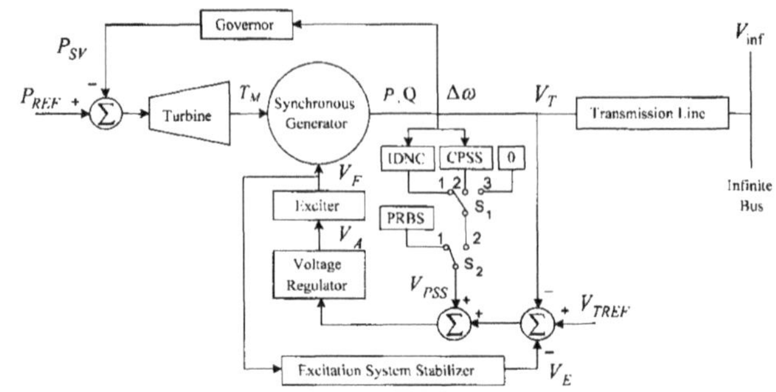

Fig. 1. System model configuration.

The SMIB consists of a synchronous generator, a turbine, a governor, an excitation system and a transmission line connected to an infinite bus. The model is built in MATLAB/SIMULINK environment using the Power System Blockset (Sybille, Brunelle, Champagne, Dessaint, & Lehuy, 2000). In Fig. 1, P_{REF} is the mechanical power reference, P_{SV} is the feedback through the governor, T_{M} is the turbine output torque, V_{inf} is the infinite bus voltage, V_{TREF} is terminal voltage reference, V_{T} is terminal voltage, V_{A} is the voltage regulator output, V_{F} is field voltage, V_{E} is the excitation system stabilizing signal, $\Delta\omega$ is the speed deviation, V_{PSS} is the PSS output signal, P is the active power and Q is the reactive power at the generator terminal.

In Fig. 1, the switch S_1 is used to carry out tests on the power system with IDNC, CPSS and without PSS (with switch S_1 in positions 1, 2 and 3, respectively). Switch S_2 is used to select between normal operation and training phase (positions 1 and 2, respectively).

The synchronous generator is described by a seventh order d–q axis set of equations with the machine current, speed and rotor angle as the state variables.

The turbine is used to drive the generator and the governor is used to control the speed and the real power. The block diagram of a separately excited turbine and a conventional governor are shown in Fig. 2.

The excitation system for the generator is modeled according to IEEE Std. 421.5 (IEEE, 1992). The block diagram of the excitation system is shown in Fig. 3.

The CPSS consists of two phase-lead compensation blocks, a signal washout block, and a gain block. The input signal is the rotor speed deviation $\Delta\omega$ (Kundur, Klein, Rogers, & Zywno, 1989). The block diagram of the CPSS is shown in Fig. 4.

The parameters for the generator, AVR, excitation system, turbine and governor are given in Appendix A (IEEE, 1992; Venayagamoorthy & Harley, 2001).

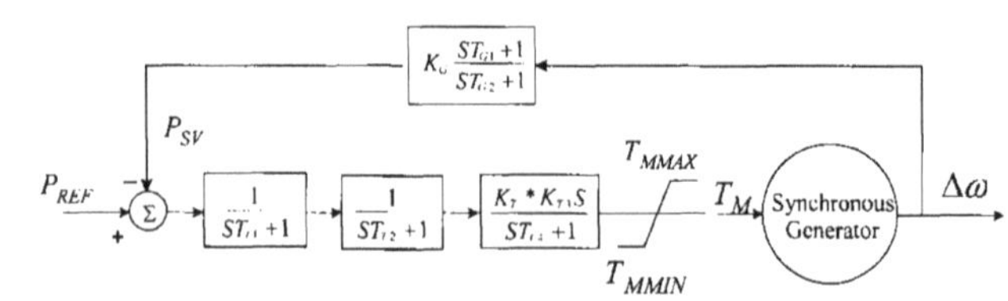

Fig. 2. Block diagram of the turbine and the governor.

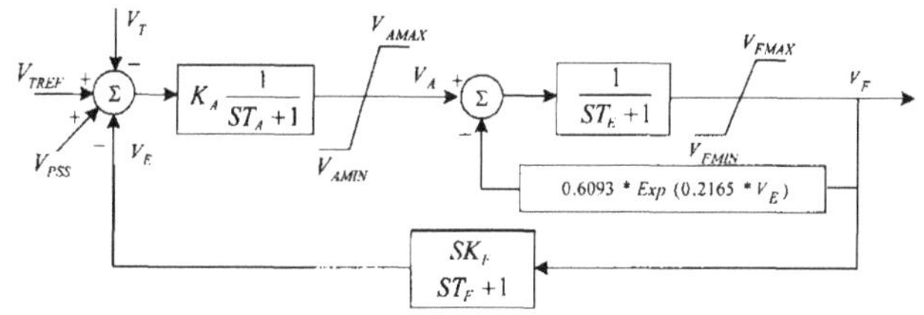

Fig. 3. Block diagram of the excitation system.

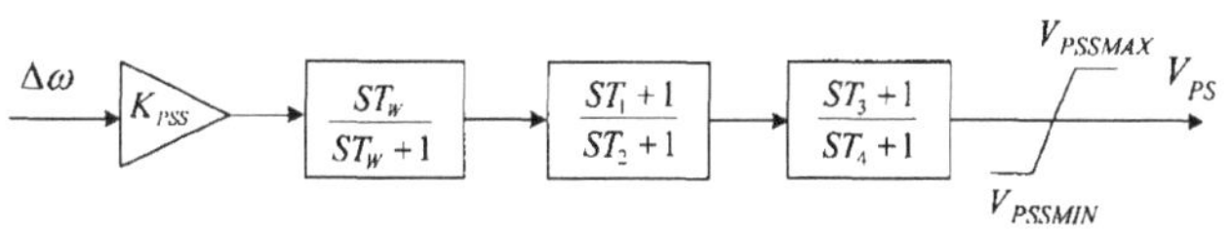

Fig. 4. Block diagram of the conventional power system stabilizer.

3. Design of the adaptive controller

IDNC design consists of two separate neural networks, namely the neuro-controller and the neuro-identifier. The structure for the training of the neuro-identifier and the neuro-controller is shown in Fig. 5. These two phases are carried out in cascade once the IDNC is connected to the plant by placing the switch S_1 at position 1 in Fig. 1. The dash lines show the backpropagation (BP) paths to update the weights of the neuro-identifier and the neuro-controller. The training processes of the neuro-identifier and neuro-controller are described in detail in Section 4.

Since the two training processes are shown in one figure, it is necessary to clarify the time step definition. Both $V_{pss}(k)$ and $\Delta\omega(k)$ signals are sampled at time step k, but $\Delta\omega(k)$ is not the response for the control signal $V_{pss}(k)$. Due to the time lag property of the plant, the impact of the control signal $V_{pss}(k)$ is reflected in the next time sample of the output signal $\Delta\omega(k+1)$. Section 3.1 describes the neuro-identifier and neuro-controller inputs and outputs for the online operation.

3.1. Neuro-Identifier

The neuro-identifier is developed using the series–parallel Nonlinear Auto Regressive Moving Average model

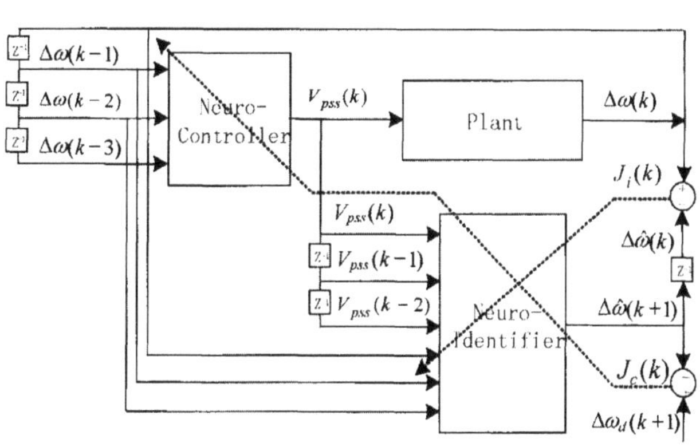

Fig. 5. Structure of the indirect neural network controller.

(Narendra & Parthasarathy, 1990). The model output $\hat{y}$ at time $k+1$ depends on both past n values of output and m past values of input. The neuro-identifier output equation takes the form given by Eq. (1)

$$\hat{y}(k+1) = f\begin{bmatrix} y(k), y(k-1), \ldots, y(k-n+1) \\ u(k), u(k-1), \ldots, u(k-m+1) \end{bmatrix} \quad (1)$$

where $y(k)$ and $u(k)$ represent the output and input of the plant to be controlled at time k. For this particular system, y, u and $\hat{y}$ are the speed deviation $\Delta\omega$ of the plant, the output of the neuro-controller V_{pss} and the estimated plant output $\Delta\hat{\omega}(k)$ by the neuro-identifier respectively. Here both m and n are chosen to be 2. One reason for choosing three time step values is because a third order model of the system is sufficient for the study of transient stability. The other reason is that more time delays means more computation and one author's previous work verified that three time delays is enough for this kind of problem (Venayagamoorthy, 2001). The neuro-identifier is a multi-layer feedforward network trained with BP algorithm. The numbers of neurons in the input, hidden and output layers are six, ten and one respectively. All the inputs and outputs signals of the neuro-identifier are normalized to the range of $[-1, 1]$.

3.2. Neuro-controller

The neuro-controller is also a multi-layer feedforward network trained with BP algorithm. The number of neurons in input, hidden and output layers is three, six and one respectively. The inputs to the neuro-controller are the speed deviation $\Delta\omega$ and its two previous values and the output of the neuro-controller is the control signal V_{pss}. The number of neurons in the hidden layers of both the neuro-identifier and the neuro-controller are arrived at heuristically.

4. Training process

The training process of the IDNC consists of two phases, namely the pre-control phase and the post-control phase. The difference between these two phases is that during the pre-control, the control signal is the PRBS while during post-control it is the output of the neuro-controller. Pre-control is used to train the IDNC to avoid the possibility of instability at the beginning of the post-control.

4.1. Pre-control phase

During this phase, the switch S_2 is at position 2 in Fig. 1. The PRBS signal is added to the voltage regulator when the plant is operating at steady state. The addition of PRBS signals excites all possible dynamics of system. The values

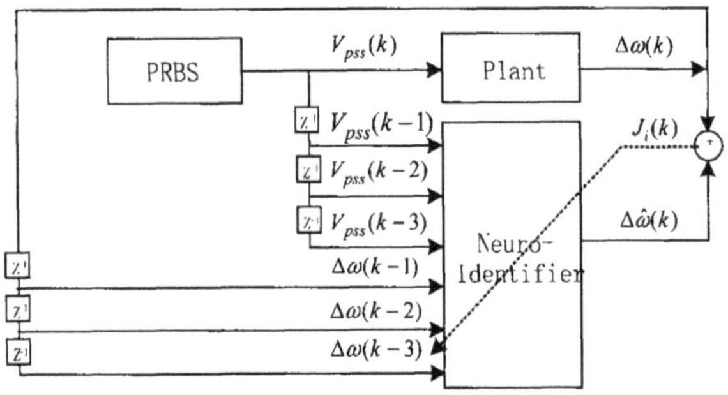

Fig. 6. Training of the neuro-identifier during pre-control.

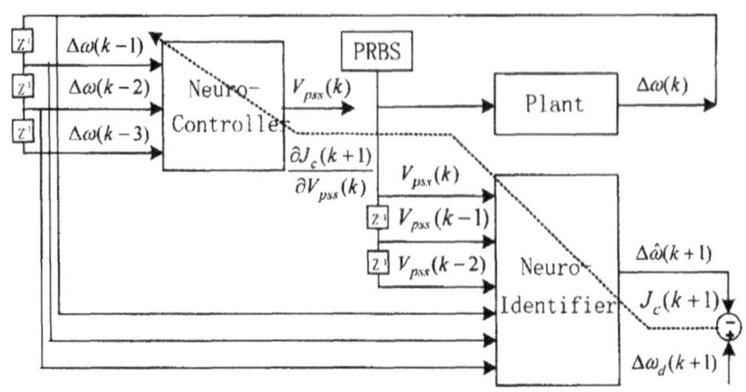

Fig. 8. Training of the neuro-controller during pre-control.

of the random signals are distributed between -0.1 and 0.1 which is the typical output range limit of a CPSS.

4.1.1. Training of the neuro-identifier

The training process of the neuro-identifier during pre-control is shown in Fig. 6. The inputs to the neuro-identifier during this phase are ($\Delta\omega(k-1)$, $\Delta\omega(k-2)$, $\Delta\omega(k-3)$, $V_{\text{pss}}(k-1)$, $V_{\text{pss}}(k-2)$, $V_{\text{pss}}(k-3)$) and its output is $\Delta\hat{\omega}(k)$. The desired output is the output of the plant $\Delta\omega(k)$. The cost function for training the neuro-identifier is given by:

$$J_i(k) = \frac{1}{2}e_i(k)^2 = \frac{1}{2}[\Delta\omega(k) - \Delta\hat{\omega}(k)]^2 \tag{2}$$

It can be seen from Fig. 7 that the neuro-identifier gives good estimation of the output of the plant after training for a period of 4 s.

4.1.2. Training of the neuro-controller

The training process of the neuro-controller is shown in Fig. 8. The training of the neuro-controller takes place with the training of the neuro-identifier in cascade. During this stage, the input to the neuro-controller is ($\Delta\omega(k-1)$, $\Delta\omega(k-2)$, $\Delta\omega(k-3)$) and the output is $\hat{V}_{\text{pss}}$, which is then fed to the neuro-identifier and evaluated against the desired output. The desired control signal is calculated through the neuro-identifier by comparing the output of the neuro-identifier with the desired system response (since the speed is expected to be constant all the time, the desired speed

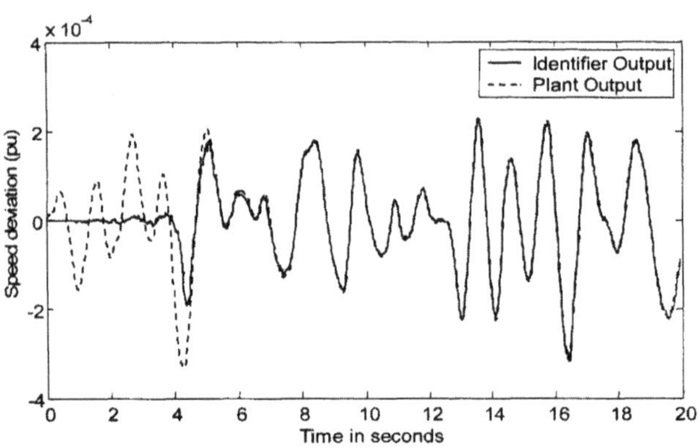

Fig. 7. Estimated and actual speed deviation of the plant.

deviation is set to zero all the time) and back propagating the error through the neuro-identifier. The desired control signal is calculated according to:

$$V^d_{\text{pss}}(k) = V_{\text{pss}}(k) + \frac{\partial J_c(k+1)}{\partial V_{\text{pss}}(k)} \tag{3}$$

During this phase the weights of the neuro-identifier are not changed. The cost function used to train the neuro-controller is given by:

$$\begin{aligned} J_c(k+1) &= \tfrac{1}{2}e_c(k+1)^2 \\ &= \tfrac{1}{2}[\Delta\omega_d(k+1) - \Delta\hat{\omega}(k+1)]^2 \end{aligned} \tag{4}$$

The cost functions (2) and (4) are also used for the training of the neuro-identifier and the neuro-controller during post-control phase. The trainings of the neuro-controller and the neuro-identifier continue for different operating points and system configurations until the weights of the neuro-controller converge.

4.2. Post-control phase

During this process, the switch S_2 in Fig. 1 is at position 1.The on-line training process includes three steps, which are the training of the neuro-identifier, training of the controller and, calculating and applying the control. The three stages are described below and also described using a flowchart listed in Appendix B.

Before the training process of post-control, the system are simulated for four time steps, so as to get the time delayed value of the control signals—$V_{\text{pss}}(k-1)$, $V_{\text{pss}}(k-2)$, $V_{\text{pss}}(k-3)$ and system states $\Delta\omega(k)$, $\Delta\omega(k-1)$, $\Delta\omega(k-2)$, $\Delta\omega(k-3)$.

4.2.1. Training of the neuro-identifier

Fig. 9 shows the training process of the neuro-identifier during post control. So far the neuro-identifier is only trained around some stable operating point, it is necessary for it to be trained online to adapt to the cases when system states change. During this phase, the input and desired output of the neuro-identifier are ($\Delta\omega(k-1)$, $\Delta\omega(k-2)$,

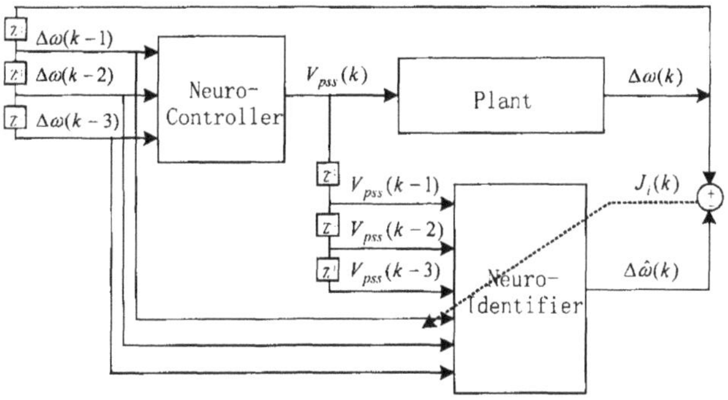

Fig. 9. Training process of the neuro-identifier.

$\Delta\omega(k-3)$, $V_{pss}(k-1)$, $V_{pss}(k-2)$, $V_{pss}(k-3)$) and $\Delta\omega(k)$, respectively, where $\Delta\hat{\omega}(k)$ is the most current system state.

4.2.2. Training of the neuro-controller

Fig. 10 shows the training process of the neuro-controller. During this phase, the neuro-controller inputs are ($\Delta\omega(k-1)$, $\Delta\omega(k-2)$, $\Delta\omega(k-3)$) and the control signal is $V_{pss}(k)$. Inputs to the neuro-identifier are ($V_{pss}(k)$, $V_{pss}(k-1)$, $V_{pss}(k-2)$, $\Delta\omega(k)$, $\Delta\omega(k-1)$, $\Delta\omega(k-2)$), and its output is $\Delta\hat{\omega}(k+1)$, which is compared with the desired plant output $\Delta\omega_d(k+1)$. The cost function in Eq. (4) is used to update the weights of the neuro-controller.

4.2.3. Applying the control signal

At the next time step, a new control signal $V_{pss}(k+1)$ is calculated by simulating the neuro-controller with ($\Delta\omega(k)$, $\Delta\omega(k-1)$, $\Delta\omega(k-2)$) and applied to the plant. The IDNC training process is repeated according to Sections 4.2.1–4.2.3 for the entire operation of the plant.

5. Simulation results

To evaluate the performance of the neuro-controller, the system response of the IDNC is compared with the cases where there is no PSS and with a CPSS in the system. The comparison is carried out under different

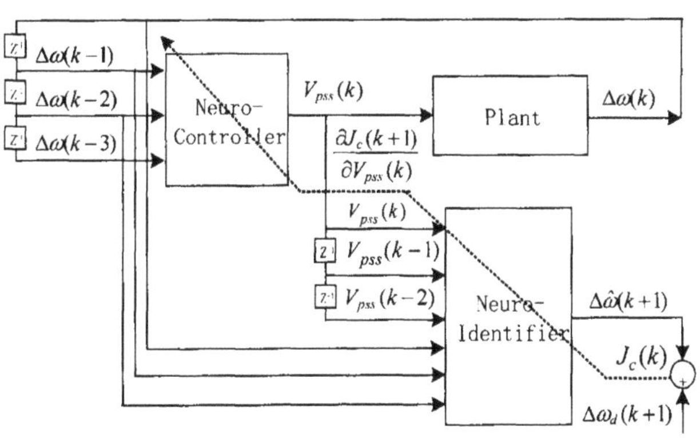

Fig. 10. Training process of the neuro-controller.

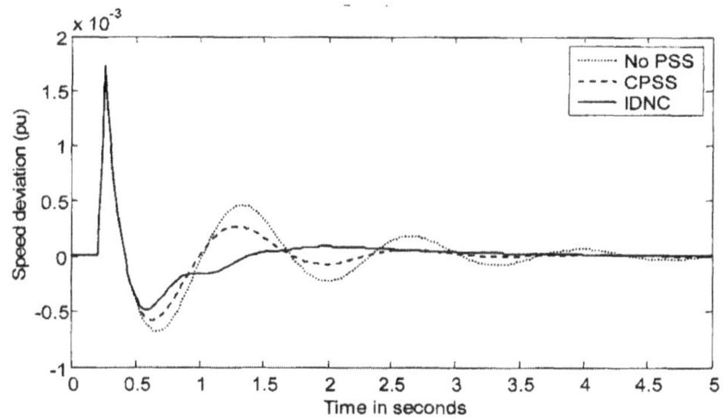

Fig. 11. System response to a three phase short circuit fault. ($P = 0.334$ pu, $Q = 0.001$ pu).

kinds of operating conditions and disturbances. These disturbances are the three phase short circuit at the infinite bus, step changes in the terminal voltage reference and a simulated transmission line fault. The comparison is carried out under two operating points, $P = 0.334$ pu, $Q = 0.001$ pu and $P = 0.50$ pu, $Q = 0.048$ pu.

5.1. Simulation results at $P = 0.334$ pu, $Q = 0.001$ pu

Fig. 11 is the comparison of the system responses under a 50 ms three phase short circuit fault occurring at 0.2 s. It can be seen that CPSS has better damping of the speed deviation than when there is no CPSS in the system but IDNC has the best damping.

Fig. 12 is the comparison of the control signal given by the CPSS and the IDNC for the 50 ms three phase short circuit fault. It can be seen that CPSS control signal output is too large at the beginning of the short circuit and hard limited to protect the excitation system. The limited control signal of CPSS can not adapt to the change in the speed deviation in time, so the oscillation magnitude of the speed is much higher than the IDNC.

Fig. 13 is the comparison of the system response to a 5% step change in V_{tref} (1.1–1.155 pu) at 0.2 s and 5% decrease (1.155–1.1pu) at 5.2 s. Again, the IDNC

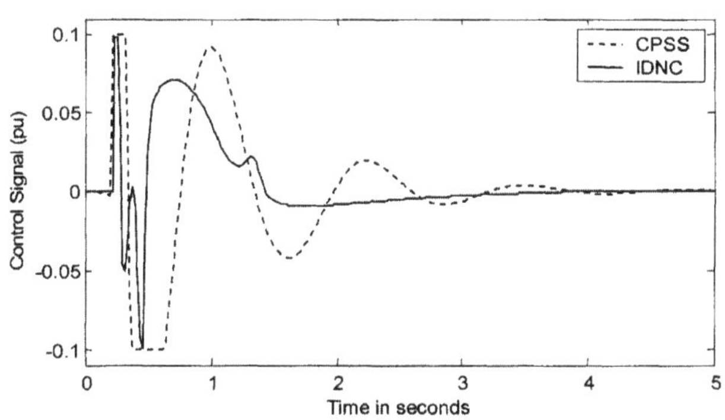

Fig. 12. Control signal response to the three phase short circuit fault. ($P = 0.334$ pu, $Q = 0.001$ pu).

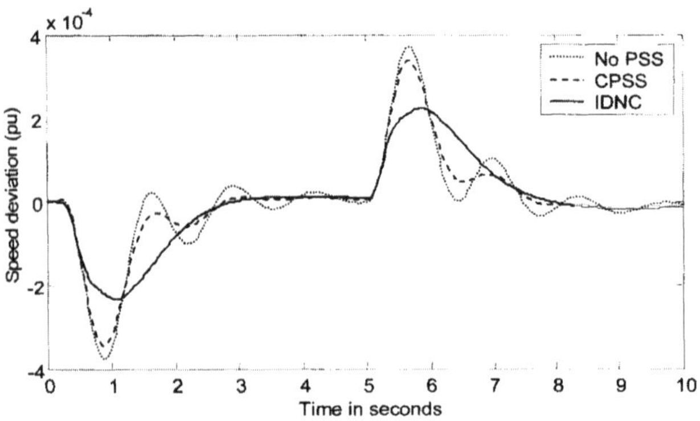

Fig. 13. System response to 5% step changes in the reference of terminal voltage ($P = 0.334$ pu, $Q = 0.001$ pu).

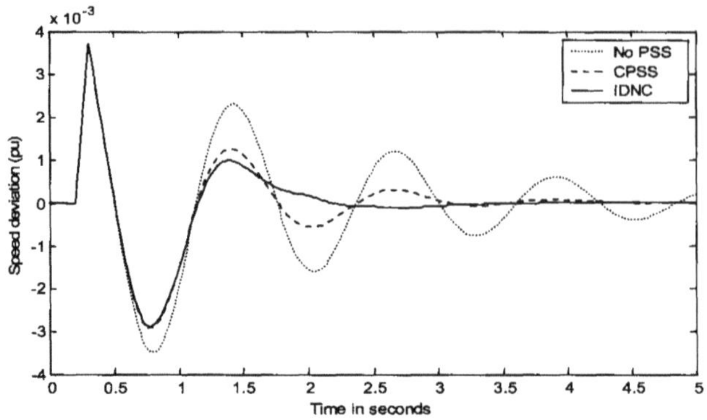

Fig. 15. System response to a three phase short circuit fault ($P = 0.50$ pu, $Q = 0.048$ pu).

provides the best damping to this disturbance. From the figure, it can be seen that the speed deviation is over-damped which can be improved by using different desired response settings, $\Delta\omega_d$.

Fig. 14 is the comparison of the system responses to a simulated transmission line fault. During this case, the impedance of the transmission line changes from $Z_1 = 0.025 + j0.7559$ pu to $Z_2 = 0.05 + j1.5$ pu at 0.2 s. Again, the IDNC provides the best damping of the three cases.

5.2. Simulation results at $P = 0.50$ pu, $Q = 0.048$ pu

Fig. 15 is a comparison of the system responses under a 100 ms three phase short circuit fault occurring at the infinite bus. Fig. 16 is the comparison of the system response to 5% step change in V_{tref}, that is 5% increase ($V_{tref} = 1.1$ pu to $V_{tref} = 1.155$ pu) at 0.2 s and 5% decrease ($V_{tref} = 1.155$ pu to $V_{tref} = 1.1$ pu) at 5.2 s. And Fig. 17 is the comparison of the system responses to a simulated transmission line fault. The impedance of the transmission line changes from $Z_1 = 0.025 + j0.7559$ pu to $Z_2 = 0.05 + j1.5$ pu at 0.2 s. For these tests, the IDNC has the best performance even though the operating point is different.

From these figures we can see that the IDNC can provide better results compared with that of CPSS under all of the three cases.

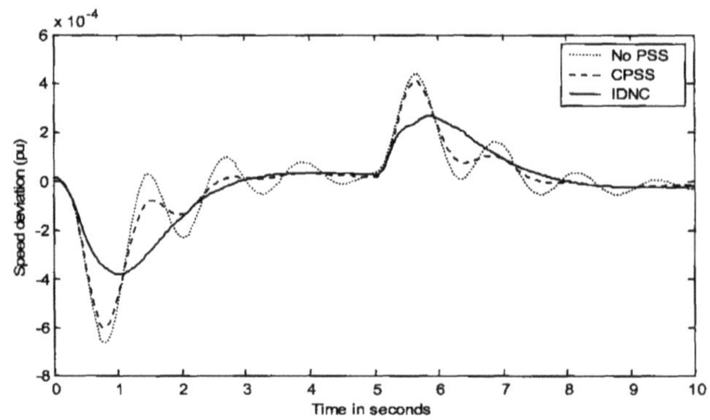

Fig. 16. System response to 5% step changes in the reference of terminal voltage ($P = 0.50$ pu, $Q = 0.048$ pu).

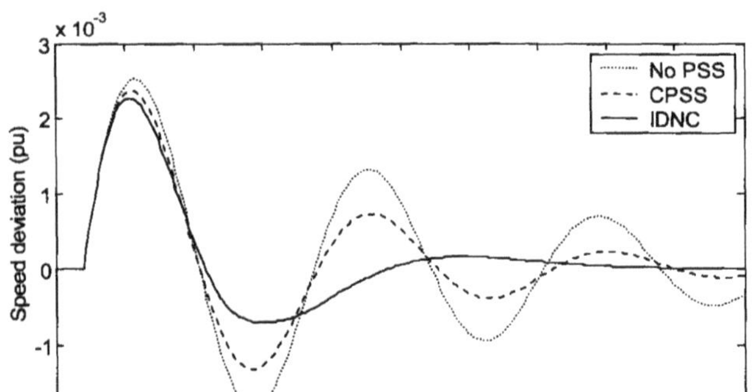

Fig. 14. System response to a simulated transmission line fault. ($P = 0.334$ pu, $Q = 0.001$ pu).

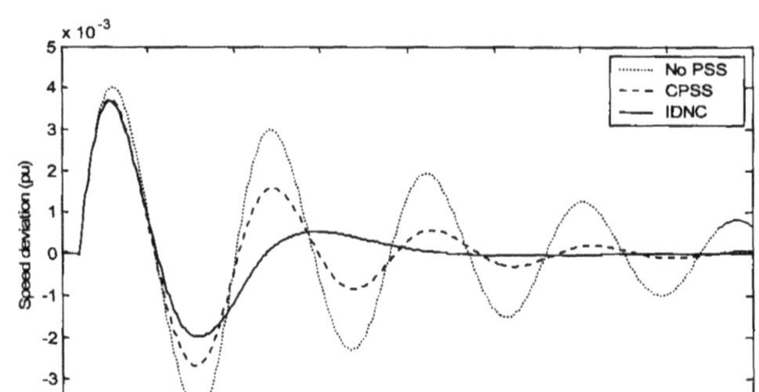

Fig. 17. System response to a simulated transmission line fault. ($P = 0.50$ pu, $Q = 0.048$ pu).

6. Conclusion

To overcome the drawbacks of CPSSs, an adaptive indirect neural network control based power system stabilizer (PSS) design is presented in this paper. The proposed method is evaluated on a SMIB. The design of the IDNC is based on only the speed deviation of the generator. Therefore, the computations involved in the neural network design are minimal. This is desirable for practical hardware implementation on the power station platforms. Simulation results for different kinds of disturbances and operating conditions demonstrate the effectiveness and robustness of the IDNC. Such a nonlinear adaptive PSS will yield better and fast damping under small and large disturbances even with changes in system operating conditions. Better and fast damping means that generators can operate more close to their maximum generation capacity. Thus, ensuring that generators remain stable under sever faults such as three phase short circuits. This means that more power generated per invested dollar.

Appendix A

Table A1.

Table A1
Parameters of the single machine infinite bus power system in Fig. 1

$T'_{d0} = 6.69$ s	$T''_{q0} = 0.25$ s	$X'_d = 0.205$ pu	$T'_d = 0.66$ s
$T''_q = 27$ ms	$X''_d = 0.164$ pu	$T''_{d0} = 33$ ms	$T_{kd} = 38$ ms
$X_q = 1.98$ pu	$T''_d = 26.4$ ms	$X_d = 2.09$ pu	$X''_q = 0.213\,pu$
$T_{T1} = 0.15$	$T_{T2} = 0.594$	$T_{T3} = 0.884$	$T_{T4} = 2.662$
$T_{\rm MMIN} = 0$	$T_{\rm MMAX} = 1.2$	$K_G = 20$	$T_{G1} = 0.264$
$T_{G2} = 0.0264$	$K_{\rm A} = 50$	$T_{\rm A} = 0.01$	$V_{\rm AMIN} = -10$
$V_{\rm AMAX} = 10$	$T_{\rm E} = 0.46$	$V_{\rm FMIN} = 0.5$	$V_{\rm FMAX} = 3$
$K_{\rm F} = 0.1$	$T_{\rm F} = 1$	$K_{\rm STAB} = 25$	$T_{\rm W} = 10$
$T_1 = 0.76$	$T_2 = 0.1$	$T_3 = 0.76$	$T_4 = 0.1$
$V_{\rm PSS\_MIN} = -0.1$	$V_{\rm PSS\_MAX} = 0.1$		

Appendix B

Fig. A1.

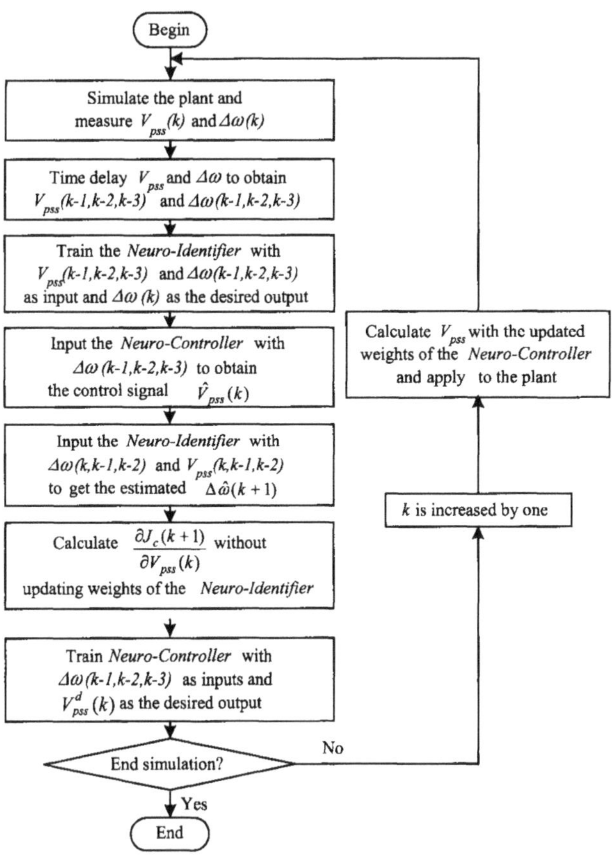

Fig. A1. Flowchart of the training of IDNC.

References

Abdel-Magid, Y. L., Abido, M. A., & Mantaway, A. H. (2000). Robust tuning of power system stabilizers in multi-machine power systems. *IEEE Transactions on Power Systems*, *15*(2), 735–740.

Abido, M. A. (2000). Robust design of multi-machine power system stabilizers using simulated annealing. *IEEE Transaction on Energy Conversion*, *15*(3), 297–304.

Changaroon, B., Srivastava, S. C., & Thukaram, D. (2000). A neural network based power system stabilizer suitable for on-line training-a practical case study for EGAT system. *IEEE Transaction on Energy Conversion*, *15*(1), 103–109.

Chapman, J. W., Ilic, M. D., King, C. A., Eng, L., & Kaufman, H. (1993). Stabilizing a multi-machine power system via decentralized feedback linearizing excitation control. *IEEE Transaction on Power System*, *8*, 830–839.

Do Bomfim, A. L. B., Taranto, G. N., & Falcao, D. M. (2000). Simultaneous tuning of power system damping controllers using genetic algorithms. *IEEE Transaction on Power Systems*, *15*(1), 163–169.

El-Metwally, K. A., Hancock, G. C., & Malik, O. P. (1996). Implementation of a fuzzy logic PSS using a micro-controller and experimental test results. *IEEE Transaction on Energy Conversion*, *11*(1), 91–96.

Hariri, A., & Malik, O. P. (1996). A fuzzy logic based power system stabilizer with learning ability. *IEEE Transaction on Energy Conversion*, *11*(4), 721–727.

He, J., & Malik, O. P. (1997). An adaptive power system stabilizer based on recurrent neural networks. *IEEE Transaction on Energy Conversion*, *12*(4), 413–418.

Hiyama, T., & Tomsovic, K. (1999). Current status of fuzzy system applications in power systems. *Proceedings of the IEEE, SMC99, Tokyo, Japan*, 527–532.

Hsu, Y. Y., & Chen, C. L. (1991). Tuning of power system stabilizers using an artificial neural network. *IEEE Transaction on Energy Conversion*, *6*(4), 612–619.

IEEE (1992). Recommended practice for excitation system models for power system stability studies. *IEEE Std. 421.5*.

Kobayashi, T., & Yokoyama, A. (1996). An adaptive neuro-control system of synchronous generator for power system stabilization. *IEEE Transaction on Energy Conversion*, *11*(3), 621–630.

Kundur, P., Klein, M., Rogers, G. J., & Zywno, M. S. (1989). Application of power system stabilizers for enhancement of overall system stability. *IEEE Transactions on Power Systems*, *4*(2), 614–626.

Larsen, E. V., & Swann, D. A. (1981). Applying power system stabilizers, Part I, II, III. *IEEE Transaction on Power Apparatus and Systems*, *PAS-100*(6), 3017–3041.

Nambu, M., & Ohsawa, Y. (1996). Development of an advanced power system stabilizer using a strict linearization approach. *IEEE Transaction on Power Systems*, *11*(2), 813–818.

Narendra, K. S. (1990). Parthasarathy. *Identification and control of dynamical systems using neural networks. IEEE Transaction on Neural Networks*, *1*(1), 4–27.

Park, Y. M., Choi, M. S., & Lee, K. Y. (1996a). A neural network-based power system stabilizer using power flow characteristics. *IEEE Transaction on Energy Conversion*, *11*(2), 435–441.

Park, Y. M., Hyun, S. H., & Lee, J. H. (1996b). A synchronous generator stabilizer design using neuro inverse controller and error reduction network. *IEEE Transactions on Power Systems*, *11*(4), 1969–1975.

Segal, R., Kothari, M. L., & Madnani, S. (2000). Radial basis function (RBF) network adaptive power system stabilizer. *IEEE Transactions on Power Systems*, *15*(2), 722–727.

Shamsollahi, P., & Malik, O. P. (1997). An adaptive power system stabilizer using on-line trained neural networks. *IEEE Transaction on Energy Conversion*, *12*(4), 382–387.

Shamsollahi, P., & Malik, O. P. (1999). Direct neural adaptive control applied to synchronous generator. *IEEE Transaction on Energy Conversion*, *14*(4), 1341–1346.

Soos, A., & Malik, O. P. (2002). An H_2 optimal adaptive power sytem stabilizer. *IEEE Transaction on Energy Conversion*, *17*(1), 143–149.

Sybille, G., Brunelle, P., Champagne, R., Dessaint, L., & Lehuy, H. (2000). *Power system blockset, version 2.0*. Mathworks.

Venayagamoorthy, G.K (2001). *Adaptive critic based neuro-controller for turbogenerators in a multi-machine power system*. PhD Thesis. University of Natal, Durban, South Africa.

Venayagamoorthy, G. K., & Harley, R. G. (2001). A continually online trained neurocontroller for excitation and turbine control of a turbogenerator. *IEEE Transactions on Energy Conversion*, *16*(16), 261–269.

Zhang, Y., Malik, O. P., Hope, G. S., & Chen, G. P. (1994). Application of an inverse input/output mapped ANN as a power system stabilizer. *IEEE Transaction on Energy Conversion*, *9*(3), 433–441.

PERGAMON

AVAILABLE AT
www.ComputerScienceWeb.com
POWERED BY SCIENCE DIRECT

Neural Networks 16 (2003) 899–905

Neural Networks

www.elsevier.com/locate/neunet

2003 Special issue

On neural network techniques in the secure management of communication systems through improving and quality assessing pseudorandom stream generators

D.A. Karras[a,*], V. Zorkadis[b]

[a]Hellenic Aerospace Industry, University of Hertfordshire (UK) and Hellenic Open University, Rodu2, Ano Iliupolis, Athens 16342, Greece
[b]Data Protection Authority, Omirou 8, Athens 10564, Greece

Abstract

Random components play an especially important role in the management of secure communication systems, with emphasis on the key management of cryptographic protocols. For this reason, the existence of strong pseudo random number generators is highly required. This paper presents novel techniques, which rely on Artificial Neural Network (ANN) architectures, to strengthen traditional generators such as IDEA and ANSI X.9 based on 3DES and IDEA. Additionally, this paper proposes a non-linear test method for the quality assessment of the required non-predictability property, which relies on feedforward neural networks. This non-predictability test method along with commonly used empirical tests based on statistics is proposed as a methodology for quality assessing strong pseudorandom stream generators. By means of this methodology, traditional and Neural Network based pseudorandom stream generators are evaluated. The results show that the proposed generators behave significantly better than the traditional ones, in particular, in terms of non-predictability.

Keywords: Secure communications systems; Secure electronic commerce; Cryptographic protocols; Security mechanisms; Authentication; Key management; Stream ciphers; Pseudorandom number generators; Multi-layer perceptrons; Recurrent artificial neural network; Unpredictability test

1. Introduction

The security of many cryptographic protocols such as electronic payment systems, authentication and integrity, digital signature scheme and key management techniques depends upon the use of random quantities, which are obtained by using true or strong pseudorandom number generators. For instance, authentication mechanisms may use nonces, i.e. random numbers to protect against replay attacks (Gollmann, Beth, & Damm, 1993) like the related mechanisms in ITU X.509 (Schneier, 1996). Symmetric and asymmetric cryptographic systems like DES, IDEA, RSA (Schneier, 1996) and AES (AES2001, 2001) that are employed for confidentiality purposes and as basic element of various security protocols require possibly real or at least strong pseudorandom cryptographic keys, should the crypto-analysis remain a hard problem.

Furthermore, integrity mechanisms such as ISO 8731-2 (Schneier, 1996) or cryptographic key exchange mechanisms such as the Diffie–Hellman Protocol (Diffie & Hellman, 1976) or the construction of digital signatures such as the Digital Signature Scheme (Schneier, 1996) require the generation and use of random numbers. In addition, random numbers are used for the generation of pseudonyms and of traffic and message padding, in order to protect against traffic analysis attacks and for the computation of strong and efficient stream ciphers (Schneier, 1996; Zeng, Yang, Wei, & Rao 1991; Simmons, 1992).

True sources of randomness are preferred for the generation of random bit sequences. Unfortunately they are not widely applied. However, in cases such sources are indeed exploited for the generation of random bit sequences, the resulting generators, i.e. bit sequences should be validated. In the absence of true random generators strong pseudorandom number generators are desired, which should lead to the production of bit sequences of good quality, i.e. of good behavior in statistical and unpredictability terms. Otherwise, it would be possible for a cryptoanalyst, given a segment of this bit sequence and reasonable computer resources, to calculate the next bits or more about them (Zeng et al., 1991). In the last two decades considerable work has been made in the design and analysis of

* Corresponding author. Tel.: +30-6944-226-018; fax: +30-2109-945-231.

E-mail addresses: dakarras@usa.net; dakarras@hol.gr; dkarras@haicorp.com (D.A. Karras), zorkadis@dpa.gr (V. Zorkadis).

0893-6080/03/$ - see front matter © 2003 Elsevier Science Ltd. All rights reserved.
doi:10.1016/S0893-6080(03)00124-2

pseudorandom number or bit generators (Karras & Zorkadis, 1998; Pfleeger, 1997; Schneier, 1996; Stallings, 1995).

In this paper, we briefly survey some of these generators, propose a methodology to enhance them and to evaluate their behavior and strength.

The level of randomness of a sequence can be defined in terms of statistical tests, which emulate computations encountered in practice, and check that the related properties of the sequence under investigation agree with those predicted if every bit (or number) was drawn from a uniform probability distribution (Stinson, 1995). The generators we consider in this paper are those used by the system-theoretic approach to the construction of stream ciphers. Secure key-stream generators have to satisfy design criteria, such as long period, ideal k-tuple distributions, large linear complexity, confusion, diffusion and nonlinearity criteria (Stinson, 1995). Most of them are contained in the proposed evaluation methodology.

In the Section 2 a method is outlined to strengthen these generators by means of neural network based mechanisms. The Section 3 is dedicated to the proposed evaluation methodology for random number generators, namely to the non-predictability test and to the appropriate statistical and non-linearity tests. In Section 4, we present evaluation results obtained by applying the proposed methodology on various traditional and strengthened generators. Finally, we conclude our paper and outline future work on this subject.

2. Strong pseudorandom stream generators

2.1. Traditional random number generators

The great majority of random number generators used for traditional applications, such as simulations, are linear congruential generators, which behave statistically very well, except in terms of non-predictability, since there exists a linear functional relation connecting the numbers of the sequence. A sequence of random numbers produced by these generators is defined as follows

$Z_i = (aZ_{i-1} + c)(\mathrm{mod}\,m)$, where m, a and c are the coefficients, i.e. the modulus, the multiplier and the increment, correspondingly. Z_0 is the seed or initialization value. All are non-negative integers. Each random number can be expressed, as mentioned above, as a function of another random number or of its predecessors or of the seed and the coefficients. Therefore, if the coefficients and the seed or any random number belonging in the sequence is known then, all numbers of the sequence can be inferred. Such generators are not appropriate for security mechanisms, since the disclosure of one of them could very easily lead to the computation of the others.

In random components of mechanisms like electronic payment systems, authentication as well as key generation and exchange, the primary concern of the used pseudorandom bit sequences is that they are unpredictable, while being uniformly and independently distributed comes as requirement next. True random numbers are independent from each other and therefore unpredictable, but they are rarely employed, since it is difficult to obtain and they are not reproducible. It is more common that numbers that behave like random numbers are obtained by means of an algorithm, i.e. a pseudo random number generator. Next, we briefly describe some of the widely used such generators, namely, the DES, the IDEA and the AES in the output feedback (OFB) mode as well as the ANSI standard X.19.

Triple Data Encryption Standard (3DES), IDEA and, recently, AES, are the most widely used symmetric encryption systems. The input to the encryption function is the plain text in blocks and the key. The plain text block is 64 bits and the key $2\times$ (or $3\times$) 56 bits in 3DES and 128 bits in IDEA. The AES is capable of using keys of 128, 192 and 256 bits to encrypt and decrypt data in blocks of 128 bits. The encryption and decryption algorithm of DES relies on permutations, substitutions and xor-operations under the control of 16 sub-keys obtained from the initial key. On the other hand, the encryption and decryption algorithms of IDEA rely on xor-operations and modular additions and multiplication. Also, the encryption and decryption functions of AES are based on modular multiplications and xor-operations. DES, IDEA and AES can operate under various modes such as Cipher Block Chaining (CBC), Cipher Feedback (CFB) and OFB. The OFB mode can be used as a pseudo random number generator for key generation and stream cipher computation.

ANSI X.9 is a generator, which is based on symmetric cryptosystems like 3DES, IDEA or AES.

Based on the OFB of such symmetric cryptosystems cryptographically strong pseudorandom number generators are some of the most commonly employed in security mechanisms of communication systems and especially in electronic commerce systems.

2.2. Improved techniques involving ANN for strengthening traditional stream cipher based pseudorandom stream generators

In this paper, we describe an approach for constructing robust random number generators to be used in security mechanisms of electronic commerce applications, which are based on feed-forward Artificial Neural Network (ANN) techniques. It is well known that ANNs possess very interesting function approximation capabilities making them a very powerful tool in many scientific disciplines. For instance, feed-forward ANNs of the MultiLayer Perceptron (MLP) type have the theoretical ability to approximate arbitrary nonlinear mappings as well as their differentials (Haykin, 1999; Cybenco, 1989; Hornik, Stinchombe, & White, 1989); there is also the possibility that such an ANN approximation is more parsimonious, i.e. it requires less parameters than other competitive techniques such as orthogonal polynomials, splines, or Fourier series. Also, since ANNs are parallel and distributed processing devices they can be implemented in parallel hardware and, consequently, they can be used for real-time applications.

Their most important and intriguing property that makes them useful for applications is their generalization capabilities, that is their ability to produce reasonable outputs when they are fed with inputs not previously encountered.

The above desired abilities, however, are acquired in MLPs by training them well with known input vectors provided overfitting has not occurred (Haykin, 1999). In the case of overfitting it is known (Haykin, 1999) that the network, on the one hand, learns very well the training samples but, on the other hand, it is unable to generalize when fed with unknown input patterns. This happens because the network draws the fitting surface of the training samples in a much more complex way, that is its fitting surface is of much higher degree, than needed to map the actual pattern population distribution. In such a case MLP response is not predictable since there is no analytic formula for describing the previously mentioned complex fitting surface. Even for unknown data with small distances from the training samples (similar inputs) network outputs will be very different from the ones obtained with the corresponding training data. Although in pattern recognition/control/prediction applications such a situation is highly undesirable, it could be exploited, however, in the case of random number generation. We demonstrate in this paper that overfitting in MLPs could be exploited as a mechanism for the generation of strong pseudorandom bit sequences as follows

1. Train an MLP of topology e.g. 4-6-6-1 in the parity-4 problem so as to learn it more than it is required, i.e. for instance for 2500 epochs even when 500 epochs are enough. The goal is that overfitting should occur in this MLP training process. Of course other binary such benchmarks as well as much more complex MLP topologies could have been involved.
2. Test the already trained MLP using test input vectors with components produced by a traditional (pseudo)random number generator, like the ones involved in the experimental section of the paper, whose values are in the interval [0,1].
3. Form a complex function of the internal representations of such an MLP and compute its value when a test input vector as previously defined is presented to the network.

In this way a sequence of (pseudo)random numbers is produced whose quality is quantitatively evaluated by utilizing the statistical tests presented in the Section 2. The complex function of MLP internal representations used in the present paper has the following analytic formula

$$y = \mathrm{mod}f\left(1000\sum\frac{|\tanh(o_k) - \tanh(o_{k+1})|}{|\tanh(o_{k+1}) - \tanh(o_{k+2})|}\right)$$

Where y is the random number obtained and o_k, o_{k+1}, o_{k+2} are the activations of the processing elements of the MLP layer preceding its output one. **modf** is a Unix-function that extracts the fractional part of a real number.

The previous discussion determines all the steps of the approach adopted here for designing strong (pseudo)random bit sequences generators employing the overfitting MLP recall properties.

Apart from MLPs we consider how Hopfield type neural networks could produce strong pseudorandom numbers for electronic commerce systems. The methodology for transforming Hopfield type recurrent ANNs into strong (pseudo)random number generators is herein depicted by exploiting their properties to minimize a cost function involving their weights and neuron activations under certain conditions concerning their weight matrix (Haykin, 1999). More specifically, a Hopfield network possesses the following important characteristics (Haykin, 1999), which are next summarized

(a) If the weight matrix of a Hopfield recurrent ANN is symmetric with zero valued diagonals and furthermore, only one neuron is activated per iteration of the recurrent recall scheme then, there exists a Liapunov type cost function involving its weights and neuron activations, which decreases after each iteration until a local optimum of this objective function is found.

(b) The final output vector of the Hopfield network, after the convergence of the above mentioned recurrent recall scheme, has minimum distance or is exactly equal to one prototype stored in the network during its weight matrix definition (learning phase) provided that the prototypes stored are orthogonal to one another and their number $M <= 0.15N$, where N is the number of neurons in the network.

(c) If the prototypes stored in the Hopfield ANN are not orthogonal or their number $M > 0.15N$ then, the recurrent recall scheme converges to a linear combination of the prototypes stored when it is fed with a variation of one of these prototype vectors, provided that the weight matrix has the properties discussed in (a) above.

(d) Hopfield net outputs are given by the following formula, which is precisely the update formula for the single neuron activated during the iterations of the recurrent recall scheme mentioned in (a) above.

$$O_k = \tanh(\Sigma W_{ki} O_i)$$

The $g = \tanh()$ non-linearity is considered in the following.

These properties lead us intuitively to the principles of the proposed random number generation methodology involving such recurrent ANNs, summarized as follows

1. If we impose a perturbation to the recurrent network weight matrix so that its symmetry is broken and its

diagonal units obtain large positive values then, the convergence property of the recurrent recall scheme will be lost. This can be achieved, for instance, by adding a positive parameter δ to every unit in the upper triangle of the matrix, including diagonal units, and subtracting the negative quantity $-\delta$ from every unit in the lower triangle of the matrix.
2. Moreover, if we let a large number of neurons (in our experiments $N/2$ neurons) update their activations by following the formula of (d) above, then, the recurrent recall scheme will loose its convergence property to a local optimum of the suitable Liapunov function associated to the network.
3. If the recurrent recall scheme is not guaranteed to converge to a network output that corresponds to the local optima of a cost function then, the behavior of the network becomes unpredictable.
4. If the network is large and the patterns stored in it are orthogonal and thus, uncorrelated (that is, they have maximum distances from one another) then, the possibility of obtaining predictable outputs after several iterations of the recurrent recall scheme is minimum compared to the one associated with storing non-orthogonal prototypes, which are correlated to one another. In our experiments we use binary valued orthogonal patterns.
5. If the history of the network outputs during its recall phase is considered for T iterations of the recurrent recall scheme then, predicting the sequence of these output vectors is much harder than trying to predict a single output vector.

The above principles lead us to use the following function of network outputs over T iterations of the recurrent recall scheme as a pseudorandom number generator. To obtain better quality pseudorandom numbers, we have considered the Unix-function **modf**, which outcomes the non-integral part of a real number, as the required mechanism for aiding Hopfield net output to acquire the desired properties, since the first digits of its decimal part are predictable, due to the fact that the sigmoidal non-linearity g is a mapping on the (0,1) interval. Consequently, the formula of the Hopfield recurrent ANN proposed random number generator is as follows

$$O = \mathrm{mod}f\left(1000(1/TN)\sum_{t=1\ldots T}\sum_{k=1\ldots N}\left(g\left(\sum W_{ki}O_i(t)\right)\right)^2\right)$$

The previous discussion determines all the steps of the approach adopted here for designing strong (pseudo)random bit sequences generators employing the recurrent recall scheme of Hopfield networks.

Additionally, the above two presented neural network based methodologies for constructing strong pseudo-random bit sequences could be involved in strengthening traditional generators as follows. The initial weights of MLP are drawn from the traditional random number generator produced bit sequence and then, the MLP is employed as previously described as a random number generator mechanism. Thus, a two-stage generator is created, which, as shown in Section 4 enhances the quality characteristics of the corresponding traditional one. On the other hand, Hopfield recurrent ANN initial input values are drawn in the same way from the traditional random number generator produced bit sequence and then, this Hopfield net is involved as a random bit generator. Thus, again, a two-stage generator with enhanced properties might be produced, which is evaluated in Section 4.

3. A methodology for quality assessing random number generators in communication systems

Several research efforts exist in the literature for developing suites of tests for evaluating random number generators to be involved in stream ciphers (Gustafson, 1994; NIST Special Publication, 2001; Rueppel, 1986). In all these methodologies two criteria are used for the evaluation of the quality of random numbers obtained by using some generator in traditional applications such as simulation studies: uniform distribution and independence. The most important requirement imposed on random number generators is their capability to produce random numbers uniformly distributed in [0,1]; otherwise the application's results may be completely invalid. The independence requires that the numbers should not exhibit any correlation with each other. Additionally, random number generators should possess further properties: to be fast in computing the random numbers, to have the possibility to reproduce a given sequence of random numbers and to be able of producing several separate sequences of random numbers. However, for random number generators involved in the implementation of security mechanisms such as authentication, key generation and exchange in electronic commerce systems the most important property might be to produce unpredictable streams. True random numbers possess this property. It is well known that pseudorandom number generators, that are used for simulations such as the linear congruential generators have not this property since each number they produce can be expressed as a function of the initialization value or of its predecessor value and the coefficients of the generator.

3.1. An MLP based non-predictability test

In addition to these traditional tests we introduce a predictability test for random bit sequences based on the MLP capabilities to approximate functions without any kind of assumption about their model, either linear or non-linear (Haykin, 1999; Hornik, Stinchombe, & White, 1989). To this end, if we consider a random bit sequence as a time series, then, by scanning it with a sliding window of length M we could form from it a series of patterns suitable for defining a training task for an MLP. Thus, M such samples comprise its inputs while their corresponding next one comprises its desired output. The training task for such an MLP is to perfectly learn these predictability patterns. If the random bit sequence has N samples then, there exist $N - M$ such patterns. The rationale underlying the suggested test is that if such a task is learnable then, obviously, there exists great possibility that future numbers of the sequence under consideration can be inferred from their present and past values in the sequence. Therefore, by applying the above discussed learning task to an MLP and estimating the corresponding Minimum Average Sum of Squared Errors (SSE) per pattern we could have a view of how difficult is to predict the given random bit sequence. This SSE based measure of non-predictability, however, provides a hint for the average performance of the generator only. There might exist portions of the sequence that could be more predictable than others. A measure, suitable to account for such a fact, is the Maximum Approximation Probability (MAP), which counts the maximum number of correctly predicted patterns, with respect to a predefined approximation error ε per pattern, within the total number of patterns. It is obtained during the above specified MLP training session. Therefore, MAP = max[predicted patterns (with SSE $< \varepsilon$)]/[total number of patterns ($= N - M$)] during the whole MLP training session. In our simulations the quantities above described take on the values $\varepsilon = 0.001, N = 5000$ and $M = 2$, respectively.

3.2. Traditional empirical tests based on statistics

Statistical tests are applied to examine whether the pseudorandom number sequences are sufficiently random (Stallings, 1995). In the following we shortly discuss the empirical tests we use to evaluate the quality of the pseudorandom numbers obtained by the generators involved in this paper, i.e. how well they resemble true random numbers.

The first empirical test we apply is the most basic technique in the suite of the methods used for evaluating pseudorandom numbers quality, namely, the chi-square test (x^2 test). According to this method the interval [0,1] is divided into k subintervals of equal length. The k should be at least 100, and n/k should be at least five, where n is the length of the sequence (Knuth, 1998; Law & Kelton, 1991). In our examples $n = 5000$ and $k = 101$. We build $x^2 = k/n \sum_{i=1}^{k} (f_i - (n/k))^2$, where f_i is the number of random quantities that fall in the jth subinterval. For large n, x^2 will have an approximate chi-square distribution with k − 1 df (degrees of freedom) under the null hypothesis that the obtained pseudorandom numbers are identically, independently and uniformly distributed in the interval $[0,1)$ (Law & Kelton, 1991; Knuth, 1998). We reject this hypothesis at level of confidence $1 - a$ if $x^2 > x^2_{k-1,1-a}$, where $x^2_{k-1,1-a}$, is the upper $1 - a$ critical point of the chi-square distribution with $k - 1$ df (Knuth, 1998; Law & Kelton, 1991). In this paper, we make use of an approximate value of the

$$x^2_{k-1,1-a} \approx (k-1)\left\{1 - \frac{2}{9(k-1)} + z_{1-a}\sqrt{2/[9(k-1)]}\right\}^3$$

suggested in (Knuth, 1998; Law & Kelton, 1991), where z_{1-a} is the upper $1 - a$ critical point of the $N(0,1)$ distribution.

The second empirical test we use is the run test. The run tests look for independence and therefore, as discussed in the introduction of this work, are the most important tests for electronic commerce applications. With these tests we examine the length of monotone (increasing) portions of the pseudorandom number sequence. The test statistic is

$$V = \frac{1}{N}\sum_{i=1}^{6}\sum_{j=1}^{6} A_{ij}(R_i - NB_i)(R_j - NB_j),$$

where N is the sequence length, R_i is the number of monotone portions of length i with $i < 6$ and R_6 is the number of the rest portions of length >5. The matrices of coefficients A_{ij} and B_i are approximate values taken from (Knuth, 1998; Law & Kelton, 1991). The statistic V should have the chi-square distribution with six degrees of freedom, when N is large, i.e. greater than 4000. If V is greater than the critical point of the x^2 distribution with six df at confidence level $1 - a$ we reject the hypothesis of independence.

Finally, concerning the classical empirical tests, the sample means and variances of the pseudorandom number sequences obtained by the generators herein employed have been computed and compared with their expected values associated to the uniform distribution in the range [0,1), i.e. 0.5 and (1/12), respectively.

4. Evaluation and discussion of results

An experimental study has been carried out in order to demonstrate the efficiency of the suggested, in Section 2, procedures for designing pseudorandom number generators. The following experiments have been conducted by applying the empirical tests depicted in Section 3, on

1. A random sequence produced by the IDEA algorithm and another one produced by the ANSI-X.9 based on the 3DES and the IDEA algorithm.
2. A random sequence produced by the Hopfield recurrent ANN using the methodology described in Section 2.
3. A random sequence produced by an overfitting MLP based pseudorandom number generator, whose initial weights and all its inputs have been computed from a random sequence resulted by running a linear congruential number generator.

Table 1
The classical empirical test results. In order to interpret the results: For the x^2 and the run tests above, in order not to reject the hypothesis of randomness the result should be less than the indicated max value of the statistics threshold

Random number generator	χ^2 test (max value = 118.499) the smallest the result the best	Run test (max value = 10.645) the smallest the result the best	Sample mean the nearest the result to 0.500 the best	Sample variance the nearest the result to 1/12 the best
IDEA	109.186	2.464	0.503	0.0836
ANSI-X.9	98.26	4.861	0.500	0.0828
Hopfield-recurrent ANN	79.837	3.745	0.498	0.0835
MLP (4-20-20-1) off-line BP	57.874	0.268	0.500	0.0832
MLP (4-6-6-1) off-line BP, parity-4 ($n = 1.0$)	80.098	1.323	0.498	0.0819
IDEA-MLP (4-6-6-1) off-line BP, parity-4 ($n = 0.4$)	92.63	1.351	0.502	0.0830
ANSI-X.9-MLP (4-6-6-1) off-line BP, parity-4 ($n = 1.0$)	83.026	0.978	0.500	0.0832
IDEA-hopfield	85.42	1.39	0.501	0.0827
ANSI-X.9-hopfield	81.60	1.65	0.501	0.0830

4. Two two-stage generators involving in their second stage an MLP generator while, at their first stage, these MLP's weights are initialized from: (a) the IDEA sequence of (1) above, (b) the ANSI-X.9 sequence of (1) above.
5. Two two-stage generators involving in their second stage a Hopfield type ANN generator while, at their first stage, the input values are initialized from: (a) the IDEA sequence of (1) above, (b) the ANSI-X.9 sequence of (1) above.

The Hopfield ANN herein employed has $N = 100$ neurons connected following the conventional feedback architecture. All the sequences herein produced and compared have 5000 points. All the results obtained from the above specified experiments concerning the statistical and the non-predictability tests are presented in Tables 1 and 2, respectively. From these tables we can derive the following

1. Indeed, it is possible to obtain strong pseudorandom numbers using the complex recurrent recall scheme of Hopfield type ANNs.
2. It is possible to obtain strong pseudorandom numbers using the complex mapping properties of overfitting feedforward ANN of the MLP type to respond unpredictably to unknown input vectors even when they are similar to the training patterns.
3. Additionally, the proposed pseudo-RNG can enhance the quality of random numbers obtained by traditional generators when they are involved in a two stage procedure.
4. These pseudorandom numbers are of good quality, passing several critical evaluation tests.

Table 2
Non-predictability test results. SSEs are considered on all the $N - M$ patterns of each random sequence, where $N = 5000$ is the sequence length and $M = 2$ is the sliding window length. It is obvious that the larger the SSE and the smaller the MAP metric the less learnable the task and thus the better the stream generator since it presents non-predictability property

Random number generator	Minimum SSE per pattern (= total min SSE/number of patterns = 4998) in a 2-35-35-1 MLP, on-line BP ($n = 0.2$, $a = 0.3$) (the larger the SSE the better)	MAP ($\varepsilon = 0.001$) (the smallest the probability the better) (1/1000)
IDEA	420.72/4998	66.07
ANSI-X.9	417.44/4998	53.82
Hopfield-recurrent ANN	425.59/4998	53.04
MLP (4-20-20-1) Off-line BP	422.74/4998	51.78
MLP (4-6-6-1) off-line_BP, parity-4 ($n = 1.0$)	422.20/4998	51.50
IDEA-MLP (4-6-6-1) off-line_BP, parity-4 ($n = 0.4$)	426.38/4998	45.02
ANSI-X.9-MLP (4-6-6-1) Off-line_BP, parity-4 ($n = 1.0$)	425.34/4998	43.14
IDEA-hopfield	423.52/4998	55.25
ANSI-X.9-hopfield	422.78/4998	52.43

5. Although it has been demonstrated that there exists at least one function of MLP weights, or Hopfield network parameters, which can be designed to have the required properties, it is not obvious how to construct it. Building such functions relies on intuition and experimentation.
6. The proposed non-linear non-predictability test can reveal hints when analyzing a given pseudorandom number sequence. To be more specific, it can provide indications about average and maximum predictability properties of such a series.

5. Conclusions and future prospects

We have studied the use of recurrent ANN of the Hopfield type with the tanh sigmoidal, output function and the use of Overfitting MLP neural network training properties as generators of pseudorandom numbers and as strengthening elements of traditional generators to be integrated in the protocols of secure communications. The first such stream cipher proposed relies on the Hopfield networks ability to perform complex mappings between their inputs and outputs during their recurrent recall phase, which are unpredictable when a suitable perturbation of the weight matrix is involved. The second novel stream cipher herein developed is exploiting the fact that Overfitting MLPs respond unpredictably to unknown inputs even when they are similar to the ones employed in their training set.

The same characteristics of the neural network architectures are exploited by their role as strengthening elements of traditional generators. The proposed non-predictability test, which is based on the time series forecasting properties of MLP, along with empirical and theoretical tests comprise an evaluation methodology of pseudorandom number generators.

The neural-network-based and the strengthened generators have been shown to behave better than the traditional ones in terms of statistical and non-predictability tests. Future work aims to extent the role of further neural network architectures as generators or as strengthening elements of generators. The evaluation of often used generators by means of the proposed methodology is, also, a pursuit of our current work. But the most practical aspect of our work is to integrate such algorithms in the protocols of multimedia communications for secure transactions in the delivery of multimedia content, which is under way and will be presented in the near future.

References

AES2001 (2001). Advanced Encryption Standard. Federal Information Processing Standards Publication (FIPS PUBS) 197. http://csrc.nist.gov/publications/

Cybenco, G. (1989). Approximation by superposition of a sigmoidal function. *Mathematics of Control, Signals and Systems*, *2*, 303–314.

Diffie, W., & Hellman, M. E. (1976). New directions in cryptography. *IEEE Transactions on Information Theory*, *22*(6), 644–654.

Gollmann, D., Beth, T., & Damm, F. (1993). Authentication services in distributed systems. *Journal of Computers and Security*, *12*, 753–764.

Gustafson, H., et al. (1994). A computer package for measuring strength of encryption algorithms. *Journal of Computers and Security*, *13*(8), 687–697.

Haykin, S. (1999). *Neural networks: A comprehensive foundation* (2nd ed). Englewood Cliffs, NJ: Prentice Hall.

Hornik, K., Stinchombe, M., & White, H. (1989). Multilayer feedforward network are universal approximators. *Neural Networks*, *2*, 359–366.

Karras, D. A., & Zorkadis, V. (1998). On applying multilayer perceptron learning to (pseudo)random number generation and evaluation. *Journal of Neural Parallel and Scientific Computations*, 513–521.

Knuth, D. (1998). *The art of computer programming* (3rd ed) (*Vol. 2*). *Seminumerical algorithms*, Reading, MA: Addison-Wesley.

Law, A. M., & Kelton, W. D. (1991). *Simulation modeling and analysis*. New York: McGraw-Hill.

NIST Special Publication 800-22 (2001). A Statistical Test Suite for Random and Pseudorandom Number Generators for Cryptographic Applications. http://csrc.nist.gov/publications/

Pfleeger, C. P. (1997). *Security in computing*. Englewood Cliffs, NJ: Prentice-Hall.

Rueppel, R. A. (1986). *Analysis and design of stream ciphers*. Berlin: Springer.

Schneier, B. (1996). *Applied cryptography*. New York: Wiley.

Simmons, G. J. (1992). *Contemporary cryptology. The science of information integrity*, IEEE Press.

Stallings, W. (1995). *Network and internetwork security*. Englewood Cliffs, NJ: Prentice-Hall.

Stinson, D. R. (1995). *Crytography: theory and practice*. CRC Press.

Zeng, K., Yang, C.-H., Wei, D.-Y., & Rao, T. R. N. (1991). Pseudo random bit generators in stream cipher cryptography. *IEEE Computer*, 8–17.

AVAILABLE AT
www.ComputerScienceWeb.com
POWERED BY SCIENCE DIRECT

PERGAMON

Neural Networks 16 (2003) 907–914

Neural Networks

www.elsevier.com/locate/neunet

2003 Special issue

Multimedia authenticity protection with ICA watermarking and digital bacteria vaccination

Harold Szu[a,*], Steven Noel[b], Seong-Bin Yim[c], Jeff Willey[d], Joe Landa[e]

[a]*Office of Naval Research, 800 N. Quincy St, Arlington, VA 22217-5660, USA*
[b]*Center for Secure Information Systems, George Mason University, VA 22030-4444, USA*
[c]*Digital Media RF Lab, ECE Department, The George Washington University, Washington, DC 20052, USA*
[d]*Code 5344, Naval Research Laboratory, Washington, DC 20375-5336, USA*
[e]*BriarTek, Inc., 112 E. Del Ray Ave., Suite A, Alexandria, VA 22301, USA*

Abstract

We propose the application of independent component analysis (ICA), via unsupervised neural networks, to authenticity protection for multimedia products. We give an overview of the current state of multimedia authenticity protection, including the requirements of various multimedia applications, current approaches to the problem, and the robustness of the approaches. For watermark security, a covert independent-component watermarking signal can serve as a 'vaccination' against a dormant digital 'bacteria' protecting the multimedia data. An unauthorized removal of the watermark triggers the bacteria payload, which then degrades the quality of the unauthorized data. We argue that such digital bacteria meet all the established requirements for beneficial virus-like programs, and their payload would merely affect pirated media. We show how these new approaches contribute to a flexible, robust, and secure system for protecting the authenticity of multimedia products.
Published by Elsevier Science Ltd.

Keywords: Multimedia watermark; Copyright protection; Internet commerce; Independent component analysis; Unsupervised neural networks

1. Introduction

The ubiquitous piracy of copyrighted digital music files over the Internet threatens the livelihood of content-providing businesses as well as the creative artists who hold the copyright. Other than the legal and practical issues related to copyright enforcement, several technology factors influence the piracy. The major technology component is the presence of easy to use Internet based peer-to-peer file-sharing technology. Another factor is the compact format and high fidelity of Moving Picture Expert Group-I (MPEG-I) Layer-3 (MP3) digitally encoded music files. The result is that peer-to-peer MP3 encoded music files can be obtained quickly over high-speed network connections.

The application of Independent Component Analyses (ICA) to digital watermarking, for the purpose of multimedia authenticity protection, was first introduced in (Noel & Szu, 2000). This has foundations in previous work in ICA for intelligent sensory processing, (i.e. Quan, Szu & Markovitz, 2000; Szu, 1999a,b).

Many other technical strategies have been both proposed and pursued to reduce the piracy problem. One approach is to embed a digital code or watermark in the music itself. The watermark can be chosen to be imperceptible to the listener or deliberately chosen to corrupt the musical audio signal.

The ideal watermarking technique for digital music files has several desirable attributes including (1) compatibility with the popular MP3 format, (2) resistance to watermark removal by the consumer, and (3) complete recovery of the music from the watermark with authorized/restricted computer codes. We explore the efficacy of a novel approach (linear mixing and blind demixing with ICA) for watermarking digital music files to fulfill these goals.

Earlier research on watermarking via ICA concentrated on either detection, (Hartung & Kutter, 1999; Jessop, 1999; Swanson, Kobayashi, & Tewfick, 1998; Szu, 1999a,b), or on application to imagery (Barnett, 1999; Noel & Szu, 2000; Kopriva & Szu, 2003; Quan et al., 2000; Seok & Hong, 2001). Instead, this paper focuses on some of the subtle and practical issues of ICA for watermarking digital music files, especially robustness with respect to noisy MP3 compression.

* Corresponding author.

0893-6080/03/$ - see front matter Published by Elsevier Science Ltd.
doi:10.1016/S0893-6080(03)00132-1

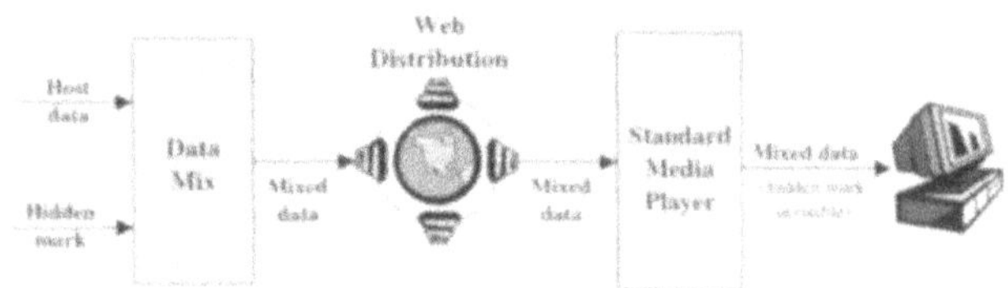

Fig. 1. Standard watermarking model.

Earlier work (Noel & Szu, 2000) described two models for watermarking of multimedia products: (1) a standard model and (2) a model for neural net ICA demix enabled media player (Figs. 1 and 2, respectively). The model in Fig. 1 uses a standard media player; therefore, the hidden watermark is invisible. On the other hand, the model in Fig. 2 uses an ICA demixed media player to recover the hidden watermark when proving copyright. Previous work (Noel & Szu, 2000) points out a critical issue: ICA needs to be able to demix signals that have been subjected to lossy compression. It also demonstrates that ICA neural networks can blindly demix media signals with relatively little distortion after the application of lossy wavelet compression.

In this paper, the idea is to non-linearly mix a watermark audio signal with the music signal, MP3 encode and decode the resulting signal, then attempt to demix the watermark signal from the music. The novelty of this method introduces difficulty in the removal of the watermark by the unsophisticated consumer. The value of restricted computer codes to restore the music from a watermarked signal will depend in part on the quality of music after blind demixing with ICA (Amari, Chichocki, & Yang, 1996; Bell & Sejnowski, 1995, 1996; Gonzalez-Serrano, Molina-Bulla, & Murillo-Fuentes, 2001; Yu & Satter, 2002; Yu, Satter, & Ma, 2002). We measure the watermark contamination of the music after blind demixing with ICA with MP3 encoding.

In ICA (Comon, 1994; Hyvärinen & Oja, 1999) sensed signals are modeled as statistically independent components, which are then linearly mixed. Here independence is over all orders of statistics, not just second-order correlations. Neural networks with unsupervised learning rules are able to estimate the signal mixing to high accuracy,

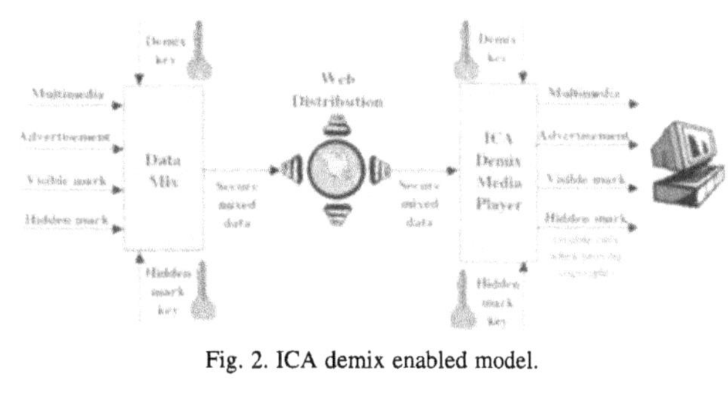

Fig. 2. ICA demix enabled model.

so that the original signals (independent components) can be recovered through inverse mixing.

The ability to blindly demix signals enables a novel form of security against those who may attack multimedia watermarks. One of the independent component signals in the mixed data stream could be a copy of an overt (visible or audible) authenticity mark on the host signal. A multimedia player enabled with an ICA neural network could then blindly demix the overt mark copy and determine whether the mark is still present in the host data.

If the overt authenticity mark has been removed, then a program triggers that degrades the quality of the unauthorized data. We call this program an electronic 'bacterium', as opposed to a 'virus', in the sense that it does not replicate indiscriminately. Moreover, there exists a 'vaccine' against this electronic bacterium, i.e. the presence of the authenticity mark. We also investigate two key requirements of the approach: (1) the robustness of ICA digital watermarking with respect to lossy compression and (2) the dynamic range of the digital watermark as clutter versus original music, for a signal coded under the MPEG-3.

In Section 2, we review ICA theory and introduce the concept of multimedia watermarks via ICA. Section 3 then applies ICA watermarks within a full framework for protecting multimedia authenticity. Sections 4–7 then perform experiments testing the robustness of the approach for MPEG-3 audio.

2. Blind demixing of multimedia data with ICA neural networks

Existing watermarking systems are essentially non-blind, in the sense that they require original versions of both the host data and watermark keystream in order to extract the watermark. This may be reasonable for applications that merely verify the existence of the watermark for proving ownership. However, non-blind schemes are inadequate for our application, in which embedded data is extracted on the consumer side, not the producer side.

A straightforward way to combine host and watermark signals is to combine them linearly. The signals could then later be demixed given the linear mixing coefficients. However, this provides little in the way of flexibility or security. It would be much better if the signals could be demixed without knowledge of the original mixing coefficients, or even of the original signals themselves. Thus, we are faced with the problem of blind demixing of source signals.

In ICA, the source signals are modeled as statistically independent signal components, which have been subsequently mixed linearly. Independence is defined such that the joint probability densities of the signal components can be factorized as the product of the marginal densities. Thus, independence is over all orders of statistics, not just second-order correlations.

Neural networks with unsupervised learning are able to estimate the signal mixing to high accuracy, so that the original signals (independent components) can be recovered through inverse mixing. The learning rules are based on maximizing the degree to which the independent components are non-gaussian. Possible measures of non-gaussianity are the absolute value of kurtosis (fourth-order cumulant), or negentropy (slightly modified version of differential entropy).

ICA assumes that there are multiple sensors, each sensing a different mix of the independent components. Thus is extends conventional single-sensor processing of signals to multiple sensors, analogous to the multiple sensors (eyes and ears) in humans. The unsupervised ICA neural networks are able to simultaneously compare sensor outputs, extracting noise so that only coherent signals remain. In the unsupervised learning rule, there is no specific desired output other than white gaussian noise. This is consistent with the idea that what is not noise must be signals.

More formally, assume n mutually independent signal sources at each time instant, represented as the vector $s = [s_1(t), s_2(t), \ldots, s_n(t)]^T$, which are then linearly mixed with an unknown mixing matrix **A** onto a vector of received signals $x = [x_1(t), x_2(t), \ldots, x_m(t)]^T$, i.e.

$$\mathbf{x} = \mathbf{A}\mathbf{s}, \tag{1}$$

where **A** is an $m \times n$ scalar matrix of full rank. Now let a neural processor with weight matrix **W** and non-linear contrast function g form the output y :

$$\mathbf{u} = \mathbf{W}\mathbf{x}, \tag{2}$$

$$y = g(\mathbf{u}), \tag{3}$$

where **W** is an $n \times m$ scalar weight matrix. Further, let the following additional assumptions hold:

1. The function g_i, is the cumulative distribution function of the source probability density function, $p(s_i(t))$.
2. The number of received signals, m, is at least equal to the number of source signals, n.
3. At most one source is normally distributed.
4. The receiver noise is negligible relative to the source signal power.

When speed of media processing is important, we recommend pixel-parallel Lagrange Constraint Neural Networks (LCNN), which solves blind source separation pixel by pixel in parallel. It has been shown (Szu, 1999a,b) that minimization of Helmholtz free energy $\mathbf{H} = \mathbf{E} - \mathbf{T}_0\mathbf{S}$ will achieve blind signal source separation, where **E** is the Lagrange constraint first-order estimation error

$$\mathbf{E} = \lambda([\mathbf{A}]\mathbf{s} - \mathbf{x}) = \mu([\mathbf{W}]\mathbf{x} - \mathbf{s}).$$

Here T_0 is the constant temperature of thermal reservoir, and S is the Shannon Boltzmann entropy. Two LCNN theorems (Theorems 1 and 2 are reviewed as follows, the first one without data, the other with data.

Theorem 1. *An equal partition law at Maximum Entropy: without being biased by pixel data, the equilibrium distribution at the maximum of entropy is an equal partition law as follows*:

$$\mathbf{S} = -\mathbf{K}_B \sum_{j=1,M} \mathbf{s}_j \log \mathbf{s}_j + \mathbf{K}_B(\lambda_0 + 1)\left(\sum_{j=1} \mathbf{s}_j - 1\right).$$

Next

$$\frac{\partial \mathbf{S}}{\partial s_j} = -\mathbf{K}_\mathbf{B}(\log \mathbf{s}_j + 1) + \mathbf{K}_\mathbf{B}(\lambda_0 + 1) = 0,$$

yields $\mathbf{s}_j = \exp(\lambda_0)$, *and imposing the unit sum* $\sum_{j=1,\mathbf{M}} \times \mathbf{s}_j = 1$ we find $\mathbf{s}_j = 1/\mathbf{M}$ *for the equal partition distribution.*

By computation of the Amari natural gradient with respect to the weight matrix **W**, and the distance metric $[A]^T[A]$, we have

$$\mathrm{d}x = (x, x) = (s, [A]^T[A]s) = d.$$

$$\frac{\partial \mathbf{A}}{\partial \mathbf{t}} = \frac{\partial \mathbf{H}(\mathbf{x})}{\partial \mathbf{A}} \mathbf{A}^T\mathbf{A}, \tag{4}$$

Theorem 2. *ANN Sigmoid Distribution Setting the derivative to zero for the minimum solution*

$$\frac{\partial \mathbf{H}}{\partial s_j} = \sum_k \lambda_k \mathbf{A}_{kj} + \log \mathbf{s}_j + 1 - (\lambda_o + 1) = 0,$$

reproduces, by the unit sum constraints $\sum_j \mathbf{s}_j = 1$, *the ANN sigmoid threshold (without assuming it for ICA post processing)*:

$$s_j = \exp\left(\frac{\lambda_j}{\mathbf{K}_\mathbf{B}\mathbf{T}_0} + \lambda_0\right) = \frac{1}{1 + \sum_{k \neq j} \exp\left(\frac{\lambda_k}{\mathbf{K}_\mathbf{B}\mathbf{T}_0} - \frac{\lambda_j}{\mathbf{K}_\mathbf{B}\mathbf{T}_0}\right)}$$

$$= \sigma\left(\frac{\lambda_j}{\mathbf{K}_\mathbf{B}\mathbf{T}_0}\right).$$

The Lagrange constraint vector could be obtained with a standard textbook in physics. Thus, we achieved single pixel blind source separation, i.e. the output would not have the pixel ensemble average led to a permutation and scaled version of the original mutually independent signal sources s.

On the other hand, a batch-mode operation uses the feed forward weight update rule (Bell & Sejnowski, 1995) to

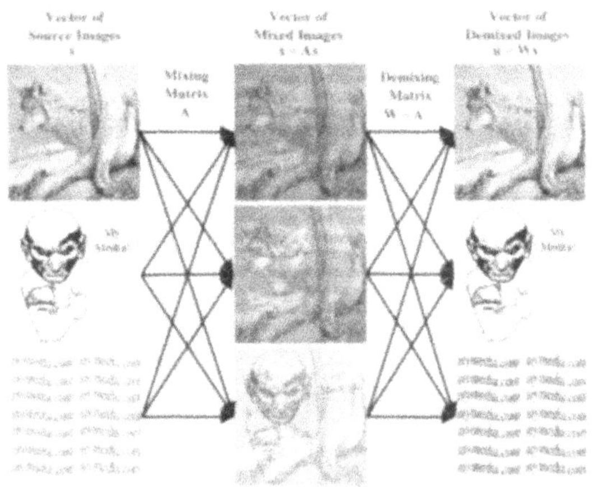

Fig. 3. Example mixing of multimedia data, with blind demixing via ICA unsupervised neural network.

have the general form

$$\frac{\partial S(y)}{\partial \mathbf{W}} = (\mathbf{W}^{\mathrm{T}})^{-1} + \left(\frac{\frac{\partial \mathbf{p}(\mathbf{u})}{\partial \mathbf{u}}}{\mathbf{p}(\mathbf{u})} \right) \mathbf{x}^{\mathrm{T}}, \tag{5}$$

Here $p(u)$ is a source probability density function. As Amari et al. (1996) shows by post multiplication of Eq. (5) by $\mathbf{W}^{\mathrm{T}}\mathbf{W}$, one has

$$\frac{\partial S(y)}{\partial \mathbf{W}} = \left[\mathbf{I} + \left(\frac{\frac{\partial \mathbf{p}(\mathbf{u})}{\partial \mathbf{u}}}{\mathbf{p}(\mathbf{u})} \right) \mathbf{u}^{\mathrm{T}} \right] \mathbf{W}. \tag{6}$$

In practice, we employ fixed-point Fast ICA Matlab code (Oja & Karhunen, 1995) to compute the gradient. Here the hyperbolic tangent function is chosen for the contrast related function, $(\mathrm{d}p(u)/\mathrm{d}u)/p(u)$, in Eq. (6).

Fig. 3 is an example of the mixing of multimedia data, with blind demixing by an ICA unsupervised neural network. The three independent data components are the host data, an advertisement, and an authenticity mark. The data are mixed to insure the various components remain together for Internet distribution. The neural network with unsupervised learning estimates with high accuracy the mixing matrix **A**, allowing blind demixing of the independent components.

3. Independent components for multimedia watermark vaccination

It is important that ICA demixing be robust with respect to various forms of signal processing. Being linear, ICA demixing is invariant with respect to linear filtering. It is also invariant with respect to various changes in sampling, which cause synchronization problems with most other watermarking techniques. Such sampling changes include cropping, line dropping, or changing the sample rate. In the ICA model, each sample point is a mix of two independent components, and the mix is same for all samples.

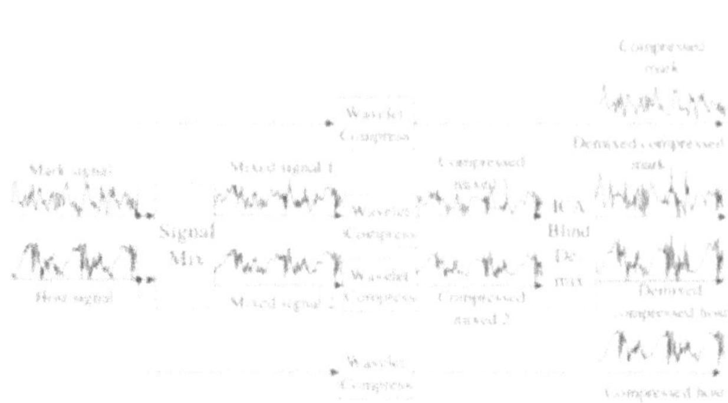

Fig. 4. Robustness of ICA neural net blind demixing with respect to non-linear wavelet audio data compression.

It is also critical that ICA neural networks be able to demix signals that have been subjected to lossy compression. In general, compression can occur either before or after mixing. Compression before mixing yields nearly lossless demixing, and avoids costly decompression of previously compressed data. As we see in Fig. 4 for audio data, ICA neural networks can blindly demix signals with minimal distortion even after they have been subjected to the non-linear transformation of lossy wavelet compression.

In Fig. 5, after the host and watermark images are mixed, the mixtures are subjected to DWT compression. ICA unsupervised neural nets are still able to blindly demix host and mark images, despite the non-linear transformation of mixed images via compression. In fact, there is little visual difference compared to the compressed versions with no mixing involved.

Once the data is demixed, it is open to attack by the consumer. For example, the consumer could attempt to remove a visible overt company logo from the demixed multimedia product, to claim ownership. We do not have the luxury of a DVD-like approach, where there is industry-wide cooperation and all multimedia players are trusted. Our approach needs to be completely autonomous.

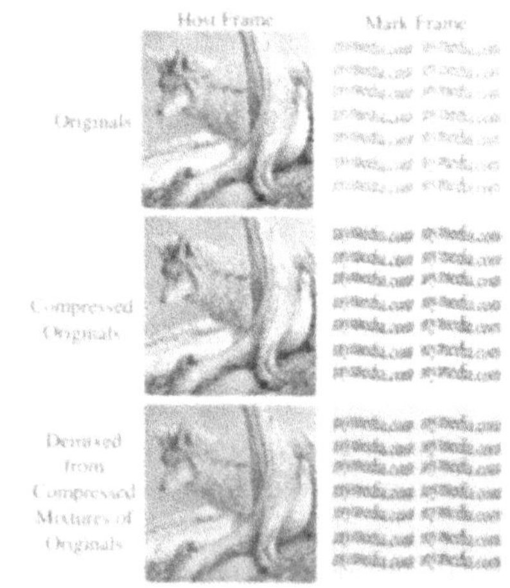

Fig. 5. Robustness of ICA neural net blind demixing with respect to non-linear wavelet image data compression.

Our approach to making product authenticity secure against someone who has the demix key is essentially a watermark 'vaccination' against digital 'bacteria'. The purpose of the bacteria is to degrade the quality of the multimedia product if it has been tampered with, e.g. its company logo is removed.

The vaccination is the actual presence of the company logo, and it has already been administered in the sense that the logo is initially part of the product. Hidden data localized to the company logo serves as the flag for the logo's presence. The level of infection (i.e. the action to take upon logo deletion) can vary from doing nothing, to degrading sound/video quality, to rendering the multimedia product unusable, depending on the choice of product owner. The infection is localized to the unauthorized multimedia file, and spreads to no other part of computer, since unauthorized content is directly recognizable via ICA demixing.

Fred Cohen pioneered research in computer viruses[1] (Cohen, 1984). His early results showed that (1) viruses could spread unhindered, even in secured networks, (2) that they could cause essentially unlimited damage with little effort by the virus writer, (3) that virus detection was undecidable, and (4) that many of the defenses that could be devised relatively quickly were ineffective against a serious virus writer. Despite subsequent advances in virus defense, it appears that it will always be possible to write effective viruses.

For various reasons, the general public usually considers computer viruses to be malicious code with no useful purpose. However, maliciousness is neither a necessary nor a sufficient property for computer viruses. Indeed, Cohen has described the potential advantages of beneficial viruses.

It is true that there have been relatively few successful examples of beneficial viruses, despite several attempts. Bontchev argues convincingly (Bontchev, 1994) that such failed attempts violate one or more important properties that beneficial viruses should have.

In particular, the technical properties that beneficial viruses should have are (1) control, (2) recognition, (3), no resource wasting, (4) bug containment, (5) compatibility, and (6) effectiveness. Such viruses should also meet ethical/legal requirements with respect to unauthorized data modification and copyrights, as well as psychological barriers involving lack of trust and negative connotations with computer viruses.

Bontchev also describes a general model for beneficial viruses that satisfies these requirements (Bontchev, 1994). This model requires the active consent of individual users, via cryptographically strong system authentication. It also requires that the virus be self-contained and propagate as a whole, and not depend on attaching itself to a host executable file. The beneficial virus must also consume negligible resources, at least compared to the benefits it provides.

Our proposed digital bacteria fit within this general model for beneficial viruses. They fulfill the control requirement because they only spread to machines that have agreed to the network policy with respect to unauthorized media. They fulfill the recognition property because they can be easily ignored by anti-virus scanners, since they can authenticate themselves as a known beneficial virus.

Our digital bacteria meet the resource-wasting criterion, since only a single instance of the virus is present on an infected machine, and assuming the media degradation process is efficient. Through public-key cryptography for authentication, digital bacteria updates can be strictly controlled, addressing the bug-containment problem.

Because the digital bacteria are self-contained and do not modify other programs, they introduce no greater risk on incompatibility than non-viral programs. Our digital bacteria meet the effectiveness requirement, since a virus-like propagation is a highly effective way to ensure multimedia authenticity protection across a participating network.

Since our proposed digital bacteria modify only unauthorized media files, there are no ethical/legal problems. The psychological barrier is largely overcome by the fact that most people would not consider such programs to be actual viruses. Some users may resent the effects of the digital bacteria if they thwart their efforts at illegally copying music or videos. But network administrators would appreciate that illegal activities are being curtailed on their network, and there would be definite monetary incentives by the media content producers and artists.

One way to implement watermark vaccination is to have the vaccination-checking executable code downloaded along with the mixed data and multimedia player. It is then executed along with the player, as shown in Fig. 6. Multimedia data, advertisement, and mark data are mixed

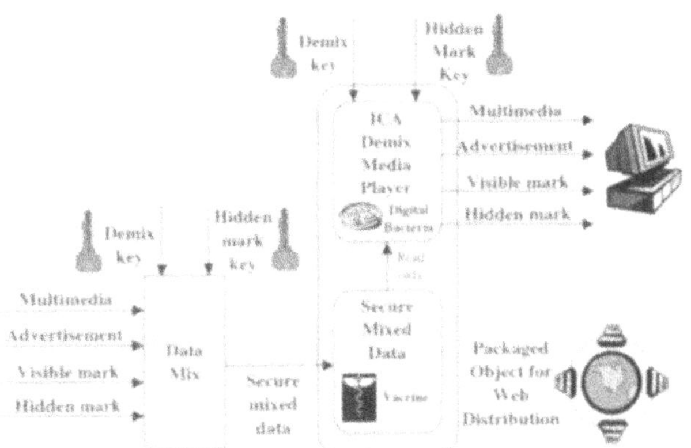

Fig. 6. Object-based model for multimedia product protection by watermark vaccination.

[1] In the early 1980s, as a PhD student at the University of Southern California, Fred Cohen got the idea of self-replicating software that spreads by attaching itself to existing programs. He shared this idea with his thesis advisor Len Adleman, who pointed out the similarity to a biological virus, leading to the term 'computer virus.'

and secured, then embedded within the object. The neural network ICA demix media player is defined as an object method, with read-only access to mixed data. The demix key allows data to be demixed, and the mark key allows the hidden mark to be accessed for copyright proof.

Another implementation is DVD-like, that is, via trusted players. Either the multimedia producers or a third party provides the player/protection software cost-free. This approach requires universal participation for complete protection; otherwise, there is protection only among trusted players. A third approach is to implement a DVD-like scheme in hardware, with an interface to the operating system.

4. Experimental background

4.1. Blind demixing with ICA

The idea is to linearly mix a watermark acoustic signal with the music signal, MP3 encode and decode the resulting signal, then attempt to demix the watermark signal from the music. The novelty of this method introduces difficulty in the removal of the watermark by the unsophisticated consumer. The value of restricted computer codes to restore the music from a watermarked signal will depend in part on the quality of music after blind demixing with ICA. We measure the watermark contamination of the music after blind demixing with ICA with MP3 encoding. The receiver noise is negligible relative to the source signal power.

4.2. MP3 encoding/decoding

The compact MP3 encoding format is a lossy compression method. It utilizes a psycho-acoustic model of human hearing to discard information (Brandenburg & Popp, 2000; Pan, 1995). As shown in Fig. 7, human hearing is subject to auditory masking, where small tones in the local frequency neighborhood of a much stronger tone are imperceptible.

Further, the human auditory system's frequency resolution is a function of absolute frequency; perceptible filter widths are narrow at the low end and significantly wider at the high end. Thus, weak tones adjacent to stronger tones may be eliminated by MP3 encoding/decoding.

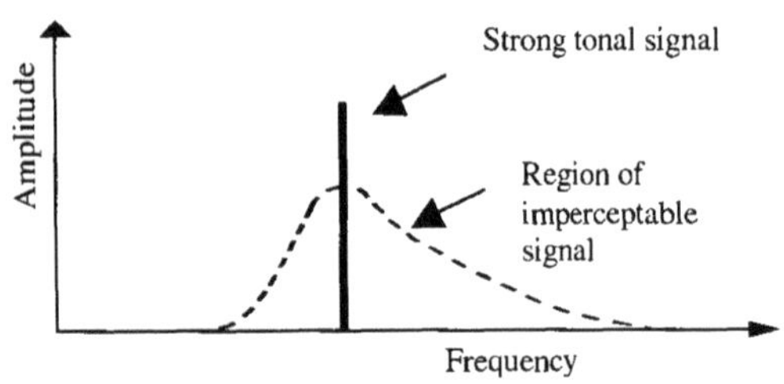

Fig. 7. Illustration of audio noise masking. Weak signals in the local frequency neighborhood of a strong tone are imperceptible.

Several issues arise (Yim, Willey, Landa & Szu, 2003) when considering ICA for blind demixing of MP3 watermarked music. First, introduction of a watermark signal must be considered in the context of the music, so that it will not be eliminated by the lossy MP3 encoding/decoding. A second issue is consideration of the statistics of the music and watermark signals after MP3 encoding/decoding. The concern is that the statistics of both the watermark and music signals may be perturbed when selected frequency components are nulled. The altered statistics may adversely affect the ICA blind demixing.

Our strategy is to measure the watermark contamination in the music signal after blind demixing with ICA. First we measure the watermark residue in the music channel without MP3 encoding/decoding. Then the measurement is repeated after MP3 encoding/decoding. Section 5 discusses the methodology and equipment configuration for our measurements.

5. Methodology

The goal is to measure the watermark contamination in the music signal after blind demixing with ICA. First a baseline is produced that measures the watermark residue in the music channel when the MP3 codec is not employed, in Fig. 8 without the dashed block. Then the residue level is measured by introducing the MP3 codec to the linearly mixed signals as in Fig. 8 with the dashed block. To control the relative contributions of the watermark and music signals, the linear mixing matrix was parameterized for a single mixture angle, ∅. In both cases, the latter are demixed using ICA to recover permuted and scaled versions of the originals (Music' and Watermark').

To facilitate simultaneous linearity and residue measurements, the watermark signal and music signals were implemented as a pair of dual tones. The Watermark signal is two equal amplitude tones at 900 and 1000 Hz and two equal amplitude tones for the Music signal are at 2100 and 2250 Hz. The linear dynamic range is determined by measuring the magnitude of the intermodulation (IM)

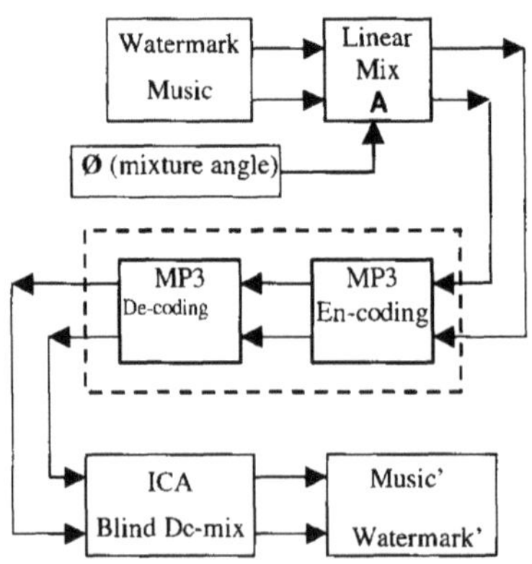

Fig. 8. Mixing and demixing procedure model with/without MP3 codec block (dashed block).

products generated by the tone pair, relative to the magnitude of the respective tone pairs. As an example, for the two tone watermark signal at 900 and 1000 Hz, any first order IM products would occur at 800 and 1100 Hz.

The MP3 codec was implemented using commercial software (Syntrillium, 2003). The following MP3 encoding options were chosen and held constant through all the experiments: 44.1 kHz sample rate, 128 kbps per channel, and stereo (no joint stereo coding).

As a check, the software MP3 decoder was checked with consumer hardware. MP3 files were burned on CDROMs, played back on a Riovolt MP3/CD Player through an RCA SA-155 Integrated Stereo Amplifier (Radio Shack catalog #31-5000) with spectrum measurements obtained from a spectrum analyzer (HP 3588A with opt. 001). The nominal 80 dB of linear dynamic range measured in the MP3 software codec was also observed with the hardware.

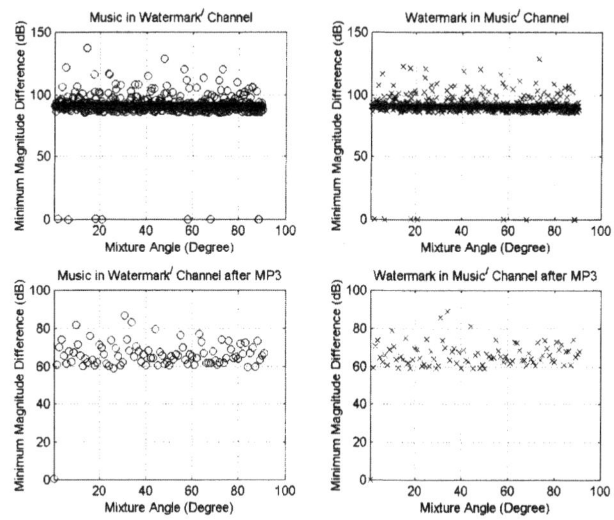

Fig. 10. Minimum magnitude differences (dB) between the residue signal and the wanted signal are shown at each mixture angle from 0 to 90°.

6. Results

An illustration of the results of demixing for a mixture angle of 30° in the absence of the MP3 codec is shown in Fig. 9. It shows more than 80 dB of isolation between the wanted signals and the residue signals. The left column is Watermark' channel with the wanted watermark tones at 900 and 1000 Hz, and the right column is Music' channel with the wanted music tones at 2100 and 2250 Hz.

Fig. 10 is the summary of minimum magnitude differences in dB for the case when the MP3 codec (the dashed block in Fig. 8) was absent and the mixture angle was varied from 0 to 90° at 0.1° increments in the top of pictures.

In the bottom of the pictures in Fig. 10 is a summary for the case when the MP3 codec (the dashed block in Fig. 8) was present, but the residues were evaluated only from 0 to 90° at every 1° increments. In this figure, the left column shows the minimal magnitude differences in dB between the residue signal and the wanted signal in the Watermark' channel, and in the same way the right column shows the minimal magnitude differences in Music' channel.

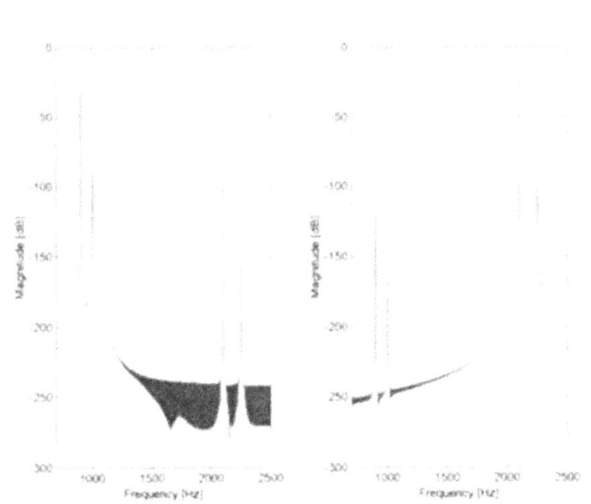

Fig. 9. The residues in both demixed channels.

7. Discussion

Without the MP3 codec, the results of blind demixing with ICA showed watermark attenuation in the music channel was more than 82 dB for a wide range of mixture angles, close to the 90 dB dynamic range of MP3 encoded music. When the linearly mixed signals were passed through the lossy MP3 codec, the residues were approximately 70 dB down from the wanted signals as measured at the 30 and 60° mixture angles. However, when we measured from 0 to 90° at every 1°, the residues were approximately larger than 59 dB down. Despite the 23 dB performance deficiency with the MP3 codec, the watermark contamination in the music channel is likely to be imperceptible by the human auditory system. The high quality of the music recovery suggests that there is value in restricted computer codes for the restoration of music from watermarked MP3 digital music files.

The lossy MP3 coding format might affect the statistics of both the watermark and music signals when selected frequency components are nulled. However, in our evaluations with the selected simple tonal pairs representing the watermark and acoustic signals, the adverse affects on blind demixing with ICA are small.

Some open research opportunities include recovery of the absolute amplitude and phase of the music signal. With ICA blind demixing an unknown scale and permutation in the re-covered outputs generally occurs. A scale change could also manifest itself as a 180° phase shift in the music channel. For stereo music, this may destroy the 'depth' perception. If some of the properties of the watermark are known a priori, then recovery of the watermark might serve as a guide to recover the music channel's absolute amplitude and sense of phase.

8. Summary and conclusions

This paper examines the application of ICA, via unsupervised neural networks, to authenticity protection for multimedia products. The blind demixing capability of these neural networks extends signal processing from a one-sensor approach to a multi-sensor approach.

For watermark security, we propose a covert watermarking signal that serves as a vaccination against a dormant digital bacterium. Removal of the watermark triggers the bacterium, which degrades the quality of the product being pirated. We show that our digital-bacteria model meets established technical and ethical requirements for beneficial virus-like programs.

We apply our novel ICA watermarking method to digitally encoded acoustic music files. A watermarked signal was linearly mixed with a music signal. The resulting mixture pair was put through an MP3 codec, and then blindly demixed with ICA to recover the music signal. The watermark contamination in the music channel was measured both when the MP3 codec was absent and when it was present.

Our experimental results show that watermark contamination in the music channel is likely to be inaudible, and that the adverse affects on blind demixing with ICA are small. We conclude that our approach can provide a flexible, robust, and secure system for protecting the authenticity of multimedia products.

References

Amari, S., Chichocki, A., & Yang, H. (1996). A new learning algorithm for blind signal separation. In D. Touretzky, M. Mozer, & M. Hasselmo (Eds.), (*Vol. 8*). *Advances in neural information processing systems*. Cambridge, MA: MIT Press.

Barnett, R. (1999). Digital watermarking: applications, techniques, and challenges. *Electronics and Communication Engineering Journal*, *11*(4), 173–183.

Bell, A., & Sejnowski, T. (1995). An information-maximization approach to blind separation and blind deconvolution. *Neural Computation*, *7*, 1129–1159.

Bell, A., & Sejnowski, T. (1996). Learning the higher-order structure of a natural sound. *Network: Computation in Neural Systems*, *7*, 261–266.

Bontchev, V. (1994). Are good computer viruses still a bad idea? *Proceedings of EICAR, London.*

Brandenburg, K., & Popp, H. (2000). An introduction to MPEG Layer-3. *EBU Technical Review*, 1–15.

Cohen, F. (1984). Computer viruses—theory and experiments. *Computers and Security*, *6*(1), 22–35.

Comon, P. (1994). Independent component analysis, a new concept? *Signal Processing*, *36*(3), 287–314.

Gonzalez-Serrano, F., Molina-Bulla, H., & Murillo-Fuentes, J. (2001). Independent component analysis applied to digital image watermarking. *Proceedings of the IEEE International Conference on Acoustics, Speech, and Signal Processing Salt Lake City*, 1997–2000.

Hartung, F., & Kutter, M. (1999). Multimedia watermarking techniques. *Proceedings of the IEEE*, *87*(7), 1079–1107.

Hyvärinen, A., & Oja, E (1999). *Independent component analysis: a tutorial.* Tutorial Notes, International Joint Conference on Neural Networks, Washington, DC.

Jessop, P. (1999). The business case for audio watermarking. *Proceedings of the IEEE International Conference on Acoustics, Speech, and Signal Processing Phoenix*, 2074–2077.

Kopriva, I., & Szu, H. (2003). Blind inversion in nonlinear space-variant imaging by using cauchy machine. *Proceedings of the SPIE Conference on Independent Component Analyses, Neural Nets and Wavelets, Orlando.*

Noel, S., & Szu, H. (2000). Multimedia authenticity with ICA watermarks. *Proceedings of Wavelet Applications VII Orlando*, 175–184.

Oja, E., & Karhunen, J. (1995). Signal separation by nonlinear hebbian learning. *Proceedings of the International Conference on Neural Networks Perth*, 417–421.

Pan, D. (1995). A tutorial on MPEG/audio compression. *IEEE Multimedia Journal*, 60–74.

Quan, A., Szu, A., & Markovitz, Z. (2000). Local ICA for the most wanted face recognition. *Proceedings of Wavelet Applications VI Orlando*, 539–551.

Seok, J., & Hong, J. (2001). Audio watermarking for copyright protection of digital audio data. *Electronics Letters*, *37*(1), 60–61.

Swanson, M., Kobayashi, M., & Tewfick, A. (1998). Multimedia data-embedding and watermarking technologies. *Proceedings of the IEEE*, *86*(6), 155–178.

Syntrillium Software Corporation (2003). Syntrillium software—Home of Cool Edit 2000 and Cool Edit Pro. Web page, http://www.syntrillium.com/. Last accessed March 21, 2003.

Szu, H. (1999a). ICA-enabling techniques for intelligent sensory processing. *IEEE Circuits and Systems Newsletters*, 14–41.

Szu, H. (1999b). Progress in unsupervised artificial neural networks for image demixing applications. *IEEE Industrial Electronics Society Newsletter*, *46*(2), 7–12.

Yim, S.-B., Willey, J., Landa, J., & Szu, H. (2003). Watermarking MP3 encoded music and ICA blind demixing. *Proceedings of the SPIE Conference on Independent Component Analyses, Neural Nets and Wavelets, Orlando.*

Yu, D., & Satter, F. (2002). Robust image watermarking based on independent component analysis. *Proceedings of the IEEE International Conference on Acoustics, Speech, and Signal Processing Orlando*, 4177.

Yu, D., Satter, F., & Ma, K.-K. (2002). Watermark detection and extraction using ICA method. *EURASIP Journal on Applied Signal Processing*, *1*, 92–104.

AVAILABLE AT
www.ComputerScienceWeb.com
POWERED BY SCIENCE DIRECT

PERGAMON

Neural Networks 16 (2003) 915–923

Neural Networks

www.elsevier.com/locate/neunet

2003 Special issue

Interpolation processes in the visual perception of objects

P.J. Kellman

University of California, 405 Hilgard Avenue, Los Angeles, CA 90095-1563, USA

Abstract

Visual perception of objects depends on segmentation and grouping processes that act on fragmentary input. This paper gives a brief overview of these processes. A simple geometry accounting for contour interpolation is described, and its applications to 2D, 3D, and spatiotemporal object interpolation processes are considered. A method is described for distinguishing interpolation based on this geometry from more global or top-down influences. Results suggest a separation between interpolation based on relatively local stimulus relations, which give rise to precise boundary representations, and processes involving recognition from partial information, which do not. Aspects of the model—especially the unified treatment of illusory and occluded objects—raise questions about the nature of seeing. Although it is often believed that illusory objects are *perceived*, while occluded objects are *inferred*, I suggest that both research and theory converge in supporting a more unified account. Illusory and occluded contours and surfaces do not divide into the real, the perceived, and the inferred, but are all *represented*, and in key respects, derive from identical perceptual processes.

Keywords: Interpolation processes; Visual perception; Objects; Occlusion; Contours; Illusory contours

1. Introduction

Few verbs have the multiplicity of meanings as 'to see.' One might see a point made in discussion, see that it's getting late, or see about dinner reservations. In understanding visual perception, one of the most important ambiguities involves what it is that we can see. A long and successful scientific tradition has characterized the eye as an optical system and described visual pathways as allowing us to see light or extract properties of light. Conversely, in common parlance and in the understanding of perception, we seem to be involved with the seeing of *objects*, as well as their arrangement in space and events involving them. Do we see light? Or objects? Assuming that the answers are 'yes' in some sense to both questions, what is the relation between these different kinds of seeing?

These questions may seem to be purely philosophical, but they become crucial in the study of perceptual organization. In this article, we consider specifically perceptual processes that create objects from what is often a fragmentary patchwork of light reflected to the eyes from a given object in the world. I will both describe some current directions in research on object perception and consider a couple of larger issues involving the dichotomy between receiving reflected light and achieving perceptual representations.

The focus will be on processes of perceptual organization that build representations of complete contours, objects, and surfaces from fragmentary input. To keep the discussion brief, I provide in most cases only the gist of research findings, referring to other published work for details.

Perceptual systems provide the information that humans and other organisms use to guide thought and action. Vision is special among these systems, in that it gives detailed knowledge of objects and the spatial layout, and it works at a distance. Understanding vision requires us to determine how visual information leads to descriptions of objects, spatial arrangements, and events.

Our descriptions of perceived reality are heavily based in a vocabulary of *objects*—bounded volumes of matter that function as units in our interactions with the world. Objects are both physical and psychological units; in fact, they may be best described as ecological units (Kellman & Arterberry, 1998). In physical reality, we believe that there exist coherent entities, such as pebbles, books, and cars. They separate from other things and cohere over movement. At the same time, our psychological notions of objects are restricted in terms of size, duration, and degree of cohesion. Neither the planet earth nor a sub-atomic particle is an object for ordinary cognition and behavior. So, objects are physical units at scales relevant to our thought and behavior.

How do we perceive objects? Although the operation of object perception is ordinarily quick and effortless,

0893-6080/03/$ - see front matter © 2003 Elsevier Science Ltd. All rights reserved.
doi:10.1016/S0893-6080(03)00101-1

the scientific explanation of object perception is extremely challenging. Many of the problems are commonly considered together as issues of *visual segmentation and grouping*. Whether the problem is segmentation or grouping depends on the description with which you start. If the starting point is an image of a scene, either on your retina or on a CRT screen, the issue is how to segment this entity into parts that correspond to different objects in the world. If instead you start with the well-known coding of visual inputs in mammalian vision into small, local patches of oriented contrast in early cortical areas, the problem is how to group together the outputs of thousands of units that might all be registering parts of a single object. Grouping is also the issue if one starts with an image description in terms of many pixels. Likewise, if we start with visible regions, parts of a single object must be grouped, as often they project to several different retinal locations, as we will consider.

A pervasive and fundamental difficulty in achieving descriptions of objects from information in reflected light may be labeled the *fragmentation problem*. Whereas the world and our representations of it contain coherent objects and continuous surfaces, the input from the world to our eyes is fragmentary. Most objects are partly occluded; their projections to the eyes are interrupted by parts of other objects. Viewing a scene through foliage, the observer's retina receives many separate patches of each object in the scene. How do we obtain representations of complete objects—a building, a car, a person—under these circumstances? The answers are important, as these circumstances are more the rule than the exception in ordinary perception. The problems become all the more complicated when observers or objects move, as patterns of occlusion continuously change.

2. Visual interpolation phenomena

Fortunately the visual system has processes that overcome fragmentation in the input and produce representations of complete objects. Shown in Fig. 1 are examples of several phenomena in which the visual system overcomes gaps in the input in perceiving objects. Fig. 1A shows a case of partial occlusion; the three black regions all appear as part of a complete object, whose shape is apparent. Fig. 1B shows an example of the phenomenon of *illusory contours* or illusory objects. Here, contours are connected across gaps such that these interpolated parts appear in front of other surfaces. In Fig. 1C, an additional effect, one of transparency, can be observed in the figure that is created across the gaps.

Fig. 1. Visual interpolation phenomena: (A) partial occlusion; (B) illusory contours; (C) transparency.

These phenomena are formally similar in that equivalent or similar visible contours and surface fragments become linked to form objects, despite intervening gaps. Research suggests that the similarity is more than formal: these phenomena share a common underlying interpolation process.

3. Visual interpolation processes

How do visual processes overcome fragmentation to achieve accurate object perception? The visual system uses relationships among visible *contour* segments to guide segmentation and derive shape. It also uses relationships of *surface* properties to establish surface continuity. Most of our focus will be on contour processes, but we will describe surface processes briefly in a later section. After giving a sketch of these processes, I will consider their implications for the nature of seeing: do these processes create illusions or give us windows into reality?

3.1. Contour extraction processes

Object perception involves a number of conceptually distinct information processing tasks and representations. (These may or may not be realized as separate processes or mechanisms in the brain.) Fig. 2 provides a schematic model of these processes, representations and their interactions. Some components and their connections reflect established findings whereas others represent newer conjectures. Considerable differences exist in how much is known about precise computations and neural implementations in the specific boxes. Rectangles indicate functions or processes, and octagons indicate representations. The model has few representations: output representations of shape and unity (labeling regions belonging to a single object) and one intermediate representation: the *visible regions representation*. Among other things, this representation marks connected visual areas, derived from depth, velocity, and luminance maps, and labels their contours as bounding or belonging to other (occluding) objects. (For this and other details of the model, see Kellman, Guttman, & Wickens, 2001).

Our immediate concern is the contour stream, which locates discontinuities in luminance, color, texture, depth, and motion, uses these to find edges and junctions, and ultimately leads to meaningful contours and object shape. The importance of contours derives from the fact that objects will tend to be relatively homogenous in their composition (and thus in their lightness, color, texture,

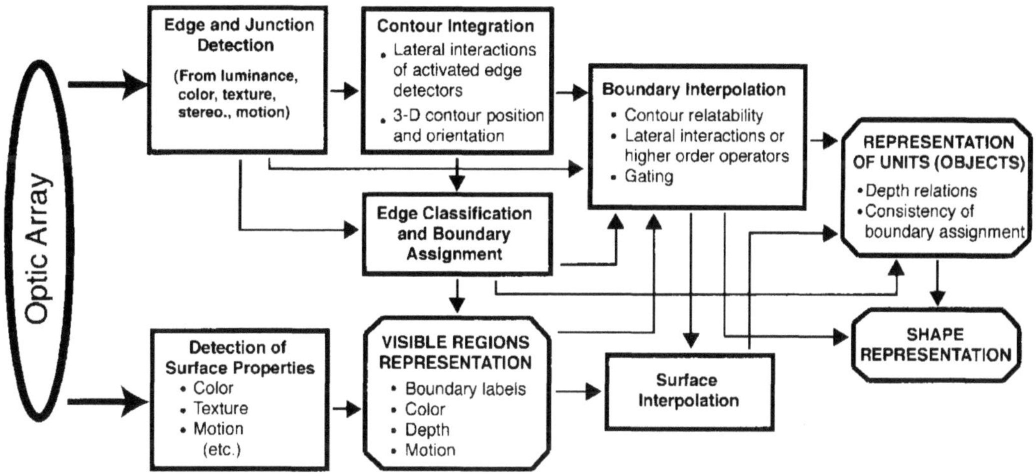

Fig. 2. A framework for object perception. Rectangles are functions; octagons are representations (see text).

depth, etc.) and will often differ from nearby objects and surfaces. Visible contours often, but not always, mark the locations of object boundaries.

Computations leading to perception of contours and edges appear to begin in the early cortical areas V1 and V2. Cells in these areas respond to oriented luminance contrast at particular spatial frequencies in particular retinal locations (Campbell, Cooper, & Enroth-Cugell, 1969; Hubel & Wiesel, 1968). By area V2, and perhaps earlier, many cells respond selectively to particular binocular disparities, providing the basis for stereoscopic depth perception (Fischer & Poggio, 1979). Some cells in the early cortical areas also respond preferentially to motion, although areas upstream, particularly area V5 (the human homologue to macaque area MT), appear to be specialized for motion processing. Numerous proposals in both biological and computational vision have been made about how early cortical responses can be utilized to detect luminance edges. The modeling of object perception based on other types of edge inputs, such as discontinuities in stereoscopic depth and motion is less advanced. Likewise, how the visual system integrates edge information arising from various sources remains relatively unknown.

Additional tasks that we will not discuss here include the classification of edges, as arising from illumination or reflectance differences, and boundary assignment of those edges determined to be occluding edges.

3.2. Contour interpolation

Although the tasks of contour finding, classification, and boundary assignment are challenging in themselves, even their complete solution does not provide reasonable representations of objects. Because of occlusion, in normal scenes, most objects are partly occluded by others. *Contour interpolation* processes connect visible contours across gaps caused by occlusion to produce perceptual units that correspond more accurately to the actual objects in a scene.

3.2.1. Tangent discontinuities and contour relatability

In recent years, we have learned a great deal about how interpolation processes proceed (for more details, see Kellman et al., 2001; Kellman & Shipley, 1991). These computations begin with contour intersections or *junctions*. Junctions are points of *tangent discontinuity*—places where contours have no unique orientation. Most often there are two orientations at image junctions. As can be seen in Fig. 1, interpolated contours begin and end at these tangent discontinuities in the image. These points include all of the places where edges go out of sight and need to be interpolated. It has been proposed that "end-stopped" cells in visual cortex (cells sensitive to the contours that end in their receptive fields) underlie junction detection (e.g., Heitger et al., 1992).

Interpolated contours not only begin at tangent discontinuities, but they agree with the slopes of visible contours that terminate at these connection points (see examples of Fig. 1). Contour interpolation can be summarized by saying that visual system interpolates according to a smoothness principle, called *contour relatability*, such that interpolated contours are smooth (differentiable at least once) and monotonic (singly inflected), and at their endpoints, they match the slopes of real contours. Fig. 3 shows a geometric construction defining relatability (Kellman & Shipley, 1991). Except for the additional constraint that interpolated edges bend by no more than 90°, relatability can be summarized by saying that edges are relatable if their linear extensions meet in their extended regions.

The notion of relatability in perceptual grouping is not the same as but is related to the principle of *good continuation*, proposed as one of several principles of perceptual organization in the early 20th century by the Gestalt psychologists (Wertheimer, 1958). Relatability

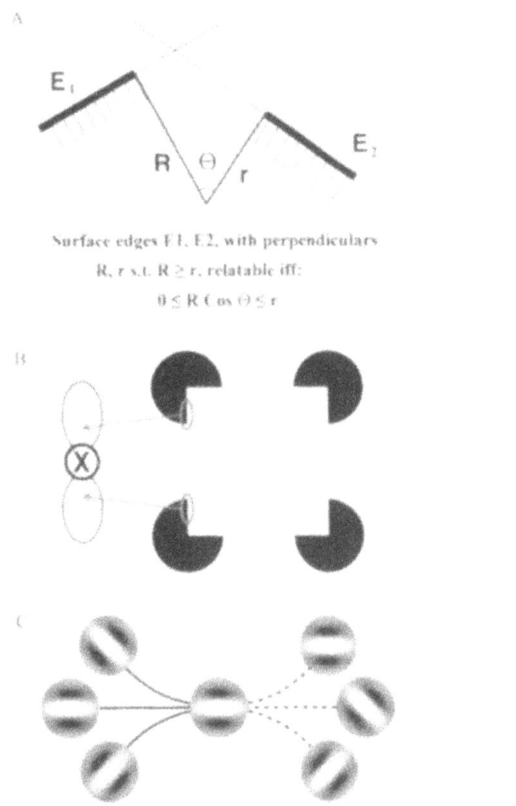

Fig. 3. (A) Relatability geometry (Kellman & Shipley, 1991); (B) bipole implementation of interpolation (Grossberg & Mingolla, 1985; Heitger et al., 1998); (C) network implementation (Field et al., 1993).

appears to tap into important regularities about the smoothness and predictability of objects (Geisler, Perry, Super, & Gallogly, 2001).

3.2.2. Quantitative variation in interpolation

The definition of relatability as given is categorical—it distinguishes contours that can be connected by interpolation from those that cannot. There is an important categorical aspect to these perceptual decisions, as perhaps their most important function is to allow us to perceive visible regions as connected or not. Even so, experimental data suggest that within the category of relatable edges, there are quantitative variations in strength (Field, Hayes, & Hess, 1993; Kellman & Shipley, 1991). Interpolation strength decreases as the angular relation between edges goes from collinear to near-zero at about 90°. It also rapidly declines with misalignment of parallel edges (Shipley & Kellman, 1992a).

Experimental results suggest that strength of contour interpolation depends not only on angular relations of edges but on their lengths and separation (Banton & Levi, 1992; Shipley & Kellman, 1992b). Specifically, over a wide range of image sizes, strength of interpolation seems to be proportional to: $(L_1 + L_2)/(L_1 + L_2 + g)$, where L_1 and L_2 are the lengths of (physically specified) relatable edges and g is the gap between them (Shipley & Kellman, 1992b).

3.2.3. Implementation of the relatability geometry

How are the relationships captured by the geometry of relatability implemented in neural mechanisms of vision? This is an active area of research. Several neural-style models of contour interpolation have been proposed (Grossberg & Mingolla, 1985; Heitger, von der Heydt, Peterhans, Rosenthaler, & K bler, 1998). There are two basic ideas about the mechanisms used by the visual system to surmount gaps. One is the use of higher-order operators, often called bipole cells. Real edge inputs on either side of a gap feed into these nonlinear grouping operators (Heitger et al., 1998). The activation of these operators, centered over a discontinuity in edge input, may be used to construct a contour that spans the gap (Fig. 3B).

Interpolation may also be carried out by an interactive network of orientation-signaling units (Field et al., 1993; Fig. 3C). According to this idea, luminance-defined edges activate some units, leading to facilitative interactions with other units that do not receive direct stimulus input. Interpolation occurs when a path of units, defined on either end by directly stimulated units, becomes active as the result of these interactions. Some models combine aspects of both bipole and network scheme (Grossberg & Mingolla, 1985).

Current models do not implement all that is known about the geometry of relatability or certain other influences on contour interpolation, such as support ratio (but see Grossberg, Mingolla & Ross, 1997). Yet, the basic concepts of cooperative (e.g. bipole) units and network interactions seem likely to be the building blocks of future advances. A virtue of both approaches is their use the outputs of orientation-sensitive cells in early cortical visual areas. The existence of extensive recurrent connections (connections feeding back from later levels to earlier ones) in the relevant cortical areas has been argued to support hybrid models (Grossberg & Mingolla, 1985) although other models (Heitger et al., 1998) have stressed purely feed-forward processing as a virtue. (For further discussion of the relation of geometric and neural models in object formation, see Kellman et al., 2001).

A controversial argument about the process as described above is the *identity hypothesis*—the claim that the same interpolation process applies to several different looking contour interpolation phenomena. These include the phenomena in Fig. 1. Occluded objects, illusory objects, and other cases of interpolation differ in appearance and involve differing assignments of depth and boundary ownership relative to adjacent surfaces. Despite these differences, in appearance, research indicates that an identical interpolation process operates in all of these cases (Kellman, Yin, & Shipley, 1998; Ringach & Shapley, 1996; Shipley & Kellman, 1992a). Some models (Grossberg & Mingolla, 1985) and recent evidence (Guttman & Kellman, 2000; Kellman et al., 2001) suggest a *promiscuous* early interpolation process that makes more connections than are realized in the final scene representation. Later

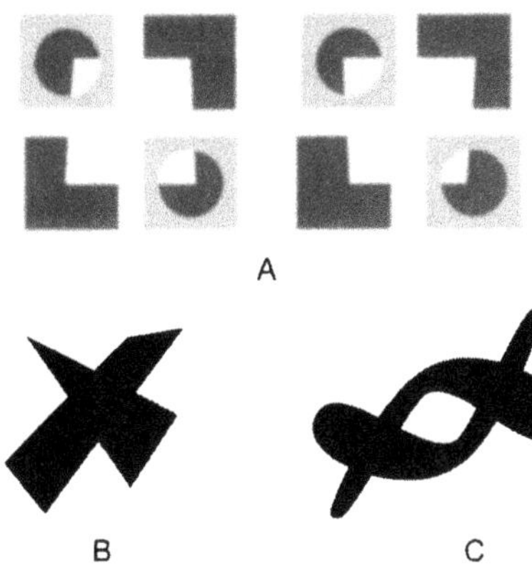

Fig. 4. (A) Illusory and occluded contours join. Display is a stereo pair; free-fuse by crossing the eyes. (B) and (C) Examples of homogeneous areas that split into two perceived objects (see text).

stages delete some interpolations and determine final depth arrangements of interpolated and other contours and surfaces.

Fig. 4 shows two phenomena that implicate a common interpolation process. Fig. 4A presents a stereo pair that may be free-fused by crossing the eyes to obtain a 3D display. (The effects to be described are also visible in each image alone, although less vividly due to all parts lying in a single depth plane.) The central white figure has 4 interpolated contours. Each one is an illusory contour for part of its length and an occluded contour along another part. That these *join* to form a single contour (or perhaps more to the point, that interpolation *occurs* between these two different kinds of endpoints) is significant and unexpected. It indicates that the interpolation process accepts either type of input, including combinations. This would be strictly prohibited in some models (Heitger et al., 1998), because of constraints on the inputs allowed to a given bipole operator. Fig. 4B (after Petter, 1956) shows a display having entirely homogeneous surface characteristics. This kind of display is an excellent demonstration and test of the basic segmentation and grouping concepts described above. Although one might expect a homogeneous region to be perceived as a single unified object, it splits into two perceived objects. The reason is the presence of the four tangent discontinuities in the concavities of the display, and the relatable edges leading into them. Once interpolation occurs, closed contours formed by real and interpolated edges define each of the two objects, the triangle and the quadrilateral.

This kind of display has some interesting properties relevant to the identity hypothesis. Where the two objects cross in the image, one appears in front, having illusory contours, and the other appears to pass behind, having occluded contours. With prolonged viewing of Fig. 4B, the depth order appears to switch, so that illusory contours become occluded ones and vice versa. There is an interesting regularity in such displays (Petter, 1956). Where interpolated boundaries cross, those crossing the smaller gap appear in front, as illusory contours, whereas the boundaries crossing the larger gap are seen behind, as occluded contours (Fig. 4C). The depth order ambiguity in Fig. 4B derives from the approximately equal lengths of interpolated edges. This claim about relative extent of interpolation, sometimes called Petter's Effect, has substantial experimental support and has been around for a long time. What has only recently been realized is that the effect provides a strong argument for an interpolation mechanism common to illusory and occluded contours. The reason is that in these displays, the determination of illusory vs. occluded appearance depends on a *comparison* of interpolated contours. Which appears in front depends on the relative lengths of crossing contours. If the illusory or occluded appearance of an interpolated contour depends on its length relative to a crossing interpolated contour, there must be, implicitly or explicitly, a length comparison process. This implies, in turn, that the locations and extents of contour interpolation are determined prior to their final appearance as illusory or occluded, at least in this case.

Several logical arguments of this kind as well as substantial experimental evidence combine to support the notion of a common underlying interpolation process, one that produces very precise and essentially identical representations of boundary locations in both illusory and occluded interpolation cases (Kellmam, Temesvary, Palmer, & Shipley, 2000; Kellman et al., 1998). Of course, different looking interpolation phenomena do involve differences in other aspects of scene representation, such as their depth relations with (projectively) adjacent surfaces.

The idea of a common perceptual process underlying illusory objects and occluded ones cuts against deep-seated assumptions in sensory and perceptual research. We will take up some of these issues in the last section.

3.2.4. Three-dimensional and spatiotemporal interpolation

Most interpolation research has addressed static, 2D displays. Some recent efforts have enlarged the domain to 3D and moving contours. It is clear that interpolation processes utilize 3D and motion-carried information and produce representations of 3D objects.

Fig. 5 shows 3D interpolation. Both rows show stereo pairs that should be free-fused by crossing the eyes.

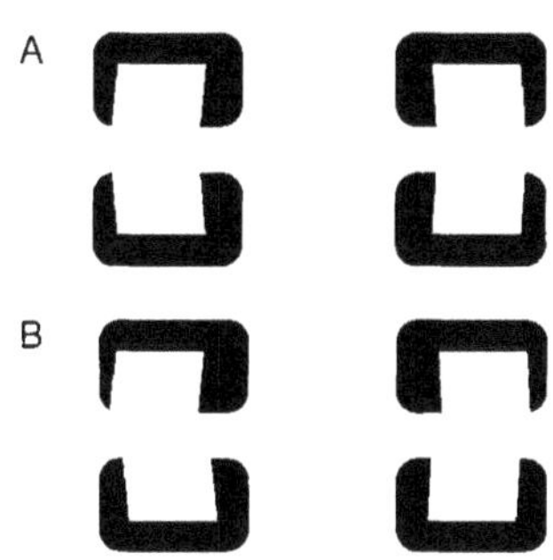

Fig. 5. 3D Interpolation displays (see text).

In Fig. 5A (and Fig. 4A above), illusory surfaces are visible. These utilize as inputs 3D orientations and positions of edges, and produce as outputs contours and surfaces traversing all three spatial dimensions. Fig. 5A and B shows one of the findings of our research (Kellman, Yin, Garrigan, Shipley, & Machado, 2003), namely that an expanded 3D principle of relatability appears to govern 3D interpolation. In Fig. 5A but not Fig. 5B, contours can be connected by a smooth, monotonic curve; an interpolated surface is seen in the former case, but not the latter. Also important for our perception of complete objects is dynamic information. Moving observers and moving objects produce changing patterns of occlusion. Our recent research (Palmer, Kellman, & Shipley, 1997) indicates that a notion of spatiotemporal relatability appears to govern which successively visible fragments get perceptually connected. It appears that briefly visible regions are encoded in a buffer, along with information about their velocity relative to the observer. The velocity information is used to extrapolate over time the positions of these stored fragments. As new contours and regions become visible, they are connected to the previously viewed regions following the geometry of spatial relatability, here applied to currently visible and previously stored regions in updated positions.

Results to date point to commonalities of interpolation processes in 2D, 3D, and dynamic object formation. Integrating these in more comprehensive accounts remains a research task of high priority.

3.3. Surface interpolation

Contour interpolation is not the only visual process that links visible areas; surface relations also play a role. In Fig. 6, note that the black circles in the display have no tangent discontinuities and therefore cannot participate in contour interpolation. Those circles that appear within interpolated edges of the surrounding black figure appear as holes. This is a manifestation of surface interpolation. In contrast, the black spot outside the figure appears as a spot on a surface. Likewise the white circles appear as holes through which the background is seen. Surface spreading behind occlusion links visible areas but provides little shape information; it is confined by real and interpolated contours. Visible regions are connected across gaps in the input based on the similarity of surface qualities (e.g. lightness, color, and texture). (For details and experimental work, see Yin, Kellman, & Shipley, 1997, 2000).

4. Separating processes in object perception

An important challenge in research on object perception is distinguishing processes that may be separate, functionally, computationally, and/or neurally. The challenge affects both the interpretation of empirical data and the construction of models. For models, separating processes improves understanding of what is going on and permits independent tests of assumptions and constructs. This becomes a high priority in the case of complicated models that incorporate large numbers of hypotheses, multiple processes, and interactions among them, perhaps including recurrent feedback and a combination of stimulus-driven processing and top-down influences (Grossberg, 1994). Although a model may simulate certain phenomena, it will also be imperfect in some respects. Tracking the sources of error and subjecting a particular theoretical construct to scientific test depend upon being able to isolate its effects. A companion problem arises empirically. Sometimes when outcomes of two experiments appear to conflict, the reason is that more than one process is at work. Different paradigms or stimuli may be differentially sensitive to the underlying processes.

In object perception, an important and instructive issue involves the contributions of relatively local, stimulus-driven processes and more global processes, involving familiarity, symmetry, or simplicity. The model we have described to this point has no influences from the latter. Interpolation based on contour relatability works equally well when the outcomes are familiar or unfamiliar, symmetric or asymmetric objects. Yet, global symmetry or familiarity have often been claimed to be important, perhaps beginning with the Gestalt notion of 'good form' (Wertheimer, 1923/1958). Kanizsa (1979) analyzed a number of cases in which local continuity conflicted with global symmetry, concluding that the latter is a weak or questionable contributor to object formation.

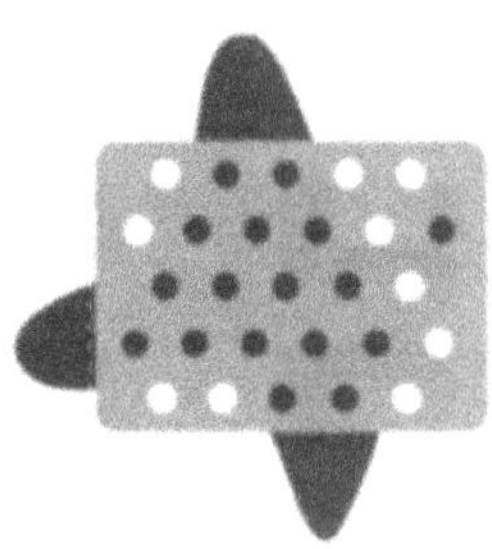

Fig. 6. Example of surface interpolation process that complements contour interpolation (see text).

Fig. 7. (A) Occlusion display sometimes claimed to support global (symmetric) interpolation. (B) Illusory contour version of occlusion display in (A). No global completion is seen.

The controversy about local vs. global effects has continued, however. Evidence from priming studies has been consistent with both local and global effects (Sekuler, Palmer, & Flynn, 1994; van Lier, van der Helm, & Leeuwenberg, 1995). Fig. 7A shows an example. Global completion entails seeing a fourth articulated part behind the occluder, making the display radially symmetric.

In the boundary interpolation process as I have described it here, there is no way to create a fourth lobe behind the occluder. Compare Fig. 7B. In this illusory contour version of the display in Fig. 7A, there is no hint of a fourth lobe. Indeed, no illusory contour studies have suggested completions based on global symmetry in this sort of situation.

Yet one can still make sense of the claim of some observers to see the symmetric completion in Fig. 7A. Specifically, in an occluded display, observers are aware that part of an object is hidden from view. Apart from relatively low-level contour interpolation processes, cognitive processes may allow the observer to recognize that the visible areas are consistent with some familiar or symmetric figure. We have called this process recognition from partial information (RPI). RPI is conceptually distinguishable from processes that fill in contours. For example, a view of a helicopter's tail protruding from behind a building is sufficient to activate a representation of a helicopter, although its hidden boundaries may not be specified by available information. RPI would be consistent with the fact that global effects seem to be reported primarily in priming paradigms, as priming is known to be influenced by processes at various levels, including high level cognitive ones (e.g. in bilinguals, the English word 'bread' can prime the French word for butter).

Reasoning in this way, we predicted that boundary interpolation and RPI might be distinguishable experimentally. The former might lead to representations of precise boundary location in hidden regions, whereas the latter might not. To measure the precision of boundary location, we used a dot localization paradigm in which an occluded display was presented, followed by a brief probe dot in front of the occluder, after which the display was masked. Subjects were instructed to respond on each trial whether the probe dot fell inside or outside the occluded object's boundaries (i.e. whether the projection of the occluded object to the eye would or would not encompass the dot).

Using adaptive staircase procedures (stimulus values change over trials depending on the subject's responses), we were able to estimate the 0.707 probability of seeing the dot as outside the boundary and 0.707 probability of seeing the dot inside the boundary (= 0.293 probability of outside), respectively. *Imprecision* was measured as the *difference* between these estimates, and accuracy as their *mean*.

Staircases for several stimulus patterns were interleaved, and screen position varied randomly.

Kellman, Temesvary, Palmer and Shipley (2000, 2003) tested occluded displays similar to those used in priming research (Sekuler et al., 1994). Different groups of subjects were instructed that the occluded display should be completed globally or locally in order to induce in each case the best possible performance.

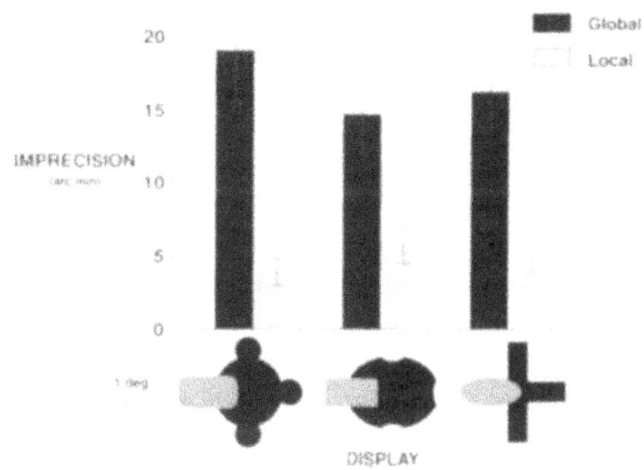

Fig. 8. Data from dot localization experiment. Imprecision in localization for the hidden boundary of each occluded figure is plotted, for global and local completion conditions (from Kellman et al., 2003).

Results showed that localization of boundaries in displays where completion is predicted by contour relatability was precise and accurate. Where completion is predicted to follow global symmetry, precision was far worse. Fig. 8 shows imprecision for several displays for both groups. Error in accuracy showed a similar pattern; subjects' judgments of the positions of boundaries predicted by global processes was very poor. This research suggests that global recognition processes may be experimentally separated from local boundary perception processes on the basis of the sorts of representations these create. Precise spatial positions of object boundaries are created in representations derived from latter process but not the former. These outcomes are consistent with the idea of separate perceptual completion and more cognitive RPI processes. Application of the dot localization method to illusory contour displays shows similar results: that real contours and illusory contours support good precision and accuracy of localization, whereas mere positional markers or displays with rounded tangent discontinuities do not (Guttman & Kellman, 2002).

5. Objects from interpolation: illusions, realities or representations?

What does it mean to say we *perceive* occluded regions of contours, surfaces, and objects? Do we really see them, or are they inferred? The issues are interesting, and they raise important questions about illusion, reality, and what it means to see.

The identity hypothesis, arguing for a common process in illusory and occluded contour completion, raises these issues directly, as these phenomena have traditionally been considered very different. Michotte (Michotte, Thines, &

Crabbe, 1964) labeled them as *modal* and *amodal* varieties of completion. Modal referred to the presence of sensory attributes, or modes, in the completed object, whereas amodal meant that the completed parts exist perceptually but without sensory attributes.

This distinction in phenomenology has most often led to a common sense conclusion. Illusory contours and surfaces are clearly *perceptual* phenomena, because we *see* them, i.e. they produce sensory experiences. Occluded contours and surfaces are out of sight, so in what sense can we be said to see them? They are *cognitive* phenomena; occluded parts are somehow known or inferred, not perceived.

Obviously, the account we sketched above clashes with this view of seeing vs. knowing. Where does the problem lie, in our unified account or in implicit conceptions of what it means to see?

The source of the problem, I believe, is confining the meaning of *seeing* to local sensory responses based on local physical data. Perceptual descriptions are functions of incoming information, but they need not be restricted to some narrow class of functions, such as a one-to-one correspondence between represented properties of objects and local sensations or stimuli.

This point has been made convincingly about once a generation in visual science, but it remains a source of abrasion between sensory and physiological approaches on one hand, and approaches to higher-order perception on the other. The Gestalt psychologists (Koffka, 1935; Wertheimer, 1958) presented a compelling case that perception is not a summation of local sensory responses. Gibson (1979) argued that sensations are actually quite incidental to perception. Rather than reviewing their arguments, perhaps the best way to sweep away the cobwebs here is to remind ourselves of the arguments for computation and representation in perception and information processing generally (Marr, 1982). On the computational/representational theory of mind, what is the principled difference between representing some contour as going behind another surface and representing some contour in front of another surface? Nothing. One is not more privileged or 'real' than the other. Characterizing one as a 'sensory' effect and the other a 'cognitive' effect reflects an epistemology that did not work out. Occluded contours are no more and no less 'inferred' than are illusory ones.

Given that there is no theoretical barrier separating represented contours and surfaces that are occluded or illusory, why do they *look* so different? What causes the robust difference in phenomenology? An answer is that this aspect of our phenomenology—the modal/amodal appearance—may simply code whether some surface or contour is nearest to the observer in some visual direction. This piece of information is important and, unlike the connectivity of objects, depends on the vantage point of the observer. Parts of an object that are nearest in a visual direction may be reached or grasped, whereas those equally real edges and surfaces behind some other object may not be reached without going around or through something.

The point is that all seeing is representational. So-called 'real' contours must be represented to be seen just as much as illusory or occluded ones. As we have seen, there is no basis for designating representations derived solely from local sensations as being the only 'real' ones. There are, however, multiple aspects of scenes that we need to represent. The connectivity of objects is one, best served by processes that are relatively indifferent to whether part of a contour goes behind or in front of something else. On the other hand, the reachability of a surface is a different aspect; it depends on the vantage point of the observer, and it is related to the phenomenology of modal/amodal. In the mind, there are not real contours, perceived contours, and inferred contours, only represented ones.

So, are interpolated parts of objects illusory or real? Our analysis brings us to a useful answer. For the representations needed for effective thought and action, encoding visible fragments alone would never do. Although faithful to local stimulation, such fragments are not the objects of the physical world. Interpolation processes pick up on basic regularities in the physical environment, probably as a result of evolutionary processes. As a result, they supply missing parts that lead to less faithful representations of the momentary image, but more accurate representations of the physical environment. In this sense they produce not illusions, but representations that bring us closer to reality.

Acknowledgements

Preparation of this paper was supported in part by a research grant from the National Eye Institute (R01 EY13518) to PJK. I thank Stephen Grossberg and an anonymous reviewer for comments on an earlier draft and Jennifer Vanyo for general assistance.

References

Banton, T., & Levi, D. M. (1992). The perceived strength of illusory contours. *Perception & Psychophysics*, *52*, 676–684.

Campbell, F. W., Cooper, G. F., & Enroth-Cugell, C. (1969). The spatial selectivity of the visual cells of the cat. *Journal of Physics*, *203*, 223–235.

Field, D., Hayes, A., & Hess, R. F. (1993). Contour integration by the human visual system: evidence for a local association field. *Vision Research*, *33*, 173–193.

Fischer, B., & Poggio, G. F. (1979). Depth sensitivity of binocular cortical neurons of behaving monkeys. *Proceedings of the Royal Society of London B*, *1157*, 409–414.

Geisler, W. S., Perry, J. S., Super, B. J., & Gallogly, D. P. (2001). Edge co-occurrence in natural images predicts contour grouping performance. *Vision Research*, *41*, 711–724.

Gibson, J. J. (1979). *The ecological approach to visual perception*. Boston: Houghton-Mifflin.

Grossberg, S. (1994). 3D vision and figure-ground separation by visual cortex. *Perception & Psychophysics, 55*(1), 48–120.

Grossberg, S., & Mingolla, E. (1985). Neural dynamics of form perception: boundary completion, illusory figures, and neon color spreading. *Psychoanalytic Review, 92,* 173–211.

Grossberg, S., Mingolla, E., & Ross, W. D. (1997). Visual brain and visual perception: how does the cortex do perceptual grouping? *Trends in Neurosciences, 20*(3), 106–111.

Guttman, S. E., & Kellman, P. J. (2000). Seeing between the lines: contour interpolation without perception of interpolated contours. *Investigative Ophthalmology and Visual Science, 41*(4), S439.

Guttman, S. E., & Kellman, P. J. (2002). Do spatial factors influence the microgenesis of illusory contours? [Abstract]. *Journal of Vision, 2*(7), 355a http://journalofvision.org/2/7/355/, DOI 10.1167/2.7.355.

Heitger, F., Rosenthaler, L., von der Heydt, R., Peterhans, E., & Kübler, O. (1992). Simulation of neural contour mechanisms: from simple to end-stopped cells. *Vision Research, 32,* 963–981.

Heitger, F., von der Heydt, R., Peterhans, E., Rosenthaler, L., & Kübler, O. (1998). Simulation of neural contour mechanisms: representing anomalous contours. *Image and Vision Computing, 16,* 407–421.

Hubel, D. H., & Wiesel, T. N. (1968). Receptive fields and functional architecture of monkey striate cortex. *Journal of Physics, 195,* 215–243.

Kanizsa, G. (1979). *Organization in vision*. New York: Praeger.

Kellman, P. J., & Arterberry, M. (1998). *The cradle of knowledge*. Cambridge, MA: MIT Press.

Kellman, P. J., Guttman, S., & Wickens, T. (2001). *Geometric and neural models of object perception. From fragments to objects: segmentation and grouping in vision (pp. 183–245)*, Amsterdam: Elsevier.

Kellman, P. J., & Shipley, T. F. (1991). A theory of visual interpolation in object perception. *Cognitive Psychology, 23,* 141–221.

Kellman, P. J., Temesvary, A., Palmer, E. M., & Shipley, T. F. (2000). Separating local and global processes in object perception: evidence from an edge localization paradigm. *Investigative Ophthalmology and Visual Science, 41*(4), S741.

Kellman, P.J., Temesvary, A., Palmer, E.M., & Shipley, T.F. (2003). Separating local and global processes in object perception, in preparation.

Kellman, P.J., Yin, C., Garrigan, P.B., Shipley, T.F., & Machado, L.J. (2003) Visual interpolation in three dimensions, in preparation.

Kellman, P. J., Yin, C., & Shipley, T. F. (1998). A common mechanism for illusory and occluded object completion. *Journal of Experimental Psychology: Human Perception and Performance, 24,* 859–869.

Koffka, K. (1935). *Principles of Gestalt Psychology*. NY: Harcourt, Brace & World.

Marr, D. (1982). *Vision*. San Francisco: W.H. Freeman.

Michotte, A., Thines, G., & Crabbe, G. (1964). *Les complements amodaux des structures perceptives*. Louvain, Belgium: Publications Universitaires de Louvain.

Palmer, E. M., Kellman, P. J., & Shipley, T. F. (1997). Spatiotemporal relatability in dynamic object completion. *Investigative Ophthalmology and Visual Science, 38*(4), S256.

Petter, G. (1956). Nuove ricerche sperimentali sulla totalizzazione percettiva. *Rivista di Psicologia, 50,* 213–227.

Ringach, D., & Shapley, R. (1996). Spatial and temporal properties of illusory contours and amodal boundary completion. *Vision Research, 36,* 3037–3050.

Sekuler, A. B., Palmer, S. E., & Flynn, C. (1994). Local and global processes in visual completion. *Psychological Science, 5,* 260–267.

Shipley, T. F., & Kellman, P. J. (1992a). Perception of partly occluded objects and illusory figures: evidence for an identity hypothesis. *Journal of Experimental Psychology: Human Perception and Performance, 18,* 106–120.

Shipley, T. F., & Kellman, P. J. (1992b). Strength of visual interpolation depends on the ratio of physically-specified to total edge length. *Perception & Psychophysics, 52,* 97–106.

van Lier, R. J., van der Helm, P. A., & Leeuwenberg, E. L. J. (1995). Competing global and local completions in visual occlusion. *Journal of Experimental Psychology: Human Perception and Performance, 21,* 571–583.

Wertheimer, M. (1958). Principles of perceptual organization. In D. C. Beardslee, & M. Wertheimer (Eds.), *Readings in perception*. Princeton, NJ: Van Nostrand, (Original work published 1923).

Yin, C., Kellman, P. J., & Shipley, T. F. (1997). Surface completion complements boundary interpolation in the visual integration of partly occluded objects. *Perception, 26,* 1459–1479.

Yin, C., Kellman, P. J., & Shipley, T. F. (2000). Surface integration influences depth discrimination. *Vision Research, 40,* 1969–1978.

PERGAMON

AVAILABLE AT
www.ComputerScienceWeb.com
POWERED BY SCIENCE @DIRECT

Neural Networks

Neural Networks 16 (2003) 925–931

www.elsevier.com/locate/neunet

2003 Special issue

Laminar cortical dynamics of visual form perception

Stephen Grossberg*,[1]

Department of Cognitive and Neural Systems, Center for Adaptive Systems, Boston University, 677 Beacon Street, Boston, MA 02215, USA

The neocortex is the seat of all higher biological intelligence. All sensory and cognitive neocortex is organized into layered circuits. How does Laminar Computing contribute to biological intelligence? A recent family of LAMINART models (Fig. 1) proposes a detailed answer to this question by characterizing how bottom–up, top–down, and horizontal interactions are organized within cortical layers to generate percepts of visual form. In particular, LAMINART shows how these interactions help visual cortex to realize: (1) stable development and learning of circuit connections and weights in response to a changing environment; (2) coherent grouping or binding of distributed information into boundary representations of objects and events without a loss of analog sensitivity—the property of *analog coherence*; and (3) attentional focusing on important object representations at the expense of less important representations (Grossberg, 1999a; Grossberg, Mingolla, & Ross, 1997; Grossberg & Raizada, 2000; Grossberg & Seitz, 2003; Grossberg & Williamson, 2001; Raizada & Grossberg, 2001, 2003; Ross, Grossberg, & Mingolla, 2000). Three exciting implications of this result are: first, biological vision systems are not merely bottom–up filtering devices, as Hubel and Wiesel (1977) had proposed in their Nobel prize winning analysis of early vision. Rather, even early processing stages of visual cortex group spatially distributed and incomplete information into 3D object representations. Second, even early visual processing is modulated by system goals via top–down expectations and attention. The laminar circuits provide an interface (in particular, between layers 6 and 4; see Fig. 1(b) and (c)) where data-driven bottom–up pre-attentive processing and task-directed top–down attentive processing fuse via a shared decision circuit. This modulatory decision circuit realizes at least three functional roles in the model: contrast normalization of bottom–up inputs; selection of winning groupings while preserving their analog coherence in response to intracortical feedback; and attentional priming in response to intercortical feedback from a higher cortical level. Third, mechanisms governing (1) in the infant lead to properties (2) and (3) in the adult. Thus, mechanisms that enable the cortex to learn stably way *define* key properties of adult visual information processing. This last result is important because it shows that learning and information processing need to be co-designed for either to work well in a novel environment. Data simulations include Gestalt grouping properties, fast synchronization, object-based attentional priming, interactions between attention and grouping, contrast–sensitive facilitation and suppression of groupings; and stable development of cortical circuits.

1. Bipole grouping, association field, and relatability conditions

One of the accomplishments of the LAMINART model has been to show how the *bipole grouping property* that was predicted in by Grossberg and colleagues in the early 1980s (Cohen & Grossberg, 1984; Grossberg, 1984; Grossberg & Mingolla, 1985a,b) is realized by horizontal interactions among identified cells in cortical layer 2/3; see Fig. 2. Since this original prediction was made, supportive evidence for the bipole prediction has come from neurophysiological experiments (von der Heydt, Peterhans, & Baumgartner, 1984; Peterhans & von der Heydt, 1989) and psychophysical experiments (Field, Hayes, & Hess, 1993; Kellman & Shipley, 1991). In particular, the 'association field' of Field et al. (1993) and the 'relatability conditions' of Kellman and Shipley (1991) are both consistent with grouping properties of the original bipole cell receptive field; see Kellman (this volume). The original Boundary Contour System (BCS) model of perceptual grouping (Grossberg & Mingolla, 1985a,b) clarified how both 'real' and 'illusory' contours could be completed by the same cortical mechanisms; see Kellman (this volume). A key difference between real and

* Tel.: +1-617-353-7858; fax: +1-617-353-7755.
E-mail address: steve@bu.edu (S. Grossberg).
[1] http://www.cns.bu.edu/Profiles/Grossberg

doi:10.1016/S0893-6080(03)00097-2

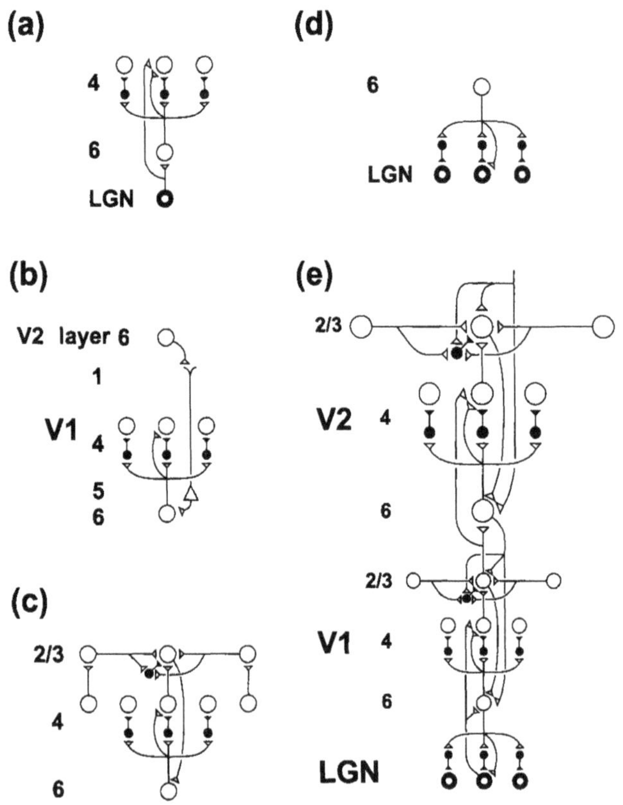

Fig. 1. How known cortical connections join the layer 6 → 4 and layer 2/3 circuits to form an entire V1/V2 laminar model. Inhibitory interneurons are shown filled-in black. (a) The LGN provides bottom–up activation to layer 4 via two routes. First, it makes a strong connection directly into layer 4. Second, LGN axons send collaterals into layer 6, and thereby also activate layer 4 via the 6 → 4 on-center off-surround path. The combined effect of the bottom–up LGN pathways is to stimulate layer 4 via an on-center off-surround, which provides divisive contrast normalization (Grossberg, 1973, 1980; Heeger, 1992) of layer 4 cell responses. (b) Folded feedback carries attentional signals from higher cortex into layer 4 of V1, via the modulatory 6 → 4 path. Corticocortical feedback axons tend preferentially to originate in layer 6 of the higher area and to terminate in layer 1 of the lower cortex (Salin and Bullier, 1995, p.110), where they can excite the apical dendrites of layer 5 pyramidal cells whose axons send collaterals into layer 6. The triangle in the figure represents such a layer 5 pyramidal cell. Several other routes through which feedback can pass into V1 layer 6 exist (see Raizada and Grossberg (2001) for a review). Having arrived in layer 6, the feedback is then 'folded' back up into the feedforward stream by passing through the 6 → 4 on-center off-surround path (Bullier, Hupé, James, & Girard, 1996). (c) Connecting the 6 → 4 on-center off-surround to the layer 2/3 grouping circuit: like-oriented layer 4 simple cells with opposite contrast polarities compete (not shown) before generating half-wave rectified outputs that converge onto layer 2/3 complex cells in the column above them. Just like attentional signals from higher cortex, as shown in (b), groupings that form within layer 2/3 also send activation into the folded feedback path, to enhance their own positions in layer 4 beneath them via the 6 → 4 on-center, and to suppress input to other groupings via the 6 → 4 off-surround. There exist direct layer 2/3 → 6 connections in macaque V1, as well as indirect routes via layer 5. (d) Top–down corticogeniculate feedback from V1 layer 6 to LGN also has an on-center off-surround anatomy, similar to the 6 → 4 path. The on-center feedback selectively enhances LGN cells that are consistent with the activation that they cause (Sillito, Jones, Gerstein, & West, 1994), and the off-surround contributes to length-sensitive (end-stopped) responses that facilitate grouping perpendicular to line ends. (e) The entire V1/V2 circuit: V2 repeats the laminar pattern of V1 circuitry, but at a larger spatial scale. In particular, the horizontal layer 2/3 connections have a longer range in V2, allowing above-threshold perceptual groupings between more widely spaced inducing stimuli to form (Amir, Harel, & Malach, 1993). V1 layer 2/3 projects up to V2 layers 6 and 4, just as LGN projects to layers 6 and 4 of V1. Higher cortical areas send feedback into V2, which ultimately reaches layer 6, just as V2 feedback acts on layer 6 of V1 (Sandell & Schiller, 1982). Feedback paths from higher cortical areas straight into V1 (not shown) can complement and enhance feedback from V2 into V1. Top–down attention can also modulate layer 2/3 pyramidal cells directly by activating both the pyramidal cells and inhibitory interneurons in that layer. The inhibition tends to balance the excitation, leading to a modulatory effect. (Reprinted with permission from Raizada and Grossberg (2001).)

illusory contours is that illusory contours, even when they are consciously recognized, may be 'amodal,' or perceptually invisible, because visibility is predicted to be a property of the surface processing stream of the visual cortex (namely the 'blob' stream from LGN through V4) rather than of the boundary processing stream of the visual cortex (namely the 'interblob' stream from LGN through V4).

2. Support for a prediction from adaptive resonance theory

Attention is realized within the LAMINART model via a top–down modulatory on-center off-surround network. For example, top–down signals from layer 6 of a higher cortical area reach layer 6 of a lower cortical area and then activate a modulatory on-center off-surround network from layer 6 to 4; see Fig. 1(b). The top–down circuit is modulatory because excitatory signals within the on-center of the network are approximately balanced by inhibitory signals. Such a circuit can prime, or sensitize, cells in the on-center to respond more effectively to expected bottom–up inputs, but cannot typically fire these cells on their own. Such a top–down circuit can also strongly inhibit cells in the off-surround. This type of network embodies a prediction of Adaptive Resonance Theory, or ART, from the 1970s that attention is realized by a modulatory top–down on-center off-surround network. Many recent psychophysical, neurophysiological, and anatomical data support this prediction; see Raizada and Grossberg (2003) for a review. This proposal of how ART mechanisms are realized within laminar cortical circuits the reason for the name LAMINART model. In addition to this *inter*cortical feedback pathway, there is an *intra*cortical feedback pathway from layer 2/3-to-6-to-4-to-2/3. Both pathways have been proposed to play an important role in stabilizing development and learning within neocortex, as well as in controlling adult perceptual grouping and attention (Grossberg, 1999a).

The modulatory top–down on-center off-surround circuit also clarifies many other data. For example, it suggests how volitional signals may allow top–down signals to fire target cells, and thereby lead to visual imagery, fantasy, and planning activities, and how breakdowns in the normal action of volition can lead to hallucinations (Grossberg, 2000).

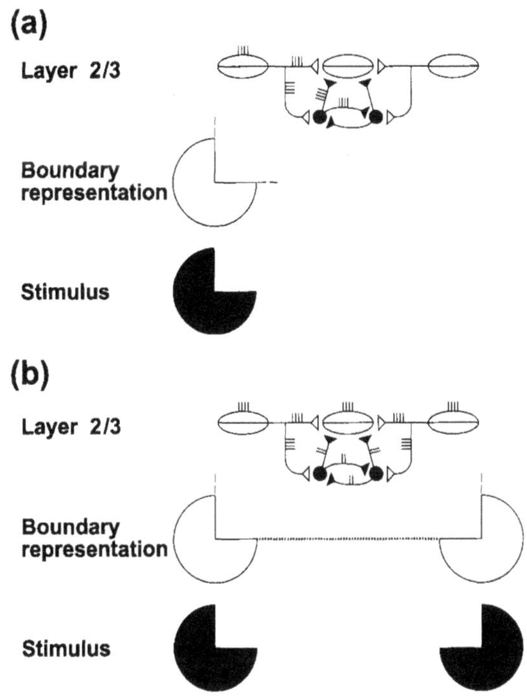

Fig. 2. Schematic of the boundary grouping circuit in layer 2/3. Pyramidal cells with colinear, coaxial receptive fields (shown as ovals) excite each other via long-range horizontal axons (Bosking, Zhang, Schofield, & Fitzpatrick, 1997; Schmidt et al., 1997), which also give rise to short-range, disynaptic inhibition via pools of interneurons, shown filled-in black (McGuire, Gilbert, Rivlin, & Wiesel, 1991). This balance of excitation and inhibition helps to implement the *bipole property*. (a) Illustration of how horizontal input coming in from just one side is insufficient to cause above-threshold excitation in a pyramidal cell (henceforth referred to as the target) whose receptive field does not itself receive any bottom–up input. The inducing stimulus (e.g. a Kanizsa 'pacman') excites the oriented receptive fields of layer 2/3 cells, which send out long-range horizontal excitation onto the target pyramidal. This excitation brings with it a commensurate amount of disynaptic inhibition. This balance of 'one-against-one' prevents the target pyramidal cell from being excited above-threshold. The boundary representation of the solitary pacman inducer produces only weak, sub-threshold colinear extensions (thin dashed lines). (b) When two colinearly aligned inducer stimuli are present, one on each side of the target pyramidal cell receptive field, a boundary grouping can form. Long-range excitatory inputs fall onto the cell from both sides, and summate. However, these inputs fall onto a shared pool of inhibitory interneurons, which, as well as inhibiting the target pyramidal, also inhibit each other (Tamas, Somogyi, & Buhl, 1998), thus normalizing the total amount of inhibition emanating from the interneuron pool, without any individual interneuron saturating. The combination of summating excitation and normalizing inhibition together create a case of 'two-against-one', and the target pyramidal is excited above-threshold. This process occurs along the whole boundary grouping, which thereby becomes represented by a line of suprathreshold-activated layer 2/3 cells (thick dotted line). Boundary strength scales in a graded analog manner with the strength of the inducing signals. (Reprinted with permission from Grossberg and Raizada (2000).)

3. D LAMINART model: stereopsis and 3D planar surface perception

The initial LAMINART model did not explain how the brain represents the 3D shape of objects, and their locations in depth. Earlier work on the Form-And-Color-And-DEpth (FACADE) model of 3D vision and figure–ground separation did propose analyses of how the boundary processing stream, modeled by the BCS, and the parallel surface processing stream, or Feature Contour System (FCS), work together during 3D vision. But this analysis was first developed without a laminar cortical interpretation (Grossberg, 1987a,b, 1994, 1997; Grossberg & Kelly, 1999; Grossberg & McLoughlin, 1997; Grossberg & Pessoa, 1998; Kelly & Grossberg, 2000; McLoughlin & Grossberg, 1998). A 3D LAMINART model (Fig. 3) has begun to synthesize the LAMINART and FACADE models to explain how the laminar circuits of visual cortex form 3D boundary and surface representations in cortical areas V2 and V4 (Grossberg & Howe, 2003).

3D vision poses challenging problems in distributed data processing and adaptive multi-dimensional data fusion because a single scenic feature causes spatially disparate inputs to the left and right eyes. The 3D LAMINART model proposes how these spatially disparate pairs of monocular features from the two eyes are spatially deformed into a single *fused* binocular representation; how, despite this spatial deformation, the fused representation achieves sharp selectivity to binocular disparity; how the fused data generate 3D boundary representations; and how 3D boundary representations capture the correct combinations of monocular brightness and color signals and trigger selective filling-in of visible 3D surface representations. In particular the model shows how to: join polarity-specific binocular matching with polarity-independent long-range grouping; implement the contrast constraint on binocular matching, whereby only similar contrasts in the two eyes can be binocularly fused; solve the classical Correspondence Problem, whereby only signals registered in the two eyes that come from the same object feature are fused; and combine monocular and binocular information to explain percepts like DaVinci stereopsis. DaVinci stereopsis is particularly important to explain because some parts of a scene are seen only monocularly due to occlusion by nearer objects. DaVinci stereopsis shows that these monocular regions inherit the depth that is computed at binocularly viewed parts of the scene. In other words, partial fusion can lead to total fusion.

As illustrated in Fig. 3, polarity-specific binocular matching in V1 occurs between layers 4 and 3B due to fusion at binocular simple cells in layer 3B of inputs from left eye and right eye signals from monocular simple cells with the same contrast–polarity sensitivity. Polarity-independent grouping begins between layers 3B and 2/3A, where inputs from like-oriented simple cells of the same disparity–sensitivity but opposite contrast polarity are fused at complex cells in layer 2/3A. The model has been used to quantitatively simulate key psychophysical data about binocular vision, including: contrast variations of dichoptic masking and the Correspondence Problem, the effect of interocular contrast differences on stereoacuity, Panum's limiting case, the Venetian blind illusion, stereopsis with

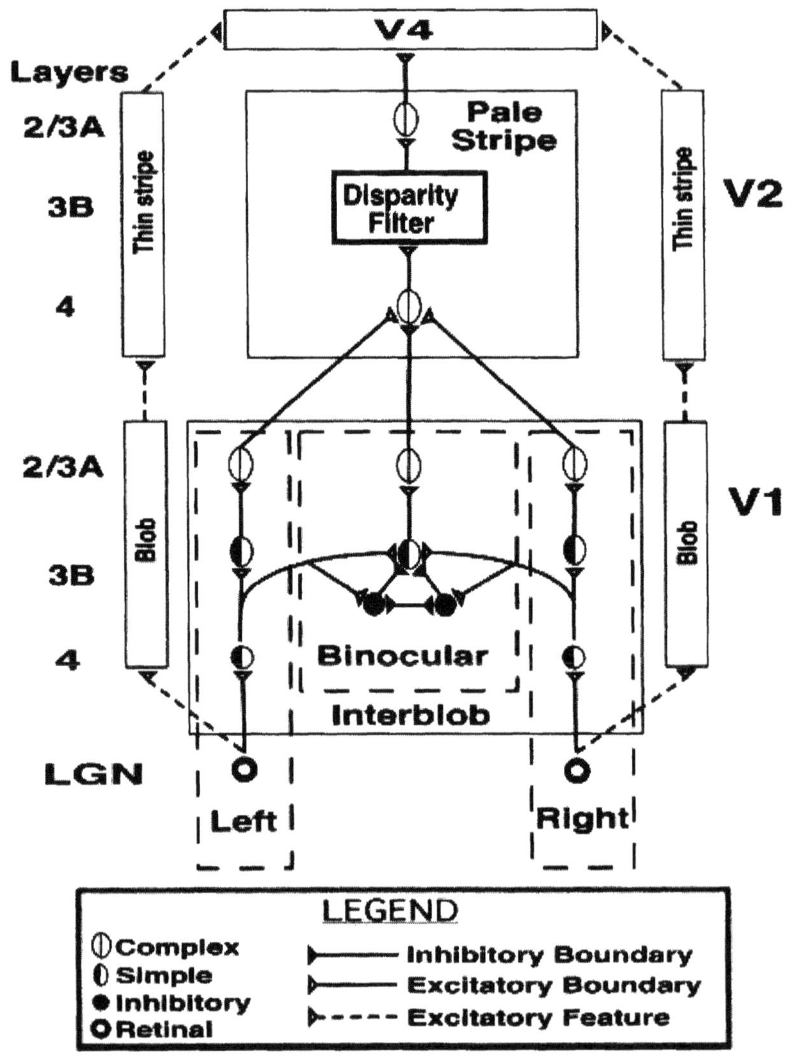

Fig. 3. 3D LAMINART model: See text for discussion. (Reprinted with permission from Grossberg and Howe (2003).)

polarity-reversed stereograms, DaVinci stereopsis, and various lightness illusions.

4. A synthesis of stereopsis, 3D planar grouping, and attention

The 3D LAMINART model has been used to explain and simulate data about stereopsis and 3D planar surface perception that do not require perceptual grouping or attention. An extension of the model that includes LAMINART model mechanisms of grouping and attention, as well as 3D mechanisms of stereopsis and 3D planar surface perception, is shown in Fig. 4. This model clarifies how displaced binocular cells in layer 2/3A can contact their monocular source cells via vertical signals from layer 2/3A to layer 5, which then contact the corresponding monocular cells in layer 6 via horizontal signals from layer 5 to 6.

5. Cross-stream learned alignment of boundary and surface representations: McCollough effect

There are many explanatory spin-offs from a sustained study of 3D vision. In particular, the process whereby depth-sensitive boundary representations are formed in V2 causes the perceived location of a fused binocular boundary to be shifted relative to the perceived positions of the individual monocular signals from the left and right eyes; e.g. at layer 3B in Fig. 3. To see this, just look at an object alternately with the left eye and right eye, with the other eye closed, and then open and close just one eye. Because of this displacement or allelotropia, the binocular boundaries are mis-aligned with respect to the monocular surface signals from each eye taken separately. In order for boundaries (within the BCS) to effectively control the filling-in of surface properties like lightness, color, and depth (within the FCS), the connections between the binocular boundaries and the corresponding monocular surface signals need to be adaptively re-aligned through

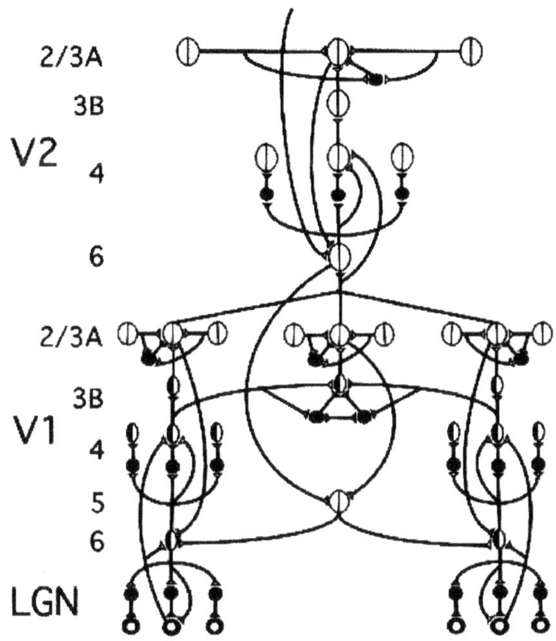

Fig. 4. 3D LAMINART synthesis of stereopsis, 3D planar perceptual grouping, and attention. (Reprinted with permission from Grossberg and Howe (2003).)

learning. This cross-stream learning process enables the model to quantitatively many challenging data about the McCollough effect, a long-term orientation-dependent chromatic aftereffect (Grossberg, Hwang, & Mingolla, 2002).

6. 3D representations of slanted and curved boundaries and surfaces: reset and bistability

Additional development of the 3D LAMINART model has clarified how laminar cortical circuits in V1 through V4 generate 3D representations of slanted and curved objects from both 2D images and 3D scenes (Grossberg & Swaminathan, 2003). A major issue here is how contextual interactions can disambiguate visual cues whose depth is locally ambiguous. For example, a parallelogram, when seen in isolation, may appear to lie on a flat plane. However, when it is part of a perspective drawing of a 3D cube, it can seem to be tilted either from near-to-far or from far-to-near in depth. The 3D interpretation of the parallelogram is disambiguated by the context in which it appears. Correspondingly, the model clarifies how: context-sensitive cell types (e.g. angle cells, colinear grouping cells, disparity-gradient cells) self-organize in cortical maps from a single set of laws (Grossberg & Williamson, 2001) and, when they interact together contextually, can activate the correct 3D boundary groupings, including groupings that can form across multiple depths. These groupings obey a 3D version of the relatability conditions; see Kellman (this volume).

This analysis also clarifies how surface filling-in can cross multiple depths without dissipating across space due to 'holes' at each depth plane in the slanted 3D boundaries that form filling-in barriers, and how 3D boundaries are formed and reset in response to rapidly changing imagery. The reset problem arises because positive feedback within and across the cortical layers (see Fig. 1) selects correct 3D boundaries from among many possible boundary groupings, while suppressing weaker or incorrect groupings. Without reset to break this positive feedback loop, hysteresis could occur, leading to massive smearing of visual representations in response to moving objects in a scene. Explanations of visual persistence, aftereffects, and bistable percepts like the Necker Cube and binocular rivalry follow from how the reset mechanism interacts with other cooperative and competitive feedforward and feedback circuits of the model (Francis & Grossberg, 1996a,b; Francis, Grossberg, & Mingolla, 1994; Grossberg, 1987b, 1994; Grossberg & Swaminathan, 2003). From a more general perspective, these results propose a radically different and new view of 3D geometry and how we use it to understand the world around us.

7. Future directions for laminar computing

A shared laminar design is found across many different parts of the neocortex. Future research may be expected to expand the number of phenomena that can be explained using a unified laminar theory, with different processes being analyzed as variations of an underlying general theory of laminar cortical design. The proposed role of ART-based mechanisms in ensuring stable development and learning of LAMINART model circuits provides a context for such additional studies. In particular, neural models of visual object learning and recognition (Bradski & Grossberg, 1995; Carpenter, 1997; Carpenter & Ross, 1995; Grossberg, 1999b; Grossberg & Williamson, 1999), visual motion perception (Chey, Grossberg, & Mingolla, 1997, 1998; Grossberg, Mingolla, & Viswanathan, 2001), visual search (Grossberg, Mingolla, & Ross, 1994), auditory perception and streaming (Grossberg, 1999b), and speech perception and word recognition (Grossberg, Boardman, & Cohen, 1997; Grossberg & Myers, 2000; Grossberg & Stone, 1986), among other competences, have been developed in which ART-based cortical mechanisms have played a central role in explaining many data which have no other explanation at the present time. It remains to be seen whether and how such mechanisms may be specialized within the laminar circuits of the other cortical areas that embody these several types of intelligent behavior.

Acknowledgements

Supported in part by the Air Force Office of Scientific Research (AFOSR F49620-01-1-0397) and the Office of Naval Research (ONR N00014-01-1-0624).

References

Amir, Y., Harel, M., & Malach, R. (1993). Cortical hierarchy reflected in the organization of intrinsic connections in Macaque monkey visual cortex. *Journal of Comparative Neurology*, *334*, 19–46.

Bosking, W. H., Zhang, Y., Schofield, B., & Fitzpatrick, D. (1997). Orientation selectivity and the arrangement of horizontal connections in the tree shrew striate cortex. *The Journal of Neuroscience*, *17*, 2112–2127.

Bradski, G., & Grossberg, S. (1995). Fast-learning VIEWNET architectures for recognizing three-dimensional objects from multiple two-dimensional views. *Neural Networks*, *8*, 1053–1080.

Bullier, J., Hupé, J. M., James, A., & Girard, P. (1996). Functional interactions between areas V1 and V2 in the monkey. *Journal of Physiology (Paris)*, *90*, 217–220.

Carpenter, G. A. (1997). Distributed learning, recognition, and prediction by ART and ARTMAP neural networks. *Neural Networks*, *8*, 1473–1494.

Carpenter, G. A., & Ross, W. D. (1995). ART-EMAP: A neural network architecture for object recognition by evidence accumulation. *IEEE Transactions on Neural Networks*, *6*, 805–818.

Chey, J., Grossberg, S., & Mingolla, E. (1997). Neural dynamics of motion grouping: From aperture ambiguity to object speed and direction. *Journal of the Optical Society of America A*, *4*, 2570–2594.

Chey, J., Grossberg, S., & Mingolla, E. (1998). Neural dynamics of motion processing and speed discrimination. *Vision Research*, *38*, 2769–2786.

Cohen, M. A., & Grossberg, S. (1984). Neural dynamics of brightness perception: Features, boundaries, diffusion, and resonance. *Perception and Psychophysics*, *36*, 428–456.

Field, D. J., Hayes, A., & Hess, R. F. (1993). Contour integration by the human visual system: Evidence for a local 'association field'. *Vision Research*, *33*, 173–193.

Francis, G., & Grossberg, S. (1996aa). Cortical dynamics of boundary segmentation and reset: Persistence, afterimages, and residual traces. *Perception*, *35*, 543–567.

Francis, G., & Grossberg, S. (1996bb). Cortical dynamics of form and motion integration: Persistence, apparent motion, and illusory contours. *Vision Research*, *36*, 149–173.

Francis, G., Grossberg, S., & Mingolla, E. (1994). Cortical dynamics of feature binding and reset: Control of visual persistence. *Vision Research*, *34*, 1089–1104.

Grossberg, S. (1982). Contour enhancement, short term memory, and constancies in reverberating neural networks. *Studies in Applied Mathematics*, *52*, 217–257. Reprinted in S. Grossberg (1982). Studies of mind and brain. Dordrecht, The Netherlands: D. Reidel Publishing Company.

Grossberg, S. (1980). How does a brain build a cognitive code? *Psychological Review*, *87*, 1–51.

Grossberg, S. (1984). Outline of a theory of brightness, color, and form perception. In E. Degreef, & J. van Buggenhaut (Eds.), *Trends in mathematical psychology*. Amsterdam: North-Holland.

Grossberg, S. (1987aa). Cortical dynamics of three-dimensional form, color, and brightness perception: I. Monocular theory. *Perception and Psychophysics*, *41*, 87–116.

Grossberg, S. (1987bb). Cortical dynamics of three-dimensional form, color, and brightness perception: II. Binocular theory. *Perception and Psychophysics*, *41*, 117–158.

Grossberg, S. (1994). 3-D vision and figure-ground separation by visual cortex. *Perception and Psychophysics*, *55*, 48–120.

Grossberg, S. (1997). Cortical dynamics of three-dimensional figure–ground perception of two-dimensional figures. *Psychological Review*, *104*, 618–658.

Grossberg, S. (1999aa). How does the cerebral cortex work? Learning, attention, and grouping by the laminar circuits of visual cortex. *Spatial Vision*, *12*, 16–185.

Grossberg, S. (1999bb). The link between brain learning, attention, and consciousness. *Consciousness and Cognition*, *8*, 1–44.

Grossberg, S. (2000). How hallucinations may arise from brain mechanisms of learning, attention, and volition. *Journal of the International Neuropsychological Society*, *6*, 583–592.

Grossberg, S., Boardman, I., & Cohen, M. A. (1997). Neural dynamics of variable-rate speech categorization. *Journal of Experimental Psychology: Human Perception and Performance*, *23*, 481–503.

Grossberg, S., & Howe, P. D. L. (2003). A laminar cortical model of stereopsis and 3D surface perception. *Vision Research*, *43*, 801–829.

Grossberg, S., Hwang, S., & Mingolla, E. (2002). Thalamocortical dynamics of the McCollough effect: Boundary-surface alignment through perceptual learning. *Vision Research*, *42*, 1259–1286.

Grossberg, S., & Kelly, F. J. (1999). Neural dynamics of binocular brightness perception. *Vision Research*, *39*, 3796–3816.

Grossberg, S., & McLoughlin, N. P. (1997). Cortical dynamics of three-dimensional surface perception: Binocular and half-occluded scenic images. *Neural Networks*, *10*, 1583–1605.

Grossberg, S., & Mingolla, E. (1985aa). Neural dynamics of form perception: Boundary completion, illusory figures, and neon color spreading. *Psychological Review*, *92*, 173–211.

Grossberg, S., & Mingolla, E. (1985bb). Neural dynamics of perceptual grouping: Textures, boundaries and emergent segmentations. *Perception and Psychophysics*, *38*, 141–171.

Grossberg, S., Mingolla, E., & Ross, W. D. (1994). A neural theory of attentive visual search: Interactions of boundary, surface, spatial, and object representations. *Psychological Review*, *101*, 470–489.

Grossberg, S., Mingolla, E., & Ross, W. D. (1997). Visual brain and visual perception: How does the cortex do perceptual grouping? *Trends in Neurosciences*, *20*, 106–111.

Grossberg, S., Mingolla, E., & Viswanathan, L. (2001). Neural dynamics of motion integration and segmentation within and across apertures. *Vision Research*, *41*, 2521–2553.

Grossberg, S., & Myers, C. W. (2000). The resonant dynamics of speech perception: Interword integration and duration-dependent backward effects. *Psychological Review*, *4*, 735–767.

Grossberg, S., & Pessoa, L. (1998). Texture segregation, surface representation, and figure–ground separation. *Vision Research*, *38*, 2657–2684.

Grossberg, S., & Raizada, R. D. S. (2000). Contrast–sensitive perceptual grouping and object-based attention in the laminar circuits of primary visual cortex. *Vision Research*, *40*, 1413–1432.

Grossberg, S., & Seitz, A. (2003). Laminar development of receptive fields, maps, and columns in visual cortex: The coordinating role of the subplate. *Cerebral Cortex*, in press.

Grossberg, S., & Stone, G. O. (1986). Neural dynamics of word recognition and recall: Attentional priming, learning, and resonance. *Psychological Review*, *93*, 46–74.

Grossberg, S., & Swaminathan, G (2003). *A laminar cortical model for the 3D perception of slanted and curved surfaces and images*. Submitted for publication.

Grossberg, S., & Williamson, J. R. (1999). A self-organizing neural system for learning to recognize textured scenes. *Vision Research*, *39*, 1385–1406.

Grossberg, S., & Williamson, J. R. (2001). A neural model of how horizontal and interlaminar connections of visual cortex develop into adult circuits that carry out perceptual grouping and learning. *Cerebral Cortex*, *11*, 37–58.

Heeger, D. J. (1992). Normalization of cell responses in cat striate cortex. *Visual Neuroscience*, *9*, 181–197.

von der Heydt, R., Peterhans, E., & Baumgartner, G. (1984). Illusory contours and cortical neuron responses. *Science*, *224*, 1260–126215.

Hubel, D. H., & Wiesel, T. N. (1977). Functional architecture of macaque monkey visual cortex. *Proceedings of the Royal Society of London, Series B*, *198*, 1–59.

Kellman, P. J., & Shipley, T. F. (1991). A theory of visual interpolation in object perception. *Cognitive Psychology*, *23*, 141–221.

Kelly, F., & Grossberg, S. (2000). Neural dynamics of 3-D surface perception: Figure–ground separation and lightness perception. *Perception and Psychophysics*, *62*, 1596–1618.

McGuire, B. A., Gilbert, C. D., Rivlin, P. K., & Wiesel, T. N. (1991). Targets of horizontal connections in macaque primary visual cortex. *The Journal of Comparative Neurology*, *305*, 370–392.

McLoughlin, N. P., & Grossberg, S. (1998). Cortical computation of stereo disparity. *Vision Research*, *38*, 91–99.

Peterhans, E., & von der Heydt, R. (1989). Mechanisms of contour perception in monkey visual cortex. II. Contours bridging gaps. *The Journal of Neuroscience*, *9*, 1749–1763.

Raizada, R. D. S., & Grossberg, S. (2001). Context-sensitive binding by the laminar circuits of V1 and V2: A unified model of perceptual grouping, attention, and orientation contrast. *Visual Cognition*, *8*(3/4/5), 341–466.

Raizada, R. D. S., & Grossberg, S. (2003). Towards a theory of the laminar architecture of cerebral cortex: Computational cues from the visual system. *Cerebral Cortex*, *13*, 100–113.

Ross, W. D., Grossberg, S., & Mingolla, E. (2000). Visual cortical mechanisms of perceptual grouping: Interacting layers, columns, and maps. *Neural Networks*, *13*, 571–588.

Salin, P., & Bullier, J. (1995). Corticocortical connections in the visual system: Structure and function. *Physiological Reviews*, *75*, 107–154.

Sandell, J. H., & Schiller, P. H. (1982). Effect of cooling area 18 on striate cortex cells in the squirrel monkey. *Journal of Neurophysiology*, *48*, 38–48.

Schmidt, K. E., Schlote, W., Bratzke, H., Rauen, T., Singer, W., & Galuske, R. A. W. (1997). Patterns of long range intrinsic connectivity in auditory and language areas of the human temporal cortex. *Society for Neuroscience Abstracts*, *415*(13), 1058.

Sillito, A. M., Jones, H. E., Gerstein, G. L., & West, D. C. (1994). Feature-linked synchronization of thalamic relay cell firing induced by feedback from the visual cortex. *Nature*, *369*, 479–482.

Tamas, G., Somogyi, P., & Buhl, E. H. (1998). Differentially interconnected networks of GABAergic interneurons in the visual cortex of the cat. *The Journal of Neuroscience*, *18*, 4255–4270.

AVAILABLE AT
www.ComputerScienceWeb.com
POWERED BY SCIENCE DIRECT

PERGAMON

Neural Networks 16 (2003) 933–938

Neural Networks

www.elsevier.com/locate/neunet

2003 Special issue

Moving objects appear to slow down at low contrasts

Stuart Anstis*

Department of Psychology, University of California, San Diego, 9500 Gilman Drive, La Jolla, CA 92093-0109, USA

Abstract

Moving cars give the illusion of slowing down in foggy conditions, because low contrast reduces perceived speed. A grey square that drifts horizontally across a surround of black and white vertical stripes appears to stop and start as it crosses each stripe, because its contrast keeps changing. A moving square whose vertical and horizontal edges have different contrasts will show illusory distortions in perceived direction. Contrast also affects the apparent amplitude and salience of back-and-forth apparent motion. Finally, a line of black and white dots on a grey surround moves in illusory directions, because of a mismatch in the contrasts along and across the dotted line. Thus, motion signals in the early parts of the visual system are profoundly altered by stimulus luminance and contrast. This suggests that motion is coded by the relative firing rates of neural channels tuned to fast and slow motion, with contrast-dependence being a motion analog of the Bezold–Brucke hue shift.

Keywords: Contrasts; Luminance; Motion perception; Speed perception

1. Introduction

Motion perception allows us to keep track not only of moving objects, but also of our own movements through space (Gibson, 1950; Nakayama, 1985). It also provides valuable raw material for neural modelers. One might guess that motion is a recent evolutionary development, but in fact, as Walls (1942) pointed out, motion perception is one of the most ancient and primitive forms of vision. A hungry frog will starve to death on a heap of plump dead flies, but if one of these flies is jerked around on a fishing line in front of the frog, it will immediately snap up the insect and eat it up. Motion plays a crucial part in the constant arms race between predators and prey. Lions and gazelles have excellent vision for motion, gazelles so that they can see the big cats creeping up on them and predators so that they can track the hasty flight of their prey. Lions will stalk their prey stealthily making minimal movements, and young gazelles will often freeze as a defensive measure, in an effort to outfox the motion perception of the other species.

The range of speeds that we can see is an impressive 1000:1. The moon's slow sail across the sky is too slow, but only just too slow, for us to see. It moves through 360° of visual angle in 24 h, or 0.25 min arc per second of time. Stated differently, it moves through its own diameter in a time of 2 min. The fastest speed we can resolve is about a thousand times faster, depending on illumination and adaptation.

We can run no faster than about 10 mph. Modern cars have increased this speed 10-fold, to a maximum of 100 mph. Nowadays we could hardly live without cars—but it is easy to die in them, since the stopping distance of a vehicle goes up with the square of the velocity, from 4 ft at 10 mph to a frightening 400 ft at 100 mph. And that is on a good dry road in ideal conditions! No wonder that car accidents are the leading cause of death for people between the ages of 5 and 44. One cause of accidents that can be avoided is driving too fast in the fog. For example, on November 4th, 2002, nearly 200 cars and big-rig trucks collided in heavy fog on the Long Beach Freeway, injuring dozens of people, including nine critically. A mangled mess of cars, vans and big-rig trucks shutdown the freeway, about 25 miles south of Los Angeles, for nearly 11 h. Authorities said some motorists were driving too fast for the foggy conditions. Estimates are that cars were moving at 25–35 mph. In the state of Wisconsin alone, about 1200 vehicle accidents occur each year when dense fog is a factor. This results in about 16 deaths and 700 injuries. Nationally, an average of 950 people die in winter-related road accidents each year. Many of these could be avoided.

What can be done? Often fog simply makes other cars invisible. Motorists do not see them and crash into them, and visual science can do nothing about this, although IQ testing

* Tel.: +1-858-534-5456; fax: +1-858-534-7190.
E-mail address: sanstis@ucsd.edu (S. Anstis).

0893-6080/03/$ - see front matter © 2003 Elsevier Science Ltd. All rights reserved.
doi:10.1016/S0893-6080(03)00111-4

might help. But at other times fog makes other cars somewhat less visible without hiding them completely, and other motorists misjudge them. Here visual science can perhaps make a useful contribution. Many anecdotes suggest that during a fog, other cars and also one's own car appear to move more slowly than their actual speeds. My recent findings attribute both phenomena to the fact that objects *appear to move more slowly when they are low in contrast*, as they are in a fog. (Note: 'Contrast' refers throughout this paper to the measurable stimulus property of differences in luminance. It does not refer to the 'simultaneous contrast', or illusory brightness induction, that is caused by lateral inhibition.) In a fog, other cars are reduced in contrast so they appear to be going more slowly than they really are. Also, a driver judges his own speed largely by visual cues from the landscape as it slides past him, often viewed through the side windows of the car in peripheral vision (Anstis, 1998). Fog reduces the contrast of the passing landscape, so it appears to slip by him more slowly and he believes that he himself is driving slowly.

2. Results

It is known that apparent speed varies with contrast (Stone & Thompson, 1992; Thompson, 1982; Thompson & Stone, 1997; Thompson, Stone, & Swash, 1996). I have found some novel and direct demonstrations of these illusory changes in apparent speed. Two squares, one of them light grey and the other one dark grey, moved horizontally at constant speed across a stationary surround of vertical stripes (Fig. 1). Each square was exactly two stripe widths in diameter, so that its front and back edges always lay on the same color (black or white). I found that the two squares appeared to stop and start in alternation, depending upon their local contrast. When the dark grey square lay on white stripes it had high contrast (dark versus white) and appeared to speed up momentarily. When it lay on black stripes it had low contrast (dark versus black) and appeared to slow down. The opposite was true for the light grey square. Consequently the two squares appeared to speed up and slow down in alternation, like a pair of walking feet. So I called this the 'footsteps illusion' (Anstis, 2001, 2003). In this display you see the contrast altering the apparent speed in real time. The illusion is very strong, particularly in peripheral vision, where the squares can appear to stop dead and re-start, about once every second or so.

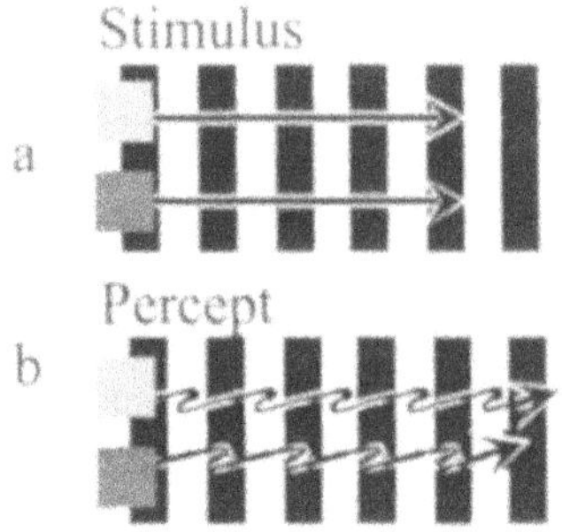

Fig. 1. The footsteps illusion. A light and a dark grey square move together at constant speed across stationary stripes. As they alternately change from high to low contrast, they seem to alternate between high and low speeds.

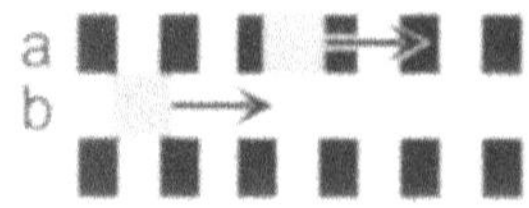

Fig. 2. The upper square shows the footsteps illusion because its leading and trailing edges change contrast as it traverses the stripes. The lower square shows no illusion because only its irrelevant top and bottom edges change in contrast.

I examined which parts of the stimulus cause the footsteps illusion. I moved the squares along a narrow horizontal 'railway track', so that only the front and back edges of the squares contacted the stripes. The illusion was still present in full force (Fig. 2a). Then I moved the squares along a narrow 'clear track' cut through the stripes, so that only the top and bottom edges of the squares contacted the stripes. The illusion vanished (Fig. 2b). Thus, motion computations are local to the moving edges (Fig. 3).

Contrast affects not only smooth real movement, but also stroboscopic apparent movement. A black square and a white square, one above the other, jumped back and forth horizontally through a distance of one-quarter of the square's width. On a dark surround, the white square appeared to jump through a greater distance, because it had a higher contrast. On a light surround, the black square appeared to jump through a greater distance, because now it was the square with higher contrast. This was particularly true in peripheral vision. Here the contrast affects the apparent amplitude of motion, not its apparent speed. This was a true motion illusion; it was not simply a misperception of the position of the two end-points of the motion, because separate experiments showed that the judged positions of stationary squares were not affected by contrast.

Here is another case of contrast affecting stroboscopic as well as real motion. In Fig. 4, two vertical bars, one black and one white, lie side by side but not touching on a grey

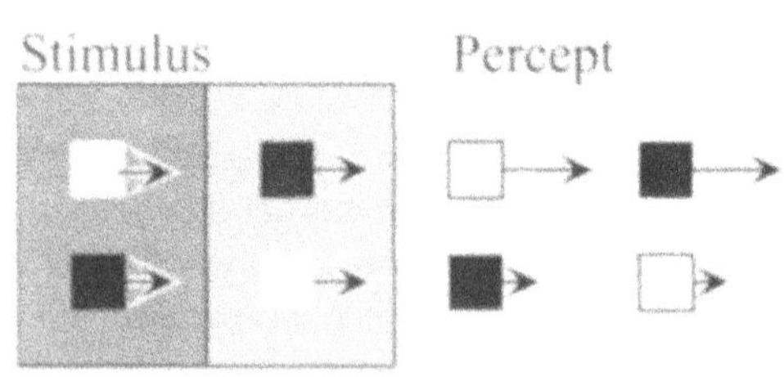

Fig. 3. All squares jump back and forth through exactly the same distance. However, the top squares have higher contrasts against their surrounds, so they appear to move further than the bottom squares.

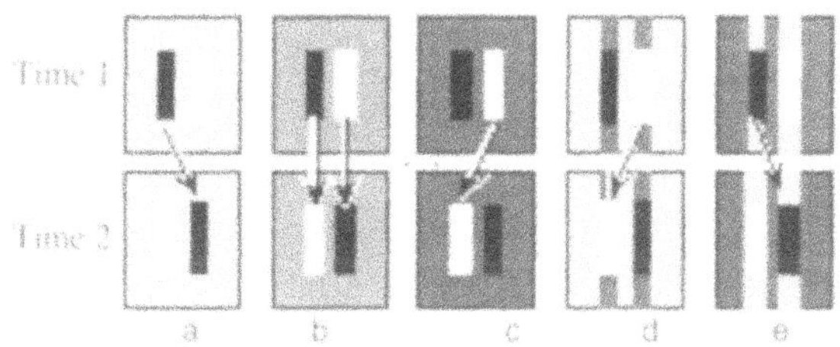

Fig. 4. A black and a white bar abruptly exchange luminances. On a light grey surround (a), the black bar appears to jump, but on a dark grey surround (c), the white bar appears to jump. A mid-grey surround (b) gives little motion. Embedding bars (d) and (e) influence motion more than the rest of the surround does. Thus the bar with the higher contrast against the surround appears to jump.

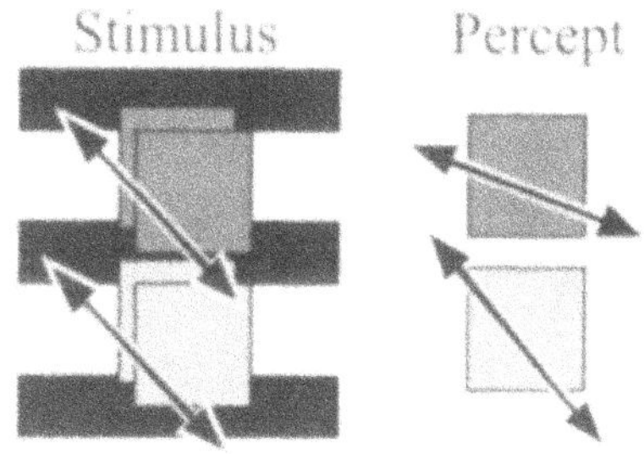

Fig. 5. Squares jumping obliquely. On left, the positions of the squares at times $T1$, $T2$ are shown overlapping. Actual jumps were oblique at 45°, but different contrasts on vertical and horizontal edges altered the perceived motion paths (right).

surround. Suddenly the black bar becomes white and at the same instant the white bar becomes black. What will this look like? Will an observer see the two bars simply exchanging luminances? Or will the black bar appear to jump to the right? Or the white bar to the left? Or will both bars appear to jump past each other in opposite directions? It turns out that the result depends upon the luminance of the surround (Anstis & Mather, 1985; Anstis, Smith, & Mather, 2000; Mather & Anstis, 1995). On a light grey surround, the black bar appears to jump, but on a dark grey surround, the white bar appears to jump. In other words the bar with the higher contrast against the surround appears to jump. I showed, in experiments that I shall not detail here, that the two bars generated motion signals in opposite directions, but the stronger signal predominated in a winner-take-all outcome. An analogous case would be two overlapping, superimposed gratings of vertical bars drifting in opposite directions. Both gratings have the same speed and spatial frequency. If they also have the same contrast, an observer sees a counterphase grating that flickers in place. However, if (say) the rightward grating has a higher contrast, one sees next motion to the right. Once again the two opposed motion signals compete and the stronger one wins.

When the black and white bars in Fig. 4 exchanged luminances, the perceived motion vanished when the surround was mid-grey, at the arithmetic mean of black and white. This mid-grey gave the black and white bars equal Michelson contrasts, defined as (Max − Min)/(Max + Min). In the footsteps illusion described earlier, the illusory accelerations also disappeared when the moving square was mid-grey, at the arithmetic mean of the black and white stripes. This meant that its Michelson contrast stayed the same as it crossed the stripes. Interestingly, only the amount of contrast mattered, not its polarity.

Contrast-based motion illusions can be applied to different parts of a single moving object. Two squares, one light grey and the other dark grey, jumped back and forth obliquely, at 45° from the vertical, across a horizontally striped surround (Fig. 5).

The squares were placed so that their top and bottom edges contacted black stripes, whereas their left and right edges contacted white stripes. So the dark grey square's top and bottom edges contacted a black surround and had low contrast. This reduced the effective vertical component of the dark square's oblique motion. Its left and right edges contacted a white surround and had high contrast. This enhanced the horizontal component of its motion. The result was that the dark square appeared to move back and forth between 10 o'clock and 4 o'clock. The opposite was true for the light square, which appeared to move back and forth between 11 o'clock and 5 o'clock. So contrast could alter the perceived direction of motion, as well as its perceived speed. Fortunately this does not usually happen on the road. It would be as if painting one fender of a car black and the other fender white made the whole car appear to move obliquely.

Ends of lines. I found two extreme cases in which different parts of an object move differently: the ends of a moving line are far more important in determining its seen motion than the middle part.

(1) In the well-known *aperture problem*, a long straight line moves behind a circular aperture. The motion of the middle of the line is ambiguous; usually the ends of the line reveal its true motion, but when the aperture hides the end-points the motion remains ambiguous (Adelson & Movshon, 1982). I have found that an aperture problem can arise even without an aperture! A new *peripheral-oblique* phenomenon shows that motion perception is more contrast-dependent in the periphery than in central vision. An oblique grey line oscillated up and down vertically on a black surround, at a rate of 1 Hz and at a retinal eccentricity of 15°, during strict fixation. Since the ends and the middle of the line were all equally visible, the line was correctly seen as moving vertically. However, if the line was made really dim its trajectory appeared to veer round toward the oblique, and by the time it was just above threshold it appears to move at 45°, at right angles to its own orientation. What mattered was the stimulus contrast of the line, not its luminance. This was shown with the photographic negative of the previous setup. A grey line on a white surround was seen correctly, but as it was made lighter and less clearly visible, it also changed its perceived direction of motion

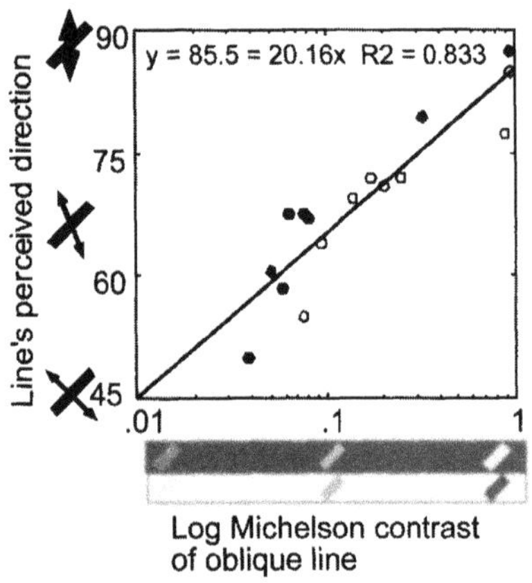

Fig. 6. An oblique peripheral line moving up and down was seen correctly at high contrasts. At low contrasts its ends became invisible and it seemed to move at 45°, at right angles to it own length. Results were the same for a white surround (filled symbols) and a black surround (open symbols).

towards 45°. So a dark line on a black surround, and a light line on a white surround, both showed the same illusory motion (Fig. 6). The reason is that at low contrast and in peripheral vision the terminators start to lose visibility, and with it their ability to influence the perceived direction of motion. The aperture problem can be solved only if the terminators reach some criterion level of contrast—otherwise they are ignored. Eccentricity makes the terminators less visible than the line center; perhaps they are under sampled and stimulate only one receptive field whilst the central portion of the line stimulates a whole row of receptive fields.

(2) Conversely, I pitted the contrast of the ends and of the middle of a line against each other by combining crossover motion with *White's effect* (1979, 1981). We saw in Fig. 4a and c that when a light and a dark bar exchanged luminances on a spatially uniform surround, motion was assigned to the bar that differed most from the surround. I now applied different surrounds to different parts of the bars, by embedding each bar in a long vertical dark line on a light surround, or vice versa (Fig. 4d and e). A titration method showed that the embedding lines were three times as important as the surround in driving apparent motion. For example, lightening (or darkening) the embedding lines by 0.1 log units shifted the motion balance in favour of the darker (lighter) test bar, and the surround had to be darkened (lightened) by as much as 0.3 log units to redress the balance. I conclude that motion strength is determined by contrast of the test bars against the embedding lines, not against the rest of the surround.

Here is another example of contrast affecting perceived direction (Cavanagh & Anstis, 2002; Ito & Anstis, 2002 and unpublished). Fig. 7a shows two lines forming a shallow V. Put a pen tip at the tail of the arrow and move the pen to the left, toward the tip of the arrow. Or simply hold the pen tip stationary and move the page to the right under the pen. Gaze at the pen tip but attend to the two lines. They will

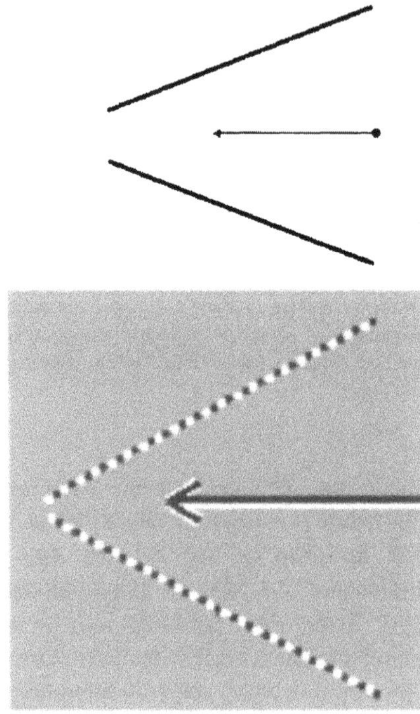

a

b

Fig. 7. (a) Move a pen tip to the left along the arrows; black lines appear to converge inwards, but (b) dotted lines appear to move outwards.

appear to move closer together. This is not surprising because the lines really are closer to the fovea when the pen is shifted to the left. But now do the same for the two dotted lines in Fig. 7b. These lines appear to move *outwards*.

Fig. 8 shows the reason. When a long, straight line moves, its motion is ambiguous because the component of

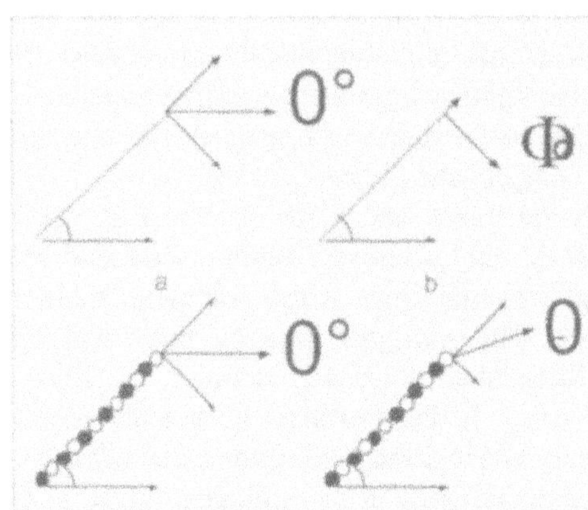

c d

Fig. 8. (a) When an oblique black line moves horizontally to the right (top arrow), its motion can be decomposed into one vector along the line and another at right angles to the line (oblique arrows). (b) Since a straight line is invariant under motion along its axis, the vector along its axis is not perceived. Only the orthogonal vector is seen, and the line appears to move at right angles to its own length in direction Ø. (c) A moving dotted line can be similarly decomposed into two vectors. (d) Now the vector along the axis is seen, or even overestimated, whilst the orthogonal vector is underestimated. Motion is perceived in a direction *O*, closer to the line's orientation.

motion along its length produces no changes at the retina. Thus a straight line is invariant under motion along its own length. If a 45° oblique black line moves horizontally to the right, its motion can be decomposed into a component along its length, which is not seen, and a component at right angles to its own length. Result: The line is perceived as moving obliquely down, at right angles to its own length (Fig. 8a and b). But when a 45° oblique dotted line moves to the right, its motion can again be decomposed into two components, one along its length and the other at right angles to its own length. For the dotted line, however, the contrast along its own length (between black dots and white dots) is about twice as high as the contrast at right angles to its own length (between black dots and the mid-grey surround, or between white dots and the mid-grey surround). So the motion along the line's length, instead of being invisible, is highly visible and high in contrast, so that it predominates over the motion across the line (Fig. 8c and d). The resulting perceived motion is the vector sum of these two components, and the line is perceived as moving almost parallel to its own length.

3. Discussion

All these contrast-based illusions of motion are compatible with models of motion coding that use velocity-tuned neural units, each tuned to a different range of speeds. Such units have been found in primate MT (Allman, Miezin, & McGuinness, 1985; Maunsell & Van Essen, 1983; Mikami, Newsome, & Wurtz, 1986; Zeki, 1974). Let us briefly compare motion coding to color coding. The retina contains three types of cones, namely R, G and B, sensitive, respectively, to long, medium and short wavelengths. The cones have broad, overlapping spectral sensitivity curves, so that a given wavelength stimulates more than one cone type, and each wavelength is coded neurally as the ratio of firing in different cones. For instance, a particular yellow might stimulate the R and G cones equally. If the luminance of the yellow increased, then so would the firing rate of the R and the G cone—in theory by an equal amount, so that the firing ratio R/G would successfully encode a particular yellow despite changes in luminance. However, this compensation for luminance changes is not perfect, and in fact hues do tend to change their appearance, moving toward yellow and blue, and away from green and purple, as the luminance is increased (Fry, 1983). This is the Bezold–Brucke illusion (Pridmore, 1999) and probably reflects a nonlinearity in which the firing rate in one cone, or more likely in one opponent-color pathway, increases more rapidly with luminance than another. The contrast illusions described in the present paper may simply be motion analogs of the Bezold–Brucke effect, in which a medium velocity might stimulate a slow and a fast detector equally. In a perfect system, changes in stimulus contrast would increase the firing of a slow and a fast detector by exactly the same amount, so that the firing ratio Fast/Slow would successfully encode a particular medium speed despite changes in contrast. However, this compensation for changes in contrast may not be perfect. I suggest that the apparent increases in speed with contrast arise because responses of fast detectors grow more rapidly with contrast than do slow detectors. Note that colors show small illusory changes with luminance, whereas in our displays motion shows large illusory changes with contrast.

A series of papers by Grossberg and his colleagues (Chey, Grossberg, & Mingolla, 1997, 1998; Grossberg & Rudd, 1992) offer a far more sophisticated approach along these lines. Their neural network model represents visual velocity as a distributed population code of speed-tuned units, in which the size of a unit's receptive field is correlated with its preferred speed. A key aspect of their model is that larger cells need to have higher thresholds, and that they compete in specific, albeit simple, ways. Their multiple broadly speed-tuned detectors explain a great deal of data about speed estimation and discrimination, and in particular the relationship between contrast and perceived speed. The authors successfully simulated data from Thompson et al. showing that higher contrast increases perceived speed. Moreover, their model can be extended to cover motion grouping and vector coding of motion (Grossberg, Mingolla, & Viswanathan, 2001).

Drive carefully in the fog.

Acknowledgements

Supported by grants from the UCSD Department of Psychology and Academic Senate.

References

Adelson, E. H., & Movshon, J. A. (1982). Phenomenal coherence of moving visual patterns. *Nature*, *300*, 523–525.

Allman, J., Miezin, F., & McGuinness, E. (1985). Direction and velocity specific response from beyond the classical receptive field in the middle temporal visual area, (MT). *Perception*, *14*, 105–126.

Anstis, S. M. (1998). Picturing peripheral acuity. *Perception*, *27*, 817–825.

Anstis, S. M. (2001). Footsteps and inchworms: illusions show that contrast affects apparent speed. *Perception*, *30*, 785–794.

Anstis, S. M. (2003). Levels of motion perception. In L. Harris, & M. Jenkin (Eds.), *Levels of Perception*. New York: Springer.

Anstis, S. M., & Mather, G. (1985). Effects of luminance and contrast on direction of ambiguous apparent motion. *Perception*, *14*, 167–179.

Anstis, S. M., Smith, D. R., & Mather, G. (2000). Luminance processing in apparent motion, Vernier offset and stereoscopic depth. *Vision Research*, *40*, 657–675.

Cavanagh, P., & Anstis, S. (2002). The boogie-woogie illusion. *Perception*, *31*, 1005–1011.

Chey, J., Grossberg, S., & Mingolla, E. (1997). Neural dynamics of motion grouping: from aperture ambiguity to object speed and direction. *Journal of the Optical Society of America*, *14*, 2570–2594.

Chey, J., Grossberg, S., & Mingolla, E. (1998). Neural dynamics of motion processing and speed discrimination. *Vision Research*, *38*, 2769–2786.

Fry, G. A. (1983). The Bezold–Brucke phenomena at the two ends of the spectrum. *American Journal of Optometry and Physiological Optics*, *60*, 977–981.

Gibson, J. J. (1950). *The Perception of the Visual World*. Boston: Houghton Mifflin.

Grossberg, S., Mingolla, E., & Viswanathan, L. (2001). Neural dynamics of motion integration and segmentation within and across apertures. *Vision Research*, *41*, 2521–2553.

Grossberg, S., & Rudd, M. (1992). Cortical dynamics of visual motion perception: short-range and long-range apparent motion. *Psychological Review*, *99*, 78–121.

Ito, H., & Anstis, S. M. (2002). *Motion after Effects from Illusory Movements of Second-Order Contours*. Glasgow, Scotland: ECVP Presentation.

Ito, H., & Anstis, S.M. Anomalous movements of dotted contours, unpublished.

Mather, G., & Anstis, S. (1995). Second-order texture contrast resolves ambiguous apparent motion. *Perception*, *24*, 1373–1382.

Maunsell, J. H. R., & Van Essen, D. C. (1983). Functional properties of neurons in idle temporal visual area of the macaque monkey. I. Selectivity for stimulus duration, speed, and orientation. *Journal of Neurophysiology*, *49*, 1127–1147.

Mikami, A., Newsome, W. T., & Wurtz, R. H. (1986). Motion selectivity in macaque visual cortex. II. Spatiotemporal range of directional interactions in MT and V1. *Journal of Neurophysiology*, *55*(6), 1328–1338.

Nakayama, K. (1985). Biological image motion processing: a review. *Vision Research*, *25*, 625–660.

Pridmore, R. W. (1999). Bezold–Brucke hue-shift as functions of luminance level, luminance ratio, interstimulus interval and adapting white for aperture and object colors. *Vision Research*, *39*, 3873–3879.

Stone, L. S., & Thompson, P. (1992). Human speed perception is contrast dependent. *Vision Research*, *32*, 1535–1549.

Thompson, P. (1982). Perceived rate of movement depends on contrast. *Vision Research*, *22*, 377–380.

Thompson, P., & Stone, L. S. (1997). Contrast affects flicker and speed perception differently. *Vision Research*, *37*, 1255–1260.

Thompson, P., Stone, L. S., & Swash, S. (1996). Speed estimates from grating patches are not contrast-normalized. *Vision Research*, *36*, 667–674.

Walls, G. E. (1942). *The Vertebrate Eye and Its Adaptive Radiation*. New York: Hafner.

Zeki, S. M. (1974). Functional organization of a visual area in the posterior bank of the superior temporal sulcus of the rhesus monkey. *Journal of Physiology*, *236*, 546–573.

AVAILABLE AT
www.ComputerScienceWeb.com
POWERED BY SCIENCE DIRECT

PERGAMON

Neural Networks 16 (2003) 939–945

Neural Networks

www.elsevier.com/locate/neunet

2003 Special issue

Neural models of motion integration and segmentation

Ennio Mingolla

Department of Cognitive and Neural Systems, Boston University, Boston, MA 02215, USA

Abstract

A neural model is developed of how motion integration and segmentation processes compute global motion percepts. Figure-ground properties, such as occlusion, influence which motion signals determine the percept. For visible apertures, a line's extrinsic terminators do not specify true line motion. For invisible apertures, a line's intrinsic terminators create veridical feature tracking signals, which are amplified before they propagate across space and are integrated with ambiguous motion signals within line interiors. This integration process is the result of several processing stages: directional transient cells respond to image transients and input to a directional short-range filter that selectively boosts feature tracking signals. Competitive interactions further boost feature tracking signals and create speed-selective receptive fields. A long-range filter gives rise to true directional cells by pooling signals over multiple orientations and opposite contrast polarities. A distributed population code of speed tuning realizes a size–speed correlation, whereby activations of multiple spatially short-range filters of different sizes are transformed into speed-tuned cell responses. These mechanisms use transient cell responses, output thresholds that covary with filter size, and competition. The model reproduces empirically derived speed discrimination curves and simulates data showing how visual speed perception and discrimination are affected by stimulus contrast.

Keywords: Neural model; Contrast-induced speed perception; Motion integration

1. Motion integration and segmentation

Perception of moving objects in cluttered scenes requires coordinated processes to solve the complementary problems of motion integration and motion segmentation (Braddick, 1993). The present treatment follows that of Grossberg, Mingolla, and Viswanathan (2001), who describe how the integration process joins disparate motion signals that belong to the same object, while the segmentation process keeps separate nearby signals that belong to different objects.

Wallach (1935) (translated by Wuerger, Shapley, and Rubin) first noted that the motion of a featureless line viewed through a circular aperture is ambiguous, and by default perceived as in a direction normal to the line's orientation. This so-called aperture problem confronts any localized detector, such as a cortical neuron with a localized receptive field (Marr & Ullman, 1981). Only when the contour within an aperture contains distinct features, such as a line end, corner, or a discrete blob or dot can a local detector accurately measure both direction and speed of motion. If, on the other hand, a partially occluded object moves in such a way that each of several measurable local motions is subject to the aperture problem, it may be that a process of integration operating at a spatial scale larger than that of the receptive fields of individual motion detectors is still able to determine the velocity of coherent object motion from the fragmented information.

To solve the twin problems of motion integration and segmentation, the visual system needs to use the relatively few unambiguous motion signals arising from image features to veto and constrain the more numerous ambiguous signals from contour interiors. In addition, the visual system uses contextual interactions to compute a consistent motion direction and velocity when the scene is devoid of any unambiguous motion signals.

The motion of a grating of parallel lines seen moving behind a circular aperture is ambiguous. However, when two such gratings are superimposed to form a plaid, the perceived motion is not ambiguous. Plaids have therefore been used extensively to study motion perception. Three major mechanisms for the perceived motion of coherent plaids have been presented in the literature. (1) *Vector average*. The vector average solution is one in which the velocity of the plaid appears to be the vector average of the normal components of the plaid's constituent gratings. (2) *Intersection of constraints*. A constraint line, first defined by Adelson and Movshon (1982), is the locus in velocity space of all possible positions of the leading edge of a bar or line after some time interval (Fig. 1). The constraint line for

0893-6080/03/$ - see front matter © 2003 Elsevier Science Ltd. All rights reserved.
doi:10.1016/S0893-6080(03)00099-6

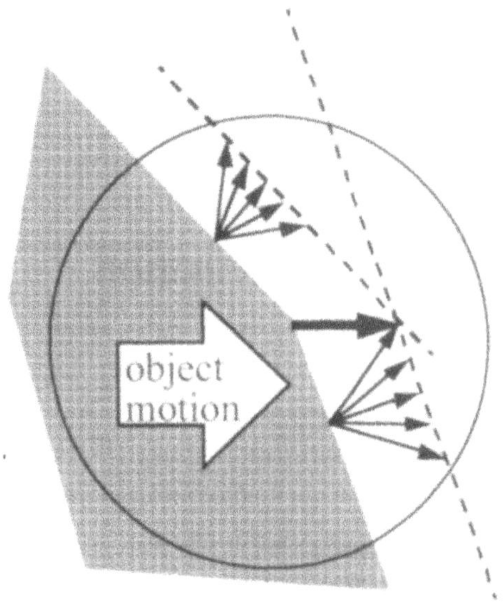

Fig. 1. Viewed through a circular aperture, the two leading edges of a polygon have different normal velocities. Dashed 'constraint lines' indicate the locus of all locations where those leading edges might appear after a small time increment. Their intersection represents the 'intersection of constraints' solution, which of necessity corresponds to the trajectory of the corner feature. Reprinted with permission from Mingolla et al. (1992).

a featureless bar, or a grating of parallel featureless bars, that is moving behind a circular aperture is parallel to the bar. The authors suggested that the perceived motion of a plaid pattern was defined by the velocity vector of the intersection in velocity space of the constraint lines of the plaid components. They named this the intersection of constraints (IOC) solution to the plaid problem. The IOC solution is the mathematically correct solution to the motion perception problem and, hence, is always veridical. However, as noted below, it does not always predict human motion perception even for coherent plaids. (3) *Feature tracking*. When two one-dimensional gratings are superimposed, they form intersections, which act as features whose motion can be reliably tracked. Other features are line endings and object corners. A third possible solution to the problem of plaid motion perception is that the visual system may be tracking features instead of computing a vector average or an IOC solution. At intersections or object corners, the IOC solution and the trajectory of the feature are always identical. However, in some non-plaid displays described below, the feature tracking solution differs from the IOC solution.

Ferrera and Wilson (1990, 1991) noted that perception of motion for certain plaids, for which the IOC prediction falls outside the arc formed by motion vectors for the two components, is not always in accordance with the IOC prediction. Mingolla, Todd, and Norman (1992) introduced a multi-aperture paradigm in order to combine two component motions without the benefit of trackable intersection features, and found that motion was thereby biased away from the IOC solution and toward the vector average. Rubin and Hochstein (1993) created displays in which moving lines could be seen to move in the direction of a vector average, rather than the IOC direction.

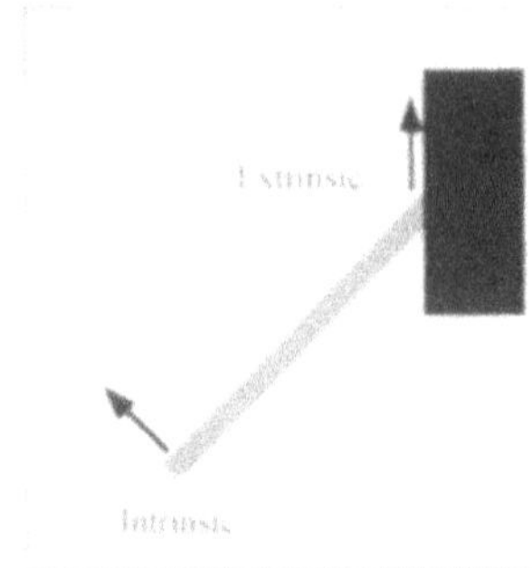

Fig. 2. Extrinsic vs. intrinsic terminators: the boundary that is caused due to the occlusion of the gray line by the black bar is an extrinsic terminator of the line. This boundary belongs to the occluder rather than the occluded object. The unoccluded terminator of the gray line is called an intrinsic terminator because it belongs to the line itself. Reprinted with permission from Grossberg et al. (2001).

A key insight of recent psychophysical research concerns the significance of line endings in motion displays. The trajectories of line ends are unambiguous, but line endings are not all created equal (Fig. 2). Nakayama, Shimojo, and Silverman (1989) introduced the terms intrinsic and extrinsic terminators to distinguish ends of lines or edges that 'belong' to an object from ends that are adventitiously formed by an occluding object. While motion signals at extrinsic terminators may over time trace out the shape of a stationary occluding object, they tell us little about the true velocity of the occluded object.

The present model accordingly ascribes a primary role to mechanisms that detect and enhance the trajectories of features such as dots, line endings or corners, by creating 'feature tracking signals.' Note that the determination of whether a part of a scene contains such a trackable feature may be better accomplished by mechanisms of the visual system's 'form' pathway, rather than by the early units of the 'motion' pathway, which may process raw spatio-temporal variations of contrast quickly into 'raw' motion estimates. Accordingly, the inputs to the model described in Fig. 3 are here taken to be the outputs of FACADE mechanisms, as described in a model of Form And Color and DEpth processing first described by Grossberg (1994).

A key property of the FACADE model is its ability to process occlusions at T-junctions in a manner that results in a weakened representation for a boundary at an extrinsic line, compared to what is registered at an intrinsic line end (Kelly & Grossberg, 2000).

2. Neural model

This model employs a cascade of six neural levels, with feedback between the last two. *Level 1*: Input to the model is not a raw spatio-temporal array of changing contrasts, but

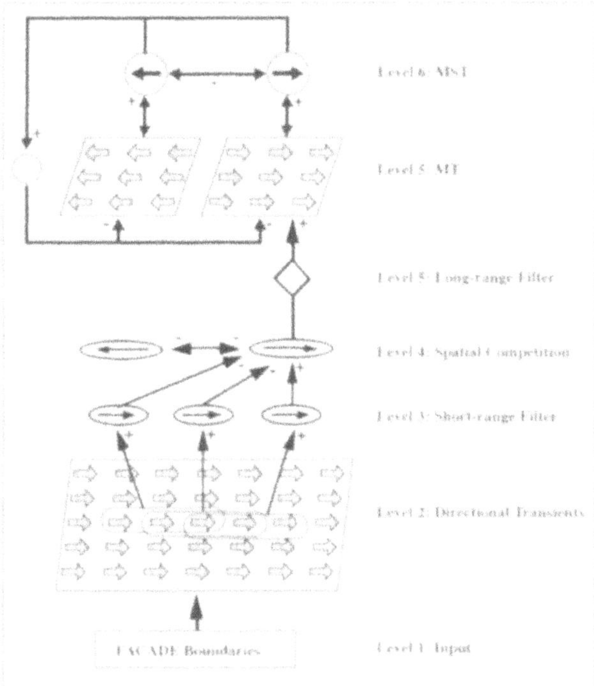

Fig. 3. Model macrocircuit. See text for details. Reprinted with permission from Grossberg et al. (2001).

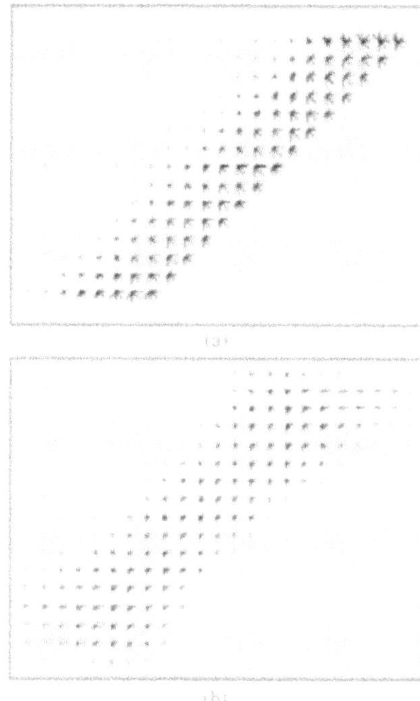

Fig. 4. (a) A diagonal line translating to the right. Output of directional transient cells of Level 2 shows aperture ambiguity at all locations. (b) The Level 4 competition network shows suppression of ambiguous interior signals and directionally unambiguous feature tracking signals at line ends.

rather the result of early boundary processing by a network called the FACADE model that is capable of distinguishing extrinsic from intrinsic terminators, based on 'static' form cues (Grossberg, 1994; Kelly & Grossberg, 2000). FACADE boundary processing thus models Pathway 1 of Fig. 4, the V1/V2 circuit that is part of the form (or 'what' as opposed to 'where') pathway. The enhanced response of FACADE boundaries to intrinsic, as compared to extrinsic, terminators yields the seeds of what will become 'feature tracking signals' in subsequent levels. *Level 2*: Here directional transient cells begin the process of forming signals sensitive to local motion, via a nulling mechanism such as first suggested by Barlow and Levick (1965) for rabbit retina. *Level 3*: A short-range filter next combines outputs of neighboring directional transient cells that are aligned, thereby gaining selectivity to feature trajectories. *Level 4*: Spatial competition and opponent direction inhibition (Albright, 1984) further overcomes the local aperture problem and enhances directionally unambiguous signals at intrinsic line ends, points, or corners. Signals along line or edge interiors remain relatively weak, because local competition among several competing directions (i.e. the aperture problem) results in normalizing, divisive inhibition. *Levels 5 and 6*: A long-range feedback cooperative/competitive circuit, identified with areas MT and MST, here reorganizes ambiguous directional signals in line or edge interiors based on information from unambiguous trackable features. The nonlinearities of this circuit permit spatially smaller (or, in network terms, numerically fewer) pools of activity that are higher in amplitude to overcome spatially larger (and numerically greater) signals along line or edge interiors.

An insight into key model mechanisms is best gotten by considering a simple example of early model stage outputs. Fig. 4a shows that the directional transient cells of Level 2 code an ambiguous array of local motion directions, with the direction normal to the moving line being preferred. The short-range filter and spatial competition stages suppress regions of homogenous, ambiguous direction signals, however, while favoring those signals at the depicted line's end that code veridically for horizontal rightward motion.

This model has successfully simulated data on the barberpole illusion and its variants involving motion capture, such as spotted barberpole patterns (Shiffrar, Li, & Lorenceau, 1995); line capture (Ramachandran & Inada, 1985); the triple barberpole illusion (Shimojo, Silverman, & Nakayama, 1989); and the chopsticks illusion (Anstis, 1990). Moreover, Pack and Born (2001) have found direct evidence that cells of MT dynamically change their directional preference to the motion of lines moving obliquely to their orientation, as predicted by the terminator-to-interior propagation of signals in the model, see Figs. 4–6.

3. Contrast and speed

The model is sensitive to speed through the use of multi-scale filters at Level 3, followed by intra-scale and

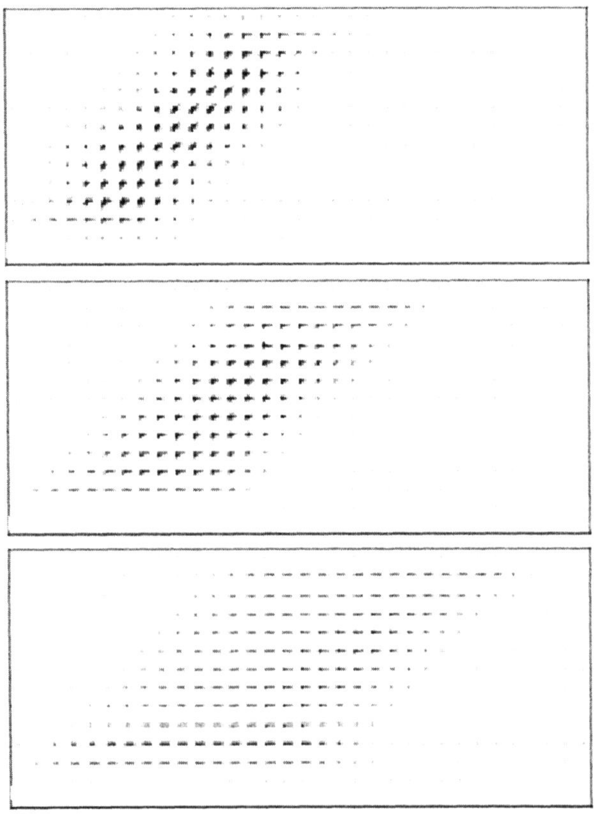

Fig. 5. Activities of long-range filters evolve over time in response to a rightward-moving diagonal line. The early distribution (top) contains ambiguous signals in the interior regions. Successive time slices (middle and bottom) show that the distribution of interior signals normal to the diagonal line is replaced by veridical horizontal signals. Reprinted with permission from Chey, Grossberg, and Mingolla (1997).

inter-scale competition, as described in Figs. 7 and 8. The present description follows that of Chey, Grossberg, and Mingolla (1998).

In the present model speed is represented through the distributed activity of speed-tuned units, or cell populations.

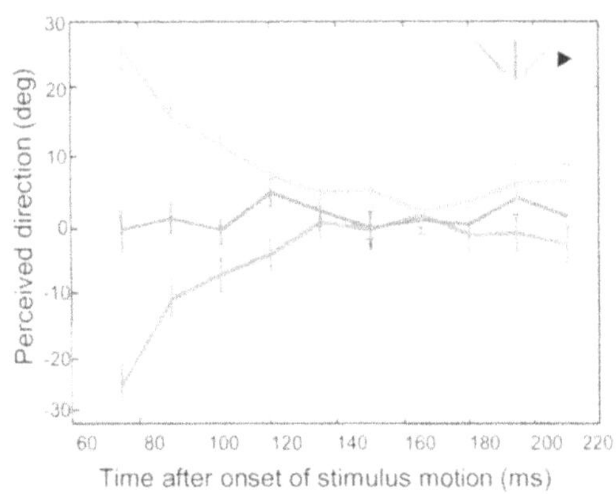

Fig. 6. The preferred directional response of MT cells of macaque changes over time. Initial responses are biased by the orientation of line segments (top right) translating through the receptive field. Over time, cell responses reflect the true horizontal motion of translating stimuli. Reprinted with permission from Pack and Born (2001).

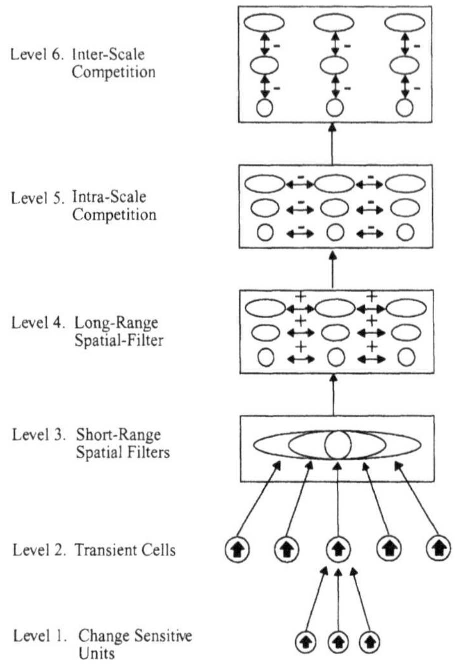

Fig. 7. See text for details. Reprinted with permission from Chey et al. (1998).

We define speed-tuned cells as those that respond preferentially to a limited, continuous range of speeds, as opposed to speed-sensitive cells, but that do not exhibit a preference for a particular speed. The speed tunings of model cells arise primarily from their different spatial scales, which determine the size of their input fields. A key model hypothesis is that larger scales respond preferentially to faster stimuli; we call this covariation the size–speed correlation.

The visual system is faced with the problem of maintaining sensitivity to a wide range of speeds, using mechanisms with limited operating ranges, without sacrificing speed resolution or spatial resolution, such as when small objects travel very fast. Since a simple 'match filter' scheme using neurons uniquely tuned to every combination of speed, size, contrast, and so forth is hopelessly impractical, units with overlapping sensitivities to spatial and temporal parameters of inputs must be used. How can the units of such a scheme be properly tuned? Each scale is turned on whenever a contrast passes through the region corresponding to the filter's spatial extent. A continuously moving contrast has a longer dwell time in the domain of a large-scale filter than in the domain of a small-scale filter centered at the same retinal location. Why does not the largest scale always win in response to all input speeds, simply because it has a larger receptive field with which to attain a higher level of activation?

Our work suggests that two simple mechanisms suffice. The first is a scale-proportionate threshold, which requires units of larger scales to have larger absolute activity (or, equivalently, similar proportions of their maximum possible

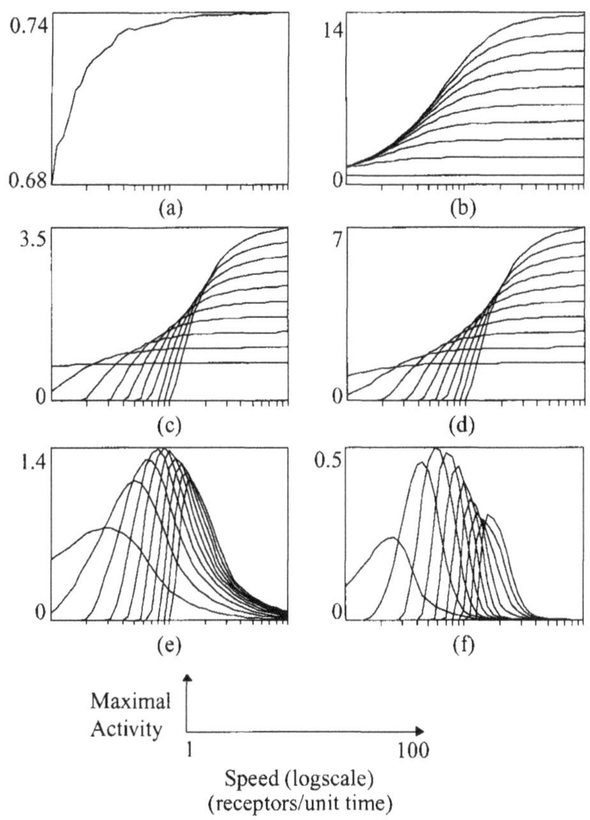

Fig. 8. Maximal responses of cells in the network to a variety of simulated speeds are plotted. From the top left, across then down, plots show (a) transient cells, (b) short-range spatial filters, (c) thresholded short-range filters, (d) long-range filters, (e) intra-scale competition, and (f) inter-scale competition. For levels where there are multiple spatial scales at a single location, activities from all scales are shown as different curves superimposed on the same plot. The smaller scales always respond less vigorously to fast speeds, so their activity profiles always show lower values, as is particularly evident at fast speeds. Vertical axis scales vary and are indicated next to each plot. Reprinted with permission from Chey et al. (1998).

activity) to transmit a signal. The second is competition, both among units of similar scales and across units of differing scales.

Fig. 7 presents a schematic outline of network layers. Level 1 consists of change-sensitive units that are transiently activated for fixed time intervals by a moving stimulus. Level 2 transient cells sum and time-average the activities from fixed, non-overlapping sets of the change-sensitive units. Multiple Level 3 short-range filters are available at each spatial position. Each filter draws input from a set of transient cells, the size of which is determined by the spatial scale of the filter. As depicted, scale 1 receives input from 1 transient cell, scale 2 from 3 and scale 3 from 5. The transient cells that each filter draws from overlap both between scales at a single location and between locations at a single scale. Thus, the largest scale depicted in the outline draws input from a superset of the transient cells that the smaller scales draw from. A long-range spatial filter at Level 4 spatially blurs the thresholded outputs of the short-range filters. The output of the long-range filters forms input to Level 5 intra-scale competition across space. This competition is enacted through spatial antagonistic center-surround mechanisms. At Level 6, inter-scale competition then takes place between all scales at each spatial location, again enacted through a center-surround mechanism. The results of this final competitive stage form the output of the network and can be interpreted as a pre-speed estimate.

This speed model has been used to simulate a wide variety of data, as described by Chey et al. (1998). To illustrate how model mechanisms interact with key psychophysical findings, one particular simulation study is reviewed here.

4. Contrast effects on speed coding

In addition to affecting discrimination performance, several studies have reported that contrast affects the perceived speed of moving objects. Thompson (1982) reported that low contrast gratings were perceived to move more slowly than high contrast gratings. Ferrera and Wilson (1990) found that contrast influenced the perceived speed of coherent plaid patterns formed from superimposed gratings. Castet, Lorenceau, Shiffrar and Bonnet (1993) found a contrast-induced reduction in perceived speed of translating lines. Anstis (2001) has provided some particularly compelling demonstrations of the importance of contrast in speed perception.

The data simulated here are from a study by Stone and Thompson (1992) in which subjects compared the speed of two simultaneously presented grating patches, a test and a reference. The contrast of the reference grating was varied and percentage of test gratings perceived as moving faster were recorded as a function of the test speed for each contrast level.

To show how the model simulates the change in relative speed judgments due to contrast variations, we used the previously defined speed measure, and calculated speed judgments on the basis of differences between speed measures obtained from two inputs which were simulated separately. We passed the difference between the two speed measures through an 'error function' to obtain a simulated probability of an observer judging one speed as faster than the other. The results of this process are shown in Fig. 9b. For inputs of the same contrast, we obtain a standard error function. Changing the simulated contrast or receptor activity amplitude causes a curve shift similar to that observed in the data. In both the data and the simulation, there is little change in the curve shapes under this shift. In addition, both data and simulation show that increasing input magnitude results in a greater shift than decreasing it, at least under this contrast range.

The effects of increasing input magnitude are ultimately bounded by the shunting properties of the transient cells. Thus, beyond a certain contrast level, the model predicts no

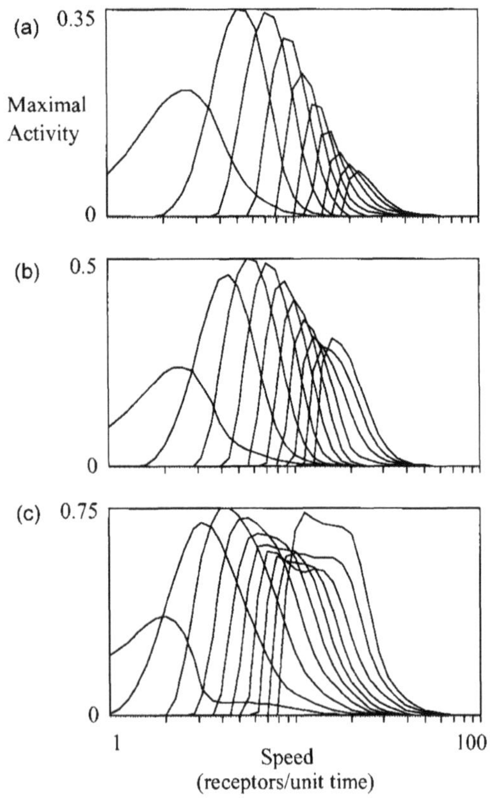

Fig. 9. Maximal network activities over speed using different receptor response amplitudes, hypothesized to correspond to different stimulus contrasts. Plot (a) shows low amplitude receptor activity (0.75), (b) shows intermediate amplitude (1) and (c) shows high amplitude (2). Increasing receptor activity amplitude causes large scales to respond more vigorously and at lower speeds. This biases the network to provide higher speed estimates. Reprinted with permission from Chey et al. (1998).

effect of increased stimulus contrast. As contrast decreases, perceived speed also decreases until the input energy is sufficiently low as to cause the stimulus to be no longer visible, or visibly in motion. At the same time as the speed measure is decreasing in the model due to decreased receptor amplitude, the total activity in the final network level is also decreasing. We predict that at very low activity levels, speed measures obtained from the network are indistinguishable from noise. Thus, it may not be the case that decreasing stimulus contrast always results in slower perceived speeds, i.e. there may be a network energy threshold below which the speed measures are no longer relevant. In summary, the range of stimulus contrasts under which a contrast-induced speed change can be effected in the model is bounded below by the energy present and above by the shunting properties of the transient cells. Failure to use stimuli in this range may result in failure to observe contrast-induced speed perception.

The model accounts for contrast-induced changes in perceived speed through the dependence of network output on the spatial and temporal summation of energy provided by receptor responses by the short-range filters of Level 3. Stimulus contrast changes translate into changes in receptor activity amplitude in the model, so that high contrast stimuli generate larger receptor activity amplitudes.

Since the model is based on spatio-temporal summation, one might expect that increasing input amplitude (by raising contrast) might result in a failure of speed estimates, by causing large-scale cells to respond at very slow speeds where they would normally be inactive. Several factors work to ensure that this is not the case. Firstly, the changes in receptor amplitude are limited in their effects by the membrane or shunting properties of the transient cells, which restrict the transient cell output ranges irrespective of their input. Secondly, normalization due to intra-scale competition limits activity at fast speeds, so that activity cannot rise beyond a certain level nor can cells ever respond at speeds beyond some high cut-off. Fig. 9 shows how contrast affects the model's activity distribution across scales.

5. Previous models

Several other methods by which the human visual system might extract speed estimates have been proposed. Correlational models, such as the Reichardt detector, incorporate speed-selectivity into directionally selective motion sensors. Human speed perception has been modelled by the elaborated Reichardt detector (van Santen & Sperling, 1985), which differs from the original Reichardt formulation in that preliminary spatial filtering is performed by the receptors before their outputs are multiplied. A similar model (shown to be formally equivalent by van Santen and Sperling) is the motion energy model (Adelson & Bergen, 1985) in which temporal filtering takes the place of the delay. An alternative model was suggested by Watson and Ahumada (1985). In their model, the temporal response patterns of directionally selective sensors were used to derive speed estimates.

The present model differs from these formulations in that it starts with simple transient cell responses and builds directionality and speed sensitivity from these. The model postulates that speed tuning is an emergent property of spatio-temporal network interactions across a series of network processing stages; it is not explicitly defined by any one operation. Support for this hypothesis is found in the fact that the emergent tuning varies with input parameters in a manner that matches changes in perceived speed in response to stimulus parameter manipulations in psychophysical experiments.

6. Conclusion

The circuits that underlie motion speed and direction processing are well described by a multi-scale, competitive network with feedback, designed to emulate the process of the V1-V2-MT-MST circuit of the primate visual system.

Acknowledgements

Supported in part by N00014-01-1-0624 (ONR).

References

Adelson, E. H., & Bergen, J. R. (1985). Spatiotemporal energy models for the perception of motion. *Journal of the Optical Society of America*, *2*(2), 284–299.

Adelson, E. H., & Movshon, A. (1982). Phenomenal coherence of moving visual patterns. *Nature*, *300*, 523–525.

Albright, T. D. (1984). Direction and orientation selectivity of neurons in visual area MT of the macaque. *Journal of Neurophysiology*, *52*(6), 1106–1130.

Anstis, S. M. (1990). Imperceptible intersections: The chopstick illusion. In A. Blake, & T. Troscianko (Eds.), *AI and the Eye, Chap. 5* (pp. 105–117). New York: Wiley.

Anstis, S. M. (2001). Footsteps and inchworms: illusions show that contrast affects apparent speed. *Perception*, *30*(7), 785–794.

Barlow, H. B., & Levick, W. R. (1965). The mechanism of directionally selective units in the rabbit's retina. *Journal of Physiology*, *178*, 477–504.

Braddick, O. (1993). Segmentation versus integration in visual motion processing. *Trends in Neurosciences*, *16*(7), 263–268.

Castet, E., Lorenceau, J., Shiffrar, M., & Bonnet, C. (1993). Perceived speed of moving lines depends on orientation, length, speed and luminance. *Vision Research*, *33*(14), 1921–1936.

Chey, J., Grossberg, S., & Mingolla, E. (1997). Neural dynamics of motion grouping: from aperture ambiguity to object speed and direction. *Journal of the Optical Society of America A*, *14*(10), 2570–2594.

Chey, J., Grossberg, S., & Mingolla, E. (1998). Neural dynamics of motion processing and speed discrimination. *Vision Research*, *38*, 2769–2786.

Ferrera, V. P., & Wilson, H. R. (1990). Perceived direction of moving two-dimensional patterns. *Vision Research*, *30*, 273–287.

Ferrera, V. P., & Wilson, H. R. (1991). Perceived speed of moving two-dimensional patterns. *Vision Research*, *31*, 877–893.

Grossberg, S. (1994). 3D vision and figure-ground separation by visual cortex. *Perception & Psychophysics*, *55*, 48–120.

Grossberg, S., Mingolla, E., & Viswanathan, L. (2001). Neural dynamics of motion integration and segmentation within and across apertures. *Vision Research*, *41*(19), 2521–2553.

Kelly, F., & Grossberg, S. (2000). Neural dynamics of 3D surface perception: figure-ground separation and lightness perception. *Perception & Psychophysics*, *62*(8), 1596–1618.

Marr, D., & Ullman, S. (1981). Directional selectivity and its use in early visual processing. *Proceedings of the Royal Society of London B*, *211*, 151–180.

Mingolla, E., Todd, J. T., & Norman, J. F. (1992). The perception of globally coherent motion. *Vision Research*, *32*, 1015–1031.

Nakayama, K., Shimojo, S., & Silverman, G. H. (1989). Stereoscopic depth: its relation to image segmentation grouping and the recognition of occluded objects. *Perception*, *18*, 55–68.

Pack, C. C., & Born, R. T. (2001). Temporal dynamics of a neural solution to the aperture problem in visual area MT of macaque brain. *Nature*, *409*(6823), 1040–1042.

Ramachandran, V. S., & Inada, V. (1985). Spatial phase and frequency in motion capture of random-dot patterns. *Spatial Vision*, *1*(1), 57–67.

Rubin, N., & Hochstein, S. (1993). Isolating the effect of one-dimensional motion signals on the perceived direction of moving two-dimensional objects. *Vision Research*, *33*, 1385–1396.

Shiffrar, M., Li, X., & Lorenceau, J. (1995). Motion integration across differing image features. *Vision Research*, *35*(15), 2137–2146.

Shimojo, S., Silverman, G. H., & Nakayama, K. (1989). Occlusion and the solution to the aperture problem for motion. *Vision Research*, *29*(5), 619–626.

Stone, L. S., & Thompson, P. (1992). Human speed perception is contrast dependent. *Vision Research*, *32*(8), 1535–1549.

Thompson, P. (1982). Perceived rate of movement depends on contrast. *Vision Research*, *22*, 377–380.

van Santen, J. P. H., & Sperling, G. (1985). Elaborated Reichardt detectors. *Journal of the Optical Society of America*, *2*(2), 300–321.

Wallach, H. (1935). On the visually perceived direction of motion. *Psychologische Forschung*, *20*, 325–380.

Watson, B., & Ahumada, A. J., Jr. (1985). Model of human visual-motion sensing. *Journal of the Optical Society of America*, *2*(2), 322–342.

www.ingramcontent.com/pod-product-compliance
Ingram Content Group UK Ltd.
Pitfield, Milton Keynes, MK11 3LW, UK
UKHW050952290926
15470UKWH00005B/1776

9 780080 443201